Ireland

Counties
Londonderry & Antrim
p598

County
Donegal
p436

Counties
Fermanagh &
Tyrone
p634

Belfast
p536

Counties
Down & Armagh
p572

Counties
Mayo & Sligo
p401

Counties Meath,
Louth, Cavan &
Monaghan
p500

The Midlands
p472

Dublin
p58

County Galway
p359

Counties Wicklow
& Kildare
p138

County Clare
p324

Counties
Limerick &
Tipperary
p302

Counties
Wexford, Waterford,
Carlow & Kilkenny
p164

County
Kerry
p256

County
Cork
p211

County
Cork
p211

Neil Wilson, Isabel Albiston, Fionn Davenport,
Damian Harper, Catherine Le Nevez

Contents

ST GEORGE'S MARKET P544

KILLARNEY NATIONAL PARK P265

Contents

ON THE ROAD

Contents

SPECIAL FEATURES

Welcome to Ireland

A small country with a big reputation: breathtaking landscapes and fascinating, friendly people, whose lyrical nature is expressed in the warmth of their welcome.

A Scenic Wonderland

Everything you've heard is true: Ireland is a stunner. The Irish need little prodding to proclaim theirs the most beautiful land in the world, and will support their claim with examples, from the brooding loneliness of Connemara to the dramatic wildness of Donegal and the world-famous scenery of counties Kerry and Cork. Northern Ireland might be in a different country, but it's very much the same land and you'll find beauty throughout the region, from the mountains of Mourne to the lakelands of Roscommon and its own scenic star turn along the Antrim Coast.

Rich Historical Heritage

History is everywhere, from the breathtaking monuments of prehistoric Ireland at Brú na Bóinne, Slea Head in Kerry and Carrowmore in Sligo, to the fabulous ruins of Ireland's rich monastic past at Glendalough, Clonmacnoise and Cashel. The island's newest tourism venture, Ireland's Ancient East, is all about the country's rich heritage. More recent history is visible in the Titanic Experience in Cobh and the forbidding Kilmainham Gaol in Dublin. And there's history so young that it's still considered the present, best experienced on a black-taxi tour of West Belfast or an examination of Derry's colourful political murals.

A Cultural Well

It's become almost trite to declare that Ireland operates a cultural surplus. Its main strengths are the literary and musical fields, where Ireland has long punched well above its weight, but Ireland is well represented in most other fields too. Wherever you go you will discover an abundance of cultural expression. You can attend a play by a literary great in Dublin, toe-tap your way through a traditional-music 'session' in a west-of-Ireland pub or get your EDM on at a club in Belfast. The Irish summer is awash with festivals celebrating everything from flowers in bloom to high literature.

A Warm Welcome

On the plane and along your travels you might hear it said: *tá Fáilte romhat* (taw fall-cha row-at) – you're very welcome. Or, more famously, *céad míle fáilte* – a hundred thousand welcomes. Irish friendliness is an over-simplification of a character that is infinitely complex, but the Irish are nonetheless warm and welcoming. But this isn't just altruism, as the comfort they seek is actually their own, for the Irish cannot be at ease in the company of those who aren't. A hundred thousand welcomes. It seems excessive, but in Ireland, excess is encouraged, so long as it's practised in moderation.

Why I Love Ireland

By Fionn Davenport, Writer

There's an unvarnished informality about Ireland that I cherish, based on an implied assumption that life is a tangled, confusing struggle that all of us – irrespective of who we are and how we worship – have to negotiate to the best of our abilities. We're all in this together, come hell or high water, so we may as well be civil and share a moment when we can.

For more about our writers, see p719

Above: Christ Church Cathedral, Dublin (p79)

Ireland

ELEVATION

700m
500m
300m
200m
100m
0

50 miles
100 km

ATLANTIC OCEAN

North Channel

Wild Atlantic Way
Coves, cliffs and stunning scenery (p47)

Causeway Coast
Fitting backdrop for *Game of Thrones* (p620)

Titanic Belfast
Museum of the world's most famous ship (p545)

Brú na Bóinne
Outstanding Neolithic passage tombs (p501)

Derry (Londonderry)
Walled city featuring music and art (p599)

Carrowmore Megalithic Cemetery
Stone Age monuments (p428)

Connemara
Brooding and beautiful landscape (p385)

Malin Head

North Channel

Rathlin Island
Ballycastle
Giant's Causeway
Bushmills
Portstewart
Portrush
Dunluce Castle
Inishowen Castle Head
Culdaff
Carndonagh
Moville
Inishowen Peninsula
Coleraine
Downhill
Limavady
Derry
Buncrana
Letterkenny

Larne
Ballymena
Slemish (438m)
Carrickfergus
Bangor
Newtownards
Ards Peninsula
Strangford Lough
Holywood
Crawfordsburn
Belfast
Lisburn
Killyleagh
Downpatrick
Lecale Peninsula
Greencastle

Ballyliffin
Fanad Peninsula
Lough Swilly
Dunfanaghy
Rosguill Peninsula
Gortahork
Glenveagh National Park
Lough Gartan

Antrim
Kells
Lurgan
Craigavon Portadown
Armagh
Banbridge

ANTRIM
Lough Neagh

Strabane
LONDONDERRY
Sperrin Mountains
Omagh
TYRONE

Monaghan
Clones
MONAGHAN
Carrickmacross

DOWN

ARMAGH

Cooley Peninsula
Carlingford
Dundalk
LOUTH

Tory Island
Bloody Foreland
Arranmore Island
Gweedore
Dunlewy
Dungloe
Kincasslagh
Ardara
Glenties
Longhrea Peninsula
Maghery
Killybegs
Carrick
Kilcar
Donegal Bay
Glencolumbcille

DONEGAL
Blue Stack Mountains
Mountcharles
Donegal
Rossnowlagh
Bundoran

Lough Finn
Bruckless
Lough Eske

Lough Derg
Lower Lough Erne
Enniskillen
FERMANAGH
Upper Lough Erne
Lough Macnean Lower
Lough Macnean Upper

Cuilcagh Mountain (667m)

Rossmore Forest Park

Cavan
CAVAN

LEITRIM
Carrick-on-Shannon

River Annagh
River Erne

Carrickmacross
Inniskeen

Battle of Boyne Site
Slane
Brú na Bóinne
Navan
Trim
Tara

Drogheda
Laytown
Newgrange

MEATH
DUBLIN

Inishmurray Island
Sligo Bay
Lough Gill
Sligo
Carrowmore Megalithic Cemetery
Ballina

SLIGO
Boyle

ROSCOMMON
Roscommon
Lough Ree
River

Strokestown
Longford
LONGFORD
Mullingar

Ireland West Airport Knock
Knock

Céide Fields
Pollatomish
Bangor Erris
Mullet Peninsula
Killala
Ballycastle
Killala
Ballycroy National Park
Newport
Castlebar
Westport

Clare Island
Clew Bay
Croagh Patrick (765m)
Doolough Valley
Leenane
Connemara National Park

MAYO
Cong

Inishturk Island
Inishbofin
Cleggan
track
Claddaghduff

Clare

ATLANTIC OCEAN

55°N
54°N

10°W
9°W
8°W
7°W
6°W

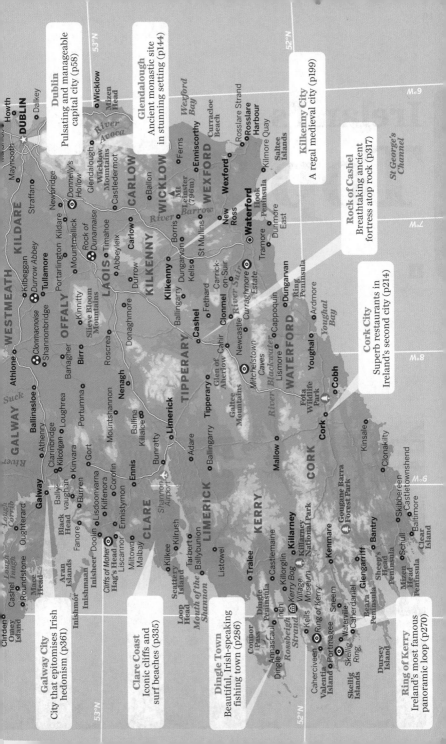

Dublin
Pulsating and manageable capital city (p58)

Glendalough
Ancient monastic site in stunning setting (p144)

Kilkenny City
A regal medieval city (p199)

Rock of Cashel
Breathtaking ancient fortress atop rock (p317)

Cork City
Superb restaurants in Ireland's second city (p214)

Ring of Kerry
Ireland's most famous panoramic loop (p270)

Dingle Town
Beautiful, Irish-speaking fishing town (p286)

Clare Coast
Iconic cliffs and surf beaches (p335)

Galway City
City that epitomises Irish hedonism (p361)

Ireland's
Top 21

Dublin

1 Ireland's capital and largest city by some stretch is the main gateway into the country, and it has enough distractions to keep visitors engaged for at least a few days. From world-class museums and entertainment, superb dining and top-grade hotels, Dublin (p58) has all the baubles of a major international metropolis. But the real clinchers are Dubliners themselves, who are friendlier, more easygoing and more welcoming than the burghers of virtually any other European capital. And it's the home of Guinness.

Below: Grand Canal Docks (p93)

Connemara, County Galway

2 A filigreed coast of tiny coves and beaches is the Connemara Peninsula (p385)'s beautiful border with the wild waters of the Atlantic. Wandering characterful roads bring you from one village to another, each with trad pubs and restaurants serving seafood chowder cooked from recipes that are family secrets. Inland, the scenic drama is even greater. In fantastically desolate valleys, green hills, yellow wildflowers and wild streams reflecting the blue sky provide elemental beauty. Rambles take you far from others and back to a simpler time.

MADRUGADA VERDE/SHUTTERSTOCK ©

GRAFXART/SHUTTERSTOCK ©

Traditional Music

3 Western Europe's most vibrant folk music is Irish traditional music, which may have earned worldwide fame thanks to the likes of *Riverdance* but is best expressed in a more sedate setting, usually an old-fashioned pub. The west of Ireland is particularly musical: from Donegal down to Kerry there are centres of musical excellence, none more so than Doolin (p348) in County Clare, the unofficial capital of Irish music. It's unlikely you'll be asked to join in, but there's nothing stopping your foot from tapping and your hands from clapping.

The Pub

4 Every town and hamlet has at least one: no matter where you go, you'll find that the social heart of the country beats loudest in the pub, which is still the best place to discover what makes the country tick. In suitable surroundings – whether a quiet traditional pub such as Morrissey's (pictured above; p496) of Abbeyleix with flagstone floors and a large peat fire or a more modern bar with flashing lights and music – take a moment or an evening to listen for that beating heart...and drink some decent beer in the process.

Glendalough, County Wicklow

5 St Kevin knew a thing or two about magical locations. When he chose a remote cave on a glacial lake nestled at the base of a forested valley as his monastic retreat (p144), he inadvertently founded a settlement that would later prove to be one of Ireland's most dynamic universities and, in our time, one of the country's most beautiful ruined sites. The remains of the settlement (including an intact round tower), coupled with the stunning scenery, are unforgettable. Bottom right: Round Tower, Glendalough (p146)

Dingle, County Kerry

6 Dingle (p286) is the name of both the picturesque peninsula jutting into the Atlantic from County Kerry, strewn with ancient ruins. Fishing boats unload fish and shellfish that couldn't be any fresher if you caught it yourself, many pubs are untouched since their earlier incarnations as old-fashioned shops, artists sell their creations (including beautiful jewellery with Irish designs) at intriguing boutiques, and toe-tapping trad sessions take place around roaring pub fires here. Top: Dingle Peninsula (p285)

Galway City

7 One word to describe Galway City (p361)? Craic! Ireland's liveliest city literally hums through the night at music-filled pubs where you can hear three old guys playing spoons and fiddles or a hot, young band. Join the locals as they bounce from place to place, never knowing what fun lies ahead but certain of the possibility. Add in local bounty such as the famous oysters and nearby adventure in the Connemara Peninsula and the Aran Islands, and the fun never ends. Bottom: Shop St, Galway City (p361)

DESIGN PICS INC/GETTY IMAGES ©

JON CHICA/SHUTTERSTOCK ©

Walking & Hiking

8 Yes, you can visit the country easily enough by car, but Ireland is best explored on foot, whether you opt for a gentle afternoon stroll along a canal towpath or to take on the challenge of any of the 43 waymarked long-distance routes. There are coastal walks (p39) and mountain hikes (p265); you can explore towns and villages along the way or steer clear of civilisation by traipsing along lonely moorland and across barren bogs. All you'll need is a decent pair of boots and, inevitably, a rain jacket. Top: Hiking Macgillycuddy's Reeks (p268)

Brú na Bóinne, County Meath

9 Looking at once ancient and yet eerily futuristic, Newgrange's immense, round, white stone walls topped by a grass dome is one of the most extraordinary sights you'll ever see. Part of the vast Neolithic necropolis Brú na Bóinne (p501) (the Boyne Palace), it contains Ireland's finest Stone Age passage tomb, predating the Pyramids by some six centuries. Most extraordinary of all is the tomb's precise alignment with the sun at the time of the winter solstice.

SEMMICK PHOTO/SHUTTERSTOCK ©

LMSPENCER/SHUTTERSTOCK ©

DESIGN PICS INC/GETTY IMAGES ©

MBRANDES/SHUTTERSTOCK ©

GABRIELL2/SHUTTERSTOCK ©

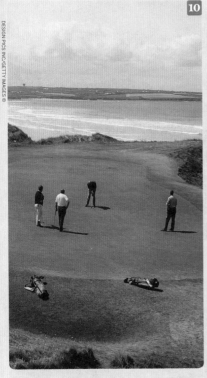

Links Golf

10 If Scotland is the home of golf, then Ireland is where it goes on holiday. And the best vacation spots are along the sea, where the country's collection of seaside links are dotted in a steady string along virtually the entire Irish coastline, each more revealed than carved in the undulating, marram-grass-covered landscapes. Some of the world's best-known courses, including 2019 Open host Royal Portrush (p615), share spectacular scenery with lesser-known gems, and each offers the golfer the opportunity to test their skills against the raw materials provided by Mother Nature. Top Left: Ballybunion Golf Club (p301)

Rock of Cashel, County Tipperary

11 Soaring up from the green Tipperary pastures, this ancient fortress (p317) takes your breath away at first sight. The seat of kings and churchmen who ruled over the region for more than a thousand years, it rivalled Tara as a centre of power in Ireland for 400 years. Entered through the 15th-century Hall of the Vicars Choral, its impervious walls guard an awesome enclosure with a complete round tower, a 13th-century Gothic cathedral and the most magnificent 12th-century Romanesque chapel in Ireland.

Cork City

12 The Republic's second city is second only in terms of size – in every other respect it will bear no competition. A tidy, compact city centre is home to an enticing collection of art galleries, museums and – most especially – places to eat. From cheap cafes to top-end gourmet restaurants, Cork city (p214) excels, although it's hardly a surprise given the county's exceptional foodie reputation. At the heart of it is the simply wonderful English Market (pictured above), a covered produce market that is an attraction unto itself.

PETE SEAWARD/LONELY PLANET ©

WESTEND61/GETTY IMAGES ©

Ring of Kerry

13 Driving around the Ring of Kerry (p270) is an unforgettable experience in itself, but you don't need to limit yourself to the main route. Along this 179km loop around the Iveragh Peninsula there are countless opportunities for detours. Near Killorglin, it's a short hop up to the beautiful, little-known Cromane Peninsula. Between Portmagee and Waterville, you can explore the Skellig Ring. The peninsula's interior offers mesmerising mountain views. And that's just for starters. Wherever your travels take you, remember to charge your camera! Top: Ladies View (p270)

Carrowmore Megalithic Cemetery, County Sligo

14 One of the most significant megalithic monuments in Europe, the collection of stone circles, passage tombs and dolmens at Carrowmore (p428) is the oldest Stone Age monument in Ireland and one of the largest cemeteries of its kind in Europe. The discovery process is ongoing, as archaeologists continue to excavate new monuments and piece together clues to the site's deeper meaning and connection to the world around it, including its mathematical relationship with the rising and setting of the sun at Halloween.

Kilkenny City

15 From its regal castle to its soaring medieval cathedral, Kilkenny (p199) exudes a permanence and culture that have made it an unmissable stop on journeys to the south and west. Its namesake county boasts scores of artisans and craftspeople and you can browse their wares at Kilkenny's classy shops and boutiques. Chefs eschew Dublin in order to be close to the source of Kilkenny's wonderful produce and you can enjoy the local brewery's brews at scores of delightful pubs.

Causeway Coast, County Antrim

16 Antrim's Causeway Coast is an especially dramatic backdrop for *Game of Thrones* filming locations. Put on your walking boots by the swaying Carrick-a-Rede rope bridge (pictured above), then follow the rugged coastline for 16.5 spectacular kilometres, passing Ballintoy Harbour (aka the Iron Islands' Lordsports Harbour) and the geological wonder of the Giant's Causeway's (p618) outsized basalt columns, as well as cliffs and islands, sandy beaches and ruined castles, before finishing with a dram at the Old Bushmills Distillery.

JOE DANIEL PRICE/GETTY IMAGES ©

ATMOSPHERE1/SHUTTERSTOCK ©

BILDAGENTUR ZOONAR GMBH/GETTY IMAGES ©

Donegal's Coast

17 Depending on what direction you travel in, the craggy, crenellated Donegal coastline is either the wildly dramatic finale of the Wild Atlantic Way (p47) or its breathtaking beginning. Ireland's northwestern corner is an untamed collection of soaring cliffs (the tallest in Europe), lonely, sheep-speckled headlands and, between them, secluded coves and long stretches of white, powdery sand: among them is Rossnowlagh in the southwest of the county, one of Europe's premier surf beaches and a mecca for big-wave surfers. Left: Fanad Head Lighthouse (p465)

Titanic Belfast

18 The construction of the world's most famous ocean liner is celebrated in high-tech, multimedia glory at this wonderful museum (p545). Not only can you explore virtually every detail of the *Titanic*'s construction – including a simulated 'fly-through' of the ship from keel to bridge – but you can place yourself in the middle of the industrial bustle that was Belfast's shipyards at the turn of the 20th century. The experience is heightened by the use of photography, audio and – perhaps most poignantly – the only footage of the actual *Titanic* still in existence.

Derry City

19 History runs deep in Northern Ireland's second city, Derry (p599). The symbols of the country's sectarian past are evident, from the 17th-century city walls built to protect Protestant settlers to the latter forcing the adoption of its Loyalist name, Londonderry. Explore its tormented past by walking the walls, visiting the Bogside and the famous murals that tell the tale of resistance and defiance, before losing yourself in Derry's superb live-music scene and terrific nightlife, an almost certain guarantee of a memorable night out. Bottom right: *Hands Across the Divide* (p604), by sculptor Maurice Harron

Irish Sport

20 It depends on whether you're in a football or hurling stronghold (some are both), but attending a match of the county's chosen sport is not just a unique Irish experience but also a key to unlocking local passions and understanding one of the cultural pillars of Ireland. Whether you attend a club football match in County Galway, an intercounty hurling battle between old foes like Kilkenny and Tipperary, or an All-Ireland final at Croke Park (p126), you cannot but be swept up in the emotion of it all. Top: Tipperary Vs. Waterford hurling match

Cliffs of Moher, County Clare

21 Bathed in the golden glow of the late-afternoon sun, the iconic Cliffs of Moher (p345) are but one of the splendours of County Clare. From a boat bobbing below, the towering stone faces have a jaw-dropping dramatic beauty that's enlivened by scores of seabirds, including cute little puffins. Down south in Loop Head, pillars of rock towering above the sea have abandoned stone cottages whose very existence is inexplicable. All along the coast are cute little villages like trad-session-filled Ennistymon and the surfer mecca of Lahinch.

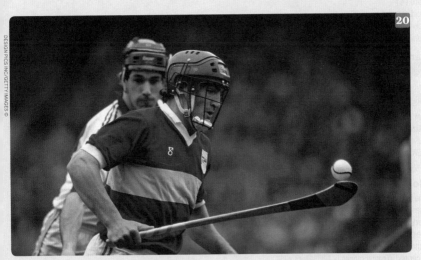

Need to Know

For more information, see Survival Guide (p683)

Currency
Republic of Ireland:
euro (€)
Northern Ireland:
pound sterling (£)

Language
English, Irish

Visas
Not required by most
citizens of Europe,
Australia, New Zealand,
USA and Canada.

Money
The Republic of Ireland
uses the euro (€), while
Northern Ireland uses
the pound sterling (£),
although the euro is also
accepted in many places.

Mobile Phones
All European and Aus-
tralasian phones work
in Ireland and Northern
Ireland; some North
American (non-GSM)
phones don't. Check with
your provider. Prepaid
SIM cards cost from €10.

Time
Western European Time
(UTC/GMT November
to March; plus one hour
April to October).

When to Go

Belfast

Galway
GO May–Sep

Dublin
GO year-round,
lots of indoor
attractions

Kerry
GO May–Sep

Cork
GO May–Sep

High Season
(Jun–mid-Sep)

➡ Weather at its
best.

➡ Accommodation
rates at their highest
(especially in
August).

➡ Tourist peak
in Dublin, Kerry,
southern and
western coasts.

Shoulder
(Easter–May,
mid-Sep–Oct)

➡ Weather often
good: sun and rain
in May.

➡ 'Indian summers'
and often warm in
September.

➡ Summer crowds
and accommodation
rates drop off.

Low Season
(Nov–Feb)

➡ Reduced opening
hours from October
to Easter; some
destinations close.

➡ Cold and wet
weather throughout
the country; fog can
reduce visibility.

➡ Big city
attractions operate
as normal.

Useful Websites

Entertainment Ireland (www.entertainment.ie) Country-wide listings for every kind of entertainment.

Failte Ireland (www.discoverireland.ie) Official tourist board website – practical info and a huge accommodation database.

Lonely Planet (www.lonelyplanet.com/ireland) Destination information, hotel bookings, traveller forum and more

Important Numbers

Include area codes only when dialling from outside the area or from a mobile phone. Drop the initial 0 when dialling from abroad.

Country code	☑ +353 Republic of Ireland; ☑ +44 Northern Ireland
International access code	☑ 00
Emergency (police, fire, ambulance)	☑ 999

Exchange Rates

The Republic of Ireland uses the euro.

Australia	A$1	€0.67
Canada	C$1	€0.68
Japan	Y100	€0.79
New Zealand	NZ$1	€0.64
UK	£1	€1.14
USA	US$1	€0.88

For current exchange rates see www.xe.com.

Daily Costs

Budget: Less than €80

➡ Dorm bed: €12–20

➡ Cheap meal in cafe or pub: €8–15

➡ Inter-city bus travel (200km trip): €12–25

➡ Pint: €5–6.50 (more expensive in cities)

Midrange: €80–150

➡ Double room in hotel or B&B: €80–180 (more expensive in Dublin)

➡ Main course in midrange restaurant: €15–30

➡ Car rental (per day): from €30

➡ Three-hour train journey: €60

Top end: More than €150

➡ Four-star hotel stay: from €200

➡ Three-course meal in good restaurant: around €70

➡ Top round of golf (midweek): from €100

Opening Hours

Banks 10am–4pm Monday to Friday (to 5pm Thursday)

Pubs 10.30am–11.30pm Monday to Thursday, 10.30am to 12.30am Friday and Saturday, noon to 11pm Sunday (30 minutes 'drinking up' time allowed); closed Christmas Day and Good Friday

Restaurants Noon–10.30pm; many close one day of the week

Shops 9.30am–6pm Monday to Saturday (to 8pm Thursday in cities), noon to 6pm Sunday

Arriving in Ireland

Dublin Airport Private coaches run every 10 to 15 minutes to the city centre (€7). Taxis take 30 to 45 minutes and cost €20 to €25.

Dun Laoghaire Ferry Port Public bus takes around 45 minutes to the centre of Dublin; DART (suburban rail) takes about 25 minutes. Both cost €3.25.

Dublin Port Terminal Buses are timed to coincide with arrivals and departures; costs €3 to the city centre.

Getting Around

Transport in Ireland is efficient and reasonably priced to and from major urban centres; smaller towns and villages along those routes are well served. Service to destinations not on major routes is less frequent and often impractical.

Car The most convenient way to explore Ireland's every nook and cranny. Cars can be hired in every major town and city; drive on the left.

Bus An extensive network of public and private buses make them the most cost-effective way to get around; there's service to and from most inhabited areas.

Bicycle Dublin operates a bike-share scheme with over 100 stations spread throughout the city.

Train A limited (and expensive) network links Dublin to all major urban centres, including Belfast in Northern Ireland.

For much more on **getting around**, see p694

First Time Ireland

For more information, see Survival Guide (p683)

Checklist

➡ Make sure your passport is valid for at least six months past your arrival date

➡ Make all necessary bookings (accommodation, events and travel)

➡ Check the airline baggage restrictions

➡ Inform your debit-/credit-card company

➡ Arrange appropriate travel insurance

➡ Check if your mobile phone is compatible

What to Pack

➡ Good walking shoes, as there's plenty of good walking to do

➡ Raincoat – you will undoubtedly need it

➡ UK/Ireland electrical adapter

➡ Finely honed sense of humour

➡ A hollow leg – all that beer has to go somewhere

➡ Irish-themed Spotify playlist

Top Tips for Your Trip

➡ Quality rather than quantity should be your goal: instead of a hair-raising race to see everything, pick a handful of destinations and give yourself time to linger. The most memorable experiences in Ireland are often the ones where you're doing very little at all.

➡ If you're driving, get off the main roads when you can: some of Ireland's most stunning scenery is best enjoyed on secondary or tertiary roads that wind their narrow way through standout photo ops.

➡ Make the effort to greet the locals: the best experiences are to be had courtesy of the Irish themselves, whose helpfulness, friendliness and sense of fun has not been overexaggerated.

What to Wear

You can wear pretty much whatever you want: smart casual is the most you'll need for fancy dinners, the theatre or the concert hall. Irish summers are warm but rarely hot, so you'll want something extra when the temperatures cool, especially in the evening. Ultimately the ever-changeable weather will determine your outfits, but a light waterproof jacket should never be beyond reach for the almost inevitable rain.

Sleeping

From basic hostels to five-star hotels, you'll find every range of accommodation in Ireland. Advance bookings are generally recommended and an absolute necessity during the busy holiday period.

Hotels From chain hotels with comfortable digs to Norman castles with rainfall shower rooms and wi-fi – with prices to match.

B&Bs From a bedroom in a private home to a luxurious Georgian townhouse, the ubiquitous B&B is the bedrock of Irish accommodation.

Hostels Every major town and city has a selection of hostels, with clean dorms and wi-fi – some have laundry and kitchen facilities.

Money

ATMs are found pretty much everywhere. They're all linked to the main international money systems, allowing you to withdraw money with your own card, but be sure to check with your bank before you travel.

Credit and debit cards can be used almost everywhere except for some rural B&Bs that only accept cash. Make sure bars or restaurants will accept cards before you order. The most popular are Visa and MasterCard; American Express is only accepted by the major chains, and virtually no one will accept Diners or JCB. Chip-and-PIN is the norm for card transactions – only a few places will accept a signature.

If you don't want to rely on plastic, banks, post offices and some of the larger hotels will change cash and travellers cheques.

Bargaining

Ireland doesn't do bargaining – unless you're buying a horse.

Tipping

Hotels €1/£1 per bag is standard; tip cleaning staff at your discretion.

Pubs Not expected unless table service is provided, then €1/£1 for a round of drinks.

Restaurants For decent service 10%; up to 15% in more expensive places.

Taxis Tip 10% or round up fare to nearest euro/pound.

Toilet Attendants Loose change; no more than €0.50/50p.

Pints of Guinness, O'Donoghue's pub (p123),

Etiquette

Although largely informal in their everyday dealings, the Irish do observe some (unspoken) rules of etiquette.

Greetings Shake hands with men, women and children when meeting for the first time and when saying goodbye. The Irish expect a firm handshake with eye contact. Female friends are greeted with a single (air) kiss.

Conversation Generally friendly but often reserved, the Irish avoid conversations that might embarrass. They are very mistrustful of 'oversharers'.

Round System The Irish generally take it in turns to buy a 'round' of drinks for the whole group and everyone is expected to take part. The next round should always be bought before the first round is drunk.

Eating

Booking ahead is recommended in cities and larger towns; same-day reservations are usually fine except for top-end restaurants – book those two weeks in advance.

Restaurants From cheap cafes to Michelin-starred feasts, covering every imaginable cuisine.

Cafes Open during the daytime (rarely at night), cafes are good for all-day breakfasts, sandwiches and basic dishes.

Pubs Pub grub ranges from toasted sandwiches to carefully crafted dishes as good as any you'll find in a restaurant.

➡ **Hotels** All hotel restaurants accept nonguests. They're a popular option in rural Ireland.

What's New

Ireland's Ancient East

The second major tourism initiative (after the Wild Atlantic Way) was officially launched in 2016, exploring 5000 years of history and heritage across 13 counties along the east coast and midlands.

Medieval Mile Museum

A former church has been transformed into this impressive celebration of Kilkenny's history, with exhibits ranging from 13th-century grave slabs to an interactive map of the medieval city. (p201)

Waterford Greenway

Running for 46km along a disused railway line between Waterford city and Dungarvan, this all-abilities cycling trail wends its way through tunnels, over viaducts and along the scenic West Waterford coastline. (p187)

Limerick Food Scene

The city of Limerick is having something of a 'foodie moment', with a fine crop of new restaurants, a thriving farmers market, and a lunchtime food truck market on the boardwalk overlooking the River Shannon. (p309)

Seamus Heaney Home Place

An excellent new museum and arts centre dedicated to Seamus Heaney, located in the poet's home town of Bellaghy, northeast of Lough Neagh in south County Londonderry. (p632)

Patrick Pearse's Cottage

A state-of-the-art visitor centre opened in 2016 in a small thatched cottage by the side of a remote lake in Connemara, which was used by the poet and patriot as a refuge where he could write poems and ruminate on Ireland's fortunes. (p389)

The Gin Craze

Ireland is on trend and has also cottoned on to the gin trend – bars have created gin libraries and put on gin tasting nights, and there are a couple of new gin distilleries, including one just outside Drogheda, County Louth. (p517)

Kells Bay House & Gardens

Ireland's longest rope bridge has recently been installed at this hunting lodge in County Kerry, a 33.5m stretch over a river at a height of 11m. (p276)

Rathlin West Light Seabird Centre

This 1919 lighthouse on Rathlin Island in County Antrim has recently opened a centre operated by the Royal Society for the Protection of Birds for the observation of the island's famous puffin colonies. (p626)

Finn Lough Bubble Domes

New transparent bubble domes have been installed at this County Fermanagh resort for that perfect view of the night sky...from the comfort of your bed. (p644)

For more recommendations and reviews, see lonelyplanet.com/ireland

If You Like...

Traditional Pubs

Everybody's got their favourite, so picking the best ones is a futile exercise. What can be done, however, is to select a handful that won't disappoint you, especially if you're looking for a traditional pub in the classic mould.

Blakes of the Hollow Ulster's best pint of Guinness in a Victorian classic. (p640)

John Benny's Stone slab floor, memorabilia on the walls and rocking trad sessions in this Dingle pub most nights. (p291)

McCarthy's A pub, restaurant and undertakers, all in one, in Fethard. (p323)

Tigh Neachtain In Galway, one of Ireland's best-known traditional pubs. (p371)

John Mulligan's The most famous of the capital's traditional pubs and a star of film and TV – where it usually plays itself. (p121)

Vaughan's Pub Superb bar in Kilfenora with outstanding reputation for trad music. (p353)

Great Views

Irish scenery is among the most spectacular in Europe, with breathtaking views and stunning landscapes throughout the whole country. There are the famous spots, of course, but they're not alone.

Binevenagh Lake Spectacular views over Lough Foyle, Donegal and the Sperrin Mountains from the cliff top at the height of Bishop's Rd. (p613)

Kilkee Cliffs Jaw-dropping views of soaring cliffs that aren't the Cliffs of Moher. (p338)

Powerscourt Estate The view of the Sugarloaf from the entrance road to this Palladian mansion is one of the best along the east coast. (p142)

Connor Pass Stand at the top of the 456m pass through the mountains of the Dingle Peninsula and inhale the views of the valley below. (p295)

Poisoned Glen The views down this Donegal valley are breathtaking; the final touch is the ruined church at the foot of the glen. (p454)

Priest's Leap A scenic mountain pass near the Beara Peninsula with sensational views of Bantry Bay and its eponymous town. (p248)

Sky Road Astonishing views over the sea from this dramatic coastal road just outside Clifden in Connemara. (p391)

Ancient Ruins

Thanks to the pre-Celts, Celts and early Christians, ancient and monastic sites are a feature of the Irish landscape. Thanks to the Vikings and Henry VIII, many of these are ruins, but no less impressive.

Glendalough The ruins of a once-powerful monastic city in tranquil Wicklow surroundings. (p148)

Brú na Bóinne Europe's most impressive Neolithic burial site. (p501)

Clonmacnoise Ireland's finest monastic site. (p492)

Athassel Priory Sublime and haunting ecclesiastical ruin. (p318)

Carrowkeel Megalithic cemetery and majestic views. (p430)

Athenry A magnificent castle, Dominican priory, an original market cross and lengthy sections of town walls. (p399)

Devenish Island Ruins of an Augustinian monastery and near-perfect round tower on the biggest island in Lough Erne. (p642)

Dun Aengus Stunning Stone Age fort perched perilously on Inishmore's cliffs in the Aran Islands. (p375)

Literary Corners

Four Nobel laureates for literature are just the highlight of a rich literary tradition. Ireland is one of the English-speaking world's most notable heavyweights of the written word, a tradition that continues to thrive through contemporary writers and literary festivals.

Cape Clear Island International Storytelling Festival The storytelling tradition is kept alive by tales tall and long from all over the world. (p242)

Seamus Heaney Home Place New museum and arts centre in Heaney's home town of Bellaghy, County Londonderry. (p632)

Cúirt International Festival of Literature Galway attracts writers from far and wide to its April literary showcase. (p365)

Dublin Literary Pub Crawl A fine selection of literary tours take full advantage of the city's rich literary reputation. (p100)

Listowel Writers' Week The Irish literary festival, held in June in the home town of John B Keane. (p301)

Town of Books Festival The Kilkenny town of Graiguenamanagh aspires to be Ireland's answer to Hay-on-Wye with this annual festival. (p210)

Traditional Music

Western Europe's most vibrant folk music is kept alive by musicians who ply their craft (and are plied with drink) in impromptu and organised sessions in pubs and music houses throughout the country; even the 'strictly for tourists' stuff will feature excellent performances.

PHB.CZ (RICHARD SEMIK)/SHUTTERSTOCK ©

PHB.CZ (RICHARD SEMIK)/SHUTTERSTOCK ©

Top: Ulster American Folk Park (p648), County Tyrone

Bottom: Powerscourt Estate (p142), County Wicklow

An Droichead Excellent music sessions at a Belfast arts centre dedicated to Irish culture. (p566)

Matt Molloy's The Chieftain's fife player owns this Westport pub where the live *céilidh* (session of traditional music and dancing) kicks off at 9pm nightly. (p412)

Miltown Malbay Every pub in this County Clare town features outstanding Irish trad sessions. (p341)

Tig Cóilí Galway's best trad sessions are held in a pub whose name means 'house of music'. (p371)

Marine Bar Wonderful music nightly during summer months at this 200-year-old pub on the Ring Peninsula. (p189)

Cobblestone The nightly sessions in this Smithfield pub are the best in the capital. (p121)

Tracing Your Roots

Roughly 80 million people worldwide can claim to be part of, or descended from, the Irish diaspora, with about 41 million of those in the USA alone. Most major towns have a heritage centre with a genealogical service.

Genealogy Office Based in the National Library in Dublin, this is the place to start your search for your Irish ancestors. (p84)

PRONI (Public Record Office of Northern Ireland) Belfast's purpose-built centre is the place to go to track down your Ulster family history. (p559)

Cobh, The Queenstown Story Cobh's superb heritage museum houses a genealogy centre. (p226)

Dún na Sí Heritage Centre A folk park 16km east of Athlone with an associated genealogical centre attached. (p482)

Ulster American Folk Park Ulster's rich links with the USA are explored in one of Northern Ireland's best museums. (p648)

Rothe House & Garden An excellent genealogical service is housed in this 16th-century merchant's house in Kilkenny city. (p203)

Family Days Out

There are plenty of family-friendly activities across the country, from heritage museums to ziplines across a forest canopy.

Castle Ward Estate *Game of Thrones* was filmed at this National Trust property, which also has an adventure playground and farm animals. (p583)

Lough Key Forest Park This 142-hectare adventure playland includes a 300m-long canopy walk and an outdoor adventure playground. (p480)

Tayto Park Lots of fun for all the family, including Europe's largest wooden inverted roller-coaster, a zoo and a 5D cinema. (p510)

Great Western Greenway Flat and popular bike path from Westport to Achill with plenty of castles and sites to see along the way. (p413)

Fota Wildlife Park Huge outdoor zoo just outside Cork city with not a cage or fence in sight; the cheetah run is especially popular. (p225)

Tralee Bay Wetlands Centre When you're done learning about the habitats of this 300-hectare reserve, you can hop aboard a boat for the 15-minute safari ride. (p297)

Golf

There are over 400 courses spread throughout the island, but for a proper Irish golfing experience, tee it up on a links course by the sea.

Ballybunion Golf Club A perennial favourite with visiting celebrities and professionals – the course is as tough as the views are beautiful. (p301)

County Sligo Golf Course Stunning links on a peninsula in the shadow of Ben Bulben. (p428)

Lahinch Golf Club One of Ireland's most beloved links was laid out by Scottish soldiers in 1892. (p342)

Royal County Down Hallowed links designed by Old Tom Morris often rated as the best course in Ireland. (p584)

Royal Portrush A stunner that hosted the Open Championship in 1951 and will do so again in 2019. (p615)

Waterville Golf Links A world-class links with views to match. (p280)

Month by Month

February

Bad weather makes February the perfect month for indoor activities. Some museums launch new exhibits, and it's a good time to visit the major towns and cities.

✥ Audi Dublin International Film Festival

Most of Dublin's cinemas participate in the capital's film festival, a two-week showcase for films by Irish and international directors, which features local flicks, arty international films and advance releases of mainstream movies. (p101)

☆ Six Nations Rugby

The Irish national rugby team (www.irishrugby.

ie) plays its three home matches at the Aviva Stadium in the southern suburb of Ballsbridge. The season runs from February to April.

March

Spring is in the air, and the whole country is getting ready for arguably the world's most famous parade. Dublin's is the biggest, but every town in Ireland holds one.

✥ St Patrick's Day

Ireland erupts into one giant celebration on 17 March (www.stpatricks day.ie), but Dublin throws a five-day party around the parade (attended by around 600,000 people), with gigs and festivities that leave the city with a giant hangover.

April

The weather is getting better, the flowers are beginning to bloom and the festival season begins anew. Seasonal attractions start to open up around the middle of the month or at Easter.

☆ Circuit of Ireland International Rally

Northern Ireland's most prestigious rally car race – known locally as the 'Circuit' (www.circuitofireland. net) – sees over 130 competitors throttle and turn through some 550km of Northern Ireland and parts of the Republic over two days at Easter.

☆ Irish Grand National

Ireland loves horse racing, and the race that's loved the most is the Grand National, the showcase of the hunt season that takes place at Fairyhouse in County Meath on Easter Monday. (p126)

☆ World Irish Dancing Championships

There's far more to Irish dancing than *Riverdance*. Every April some 4500 competitors from all over the world gather to test their steps and skills against the very best. The location varies from year to year; see www.irishdancingorg.com.

May

The May Bank Holiday (on the first Monday) sees the first of the busy summer weekends as the Irish take to the roads to enjoy the budding good weather.

⚜ Cork International Choral Festival

One of Europe's premier choral festivals (www. corkchoral.ie), with the winners going on to the Fleischmann International Trophy Competition, is held over four days at the beginning of May.

☆ North West 200

Ireland's most famous road race is also the country's biggest outdoor sporting event; 150,000-plus people line the triangular route to cheer on some of the biggest names in motorcycle racing. Held in mid-May. (p614)

⚜ Fleadh Nua

The third week of May sees the cream of the traditional music crop come to Ennis, County Clare, for one of the country's most important festivals. (p326)

⚜ Cathedral Quarter Arts Festival

Belfast's Cathedral Quarter hosts a multidisciplinary arts festival, including drama, music, poetry and street theatre over 10 days at the beginning of the month. (p557)

⚜ Listowel Writers' Week

Well-known writers engaged in readings, seminars and storytelling are the attraction at the country's premier festival (www.writersweek.ie) for bibliophiles, which runs over five days in the County Kerry town of Listowel

at the end of the month. There's also poetry, music and drama.

June

The bank holiday at the beginning of the month sees the country spoilt for choice as to what to do. Weekend traffic gets busier as the weather gets better.

⚜ Cat Laughs Comedy Festival

Kilkenny gets very, very funny in early June (or sometimes late May) with the country's premier comedy festival, which draws comedians both known and unknown from the four corners of the globe. (p204)

⚜ Dublin Pride

Ireland's most important LGBTQI celebration sees two weeks of events, gigs, screenings and talks that culminate in a huge colourful parade through the capital. (p101)

☆ Ireland BikeFest Killarney

The country's largest gathering of motorcycle enthusiasts (www.irelandbike fest.com) takes place over the first weekend of the month in Killarney, where riders can then do a loop along the famous Wild Atlantic Way.

☆ Irish Derby

Wallets are packed and fancy hats donned for the best flat-race festival in the country (www.curragh. ie), run during the first week of the month.

⚜ Bloomsday

Edwardian dress and breakfast of 'the inner organs of beast and fowl' are but two of the elements of the Dublin festival celebrating 16 June, the day on which Joyce's *Ulysses* takes place; the real highlight is retracing Leopold Bloom's steps.

🏃 Mourne International Walking Festival

The last weekend of the month plays host to a walking festival (www. mournewalking.co.uk) in the Mourne Mountains of County Down, designated an Area of Outstanding Natural Beauty.

⚜ Cork Midsummer Festival

Cork city's largest celebration of the arts (www.cork midsummer.com) takes place over 10 days in mid-month at various venues throughout the city.

July

There isn't a weekend in the month that a major festival doesn't take place, while visitors to Galway will find that the city is in full swing for the entire month.

⚜ Willie Clancy Summer School

Inaugurated to celebrate the memory of a famed local piper, this exceptional festival of traditional music sees the world's best players show up for gigs, pub sessions and workshops over nine days in Miltown Malbay, County Clare. (p341)

★☆ Galway International Arts Festival

Music, drama and a host of artistic endeavours are on the menu at the most important arts festival in the country, which sees Galway go merriment mad for the last two weeks of the month. (p361)

☆ Galway Film Fleadh

Irish and international releases make up the program at one of the country's premier film festivals, held in early July. (p366)

☆ Longitude

A mini-Glastonbury in Dublin's Marlay Park, Longitude packs them in over three days in mid-July for a feast of EDM, nu-folk, rock and pop. In 2017 Stormzy, The Weeknd and Mumford & Sons were the headliners. (p101)

★☆ Killarney Summerfest

Killarney gets all folksy in early July for this festival (http://folkfestkillarney.com) featuring music, beards and flannel from all over Ireland and abroad, including performers from Britain, the USA and elsewhere.

August

Schools are closed, the sun is shining (or not!) and Ireland is in holiday mood. Seaside towns and tourist centres are at their busiest as the country makes the most of its time off.

★☆ Féile An Phobail

The name translates simply as the 'people's festival' and it is just that: Europe's largest community arts festival takes place on the Falls Rd in West Belfast over 10 days. (p557)

★☆ Fleadh Cheoil na hÉireann

The mother of all Irish music festivals (www.fleadh cheoil.ie), held at the end of the month, attracts in excess of 400,000 music-lovers and revellers to whichever town is playing host (for the last couple of years it's been Ennis, County Clare) – there's some great music amid the drinking.

☆ Galway Race Week

The biggest horse-racing festival west of the Shannon is not just about the horses; it's also a celebration of Irish culture, sporting gambles and elaborate hats. (p366)

★☆ Mary From Dungloe Festival

Ireland's second-most important beauty pageant takes place in Dungloe, County Donegal, at the beginning of the month – although it's an excuse for a giant party, the young women really do want to be crowned the year's 'Mary'. (p451)

★☆ Puck Fair

Ireland's oldest festival is also its quirkiest: crown a goat king and celebrate for three days. Strange idea, but a brilliant festival that takes place in Killorglin, County Kerry in mid-August. (p271)

★☆ Rose of Tralee

The country's biggest beauty pageant divides critics between those who see it as an embarrassing throwback to older days and those who see it as a throwback to older days. Wannabe Roses plucked from Irish communities throughout the world compete for the ultimate prize. (p299)

★☆ Kilkenny Arts Festival

One of Ireland's most important arts festivals brings musicians, artists, performers and writers to a variety of sites across Kilkenny city, including churches, castles, courtyards, townhouses and gardens. The 10-day event takes place in the middle of the month. (p204)

September

Summer may be over, but September weather can be surprisingly good, so it's often the ideal time to enjoy the last vestiges of the sun as the crowds dwindle.

✕ Galway International Oyster & Seafood Festival

Over the last weekend of the month Galway kicks off its oyster season with a festival celebrating the local catch. Music and beer have been the accompaniment since its inception in 1953. (p43)

✦ Dublin Fringe Festival

Upwards of 100 different performances take the stage, the street, the bar and the car in the fringe festival that is unquestionably more innovative than the main theatre festival that follows it. (p102)

☆ All-Ireland Finals

The second and fourth Sundays of the month see the finals of the hurling and Gaelic football championships respectively, with 80,000-plus crowds thronging into Dublin's Croke Park for the biggest sporting days of the year.

October

The weather starts to turn cold, so it's time to move the fun indoors again. The calendar is still packed with activities and distractions, especially over the last weekend of the month.

✦ Dublin Theatre Festival

The most prestigious theatre festival in the country sees new work and new versions of old work staged in theatres and venues throughout the capital. (p102)

✦ Wexford Opera Festival

Opera fans gather in the Wexford Opera House, the country's only theatre built for opera, to enjoy Ireland's premier lyric festival, which tends to eschew the big hits in favour of lesser-known works. (p169)

✦ Cork Jazz Festival

Ireland's best-known jazz festival sees Cork taken over by more than a thousand musicians and their multitude of fans during the last weekend of the month – even if some of the music sounds suspiciously like blues and rock. (p218)

✦ Belfast International Arts Festival

Northern Ireland's top arts festival attracts performers from all over the world for the second half of the month; on offer is everything from visual arts to dance. (p557)

December

Christmas dominates the calendar as the country prepares for the feast with frenzied shopping and after-work drinks with friends and family arrived home from abroad. On Christmas Day nothing is open.

✦ Christmas

This is a quiet affair in the countryside, though on 26 December (St Stephen's Day) the ancient custom of Wren Boys is re-enacted, most notably in Dingle, County Kerry, when groups of children dress up and go about singing hymns.

☆ Christmas Dip

A traditional Christmas Day swim at the Forty Foot in the Dublin suburb of Sandycove sees a group of very brave swimmers go for a 20m swim to the rocks and back.

Itineraries

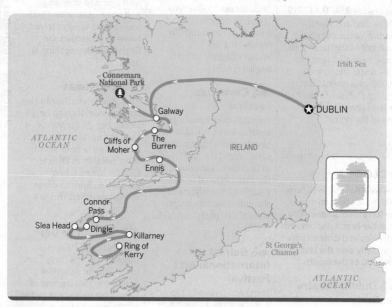

Ireland Highlights

This 300km tourist trail takes you past some of Ireland's most famous attractions and through spectacular countryside.

Start with a whistle-stop tour of **Dublin**, including visits to Trinity College and the **Book of Kells** as well as a sample of Guinness in its home town. The next day, head west to **Galway**, from where you should take a drive through stunning, brooding **Connemara National Park** (which can be driven in a nice loop) before heading south through the moonlike landscape of **The Burren**. Take a detour to the **Cliffs of Moher**, then head to **Ennis**, a good spot to enjoy a bit of traditional Irish music. Keep going south through the **Connor Pass** into County Kerry, stopping for a half-day in **Dingle** before setting out to visit its peninsula, taking in the views and prehistoric monuments of **Slea Head**. Via the ferry, continue on to **Killarney**, the perfect base from which to explore the famous **Ring of Kerry**, a much-trafficked 179km loop around the Iveragh Peninsula.

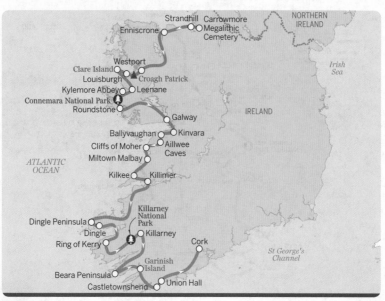

Best of the West

2 WEEKS

The west of Ireland is where you'll find the best scenery and the best traditional music pubs.

Start in County Sligo, where prehistory and panorama combine to wonderful effect at **Carrowmore Megalithic Cemetery**. Wind your way south along the coast, stopping at some of Ireland's best surf beaches like **Strandhill** and **Enniscrone**. Continue south to the pub-packed heritage town of **Westport**. Southwest of here is magnificent **Croagh Patrick**, worth a climb if only to feast your eyes from a height on island-studded Clew Bay. Go west to Louisburgh, from where you can head offshore to craggy **Clare Island** (home of the pirate queen Grace O'Malley), before turning south along the beautiful Doolough Valley to **Leenane**, situated on Ireland's only fjord. This is the northern gateway to **Connemara National Park**, which you can explore via the beautiful coastal route, passing Kylemore Abbey, venturing onto Clifden's scenic Sky Road and then winding your way around the coast through pretty **Roundstone**. Alternatively, you could savour the stunning wilderness of the inland route to **Galway**, where you should devote at least a day to exploring its colourful streets and wonderful pubs.

South of Galway, the fishing villages of **Kinvara** and **Ballyvaughan** are at the edge of the karst landscape of **The Burren**, home to all manner of flora and fauna, as well as attractions such as the ancient **Aillwee Cave** and the **Cliffs of Moher**. Going south, experience some of Ireland's traditional music by attending a session in one of the pubs of **Miltown Malbay**; beach-lovers should also opt for a stop in **Kilkee**, a favourite with surfers.

The easiest way to cross into County Kerry is via the ferry at **Killimer**. Take a day to explore the **Dingle Peninsula**, with its rich menu of ancient sites and stunning views, before overnighting in **Dingle** – one of the prettiest towns along the entire west coast. Take another day to explore the world-famous **Ring of Kerry**, ending in **Killarney National Park**, right on the edge of **Killarney** itself. Take the scenic route across the middle of the **Beara Peninsula** and make your way to the Italianate **Garinish Island**, with its exotic flowers. Then follow the coast through **Castletownshend** and the fishing village of **Union Hall** to the city of **Cork**.

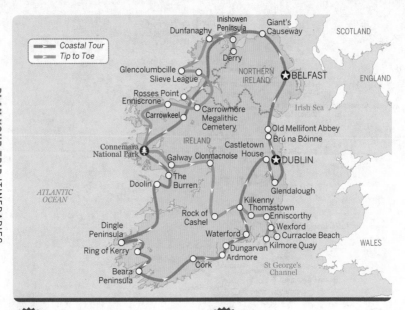

3 WEEKS Coastal Tour

This round-the-island tour takes in a big chunk of Ireland's major scenic and heritage highlights.

From **Dublin**, head north to the Neolithic necropolis at **Brú na Bóinne**. Continue on to the atmospheric **Old Mellifont Abbey** before crossing into Northern Ireland and heading to **Belfast**. Go northwest along the Antrim coast to the **Giant's Causeway**. Continue around the coastline and head south into Sligo to climb the Stone Age passage grave at **Carrowkeel** for views of Lough Arrow. Go southwest via **Connemara National Park**. Wonder at **The Burren** and check out traditional music in **Doolin** before crossing into County Kerry for music, scenery and heritage on the **Dingle Peninsula** and the **Ring of Kerry**. See gorgeous landscapes on the **Beara Peninsula**, then visit Ireland's second city, **Cork**. Discover County Waterford from seaside **Ardmore**, visit **Dungarvan** and its castle, and the Museum of Treasures in **Waterford**. Go north through medieval **Kilkenny** and then check out handsome **Castletown House** in County Kildare. Cut east to see the monastic site at **Glendalough**. Finally, head back to Dublin.

2 WEEKS Tip to Toe

The full range of Ireland – from north to south – is on the menu in this itinerary.

Begin in Northern Ireland's second city, **Derry**, walking the city walls and exploring the Bogside district. Cross into County Donegal and explore the **Inishowen Peninsula** before overnighting in **Dunfanaghy**. As you move down Donegal's coastline, visit the monastic ruins of **Glencolumbcille** and the sea cliffs at **Slieve League**. Cross into County Sligo and visit the **Carrowmore Megalithic Cemetery**. The next day, play a round of golf at the County Sligo Golf Course at **Rosses Point** or a seaweed bath in **Enniscrone**. You'll skirt the eastern edge of **Connemara National Park** as you travel south to **Galway**, from where you should strike out for **Clonmacnoise**. From here, move through the heart of the Midlands to another monastic gem, the **Rock of Cashel**. Medieval **Kilkenny** is only an hour away – visit its stunning castle before exploring nearby **Thomastown** and Jerpoint Abbey. Using **Wexford** as a base, explore **Curracloe Beach** and visit **Enniscorthy** and the excellent National 1798 Rebellion Centre. Or you could chill out and watch the fishermen draw in their lines in **Kilmore Quay**.

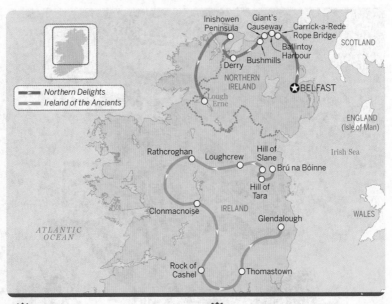

Northern Delights

1 WEEK

Explore the gorgeous landscapes and discover the fascinating history of this much-misunderstood province.

Start in **Belfast**, where you should visit the Titanic Experience and take a black-taxi tour, before heading north towards the Antrim Coast and on to the **Carrick-a-Rede Rope Bridge**. Head west towards the Unesco World Heritage–listed **Giant's Causeway**, a highlight of any trip to Northern Ireland; along the way, *Game of Thrones* fans can check out **Ballintoy Harbour**, which stood in for the Iron Islands' Lordsport Harbour in the TV series. The causeway coast finishes in the fascinating village of **Bushmills**, home to the famous distillery. **Derry** is worth a day – walk the city's walls and explore its more recent past in the Bogside district, and then cross the invisible border into the Republic by visiting the **Inishowen Peninsula** in County Donegal. Back in the North, finish your visit southeast in **Lough Erne**, taking in both White Island and the carved stones of Devenish Island.

Ireland of the Ancients

1 WEEK

Discover the majesty and mystery of Ireland's ancient history on this one-week route.

Begin at the stunning Neolithic tombs of Newgrange and Knowth in County Meath, in the heart of **Brú na Bóinne**. Nearby, stand at the top of the **Hill of Tara**, a site of immense folkloric significance and seat of the high kings of Ireland until the 11th century. Across the plain is the **Hill of Slane**, where St Patrick lit a fire in 433 to proclaim Christianity throughout the land. To the west is the Neolithic monument of **Loughcrew** – a quieter alternative to Brú na Bóinne. Keep going west to County Roscommon. Just outside Tulsk village is **Rathcroghan**, the most important Celtic site in Europe. Head south to **Clonmacnoise**, the 6th-century monastic site in County Offaly, then continue through the heart of the country to the impressive **Rock of Cashel** in County Tipperary. Turn east and head through County Kilkenny, stopping at the Cistercian Jerpoint Abbey, at the pretty village of **Thomastown**. From here, travel northeast to Wicklow and magnificent **Glendalough**, where the substantial remains of a monastic settlement linger by two beautiful lakes.

Top: Clonmacnoise (p492), County Offaly

Bottom: Connor Pass (p295), County Kerry

Plan Your Trip
The Great Outdoors

There's no better way of experiencing this wildly beautiful country than by exploring its varied landscapes – and the rewards can be spectacular. From majestic craggy mountains to lush lakeside woods, from broad sandy beaches to blankets of wild bog stretching as far as the eye can see, Ireland's great outdoors will never disappoint.

Walking

Gentle hills, rocky ridges, wild moorlands, spectacular sea cliffs, remote islands, warm hospitality and the gloriously unpredictable weather – all are part of the wonderful experience of exploring Ireland on foot. There is something for everyone, from post-prandial strolls to challenging 1000m peaks.

What to Bring

For short walks on waymarked trails all you will need is comfortable footwear, a rain jacket and some food and water.

Hikers venturing further into Ireland's hills and bogs should be properly equipped and cautious, as the weather can become vicious at any time of year.

➡ After rain, peaty soil can become boggy, so always wear stout shoes or boots and carry good waterproofs and extra food and drink.

➡ Always take a map and compass (and know how to use them). Don't depend on mobile phones (although carrying one with you is a good idea).

➡ Leave a note with your route and expected time of return with a trusted person (either at your accommodation, or via email or text to a friend or family member), and let them know when you have returned safely.

Top Outdoor Tips

Best Time to Go

May, June and September are the best months for hiking and biking – best chance of dry weather and less chance of midges.

Best Outdoor Experiences

Hike the Wicklow Way (Wicklow), climb Carrauntoohil (Kerry), cycle the Great Western Greenway (Mayo), mountain-bike at Davagh Forest (Tyrone), tee off at Royal Portrush (Antrim), sea kayak in Lough Hyne (Cork) and canoe the Lough Erne Canoe Trail (Fermanagh).

Essential Hill-Walking Gear

Good waterproofs, spare warm clothing, map and compass, mobile phone (but don't rely on it), first-aid kit, head torch, whistle (for emergencies), spare food and drink.

Safety Checklist

Check the weather forecast first, let someone know your plans, set your pace and objective to suit the slowest member of your party, and don't be afraid to turn back if it's too difficult.

Walking Guides & Maps

There are several good hiking guidebooks that cover Ireland, notably the Collins Press (www.collinspress.ie) series of walking guides.

The Ordnance Survey of Ireland (www.ose.ie) and the Ordnance Survey of Northern Ireland (www.nidirect.gov.uk/ordnance-survey-of-northern-ireland) cover the entire island with their 1:50,000 *Discovery/Discoverer* series (€8.99/£6.50 per sheet). There are also more detailed 1:25,000 *Adventure/Activity* maps (€12.99/£7.80) covering popular areas such as MacGillicuddy's Reeks & Killarney National Park, the Wicklow Mountains, the Mournes and the Causeway Coast.

Maps produced specifically for walkers include the following:

Harveys Superwalker (www.harveymaps.co.uk) Waterproof 1:30,000 hill-walking maps covering Connemara, the Mournes, the Wicklow Mountains and MacGillicuddy's Reeks.

EastWest Mapping (www.eastwestmapping.ie) Walkers' maps of the Wicklow Mountains, the Wicklow Way and the Blackstairs Mountains & Barrow Valley.

Access to the Countryside

Unlike Scotland, England and Wales (and most other European countries) where there are public rights of way and/or a public right of access to most areas of uncultivated land, walkers and cyclists in Ireland have no rights of access to privately owned land, not even on wild moorland and mountain (unless it is part of a national park).

The absence of a legal framework has led to a rather fraught situation in recent years as the popularity of walking, mountaineering and off-road biking has increased, and numerous disputes have blown up across the country, forcing the closure or re-routing of some traditional walking routes.

Access has been negotiated with landowners for many national trails and waymarked walks (disputes over access is why many of these trails follow public roads for long distances). However, you will occasionally come across locked gates, barbed wire fences or 'no walkers allowed' signs – these are legal and must be obeyed.

For more information on access rights and responsible walking see the following:

Keep Ireland Open (www.keepirelandopen.org) Voluntary body campaigning for rights of access to the countryside.

Leave No Trace (www.leavenotraceireland.org) Educational charity promoting responsible use of the outdoors.

Mountaineering Ireland (www.mountaineering.ie) Good information and advice on the Access Policy page.

Where to Walk

For a small country, Ireland is packed with choice – from seaside ambles to long-distance treks in mountain ranges.

Day Walks

You can take a leisurely day hike in just about any part of Ireland. Some suggestions:

Barrow Towpath (p196) Along the River Barrow in Counties Carlow and Kilkenny, pleasant walks can

---

TOP FIVE IRISH HILL WALKS

What Ireland's mountains lack in height (its tallest peak is a meagre 1040m) they more than make up for in stunning scenery and superb hill-walking opportunities.

Carrauntoohil (1040m; MacGillicuddy's Reeks, County Kerry) The ascent of Ireland's highest summit involves scrambling and challenging navigation; inexperienced hill walkers should hire a guide.

Slieve Donard (853m; Mourne Mountains, County Down) Northern Ireland's highest hill is a straightforward climb; its near-neighbour Slieve Binnian is more interesting.

Errigal Mountain (752m; County Donegal) This pyramidal quartzite peak is one of Ireland's shapeliest hills.

Twelve Bens (729m; County Galway) Though small in stature, Connemara's craggy hills offer some of Ireland's toughest terrain. The Glencoaghan Horseshoe is often cited as the country's finest hill-walk.

Mt Brandon (951m; County Kerry) The highest peak on the Dingle Peninsula has rugged trails that yield jaw-droppingly spectacular views.

be had along the towpath from Borris to Graiguena-managh and on to St Mullins.

Glendalough (p150) The wooded trails around this ancient monastic site in County Wicklow lure many a traveller from nearby Dublin for a few hours' rambling.

Lough Key Forest Park (p480) The woods around this lake in County Roscommon have a wonderful canopied trail.

Sky Road (p391) In County Galway, Clifden's Sky Road yields views of the Connemara coast; it's suitable for walking or cycling.

South Leinster Way (p210) The prettiest section of this waymarked way is a 13km hike between the charming villages of Graiguenamanagh and Inistioge in County Kilkenny.

Brandon Way (p210) Not to be confused with Mt Brandon in County Kerry, the smaller Brandon Hill (516m) in County Kilkenny has a path that wends up to the summit from woodlands and moorlands along the River Barrow.

Killarney National Park (p265) Superb short walks on the shores of Lough Leane in County Kerry, plus the slightly longer Muckross Lake Loop.

Killary Harbour (p397) Scenic walks along the shore of this long, fjord-like inlet of the sea in County Galway.

Glen of Aherlow (p315) Fine walking amid lush woodland and low hills in County Tipperary with grand views towards the high Galtee Mountains.

Fair Head (p627) Easy paths lead to the top of huge basalt sea cliffs in county Antrim, with a panorama that takes in Rathlin Island and the Scottish coast.

Coastal Trails

Ireland's coastlines are naturally conducive to long and reflective walks with or without shoes on. Here are five to get you started:

Arranmore Way (p453; County Donegal) This 14km trail makes a circuit of the wild seacliff scenery of this rocky island off the Donegal coast.

Causeway Coast Way (www.walkni.com; County Antrim) A waymarked trail that follows Antrim's north coast. Particularly spectacular is the final 16.5km of this waymarked way, from Carrick-a-Rede to the Giant's Causeway.

Wexford Coastal Walk (County Wexford) Follow 221km of trails overlooking vast sandy beaches, bird-haunted backwaters and the bones of old shipwrecks.

Sheep's Head Lighthouse (p246; County Cork) A superb short walk leads from the road-end to one of the country's most spectacularly sited lighthouses.

Tory Way (p459; County Donegal) A 12km looped trail around the rocky coast of Tory Island

Waymarked Trails

The opening of the 1000km Ulster Way in the 1970s followed by the Wicklow Way in 1982 prompted the establishment of a network of 44 long-distance walking trails that total over 5000km in length. Though many of these would take several days, or even weeks, to complete, you can easily walk shorter sections of each trail as you see fit.

Our top 10 of Ireland's long-distance trails:

Barrow Way A 114km wander through some of Ireland's loveliest riverside scenery between Lowtown in County Kildare and St Mullins in County Carlow.

Beara Way A moderately easy loop of 196km that follows historic routes and tracks on a stunning peninsula in West Cork.

Burren Way This 123km walk takes in County Clare's unique rocky landscape, the Cliffs of Moher and the musical town of Doolin.

Cavan Way Impressive topographic variety is packed into this short (26km) route, taking in bogs, Stone Age monuments and the source of the River Shannon.

Dingle Way A popular 168km route in County Kerry that loops around one of Ireland's most beautiful peninsulas.

East Munster Way Starting in County Tipperary and ending up in County Waterford, a 70km walk through forest and open moorland, and along the towpath of the River Suir.

Kerry Way A 214km route that takes in Killarney National park, the spectacular Macgillycuddy's Reeks and the Ring of Kerry coast.

Sheep's Head Way Sweeping seascapes and splendid isolation mark out this 88km off-the-beaten-track peninsular circuit.

Ulster Way A route totalling 1000km, making a circuit around the six counties of Northern Ireland and Donegal. It can easily be broken down into smaller sections.

Wicklow Way Ireland's most popular walking trail is this 132km route, which starts in southern Dublin and ends in Clonegal in County Carlow.

Golf

With over 400 courses dotted around the island, golf is one of Ireland's most popular pastimes and – for the most part – lacks the exclusivity that comes with the game in other parts of the world. There are plenty of parkland courses, but the more memorable golf experiences are to be had on a seaside links – the Irish coastline is home to 30% of the world's links courses.

Most golf courses are privately owned, but all welcome non-member bookings and walk-ins: to avoid disappointment, book the better-known courses in advance. For the top courses, expect to pay €100 to €250 or more per round; lesser-known courses charge as little as €25, depending on when you play. Some courses will insist that you have a registered handicap from your home country. Most courses will also rents out clubs, but they're not usually very good.

A great option is to rent a customised set of clubs at Dublin or Cork airport through www.clubstohire.com, which you can drop back at the airport when you leave.

Our favourite courses include:

Ballybunion Golf Club (p301), County Kerry

Royal Portrush Golf Club (p615), County Londonderry

County Sligo Golf Course (p428), County Sligo

Portmarnock Golf Club (p134), County Dublin

Waterville Golf Links (p280), County Kerry

Lahinch Golf Club (p342), County Clare

Killeen Castle (www.killeencastle.com; Dunsany, Co Meath; green fee €50-90), County Meath

For more information, check out **Golf Ireland** (www.golf.discoverireland.ie), or the **Golfing Union of Ireland** (www.golfnet.ie), both of which offer booking services.

There are specials and discounted green fees available throughout the year: a good online resource is www.teetimes.ie, where you can book heavily discounted green fees at dozens of courses throughout the country.

MIDGES

Midges are tiny, 2mm-long blood-sucking flies that appear in huge swarms in summer, and can completely ruin a holiday if you're not prepared to deal with them.

They proliferate from late May to mid-September, but especially mid-June to mid-August – which unfortunately coincides with the main tourist season – and are most common in the western and northern parts of Ireland, especially in boggy areas such as Connemara and Donegal.

Midges are at their worst during the twilight hours, and on still, overcast days – strong winds and bright sunshine tend to discourage them. The only way to combat them is to cover up, particularly in the evening. Wear long-sleeved, light-coloured clothing (midges are attracted to dark colours) and, most importantly, use a reliable insect repellent.

Cycling

Ireland has a lot to offer the cycle tourist, not least in the huge network of minor roads that criss-cross even the wildest parts of the island. Take along a good map and a spirit of adventure (and decent waterproofs, of course), and you can clock up hundreds of kilometres of happy exploration.

Several operators offer guided and self-guided cycling tours in Ireland, including the following:

Iron Donkey (www.irondonkey.com)

Ireland by Bike (www.irelandbybike.com)

Where to Cycle

Great Western Greenway (p413) This 42km-long, mostly off-road and hugely popular cycleway stretches from Westport to Achill Island in County Mayo.

Killarney National Park (p265) The park offers an adventurous boat-and-bike adventure via the lakes of Killarney and up through the impressive Gap of Dunloe.

Kingfisher Trail (p639) A waymarked, long-distance cycling trail stretching some 370km along the back roads of Counties Fermanagh, Leitrim, Cavan and Monaghan.

Clifden Cycle Hub The 'capital' of Connemara in County Galway is the focus of four looped cycle routes, ranging from 16km to 40km in length, including the scenic Sky Road.

Waterford Greenway (p187) A 46km, all-abilities trail that opened in in 2017 along the lines of a railway track between Waterford city and Dungarvan.

Mountain Biking

The lack of a legal right of access to private land has meant that off-road biking in Ireland lags behind the UK. That said, there are some excellent purpose-built trail centres, mostly in state forest parks on both sides of the border.

In many areas, local riders quietly work away at their own network of self-built trails; the local bike shop is a great source of information on these.

For more details, check out the following:

Mountain Bike NI (www.mountainbikeni.com) Full details of MTB centres in Northern Ireland.

TrailBadger (www.trailbadger.com) Useful database of mountain-bike trails in Ireland.

Biking.ie (www.biking.ie) Excellent resource including trail details, rentals and tours in the Republic.

Top MTB Trail Centres

Davagh Forest (p648) Forest trails for beginners, rock slabs and drop-offs for experts, in the heart of County Tyrone.

Rostrevor (p588) With a thigh-crunching 27km red trail and a terrifying 19km black, Rostrevor in County Down is reckoned by some to offer the best mountain-biking in Ireland.

Ballyhoura (www.trailriders.ie) This MTB centre in County Limerick has the biggest network of trails in the country, ranging from green to black, with the longest at more than 50km.

Ballinastoe (www.coillteoutdoors.ie) This trail centre on the edge of the Wicklow Mountains south of Dublin has a superbly flowing, 14km blue trail. There are plenty more trails to explore in the nearby hills.

Bike Park Ireland (http://bikeparkireland.ie) This purpose-built centre in County Tipperary has an uplift service to the top of the hill, and downhill trails for all levels of rider.

Ticknock MTB (www.dublinmountains.ie; Ticknock Forest, Sandyford) (www.dublinmountains.ie) A 13km-long network of purpose-built single track

trails and forest roads in the Dublin Mountains offering varying degrees of gradient and difficulty. Access is at the bottom of Three Rock Mountain.

Water Sports
Surfing & Windsurfing

Surfing is all the rage on the coast, especially in the west. The most popular spots include the following:

County Donegal Bundoran, the unofficial capital of Irish surfing, hosts the Irish national championships in April. Along the coast there are at least half a dozen top-rated spots for beginners and advanced surfers. Windsurfing and kitesurfing are equally popular around Port-na-Blagh.

County Sligo Easkey and Strandhill are famous for their year-round surf, and have facilities for travellers who seek room and board (with the room being optional).

County Clare Nice breaks at Kilkee, Lahinch and Fanore.

County Waterford Tramore Beach is a coastal resort that's home to Ireland's largest surf school.

County Kerry Surfers flock to massive Inch Strand for its nicely sized, well-paced waves. Brandon Bay and Ballybunion are also top spots.

County Antrim The beaches around Portrush afford good surfing and body-surfing. The swells are highest and the water warmest in September and October.

Canoeing & Sea Kayaking

Ireland's long, indented coastline provides some of the finest sea kayaking in the world. There are sheltered inlets ideal for beginners, long and exciting coastal and island tours, and gnarly tidal passages that will challenge even the most expert paddler, all amid spectacular scenery and wildlife – encounters with seals, dolphins and even whales are relatively common. The **Irish Sea Kayaking Association** (www.iska.ie) lists providers of kayak tours and courses.

The country's inland lakes and waterways offer excellent Canadian canoeing. Northern Ireland has established a network of official **canoe trails** (www.canoeni.com), with infrastructure that includes access points, information boards, toilets and campsites. South of the border, waterways such as the Shannon, Barrow and Grand Canal (see www.waterwaysireland.org) all offer long-distance canoe touring possibilities.

Scuba Diving

Ireland's west coast has some of the best scuba diving in Europe. The best period for diving is roughly March to October, when visibility averages more than 12m, but can increase to 30m on good days.

Top dive locations include Kilkee (Mayo), Baltimore (Cork), Castlegregory (Kerry) and Arranmore Island and Rosguill (Donegal).

For more details about diving, contact Comhairle Fó-Thuinn (CFT), also known as the **Irish Underwater Council** (www.diving.ie); it publishes the dive magazine *SubSea* (available online).

Coasteering

If sometimes a simple clifftop walk doesn't cut the mustard, then coasteering might appeal. It's like mountaineering, but instead of going up a mountain, you go sideways along a coast – a steep and rocky coast – with waves breaking around your feet. And if the rock gets too steep, no problem – you jump in and start swimming. Coasteering centres provide wetsuits, helmets and buoyancy aids; you provide an old pair of training shoes and a sense of adventure.

Providers include the following:

Coasteering Ireland (www.coasteering-ireland.com) Operates mostly in the Beara Peninsula (Cork) and the Ring of Kerry.

Coasteering NI (www.coasteeringni.co.uk) Operates in County Antrim near the Giant's Causeway, and at Glencolumbkille in Donegal.

Fishing

Fishing – whether in sea, lough or river – is one of Ireland's most popular pastimes. Ireland is justly famous for its salmon, sea trout and brown trout fishing, and for its superb sea angling.

Top Irish angling experiences:

➡ Fly fishing for brown trout on the big limestone loughs of Corrib and Mask (County Galway); the annual mayfly hatch here attracts thousands of anglers from all over the world.

➡ Sea trout fishing on Lough Currane in County Kerry, one of the best sea trout fisheries in all of Britain and Ireland.

➡ Fishing for salmon on the Blackwater (Cork), Laune (Kerry) or Roe (Londonderry), three of Ireland's top salmon rivers.

➡ Shore fishing for sea bass in the southwest, or boat fishing for blue shark out of Kinsale – Ireland has some of Europe's finest sea angling.

The books *Rivers of Ireland* and *Loughs of Ireland* by Peter O'Reilly provide a comprehensive guide to fishing for trout and salmon in both Northern Ireland and the Republic of Ireland.

Permits & Rod Licences

Neither a permit nor a licence is needed for sea angling.

Permits Fishing for brown trout in many of Ireland's most famous loughs, including Corrib, Mask and the Killarney lakes, is free. However, most loughs and rivers require a permit (ask at the local hotel or tackle shop). Day ticket prices range from €3 to €20.

Rod licences In addition to a permit, a rod licence is required for all freshwater fishing in Northern Ireland (three days/14 days £3.50/9). In the Republic, a rod licence is needed only for salmon and sea trout fishing (one day/three weeks €20/40). You can buy them from local tackle shops and from some tourist offices.

For more information, see www.fishinginireland.info.

Rock Climbing

Ireland's mountain ranges aren't high – Mt Carrantuohil in Kerry's Macgillycuddy's Reeks is the highest peak in Ireland at only 1040m – but they offer some excellent rock climbing, notably in the Mournes, the Reeks and around Glendalough in the Wicklow Mountains.

However, the cream of the country's climbing is on its superb sea cliffs – from Malin Beg in Donegal and the cliffs of Achill Island, to the soaring basalt columns of Fair Head and perfect limestone crags of the Burren. *Rock Climbing in Ireland* (2014; €25) by David Flanagan covers 400 of the country's best routes. For all other information, check out **Irish Climbing Online** (www.climbing.ie).

Plan Your Trip

Eat & Drink Like a Local

In the last couple of decades Ireland has 'rediscovered' its own native cuisine. A host of chefs and producers have led a foodie revolution that, at its heart, is about bringing to the table the kind of meals that have long been taken for granted on well-run Irish farms. This 'local food' movement has gone from strength to strength, with farmers markets showcasing local produce, and restaurants all over the country increasingly highlighting local sourcing of ingredients.

Food Experiences

Meals of a Lifetime

Restaurant Patrick Guilbaud (p111), Dublin

Finn's Table (p234), Kinsale, County Cork

Nash 19 (p219), Cork City

Campagne (p206), Kilkenny City

Wilde's at the Lodge (p406), Cong, County Mayo

Jacks' Coastguard Restaurant (p271), Cromane Peninsula, County Kerry

Olde Post Inn (p527), Butlersbridge, County Cavan

Restaurant 1826 Adare (p313), County Limerick

MacNean House & Restaurant (p528), County Cavan

Loam (p370), Galway City

Dare to Try

Ironically, while the Irish palate has become more adventurous, it is the old-fashioned Irish menu that features some fairly challenging dishes:

Black pudding Made from cooked pork blood, suet and other fillings; a ubiquitous part of an Irish cooked breakfast.

The Year in Food

April–June

Freshly picked fruit and vegetables, such as asparagus and rhubarb, make an appearance.

West Waterford Festival of Food (p187) Three days of local produce and fine food in Dungarvan, including a seaside barbecue and a craft beer garden.

Taste of Dublin (p101) The capital's best restaurants combine to serve up sample platters of their best dishes amid music and other entertainment.

July–September

First of the season's new potatoes appear, along with jams and pies with gooseberries, blackberries and loganberries.

Taste of West Cork Food Festival (p239) Skibbereen brings together its best producers to put on this week-long festival.

Galway International Oyster & Seafood Festival (www.galwayoysterfest.com; ☉late Sep) Last weekend in September sees plenty of oysters, washed down with lashings of Guinness.

October–December

October is apple-picking month, and the main potato crop is dug up.

Kinsale Gourmet Festival (p233) The unofficial gourmet capital struts its stuff over three days.

THE BEST IRISH CHEESES

Ardrahan Flavoursome farmhouse creation with a rich, nutty taste.

Corleggy Subtle, pasteurised goat's cheese.

Gubbeen The oak-smoked variety is superb.

Durrus (p246) A creamy, fruity cheese, beloved of fine-food fans.

Cashel Blue Creamy blue cheese from Tipperary.

Cooleeney Award-winning Camembert-style cheese.

Boxty A Northern Irish starchy potato cake made with a half-and-half mix of cooked mashed potatoes and grated, strained raw potato.

Carrageen The typical Irish seaweed that can be found in dishes as diverse as salad and ice cream.

Corned beef tongue Usually accompanied by cabbage, this dish is still found on a traditional Irish menu.

Lough Neagh eel A speciality of Northern Ireland, typically eaten around Halloween; it's usually served in chunks with a white onion sauce.

Poitín It's rare for you to be offered a drop of the 'cratur', as illegally distilled whiskey (made from malted grain or potatoes) is called here. Still, there are pockets of the country with secret stills – in Donegal, Connemara and West Cork.

Local Specialities

To Eat

Potatoes Still a staple of most traditional meals and presented in a variety of forms. The mashed potato dishes colcannon and champ (with cabbage and spring onion, respectively) are two of the tastiest recipes in the country.

Meat and seafood Beef, lamb and pork are common options. Seafood is widely available in restaurants and is often excellent, especially in the west. Oysters, trout and salmon are delicious, particularly if they're direct from the sea or a river rather than a fish farm.

Soda bread The most famous Irish bread is made with bicarbonate of soda, to make up for soft Irish flour that traditionally didn't take well to yeast. Combined with buttermilk, it makes a superbly tasty bread, and is often on the breakfast menus at B&Bs.

The fry Who can say no to a plate of fried bacon, sausages, black pudding, white pudding, eggs and tomatoes? For the famous Ulster fry, common throughout the North, simply add fadge (potato bread).

To Drink

Stout While Guinness has become synonymous with stout the world over, few outside Ireland realise that there are two other major producers competing for the favour of the Irish drinker: Murphy's and Beamish & Crawford, both based in Cork city.

Tea The Irish drink more tea, per capita, than any other nation in the world and you'll be offered a cup as soon as you cross the threshold of any Irish home. Taken with milk (and sugar, if you want) rather than lemon, preferred blends are very strong, and nothing like the namby-pamby versions that pass for Irish breakfast tea elsewhere.

Whiskey At last count, there were almost 100 different types of Irish whiskey, brewed by only three distilleries – Jameson's, Bushmills and Cooley's. A visit to Ireland reveals a depth of excellence that will make the connoisseur's palate spin while winning over many new friends to what the Irish call *uisce beatha* (water of life).

Craft Distilleries

A handful of independently owned distilleries have opened in the last few years, producing whiskies (and, in some cases, other spirits) that have added a fine bit of diversity to the range of Irish spirits.

Blackwater Distillery (☎058-52621; www.blackwaterdistillery.ie; Unit 3, Cappoquin Enterprise Park) A distillery in Cappoquin, County Waterford, that produces around 50 casks of whisky (without the 'e' in accordance with Munster tradition) a year.

Dingle Distillery (p287) Whiskey, a quintuple-distilled vodka and a London dry gin made on the edge of town.

Listoke Distillery & Gin School (p517) Local gin distillery that gives you the chance to make your own.

West Cork Distillers (p239) Blended, pot still and single malt whiskies, as well as liqueurs and vodka.

Slane Distillery (p507) The first batch of triple cask matured whiskey was made in 2017 at this brand new distillery.

Teeling Distillery (p85) Dublin's first new distillery in 125 years was opened in 2015 by the same family that owns the Cooley Distillery in County Louth.

How to Eat & Drink

When to Eat

Irish eating habits have changed over the last couple of decades, and there are differences between urban and rural practices.

Breakfast Usually eaten before 9am (although hotels and B&Bs will serve until 11am Monday to Friday, and to noon at weekends in urban areas), as most people rush off to work. Weekend brunch is popular in bigger towns and cities.

Lunch Urban workers eat on the run between 12.30pm and 2pm (most restaurants don't begin to serve lunch until at least midday). At weekends, especially Sunday, the midday lunch is skipped in favour of a substantial mid-afternoon meal (called dinner), usually between 2pm and 4pm.

Tea Not the drink, but the evening meal – also confusingly called dinner. This is the main meal of the day for urbanites, usually eaten around 6.30pm. Rural communities eat at the same time but with a more traditional tea of bread, cold cuts and, yes, tea. Restaurants follow

international habits, with most diners not eating until at least 7.30pm.

Supper A before-bed snack of tea and toast or sandwiches, still enjoyed by many Irish, although urbanites increasingly eschew it for health reasons. Not a practice in restaurants.

Where to Eat

Restaurants From cheap 'n' cheerful to Michelin-starred, Ireland has something for every palate and budget.

Cafes Ireland is awash with cafes of every description, many of which are perfect for a quick, tasty bite.

Hotels Even if you're not a guest, most hotel restaurants cater to outside diners. Top hotels usually feature good restaurants with prices to match.

Pubs Pub grub is ubiquitous, mostly of the toasted-sandwich variety. However, a large number also have full menu service, with some of them being as good as any top restaurant.

Dining Etiquette

The Irish aren't big on restrictive etiquette, preferring friendly informality to any kind of stuffy to-dos. Still, the following are a few tips to dining with the Irish:

Children All restaurants welcome kids up to 7pm, but pubs and some smarter restaurants don't allow them in the evening. Family restaurants have

IRELAND'S CRAFT BEERS

Although mainstream lagers like Heineken, Carlsberg and Coors Lite are most pubs' best-selling beers, the craft-beer revolution has resulted in dozens of microbreweries springing up all over the island, making artisan beers that are served in more than 600 of Ireland's pubs and bars. Here's a small selection to whet the tastebuds:

Devil's Backbone (4.9% Alcohol by volume) Rich amber ale from County Donegal brewer Kinnegar.

The Full Irish (6% ABV) Pale ale by Eight Degrees Brewery outside Mitchelstown, County Cork, voted Irish beer of the year in 2015.

O'Hara's Leann Folláin (6% ABV) Dry stout with vaguely chocolate notes produced by Carlow Brewing Company.

Metalman Pale Ale (4.3% ABV) American-style pale ale by the much-respected Metalman Brewing Company in County Waterford – now available in cans.

Puck Pilsner (4.5% ABV) A light lager brewed by Jack Cody's Brewery in Drogheda, County Louth.

Twisted Hop (4.7% ABV) Blond ale produced by Hilden just outside Lisburn, Ireland's oldest independent brewery.

Soda bread (p44)

children's menus; others have reduced portions of regular menu items.

Returning a dish If the food is not to your satisfaction, it's best to politely explain what's wrong with it as soon as you can; any respectable restaurant will endeavour to replace the dish immediately.

Paying the bill If you insist on paying the bill for everyone, be prepared for a first, second and even third refusal to countenance such an exorbitant act of generosity. But don't be fooled: the Irish will refuse something several times even if they're delighted with it. Insist gently but firmly and you'll get your way!

Finding the Best of Irish Food & Drink

www.guides.ie Extensive coverage of artisan producers and the best restaurants serving their produce.

www.bordbia.ie Irish Food Board website, with a few local producers listed, as well as a comprehensive list of farmers markets.

www.irishcheese.ie The Association of Irish Farmhouse Cheesemakers, with every small dairy covered.

www.slowfoodireland.com Organisation supporting small producers, with social events across Ireland.

Wild Atlantic Way

Ireland's western coastline is one of the world's most stunning stretches, a 2500km-long necklace of jagged cliffs, crescent strands and latticed fields strung out from west Cork to northeastern Donegal. This official driving route is richly decorated with the panoramic pit stops you came to Ireland to experience.

Cork to Kerry

Ireland's southwestern corner is packed with scenic highlights along its 463km coastline, skirting around the best known (and explored) peninsulas in the country.

Highlights

Mizen Head (p243; Cork) The spectacular views from the rugged clifftop (cross the Mizen footbridge to get right to the edge) include the Fastnet Lighthouse, perched on a rock known as Ireland's Teardrop; as this was the last sight of the country for emigrants embarked for America during the Famine.

Slea Head Drive (p292; Kerry) Only 50km long, this circular route around the tip of the peninsula is one of Ireland's best scenic drives. The main distraction from the stunning scenery is the heavy concentration of prehistoric sites dotted throughout the hills.

Worth Discovering

Dursey Island (p253) (Cork) At the tip of the remote Beara Peninsula is a quiet island, blissfully free of shops, pubs and restaurants but worth visiting for its lighthouse, castle ruins and standing stones. Get here via a 10-minute ride on the cable car, but remember that the handful of residents take precedence over tourists!

Need to Know

The Route

Split into five connected sections spread across nine counties: Cork, Kerry, Clare, Limerick, Galway, Mayo, Sligo, Leitrim and Donegal.

Clearly marked by nearly 4000 signposts featuring an aquamarine-coloured wave and punctuated by 157 'Discovery Points' where you can stop and learn about must-sees and lesser-known diversions of each area.

Direction

Car You can do the route in either direction, but to stay closer to the sea – with the best views – drive south to north.

Bicycle The prevailing wind is southerly, so north to south is easier (even if the wind can't be relied to cooperate).

Information

For up-to-date information on everything to do with the Wild Atlantic Way, check out Fáilte Ireland's designated website at www.wildatlantic way.com or download the terrific app, which is available for Android and iPhone.

0   50 km
0   25 miles

COUNTY DONEGAL

Ireland's wild and rugged north-western corner is a county of largely unspoilt scenic splendour, with virtually every part of its long coastline worth stopping to feast on. (p436)

COUNTIES MAYO & SLIGO

Lonely peninsulas, surf beaches and the country's most distinctive peak are an inspiration to artists and poets. (p401)

COUNTY GALWAY

A beautiful interior wrapped in a ribbon of hidden coves and traditional fishing villages, while the offshore islands are the stuff of myth. (p359)

COUNTY CLARE

Ireland's most famous cliffs, a moon-like limestone landscape, beautiful surf beaches and the heartland of Irish traditional music. (p324)

COUNTIES CORK & KERRY

The bright stars of Irish tourism, packed with stunning scenery, ancient sites, buzzing towns and a terrific foodie scene. (p211, 256)

ATLANTIC OCEAN

Malin Head
Tory Island
Ballyliffin
Culdaff
Dunfanaghy
Arranmore Island
Buncrana
Coleraine
Letterkenny
Derry
Dungloe
DONEGAL
LONDONDERRY
Tramore Beach
Strabane
Ardara
Carrick
Donegal
TYRONE
Slieve League
Omagh
Lough Neagh
Bundoran
FERMANAGH
Benbulben (625m)
Armagh
Pollatomish
Ballycastle
Strandhill
Enniskillen
Mullet Peninsula
Bangor Erris
Ballina
Sligo
Monaghan
Achill Island
SLIGO
Newport
MAYO
Boyle
Clew Bay
Castlebar
Inishturk Island
Westport
Croagh Patrick (765m)
Inishbofin
Roscommon
MEATH
Sky Road
Leenane
Mullingar
Clifden
Oughterard
GALWAY
Athlone WESTMEATH
Roundstone
Galway
Kilcolgan
Loughrea
Aran Islands
Inishmór Fanore
Inishmaan
The Burren
Gort
Inisheer
Doolin
Cliffs of Moher
Ennistymon
Lahinch
Ennis
Nenagh
Carlow
CLARE
KILKENNY
CARLOW
Kilkee
Kilrush
Limerick
Kilkenny
Loop Head
Kilrush
Foynes
Ballybunion
Tarbert
Adare
Listowel
LIMERICK
Slea Head Drive
Tralee
Mallow
Dungarvan
Dingle
Killorglin
Killarney
CORK
Cork
Youghal
Kells
KERRY
Cobh
Sneem
Kenmare
Portmagee
Beara Peninsula
Glengarriff
Kinsale
Skellig Islands
Bantry
Clonakilty
Dursey Castletownbere
Island
Schull
Skibbereen
Mizen Head

SIGNATURE EXPERIENCES

The Wild Atlantic Way is interspersed with a series of 'signature experiences' designed to enhance your visit. They include the following:

Cork & Kerry A visit to Skellig Michael (p278), a rocky crag with the beehive huts of 8th-century monks; described by George Bernard Shaw as 'part of our dream world'.

Clare Take a guided tour (p347) of The Burren, as the local guides will give you a remarkable insight into 'Europe's largest rock garden' – an area rich in flora and home to neolithic monuments that predate the Egyptian pyramids.

Clare/Galway Explore Inisheer, the smallest of the Aran Islands, by pony and trap. If it suits, catch the ferry (p375) to Doolin, in County Clare: if you time it right, you'll go by the Cliffs of Moher just as the sun is going down.

Sligo Take an oily soak in hand-harvested Atlantic seaweed and briny water, the traditional organic cure for stress and other ailments due to the high concentration of iodine in the seaweed. Voya Seaweed Baths (p430) in Strandhill are renowned.

Donegal Take the ferry out to the remote island of Tory, where nearly everybody is a painter in the native art style developed in the 1950s; you'll most likely be met at the dock by the 'King' of the island, Patsy Dan...who happens to be a painter too.

County Clare

Clare's coastline is justifiably renowned throughout Europe for its dramatic cliffs, shaped over aeons by the crashing waves of the relentless Atlantic.

Highlights

Loop Head (p337) This narrow shelf of headland, surrounded on both sides by the sea, has a long hiking trail between the tip and Kilkee. The views – of the Dingle Peninsula to the south and Galway and the Aran Islands to the north – are mesmerising.

Cliffs of Moher (p345) Ireland's most famous cliffs rise vertically from the sea to 203m and their majesty entirely justifies the busloads of visitors that come, gawp and leave in wonder. For the best views, head south for about 5km along the southerly trail to Hag's Head.

Worth Discovering

Lahinch (p341) The Blue Flag beach at Lahinch is a surfer's paradise thanks to its flooding tide. Nearby is one of the best golf courses in Ireland, and, a little further afield, Ennistymon is a fine spot for traditional music.

County Galway

Wildness abounds in Galway, even beyond the crazy nights in its namesake city. Connemara is a stunning wilderness of bog, mountain and glacial lakes while the Aran Islands' dramatic desolation is at the heart of their beguiling beauty.

Highlights

Sky Road (p391) A 12km circular route from Clifden, Connemara's 'capital': the scenery is staggering, especially northward towards Inishboffin and the islands of Clew Bay in Mayo. It's also a popular cycling route; you can hire bikes in Clifden.

Aran Islands (p374) Forty minutes by ferry (or 10 by plane) and you're in another century: take your pick of three islands, each with their distinctive features (Inishmor the most visited, Inisheer the smallest and Inishmaan the most isolated) but each giving the feeling of living at the edge of the world.

Worth Discovering

Dog's Bay/Gurteen Bay (p389) About 3km from Roundstone, the twin beaches of Dog's Bay and Gurteen are among Ireland's most beautiful: two back-to-back crescents of brilliant white sand made entirely of tiny bits of seashells rather than the crushed limestone common in other beaches.

County Mayo to County Sligo

Less visited than their southern counterparts, Mayo and Sligo adorn the Wild Atlantic crown with some truly stunning and desolate landscapes, beautiful islands and a handful of superb beaches that are surfers' favourites.

Highlights

Achill Island (p414) (Mayo) Ireland's largest offshore island is easily reached by causeway from the mainland. Once there, you'll have soaring cliffs and sandy beaches to explore as well as blanket bogs and even a mountain range.

Benbulben (p433) (Sligo) On a clear day, you won't miss the distinctive peak of Sligo's most famous mountain, which is like a table covered in a pleated tablecloth. Its beguiling look inspired WB Yeats.

Worth Discovering

Mullet Peninsula (p418) (Mayo) Few spots in Ireland are as unspoilt and as unpopulated as this beautiful peninsula, which juts out into the Atlantic for about 30km. The eastern shores are lined with pristine beaches and the few people there speak Irish.

County Donegal

Wild, remote in parts but beautiful throughout, Donegal is the fitting end (or start) to the Wild Atlantic Way. Its jagged coastline of sheer cliffs, hidden coves and long stretches of golden sand are the stuff of myth and postcard – and an easy rival to any other county in the natural beauty stakes.

Highlights

Slieve League (p447) These spectacular, monochrome cliffs in southwestern Donegal get far less press than their southern equivalent, but they're taller, at 600m, and every bit as dramatic.

Malin Head (p468) Ireland's northernmost point is a rocky, weather-battered promontory topped by an early-19th-century martello tower called Banba's Crown.

Worth Discovering

Tramore Beach (p185) An exhilarating 2km hike from the pretty village of Dunfanaghy takes you through some impressive dunes to a beautiful, usually empty strand; at the far end a path leads to Pollaguill Bay.

Regions at a Glance

The historic counties of Antrim, Armagh, Down, Fermanagh, Londonderry and Tyrone form Northern Ireland, which is part of the United Kingdom and (despite the lack of border controls) separate from the Republic of Ireland.

Dublin

Museums
Entertainment
History

Cultural Exhibits

The capital is the nation's primary repository of archaeological artefacts, artistic treasures and other cultural treasures. The National Museum's three Dublin branches are the place to start, while the city's multitude of galleries have art on their walls from the Renaissance to the current day.

Pubs & Nightlife

With a thousand-odd pubs to choose from, there is plenty of choice when deciding where to enjoy a pint of Dublin's most celebrated produce. But beyond Guinness and pub chatter there is theatre old and new, all manner of gigs and a host of sporting distractions.

History & Heritage

Virtually every Dublin street is lined with monuments to its history, from the cobbled grounds of Trinity College to the bloodied walls of Kilmainham Gaol. Its finest buildings and most elegant streets belong to its golden Georgian age, when Dublin was the second city of the British empire.

p58

Counties Wicklow & Kildare

Scenery
Monastic Ruins
Activities

Mountain Views

There are splendid views pretty much everywhere in the Wicklow Mountains, especially at the top of the passes that cut through the range; on a clear day you can see five counties. In Kildare, the fecund Bog of Allen offers another classic Irish landscape.

Ancient Monasteries

Not only are the ruins of Glendalough utterly absorbing, but their location, at the bottom of a glacial valley by two lakes, is absolutely enchanting and well worth the visit alone.

Walking Routes

Ireland's most popular walking trail, the Wicklow Way, cuts through the county north to south. Kildare is horse-breeding country, where the walking paths are a little bit gentler but no less enjoyable.

p138

Counties Wexford, Waterford, Carlow & Kilkenny

Scenery
History
Food

Seaside Vistas

Iconic emerald-green fields above ragged ebony cliffs that end in a cerulean sea: you will never tire of the vista. Should you need a break, perfect pockets of sand dot the coast, while Wexford's beaches stretch beyond the horizon. Inland, rural Ireland includes wild rivers and bucolic farms.

Viking Trails

You half expect to encounter a Viking as you wander the streets of Waterford and Wexford, where traces of the Middle Ages are all around you. Kilkenny's medieval past is impossible to miss, from its soaring cathedral to its great castle.

Local Produce

Head to Dungarvan, County Waterford, to enjoy Irish cooking at its best, and enjoy the region's wonderful produce in all towns, big and small.

p164

County Cork

Food
Scenery
History

Gourmet Treats

County Cork is the unofficial gourmet heartland of Ireland, from the fabulous eateries of Cork city to the wealth of local producers and foodie artisans of West Cork, where you can buy directly at source and eat like a lord.

Peninsular Panoramas

The county's three western peninsulas – Mizen Head, Sheep's Head and Beara – have it all: mountain passes, lonely windswept hills, beautiful beaches and views that will stay with you long after you've left for home.

Story of Rebellion

'The Rebel County' wears its history with pride, even the sorrowful kind. You can explore it all, from Famine memorials and scenes of 17th-century battles to the powerful tribute to its more recent fallen heroes.

p211

County Kerry

Scenery
Seafood
Traditional Music

An Irish Postcard

County Kerry is the very definition of scenic Ireland – the Connor Pass, the Dingle Peninsula and, particularly, the Ring of Kerry are the gold standard by which Irish landscapes are judged. Decide for yourself by picking up a postcard.

Fresh from the Sea

Kerry's intimate relationship with the sea means that the fresh catch of the day is exactly that: throughout the Dingle Peninsula you can eat fish fresh off the boat you've just watched land.

Traditional Sound

No Kerry town or village is complete without at least one pub featuring traditional music, played by musicians schooled in the respective styles of their region. It's the proper accompaniment to a visit to the county.

p256

Counties Limerick & Tipperary

Walking
History
Scenery

Heritage Trails

It's a long way to Tipperary, but keep going once you get there, tramping through the chequered Glen of Aherlow and along the more challenging Tipperary Heritage Trail, a 56km walk through beautiful river valleys dotted with ancient ruins.

Castles & Monasteries

From the mighty monastic city of Cashel in County Tipperary to the impressive fortifications of King John's Castle in Limerick city, the varied fortunes of the region's history are easily discernible throughout the two counties.

Atmospheric Ruins

At its broadest point, the mighty Shannon makes for some beautiful vistas, while the rolling hills and farmland of County Tipperary, peppered with ancient ruins, offer the kind of views for which Ireland is renowned.

p302

County Clare

Scenery
Music
Pubs

Dramatic Cliffs

Rising from the stormy Atlantic in all their sheer dramatic glory, the Cliffs of Moher are an arresting sight not to be missed. Elsewhere on the Clare coast are similar levels of drama and beauty, especially at Loop Head and the coastal roads leading to and from its spectacular views of the restless Atlantic.

Traditional Sessions

Clare plays Ireland's most traditional music, with few modern influences. At festivals, in pubs or even just around any corner, you can hear brilliant trad sessions by the county's surfeit of musicians.

Old-style Drinking

There is *no* town in Clare that doesn't have at least one wonderful old pub where the Guinness is ready, the peat is lit and the craic never ends.

p324

County Galway

Scenery
Food
Culture

Islands & Mountains

Hundreds of years of ceaseless toil have brought green accents to the otherwise barren rocks of the Aran Islands. The results are gorgeous, and a walk around these windswept and intriguing islands is one of Ireland's highlights. In spring, when the gorse blooms in brilliant yellow, the Connemara Peninsula's beauty astounds.

Fresh Oysters

Even as you read this, millions of succulent oysters are growing to the perfect size out in the tidal waters of Galway Bay. Local chefs excel at creating tasty treats with the water's bounty.

Gigs Everywhere

On any given night, Galway city's pubs and clubs hum with trad sessions, brilliant rock and tomorrow's next big band. It's a feast for the ears.

p359

Counties Mayo & Sligo

Islands
Megalithic Remains
Yeats Country

Scenery

There are reputed to be 365 islands in Mayo's Clew Bay, including one once owned by John Lennon. There's also Craggy Island, which isn't the island of *Father Ted* fame but rather the home of the notorious pirate queen, Grace O'Malley (or Granuaile).

Ancient Ruins

From the world's most extensive Stone Age monument at Céide Fields to the megalithic cemeteries at Carrowmore and Carrowkeel, the environs of Mayo's Ballycastle are a step back into prehistory.

Poetic Inspiration

County Sligo is Yeats country: he's buried in the church at Drumcliff, in the shadow of Benbulben; and throughout the county you'll find tributes to him in museums and heritage centres, while the landscapes are reflected in his poetry.

p401

County Donegal

Wild Landscapes
Pristine Beaches
Surfing

Mountains & Cliffs

Untamed and almost impossibly wild, Donegal is the ultimate frontier country; from the wave- and windlashed cliffs and beaches of the coast to the mountainous interior, it's as brooding as it is beautiful.

Sweeping Coastlines

The county with the second-longest coastline has the country's best beaches, including surf-friendly Rossnowlagh, unspoilt Tramore and the red-tinged sands of Malinbeg. The multitude of coves hides an astonishing number of sandy hideaways.

Sea Activities

In Donegal you can learn to surf as well as take on some of the world's toughest breaks – the county is arguably the best place in the country to ride the waves due to its great mix of beaches and abundance of surf centres.

p436

The Midlands

Traditional Pubs
The Mighty River
Saints & Scholars

Authentic Atmosphere

Spread almost innocuously across the Midlands are some of the most atmospheric pubs in the country, including Morrissey's of Abbeyleix in County Laois, perhaps the most perfect pub in Ireland.

Cruise the Shannon

What better way to explore the length and breadth of the country's belly than by cruiser along Ireland's longest river? See the sights and stop off along the way to eat in the riverbank restaurants that have sprouted for that purpose.

Saints & Scholars

The top monastic site in Ireland is Clonmacnoise, perched on the edge of the Shannon in County Offaly. Within its walled enclosure you'll find early churches, high crosses, round towers and graves in astonishingly good condition.

p472

Counties Meath, Louth, Cavan & Monaghan

History
Fishing
Scenery

Chieftains & Conflict

Irish history was lived and written across these counties, at the Hill of Tara, the Neolithic monuments of Brú na Bóinne and Loughcrew (all in Meath), and in the magnificent abbeys of Mellifont and Monasterboice, and in towns such as Drogheda (all in Louth).

Casting a Line

County Cavan's myriad lakes are famed for coarse fishing. County Monaghan isn't far behind, and if you fancy a little sea angling, towns such as Clogherhead and Carlingford in County Louth are the places to go.

Lakelands & Hills

These counties offer all kinds of scenery, from the lakelands of Cavan and Monaghan to the fecund hills of County Meath. There are beautiful seaside views too, along the Louth coast as far up as scenic Carlingford.

p501

Belfast

History
Pubs
Music

Titanic Belfast

Belfast's shipbuilding heritage has been salvaged and transformed into Northern Ireland's most-visited museum – a fabulous multimedia experience centred on the construction of the world's most famous maritime disaster, which you can explore in virtual detail.

Victorian Gems

The Victorian classic pubs of the city centre are Belfast's most beloved treasure – the Crown might be the most famous, but equally beautiful are the John Hewitt and the Garrick, while older taverns such as White's and Kelly's have even more atmosphere.

Banging Tunes

From DJs spinning tunes in the Eglantine to sell-out gigs at the Odyssey, Belfast's music scene is top-notch. Best of the lot is probably the Belfast Empire, which features new bands and established acts nightly.

p536

Counties Down & Armagh

Activities
Wildlife
Food

Walking Festivals

With an impressive calendar of yearly events including birdwatching meets, walking festivals and more-strenuous activities such as rock climbing and canoeing, there's enough to do here to keep you busy every day of the year.

Birds & Seals

The bird-filled mudflats of Castle Espie in County Down are home to a wildfowl and wetlands centre that will entice even the most indifferent of ornithologists, while large colonies of grey seals are but the most obvious of visitors to Strangford Lough in County Armagh.

Gastro-goodness

You'll find first-rate dining in the restaurants and gastropubs of Hillsborough, Bangor and Warrenpoint. Many of the best places to eat are in the countryside, and use seafood, beef, apples and other local ingredients.

p572

Counties Londonderry & Antrim

History
Scenery
Pop culture

A Walled City

Derry, Ireland's only walled city, has a rich historical past, poignantly told along the walls that withstood a siege in 1688–89, in its storied museums and, most tellingly, in the political murals of the Bogside district, where history was played out on its very streets.

Giant's Footsteps

Virtually the entire length of the Antrim coast is scenic gold, but the real stars are the southern section around Carnlough Bay and the North's most outstanding tourist attraction, the surreal geological formations of the Giant's Causeway.

Game of Thrones

Game of Thrones fans will recognise Antrim's Dark Hedges as the Kingsroad; Mussenden Temple on the Causeway Coast as Dragonstone; Cushenden Caves as the spot where Melisandre gave birth to the shadow baby in Season 2; and Ballintoy Harbour as the Iron Islands' Lordsports Harbour.

p598

Counties Fermanagh & Tyrone

Activities
Scenery
History

Walking & Fishing

Need something to do? How about fishing in the waters of County Fermanagh, or taking part in the Ulster American Folk Park's annual Appalachian and bluegrass festival? Or, for something more spiritual, why not climb to the summit of Mullaghcarn, County Tyrone, along with other pilgrims?

From a Height

Whether you're boating on Lough Erne, staring out the windows at the top of the round tower on Devenish Island (both in County Fermanagh) or hiking across th-Tyrone's Sperrin Mountains, the scenery is beguiling, especially in decent weather.

Conflict & onnections

The towns of Omagh (County Tyrone) and Enniskillen (County Fermanagh) speak volumes about the atrocities of violence, but Northern Ireland's history isn't just one of conflict: Tyrone's Ulster American Folk Park expertly tells the story of the province's strong links with the USA.

p634

On the Road

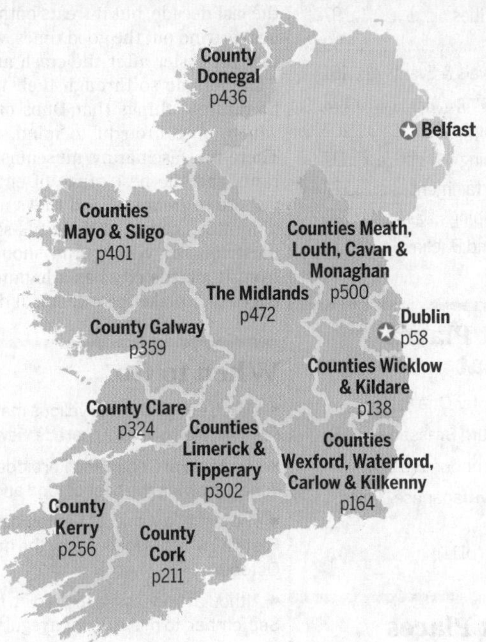

County Donegal
p436

★ Belfast

Counties Mayo & Sligo
p401

Counties Meath, Louth, Cavan & Monaghan
p500

The Midlands
p472

County Galway
p359

Dublin
★ p58

Counties Wicklow & Kildare
p138

County Clare
p324

Counties Limerick & Tipperary
p302

Counties Wexford, Waterford, Carlow & Kilkenny
p164

County Kerry
p256

County Cork
p211

Dublin

POP 1,345,402 / AREA 114.99 SQ KM

Best Places to Eat

➡ Chapter One (p116)

➡ Coburg Brasserie (p111)

➡ Greenhouse (p110)

➡ Banyi Japanese Dining (p112)

➡ Etto (p111)

Best Places to Sleep

➡ Merrion (p104)

➡ Conrad Dublin (p105)

➡ Aberdeen Lodge (p107)

➡ Merrion Mews (p104)

➡ Isaacs Hostel (p106)

Why Go?

Sultry rather than sexy, Dublin exudes personality as only one who has managed to turn careworn into carefree can. The city has seen its fair share of triumph and disaster in the last decade, but it treats both as imposters and continues to grind out the good times, which have finally become that bit easier after the crash and burn of the recession. Dubliners do so through their music, their art and their literature – things that Dubs often take for granted but which, once brought to mind, generate immense pride. There are fascinating museums, mouth-watering restaurants and the best range of entertainment available anywhere in Ireland – and that's not including the pub, the ubiquitous centre of the city's social life and an absolute must for any visitor. And should you wish to get away from it all, the city has a handful of seaside towns at its edges that make for wonderful day trips.

When to Go

➡ March brings the marvellous mayhem of St Patrick's Festival, with 600,000 parade viewers.

➡ The Taste of Dublin and Forbidden Fruit festivals are in June, featuring the best of food and music.

➡ The last two weeks of September host the Dublin Fringe Festival, which is followed by the main theatre festival in October.

➡ Although impossible to predict, the best weather is often in September, to make up for a regularly disappointing August!

History

Dublin's been making noise since around 500 BC, when a bunch of intrepid Celts camped at a ford over the River Liffey, which is the provenance of the city's tough-to-pronounce Irish name, Baile Átha Cliath (Bawlya Aw-ha Klee-ya; Town of the Hurdle Ford). The Celts went about their merry way for a thousand years or so, but it wasn't until the Vikings showed up that Dublin was urbanised in any significant way. By the 9th century raids from the north had become a fact of Irish life, and some of the fierce Danes chose to stay rather than simply rape, pillage and depart. They intermarried with the Irish and established a vigorous trading port at the point where the River Poddle joined the Liffey in a dubh linn (black pool). Today there's little trace of the Poddle, which has been channelled underground and flows under St Patrick's Cathedral to dribble into the Liffey by the Capel St (Grattan) Bridge.

The Normans arrived in the 12th century, and so began the slow process of subjugating Ireland to Anglo-Norman (and then British) rule, during which Dublin generally played the role of Anglo-Norman, later British, bandleader. By the beginning of the 18th century, the squalid city packed with poor Catholics hardly reflected the imperial pretensions of its Anglophile burghers. The great and the good – aka the Protestant ascendancy – wanted big improvements, and they set about transforming what was in essence still a medieval town into a modern, Anglo-Irish metropolis. Roads were widened, landscaped squares laid out and new townhouses built, all in a proto-Palladian style that soon became known as Georgian, after the kings then on the English throne. For a time Dublin was the second largest city in the British Empire and all was very, very good – unless you were part of the poor, mostly Catholic masses living in the city's ever-developing slums.

The Georgian boom came to a sudden and dramatic halt after the Act of Union (1801), when Ireland was formally united with Britain and its separate parliament closed down. Dublin went from being the belle of the imperial ball to the annoying cousin who just wouldn't take the hint, and slid quickly into economic turmoil and social unrest. During the Potato Famine (1845–51), the city's population was swollen by the arrival of tens of thousands of starving refugees from the west, who joined the ranks of an already downtrodden working class. As Dublin entered the 20th century, it was a dispirited place plagued by poverty, disease and more social problems than anyone cared to mention. It's hardly surprising that the majority of Dublin's citizenry were disgruntled and eager for change.

The first fusillade of transformation came during the Easter Rising of 1916, which caused considerable damage to the city centre. At first, Dubliners weren't too enamoured of the rebels, who caused more chaos and disruption than most locals were willing to put up with, but they soon changed their tune when the leaders were executed – Dubliners being natural defenders of the underdog.

As the whole country lurched radically towards full-scale war with Britain, Dublin, surprisingly, was not part of the main theatre of events. In fact, although there was an increased military presence, the odd shooting and the blowing up of some notable buildings – such as the Custom House in 1921 – in the capital it was business as usual for much of the War of Independence.

A year later, Ireland – minus its northern bit – was independent, but it then tumbled into the Civil War, which led to the burning of more notable buildings, including the Four Courts in 1922. Ironically the war among the Irish was more brutal than the struggle for independence – O'Connell St became 'sniper row' and the violence left deep scars that took most of the 20th century to heal.

When the new state finally started doing business, Dublin was an exhausted capital. Despite slow and steady improvements, the city – like the rest of Ireland – continued to be plagued by rising unemployment, high emigration rates and a general stagnation that hung about like an impenetrable cloud. Dubliners made the most of the little they had, but times were tough.

The city has been in and out of recession for decades, but the dramatic dip that followed the sky-high good times of the Celtic Tiger was especially severe: Dublin is recovering more than the rest of the country, but recuperation has still been slow.

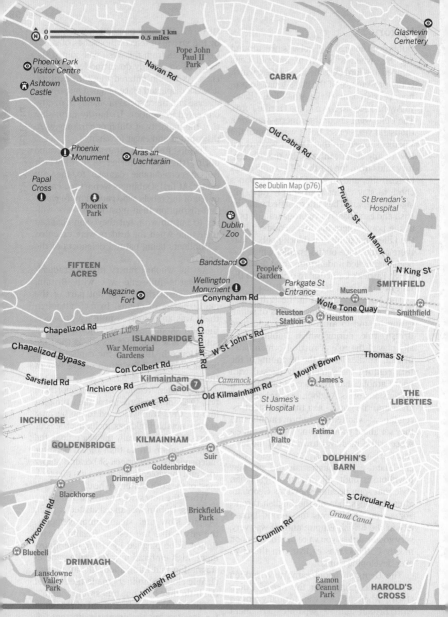

Dublin Highlights

① Strolling the Elizabethan grounds of **Trinity College** (p64).

② Poring over ancient books and treasures in the **Chester Beatty Library**. (p69)

③ Exploring your thespian side by taking in a play at one of Dublin's theatres, such as the **Abbey** (p125) or the **Gate** (p125).

④ Getting to grips with Ireland's historic treasures and ancient past with a visit to the **National Museum of Ireland – Archaeology** (p75).

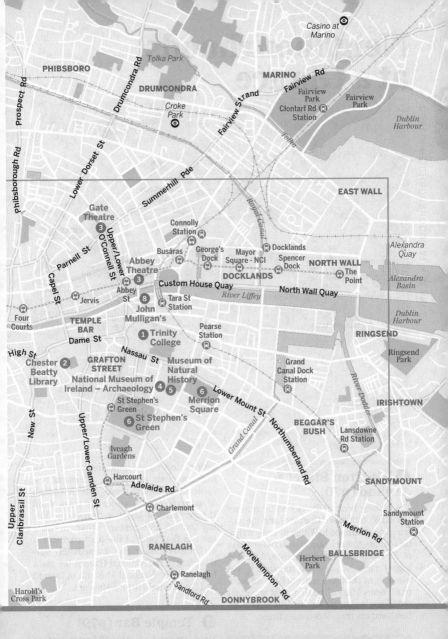

Casino at Marino

PHIBSBORO

Tolka Park

DRUMCONDRA

MARINO

Fairview Rd

Fairview Park

Clontarf Rd Station

Fairview Park

Dublin Harbour

Prospect Rd

Drumcondra Rd

Croke Park

Fairview Strand

Tolka

Phibsborough Rd

Lower Dorset St

Summerhill Pde

EAST WALL

Royal Canal

3 Gate Theatre

Connolly Station

Alexandra Quay

Parnell St

Upper/Lower O'Connell St

Busáras

George's Dock

Mayor Square - NCI

Docklands

Spencer Dock

NORTH WALL

Capel St

3 Abbey Theatre

Custom House Quay

DOCKLANDS

Alexandra Basin

The Point

Jervis

Abbey St

8 John Mulligan's

Tara St Station

River Liffey

North Wall Quay

Dublin Harbour

Four Courts

TEMPLE BAR

Dame St

1 Trinity College

Pearse Station

RINGSEND

Ringsend Park

High St

2 Chester Beatty Library

GRAFTON STREET

Nassau St

Museum of Natural History

National Museum of Ireland – Archaeology

4 **5**

6 Merrion Square

Lower Mount St

Grand Canal Dock Station

River Dodder

IRISHTOWN

New St

St Stephen's Green

6 St Stephen's Green

Northumberland Rd

BEGGAR'S BUSH

Lansdowne Rd Station

Iveagh Gardens

Grand Canal

Upper/Lower Camden St

Harcourt

Adelaide Rd

SANDYMOUNT

Upper Clanbrassil St

Charlemont

Sandymount Station

RANELAGH

Morehampton Rd

Merrion Rd

BALLSBRIDGE

Herbert Park

Harold's Cross Park

Ranelagh

Sandford Rd

DONNYBROOK

5 Tapping into your inner Victorian botanist (and watching the kids go 'wow') with a visit to the 'dead zoo', the **Museum of Natural History** (p78).

6 Enjoying Georgian gems surrounding the landscaped **Merrion Square** (p75) and **St Stephen's Green** (p70).

7 Seeing the past up close at **Kilmainham Gaol** (p84).

8 Quaffing a pint or five in one of Dublin's many pubs – our favourite is **John Mulligan's** (p121).

Neighbourhoods at a Glance

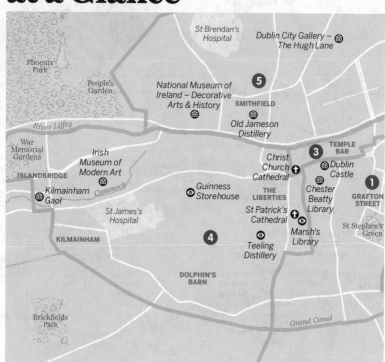

❶ Grafton Street & Around (p70)

The bustling heart of the city centre revolves around pedestrianised Grafton St and the warren of streets around it. Within its easily walkable confines, this neighbourhood is where most of the action takes place, where you'll find the biggest range of pubs and restaurants, and where most Dubliners come to blow off some retail steam. Many of the city's most important sights and museums are here, as is Dublin's best-loved city park, St Stephen's Green.

❷ Merrion Square & Around (p74)

Genteel, sophisticated and elegant, the exquisite Georgian architecture spread around handsome Merrion Sq is a near-perfect mix of imposing public buildings, museums, and private offices and residences. It is round these parts that much of moneyed Dublin works and plays, amid the neoclassical beauties thrown up during Dublin's 18th-century prime. Beauties such as the home of the Irish parliament at Leinster House and, immediately surrounding it, the National Gallery, the main branch of the National Museum of Ireland and the Natural History Museum.

❸ Temple Bar (p79)

Many weekend visitors will barely venture beyond the cobbled borders of Dublin's so-called 'cultural quarter', such is the nature of the distractions on offer. Temple Bar is all about fun – mostly in the pubs – and on summer evenings the party spills out onto the street, lending the whole place some

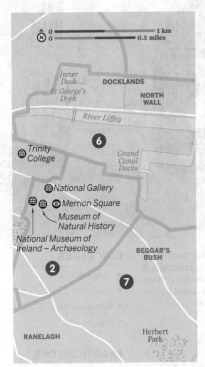

5 North of the Liffey (p86)

Grittier than its more genteel southside counterpart, the neighbourhoods immediately north of the River Liffey offer a fascinating mix of 18th-century grandeur, traditional city life and the multicultural melting pot that is contemporary Dublin. Beyond its widest, most elegant boulevard you'll find art museums and whiskey museums, bustling markets and some of the best ethnic eateries in town. Oh, and Europe's largest enclosed park – home to the president, the US Ambassador and the zoo.

6 Docklands (p93)

If it was built in the last 15 years, the chances are it's in the docklands (jokingly called 'Canary Dwarf' in reference to London's own dockland development), east of the city centre towards Dublin Bay. The most interesting area is around Grand Canal Dock, just south of the Liffey, which is home to affluent apartment dwellers, a handful of nice eateries and the city's biggest theatre, designed by Daniel Libeskind.

thing of a carnival atmosphere. There are plenty of restaurants as well as some interesting art galleries and shops that do provide a change of pace.

4 Kilmainham & the Liberties (p83)

Dublin's oldest and most traditional neighbourhoods would scarcely attract any visitors were it not for the presence of the Guinness Brewery, which dominates the city centre's western edge and is home to its most visited museum. Dublin's two medieval cathedrals are here too, while further west are the country's premier modern-art museum and a historic site that is worth every effort to visit.

7 Southside (p95)

The neighbourhoods that border the southern bank of the Grand Canal are less about sights and more about the experience of affluent Dublin – dining, drinking and sporting occasions, both watching and taking part. Here are the city's most desirable neighbourhoods and most precious postcodes: Dublin 4, which includes fancy schmancy Ballsbridge and Donnybrook, home to embassies and local potentates; and Dublin 6, covered by the elegant residential districts of Ranelagh, Rathgar and Rathmines, where the professional classes who still want a slice of city life reside.

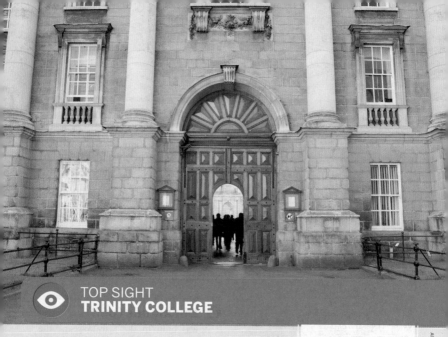

TOP SIGHT
TRINITY COLLEGE

This calm and cordial retreat from the bustle of contemporary Dublin is Ireland's most prestigious university, a collection of elegant Georgian and Victorian buildings, cobbled squares and manicured lawns that is among the most delightful places to wander.

History

The college was established by Elizabeth I in 1592 on land confiscated from an Augustinian priory in an effort to stop the brain drain of young Protestant Dubliners, who were skipping across to continental Europe for an education and becoming 'infected with popery'. Trinity went on to become one of Europe's most outstanding universities, producing a host of notable graduates – how about Jonathan Swift, Oscar Wilde and Samuel Beckett at the same alumni dinner?

Front Square & Parliament Square

The elegant **Regent House** entrance on College Green is guarded by statues of the writer **Oliver Goldsmith**, 1728–74, and the orator **Edmund Burke**, 1729–97. The railings outside are a popular meeting spot.

Through the entrance, past the Students Union, are Front Sq and Parliament Sq, the latter dominated by the 30m-high **Campanile**, designed by Edward Lanyon and erected from 1852 to 1853 on what was believed to be the centre of the monastery that preceded the college. According to superstition, students who pass beneath it when the bells toll will fail their exams. To the north of the Campanile is a statue of **George Salmon**, the college provost from 1886 to 1904, who fought bitterly to keep women out of the college. He carried out his threat to permit them in 'over his dead body' by dropping dead when the worst happened. To the south of the Campanile is a statue of historian **WEH Lecky** (1838–1903).

DON'T MISS

→ Long Room
→ *Book of Kells*
→ Science Gallery
→ Walking Tour

PRACTICALITIES

→ Map p71
→ ☎ 01-896 1000
→ www.tcd.ie
→ College Green
→ ⊘ 8am-10pm
→ 🚌 all city centre;
🚊 College Green

Library Square & Old Library

On the far east of Library Sq, the red-brick Rubrics Building (⊘ closed to the public) dates from around 1690, making it the oldest building in the college. Extensively altered in an 1894 restoration, it underwent serious structural modification in the 1970s.

If you are following the less-studious-looking throng, you'll find yourself drawn south of Library Sq to the Old Library (Library Sq; adult/student/family €11/9.50/22, fast-track €14/12/28; ⊙ 8.30am-5pm Mon-Sat, 9.30am-5pm Sun May-Sep, 9.30am-5pm Mon-Sat, noon-4.30pm Sun Oct-Apr), home to Trinity's prize possession and biggest crowd-puller, the astonishingly beautiful *Book of Kells*.

Upstairs is the highlight of Thomas Burgh's building, the magnificent 65m Long Room with its barrel-vaulted ceiling. It's lined with shelves containing 200,000 of the library's oldest manuscripts, busts of scholars, a 14th-century harp and an original copy of the Proclamation of the Irish Republic.

Fellows' Square

West of the brutalist, brilliant Berkeley Library (Fellows' Sq; ⊘ closed to the public), designed by Paul Koralek in 1967, the Arts & Social Science Building (⊘ closed to the public) is home to the Douglas Hyde Gallery (www.douglashydegallery.com; ⊙ 11am-6pm Mon-Wed & Fri, to 7pm Thu, to 4.45pm Sat) FREE, one of the country's leading contemporary galleries. It hosts regularly rotating shows presenting the works of top-class Irish and international artists across a range of media.

Science Gallery

Although it's part of the campus you'll have to walk along Pearse St to get into Trinity's newest attraction, the Science Gallery (www.sciencegallery.ie; Naughton Gallery, Pearse St; ⊘ exhibitions usually noon-8pm Tue-Fri, to 6pm Sat & Sun) FREE. Since opening in 2008, it has proven immensely popular with everyone for its refreshingly lively and informative exploration of the relationship between science, art and the world we live in. Exhibits have touched on a range of fascinating topics including the science of desire and an exploration of the relationship between music and the human body. The ground-floor cafe (Map p94; Pearse St; sandwiches €4-8; ⊙ 8am-8pm Tue-Fri, noon-6pm Sat & Sun; 🚇 all city centre), bathed in floor-to-ceiling light, is a pretty good spot to take a load off.

DUBLIN TRINITY COLLEGE

A CATHOLIC BAN

Trinity was exclusively Protestant until 1793, but even when the university relented and began to admit Catholics, the Catholic Church forbade it; until 1970, any Catholic who enrolled here could consider themselves excommunicated.

For nearly two centuries students weren't allowed through the grounds without a sword – and duels with pistols were not uncommon in the 17th and 18th centuries.

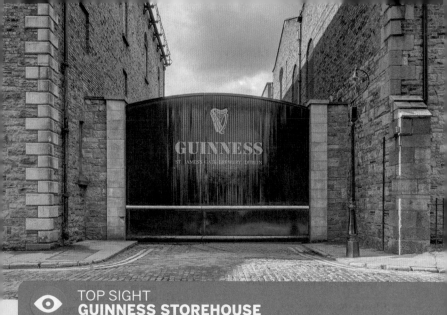

TOP SIGHT
GUINNESS STOREHOUSE

More than any beer produced anywhere in the world, Guinness has transcended its own brand and is not just the best-known symbol of the city but a substance with near spiritual qualities, according to its legions of devotees the world over. A visit to the factory museum where it's made is therefore something of a pilgrimage for many of its fans.

The mythology around Guinness is remarkably durable: it doesn't travel well; its distinctive flavour comes from Liffey water; it is good for you – not to mention the generally held belief that you will never understand the Irish until you develop a taste for the black stuff. All absolutely true, of course, so it should be no surprise that the Guinness Storehouse, in the heart of the St James's Gate Brewery, is the city's most-visited tourist attraction, an all-singing, all-dancing extravaganza that combines sophisticated exhibits, spectacular design and a thick, creamy head of marketing hype.

From Humble Beginnings to World Domination

In the 1770s, while other Dublin brewers fretted about the popularity of a new English beer known as porter – which was first created when a London brewer accidentally burnt his hops – Arthur Guinness started making his own version. By 1799 he decided to concentrate all his efforts on this single brew. He died four years later, aged 83, but the foundations for world domination were already in place.

DON'T MISS

➡ A drink of Guinness

➡ Gravity Bar view

➡ 1837 Bar & Brasserie

➡ Advertising exhibit

➡ Connoisseur Experience

PRACTICALITIES

➡ Map p76

➡ www.guinness-storehouse.com

➡ St James's Gate, South Market St

➡ adult/child €18/16.50, Connoisseur Experience €48

➡ ⊙9.30am-5pm Sep-Jun, to 6pm Jul & Aug

➡ 🚌 21A, 51B, 78, 78A, 123 from Fleet St, 🚃 James's

At one time a Grand Canal tributary was cut into the brewery to enable special Guinness barges to carry consignments out onto the Irish canal system or to the Dublin port. When the brewery extensions reached the Liffey in 1872, the fleet of Guinness barges became a familiar sight. Pretty soon Guinness was being exported as far afield as Africa and the West Indies. As the barges chugged their way along the Liffey towards the port, boys used to lean over the wall and shout, 'Bring us back a parrot'. Old-school Dubliners still say the same thing to each other when they're going off on holiday.

The Essential Ingredients

One link with the past that hasn't been broken is the yeast used to make Guinness, essentially the same living organism that has been used since 1770. Another vital ingredient is a hop by the name of fuggles, which used to be grown exclusively around Dublin but is now imported from Britain, the USA and Australia (everyone take a bow).

Guinness Storehouse Museum

The brewery is far more than just a place where beer is manufactured. It is an intrinsic part of Dublin's history and a key element of the city's identity. Accordingly, the quasi-mythical stature of Guinness is the central theme of the brewery's museum, the Guinness Storehouse, which is the only part of the brewery open to visitors.

It occupies the old Fermentation House, built in 1904. As it's a listed building, the designers could only adapt and add to the structure without taking anything away. The result is a stunning central atrium that rises seven storeys and takes the shape of a pint of Guinness. The head is represented by the glassed Gravity Bar, which provides panoramic views of Dublin to savour with your complimentary half-pint.

Before you race up to the top, however, you might want to check out the museum for which you've paid so handsomely. Actually, it's designed as more of an 'experience' than a museum. It has nearly 1.5 hectares of floor space, featuring a dazzling array of audiovisual and interactive exhibits, which cover most aspects of the brewery's story and explain the brewing process in overwhelming detail.

On the ground floor, a copy of Arthur Guinness' original lease lies embedded beneath a pane of glass in the floor. Wandering up through the various exhibits, including 70-odd years of advertising, you can't help feeling that the now wholly foreign-owned company has hijacked the mythology Dubliners attached to the drink, and it has all become more about marketing and manipulation than mingling and magic.

THE GRAVITY BAR

Whatever reservations you may have, however, can be more than dispelled at the top of the building in the circular Gravity Bar, where you get a complimentary glass of Guinness. The views from the bar are superb, but the Guinness itself is as near-perfect as a beer can be.

St Patrick's Tower, the large smock windmill on the extensive factory grounds, was originally built as part of the Roe Distillery, which once occupied 7 hectares on the north side of James's St and was Europe's largest producer of whiskey. Arthur Guinness didn't much care for whiskey, branding it the 'curse of the nation' (and his own brew the 'nurse of the nation'). The Roe distillery stopped producing whiskey in 1926 and was taken over by Guinness in 1949.

TOP SIGHT
DUBLIN CASTLE

If you're looking for a medieval castle straight out of central casting you'll be disappointed; the stronghold of British power here for 700 years is principally an 18th-century creation that is more hotchpotch palace than turreted castle.

Guided Tours

The 70-minute **guided tours** (departing every 20 to 30 minutes, depending on numbers) are pretty dry, seemingly pitched at tourists more likely to ooh and aah over period furniture than historical anecdotes, but they're included in the entry fee. You get to visit the **State Apartments**, many of which are decorated in dubious taste. There are beautiful chandeliers (ooh!), plush Irish carpets (aah!), splendid rococo ceilings, a Van Dyck portrait and the throne of King George V. You also get to see **St Patrick's Hall**, where Irish presidents are inaugurated and foreign dignitaries toasted, and the room in which the wounded James Connolly was tied to a chair while convalescing after the 1916 Easter Rising – brought back to health to be executed by firing squad.

The highlight is a visit to the **subterranean excavations** of the old castle, discovered by accident in 1986. They include foundations built by the Vikings (whose long-lasting mortar was made of ox blood, eggshells and horsehair), the hand-polished exterior of the castle walls that prevented attackers from climbing them, the steps leading down to the moat and the trickle of the historic River Poddle, which once filled the moat on its way to join the Liffey.

DON'T MISS

➡ Chapel Royal
➡ State Apartments
➡ Upper Yard

PRACTICALITIES

➡ Map p80
➡ ☏ 01-677 7129
➡ www.dublincastle.ie
➡ Dame St
➡ guided tours adult/child €10/4, self-guided tours €7/3
➡ ⊙ 9.45am-5.45pm, last admission 5.15pm
➡ 🚌 all city centre

CHESTER BEATTY LIBRARY

The world-famous Chester Beatty Library, housed in the Clock Tower at the back of Dublin Castle (p68), is not just Ireland's best small museum, but one of the best you'll find anywhere in Europe.

This extraordinary collection, so lovingly and expertly gathered by New York mining magnate Alfred Chester Beatty, is breathtakingly beautiful and virtually guaranteed to impress.

Arts of the Book

The collection is spread over two levels. On the ground floor you'll find *Arts of the Book*, a compact but stunning collection of artworks from the Western, Islamic and East Asian worlds. Highlights include the finest collection of Chinese jade books in the world and illuminated European texts featuring exquisite calligraphy that stand up in comparison with the *Book of Kells*. Audiovisual displays explain the process of bookbinding, paper-making and printing.

Sacred Traditions

The 2nd floor is home to Sacred Traditions, a wonderful exploration of the world's major religions through decorative and religious art, enlightening text and a cool cultural-pastiche video at the entrance. The collection of Qu'rans dating from the 9th to the 19th centuries (the library has more than 270 of them) is considered by experts to be the best example of illuminated Islamic texts in the world. There are also outstanding examples of ancient papyri, including renowned Egyptian love poems from the 12th century, and some of the earliest illuminated gospels in the world, dating from around AD 200.

DON'T MISS

➡ Nara e-hon scrolls (East Asian Collection, Sacred Traditions)

➡ Ibn al-Bawwab Qu'ran (Qu'ran Collection, Sacred Traditions)

➡ New Testament papyri (Western Collection, Sacred Traditions)

PRACTICALITIES

➡ Map p80

➡ ☎ 01-407 0750

➡ www.cbl.ie

➡ Dublin Castle

➡ ⊙ 10am-5pm Mon-Fri, 11am-5pm Sat, 1-5pm Sun year-round, closed Mon Nov-Feb, free tours 1pm Wed, 2pm Sat & 3pm Sun

➡ 🚌 all city centre

⊙ Sights

⊙ Grafton Street & Around

Trinity College   HISTORIC BUILDING
See p64.

Dublin Castle   HISTORIC BUILDING
See p68.

Chester Beatty Library   MUSEUM
See p69.

★ Little Museum of Dublin   MUSEUM
(Map p80; ☑01-661 1000; www.littlemuseum.
ie; 15 St Stephen's Green N; adult/student €8/6;
☺9.30am-5pm Mon-Wed & Fri, to 8pm Thu;
▣all city centre, ▣St Stephen's Green) This
award-winning museum tells the story of
Dublin over the last century via memorabilia, photographs and artefacts donated
by the general public. The impressive collection, spread over the rooms of a handsome Georgian house, includes a lectern
used by JFK on his 1963 visit to Ireland
and an original copy of the fateful letter
given to the Irish envoys to the treaty negotiations of 1921, whose contradictory
instructions were at the heart of the split
that resulted in the Civil War.

There's a whole room on the 2nd floor
devoted to the history of U2, as well as the
personal archive of Alfred 'Alfie' Byrne (1882–
1956), mayor of Dublin a record 10 times and
known as the 'Shaking Hand of Dublin'. Vis-

it is by guided tour, which goes on the hour
every hour. The museum also runs the Green
Mile walking tour (p99) of St Stephen's Green.

★ St Stephen's Green   PARK
(Map p72; ☺dawn-dusk; ▣all city centre, ▣St
Stephen's Green) As you watch the assorted groups of friends, lovers and individuals splaying themselves across the nine
elegantly landscaped hectares of Dublin's
most popular green lung, St Stephen's
Green, consider that those same hectares
once formed a common for public whip-
pings, burnings and hangings. These days,
the harshest treatment you'll get is the
warden chucking you off the grass for playing football or Frisbee.

The buildings around the square date
mainly from the mid-18th century, when the
green was landscaped and became the centrepiece of Georgian Dublin. The northern
side was known as the Beaux Walk and it's
still one of Dublin's most esteemed stretches,
home to Dublin's original society hotel, the
Shelbourne (p105). Nearby is the tiny **Huguenot Cemetery** (☺closed to public), established in 1693 by French Protestant refugees.

Railings and locked gates were erected
in 1814, when an annual fee of one guinea
was charged to use the green. This private
use continued until 1877 when Sir Arthur Edward Guinness pushed an act through parliament opening the green to the public once
again. He also financed the central park's
gardens and ponds, which date from 1880.

BOOK OF KELLS

The history of the *Book of Kells* is almost as fascinating as its illuminations. It is thought
to have been created around AD 800 by the monks at St Colmcille's Monastery on Iona, a
remote island off the coast of Scotland; repeated looting by marauding Vikings forced the
monks to flee to Kells, County Meath, along with their masterpiece. It was stolen in 1007,
then rediscovered three months later buried underground. The *Book of Kells* was brought
to Trinity College for safekeeping in 1654, and is now housed in the **Old Library** (p65), with
over half a million visitors queueing up to see it annually. The 680-page (340-folio) book
was rebound in four calfskin volumes in 1953.

And here the problems begin. Of the 680 pages, only two are on display – one showing
an illumination, the other showing text – hence the 'page of Kells' moniker. No getting
around that one, though: you can hardly expect the right to thumb through a priceless
treasure at random. No, the real problem is its immense popularity, which makes viewing
it a rather unsatisfactory pleasure. Punters are herded through the specially constructed
viewing room at lightning pace, making for a quick-look-and-move-along kind of experience.

To really appreciate the book, you can get your own reproduction copy for a mere
€22,000. Failing that, the Old Library bookshop stocks a plethora of souvenirs and other
memorabilia, including Bernard Meehan's *The Book of Kells* (€17), which includes plenty of
reproductions plus excellent accompanying text.

Trinity College

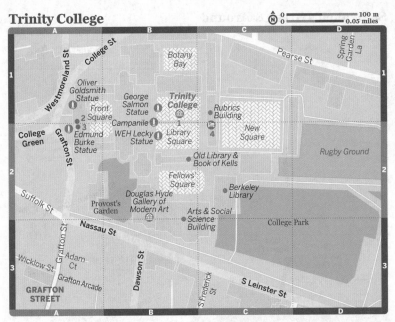

The main entrance to the green today is beneath **Fusiliers' Arch** (Map p80), at the top of Grafton St. Modelled to look like a smaller version of the Arch of Titus in Rome, the arch commemorates the 212 soldiers of the Royal Dublin Fusiliers who were killed fighting for the British in the Boer War (1899–1902).

Spread across the green's lawns and walkways are some notable artworks; the most imposing of these is a **monument to Wolfe Tone** (Map p72), the leader of the abortive 1798 Rising. Occupying the northeastern corner of the green, the vertical slabs serving as a backdrop to the statue have been dubbed 'Tonehenge'. At this entrance is a **memorial** (Map p72) to all those who died in the Potato Famine (1845–51).

On the eastern side of the green is a **children's playground** (Map p72; ⊘dawn-dusk) and to the south there's a fine old **bandstand**, erected to celebrate Queen Victoria's jubilee in 1887. Musical performances often take place here in summer. Near the bandstand is a **bust of James Joyce** (Map p72).

Bank of Ireland   NOTABLE BUILDING
(Map p80; ☑01-671 1488; College Green; ⊘10am-4pm Mon-Wed & Fri, to 5pm Thu; ☐all city centre) A sweeping Palladian pile occupying one side of

Trinity College

College Green, this magnificent building was the Irish Parliament House until 1801 and was the first purpose-built parliament building in the world. The original building – the central colonnaded section that distinguishes the present-day structure – was designed by Sir Edward Lovett Pearce in 1729 and completed by James Gandon in 1733.

When the parliament voted itself out of existence through the 1801 Act of Union, the building was sold under the condition that the interior would be altered to prevent it ever again being used as a debating chamber. It was a spiteful strike at Irish parliamentary aspirations, but while the central House of Commons was remodelled and offers little hint of its former role, the smaller **House of Lords** (admission free) survived

St Stephen's Green & Around

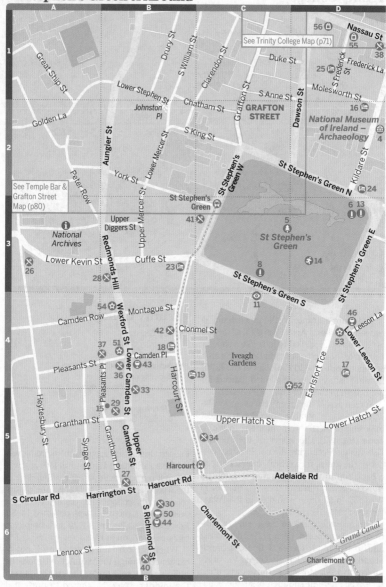

and is much more interesting. It has Irish oak woodwork, a mahogany longcase parliament clock and a late-18th-century Dublin crystal chandelier. Its design was copied for the construction of the original House of Representatives in Washington, DC, now the National Statuary Hall. The House of Lords is open to visitors during banking hours and Dublin historian Sean Ó Laocha does prearranged tours of the chamber on Tuesdays between 10.30am and 12.30pm.

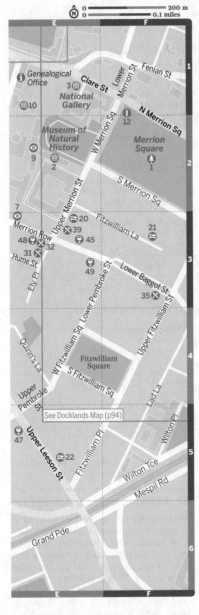

and 1779, and botched in the mid-19th century when it became the offices of the local government (hence its name). Thankfully, a more recent renovation (2000) has restored it to its gleaming Georgian best. The basement has an exhibit on the city's history.

The rotunda and its ambulatory form a breathtaking interior, bathed in natural light from enormous windows to the east. A vast marble statue of former mayor and Catholic emancipator Daniel O'Connell stands here as a reminder of the building's links with Irish nationalism (the funerals of both Charles Stewart Parnell and Michael Collins were held here). Dublin City Council still meets here on the first Monday of the month, gathering to discuss the city's business in the Council Chamber, which was the original building's coffee room.

There was a sordid precursor to City Hall on this spot in the shape of the Lucas Coffee House and the adjoining Eagle Tavern, in which the notorious Hellfire Club was founded by Richard Parsons, Earl of Rosse, in 1735. Although the city abounded with gentlemen's clubs, this particular one gained a reputation for messing about in the arenas of sex and Satan, two topics that were guaranteed to fire the lurid imaginings of the city's gossip-mongers.

Located in the striking vaulted basement, **The Story of the Capital** is a multimedia exhibition that traces the history of the city from its earliest beginnings to its hoped-for future – with ne'er a mention of sex and Satan. More's the pity, as the info is quite overwhelming and the exhibits are a little text-heavy. Still, it's a pretty slick museum with informative audiovisual displays.

Royal College of Surgeons   UNIVERSITY
(Map p80; www.rcsi.ie; 123 St Stephen's Green W; ⊘ closed to the public; 🚌 all city centre) The early 19th-century Royal College of Surgeons has one of the finest facades on St Stephen's Green. During the 1916 Easter Rising, the building was occupied by rebel forces led by the colourful Countess Markievicz (1868–1927), an Irish Nationalist married to a supposed Polish count. The columns are scarred with bullet holes. Today it continues to produce doctors, and is especially popular with students from overseas.

Newman House   NOTABLE BUILDING
(Map p72; 📞 01-477 9810; www.ucd.ie; 85-86 St Stephen's Green S; ⊘ closed; 🚌 all city centre, 🚆 St Stephen's Green) Among the finest examples

City Hall   MUSEUM
(Map p80; www.dublincity.ie/dublincityhall; Dame St; adult/student/child €4/2/1.50; ⊘ 10am-5.15pm Mon-Sat; 🚌 all city centre) This beautiful Georgian structure was originally built by Thomas Cooley as the Royal Exchange between 1769

St Stephen's Green & Around

of Georgian architecture in Dublin are these two townhouses, founded by Cardinal Newman as the Catholic University of Ireland in 1865, along with an adjoining Victorian hall. The alma mater of James Joyce, Pádraig Pearse and Eamon de Valera is currently closed pending a major restoration that will also see the opening of a new museum dedicated to Irish writers in 2019.

City Assembly House   HISTORIC BUILDING
(Map p80; www.igs.ie; 58 South William St; ☉10am-6pm Mon-Sat; 🚇all city centre) FREE
This Georgian townhouse was built between 1766 and 1771 by the Society of Artists as the first purpose-built public exhibition room in the British Isles. During the 19th century it served as an unofficial city hall but it is now the headquarters of the Irish Georgian

Society, who are restoring it to its original purpose. It now hosts exhibitions.

◎ Merrion Square & Around

Georgian Dublin's apotheosis occurred in the exquisite architecture and elegant spaces of Merrion and Fitzwilliam Sqs. Here you'll find the perfect mix of imposing public buildings, museums, and private offices and residences. It is round these parts that much of moneyed Dublin works and plays, amid the neoclassical beauties thrown up during Dublin's 18th-century prime. These include the home of the Irish parliament at Leinster House and, immediately surrounding it, the National Gallery, the main branch of the National Museum of Ireland and the Museum of Natural History.

★ **Merrion Square** PARK

(Map p72; ☉ dawn-dusk; ☐ all city centre) Merrion Sq is the most prestigious and, arguably, the most elegant of Dublin's Georgian squares. Its well-kept lawns and tended flower beds are flanked on three sides by gorgeous Georgian houses with colourful doors, peacock fanlights, ornate door knockers and, occasionally, foot-scrapers, used to remove mud from shoes. Over the last two centuries they've been used by some notable residents.

The square, laid out in 1762, is bordered on its fourth side by the National Gallery (p75) and Leinster House (p78) – all of which, apparently, isn't enough for some. One former resident, W B Yeats (1865–1939), was less than impressed and described the architecture as 'grey 18th century'; there's just no pleasing some people.

Just inside the northwestern corner of the square is a flamboyant **statue of Oscar Wilde** (Map p72; ☉ dawn-dusk; ☐ 7, 8 & 46A from city centre).

★ **National Museum of Ireland – Archaeology** MUSEUM

(Map p72; www.museum.ie; Kildare St; ☉ 10am-5pm Tue-Sat, 2-5pm Sun; ☐ all city centre) **FREE** Ireland's most important cultural institution was established in 1877 as the primary repository of the nation's archaeological treasures. These include the most famous of Ireland's crafted artefacts, the **Ardagh Chalice** and the **Tara Brooch**, dating from the 12th and 8th centuries respectively. They are part of the **Treasury**, itself part of Europe's finest collection of Bronze and Iron Age gold artefacts, and the most complete assemblage of medieval Celtic metalwork in the world.

Also part of the Treasury is the exhibition **Ór-Ireland's Gold**, featuring stunning jewellery and decorative objects created by Celtic artisans in the Bronze and Iron Ages. Among them are the **Broighter Hoard**, which includes a 1st-century-BC large gold collar, unsurpassed anywhere in Europe, and an extraordinarily delicate gold boat. There's also the wonderful Loughnashade bronze war trumpet, which also dates from the 1st century BC.

The other showstopper is the collection of Iron Age 'bog bodies' in the **Kingship and Sacrifice** exhibit – four figures in varying states of preservation dug out of the midland bogs. The bodies' various eerily preserved details – a distinctive tangle of hair, sinewy legs and fingers with fingernails intact – are memorable, but it's the accompanying detail that will make you pause: scholars now believe that all of these bodies were victims of the most horrendous ritualistic torture and sacrifice – the cost of being notable figures in the Celtic world.

Upstairs are **Medieval Ireland 1150 – 1550, Viking Ireland** – which features exhibits from the excavations at Wood Quay, the area between Christ Church Cathedral and the river – and **Ancient Egypt**, featuring items acquired from excavations conducted between 1890 and 1930.

The museum has three sister museums throughout the country: the stuffed beasts of the Museum of Natural History (p78), the decorative arts section at Collins Barracks (p87), and a country life museum (p422) in County Mayo, on Ireland's west coast.

★ **National Gallery** MUSEUM

(Map p72; www.nationalgallery.ie; West Merrion Sq; ☉ 9.15am-5.30pm Mon-Wed, Fri & Sat, to 8.30pm Thu, 11am-5.30pm Sun; ☐ 4, 7, 8, 46A from city centre) **FREE** A magnificent Caravaggio and a breathtaking collection of works by Jack B Yeats – William Butler's younger brother – are the main reasons to visit the National Gallery, but not the only ones. Its excellent collection is strong in Irish art, and there are

---

LITERARY ADDRESSES

Merrion Sq has long been the favoured address of Dublin's affluent intelligentsia. **Oscar Wilde** spent much of his youth at 1 North Merrion Sq, now the campus of the American College Dublin. Grumpy **WB Yeats** (1865–1939) lived at 52 East Merrion Sq and later, from 1922 to 1928, at 82 South Merrion Sq. **George (AE) Russell** (1867–1935), the self-described 'poet, mystic, painter and cooperator', worked at No 84. The great Liberator **Daniel O'Connell** (1775–1847) was a resident of No 58 in his later years. Austrian **Erwin Schrödinger** (1887–1961), he of the alive, dead or simultaneously both cat paradox and co-winner of the 1933 Nobel Prize for Physics, lived at No 65 from 1940 to 1956. Dublin seems to attract writers of horror stories and **Joseph Sheridan Le Fanu** (1814–73), who penned the vampire classic *Camilla*, was a resident of No 70.

Dublin

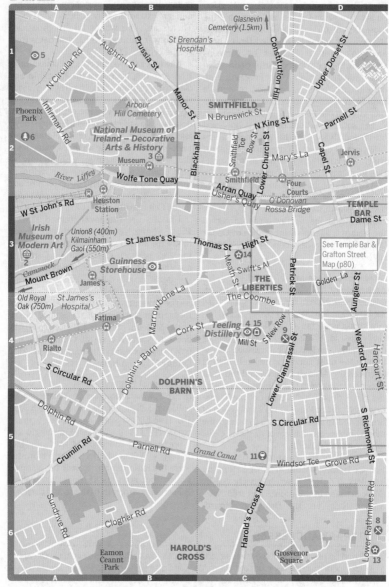

Glasnevin ↑
Cemetery (1.5km)

St Brendan's
Hospital

Phoenix
Park

6

N Circular Rd

Aughrim St

Prussia St

Infirmary Rd

Arbour
Hill Cemetery

Manor St

SMITHFIELD

N Brunswick St

Constitution Hill

Upper Dorset St

Parnell St

**National Museum of
Ireland – Decorative
Arts & History**
Museum **3**

Blackhall Pl

Smithfield
Tce

Bow St

N King St

Lower Church St

Capel St

Jervis

River Liffey

Wolfe Tone Quay

Arran Quay

Mary's La

Four
Courts

TEMPLE
BAR
Dame St

W St John's Rd

Heuston
Station

Usher's Quay

O'Donovan
Rossa Bridge

Irish
Museum of
Modern Art
2

Union8 (400m)
Kilmainham
Gaol (550m)

St James's St

Thomas St

High St

See Temple Bar &
Grafton Street
Map (p80)

Camnock

Mount Brown

**Guinness
Storehouse 1**

Meath St

Swift's Al

Patrick St

Golden La

Aungier St

Old Royal
Oak (750m)

James's

St James's
Hospital

THE
LIBERTIES

Fatima

Marrowbone La

The Coombe

Wexford St

Harcourt St

Rialto

S Circular Rd

Cork St

Teeling 4 15
Distillery 9
Mill St

S New Row

Lower Clanbrassil St

S Richmond St

Dolphin's Barn

**DOLPHIN'S
BARN**

Dolphin Rd

Crumlin Rd

Parnell Rd

Grand Canal **11**

S Circular Rd

Windsor Tce

Grove Rd

Sundrive Rd

Clogher Rd

**HAROLD'S
CROSS**

Harold's Cross Rd

Lower Rathmines Rd

8

13

Eamon
Ceannt
Park

Grosvenor
Square

also high-quality collections of every major European school of painting.

Spread about its four wings you'll find: works by Rembrandt and his circle; a Spanish collection with paintings by El Greco, Goya and Picasso; and a well-represented display of Italian works dating from the early Renaissance to the 18th century. Fra Angelico, Titian and Tintoretto are among the artists represented, but the highlight is undoubtedly Caravaggio's *The Taking of Christ* (1602), which lay for over 60 years

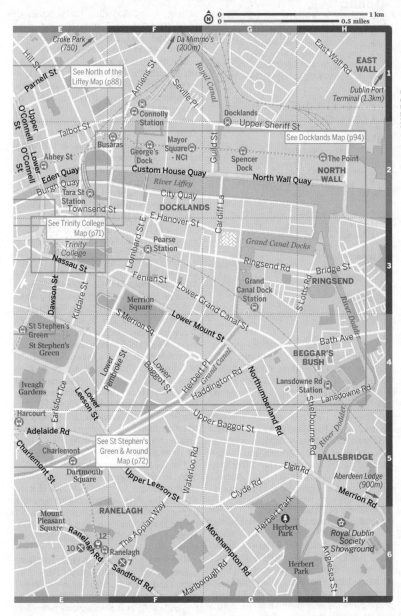

in a Jesuit house in Leeson St and was accidentally discovered by chief curator Sergio Benedetti.

The ground floor displays the gallery's fine Irish collection, plus a smaller British collection, with works by Reynolds, Hogarth, Gainsborough, Landseer and Turner. Absolutely unmissable is the **Yeats Collection** at the back of the gallery, displaying more than 30 works by Irish Impressionist Jack B Yeats (1871–1957), Ireland's most important 20th-century painter.

Dublin

Pending ongoing restorations to the main building, entrance is via the light-filled modern **Millennium Wing** on Clare St. Here you'll also find a small collection of 20th-century Irish art, high-profile visiting collections (for which there are admission charges), an art reference library, a lecture theatre, a good bookshop and Fitzer's Café.

There are free tours at 12.30pm on Saturdays and at 11.30am, 12.30pm and 1.30pm on Sundays. The gallery also has a free Masterpieces app (available for both Android and iPhone) featuring 80% of its collection.

★ **Museum of Natural History**   MUSEUM
(National Museum of Ireland – Natural History; Map p72; www.museum.ie; Upper Merrion St; ⊙10am-5pm Tue-Sat, 2-5pm Sun; 🚌7, 44 from city centre) FREE Dusty, weird and utterly compelling, this window into Victorian times has barely changed since Scottish explorer Dr David Livingstone opened it in 1857 – before disappearing into the African jungle for a meeting with Henry Stanley. It is a fine example of Victorian charm and scientific wonderment, and its enormous collection is a testament to the skill of taxidermy.

The **Irish Room** on the ground floor is filled with mammals, sea creatures, birds and some butterflies all found in Ireland at some point, including the skeletons of three 10,000-year-old Irish elk that greet you as you enter. The **World Animals Collection**, spread across three levels, has as its centrepiece the skeleton of a 20m-long fin whale found beached in County Sligo. Evolutionists will love the line-up of orang-utan, chimpanzee, gorilla and human skeletons on the 1st floor.

A more recent addition is the **Discovery Zone**, where visitors can do some firsthand exploring of their own, handling taxidermy specimens and opening drawers. Other notables include a Tasmanian tiger (an extinct Australian marsupial, mislabelled as a Tasmanian wolf), a giant panda from China, and several African and Asian rhinoceros. The wonderful **Blaschka Collection** comprises finely detailed glass models of marine creatures whose zoological accuracy is incomparable.

Leinster House   NOTABLE BUILDING
(Oireachtas Éireann; Map p72; 📞01-618 3271; www.oireachtas.ie; Kildare St; ⊙observation galleries 2.30-8.30pm Tue, 10.30am-8.30pm Wed, 10.30am-5.30pm Thu Nov-May; 🚌all city centre) All the big decisions are made at the Oireachtas (parliament). This Palladian mansion was built as a city residence for James Fitzgerald, the Duke of Leinster and Earl of Kildare, by Richard Cassels between 1745 and 1748. Prearranged free **guided tours** (Map p72; www.oireachtas.ie; Kildare St; ⊙10.30am, 11.30am, 2.30pm & 3.30pm Mon-Fri; 🚌all city centre) FREE are available when parliament is in session (but not sitting); entry tickets to the observation galleries are available.

The Kildare St facade looks like a townhouse (which inspired Irish architect James Hoban's design for the US White House), whereas the Merrion Sq frontage resembles a country mansion. The obelisk in front of the building is dedicated to Arthur Griffith, Michael Collins and Kevin O'Higgins, the architects of independent Ireland.

The first government of the Irish Free State moved in from 1922, and both the Dáil (lower house) and Seanad (senate, or upper house) still meet here to discuss the affairs of the nation and gossip at the exclusive members bar. The 60-member Seanad meets for fairly low-key sessions in the north-wing saloon, while there are usually more sparks and tantrums when the 166-member Dáil bangs heads in a less-interesting room, formerly a lecture theatre, which was added to the original building in 1897. Parliament sits for 90 days a year.

⊙ Temple Bar

You can visit all of Temple Bar's attractions in less than half a day, but that's not really the point: this cobbled neighbourhood, for so long the city's most infamous party zone, is really more about ambience than attractions. If you visit during the day, the district's bohemian bent is on display. You can browse for vintage clothes, get your nipples pierced, nibble on Mongolian barbecue, buy organic food, pick up the latest musical releases and buy books on every conceivable subject. You can check out the latest art installations or join in a pulsating drum circle. By night – or at the weekend – it's a different story altogether, as the area's bars are packed to the rafters with revellers looking to tap into their inner Bacchus: it's loud, raucous and usually a lot of fun. Temple Bar is also Dublin's official 'cultural quarter', so you shouldn't ignore its more high-minded offerings like the progressive Project Arts Centre (p124), **Temple Bar Gallery & Studios** (Map p80; ☑01-671 0073; www.templebargallery.com; 5 Temple Bar; ⊙11am-6pm Tue-Sat; ☒all city centre) **FREE** and the Irish Film Institute (p125).

★**Christ Church Cathedral**   CHURCH
(Church of the Holy Trinity; Map p80; www.christchurchcathedral.ie; Christ Church Pl; adult/student/child €6.50/4/2.50, with Dublinia €14.50/12/7.50; ⊙9am-5pm Mon-Sat, 12.30-2.30pm Sun year-round, longer hours Mar-Oct; ☒50, 50A, 56A from Aston Quay, 54, 54A from Burgh Quay) Its hilltop location and eye-catching flying buttresses make this the most photogenic of Dublin's cathedrals. It was founded in 1030 and rebuilt from 1172, mostly under the impetus of Richard de Clare, Earl of Pembroke (better known as Strongbow), the Anglo-Norman noble who invaded Ireland in 1170 and whose monument has pride of place inside.

Guided tours (Map p80; www.christchurch cathedral.ie; Christ Church Pl; adult/family €4/12; ⊙12.10pm, 2pm & 4pm Mon-Fri, 2pm, 3pm & 4pm Sat; ☒50, 50A, 56A from Aston Quay, 54, 54A from Burgh Quay) include the belfry, where a campanologist explains the art of bell-ringing and you can even have a go.

Once the original wooden church was replaced by the building you see today, the cathedral vied for supremacy with nearby St Patrick's Cathedral, but like its sister church it fell on hard times in the 18th and 19th centuries – the nave was been used as a market and the crypt housed taverns – and was virtually derelict by the time restoration took place. Today, both Church of Ireland cathedrals are outsiders in a largely Catholic nation.

From the southeastern entrance to the churchyard, walk past ruins of the **chapter house**, which dates from 1230. The entrance to the cathedral is at the southwestern corner and as you enter you face the northern wall. This survived the collapse of its southern

---

DUBLIN IN...

Two Days

If you've only got two days (whatever is taking you away better be worth it!), start with **Trinity College** (p64) and the **Book of Kells** (p65) before venturing into the Georgian heartland – amble through **St Stephen's Green** (p70) and **Merrion Square** (p75), and be sure to visit both the **National Museum of Ireland – Archaeology** (p75) and the **National Gallery** (p75). In the evening, try an authentic Dublin pub – **Kehoe's** (p117) off Grafton St will do nicely. The next day go west, stopping at the **Chester Beatty Library** (p69) on your way to the **Guinness Storehouse** (p66); if you still have the legs for it, the **Irish Museum of Modern Art** (p85) and **Kilmainham Gaol** (p84) will round off your day perfectly. Take in a traditional Irish music session at the **Cobblestone** (p121).

Four Days

Follow the two-day itinerary, but stretch it out with refuelling stops at some of the city's better pubs. Visit **Glasnevin Cemetery** (p95) and the **Dublin City Gallery – Hugh Lane** (p86). Become a whiskey expert at the **Old Jameson Distillery** (p87) and a literary (or beer) ace with a **Dublin Literary Pub Crawl** (p100). Explore the north side's blossoming foodie scene – there's superb Italian at **Da Mimmo's** (☑01-856 1714; www. damimmo.ie; 148 North Strand Rd; mains €10-16; ⊙noon-10pm; ☒53 from Talbot St). Oh, and don't forget Temple Bar, where there are distractions for every taste.

Temple Bar & Grafton Street

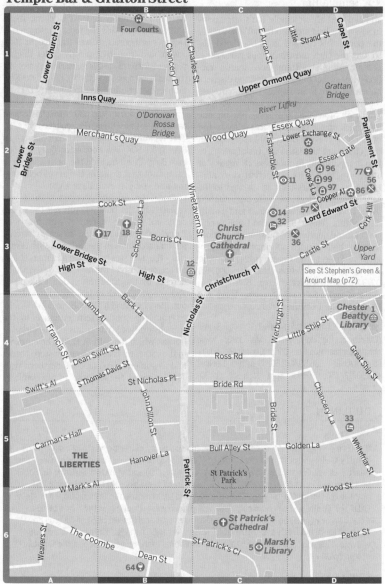

counterpart but has also suffered from subsiding foundations.

The monument to Strongbow is in the southern aisle. The armoured figure on the tomb is unlikely to be Strongbow (it's more probably the Earl of Drogheda), but his internal organs may have been buried here. A popular legend relates that the half figure beside the tomb is Strongbow's son, who was cut in two by his father when his bravery in battle was suspect.

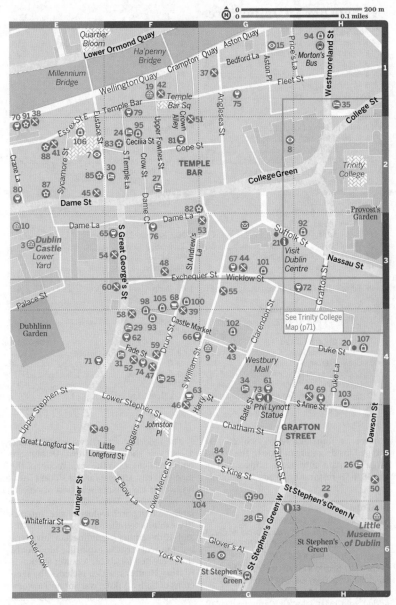

The southern transept contains the superb baroque **tomb** of the 19th Earl of Kildare (died 1734). His grandson, Lord Edward Fitzgerald, was a member of the United Irishmen and died in the abortive 1798 Rising.

An entrance just by the south transept descends to the unusually large arched **crypt**, which dates back to the original Viking church. Curiosities in the crypt include a glass display case housing a mummified cat chasing a mummified rat

Temple Bar & Grafton Street

(known as Tom and Jerry), which were trapped inside an organ pipe in the 1860s! From the main entrance, a bridge, part of the 1871–78 restoration, leads to Dublinia (p82).

Dublinia: Experience Viking & Medieval Dublin MUSEUM
(Map p80; ☏01-679 4611; www.dublinia.ie; Christ Church Pl; adult/student/child €9.50/8.50/6, with Christchurch Cathedral €14.50/12/7.50; ⊙10am-5.30pm Mar-Sep, to 4.30pm Oct-Feb; 🚌50, 50A, 56A from Aston Quay, 54, 54A from Burgh Quay) A must for the kids, the old Synod Hall, added to Christ Church Cathedral (p79) during its late 19th-century restoration, is home to the seemingly perennial Dublinia, a lively and kitschy attempt to bring Viking and medieval Dublin to life. Models, streetscapes and somewhat old-fashioned interactive displays do a fairly decent job of it, at least for kids.

The model of a medieval quayside and a cobbler's shop in **Medieval Dublin** are both excellent, as is the scale model of the medieval city. Up one floor is **Viking Dublin**, which has a large selection of objects recovered from Wood Quay, the world's largest Viking archaeological site. Interactive exhibits tell the story of Dublin's 9th- and 10th-century Scandinavian invaders, but the real treat is exploring life aboard the re-created longboat. A newer section is **History Hunters**, which includes the skeletons of both a Viking warrior and a woman who died in the Middle Ages. You'll also hear the languages of old Dublin. Finally, you can climb neighbouring **St Michael's Tower** and peek through its grubby windows for views over the city to the Dublin hills. There is also a pleasant cafe and the inevitable souvenir shop.

Icon Factory
ARTS CENTRE

(Map p80; ☑086 202 4533; www.iconfactory
dublin.ie; 3 Aston Pl; ☺11am-6pm; ☒all city centre) FREE This fantastic artists collective in
the heart of Temple Bar hosts exhibitions
on Ireland's cultural heritage. You'll find
colourful, unique souvenirs celebrating the
very best in Irish music and literature and
every sale goes towards the artists themselves. Take a stroll around their Icon Walk
outside and get better acquainted with
Irish playwrights, rock stars, sporting heroes and actors.

Ha'penny Bridge
BRIDGE

(Map p88; ☒all city centre) Dublin's most famous bridge is the Ha'penny Bridge, built
in 1816. One of the world's oldest cast-iron
bridges, it was built to replace the seven
ferries that plied a busy route between the
two banks of the river. Officially known
as the Liffey Bridge, it gets its name from
the ha'penny toll that was charged until
1919 (for a time the toll was one and a
half pence, and so it was called the Penny
Ha'penny Bridge).

Contemporary Music Centre
ARTS CENTRE

(Map p80; ☑01-490 1857; www.cmc.ie; 19
Fishamble St; ☺10am-5.30pm Mon-Fri; ☒all
city centre) FREE Anyone with an interest
in Irish contemporary music must visit
the CMC's national archive where you can
hear (and play around with on an electronic organ) 10,000 samples from composers
of this and the last century. There's also a
good reference library where you can attend courses and meet composers.

◉ Kilmainham & the Liberties

Guinness Storehouse
BREWERY, MUSEUM

See p66.

TRACING YOUR ANCESTORS

The **Genealogical Office** (Map p72; ☑ 01-603 0200; Kildare St, 2nd fl, National Library; ⊘ 9.30am-5pm Mon-Fri, 9.30am-1pm Sat; ☐ all city centre) at the **National Library** (Map p72; www.nli.ie; Kildare St; ⊘ 9.30am-7.45pm Mon-Wed, to 4.45pm Thu & Fri, 9.30am-12.45pm Sat; ☐ all city centre) **FREE** will advise you on how to trace your ancestry, which is a good way to begin your research if you have no other experience. For information on commercial agencies that will do the research for you, contact the **Association of Professional Genealogists** (AGI; www.accreditedgenealogists.ie; c/o the Genealogy Advisory Service, Kildare St; ☐ all city centre) in Ireland. The files of the National Library and the **National Archives** (Map p72; ☑ 01-407 2300; www.nationalarchives.ie; Bishop St, Dublin 8; ⊘ 10am-5pm Mon-Fri; ☐ all city centre) are all potential sources of genealogical information.

★ **Kilmainham Gaol**   MUSEUM
(☑ 01-453 2037; www.kilmainhamgaolmuseum.ie; Inchicore Rd; adult/child €8/4; ⊘ 9.30am-6.45pm Jul & Aug, to 5.30pm rest of year; ☐ 69, 79 from Aston Quay, 13, 40 from O'Connell St) If you have *any* desire to understand Irish history – especially the juicy bits about resistance to British rule – then a visit to this former prison is an absolute must. This threatening grey building, built between 1792 and 1795, played a role in virtually every act of Ireland's painful path to independence, and even today, despite closing in 1924, it still has the power to chill.

The uprisings of 1798, 1803, 1848, 1867 and 1916 ended with the leaders' confinement here. Robert Emmet, Thomas Francis Meagher, Charles Stewart Parnell and the 1916 Easter Rising leaders were all visitors, but it was the executions in 1916 that most deeply etched the jail's name into the Irish consciousness. Of the 15 executions that took place between 3 May and 12 May after the revolt, 14 were conducted here. As a finale, prisoners from the Civil War were held here from 1922.

An excellent audiovisual introduction to the building is followed by a thought-provoking tour of the eerie prison, the largest unoccupied building of its kind in Europe.

Sitting incongruously outside in the yard is the *Asgard*, the ship that successfully ran the British blockade to deliver arms to Nationalist forces in 1914. The tour finishes in the gloomy yard where the 1916 executions took place. Entrance is via the Kilmainham Courthouse next door.

★ **St Patrick's Cathedral**   CATHEDRAL
(Map p80; www.stpatrickscathedral.ie; St Patrick's Close; adult/child €6.50/free; ⊘ 9.30am-5pm Mon-Fri, 9am-6pm Sat, 9-10.30am & 12.30-2.30pm Sun; ☐ 50, 50A, 56A from Aston Quay, 54, 54A from Burgh Quay) Ireland's largest church is St Patrick's Cathedral, built between 1191 and 1270 on the site of an earlier church that had stood here since the 5th century. It was here that St Patrick himself reputedly baptised the local Celtic chieftains, making this bit of ground some fairly sacred turf: the well in question is in the adjacent **St Patrick's Park**, which was once a slum but is now a lovely spot to sit and take a load off.

Like Christ Church Cathedral, the building has suffered a rather dramatic history of storm and fire damage and has been altered several times (most questionably in 1864 when the flying buttresses were added, thanks to the neo-Gothic craze that swept the nation). Oliver Cromwell, during his 1649 visit to Ireland, converted St Patrick's to a stable for his army's horses, an indignity to which he also subjected numerous other Irish churches. Jonathan Swift, author of *Gulliver's Travels*, was the dean of the cathedral from 1713 to 1745, but after his tenure the cathedral was very neglected until its restoration in the 1860s. Also like Christ Church, St Patrick's is a Church of Ireland cathedral – which means that overwhelmingly Catholic Dublin has two Anglican cathedrals!

Entering the cathedral from the southwestern porch you come almost immediately, on your right, to the **graves of Swift and his long-time companion Esther Johnson**, aka Stella. On the wall nearby are Swift's own (self-praising) Latin epitaphs to the two of them, and a bust of Swift.

The huge, dusty **Boyle Monument** to the left was erected in 1632 by Richard Boyle, Earl of Cork, and is decorated with numerous painted figures of members of his family. The figure in the centre on the bottom level is the earl's five-year-old son Robert Boyle (1627–91), who grew up to become a noted scientist. His contributions to physics include Boyle's Law, which relates to the pressure and volume of gases.

★ Marsh's Library   LIBRARY

(Map p80; www.marshlibrary.ie; St Patrick's Close; adult/child €3/free; ⊙ 9.30am-5pm Mon & Wed-Fri, 10am-5pm Sat; 🚌 50, 50A, 56A from Aston Quay, 54, 54A from Burgh Quay) This magnificently preserved scholars' library, virtually unchanged in three centuries, is one of Dublin's most beautiful open secrets and an absolute highlight of any visit. Atop its ancient stairs are beautiful, dark-oak bookcases, each topped with elaborately carved and gilded gables, and crammed with 25,000 books, manuscripts and maps dating back to the 15th century.

Founded in 1701 by Archbishop Narcissus Marsh (1638–1713) and opened in 1707, the library was designed by Sir William Robinson, the man also responsible for the Royal Hospital Kilmainham (p85). It's the oldest public library in the country, and contains 25,000 books dating from the 16th to the early 18th century, as well as maps, manuscripts (including one in Latin dating back to 1400) and a collection of incunabula (books printed before 1500).

★ Irish Museum of Modern Art   MUSEUM

(IMMA; Map p76; www.imma.ie; Military Rd; ⊙ 11.30am-5.30pm Tue-Fri, 10am-5.30pm Sat, noon-5.30pm Sun, tours 1.15pm Wed, 2.30pm Sat & Sun; 🚌 51, 51D, 51X, 69, 78, 79 from Aston Quay, 🚆 Heuston) FREE Ireland's most important collection of modern and contemporary Irish and international art is housed in the elegant, airy expanse of the Royal Hospital Kilmainham, designed by Sir William Robinson and built between 1684 and 1687 as a retirement home for soldiers. It fulfilled this role until 1928, after which it languished for nearly 50 years until a 1980s restoration saw it come back to life as this wonderful repository of art.

The building, which was inspired by Les Invalides in Paris, is a marvellous example of the Anglo-Dutch style that preceded the Georgian Age; at the time of its construction there were mutterings that it was altogether too fine a place for its residents.

Following Irish independence it was briefly considered as a potential home for the new Irish parliament, but it ended up as a storage facility for the National Museum of Ireland. Restorations began on the

occasion of its 300th birthday in 1984 and it opened in 1991. A major restoration between 2012 and 2013 gave it an extra bit of sparkle.

The blend of old and new comes together wonderfully, and you'll find such contemporary Irish artists as Louis Le Brocquy, Sean Scully, Barry Flanagan, Kathy Prendergrass and Dorothy Cross featured here, as well as a film installation by Neil Jordan. The permanent exhibition also features paintings from heavy-hitters Pablo Picasso and Joan Miró, and is topped up by regular temporary exhibitions. There's a good cafe and bookshop on the grounds.

There are free guided tours of the museum's exhibits throughout the year.

★ Teeling Distillery   DISTILLERY

(Map p76; www.teelingwhiskey.com; 13-17 Newmarket; tours €15-30; ⊙ 9.30am-5.30pm Mon-Fri; 🚌 27, 77A & 151 from city centre) FREE The first new distillery in Dublin for 125 years, Teeling only began production in 2015 and it will be several years before any of the distillate can be called whiskey. In the meantime, you can explore the visitor centre and taste (and buy) whiskeys from the family's other distillery on the Cooley Peninsula.

You'll get a taste of whiskey at the end of the tour, but to try the really good stuff you'll have to upgrade to one of the organised tastings, which range from the Teeling Tasting (€15) to the Single Malt Reserve Tasting (€30), where you'll indulge in three special whiskeys, including the exceptional 21-year-old Reserve Single Malt, voted the world's best at the Whiskey Awards in 2014.

There's also an excellent cafe on the premises.

ⓘ DUBLIN PASS

For heavy-duty sightseeing, the **Dublin Pass** (adult/child one day €52/31, three day €83/52) will save you a packet. It provides free entry to over 25 attractions (including the Guinness Storehouse), discounts at 20 others and guaranteed fast-track entry to some of the busiest sights. To avail of the free Aircoach transfer to and from the airport, order the card online so you have it when you land. Otherwise it's available from any Discover Ireland Dublin Tourism Centre.

War Memorial Gardens
PARK

(www.heritageireland.ie; South Circular Rd, Island-bridge; ☺8am-dusk Mon-Fri, 10am-dusk Sat & Sun; ☒69, 79 from Aston Quay, 13, 40 from O'Connell St) **FREE** Hardly anyone ever ventures this far west, but they're missing a lovely bit of landscaping in the shape of the War Memorial Gardens – by our reckoning as pleasant a patch of greenery as any you'll find in the heart of the Georgian centre. Designed by Sir Edwin Lutyens, the memorial commemorates the 49,400 Irish soldiers who died during WWI – their names are inscribed in the two huge granite bookrooms that stand at one end.

St Audoen's Church of Ireland
CHURCH

(Map p80; ☑01-677 0088; www.heritageireland. ie; Cornmarket, High St; ☺9.30am-5.30pm May-Oct; ☒50, 50A, 56A from Aston Quay, 54, 54A from Burgh Quay) Two churches, side-by-side, each bearing the same name, a tribute to St Audoen, the 7th-century bishop of Rouen (aka Ouen) and patron saint of the Normans. They built the older of the two, the Church of Ireland, between 1181 and 1212, and today it is the only medieval church in Dublin still in use. A free 30-minute guided tour departs every 30 minutes from 9.30am to 4.45pm. Attached to it is the newer, bigger, 19th-century **Catholic St Audoen's** (Map p80; www.heritageireland.ie; Cornmarket, High St; ☺9.30am-4.45pm May-Oct; ☒50, 50A, 56A from Aston Quay, 54, 54A from Burgh Quay) **FREE**.

Through the Norman church's heavily moulded Romanesque Norman door, you can touch the 9th-century 'lucky stone' that was believed to bring good luck to business, and check out the 9th-century slab in the porch that suggests it was built on an even older church. As part of the tour you can explore the ruins as well as the present church, which has funerary monuments that were beheaded by Cromwell's purists. Its tower and door date from the 12th century and the aisle from the 15th century, but the church today is mainly a product of a 19th-century restoration.

St Anne's Chapel, the visitor centre, houses a number of tombstones of leading members of Dublin society from the 16th to 18th centuries. At the top of the chapel is the tower, which holds the three oldest bells in Ireland, dating from 1423. Although the church's exhibits are hardly spectacular, the building itself is beautiful and a genuine slice of medieval Dublin.

The church is entered from the south off High St through **St Audoen's Arch**, which was built in 1240 and is the only surviving reminder of the city gates. The adjoining park is pretty but attracts many unsavoury characters, particularly at night.

◉ North of the Liffey

★ Dublin City Gallery – the Hugh Lane
GALLERY

(Map p88; ☑01-222 5550; www.hughlane.ie; 22 N Parnell Sq; ☺9.45am-6pm Tue-Thu, to 5pm Fri & Sat, 11am-5pm Sun; ☒7, 11, 13, 16, 38, 40, 46A, 123 from city centre) **FREE** Whatever reputation Dublin has as a repository of world-class art has a lot to do with the simply stunning collection at this exquisite gallery, housed in the equally impressive Charlemont House, designed by William Chambers in 1763. Within its walls you'll find the best of contemporary Irish art, a handful of Impressionist classics and Francis Bacon's relocated studio.

The gallery owes its origins to one Sir Hugh Lane (1875–1915). Born in County Cork, Lane worked in London art galleries before setting up his own gallery in Dublin in 1908. He had a connoisseur's eye and a good nose for the directions of the market, which enabled him to build up a superb collection, particularly strong in Impressionists.

Unfortunately for Ireland, neither his talents nor his collection were much appreciated. Irish rejection led him to rewrite his will and bequeath some of the finest works in his collection to the National Gallery in London. Later he relented and added a rider to his will leaving the collection to Dublin but failed to have it witnessed, thus causing a long legal squabble over which gallery had rightful ownership.

The collection of eight paintings (known as the **Hugh Lane Bequest 1917**) was split in two in a 1959 settlement that sees half of them moving back and forth every six years. From 2015 the gallery has *Les Parapluies* by Auguste Renoir, *Portrait of Eva Gonzales* by Edouard Manet, *Jour d'Été* by Berthe Morisot and *View of Louveciennes* by Camille Pissarro.

Impressionist masterpieces notwithstanding, the gallery's most popular exhibit is the **Francis Bacon Studio**, which was painstakingly moved, in all its shambolic mess, from 7 Reece Mews, South Kensington, London, where the Dublin-born artist (1909–92) lived for 31 years. The display features some 80,000 items madly strewn about the place, including slashed canvases and the last painting he was working on.

The gallery is also home to a permanent collection of seven abstract paintings by Irish-born, New York–based Sean Scully, probably Ireland's most famous living painter.

At noon on Sundays, from September to June, the art gallery hosts up to 30 concerts of contemporary classical music.

★ **National Museum of Ireland – Decorative Arts & History** MUSEUM
(Map p76; www.museum.ie; Benburb St; ☺10am-5pm Tue-Sat, 2-5pm Sun; ☐ 25, 66, 67, 90 from city centre, ☐ Museum) FREE Once the world's largest military barracks, this splendid early neoclassical grey-stone building on the Liffey's northern banks was completed in 1704 according to the design of Thomas Burgh (he of Trinity College's Old Library). It is now home to the Decorative Arts & History collection of the National Museum of Ireland, with a range of superb permanent exhibits ranging from a history of the **Easter Rising** to the work of iconic Irish designer **Eileen Gray** (1878–1976).

The building's central square held six entire regiments and is a truly awesome space, surrounded by arcaded colonnades and blocks linked by walking bridges. Following the handover to the new Irish government in 1922, the barracks was renamed to honour Michael Collins, a hero of the struggle for independence, who was killed that year in the Civil War; to this day most Dubliners refer to the museum as the **Collins Barracks**. Indeed, the army coat Collins wore on the day of his death (there's still mud on the sleeve) is part of the **Soldiers and Chiefs** exhibit, which covers the history of Irish soldiery at home and abroad from 1550 to the 21st century.

The museum's exhibits include a treasure trove of artefacts ranging from silver, ceramics and glassware to weaponry, furniture and folk-life displays. The fascinating **Way We Wore** exhibit displays Irish clothing and jewellery from the past 250 years. An intriguing sociocultural study, it highlights the symbolism jewellery and clothing had in bestowing messages of mourning, love and identity. The old Riding School is home to **Proclaiming a Republic: The 1916 Rising**, which opened in 2016 as an enhanced and updated version of the long-standing exhibit dedicated to the rebellion. The exhibit explores the complicated socio-historical background to the

Rising and also includes visceral memorabilia such as firsthand accounts of the violence of the Black and Tans and post-Rising hunger strikes, and the handwritten death certificates of the Republican prisoners and their postcards from Holloway prison. Some of the best pieces are gathered in the **Curator's Choice** exhibition, which is a collection of 25 objects hand-picked by different curators and displayed alongside an account of why they were chosen.

★ **Old Jameson Distillery** MUSEUM
(Map p88; www.jamesonwhiskey.com; Bow St; adult/student/child €18/15/9, masterclasses €55; ☺10am-5pm Mon-Sat, 10.30am-5pm Sun; ☐ 25, 66, 67, 90 from city centre, ☐ Smithfield) Smithfield's biggest draw is devoted to *uisce beatha* (ish-kuh ba-ha, 'the water of life'); that's Irish for whiskey. To its more serious devotees, that is precisely what whiskey is, although they may be put off by the slickness of this museum (occupying part of the old distillery that stopped production in 1971), which shepherds visitors through a compulsory tour of the re-created factory (the tasting at the end is a lot of fun) and into the ubiquitous gift shop.

If you're really serious about whiskey, you can deepen your knowledge with the Whiskey Makers or the Whiskey Shakers, two 90-minute masterclasses that deconstruct the creation of Jameson whiskies and teach how to make a range of whiskey-based cocktails. If you're just buying whiskey, go for the stuff you can't buy at home, such as the excellent Red Breast or the superexclusive Midleton, a very limited reserve that is appropriately expensive.

General Post Office HISTORIC BUILDING
(Map p88; ☏ 01-705 7000; www.anpost.ie; Lower O'Connell St; ☺8am-8pm Mon-Sat; ☐ all city centre, ☐ Abbey) It's not just the country's main post office, or an eye-catching neoclassical building: the General Post Office is at the heart of Ireland's struggle for independence. The GPO served as command HQ for the rebels during the Easter Rising of 1916 and as a result has become the focal point for all kinds of protests, parades and remembrances, as well as home to an interactive visitor centre.

The building – a neoclassical masterpiece designed by Francis Johnston in 1818 – was burnt out in the siege that resulted from the rising, but that wasn't the end of it. There was bitter fighting in and around the GPO

North of the Liffey

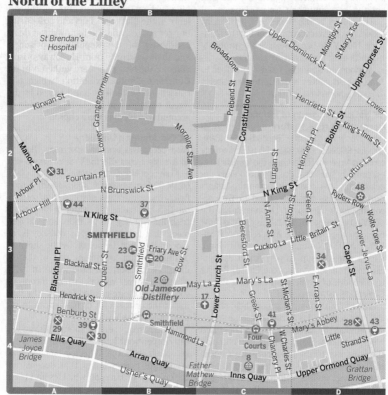

during the Civil War of 1922; you can still see the pockmarks of the struggle in the Doric columns. Since its reopening in 1929 it has lived through quieter times, although its role in Irish history is commemorated inside the visitor centre. For €10, you can take a self-guided tour of an exhibition that brings you through the causes, action and aftermath of the armed rebellion.

James Joyce
Cultural Centre   CULTURAL CENTRE
(Map p88; www.jamesjoyce.ie; 35 N Great George's St; adult/student/child €4.50/3.50/free; ⊙10am-5pm Tue-Sat, noon-5pm Sun; ◻3, 10, 11, 11A, 13, 16, 16A, 19, 19A, 22 from city centre) Denis Maginni, the exuberant, flamboyant dance instructor and 'confirmed bachelor' immortalised by James Joyce in *Ulysses,* taught the finer points of dance out of this beautifully restored Georgian house, now a centre devoted to promoting and preserving the Joycean heritage. Inside are a

handful of exhibits that will pique the interest of a Joyce enthusiast.

The exhibits include some of the furniture from Joyce's Paris apartment; a life-size re-creation of a typical Edwardian bedroom (not Joyce's, but one similar to what James and Nora would have used); and the original door of 7 Eccles St, the home of Leopold and Molly Bloom in *Ulysses,* which was demolished in real life to make way for a private hospital.

It's not much, but the absence of period stuff is more than made up for by the superb interactive displays, which include three short documentary films on various aspects of Joyce's life and work, and – the highlight of the whole place – computers that allow you to explore the content of *Ulysses* episode by episode and trace Joyce's life year by year. It's enough to demolish the myth that Joyce's works are an impenetrable mystery and render him as he should

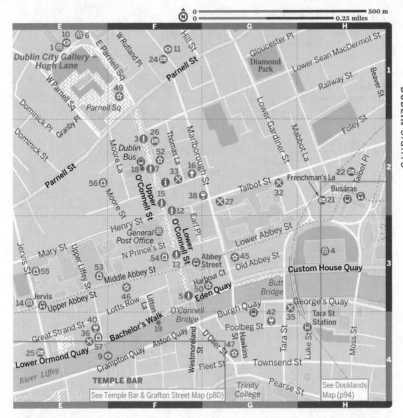

N 0 ___ 500 m
0 ___ 0.25 miles

See Temple Bar & Grafton Street Map (p80)

See Docklands Map (p94)

be to the contemporary reader: a writer of enormous talent who sought to challenge and entertain his audience with his breathtaking wit and use of language.

While here, you can also admire the fine plastered ceilings; some are restored originals while others are meticulous reproductions of Dublin stuccodore Michael Stapleton's designs. The street has also been given a facelift and now boasts some of the finest Georgian doorways and fanlights in the city.

St Michan's Church   CHURCH
(Map p88; ☎ 01-872 4154; Lower Church St; adult/child €5/3.50; ⊙ 10am-12.45pm & 2-4.45pm Mon-Fri, 10am-12.45pm Sat; ⓢ Smithfield) Macabre remains are the main attraction at this church, which was founded by the Danes in 1095 and named after one of their saints. Among the 'attractions' is an 800-year-old Norman crusader who was so tall that his feet were lopped off so he could fit in a coffin. Visits are by guided tour only.

St Michan's was the northside's only church until 1686, a year after it was almost completely rebuilt (it was remodelled in 1825 and again after the Civil War), leaving only the 15th-century battlement tower as its oldest bit. The courtroom-like interior hasn't changed much since the 19th century: still in place is the organ from 1724, which Handel may have played for the first-ever performance of his *Messiah*. The organ case is distinguished by the fine oak carving of 17 entwined musical instruments on its front. A skull on the floor on one side of the altar is said to represent Oliver Cromwell. On the opposite side is the Stool of Repentance, where 'open and notoriously naughty livers' did public penance.

The tours of the underground vaults are the real draw, however. The bodies within are aged between 400 and 800 years, and have been preserved by a combination of methane gas coming from rotting vegetation beneath

North of the Liffey

the church, the magnesium limestone of the masonry (which absorbs moisture from the air) and the perfectly constant temperature. Although there are caskets strewn about the place, the main attractions are 'the big four' – mummified bodies labelled The Unknown (a female about whom nothing is known), The Thief (his hands and feet are missing; some say as punishment for his crimes), The Nun and The Crusader: if he is indeed 800 years old then he may have participated in the piratical free-for-all crusades of the 13th century that resulted in the sack of Constantinople but which weren't sanctioned by the church. Also in the crypt are the bodies of John and Henry Sheares, two brothers executed following the Rising of 1798 and – it

is claimed – the remains of Robert Emmett, the fallen leader of the 1803 rebellion. Bram Stoker is said to have visited the crypt, which may have inspired him to write a story about a certain vampire who slept in a coffin...

Dublin Writers Museum   MUSEUM
(Map p88; www.writersmuseum.com; 18 N Parnell Sq; adult/child €8/5; ⊙9.45am-4.45pm Mon-Sat, 11am-4.30pm Sun; ▣3, 7, 10, 11, 13, 16, 19, 46A, 123 from city centre) Memorabilia aplenty and lots of literary ephemera line the walls and display cabinets of this elegant museum devoted to preserving the city's rich literary tradition up to 1970. The building, comprising two 18th-century houses, is worth exploring on its own; Dublin stuccodore Michael Stapleton decorated the upstairs gallery.

However, the curious decision to omit living writers limits its appeal – no account at all is given to contemporary writers, who would arguably be more popular with today's readers.

Although the busts and portraits of the greats in the gallery upstairs warrant more than a cursory peek, the real draws are the ground-floor displays, which include Samuel Beckett's phone (with a button for excluding incoming calls, of course), a letter from the 'tenement aristocrat' Brendan Behan to his brother, and a 1st edition of Bram Stoker's *Dracula*.

The **Gorham Library** next door is worth a visit, and there's also a calming Zen garden. The basement restaurant, Chapter One (p116), is one of the city's best.

While the museum focuses on the dearly departed, the **Irish Writers Centre** (Map p88; ☑ 01-872 1302; www.irishwriterscentre.ie; 19 N Parnell Sq; ☺10am-9pm Mon-Thu, to 5pm Fri; 🚍3, 7, 10, 11, 13, 16, 19, 46A, 123 from city centre) next door provides a meeting and working place for their living successors.

National Leprechaun Museum　MUSEUM
(Map p88; www.leprechaunmuseum.ie; Twilfit House, Jervis St; adult/child €14/10, Darkland Tour €16; ☺10am-6.30pm, also 7-8.30pm Fri & Sat May-Jun; 🚍 all city centre, 🚇 Jervis) Ostensibly designed as a child-friendly museum of Irish folklore, this is really a romper-room for kids sprinkled with bits of fairy tale. Which is no bad thing, even if the picture of the leprechaun painted here is more Lucky Charms and Walt Disney than sinister creature of pre-Christian mythology.

There's the optical illusion tunnel (which makes you appear smaller to those at the other end), the room full of oversized furniture, the wishing wells and, inevitably, the pot of gold; all of which is strictly for the kids. But if Walt Disney himself went on a leprechaun hunt when visiting Ireland during the filming of *Darby O'Gill and the Little People* in 1948, what the hell do we know? They've recently added the summertime Darkland Tour, a night-time storytelling session of dark and haunting tales of folklore.

DUBLIN SIGHTS

O'CONNELL STREET STATUARY

O'Connell St is lined with statues of Irish history's good and great. The big daddy of them all is the 'Liberator' himself, **Daniel O'Connell** (1775–1847; statue 1880, unveiled 1882; Map p88; Lower O'Connell St; 🚍 all city centre, 🚇 Abbey) whose massive bronze bulk soars above the street at the bridge end. The four winged figures at his feet represent O'Connell's supposed virtues: patriotism, courage, fidelity and eloquence. Dubs began to refer to the street as O'Connell St soon after the monument was erected; its name was officially changed after independence.

Heading away from the river, past a monument to **William Smith O'Brien** (1803–64), leader of the Young Irelanders, is a statue that easily rivals O'Connell's for drama: just outside the GPO is the spread-armed figure of trade-union leader **Jim Larkin** (1876–1947) (Map p88; Lower O'Connell St; 🚍 all city centre, 🚇 Abbey). His big moment came when he helped organise the general strike in 1913 – the pose catches him in full flow, urging workers to rise up for their rights. We're with you, comrade.

Next up and difficult to miss is the **Spire** (Map p88; O'Connell St; 🚍 all city centre, 🚇 Abbey), but just below it, on pedestrianised North Earl St, is the detached figure of **James Joyce** (Map p88; N Earl St; 🚍 all city centre, 🚇 Abbey), looking on the fast and shiny version of 21st-century O'Connell St with a bemused air. Dubs have lovingly dubbed him the 'prick with the stick' and we're sure Joyce would have loved the vulgar rhyme.

Further on is **Father Theobald Mathew** (Map p89; Upper O'Connell St; 🚍 all city centre, 🚇 Abbey) the 'apostle of temperance' (1790–1856). There can't have been a tougher gig in Ireland, but he led a spirited campaign against 'the demon drink' in the 1840s and converted hundreds of thousands to teetotalism.

The top of the street is completed by the imposing statue of **Charles Stewart Parnell** (Map p89; Upper O'Connell St; 🚍 all city centre, 🚇 Abbey) the 'uncrowned king of Ireland' (1846–91), who was an advocate of Home Rule and became a political victim of Irish intolerance.

St Mary's Pro-Cathedral   CHURCH

(Map p88; www.procathedral.ie; Marlborough St; ⊙8am-6.30pm; ☐all city centre, ☐Abbey) **FREE** Dublin's most important Catholic church is not quite the showcase you'd expect. It's in the wrong place for starters. The large neoclassical building, built between 1816 and 1825, was intended to stand where the GPO is, but Protestant objections resulted in its location on a cramped street that was then at the heart of Monto, the red-light district.

In fact, it's so cramped for space around here that you'd hardly notice the church's six Doric columns, which were modelled on the Temple of Theseus in Athens, much less be able to admire them. The interior is fairly functional, and its few highlights include a carved altar by Peter Turnerelli and the high relief representation of the Ascension by John Smyth. The best time to visit is 11am on Sunday when the Latin Mass is sung by the Palestrina Choir, with whom Ireland's most celebrated tenor, John McCormack, began his career in 1904. If you log on to the website during mass times you'll hear a live stream of the service.

★ Phoenix Park   PARK

(Map p76; www.phoenixpark.ie; ⊙24hr; ☐10 from O'Connell St, 25, 26 from Middle Abbey St) **FREE** Measuring 709 glorious hectares, Phoenix Park is one of the world's largest city parks; you'll find MP3-rigged joggers, grannies pushing buggies, ladies walking poodles, gardens, lakes, a sporting oval, and 300 deer. There are also cricket and polo grounds, a motor-racing track and some fine 18th-century residences, including those of the Irish president and the US ambassador.

The deer were first introduced by Lord Ormond in 1662, when lands once owned by the Knights of Jerusalem were turned into a royal hunting ground. In 1745 the viceroy Lord Chesterfield threw it open to the public and it has remained so ever since. (The name 'Phoenix' has nothing to do with the mythical bird; it is a corruption of the Irish *fionn uisce*, meaning 'clear water'.)

In 1882 the park played a crucial role in Irish history, when Lord Cavendish, the British chief secretary for Ireland, and his assistant were murdered outside what is now the Irish president's residence by an obscure nationalist group called the Invincibles. Lord Cavendish's home is now called Deerfield and is used as the official residence of the US ambassador.

➡ Garda Síochána Headquarters

(Map p76; Phoenix Park; ⊙closed to the public; ☐10 from O'Connell St, 25, 26 from Middle Abbey St) The large Victorian building behind Dublin Zoo, on the edge of the park, is the 19th-century Garda Síochána Headquarters, designed by Benjamin Woodward (also author of the Old Library in Trinity College).

➡ Papal Cross

(Phoenix Park; ☐10 from O'Connell St, 25, 26 from Middle Abbey St) In the centre of Phoenix Park, the Papal Cross marks the site where Pope John Paul II preached to 1.25 million people in 1979.

➡ Phoenix Monument

(Phoenix Park; ☐10 from O'Connell St, 25, 26 from Middle Abbey St) The Phoenix Monument, a Corinthian column topped by a very unphoenix-like bird, was erected by Lord Chesterfield in 1747, and is often referred to as the Eagle Monument. In the early years of the 20th century it was removed to facilitate motor racing in the park, but returned to its original spot in the 1990s.

➡ Magazine Fort

(Phoenix Park; ☐10 from O'Connell St, 25, 26 from Middle Abbey St) Towards Phoenix Park's Parkgate entrance is Magazine Fort on Thomas' Hill. Built between 1734 and 1801, the fort served as an occasional arms depot for the British and later the Irish armies. It was a target during the 1916 Easter Rising and again in 1940, when the IRA made off with the entire ammunitions reserve of the Irish army.

Dublin Zoo   ZOO

(www.dublinzoo.ie; Phoenix Park; adult/child/family €17.50/13/49; ⊙9.30am-6pm Mar-Sep, to dusk Oct-Feb; ☐10 from O'Connell St, 25, 26 from Middle Abbey St) Established in 1831, the 28-hectare Dublin Zoo just north of the Hollow is one of the oldest in the world. It is well known for its lion-breeding program, which dates back to 1857, and includes among its offspring the lion that roars at the start of MGM films. You'll see these tough cats, from a distance, on the 'African Savannah', just one of several habitats created in the last decade or so.

The zoo is home to roughly 400 animals from 100 different species, and you can visit all of them across the eight different habitats, which range from an Asian jungle to a family farm, where kids get to meet the inhabitants up close and milk a (model) cow. Sadly, a strain of avian flu in 2017 meant that all of the zoo's birds were moved indoors so as to avoid interaction with native, wild species.

There are restaurants, cafes and even a train to get you round.

Áras an Uachtaráin HISTORIC BUILDING

(www.president.ie; Phoenix Park; ⊙ guided tours hourly 10.30am-3.30pm Sat; ⊒ 10 from O'Connell St, 25, 26 from Middle Abbey St) **FREE** The residence of the Irish president is a Palladian lodge that was built in 1751 and enlarged a couple of times since, most recently in 1816. Tickets for the free one-hour tours (hourly 10.30am to 3.30pm Saturday) can be collected from the **Phoenix Park Visitor Centre** (☑ 01-677 0095; www.phoenixpark.ie; ⊙ 10am-6pm Apr-Dec, 9.30am-5.30pm Wed-Sun rest of year; ⊒ 10 from O'Connell St, 25 & 26 from Middle Abbey St) **FREE**, the converted former stables of the papal nunciate (embassy), where you'll see a 10-minute introductory video before being shuttled to the Áras itself to inspect five state rooms and the president's study.

It was home to the British viceroys from 1782 to 1922, and then to the governors general until Ireland cut ties with the British Crown and created the office of president in 1937. Queen Victoria stayed here during her visit in 1849, when she appeared not to even notice the Famine. The candle burning in the window is an old Irish tradition, to guide 'the Irish diaspora' home.

◉ Docklands

Custom House MUSEUM

(Map p88; Custom House Quay; ⊙ 9am-5pm Mon-Fri; ⊒ all city centre) Georgian genius James Gandon (1743–1823) announced his arrival on the Dublin scene with this magnificent building (1781–91), constructed just past Eden Quay at a wide stretch in the River Liffey. It's a colossal, neoclassical pile that stretches for 114m topped by a copper dome, beneath which the **visitor centre** (Map p88; €1.50; ⊙ 10am-12.30pm Mon-Fri, 2-5pm Sat & Sun mid-Mar–Oct, closed Mon, Tue & Sat Nov–mid-Mar) features a small museum on Gandon and the history of the building.

Best appreciated from the south side of the Liffey, its fine detail deserves closer inspection. Below the frieze are heads representing the gods of Ireland's 13 principal rivers; the sole female head, above the main door, represents the River Liffey. The cattle heads honour Dublin's beef trade, and the statues behind the building represent Africa, America, Asia and Europe. Set into the dome are four clocks and, above that, a 5m-high statue of Hope.

EPIC The Irish Emigration Museum MUSEUM

(Map p94; ☑ 01-906 0861; www.epicchq.com; CHQ Bldg, Custom House Quay; adult/child €14/7; ⊙ 10am-6.45pm, last entrance 5pm; ⊒ George's Dock) This is a high-tech, interactive exploration of emigration and its effect on Ireland and the 70 million or so people spread throughout the world who claim Irish ancestry. Start your visit with a 'passport' and proceed through 20 interactive – and occasionally moving – galleries examining why they left, where they went and how they maintained their relationship with their ancestral home.

Famine Memorial MEMORIAL

(Map p94; Custom House Quay; ⊒ all city centre) Just east of the Custom House (p93) is one of Dublin's most thought-provoking examples of public art: the set of life-size bronze figures (1997) by Rowan Gillespie known simply as *Famine*. Designed to commemorate the ravages of the Great Hunger (1845–51), their haunted, harrowed look testifies to a journey that was both hazardous and unwelcome.

The location of the sculptures is also telling, for it was from this very point in 1846 that one of the first 'coffin ships' (as they came to be known) set sail for the USA. Steerage fare on the *Perseverance* was £3 and 210 passengers made that first journey, landing in New York on 18 May 1846, with all passengers and crew intact.

In June 2007 a second series of *Famine* sculptures by Rowan Gillespie was unveiled on the quayside in Toronto's Ireland Park by Irish president Mary McAleese to commemorate the arrival of Famine refugees in the New World.

Jeanie Johnston MUSEUM

(Map p94; www.jeaniejohnston.ie; Custom House Quay; adult/student/child/family €10/9/5.50/25; ⊙ tours hourly 10am-4pm Apr-Oct, 11am-3pm Nov-Mar; ⊒ all city centre, ⊒ George's Dock) One of the city's most original tourist attractions is an exact working replica of a 19th-century 'coffin ship', as the sailing boats that transported starving emigrants away from Ireland during the Famine were gruesomely known. A small on-board museum details the harrowing plight of a typical journey, which usually took around 47 days.

DUBLIN SIGHTS

Docklands

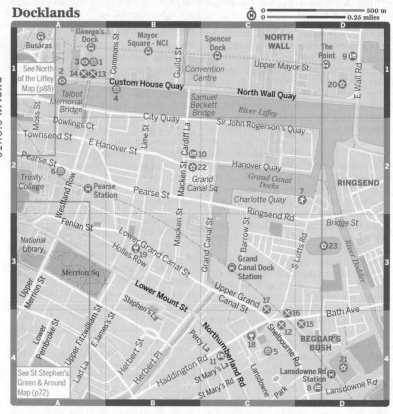

Docklands

⊙ Sights

1 EPIC The Irish Emigration
  Museum A1
2 Famine Memorial A1
3 Irish Family History Centre A1
4 Jeanie Johnston B1
5 National Print Museum C4
6 Science Gallery A2

⊕ Activities, Courses & Tours

7 Wakedock D2

🛏 Sleeping

8 Ariel House D4
9 Gibson Hotel D1
10 Marker B2
11 Schoolhouse Hotel C4

⊗ Eating

12 Chophouse C4
13 CHQ Farmers' Market A1
14 Ely Bar & Brasserie A1
15 Farmer Brown's D4
16 Juniors Deli & Cafe C4
17 Paulie's Pizza C3
  Science Gallery Café .... (see 6)

⊖ Drinking & Nightlife

18 Beggar's Bush C4
19 Square Ball B3

⊕ Entertainment

20 3 Arena D1
21 Aviva Stadium D4
22 Bord Gáis Energy Theatre B2
23 Shelbourne Park Greyhound
  Stadium D3

This particular ship, a three-masted barque originally built in Quebec in 1847, made 16 transatlantic voyages, carrying more than 2500 people, and never suffered a single death. The ship also operates as a Sail Training vessel, with journeys taking place from May to September. If you are visiting during these times, check the website for details of when it will be in dock.

Irish Family History Centre CULTURAL CENTRE
(Map p94; ☑01-671 0338; www.irishfamily historycentre.com; CHQ Bldg, Custom House Quay; €9.50, incl EPIC The Irish Emigration Museum €22; ☺10am-5pm; ☒George's Dock) Discover your family history with interactive screens where you can track your surname and centuries of Irish emigration. The ticket price also includes a 15-minute consultation with a genealogist. You can visit as part of the EPIC (p93) exhibition or buy a separate ticket.

◉ Southside

National Print Museum MUSEUM
(Map p94; ☑01-660 3770; www.nationalprint museum.ie; Haddington Rd, Garrison Chapel, Beggar's Bush; adult/concession €3.50/2; ☺9am-5pm Mon-Fri, 2-5pm Sat & Sun; ☒4, 7 from city centre, ☒Grand Canal Dock, Lansdowne Rd) You don't have to be into printing to enjoy this quirky little museum, where personalised guided tours (11.30am daily and 2.30pm Monday, Tuesday, Thursday and Friday) are offered in a delightfully casual and compelling way. A video looks at the history of printing in Ireland and then you wander through the various (still working) antique presses amid the smell of ink and metal.

The guides are excellent and can tailor the tours to suit your special interests – for example, anyone interested in history can get a detailed account of the difficulties encountered by the rebels of 1916 when they tried to have the proclamation printed. Upstairs there are lots of old newspaper pages recording important episodes in Irish history over the last century.

Herbert Park PARK
(Map p76; Ballsbridge; ☺dawn-dusk; ☒5, 7, 7A, 8, 45, 46, ☒Sandymount, Lansdowne Rd) A gorgeous swath of green lawns, ponds and flower beds near the Royal Dublin Society Showground (p126). Sandwiched between prosperous Ballsbridge and Donnybrook, the park runs along the River Dodder. There are tennis courts and a kids' playground here too.

WORTH A TRIP

POOLBEG LIGHTHOUSE

One of the city's most rewarding walks is a stroll along the Great South Wall to the **Poolbeg Lighthouse** (South Wall; ☺24hr; ☒1, 47, 56A, 77A, 84N from city centre), that red tower visible in the middle of Dublin Bay. The lighthouse dates from 1768, but it was redesigned and rebuilt in 1820. To get there, take the bus to Ringsend from the city centre, and then make your way past the power station to the start of the wall (it's about 1km). It's not an especially long walk out to the lighthouse – about 800m or so – but it will give you a stunning view of the bay and the city behind you, a view best enjoyed just before sunset on a summer's evening.

◉ Beyond the City Centre

Croke Park Experience MUSEUM
(www.crokepark.ie; Clonliffe Rd, New Stand, Croke Park; adult/child museum €7/5, museum & tour €14/9; ☺9.30am-6pm Mon-Sat, 10.30am-5pm Sun Jun-Aug, 9.30am-5pm Mon-Sat, 10.30am-5pm Sun Sep-May; ☒3, 11, 11A, 16, 16A, 123 from O'Connell St) This museum is all about the history and importance of Gaelic sports in Ireland and the role of the Gaelic Athletic Association (GAA) as the stout defender of a proud cultural identity. It helps if you're a sporting enthusiast.

The twice-daily tours (except match days) of the impressive Croke Park stadium are excellent, and well worth the extra cost. Admission to the tour includes a museum visit.

The stadium's other attraction is the **Skyline** (www.crokepark.ie; Croke Park; adult/child €20/12; ☺half-hourly 10.30am-3.30pm Mon-Sat, from 11.30am Sun Jul & Aug, 11.30am & 2.30pm Mon-Fri, half-hourly 10.30am-2.30pm Sat, from 11.30am Sun rest of year.; ☒3, 11, 11A, 16, 16A, 123 from O'Connell St).

Glasnevin Cemetery Museum MUSEUM
(www.glasnevintrust.ie; Finglas Rd; museum €4.50, museum & tour €10; ☺10am-6pm Mon-Fri; ☒40, 40A, 40B from Parnell St) The history of **Glasnevin Cemetery** (Prospect Cemetery; www.glasnevintrust.ie; Finglas Rd; tours €10; ☺10am-5pm, tours hourly 10.30am-3.30pm; ☒40, 40A, 40B from Parnell St) FREE is told in wonderful, award-winning detail in this museum, which tells the social and political story of Ireland

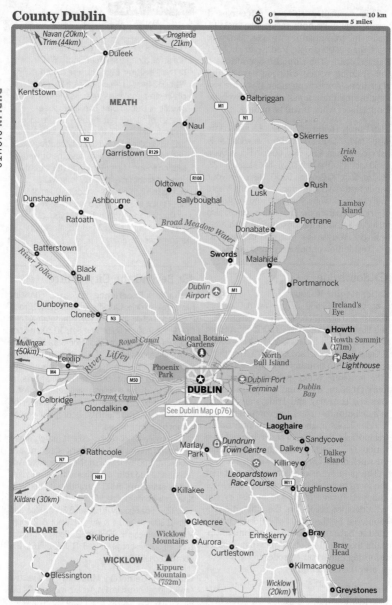

through the lives of the people, known and unknown, buried here. The City of the Dead covers the burial practice and religious beliefs of the roughly 1½ million people whose final resting place this is, while the Milestone Gallery features a 10m-long digitally interactive timeline outlining the lives of the cemetery's most famous residents.

The superb **tours** include a general history of the cemetery and an in-depth look at the lives of some of its residents (the Dead Interesting tour).

National Botanic Gardens GARDENS
(Botanic Rd; ⊙9am-6pm Mon-Sat, 11am-6pm Sun Apr-Oct, 10am-4.30pm Mon-Sat, 11am-4.30pm Sun Nov-Mar; ☐13, 13A, 19 from O'Connell St, 34, 34A from Middle Abbey St) FREE Founded in 1795, the 19.5-hectare botanic gardens are home to a series of curvilinear glasshouses, dating from 1843 to 1869, created by Richard Turner, who was also responsible for the glasshouse at Belfast Botanic Gardens and the Palm House in London's Kew Gardens. Within these Victorian masterpieces you will find the latest in botanical technology, including a series of computer-controlled climates reproducing environments of different parts of the world.

Casino at Marino MUSEUM
(www.casinomarino.ie; Malahide Rd; adult/child €7/3; ⊙10am-5pm Mar-May & Oct, to 6pm Jun-Sep; ☐20A, 20B, 27, 27B, 42, 42C, 123 from city centre) It's not the roulette-wheel kind of casino but the original Italian kind, the one that means 'summer home' (it literally means 'small house'), and this particular casino is one of the most enchanting constructions in all of Ireland. Entrance is by guided tour only; the last tour is 45 minutes before closing.

It was built in the mid-18th century for the Earl of Charlemont, who returned from his grand tour of Europe with more art than he could store in his own home, Marino House, which was on the same grounds but was demolished in the 1920s. He also came home with a big love of the Palladian style – hence the architecture of this wonderful folly.

The exterior of the building, with a huge entrance doorway, and 12 Tuscan columns forming a templelike facade, creates the expectation that its interior will be a simple single open space. But instead it is an extravagant convoluted maze: flights of fancy include chimneys for the central heating that are disguised as roof urns, downpipes hidden in columns, carved draperies, ornate fireplaces, beautiful parquet floors constructed of rare woods, and a spacious wine cellar. A variety of statuary adorns the outside, but it's the amusing fakes that are most enjoyable. The towering front door is a sham – a much smaller panel opens to reveal the secret interior. The windows have blacked-out panels to hide the fact that the interior is a complex of rooms, not a single chamber.

Activities

Experience Gaelic Games ADVENTURE SPORTS
(☑01-254 4292; www.experiencegaelicgames.com; Saint Mobhi Rd; per person €25-35; ⊙Mon-Sat Mar-Oct, Fri & Sat Nov- Feb; ☐4, 9 from O'Connell St) Easily reachable from the city centre, this is the only place in Dublin to experience the unique trio of Gaelic games: hurling, Gaelic football and handball. The staff have an enormous passion for the sports and their pride and delight at showing visitors is infectious. You can join one of the open sessions or groups of six or more can book a private session.

National Aquatic Centre SWIMMING
(☑01-646 4300; www.nationalaquaticcentre.ie; Snugborough Rd; adult/child & student €7.50/5.50, incl AquaZone €15/13; ⊙6am-10pm Mon-Fri, 9am-8pm Sat & Sun; ☐38 & 38A from O'Connell St) The National Aquatic Centre is the largest indoor water park in the country. Besides its Olympic-sized competition pool, there's the AquaZone, with water rollercoasters, wave and surf machines, a leisure pool and all types of flumes. It's a great day out for the family, but at weekends be prepared to join the line of shivering children queuing for slides.

Wakedock ADVENTURE SPORTS
(Map p94; ☑01-664 3883; www.wakedock.ie; Grand Canal Dock; 30min tuition adult/student €60/45; ⊙noon-8pm Tue-Fri, 10am-8pm Sat & Sun; ☐1, 15A, 15B, 56A, 77A from city centre, ☐Grand Canal Dock) Try the relatively new sport of cable wakeboarding – waterskiing by holding on to a fixed overhead cable instead of a motorboat. The sport is shortlisted for the 2020 Olympics. You can also rent wetsuits (€2).

> ### ⓘ A WORD IN YOUR EAR
> Dublin's best-known tour guide is local historian **Pat Liddy** (p100), who leads a variety of guided walks including Dublin Highlights and The Best of Dublin – The Complete Heritage Walking Tour. He is also available for private guided walks (check the website for timings) and has a bunch of podcast walks (www.visitdublin.com/iwalks) available for download.

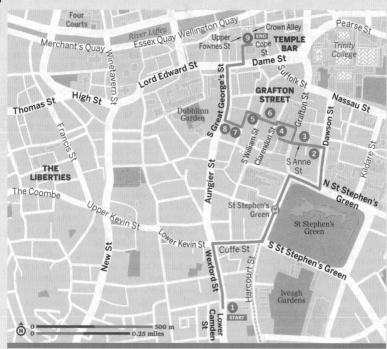

Walking Tour
Dublin Pub Crawl

START LOWER CAMDEN ST
END CROWN ALLEY
LENGTH 2KM; ONE HOUR TO TWO DAYS

Dubliners of old would assure their 'bitter halves' that they were 'going to see a man about a dog' before retreating to the nearest watering hole. Visiting barflies need no excuse to enjoy the social and cultural education – ahem – of a tour of Dublin's finest, most charming and most hard-core bars.

Start in the always excellent ❶ **Anseo** (p118), where hipsters rub shoulders with the hoi polloi and everyone toe-taps to the great bag of DJ tunes. Head deep into the city centre and rub shoulders with the beautiful people at ❷ **Sam's Bar** (p118). Go old school by sinking a pint of plain in the snug at South Anne St's ❸ **Kehoe's** (p117), one of the city centre's most atmospheric bars. Find a spot out front of ❹ **Bruxelles** (p118): the bronze statue of Thin Lizzy's Phil Lynott outside is testament to the bar's reputation as a great spot for rock music,

even if it's just on the stereo. Discuss the merits of that unwritten masterpiece with a clutch of frustrated writers and artists in ❺ **Grogan's Castle Lounge** (p117), a traditional haunt that admirably refuses to modernise. Directly across the street in the basement of the Powerscourt Townhouse Shopping Centre is ❻ **Pygmalion** (p118), which is all about now. A couple of streets away, on Fade St, a couple of bars vie for hipster euros: the upstairs ❼ **No Name Bar** (p118) is elegant and discreet, while ❽ **Hogan's** (p102), at the corner with South Great George's St, has been one of the most popular watering holes in the city for longer than its clientele have been alive.

Finally, make your way into Temple Bar and ring the doorbell to access the ❾ **Vintage Cocktail Club** (p119), upstairs behind a plain steel door on Crown Alley, where the in-crowd sips cocktails and eats delicious titbits in a speakeasy atmosphere. If you've followed the tour correctly, it's unlikely that you'll now be referring to this guide. How many fingers?

DUBLIN FOR CHILDREN
....

Kid-friendly? You bet. Dublin loves the little 'uns, and will enthusiastically 'ooh' and 'aah' at the cuteness of your progeny. But alas such admiration hasn't fully translated into child services such as widespread and accessible baby-changing facilities.

If your kids are between three and 14, spend an afternoon at **Ark Children's Cultural Centre** (Map p80; www.ark.ie; 11a Eustace St; 🔲 all city centre), which runs activities aimed at stimulating participants' interests in science, the environment and the arts – but be sure to book well in advance.

There are loads of ways to discover Dublin's Viking past, but **Dublinia** (p82), the city's Viking and medieval museum, has interactive exhibits that are specifically designed to appeal to younger visitors.

Kids of all ages will love a **Viking Splash Tour** (p100), where you board an amphibious vehicle, put on a plastic Viking hat and roar at passersby as you do a tour of the city before landing in the water at the Grand Canal basin.

A perennial favourite is **Dublin Zoo** (p92), while the **National Leprechaun Museum** (p91) lets the kids' imaginations run wild among the optical illusions and oversized furniture. On the 2nd floor of the Powerscourt Townhouse Shopping Centre is the **Dolls Store** (Map p80; www.dollstore.ie; ⊙10am-6pm Mon-Sat; 🔲 all city centre), which sells all kinds of dolls and doll's houses; should your little one's doll or teddy get 'ill', this is also the home of Ireland's only doll and teddy-bear hospital.

All but a few hotels will provide cots (cribs), and most top-range hotels have babysitting services (€12 to €20 per hour). Restaurants are generally accommodating until 7pm, after which things can get difficult, especially for babies: check while making a booking.

👉 Tours

★ Green Mile   WALKING
(Map p80; 📞 01-661 1000; www.littlemuseum.ie; Little Museum of Dublin, 15 St Stephen's Green N; adult/student €7/5; ⊙11am Sat & Sun; 🔲 all city centre, 🚉 St Stephen's Green) Excellent one-hour tour of St Stephen's Green led by local historian Donal Fallon. Along the way you'll hear tales of James Joyce, the park's history and the drafting of the Irish Constitution. Book ahead as tours fill up pretty quickly. The tour also includes admission to and a guided tour of the Little Museum of Dublin (p70).

★ Fab Food Trails   WALKING
(www.fabfoodtrails.ie; tours €55; ⊙10am Sat) Highly recommended 2½-hour tasting walks through the city centre's choicest independent producers. You'll visit up to eight bakeries, cheesemongers, markets and delis, learning about the food culture of each neighbourhood you explore. There is also a Coffee Walk (exploring the best artisanal coffee shops) and a Food & Fashion walk. You meet in the city centre.

★ Historical Walking Tour   WALKING
(Map p71; 📞 01-878 0227; www.historicaltours.ie; Trinity College Gate; adult/student/child €12/10/ free; ⊙11am & 3pm May-Sep, 11am Apr & Oct, 11am Fri-Sun Nov-Mar; 🔲 all city centre) Trinity College history graduates lead this 'seminar on the street' that explores the Potato Famine, Easter Rising, Civil War and Partition. Sights include Trinity, City Hall, Dublin Castle and Four Courts. In summer, themed tours on architecture, women in Irish history and the birth of the Irish state are also held. Tours depart from the College Green entrance.

★ Dublin Musical Pub Crawl   WALKING
(Map p80; 📞 01-478 0193; www.discoverdublin.ie; 58-59 Fleet St; adult/student €14/12; ⊙7.30pm daily Apr-Oct, 7.30pm Thu-Sat Nov-Mar; 🔲 all city centre) The story of Irish traditional music and its influence on contemporary styles is explained and demonstrated by two expert musicians in a number of Temple Bar pubs over 2½ hours. Tours meet upstairs in the **Oliver St John Gogarty** (Map p80; www.gogartys.ie; 58-59 Fleet St; ⊙10.30am-11.30pm Mon-Thu, to 12.30am Fri & Sat, noon-11pm Sun; 🔲 all city centre) pub and are highly recommended.

Dublin Bus Tours   BUS
(Map p88; 📞 01-872 0000; www.dublinsightseeing.ie; 59 Upper O'Connell St; adult €15-28; 🔲 all city centre, 🚉 Abbey) A selection of bus tours including a hop-on, hop-off city tour (€22), a ghost-bus tour (€28) and two half-day

DUBLIN ACTIVITIES

EVENSONG AT THE CATHEDRALS

In a rare coming together, the choirs of St Patrick's Cathedral and Christ Church Cathedral both participated in the first-ever performance of Handel's *Messiah* in nearby Fishamble St in 1742, conducted by the great composer himself. Both houses of worship carry on their proud choral traditions, and visits to the cathedrals during evensong will provide enchanting and atmospheric memories. The choir performs evensong in St Patrick's at 5.45pm Monday to Friday (not on Wednesday in July and August), while the Christ Church choir performs at 5.30pm on Sunday, 6pm on Wednesday and Thursday, and 5pm Saturday. If you're going to be in Dublin around Christmas, do not miss the carols at St Patrick's; call ahead for the hard-to-get tickets on ☎ 01-453 9472.

tours: the four-hour South Coast & Gardens Tour (€27; including Powerscourt) and the North Coast & Castle Tour (€25; including Malahide Castle). In 2016 they added a 1916 anniversary tour (€15) that covers the sights associated with the Easter Rising.

See Dublin by Bike CYCLING
(Map p72; ☎ 01-280 1899; www.seedublinbybike.ie; Daintree Bldg, Pleasants Pl; tours €25; ☐ all city centre) Three-hour themed tours that start outside the Daintree Building on Pleasants Pl and take in the city's highlights and not-so-obvious sights. The Taste of Dublin is the main tour, but you can also take a U2's Dublin tour and a Literary Dublin tour. Bikes, helmets and hi-vis vests included.

1916 Rebellion Walking Tour WALKING
(Map p80; ☎ 086 858 3847; www.1916rising.com; 23 Wicklow St; €13; ☉ 11.30am Mon-Sat, 1pm Sun Mar-Oct; ☐ all city centre) Superb two-hour tour starting in the International Bar (Map p80; www.international-bar.com; 23 Wicklow St; ☉ 10.30am-11.30pm Mon-Thu, to 12.30am Fri & Sat, noon-11pm Sun; ☐ all city centre), Wicklow St. Lots of information, humour and irreverence to boot. The guides – all Trinity graduates – are uniformly excellent and will not say no to the offer of a pint back in the

International at tour's end. The also have a tour based around Michael Collins, hero of the War of Independence.

Dublin Literary Pub Crawl WALKING
(Map p80; ☎ 01-670 5602; www.dublinpubcrawl.com; 9 Duke St; adult/student €13/11; ☉ 7.30pm daily Apr-Oct, 7.30pm Thu-Sun Nov-Mar; ☐ all city centre) A tour of pubs associated with famous Dublin writers is a sure-fire recipe for success, and this 2½-hour tour-performance by two actors is a riotous laugh. There's plenty of drink taken, which makes it all the more popular. It leaves from the Duke on Duke St; get there by 7pm to reserve a spot for the evening tour.

James Joyce Walking Tours WALKING
(Map p88; ☎ 01-878 8547; www.jamesjoyce.ie; 35 N Great George's St; adult/student €10/8; ☉ 2pm Tue, Thu & Sat May-Sep, Sat only Oct-Apr; ☐ 3, 10, 11, 11A, 13, 16, 16A, 19, 19A, 22 from city centre) A series of 90-minute tours run by the James Joyce Cultural Centre (p88) cover the life and work of the artist who lived, was schooled and lost his virginity on the northside. You have a choice between Joyce's Dublin, the Footsteps of Leopold Bloom (based on *Ulysses*) and a *Dubliners* tour.

Pat Liddy Walking Tours WALKING
(Map p80; ☎ 01-831 1109; www.walkingtours.ie; Visit Dublin Centre, 25 Suffolk St; tours €10-15; ☐ all city centre) Local historian Pat Liddy leads a variety of guided walks including Dublin Highlights & Hidden Corners and The Best of Dublin – The Complete Heritage Walking Tour. He is also available for private guided walks. Check the website for timings.

Dublin Discovered Boat Tours BOATING
(Map p88; ☎ 01-473 4082; www.dublindiscovered.ie; Bachelor's Walk; adult/student/child €15/13/9; ☉ 10.30am-4.15pm Mar-Oct; ☐ all city centre, ☐ Abbey) 'See the sights without the traffic' is the pitch; you get to hear the history of Dublin from a watery point of view aboard an (all-important) all-weather cruiser.

Viking Splash Tours TOURS
(Map p80; ☎ 01-707 6000; www.vikingsplash.com; St Stephen's Green N; adult/child Sep-Jun €22/12, Jul-Aug €25/12; ☉ every 30-90min 10am-3pm; ☐ all city centre, ☐ St Stephen's Green) Go on, what's the big deal? You stick a plastic Viking's helmet on your head and yell 'yay' at the urging of your guide, but

the upshot is you'll get a 1¼-hour semiamphibious tour that ends up in the Grand Canal Dock. 'Strictly for tourists' seems so...superfluous.

Trinity College Walking Tour   WALKING
(Authenticity Tours; Map p71; www.tcd.ie/visitors/tours; Trinity College; tours €6, incl Book of Kells €14; ⊙ 10.15am-3.40pm Mon-Sat, to 3.15pm Sun May-Sep, fewer midweek tours Oct & Feb-Apr; 🚌 all city centre, 🚌 College Green) A great way to see Trinity's grounds is on a student-led walking tour, which depart from the College Green entrance every 20 to 40 minutes.

✨ Festivals & Events

Temple Bar Trad Festival   MUSIC
(www.templebartrad.com; ⊙ Jan; 🚌 all city centre) Traditional music festival in the pubs of Temple Bar over the last weekend in January.

Audi Dublin International Film Festival   FILM
(www.diff.com; ⊙ mid-Mar) Local flicks, arty international films and advance releases of mainstream movies make up the menu of the city's film festival, which runs over two weeks in mid-March.

★ St Patrick's Festival   PARADE
(www.stpatricksfestival.ie; ⊙ Mar) The mother of all festivals; 600,000-odd gather to 'honour' St Patrick over four days around 17 March on city streets and in venues.

Forbidden Fruit   MUSIC
(www.forbiddenfruit.ie; 1-/2-day ticket from €60/110; ⊙ Jun; 🚌 51, 51D, 51X, 69, 78, 79 from Aston Quay) A two-day alternative-music festival over the first weekend in June in the grounds of the Irish Museum of Modern Art.

Taste of Dublin   FOOD & DRINK
(www.tasteofdublin.ie; Iveagh Gardens; €17.50, VIP ticket €64.50; ⊙ mid-Jun; 🚌 Harcourt) The capital's best restaurants combine to serve up sample platters of their finest dishes amid music and other entertainment over three food-filled days. It's so popular that tickets are limited to four-hour increments; VIP tickets include access to the champagne lounge, where you'll get a glass of bubbly and some chocolates.

Dublin Pride   LGBT
(www.dublinpride.ie; ⊙ mid-Jun) Two weeks of events, gigs, screenings and talks that culminate in a huge colourful parade through the city centre.

Bloomsday   LITERATURE
(www.jamesjoyce.ie; ⊙ 16 Jun) Every 16 June a bunch of weirdos wander around the city dressed in Edwardian gear, talking nonsense in dramatic tones. They're not mad – at least not clinically – they're only Bloomsdayers committed to commemorating James Joyce's epic novel *Ulysses* through readings, performances and re-created meals, including Leopold Bloom's famous breakfast of 'kidneys with the faint scent of urine'. Yummy.

★ Longitude   MUSIC
(www.longitude.ie; Marlay Park; ⊙ Jul; 🚌 14, 14A, 16, 48A or 75 from city centre) A three-day alt-music festival in mid-July featuring old and new acts, art installations and food stalls.

JAMES JOYCE & ULYSSES

Ulysses is the ultimate chronicle of the city in which, Joyce once said, he intended to 'give a picture of Dublin so complete that if the city suddenly one day disappeared from the earth it could be reconstructed out of my book'. It is set here on 16 June 1904 – the day of Joyce's first date with Nora Barnacle – and follows its characters as their journeys around town parallel the voyage of Homer's *Odyssey*.

The experimental literary style makes it difficult to read, but there's much for even the slightly bemused reader to relish. It ends with Molly Bloom's famous stream of consciousness discourse, a chapter of eight huge, unpunctuated paragraphs. Because of its sexual explicitness, the book was banned in the USA and the UK until 1933 and 1937 respectively.

In testament to the book's enduring relevance and extraordinary innovation, it has inspired writers of every generation since. Joyce admirers from around the world descend on Dublin every year on 16 June to celebrate Bloomsday and retrace the steps of *Ulysses'* central character, Leopold Bloom. It is a slightly gimmicky and touristy phenomenon that is aimed at Joyce fanatics and tourists, but it's plenty of fun and a great way to lay the groundwork for actually reading the book.

★ **Dublin Fringe Festival** THEATRE
(www.fringefest.com; ◷Sep) Initially a festival
for those shows too 'out there' or insignificant to be considered for the main Dublin
Theatre Festival, this is now a three-week extravaganza in its own right, with more than
100 events and over 700 performances held
in September.

★ **Culture Night** ART
(www.culturenight.ie; Sep) For one night a year,
museums, galleries, artists' studios, historic
homes and churches open their doors and
host performances, lectures and workshops
for the public. Everything is free and fabulous.

Dublin Theatre Festival THEATRE
(www.dublintheatrefestival.com; ◷Oct) For two
weeks in October most of the city's theatres
participate in this festival, originally founded in 1957 and today a glittering parade of
quality productions and elaborate shows.

Dublin Book Festival LITERATURE
(www.dublinbookfestival.com; ◷mid-Nov) A three-
day festival of literature with readings and
talks. In collaboration with the city's public
libraries and the UNESCO city of literature
office.

🛌 Sleeping

The surge in tourist numbers and the relative lack of beds means hotel prices are
higher than they were during the Celtic Tiger years. There are good midrange options
north of the Liffey, but the biggest spread of
accommodation is south of the river, from
midrange Georgian townhouses to the city's
top hotels. Budget travellers rely on the selection of decent hostels.

🛌 Grafton Street & Around

Grafton St itself has only one hotel – one of
the city's best – but you'll find a host of choices
in the area surrounding it. Not surprisingly,
being so close to the choicest street in town
comes at a premium, but the competition for
business is fierce, which ensures top quality.

Kelly's Hotel BOUTIQUE HOTEL €
(Map p80; www.kellysdublin.com; 36 S Great
George's St; r from €110; ❉@ 令; 🚇all city centre)
A trendy boutique hotel in an original Victorian red-brick. The interiors are thoroughly modern: rooms are small and tastefully
decorated with polished wooden floors and
elegant minimalist furnishings. It's part of a
complex that includes Grafton House, two

bars – **Hogan's** (Map p80; 35 S Great George's
St; ◷1.30pm-11.30am Mon-Wed, to 1am Thu, to
2.30am Fri & Sat, 2-11pm Sun), and the No Name
Bar (p118) – and L'Gueuleton (p110) next
door. Front-facing rooms can be quite noisy.

Grafton House BOUTIQUE HOTEL €
(Map p80; ☑01-648 0010; www.graftonguest
house.com; 27 S Great George's St; s/d from
€90/140; @ 令; 🚇all city centre, 🚇St Stephen's
Green) Pine furnishings, pristine white linen
and thoroughly modern bathrooms are the
defining features of the smallish rooms at
this boutique hotel that is a good choice for
location and price. Check in at Kelly's Hotel (p102), a couple of doors down; (continental) breakfast is served in L'Gueuleton
(p110), just around the corner. Street-facing
rooms are noisy, especially at weekends.

Avalon House HOSTEL €
(Map p80; ☑01-475 0001; www.avalon-house.ie; 55
Aungier St; dm/s/d from €10/34/54; @ 令; 🚇15,16,
16A, 16C, 19, 19A, 19C, 65, 65B, 83, 122) Pared-back
dorms with high ceilings and old-fashioned
sinks, metal-framed bunks and shared bathrooms give this an old-school look at odds
with newer hostels, but it's popular – because
of its location and nice common room. In
2017 the downstairs cafe was taken over by
Starbucks. Book well in advance.

Radisson Blu Royal Hotel HOTEL €€
(Map p80; ☑01-898 2900; www.radissonblu.
ie/royalhotel-dublin; Golden Lane; r from €200;
🅿❉@ 令; 🚇all city centre, 🚇St Stephen's Green)
A business hotel that is an excellent example of how sleek lines and muted colours
combine beautifully with luxury, ensuring a
memorable night's stay. From hugely impressive public areas to sophisticated bedrooms –
each with a flat-screen digital TV embedded
in the wall to go along with all the other little
touches – this hotel will not disappoint.

Trinity Lodge GUESTHOUSE €€
(Map p72; ☑01-617 0900; www.trinitylodge.com;
12 S Frederick St; r from €170; 令; 🚇all city centre,
🚇St Stephen's Green) Martin Sheen's grin greets
you upon entering this award-winning guesthouse, which he declared his favourite spot
for an Irish stay. Marty's not the only one:
this place is so popular they've added a second townhouse across the road, which has
also been kitted out to the highest standards.
Room 2 of the original house has a lovely bay
window.

Discounted parking (€17.50) is available
in an adjacent covered car park.

Dawson
BOUTIQUE HOTEL **€€**

(Map p80; ☑01-612 7900; www.thedawson.ie; 35 Dawson St; r from €160; @☎; ⬜all city centre, ⬚St Stephen's Green) A boutique hotel with a range of elegant rooms designed in a variety of styles, from classical French to more exotic Moroccan. Crisp white sheets throughout and luxe amenities in the bathrooms. There's also a fancy spa and the trendy Sam's Bar (p118) below.

Dean
HOTEL **€€**

(Map p72; ☑01-607 8110; www.deanhoteldublin. ie; 33 Harcourt St; r/ste from €150/370; P@☎; ⬜10, 11, 13, 14, 15A, ⬚St Stephen's Green) Every room at this newish designer hotel comes with earplugs, vodka, wine and Berocca – so you know what to expect. Take your pick from well-appointed and elegant Mod Pods (single bed on a couch), Punk Bunks (yup, bunk beds) or deluxe doubles (SupeRooms or Hi-Fis) and suites. The more expensive rooms come with Netflix and a turntable.

The hotel deliberately advertises as an upmarket party hotel that borrows its ethos (if not its look) from the Ace Hotel in New York and the Hoxton in London: sandwiched between two of the most popular nightclubs in town the rooms can get very noisy indeed, especially those on the 1st floor. The top floor is home to **Sophie's** (Map p72; www.sophies.ie; 33 Harcourt St; mains €14-29; ⊙7am-midnight; ⬜10, 11, 13, 14, 15A, ⬚Harcourt), a brasserie that turns into a popular bar after 11pm.

It has discounted parking arrangements with a car park five-minutes' walk away.

Harrington Hall
GUESTHOUSE **€€**

(Map p72; ☑01-475 3497; www.harringtonhall.com; 69-70 Harcourt St; r from €180; @☎; ⬚Harcourt) Want to fluff up the pillows in the home of a former Lord Mayor of Dublin? The traditional Georgian style of Timothy Charles Harrington's home – he wore the gold chain from 1901 to 1903 – has thankfully been retained and this smart guesthouse stands out for its understated elegance. The 1st- and 2nd-floor rooms have their original fireplaces and ornamental ceilings.

Brooks Hotel
HOTEL **€€**

(Map p80; ☑01-670 4000; www.brookshotel.ie; 59-62 Drury St; r from €200; P❉@☎; ⬜all cross-city, ⬚St Stephen's Green) About 120m west of Grafton St, this small, plush place has an emphasis on familial, friendly service. The decor is nouveau classic with high-veneer-panelled walls, decorative bookcases and old-fashioned sofas, while bedrooms are extremely comfortable and come fitted out in subtly coloured furnishings. The clincher though, is the king- and superking-size beds in all rooms, complete with...a pillow menu.

O'Callaghan Stephen's Green
HOTEL **€€**

(Map p72; ☑01-607 3600; www.stephensgreen hotel.ie; 1-5 Harcourt St; r from €180; P@☎; ⬜all cross-city, ⬚St Stephen's Green) Past the glass-fronted lobby are 75 thoroughly modern rooms that make full use of the visual impact of primary colours, most notably red and blue. This is a business hotel par excellence: everything here is what you'd expect from a top international hotel (including a gym and a business centre). There are extraordinary online deals available.

Buswell's Hotel
HOTEL **€€**

(Map p72; ☑01-614 6500; www.buswells.ie; 23-27 Molesworth St; s/d from €165/180; P❉@; ⬜all cross-city, ⬚St Stephen's Green) This Dublin institution, open since 1882, has a long

---

ℹ **BOOKING SERVICES**

Getting the hotel of your choice without a reservation can be tricky in high season (May to September), so always book your room in advance. You can book through Dublin Tourism's online booking service (www.visitdublin.com). Advance internet bookings are your best bet for deals.

All Dublin Hotels (www.irelandhotels.com/hotels) Decent spread of accommodation in the city centre and suburbs.

Daft.ie (www.daft.ie) If you're looking to rent in Dublin, this is the site to search.

Dublin Hotels (www.dublinhotels.com) Hotels in the city centre and beyond.

Dublin Tourism (www.visitdublin.com) Good selection of rated accommodation.

Hostel Dublin (www.hosteldublin.com) Good resource for hostel accommodation.

Lonely Planet (www.lonelyplanet.com/ireland/dublin/hotels) Recommendations and bookings.

CAMPUS ACCOMMODATION

During the summer months, visitors can opt to stay in campus accommodation, which is both convenient and comfortable.

Trinity College (Map p71; ☑ 01-896 1177; www.tcd.ie/summeraccommodation; Accommodations Office, Trinity College; s/d from €79/129; ☺ May–mid-Sep; 🅿 @ 🛜; 🖳 all cross-city) The extensive range of student accommodation includes modern apartments with all mod cons and older (more atmospheric) rooms with shared bathroom. They're on campus and just off it, on Pearse St.

Dublin City University (DCU; ☑ 01-700 5736; www.summeraccommodation.dcu.ie; Larkfield Apartments, Campus Residences, Dublin City University; s/d from €80/120; ☺ mid-Jun–mid-Sep; 🖳 11, 11A, 11B, 13, 13A, 19, 19A from city centre) This accommodation is proof that students slum it in relative luxury. The modern rooms have plenty of amenities at hand, including a kitchen, a common room and a fully equipped health centre. The Glasnevin campus is only 15 minutes by bus or car from the city centre.

association with politicians, who wander across the road from Dáil Éireann (Irish Assembly) to wet their beaks at the hotel bar. The 69 bedrooms have all been given the once-over, but have kept their Georgian charm intact.

⭐**Fitzwilliam Hotel**   HOTEL €€€
(Map p80; ☑ 01-478 7000; www.fitzwilliam-hotel.com; St Stephen's Green W; r from €230; 🅿 ✳ @ 🛜; 🖳 all cross-city, 🖳 Stephen's Green) You couldn't pick a more prestigious spot on the Dublin Monopoly board than this minimalist Terence Conrad–designed number overlooking the Green. Ask for a corner room on the 5th floor (502 or 508), with balmy balcony and a view. The mezzanine-level Citron restaurant serves modern Irish cuisine. It's contemporary elegance at its very best.

Westbury Hotel   HOTEL €€€
(Map p80; ☑ 01-679 1122; www.doylecollection.com; Grafton St; r/ste from €250/380; 🅿 @ 🛜; 🖳 all city centre, 🖳 St Stephen's Green) Tucked away just off Grafton St is one of the most elegant hotels in town, although you'll need to upgrade to a suite to really feel the luxury. The standard rooms are perfectly comfortable but not really of the same theme as the luxurious public space – the upstairs lobby is a great spot for afternoon tea or a drink.

Westin Dublin   HOTEL €€€
(Map p80; ☑ 01-645 1000; www.thewestindublin.com; Westmoreland St; r from €250; 🅿 @ 🛜; 🖳 all city centre) Once a fancy bank branch, now a fancier hotel: rooms are decorated in elegant mahogany and soft colours that are reminiscent of the USA's finest. You will sleep on 10 layers of the Westin's own trade-

mark Heavenly Bed, which is damn comfortable indeed. The old bank vault is now the basement bar.

🛏 Merrion Square & Around

⭐**Merrion Mews**   GUESTHOUSE €€€
(Irish Landmark Trust; Map p72; www.irishlandmark.com; Fitzwilliam Lane; 2 nights from €822; 🅿 🛜; 🖳 7, 46A from city centre) This carefully restored Georgian mews dating from 1792 is managed by the Irish Landmark Trust. There are three beautifully appointed double bedrooms that sleep six, a living area and a fully equipped kitchen above a stables – which is still used by the mounted unit of the police. Outside is a garden, one of the few left in the area.

Bookings are for a minimum of two nights and as it's a period home – with thick walls – the wi-fi can be a bit sketchy.

⭐**Merrion**   HOTEL €€€
(Map p72; ☑ 01-603 0600; www.merrionhotel.com; Upper Merrion St; r/ste from €400/750; 🅿 @ 🛜 ✖; 🖳 all city centre) This resplendent five-star hotel, in a terrace of beautifully restored Georgian townhouses, opened in 1988 but looks like it's been around a lot longer. Try to get a room in the old house (with the largest private art collection in the city), rather than the newer wing, to sample its truly elegant comforts.

Located opposite Government Buildings, its marble corridors are patronised by politicos, visiting dignitaries and the odd celeb. Even if you don't stay, book a table for the superb Art Afternoon Tea (€85 for two), with endless cups of tea served out of silver pots by a raging fire.

★ **Number 31** GUESTHOUSE €€€

(Map p72; ☑ 01-676 5011; www.number31.ie; 31 Leeson Close; s/d €220/260; P 🛜; 🖵 all city centre) The city's most distinctive property is the former home of modernist architect Sam Stephenson, who successfully fused '60s style with 18th-century grace. Its 21 bedrooms are split between the retro coach house, with its coolly modern rooms, and the more elegant Georgian house, where rooms are individually furnished with tasteful French antiques and big comfortable beds. Breakfast included.

Gourmet breakfasts with kippers, homemade breads and granola are served in the conservatory.

★ **Conrad Dublin** HOTEL €€€

(Map p72; ☑ 01-602 8900; www.conradhotels.com; Earlsfort Tce; r from €269; P @ 🛜; 🖵 all city centre) A €13-million refit has transformed this standard business hotel into an exceptional five-star property. The style is contemporary chic – marble bathrooms, wonderfully comfortable beds and a clutter-free aesthetic that doesn't skimp on mod cons (bedside docking stations for iPhones, USB sockets and HD flat-screen TVs) – and it works. The Coburg Brasserie (p111) is exceptional.

The Conrad's one/three/five 'Stay Inspired' concept – where guests can avail of tailored one-, three- and five-hour itineraries based on their interests – is a tad overambitious: it would be miraculous to reach Powerscourt in Wicklow in the 20 minutes allotted in the five-hour itinerary, but the recommendation of Catch 22 in the three-hour itinerary is spot-on.

Shelbourne HOTEL €€€

(Map p72; ☑ 01-676 6471; www.theshelbourne.ie; 27 St Stephen's Green N; r from €385; P @ 🛜; 🖵 all city centre, 🚆 St Stephen's Green) Dublin's most famous hotel was founded in 1824 and has been the preferred halting post of the powerful and wealthy ever since. Several owners and refurbs later it is now part of Marriott's Renaissance portfolio, and while it has a couple of rivals in the luxury stakes, it cannot be beaten for heritage.

Guests are staying in a slice of history: it was here that the Irish Constitution was drafted in 1921, and this is the hotel in Elizabeth Bowen's eponymous novel. Afternoon tea in the refurbished Lord Mayor's Lounge remains one of the best experiences in town.

🛏 Temple Bar

If you're here for a weekend of wild abandon and can't fathom anything more than a quick stumble into bed, then Temple Bar's choice of hotels and hostels will suit you perfectly. Generally speaking the rooms are small, the prices are large and you must be able to handle the late-night symphonies of revellers.

Barnacles HOSTEL €

(Map p80; ☑ 01-671 6277; www.barnacles.ie; 19 Temple Lane S; dm/d from €20/130; P 🛜; 🖵 all city centre) If you're here for a good time, not a long time, then this bustling Temple Bar hostel is the ideal spot to meet fellow revellers and tap up the helpful and knowledgable staff for the best places to cause mischief. Rooms are quieter at the back.

Kinlay House HOSTEL €

(Map p80; ☑ 01-679 6644; www.kinlaydublin.ie; 2-12 Lord Edward St; dm/d from €20/90; 🛜; 🖵 all city centre) This former boarding house for boys has massive, mixed dormitories (for up to 24), and smaller rooms, including doubles. It's in Temple Bar, so it's occasionally raucous. Staff are friendly, and there are cooking facilities and a cafe. Breakfast is included.

Dublin Citi Hotel HOTEL €

(Map p80; ☑ 01-679 4455; www.dublincitihotel.com; 46-49 Dame St; r from €109; @ 🛜; 🖵 all city centre) An unusual turreted 19th-century building right next to the Central Bank is home to this midrange hotel. Rooms aren't huge, are simply furnished and have fresh white quilts. It's only a stagger (literally) from the heart of Temple Bar, hic.

★ **Irish Landmark Trust** HERITAGE HOTEL €€€

(Map p80; ☑ 01-670 4733; www.irishlandmark.com; 25 Eustace St; 2 nights for 7 people €820; 🖵 all city centre) This 18th-century heritage house has been gloriously restored to the highest standard by the Irish Landmark Trust. Furnished with tasteful antiques and authentic furniture and fittings (including a grand piano in the drawing room), it sleeps up to seven in its three bedrooms, which must be booked for a minimum of two nights.

The house was built in 1720 and was home to a wealthy wool merchant and later to author and historian Standish O'Grady (1846–1928), whom WB Yeats called the 'Father of the Irish Revival' for works like *The Story of Ireland* (1894; written while he lived in the house), despite being a Protestant and a staunch unionist!

🛏 North of the Liffey

There is a scattering of good midrange options between O'Connell St and Smithfield. Gardiner St, to the east of O'Connell St, was the traditional B&B district of town, but with only a few exceptions it has been rendered largely obsolete by chain hotels elsewhere throughout the city.

⭐ Isaacs Hostel   HOSTEL €

(Map p88; 📞 01-855 6215; www.isaacs.ie; 2-5 Frenchman's Lane; dm/tw from €16/70; @🛜; 🚇 all city centre, 🚆 Connolly) The northside's best hostel – hell, for atmosphere alone it's the best in town – is in a 200-year-old wine vault just around the corner from the main bus station. With summer barbecues, live music in the lounge, internet access, colourful dorms and even a sauna, this terrific place generates consistently good reviews from backpackers and other travellers.

⭐ Generator Hostel   HOSTEL €

(Map p88; 📞 01-901 0222; www.generator hostels.com; Smithfield Sq; dm/tw from €16/70; @🛜; 🚆 Smithfield) This European chain brings its own brand of funky, fun design to Dublin's hostel scene, with bright colours, comfortable dorms (including women-only) and a lively social scene. It even has a screening room for movies. Good location right on Smithfield Sq, next to the Old Jameson Distillery (p87).

MEC Hostel   HOSTEL €

(Map p88; 📞 01-873 0826; www.mechostel.com; 42 N Great George's St; dm/d from €14/70; 🛜; 🚌 36, 36A) A Georgian classic on one of Dublin's most beautiful streets, this popular hostel has a host of dorms and doubles, all with private bathroom. Facilities include a full kitchen, two lounges and a bureau de change. Breakfast is only €2 and there's decent wi-fi throughout.

Jacob's Inn   HOSTEL €

(Map p88; 📞 01-855 5660; www.jacobsinn.com; 21-28 Talbot Pl; dm/d from €11/70; 🛜; 🚇 all city centre, 🚆 Connolly) Sister hostel to Isaacs (p106) around the corner, this clean and modern hostel offers spacious accommodation with private bathrooms and outstanding facilities, including some wheelchair-accessible rooms, a bureau de change, bike storage and a self-catering kitchen.

Riu Plaza Gresham Hotel   HOTEL €€

(Map p88; 📞 01-874 6881; www.gresham-hotels.com; 23 Upper O'Connell St; r from €200; 🅿🌣@🛜; 🚇 all city centre) In 2016 the landmark Gresham was purchased by Spanish hotel giants Riu, who so far have not altered a building that has been hosting guests since 1817. Its 323 rooms and 10 suites are spacious and well-serviced. The fabulous open-plan foyer is one of the city's most impressive hotel lobbies.

Maldron Hotel Smithfield   HOTEL €€

(Map p88; 📞 01-485 0900; www.maldron hotels.com; Smithfield Village; r/ste from €180/220; 🛜; 🚌 25, 25A, 25B, 66, 66A, 66B, 67, 90, 151 to Upper Ormond Quay, 🚆 Smithfield) With big bedrooms and plenty of earth tones to soften the contemporary edges, this functionally modern hotel is your best bet in this part of town. We love the floor-to-ceiling windows: great for checking out what's going on below in the square.

Morrison Hotel   HOTEL €€€

(Map p88; 📞 01-887 2400; www.morrisonhotel.ie; Lower Ormond Quay; r from €260; 🅿@🛜; 🚇 all city centre, 🚆 Jervis) Space-age funky design is the template at this hip hotel, part of the Hilton Doubletree group. King-size beds (with fancy mattresses), 40in LCD TVs, free wi-fi and deluxe toiletries are just some of the hotel's offerings. Easily the northside's most luxurious address.

🛏 Docklands

Staying in the Docklands area means you'll be relying on public transport or taxis to get you in and out of the city centre.

⭐ Marker   HOTEL €€€

(Map p94; 📞 01-687 5100; www.themarker hoteldublin.com; Grand Canal Sq; r/ste from €350/520; 🅿@🛜; 🚆 Grand Canal Dock) Behind the eye-catching chequerboard facade created by Manuel Aires Mateus are 187 swanky rooms and suites decked out in a wintry palette (washed out citruses and cobalts) and starkly elegant furnishings, which give them an atmosphere of cool sophistication. The public areas are a little wilder and the rooftop bar is a summer favourite with the 'in' crowd.

Gibson Hotel   HOTEL €€€

(Map p94; 📞 01-618 5000; www.thegibsonhotel.ie; Point Village; r from €250; 🅿@🛜; 🚌 151 from city centre, 🚆 The Point) Built for business travellers and out-of-towners taking in a gig at the 3 Arena (p124) next door, the Gibson is impressive: 250-odd ultramodern rooms decked out in deluxe beds, flat-screen TVs and internet work stations. You might catch last night's star act having breakfast the next morning in the snazzy restaurant area.

🛏 Southside

Some of the city's most elegant B&Bs are scattered about these leafy suburbs, including a handful that can rival even the best hotels in town for comfort and service.

★ Ariel House
INN €

(Map p94; ☑01-668 5512; www.ariel-house.net; 52 Lansdowne Rd; r from €130; ℗�/?; ☑4, 7, 8, 84 from city centre) Our favourite lodging in Ballsbridge is this wonderful Victorian-era property that is somewhere between a boutique hotel and a luxury B&B. Its 28 rooms are all individually decorated with period furniture, which lends the place an air of genuine luxury. A far better choice than most hotels.

★ Aberdeen Lodge
GUESTHOUSE €€

(☑01-283 8155; www.aberdeenlodgedublin.com; 53-55 Park Ave; r from €160; ℗@?; ☑2, 3, ☒Sydney Parade) Not only is this absolutely one of Dublin's best guesthouses, but it's also a carefully guarded secret, known only to those who dare stay a short train ride away from the city centre. Their reward is a luxurious house with a level of personalised service as good as you'll find in one of the city's top hotels.

Most of the stunning rooms have either a four-poster, a half-tester or a brass bed to complement the authentic Edwardian furniture and tasteful art on the walls. The suites even have fully working Adams fireplaces. As there is one member of staff for every two rooms, the service is exceptional, not to mention totally hands-on and very courteous. An added touch for international guests is the 'meet and greet' service at Dublin Airport, where a driver will collect you and your baggage and escort you to the hotel in a town car (book it in advance).

Schoolhouse Hotel
BOUTIQUE HOTEL €€

(Map p94; ☑01-667 5014; www.schoolhousehotel.com; 2-8 Northumberland Rd; r from €170; ℗?; ☑5, 7, 7A, 8, 18, 27X, 44 from city centre) A Victorian schoolhouse dating from 1861, this beautiful building has been successfully converted into an exquisite boutique hotel that is (ahem) ahead of its class. Its 31 cosy bedrooms, named after famous Irish people,

all have king-sized beds, big white quilts and loudly patterned headboards. The Canteen bar and patio bustles with local businessfolk in summer.

✕ Eating

The choice of restaurants in Dublin has never been better. Every cuisine and every trend – from doughnuts on the run to kale with absolutely everything – is catered for, as the city seeks to satisfy the discerning taste buds of its diners.

✕ Grafton Street & Around

Grafton St's only food offerings are of the fast variety, but the real treats are in the streets around it, which are full of food joints of every hue and flavour, from funky cafes to fancy restaurants. The diversity in taste is matched by a range in prices.

Meet Me in the Morning
CAFE €

(Map p72; 50 Pleasants St; mains €5-8; ⊗8am-5pm Tue-Fri, 10am-5pm Sat & Sun; ☑14, 15, 65, 83) Scrummy breakfasts (there's eggs done just right, but try the nut eile, a toasted hazelnut and cacao spread on toast with sea salt) and lunches with a Middle Eastern flavour to them (puy lentil tabouli with shaved fennel) make this one of the nicest cafes in town. It's named after a Dylan song.

Wow Burger
BURGERS €

(Map p80; www.wowburger.ie; 8 Wicklow St; burgers €6-7; ⊗noon-9.30pm; ☑all city centre) The basement of Mary's Bar (Map p80; 8 Wicklow St; ⊗11am-11.30pm Mon-Wed, to 12.30am Thu, to 1.30am Fri & Sat, noon-11pm Sun; ☑all city centre) is home to the hottest burger joint in town: hamburgers, cheeseburgers and a sinful bacon cheeseburger come in two sizes (double or single) and with a side of choice – the garlic butter fries are terrific. Order at the bar, pick up at the counter and eat in the '50s diner–styled room.

Assassination Custard
CAFE €

(Map p72; 19 Kevin St; mains €4-6; ⊗8am-3.30pm Mon-Fri; ☑all city centre) It doesn't look like much, but this is one of the tastiest treats in town – how about roasted cauliflower with toasted dukkah, or broccoli with spicy Italian 'nduja pork sausage and Toonsbridge ricotta? And if you're feeling really adventurous, try the tripe sandwich. The name comes from a phrase coined by Samuel Beckett.

Azteca
MEXICAN €

(Map p80; 19 Lord Edward St; burritos €9-11; ☉10am-10pm Mon-Fri, noon-10pm Sat, noon-6pm Sun; 🚇all city centre) This spot near Dublin Castle has been around for a few years but rarely features on anyone's 'must-eat' list. It's their loss, because the burritos here are excellent.

Bunsen
BURGERS €

(Map p80; ☎01-652 1022; www.bunsen.ie; 3 S Anne St; burgers €7-9; ☉noon-9.30pm Mon-Wed, noon-10.30pm Thu-Sat, 1-9.30pm Sun; 🚇all city centre, 🚉St Stephen's Green) Artisanal burgers that are so popular, the queues go out the door.

Silk Road Café
MIDDLE EASTERN €

(Map p80; Chester Beatty Library, Dublin Castle; mains €12; ☉10am-4.45pm Mon-Fri, 11am-4.45pm Sat & Sun May-Oct, closed Mon Nov-Apr; 🚉50, 51B, 77, 78A, 123) This vaguely Middle Eastern–North African–Mediterranean gem on the ground floor of the Chester Beatty Library (p69) is no ordinary museum cafe. Complementing house specialities including Greek moussaka and spinach lasagne are daily specials such as *djaj mehshi* (chicken stuffed with spices, rice, dried fruit, almonds and pine nuts). All dishes are halal and kosher.

Fallon & Byrne
DELI €

(Map p80; www.fallonandbyrne.com; Exchequer St; mains €5-10; ☉8am-9pm Mon-Fri, 9am-9pm Sat, 11am-7pm Sun; 🚇all city centre) Dublin's answer to the American Dean and DeLuca chain is this upmarket food hall and wine cellar, which is where discerning Dubliners come to buy their favourite cheeses and imported delicacies, as well as to get a superb takeaway lunch from the deli counter.

Upstairs in an elegant brasserie (Map p80; ☎01-472 1000; www.fallonandbyrne.com; Exchequer St; mains €12-17; ☉noon-3pm & 5.30-9pm Sun-Tue, to 10pm Wed & Thu, to 11pm Fri & Sat; 🚇all city centre) that serves Irish-influenced Mediterranean cuisine.

Simon's Place
CAFE €

(Map p80; George's St Arcade, S Great George's St; sandwiches €5-6; ☉8.30am-5pm Mon-Sat; ☎; 🚇all city centre) Simon's soup-and-sandwich joint is a city stalwart, impervious to the fluctuating fortunes of the world around it, mostly because its doorstep sandwiches and wholesome vegetarian soups are delicious and affordable. As trustworthy cafes go, this is the real deal.

★ Pichet
FRENCH €€

(Map p80; ☎01-677 1060; www.pichetrestaurant.ie; 15 Trinity St; mains €19-27; ☉noon-3pm & 5-10pm Mon-Sat, 11am-4pm & 5-9pm Sun; 🚇all city centre) Head chef Stephen Gibson (formerly of L'Ecrivain) delivers his version of modern French cuisine to this newly refurbished dining room, whose elegance matches the fabulous food and service. Load up on an expertly made cocktail before feasting on as good a meal as you'll find at this price anywhere in the city centre.

Little Jerusalem
MIDDLE EASTERN €€

(Map p72; ☎01-424 4001; 77 Lower Camden St; mains €12-17; ☉noon-midnight; ☎; 🚉14, 15, 65, 83) A candidate for best ethnic cuisine in town, this friendly spot serves up a mix of Lebanese and Palestinian dishes that range from the familiar (hummus, felafel, lamb shwarma) to the exotic – how about *makloubet* (chicken, aubergine, cauliflower, potatoes and onions...served 'upside down')? The extensive menu requires repeat visits. It's strictly BYOB.

Hang Dai
CHINESE €€

(Map p72; ☎01-545 8888; www.hangdaichinese.com; 20 Lower Camden St; mains €16-29; ☉5pm-midnight Tue-Sat; 🚉14, 15, 65, 83) You'll need a reservation to get a seat at the bar or in one of the carriage booths of this super-trendy spot, designed to look like the inside of a railway carriage. The low red lighting and soulful tunes give off the ambience of a '70s porn theatre. The food, however – contemporary versions of Chinese classics – is excellent.

Port House
TAPAS €€

(Map p80; ☎01-677 0298; www.porthouse.ie; 64a South William St; tapas €7-10; ☉11am-midnight; 🚇all city centre) This dark cavern restaurant is full of flickering candlelight. The extensive, delicious Spanish tapas menu is best enjoyed with the impressive Iberian wines (which the friendly staff can help you navigate). It doesn't take bookings, so if you go at the weekend prepare to wait for a table.

Camden Kitchen
BISTRO €€

(Map p72; ☎01-476 0125; www.camdenkitchen.ie; 3 Camden Market, Grantham St; mains €16-26; ☉noon-2.30pm & 5.30-10pm Wed-Fri, 5.30-10pm Tue & Sat; 🚉14, 15, 65, 83) Tucked away off busy Camden St, this inviting little bistro prides itself on its fresh, seasonal menu of changing and beautifully presented dishes like handmade gnocchi with organic spinach and greens and wild mushrooms topped with a free-range egg; or wild Wicklow venison saddle with a pressed potato terrine. The somewhat expensive wine menu complements the reasonably priced food.

Richmond   MODERN IRISH €€

(Map p72; ☑ 01-478 8783; www.richmondrestaurant.ie; 43 S Richmond St; mains €16-27; ☺ 5.30-9.30pm Wed-Sun, 11am-3pm Sat & Sun; ☐ 14, 15, 65, 83) At first glance the menu offers nothing particularly novel, just a nice selection of favourites from a burger to a roasted breast of duck. But it's the way it's prepared and presented that makes this place one of the best in town, and proof that expertise in the kitchen trumps everything else. Brunch is a particular favourite.

Dada   MOROCCAN €€

(Map p80; www.dadarestaurant.ie; 45 S William St; mains €14-25; ☺ 5-11pm Mon-Thu, 1.30pm-12.30am Fri & Sat, 2.30-11pm Sun; ☐ all city centre) This bustling Moroccan restaurant has an atmospheric, low-lit dining room, spread about lots of alcoves so as to give the feel of a medina, and a substantial menu of North African favourites. The emphasis is on lamb (three separate tagines and a seven-hour roasted lamb shoulder) but there's also fish, chicken and decent vegetarian options.

Super Miss Sue   SEAFOOD €€

(Map p80; www.supermisssue.com; 2-3 Drury St; mains €15-28; ☺ noon-9pm Mon-Wed, to 11pm Thu-Sat, to 4pm Sun; ☐ all city centre) Super Miss Sue is not one restaurant, but three: on the ground floor is a bright cafe-style dining room that serves mostly seafood, including lots of types of oysters and a

shellfish platter to die for. Downstairs is Luna (open 5pm to 11pm, Wednesday to Saturday), where the focus is Italian and the menu favours meat dishes. There's also Cerva, a takeaway fish-and-chip shop.

Pitt Bros BBQ   BARBECUE €€

(Map p80; www.pittbrosbbq.com; Unit 1, Wicklow House, S Great George's St; mains €14-16; ☺ noon-midnight Mon-Fri, 12.30pm-late Sat & Sun; ☐ all city centre) Delicious, Southern-style barbecue – you have a choice of pulled pork, brisket, ribs, sausage or half a chicken – served amid loud music and a hipster-fuelled atmosphere that says Brooklyn, New York, rather than Birmingham, Alabama. For dessert, there's a DIY ice-cream dispenser. Locals grumble that it's a straight rip-off of Bison Bar, but the happy clientele doesn't care.

Fade Street Social   MODERN IRISH €€

(Map p80; ☑ 01-604 0066; www.fadestreetsocial.com; 4-6 Fade St; mains €18-32, tapas €5-12; ☺ 12.30-10.30pm Mon-Fri, 5-10.30pm Sat & Sun; ☎; ☐ all city centre) 🍴 Two eateries in one, courtesy of renowned chef Dylan McGrath: at the front, the buzzy tapas bar, which serves up gourmet bites from a beautiful open kitchen. At the back, the more muted restaurant specialises in Irish cuts of meat – from veal to rabbit – served with homegrown, organic vegetables. There's a bar upstairs too. Reservations suggested.

Pig's Ear   MODERN IRISH €€

(Map p72; ☑ 01-670 3865; www.thepigsear.com; 4 Nassau St; mains €18-28; ☺ noon-2.45pm & 5.30-10pm Mon-Sat; ☐ all city centre) Looking over the playing fields of Trinity College – which

---

FARMERS & ORGANIC MARKETS

For more info on local markets, check out www.irishfarmersmarkets.ie, www.irishvillagemarkets.com or local county council sites such as www.dlrcoco.ie/markets.

Dublin Food Co-op (p128) Eco friendly and organic market that is especially popular on Saturday.

Coppinger Row Market (Map p80; Coppinger Row; ☺ 11am-7pm Thu; ☐ all city centre) Tiny street market with fresh breads and other homemade products.

Harcourt Street Food Market (Map p72; www.irishfarmersmarkets.ie; Park Pl, Station Bldgs, Upper Hatch St; ☺ noon-2pm Thu; ☐ all city centre, ☐ Harcourt) Organic produce used to make products representing cuisines from all over the world.

CHQ Farmers' Market (Map p94; www.irishfarmersmarkets.ie; CHQ Bldg; ☺ 11am-3pm Fri; ☐ George's Dock) Local producers hawking everything from chocolate to homemade sauce.

People's Park Market (☑ 087 957 3647; People's Park, Dun Laoghaire; ☺ 11am-4pm Sun; ☐ Dun Laoghaire) Seafood, meat and locally sourced veg.

counts as a view in Dublin – this fashionably formal restaurant is spread over two floors and is renowned for its exquisite and innovative Irish cuisine, including dishes such as barbecued pork belly, short rib of Irish beef and a superb slow-cooked Lough Erne shepherd's pie.

L'Gueuleton   FRENCH €€

(Map p80; www.lgueuleton.com; 1 Fade St; mains €25-28; ⊗12.30-4pm & 5.30-10pm Mon-Wed, to 10.30pm Thu-Sat, noon-4pm & 5.30-9pm Sun; ⊒all city centre) Despite the tongue-twister name (it means 'gluttonous feast' in French), L'Gueuleton is a firm favourite with locals for its robust (meaty, filling) take on French rustic cuisine – it does a mean onion soup and the steak frites is a big crowd pleaser. It has a no-reservations, leave-your-name-at-the-door policy; just go for a drink and wait for the call.

Yamamori   JAPANESE €€

(Map p80; ☑01-475 5001; www.yamamorinoodles.ie; 71 S Great George's St; mains €15-28, lunch bentos €10; ⊗12.30-11pm; ☑; ⊒all city centre) Yamamori rarely disappoints with its bubbly service and vivacious cooking that swoops from sushi and sashimi to whopping great plates of noodles, with plenty in-between. The lunch bento is one of the best deals in town. There's another branch (p116) north of the river.

★Greenhouse   SCANDINAVIAN €€€

(Map p80; ☑01-676 7015; www.thegreenhouserestaurant.ie; Dawson St; 2-3-course lunch menu €29.50/38, 4-6-course dinner menu €79/95; ⊗noon-2.15pm & 6-9.30pm Tue-Sat; ⊒all city centre, ⊠St Stephen's Green) Chef Mickael Viljanen might just be the most exciting chef working in Ireland today thanks to his Scandi-influenced tasting menus, which have made this arguably Dublin's best restaurant. Wine selections are in the capable hands of Julie Dupouy, who in 2017 was voted third-best sommelier in the world, just weeks before the restaurant was awarded a Michelin star. Reservations necessary.

Shanahan's on the Green   STEAK €€€

(Map p72; ☑01-407 0939; www.shanahans.ie; 119 St Stephen's Green W; mains €42-49; ⊗6-10pm Sat-Thu, noon-10pm Fri; ⊒all city centre, ⊠St Stephen's Green) You could order seafood or a plate of vegetables, but you'd be missing the point of this supremely elegant steakhouse: the finest cuts of juicy and tender Irish Angus beef you'll find anywhere. The ambience is upscale Americana – the bar downstairs is called the Oval Office and pride of place goes to a rocking chair owned by JFK.

✖ Merrion Square & Around

The area around Merrion Row is a culinary hotbed, whether it's casual lunches for the business trade or upmarket dining at restaurants that hold most of the city's Michelin

---

VEGETARIAN FOOD

Vegetarians are finding it increasingly easier in Dublin as the capital has veered away from the belief that food isn't food until your incisors have ripped flesh from bone, and towards an understanding that healthy eating leads to, well, longer lives.

There's a selection of general restaurants that cater to vegetarians beyond the token dish of mixed greens and pulses – places such as **M&L** (p113), **Yamamori** (p110) and **Chameleon** (Map p80; ☑01-671 0362; www.chameleonrestaurant.com; 1 Lower Fownes St; set menus €30-40, tapas €7.50-11; ⊗4-11pm Wed-Sun; ☑; ⊒all city centre). The Wednesday night dinner at the **Fumbally** (p112) always includes a tasty vegetarian option, while **Assassination Custard** (p107) strikes an even balance between meat and vegetarian dishes.

Solidly vegetarian places include **Blazing Salads** (Map p80; 42 Drury St; salads €5-10; ⊗10am-6pm Mon-Wed, Fri & Sat, to 8pm Thu; ☑; ⊒all city centre), with organic breads, Californian-style salads and pizza; **Cornucopia** (Map p80; www.cornucopia.ie; 19-20 Wicklow St; salads €5.50-11, mains €12.50-14; ⊗8.30am-9pm Mon, 8.30am-10pm Tue-Sat, noon-9pm Sun; ☑; ⊒all city centre), Dublin's best-known vegetarian restaurant, serving wholesome salads, sandwiches and a selection of hot main courses; and **Govinda's** (Map p80; www.govindas.ie; 4 Aungier St; mains €10.45; ⊗noon-9pm Mon-Sat; ☑; ⊒all city centre), an authentic beans-and-pulses place run by the Hare Krishna.

stars. Sandwich bars and nondescript cafes make up the rest of the dining landscape.

★ Etto

ITALIAN €€

(Map p72; ✐01-678 8872; www.etto.ie; 18 Merrion Row; mains €18-23; ⊘noon-10pm Mon-Fri, 12.30-10pm Sat; ☐all city centre) Award-winning restaurant and wine bar that does contemporary versions of classic Italian cuisine. All the ingredients are fresh, the presentation is exquisite and the service is just right. Portions are small, but the food is so rich you won't leave hungry. The only downside is the relatively quick turnover; lingering over the excellent wine would be nice. Book ahead.

★ Coburg Brasserie

FRENCH €€

(Map p72; ✐01-602 8900; www.thecoburgdublin. com; Conrad International, Earlsfort Tce; mains €11-18; ☐all city centre) The French-inspired, seafood-leaning cuisine at this revamped hotel brasserie puts the emphasis on shellfish: the all-day menu offers oysters, mussels and a range of 'casual' lobster dishes, from lobster rolls to lobster cocktail. The bouillabaisse is chock-full of sea flavours, and you can also get a shrimp burger and a fine plate of Connemara whiskey-cured organic salmon. Top-notch.

House

MEDITERRANEAN €€

(Map p72; www.housedublin.ie; 27 Lower Leeson St; tapas €9-11, mains €14-26; ⊘8am-midnight Mon-Wed, 8am-3am Thu & Fri, 4pm-3am Sat; ☐11, 46, 118, 145) This gorgeous bar does a limited selection of main courses, but the real treats are the tapas-style sharing plates, which cover the full Mediterranean spread, from wild mushroom risotto and pulled pork to grilled halloumi and salt and pepper calamari.

Ely

MODERN IRISH €€

(Map p72; ✐01-676 8986; www.elywinebar.ie; 22 Ely Pl; mains €15-29; ⊘noon-11.30pm Mon-Fri, 5pm-12.30am Sat; ☐all city centre) ✿ Scrummy homemade burgers, bangers and mash, and braised wild mushroom are some of the dishes you can find in this basement restaurant. Meals are prepared with organic and free-range produce from the owner's family farm in County Clare, so you can rest assured of the quality. There's another **branch** (Map p94; ✐01-672 0010; www.elywinebar.ie; Custom House Quay; mains €16-28; ⊘noon-11pm Mon-Fri, 4pm-midnight Sat; ☐George's Dock) ✿ in the Docklands.

★ Restaurant Patrick Guilbaud

FRENCH €€€

(Map p72; ✐01-676 4192; www.restaurantpatrick guilbaud.ie; 21 Upper Merrion St; 2-/3-course set lunch €50/60, dinner menus €90-185; ⊘12.30-2.30pm & 7.30-10.30pm Tue-Sat; ☐7, 46 from city centre) Ireland's only Michelin two-star is understandably considered the best in the country by its devotees, who proclaim Guillaume Lebrun's French haute cuisine the most exalted expression of the culinary arts. If you like formal dining, this is as good as it gets: the lunch menu is an absolute steal, at least in this stratosphere. Innovative and beautifully presented.

The room itself is all contemporary elegance and the service expertly formal yet surprisingly friendly – the staff are meticulously trained and as skilled at answering queries and addressing individual requests as they are at making sure not one breadcrumb lingers too long on the immaculate tablecloths. Owner Patrick Guilbaud usually does the rounds of the tables himself in the evening to salute regular customers and charm first-timers into returning. Reservations are absolutely necessary.

★ L'Ecrivain

FRENCH €€€

(Map p72; ✐01-661 1919; www.lecrivain.com; 109a Lower Baggot St; 3-course lunch menus €45, 8-course tasting menus €90, mains €45; ⊘12.30-2pm Wed-Fri, 6.30-10pm Mon-Sat; ☐38, 39 from city centre) Head chef Derry Clarke is considered a gourmet god for the exquisite simplicity of his creations, which put the emphasis on flavour and the best local ingredients – all given the French once over and turned into something that approaches divine dining. The Michelin people like it too and awarded it one of their stars.

✕ Temple Bar

Scattered among the panoply of overpriced and underwhelming eateries in Temple Bar are some excellent spots to get a bite that will suit a variety of tastes and pocket depths.

Klaw

SEAFOOD €

(Map p80; www.klaw.ie; 5a Crown Alley; mains €8-15; ⊘noon-10pm Mon-Wed & Sun, to 11pm Thu-Sat; ☐all city centre) There's nothing sophisticated about this crabshack-style place except the food: Irish oysters served naked, dressed or torched; Lambay Island crab claws served with a yuzu aioli; or half a lobster. Whatever you go for it's all delicious; the 'shucknsuck' oyster happy hour is a terrific deal with all oysters €1.50.

Bison Bar & BBQ
BARBECUE €

(Map p80; 086 056 3144; www.bisonbar.ie; 11 Wellington Quay; mains €14-17; noon-9pm; all city centre) Beer, whiskey sours and finger-lickingly good Texas-style barbecue – served on throwaway plates along with tasty sides such as slaw or mac 'n' cheese – is the fare at this boisterous restaurant. The cowboy theme is taken to the limit with the saddle chairs (yes, actual saddles); this is a place to eat, drink and be merry.

Bunsen
BURGERS €

(Map p80; www.bunsen.ie; 22 Essex St E; burgers €7-10; noon-9.30pm Mon-Wed, noon-10.30pm Thu-Sat, 1-9.30pm Sun; all city centre) The tag line says Straight Up Burgers, but Bunsen serves only the tastiest, most succulent lumps of prime beef cooked to perfection and served between two halves of a homemade bap. Want fries? You've a choice between skinny, chunky or sweet potato. Order the double at your peril. There are two other branches: on Wexford St (Map p72; www.bunsen.ie; 36 Wexford St; burgers €7-9; noon-9.30pm Mon-Wed, noon-10.30pm Thu-Sat, 1-9.30pm Sun; all city centre) and S Anne St (p108).

Queen of Tarts
CAFE €

(Map p80; 01-670 7499; www.queenoftarts. ie; 4 Cork Hill; mains €5-10; 8am-8pm Mon-Fri, 8.30am-8pm Sat, 9am-7pm Sun; all city centre) This cute little cake shop does a fine line in tarts, meringues, crumbles, cookies and brownies, not to mention a decent breakfast: the smoked bacon and leek potato cakes with eggs and cherry tomatoes are excellent. There's another, bigger, branch around the corner on Cow's Lane (Map p80; www.queenoftarts.ie; 3-4 Cow's Lane; mains €5-10; 8am-8pm Mon-Fri, 8.30am-8pm Sat, 9am-7pm Sun; all city centre).

★ Banyi Japanese Dining
JAPANESE €€

(Map p80; 01-675 0669; www.banyijapanese dining.com; 3-4 Bedford Row; lunch bento €11, small/large sushi platter €15/27; noon-11pm; all city centre) This compact restaurant in the heart of Temple Bar has arguably the best Japanese cuisine in Dublin. The rolls are divine, and the sushi as good as any you'll eat at twice the price. If you don't fancy raw fish, the classic Japanese main courses are excellent, as are the lunchtime bento

boxes. Dinner reservations are advised, particularly at weekends.

Crackbird
FAST FOOD €€

(Map p80; www.joburger.ie; 60 Dame St; half/full roast chicken €12.50/22; noon-10pm Mon-Wed, to 11pm Thu-Sat, to 9pm Sun; ; all city centre) It's a trendy version of fried chicken in a bucket, but it's oh so tasty. Choose between a half or full portion (half is enough for most humans) and add some sides – potato salad, chipotle baked beans, couscous or carrot and cranberry salad – for extra flavour and variety.

✕ Kilmainham & the Liberties

★ 1837 Bar & Brasserie
BRASSERIE €

(Map p76; 01-471 4602; www.guinness-storehouse.com; Guinness Storehouse, St James's Gate; mains €9-14; noon-3pm; 21A, 51B, 78, 78A, 123 from Fleet St, James's) This lunchtime brasserie serves up tasty dishes, from really fresh oysters to an insanely good Guinness burger, with skin-on fries and red-onion chutney. The drinks menu features a range of Guinness variants such as West Indian porter and Golden Ale. Highly recommended for lunch if you're visiting the museum.

★ Fumbally
CAFE €

(Map p76; 01-529 8732; www.thefumbally.ie; Fumbally Lane; mains €5-9.50; 8am-5pm Tue-Fri, 10am-5pm Sat, plus 7-9.30pm Wed; 49, 54A from city centre) A bright, airy warehouse cafe that serves healthy breakfasts, salads and sandwiches – while the occasional guitarist strums away in the corner. Its Wednesday dinner (mains €16) is an organic, locally sourced exploration of the cuisines of the world that includes a single dish (and its vegetarian variant) served in a communal dining experience; advance bookings suggested.

Union8
MODERN IRISH €€

(01-677 8707; www.union8.ie; 740 South Circular Rd; mains €18-27; 9am-9pm Sun-Tue, to 9.30pm Wed, to 10pm Thu-Sat; 69, 79 from Aston Quay, 13, 40 from O'Connell St) A hub for the local community of Dublin 8 (hence the name), this terrific spot serves tasty breakfasts and contemporary Irish cuisine (beautifully presented fish dishes, succulent lamb, tasty pork belly and the like) for lunch and dinner. Highly recommended if you're in this part of town.

✖ North of the Liffey

★Oxmantown
CAFE €

(Map p88; www.oxmantown.com; 16 Mary's Abbey, City Markets; sandwiches €5.50; ⊙7.30am-4pm Mon-Fri; 🚋Four Courts, Jervis) Delicious breakfasts and excellent sandwiches make this cafe one of the standout places for daytime eating on the north side of the Liffey. Locally baked bread, coffee supplied by Cloud Picker (Dublin's only microroastery) and meats sourced from Irish farms are the ingredients, but it's the way it's all put together that makes it so worthwhile.

★M&L
CHINESE €

(Map p88; ☑01-874 8038; www.mlchinese restaurant.com; 13/14 Cathedral St; mains €9-13; ⊙11.30am-10pm Mon-Sat, noon-10pm Sun; 🚋all city centre) Beyond the plain frontage and the cheap-looking decor is Dublin's best Chinese restaurant...by some distance. It's usually full of Chinese people, who come for the authentic Szechuan-style cuisine – spicier than Cantonese and with none of the concessions usually made to Western palates (no prawn crackers or curry chips).

Brother Hubbard
CAFE €

(Map p88; ☑01-441 6595; www.brotherhubbard. ie; 153 Capel St; dishes €7-11; ⊙8am-4.30pm Mon & Tue, 8am-10pm Wed-Fri, 9am-10pm Sat, 9am-4.30pm Sun; 🚋all city centre, 🚋Jervis) Anchored by its excellent baristas (beans by coffee experts 3FE), this cafe with a small garden at the back also does a nice menu of sandwiches, flatbreads and salads. The evening Mezze and Middle Eastern Feast menus are a sharing experience made up of a variety of small plates (reservations recommended). There's another branch (www. brotherhubbard.ie; 46 Harrington St; mains €5-10; ⊙7.45am-4.30pm Mon-Fri, 9am-4.30pm Sat & Sun; 🚋15A, 122 from city centre) south of the river.

★Fish Shop
SEAFOOD €€

(Map p88; ☑01-430 8594; www.fish-shop.ie; 6 Queen St; 4-course/tasting menu €39/55; ⊙noon-2.30pm & 5-10pm Wed-Fri, 5-10pm Tue & Sat; 🚋25, 25A, 66, 67 from city centre, 🚋Smithfield) The menu changes daily at this tiny restaurant (it has only 16 seats) to reflect what's good and fresh, but you'll have to trust them: your only choice is a four-course or tasting menu. One day you might fancy line-caught mackerel with a green sauce, another day slip sole with caper butter. Maybe the best seafood restaurant in town.

Fish & Chip Shop
FISH & CHIPS €€

(Map p88; ☑01-557 1473; www.fish-shop.ie; 76 Benburb St; mains €12.50-14.50; ⊙noon-1pm Tue-Fri, 4-10pm Sat & Sun; 🚋25, 25A, 66, 67 from city centre, 🚋Museum) A classic fish-and-chip shop with a gourmet, sit-down twist – not only is the fish the best you'll taste in battered form, but you'll wash it down with a fine wine from their carefully selected list. It's the original Fish Shop that moved from Queen St, where its fancier sister restaurant (p113) is now installed.

Le Bon Crubeen
IRISH €€

(Map p88; ☑01-704 0126; www.leboncrubeen.ie; 81-82 Talbot St; mains €15-24; ⊙noon-10.30pm; 🚋Abbey) This is modern Irish cuisine with a subtle French twist, managing to combine hearty comfort food with classic elegance. The saloon-style restaurant is comfortable and cosy, despite its large size, and the menu is top quality, including good vegetarian options.

It's a great pre-theatre option if you're visiting the nearby Abbey Theatre (p125).

101 Talbot
MODERN IRISH €€

(Map p88; www.101talbot.ie; 100-102 Talbot St; mains €18-24; ⊙noon-3pm & 5-11pm Tue-Sat; 🚋all city centre) This Dublin classic has expertly resisted every trendy wave and has been a stalwart of good Irish cooking since opening more than two decades ago. Its speciality is traditional meat-and-two-veg dinners, but with Mediterranean influences: chargrilled swordfish with roasted sweet potato and chorizo; pan-roasted duck breast with fondant potato and grilled plums. Superb.

L Mulligan Grocer
MODERN IRISH €€

(Map p88; ☑01-670 9889; www.lmulligangrocer. com; 18 Stoneybatter; mains €15-29; ⊙4-10pm Mon-Fri, 12.30-10pm Sat & Sun; 🚋25, 25A, 66, 67 from city centre, 🚋Museum) 🌿 It's a great traditional pub, but the main reason to come here is for the food, all sourced locally and made by expert hands. The menu includes slow-cooked free-range pork belly and herb-crumbed haddock, as well as a particularly tasty lamb burger. There are about a dozen craft beers on draught and as many again in a bottle.

Winding Stair
MODERN IRISH €€

(Map p88; ☑01-873 7320; www.winding-stair.com; 40 Lower Ormond Quay; 2-course lunch €22, mains €22-28; ⊙noon-5pm & 5.30-10.30pm; 🚋all city centre) In a beautiful Georgian building that once housed the city's most beloved bookshop – the

FAITHIE/SHUTTERSTOCK ©

1. Live Music (p123)
From street musicians to trad-music sessions, Dublin has plenty of music on offer.

2. Docklands (p93)
The revamped Docklands precinct sports an impressive array of contemporary architecture, including the Bord Gáis Energy Theatre, designed by Daniel Libeskind.

3. Howth (p136)
Howth's beautiful coastal scenery is easily accessible from Dublin.

4. St Patrick's Park (p84)
The park adjacent to St Patrick's Cathedral is the perfect place to sit and take it all in.

XIN TAN/500PX ©

ground floor still is one (p129) – the Winding Stair's conversion to elegant restaurant has been faultless. The wonderful Irish menu (creamy fish pie, bacon and organic cabbage, steamed mussels, and Irish farmyard cheeses) coupled with an excellent wine list makes for a memorable meal.

Yamamori Sushi
JAPANESE €€

(Map p88; www.yamamorinoodles.ie; 38-39 Lower Ormond Quay; sushi €4-4.50, mains €17-35; ⊗noon-10.30pm; 🖫all city centre) A sibling of the long-established Yamamori (p110) on South Great George's St, this large restaurant – spread across two converted Georgian houses and including a bamboo garden – does Japanese with great aplomb, serving up all kinds of favourites from steaming bowls of ramen to a delicious *nami moriawase* (sushi platter).

★ Chapter One
MODERN IRISH €€€

(Map p88; ☑01-873 2266; www.chapterone restaurant.com; 18 N Parnell Sq; 2-course lunch €32.50, 4-course dinner €75; ⊗12.30-2pm Tue-Fri, 7.30-10.30pm Tue-Sat; 🖫3, 10, 11, 13, 16, 19, 22 from city centre) Flawless haute cuisine and a relaxed, welcoming atmosphere make this Michelin-starred restaurant in the basement of the Dublin Writers Museum our choice for best dinner experience in town. The food is French-inspired contemporary Irish, the menus change regularly and the service is top-notch. The three-course pre-theatre menu (€39.50) is great if you're going to the Gate (p125) around the corner.

✖ Docklands

★ Juniors Deli & Cafe
ITALIAN €€

(Map p94; ☑01-664 3648; www.juniors.ie; 2 Bath Ave; mains €18-21; ⊗8.30am-2.30pm & 5.30-10pm Mon-Fri, 11am-3pm & 5.30-10.30pm Sat, 11am-3.30pm Sun; 🖫3 from city centre, 🖫Grand Canal Dock) Cramped and easily mistaken for any old cafe, Juniors is anything but ordinary. Designed to imitate a New York deli, the food (Italian-influenced, all locally sourced produce) is delicious, the atmosphere always buzzing (it's often hard to get a table) and the ethos top-notch, which is down to the two brothers who run the place.

Paulie's Pizza
ITALIAN €€

(Map p94; www.juniors.ie; 58 Upper Grand Canal St; pizzas €12-18; ⊗6-10pm; 🚼; 🖫3 from city centre, 🖫Grand Canal Dock) At the heart of this lovely, occasionally boisterous restaurant is a Neapolitan pizza oven, used to create some

of the best pizzas in town. Margheritas, *biancas* (no tomato sauce), calzoni and other Neapolitan specialities are the real treat, but there's also room for a classic New York slice and a few local creations.

Workshop Gastropub
MODERN IRISH €€

(Kennedy's; Map p88; ☑01-677 0626; www.the workshopgastropub.com; 10 George's Quay; mains lunch €7-9, dinner €10-24; ⊗noon-3pm Mon-Fri, to 4.45pm Sat & Sun; 🖉; 🖫all city centre, 🖫Tara St) Take a traditional pub and introduce a chef with a vision: hey presto, you've got a gastropub (surprisingly one of the few in the city) serving burgers, *moules frites* (mussels served with French fries) and sandwiches, as well as a good range of salads.

✖ Southside

★ Farmer Brown's
INTERNATIONAL €€

(Map p94; ☑01-660 2326; www.farmerbrowns. ie; 25a Bath Ave; brunch €10-12, dinner €14-26; ⊗11am-10pm Mon-Fri, 10am-10pm Sat & Sun; 🖀; 🖫7, 8 from city centre, 🖫Grand Canal Dock) The hicky-chic decor and mismatched furniture won't be to everyone's liking, but there's no disagreement about the food, which makes this spot our choice for best brunch in Dublin. From healthy smashed avocado to a stunning Cuban pork sandwich, it has all your lazy breakfast needs covered. Very much worth the effort. There's another branch (Map p76; ☑086-046 8837; 170 Lower Rathmines Rd; mains €10-26; ⊗10am-10pm Mon-Sat, to 9pm Sun; 🖫14, 15 from city centre) in Rathmines.

Butcher Grill
INTERNATIONAL €€

(Map p76; ☑01-498 1805; www.thebutchergrill.ie; 92 Ranelagh Rd; mains €20-28; ⊗5.30-9.30pm Sun-Wed, to 10.30pm Thu-Sat, plus noon-3pm Sat & Sun; 🖫Ranelagh) No surprise that this terrific spot specialises in meat, which is locally sourced and cooked to perfection in its wood-smoked grill. From barbecued baby back ribs to a superb *côte de boeuf* (rib steak) to share – there are few spots in town where the meat sweats are so welcome. Locals will also argue that the brunch is the best in the city.

Kinara
PAKISTANI €€

(Map p76; ☑01-406 0066; www.kinarakitchen.ie; 17 Ranelagh Rd; mains €19-30; ⊗5-11pm daily, plus noon-3pm Thu & Fri, 1-5pm Sun; 🖫Ranelagh) Connoisseurs of the various cuisines of South Asia can distinguish between Indian and Pakistani fare; this exceptional restaurant specialising in the latter will soon educate even the most inexperienced palate. Curries such as the *nehari gosht* (made with beef) are superb, as are fish dishes, including the *machali achari* (fillet of red snapper simmered with pickles).

Chophouse

GASTROPUB €€

(Map p94; 01-660 2390; www.thechophouse. ie; 2 Shelbourne Rd; lunch €12-25, dinner €19-35; ⊙restaurant noon-2.30pm & 6-10pm Mon-Fri, 5-10pm Sat, 1-8pm Sun; 4, 7, 8, 120 from city centre) This fine sprawling bar is a terrific gastropub where the focus is on juicy cuts of steak, but reluctant carnivores also have a choice of fish, chicken or lamb dishes. It does an excellent Sunday lunch – the slow-braised pork belly is delicious. It's a popular watering hole when there's a match on at the Aviva Stadium (p126).

Drinking & Nightlife

If there's one constant about life in Dublin, it's that Dubliners will always take a drink. Come hell or high water, the city's pubs will never be short of customers, and we suspect that exploring a variety of Dublin's legendary pubs and bars ranks pretty high on the list of reasons you're here.

Last orders are at 11.30pm Monday to Thursday, 12.30am Friday and Saturday and 11pm Sunday, with 30 minutes' drinking-up time each night. However, many central pubs have secured late licences to serve until 1.30am or even 2.30am (usually pubs that double up as dance clubs).

Grafton Street & Around

★Kehoe's

PUB

(Map p80; 9 S Anne St; ⊙10.30am-11.30pm Mon-Thu, to 12.30am Fri & Sat, noon-11pm Sun; all city centre) This classic bar is the very exemplar of a traditional Dublin pub. The beautiful Victorian bar, wonderful snug and side room have been popular for Dubliners and visitors for generations, so much so that the publican's living quarters upstairs have since been converted into an extension – simply by taking out the furniture and adding a bar.

★Grogan's Castle Lounge

PUB

(Map p80; www.grogganspub.ie; 15 S William St; ⊙10.30am-11.30pm Mon-Thu, to 12.30am Fri & Sat, 12.30-11pm Sun; all city centre) This place, known simply as Grogan's (after the original owner), is a city-centre institution. It has long been a favourite haunt of Dublin's writers and painters, as well as others from the alternative bohemian set, who enjoy a fine Guinness while they wait for that inevitable moment when they're discovered.

★Long Hall

PUB

(Map p80; 51 S Great George's St; ⊙10.30am-11.30pm Mon-Thu, to 12.30am Fri & Sat, noon-11pm Sun; all city centre) A Victorian classic that is one of the city's most beautiful and best-loved pubs. Check out the ornate carvings in the woodwork behind the bar and the elegant chandeliers. The bartenders are experts at their craft, an increasingly rare attribute in Dublin these days.

Stag's Head

PUB

(Map p80; www.louisfitzgerald.com/stagshead; 1 Dame Ct; ⊙10.30am-1am Mon-Sat, to midnight Sun; all city centre) The Stag's Head was built in 1770, remodelled in 1895 and thankfully not changed a bit since then. It's a superb pub: so picturesque that it often appears in films (p119) and also featured in a postage-stamp series on Irish bars. A bloody great pub, no doubt.

Chelsea Drug Store

BAR

(Map p80; 25 S Great George's St; ⊙4pm-midnight Mon-Fri, noon-1.30am Sat, 4-11pm Sun; all city centre) It doesn't matter that its name seems plucked out of a trendy focus group and the decor carefully curated to reflect current trends (art-deco elements, old-looking-like-new), this is actually a beautiful bar that, at the time of research, was full of young

DUBLIN DRINKING & NIGHTLIFE

CAFE CULTURE

Dublin's coffee junkies are everywhere, looking for that perfect barista fix that will kill the cravings until the next one. You can top-up at any of the chains – including that one from Seattle (with multiple branches throughout the city centre) – but we reckon you'll get the best fix at places such as **Clement & Pekoe** (Map p80; www.clementandpekoe.com; 50 S William St; ⊙8am-7pm Mon-Fri, 10am-6pm Sat, noon-6pm Sun; all city centre), **Brother Hubbard** (p113), **Wall and Keogh** (Map p72; www.wallandkeogh.ie; 45 S Richmond St; ⊙8am-8pm Mon-Fri, 10.30am-7pm Sat & Sun; all city centre) and **Kaph** (Map p80; 31 Drury St; ⊙9am-6pm Mon-Sat, noon-6pm Sun; all city centre).

creatives ordering cocktails with names like The Truth Behind Augustus and Penicillin.

No Name Bar
BAR

(Map p80; 3 Fade St; ⊙12.30-11.30pm Sun-Wed, to 1am Thu, to 2.30am Fri & Sat; ▣all city centre) A low-key entrance just next to the trendy French restaurant L'Gueuleton (p110) leads upstairs to one of the nicest bar spaces in town, consisting of three huge rooms in a restored Victorian townhouse plus a sizeable heated patio area for smokers. There's no sign or a name – folks just refer to it as the No Name Bar.

Bernard Shaw
BAR

(Map p72; www.bodytonicmusic.com; 11-12 S Richmond St; ⊙8am-11.30pm Mon-Thu, to 1am Fri, 10am-1am Sat, 2-11.30pm Sun; ▣14, 15, 65, 83) This deliberately ramshackle boozer is probably the coolest bar in town for its marvellous mix of music (courtesy of its owners, the Bodytonic production crew) and diverse menu of events such as afternoon car-boot sales, storytelling nights and fun competitions like having a 'tag-off' between a bunch of graffiti artists. They also run the excellent **Eatyard** (Map p72; www.the-eatyard.com; 9-10 South Richmond St; before/after 5pm free/€2; ⊙noon-8pm Thu-Sun; ▣14, 15, 44, 65, 140, 142 from city centre, ▣Harcourt).

Anseo
BAR

(Map p72; 18 Lower Camden St; ⊙10.30am-11.30pm Mon-Thu, to 12.30am Fri & Sat, 11am-11pm Sun; ▣14, 15, 65, 83) Unpretentious, unaffected and incredibly popular, this cosy alternative bar – which is pronounced 'an-*shuh*', the Irish for 'here' – is a favourite with those who live by the credo that to try too hard is far worse than not trying at all. The pub's soundtrack is an eclectic mix; you're as likely to hear Peggy Lee as Lee Perry.

McDaid's
PUB

(Map p80; ☑01-679 4395; 3 Harry St; ⊙10.30am-11.30pm Mon-Thu, to 12.30am Fri & Sat, 12.30-11pm Sun; ▣all city centre) One of Dublin's best-known literary pubs, this classic boozer was popular with the likes of Patrick Kavanagh and Brendan Behan (both of whom were eventually barred) and it still oozes character. The pints are perfect, and best appreciated during the day when it's less busy. Thankfully, there's no music – just conversation and raucous laughter.

Swan
PUB

(Map p80; ☑01-647 5272; 70 Aungier St; ⊙11am-11.30pm Mon-Thu, to 12.30am Fri & Sat, noon-11pm Sun; ▣all city centre) Ex-rugby international John Lynch's pub is home to two kinds of punter: the in-for-a-pint-and-a-chat tippler who doesn't venture far from the Victorian front bar; and the more animated younger person, who finds solace and music in the side bar. It's a beautiful marriage that works because neither troubles the other.

Sam's Bar
BAR

(Map p80; 36 Dawson St; ⊙4pm-2am Mon-Thu, 1pm-2.30am Fri-Sun; ▣all city centre, ▣St Stephen's Green) A posh Dawson St drinking spot, Sam's has decor that is Middle Eastern (a hangover of its previous incarnation as an Asian-themed bar) meets art-college graffiti. An odd mix, but it doesn't bother the young professional clientele, who come to share tales of success over fancy cocktails.

Bruxelles
PUB

(Map p80; 7-8 Harry St; ⊙9.30am-1.30am Sun-Thu, to 2.30am Fri & Sat; ▣all city centre) Bruxelles is a raucous music bar split across different areas. It's comparatively trendy on the ground floor, while downstairs is a great, loud and dingy rock bar with live music each weekend.

Pygmalion
BAR

(Map p80; ☑01-674 6712; www.bodytonicmusic.com; Powerscourt Townhouse Shopping Centre, 59 S William St; ⊙10am-midnight; ▣all city centre) The 'Pyg', with its craft beers, flavoured cocktails, excellent, pounding music and myriad nooks and crannies, is hugely popular with younger drinkers and partygoers. By day, those same revellers work out the previous night's shenanigans over coffee at the covered outside tables.

Merrion Square & Around

★Toner's
PUB

(Map p72; ☑01-676 3090; www.tonerspub.ie; 139 Lower Baggot St; ⊙10.30am-11.30pm Mon-Thu, to 12.30am Fri & Sat, 11.30am-11pm Sun; ▣7, 46 from city centre) Toner's, with its stone floors and antique snugs, has changed little over the years and is the closest thing you'll get to a country pub in the heart of the city. Next door, Toner's Yard is a comfortable outside space. The shelves and drawers are reminders that it once doubled as a grocery shop.

★ **O'Donoghue's**   PUB
(Map p72; www.odonoghues.ie; 15 Merrion Row; ⊙10.30am-11.30pm Mon-Thu, to 12.30am Fri & Sat, noon-11pm Sun; ▣ all city centre) The pub where traditional music stalwarts The Dubliners made their name in the 1960s still hosts live music nightly, but the crowds would gather anyway – for the excellent pints and superb ambience, in the old bar or the covered coach yard next to it.

Square Ball   BAR
(Map p94; ☑01-662 4473; www.the-square-ball. com; 45 Hogan Pl; ⊙4-11.30pm Mon, noon-11.30pm Tue-Thu, noon-12.30am Fri & Sat, noon-11pm Sun; ▣4, 7 from city centre) This bar is many things to many people: craft beer and cocktail bar in front, sports lounge and barbecue pit in the back and an awesome vintage arcade upstairs. There are also plenty of board games, so bring your competitive spirit.

House   BAR
(Map p72; ☑01-905 9090; www.housedublin.ie; 27 Lower Leeson St; ⊙8am-midnight Mon-Wed, 8am-3am Thu & Fri, 4pm-3am Sat; ▣11, 46, 118, 145) Spread across two Georgian townhouses, this could be Dublin's most beautiful modern bar, with gorgeous wood-floored rooms, comfortable couches and even log fires in winter to amp up the cosiness. In the middle there's a lovely glassed-in outdoor space that on a nice day bathes the rest of the bar with beautiful natural light. There's also an excellent menu.

Hartigan's   PUB
(Map p72; 100 Lower Leeson St; ⊙10.30am-11.30pm Mon-Thu, to 12.30am Fri & Sat, noon-11pm Sun; ▣ all city centre) This is about as spartan a bar as you'll find in the city, and the daytime home of some serious drinkers, who appreciate the quiet, no-frills surroundings. In the evening it's popular with students from the medical faculty of University College Dublin (UCD).

Doheny & Nesbitt's   PUB
(Map p72; ☑01-676 2945; www.dohenyand nesbitts.ie; 5 Lower Baggot St; ⊙10am-11.30pm Mon-Thu, 10am-2am Fri & Sat, noon-11pm Sun; ▣ all city centre) A standout, even in a city of wonderful pubs, Nesbitt's is equipped with antique snugs and is a favourite place for the high-powered gossip of politicians and journalists; Leinster House is only a short stroll away.

THE STAG'S & HOLLYWOOD

The **Stag's Head** (p117) is justifiably famous as one of Dublin's most beautiful traditional bars, which has led to it featuring in a couple of Hollywood movies: *Educating Rita* (1983) and *A Man of No Importance* (1994). Not bad on the resumé, but its most loyal patrons are far more thrilled by another, less successful brush with Hollywood: Quentin Tarantino was looking for a pint after the call for last orders had gone out, but he pulled the 'do you know who I am?' card and scuppered his chances of swaying the bartender's sympathies.

 Temple Bar

Liquor Rooms   COCKTAIL BAR
(Map p80; ☑087 339 3688; www.theliquorrooms. com; 5 Wellington Quay; ⊙5pm-2am Mon-Thu & Sun, to 3am Fri & Sat; ▣ all city centre) A subterranean cocktail bar decorated in the manner of a Prohibition-era speakeasy. There's lots of rooms – and room – for hip lounge cats to sprawl and imbibe both atmosphere and a well-made cocktail. There's dancing in the Boom Room, classy cocktails in the Blind Tiger Room and art-deco elegance in the Mayflower Room.

Vintage Cocktail Club   BAR
(Map p80; www.vintagecocktailclub.com; Crown Alley; ⊙5pm-1.30am Mon-Fri, 12.30pm-1.30am Sat & Sun; ▣ all city centre) The atmosphere behind this inconspicuous, unlit doorway initialled with the letters 'VCC' is that of a Vegas rat pack hang-out or a '60s-style London members' club. It's so popular you'll need to book for one of the 2½-hour evening sittings, which is plenty of time to sample some of the excellent cocktails and finger food.

Temple Bar   BAR
(Map p80; ☑01-677 3807; 48 Temple Bar; ⊙10.30am-1.30am Mon-Wed, to 2.30am Thu-Sat, 11.30am-1am Sun; ▣ all city centre) The most photographed pub facade in Dublin, perhaps the world, the Temple Bar (aka Flannery's) is smack bang in the middle of the tourist precinct and is usually chock-a-block with visitors. It's good craic, though, and presses all the right buttons, with traditional musicians, a buzzy atmosphere and even a beer garden.

The Oak BAR
(Map p80; ☑01-670 7220; www.theoak.ie; 1 Parliament St; ⊙noon-12.30am Sun-Wed, to 1.30am Thu-Sat; ☒all city centre) Blue velvet chairs, handsome leather booths and walls adorned with prints of Georgian Dublin set a sophisticated tone for this bar, which has a whole shelf devoted to negronis and a cocktail menu straight out of the roaring '20s. A touch of class.

Kilmainham & the Liberties

★ Old Royal Oak PUB
(11 Kilmainham Lane; ⊙10.30am-11.30pm Mon-Thu, to 12.30am Fri & Sat, noon-11pm Sun; ☒68, 79 from city centre) Locals are fiercely protective of this gorgeous traditional pub, which opened in 1845 to serve the patrons and staff of the Royal Hospital (now the Irish Museum of Modern Art). The clientele has changed, but everything else has remained the same, which makes this one of the nicest pubs in the city in which to enjoy a few pints.

MVP BAR
(Map p76; ☑01-558 2158; www.mvpdublin.com; 29 Upper Clanbrassil St; ⊙4-11.30pm Mon-Thu, to 12.30am Fri & Sat, to 11pm Sun; ☒49, 54A, 77X from city centre) A small and friendly bar just off the beaten path that is home to potent and inventive cocktails. The menu is pure comfort food; baked and roast potatoes in all varieties are designed to warm your belly.

Fallon's PUB
(Map p80; ☑01-454 2801; 129 The Coombe; ⊙10.30am-11.30pm Mon-Thu, to 12.30am Fri & Sat, noon-11pm Sun; ☒123, 206, 51B from city centre) A fabulously old-fashioned bar that has been serving a great pint of Guinness since the end of the 17th century. Prizefighter Dan Donnelly, the only boxer ever to be knighted, was head bartender here in 1818. A local's local.

POURING THE PERFECT GUINNESS

Like the Japanese Tea Ceremony, pouring a pint of Guinness is part ritual, part theatre and part logic. It's a five-step process that every decent Dublin bartender will use to serve the perfect pint.

The Glass
A dry, clean 20oz (568mL) tulip pint glass is used because the shape allows the nitrogen bubbles to flow down the side, and the contour 'bump' about halfway down pushes the bubbles into the centre of the pint on their way up.

The Angle
The glass is held beneath the tap at a 45-degree angle – and the tap faucet shouldn't touch the sides of the glass.

The Pour
A smooth pour should fill the glass to about three-quarters full, after which it is put on the counter 'to settle'.

The Head
As the beer flows into the glass its passes through a restrictor plate at high speed that creates nitrogen bubbles. In the glass, the agitated bubbles flow down the sides of the glass and – thanks to the contour bump – back up through the middle, settling at the top in a nice, creamy head. This should take a couple of minutes to complete.

The Top-Off
Once the pint is 'settled', the bartender will top it off, creating a domed effect across the top of the glass with the head sitting comfortably just above the rim. Now it's the perfect pint.

Where to Find It?
Most Dublin pubs know how to serve a decent pint of Guinness. But for something really special, you'll need the expertise of an experienced bartender and the appropriate atmosphere in which to savour their creations. Everyone has their favourites: we recommend Kehoe's (p117), the Stag's Head (p117) and John Mulligan's (p121) on the south side; and Walshe's on the north side.

North of the Liffey

★ Cobblestone
PUB

(Map p88; www.cobblestonepub.ie; N King St; ⊘ 4.30-11.30pm Mon-Thu, to 12.30am Fri & Sat, 1.30-11.30pm Sun; 🚇 Smithfield) It advertises itself as a 'drinking pub with a music problem', which is an apt description for this Smithfield stalwart – although the traditional music sessions that run throughout the week can hardly be described as problematic. Wednesday's Balaclava session (from 7.30pm) is for any musician who is learning an instrument, with musician Síomha Mulligan on hand to teach.

Confession Box
PUB

(Map p88; ⏺ 01-874 7339; www.c11407968.wixsite. com/ryan; 88 Marlborough St; ⊘ 11am-11pm Mon-Fri, 10am-midnight Sat & Sun; 🚇 Abbey) This historic pub is popular with tourists and locals alike. Run by some of the friendliest bar staff you're likely to meet, it's also a good spot to brush up on your local history: the pub was a favourite spot of Michael Collins, one of the leaders in the fight for Irish independence.

Walshe's
PUB

(Map p88; 6 Stoneybatter; ⊘ 10.30am-11.30pm Mon-Thu, to 12.30am Fri & Sat, noon-11pm Sun; 🚇 25, 25A, 66, 67 from city centre, 🚇 Museum) If the snug is free, a drink in Walshe's is about as pure a traditional experience as you'll have in any pub in the city; if it isn't, you'll have to make do with the old-fashioned bar, where the friendly staff and brilliant clientele (a mix of locals and trendsetting imports) are a treat. A proper Dublin pub.

Dice Bar
BAR

(Map p88; ⏺ 01-633 3936; www.dicebar.com; 79 Queen St; ⊘ 4pm-midnight Mon-Thu, 3pm-1am Fri & Sat, 3-11.30pm Sun; 🚇 25, 25A, 66, 67 from city centre, 🚇 Museum) More of a New York dive bar than a traditional Dublin pub, Dice Bar was originally owned by Huey from the Fun Lovin' Criminals. He's since sold his interest, but the look has stayed the same: black-and-red painted interior, dripping candles and stressed seating. Add the rocking DJs and you've got one of the northside's most popular bars.

Grand Social
BAR

(Map p88; ⏺ 01-874 0076; www.thegrandsocial. ie; 35 Lower Liffey St; ⊘ 4pm-2.30am Thu-Sat, to 11.30pm Sun-Wed; 🚇 all city centre, 🚇 Jervis) This multipurpose venue hosts club nights, comedy and live-music gigs, and is a decent bar for a drink. It's spread across three floors, each of which has a different theme: the Parlour downstairs is a cosy, old-fashioned bar; the midlevel Ballroom is where the dancing is; and the upstairs Loft hosts a variety of events.

Hughes' Bar
PUB

(Map p88; 19 Chancery St; ⊘ 10.30am-11.30pm Mon-Thu, to 12.30am Fri & Sat, noon-11pm Sun; 🚇 25, 66, 67, 90 from city centre, 🚇 Four Courts) Traditional purists love the music sessions at this pub, which kick off at around 9.30pm nightly Saturday through Tuesday. By day, the pub caters to the sobering conversations of barristers, solicitors and their clients from the nearby **Four Courts** (Map p88; ⏺ 01-886 8000; Inns Quay; ⊘ 9am-5pm Mon-Fri; 🚇 25, 66, 67, 90 from city centre, 🚇 Four Courts) **FREE**.

Docklands

★ John Mulligan's
PUB

(Map p88; www.mulligans.ie; 8 Poolbeg St; ⊘ 10.30am-11.30pm Mon-Thu, to 12.30am Fri & Sat, noon-11pm Sun; 🚇 all city centre) This brilliant old boozer is a cultural institution, established in 1782 and in this location since 1854. A drink (or more) here is like attending liquid services at a most sacred, secular shrine. John F Kennedy paid his respects in 1945, when he joined the cast of regulars that seems barely to have changed since.

Southside

Taphouse
BAR

(Map p76; ⏺ 01-491 3436; www.taphouse.ie; 60 Ranelagh Rd; ⊘ 12.30pm-12.30am Mon-Sat, to 11pm Sun; 🚇 Ranelagh) Locals refer to it by its original name of Russell's, but that doesn't mean that the regulars aren't delighted with the spruce-up the new owners have brought to a village favourite. What they didn't change was the beloved balcony – the best spot to have a drink on a warm day.

Beggar's Bush
PUB

(Jack Ryan's; Map p94; 115 Haddington Rd; ⊘ 11am-11pm; 🚇 4, 7, 8, 120 from city centre, 🚇 Grand Canal Dock) A staunch defender of the traditional pub aesthetic, Ryan's (as it's referred to by its older clientele) has adjusted to the modern age by adding an outside patio for good weather. Everything else, though, has remained the same, which is precisely why it's so popular with flat-capped pensioners and employees from nearby Google.

GAY & LESBIAN DUBLIN

Dublin is a pretty good place to be LGBTQ. Being gay or lesbian in the city is completely unremarkable, while in recent years members of the trans community have also found greater acceptance. However, LGBTQ people can still be harrassed or worse, so if you do encounter any sort of trouble, call the **Garda LGBTQ Liaison Officer** (☑116006; ⊙24hr) or the **Sexual Assault Unit** (☑01-666 3430; ⊙24hr).

Resources include the following:

Gaire (www.gaire.com) Online message board and resource centre.

Gay Men's Health Project (☑01-660 2189; www.hse.ie/go/GMHS) Practical advice on men's health issues.

Gay Switchboard Dublin (☑01-872 1055; www.gayswitchboard.ie; ⊙6.30am-4pm Mon-Fri, to 6pm on Sat & Sun) A friendly and useful voluntary service that provides information on matters such as legal issues and where to find accommodation.

National Lesbian & Gay Federation (NLGF; ☑01-675 5025; www.nxf.ie; 2 Upper Exchange St, Temple Bar; ☐all city centre) Publishers of *Gay Community News*.

Outhouse (☑01-873 4932; www.outhouse.ie; 105 Capel St; ☐all city centre) Top gay, lesbian and bisexual resource centre, and a great stop-off point to see what's on, check noticeboards and meet people. It publishes the free *Ireland's Pink Pages*, a directory of gay-centric services, which is also accessible on the website.

Festivals & Events

International Dublin Gay Theatre Festival (www.gaytheatre.ie; ⊙May) The only event of its kind anywhere in the world, with more than 30 gay- and lesbian-themed productions over two weeks in May.

Gaze International LGBT Film Festival (www.gaze.ie; ⊙Aug; ☐all city centre) An international film and documentary festival held at the **Irish Film Institute** (p125).

Drinking & Nightlife

Pantibar (Map p88; www.pantibar.com; 7-8 Capel St; ⊙5-11.30pm Mon, Wed & Sun, to 2am Tue, to 2.30am Thu-Sat; ☐all city centre) A raucous, fun gay bar owned by Rory O'Neill, aka Panti, star of 2015's acclaimed documentary *The Queen of Ireland*, about the struggle for equality that climaxes in the historic marriage referendum of May 2015. The bar has since become a place of LGBTQ pilgrimage – and no-holds-barred enjoyment.

Street 66 (Map p80; www.street66.bar; 33 Parliament St; ⊙8.30am-midnight Mon-Thu, to 2.30am Fri & Sat, noon-11pm Sun; ☐all city centre) In late 2016 this place replaced the very popular LGBT Front Lounge and promised to be all things to all people: a dog-friendly coffee shop and bar dressed in upcycled chic that is LGBTQ friendly. The front is the Dive Bar, the back the Disco Lounge. Better than most Temple Bar joints.

George (Map p80; www.thegeorge.ie; 89 S Great George's St; weekends after 10pm €5-10, other times free; ⊙2pm-2.30am Mon-Fri, 12.30pm-2.30am Sat, 12.30pm-1.30am Sun; ☐all city centre) The purple mother of Dublin's gay bars is a long-standing institution, having lived through the years when it was the only place in town where the gay crowd could, well, be gay. Shirley's legendary Sunday-night bingo is as popular as ever, while Wednesday's Space N Veda is a terrific night of cabaret and drag.

Mother (Map p80; www.twitter.com/motherdublin; Copper Alley, Exchange St; €10; ⊙11pm-3.30am Sat; ☐all city centre) The best club night in the city is ostensibly a gay night, but it does not discriminate: clubbers of every sexual orientation come for the sensational DJs – mostly local but occasionally brought in from abroad – who throw down a mixed bag of disco, modern synth-pop and other danceable styles.

☆ Entertainment

Believe it or not, there is life beyond the pub. There are comedy clubs and classical concerts, recitals and readings, marionettes and music – lots of music. The other great Dublin treat is the theatre, where you can enjoy a light-hearted musical alongside the more serious stuff by Beckett, Yeats and O'Casey – not to mention a host of new talents.

Theatre, comedy and classical concerts are usually booked directly through the venue. Otherwise you can buy through booking agencies such as **Ticketmaster** (Map p80; ✆ 0818 719 300; www.ticketmaster.ie; Stephen's Green Shopping Centre; ⬚ all city centre, ⬚ St Stephen's Green), which sells tickets to every genre of big- and medium-sized show – but be aware that it charges between 9% and 12.5% service charge *per ticket*.

Live Music

O'Donoghue's   TRADITIONAL MUSIC
(Map p72; ✆ 01-660 7194; www.odonoghues.ie; 15 Merrion Row; ⊙ from 7pm; ⬚ all city centre) There's traditional music nightly in the old bar of this famous boozer. Regular performers include local names such as Tom Foley, Joe McHugh, Joe Foley and Maria O'Connell.

★ Devitt's   LIVE MUSIC
(Map p72; ✆ 01-475 3414; www.devittspub.ie; 78 Lower Camden St; ⊙ from 9pm Thu-Sat; ⬚ 14, 15, 65, 83) Devitt's – aka the Cusack Stand – is one of the favourite places for the city's talented musicians to display their wares, with sessions as good as any you'll hear in the city centre. Highly recommended.

Bowery   LIVE MUSIC
(Map p76; www.thebowery.ie; 196 Lower Rathmines Rd; ⊙ 5pm-midnight Sun-Thu, to 12.30am Fri & Sat; ⬚ 14, 65, 140) With its burnished wood, intricate chandeliers and ship-shaped stage, this music venue is one of the best-looking bars in the city. It features live performances every night of the week, from ska to disco to reggae, and upstairs is an excellent people-watching spot.

Whelan's   LIVE MUSIC
(Map p72; ✆ 01-478 0766; www.whelanslive.com; 25 Wexford St; ⬚ 16, 122 from city centre) Perhaps the city's most beloved live-music venue is this midsize room attached to a traditional bar. This is the singer-songwriter's spiritual home: when they're done pouring out the contents of their hearts on stage, you can find them filling up in the bar along with their fans.

Workman's Club   LIVE MUSIC
(Map p80; ✆ 01-670 6692; www.theworkmansclub.com; 10 Wellington Quay; free-€20; ⊙ 5pm-3am; ⬚ all city centre) A 300-capacity venue and bar in the former working-men's club of Dublin. The emphasis is on keeping away from the mainstream, which means everything from singer-songwriters to electronic cabaret. When the live music at the Workman's Club (Twitter: @WorkmansClubs) is over, DJs take to the stage, playing rockabilly, hip hop, indie, house and more.

Vicar Street   LIVE MUSIC
(Map p76; ✆ 01-454 5533; www.vicarstreet.com; 58-59 Thomas St; tickets €25-60; ⊙ 7pm-midnight; ⬚ 13, 49, 54A, 56A from city centre) Vicar Street is a midsized venue with a capacity of around 1000, spread between the table-serviced group-seating downstairs and a theatre-style balcony. It offers a varied program of performers, from comedians to soul, jazz, folk and world music.

Sugar Club   LIVE MUSIC
(Map p72; ✆ 01-678 7188; www.thesugarclub.com; 8 Lower Leeson St; €7-20; ⊙ 7pm-late; ⬚ 7, 46 from city centre) There's live jazz, cabaret and soul music on weekends in this comfortable theatre-style venue on the corner of St Stephen's Green.

Academy   LIVE MUSIC
(Map p88; ✆ 01-877 9999; www.theacademydublin.com; 57 Middle Abbey St; ⬚ all city centre, ⬚ Abbey) A terrific midsize venue, the Academy's stage has been graced by an impressive list of performers on the way up – and down – the ladder of success, from Ron Sexsmith to the Wedding Present.

---

❶ ONLINE LISTINGS

Entertainment.ie (www.entertainment.ie) For all events.

MCD (www.mcd.ie) Biggest promoter in Ireland.

Nialler9 (www.nialler9.com) Excellent indie blog with listings.

Sweebe (www.sweebe.com) More than 200 venues listed.

Totally Dublin (http://totallydublin.ie) Comprehensive listings and reviews.

What's On In (www.whatsonin.ie) From markets to gigs and club nights.

Button Factory
LIVE MUSIC

(Map p80; ☑ 01-670 0533; www.buttonfactory.ie; Curved St; €10-20; ⊙ 7.30-11.30pm Mon-Thu, to 2.30am Fri-Sun; ☐ all city centre) A multipurpose venue where one night you might be shaking your glow light to a thumping live set by a top DJ, and the next you'll be shifting from foot to foot as an esoteric Finnish band drag their violin bows over their electric guitar strings. Live gigs are usually followed by club nights.

3 Arena
LIVE MUSIC

(Map p94; ☑ 01-819 8888; www.3arena.ie; East Link Bridge, North Wall Quay; tickets €30-90; ⊙ 6.30-11pm; ☐ The Point) The premier indoor venue in the city has a capacity of 23,000 and plays host to the brightest touring stars in the firmament. Radiohead, Bob Dylan and Take That performed here in 2017.

Classical

Bord Gáis Energy Theatre
THEATRE

(Map p94; ☑ 01-677 7999; www.grandcanaltheatre.ie; Grand Canal Sq; ☐ Grand Canal Dock) Forget the uninviting sponsored name: Daniel Libeskind's masterful design is a three-tiered, 2100-capacity auditorium where you're as likely to be entertained by the Bolshoi or a touring state opera as you are to see *Disney on Ice* or Barbra Streisand. It's a magnificent venue – designed for classical, paid for by the classics.

National Concert Hall
LIVE MUSIC

(Map p72; ☑ 01-417 0000; www.nch.ie; Earlsfort Tce; ☐ all city centre) Ireland's premier orchestral hall hosts a variety of concerts year-round, including a series of lunchtime concerts from 1.05pm to 2pm on Tuesdays from June to August.

Theatre

Smock Alley Theatre
THEATRE

(Map p80; ☑ 01-677 0014; www.smockalley.com; 6-7 Exchange St) One of the city's most diverse theatres is hidden in this beautifully restored 17th-century building. It boasts a diverse program of events (expect anything from opera to murder mystery nights, puppet shows and Shakespeare) and many events also come with a dinner option.

The theatre was built in 1622 and was the only Theatre Royal to ever be built outside London. It's been reinvented as a warehouse and a Catholic church and was lovingly restored in 2012 to become a creative hub once again.

Project Arts Centre
THEATRE

(Map p80; ☑ 1850 260 027; www.projectartscentre.ie; 39 Essex St E; ⊙ 45min before showtime; ☐ all city centre) The city's most interesting venue for challenging new work – be it drama, dance, live art or film. Three separate spaces allow for maximum versatility. You never know what to expect, which makes it all that more fun: we've seen some awful rubbish here, but we've also seen some of the best shows in town.

Olympia Theatre
THEATRE

(Map p80; ☑ 01-677 7744; www.olympia.ie; 72 Dame St; tickets €30-60; ⊙ shows from 7pm; ☐ all city centre) This lovely Victorian-era theatre

---

DUBLIN THEATRE TODAY

Despite Dublin's rich theatrical heritage, times are tough for the city's thespians. Once upon a time, everybody went to the theatre to see the latest offering by Synge, Yeats or O'Casey. Nowadays a night at the theatre is the preserve of the passionate few, which has resulted in the city's bigger theatres taking a conservative approach to their programming and many fringe companies having to make do with non-theatrical spaces to showcase their skills.

In 2016 the theatrical establishment was taken to task by the #wakingthefeminists pressure group, who led a hugely successful campaign to highlight the institutional discrimination against women in the industry: its 2017 report revealed that there was an inverse relationship between levels of state funding and female representation. The two biggest sinners, the Abbey and the Gate, have made wholesale changes to their programs and staffing to address the imbalance.

As a result, future programs will see the city's bigger theatres strike more of a balance between traditional plays and newer work reflecting the broad range of experiences and perspectives.

Theatre bookings can usually be made by quoting a credit-card number over the phone, then you can collect your tickets just before the performance. Expect to pay anything between €12 and €25 for most shows, with some costing as much as €30. Most plays begin between 8pm and 8.30pm. Check www.irishtheatreonline.com to see what's playing.

specialises in light plays and, at Christmastime, pantomimes. It also hosts some terrific live gigs.

Abbey Theatre   THEATRE
(Map p88; ☎01-878 7222; www.abbeytheatre.ie; Lower Abbey St; ☐all city centre, ☐Abbey) Ireland's national theatre was founded by WB Yeats in 1904 and was a central player in the development of a consciously native cultural identity. In 2017 it appointed Neil Murray and Graham McLaren of the National Theatre of Scotland as its new directors, and they have promised an exciting new program that will fuse traditional and contemporary fare.

The Abbey's contemporary relevance is a popular subject of debate in the Irish cultural scene, but for visitors it offers the best chance of seeing classic Irish plays (as well as the work of new dramatists) in an established theatrical context.

Gaiety Theatre   THEATRE
(Map p80; ☎01-677 1717; www.gaietytheatre. com; S King St; ⊕7-10pm; ☐all city centre) The 'Grand Old Lady of South King St' is more than 150 years old and has for much of that time thrived on a diet of fun-for-all-the-family fare: West End hits, musicals, Christmas pantos and classic Irish plays keep the more serious-minded away, leaving more room for those simply looking to be entertained.

Gate Theatre   THEATRE
(Map p88; ☎01-874 4045; www.gatetheatre.ie; 1 Cavendish Row; ⊕performances 7.30pm Mon-Sat, 2.30pm Wed; ☐all city centre) The city's most elegant theatre, housed in a late 18th-century building, features a generally unflappable repertory of classic Irish, American and European plays. Orson Welles and James Mason played here early in their careers. Even today it is the only theatre in town where you might see established international movie stars work on their credibility with a theatre run.

Comedy
Chaplins Comedy Club   COMEDY
(Map p88; www.chaplinscomedy.com; Chaplin's Bar, 2 Hawkins St; €10; ⊕8-11pm Fri & Sat; ☐all city centre) A regularly changing line-up of up-and-coming and local talent look for laughs at this all-seater club; failing that, there's always pizza and craft beer to guarantee a decent night out. Shows start at 9pm.

Laughter Lounge   COMEDY
(Map p88; ☎01-878 3003; www.laughterlounge. com; 4-8 Eden Quay; from €20; ⊕doors open 7.30pm; ☐all city centre) Dublin's only specially designated comedy theatre is where you'll find those comics too famous for the smaller pub stages but not famous enough to sell out the city's bigger venues. Think comedians on the way up (or on the way down).

Banker's Comedy Club   COMEDY
(Map p80; ☎01-679 3697; 16 Trinity St; €8; ⊕9-11pm Fri & Sat; ☐all city centre) The basement room of this decent bar hosts two nights of comedy: the Craic Club on Fridays and the usually excellent Stand Up at the Banker's on Saturday nights. There's decent talent on stage – some of whom have made it onto TV.

Cinema
Light House Cinema   CINEMA
(Map p88; ☎01-872 8006; www.lighthousecinema. ie; Smithfield Plaza; ☐all city centre, ☐Smithfield) The most impressive cinema in town is this snazzy four-screener in a stylish building just off Smithfield Plaza. The menu offers a mix of art-house and mainstream releases, documentaries and Irish films.

Irish Film Institute   CINEMA
(IFI; Map p80; ☎01-679 5744; www.ifi.ie; 6 Eustace St; ⊕11am-11pm; ☐all city centre) The IFI has a couple of screens and shows classics and new art-house films. The complex also has a bar, a cafe and a bookshop.

Savoy   CINEMA
(Map p88; ☎01-874 6000; Upper O'Connell St; ⊕from 2pm; ☐all city centre) The Savoy is a five-screen, first-run cinema, and has late-night shows at weekends. Savoy Cinema 1 is the largest in the city and its enormous screen is the perfect way to view really spectacular blockbuster movies.

HANDEL IN DUBLIN

The clue is the name: on the site of the **Handel's Hotel** (Map p80; 16-18 Fishamble St; ☐all city centre) was once Neal's New Musick Hall, where on 13 April 1742, the nearly broke GF Handel conducted the very first performance of his epic work *Messiah*. All that's left now is the original arch, restored to something like its elegant original. Every year the *Messiah* is performed in an open-air concert on Fishamble St – Dublin's oldest street – to commemorate the event.

Cineworld Multiplex CINEMA
(Map p88; ☑ 0818 304 204; www.cineworld.ie; Parnell Centre, Parnell St; ☐ all city centre) This 17-screen cinema shows only commercial releases. The seats are comfy, the concession stand is huge and the selection of pick 'n' mix could induce a sugar seizure. It lacks the charm of the older-style cinemas, but we like it anyway.

Sport

Croke Park SPECTATOR SPORT
(☑ 01-836 3222; www.crokepark.ie; Clonliffe Rd; ☐ 3, 11, 11A, 16, 16A, 123 from O'Connell St) Hurling and Gaelic football games are held from February to November at Europe's fourth-largest stadium (capacity around 82,000), north of the Royal Canal in Drumcondra; see www.gaa.ie for schedules.

The stadium is also the administrative HQ of the Gaelic Athletic Association (GAA), the body that governs them. To get an idea of just how important the GAA is here, a visit to the Croke Park Experience (p95) is a must, though it will help if you're a sporting enthusiast. The twice-daily tours (except match days) of the impressive stadium are excellent.

Aviva Stadium STADIUM
(Map p94; ☑ 01-238 2300; www.avivastadium.ie; 11-12 Lansdowne Rd; ☐ Lansdowne Rd) Gleaming 50,000-capacity ground with an eye-catching curvilinear stand in the swanky neighbourhood of Donnybrook. Home to Irish rugby and football internationals.

Fairyhouse HORSE RACING
(☑ 01-825 6167; www.fairyhouse.ie; Fairyhouse Rd, Ratoath, Co Meath; €15-25; ☐ special from Busáras) The National Hunt season has its yearly climax with the Grand National, held here on Easter Monday. The course is 25km north of Dublin.

Leopardstown Race Course HORSE RACING
(☑ 01-289 3607; www.leopardstown.com; Foxrock, Dublin 18; tickets from €12.50; ☐ special from Eden Quay, ☐ Sandyford) The Irish love of horse racing can be observed about 10km south of the city centre in Foxrock. Special buses depart from the city centre on race days; call the racecourse for details.

Shelbourne Park Greyhound Stadium SPECTATOR SPORT
(Map p94; ☑ 1890 269 969; www.igb.ie; South Lotts Rd; packages €12-45; ☺ 6.30-10.30pm Tue & Thu-Sat; ☐ 3, 7, 7A, 8, 45, 84 from city centre) A top-class dog track with terrific vantage points from the glassed-in restaurant, where you can eat, bet and watch without leaving your seat. There's a free **shuttle service** (Map p88; Burgh Quay; ☺ 7pm Fri & Sat) FREE Friday and Saturday only from Burgh Quay.

Royal Dublin Society Showground SPECTATOR SPORT
(RDS Showground; Map p76; ☑ 01-668 9878; Merrion Rd, Ballsbridge; ☐ 7 from Trinity College) This impressive, Victorian-era showground is used for various exhibitions throughout the year. The most important annual event here is the late-July **Dublin Horse Show**, which includes an international showjumping contest. Leinster rugby also plays its home matches in the 35,000-capacity arena. Ask at the tourist office for other events.

The Royal Dublin Society Showground was founded in 1731 and has had its headquarters in a number of well-known Dublin buildings, including Leinster House from 1814 to 1925. The society was involved in the foundation of the National Museum, National Library, National Gallery and National Botanic Gardens.

Parnell Park SPECTATOR SPORT
(www.dublingaa.ie; Clantarkey Rd, Donnycarney; adult/child €11/8; ☐ 20A, 20B, 27, 27A, 42, 42B, 43, 103 from Lower Abbey St or Beresford Pl) The Dublin Gaelic team plays its league matches at Parnell Park.

🔒 Shopping

If it's made in Ireland – or pretty much anywhere else – you can find it in Dublin. Grafton St is home to a range of largely British-owned high-street chain stores; you'll find the best local boutiques in the surrounding streets. On the north side, pedestrianised Henry St has international chain stores, as well as Dublin's best department store, Arnott's.

Traditional Irish products such as crystal and knitwear remain popular choices, and you can increasingly find innovative modern takes on the classics. But steer clear of the mass-produced junk whose joke value isn't worth the hassle of carting it home on the plane: trust us, there's no such thing as a genuine *shillelagh* (Irish fighting stick) for sale anywhere in town.

Citizens of non-EU countries can reclaim the VAT paid on purchases made at stores that display a cash-back sticker.

Most shops open from 9.30am to 6pm Monday to Saturday, with later hours – usually to 8pm – on Thursday. Many also open on Sunday, usually from noon to 6pm.

🏠 Grafton Street & Around

⭐**Irish Design Shop**   ARTS & CRAFTS
(Map p80; ☑01-679 8871; www.irishdesignshop.
com; 41 Drury St; ☺10am-6pm Mon-Wed, Fri & Sat,
to 7pm Thu, 1-5pm Sun; ☐all city centre) Beautiful, imaginatively crafted items – from jewellery to kitchenware – carefully curated by
owners Clare Grennan and Laura Caffrey. If
you're looking for a stylish, Irish-made me-
mento or gift, you'll surely find it here.

⭐**Article**   HOMEWARES
(Map p80; ☑01-679 9268; www.articledublin.com;
1st fl, Powerscourt Townhouse Shopping Centre, S
William St; ☺10.30am-6pm Mon-Wed, Fri & Sat, to
7pm Thu, 1-5pm Sun; ☐all city centre) Beautiful
tableware and decorative home accessories
all made by Irish designers. Ideal for unique,
tasteful gifts that you won't find elsewhere.

⭐**Avoca Handweavers**   ARTS & CRAFTS
(Map p80; ☑01-677 4215; www.avoca.ie; 11-13 Suffolk
St; ☺9.30am-6pm Mon-Wed & Sat, to 7pm Thu & Fri,
11am-6pm Sun; ☐all city centre) Combining clothing, homewares, a basement food hall and an
excellent top-floor cafe (Map p80; www.avoca.
ie; 11-13 Suffolk St; mains €9-16; ☺9.30am-5.30pm
Mon-Wed & Sat, to 7pm Thu & Fri, 11am-6pm Sun;
☐all city centre), Avoca promotes a stylish but
homey brand of modern Irish life – and is one
of the best places to find an original present.
Many of the garments are woven, knitted and
naturally dyed at its Wicklow factory. There's
a terrific kids' section.

⭐**Barry Doyle Design Jewellers**   JEWELLERY
(Map p80; ☑01-671 2838; www.barrydoyde-
sign.com; 30 George's St Arcade; ☺10am-6pm
Mon-Wed, Fri & Sat, to 7pm Thu; ☐all city centre)
Goldsmith Barry Doyle's upstairs shop is
one of the best of its kind in Dublin. The
handmade jewellery – using white gold, silver, and some truly gorgeous precious and
semiprecious stones – is exceptional in its
beauty and simplicity. Most of the pieces
have Afro-Celtic influences.

⭐**Ulysses Rare Books**   BOOKS
(Map p80; ☑01-671 8676; www.rarebooks.ie; 10
Duke St; ☺9.30am-5.45pm Mon-Sat; ☐all city

SHOPPING CENTRES

Dublin offers a handful of 'under-the-one-roof' shopping experiences.

Powerscourt Townhouse Shopping Centre (Map p80; ☑01-679 4144; 59 S William St;
☺10am-6pm Mon-Wed & Fri, to 8pm Thu, 9am-6pm Sat, noon-6pm Sun; ☐all city centre) This
absolutely gorgeous and stylish centre is in a carefully refurbished Georgian townhouse,
built between 1741 and 1744. These days it's best known for its cafes and restaurants but
it also does a top-end, selective trade in high fashion, art, exquisite handicrafts and other
chichi sundries.

George's Street Arcade (Map p80; www.georgesstreetarcade.ie; btwn S Great George's &
Drury Sts; ☺9am-6.30pm Mon-Wed, to 7pm Thu-Sat, noon-6pm Sun; ☐all city centre) Dublin's
best nonfood market is sheltered within an elegant Victorian Gothic arcade. Apart from
shops and stalls selling new and old clothes, secondhand books, hats, posters, jewellery and
records, there's a fortune teller, some gourmet nibbles, and a fish and chipper that does a
roaring trade.

St Stephen's Green Shopping Centre (Map p80; ☑01-478 0888; St Stephen's Green W;
☺9am-7pm Mon-Wed, Fri & Sat, 9am-9pm Thu, 11am-6pm Sun; ☐all city centre) A 1980s version
of a 19th-century shopping arcade; the dramatic, balconied interior and central courtyard
are a bit too grand for the nondescript chain stores within. There's Boots, Benetton and
a large Dunnes Store with a supermarket, as well as last-season designer warehouse TK
Maxx.

Jervis Centre (Map p88; ☑01-878 1323; www.jervis.ie; Jervis St; ☺9am-6.30pm Mon-Wed, Fri
& Sat, to 7pm Thu, 11am-6.30pm Sun; ☐all city centre) This modern, domed mall is a veritable
shrine to the British chain store. Boots, Topshop, Debenhams, Argos, Dixons, M&S and Miss
Selfridge all get a look-in.

Dundrum Town Centre (☑01-299 1700; www.dundrum.ie; Sandyford Rd; ☺9am-9pm Mon-
Fri, to 7pm Sat, 10am-7pm Sun; ☐17, 44C, 48A, 75 from city centre, ☐Dundrum, Ballaly) Modern
Ireland's grandest retail cathedral is this huge shopping and entertainment complex in the
southern suburb of Dundrum. Over 100 retail outlets are represented.

centre) Our favourite bookshop in the city stocks a rich and remarkable collection of Irish-interest books, with a particular emphasis on 20th-century literature and a large selection of first editions, including rare ones by the big guns: Joyce, Yeats, Beckett and Wilde.

★ Sheridan's Cheesemongers   FOOD
(Map p80; ☑01-679 3143; www.sheridans cheesemongers.com; 11 S Anne St; ◎10am-6pm Mon-Fri, 9.30am-6pm Sat; ▣all city centre) If heaven were a cheese shop, this would be it. Wooden shelves are laden with rounds of farmhouse cheeses, sourced from around the country by Kevin and Seamus Sheridan, who have almost single-handedly revived cheese-making in Ireland.

Design Centre   CLOTHING
(Map p80; ☑01-679 5718; www.designcentre.ie; Powerscourt Townhouse Shopping Centre, S William St; ◎10am-6pm Mon-Wed, Fri & Sat, to 8pm Thu; ▣all city centre) Mostly dedicated to Irish designer womenswear, featuring well-made classic suits, evening wear and knitwear. Irish labels include Jill De Burca, Philip Treacy, Aoife Harrison and Erickson Beamon – a favourite with Michelle Obama.

Kilkenny Shop   ARTS & CRAFTS
(Map p72; ☑01-677 7066; www.kilkennyshop.com; 6 Nassau St; ◎8.30am-7pm Mon-Wed, Fri & Sat, to 8pm Thu, 10am-6.30pm Sun; ▣all city centre) A large, long-running repository for contemporary, innovative Irish crafts, including multicoloured, modern Irish knits, designer clothing, Orla Kiely bags and lovely silver jewellery. The glassware and pottery is beautiful and sourced from workshops around the country. A great source for traditional presents.

Stokes Books   BOOKS
(Map p80; ☑01-671 3584; 19 George's St Arcade; ◎11am-6pm Mon-Sat; ▣all city centre) A small bookshop specialising in Irish history books, both old and new. Other titles, covering a

---

DUBLIN MARKETS

In recent years Dublin has gone gaga for markets. Which is kind of ironic, considering the city's traditional markets, such as Moore St, were ignored by those same folks who now can't get enough of the homemade hummus on sale at the new gourmet spots. It's all so... continental.

Cow's Lane Designer Mart (Map p80; Cow's Lane; ◎10am-5pm Sat Jun-Sep; ▣all city centre) A real market for hipsters, on the steps of Cow's Lane, this market brings together over 60 of the best clothing, accessory and craft stalls in town. It's open from June to September; the rest of the year it moves indoors to St Michael's and St John's Banquet Hall (Map p80; St Michael's & St John's Banquet Hall, Essex St W; ◎10am-5pm Oct-May; ▣all city centre), just around the corner.

Buy cutting-edge designer duds from the likes of Drunk Monk, punky T-shirts, retro handbags, costume jewellery by Kink Bijoux and even clubby babywear.

Temple Bar Food Market (Map p80; www.facebook.com/TempleBarFoodMarket; Meeting House Sq; ◎10am-5pm Sat; ▣all city centre) From sushi to salsa, this is the city's best open-air food market; pick, prod and poke your way through the organic foods of the world with a compact stroll through gourmet lane. There are tastes of everywhere, from cured Spanish chorizo and paellas to Irish farmhouse cheeses, via handmade chocolates, freshly made crêpes, homemade jams and freshly squeezed juices.

Dublin Food Co-op (Map p76; www.dublinfood.coop; 12 Newmarket; ◎10am-7pm Wed & Fri, to 8pm Thu, 9.30am-5pm Sat, 11am-5pm Sun; ▣49, 54A, 77X from city centre) From dog food to detergent, everything in this member-owned co-op is organic and/or ecofriendly. Thursday has a limited selection of local and imported fair-trade products, but Saturday is when it's all on display – Dubliners from all over drop in for their responsible weekly shop. There's an on-the-premises baker and even baby-changing facilities.

Moore Street Market (Map p88; Moore St; ◎8am-4pm Mon-Sat; ▣all city centre) A shadow of its vibrant former self, this is the most traditional of Dublin street markets. You can get fruit, fish and flowers, while other vendors hawk cheap cigarettes and other products. Don't try to buy just one banana though – if it says 10 for €1, that's what it is.

range of subjects, include a number of beautiful, old, leather-bound editions.

Knobs & Knockers ARTS & CRAFTS
(Map p72; 01-671 0288; 19 Nassau St; 9.30am-5.30pm Mon-Sat; all city centre) Replica Georgian door-knockers are a great souvenir of your Dublin visit, and there are plenty of other souvenir door adornments to look at here too.

🏠 Temple Bar

★**Gutter Bookshop** BOOKS
(Map p80; 01-679 9206; www.gutterbookshop.com; Cow's Lane; 10am-6.30pm Mon-Wed, Fri & Sat, to 7pm Thu, 11am-6pm Sun; all city centre) Taking its name from Oscar Wilde's famous line from *Lady Windermere's Fan* – 'We are all in the gutter, but some of us are looking at the stars' – this fabulous place is flying the flag for the downtrodden independent bookshop, stocking a mix of new novels, children's books, travel literature and other assorted titles.

★**Claddagh Records** MUSIC
(Map p80; 01-677 0262; www.claddaghrecords.com; 2 Cecilia St; 10am-6pm Mon-Sat, noon-6pm Sun; all city centre) An excellent collection of good-quality traditional and folk music is the mainstay at this centrally located record shop. The profoundly knowledgable staff should be able to locate even the most elusive recording for you. There's also a decent selection of world music. There's another **branch** (Map p80; 01-888 3600; www.claddaghrecords.com; 5 Westmoreland St; 10am-6pm Mon-Sat, noon-6pm Sun; all city centre) on Westmoreland St; you can also shop online.

🏠 North of the Liffey

Winding Stair BOOKS
(Map p88; 01-872 6576; www.winding-stair.com; 40 Lower Ormond Quay; 10am-6pm Mon-Wed & Fri, to 7pm Thu & Sat, noon-6pm Sun; all city centre) This handsome old bookshop is in a ground-floor room when once upon a time it occupied the whole building, which is now given over to an excellent restaurant (p113) of the same name. Smaller selection, but still some excellent quality new and old-book perusals.

Arnott's DEPARTMENT STORE
(Map p88; 01-805 0400; www.arnotts.ie; 12 Henry St; 10am-6pm Mon-Wed, Fri & Sat, to 7pm Thu, noon-6pm Sun; all city centre) Occupying

GUARANTEED IRISH ARTS & CRAFTS

Avoca Handweavers (p127) Our favourite department store in the city has myriad homemade gift ideas.

Irish Design Shop (p127) Wonderful handicrafts carefully sourced.

Barry Doyle Design Jewellers (p127) Exquisite handcrafted jewellery with unique contemporary designs.

Ulysses Rare Books (p127) For that priceless first edition or a beautiful, leather-bound copy of Joyce's *Dubliners*.

Louis Copeland (Map p80; 01-872 1600; www.louiscopeland.com; 19-21 Wicklow St; 9am-5.30pm Mon-Wed, Fri & Sat, to 7.30pm Thu; all city centre) Dublin's very own top tailor with made-to-measure suits.

a huge block with entrances on Henry, Liffey and Abbey Sts, this is our favourite of Dublin's department stores. It stocks virtually everything, from garden furniture to high fashion, and it's all relatively affordable.

Eason's BOOKS
(Map p88; 01-873 3811; www.easons.com; 40 Lower O'Connell St; 8am-7pm Mon-Wed & Sat, to 9pm Thu, to 8pm Fri, noon-6pm Sun; all city centre, Abbey) The biggest selection of magazines and foreign newspapers in the whole country can be found on the ground floor of this huge bookshop near the GPO, along with literally dozens of browsers leafing through mags with ne'er a thought of purchasing one.

ℹ️ Information

DANGERS & ANNOYANCES

Dublin is a safe city by any standards, except maybe those set by the Swiss. Basically, act as you would at home.

➡ Don't leave anything visible in your car when you park.

➡ Skimming at ATMs is an ongoing problem; be sure to cover the keypad with your hand when you input your PIN.

➡ Take care around the western edge of Thomas St (onto James St), where drug addicts are often present.

➡ The northern end of Gardiner St and the areas northeast of there have crime-related problems.

EMERGENCY

Drugs Advisory & Treatment Centre (☎01-648 8600; www.dtcb.ie; Trinity Ct, 30-31 Pearse St; ⊙9.30am-12.30pm & 2-4.30pm Mon-Fri, 10am-2.30pm Sat & Sun; ▣all city centre) Walk-in clinic for those battling substance abuse.

Garda Station (☎01-676 3481; Harcourt Tce; ⊙24hr; ▣Harcourt) Largest police station in southside city centre.

Rape Crisis Centre (☎01-661 4911, 24hr 1800 778 888; www.drcc.ie; 70 Lower Leeson St; ⊙8am-7pm Mon-Fri, 9am-4pm Sat; ▣all city centre) In the unlikely event of a sexual assault, get in touch with the police and the Rape Crisis Centre.

INTERNET ACCESS

Wi-fi and 3G/4G networks are making internet cafes largely redundant (except to gamers); the few that are left will charge around €6 per hour. Most accommodation has wi-fi service, either free or for a daily charge (up to €10 per day).

MEDICAL SERVICES

Should you experience an immediate health problem, contact the A&E (accident and emergency) department of the nearest public hospital; in an emergency, call an ambulance (☎999). There are no 24-hour pharmacies in Dublin; the latest any stay open is 10pm.

Caredoc (☎1850 334 999; www.caredoc.ie; ⊙6pm-8am Mon-Fri, 24hr Sat & Sun) Doctors on call; available only out of regular surgery hours.

City Pharmacy (☎01-670 4523; 14 Dame St; ⊙9am-10pm; ▣all city centre) Late-night pharmacy.

Dental Hospital (☎01-612 7200; 20 Lincoln Pl; ⊙9am-5pm Mon-Fri; ▣7, 44) If you don't have an appointment, head in after noon.

Grafton Medical Centre (☎01-671 2122; www.graftonmedical.ie; 34 Grafton St; ⊙8.30am-6pm Mon-Fri, 11am-2pm Sat; ▣all city centre) One-stop shop with male and female doctors as well as physiotherapists. They'll usually require a day's advance notice, but same-day appointments are often available.

Health Service Executive (☎01-679 0700, 1800 520 520; www.hse.ie; Dr Steevens' Hospital, Steevens' Lane; ⊙9.30am-5.30pm Mon-Fri) Central health authority with Choice of Doctor Scheme, which can advise you on a suitable GP from 9am to 5pm Monday to Friday. Also has information services for those with physical and mental disabilities.

Hickey's Pharmacy (☎01-873 0427; 55 Lower O'Connell St; ⊙8am-10pm Mon-Fri, 8.30am-10pm Sat, 10am-10pm Sun; ▣all city centre) Late-night pharmacy.

Mater Misericordiae Hospital (☎01-830 1122; Eccles St; ▣120, 122 from city centre) Northside city centre, off Lower Dorset St.

St James's Hospital (☎01-410 3000; www.stjames.ie; James's St; ▣James's) Dublin's main 24-hour accident and emergency department.

MONEY

The best exchange rates are at banks, although bureaux de change and other exchange facilities usually open for more hours. There's a cluster of banks located around College Green opposite Trinity College and all have exchange facilities.

POST

The Irish postal service, An Post, is reliable, efficient and generally on time. Postboxes in Dublin are usually green and have two slots: one for 'Dublin only', the other for 'All Other Places'. There are a couple of post offices in the city centre, including **An Post** (Map p80; ☎01-705 8206; www.anpost.ie; St Andrew's St; ⊙8.30am-5pm Mon-Fri; ▣all city centre) and the **General Post Office** (p87).

TOURIST INFORMATION

A handful of official-looking tourism offices on Grafton and O'Connell Sts are actually privately run enterprises where members pay to be included.

Visit Dublin Centre (Map p80; www.visitdublin.com; 25 Suffolk St; ⊙9am-5.30pm Mon-Sat, 10.30am-3pm Sun; ▣all city centre) The main tourist information centre, with free maps, guides and itinerary planning, plus booking services for accommodation, attractions and events.

Dublin Discover Ireland Centre (Map p88; 14 Upper O'Connell St; ⊙9am-5pm Mon-Sat; ▣all city centre) Failte Ireland's walk-in information centre for Dublin.

USEFUL WEBSITES

Dublin Tourism (www.visitdublin.com) Official website of Dublin Tourism.

Dublintown (www.dublintown.ie) Comprehensive list of events and goings on.

Failte Ireland (www.discoverireland.ie) Official tourist-board website.

Lonely Planet (www.lonelyplanet.com/dublin) Destination information, hotel bookings, traveller forums and more.

Lovin Dublin (www.lovindublin.com) Honest, sometimes scathing, reviews of bars, restaurants and other Dublin-related activities.

Old Dublin Town (www.olddublintown.com) In a city in flux, this haphazard-looking website is an excellent resource.

Totally Dublin (www.totallydublin.ie) Latest news and reviews.

ℹ Getting There & Away

AIR

Dublin Airport (Map p96; ✆ 01-814 1111; www.dublinairport.com) Dublin Airport, 13km north of the centre, is Ireland's major international gateway airport. It has two terminals: most international flights (including most US flights) use the newer Terminal 2; Ryanair and select others use Terminal 1. Both terminals have the usual selection of pubs, restaurants, shops, ATMs and car-hire desks.

BOAT

Dublin Port Terminal (Map p96; ✆ 01-855 2222; Alexandra Rd; 🚌 53 from Talbot St) The Dublin Port Terminal, 3km northeast of the city centre, serves Holyhead (in Wales) and Liverpool.

An express bus transfer to and from Dublin Port is operated by Morton's (Map p80; www.mortonscoaches.ie; adult/child €3/1.50; ⏰ 7.15am, 1.30pm & 7pm), departing from Westmoreland St at 7.15am, 1.30pm and 7pm (timed to coincide with ferry departures). Fares are adult/child €3/1.50. Otherwise, regular bus 53 serves the port from Talbot St. Inbound ferries are met by timed bus services that serve the city centre.

BUS

Dublin's central bus station, **Busáras** (Map p88; ✆ 01-836 6111; www.buseireann.ie; Store St; 🚊 Connolly) is just north of the river behind the Custom House; it has different-sized luggage lockers costing €6 to €10 per day.

It's possible to combine bus and ferry tickets from major UK centres to Dublin on the bus network. The journey between London and Dublin takes about 12 hours and costs from €29 return (€41 for a single!). For details in London, contact **Eurolines** (✆ 0870 514 3219; www.eurolines.com).

From here, **Bus Éireann** (✆ 1850 836 6111; www.buseireann.ie) buses serve the whole national network, including buses to towns and cities in Northern Ireland.

CAR & MOTORCYCLE

Road access to and from Dublin is pretty straightforward. A network of motorways radiate outward from the M50 ring road that surrounds Dublin, serving the following towns and cities:

M1 North to Drogheda, Dundalk and Belfast

M3 Northwest to Navan, Cavan and Donegal

M4 West to Galway and Sligo

M7 Southwest to Limerick; also (via M8) to Cork

M9 Southeast to Kilkenny and Waterford

M11 Southeast to Wexford

TRAIN

All trains in the Republic are run by **Irish Rail** (Iarnród Éireann; ✆ 1850 366 222; www.irishrail.ie). Dublin has two main train stations: **Heuston Station** (✆ 01-836 5421; 🚊 Heuston), on the western side of town near the Liffey; and **Connolly Station** (✆ 01-836 3333; 🚊 Connolly, 🚊 Connolly Station), a short walk northeast of Busáras, behind the Custom House.

Connolly Station is a stop on the DART line into town; the Luas Red Line serves both Connolly and Heuston stations.

ℹ Getting Around

TO/FROM THE AIRPORT

Bus

It takes about 45 minutes to get into the city by bus.

Aircoach (✆ 01-844 7118; www.aircoach.ie; One way/return €7/12) Private coach service with three routes from the airport to more than 20 destinations throughout the city, including the main streets of the city centre. Coaches run every 10 to 15 minutes between 6am and midnight, then hourly from midnight until 6am.

Airlink Express Coach (✆ 01-873 4222; www.dublinbus.ie; One way/return €6/10) Bus 747 runs every 10 to 20 minutes from 5.45am to 12.30am between the airport, the central bus station (Busáras) and the Dublin Bus office on Upper O'Connell St. Bus 757 runs every 15 to 30 minutes from 5am to 12.25am between the airport and various stops in the city, including Grand Canal Dock, Merrion Sq and Camden St.

Dublin Bus (Map p88; ✆ 01-873 4222; www.dublinbus.ie; 59 Upper O'Connell St; ⏰ 8.30am-5.30pm Tue-Fri, to 2pm Sat, 9am-5.30pm Mon; 🚌 all city centre) A number of buses serve the airport from various points in Dublin, including buses 16 (Rathfarnham), 41 (Lower Abbey St) and 102 (Sutton/Howth); all cross the city centre on their way to the airport.

Taxi

There is a taxi rank directly outside the arrivals concourse of both terminals. It should take about 25 minutes to get into the city centre by taxi and should cost around €25, including an initial charge of €3.60 (€4 between 10pm and 8am and on Sundays and bank holidays). Make sure the meter is switched on.

BICYCLE

Dublin is relatively flat and compact, making it ideal cycling territory. You can zip from one side of the city to the other in double-quick time, and a bike makes the suburbs much more accessible. The city does have a growing network of cycle lanes, especially south of the Liffey, but getting around the centre itself can be a bit of an obstacle course as larger vehicles such as buses

ⓘ DUBLIN BY BIKE

One of the most popular ways to get around the city is with the blue bikes of Dublinbikes (www.dublinbikes.ie), a public bicycle-rental scheme with more than 100 stations spread across the city centre. Purchase a €10 smart card (as well as pay a credit-card deposit of €150) or a three-day card online or at any station before 'freeing' a bike for use, which is then free of charge for the first 30 minutes and €0.50 for each half-hour thereafter.

and trucks are forced to encroach on lanes nominally reserved for two wheels due to the narrowness of the streets.

There are plenty of spots to lock your bike throughout the city, but be sure to do so thoroughly as bike theft can be a problem – and never leave your bike on the street overnight as even the toughest lock can be broken. Dublin City Cycling (www.cycledublin.ie) is an excellent online resource.

Bikes are only allowed on suburban trains (not the DART), either stowed in the guard's van or in a special compartment at the opposite end of the train from the engine.

Bike rental has become tougher due to the Dublinbikes scheme. Typical rental for a hybrid or touring bike is around €25 a day or €140 per week.

Cycleways (www.cycleways.com; 185-187 Parnell St; ⊙8.30am-6.30pm Mon-Wed & Fri, to 8pm Thu, 9.30am-6pm Sat; ⊠all city centre) An excellent bike shop that rents out hybrids and touring bikes during the summer months (May to September).

2Wheels (www.2wheels.ie; 57 S William St; ⊙10am-6pm Mon, Tue & Sat, to 8pm Wed, Thu & Fri, noon-6pm Sun; ⊠all city centre) New bikes, all the gear you could possibly need and a decent repair service; but be sure to book an appointment as it is generally quite busy.

MacDonald Cycles (☑01-475 2586; www.macdonaldcycles.ie; 38 Wexford St; ⊙9am-6pm Mon-Fri, 9.30am-6pm Sat; ⊠14, 15, 65, 83) Does repairs, and will have your bike back to you within a day or so (barring serious damage).

CAR & MOTORCYCLE

Traffic in Dublin is a nightmare and parking is an expensive headache. There are no free spots to park anywhere in the city centre during business hours (7am to 7pm Monday to Saturday), but there is plenty of paid parking, priced according to zone: €2.90 per hour in the yellow (central) zone down to €0.60 in the blue (suburban). Supervised and

sheltered car parks cost around €4 per hour, with most offering a low-cost evening flat rate.

Clamping of illegally parked cars is thoroughly enforced, and there is an €80 charge for removal. Parking is free after 7pm Monday to Saturday, and all day Sunday, in most metered spots (unless indicated) and on single yellow lines.

Car theft and break-ins are an occasional nuisance, so never leave anything visible or of value in the car. When you're booking accommodation, check on parking facilities.

The **Automobile Association of Ireland** (AA; ☑01-617 9999, breakdown 1800 667 788; www.aaireland.ie; 61 S William St; ⊠all city centre) is located in the city centre.

Car Rental

All the main agencies are represented in Dublin. Book in advance for the best fares, especially at weekends and during summer months, when demand is highest.

Motorbikes and mopeds are not available for rent. People aged under 21 are not allowed to hire a car; for the majority of rental companies you have to be at least 23 and have had a valid driving licence for a minimum of one year. Many rental agencies will not rent to people over 70 or 75.

The following rental agencies have several branches across the capital and at the airport:

Avis Rent-a-Car (☑01-605 7500; www.avis.ie; 35 Old Kilmainham Rd; ⊙8.30am-5.45pm Mon-Fri, 8.30am-2.30pm Sat & Sun; ⊠23, 25, 25A, 26, 68, 69 from city centre)

Budget Rent-a-Car (☑01-837 9611; www.budget.ie; 151 Lower Drumcondra Rd; ⊙9am-6pm; ⊠41 from O'Connell St)

Europcar (☑01-812 2800; www.europcar.ie; 1 Mark St; ⊙8am-6pm Mon-Fri, 8.30am-3pm Sat & Sun; ⊠all city centre)

Hertz Rent-a-Car (☑01-709 3060; www.hertz.com; 151 South Circular Rd; ⊙8.30am-5.30pm Mon-Fri, 9am-4.30pm Sat, 9am-3.30pm Sun; ⊠9, 16, 77, 79 from city centre)

Thrifty (☑01-844 1944; www.thrifty.ie; 26 Lombard St E; ⊙8am-6pm Mon-Fri, to 3pm Sat & Sun; ⊠all city centre)

PUBLIC TRANSPORT
Bus

The **Dublin Bus Office** (p131) has free single-route timetables for all its services. Buses run from around 6am (some start at 5.30am) to about 11.30pm. Fares are calculated according to stages (stops):

Stages	Cash Fare (€)	Leap Card (€)
1-3	2	1.50
4-13	2.70	2.05
over 13	3.30	2.60

A Leap Card (www.leapcard.ie), available from most newsagents, is not just cheaper but also more convenient as you don't have to worry about tendering exact fares (required with cash, otherwise you will get a receipt for reimbursement, which is only possible at the Dublin Bus main office). Register the card online and top it up with whatever amount you need. When you board a bus, DART, Luas (light rail) or suburban train, just swipe your card and the fare is automatically deducted.

If you're travelling within the College Green Bus Corridor (roughly between Parnell Sq to the north and St Stephen's Green to the south) you can use the €0.50 special City Centre fare.

Nitelink

Nitelink late-night buses run from the College, Westmoreland and D'Olier Sts triangle. On Fridays and Saturdays, departures are at 12.30am, then every 20 minutes until 4.30am on the more popular routes, and until 3.30am on the less frequented ones; there are no services Sunday to Thursday. Fares are €6.50 (€5.20 with Leap card). See www.dublinbus.ie for route details.

Luas (Light Rail)

The Luas (www.luas.ie) light-rail system has two lines: the green line (running every five to 15 minutes) connects St Stephen's Green with Sandyford in south Dublin via Ranelagh and Dundrum; the red line (every 20 minutes) runs from the Point Village to Tallaght via the north quays and Heuston Station.

There are ticket machines at every stop or you can use a tap-on, tap-off Leap Card, which is available from most newsagents. A typical short-hop fare (around four stops) is €2.30. Services run from 5.30am to 12.30am Monday to Friday, from 6.30am to 12.30am Saturday and from 7am to 11.30pm Sunday.

From 2018, a new cross-city line will connect the green and red lines with a route from St Stephen's Green through Dawson St and around Trinity College and over the river.

Taxi

All taxi fares begin with a flagfall of €3.60 (€4 from 10pm to 8am), followed by €1.10 per kilometre thereafter (€1.40 from 10pm to 8am). In addition to these, there are a number of extra charges – €1 for each extra passenger and €2 for telephone bookings. There is no charge for luggage.

Taxis can be hailed on the street and found at taxi ranks around the city, including on the corner of Abbey and O'Connell Sts; College Green, in front of Trinity College; and St Stephen's Green at the end of Grafton St.

Numerous taxi companies, such as **National Radio Cabs** (☑ 01-677 2222; www.nrc.ie),

dispatch taxis by radio. You can also try MyTaxi (www.mytaxi.com), a taxi app.

Train (DART)

The **Dublin Area Rapid Transport** (DART; ☑ 01-836 6222; www.irishrail.ie) provides quick train access to the coast as far north as Howth (about 30 minutes) and as far south as Greystones in County Wicklow. Pearse Station is convenient for central Dublin south of the Liffey, and Connolly Station for north of the Liffey. There are services every 10 to 20 minutes, sometimes more frequently, from around 6.30am to midnight Monday to Saturday. Services are less frequent on Sunday. A one-way DART ticket from Dublin to Dun Laoghaire or Howth costs €3.25.

There are also suburban rail services north as far as Dundalk, inland to Mullingar and south past Bray to Arklow.

AROUND DUBLIN

Without even the smallest hint of irony Dubliners will tell you that one of the city's best features is how easy it is to get out of – and they do, whenever they can. But they don't go especially far: for many the destination is one of the small seaside villages that surround the capital. To the north are the lovely villages of Howth and Malahide – slowly and reluctantly being sucked into the Dublin agglomeration – while to the south is Dalkey, which has long since given up the fight but still manages to retain that village vibe.

> ### ℹ FARE SAVER PASSES
>
> Fare-saver passes include the following:
>
> **Freedom of the City** (adult/child €33/16) Three-day unlimited travel on all bus services, including Airlink and Dublin Bus Hop-On, Hop-Off tours as well as entry to the Little Museum of Dublin and a Pat Liddy walking tour.
>
> **Luas Flexi Ticket** (one/seven/30 days €7/26/100) Unlimited travel on all Luas services.
>
> **Rambler Pass** (five/30 days €31.50/157.50) Valid for unlimited travel on all Dublin Bus and Airlink services, except Nitelink.
>
> **Visitor Leap Card** (one/three/seven days €10/19.50/40) Unlimited travel on bus, Luas and DART, including Airlink, Nitelink and Xpresso bus.

Malahide

POP 15,846

Malahide (Mullach Íde) was once a small village with its own harbour, a long way from the urban jungle of Dublin. The only thing protecting it from the northwards expansion of Dublin's suburbs is Malahide Demesne, 101 well-tended hectares of parkland dominated by a castle once owned by the powerful Talbot family.

The handsome village remains relatively intact, but the once-quiet marina has been massively developed and is now a bustling centre with a pleasant promenade and plenty of restaurants and shops.

◎ Sights & Activities

Malahide Castle   CASTLE

(☑ 01-816 9538; www.malahidecastleandgardens.ie; Malahide; adult/child €12.50/6.50; ⊘ 9.30am-5.30pm; ◻ 42, 142 from city centre, ◪ Malahide) The oldest part of this hotchpotch castle, which was in the hands of the Talbot family from 1185 to 1976, is the three-storey 12th-century tower house. The facade is flanked by circular towers that were tacked on in 1765. The castle, now owned by Fingal County Council, is accessible via guided tour only (last tour 4.30pm; 3.30pm November to March); the impressive gardens are self-guided.

The castle is packed with furniture and paintings; highlights are a 16th-century oak room with decorative carvings, and the medieval Great Hall, which has family portraits, a minstrel's gallery and a painting of the Battle of the Boyne. Puck, the Talbot family ghost, is said to have last appeared in 1975.

★ Portmarnock Golf Club   GOLF

(☑ 01-846 2968; www.portmarnockgolfclub.ie; Golf Links Rd, Portmarnock; green fee weekday/weekend €200/225) Founded in 1894, this is one of the world's outstanding links courses and a former long-time host of the Irish Open. Visitor tee-times are spread out throughout the day, with 11.30am to 2.30pm reserved exclusively for members.

✕ Eating & Drinking

Malahide is one of north Dublin's great culinary hot spots, chock-full of excellent restaurants serving virtually every kind of cuisine. The competition is so fierce and the expectations so high that it's hard to eat badly here. All of the best places are divided between town and the marina.

Greedy Goose   INTERNATIONAL €€

(www.greedygoose.ie; 15 Townyard Lane; menus €24-30; ⊘ 5-11pm Mon-Fri, 1-11pm Sat & Sun; ◻ 42, 142 from city centre, ◪ Malahide) The menu at this pleasant restaurant overlooking the marina has dishes from all over the globe: take your pick of barbecued chicken wings, chana masala, Cajun-style Irish salmon and others. The food is best enjoyed as part of three separate menus: pick three dishes from one and eat portions roughly equivalent to Spanish raciones – bigger than starters, smaller than mains.

Chez Sara   FRENCH €€

(☑ 01-845 1882; www.chezsara.ie; 3 Old St; mains €16-24; ⊘ 5pm-midnight Tue-Sun; ◻ 42, 142 from city centre, ◪ Malahide) Irish lamb, red snapper and a beautifully cooked steak are just three of the highlights of this cosy French restaurant in the middle of the village.

Sale e Pepe   INTERNATIONAL €€

(☑ 01-845 4600; www.saleepepe.ie; The Diamond, Main St; mains €17-28; ⊘ 5-11pm Mon-Sat, 4-11pm Sun; ◻ 42, 142 from city centre, ◪ Malahide) Despite the name, there's only a handful of Italian dishes on a menu that emphasises well-prepared steaks, fish and chips, and homemade organic burgers.

Gibney's   PUB

(6 New St; ⊘ 10.30am-11.30pm Mon-Wed, to 12.30am Thu-Sat, to 11pm Sun; ◻ 42, 142 from city centre, ◪ Malahide) Malahide's best-known, best-loved pub is a huge place, spread over a number of rooms and outdoor areas. At weekends it's always packed with locals.

❶ Getting There & Away

Malahide is 13km north of Dublin.

Bus Services 42 and 142 (€3.25) from Talbot St take around 45 minutes.

DART Stops in Malahide (€3.25).

If travelling by DART, be sure to get on the right train from Dublin city centre as the line splits at Howth Junction.

Dalkey

POP 8083

Dublin's most important medieval port has long since settled into its role as an elegant dormitory village, but there are some revealing vestiges of its illustrious past, most

SANDYCOVE

Sandycove has a pretty little beach and a Martello tower – built by British forces as a look-out for signs of a Napoleonic invasion – now home to the James Joyce Museum.

There are really only two things to do here: visit the Martello Tower and, if you're brave enough, get into the water at the adjacent Forty Foot Pool

If you want to swim in the Forty Foot Pool in your birthday suit, do so before 9am; later swims are generally done wearing bathing suits.

DART Easily reached from Dublin.

Walk It's a 1km walk north of Dalkey.

James Joyce Tower & Museum (☑ 01-280 9265; www.joycetower.ie; Joyce Tower; ☉ 10am-6pm May-Sep, to 4pm Oct-Apr; ⊠ Sandycove & Glasthule) This tower is where the action begins in Joyce's epic novel *Ulysses*. The museum was opened in 1962 by Sylvia Beach, the Paris-based publisher who first dared to put *Ulysses* into print, and has photographs, letters, documents, various editions of Joyce's work and two death masks of Joyce on display.

Forty Foot Pool (Sandycove; ⊠ Sandycove & Glasthule) The Forty Foot Pool is an open-air, seawater bathing pool that took its name from the army regiment, the Fortieth Foot, that was stationed at the tower until the regiment was disbanded in 1904. At the close of the first chapter of *Ulysses*, Buck Mulligan heads off to the Forty Foot Pool for a morning swim. A morning wake-up here is still a local tradition, in summer and winter: the Christmas Day Dip is one of Dublin's most enduring traditions.

Pressure from female bathers eventually opened this public stretch of water – originally nudist and for men only – to both sexes, despite strong opposition from the 'forty foot gentlemen', who eventually agreed.

notably the remains of three of the eight castles that once lorded over the area.

Dalkey is small enough that you can get around on foot. Most visitors will be arriving by DART, so start your exploration in the middle of town: the main sights are on Castle St, as are most of the cafes (or on the streets just off it). Coliemore Harbour is where you can get boat trips; overlooking the adjoining Bullock Harbour are the remains of Bullock Castle.

The waters around the island are popular with scuba divers; qualified divers can rent gear in Dun Laoghaire, further north, from **Ocean Divers** (www.oceandivers.ie; The Boat Yard, Dun Laoghaire Harbour, Dun Laoghaire; boat dives €35-55; ☉ 9.30am-5pm Tue-Sat; ⊠ Dalkey).

To the south there are good views from the small park at Sorrento Point and from Killiney Hill. A number of rocky swimming pools are also found along the Dalkey coast.

⊙ Sights & Activities

Dalkey Castle & Heritage Centre   MUSEUM
(☑ 01-285 8366; www.dalkeycastle.com; Castle St, Dalkey; adult/child €9/7; ☉ 10am-5.30pm Mon-Fri, 11am-5.30pm Sat & Sun Jun-Aug, closed Tue Sep-May; ⊠ Dalkey) Spread across Goat Castle and St Begnet's Church, this heritage centre has models, displays and exhibitions on Dalkey's history; a Living History tour in the format of a theatre performance; and a Writers' Gallery, covering the town's rich literary heritage – from Samuel Beckett (who was born here) to Joseph O'Connor (who lives here). The centre also organises walking tours (p135).

Dalkey Island   ISLAND
Dalkey Island's main sight is **St Begnet's Holy Well** (ferry from Coliemore Harbour adult/child €8/5; ⊠ Dalkey) **FREE**, but it's also a popular spot for fishing, with shoals of pollock, mackerel and coalfish feeding in its waters. It's also a lovely spot to spend a couple of hours with a picnic – but be sure to take everything off the island with you when you leave. **Ken the Ferryman** (www.kentheferryman.com; Coliemore Harbour; adult/child €8/5; ☉ 10am-6pm) provides transport to and from the island.

Dalkey Guided Tours   TOURS
(www.dalkeycastle.com; Dalkey Castle & Heritage Centre; €9; ☉ 11am & noon Wed & Fri Jun-Aug) Historical and literary tours of Dalkey, including a Maeve Binchy–themed walk (the writer lived here) and a Joyce-themed one.

WORTH A TRIP

IRELAND'S EYE

A short distance offshore from Howth is **Ireland's Eye** (☏ 01-831 4200) a rocky seabird sanctuary with the ruins of a 6th-century monastery. There's a Martello tower at the northwestern end of the island, where boats from Howth land, while a spectacularly sheer rock face plummets into the sea at the eastern end. It's really only worth exploring if you're interested in birds, although the boat trip out here, with **Doyle & Sons** (☏ 01-831 4200; www.howth-boats.com; from €15; 🚍 31, 31A from Beresford Pl, 🚆 Howth), affords some lovely views of Dublin Bay.

As well as the seabirds overhead, you can see young birds on the ground during the nesting season. Seals can also be spotted around the island. Further north from Ireland's Eye is Lambay Island, an important seabird sanctuary that cannot be visited.

They're run out of Dalkey Castle & Heritage Centre (p135).

★ **Dalkey Book Festival**   LITERATURE
(www.dalkeybookfestival.org; ⊙ mid-Jun) Salman Rushdie is an acknowledged fan, which must help its organisers, Sian Smyth and David McWilliams, to always draw some big award-winning names – in 2017 Louis de Bernières, Marlon James and Bernie Sanders were speakers.

✖ Eating & Drinking

Dalkey's culinary credentials are excellent, mostly because its affluent population wouldn't stand for anything else. There's a good choice of everything from healthy cafe bites to fine dining.

★ **Select Stores**   HEALTH FOOD €
(www.selectstores.ie; 1 Railway Rd; mains €4-12; ⊙ 8am-6pm, closed Sun Oct-Apr; 🚆 Dalkey) This long-established food emporium has been transformed into a one-stop shop for all things good for you: the award-winning kitchen rolls out veggie burgers, fresh juices, salads and, in the mornings, a range of healthy breakfasts. Bono is a fan, apparently.

Magpie Inn   PUB FOOD €€
(☏ 01-202 3909; www.magpieinn.com; 115-116 Coliemore Rd; mains €12-25; ⊙ noon-11.30pm;

🚆 Dalkey) The excellent menu's main strength is, obviously, seafood, including a range of mouth-watering lunch options like fresh Sligo mussels marinière with toasted sourdough bread and more substantial dinner mains like a seafood skillet of pan-fried salmon, cod, langoustine, mussels, tomatoes, potatoes, onions and garlic in a white-wine sauce. Wash it all down with a choice of craft beer.

Finnegan's   PUB
(www.finnegans.ie; 1 Sorrento Rd; ⊙ noon-11.30pm Mon-Thu, to 12.30am Fri & Sat, noon-11pm Sun; 🚆 Dalkey) There's a fabulous local atmosphere in this lovely traditional pub, which has been a staple here for over 40 years.

ℹ Getting There & Away

DART The best way to get to Dalkey is by train from Pearse or Connolly stations – a one-way ticket costs €3.25.

Bus Service 7 takes a slow route from Mountjoy Sq through Dublin city centre to Dalkey – fare is €3.25.

Howth

POP 8277

Tidily positioned at the foot of a bulbous peninsula, the pretty port village of Howth (the name rhymes with 'both') is a major fishing centre, a yachting harbour and one of the most sought-after addresses in town.

Howth is divided between the upper headland – where the best properties are, discreetly spread atop the gorse-rich hill where there are some fine walks and spectacular views of Dublin Bay – and the busy port town, where all the restaurants are (as well as an excellent weekend farmers market).

⊙ Sights & Activities

Howth Castle   CASTLE
(🚍 31, 31A from Beresford Pl, 🚆 Howth) **FREE** Most of Howth backs onto the extensive grounds of Howth Castle, built in 1564 but much changed over the years, most recently in 1910 when Sir Edwin Lutyens gave it a modernist makeover. Today the castle is divided into four very posh and private residences (the grounds are open to the public). The **castle gardens** (⊙ 24hr; 🚍 31, 31A from Beresford Pl, 🚆 Howth) **FREE** are worth visiting, as they're noted for their rhododendrons (which bloom in May and June), azaleas and a long, 10m-high beech hedge planted in 1710.

The original estate was acquired in 1177 by the Norman noble Sir Almeric Tristram, who changed his surname to St Lawrence after winning a battle at the behest (or so he believed) of his favourite saint. The family has owned the land ever since, though the unbroken chain of male succession came to an end in 1909.

On the grounds are the ruins of the 16th-century Corr Castle and an ancient dolmen (a tomb chamber or portal tomb made of vertical stones topped by a huge capstone) known as Aideen's Grave. Legend has it that Aideen died of a broken heart after her husband was killed at the Battle of Gavra near Tara in AD 184, but the legend is rubbish because the dolmen is at least 300 years older than that.

Also within the grounds are the ruins of **St Mary's Abbey** (Abbey St; 🚌31, 31A from Beresford Pl, 🚉Howth) FREE, originally founded in 1042 by the Viking King Sitric, who also founded the original church on the site of Christ Church Cathedral. The abbey was amalgamated with the monastery on Ireland's Eye in 1235. Some parts of the ruins date from that time, but most are from the 15th and 16th centuries. The tomb of Christopher St Lawrence (Lord Howth), in the southeastern corner, dates from around 1470. See the caretaker or read the instructions on the gate for opening times.

★Howth Summit Walk WALKING
(Howth DART station; 🚌31, 31A from Beresford Pl, 🚉Howth) A 6km looped walk around the headlands begins at Howth DART station – follow the green arrow along the promenade and then turn right onto the cliff path. The walk takes you up to the summit before looping back down again. There are other, longer, walks marked by blue, red and purple arrows (which partially overlap the green route).

Eating

Howth Market MARKET €
(📌01-839 4141; www.howthmarket.ie; 3 Harbour Rd, Howth Harbour; ⊙9am-6pm Sat, Sun & bank holidays; 🚌31, 31A from Beresford Pl, 🚉Howth) One of the best in greater Dublin, this is the place to come not only for fresh fish (obviously) but also for organic meat and veg, and homemade everything else, including jams, cakes and breads. A great option for Sunday lunch.

★House IRISH €€
(📌01-839 6388; www.thehouse-howth.ie; 4 Main St; mains €13-22; ⊙8.45am-4pm Mon, to 9.30pm Tue-Fri, 10am-10pm Sat & Sun; 🚌31, 31A from Beresford Pl, 🚉Howth) Wonderful spot on the main street leading away from the harbour where you can feast on dishes such as crunchy Bellingham blue-cheese polenta or wild Wicklow venison stew, as well as a fine selection of fish. The brunch is one of the best you'll find on the north side of the city.

Octopussy's Seafood Tapas SEAFOOD €€
(📌01-839 0822; www.octopussys.ie; 7-8 West Pier; tapas €8-16; ⊙noon-10pm; 🚌31, 31A from Beresford Pl, 🚉Howth) Best known for its tasty seafood tapas, Octopussy's is a firm local favourite. All of the seafood comes from the fish shop next door, which in turn buys it from the fishing boats that dock right in front. You can't get any fresher than that.

ⓘ Getting There & Away

DART The 20-minute train ride from Dublin city centre to Howth Village costs €3.25.

Bus Services 31 and 31A from Beresford Pl near Busáras run up to Howth Summit for €2.70.

Counties Wicklow & Kildare

POP 364,930 / AREA 3718 SQ KM

Best Places to Eat

➡ Kennedy's (p144)

➡ Wicklow Heather (p151)

➡ Strawberry Tree (p154)

➡ Grangecon Café (p158)

➡ Byrne & Woods (p144)

➡ Happy Pear (p153)

Best Places to Sleep

➡ Heather House (p151)

➡ Hunter's Hotel (p153)

➡ Powerscourt Hotel & Spa (p143)

➡ Martinstown House (p160)

➡ Tinakilly Country House (p153)

Why Go?

Wicklow and Kildare may be neighbours and have a boundary with Dublin in common, but that's where the similarities end.

Immediately south of the capital is wild, scenic Wicklow. Its most dramatic natural feature is a gorse-and-bracken mountain spine that is the east coast's most stunning landscape, complete with deep glacial valleys, isolated mountain passes and, dotted throughout, some important historic treasures, including one of Ireland's most important early-Christian sites and a couple of 18th-century Palladian mansions.

To the west is flat, fertile Kildare, which also has a handful of elegant Palladian piles but is best known as horse country – of the thoroughbred kind. Some of the world's most lucrative stud farms are here, many with links to the horse-breeding centre of Kentucky in the USA. Kildare is also home to some of the best golf courses in Ireland and, in recent years, the country's largest outlet mall.

When to Go

➡ Your best chance of witnessing the birth of a thoroughbred foal at the Irish National Stud is between February and June.

➡ The Irish Derby takes place at the Curragh racecourse in June; meets continue right up to October.

➡ The best weather for walking the Wicklow Way or exploring Wicklow's gardens is from June to September.

COUNTY WICKLOW

Just south of Dublin, County Wicklow (Cill Mhantáin) is the capital's favourite playground, a wild pleasure garden of coastline, woodland and daunting mountains through which runs the country's most popular walking trail. Stretching 127km from Dublin's southern suburbs to the rolling fields of County Carlow, the Wicklow Way (p149) leads walkers along disused military supply lines, old bog roads and forest trails. Along the way you can explore monastic ruins, handsome gardens and magnificent 18th-century mansions.

Wicklow Mountains National Parks

Wicklow Mountains National Park (www. wicklowmountainsnationalpark.ie) covers just over 200 sq km of mountain, blanket bog and woodland. Within its boundaries are two nature reserves, owned and managed by the Heritage Service and legally protected by the Wildlife Act 1976. The larger reserve, west of the Glendalough Visitor Centre (p148), conserves the extensive heath and bog of the Glendalough Valley plus the Upper Lake and valley slopes on either side. The second, Glendalough Wood Nature Reserve, protects oak woods stretching from the Upper Lake as far as the Rathdrum road to the east.

Most of Ireland's native mammal species can be found within the confines of the park. Large herds of deer roam on the open hill areas, though these were introduced in the 20th century as the native red-deer population became extinct during the first half of the 18th century. The uplands are the preserve of foxes, badgers and hares. Red squirrels are usually found in the pine woodlands – look out for them around the Upper Lake.

The bird population of the park is plentiful. Birds of prey abound, the most common being peregrine falcons, merlins, kestrels, hawks and sparrowhawks. Hen harriers are a rarer sight, though they too live in the park. Moorland birds found in the area include meadow pipits and skylarks. Less common birds such as whinchats, ring ouzels and dippers can be spotted, as can red grouse, which are quickly disappearing in other parts of Ireland.

ⓘ Getting There & Away

BUS

St Kevin's Bus runs twice daily from Dublin and Bray to Roundwood and Glendalough. Dublin Bus 65 runs regularly as far as Blessington.

CAR

The main routes are the N11/M11, which runs north–south through the county from Dublin to Wexford, and the N81, which runs down the western side of the Wicklow Mountains through Blessington into County Carlow.

TRAIN

The **Dublin Area Rapid Transport (DART)** (p133) suburban rail line runs southward from Dublin as far as Bray, and there are regular train and bus connections from the capital to Wicklow town and Arklow.

Wicklow Mountains

As you leave Dublin and cross into Wicklow, the landscape changes dramatically. From Rathfarnham, still within the city limits, the Military Rd begins a 40km southward journey along the spine of the Wicklow Mountains, crossing vast sweeps of gorse-, bracken- and heather-clad moors, bogs and hills, dotted with small corrie lakes.

The highest peak in the range, Lugnaquilla (924m), is really more of a very large hill, but that hardly matters here. This vast granite intrusion, an upwelling of molten rock that solidified some 400 million years ago, was shaped during the ice ages into the schist-capped mountains visible today. The peaks are marvellously desolate and as raw as only nature can be. Between the mountains are a number of deep glacial valleys – most notably Glenmacnass, Glenmalure and Glendalough – while corrie lakes such as Lough Bray Upper and Lower, and Lough Tay, gouged by ice at the head of the glaciers, complete the wild topography.

The Military Road

The R115, better known as the Military Road, was first built in the early 1800s by British forces to help suppress rebels in the wake of the 1798 rising. The narrow road winds its way through the most remote parts of the mountains, offering some extraordinary views of the surrounding countryside. The best place to join it is at Glencree (from Enniskerry). It then runs south through the Sally Gap, Glenmacnass Valley and Laragh, then on to Glenmalure and Aghavannagh.

On the trip south you can divert east at the Sally Gap to look at Lough Tay and Lough Dan. Further south you pass the great waterfall at Glenmacnass before dropping

Counties Wicklow & Kildare Highlights

1 Glendalough (p144) Stepping back in time at this evocative and scenic early-Christian monastic site.

2 Powerscourt Estate (p142) Admiring the gorgeous Italianate gardens, glorious views and impressive waterfall at this Enniskerry estate.

3 Castletown House (p159) Taking the tour at Ireland's most impressive Palladian mansion, once owned by the country's richest man.

4 Wicklow Way (p149) Hiking at least part of Ireland's most popular long-distance hiking trail.

5 Russborough House (p157) Examining the art and absorbing the aristocratic atmosphere of this magnificent mansion.

6 Irish National Stud (p158) Learning about Ireland's long association with thoroughbred racehorses.

7 Avoca Handweavers (p155) Shopping for crafts at the birthplace of one of the country's best-known brands.

8 Bog of Allen (p162) Learning about conservation and biodiversity amid County Kildare's huge tracts of exploited peat bog.

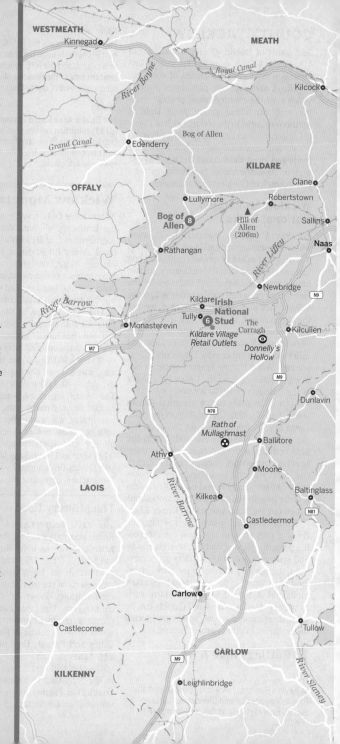

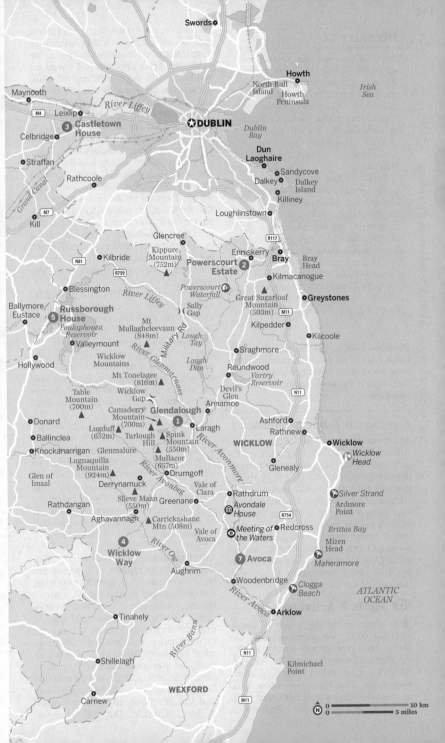

THE SALLY GAP

One of the two main east–west passes across the Wicklow Mountains, the Sally Gap is surrounded by some spectacular countryside. From the turn-off on the lower road (R755) a few kilometres north of Roundwood, the narrow R759 passes above the dark and dramatic Lough Tay, backed by steep scree slopes descending from Luggala (Fancy Mountain).

The almost fairy-tale estate of Luggala is owned by one Garech de Brún, member of the Guinness family and founder of Claddagh Records, a leading producer of Irish traditional and folk music. The small River Cloghoge links Lough Tay with Lough Dan just to the south. The R759 then continues to the Sally Gap crossroads, where it cuts across the Military Rd and heads northwest to Kilbride and the N81, following the young River Liffey, still only a stream here.

down into Laragh, with the magnificent monastic ruins of Glendalough nearby. Continue south through the valley of Glenmalure and, if you're fit enough, climb to the top of Lugnaquilla.

Powerscourt Estate & Enniskerry

At the top of the '21 Bends', as the steep and winding R117 road from Bray is known, the handsome village of Enniskerry is home to upmarket shops and the kind of all-organic gourmet cafes that would treat you as a criminal if you admitted to eating battery eggs. Such self-regard is a far cry from the village's origins, when Richard Wingfield, earl of nearby Powerscourt, commissioned a row of terraced cottages for his labourers in 1760. These days, you'd need to have laboured pretty successfully to get your hands on one of them.

◉ Sights & Activities

★ **Powerscourt Estate** GARDENS
(☑ 01-204 6000; www.powerscourt.com; Enniskerry; house free, gardens adult/child €10/5; ⊙ 9.30am-5.30pm Mar-Oct, to dusk Nov-Feb; P ⊕) Wicklow's most visited attraction is this magnificent 64-sq-km estate, whose main entrance is 500m south of Enniskerry town. At the heart of it is an elegant Palladian man-

sion, but the real draw is the formal gardens and the stunning views that accompany them. Most of the house is not open to the public, but there's a fine cafe and several gift and homewares shops to be enjoyed, while the grounds are home to two golf courses and the best hotel (p143) in Wicklow.

The estate has existed more or less since 1300, when the LePoer (later anglicised to Power) family built themselves a castle here. The property changed Anglo-Norman hands a few times before coming into the possession of Richard Wingfield, newly appointed Marshall of Ireland, in 1603. His descendants were to live here for the next 350 years. In 1730 the Georgian wunderkind Richard Cassels (or Castle) was given the job of building a 68-room Palladian-style mansion around the core of the old castle. He finished the job in 1741, but an extra storey was added in 1787 and other alterations were made in the 19th century.

The Wingfields left during the 1950s, after which the house had a massive restoration. Then, on the eve of its opening to the public in 1974, a fire gutted the whole building. The estate was eventually bought by the Slazenger sporting-goods family who have overseen a second restoration as well as the addition of all the amenities the estate now has to offer, including the two golf courses and the fabulous hotel, now part of Marriott's Autograph collection.

The star of the show is the 20-hectare landscaped gardens, originally laid out in the 1740s but redesigned in the 19th century by gardener Daniel Robinson. Robinson was one of the foremost horticulturalists of his day, and his passion for growing things was matched only by his love of booze: the story goes that by a certain point in the day he was too drunk to stand and so insisted on being wheeled around the estate in a barrow.

Perhaps this influenced his largely informal style, which resulted in a magnificent blend of landscaped gardens, sweeping terraces, statuary, ornamental lakes, secret hollows, rambling walks and walled enclosures replete with more than 200 types of trees and shrubs, all designed to frame the stunning natural backdrop of the Great Sugarloaf Mountain. Tickets come with a map laying out 40-minute and hour-long walks around the gardens. Don't miss the exquisite Japanese Gardens or the Pepperpot Tower, modelled on a 3in actual pepper pot owned by Lady Wingfield. Our own favourite, however, is the **animal cemetery**, final resting place of the Wingfield pets and even one of the family's favourite milking cows. Some of the epitaphs are surprisingly personal.

The house itself is every bit as grand as the gardens, but ongoing renovation means there's not much to see beyond the bustle of the ground-floor cafe and gift shop. The sole exception is the **Museum of Childhood** (Tara's Palace; ☑ 01-274 8090; www.childhoodmuseum.org; adult/child/family €5/3/12; ☉ 10am-5pm Mon-Sat, noon-5pm Sun), full of period miniature dolls and dolls' houses, including Tara's Palace, a 22-room house designed to one-twelfth scale and inspired by the Palladian piles of Castletown House, Leinster House and Carton House. Each of the rooms is decorated in exquisite, hand-crafted miniatures.

A 6km drive to a separate part of the estate takes you to the 121m-high **Powerscourt Waterfall** (www.powerscourt.com/waterfall; Powerscourt Estate; adult/child €6/3.50; ☉ 9.30am-7pm May-Aug, 10.30am-5.30pm Mar-Apr, Sep & Oct, to 4.30pm Nov-Feb; P) – walking from house to falls is not recommended, because the route lies on narrow roads with no footpath. It's the highest waterfall in Ireland, and at its most impressive after heavy rain. A nature trail has been laid out around the base of the waterfall, taking you past giant redwoods, ancient oaks, beech, birch and rowan trees. There are plenty of birds in the vicinity, including chaffinch, cuckoo, chiffchaff, raven and willow warbler.

Great Sugarloaf HILL

At 503m it's nowhere near Wicklow's highest summit, but the Great Sugarloaf is one of the most distinctive hills in Ireland, its conical peak visible for many kilometres around. The mountain towers over the small village of Kilmacanogue, on the N11 about 35km south of Dublin, and can be climbed from a car park on the L1031 minor road (off the R755 road, 7.5km south of Enniskerry). It's a steep but straightforward hike (one hour return trip).

Powerscourt Golf Club GOLF

(☑ 01-204 6033; http://powerscourtgolfclub.com; Powerscourt Estate, Enniskerry; green fees €75 Apr-Oct, Nov-Mar €55) You have your choice of two stunning courses here: the West Course was designed by David McLay Kidd (who also designed Bandon Dunes in Oregon) and is a shade tougher than the East Course, which is arguably the more scenic.

⌖ Tours

All tours that take in Powerscourt start in Dublin.

DoDublin Bus Tour BUS

(www.dodublin.ie; adult/child €21.60/9.60; ☉ 10.30am daily Apr-Oct) Departing at 10.30am from the Dublin Bus office at 59 Upper O'Connell St in Dublin, this tour takes in both Glendalough and Powerscourt, returning to Dublin at 5pm.

🛏 Sleeping & Eating

Summerhill House Hotel HOTEL €€

(☑ 01-286 7928; www.summerhillhousehotel.com; r from €99; P🖤) This country mansion about 700m south of town just off the N11 is a great place to lay your head – on soft cotton pillows surrounded by delicate antiques and pastoral views in oils. Everything about the place, including the top-notch breakfast, is memorable. It's a popular wedding venue so call ahead and check if you're looking for peace and quiet.

Coolakay House B&B €€

(☑ 01-286 2423; www.coolakayhouse.ie; Waterfall Rd, Coolakay; s/d from €55/75; P🖤) A modern working farm about 3km south of Enniskerry (it is signposted along the road), this is a great option for walkers along the Wicklow Way. The bedrooms are all well appointed and comfortable, the views are terrific and the breakfast sensational. March and April is lambing season and guests are encouraged to observe – and even name – a newborn lamb!

★ Powerscourt Hotel & Spa HOTEL €€€

(☑ 01-274 8888; www.powerscourthotel.com; Powerscourt Estate, Enniskerry; r from €265; P🖤🏊) Wicklow's most luxurious hotel is this 200-room stunner on the grounds of the Powerscourt Estate (p142). Inside this Marriott-managed property all is over-the-top luxury, and the decor is a thoroughly contemporary version of the estate's Georgian style. The rooms are massive. Downstairs there's a decent restaurant and a superb spa.

Kennedy's CAFE €

(www.kennedysofenniskerry.com; Church Hill; mains €5-12; ☉ 8.30am-5pm; 🖤) A lovely cafe with old-fashioned furniture in cool pastel shades, this is the place to get excellent breakfasts (it does great poached eggs on sourdough toast) and homemade soups and sandwiches. It also sells delicious artisan bread made by the Bretzel Bakery in Dublin.

Johnnie Fox's
SEAFOOD €€

(☎ 01-295 5647; www.jfp.ie; Glencullen; mains €11-30; ☺ food served 12.30-9.30pm; P 🤖 ♿) Busloads of tourists fill this place nightly throughout the summer, mostly for the knees-up, faux-Irish Hooley Show of music and dancing. But there's nothing contrived about the seafood, which is so damn good we'd happily sit through yet another chorus of 'Danny Boy' and even consider joining in the jig. The pub is 3km northwest of Enniskerry.

Shopping

Avoca Handweavers
ARTS & CRAFTS

(☎ 01-286 7466; www.avoca.ie; Main St, Kilmacanogue; 9am-6pm Mon-Fri, 9.30am-6pm Sat & Sun; 🤖 ♿) Avoca is one hell of an operation, with seven branches nationwide and a widespread reputation for adding elegance and style to traditional rural handicrafts. Operational HQ is set in a 19th-century arboretum 5km southeast of Enniskerry, and the bustling shop crammed with knitwear, textiles, ceramics, toys, homewares and gourmet foodstuffs will leave you in no doubt as to the company's incredible success.

The attached **cafe** (mains €7 to €15) is excellent and you can bring a little of it home with you by purchasing one (or all) of the Avoca cookbooks.

ℹ Getting There & Away

Enniskerry is 18km south of Dublin, just 3km west of the M11 along the R117. From here, getting to Powerscourt House on foot is not a problem (it's 500m from the town).

Bus Éireann (☎ 01-836 6111; www.buseireann.ie) No 133 from Dublin to Wicklow town stops in Kilmacanogue (one way/return €4.90, 45 minutes, 10 daily).

Roundwood
POP 948

Roundwood's greatest boast is that it's the highest village in Ireland – hardly impressive at 238m – but it is a handy staging post for a meal and a rest for walkers on the Wicklow Way, which runs 2.5km past the town to the west.

Sleeping & Eating

Roundwood Caravan & Camping Park
CAMPGROUND €

(☎ 01-281 8163; www.dublinwicklowcamping.com; campsites per adult/child €8/4, plus per tent/ campervan €8; ☺ Apr-Sep; 🤖) Good shelter (though no views) and top-notch facilities, including a kitchen, dining area and TV lounge, make this one of the better camp grounds in Wicklow. It is about 500m north of the village and is served by the daily St Kevin's Bus (p144) service between Dublin and Glendalough.

Byrne & Woods
MODERN IRISH €€

(☎ 01-281 7078; www.byrneandwoods.com; Main St; mains €14-26; ☺ 12.30-9pm Mon-Sat, to 8pm Sun Apr-Sep, shorter hours Oct-Mar; ♿) Everything that is admirable about contemporary Irish cuisine – a focus on locally sourced produce, inventive reinterpretations of classic dishes and beautiful presentation – is on hand at this elegant restaurant housed in an old cottage. Excellent service and a fine collection of wines round out a satisfying meal.

Coach House
INTERNATIONAL €€

(☎ 01-281 8157; http://thecoachhouse.ie; Main St; mains €12-25; ☺ 9am-11.30pm; P 🤖 ♿) A black-and-white timbered coaching inn, this is a terrific spot to take a load off and refuel. The fare on offer is pretty standard – burgers, salads, fish and chips and a nice steak sandwich – but everything is perfectly made and tastes delicious. Food is served till 9pm. There's live music at weekends.

ℹ Getting There & Away

St Kevin's Bus (☎ 01-281 8119; www.glendaloughbus.com) passes through Roundwood on its twice-daily jaunt between Dublin and Glendalough (one way/return €8/14, 1¼ hours).

Glendalough

If you've come to Wicklow, the chances are that a visit to Glendalough (Gleann dá Loch, meaning 'Valley of the Two Lakes') is one of your main reasons. And you're not wrong, for this is one of the most beautiful corners of the whole country and the epitome of the kind of rugged, romantic Ireland that probably drew you to the island in the first place.

The substantial remains of this important monastic settlement are certainly impressive, but an added draw is the splendid setting: two dark and mysterious lakes tucked into a long, glacial valley fringed by forest. It is, despite its immense popularity, a deeply tranquil and spiritual place, and you will have little difficulty in understanding why those solitude-seeking monks came here in the first place.

Glendalough

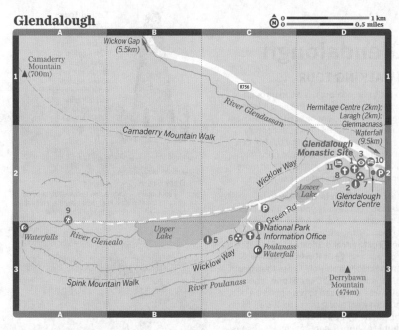

Glendalough

◎ **Top Sights**
1 Glendalough Monastic Site D2

◎ **Sights**
   Cathedral of St Peter and St
   Paul .... (see 1)
2 Deer Stone D2
3 Monastery Gatehouse D2
   Priest's House .... (see 1)
4 Reefert Church C3
   Round Tower .... (see 1)
5 St Kevin's Bed C3

6 St Kevin's Cell C3
   St Kevin's Kitchen .... (see 7)
7 St Kieran's Church D2
8 St Mary's Church D2
   Teampall na Skellig .... (see 5)

⊙ **Activities, Courses & Tours**
9 Mine Workings Walk A2

⊜ **Sleeping**
10 Glendalough Hotel D2
11 Glendalough International Hostel D2

History

In AD 498 a young monk named Kevin arrived in the valley looking for somewhere to kick back, meditate and be at one with nature. He pitched up in what had been a Bronze Age tomb on the southern side of the Upper Lake and for the next seven years slept on stones, wore animal skins, maintained a near-starvation diet and – according to the legend – became bosom buddies with the birds and animals. Kevin's ecofriendly lifestyle soon attracted a bunch of disciples, all seemingly unaware of the irony that they were flocking to hang out with a hermit who wanted to live as far away from other people as possible. Over the next

couple of centuries his one-man operation mushroomed into a proper settlement and by the 9th century Glendalough rivalled Clonmacnoise as the island's premier monastic city. Thousands of students studied and lived in a thriving community that was spread over a considerable area.

Inevitably Glendalough's success made it a key target for Viking raiders, who sacked the monastery at least four times between 775 and 1071. The final blow came in 1398, when English forces from Dublin almost destroyed it. Efforts were made to rebuild and some life lingered on here as late as the 17th century when, under renewed repression, the monastery finally died.

Glendalough

A WALKING TOUR

A visit to Glendalough is a trip through ancient history and a refreshing hike in the hills. The ancient monastic settlement founded by St Kevin in the 5th century grew to be quite powerful by the 9th century, but it started falling into ruin from 1398 onwards. Still, you won't find more evocative clumps of stones anywhere.

Start at the **1 Main Gateway** to the monastic city, where you will find a cluster of important ruins, including the (nearly perfect) 10th-century **2 Round Tower**, the **3 cathedral** dedicated to Sts Peter and Paul, and **4 St Kevin's Kitchen**, which is really a church. Cross the stream past the famous **5 Deer Stone**, where Kevin was supposed to have milked a doe, and turn west along the path. It's a 1.5km walk to the **6 Upper Lake**. On the lake's southern shore is another cluster of sites, including the **7 Reefert Church**, a plain 11th-century Romanesque church where the powerful O'Toole family buried their kin, and **8 St Kevin's Cell**, the remains of a beehive hut where Kevin is said to have lived.

ST KEVIN

St Kevin came to the valley as a young monk in AD 498, in search of a peaceful retreat. He was reportedly led by an angel to a Bronze Age tomb now known as St Kevin's Bed. For seven years he slept on stones, wore animal skins, survived on nettles and herbs and – according to legend – developed an affinity with the birds and animals. One legend has it that, when Kevin needed milk for two orphaned babies, a doe stood waiting at the Deer Stone to be milked.

Kevin soon attracted a group of disciples and the monastic settlement grew, until by the 9th century Glendalough rivalled Clonmacnoise as Ireland's premier monastic city. According to legend, Kevin lived to the age of 120. He was canonised in 1903.

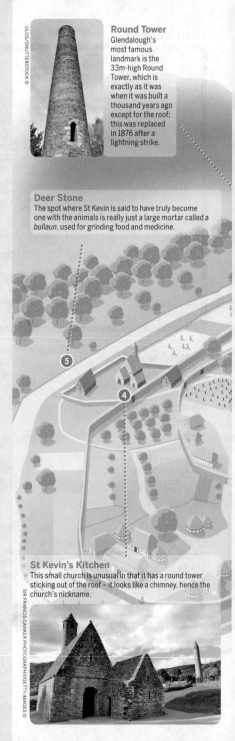

Round Tower
Glendalough's most famous landmark is the 33m-high Round Tower, which is exactly as it was when it was built a thousand years ago except for the roof; this was replaced in 1876 after a lightning strike.

OLOS/SHUTTERSTOCK ©

Deer Stone
The spot where St Kevin is said to have truly become one with the animals is really just a large mortar called a *bullaun*, used for grinding food and medicine.

St Kevin's Kitchen
This small church is unusual in that it has a round tower sticking out of the roof – it looks like a chimney, hence the church's nickname.

SIR FRANCIS CANKER PHOTOGRAPHY/GETTY IMAGES ©

St Kevin's Cell
This beehive hut is reputedly where St Kevin would go for prayer and meditation; not to be confused with St Kevin's Bed, a cave where he used to sleep.

Reefert Church
Its name derives from the Irish *righ fearta*, which means 'burial place of the kings'. Seven princes of the powerful O'Toole family are buried in this simple structure.

Upper Lake
The site of St Kevin's original settlement is on the banks of the Upper Lake, one of the two lakes that give Glendalough its name – the 'Valley of the Lakes'.

INFORMATION
At the eastern end of the Upper Lake is the National Park Information Point, which has leaflets and maps on the site, local walks etc. The grassy spot in front of the office is a popular picnic spot in summer.

← NORTH

Cathedral of Sts Peter & Paul
The largest of Glendalough's seven churches, the cathedral was built gradually between the 10th and 13th centuries. The earliest part is the nave, where you can still see the *antae* (slightly projecting column at the end of the wall) used for supporting a wooden roof.

Main Gateway
The only surviving entrance to the ecclesiastical settlement is a double arch; notice that the inner arch rises higher than the outer one in order to compensate for the upward slope of the causeway.

◉ Sights

While the Upper Lake has the best scenery, the most fascinating buildings lie in the lower part of the valley east of the Lower Lake, huddled together around the heart of the ancient monastic site. A woodland trail and boardwalk link the two lakes; it takes about 20 to 30 minutes to walk from one to the other.

★ Glendalough
Monastic Site
CHRISTIAN SITE

(www.glendalough.ie; 25km south of Dublin; ⊘24hr; P; ☐St Kevin's Bus (www.glendalough bus.com;one-way/return €9/15)) FREE Nestled between two lakes, haunting Glendalough (Gleann dá Loch, meaning 'Valley of the Two Lakes') is one of the most significant monastic sites in Ireland and one of the loveliest spots in the country, centred on a 1000-year-old round tower, a ruined cathedral and the tiny church known as St Kevin's Kitchen.

The site is entered through the only surviving monastic gateway (p148) in Ireland. The **Glendalough Visitor Centre** (✆0404-45352; www.heritageireland.ie; adult/child €5/3; ⊘9.30am-6pm mid-Mar–mid-Oct, to 5pm mid-Oct–mid-Mar; P), opposite the Lower Lake car park, has historical displays and a good 20-minute audiovisual show. From the Upper Lake (1.5km west of the visitor centre), several good hiking trails (p150) head into the hills.

Visitors swarm to Glendalough in summer, so it's best to arrive early and/or stay late, preferably on a weekday, as the site is free and open 24 hours. The lower car park gates are locked when the visitor centre closes.

LOWER LAKE
Monastery Gatehouse
GATE

The stone arch of the monastery gatehouse is the only surviving example of a monastic entranceway in the country. Just inside the entrance is a large slab with an incised cross.

Round Tower
TOWER

The 10th-century Round Tower is 33m tall and 16m in circumference at the base. The upper storeys and conical roof were reconstructed in 1876.

Cathedral of St Peter and St Paul
CHURCH

The Cathedral of St Peter and St Paul, just southeast of the Round Tower, has a 10th-century nave; the chancel and sacristy date from the 12th century.

Priest's House
ARCHITECTURE

At the centre of Glendalough's graveyard, to the southwest of the cathedral, is the Priest's House. This odd building dates from 1170 but has been heavily reconstructed. It may have been the location of shrines to St Kevin. Later, during penal times, it became a burial site for local priests – hence the name.

St Kevin's Kitchen
CHURCH

Glendalough's trademark is St Kevin's Kitchen or Church, at the southern edge of the monastic site. This compact structure, with a miniature round towerlike belfry, protruding sacristy and steep stone roof, is a masterpiece. It was never a kitchen, instead getting its name because its belfry resembles a kitchen chimney. The oldest parts of the building date from the 11th century – the structure has been remodelled since; but it's still a classic early Irish church.

Deer Stone
MONUMENT

At the junction with Green Rd as you cross the river just south of the monastic site (p148) is the Deer Stone, set in the middle of a group of rocks. Legend claims that, when St Kevin needed milk for two orphaned babies, a doe stood here waiting to be milked. The stone is actually a *bullaun* (a stone used as a mortar for grinding medicines or food).

Many such stones are thought to be prehistoric, and they were widely regarded as having supernatural properties: women who bathed their faces with water from the hollow were supposed to keep their looks forever. The early churchmen brought the stones into their monasteries, perhaps hoping to inherit some of their powers.

St Mary's Church
CHURCH

The 10th-century St Mary's Church, to the southwest of the round tower, stands outside the walls of the monastic site and belonged to local nuns. It has a lovely western doorway.

St Kieran's Church
RUINS

There are but scant remains of St Kieran's Church, the smallest at Glendalough. It's to the east of St Mary's Church.

UPPER LAKE
Reefert Church
CHURCH

The considerable remains of Reefert Church sit above the tiny River Poulanass, south of the Upper Lake car park. It's a small, plain, 11th-century Romanesque nave-and-chancel church with some reassembled arches and

WALK: THE WICKLOW WAY – GLENDALOUGH TO AUGHRIM

The 127km Wicklow Way is one of Ireland's most popular long-distance walks because of its remarkable scenery and its relatively fluid and accessible starting and finishing points – there are plenty of half- and full-day options along the way.

This section is 37km long and takes you through some of the more remote parts of the Wicklow Mountains and down into the southeastern foothills. There's relatively little road walking; the greater part of the day is through conifer plantations. The walk should take between 7½ and eight hours, with an ascent of 1035m.

From the National Park Information Office on the southern side of Glendalough's Upper Lake, climb the yellow-waymarked trail beside Lugduff Brook and **Poulanass Waterfall**. Veer left when you meet a forest track, then left again at a junction and cross two bridges. The Way leads northeast for about 600m then, from a tight right bend, heads almost directly southwards (via a series of clearly marked junctions), up through the conifer plantations, across Lugduff Brook again and beside a tributary, to open ground on the saddle between **Mullacor** (657m) and **Lugduff** (652m; 1¾ hours from Glendalough). From here on a good day, massive Lugnaquilla sprawls across the view to the southwest; in the opposite direction is Camaderry's long ridge above Glendalough, framed against the bulk of Tonelagee. Follow the raised boardwalk down, contour above a plantation and drop into it where a steep muddy and rocky path descends to a forest road; turn left.

If you're planning to stay at **Glenmalure Hostel** (p152), rather than go all the way down to the crossroads in Glenmalure, follow the Way from the left turn for about 1km southwards. At an oblique junction where the Way turns southeast, bear left in a westerly direction and descend steeply to the road in Glenmalure. The hostel is about 2km northwest.

To continue straight on along the Way from the left turn, follow forest roads south then southeast for 1.6km to a wide zigzag above open ground, then contour the steep slope, swing northeast and drop down to a minor road beside two bridges. Continue down to an intersection and Glenmalure; it's about 1¼ hours from the saddle.

The Way presses straight on (south) through the crossroads for 500m, across the River Avonbeg and past silent **Drumgoff Barracks**, built in 1803 but long since derelict, then right along a forest track. Keep left past a ruined cottage and start to gain height in two fairly long reaches; go through two left turns then it's down and across a stream. About 800m further on, turn right along a path to start the long ascent almost to the top of **Slieve Maan** (550m) via four track junctions, maintaining a southwesterly to south-southwesterly direction. Back on a forest track, the Way turns left (southeast) close to unforested ground to the west. With a few more convoluted turns, you're out of the trees and on a path between the plantation and the road (mapped as the Military Rd). The Way eventually meets the latter beside a small tributary of the River Aghavannagh (two hours from Glenmalure).

Walk down the road for about 250m, then turn off left along a forest track, shortly bearing left to gain height steadily on a wide path over **Carrickashane Mountain** (508m). Descend steeply to a wide forest road and continue down for about 1km. Bear right to reach a minor road and turn right. Leave the road 500m further on and drop down to another road – Iron Bridge is just to the right (an hour from Military Rd).

Walk 150m up to a road and turn left; follow this road down the valley of the River Ow for 7.5km to a junction – Aughrim is to the left, another 500m. Buses on the Dublin to Wexford route stop here.

walls. Traditionally, Reefert (literally 'Royal Burial Place') was the burial site of the chiefs of the local O'Toole family. The surrounding graveyard contains a number of rough stone crosses and slabs, most made of shiny mica schist.

St Kevin's Cell RUINS

Climb the steps at the back of the Reefert Churchyard and follow the path to the west and you'll find, at the top of a rise overlooking the Upper Lake, the scant remains of St Kevin's Cell, a small beehive hut.

Teampall na Skellig · RUINS

The original site of St Kevin's settlement, Teampall na Skellig is at the base of the cliffs towering over the southern side of the Upper Lake and accessible only by boat; unfortunately, there's no boat service to the site so you'll have to settle for looking at it from across the lake. The terraced shelf has the reconstructed ruins of a church and early graveyard. Rough wattle huts once stood on the raised ground nearby. Scattered around are some early grave slabs and simple stone crosses.

St Kevin's Bed · MONUMENT

Just east of Teampall na Skellig, and 10m above the Upper Lake's waters, is the 2m-deep artificial cave called St Kevin's Bed, said to be where Kevin lived. The earliest human habitation of the cave was long before St Kevin's era – there's evidence that people lived in the valley for thousands of years before the monks arrived.

Activities & Tours

The Glendalough Valley is all about walking. There are nine waymarked trails in the valley, the longest of which is about 10km, or about four hours' walking. Before you set off, drop by the National Park Information Point (p151) and pick up the relevant leaflet and trail map (around €1). It also has a number of excellent guides for sale – you won't go far wrong with Joss Lynam's *Easy Walks Near Dublin* (€10) or Helen Fairbairn's *Dublin & Wicklow: A Walking Guide* (€15).

A word of warning: don't be fooled by the relative gentleness of the surrounding countryside or the fact that the Wicklow Mountains are really no taller than big hills. The weather can be merciless here, so be sure to take the usual precautions, have the right equipment and tell someone where you're going and when you should be back. For Mountain Rescue call ☑ 112 or ☑ 999.

The easiest and most popular walk is the gentle hike along the northern shore of the Upper Lake to the old lead and zinc mine workings, which date from 1800. The better route is along the lake shore rather than on the road (which runs 30m in from the shore), a distance of about 2.5km one way from the Glendalough Visitor Centre. Continue up to the head of the valley if you wish.

Alternatively you can walk up the Spink (from the Irish for 'pointed hill'; 380m), the steep ridge with vertical cliffs running along the southern flanks of the Upper Lake. You can go part of the way and turn back, or complete a circuit of the Upper Lake by following the top of the cliff, eventually coming down by the mine workings and going back along the northern shore. This circuit is about 6km long and takes about three hours.

The third option is a hike up Camaderry Mountain (700m), hidden behind the hills that flank the northern side of the valley. The path (not waymarked) begins opposite the entrance to the Upper Lake car park (near a 'Wicklow Mountains National Park' sign). Head straight up the steep hill to the north and you come out on open mountains with sweeping views in all directions. You can then continue west up the ridge to Camaderry summit. To the top of Camaderry and back is about 7.5km and takes about four hours.

Wild Wicklow Tour · BUS TOUR

(☑ 01-280 1899; www.wildwicklow.ie; adult €28, student/child €25; ⊙ departs 9am) These award-winning day trips from Dublin to Glendalough via Avoca Handweavers (p155) and the Sally Gap (p142) never fail to generate rave reviews for atmosphere and all-round fun. The first pick-up is at the Shelbourne and then the Molly Malone statue on Suffold St, but there are a variety of pick-up points throughout Dublin. The tour returns to Dublin about 5.30pm.

🛏 Sleeping & Eating

Glendalough International Hostel · HOSTEL €

(☑ 0404-45342; www.anoige.ie; The Lodge; dm/tw from €17/50; P @ 🛜) Conveniently, this modern hostel is situated near Glendalough's ancient monastic site, set within the scenic Glendalough Valley. All dorms have ensuite bathrooms and there's a decent cafeteria on the premises.

Glendalough Hermitage Centre · COTTAGE €

(☑ 087 935 6696; www.glendaloughhermitage.ie; Laragh; s/d €50/80) Five hermitages (really just plain one- and two-bed cottages) are rented out by St Kevin's Parish Church to anyone looking for a little spiritual R&R. Facilities are pretty basic but comfortable: there's a bathroom, a small kitchen and an open fire supplemented by a storage heater. The cottages are 1km east of Glendalough on the road to Laragh.

Visitors are welcome to join in morning and evening prayer, but the venture is not exclusively Catholic and all faiths and denominations are welcome.

★**Heather House** B&B €€
(✆0404-45157; www.heatherhouse.ie; Glendalough Rd, Laragh; r from €80; [P][🖙][❄]) Understated country-style elegance radiates from the luxurious bedrooms at this superb-value B&B, just 2km east of Glendalough. There's a lovely garden at the back with a view along the wooded valley (two of the bedrooms are in self-contained garden chalets), and it's just next door to the Wicklow Heather restaurant (under the same ownership).

Glendalough Hotel HOTEL €€
(✆0404-45135; www.glendaloughhotel.com; r from €69; [P][@][🖙]) There's no mistaking Glendalough's only hotel, conveniently located next door to the visitor centre. There is also no shortage of takers for its 44 chintzy bedrooms – it's a popular venue for weddings and tour groups.

Wicklow Heather INTERNATIONAL €€
(✆0404-45157; www.wicklowheather.ie; Glendalough Rd, Laragh; mains €13-29; ⊙8am-9.30pm Mon-Thu, to 10pm Fri & Sat, to 9pm Sun; [P][🖙]) This rustic family restaurant has been around for 40 years, serving everything from breakfast to dinner amid the honeyed glow of polished wood. The dinner menu offers Wicklow lamb, wild venison, Irish beef and fresh fish (the trout is excellent) – most of it sourced locally and all of it traceable from farm to fork.

There's also a Writers Room that houses a display of Irish literary memorabilia and a well-stocked Irish whiskey bar.

ℹ Information

The National Park Information Office
(✆0404-45425; www.wicklowmountains nationalpark.ie; Bolger's Cottage, Upper Lake Car Park; ⊙10am-5.30pm May-Sep, to dusk Sat & Sun Oct-Apr) provides information about Wicklow Mountains National Park, and is the place to pick up maps and leaflets about local hiking trails. It's located by the Upper Lake car park, about 2km west of the **Glendalough Visitor Centre** (p148). There's usually someone on hand to help; if you find it closed the staff may be out running guided walks.

ℹ Getting There & Away

St Kevin's Bus (✆01-281 8119; www. glendaloughbus.com) departs from the bus stop on St Stephen's Green North in Dublin at 11.30am and 6pm daily (one way/return €13/20, 1½ hours); from March to October

OFF THE BEATEN TRACK

GLENMACNASS

Desolate and utterly deserted, the Glenmacnass valley, a stretch of wild bogland between the Sally Gap crossroads and Laragh, is one of the most beautiful parts of the mountains, and the sense of isolation is quite dramatic. The highest mountain to the west is Mullaghcleevaun (848m), and River Glenmacnass flows south and tumbles over the edge of the mountain plateau in a great foaming cascade. There's a car park near the top of the waterfall.

Be careful when walking on rocks near Glenmacnass Waterfall as a few people have slipped to their deaths. There are fine walks up Mullaghcleevaun and in the hills to the east of the car park.

the evening bus leaves at 7pm on Saturday and Sunday. It also stops at the Town Hall in Bray. Departures from Glendalough are at 7.15am and 4.30pm weekdays, and 9.45am and 5.40pm on weekends. Buy your ticket on the bus.

During the week in July and August there is an additional service from Glendalough to Dublin departing at 9.45am.

Glenmalure

As you head deeper into the mountains southwest of Glendalough, near the southern end of the Military Rd, everything gets a bit wilder and more remote. Beneath the eastern slopes of Wicklow's highest peak, Lugnaquilla (925m), is Glenmalure, a dark and sombre valley flanked by scree slopes.

◉ Sights & Activities

After coming over the mountains from Laragh to Glenmalure, turn northwest at the Drumgoff bridge. From there it's about 6km up the road beside the River Avonbeg to a car park where trails lead off in various directions.

You can walk up the hidden Fraughan Rock Glen west of the car park, and – for experienced hill walkers only – continue to the summit of **Lugnaquilla Mountain** (allow six hours return trip).

The head of Glenmalure and parts of the neighbouring Glen of Imaal are off-limits. It's military land that's well posted with warning signs.

Cullen's Rock — MEMORIAL

(⊙24hr) FREE About 500m northwest of Drumgoff bridge, at the side of the Glenmalure road, is Dwyer's or Cullen's Rock, which commemorates both the Glenmalure battle and Michael Dwyer, a member of the United Irishmen who fought unsuccessfully against the English in the Rising of 1798 and holed up here. Men were hanged from the rock during the Rising.

🛏 Sleeping

Glenmalure Hostel — HOSTEL €

(☑01-830 4555; www.anoige.ie; Baravore; dm €17-18.50; ⊙daily Jun-Aug, Sat only Sep-May) No telephone (the listed number is An Oige head office), no electricity (lighting is by gas) and no running water, just a rustic two-storey former hunting lodge with 19 beds, a gas stove, water from the stream, and an open log fire. And a top literary connection – this place was the setting for JM Synge's play *Shadow of a Gunman*.

You can take a car to the hostel if the river is low enough to drive across; if not, it's a 10-minute walk from the parking area by the bridge. Otherwise, you can hike here from Laragh, following the Wicklow Way south over the hills to the Glenmalure Lodge Hotel, then continuing up the valley (total 14km).

Twelve Glenmalure Pines — CABIN €€

(☑01-269 6979; www.glenmalurepines.com; 12 Glenmalure Pines, Greenane; per week €450-600; P 🛜) At the lower end of Glenmalure, this modern, Scandinavian-style lodge has two rooms with private bathrooms, a fully equipped kitchen, a living room kitted out with all kinds of electronics, and a balcony with gorgeous views. During the summer it's only available as a weekly rental; from September to May you can get a three-night weekend stay for €300.

❶ Getting There & Away

The privately run Wicklow Way Bus (www.wicklowwaybus.com) picks up hikers from Rathdrum train station (trains from Dublin) and drops off at various places, including Laragh, **Glendalough Visitor Centre** (p148) and Glenmalure Lodge Hotel (€8, one hour, twice daily). It is not a scheduled service, and must be booked in advance.

Eastern Wicklow

The coastal towns and rolling valleys of eastern Wicklow play second fiddle to the mountains in terms of dramatic scenery, but its largely unassuming villages and seaside resorts have a subtle charm. Highlights include the upmarket seaside town of Greystones, the historic jail in Wicklow town and the beautiful Vale of Avoca.

A string of beaches – Silver Strand, Brittas Bay and Maheramore – starts 16km south of Wicklow town. With high dunes, safe bathing and powdery sand, the beaches attract droves of Dubliners in good weather.

Greystones to Wicklow Town

The coastal town of Greystones, 25km south of Dublin, was originally a fishing village and Victorian seaside resort, and the seafront around the little harbour is idyllic. In summer the bay is dotted with dinghies and windsurfers, and there are two sandy beaches – the South Beach is a Blue Flag one. The town itself rewards a little exploration with vintage shops, boutiques, cafes and a couple of excellent restaurants.

◎ Sights

★Kilruddery House & Gardens — HOUSE

(☑01-286 3405; www.killruddery.com; Southern Cross, Bray; adult/child €7.50/2; ⊙9.30am-6pm daily May-Sep, weekends only Apr & Oct; P 🐾) A stunning mansion in the Elizabethan Revival style, Killruddery has been home to the Brabazon family (earls of Meath) since 1618 and has one of the oldest gardens in Ireland. The house is impressive, but the prizewinner here is the magnificent orangery, built in 1852 and chock-full of statuary and plant life. If you like fancy glasshouses, this is the one for you. It's 6km north of Greystones just off the R761 coast road.

The house was designed by trendy 19th-century architects Richard Morrisson and his son William in 1820, and it was reduced to its present-day merely huge proportions by the 14th earl in 1953; he was obviously looking for something a little more bijou. There are guided tours of the house daily except Friday (€16 per person, in the afternoon), as well as an excellent farmers market every Saturday (10am to 3pm).

Mt Usher Gardens — GARDENS

(☑0404-40205; www.mountushergardens.ie; Ashford; adult/child €7.50/3.50; ⊙10am-6pm) Wicklow's nickname, 'the Garden of Ireland', is justified by green idylls such as the 8-hectare Mt Usher Gardens, just outside the unremarkable town of Ashford about 10km south of Greystones on the N11. Trees, shrubs and herbaceous plants from around the world are laid out in Robinsonian style – ie according to the naturalist principles of famous Irish gardener William Robinson (1838–1935) – rather than in the formalist manner of preceding gardens.

There's also an Avoca cafe on the premises, as well as a 'shopping courtyard' where you can buy freshly baked goods, plants, furniture, clothing, as well as ice cream and photographs.

Sleeping & Eating

★ Tinakilly Country House & Restaurant
HERITAGE HOTEL €€

(☎ 0404-69274; www.tinakilly.ie; Rathnew; r from €130; P ☎) This magnificent Victorian Italianate house between Rathnew and Wicklow town is one of the most elegant country homes in the county. You have a choice between a period room in the west wing (original antiques, and four-poster and half-tester canopy beds) and a sumptuous suite with a view in the east wing. Massage and beauty treatments are available.

The restaurant takes country-house cuisine to a whole new level of sophistication (dinner mains €18 to €32).

★ Hunter's Hotel
HOTEL €€

(☎ 0404-40106; www.hunters.ie; Newrath Bridge, Rathnew; r from €130; P ☎) This exquisite property on the R761 just outsidAVON-DAe Rathnew is an absolute find, with 16 stunning rooms, each decorated with unerringly good taste. The house, one of Ireland's oldest coaching inns, is surrounded by an award-winning garden. The attached fine-dining restaurant (two/three courses for €29.50/€36.50) is also excellent.

★ Happy Pear
CAFE €

(☎ 01-287 3655; http://thehappypear.ie; Church Rd; ⊗ 9am-6pm Mon-Thu, to 9pm Fri & Sat, to 7pm Sun; ☎ ☎) ⦿ Half of Greystones seem to meet each other for a chat at this hugely popular cafe, deli and organic grocery. Enjoy your fancy porridge with fruit and seeds, washed down with a soy latte, in the cool upstairs seating area, in the cosy outdoor courtyard, or on a pavement table where you can watch the world go by.

Three Q's
INTERNATIONAL €€

(☎ 01-287 5477; www.thethreeqs.com; Church Rd; mains €10-25; ⊗ 9.30am-10pm Mon-Fri, 9am-10pm

WORTH A TRIP

BALLYKNOCKEN HOUSE

This is a beautiful ivy-clad Victorian **home and cookery school** (☎ 0404-44627; www.ballyknocken.com; Glenealy, Ashford; r from €110; P ☎), where each of the seven carefully appointed bedrooms has original furnishings, and some come with original, stencilled claw-foot tubs. Besides the home itself, the big draw is Catherine Fulvio's cooking classes (from €125), which run throughout the year; check the website for details. It's 5km south of Ashford on the R752 to Glenealy.

Sat & Sun; ⦿) This elegant, award-winning restaurant is a neighbourhood favourite, serving brunch as well as lunch and dinner. The eclectic menu ranges from across the globe with dishes such as Peruvian chicken salad with quinoa and pomegranate tabouli, and baked Moroccan fish with chickpea and coriander stew. The early-bird menu (two/three courses for €19/23) is available from 5.30pm to 7pm.

❶ Getting There & Away

Bus Éireann (☎ 01-836 6111; www.buseireann.ie) operates bus 133 from Dublin (Georges Quay) to Wicklow town (€11, 1½ hours, hourly). It stops at Kilmacanogue, Newtownmountkennedy, Ashford and Rathnew.

DART (www.irishrail.ie) commuter trains run from Dublin Connolly station to Greystones (€5.95, 55 minutes, at least twice hourly).

Rathdrum

POP 1663

The quiet village of Rathdrum, sitting above the River Avonmore at the foot of the Vale of Clara, is famed as the birthplace of nationalist hero Charles Stewart Parnell (1846–91), whose story is told at nearby Avondale House and in the memorial park at the south end of the main street.

Apart from the park, there's little of interest in the village itself, which was a victim of the property crash that followed the boom of the Celtic Tiger years – there are more than a few boarded-up buildings and abandoned construction sites scarring the streets – but there are a couple of worthwhile sights and some good walks in the surrounding area.

COUNTIES WICKLOW & KILDARE EASTERN WICKLOW

⊙ Sights & Activities

Kilmacurragh Botanic Gardens　　GARDENS
(✏ 0404-48844; www.botanicgardens.ie; Kilbride; ⊙ 9am-6pm mid-Feb–Oct, to 4.30pm Nov–mid-Feb) **FREE** Surrounding the ruins of an 18th-century mansion are these ornamental gardens originally laid out in 1712 and replanted in the 19th century to reflect the wilder, antiformal style of William Robinson (1838–1935); particularly notable are the South American conifers, the colourful rhododendrons and the avenue of yews. The gardens are 3km east of Rathdrum, but poorly signposted; get directions from the website.

Avondale House　　HOUSE
(✏ 0404-46111; www.heritageisland.com; Avondale Forest Park; adult/child €7/4.50; ⊙ 11am-6pm Thu-Sun Jun-Aug; P) This fine Palladian mansion was the birthplace and Irish headquarters of Charles Stewart Parnell (1846–91), the 'uncrowned king of Ireland' and one of the key figures in the Irish independence movement. Designed by James Wyatt in 1779, the house's many highlights include a stunning vermilion-hued library and the American Room, dedicated to Parnell's eponymous grandfather, admiral of the USS *Constitution* during the War of 1812. Tours are self-guided. Though the house has limited opening hours, and the gardens are open dawn to dusk year-round.

From 1880 to 1890 Avondale was synonymous with the fight for Home Rule, which was brilliantly led by Parnell until 1890, when a member of his own Irish Parliamentary Party, Captain William O'Shea, sued his wife Kitty for divorce and named Parnell as co-respondent. Parnell's affair with Kitty O'Shea scandalised this 'priest-ridden' nation, and the ultraconservative clergy declared that Parnell was 'unfit to lead' – despite the fact that as soon as the divorce was granted the two lovers were quickly married. Parnell resigned as leader of the party and withdrew in despair to Avondale, where he died the following year.

The magnificent 209-hectare estate that surrounds the house is managed by the Irish Forestry Service, Coillte (www.coillte.ie), and there are a number of hiking trails download a trail map from the website.

Railway Walk　　WALKING
(www.coillte.ie) You can hike to Avondale House (p154) from Rathdrum village via this 2km-long trail. The start is hard to find, at the back of a small industrial estate on the far side of the tracks from Rathdrum train station, but

thereafter it's a pleasant woodland walk along the banks of the River Avonmore, passing beneath two impressive railway viaducts.

🛏 Sleeping & Eating

Brook Lodge & Wells Spa　　HOTEL €€
(✏ 0402-36444; www.brooklodge.com; Macreddin; r/ste from €130/210; P 🛜) 🍴 This luxurious country-house hotel has 86 beautifully appointed rooms ranging from standard bedrooms with sleigh beds and deep baths to mezzanine suites that wouldn't seem out of place in a New York penthouse. The accommodation is pure luxury, and the other big selling point is the sumptuous Wells Spa (treatments from €40). It's 3km west of Rathdrum.

Also on site is the superb **Strawberry Tree** (dinner menu €65; ⊙ 7pm-midnight Tue-Sun year-round, daily in Aug 🍴) restaurant, renowned for its locally sourced, organic cuisine.

Bates Restaurant　　PUB FOOD €€
(✏ 0404-29988; www.batesrestaurant.com; 3 Market Sq, Rathdrum; mains €17-27; ⊙ 6-9pm Tue-Fri, 5.30-9.30pm Sat, 12.30-8pm Sun) Housed in a coaching inn that first opened its doors in 1785, this outstanding restaurant is hidden down a side alley beside a pub. It puts a premium on exquisitely prepared beef and lamb dishes; the chargrilled beef options are particularly good, including a 17oz chateaubriand steak for two at €47. Bookings recommended for weekend evenings.

ⓘ Information

The small **tourist office** (✏ 0404-46262; http://visitwicklow.ie; 29 Main St; ⊙ 9.30am-5pm Mon-Fri) has leaflets and information on the town and surrounding area, including the Wicklow Way (p149).

ⓘ Getting There & Away

Trains serve Rathdrum from Dublin Connolly (€16.35, 1½ hours, five daily) on the main Dublin to Rosslare Harbour line.

Bus Éireann (✏ 01-836 6111; www.buseireann.ie) service 133 runs hourly from Dublin (Georges Quay) to Wicklow town, with two buses a day continuing to Rathdrum (€14, 1¾ hours) and on to Avoca and Arklow.

Vale of Avoca

One of the most scenic spots in the county is the Vale of Avoca, a darkly wooded valley that begins where the Rivers Avonbeg and Avonmore come together to form the

WICKLOW'S HISTORIC GAOL

Wicklow's infamous **jail** (☎ 0404-61599; www.wicklowshistoricgaol.com; Kilmantin Hill; adult/child incl tour €7.90/5, night tour €15; ☉10.30am-4.30pm; P) was notorious throughout Ireland for the brutality of its keepers and the harsh conditions suffered by its inmates. The smells, vicious beatings, shocking food and disease-ridden air have long since gone, but adults and children alike can experience a sanitised version of what the prison was like – and stimulate the secret sadist buried deep within – on a highly entertaining tour of the prison, now one of Wicklow's most popular tourist attractions.

The prison was opened in 1702 to house inmates sentenced under the repressive Penal Laws and continued in the role until 1877, when it was reduced to the status of a remand prison (bridewell), before closing in 1924. The building fell into ruin before finally being restored in the 1990s in recognition of its historic significance.

Actors play the roles of the various jailers and prisoners, adding to the sense of drama already heightened by the various exhibits on show, including a life-size treadmill that prisoners would have to turn for hours on end as punishment; and the gruesome dungeon.

The prison also has a **genealogical library**, where you can scour Irish digital data-bases for details of Irish ancestry. Tours are every 10 minutes except between 1pm and 2pm; on the last Friday of every month there are adult-only night tours of the prison, complete with ghouls, finger food and a glass of wine.

River Avoca. Bearing the literal name the Meeting of the Waters, this watery junction was made famous by Thomas Moore's 1808 poem of the same name.

Tiny Avoca (Abhóca) village is a pleasant spot, that's best-known as the birthplace of the superstar of all Irish cottage industries, Avoca Handweavers. Ask at the **tourist office** (☎ 0402-35022; Old Courthouse; ☉ 10am-5pm Mon-Sat) for details of nearby walks.

Sleeping & Eating

★ **River Valley Park** CAMPGROUND €
(☎ 0404-41647; www.rivervalleypark.com; Redcross; campsites €26, microlodges €80-100; 🛜🐕) With six different kinds of camping options, this award-winning site is probably the best-equipped campground in the county; it even has its own microbrewery! Besides the family campsites, there are self-catering chalets, mobile homes, glamping microlodges and an adults-only section. It's about 1km south of the village of Redcross and 7km northeast of Avoca on the R754 country road.

Meetings PUB
(☎ 0402-35226; www.themeetings.ie; Meeting of the Waters; ☉ noon-11pm; 🛜) The meeting of the Avonmore and Avonbeg rivers is marked by this excellent pub, which has music at weekends year-round. There's also a cafe and crafts gallery with a lovely terrace overlooking the river, Lily's Restaurant (open Friday to Sunday) and a choice of sleek modern guest bedrooms (doubles from €95).

Shopping

★ **Avoca Handweavers** ARTS & CRAFTS
(☎ 0402-35105; www.avoca.ie; Main St; ☉ shop 9.30am-6pm May-Sep, to 5.30pm Oct-Apr) Ireland's oldest working mill is the birthplace of Avoca Handweavers, a company that is now famous across Ireland and the world. The mill (open from 10am to 4.30pm) has been turning out woollens and other fabrics since 1723, and a lot of Avoca's much-admired line is produced here and sold in the neighbouring shop.

You are free to wander around the weaving sheds and chat to the weavers, or have lunch in the excellent cafe. Arrive early or late to avoid coach tour groups.

Getting There & Away

Bus Éireann (☎ 01-836 6111; www.buseireann. ie) service 133 runs hourly from Dublin (Georges Quay) to Wicklow town, with two buses a day continuing to Avoca (€11, two hours), with stops at Rathdrum and the Meeting of the Waters.

Western Wicklow

West of the Wicklow Mountains the landscape is more rural than rugged, especially towards the borders of Kildare and Carlow. The wild terrain of the county's east gives way to rich pastures; east of Blessington the countryside is dotted with private stud farms where some of the world's most expensive horses are trained in jealously guarded secrecy.

IRELAND'S ANCIENT EAST

Capitalising on the success of the Wild Atlantic Way (p47), the Irish tourist board's latest promotional venture is Ireland's Ancient East (www.irelandsancienteast.com). However, this is not a driving route, like the Wild Atlantic Way, but more of a branding and signposting exercise. As well as taking in big-name attractions such as **Newgrange** (p501), **Glendalough** (p148) and the **Rock of Cashel** (p317), the campaign encourages visitors to visit central and eastern Ireland's lesser-known historical attractions.

Hundreds of sights spread over 17 counties have been grouped into stories and themes. The website (and smartphone app) allows you to explore each theme (such as Sacred Ireland, Castles & Conquests, and Vikings) along with related background stories, and then click through to travel itineraries that you can customise and download.

You'll see new road signs with the Ancient East logo dotted all over the country, pointing the way to various sights; unfortunately, once you get off the main road and reach the next minor road junction...all too often there are no more signs. So be prepared to use a road map, satnav or a mapping app on your phone if you want to be sure of getting to the lesser-known spots.

Here are five of the most popular Ancient East themes with a list of the best off-the-beaten track attractions in each one.

Ancient Ireland

Ireland's 5000-year-old history has left an abundance of prehistoric sites scattered across the country. The richly decorated passage tombs of Newgrange and Howth at Brú na Bóinne (p501) are the most famous, but there are thousands more to be discovered, from impressive burial cairns to simple dolmens and standing stones:

Browne's Hill Dolmen (p195)

Loughcrew Megalithic Centre (p515)

Uisneach (p484)

Corlea Trackway (p481)

Cavan Burren Park (p528)

Vikings

Viking raiders arrived in southeast Ireland in the 9th century, burning villages, carrying off prisoners and robbing monasteries of their gold. But eventually they settled in the country, establishing harbour towns such as Waterford and Wexford and setting up a rich trading economy. Their influence can be seen in many parts of Ireland:

Irish National Heritage Park (p169)

Lough Gur Heritage Centre (p314)

Reginald's Tower (p180)

Waterford Medieval Museum (p180)

The main attraction in this part of Wicklow is the magnificent Palladian pile at Russborough House, just outside Blessington. If it's wild scenery you're after, you'll find it around Kilbride and the upper reaches of the River Liffey, as well as further south in the Glen of Imaal.

Blessington

POP 5520

Lined with pubs, shops and 18th-century townhouses, Blessington makes a convenient base for exploring western Wicklow.

The main attractions nearby are Russborough House and Poulaphouca Reservoir. Also known as Blessington Lake, the reservoir is Ireland's biggest artificial lake, created in 1940 by damming the River Liffey to generate hydroelectric power and provide water for the growing city of Dublin. It's a major venue for fishing and boating.

🔵 Sights & Activities

Russborough House HISTORIC BUILDING
(☎ 045-865 239; www.russboroughhouse.ie; guided tours adult/child €12/6; ⊙ 10am-6pm daily Mar-

Dunmore Cave (📞056-776 7726; www.heritageireland.ie; Ballyfoyle; adult/child €5/3; ⊘9.30am-6.30pm mid Jun–mid Sep, shorter hours rest of year; Ⓟ)

Castles & Conquests

Beginning in the 12th century, Norman invaders from England and Wales sought to occupy Ireland and subdue the native people, building a network of impressive castles to help control their territories:

Rock of Dunamaise (p499)

Trim Castle (p511)

Cahir Castle (p319)

Athlone Castle (p482)

Birr Castle (p487)

Sacred Ireland

Famously known as the 'land of saints and scholars', Ireland was a cradle of early Christianity. From the arrival of St Patrick in the 5th century to the dissolution of the monasteries in the 16th, there is a fantastic legacy of high crosses, churches, abbeys and monasteries, many in a state of picturesque ruin:

Clonmacnoise (p492)

St Declan's Monastery (p189)

Monasterboice (p519)

Fore Valley (p486)

Hill of Tara (p509)

Big Houses & Hard Times

Aristocrats of the 18th and 19th centuries competed with each other to show off how wealthy they were, commissioning fashionable architects to design ever-larger and more extravagant mansions. When the aristocracy fell on hard times in the 20th century, many properties were bequeathed to the state and opened to the public:

Castletown House (p159)

Curraghmore Estate (📞bookings 086 821 1917; www.curraghmorehouse.ie; Portlaw; house tours €10, shell house tours €7.50, gardens €5; ⊘10.30am-4.30pm Wed-Sun Easter-Sep; Ⓟ)

Huntington Castle (p199)

Russborough House (p157)

Belvedere House & Gardens (p485)

23 Dec; Ⓟ) Magnificent Russborough House is one of Ireland's finest stately homes, a Palladian palace built for Joseph Leeson (1705–83), later the first Earl of Milltown and, later still, Lord Russborough. Since 1952 the house has been owned by the Beit family, who founded the DeBeers diamond-mining company and stocked the mansion with a remarkable art collection, including masterpieces by Velázquez, Vermeer, Goya, Rubens and others. The admission price includes a 45-minute guided tour of the house, which lies 4km south of Blessington.

Russborough was built between 1741 and 1751 to the design of Richard Cassels, who was at the height of his fame as an architect. Poor old Richard didn't live to see it finished, but the job was well executed by Francis Bindon. The house remained in the Leeson family until 1931, but it was only after the Beits bought the pile that the drama began.

In 1974 the IRA stole 16 of the paintings, all of which were later recovered. In 1984 Loyalist paramilitaries followed suit, hiring Dublin criminal Martin Cahill to mastermind the heist. Although most of that haul was also recovered, some pieces were damaged beyond repair. In 1988 Beit donated the most valuable works to the National Gallery, but that didn't stop two more break-ins, in 2001 and 2002: one of the stolen paintings was a Gainsborough that had already been taken – and recovered – twice before. Thankfully all of the paintings were recovered after both attempts, but where a succession of thieves couldn't succeed, the cost of upkeep did: in 2015 the owners announced they were going to auction off 10 of the paintings, a decision that caused much consternation as the family had always maintained that the collection was to be held in trust for the Irish people.

On the tour of the house, which is decorated in typical Georgian style, you'll see all the (remaining) important paintings, which, given the history, is a monumental exercise in staying positive.

Blessington Lake Boat Hire　FISHING
(☑087 355 2403; www.blessingtonlakeboathire.com; Bog Rd, Ballyknockan; boat hire per day €75) This outfit rents out boats with outboard motors for fishing or cruising on Blessington Lake, which is home to brown and rainbow trout as well as being one of Ireland's prime pike fisheries. It sells fishing permits (€5 per day) and rents out fishing tackle (€15). You can also get information on fishing and buy permits at Charles Camping on Blessington's Main St.

🍽 Sleeping & Eating

Rathsallagh House & Country Club　HOTEL €€€
(☑045-403 112; www.rathsallagh.com; Dunlavin; s/d from €150/200; P🛜🐾) This fabulous country manor, converted from Queen Anne stables after the main house was burnt down during 1798 Rising, is more than just a fancy hotel. Luxury is par for the course here, from the splendidly appointed rooms to the exquisite country-house dining (mains €20 to €27) and the highly rated golf course that surrounds the estate. It's 22km south of Blessington, off the R756.

Grangecon Café　INTERNATIONAL €
(☑045-857 892; Kilbride Rd; mains €6-13; ◷10am-5pm Tue-Sat; 🛜) Salads, home-baked dishes and a full menu of Irish cheeses are the staples at this tiny, terrific cafe set in a converted schoolhouse. Everything here – from the pasta to the delicious apple juice – is made on the premises, and many of the ingredients are organic. A short but solid menu represents the best of Irish cooking.

ⓘ Information

The **tourist office** (☑045-865 850; blessingtontouristoffice@eircom.net; Unit 5, Blessington Craft Centre, Main St; ◷9.30am-5pm Mon-Fri year-round, 10am-2pm Sat-Sun Jul-Aug) is tucked away behind the Credit Union building, just west of the main street.

ⓘ Getting There & Away

Dublin Bus (www.dublinbus.ie) service 65 runs from Poolbeg St in Dublin to Blessington (€3.30, 1½ hours, every two hours).

COUNTY KILDARE

Some of Ireland's best grazing farmland has made County Kildare (Cill Dara) prime agricultural real estate, especially for the horse-racing set: the county is dotted with stud farms where champion racehorses are reared and trained as a matter of course. In recent decades it has had to contend with Dublin's ever-expanding commuter belt, which has swallowed up many of its towns and villages.

The county isn't especially stuffed with must-see attractions, but there are enough diversions to justify a day trip from the capital or a stop on your way out west.

Kildare Town

POP 8634

Built around a compact, triangular square beneath an impressive cathedral, Kildare town is closely associated with Ireland's second-most important saint, Brigid. Although there aren't a lot of attractions within the town itself, it's a shopping destination and a centre for equestrian enthusiasts, with the Irish National Stud (p158) and the Curragh racecourse (p160) both nearby.

◉ Sights

Irish National Stud & Gardens　GARDENS
(☑045-521 617; www.irishnationalstud.ie; Tully; adult/child €12.50/7; ◷9am-6pm Feb-Oct, last admission 5pm) The Irish National Stud, about 3km south of town, is the big attraction in Kildare – horse-mad Queen Elizabeth II dropped in during her historic 2011 visit. This immaculately kept centre is owned and managed by the Irish government, and breeds high-quality stallions to mate with mares from all over the world. You can wander the paddocks and go eye-to-eye

CASTLETOWN HOUSE

Magnificent **Castletown House** (☑ 01-628 8252; www.castletown.ie; Celbridge; adult/child €8/3.50, with guided tour €10/5; ⊙ 10am-6pm mid-Mar–Oct) simply has no peer. It is Ireland's most imposing Georgian estate, and a testament to the vast wealth enjoyed by the Anglo-Irish gentry during the 18th century. Hour-long guided tours begin at noon and 3pm, offering an insight into how the 1% made out in the 18th century; otherwise you can wander at will. Don't miss a stroll down to the river for grand views back to the house. Castletown is signposted from junction 6 on the M4.

The house was built between the years 1722 and 1732 for William Conolly (1662–1729), speaker of the Irish House of Commons and, at the time, Ireland's richest man. Born into relatively humble circumstances in Ballyshannon, County Donegal, Conolly made his fortune through land transactions in the uncertain aftermath of the Battle of the Boyne (1690).

The job of building a palace fit for a prince was entrusted to Sir Edward Lovett Pearce (1699–1733) – hence the colonnades and terminating pavilions. Lovett's design was an extension of a preexisting 16th-century Italian palazzo-style building, created by Italian architect Alessandro Galilei (1691–1737) in 1718, but Conolly wanted something even grander, hence Lovett's appearance on the job in 1724. A highlight of the opulent interior is the Long Gallery, replete with family portraits and exquisite stucco work by the Francini brothers.

Conolly didn't live to see the completion of his wonder-palace. His widow, Katherine, continued to live at the unfinished house after his death in 1729, and instigated many improvements. Her main architectural contribution was the curious 42.6m obelisk, known locally as the Conolly Folly. Her other offering was the Heath Robinson–esque (or Rube Goldberg–esque, if you prefer) **Wonderful Barn** (Leixlip; ⊙ dawn-dusk), six teetering storeys wrapped by an exterior spiral staircase, on private property just outside Leixlip.

Castletown House remained in the family's hands until 1965, when it was purchased by Desmond Guinness, who restored the house to its original splendour. His investment was continued from 1979 by the Castletown Foundation. In 1994 Castletown House woughteras transferred to state care and today it is managed by the Heritage Service.

with famous stallions, or take a guided tour. Around 3pm in the spring, you can watch the foals being walked back to their stables.

The stud was founded by Colonel Hall Walker (of Johnnie Walker whiskey fame) in 1900. He was remarkably successful with his horses, but his eccentric breeding technique relied heavily on astrology: the fate of a foal was decided by its horoscope and the roofs of the stallion boxes opened on auspicious occasions to reveal the stars above and hopefully influence the horses' fortunes.

Guided tours take place every hour on the hour, with access to the intensive-care unit for newborn foals. If you visit between February and June, you might even see a foal being born. Alternatively, the foaling unit shows a 10-minute video with all the action. Given that most of those foals are now geldings, they probably have dim memories of their time in the Teasing Shed, the place where stallions are stimulated before 'covering' a mare. The fee for having a mare inseminated by the stud's top stallion can be as much as €120,000.

Other attractions on site include lakeside walks, a 'fairy trail' for kids and the Irish Horse Museum, a celebration of championship horses and the history of horse racing. You can also visit Colonel Hall Walker's Japanese Gardens (part of the complex), considered to be the best of their kind in Europe. Created between 1906 and 1910, they trace the journey from birth to death through 20 landmarks, including the Tunnel of Ignorance, the Hill of Ambition and the Chair of Old Age.

St Brigid's Cathedral   CATHEDRAL
(☑ 045-521 229; Market Sq; cathedral/round tower €2/7; ⊙ 10am-1pm Mon-Sat, 2-5pm Mon-Sun May-Sep) The solid presence of 13th-century St Brigid's Cathedral looms over Kildare's Market Sq. Look out for a fine stained-glass window that depicts Ireland's three principal saints: Patrick, Brigid and Colmcille. The church also contains the restored tomb of Walter Wellesley, Bishop of Kildare, which disappeared soon after his death in 1539 and was found in 1971. One of its carved figures

has been variously interpreted as an acrobat or a sheila-na-gig (a carved female figure with exaggerated genitalia).

The 10th-century **round tower** in the grounds is Ireland's second highest at 32.9m, and one of only two in Ireland that you can climb (the other is in Kilkenny), provided the guardian is around. Its original conical roof has been replaced with an unusual Norman battlement. Near the tower is a **wishing stone** – put your arm through the hole and touch your shoulder and your wish will be granted. On the north side of the cathedral are the heavily restored foundations of an ancient **fire temple**.

🛏 Sleeping & Eating

★ Martinstown House HOTEL €€€
(☑045-441 269; www.martinstownhouse.com; Ballysax; r from €175; ☺mid-Jan–mid-Dec; ℙ) This beautiful 18th-century country manor is built in the frilly Strawberry Hill Gothic style and set in a 170-acre estate and farm surrounded by attractive woodland. The house has four rooms filled with antiques; children are banned – darn. You can arrange for memorable dinners in advance (€49.50); ingredients are drawn from the kitchen garden. It's 10km southeast of town

Agapé CAFE €
(☑045-533 711; Station Rd; meals €6-12; ☺9am-6pm Mon-Sat) That's *ah-gap-ay* (as in Greek for unconditional love), not *ah-gayp* (as in open-mouthed in astonishment), though the quality of the freshly prepared food in this trendy little cafe will leave you pleasantly surprised. There's a full coffee bar and a menu of salads, soups, sandwiches and tasty hot specials.

🛍 Shopping

Kildare Village SHOPPING CENTRE
(www.kildarevillage.com; Nurney Rd; ☺10am-7pm Mon-Wed & Sun, 10am-8pm Thu-Fri, 9am-8pm Sat) Shoppers come from all over the country to buy discounted versions of their favourite brands at this designer outlet mall, the biggest of its kind in Ireland: more than a hundred high-street brands are represented. The architecture is supposedly inspired by the county's stud farms, and you can buy lunch from gourmet food trucks that are converted horse boxes.

ℹ Information

The **Tourist Office & Heritage Centre** (☑045-521 240; www.kildare.ie; Market Sq; ☺9.30am-1pm & 2-5.30pm Mon-Sat May-Sep) has an exhibition (admission free) outlining Kildare's history. There's also local art for sale.

ℹ Getting There & Away

Bus Éireann (www.buseireann.ie) service 126 runs between Dublin (Connoly Luas stop) and Kildare (€14.30, 1½ hours, hourly). Some Dublin buses also service the **National Stud** (p158).

Trains run from Dublin Heuston to Kildare (€16.60, 30 minutes, one to four per hour). This is a major junction and trains continue to numerous places including Ballina, Galway, Limerick and Waterford.

The Curragh

Stretching from Kildare town to Newbridge, the Curragh is one of the country's largest tracts of unfenced grassland and the centre of the Irish horse-racing industry. The name derives from the Irish for 'place of the running horse', and they've been doing just that on this rolling sward since the 1700s, although there are tales of chariot races as far back as the 13th century.

If you get up early or pass by in the late evening, you'll see the thoroughbreds exercising on the wide-open spaces surrounding the world-famous **Curragh racecourse** (☑045-441 205; www.curragh.ie; €15-30; ☺mid-Apr–Oct) The Curragh is the oldest and most prestigious racecourse in the country, and one of the finest flat-racing courses in the world; even if you're not a horsey type, it's well worth experiencing the passion and atmosphere of a day at the races here. The complex is in the midst of a major redevelopment, scheduled for completion in early 2019.

Unremarkable Newbridge (Droichead Nua), at the east end of the Curragh, is best known for its shopping centres and silverware.

◉ Sights

Museum of Style Icons MUSEUM
(☑045-431 301; http://newbridgesilverware.com/mosi; Newbridge Silverware, Athgarvan Rd; ☺9am-6pm Mon-Sat, 10am-6pm Sun; ℙ) **FREE** Housed inside the Newbridge Silverware showroom, beneath a sparkle of glitter balls, is this unexpected display of star-studded

memorabilia. There are exhibits showcasing dresses, suits and stage costumes that were once worn by Audrey Hepburn, The Beatles, Victoria Beckham, Michael Jackson, Elizabeth Taylor and Princess Diana, among others. Guided tours (€5) at 10.30am Tuesday and Thursday provide added context.

Shopping

Newbridge Silverware   ARTS & CRAFTS
(☑ 045-431 301; www.newbridgesilverware.com; ⊙ 9am-6pm Mon-Sat, 10am-6pm Sun) The Newbridge Silverware Showroom is a purely commercial venture that trades on the area's metalwork heritage as it peddles vast quantities of silver jewellery, silver-plated cutlery, homewares and engravable gift items. Just inside the main entrance is the unexpected Museum of Style Icons.

Getting There & Away

The M7 from Dublin cuts through the middle of the Curragh (take exit 12 for the racecourse and Newbridge).

Bus Éireann (www.buseireann.ie) service 126 runs between Dublin's Busáras bus station and Newbridge (€11, 1¼ hours, hourly), continuing to Kildare town. Dublin Coach (http://dublincoach.ie) runs special buses from Dublin Airport and Dublin to the Curragh on race days.

Trains between Dublin Heuston station and Kildare stop in Newbridge (€15, 30 minutes, hourly).

Maynooth

POP 14,585

Bustling Maynooth (Maigh Nuad) is dominated by the local campus of the National University of Ireland (NUIM), whose students make up two-thirds of its population and add a touch of liveliness to this otherwise demure country town lined with stone-fronted houses and shops.

The main sights – the castle, college and museum – are clustered together at the western end of Main St, a 10-minute walk north from the train station.

Sights & Activities

St Patrick's College   UNIVERSITY
(☑ 01-708 6404; www.visitmaynooth.com/tours; Main St; guided tours adult/child/student €8/4/6; ⊙ tours 11am-5.30pm Jun-Aug) Part of NUI Maynooth (p162), and turning out Catholic priests since 1795, St Patrick's College & Seminary is Ireland's second-oldest uni-

ARTHUR'S LAST RESTING PLACE

The 10m-tall stump of an 8th-century round tower marks the ancient Christian site (Oughterard; ⊙ dawn-dusk) 7km southeast of Straffan. The name in Gaelic means 'high place', and the view of the green Kildare countryside is sweeping. But the cemetery is best known for its most famous resident – a vault amid the ruins of the 14th-century church is the last resting place of Arthur Guinness (1724–1803), the brewer who created the world-famous black beer.

versity (after Trinity College, Dublin). The college buildings are impressive – Gothic architect Augustus Pugin had a hand in designing them – and well worth an hour's ramble. The college grounds contain a number of lofty Georgian and neo-Gothic buildings, gardens and squares, and it's worth taking the guided tour to see the **College Chapel**, the world's largest choir chapel with stalls for more than 450 choristers.

The college was founded so that aspiring priests didn't have to skip off to seminary school in France – and so get infected with strains of republicanism and revolution. In 1898 it was made a Pontifical College (which meant that its curriculum was determined and controlled by the Holy See) and in 1910 it became part of the then recently established National University of Ireland. The college's student body remained exclusively clerical until 1966 when lay students were finally admitted, but even today, despite being part of the bigger university, it remains largely autonomous and its 80-odd male seminarians are distinct from the university's 8500 other students.

National Science & Ecclesiology Museum   MUSEUM
(☑ 01-708 3576; http://maynoothcollege.ie/national-museum-maynooth; St Patrick's College; admission by donation; ⊙ 2-4pm Wed & 2-6pm Sun Jun-Aug) Father Nicholas Callan (1799–1864), Professor of Natural Philosophy at St Patrick's College in the mid-19th century, was a pioneer of research into electromagnetism and the inventor of the induction coil. This small museum preserves his original experimental

apparatus, along with a large collection of historic scientific instruments and three centuries worth of ecclesiastical objects associated with the college.

Maynooth Castle CASTLE
(☑ 01-628 6744; www.heritageireland.ie; Parson St; ⊙ 10am-6pm Wed-Sun late-May–Sep) **FREE**
At the west end of the town centre you can see the ruined gatehouse, keep and great hall of this 13th-century castle, once home to the Fitzgerald family. The castle was dismantled in Cromwellian times, when the Fitzgeralds moved to Kilkea Castle (now closed). Entry is by a 45-minute guided tour only; there's a small exhibition on the castle's history in the keep.

Carton House GOLF
(☑ 01-651 7727; www.cartonhousegolf.com; Carton House; green fees €75-95) Two outstanding courses make Carton House one of eastern Ireland's premier golfing destinations. The O'Meara Course has broad fairways and strategically placed greens; the Montgomerie Course is more challenging, with bunkers positioned to swallow all but the best-hit shots.

🛏 Sleeping & Eating

NUI Maynooth ACCOMMODATION SERVICES €
(☑ 01-708 6400; www.maynoothcampus.com; accommodation centre, St Patrick's College; s/d from €33/54; **P** 🛜) The university campus can accommodate 1000 guests in seven types of room, ranging from a traditional college room to doubles in an apartment

---

THE GRAND CANAL TOWPATH

The **Grand Canal towpath** is ideal for leisurely walkers and there are numerous access points, with none better than Robertstown if you fancy a canalside ramble. The village is the hub of the Kildare Way and the Barrow towpath trails, the latter stretching all the way to St Mullins, 95km to the south in County Carlow. From there it's possible to connect with the South Leinster Way at Graiguenamanagh, or the southern end of the Wicklow Way at Clonegal, north of Mt Leinster.

A variety of leaflets detailing the paths can be picked up at most regional tourist offices. **Waterways Ireland** (www.waterwaysireland.org) is also a good source.

---

in the purpose-built university village. Most are in the mid-1970s North Campus, but rooms are better in the South Campus, where the accommodation office is. These are strewn around the courts and gardens of atmospheric St Patrick's College. Availability is best in the summer months.

Carton House HOTEL €€€
(☑ 01-505 2000; www.cartonhouse.com; r from €250; **P** 🅿 🛜 🏊) Dating from 1739, the former country manor of the Fitzgerald earls of Kildare (their city pile was Leinster House, now the Irish Parliament) is now an exquisite luxury hotel. Rooms are split between the grander suites of the original Richard Cassels–designed mansion and the neat, business-style accommodations in the modern extension. To reach the hotel, follow the R148 east towards Leixlip along the Royal Canal.

Gatehouse INTERNATIONAL €€
(☑ 01-629 1522; www.thegatehouse.ie; Main St; mains lunch €8-14, dinner €16-23; ⊙ 8.30am-10pm Mon-Sat, 10am-9pm Sun; 🛜) The Gatehouse's catch-all menu – breakfast dishes, seafood chowder, pizza and pasta, plus interesting choices such as teriyaki salmon, and venison with rosemary and honey jus – is a crowd-pleaser, but what makes this spot stand out is the quality of the ingredients. Everything is fresh and, wherever possible, locally sourced.

ℹ Getting There & Away

Dublin Bus (☑ 01-873 4222; www.dublinbus.ie) runs a service to Maynooth (€3.30, one hour, every 30 minutes) departing from Merrion Sq in Dublin.

Maynooth is on the main Dublin–Sligo line, with regular trains in each direction: to Dublin (€5.95, 40 minutes, one to four per hour), and to Sligo (€38, 2¾ hours, four per day).

Bog of Allen

Bog of Allen Nature Centre MUSEUM
(☑ 045-860 133; www.ipcc.ie; R414, Lullymore; adult/child €5/free; ⊙ 9am-5pm Mon-Fri year-round, occasional weekends May-Sep; **P** 🚻) 🌿 A fascinating institution run by the nonprofit Irish Peatland Conservation Council, this interpretive centre celebrates the amazing biodiversity of Ireland's bogs, and traces the history of peat extraction and the threat it poses to wildlife and the environment. The garden at the back has the largest carnivo-

rous plant collection in Ireland, including sundews, butterworts and pitcher plants, and ponds filled with frogs and newts. A nearby boardwalk extends into Lodge Bog, one of the last surviving untouched fragments of the Bog of Allen.

Lullymore Heritage &
Discovery Park   NATURE RESERVE
(✏ 045-870 238; www.lullymoreheritagepark.com; Lullymore; adult/family €9/30; ⊘ 10am-6pm daily Apr-Sep, Sat & Sun only Feb-Mar; P 🖶) Developed on an area of cutaway bog, where peat has been extracted for commercial purposes, this award-winning, family-oriented park offers a huge range of activities. A woodland trail leads past various points of interest including a re-creation of an Iron Age hut and an enchanting fairy village. Boardwalks lead out over the half-drowned bog to wildlife hides. There's also a pet farm, crazy golf, a miniature railway and an adventure playground. Put aside at least half a day to make the most of a visit.

Ballitore to Castledermot

The R448 road between Kilcullen and Carlow runs just east of the M9, linking the small villages of Ballitore, Moone and Castledermot and a handful of off-the-beaten-track sights.

Quaker Museum   MUSEUM
(✏ 059-862 3344; www.kildare.ie; Main St, Mary Leadbeater House; admission by donation; ⊘ 10am-1pm & 2-5pm Wed, Fri & Sat, 12.30-4pm Thu) Low-key Ballitore is the only planned and permanent Quaker settlement in Ireland, founded by incomers from Yorkshire in 1726. This small museum, in a tiny restored Meeting House of the Society of Friends (which also houses the local library), documents the lives of Ballitore's Quaker community (including the former owner, Mary Leadbeater, who was known

for her aversion to war). There's also a Quaker cemetery on the southern edge of the village.

Moone High Cross   CHRISTIAN SITE
(www.kildare.ie; Moone; ⊘ dawn-dusk) **FREE** One of Ireland's most magnificent early Christian monuments, the unusually tall and slender Moone High Cross is an 8th- or 9th-century masterpiece, housed within the ruins of a 13th-century abbey. It displays carved biblical scenes with the confidence and exuberance of a comic strip, among them Daniel in the lions' den and the flight into Egypt. The cross can be found on a minor road 1km west of Moone village, via an inconspicuous wooden door in a stone wall.

Castledermot Monastery   RUINS
(St James' Church, Church Lane, Castledermot; ⊘ dusk-dawn) **FREE** Castledermot village was once home to a vast ecclesiastical settlement, but all that remains of St Diarmuid's 9th-century monastery is a 20m round tower topped with a medieval battlement. Nearby are two well-preserved, 10th-century granite high crosses, a 12th-century Romanesque doorway and a medieval Scandinavian 'hogsback' gravestone, the only one in Ireland. Reach the ruins by passing through the rusty gate on all-too-busy Main St (N9), then walking along the tree-lined avenue to St James' church.

Moone High Cross Inn   INN
(✏ 059-862 4112; www.moonehighcrossinn.com; Bolton Hill; ⊘ 10am-11pm Sun-Thu, to midnight Fri & Sat) This charming 18th-century inn, 2km south of Moone, is famed for its craic and live music, which have attracted an impressive list of celebrity visitors including Bono, Sandra Bullock and Clint Eastwood (not all at the same time!). It serves good pub grub (there's always a pot of leek and potato soup on the stove), and also has five B&B bedrooms (from €85).

COUNTIES WICKLOW & KILDARE BALLITORE TO CASTLEDERMOT

Counties Wexford, Waterford, Carlow & Kilkenny

POP 422,000 / AREA 7194 SQ KM

Best Historic Buildings

➡ Hook Lighthouse (p175)

➡ Kilkenny Castle (p200)

➡ Ardmore Cathedral (p189)

➡ Jerpoint Abbey (p208)

➡ Kells Priory (p207)

Best Gardens

➡ Johnstown Castle & Gardens (p165)

➡ Lismore Castle Gardens (p191)

➡ Altamont Gardens (p195)

➡ Woodstock Gardens (p209)

➡ Huntington Castle Gardens (p199)

Why Go?

Counties Wexford, Waterford, Carlow and Kilkenny are (along with the southern chunk of Tipperary) referred to collectively as the 'sunny southeast'. This being Ireland the term is, of course, relative. But it *is* the country's warmest, driest region. A tiara of golden-sand beaches adorns the counties of Wexford and Waterford, and there are plenty more eye-catching gems, including picturesque thatched cottages, elegant seaside towns and dramatic windswept peninsulas. If you're looking for real sparkle, check out the world-acclaimed Waterford crystal. Deeper inland, the verdant valley of the River Barrow separates the riverside villages and arts and crafts studios of County Kilkenny from the country houses and flower-filled gardens of County Carlow. Kilkenny city is the urban star with its imposing castle, cathedral, medieval lanes and cracking pubs and restaurants. And thanks to that 'sunny southeast' climate, these four counties offer some of Ireland's best outdoor pursuits.

When to Go

➡ From June to September is the best time for enjoying the region's superb beaches, seafront cafes and restaurants.

➡ April to October is good for hiking and walking, although be sure to pack waterproof gear and warm clothing.

➡ October to November is great for music lovers with Wexford's world-acclaimed opera festival and Kilkenny's trad music Celtic Festival.

COUNTY WEXFORD

County Wexford's navigable rivers and fertile farmland have long lured invaders and privateers. The Vikings founded Ireland's first major town on the wide, easy-flowing River Slaney, which cuts through the middle of the county. Today the Viking city of Wexford is a centre for opera and art, complementing a beach-fringed coastline and a rural hinterland dotted with cute villages and thatched cottages.

Wexford Town & Around

POP 20,188

A fine example of the contrasts conjured up by the economic boom and bust of the last few decades, Wexford's claustrophobic maze of medieval streets is lined with a mixture of old-time pubs, posh boutiques, boarded-up buildings and modern steel-and-glass facades. The town's rich and bloody history includes being founded by the Vikings and nearly obliterated by Oliver Cromwell.

It's an arty town, with plenty of craft shops and galleries – and good restaurants – but the big cultural attraction is the world-famous Wexford Opera Festival (p169), a 12-day autumn extravaganza that presents rarely performed works to packed audiences in the town's shiny national opera house.

History

The Vikings named it Waesfjord (meaning 'harbour of mud flats') and its handy location near the mouth of the River Slaney encouraged landings as early as AD 850. The town was captured by the Normans in 1169; traces of their fort can still be seen in the grounds of the Irish National Heritage Park (p169).

Cromwell included Wexford in his destructive Irish tour of 1649–50. Around 1500 of the town's then 2000 inhabitants were killed, including all the Franciscan friars. During the 1798 Rising, rebels made a determined, bloody stand here before being defeated.

◎ Sights

Wexford doesn't have any don't-miss museums, but you can get a feeling for its long history on a leisurely stroll.

Selskar Abbey   RUINS
(Westgate, Spawell Rd; adult/child €3/1; ⊘tours 3pm Mon-Sat Mar-Oct) After Henry II murdered his former ally Thomas Becket, he did penance at Selskar Abbey, founded in

1190. Basilia, the sister of Richard Fitz Gilbert de Clare (better known as Strongbow), is thought to have married one of Henry II's lieutenants in the abbey. Its present ruinous state is a result of Cromwell's visit in 1649. Admission is by guided tour only – gather at the Westgate, off Spawell Rd.

St Iberius' Church   CHURCH
(North Main St; ⊘10am-5pm May-Sep, to 3pm Oct-Apr) FREE St Iberius' Church was built in 1660. The Renaissance-style frontage is worth a look, but the real treat is the Georgian interior with its finely crafted altar rails and 18th-century monuments in the gallery. Oscar Wilde's forebears were rectors here. The church is also famed for its superb acoustics, and is an occasional venue for concerts.

Bull Ring   SQUARE
The Bull Ring is a small, open square in the city centre that gets its name from having been used as a venue for bull baiting in medieval times. These days the Bull Ring is the site of the city's weekly market (p171).

The Lone Pikeman statue commemorates the rebels of the 1798 Rising, who used the place as an open-air armaments factory.

Westgate   HISTORIC BUILDING
The only survivor of the six original town gates is the 14th-century Westgate. It was originally a toll gate, and the recesses used by the toll collectors are still intact, as is the lock-up used to incarcerate 'runagates' – those who tried to avoid paying.

★ Johnstown Castle Gardens   GARDENS
(www.irishagrimuseum.ie; Johnstown Castle Estate; adult/child €3/1, incl museum €8/4; ⊘9am-5.30pm Apr-May & Sep, to 7pm Jun-Aug, to 4.30pm Oct-Mar; P) Parading peacocks guard the splendid 19th-century Johnstown Castle, the former home of the once-mighty Fitzgerald and Esmonde families (the estate was gifted to the nation in 1945). The empty castle (not open to public) is surrounded by 20 hectares of beautiful wooded gardens complete with an ornamental lake, a sunken Italian garden, statues and waterfalls. The castle is 7km southwest of Wexford town.

The outbuildings of the castle house the **Irish Agricultural Museum** (☑053-918 4671; adult/child incl castle gardens €8/4; ⊘9am-5pm Mon-Fri, 11am-5pm Sat & Sun Apr-May & Sep-Oct, to 6.30pm Jun-Aug, to 4pm Nov-Mar), a fascinating collection of early Ferguson tractors, farm machinery, Irish country furniture and re-created farmhouse kitchens. The

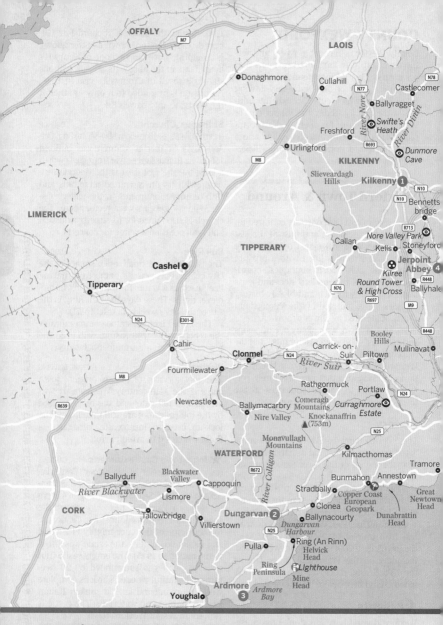

Counties Wexford, Waterford, Carlow & Kilkenny

Highlights

① **Kilkenny** (p199) Revelling in the urban pleasures of one of Ireland's most vibrant cities.

② **Dungarvan** (p187) Savouring the gourmet delights of this lively, west Waterford town's restaurants, farmers market and food festival.

③ **Ardmore** (p189) Immersing yourself in County Waterford's coastal beauty around historic Ardmore.

④ **Jerpoint Abbey** (p208) Getting into monk mode at the abbey's evocative ruins in County Kilkenny.

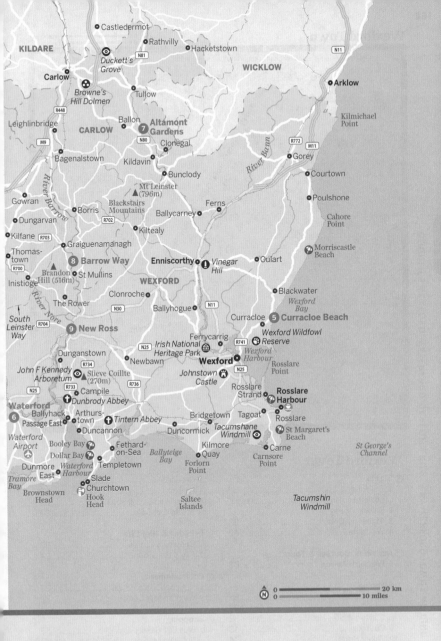

KILDARE
Castledermot
Rathvilly
Hacketstown
WICKLOW
Duckett's Grove
Carlow
Arklow
Browne's Hill Dolmen
Tullow
Kilmichael Point
Leighlinbridge
Ballon
Altamont Gardens
CARLOW
Clonegal
Gorey
Bagenalstown
Kildavin
Courtown
Bunclody
Poulshone
Mt Leinster (796m)
Gowran
Blackstairs Mountains
Ferns
Cahore Point
Dungarvan
Borris
Ballycarney
Kilfane
Graiguenamanagh
Kiltealy
Morriscastle Beach
Thomastown
Barrow Way
Enniscorthy
Vinegar Hill
Oulart
Brandon Hill (516m)
St Mullins
WEXFORD
Inistioge
Clonroche
Blackwater
The Rower
Ballyhogue
Wexford Bay
South Leinster Way
New Ross
Curracloe
Curracloe Beach
Ferrycarrig
Wexford Wildfowl Reserve
Dunganstown
Irish National Heritage Park
Wexford
Newbawn
Wexford Harbour
John F Kennedy Arboretum
Slieve Coillte (270m)
Johnstown Castle
Rosslare Point
Campile
Rosslare Strand
Rosslare Harbour
Waterford
Dunbrody Abbey
Arthurstown
Tintern Abbey
Bridgetown
Tagoat
Rosslare
Ballyhack
Passage East
Duncannon
Duncormick
Tacumshane Windmill
St Margaret's Beach
Waterford Airport
Booley Bay
Fethard-on-Sea
Kilmore Quay
Carne
Dollar Bay
Ballyteige Bay
Forlorn Point
Carnsore Point
St George's Channel
Dunmore East
Waterford Harbour
Templetown
Tramore Bay
Slade
Brownstown Head
Churchtown
Hook Head
Saltee Islands
Tacumshin Windmill

0 20 km
0 10 miles

5 Curracloe Beach (p170)
Walking along a seemingly endless vision of white powder.

6 Waterford City (p178)
Reliving the days of the Vikings and Normans in excellent museums.

7 Altamont Gardens (p195)
Tiptoeing through tulips, azaleas, roses and geraniums in County Carlow.

8 Barrow Way (p196)
Cycling along the verdant towpath between

Graiguenamanagh and St Mullins.

9 Dunbrody Famine Ship (p176) Learning about Ireland's poignant history aboard this replica immigrant ship.

Wexford Town

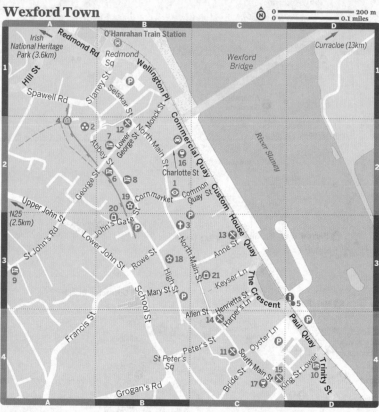

Wexford Town

⊙ Sights

1 Bull Ring	B2
Lone Pikeman Statue	(see 1)
2 Selskar Abbey	A2
3 St Iberius' Church	B3
4 Westgate	A2

✪ Activities, Courses & Tours

5 Wexford Walking Tours	D3

🛏 Sleeping

6 Abbey B&B	B2
7 Blue Door	B2
8 Clayton Whites Hotel	B2
9 Cuasnog	A3
10 Talbot Hotel	D4

✕ Eating

11 Cistín Eile	C4

12 Greenacres	B2
13 La Côte	C3
14 Simon Lambert & Sons	C4
15 Stable Diet Cafe	C4

🍷 Drinking & Nightlife

16 Centenary Stores	B2
17 Sky & the Ground	C4

✦ Entertainment

18 National Opera House	B3
19 Wexford Arts Centre	B2

🛍 Shopping

20 Blue Egg Gallery	B3
Bull Ring Market	(see 1)
21 Wexford Book Centre	C3

exhibition on the Great Famine is one of the best explanations of this national tragedy anywhere in Ireland.

Irish National Heritage Park   MUSEUM

(☑053-912 0733; www.inhp.com; Ferrycarrig; adult/family €9.50/25; ☺9.30am-6.30pm May-Aug, to 5.30pm Sep-Apr; P ♿) Over 9000 years of Irish history are squeezed together at this open-air museum. After a short audiovisual presentation, choose a guided or audio self-guided tour, taking in re-creations of a Neolithic farmstead, stone circle, ring fort, monastery, *crannóg* (artificial island), Viking shipyard and Norman castle (on the site of original Norman fort remains). Activities include archery and an adventure playground. The park is off the N11 on the western edge of Wexford town.

Wexford Wildfowl Reserve   NATURE RESERVE

(☑076 100 2660; www.wexfordwildfowlreserve.ie; North Slob; guided tours on request; ☺9am-5pm; P ♿) **FREE** The North Slob (from the Irish *slab*, meaning 'mud or mire') is a large area of reclaimed land to the north of Wexford harbour, drained by ditches and protected by Dutch-style dykes. It's prime birdwatching territory – each winter, it's home to 35% of the world's population of Greenland white-fronted geese – some 10,000 in total. There's an observation tower, assorted hides and a visitor centre with detailed exhibits. It's signposted 3km north of Wexford on the R741.

🧭 Tours

Wexford Walking Tours   WALKING

(☑087 265 8276; www.wexfordwalkingtours.net; €7; ☺11am Mon-Sat Mar-Oct) A guided walking tour is the best way to understand Wexford's complicated past and confusing remains. These 90-minute walks depart from the tourist office (p171).

🎊 Festivals & Events

Wexford Opera Festival   OPERA

(www.wexfordopera.com; tickets €60-150; ☺late Oct–early Nov) This 12-day festival is the country's premier opera event with rarely performed operas and shows playing to packed audiences. Fringe street theatre, poetry readings and exhibitions give the town a festive atmosphere, and many local bars run amateur singing competitions. Book tickets in advance.

🛏 Sleeping

★ Cuasnog   B&B $$

(☑053-912 3637; www.cuasnog.com; St John's Rd; s/d €75/120; P 🤝🐾) Hosts Caitríona and Theo not only extend a warm welcome, but also treat you to a pot of tea with smoked salmon and soda bread on arrival. The compact rooms have a comfortable feel with rustic furniture and fireplaces; breakfast includes homemade scones and local organic produce. Located a few minutes' walk from the centre on a sleepy residential street.

Blue Door   B&B $$

(☑053-912 1047; www.bluedoor.ie; 18 Lower George St; s/d/f from €50/70/100; 🤝) Behind the eponymous cobalt-blue door of this 200-year-old Georgian townhouse, homely bedrooms with a period feel are brightened by tall windows; they're quiet despite the central location.

Abbey B&B   B&B $$

(☑053-912 4408; www.abbeyhouse.ie; 34-36 Abbey St; s/d €45/80; P 🤝) This cute, black-and-white B&B blazes with window boxes trailing red blooms in summer. Its seven rooms vary considerably in size, but all have private bathrooms with walk-in showers. Breakfast is served in a cheery floral-themed dining room.

Clayton Whites Hotel   HOTEL $$

(☑053-912 2311; www.claytonwhiteshotel.com; Abbey St; s/d from €79/94; P @ 🤝🏊) Recently rebranded and revamped, this super-cool hotel with its high-tech spa enjoys a prime location in the city centre. Warm up at one of the welcoming bars, enjoy a choice of restaurants or just retreat to your room. Pay a bit more (from €129) for a slickly decorated executive room with an estuary view – all metal right-angles, tech touches and sparkling glass.

Talbot Hotel   HOTEL $$

(☑053-912 2566; www.talbotwexford.ie; Trinity St; s/d from €75/90; P @ 🤝🏊) A landmark on Wexford's waterfront, this modern hotel has water views from many of its revamped rooms. Facilities include a steam room, sauna, gym and indoor pool. The stylish, high-ceilinged Ballast Bank bar and grill dishes up traditional pub grub along with regular live music.

COUNTIES WEXFORD, WATERFORD, CARLOW & KILKENNY WEXFORD TOWN & AROUND

CURRACLOE BEACH

Soft white sand, gentle surf and lack of development are the most appealing features of the 11km-long, Blue Flag–rated Curracloe Beach. On sunny days families flock to the beach, but due to its vast size you can easily find a half-acre to call your own. The strand doubled for Omaha Beach in the famous D-Day opening scenes of the movie *Saving Private Ryan* (1998). The beach is 13km northeast of Wexford, signposted at various points along the R741 and R742 roads.

There are good walking trails through the pine forests and sand dunes of **Raven Nature Reserve** at the south end, and it's possible to cycle to the beach from Wexford town, via waymarked cycle route 2 – ask for a map at the Wexford tourist office.

✗ Eating

Stable Diet Cafe CAFE $

(☎053-914 9012; http://stabledietcafe.com; 100 South Main St; mains €8-12; ⊗8.30am-5pm Mon-Sat; ▥) ⚲ This bright and busy cafe is a Wexford institution, famous for its home-baked breads, scones and cakes; the lunch menu consists of freshly made soups and sandwiches, while breakfast choices include homemade granola and French toast with bacon and maple syrup.

Simon Lambert & Sons PUB FOOD $

(Simon's Place; ☎053-918 0041; http://simon-lambertandsons.ie; 37 South Main St; mains €8-10; ⊗food served 9.30am-noon & 12.30-4pm Mon-Sat; ☏) This atmospheric, low-ceilinged pub serves good food during the day, with breakfast offerings that run from scrambled eggs and toast to the full Irish fry-up, complete with excellent coffee. The lunch menu includes tasty and inventive sandwiches, gourmet burgers and pulled pork rolls, and a grand selection of craft beers to wash it all down.

★ Cistín Eile MODERN IRISH $$

(☎053-912 1616; 80 South Main St; lunch mains €8-17, 3-course dinner €35; ⊗noon-3pm Mon-Sat, 6-9pm Wed-Sat; ☏) ⚲ Bring a hearty appetite when you visit this always-busy restaurant – as the motto on the wall says, *Is maith an t-anlann an t-ocras* (hunger makes a great sauce). Expect the daily menu of locally sourced artisan produce to include slow-cooked beef, bacon and cabbage, mashed potatoes, foraged salad leaves, intense flavours and generous helpings.

★ Greenacres BISTRO, DELI $$

(☎053-912 2975; www.greenacres.ie; 7 Selskar St; mains €10-25, 3-course set menu €37.50; ⊗bistro 9am-5pm Mon-Sat; ☏) Eating, shopping, culture...this place has it covered! Irish cheeses and local produce are beautifully displayed in the food hall, the wine selection is the best south of Dublin, and the gourmet bistro gets star rating for innovative ingredients such as wild pigeon, rock oysters and smoked rabbit. The upper floors house an excellent art gallery.

La Côte SEAFOOD $$

(☎053-912 2122; http://lacote.ie; Custom House Quay; 3-course dinner menu €34; ⊗5.30-9.30pm Tue-Sat; ☏) ⚲ This place has been raking in various awards – notably Irish Seafood Restaurant of the Year – and delighting diners with its unpretentious and affordable take on the finest of local seafood. And there's always at least one inventive vegetarian dish on the menu, such as toasted oat and pearl barley risotto with ramsons, roast garlic and crème fraîche.

🍷 Drinking & Nightlife

Centenary Stores PUB

(☎053-912 4424; www.thestores.ie; Charlotte St; ⊗10am-11pm) One of Wexford's livelier spots, this former warehouse is a mix of old and new. A downstairs dark-wood pub with basic food and a crusty local clientele contrasts with a pulsating modern designer nightclub, the Backroom (open 9pm to 2am Thursday to Sunday), that attracts a spirited, youthful crowd at weekends. Sunday lunchtime trad music sessions in summer.

Sky & the Ground PUB

(www.facebook.com/TheSkyAndTheGround; 112-113 South Main St; ⊗2-11.30pm Mon-Thu, to 12.30am Fri & Sat, to 11pm Sun) A long-standing Wexford favourite, the Sky & the Ground's decor is classic, with a roaring fire and walls covered in old enamel signs. Live music sessions often take place on Thursday and Sunday, and during the summer there's an outdoor deck upstairs.

⭐ Entertainment

★ National Opera House
OPERA

(📞 box office 053-912 2144; www.nationalopera house.ie; High St; tickets €20-150; 🎧) Opened in 2008 Wexford's gleaming opera house packs more architectural punch inside than out, but sports state-of-the-art acoustics and superb views from the top-floor bar. In addition to hosting the opera festival (p169) in autumn, it stages theatre productions and concerts all year round.

Wexford Arts Centre
DANCE

(📞 053-912 3764; www.wexfordartscentre.ie; Cornmarket; tickets €10-20; 🎧📶) Housed in the 18th-century market hall, this centre hosts exhibitions, theatre (including occasional productions in Irish), dance and music, and has a good cafe.

🛍 Shopping

Wexford Book Centre
BOOKS

(📞 053-912 3543; www.thebookcentre.ie; 5 South Main St; ⏱ 9am-6pm Mon-Sat, 1-5pm Sun) Lots of worthwhile Irish titles plus local guides and maps.

Blue Egg Gallery
ARTS & CRAFTS

(📞 053-914 5862; www.facebook.com/blueegg gallery; John's Gate St; ⏱ 11am-5.30pm Tue-Sat) One of several commercial galleries and craft shops in town – ask the tourist office (p171) for a full list – the Blue Egg concentrates on contemporary Irish crafts in a range of materials, including ceramics, metal and glass.

Bull Ring Market
ARTS & CRAFTS

(www.facebook.com/TheBullringMarketWexford; Bull Ring; ⏱ 9.30am-4pm Fri & Sat) There is a lively weekly market at the Bull Ring (p165) with food and drink stalls, crafts, vintage clothes, antiques, jewellery, homewares, toys and accessories.

ℹ Information

Wexford Tourist Office (📞 053-912 3111; www. visitwexford.ie; Quay Front; ⏱ 9am-5.15pm Mon-Sat; 🎧) Has maps and leaflets showing local walks and cycling routes.

ℹ Getting There & Around

BUS
Buses depart from the **train station**.
Dublin €20, 1¼ hours, hourly
Enniscorthy €8, 20 minutes, hourly
Rosslare Harbour €6.20, 25 minutes, six daily
Waterford €12.50, one hour, seven daily

Wexford Bus (www.wexfordbus.com) operates to/from Dublin Airport (€20, 2¾ hours, hourly) via Enniscorthy, Ferns and Dublin city centre.

TAXI
Wexford Cabs (📞 053-9 123 123; www.wexford cabs.ie) A 24-hour taxi service, including to Rosslare Harbour and Dublin Airport.

TRAIN
Trains from **O'Hanrahan Station** (📞 053-912 2522; Redmond Sq) service **Dublin Connolly Station** (p131) (€27.65, four daily, 2½ hours) and Rosslare Harbour (€5.95, four daily, 25 minutes).

Rosslare Harbour

POP 1200

Busy, functional Rosslare Harbour has connections to Wales and France from the **Europort ferry terminal**, home also to **Rosslare Europort train station**. The road leading uphill from the harbour is the N25. The only reason to stay here is if you have to catch an early ferry.

🛏 Sleeping

St Martin's Rd (signposted Rosslare Harbour Village, on the right approaching from Wexford) is lined with B&Bs that cater to ferry passengers with early/late starts.

★ O'Leary's Farm B&B
B&B $$

(📞 053-913 3134; www.olearysfarm.com; Killilane, Kilrane; s/d from €45/76; 🅿🎧🐾) This working organic farm offers four homely guest rooms, three with sea views. The delightful sitting room has a fireplace, a piano and plenty of books. Breakfast includes vegan, vegetarian and coeliac options, the farm's produce and homemade bread. Follow the N25 and turn off at the Kilrane Inn, then follow signs south and then east for 4km. No credit cards.

ℹ Getting There & Away

Buses and trains depart from the Rosslare Europort station, beside the ferry terminal.

BOAT
Rosslare ferries link Ireland to Wales and France (note that the frequency of sailings may be reduced in winter). Destinations include the following:

Cherbourg (France) Both Stena Line (www. stenaline.ie) and Irish Ferries (www.irishferries. com) sail this route, with three or four crossings a week between them (foot passenger from €54, car and driver from €139, 19 hours).

GUINNESS BOOK OF RECORDS

During a wildfowling trip to the Slobs near Wexford in 1951, the chairman of Guinness Brewery, Sir Hugh Beaver, shot at but missed a golden plover. This provoked a spirited debate over whether it, or the red grouse, was Europe's fastest game bird. Sir Hugh realised that similar debates regularly cropped up all over the world, and that publishing definitive answers could prove profitable.

He was right about that – the first *Guinness Book of Records* was an immediate bestseller when it was published in 1955, and today it is itself a record-holder, as the world's biggest-selling copyrighted book – but wrong about Europe's fastest game bird (it's actually the spur-wing goose).

Fishguard (Wales) Stena Line runs to Wales twice daily (foot passenger from €39, car and driver from €119, 3¼ hours).

Pembroke (Wales) Irish Ferries offers two crossings daily (foot passenger €39, car and driver from €115, four hours).

Roscoff (France) Irish Ferries runs this route once or twice a week from May to September only (foot passenger from €61, car and driver from €139, 17½ hours).

BUS

Bus Éireann (www.buseireann.ie) has services to numerous Irish towns and cities, including Dublin (€24, three hours, six daily), changing at Wexford (€6.20, 25 minutes), and Cork (€29, 4½ hours, six daily) via Waterford (€20.80, 1½ hours).

TRAIN

Irish Rail runs four trains daily on the Rosslare Europort–Dublin Connolly Station route (€29.20, 2¾ hours) via Wexford (€5.95, 25 minutes).

South of Rosslare Harbour

A maze of minor roads meanders among the flatlands and tidal lagoons that spread from Rosslare Harbour to Kilmore Quay. Traditional Wexford thatched cottages – with mud walls, half-hipped roofs and trademark small, square porches – brighten the roadsides, and a sandy beach is never far away.

Sights

Lady's Island Lake LAKE
This lake's brackish waters, separated from the sea by a barrier beach, are an important breeding ground for rare roseate terns. The lake encloses **Our Lady's Island** (www.ourladysisland.ie), the site of an early Augustinian priory and still the focus of an annual pilgrimage in August/September. Pilgrims make nine circuits of the island, many of them barefoot (in olden times they used to crawl). Outside of pilgrimage season the pilgrim path makes for a lovely walk (2km); don't miss the picturesque priory graveyard, awash with wild garlic in spring.

Tacumshane Windmill HISTORIC BUILDING
(http://meylersmillhouse.com/the-windmill; Tacumshane) FREE Tacumshane Windmill is a rare survivor of the mills that once dotted this landscape, and the only complete windmill in the Republic of Ireland. Built in the 19th century using timber washed up on local beaches, it sports a cute thatched cap. It's on a minor road, a few kilometres west of Our Lady's Island; ask for the key at the neighbouring Millhouse pub.

Eating

Meyler's Millhouse Bar & Restaurant PUB FOOD $$
(053-913 1700; http://meylersmillhouse.com; Tacumshane; mains €12-19; food served 5-9pm Fri-Sat, 12.30-8pm Sun; P) This country pub has a good beer garden overlooked by Tacumshane Windmill (p172), and serves fish and chips, homemade burgers and other pub grub (kids' menu available). It's 5km southwest of Rosslare Harbour, and a bit hard to find; look out for the pub's own signposts.

Kilmore Quay

Pop 372
Kilmore Quay is part commercial fishing port, and part picturesque village lined with thatched cottages, where the cry of gulls and smell of the ocean provide the appropriate atmosphere for sampling the local seafood. The harbour is the jumping-off point for Ireland's largest bird sanctuary, the Saltee Islands.

Sea anglers can fish for sea bass, plaice and flounder from the shore, or charter a boat from the harbour (details at www.visitkilmorequay.com) for wreck and reef fishing.

☉ Sights

Ballyteigue Burrow
Nature Reserve NATURE RESERVE
(www.npws.ie; ⊙24hr) FREE The beach and
sand dunes of Ballyteigue Burrow Nature
Reserve stretch for 9km northwest from
Kilmore Quay, and are the summer home
of chattering terns and serenading skylarks. The salt marsh and mudflats behind
the dunes are an important habitat for
overwintering birds such as golden plovers, black-tailed godwits and pale-bellied
brent geese.

Ballycross Apple Farm FARM
(☎053-913 5160; www.ballycross.com; Bridgetown; adult/child €3.50/2.50; ⊙noon-6pm Sat &
Sun Apr-Oct, call for hours Nov-Mar; ℗⑉) This
working farm gets top marks from the kids
for its pedal-powered tractors and go-karts,
animal-feeding sessions and signposted
walking trails that run via riverbanks, woodland and orchards. The farm shop sells apples, apple juice, chutneys and jams, and the
cafe serves delicious homemade waffles and
pancakes. It's about 9km north of Kilmore
Quay, on a minor road 2km southwest of
Bridgetown.

Saltee Islands ISLAND
(www.salteeislands.info; ⊙11.30am-4.30pm)
Once the haunt of privateers, smugglers and
'dyvers pyrates', the Saltee Islands now have
a peaceful existence as one of Europe's most
important bird sanctuaries. More than 220
species have been recorded here, most of
them passing migrants; the main breeding
populations include chough, gannet, guillemot, razorbill, kittiwake, puffin and Manx
shearwater. Boats make the 4km trip from
Kilmore Quay harbour, but landing is weather-dependent. Book through **Declan Bates**
(☎053-912 9684, 087 252 9736; declanbates@
eircom.net; Kilmore Quay Harbour; day trips €30).

The 90-hectare Great Saltee and the
40-hectare Little Saltee (closed to visits)
were inhabited as long ago as 3500 to 2000
BC. From the 13th century until the dissolution of the monasteries, they were the property of Tintern Abbey (p174), after which
various owners were granted the land. The
islands are now privately owned.

The best time to visit is the spring and
early-summer nesting season. The birds
leave once the chicks can fly; by early August
it's eerily quiet. There are no toilets or other
facilities on the islands.

✺ Festivals & Events

Seafood Festival FOOD & DRINK
(www.kilmorequayseafoodfestival.com; ⊙Jul; ⑉)
A four-day festival of music, exhibitions,
guided nature walks, kayak races and, of
course, local seafood.

🍴 Sleeping & Eating

Mill Road Farm B&B $
(☎053-912 9633; www.millroadfarm.com; R739;
s/d €50/80; ℗⑈) About 2km northeast of
Kilmore Quay, this dairy farm has four
daintily decorated guest rooms (three with
sea views beyond the paddock) with lots
of floral fabrics; the owner breeds horses
for racing. The sitting room has plenty of
games and books for wet days. Breakfast
includes homemade bread and free-range
eggs.

Silver Fox Seafood Restaurant SEAFOOD $$$
(☎053-912 9888; www.thesilverfox.ie; Kilmore
Quay; mains lunch €9-20, dinner €18-35; ⊙noon-
8pm Easter-Oct, shorter hours Fri-Sun only rest of
year, closed Jan–mid-Feb; ⑉) ✦ The Silver Fox's
fresh-from-the-ocean offerings include locally landed plaice, langoustines, crab and mussels, plus daily specials depending on what
arrives at the quay. The dining room exudes
white-table clothed elegance; don't arrive in
flip-flops. Booking advised at weekends.

ℹ Getting There & Away

Wexford Bus (www.wexfordbus.com) runs to/
from Wexford four times daily except Sunday
(€8, 30 minutes).

Hook Peninsula

The road that leads around the long, tapering finger of the Hook Peninsula is signposted as the **Ring of Hook coastal drive**.
Around every other bend is a quiet beach,
a crumbling fortress, a stately abbey or a
seafood restaurant, and the world's oldest working lighthouse stands tall at the
peninsula's tip.

Strongbow passed here on his way to
capture Waterford in 1170, reputedly in-
structing his men to land 'by Hook or by
Crooke' (the latter referring to the nearby
settlement of Crooke) – the origin of the
popular phrase.

There is limited public transport as far as
Fethard; beyond that you'll need a car or bike.

TINTERN ABBEY

Named after its Welsh counterpart, from where its first monks hailed, the atmospheric remains of **Tintern Abbey** (☑ 051-562 650; www.heritageireland.ie; Saltmills; adult/child €5/3; ⊙ 10am-5pm Apr-Oct; ℗) enjoy a lovely setting amid 40 hectares of woodland. Unusually for an abbey, it has a long history as a private residence. Following the dissolution of the monasteries in the early 16th century, Tintern was granted to Staffordshire nobleman Anthony Colclough, and his descendants continued to live here until 1959. The abbey is signposted off the R734, 5km north of Fethard.

William Marshal, Earl of Pembroke, founded the Cistercian abbey in the early 13th century after he nearly perished at sea and swore to establish a church if he made it ashore. The cloister walls, nave, crossing tower, chancel and south transept still stand tall, along with the conversions made by generations of Colcloughs to create a country residence out of a ruined abbey.

Walking trails wind into the surrounding woods, past lakes, streams and more crumbling ruins, including a small single cell church, to the beautiful, 200-year-old **Colclough Walled Garden** (☑ 083 306 4159; www.colcloughwalledgarden.com; Saltmills; adult/child €5/3; ⊙ 10am-6pm Apr-Sep, to 4pm Oct-Mar), which has been replanted and restored to its former glory.

Duncannon & Around

POP 305

The small, dusty holiday town of Duncannon slopes down to a sandy beach that's transformed into a surrealist canvas during August's **Duncannon Sand Sculpting Festival**.

About 4km northwest of Duncannon is pretty **Ballyhack**, where a car ferry (p184) makes the short crossing to Passage East in County Waterford. It's dominated by the 15th-century **Ballyhack Castle** (☑ 051-389 468; www.heritageireland.ie; ⊙ 9.30am-5pm Sat-Wed mid-May–late Aug) FREE, a Knights Hospitallers' tower house containing a small exhibition on the Crusades.

⊙ Sights

Duncannon Fort   FORT
(☑ 051-389 530; www.duncannonfort.ie; Duncannon; tours adult/child €6/1.50; ⊙ 10am-5.30pm mid-May–Aug) Star-shaped Duncannon Fort, just west of Duncannon village, was built in 1588 to stave off a feared attack by the Spanish Armada, and was later used by the Irish army as a WWI training base (most buildings here date from this period). There are four guided tours a day, each lasting around 45 minutes.

Dunbrody Abbey   HISTORIC BUILDING
(☑ 086 275 9149; www.dunbrodyabbey.com; Campile; abbey ruin adult/child €4/1, maze & museum €7/4; ⊙ 11am-5.30pm May, Jun & Sep, to 6pm Jul & Aug; ℗) Beside the R733, 9km north of Duncannon, ruined Dunbrody Abbey is a remarkably intact Cistercian abbey founded by Strongbow in 1170 and completed in 1220. Across the road from the ruins is a museum with a huge doll's house, minigolf and an entertaining yew-hedge maze made up of over 1500 trees. There are also tearooms and a craft shop.

🛏 Sleeping & Eating

★ **Glendine Country House**   GUESTHOUSE $$
(☑ 051-389 500; www.glendinehouse.com; Arthurstown; r €110; ℗ 🕿 🐾) Staying at this 19th-century country house is like staying with friends who have impeccable taste. Bay windows overlook grounds populated by deer, cattle and sheep, and paintings by local artists adorn the walls. The rooms typically have hardwood floors, chandeliers and antiques; request room 9 with its princely proportions and king-sized bed. The house is 5km north of Duncannon.

Aldridge Lodge Restaurant & Guesthouse   INN $$
(☑ 051-389 116; www.aldridgelodge.com; Duncannon; s/d from €50/90; ℗ 🕿) In a windswept spot amid open fields above Duncannon beach, Aldridge takes a bit of finding. But it's worth it for the elegant, contemporary guest rooms and fresh local seafood such as Hook Head crab claws or Kilmore cod (dinner €40; served 7pm till late Wednesday to Sunday). Two caveats: book your table in advance, and children aged under seven aren't allowed.

Dunbrody Country
House Hotel   HOTEL $$$

(☑ 051-389 600; www.dunbrodyhouse.com; Arthurstown; s/d €190/310; P ☎) Chef Kevin
Dundon is a familiar face on Irish TV and
author of several cookbooks; he even has
his own line of cookware. His spa hotel, in a
period-decorated 1830s Georgian manor in
120-hectare grounds, is the stuff of foodies'
fantasies, with a gourmet restaurant (dinner
around €65 to €80 per head) and cookery
school (one-day courses from €175).

Sqigl Restaurant &
Roche's Bar   MODERN IRISH $$

(☑ 051-389 188; www.sqiglrestaurant.com; Quay
Rd, Duncannon; mains restaurant €20-25, bar €7-
13; ☺ restaurant 6-9pm Wed-Sat, bar noon-9pm
daily; ☎) Local produce is the mainstay
of Sqigl, where dishes range from spring
lamb to local seafood (bookings essential).
Roche's Bar adjoins and has excellent bar
food – try the seafood chowder – and an inviting atmosphere with vintage advertising
posters. Trad music sessions on Fridays.

Hook Head

The journey from Fethard to Hook Head
takes in a hypnotic stretch of horizon, with
few houses between the flat, open fields of
the tapering peninsula. Views extend across
Waterford Harbour and, on a clear day, to
the Comeragh and Galtee Mountains.

This is prime day-trip country, from
Wexford or Waterford. Villages such as
Slade (where most of the activity is in
the swirl of seagulls above the ruined castle and harbour) beguile. Beaches include
the wonderfully secluded Dollar Bay and
Booley Bay, just beyond Templetown en
route to Duncannon.

◉ Sights

★ Hook Lighthouse   LIGHTHOUSE

(☑ 051-397 055; www.hookheritage.ie; Hook
Head; adult/child under 5yr €9/free; ☺ 9.30am-
6pm Jun-Aug, to 5.30pm Sep-May; P 🖶) On
its southern tip, Hook Head is capped by
the world's oldest working lighthouse, a
modern light flashing atop a 13th-century
tower. Access is by half-hour guided tour,
which includes a climb up the 115 steps
for great views. The visitor centre has a
good cafe while the grassy grounds and
surrounding shore are popular for picnics
and walks.

It's said that monks first lit a beacon on
the head in the 5th century, and that the
first Viking invaders were so happy to have
a guiding light that they left them alone.
In the early 13th century William Marshal erected a more permanent structure,
which is still standing today beneath the
lighthouse's neat, black-and-white exterior.

Loftus Hall   HISTORIC BUILDING

(☑ 051-397 728; www.loftushall.ie; Hook Peninsula;
adult/child daytime €10/5, nighttime €18; ☺ noon-
5pm & 7-10pm Jul & Aug, weekends only Apr-Jun,
school holidays Sep-Mar; P) About 3.5km northeast of Hook Head, this crumbling manor
house gazes over to Dunmore East across the
mouth of Waterford Harbour. Dating from
the 1600s and rebuilt in the 1870s, Loftus
Hall is reputed to be one of the most haunted
houses in Ireland. Daytime tours are historical, while evening tours are 'scary' – for adults
only – and comprise an hour-long interactive
visit where the guide recounts the ghostly
history of the building. Check the website for
special events.

🏃 Activities

There are brilliant, blustery walks on both
sides of Hook Head. Poke around the tide
pools while watching for surprise showers
from blowholes on the western side of the
peninsula. The rocks here are carboniferous
limestone, rich in fossils. Search carefully
and you may find 350-million-year-old bra-
chiopod shells, lacy bryozoans and tiny disc-
like pieces of crinoids, ancient relatives of the
sea urchin. The slabs beneath the seaward
side of Hook Lighthouse are a good place to
look.

At low tide there's a good walk between
Grange and Carnivan beaches, past caves,
rock pools and Baginbun Head which,
surmounted by a 19th-century Martello
tower, is where the Normans first landed
in 1169 to begin their conquest of Ireland.
It's a good vantage point for birdwatching: more than 200 species have been recorded passing through. You might even
spot dolphins or whales in the estuary.

New Ross

POP 8040

The big attraction at New Ross (Rhos
Mhic Triúin) is the opportunity to board a
19th-century Famine ship. But New Ross'
historical links stretch back much further –

to the 12th century, when it developed as a Norman port on the River Barrow. A group of rebels tried to seize the town during the 1798 Rising. They were repelled by the defending garrison, leaving 3000 dead and much of the place in tatters.

Today it's not a pretty town, but the eastern bank retains some intriguingly steep and narrow streets, and the remains of a medieval abbey. Ask at the tourist office for a map of the town's history trail (allow 1½ hours).

Sights & Activities

★ **Dunbrody Famine Ship** MUSEUM
(☑ 051-425 239; www.dunbrody.com; The Quay; adult/child €10/6; ☺ 9am-6pm Apr-Sep, to 5pm Oct-Mar;) Called 'coffin ships' due to their fatality rate, the leaky, smelly boats that hauled a generation of Irish emigrants to America are reimagined on board this replica ship on the New Ross waterfront. The emigrants' sorrowful yet often inspiring stories are brought to life by costumed actors during 45-minute tours. A 10-minute introductory film provides historical background about the mid-19th-century Ireland they were leaving.

Galley River Cruising Restaurant BOATING
(☑ 051-421 723; www.rivercruises.ie; North Quay; lunch/afternoon/dinner €25/12/40; ☺ Apr-Oct) This floating restaurant offers scenic cruises along the 'Three Sisters' rivers – the Suir, Nore and Barrow – heading upstream to Inistioge or St Mullins or downstream towards Waterford depending on the tide. Two-hour lunch cruises depart at 12.30pm, 1½-hour afternoon tea cruises set off at 3pm, and three-hour dinner cruises leave at 6pm.

Sleeping & Eating

MacMurrough Farm Cottages COTTAGE $$
(☑ 051-421 383; www.macmurrough.com; MacMurrough; 2-person cottages from €60; ☺ mid-Mar–Oct;) A strutting rooster serves as an alarm clock at Brian and Jenny's remote hilltop farm. These well-priced self-catering cottages are located in the former stables and pleasantly furnished with good facilities. Turn off the N30 at the Topaz petrol station 3.5km northeast of New Ross and follow the signs up a series of tracks.

Brandon House Hotel HOTEL $$
(☑ 051-421 703; www.brandonhousehotel.ie; N25 Ring Rd; r from €87;) This sympathetically extended Victorian red-brick

manor certainly lives up to its reputation as family-friendly, with kids happily bounding around the place. Winning elements include river views, open log fires, a library bar and spacious modern rooms, as well as a spa. It's signposted off the N25 Ring Rd on the southern edge of New Ross.

★ **Cafe Nutshell** CAFE $
(☑ 051-422 777; inanutshell8@gmail.com; 8 South St; mains €6-16; ☺ 9am-6pm Mon-Sat;) Scones, breads and buns are all baked on the premises, inventive hot lunch specials utilise local produce and there's a great range of smoothies, juices and organic wines. Mains come with an array of fresh salads. The adjacent health food shop and deli are perfect for picnic provisions.

Information

New Ross Tourist Office (☑ 051-425 239; jfktrust@iol.ie; The Quay; ☺ 9am-6pm Apr-Sep, to 5pm Oct-Mar) Located in the same building as the Dunbrody Famine Ship ticket office.

Getting There & Away

Buses depart from The Quay and travel to Waterford (€9.40, 30 minutes, eight to 12 daily), Wexford (€9.60, 45 minutes, three to four daily) and Dublin (€18, three hours, at least four daily).

Enniscorthy

POP 11,381

County Wexford's second-largest town, Enniscorthy (Inis Coirthaidh) has a warren of steep streets descending from Augustus Pugin's cathedral to a Norman castle and the River Slaney. The town is inextricably linked to some of the fiercest fighting of the 1798 Rising, when rebels captured the town and set up camp at Vinegar Hill.

Sights

National 1798 Rebellion Centre MUSEUM
(☑ 053-923 4699; www.1798centre.ie; Parnell Rd; adult/child €7/3; ☺ 9.30am-5pm Mon-Fri Apr-Sep, 10am-4pm Mon-Fri Oct-Mar;) This exhibition does a fine job of explaining the background to one of Ireland's pivotal historical events. It covers the French and American revolutions, which helped spark Wexford's abortive uprising against British rule in Ireland, before chronicling the Battle of Vinegar Hill. One of the most bloodthirsty battles of the 1798 Rising and a turning point in the struggle, it took place just outside

WEXFORD & THE KENNEDYS

In 1848 Patrick Kennedy escaped a famine-stricken County Wexford aboard an emigrant ship similar to the **Dunbrody Famine Ship** in New Ross. Hoping to find better prospects in America, he succeeded beyond his wildest dreams: his descendants included rum-runners, senators and a US president. The family's Irish roots are remembered at two sites near New Ross, signposted from the Famine ship on a 24km driving route known as the Emigrant Trail.

John F Kennedy Arboretum (051-388 171; www.heritageireland.ie; Ballysop; adult/child €5/3; 10am-8pm May-Aug, to 6.30pm Apr & Sep, to 5pm Oct-Mar; P) This beautiful woodland park, dedicated to the memory of JFK, has 4500 species of trees and shrubs spread across 252 hectares of woods and gardens, where walking trails meander among groves of eucalyptus, redwood, oak, magnolia and many other iconic species. The park has a small visitor centre, a tearoom (May to September) and a picnic area; a miniature train tootles around in the summer months. It's 12km south of New Ross, signposted off the R733.

Kennedy Homestead (051-388 264; www.kennedyhomestead.ie; Dunganstown; adult/child €7.50/6; 9.30am-5.30pm; P) The birthplace of Patrick Kennedy, great-grandfather of John F Kennedy, is a farm that still looks much as it must have done 160 years ago. When JFK visited the farm in 1963 and hugged the current owner's grandmother, it was his first public display of affection, according to his sister Jean. A small museum examines the Kennedy dynasty's history on both sides of the Atlantic. It's on a minor road 7km south of New Ross, signposted from R733.

Enniscorthy. A visit here provides context for a walk up Vinegar Hill itself.

From April to September, joint tickets for the centre and Enniscorthy Castle (p177) are available (adult/child €10/5).

Vinegar Hill
HISTORIC SITE
(www.vinegarhill.ie; dawn-dusk) **FREE** Scene of one of the most important battles of Ireland's 1798 rebellion against British rule, this hill just outside Enniscorthy is topped with a memorial to the Rising, and dotted with explanatory signs about the battlefield. A battle reenactment takes place each year on the first weekend in August. Access is from a car park on the east side of the hill, reached via Drumgoold Rd; it's about 2km east of Enniscorthy Castle, a 30-minute walk.

Enniscorthy Castle
CASTLE
(053-923 4699; www.enniscorthycastle.ie; Castle Hill; adult/child €5/3; 9.30am-5pm Mon-Fri Apr-Sep, 10am-4pm Mon-Fri Oct-Mar, noon-5pm Sat & Sun year-round) This stout, four-towered keep was originally built by the Normans; like much else in these parts, it was surrendered to Cromwell in 1649. During the 1798 Rising, rebels used this castle as a prison, and from 1901 to 1953 it was the family home of local businessman and landowner Henry J Roche. It now houses a museum about the history of both town and castle,

and has a rooftop deck with spectacular views.

From April to September, joint tickets for the castle and the National 1798 Rebellion Centre are available (adult/child €10/5).

Festivals & Events

Strawberry Festival
FOOD & DRINK
(www.enniscorthytourism.com/events; Jun) Celebrating the favourite crop of Ireland's sunny southeast, this eclectic event celebrated its 50th year in 2017 and includes an agricultural show, a farmers market, cookery demonstrations, live music, children's events and the crowning of the Strawberry Queen. Pubs extend their hours, bands are booked, and strawberries and cream are on sale everywhere.

Sleeping

Clone House
B&B $$
(053-936 6113; www.clonehouse.ie; Clone; s/d from €50/90; P) Stepping into this ivy-clad Georgian farmhouse is like stepping back in time, with the smell of beeswax polish wafting from glowing mahogany furniture, and light sparkling from antique gilt mirrors and hand-cut Irish crystal; bedrooms have all mod cons, though. It's set in beautiful gardens beside the River Bann, on a quiet back road 9km north of Enniscorthy.

Riverside Park
HOTEL $$

(☑ 053-923 7800; www.riversideparkhotel.com; The Promenade; r from €96; P 🛜 🌊) Enjoy strolls along the grassy banks of the river from this superbly positioned hotel where a dramatic lobby in a circular tower sets the scene. Comfortable rooms are decorated in neutral creams and browns, and most have balconies and river views. This is a popular hotel for weddings so Saturdays may be booked up and/or noisy!

Woodbrook House
GUESTHOUSE $$

(☑ 053-925 5114; www.woodbrookhouse.ie; Killanne; s/d €105/170; ⊙ Easter-Jun & Aug-Sep; P 🛜) 🚲 Rebuilt after sustaining damage in the 1798 Rising, this glorious Georgian country house has a superb setting beneath the Blackstairs Mountains. The lobby features a gravity-defying spiral staircase that amazes now just as it did over 200 years ago. Green practices are used throughout and you can make arrangements for dinner (€50; organic, of course). It is 13km west of Enniscorthy.

✗ Eating & Drinking

★ Cotton Tree Cafe
CAFE $

(☑ 053-923 4641; Slaney Pl; mains €5-13; ⊙ 8.30am-5pm Mon-Sat, 10am-5pm Sun; ♿) A pleasantly informal cafe charmingly decorated with homely and historical artwork. The menu includes gourmet soups and sandwiches with ingredients such as roast Irish beef and hummus. There's also a choice of imaginative salads and daily lunch specials such as fish pie, Asian pork burger and Indonesian curry.

Farmers Market
MARKET $

(www.wexfordfarmersmarkets.com; Abbey Sq Car Park; ⊙ 9am-2pm Sat) Enniscorthy's farmers market sells local and organic goods and prepared foods. Look for Carrigbyrne cheese.

Galo Chargrill Restaurant
PORTUGUESE $$

(☑ 053-923 8077; 19 Main St; mains €15-23; ⊙ noon-2.30pm & 5-10pm Wed-Sat, noon-9pm Sun) This small Portuguese restaurant has a big reputation. On balmy days the front opens up like the lid on a can of anchovies, and even on dull days the spicy chargrills – such as fillet of pork marinated in garlic and peri-peri, or prawn and squid skewer – provide a burst of Mediterranean sunshine.

Antique Tavern
PUB

(☑ 053-923 3428; www.facebook.com/the antiquetavern; 14 Slaney St; ⊙ 5-11.30pm Mon-Fri, 11am-midnight Sat & Sun) Slanted on the side of a steep street sloping up from the river, this creaky black-and-white pub dates from 1790 and falls somewhere between twee and rustic. It attracts a rousing crowd of locals, and has an upstairs glassed-in terrace for warm-weather tippling accompanied by great river views.

❶ Information

Tourist Office (☑ 053-923 4699; www.enniscorthytourism.com; Castle Hill; ⊙ 10am-5pm Mon-Fri, noon-5pm Sat & Sun Apr-Sep, 9.30am-4pm Mon-Fri Oct-Mar) Inside Enniscorthy castle.

❶ Getting There & Away

BUS

Bus Éireann (p694) runs to Dublin (€18, two hours, hourly) and Wexford (€5, 20 minutes, hourly).

Wexford Bus (www.wexfordbus.com) service 376 runs from Wexford town to Enniscorthy (€8, 25 minutes, three daily) and continues to Carlow via Bunclody and Ballon.

TRAIN

The train station is on the eastern bank of the river.

Trains run to Dublin Connolly (€25.85, 2¼ hours, four daily) and Wexford (€8.10, 20 minutes, five daily).

COUNTY WATERFORD

Diverse County Waterford harbours seaside resorts of all flavours along its sandy coastline; historic churches, cathedrals and castles; a warren of walking trails in the beautiful Nire Valley, concealed among the Comeragh and Monavullagh Mountains; and lively Waterford city, with its maze of medieval lanes and well-preserved Georgian architecture.

Waterford City

POP 53,504

Waterford (Port Láirge) is Ireland's oldest city – it celebrated its 1100th anniversary in 2014 – with a history that dates back to Viking times. Taking its name from the Old Norse *vedrarfjord* ('winter haven' or 'windy harbour') are just two of several possible translations), it remains a busy port city on a tidal reach of the River Suir, and is famous as the home of Waterford crystal.

Waterford

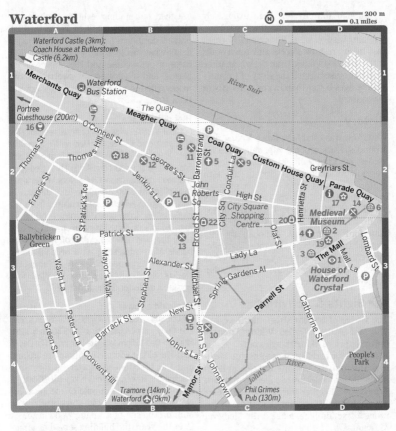

N
0 ————————— 200 m
0 ————————— 0.1 miles

Waterford

◎ Top Sights
1	House of Waterford Crystal	D3
2	Medieval Museum	D3

◎ Sights
3	Bishop's Palace	D3
4	Christ Church Cathedral	D3
5	Holy Trinity Cathedral	C2
6	Reginald's Tower	D2

🛏 Sleeping
7	Dooley's Hotel	A1
8	Granville Hotel	B2

😣 Eating
9	Berfranks	C2
10	Bodega!	C4
11	Carter's Chocolate Cafe	B2
12	La Bohème	B2
13	Momo	B3
14	Munster Bar	D2

😀 Drinking & Nightlife
15	Geoff's	B4
16	Henry Downes Bar	A2

✪ Entertainment
17	Central Arts	D2
18	Garter Lane Arts Centre	B2
19	Theatre Royal	D3

🛍 Shopping
20	Kite Design Studios	C3
21	Waterford Book Centre	B2
22	Waterford City Food & Craft Market	C3

Although the city has been extensively redeveloped, notably along the waterfront, it retains vestiges of its Viking and Norman past in the narrow streets and town walls of the so-called Viking Triangle, where three excellent museums tell the story of Ireland's Middle Ages better than in any other city in the country.

History

Waterford was established as a Viking port around 914. Its original city walls were extended by King John in 1210, making it Ireland's most powerful city. In the 15th century it resisted the forces of two pretenders to the English Crown, Lambert Simnel and Perkin Warbeck, and in 1649 defied Cromwell. In 1650 his forces returned and Waterford surrendered. Although the city escaped the customary slaughter, Catholics were either exiled to the west or shipped as slaves to the Caribbean, and the population dramatically declined.

◉ Sights & Activities

The wedge of ancient streets northwest of The Mall – the so-called **Viking Triangle** (www.waterfordvikingtriangle.com) – is home to three excellent museums: the Medieval Museum, the Bishop's Palace and Reginald's Tower, collectively called **Waterford Treasures**. Together they cover 1000 years of local history. If you only have time to visit one attraction here, make it the Medieval Museum.

The newly opened Waterford Greenway (p187) links the city to Dungarvan via a 46km all-abilities walking and cycling trail.

★**Medieval Museum**   MUSEUM
(www.waterfordtreasures.com; Greyfriars St; adult/child €7/free; ⊙9.15am-5pm Mon-Fri, 10am-5pm Sat, 11am-5pm Sun, longer hours Jun-Aug) Housed in a stunning modern building that incorporates several medieval buildings and part of the city wall in its basement (all on display), this museum documents Waterford's medieval history in glowing detail. The highlights of the collection are the extraordinary 15th-century **cloth-of-gold church vestments**, made from silk woven in Florence and embroidered in Bruges around 1460. Hidden beneath Christ Church Cathedral and forgotten for 123 years, they are a rare survivor and one of the great treasures of medieval Europe.

Other outstanding exhibits include the **Great Parchment Book of Waterford**, an original document that records in fascinating detail what medieval life was like, including cases of petty crime and the impact of the plague, and a **ceremonial sword** and two maces gifted to the city by England's Edward IV in 1462.

Bishop's Palace   MUSEUM
(🖉0761 102501; www.waterfordtreasures.com; The Mall; adult/child €7/free, with Medieval Museum €10/free; ⊙9.15am-5pm Mon-Fri, 10am-5pm Sat, 11am-5pm Sun, longer hours Jun-Aug) This Georgian mansion dating from 1741 covers Waterford's history from 1700 to 1970, and displays a wide-ranging selection of treasures from the city's coffers, from period furniture, oil paintings and Georgian silverware to old photos recording the 1960s heyday of Irish showbands. Most interesting is the original dining room set with period tableware including the world's oldest surviving piece of Waterford crystal, a decanter dating from 1789.

Reginald's Tower   MUSEUM
(🖉051-304 220; www.waterfordtreasures.com; The Quay; adult/child €5/3; ⊙9.30am-5.30pm late Mar–Dec, to 5pm Jan–late Mar, closed 24 Dec–6 Jan) The oldest complete building in Ireland and the first to use mortar, 13th-century Reginald's Tower, the city's key fortification, is an outstanding example of medieval architecture. Its 3m- to 4m-thick walls were built on the site of a Viking wooden tower. Over the years the building served as an arsenal, a prison and a mint; it now houses a museum recording the city's Viking and early medieval history. The sparse exhibits include the tiny but exquisite **Waterford Kite Brooch**, made around 1100.

★**House of Waterford Crystal**   FACTORY
(🖉051-317 000; www.waterfordvisitorcentre.com; The Mall; adult/child €13.50/5; ⊙9am-6pm Mon-Sat, 9.30am-6pm Sun Apr-Oct, shorter hours Nov-Mar) This large modern complex combines a retail shop and cafe with a factory offering a tour that shows how world-famous Waterford crystal is produced. The highlight is the blowing room where you can watch skilled artisans transform blobs of red-hot molten glass into delicate crystalware. The tour ends, inevitably, in the shop, where you can wonder at the twinkling displays that range from a €30 bottle coaster to a €30,000 crystal version of Cinderella's carriage.

The first Waterford glass factory was established at the western end of the riverside quays in 1783. Centuries later, after the boom of the 1980s and 1990s, the company fell on hard times and in 2009 was purchased by an American investment firm. Today around 60,000 pieces are made annually in Ireland, around 55% of the total output; the remainder is manufactured in Europe to strict Waterford standards.

Christ Church Cathedral CATHEDRAL
(☏ 051-858 958; www.christchurchwaterford.com; Cathedral Sq; ⊙ 10am-5pm Mon-Sat Easter-Oct, noon-3pm Mon-Sat Nov-Easter) **FREE** Christ Church Cathedral is Ireland's only neoclassical Georgian cathedral. Designed by local architect John Roberts, it was built on the site of an 11th-century Viking church, where the historic 12th-century marriage of Strongbow and Aoife took place. The rather grim highlight is the 15th-century **tomb of James Rice**, seven times Lord Mayor of Waterford: sculpted worms and frogs crawl over the effigy of his decaying corpse.

Holy Trinity Cathedral CATHEDRAL
(☏ 051-875 166; www.waterford-cathedral.com; Barronstrand St; ⊙ hrs vary depending on services) **FREE** The sumptuous interior of the city's Roman Catholic cathedral boasts a carved-oak baroque pulpit, painted pillars with Corinthian capitals and 10 Waterford crystal chandeliers. It was built between 1792 and 1796 by John Roberts, who also designed Christ Church Cathedral, making Waterford the only city where both the Catholic and Protestant cathedrals were designed by the same architect.

☞ Tours

★ Jack Burtchaell's
Guided Walking Tour WALKING
(☏ 051-873 711; www.jackswalkingtours.com; adult/ child €7/free; ⊙ 11.45am & 1.45pm mid-Mar–mid-Oct; ⋈) Jack's 'gift of the gab' brings Waterford's nooks and crannies to life, effortlessly squeezing 1000 years of history into one hour. Tours leave from near the tourist office (p183) – confirm the exact location there – picking up walkers from various hotels en route.

⊨ Sleeping

★ Granville Hotel HOTEL $$
(☏ 051-305 555; www.granville-hotel.ie; Meagher Quay; r from €99; ᴘ ⬡) The flood-lit 18th-century building overlooking the waterfront is the Granville, one of Ireland's oldest hotels.

Brocaded bedrooms maintain a touch of Georgian elegance, as do the public areas with their showstopping stained glass, historical prints and antiques. Star turns at breakfast are the organic porridge with Baileys and a perfect eggs Benedict.

Portree Guesthouse B&B $$
(☏ 051-874 574; www.portreeguesthouse.ie; Mary St; s/d from €65/109; ᴘ ⬡) This large, 24-room Georgian B&B is on a quiet street, but close to the city centre. It is well run by a couple of Londoners, and the rooms are spick and span, if not particularly memorable. There's a garden and library, a cosy sitting room with plenty of tourist information and brochures, plus 24-hour coffee and tea on offer. Popular with groups.

Dooley's Hotel HOTEL $$
(☏ 051-873 531; www.dooleys-hotel.ie; Merchants Quay; s/d from €109/119; @ ⬡) Locally owned and run like clockwork, Dooley's is a Waterford institution that has hosted family holidays, weddings and social gatherings for more than 70 years. It sports smartly refurbished bedrooms, and the breakfast is a belt-notch up from most hotel buffets, including organic porridge, fresh fruit compote and cooked options. The on-site Thai Therapy Centre offers various treatments.

Coach House at
Butlerstown Castle B&B $$
(☏ 051-384 656; www.butlerstowncastle.com; Butlerstown; r from €101; ⊙ Apr-Oct; ᴘ ⬡) This 19th-century stone-built B&B is as appealing inside as it is out, with deep, studded leather armchairs to sink into, toasty open fires to warm up by, canopied beds to drift off in, and pancakes to wake up to. It's a 10-minute drive from Waterford, 6km west of town on the L4047, signposted off the R680.

★ Waterford Castle HERITAGE HOTEL $$$
(☏ 051-878 203; www.waterfordcastleresort.com; The Island, Ballinakill; s/d from €169/398, lodges from €189; ᴘ @ ⬡) Getting away from it all is an understatement at this turreted mid-19th-century castle set on its own private island (a free car ferry at Ballinakill on the eastern edge of town provides round-the-clock access). All 19 castle rooms have hand-painted tiles and claw-foot baths, and some have four-poster beds. There are also 48 contemporary self-catering lodges on the island.

Both guests and nonguests can dine on organic fare in head chef Michael Thomas's sublime oak-panelled Munster Restaurant (three-course dinner €60), or play a round of golf on the hotel's own course (green fees €30 to €50).

Eating

★ Berfranks
CAFE, DELI $

(☑ 051-306 032; www.facebook.com/Berfranks; 86 The Quay; meals €8-11; ⊙ 8.30am-5pm Mon-Sat; 🕤) Irish artisan foods line the shelves in the deli section, while mouth-watering creations adorn the menu on the cafe side, its cosy back room lined with bookcases and sofas. This is an ideal place for a pit stop while you unravel Waterford's medieval past over daily lunch specials such as pulled beef brisket in Guinness barbecue sauce.

Carter's Chocolate Cafe
CAFE $

(☑ 051-841 802; www.facebook.com/thechoc cafe; 8 Barronstrand St; mains €4-6; ⊙ 8am-6.30pm Mon-Sat, 11am-6pm Sun; 🚼) The mint-chocolate colour scheme here is lip-smackingly apt for this shop and cafe selling not just Ireland's famous Lily O'Brien's chocolate (six chocs for €2), but also such sweet treats as berry crumble, macaroons and slices of rich dark carrot cake. Savoury snacks include gourmet sandwiches.

★ Momo
BISTRO $$

(☑ 051-581 509; www.momorestaurant.ie; 47 Patrick St; mains lunch €8-15, dinner €17-25; ⊙ noon-9pm Tue-Thu, to 10pm Fri & Sat, 1-8pm Sun; 🕤🥗🚼) 🍴 This buzzing bistro goes from strength to strength, and is so popular that you might struggle to find a table. The big draw is freshly made, flavoursome food based on quality local produce, with a menu that takes in Cajun chicken burgers, slow-cooked beef ribs and crisp fish and chips, plus a tempting range of vegetarian dishes.

★ La Bohème
FRENCH $$

(☑ 051-875 645; www.labohemerestaurant.ie; 2 George's St; mains €19-31; ⊙ 5.30pm-late Mon-Sat, noon-3pm Fri) 🍴 This dress-for-dinner kind of place combines French flair with fresh Irish produce. Set in the kitchen basement of a Georgian townhouse, the dining rooms are intimate spaces with barrel vault roofs and arches; the wine cellar is more extensive than most. The early-bird menu (all night Monday to Wednesday, till 6.45pm Thursday and Friday, and till 6.30pm Saturday) offers three courses for €29.50.

Bodega!
MODERN IRISH $$

(☑ 051-844 177; www.bodegawaterford.com; 54 John St; mains lunch €8-15, dinner €16-29; ⊙ noon-10pm Mon-Sat) 🍴 Although the colourful Mediterranean-style decor lends it a Spanish air, the latest Bodega! incarnation is contemporary Irish with an emphasis on local produce. The menu has a healthy mix of fish and meat dishes, as well as some lighter fare, such as goat's cheese tartlets and innovative salads. Keeping it local is a long list of Irish craft brews.

Munster Bar
PUB FOOD $$

(www.themunsterbar.com; Bailey's New St; mains €10-15; ⊙ food served noon-9pm; 🚼) Set in a building dating from 1822, this historic pub and restaurant has a snug complete with roaring fire and a spacious bar in the former coach house. Enjoy traditional pub food such as Irish stew with bread and butter, and sausages with colcannon. It's the perfect casual end to a long day's touring.

🍺 Drinking & Nightlife

★ Phil Grimes Pub
IRISH PUB

(☑ 051-875 759; 60 Johnstown; ⊙ 4-11.30pm Sun-Thu, to 12.30am Fri & Sat) Located on the edge of the city centre, this is a genuine local boozer with a friendly atmosphere and a loyal clientele who throng here to enjoy a range of Irish and international craft beers, live music gigs, and regular quiz and movie nights.

Henry Downes Bar
PUB

(☑ 051-874 118; Thomas St; ⊙ 5pm-11.30pm Mon-Thu, to midnight Fri-Sun, noon-2.30pm Sat & Sun; 🕤) For a change from stout, drop into Downes, which has been blending and bottling its own No 9 Irish whiskey for over two centuries. Have a dram in one of a series of character-filled rooms, or buy a bottle to take away (€45). This place is a real one-off – they even have a squash court out the back, as well as a full-sized billiard table.

Geoff's
BAR

(☑ 051-874 787; www.facebook.com/geoffscafebar waterford; 9 John St; ⊙ 11.30am-12.30pm) Geoff's bar is full of character with wood-panelled nooks and crannies, heavy wooden furniture and lofty ceilings (head for the atmospheric so-called 'church bar' out the back). Decent food is served, and there's occasional live music and DJ sessions.

⭐ Entertainment

Theatre Royal THEATRE
(📞051-874 402; www.theatreroyal.ie; The Mall; ⏱box office 10am-4pm Tue-Fri, noon-4pm Sat & performance days 6-8pm) A beautifully refurbished Georgian building, Waterford's flagship theatre stages plays, musicals and dance.

Garter Lane Arts Centre THEATRE
(📞051-855 038; www.garterlane.ie; 22a O'Connell St) This excellent theatre stages art-house films, music, dance and plays in an atmospheric 18th-century building set in a courtyard off O'Connell St.

Central Arts ARTS CENTRE
(📞086 454 3246; www.centralarts.ie; 123a Parade Quay) An intimate arts venue that stages exhibitions, drama, live music gigs and open mike nights; check the website for the listings.

🛍 Shopping

Waterford City Food & Craft Market MARKET
(John Roberts Sq; ⏱10am-4pm Sat) An excellent market featuring many prepared foods. Watch for the irresistible baked goods by Mary Doherty of Granny Maddock's Pantry. Crafts on sale include pottery, jewellery and hand-turned wood.

Waterford Book Centre BOOKS
(📞051-873 823; www.thebookcentre.ie; 25 John Roberts Sq; ⏱9am-6pm Mon-Sat, 1-5pm Sun) Three floors of books – with an excellent selection of Irish classics – and a cafe.

Kite Design Studios ARTS & CRAFTS
(📞051-858 914; www.kitedesignstudios.ie; 11 Henrietta St; ⏱9.30am-5pm Mon-Sat) This combination studio and shop provides a workshop and display space for some of Waterford's best artists and craftspeople. As well as watching the artisans at work, you can shop for locally made glassware, textiles, jewellery and more.

ℹ Information

Tourist Office (📞051-875 823; www.discoverireland.ie; 120 Parade Quay; ⏱9am-5.15pm Mon-Sat) Best source of info in Counties Waterford and Wexford.

ℹ Getting There & Away

AIR
Waterford's **airport** (📞051-846 600; www.flywaterford.com; Killowen) is some 9km south of the city centre, offering limited flights to London Luton and Birmingham. There is no public transport to the airport; a taxi costs around €20.

BUS
There are frequent Bus Éireann services to Tramore (€3.90, 45 minutes, twice hourly), Dublin (€17, 2½ hours, every two hours) and Wexford (€12.50, one hour, six daily).

The DublinCoach (www.dublincoach.ie) M9 Express service runs every two hours, linking Waterford to Cork (€10, two hours), Dungarvan (€5, 50 minutes), Kilkenny (€5, 45 minutes) and Dublin (€10, 2½ hours).

Suirway (www.suirway.com) buses to Dunmore East (€4, 25 minutes, seven or eight daily Monday to Saturday year-round, plus five Sunday late June to August) depart from the bus stop on Merchants Quay, outside the **main bus station** (📞051-879 000; www.buseireann.ie; Merchants Quay).

TRAIN
Waterford's Plunkett train station is across the river from the city centre. Direct trains:
Carlow €17.70, 1¼ hours, seven daily
Dublin Heuston €32, 2¼ hours, seven daily
Kilkenny €13.85, 35 minutes, six daily
Tipperary €17.70, 1½ hours, two daily

COUNTIES WEXFORD, WATERFORD, CARLOW & KILKENNY DUNMORE EAST

> ### ℹ FINDING WATERFORD'S ARTISANS
>
> Crystal aside, Waterford has a wealth of local craftspeople creating textiles, paintings, jewellery, pottery, papier mâché, candles, and furniture built from recycled materials. The website www.waterforddesignermakers.com maintains an up-to-date list.

Dunmore East

POP 1808
Strung out above a coastline of red sandstone cliffs scalloped with concealed coves full of screaming kittiwakes, Dunmore East (Dún Mór) is some 19km southeast of Waterford. A long-time weekend and summer retreat for Waterford locals, the village is cashing in on a newfound popularity on the back of its starring role in the 2017 BBC drama, *Redwater*.

There are two parts, separated by the town park – the **Upper Village** is poised above the fishing harbour to the south, while the **Lower Village** clusters in a hollow behind Lawlors Strand to the north.

In the 19th century, the town was a port of call for the steam packets that carried mail between England and the south of

ⓘ WATERFORD–WEXFORD FERRY

If you're driving or cycling between Wexford and Waterford along the coast, the **Passage East Ferry** (🖉 051-382 480; www.passageferry.ie; bicycle/car one way €2/8; ⊙ 7am-10pm Mon-Sat, 9.30am-10pm Sun Apr-Sep, 7am-8pm Mon-Sat, 9.30am-8pm Oct-Mar) from Ballyhack to Passage East saves a long detour via New Ross. The crossing takes five minutes, with several departures per hour.

Ireland. Legacies include picturesque thatched cottages along the main street and an unusual Doric **lighthouse** (1825) overlooking the commercial fishing harbour.

◉ Sights & Activities

The town slumbers through the winter months but comes alive in summer when bathers congregate at a series of half a dozen tiny cove beaches beneath the cliffs. Among them, **Lawlors Strand** (the largest) and neighbouring **Councillor's Strand** at the north end of town are close to pubs and cafes, while the smaller **Mens Cove** and **Ladies Cove** – at either end of the town's central park – speak of earlier, more prudish times (no segregation today, though). They offer safe swimming, and good snorkelling along the rocks between the coves.

Going west, the 16.5km **scenic drive** to the seaside frivolities of Tramore is packed with enough natural thrills (rolling green hills, soaring coastal vistas, herds of cattle crossing the road...) to more than match the resort's carnival appeal.

Dunmore East
Adventure Centre   ADVENTURE SPORTS
(🖉 051-383 783; www.dunmoreadventure.com; Stoney Cove; 2hr sessions per person €40; 🖐) Set in the first cove north of the fishing harbour, this place hires out equipment for kayaking, surfing and snorkelling. It also runs sailing, kayaking, canoeing and windsurfing courses for children and adults, plus land-based activities such as archery and rock climbing.

⁑ Festivals & Events

Bluegrass Festival   MUSIC
(🖉 051-878 832; www.discoverdunmore.com/events; ⊙ late Aug) In high summer the air

thrums with the beat of banjos as local pubs provide the stage for one of Ireland's liveliest music festivals.

⛱ Sleeping

Avon Lodge B&B   B&B $$
(🖉 051-385 775; www.avonlodgebandb.com; s/d €50/80; 🅿 �🛜) Although the exterior of this suburban-style house looks perfectly ordinary, it's run by traditional musician Richie Roberts, who is a font of knowledge about the local area. The recently refurbished rooms are clean, comfortable and brightened by punchy colour schemes with coordinated fabrics. It's on the Waterford road, a five-minute walk west of Lawlors beach.

Haven Hotel   HOTEL $$
(🖉 051-383 150; www.thehavenhotel.com; s/d from €50/100; ⊙ Mar-Oct; 🅿 🛜) Built in the 1860s as a summer house for the Malcolmson family, whose coat of arms can still be seen on the fireplaces, the Haven remains an elegant retreat with wood-panelled bathrooms and, in two rooms, four-poster beds. Local produce underpins dishes in the casual restaurant (open 5.30pm to 10pm Monday to Saturday, 10am to 3pm Sunday, March to October) and the low-lit crimson-toned bar.

✕ Eating & Drinking

Bay Cafe   CAFE $
(🖉 051-383 900; Dock Rd, Upper Village; mains €7-11; ⊙ 9am-5pm) This arty cafe, with views over the harbour and out to sea, serves interesting twists on casual cafe fare. The open-faced seafood sandwiches come highly recommended, while the guacamole-stuffed bagel is something of a novelty.

Lemon Tree Cafe   IRISH $$
(🖉 051-383 164; www.lemontreecatering.ie; Coxtown; mains €12-21; ⊙ 10am-6pm Tue-Thu, to 9pm Fri & Sat, 9.30am-4pm Sun; 🅿 🖐) ⚑ Come here for organic coffee, delectable baked goods and a deli counter (and freezer) with takeaway dishes ranging from nut and lentil loaf to seafood pie. There's plenty of seating, inside and out, and a menu of dishes with an emphasis on seafood. There's also a play section for children. It's on the southern edge of town.

Spinnaker Bar   SEAFOOD $$
(🖉 051-383 133; www.thespinnakerbar.ie; Glenville Tce, Lower Village; mains €15-29; ⊙ food served noon-

9pm;) Eat at pavement tables watching beach-goers pass by on their way to nearby Lawlors Strand, inside amid nautical knick-knacks, or out the back in the sheltered beer garden. Wherever you choose to sit, you'll enjoy top-notch casual seafood fare. Chowders, fish and chips, salads and fresh specials are expertly prepared. There's live music on summer weekends.

Power's Bar
PUB

(☑ 051-383 318; www.facebook.com/PowersBar DunmoreEast; Dock Rd, Upper Village; ⊙ noon-11.30pm Mon-Thu, to 12.30am Fri & Sat, 11.30am-11.30pm Sun) Toe-tapping trad sessions take place on Tuesday nights year-round at this butter-yellow corner pub. It's nicknamed 'the Butcher's' after its former incarnation as a meat and grocery store.

ⓘ Getting There & Away

Suirway (www.suirway.com) buses connect Waterford with Dunmore East (€4, 30 minutes, seven or eight daily Monday to Saturday year-round, five on Sunday July and August).

Tramore

POP 10,381

In summer the seafront that stretches below the steep town of Tramore (Trá Mhór in Irish, meaning 'big beach') is a whirl of fairground rides, amusement arcades, candy floss stalls and all the other tack of an old-style seaside resort. In winter, it's considerably quieter.

⊙ Sights

Tramore Bay is hemmed in by **Great Newtown Head** to the west and **Brownstown Head** to the east. Their 20m-high concrete pillars (three on Great Newtown and two on Brownstown) were erected by Lloyds of London in 1816 after a shipping tragedy: 363 lives were lost when the *Seahorse* mistook Tramore Bay for Waterford Harbour and was wrecked.

Atop the central pillar on Great Newtown Head stands the **Metal Man**, a 12ft-tall sailor made of iron, added in 1819. In white breeches and blue jacket, he points dramatically seawards as a warning to approaching ships. Legend has it that if a girl hops around the base of the statue three times on one leg, she will be married within a year (and no, it doesn't work in reverse for divorce!).

🏃 Activities

Tramore's broad, 5km-long **beach** is backed by 30m-high sand dunes at the eastern end, and is one of Ireland's premier **surfing** spots, suitable for all levels of experience, thanks to slow-forming waves. The town has year-round surf schools that also offer **eco-walks** around the Back Strand, one of Europe's largest intertidal lagoons, and various other activities.

Several places along the prom offer **surfing** lessons and equipment hire, including wetsuits and (much-needed) boots, gloves and hoods during winter.

There's a delightful, sheltered swimming spot at **Guillamene Cove** on the west side of the bay. Access is from Newtown Glen Rd (signposted Newtown & Guillamene Swimming Club); there's a car park, toilets and picnic tables.

T-Bay Surf & Eco Centre
SURFING

(☑ 051-391 297; www.tbaysurf.com; The Prom; ⊙ lessons from €35; 🖶) Ireland's largest surf school organises a wide range of courses aimed at all levels, including summer surfing camps for children. Also rents out surfboards, bodyboards and wetsuits.

Oceanics Surf School
SURFING

(☑ 051-390 944; www.oceanics.ie; Red Cottage, Old Crobally Rd; lessons from €35; 🖶) Besides providing lessons and courses, Oceanics organises surf parties and summer camps for teens and younger children.

Freedom Surf School
SURFING

(☑ 086 391 4908; www.freedomsurfschool.com; The Gap, Old Crobally Rd; lessons from €30; 🖶) As well as surfing courses, this school runs lessons in bodyboarding and stand-up paddleboarding.

Lake Tour Stable
HORSE RIDING

(☑ 086 812 8631; www.laketourstables.ie; Carrigavantry; treks adult/child from €25/20; 🖶) Tramore's pony trekking and riding centre offers a daily one-hour trek to a nearby lake, and a weekly two-hour canter (on Sundays) along Tramore Beach. About 1.5km west of Tramore, off the R682.

Tramore Golf Club
GOLF

(☑ 051-386 170; www.tramoregolfclub.com; Newtown Hill; green fees €35-45) One of Ireland's oldest courses, established in 1894, with a new nine-hole course (to add to the 18-hole championship course). Home to several championships, including the Irish Close Championship on four occasions, most recently in 2015.

🛏 Sleeping & Eating

★ Beach Haven House
HOSTEL, B&B **$**

(☑ 051-390 208; www.beachhavenhouse.com; Waterford Rd; hostel dm €20, B&B s/d €70/80, 2-person apt from €80; ☺ B&B & apts all year, hostel Mar-Nov; P 🐾) American Avery and his Irish wife Niamh have all budgets covered with their B&B, hostel and apartments (two-night minimum stay). The B&B and apartments are tastefully decorated with light wood and earth colours, while the hostel is basic but has excellent facilities, including a comfortable sitting room. In true Californian fashion Avery fires up the barbecue during the summer months.

O'Shea's Hotel
HOTEL **$$**

(☑ 051-381 246; www.osheas-hotel.com; Strand St; s/d from €55/95; 🐾) O'Shea's rooms are not quite as classy as the flower-emblazoned, black-and-white exterior suggests. Still, this family-run hotel offers decent value and a desirable location close to the beach; several of the rooms have sea views.

Vee Bistro
INTERNATIONAL **$$**

(☑ 051-386 144; www.facebook.com/thevee bistro; 1 Lower Main St; mains €8-18; ☺ 9am-4.30pm Mon-Wed, to 9.30pm Thu-Sat, to 5pm Sun; 🐾) This busy restaurant with tribal art and abstract canvases on the walls dishes up casual bistro-style fare such as barbecued ribs, fish and chips, and chicken chilli wraps, plus some superb bakery goodies, daily specials, and a good breakfast menu that includes a stack of pancakes with bacon and maple syrup.

Banyan
THAI **$$**

(☑ 051-330 707; http://thebanyanthai.ie; 3 Strand St; mains €11-15; ☺ 5-10pm Tue-Sun; 🐾) For for delicious Thai food, come to this cosy bar and restaurant (with live music in the bar on weekends). Dishes such as tom yam soup, massaman curry and satay chicken are delicately spiced with just enough heat. As usual the kitchen has to cater to Irish taste buds with a choice of rice, noodles – or chips – to accompany the main dishes.

☆ Entertainment

Waterford & Tramore Racecourse
HORSE RACING

(☑ 051-381 425; www.tramore-racecourse.com; Graun Hill) The first European horse-racing event of the year takes place on 1 January at Tramore Racecourse, one of many race meetings held here throughout the year.

ℹ Getting There & Away

Bus Éireann (p694) runs buses between Waterford and Tramore (€3.90, 45 minutes, twice hourly).

The Copper Coast

On a sunny day, the azure waters, impossibly green hills and grey-green, rust-red and yellow-ochre sea cliffs create a vibrant palette of colour along the beautiful **Copper Coast**, as the R675 winds its way from one stunning vista to another between Tramore and Dungarvan.

There are lots of little coves and beaches to discover – **Stradbally Cove** is a hidden gem – and, just before you reach Dungarvan, there is the beautiful, pristine stretch of sand that is **Clonea Strand**, near Ballynacourty.

◉ Sights & Activities

Copper Coast European Geopark
NATURE RESERVE

(www.coppercoastgeopark.com) This 20km stretch of rugged coastline, centred on the village of Bunmahon, takes its name from the copper-mining industry that flourished here in the 19th century. The most visible legacy of the area's mining industry is the Cornish-style winding-engine house at Tankardstown, 1km east of Bunmahon, and you'll find a Geological Garden on the eastern edge of Bunmahon.

Up the hill from here is the **Copper Coast Geopark Centre** (www.coppercoast geopark.com; Knockmahon Church, Bunmahon; adult/child €3.50/2.50; ☺ 11am-5pm Fri-Sun), housing an exhibition about the history and geology of copper mining. You can pick up information on the self-guided Copper Coast Trail, as well as trail cards describing walks in the area.

The area's 460-million year-old mudstones, sandstones and lavas were contorted by an ancient continental collision, and invaded by hot, metal-rich fluids, which cooled to form quartz veins rich in copper minerals.

Sea Paddling
KAYAKING

(☑ 051-393 314; www.seapaddling.com; half-/full-day tours €45/75; 🐾) Leads guided kayak tours (including instruction) of the Copper Coast, exploring remote sea cliffs, coves, caves and arches, plus personalised kayak training (€65 per hour).

Dungarvan

POP 9227

Brightly painted buildings ring Dungarvan's picturesque harbour, where the River Colligan meets the sea. This famously foodie town is home to some outstanding restaurants, a renowned cookery school and the annual West Waterford Festival of Food.

St Garvan founded a monastery here in the 7th century, but most of the centre dates from the early 19th century when the Duke of Devonshire rebuilt the streets around Grattan Sq. Overlooking the bay are a dramatic ruined castle and an Augustinian abbey.

⊙ Sights

Dungarvan Castle CASTLE
(☑058-48144; www.heritageireland.ie; Castle St; ⊙10am-6pm late May-late Sep) FREE Ongoing renovation is helping to restore this stone fortress to its former Norman glory. The oldest part of the castle, once inhabited by King John's constable Thomas Fitz Anthony, is the unusual 12th-century shell keep, built to defend the mouth of the river. The 18th-century British army barracks house a visitor centre with various exhibits. Admission is by (free) guided tour only.

Waterford County Museum MUSEUM
(☑058-45960; www.waterfordcountymuseum.org; St Augustine St; ⊙10am-5pm Mon-Fri) FREE This small well-presented museum covers maritime heritage (with relics from shipwrecks), Famine history, local personalities and various other titbits, all displayed in an 18th-century grain store.

Old Market House Arts Centre GALLERY
(☑058-48944; Lower Main/Parnell St; ⊙11am-1.30pm & 2.30-5pm Tue-Fri, 1-5pm Sat) FREE Housed in a handsome building dating from the 17th century, these light airy galleries showcase contemporary art by local artists.

🏃 Activities & Courses

Waterford Greenway CYCLING
(www.visitwaterfordgreenway.com) Completed in 2017, the Waterford Greenway is a 46km, all-abilities cycle trail that follows the line of an old railway between Waterford city (car park near WIT Arena, just off N25 at ring road) and Dungarvan (car park near Shandon roundabout). The route takes in three spectacular viaducts and a tunnel, and has great sea views at Knock, 8km east of Dungarvan.

A good short trip is to cycle east from Dungarvan along the coast to Clonea, through the Ballyvoyle tunnel to O'Mahony's pub (30 to 40 minutes' riding), and back again.

Waterford Greenway Bike hire CYCLING
(☑085 111 3850; http://waterfordgreenway.com; 1 Davitt's Quay; per day €20; ⊙9am-5pm) This place rents out bikes (hybrid or mountain), and can deliver bikes to, or pick them up from, your accommodation.

★Tannery Cookery School COOKING
(☑058-45420; www.tannery.ie; 6 Church St; courses from €75) Looking like a futuristic kitchen showroom (you can see it through the huge windows on the side street), this school is run by best-selling author and chef Paul Flynn. Courses range from the four-hour 'Cooking for Friends' (€75) to the popular three-day 'Masterclass' (€550), while others cover bread making, seafood, Italian cuisine, and cooking on an Aga.

🎊 Festivals & Events

**★West Waterford
Festival of Food** FOOD & DRINK
(www.waterfordfestivaloffood.com; ⊙mid-Apr) West Waterford's fresh produce is celebrated at this hugely popular festival that features cooking workshops and demonstrations, talks by local producers, farmers markets, guided walks and a craft-brew beer garden.

Dungarvan TradFest MUSIC
(www.comeraghs.com/tradfest; ⊙Jun) A lively festival of traditional music and dance on the June bank holiday weekend, staged in local pubs and hotels, and on a public stage

> ### TRIANGLE OF GOLF
>
> There are three championship golf courses within five minutes' drive of Dungarvan: **West Waterford Golf & Country Club** (www.westwaterfordgolf.com), **Dungarvan Golf Club** (www.dungarvangolfclub.com) and the **Gold Coast Golf Club** (www.goldcoastgolf-club.com). All three are part of the Dungarvan Golf Triangle initiative whereby keen golfers can play three courses for the price of two (€69). Check the website www.golftriangle.com for more information, including directions and maps.

in Grattan Sq. Famous for its annual bucket singing competition (look it up!).

🛏 Sleeping

★ Cairbre House
B&B $$

(☑ 058-42338; www.cairbrehouse.com; Strandside North; s/d €50/88; ⊙ closed mid-Dec–mid-Jan; 🅿🛜) Blazing with colourful flowers in summer, this four-room B&B is set on a half-hectare of riverside gardens. The gardens come into their own at breakfast, providing many of the ingredients including fragrant herbs; a small terrace and conservatory overlook the water. It's 1km north of the town centre, on the east side of the river.

Tannery Townhouse
GUESTHOUSE $$

(☑ 058-45420; www.tannery.ie; 2 Church St; s/d from €75/115; 🅿🛜) Under the same management as the Tannery restaurant (p188), this boutique guesthouse spans two buildings just across the street. Its 14 rooms are modern and stylish, and have fridges stacked with juices, fruit and muffins so you can enjoy a continental breakfast in your own time (freshly baked pastries are left outside your door in the morning).

Park Hotel
HOTEL $$

(☑ 058-42899; www.flynnhotels.com; Shandon Rd; s/d from €109/120; 🅿🛜🏊) This smart, modern hotel sprawls along the western bank of the River Colligan just north of the town centre. Rooms are bright and spacious, service is polite and attentive, and guests can make use of the attached leisure centre. It's a major venue for the Dungarvan TradFest, so book well ahead if you plan on attending the festival.

🍴 Eating & Drinking

Look for Dungarvan Brewing's locally produced craft **beers** (☑ 058-24000; http://dungarvanbrewingcompany.com; Westgate Business Park; ⊙ tours by appointment) in the pubs here, including the crisp and hoppy Helvick gold blonde ale.

★ Meades
CAFE $

(☑ 087 411 6714; www.meadescafe.com; 22 Grattan Sq; mains €5-9; ⊙ 8am-6pm Mon-Sat, 11am-5pm Sun; 🛜🍴) Enjoying an ace position on the town's main square, this cafe has a cheerful vibe with a kids' corner, sofas to lounge on, papers to read and a menu of scrumptious baked goods, as well as savoury tartlets,

homemade soups, salads and cottage pie. Breakfast special is a *blaa* (local floury bread roll) with crispy bacon, black pudding and country relish.

Merry's Gastro Pub
PUB FOOD $$

(☑ 058-24488; Lower Main/Parnell St; mains €10-24; ⊙ food served noon-9.30pm; 🍴) Lots of polished, dark wood and gleaming brass and copper reflected in antique mirrors create a pleasantly old-fashioned atmosphere in this traditional pub gone gastro – the menu runs from barbecued ribs and fish and chips, to pork belly with cumin and fennel braised in local ale. Speaking of which, there's a fine selection of craft beers too.

★ Tannery
MODERN IRISH $$$

(☑ 058-45420; www.tannery.ie; 10 Quay St; mains €26-33; ⊙ 12.30-2.30pm Fri, to 4.30pm Sun, 5.30-9pm Tue-Sat) 🍴 An old tannery building houses this innovative and much-lauded restaurant, where Paul Flynn creates seasonally changing dishes that focus on just a few flavours and celebrates them through preparations that are at once comforting yet surprising. There's intimate seating downstairs and in the buzzing, loftlike room upstairs. Service is excellent. Book ahead.

Moorings
PUB

(☑ 058-41461; www.mooringsdungarvan.com; Davitt's Quay; ⊙ 11am-midnight) Beautiful original wood panelling and a snug are the main features of the creaky period interior at this waterfront bar. Outside there's a vast beer garden beneath the walls of Dungarvan Castle where you can enjoy local beers on tap and a DJ at weekends. Also offers solid traditional food and B&B accommodation (double room €90).

🛍 Shopping

Dungarvan Farmers Market
MARKET

(www.dungarvanfarmersmarket.com; Grattan Sq; ⊙ 9.30am-2pm Thu) As you'd expect, Dungarvan farmers market is a good one, a minor festival of artisan breads, cheeses, bacon, farm vegetables and hot food.

ℹ Information

Tourist Office (☑ 058-41741; www.dungarvantourism.com; Main/Parnell St; ⊙ 9.30am-5pm Mon-Fri year-round, plus 10am-5pm Sat Apr-Sep) A helpful resource with stacks of informative brochures; the inconspicuous entrance is next to SuperValu supermarket.

ⓘ Getting There & Away

Buses pick up and drop off on Davitt's Quay on the way to and from Waterford (€5, 50 minutes, hourly) and Cork (€7, 1½ hours, hourly).

Ring Peninsula

Just 15 minutes' drive from Dungarvan, the Ring Peninsula (An Rinn, meaning 'the headland') is one of Ireland's best-known Gaeltacht (Irish speaking) areas. En route, views across Dungarvan Bay to the Monavullagh Mountains and the cliffs of the Copper Coast drift away to the northeast. You could easily spend a day exploring quiet country lanes here, with the promise of a hidden beach or fine old pub around the next corner, or hiking out to enjoy the panorama from Helvick Head.

Pubs, accommodation and shops are scattered about the peninsula; you'll need your own wheels to get around.

🛏 Sleeping & Eating

★**Dún Ard**   B&B **$$**
(☑ 058-46782; www.dunard.ie; Na Céithre Gaotha, Ring; r from €105; P 🛜) Perched high above Dungarvan Bay on the western edge of Ring village, the plain exterior of this B&B, set in an upmarket development, is deceiving. Rates may seem high, but the four rooms here really do equal the quality, spaciousness and finish you find in a top-end hotel. Breakfasts are superb, and there's a movie library for the use of guests.

Seaview   B&B **$$**
(☑ 058-41583; www.seaviewdungarvan.com; Pulla; s/d from €35/70; P 🛜🐾) This light-filled, pink-hued guesthouse has eight well-appointed rooms, self-catering facilities, and sweeping views across Dungarvan Bay from the conservatory and breakfast room. Good walks begin at the front door. It's on the N25, 8km southwest of Dungarvan.

An Seanachaí   PUB FOOD **$$**
(☑ 058-46755; www.seanachai.ie; Pulla; mains €13-25; ⊙ food served 11am-9pm Mon-Thu, to 9.30pm Fri-Sun; P 🛜) The rough-hewn walls of the 'Old Storyteller' could certainly tell a few stories of their own. Parts of this thatched-roof pub date back to its earliest incarnation as an 18th-century farm. It's an atmospheric spot for a pint, a meal (try the house speciality: Irish stew), regular live music, or their fortnightly storytelling sessions (9pm

Saturday). Just off the N25, 8km southwest of Dungarvan.

★**Marine Bar**   PUB
(☑ 058-46520; www.marinebar.ie; Pulla; ⊙ 4pm-midnight Mon-Fri, 2pm-1am Fri & Sat, 2-11.30pm Sun) Sure, there's good traditional food at this two-centuries-old pub, but the real reason to stop by is the craic. Year-round, traditional sessions rock the place from 9.30pm on Mondays and Saturdays (plus Fridays from June to September), while locals contest the traditional Irish card game '45' on Wednesday evenings (anyone can join in). Just off the N25, 8km southwest of Dungarvan.

🔒 Shopping

Criostal na Rinne   ARTS & CRAFTS
(☑ 058-46174; www.criostal.ie; Baile na nGall, Ring; ⊙ 9.30am-5.30pm Mon-Fri year-round, plus 10am-5pm Sat & noon-5pm Sun Apr-Oct) Former Waterford Crystal craftsman Eamonn Terry returned home to the Ring Peninsula to set up his own workshop, where you can buy deep-prismatic-cut, full-lead crystal vases, bowls, clocks, jewellery and even chandeliers. The studio is signposted off the main road in An Rinn village, near the Spar grocery store.

Ardmore

POP 434

The appealing seaside village of Ardmore may look unassuming these days, but it was once one of the most important Christian settlements in Ireland. St Declan is thought to have introduced Christianity to southeast Ireland in the 5th century, well before St Patrick arrived, establishing his monastery on the hill above the harbour. The cathedral that was built here in the 12th century is among Ireland's most remarkable examples of Romanesque architecture.

Today's visitors come mainly to enjoy the local beaches – as well as the town strand, there's secluded Ballyquin Beach, 4km north – water sports, bracing coastal walks and one of the country's best small luxury hotels.

◉ Sights & Activities

★**St Declan's Monastery**   RUINS
(Tower Hill; ⊙ 24hrs) 🆓 The ruins of Ireland's oldest Christian settlement occupy a striking setting on a hill above the town, strewn with gravestones both ancient

and new. The most prominent landmark is the 30m-high round tower, one of the best examples in Ireland. But the most remarkable is the roofless shell of Ardmore Cathedral, in particular the Romanesque arcading on the west gable, decorated with worn but still wonderful 12th-century stone carvings of biblical scenes – very unusual in Ireland.

Inside the cathedral are two Ogham stones featuring the earliest form of writing in Ireland, one with the longest such inscription in the country, and a number of medieval grave slabs. The oldest building on the site is the 8th-century Oratory of St Declan, which was restored in 1716; the saint is said to be buried beneath a hollow in its southeast corner.

Ardmore Cliff Walk
WALKING

An excellent, 5km loop walk leads from St Declan's Monastery – follow 'cliff walk' signs – to the 19th-century lookout tower on Ardmore Head, from where a clifftop path leads back into town along the coast. The footpath passes the wreck of the *Samson*, a crane barge that was blown ashore in 1987, wedged at the foot of the cliffs, and St Declan's Well, a sacred spring set within a ruined chapel.

Ardmore Adventures
ADVENTURE SPORTS

(☑083 374 3889; www.ardmoreadventures.ie; Main St; half day tours €45; ⊞) Operates half-day kayak tours around Ardmore Head, as well as surfing, coasteering, canyoning, climbing and more.

🛏 Sleeping & Eating

Newtown Farm Guesthouse
B&B $$

(☑024-94143; www.newtownfarm.com; Grange; s/d from €50/84; P🖭) Homemade scones, local cheeses and smoked salmon are on the breakfast menu at this stylish and peaceful B&B on a dairy farm 9km northwest of Ardmore, with views over gardens, fields and the distant sea. Coming from Dungarvan on the N25, go past the Ardmore turn-off and take the next left (signposted An Rinn); it's 100m along the side road.

★ Cliff House Hotel
LUXURY HOTEL $$$

(☑024-87800; www.thecliffhousehotel.com; Cliff Rd; r €205-370, ste €325-550; P🖭🌊) All bedrooms at this cutting-edge hotel, built into the hillside, overlook Ardmore Bay. Some suites even have two-person floor-to-ceiling glass showers so you don't miss those sea views. There are more sea views from the indoor swimming pool, the outdoor jacuzzi and spa, the bar and the much-lauded modern Irish restaurant (menu from €65), which has a Michelin star to its name.

Ardmore Gallery & Tearoom
CAFE $

(☑024-94863; www.ardmoregalleryandtearoom.ie; Main St; dishes €5-12; ⊕9.30am-6pm daily Apr-Sep, 1-5pm Sat & Sun only Oct-Mar) Always a winning combination, the gallery displays local art while the teashop sells delicious cakes, plus soup and savoury treats during the summer months. Jewellery, hand-painted silk scarves and knitwear are also for sale.

White Horses
SEAFOOD $$$

(☑024-94040; Main St; mains lunch €9-15, dinner €25-35; ⊕12.30-3.30pm & 6-10pm Tue-Sun May-Sep, Fri-Sun only Oct-Apr, closed Jan–mid-Feb) Energetically run by three sisters, this bistro set in a former grocery shop concentrates on fresh local seafood. Push the boat out and try the Dublin Bay prawns, served on plates handmade in the village. Enjoy a drink on the bench the front, or a meal at a sunny lawn table out the back.

🛍 Shopping

Ardmore Pottery & Gallery
CERAMICS

(☑024-94152; www.ardmorepottery.com; Cliff Rd; ⊕10am-6pm Mon-Sat, 2-6pm Sun Mar-Nov, hours can vary) This cosy little house above the harbour sells beautiful pottery, much of it in lovely shades of blue and cream. Other locally produced goods include warm hand-knitted socks.

❶ Getting There & Away

Bus Éireann (p694) service 260 runs one to three times daily to Youghal (€5.30, 20 minutes) and Cork (€17.50, 1½ hours); there are no connections east to Dungarvan except via Youghal.

Cappoquin & Around

Slinking up a steep hillside, the small market town of Cappoquin sits at the foot of the rounded, heathery Knockmealdown Mountains. To the west lies the picturesque valley of the River Blackwater, one of Ireland's most famous and prolific salmon fisheries.

⊙ Sights & Activities

Cappoquin House and Gardens
HISTORIC BUILDING

(www.cappoquinhouseandgardens.com; garden €5, house & garden €10; ⊙ garden 10am-4pm Mon-Sat; P) This magnificent 1779 Georgian mansion with formal gardens overlooking the River Blackwater is the private residence of the Keane family, who have lived here for 200 years. The best time to visit is May and June, when the gardens are ablaze with colourful rhododendron, azalea and oleander blossoms. The house is open at limited times – check the website. The entrance to the estate is just north of Cappoquin, at a set of huge black iron gates.

Dromana Gate
HISTORIC BUILDING

(Dromana Estate) The Dromana Drive from Cappoquin to Villierstown, 9km to the south, follows the Blackwater valley through the Dromana Estate. At a bridge over the River Finisk stands this remarkable Hindu-Gothic gate, inspired by the Brighton Pavilion in England. A temporary version was erected here in 1826 to welcome home the estate's owner, Henry Villiers-Stuart, and his wife after their honeymoon (part of which was spent in Brighton). He liked it so much, he had a permanent version built in 1830.

River Blackwater
FISHING

(www.cappoquinsalmonandtroutanglers.com; day tickets €12-40) The Blackwater is one of Ireland's finest salmon rivers, and the 6km stretch around Cappoquin offers good value and easy access. You can get advice, permits, licences and fishing tackle from the **post office** (⊘058-54152; 19 Main St; ⊙9am-1pm & 2-5.30pm Mon-Fri, 9am-1pm Sat).

⊨ Sleeping & Eating

Richmond House
GUESTHOUSE $$

(⊘058-54278; www.richmondhouse.net; Carigeen; s/d from €70/120; ⊙restaurant 6-9pm daily, noon-3pm Sun; P⊛) Dating from 1704 Richmond House is set in 6 hectares of parkland. All the same, its nine guest rooms – furnished with countrified plaids, prints and mahogany – are cosy rather than imposing, and service is genuinely friendly. Nonguests are welcome at its restaurant (dinner €55 per person; Sunday lunch €30), where local produce includes West Waterford lamb and Helvick harbour monkfish.

Barron's Bakery
BAKERY $

(⊘058-54045; www.barronsbakery.ie; The Square; mains €4-9; ⊙8.30am-5.30pm Mon-Sat) This famous local bakery has used the same brick Scotch ovens since 1887. Sandwiches, light meals and a mouth-watering selection of cakes and buns baked on the premises are available in the cafe, while its handmade breads are famed throughout the area.

❶ Getting There & Away

Bus Éireann (p694) service 366 runs from Waterford to Cappoquin (€18.10, 1½ hours, once daily Sundays only) en route to Lismore.

Lismore
POP 1374

The quiet, elegant town of Lismore on the River Blackwater was once the location of a great monastic university founded in the 7th century, frequented by statespeople and luminaries from all over Europe. Prince John of England built the first castle here in 1182, and in the 17th century the estate belonged for a while to the family of Robert Boyle, the father of modern chemistry, before passing through marriage to the dukes of Devonshire.

Present-day Lismore Castle – more of a vast, battlemented mansion, spreading along a steep slope above the river – dates mostly from the 19th century, and is still the family home of the 12th Duke of Devonshire. Adele Astaire, sister of dance legend Fred, married the son of the 9th Duke and lived in Lismore Castle from 1932 to 1944. The castle is not open to the public, but the gardens (p191) are one of the most popular attractions in County Waterford.

⊙ Sights & Activities

★ Lismore Castle Gardens
CASTLE

(⊘058-54061; www.lismorecastlegardens.com; gardens adult/child €8/6.50; ⊙10.30am-5.30pm mid-Mar–mid-Oct, last entry 4.30pm; P⊛) Although Lismore Castle itself is not open to the public, the 3 hectares of ornate and manicured gardens are well worth a visit. Thought to be the oldest landscaped gardens in Ireland, they are divided into the walled Jacobean upper garden and the less formal lower garden, the latter dotted with **modern sculpture** including two chunks of the Berlin Wall. Highlights include a splendid **yew walk** where Edmund Spenser is said to have written *The Faerie Queen*.

COUNTIES WEXFORD, WATERFORD, CARLOW & KILKENNY LISMORE

There's a contemporary **art gallery** beside the upper garden, and the castle stables and gardens are used as an opera venue during the annual **Lismore Opera Festival** (www.lismoreoperafestival.com) in June.

St Carthage's Cathedral CATHEDRAL
(North Mall; ⊙9am-6pm Apr-Sep, to 4pm Oct-Mar) FREE 'One of the neatest and prettiest edifices I have seen', commented William Thackeray in 1842 after visiting Lismore's 17th-century cathedral. And that was before the addition of the Edward Burne-Jones **stained-glass window**, which features all the Pre-Raphaelite hallmarks: an effeminate knight and a pensive maiden against a sensuous background of deep-blue velvet and intertwined flowers. There are some noteworthy 16th-century **tombs**, including the elaborately engraved MacGrath family crypt dating from 1557, with the 12 apostles carved around the sides.

Lismore Heritage Centre MUSEUM
(⬛058-54975; www.discoverlismore.com; Main St; adult/child €5/3.50; ⊙9am-5.30pm Mon-Fri, 10am-5pm Sat & noon-5pm Sun Mar-Oct, weekdays only Nov-Feb; ⬛) Features a 30-minute audiovisual presentation taking you from the arrival of St Carthage in AD 636 to the present day, via the discovery of the *Book of Lismore* behind a wall in the castle in 1814 and John F Kennedy's visit in 1947. There's also the Family Fun Experience, which is part nature trail and part treasure hunt, and which takes you around town. The information 'pack' costs €10; the kids will love it.

Lismore Cycling Holidays CYCLING
(⬛087 935 6610; www.cyclingholidays.ie; rental per day €18; ⬛) This outfit will deliver rental bikes to your accommodation, and can arrange cycling tours based around Lismore.

🛏 Sleeping & Eating

Ballyrafter Country House Hotel HOTEL $$
(⬛058-54002; http://ballyrafterhouse.com; Ballyrafter; s/d from €90/110; ⬛) Built for the Duke of Devonshire in the early 19th century, this gorgeous country-house hotel sits just across the river from Lismore, with grand views over the river and the castle (just 10 minutes' walk away). Traditionally furnished rooms offer pampering without pretension, and the owners can arrange salmon fishing on the nearby River Blackwater.

★**Lismore Farmers Market** MARKET $
(www.facebook.com/LismoreMarket; Castle Ave; ⊙11am-4pm Sun Apr-Sep) ⬛ The upmarket surrounds on the approach to the castle attract a fab collection of vendors to this market, with stalls selling artisan food and local arts and crafts. You can enjoy freshly prepared sandwiches, barbecued sausages and other goodies in the park or at tables set up on the gravel path.

Foley's IRISH $$
(⬛058-72511; www.foleysonthemall.ie; Main St; mains lunch €8-13, dinner €14-28; ⊙food served 12.30-8.30pm; ⬛) This inviting Victorian pub – complete with decorative wallpaper, leather-backed benches, an open fire, and a beer garden out the back – serves good steaks, fish and chips, hamburgers and chilli nachos.

☆ Entertainment

Booley House TRADITIONAL MUSIC
(⬛058-60456; www.thebooleyhouse.com; St Michael's Hall, Ballyduff; adult/child €15/10; ⊙8.30pm Wed Jul & Aug) This weekly show of traditional Irish music and dance takes place in St Michael's Hall in the village of Ballyduff, 10km west of Lismore.

ℹ Information

Tourist Office (⬛058-54975; www.discoverlismore.com; Main St; ⊙9am-5.30pm Mon-Fri, 10am-5pm Sat & noon-5pm Sun Mar-Oct, weekdays only Nov-Feb) Inside the **Lismore Heritage Centre** (p192); pick up the info-packed *Lismore Walking Tour Guide* (€3).

ℹ Getting There & Away

Bus Éireann (p694) service 366 runs from Lismore to Cappoquin (€3.30, 10 minutes) and Waterford (€19, 1¾ hours) once daily on Sundays only.

Northern County Waterford

Some of the most scenic parts of County Waterford are in the north around Ballymacarbry. The **Nire Valley Drive** (signposted from Ballymacarbry) leads deep into the Comeragh and Monavullagh Mountains; the last few kilometres of narrow, twisting road end at a car park where there are several waymarked walks into the hills (see www.walkingwaterford.com).

The Sgilloge Lakes walk is an easy two-hour return trip to a pair of tiny glacial lakes in one of the dramatic corries, or *coums* (glacial hollows), that give the Comeragh hills their name. The views west to the Galtee Mountains are dramatic, especially towards sunset.

There is no public transport; this region is best explored by car or bike.

 Activities

Clonanav Fly-Fishing Centre   FISHING
(☑ 052-613 6765; www.flyfishingireland.com; Clonanav, Ballymacarbry; guided fishing per day €320; ☺ 9am-5pm Tue-Sat) From March to September, the Rivers Nire, Tar and Suir offer superb trout fishing. Permits (€30 per day) can be arranged through this centre, which also has a fly-fishing school and guesthouse, and leads guided trips.

Festivals

Nire Valley Walking Festival   CULTURAL
(www.nirevalley.com; ☺ Oct) Takes place on the second weekend in October, with guided walks for all and traditional music in pubs.

Sleeping

★ **Hanora's Cottage**   GUESTHOUSE $$
(☑ 052-613 6134; www.hanorascottage.com; Nire Valley Dr, Ballymacarbry; r from €125; ⓟ🛜) This gorgeous 19th-century cottage sits between the bubbling River Nire and a picturesque church. The rooms are plush and luxurious with jacuzzi baths, and there's an outdoor deck overlooking the river. Everything in the gourmet restaurant (three-course dinner €39; 6.30pm to 8.30pm Monday to Saturday) is made on the premises. It's signposted 6.5km east of Ballymacarbry. No children.

Glasha Farmhouse B&B   B&B $$
(☑ 052-613 6108; www.glashafarmhouse.com; Ballymacarbry; s/d/f from €70/110/130; ⓟ🛜) Olive O'Gorman takes meticulous pride in maintaining the Regency-style bedrooms at her luxury farmhouse overlooking the Comeragh and Knockmealdown Mountains. Some wonderful walks fan out around the farm (including one that takes in the local pub!); afterwards, reward yourself with dinner served by candlelight (€35 to €40) in the conservatory. The farm is signposted 2km northwest of Ballymacarbry.

COUNTY CARLOW

The focus of Ireland's second-smallest county is the River Barrow, Ireland's second-longest river, which flows south from Carlow town through several picturesque villages to the monastic hamlet of St Mullins, its towpath followed by the lovely Barrow Way (p196) walking trail. The Blackstairs Mountains dominate the southeast, their rounded ridges forming the backdrop to many a view, and their underlying granite cropping up everywhere as building stone – most notably as the capstone for Europe's largest prehistoric dolmen.

The county's landed gentry have left a legacy of grand estates and country houses, many of which are now home to some of Ireland's most interesting gardens (p194).

Carlow Town

POP 24,272

The narrow streets of Carlow's compact town centre stretch along the main drag of Tullow St, from the ruins of the castle on the banks of the River Barrow to the cathedral.

◉ Sights

Carlow County Museum   MUSEUM
(☑ 059-913 1554; www.carlow.ie; cnr College & Tullow Sts; ☺ 10am-5pm Mon-Sat, 2-4.30pm Sun Jun-Aug, 10am-4.30pm Mon-Sat Sep-May) **FREE** This thoroughly engaging museum focuses on the lives of local people through the ages. There are some real one-offs, such as the trapdoor from the county gallows, dating from the early 1800s, and a 6m-high exquisitely carved pulpit from Carlow Cathedral, which the bishop apparently decided to replace with a more modern version (to the chagrin of many locals). The museum is housed in an atmospheric former convent with original stained-glass windows.

**Visual Centre for
Contemporary Art**   GALLERY
(☑ 059-917 2400; www.visualcarlow.ie; Old Dublin Rd; ☺ 11am-5.30pm Tue-Sat, 2-5pm Sun; ⓟ) **FREE** British architect Terry Pawson was behind the factory-inspired industrial design of this concrete, steel and glass cultural centre which, some consider, sits in uneasy alliance with the historic cathedral across the way. The Main Gallery is the largest single exhibition space in Ireland; changing exhibits highlight local and

COUNTIES WEXFORD, WATERFORD, CARLOW & KILKENNY CARLOW TOWN

international artists. The complex also houses the **George Bernard Shaw Theatre**.

Delta Sensory Gardens GARDENS
(☎ 059-914 3527; www.deltasensorygardens. com; Cannery Rd, Strawhall Industrial Estate; adult/child €5/free; ⊙9am-5.30pm Mon-Fri, 11am-5.30pm Sat & Sun, closed weekends Nov, Jan & Feb; 🅿 ♿) A dozen or so interconnecting, themed gardens span the five senses – from sculpture garden to formal rose garden, water and woodland garden, willow garden and even a musical garden with mechanical fountains. Admission proceeds benefit the adjoining Delta Centre, which provides services and respite for adults with learning disabilities. The gardens are hidden in an industrial estate on the northern edge of Carlow town.

Carlow Castle RUINS
(Castle Hill; 🅿) Built by William Marshal on the site of an earlier Norman motte-and-bailey fort, this 13-century castle survived Cromwell's attentions. It later succumbed to the grand plans of a certain Dr Middleton, who decided to convert it into a lunatic asylum and demolished much of the fortress in 1814 in order to 'remodel' it. The portion that survives is part of the keep flanked by two towers.

Carlow Cathedral CATHEDRAL
(Cathedral of the Assumption; ☎ 059-916 4086; www. carlowcathedral.ie; College St; ⊙9am-5pm Mon-Sat, to 7pm Sun) FREE This elegant Regency Gothic cathedral dating from 1833 was the brainchild of Bishop James Doyle, a staunch supporter of Catholic emancipation. On the right of the nave a statue of the bishop is flanked by a crowned, kneeling woman said to represent Ireland in an attitude of hope. The church also has an elaborate pulpit and some fine stained-glass windows.

CARLOW GARDENS

Carlow's soft green landscape lends itself to horticulture, and the county is patch-worked with old aristocratic estates, grand country houses – both ruined and renovated – and some of Ireland's finest flower-filled gardens. Green-fingered visitors can pick up or download a copy of the Carlow Garden Trail booklet (www.carlowgardentrail.com). Seasonal highlights include the following:

Winter
Altamont Gardens (p195) Snowdrop Week in February showcases Ireland's largest collection of snowdrops, with more than 100 varieties flowering among the trees in this venerable demesne.

Spring
Delta Sensory Gardens (p194) This community garden in Carlow town holds a daffodil weekend in late March, with around 10,000 of the bright yellow flowers creating an impressive display.

Huntington Castle (p199) The magnificent grounds of this 17th-century stately home caught the eye of film director Stanley Kubrick, who shot the movie *Barry Lyndon* here in 1975. Ancient avenues of lime and yew are set off in late April and early May by colourful bluebell woods.

Summer
Altamont Gardens (p195) Rhododendrons and azaleas create a blaze of pink, purple, red and orange blooms from May into June, followed by a profusion of roses in midsummer, with varieties both traditional and modern.

Duckett's Grove (p196) From June to August the walled gardens at this former aristocratic estate are a riot of colourful perennials and flowering shrubs including watsonia, acanthus, arbutus, euphorbia, azaleas and rhododendrons.

Autumn
Borris House (p197) The ornamental woodlands surrounding the ancestral home of the McMorrough Kavanaghs, High Kings of Leinster, put on a grand display of autumn colours in late October and November.

Browne's Hill Dolmen ARCHAEOLOGICAL SITE
(⊙dawn-dusk) **FREE** This 5000-year-old granite portal dolmen (tomb chamber) is one of Ireland's most famous prehistoric monuments, sporting the largest capstone in Europe (it weighs more than 100 tonnes). It's signposted 3km east of Carlow on the R726.

🎉 Festivals & Events

Carlow Arts Festival ART
(www.carlowartsfestival.com; ⊙Jun) The county's biggest cultural event, when musicians, writers, actors and street performers take over town for a week in early June. Lots of free and family-oriented events.

Carlow Garden Festival GARDEN
(www.carlowgardentrail.com; ⊙Jul) Talks and tours by Irish and international gardening personalities.

🛏 Sleeping

Red Setter Guest House B&B $$
(☑059-914 1848; http://redsetterbandb.ie; 14 Dublin St; s/d/tr from €40/70/99; P⟨P⟩⟨🛜⟩) Great attention to detail, simply furnished but comfortable rooms, and extra touches such as fresh flowers make this otherwise humble B&B the town centre's winning choice.

Barrowville Townhouse B&B $$
(☑059-914 3324; www.barrowville.com; Kilkenny Rd; per person €40-49; P⟨P⟩⟨🛜⟩) This 18th-century townhouse has been meticulously converted into a classy B&B with elegant rooms. Enjoy local free-range eggs for breakfast in the airy conservatory overlooking the semiformal gardens.

🍴 Eating & Drinking

BeaNice Cafe CAFE $
(☑059-913 1921; beanicecafe@gmail.com; 17 Dublin St; mains €5-11; ⊙8am-4pm Mon-Sat) Describing itself as an 'artisan food and drink emporium', this cute cafe serves delicious breakfasts, homemade soups, deli sandwiches, cupcakes and more.

★Lennons MODERN IRISH $$
(☑059-917 9245; www.lennons.ie; Visual Centre for Contemporary Art, Old Dublin Rd; mains lunch €8-12, dinner €17-27; ⊙10.30am-5pm Mon-Sat, 6-9.30pm Thu-Sat, noon-4pm Sun; P⟨P⟩⟨🛜⟩) Carlow's best dining is found amid the arty surrounds of the Visual Centre for Contemporary Art (p193). It's a sleek and stylish space with a patio bordering the grassy grounds of St Patrick's College. Lunch features creative sandwiches, salads and hot specials, while dinner is more refined with a seasonal menu that showcases local artisan produce. Book at weekends.

Teach Dolmain PUB
(☑059-913 0911; 76 Tullow St; ⊙9.30am-11.30pm Mon-Thu & Sun, to 1.30am Fri & Sat) Set on a strip of lively pubs, this friendly local has live trad music on Thursdays at 10pm, while Sunday is more of a mix, ranging from jazz to blues (7pm). Good food is also served.

🛍 Shopping

Carlow Farmers Market MARKET
(☑086 811 1108; www.carlowfarmersmarket.com; ⊙9am-2pm Sat) Fittingly held at the old Potato Market; look out for Elizabeth Bradley's Carlow cheese, homemade pesto at the olive stall, plus handcrafted chocolates, organic vegetables, ready-prepared meals and more.

ⓘ Information

Carlow Tourist Office (☑059-913 0411; www.carlowtourism.com; cnr Tullow & College Sts; ⊙9.30am-5.30pm Mon-Sat) A useful source of county-wide information.

ⓘ Getting There & Around

BUS
Buses run to Dublin (€15, 1½ hours, every two hours), Kilkenny (€11, 35 minutes, three daily) and Waterford (€15, 1½ hours, seven daily).

TAXI
Carlow Cabs (☑059-914 0000; www.carlowcabs.com)

TRAIN
The train station is on Station Rd, northeast of the town centre. Trains run to Dublin Heuston (€17.70, one hour), Waterford (€17.70, 1¼ hours) and Kilkenny (€10.35, 30 minutes), with seven to 10 departures daily.

Around Carlow Town

Although the entire county could be considered a day trip from Carlow town, the following places are quite close.

◉ Sights

★Altamont Gardens GARDENS
(☑059-915 9444; www.heritageireland.ie; Kilbride, near Ballon; parking €2; ⊙9am-6.30pm Apr-Sep, to 5pm Mar & Oct, to 4.30pm Feb & Nov, to 4pm Dec & Jan; P) **FREE** One of Ireland's most magnificent landscaped gardens, Altamont covers

THE BARROW WAY

The River Barrow, Ireland's second-longest river (after the Shannon), flows for 192km from the Slieve Bloom hills of Laois to meet the tide at St Mullins, and flow on into the sea at Waterford harbour. Made navigable in the 18th century, and linked to Dublin's Grand Canal via the Barrow Line canal, its towpath is followed by the **Barrow Way** (www.irishtrails.ie).

This national waymarked trail leads for 114km from Lowtown (near Robertstown) in County Kildare to St Mullins, with more than half of its length in County Carlow. It passes through a bucolic landscape of riverside villages, Victorian lock-keepers cottages, old stone bridges and boat-crowded quays, offering the chance of spotting wildlife such as otter, heron, little egret and kingfisher.

It would take four days to hike the whole way, but shorter sections make for a great half-day hike or bike route, notably the lovely 7.5km stretch between St Mullins and Tinnahinch (across the river from Graiguenamanagh in County Kilkenny; allow 1½ hours walking or 30 minutes cycling, each way).

16 hectares on the banks of the River Slaney, with carefully selected plantings arranged in naturalistic settings where peacocks, swans, squirrels and wild hare abound, surrounding an ornamental water-lily lake. The gardens are off the N80 at Kilbride Cross, 24km southeast of Carlow town.

Walkways meander among flower beds, shrubberies, mature trees (some more than 250 years old), rhododendrons and azaleas, before finally leading down a flight of 100 granite steps to a gorgeous bluebell wood beside the river – a great spot for a picnic.

First laid out in the 18th century, the present gardens are largely the work of plant collector Fielding Lecky Watson, who bought the estate in 1924, and his daughter Corona North, who bequeathed them to the nation after her death in 1999. There are plans to open the rather neglected Altamount House to the public once it has been restored.

Duckett's Grove
GARDENS

(☑085 113 6075; www.facebook.com/TheTeaRooms AtDuckettsGrove; ☉dawn-dusk; P) FREE Dominated by the jackdaw-haunted ruins of a Gothic fantasy of a country house, the former seat of the Duckett family (the house burned down in 1933) was taken over by Carlow County Council in 2005. The walled gardens have been restored as a public park, filled with the scents of lavender and fruit blossom in early summer, while the outbuildings house craft workshops and a tearoom (open noon to 5pm Saturday, May to September). The gardens are 12.5km northeast of Carlow, signposted off the R726 and R418.

Killeshin Church
RUINS

(Killeshin; ☉dawn-dusk) FREE One of the tallest round towers in Ireland once dominated this former monastery, but was destroyed early in the 18th century by a farmer worried that it might collapse and kill his cows. The ruins of a 12th-century church remain, including a beautifully decorated Romanesque doorway; look for the bearded face on the capstone. The church is 5km west of Carlow on the R430.

🛏 Sleeping & Eating

★ Sherwood Park House
GUESTHOUSE $$

(☑059-915 9117; www.sherwoodparkhouse.ie; Kilbride Cross, near Ballon; s/d from €65/100; P) This grey-stone Georgian manor dates from 1730. The five guest rooms are huge with period niceties such as satin- and velvet-adorned four-poster beds. You can make arrangements for dinner (€40 per person); breakfast is included. The house is on the minor road leading to Altamont Gardens (p195), which is just 600m away.

Forge
CAFE $

(www.theforgekilbride.ie; Kilbride Cross, near Ballon; mains €5-10; ☉9.30am-4.30pm Mon-Sat, to 5pm Sun; P🛜🛗) Mary Jordan cooks up delicious healthy soups and hot lunch specials using local produce at this former blacksmith's forge near Altamont Gardens (p195). There are baked goods to take away plus deli items and crafts for sale; try to get there around 10am as the scones are coming out of the oven.

Borris & Around

This Georgian village has a charming main street running uphill from the Black River, lined on one side with pastel-painted Georgian cottages and on the other by the grounds of Borris House, ancestral home of the High Kings of Leinster.

◉ Sights

Borris House   HISTORIC BUILDING
(☑ 059-977 1884; www.borrishouse.com; Borris; adult/child €12/2; ⊘ grounds noon-4pm Tue-Thu May-Sep) This impressive Tudor Gothic mansion, the ancestral home of the Mc-Morrough Kavanaghs, High Kings of Leinster, was modelled in 1810–20 around the earlier shells of an 18th-century house and a 15th-century castle. The highlight of the interior is the ornate stucco plasterwork by Michael Stapleton, whose work can also be seen in Trinity College and Powerscourt House in Dublin. Visits to the house are by guided tour only (begins 2pm), which must be booked in advance.

Kilgraney House Herb Gardens   GARDENS
(☑ 059-977 5283; www.kilgraneyhouse.com; Borris Rd, Kilgraney; €3; ⊘ 2-6pm Fri-Sun May-Aug; **P**) These delightful gardens are home to a heady cocktail of medicinal and kitchen herbs growing in orderly profusion; the re-created medieval monastic herb garden is a favourite. The herbs are used in the kitchens of the inn and restaurant here, and admission includes a complimentary herbal tea in the cafe. Kilgraney House is signposted off the R705 halfway between Borris and Bagenalstown.

⌘ Sleeping & Eating

Forge   B&B $
(☑ 059-9725740; www.ullardforgeaccommodation.eu; Ullard, Milltown; per person €35; ⊘ mid Feb–Oct; **P** ⬤) This modern, purpose-built guesthouse offers great value accommodation in a quiet rural location near the River Barrow. It's just across the border in County Kilkenny, a 10-minute drive from Borris along a single-track road off the R705 towards Graiguenamanagh.

Lorum Old Rectory   B&B $$$
(☑ 059-977 5282; www.lorum.com; Borris Rd, Kilgraney; s/d from €100/160; ⊘ Feb–Nov; **P** ⬤) Halfway between Borris and Bagenalstown off the R705, this historic manor house, dating from the 1800s, sits on a prominent knoll to the east of the road. The gardens provide peaceful views from each of the four rooms, some of which have four-poster beds. The largely organic cooking here is renowned; confirm your four-course dinner when you book (€45 per person).

★**Step House Hotel**   IRISH $$
(☑ 059-977 3209; www.stephousehotel.ie; 66 Main St, Borris; mains €14-24; **P** ⬤) The handsome 1808 Brasserie & Bar in the Step House Hotel, all polished mahogany, red leather benches and green glass lampshades, is an elegant but relaxed place to enjoy some of County Carlow's best food. Expect inventive dishes such as cured mackerel with cucumber chutney and black-sesame-seed wafer, and roast Kilmore cod with mussel vinaigrette and pickled fennel.

M O'Shea   PUB
(☑ 059-977 3106; Main St, Borris; ⊘ noon-11pm) Surprises abound in this tidy warren of rooms, which combines a general store, a modern grocery shop, and an old-fashioned pub where spare electrical parts, wellies and bits of machinery hang from the ceiling. Decent food and occasional live music sessions.

ⓘ Getting There & Away

Borris is on the east–west R702 road, which links the M9 with the N11 in County Wexford. **Kilbride Coaches** (www.kilbridecoaches.com) run twice daily Monday to Saturday from Kilkenny to Borris (€6, 40 minutes) and on to Graiguenamanagh (€3.50, 15 minutes).

Trains run between Carlow town and Bagenalstown (€5.95, 12 minutes, seven to 10 daily) en route to Kilkenny.

St Mullins

POP 100

The tranquil hamlet of St Mullins, just a few houses and a pub scattered around a hummocky village green, gives no indication of its illustrious past. Founded by St Moling (St Mullin) in the 7th century, near the holy waters of **St Moling's Well** (signposted from the village car park), this was once an important monastic site. In the 12th and 13th centuries it became a major Anglo-Norman settlement (those hummocks on the green are the remains of a motte-and-bailey castle), but for some reason the village never grew into a town. Today it's a beautiful and peaceful place, a centre for angling, canoeing, and walks and bike rides along the river.

The village hosts **St James Pattern Day**, an annual pilgrimage and Mass held on the Sunday preceding (or falling on) 25 July.

There is no public transport to St Mullins; the nearest bus stop is in Graiguenamanagh, 7km north.

◉ Sights & Activities

★ St Mullins Monastery   RUINS
(⊙ dawn-dusk) **FREE** This important monastic site, founded in the 7th century by St Moling, was the legendary burial place of the Kings of Leinster. The remains include four church buildings dating from the 10th to the 15th centuries, the stump of a round tower and a 9th-century high cross. Nearby is the grave of General Thomas Cloney, a hero of the 1798 Rising, and a monument raised by 'St Mullins exiles in New York' marking the tomb of Art, King of Leinster (1357–1416).

St Mullins Heritage Centre   MUSEUM
(☏ 059-865 0503; www.stmullinsheritagecentre. com; adult/child €2/free; ⊙ 11am-4pm Tue-Fri year-round, plus 2-6pm Sat & Sun Jun-Sep) The former Church of Ireland in the heart of the St Mullins monastic site houses an exhibition on the life of St Moling, and on the history of the monastery and the village. Opening hours can vary; call ahead to check.

Go with the Flow   CANOEING
(☏ 056-780 1299; www.gowiththeflow.ie; canoe hire per day €40) Can organise one-day experiences, canoe rental, or a five- or six-day, self-guided canoe tour along the River Barrow from Athy in County Kildare to St Mullins in County Carlow, either wild camping (from €160 per person) or staying in B&Bs or hotels (from €299 per person). One of the classic Irish canoe tours.

🛏 Sleeping & Eating

★ Mulvarra House   B&B $$
(☏ 051-424 936; www.mulvarra.com; St Mullins; s/d from €45/75; ᴾ ⊛) Most of the bedrooms in this modern, comfortable B&B have balconies with glorious views over the River Barrow, which offers lovely evening walks along its banks. You can also indulge in body treatments such as hot stone massages and facials, while breakfasts cater to all dietary needs. It's just east of the village on the road towards New Ross.

Old Grainstore   COTTAGE $$
(☏ 051-424 440; www.oldgrainstorecottages.ie; The Quay; cottages per week €550; ᴾ) Martin and Emer O'Brien have eschewed corporate life to convert this former grain warehouse on the River Barrow into three self-catering cottages sleeping two to five people. The interiors are stylish yet homely, with shelves of books and wood-burning stoves. Shorter stays are sometimes possible on request, and guests can borrow bikes and kayaks free of charge.

Mullicháin Café   CAFE $
(☏ 051-424 440; www.oldgrainstorecottages. ie; The Quay; mains €5-12; ⊙ 11am-6pm Tue-Sun Mar-Oct; ⊕) Fabulous riverside cafe serving home-baked bread and cakes, soups, deli platters and lunch specials such as prawn and crab salad.

MT LEINSTER HERITAGE DRIVE

Borris is the starting point for the Mt Leinster Heritage Drive, a signposted 75km scenic loop through south Carlow taking in the villages of Bunclody (just over the border in Wexford), Clonegal, Kildavin, Myshall, Fenagh and Bagenalstown; pick up a free leaflet at any tourist office.

The route climbs across the Blackstairs Mountains, where the **Nine Stones viewpoint** offers a breathtaking panorama that takes in eight counties – on a clear day even the coast of Wales can be seen far to the east. Nine Stones is also a popular hang-gliding and paragliding site, and is the starting point for the easiest walking route to the top of **Mt Leinster** (796m), along a road that leads to the telecommunications mast on the summit (5km return trip; allow 1½ hours).

Clonegal

POP 278

The picturesque village of Clonegal has a tiny green beside an 18th-century stone bridge over the River Derry, whose crystal-clear, limestone-fed waters are thick with waving ribbons of green ranunculus and plump brown trout.

It is the southern terminus of Ireland's inaugural long-distance walking trail, the

Wicklow Way (p149), and is home to Huntington Castle (p199), the atmospheric setting for Stanley Kubrick's 1975 movie *Barry Lyndon*.

◉ Sights

Huntington Castle CASTLE
(☑ 053-937 7160; www.huntingtoncastle.com; Clonegal; house tours adult/child €9/4, gardens only €5/2.50; ⊘ gardens 10am-5pm May-Sep; ℗) The core of Huntington Castle is a spooky, dusty old tower house built in 1625 by Sir Laurence Esmonde, now surrounded by Georgian terraces and flamboyantly castellated Victorian extensions. Related to the Esmondes by marriage, the Durdin-Robertson family still live here today and offer 45-minute guided tours of the house's Jacobean hall, Victorian kitchens and living quarters between 2pm and 5pm, complete with entertaining ghost stories.

The oddest part of the tour is the **Temple of Isis** in the basement, the idiosyncratic headquarters of the Fellowship of Isis, an order dedicated to the worship of the 'divine feminine' founded by family member Olivia Robertson in 1976.

The **gardens** combine the formal with rural fantasy and include a fabulous 500-year-old Yew Walk, an avenue of lime trees planted in 1680 and a 17th-century fish pond. Facilities include an adventure playground, a tearoom and a gift shop.

✖ Eating & Drinking

★ **Sha-Roe Bistro** MODERN IRISH $$
(☑ 053-937 5636; http://sha-roe.ie; Main St, Clonegal; mains €18-26; ⊘ 7-8.30pm Thu, 7-9.30pm Fri & Sat, 12.30-2.30pm Sun, closed Jan) Tucked inside an 18th-century building and run by award-winning chef Henry Stone, this is one of Carlow's top restaurants. A huge open fireplace and a pretty courtyard at the back provide a rustic setting for standout contemporary cuisine based on local produce fresh from the surrounding orchards and farms. Book at least two weeks ahead.

Osborne's PUB
(☑ 053-937 7359; Main St, Clonegal; ⊘ noon-11pm Mon-Sat, 12.30-10pm Sun) A traditional finishing point for Wicklow Way walkers, Osborne's pub is an atmospheric low-ceilinged hostelry, with a bar-top reputedly made from coffin lids.

❶ Getting There & Away

Drivers will find Clonegal signposted along a series of winding local roads 4.5km east of Kildavin on the N80. Hikers can take Bus Éireann service 132 from Dublin to Kildavin (€18, 2¼ hours, twice daily) and walk the 4.5km (one hour) to Clonegal.

COUNTY KILKENNY

County Kilkenny's centrepiece is, of course, its namesake city. An enduring gift from the Normans, it seduces visitors with medieval alleys winding between imposing castle and historic cathedral, craft studios, traditional pubs and riverside walks.

The county too is a delight, a place of rolling hills where you'll soon run out of adjectives for shades of green. Tiny roads navigate the valleys alongside trout-filled rivers, moss-covered stone walls and relics of centuries of Irish religious history. Shamrock-cute Inistioge village may be star of many a movie but it is the real deal, as are country towns such as Graiguenamanagh, Bennettsbridge and Thomastown. It's no surprise that so many artists and craftspeople have set up shop here.

Much of the county is easily visited on a day trip from the city, but you'll need your own wheels, as public transport is limited.

Kilkenny City

POP 26,512

Kilkenny is the Ireland of many visitors' imaginations. Built from dark-grey limestone flecked with fossil seashells, Kilkenny (from the Gaelic 'Cill Chainnigh', meaning the Church of St Canice) is also known as 'the marble city'. Its picturesque 'Medieval Mile' of narrow lanes and historic buildings strung between castle and cathedral along the bank of the River Nore is one of the southeast's biggest tourist draws. It's worth braving the crowds to soak up the atmosphere of one of Ireland's creative crucibles – Kilkenny is a centre for arts and crafts, and home to a host of fine restaurants, cafes, pubs and shops.

History

In the Middle Ages Kilkenny was intermittently the unofficial capital of Ireland, with its own Anglo-Norman parliament.

Kilkenny

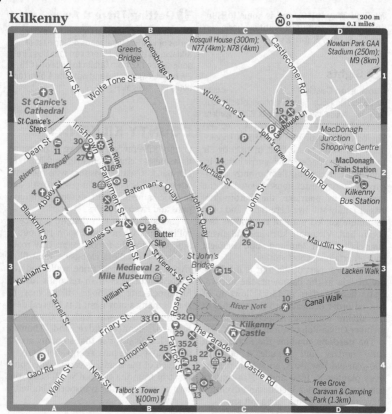

In 1366 the parliament passed the Statutes of Kilkenny aimed at preventing the adoption of Irish culture and language by the Anglo-Norman aristocracy – they were prohibited from marrying the native Irish, taking part in Irish sports, speaking or dressing like the Irish or playing any Irish music. Although the laws remained on the books for more than 200 years, they were never enforced with any great effect and did little to halt the absorption of the Anglo-Normans into Irish culture.

During the 1640s Kilkenny sided with the Catholic royalists in the English Civil War. The 1641 Confederation of Kilkenny, an uneasy alliance of native Irish and Anglo-Normans, aimed to bring about the return of land and power to Catholics. After Charles I's execution, Cromwell besieged Kilkenny for five days, destroying much of the southern wall of the castle before the ruling Ormonde family surrendered. The defeat signalled a permanent end to Kilkenny's political influence over Irish affairs.

Today tourism is Kilkenny's main economic focus, but the city is also the regional centre for more traditional pursuits such as agriculture – you'll see farmers on tractors stoically dodging tour buses.

Sights & Activities

★ Kilkenny Castle
CASTLE
(☎ 056-770 4100; www.kilkennycastle.ie; The Parade; adult/child €8/4; ☉ 9.30am-5.30pm Apr-Sep, to 5pm Mar, to 4.30pm Oct-Feb) Rising above the River Nore, Kilkenny Castle is one of Ireland's most visited heritage sites. Stronghold of the powerful Butler family, it has a history dating back to the 12th century, though much of its present look dates from Victorian times.

During the winter months (November to January) visits are by 40-minute guided tours only, which shift to self-guided tours

Kilkenny

from February to October. Highlights include the Long Gallery with its painted roof and carved marble fireplace. There's an excellent tearoom in the former castle kitchens, all white marble and gleaming copper.

The first structure on this strategic site was a wooden tower built in 1172 by Richard Fitz Gilbert de Clare, the Anglo-Norman conqueror of Ireland better known as Strongbow. In 1192 Strongbow's son-in-law, William Marshal, erected a stone castle with four towers, three of which survive. The castle was bought by the powerful Butler family (later earls and dukes of Ormonde) in 1391, and their descendants continued to live here until 1935. Maintaining the castle became such a financial strain that most of the furnishings were sold at auction. The property was handed over to the city in 1967 for the princely sum of £50.

For most visitors, the focal point of a visit is the Long Gallery, which showcases portraits of Butler family members, the oldest dating from the 17th century. It is an impressive hall with a 19th-century timber roof vividly painted with Celtic, medieval and Pre-Raphaelite motifs by John Hungerford Pollen (1820–1902), who also created the magnificent Carrara marble fireplace, delicately carved with scenes from Butler family history.

The castle basement is home to the **Butler Gallery** (☑056-776 1106; www.butlergallery.com; ☺10am-5.30pm May-Sep, 10am-1pm & 2-4.30pm Oct-Apr) **FREE**, featuring contemporary artwork in temporary exhibitions, and to a popular summertime tearoom housed in the castle kitchen. You can access the Butler Gallery and cafe without paying admission.

About 20 hectares of **public parkland** (Castle Rd; ☺8.30am-8.30pm May-Aug, to 7pm Apr & Sep, shorter hours Oct-Mar) extend to the southeast of Kilkenny Castle, framing a fine view of Mt Leinster, while a Celtic-cross-shaped rose garden lies northwest of the castle. A gate on the north side of the park leads steeply down to the riverside, where you can walk back into town at St John's Bridge.

★ **Medieval Mile Museum** MUSEUM
(☑056-781 7022; www.medievalmilemuseum.ie; 2 St Mary's Lane; adult/child €7/3; ☺10am-6pm Apr-Oct, 11am-4.30pm Nov-Mar) Dating from the early 13th century, St Mary's Church has been converted into a fascinating modern museum that charts the history of Kilkenny in medieval times. Highlights include the Rothe Chapel, lined with ornate 16th- and 17th-century tombs carved from local limestone, remnants of the 17th-century timber roof above the crossing, and a selection of

13th- and 14th-century grave slabs. A huge interactive map of Kilkenny allows you to explore maps and documents relating to the medieval city.

★ **St Canice's Cathedral** CATHEDRAL
(☎ 056-776 4971; www.stcanicescathedral.ie; St Canice's Pl; cathedral/ round tower/ combined €4/3/6; ⊙ 9am-6pm Mon-Sat, 1-6pm Sun Jun-Aug, shorter hours Sep-May) Ireland's second-largest medieval cathedral (after St Patrick's in Dublin) has a long and fascinating history. The first monastery was built here in the 6th century by St Canice, Kilkenny's patron saint. The present structure dates from the 13th to 16th centuries, with extensive 19th-century reconstruction, its interior housing ancient grave slabs and the tombs of Kilkenny Castle's Butler dynasty. Outside stands a 30m-high round tower, one of only two in Ireland that you can climb.

Records show that a wooden church on the site was burned down in 1087. The existing structure was raised between 1202 and 1285, but then endured a series of catastrophes and resurrections. The first disaster, the collapse of the church tower in 1332, was associated with Dame Alice Kyteler's conviction for witchcraft. Her maid

Petronella was also convicted, and her nephew, William Outlawe, was implicated. The unfortunate maid was burned at the stake, but Dame Alice escaped to London and William saved himself by offering to reroof part of St Canice's Cathedral with lead tiles. His new roof proved too heavy, however, and brought the church tower down with it.

In 1650 Cromwell's forces defaced and damaged the church, using it to stable their horses. Repairs began in 1661; the beautiful roof in the nave was completed in 1863.

Inside, highly polished ancient **grave slabs** are set on the walls and the floor. On the northern wall, a slab inscribed in Norman French commemorates Jose de Keteller, who died in 1280; despite the difference in spelling he was probably the father of Alice Kyteler. The **stone chair of St Kieran** embedded in the wall dates from the 13th century. The fine 1596 monument to Honorina Grace at the western end of the southern aisle is made of beautiful local black limestone. In the southern transept is the handsome black **tomb of Piers Butler**, who died in 1539, and his wife, Margaret Fitzgerald. Tombs and monuments (listed on a board in the southern aisle) to other notable Butlers crowd this corner of

COUNTIES WEXFORD, WATERFORD, CARLOW & KILKENNY KILKENNY CITY

KILKENNY ARTS & CRAFTS

At least 130 full-time craftspeople and artists work commercially in County Kilkenny – one of the highest concentrations in Ireland – thanks to its fine raw materials and inspirational scenery.

Among the best places to see their work:

Kilkenny Design Centre (p206) Has works by more than a dozen local craftspeople.

National Craft Gallery (p203) Features furniture, jewellery and textiles from all over Ireland.

Rudolf Heltzel Goldsmith (☎ 056-772 1497; http://rudolfheltzel.com; 10 Patrick St; ⊙ 9.30am-1pm & 2-5.30pm Mon-Sat) Fine-art jewellery.

Grennan Mill Craft School (p208) Exhibitions of students' pottery, prints and drawings.

Jerpoint Glass Studio (www.jerpointglass.com; Glenmore, Stoneyford; ⊙ 10am-6pm Mon-Sat, noon-5pm Sun Mar-Oct, shorter hours Nov-Feb) FREE Watch skilled glass-blowers at work.

Moth to a Flame (p208) Handmade art candlpassaes.

Nicholas Mosse (p208) Brightly coloured ceramics and tableware.

Bridge Pottery (p207) Small studio creating gorgeous ceramics.

Cushendale Woollen Mill (☎ 059-972 4118; www.cushendale.ie; Mill Rd, Graignamanagh; ⊙ 8.30am-12.30pm & 1.30-5.30pm Mon-Fri, 10am-1pm Sat) High-quality Irish textiles.

Clay Creations (p209) Gallery of original and unusual ceramic pieces.

Pick up a copy of the **Made in Kilkenny craft trail** (www.madeinkilkenny.ie) for a comprehensive list of studios and shops.

the church. Also worth a look is a model of Kilkenny as it was in 1642.

Apart from missing its crown, the 9th-century **round tower** is in excellent condition. Inside is a tight squeeze and you'll need both hands to climb the 100 steps up steep ladders (under 12s not admitted).

Walking to the cathedral from Parliament St leads you over Irishtown Bridge and up **St Canice's Steps**, which date from 1614; the wall at the top contains fragments of medieval carvings. The leaning tombstones scattered about the grounds prompt you to look, at the very least, for a black cat.

Rothe House & Garden   MUSEUM
(📞 056-772 2893; www.rothehouse.com; Parliament St; adult/child €5.50/4.50; ⊙ 10.30am-5pm Mon-Sat, noon-5pm Sun Apr-Oct, 10.30am-4.30pm Mon-Sat Nov-Mar) Dating from 1594 this is Ireland's finest example of a Tudor merchant's house, complete with restored medieval garden. Built around a series of courtyards, it now houses a museum with a rather sparse display of local artefacts including a rusted Viking sword and a grinning stone head sculpted by a Celtic artist. The highlight is the delightful walled garden, divided into fruit, vegetable and herb sections and a traditional orchard, as it would have been in the 17th century.

In the 1640s the wealthy Rothe family played a part in the Confederation of Kilkenny, and Peter Rothe, son of the original builder, had all his property confiscated. His sister was able to reclaim it, but just before the Battle of the Boyne (1690) the family supported James II and so lost the house permanently. In 1850 a Confederation banner was discovered in the house; it's now in the National Museum in Dublin.

National Craft Gallery   GALLERY
(📞 056-779 6147; www.nationalcraftgallery.ie; Castle Yard; ⊙ 10am-5.30pm Tue-Sun; 👶) FREE Contemporary Irish crafts are showcased at these imaginative galleries, set in former stables across the road from Kilkenny Castle, next to the shops of the Kilkenny Design Centre (p206). Ceramics dominate, but exhibits often feature furniture, jewellery and weaving from the members of the Crafts Council of Ireland. Family days are held the third Saturday of every month, with a tour of the gallery and free hands-on workshops for children. For additional workshops and events, check the website.

Behind the complex, look for the gate that leads into the beautiful **Butler House Gardens** (The Parade; ⊙ 10am-5pm Mon-Fri, to noon Sat & Sun) FREE, with an unusual water feature constructed from remnants of the British-built Nelson Pillar, which once stood in Dublin's O'Connell St but was blown up by the IRA in 1966.

Black Abbey   CHURCH
(http://visitkilkenny.ie/black_abbey; Abbey St; ⊙ 7.30am-7pm Mon-Sat, 9am-7pm Sun Apr-Sep, 7.30am-5.30pm Mon-Sat, 9am-5.30pm Sun Oct-Mar) FREE This Dominican abbey was founded in 1225 by William Marshal and takes its name from the monks' black habits. Much of what survives dates from the 18th and 19th centuries, but remnants of more ancient archways are still evident, and the stained glass is glorious. When services are not being held (check website for Mass times), you can pick up an information leaflet in exchange for a donation and explore; look for the 13th-century coffins near the entrance.

Smithwick's Experience   BREWERY
(📞 056-778 6377; www.smithwicksexperience.com; Parliament St; adult/child €13/7; ⊙ 10am-6pm Mar-Oct, 11am-5pm Nov-Feb) Until its closure, Smithwick's was Ireland's oldest working brewery. John Smithwick founded the business in 1710 on the site of Kilkenny's 13th-century St Francis Abbey (the abbey ruins remain within the complex). Smithwick's is now owned by drinks giant Diageo (Guinness, Harp et al), which moved production to Dublin in 2014.

The old brewery complex now functions as a tourist attraction, offering one-hour tours where you can learn about the brewing process and the history of the brewery, and do some tasting.

Nore Linear Park   WALKING
This network of footpaths allows walkers to hike southeast along the banks of the River Nore as far as the ring road (2.5km) and return on the opposite side. Ask the tourist office (p206) for a map or see http://trail kilkenny.ie.

The **Canal Walk**, on the southwest bank, leads under the castle and on past mill races, weirs and the ruins of 19th-century woollen mills, some of which continued working until the 1960s. The **Lacken Walk**, on the northeast side, begins on Maudlin St.

👉 Tours

Kilkenny Cycling Tours   CYCLING
(📞086 895 4961; www.kilkennycyclingtours.com; adult/child from €25/16; 🚲) Explore the city and surrounds on a bike over a 2½-hour tour that can include a lunch option; prebooking is essential, at least 48 hours in advance. Bikes are delivered to your accommodation.

Pat Tynan Walking Tours   WALKING
(📞087 265 1745; www.kilkennywalkingtours.ie; €7; 🕙11am & 2pm daily mid-Mar–Oct) Entertaining, informative 70-minute walking tours through Kilkenny's narrow lanes, steps and pedestrian passageways. Meet at the tourist office (p206).

🎉 Festivals & Events

★Cat Laughs Comedy Festival   COMEDY
(📞056-776 3837; www.thecatlaughs.com; 🕙May-Jun) An acclaimed gathering of world-class comedians, including Irish stars such as Dara O'Briain and Aisling Bea, in Kilkenny's hotels and pubs over a long weekend in late May/early June.

Kilkenny Rhythm & Roots   MUSIC
(📞056-776 3669; www.kilkennyroots.com; 🕙Apr-May) More than 30 pubs and other venues participate in hosting this major music festival in late April/early May, with an emphasis on country and 'old-time' American roots music.

Kilkenny Arts Festival   ART
(📞056-776 3663; www.kilkennyarts.ie; 🕙Aug; 🚲) In August the city comes alive with theatre, cinema, music, literature, visual arts, children's events and street spectacles for 10 action-packed days.

🛏 Sleeping

If you're arriving in town with no room booked (an unwise move at weekends, in summer and during festivals), the tourist office (p206) runs an efficient accommodation booking service (€4).

Tree Grove Caravan
& Camping Park   CAMPGROUND $
(📞086-830 8845; www.treegrovecamping.com; New Ross Rd; sites campervan €17-28, hiker €8-9; 🕙Mar–mid-Nov; 🛜) An attractive camp ground set in a small park 1.5km south of Kilkenny off the R700, a pleasant half-hour walk along the river from the city centre.

Kilkenny Tourist Hostel   HOSTEL $
(📞056-776 3541; www.kilkennyhostel.ie; 35 Parliament St; dm/tw from €17/42; @🛜) Inside an ivy-covered 1770s Georgian townhouse, this fairly standard, 60-bed IHH hostel has a sitting room warmed by an open fireplace, and a timber- and leadlight-panelled dining room adjoining the self-catering kitchen. Excellent location, but a place for relaxing rather than partying.

★Rosquil House   GUESTHOUSE $$
(📞056-772 1419; www.rosquilhouse.com; Castlecomer Rd; r from €95, 2-person apt from €80; 🅿🛜) Rooms at this immaculately maintained guesthouse are decorated with dark-wood furniture and pretty paisley fabrics, while the guest lounge is similarly tasteful with sink-into sofas, brass-framed mirrors and leafy plants. The breakfast is above average with homemade granola and fluffy omelettes. There's also a well-equipped and comfortable self-catering apartment (minimum three-night stay).

★Pembroke Hotel   HOTEL $$
(📞056-780 2111; www.pembrokekilkenny.com; Patrick St; r from €120; 🅿@🛜) Wake up to castle views (from some of the rooms) at this stylish, modern and central hotel. Good-value deluxe rooms feature balconies, and the overall room decor is easy on the eye with a muted moss-green, soft-blue and dark-red colour scheme. There's a leather sofa–filled bar, and the use of swimming and leisure facilities just around the corner.

Butler House   HOTEL $$
(📞056-772 2828; www.butler.ie; 16 Patrick St; r from €139; 🅿@🛜) You can't stay in Kilkenny Castle, but this historic mansion is the next best thing. Once the home of the earls of Ormonde, today it houses a hotel that combines modern design with aristocratic trappings including sweeping staircases, marble fireplaces, an art collection and impeccable gardens. The generous rooms are individually decorated and, to remind you you're staying amid history, the floors creak.

Butler Court   INN $$
(📞056-776 1178; www.butlercourt.com; Patrick St; r €85-130; 🅿🛜) Not to be confused with the grand Butler House, this was originally the mail-coach yard for Kilkenny Castle. Wrapping around a flower-filled courtyard, contemporary rooms have Canadian-cherry parquet floors, and eye-catching photography

or Celtic art on the walls. A continental breakfast, including fresh fruit and filtered coffee, is stocked in your in-room fridge.

Bregagh House
B&B $$

(☑056-772 2315; www.bregaghhouse.com; Dean St; s/d from €60/100; ℗) If you want the cosiness that comes with staying in a family home, this B&B is a good bet. It offers a convenient location near the cathedral, comfortable soundproof guest rooms and filling hot breakfasts (or continental). There's ample on-site parking and a conservatory overlooking a pretty back garden with a magnificent copper beech tree.

Celtic House
B&B $$

(☑056-776 2249; www.celtic-house-bandb.com; 18 Michael St; r €60-80; ℗@🛜) Artist and author Angela Byrne extends one of Ireland's warmest welcomes at this homely and comfortable B&B. Some of the brightly decorated bedrooms have sky-lit bathrooms, others have views of the castle, and Angela's landscapes adorn many of the walls. Book ahead.

Langton House Hotel
HOTEL $$

(☑056-776 5133; www.langtons.ie; 67 John St; s/d from €85/150; ℗🛜) In the same family since the 1930s, but constantly evolving, this Kilkenny icon has 34 corporate-style rooms with dark wood and sombre-toned furnishings. The beige-tiled bathrooms have superb high-power pressure showers. There's a fine restaurant and a popular pub.

Kilkenny River Court
HOTEL $$$

(☑056-772 3388; www.rivercourthotel.com; John St; s/d from €126/130; ℗@🛜♨) When not unwinding in your spacious modern room, you can dine at the respected restaurant, swim laps in the award-winning health club's sunlit indoor pool, or sip a cocktail on the cobblestone terrace of the wraparound bar overlooking the river beneath the castle. Staff are consistently helpful. Rates increase by 25% to 50% at weekends.

Eating

From simple cafe to Michelin-starred restaurant, Kilkenny city offers a huge choice of places to eat; in the top-end restaurants it's best to book a table at weekends.

Mocha's Vintage Tearooms
CAFE $

(www.facebook.com/thevintagetearoomsby mocha; 4 The Arches, Gashouse Lane; mains €7-14; ⊙8.30am-5.30pm Mon-Sat) Cute retro tearoom with picture-cluttered walls and rose-patterned

china. As well as tea and cakes, there's a breakfast menu (until 11.30am) with a choice of bagels or a full Irish fry-up, and hot lunch specials including fish and chips.

Gourmet Store
SANDWICHES $

(☑056-777 1727; 56 High St; sandwich & coffee €5; ⊙8am-6pm Mon-Sat) In this crowded little deli, takeaway sandwiches are assembled from choice imported meats and cheeses (plus a few top-notch local varieties).

★Zuni
IRISH $$

(☑056-772 3999; http://zuni.ie; 26 Patrick St; mains lunch €8-14, dinner €20-27; ⊙12.30-2.30pm daily, 6-9.30pm Mon-Sat, 6-9pm Sun; 🛜) ✿ Among Kilkenny's most stylish and busiest restaurants, Zuni manages to hold its place on the cutting edge it pioneered when it opened just before the turn of the millennium. It's sophisticated yet informal, with a menu that lends a gourmet touch to hearty, lip-smacking comfort food such as strip steak with onions and roast mushroom gravy on focaccia. Yum.

★Foodworks
BISTRO, CAFE $$

(☑056-777 7696; www.foodworks.ie; 7 Parliament St; lunch mains €14, 3-course dinner €30; ⊙noon-4.30pm Sun-Wed, noon-9.30pm Thu-Sat; 🛜🍴) ✿ The owners of this cool and casual bistro keep their own pigs and grow their own salad leaves, so it would be churlish not to try their pork belly stuffed with black pudding, or confit pig's trotter – and you'll be glad you did. Delicious food, excellent coffee and friendly service make this a justifiably popular venue; it's best to book a table.

Rinuccini
ITALIAN $$

(☑056-776 1575; www.rinuccini.com; 1 The Parade; dinner mains €17-29; ⊙noon-2.30pm & 5-10pm Mon-Sat, noon-9pm Sun) Follow a short flight of steps down to a candlelit basement to bliss out on Antonio Cavaliere's classic Italian cuisine, including house special *gamberoni Rinuccini* (fresh Kilmore Quay langoustines with a cream, brandy and Dijon mustard sauce). The two-/three-course lunch and early-bird menu costs €24/29.

Kilkenny Design Centre Foodhall & Restaurant
CAFETERIA $$

(www.kilkennydesign.com; Castle Yard; mains €7-15; ⊙10am-6pm; 🛜🍴) Upstairs from the craft shops, this arty, organic-oriented, self-service cafeteria offers home-baked breads and scones, tasty seafood chowder, salads in vast variety, gourmet sandwiches, hot specials and sumptuous desserts.

★ Campagne
MODERN IRISH $$$

(☑056-777 2858; www.campagne.ie; 5 Gashouse Lane; mains €30-33; ⊙12.30-2.30pm Fri-Sun, 6-10pm Tue-Thu, 5.30-10pm Fri & Sat) 🍴 Chef Garrett Byrne was awarded a Michelin star for this bold, stylish restaurant in his native Kilkenny. He's passionate about supporting local and artisan producers, and serves ever-changing, ever-memorable meals, adding a French accent to every culinary creation. The three-course lunch and early bird menu (till 7pm Tuesday to Thursday, till 6pm Friday and Saturday) is €34.

Drinking & Nightlife

★ Kyteler's Inn
PUB

(☑056-772 1064; www.kytelersinn.com; 27 St Kieran's St; ⊙11am-midnight Sun-Thu, to 2am Fri & Sat) Dame Alice Kyteler's old house was built back in 1224 and has seen its share of history: she was charged with witchcraft in 1323. Today the rambling bar includes the original building, complete with vaulted ceiling and arches. There is a beer garden, a courtyard and a large upstairs room for the live bands (nightly March to October), ranging from trad to blues.

O'Hara's Brewery Corner
PUB

(☑056-780 5081; www.carlowbrewing.com/our-pub; 29 Parliament St; ⊙1-11.30pm Mon-Thu, to 12.30am Fri & Sat, to 11pm Sun) Kilkenny's best venue for craft brews is a long, narrow beer hall of a place owned by Carlow Brewing Company. Service can be a bit hit or miss, especially at quiet times, but there's a wide selection of ale to choose from, including Carlow's own IPA.

John Cleere's
PUB

(☑056-776 2573; www.cleeres.com; 22 Parliament St; ⊙11.30am-11.30pm Mon-Thu, to 12.30am Fri & Sat, 1-11pm Sun) One of Kilkenny's finest venues for live music, theatre and comedy, this long bar has blues, jazz and rock, as well as trad music sessions on Monday and Wednesday. Food is served throughout the day, including soup, sandwiches, pizza and Irish stew.

Left Bank
BAR

(☑056-775 0016; www.leftbank.ie; The Parade; ⊙noon-11.30pm Mon-Thu, to 12.30am Fri & Sat, 12.30-11pm Sun) This former Bank of Ireland building has been resurrected as undoubtedly the most eye-catching bar in town. Dating from the 1870s, the interior is magnificent with original portico columns, carved-wood detail, exposed brick walls and chandeliers. Snacks also served.

Bridie's General Store
PUB

(☑056-776 5133; John St; ⊙11am-10pm Sun-Wed, 6pm-2am Thu-Sat) Top design talent was employed by the Langton's empire to create this reproduction trad grocery-cum-pub; the results are worth it. The front is a beguiling retail potpourri of souvenirs, jokes, toys, preserves and deli items. Step through the swinging doors to arrive at a new/old pub with beautiful tiles, while outback is a fittingly classy beer garden.

☆ Entertainment

Watergate Theatre
THEATRE

(☑box office 056-776 1674; www.watergate theatre.com; Parliament St) Kilkenny's top theatre venue hosts drama, comedy and musical performances. If you're wondering why intermission lasts 18 minutes, it's so patrons can nip into John Cleere's pub for a pint.

Nowlan Park GAA Stadium
SPECTATOR SPORT

(www.kilkennygaa.ie; O'Loughlin Rd) One of the classic experiences of a trip to Ireland is catching a game of hurling at the Kilkenny Cats' hallowed home stadium.

🛍 Shopping

★ Kilkenny Design Centre
ARTS & CRAFTS

(☑056-772 2118; www.kilkennydesign.com; Castle Yard; ⊙10am-7pm) Sells top-end Irish crafts and artworks, from county-wide artisans. Look for John Hanly wool blankets, Cushendale woollen goods, Foxford scarves and Bunbury cutting boards.

Farmers Market
MARKET

(☑056-779 4515; Mayors Walk, The Parade; ⊙9.30am-2.30pm Thu) Kilkenny's weekly farmers market is a showcase for local produce.

Kilkenny Book Centre
BOOKS

(☑056-776 2117; http://thebookcentre.ie; 10 High St; ⊙10am-5pm Mon-Sat) The largest bookshop in town, stocking plenty of Irish-interest fiction and nonfiction, periodicals and a good range of maps. There's a cafe upstairs.

ⓘ Information

Kilkenny Tourist Office (☑056-775 1500; www.visitkilkenny.ie; Rose Inn St; ⊙9am-6pm Mon-Sat, 10.30am-4pm Sun) Stocks guides and walking maps. Located in Shee Alms House, dating from 1582 and built in local stone by benefactor Sir Richard Shee to help the poor.

ℹ Getting There & Away

BUS

Bus Éireann (p694) and DublinCoach (http://www.dublincoach.ie/) services **stop** at the train station and on Ormonde Rd (nearer the town centre); JJ Kavanagh (www.jjkavanagh.ie) buses to Dublin airport stop on Ormonde Rd only.

Carlow (€10.40, 35 minutes, four daily) Bus Éireann

Cork (€15, 2½ hours, every two hours) Dublin-Coach M9 Express

Dublin (€14.50, 2¼ hours, two daily) Bus Éireann X4

Dublin airport (€20, two to three hours, seven daily) JJ Kavanagh

Waterford (€5, 40 minutes, every two hours) DublinCoach M9 Express

TRAIN

Kilkenny's **MacDonagh train station** (Dublin Rd) is a 10-minute walk northeast of the town centre, with trains to Dublin Heuston (€25.85, 1½ hours, six daily) and Waterford (€13.85, 40 minutes, seven daily).

Kells & Around

Kells (not to be confused with Kells in County Meath) is a mere hamlet with a fine stone bridge on a tributary of the Nore. However, in Kells Priory, the village has one of Ireland's most evocative monastic sites. The village is 13km south of Kilkenny city on the R697.

◉ Sights

★**Kells Priory**   RUINS

(☉ dawn-dusk; Ⓟ) FREE This fortified Augustinian monastery is the best sort of ruin, where you can amble around whenever you like, with no tour guides, set hours or fees. Most days you stand a chance of exploring the site alone (apart from some nosy sheep); at dusk with a clear sky the old priory is simply beautiful. The ruins are 500m east of Kells on the Stoneyford road; from the car park, head to the right of the walls to find the main entrance.

The earliest remains of the monastic site date from the late 12th century, while the bulk of the present ruins are from the 15th century. In a sea of rich farmland, a carefully restored protective wall connects seven dwelling towers. Within the walls are the remains of an **Augustinian abbey** and the foundations of several chapels and houses. It's unusually well fortified and the heavy curtain walls hint at a troubled history. Indeed, within a single century

from 1250, the abbey was twice fought over and burned down by squabbling warlords. Its permanent decline began when it was suppressed in 1540 as part of King Henry VIII's campaign to dissolve all Catholic monasteries in England, Wales and Ireland.

Kilree Round Tower & High Cross   HISTORIC SITE

(☉ dawn-dusk) FREE About 2km south of Kells, signposted across the road from Kells Priory car park, there's a 29m-high round tower, an ancient church and a Celtic high cross, said to mark the grave of a 9th-century Irish high king, Niall Caille. He apparently drowned in the Kings River at Callan some time in the 840s while attempting to save a servant, and his body washed up near Kells. His final resting place lies outside the church grounds because he wasn't a Christian.

🛏 Sleeping & Eating

★**Lawcus Farm**   GUESTHOUSE $$

(☎ 056-772 8949; www.lawcusfarmguesthouse.com; Lawcus, Stoneyford; s/d/f from €80/100/150; Ⓟ 🤶) 🍴 Bought as a thatched ruin, this 18th-century farmhouse has been rebuilt and expanded to create an enchanting place to stay. Rooms typically have stone walls, rustic antiques and quirky curiosities, while breakfast features the farm's own eggs, sausages and ham. The farm is bordered by the Kings River (fishing available for guests) and signposted off the minor road between Kells and Stoneyford.

Jen's at Knockdrinna   DELI, CAFE $

(☎ 083 800 7474; www.facebook.com/jensknockdrinna; Main St, Stoneyford; cafe mains €6-10, 3-course dinner €28; ☉ 10am-4.30pm Tue-Sat, 7-10.30pm Sat, 10am-2.30pm Sun; 🍴) 🍴 This gourmet cafe and deli is a tiny tour de force of locally produced cheese, cured meats, smoked fish, salads and much more. Assemble a meal that will outclass your previous best picnic, or settle down at a table for an all-day breakfast, sit-in lunch or Saturday dinner (bookings essential for dinner). Stoneyford is 9km northwest of Thomastown.

🛍 Shopping

Bridge Pottery   CERAMICS

(☎ 056-772 9156; www.thebridgepottery.com; Burnchurch; ☉ 10am-6pm Mon-Sat) Hidden away on a country lane 8km northwest of Kells, this rural pottery is the base for Mark Campden, who turns out colourful majolica pieces with meticulous hand-painted decoration, while his partner Caroline Dolan creates elegant vases, bowls, mugs and jugs in tin-glazed earthenware.

Bennettsbridge & Around

Bennettsbridge is home to a couple of craft studios and shops. Just 7km south of Kilkenny city on the R700, the village takes its name from the elegant 18th-century stone bridge that spans the River Nore.

Nore Valley Park FARM
(☑ 056-772 7229; www.norevalleypark.com; Annamult; adult/child €7/6.50; ☺ park 9am-6pm Mon-Sat Mar-Oct; ℗ ⓘ) A 180-acre farm where children can pet goats, cuddle rabbits, navigate a maze (in the former barn), play crazy golf and jump on a straw bounce. There's also a tearoom and picnic area. It's 4km south of Bennettsbridge, along Annamult Rd on the west side of the river.

Nicholas Mosse Irish Country Shop CERAMICS
(☑ 056-772 7505; www.nicholasmosse.com; Bennettsbridge; ☺ 10am-6pm Mon-Sat, 1.30-5pm Sun) Housed in an old mill across the river from the village, this pottery shop specialises in handmade spongeware – ceramics decorated with sponged patterns – which is exported worldwide to retail outlets such as Tiffany's. Short audiovisual displays explain the manufacturing process.

The cafe here is the best choice locally for lunch, with a range of soups, sandwiches and hot dishes, plus its renowned scones.

Moth to a Flame ARTS & CRAFTS
(☑ 056-772 7826; www.mothtoaflame.ie; Kilkenny Rd, Bennettsbridge; ☺ 9am-6pm Mon-Sat) Established in 1999 this workshop creates beautifully coloured and textured candles of all sizes, from bedside table to church altar scale.

Thomastown & Around

Named after 14th-century Welsh mercenary Thomas de Cantwell, who became a local lord, Thomastown retains some fragments of its medieval town walls. Down by the bridge over the River Nore (built in 1792) you can find **Mullin's Castle**, the

most prominent survivor of no fewer than 14 towers that once stood along the town perimeter. There's good **trout fishing** here; get a permit at Simon Treacy Hardware, just along from the bridge.

Like the rest of Kilkenny, the area has a vibrant craft scene – look out for Clay Creations.

⊙ Sights & Activities

★**Jerpoint Abbey** RUINS
(☑ 056-772 4623; www.heritageireland.ie; Jerpoint, Thomastown; adult/child €5/3; ☺ 9am-5.30pm Mar-Sep, to 5pm Oct, 9.30am-4pm Nov, closed Dec-Feb) One of Ireland's finest Cistercian ruins, Jerpoint Abbey was established in the 12th century, with the tower and cloister dating from the late-14th or early-15th century. It is famous for its unusually large number of medieval stone carvings – look for the series of unusual and often amusing figures, both human and animal, carved on the pillars around the cloister. The abbey enjoys a lovely rural setting about 2.5km southwest of Thomastown on the N9.

Faint traces of a 15th- or 16th-century painting remain on the northern wall of the church. This chancel area also contains a tomb thought to belong to hard-headed Felix O'Dulany, Jerpoint's first abbot and bishop of Ossory, who died in 1202.

Jerpoint Park HISTORIC SITE
(☑ 086 606 1449; www.jerpointpark.com; Belmore House, Jerpoint, Thomastown; admission €8, sheepdog demos €5; ☺ 10am-5pm May-Sep, hours can vary; ℗) Jerpoint Park is a working farm on the site of a 12th-century medieval town, where 90-minute guided tours (10am, noon and 3pm) use cutting-edge archaeological techniques to reveal in detail the settlement that once stood here. This includes the ruined Church of St Nicholas where, according to local legend, St Nicholas (or Santa Claus) is buried. There are also sheepdog demonstrations, angling on the River Nore, and a tearoom (open July and August) famed for its homemade scones. It's 3km southwest of Thomastown.

Grennan Mill Craft School ART STUDIO
(☑ 056-772 4557; www.grennanmillcraftschool.com; Island Mill, Thomastown; ☺ 10am-6pm, hours vary) FREE Housed in an old mill building, this craft school runs courses in ceramics, metalwork, batik and drawing, and stages regular exhibitions of arts and crafts includ-

ing an annual graduate show in June. It also runs three-day weekend courses in summer (€220 per person, beginners welcome) where you can learn how to use a potter's wheel.

Kilfane Church RUINS

(Kilfane; ⊘24hr) **FREE** About 3km north of Thomastown, east of the R448, is a small, ruined 13th-century church and Norman tower, signposted 50m off the road. The church contains a remarkable, life-size **stone effigy of Thomas de Cantwell** called the Cantwell Fada or Long Man. It depicts a tall, thin knight in detailed chain-mail armour brandishing a shield decorated with the Cantwell coat of arms.

Mount Juliet GOLF

(☑056-777 3071; www.mountjuliet.ie; Mount Juliet Estate, Jerpoint; green fees €65-115) Just 4km southwest of Thomastown, high-fliers tee off at the Jack Nicklaus–designed Mount Juliet. Set over 600 wooded acres, it also has its own equestrian centre, a gym and spa, two restaurants, wine masterclasses, and palatial rooms catering to every whim, right down to a pillow menu (accommodation from €150).

Eating

★ Blackberry Cafe CAFE $

(www.theblackberrycafe.ie; Market St, Thomastown; mains €5-9; ⊘9.30am-5.30pm Mon-Fri, 10am-5.30pm Sat; ⊞) Superb thick-cut sandwiches, toasties, quiche and warming soups are served with pumpkin-seed-speckled soda bread here. Much is organic, and the tarts and cakes are baked daily. Between noon and 2pm, great-value hot lunches see the place packed to bursting.

Shopping

Clay Creations CERAMICS

(☑087 257 0735; www.bridlyonsceramics.com; Low St, Thomastown; ⊘10am-5.30pm Wed-Sat, by appointment Mon & Tue) Clay Creations displays the quixotic ceramics and sculptures of local artist Brid Lyons.

Getting There & Away

➜ Kilbride Coaches (www.kilbridecoaches. com) runs buses from Kilkenny to Thomastown (€4.50, 25 minutes, twice daily except Sunday), continuing to Inistioge and New Ross.

➜ Trains on the Dublin to Waterford route via Kilkenny stop at Thomastown station, 1km west of town.

Inistioge
POP 285

Tiny Inistioge (*in*-ish-teeg) is a delight, with its tranquil village square, riverside park and 18th-century, 10-arch stone bridge spanning the River Nore (fishing permits available from O'Donnell's pub on the square). The **Nore Valley Walk** heads north along the riverbank to Thomastown, or try the **Nature Walk** signposted south from the square.

The R700 from Thomastown makes for a lovely scenic drive along the Nore valley, and features views of the ruined 13th-century **Grennan Castle**.

Kilbride Coaches (www.kilbridecoaches. com) runs buses from Kilkenny to Inistioge (€5, 35 minutes, twice daily except Sunday), continuing to New Ross.

Woodstock Gardens GARDENS

(☑056-779 4373; www.woodstock.ie; parking €4; ⊘9am-7pm Apr-Sep, 10am-4pm Oct-Mar) **FREE** Thickly wooded Woodstock Gardens is a beauty of a park with huge landscaped terraces, a walled garden, an arboretum (including two 40m-tall redwoods), walking trails and a cafe (open 11am to 5pm at weekends only). From Inistioge, follow Main St (opposite the Woodstock Arms) for 1km to signs for Woodstock Estate and enter the large gates (despite appearances, it's a public road) then continue along the road for another 2km until you reach the car park.

Woodstock Arms B&B $$

(☑056-775 8440; www.woodstockarms.ie; The Square; s/d/tr from €40/70/90; ☏) This picturesque pub has tables on the square and seven basic bedrooms that are squeaky clean; the triples are particularly spacious. Breakfast is served in a pretty little room out the back with wooden tables and traditional local china.

Circle of Friends CAFE $

(☑056-347 9503; rudd_dennis@yahoo.ie; High St; mains €7-14; ⊘11am-5pm Tue-Fri, to 6pm Sat & Sun, longer hours Jun-Aug) With tables on the street, this cheerful cafe has flavoured coffees (mint, caramel and so on), all-day breakfasts, hot dishes such as beer-battered cod and chips and – the reason everyone's really here – gargantuan servings of homemade desserts such as pavlova. It's named for the 1995 film of the Maeve Binchy novel, parts of which were shot in the village.

COUNTIES WEXFORD, WATERFORD, CARLOW & KILKENNY INISTIOGE

COUNTY KILKENNY WALKS

The **South Leinster Way** (www.irish trails.ie) slices through the hilly southern part of County Kilkenny, from Graiguenamanagh to Inistioge, down to Mullinavat and westward to Piltown. By far the prettiest part, a stretch of some 13km, links the two charming villages of Graiguenamanagh and Inistioge; in either you can reward yourself with a tasty meal.

Along this path, 4km south of Graiguenamanagh, you can branch off onto the **Brandon Hill Loop** (purple waymarks; www.trailkilkenny.ie), which scales Brandon Hill (516m). The broad moorland summit is easily reached and affords a lovely view of the Blackstairs Mountains and Mt Leinster to the east. The return trip from Graiguenamanagh is a fairly relaxed 12km walk.

Graiguenamanagh

POP 1475

Graiguenamanagh (greg-nuh-*mah*-na; known locally as just Graig) is the kind of place where you could easily find yourself staying longer than planned. Spanning the Barrow, an ancient six-arch stone bridge is illuminated at night and connects the village with the smaller township of Tinnahinch on the County Carlow side of the river (look for the darker stones at the Carlow end of the bridge – a legacy of being rebuilt after getting blown up during the 1798 Rising).

There are good walks near town, notably the riverside Barrow Way (p196).

◉ Sights & Activities

Duiske Abbey CHURCH

(☑059-972 4238; Main St; ☉9am-6pm May-Sep, to 5pm Oct-Apr) FREE This was once Ireland's largest Cistercian abbey, founded in 1204, and is still very much a working parish church. In the grounds stand two Celtic **high crosses** (7th century and 9th century), brought here in the last century for protection. Around the corner, the **Abbey Centre** (open 9am to 1pm weekdays only) houses a small exhibition of Christian art, plus pictures of the abbey in its unrestored state.

Waterside Bike & Hike CYCLING, WALKING

(☑086-408 4008; www.watersideguesthouse.com; The Quay; pedal/electric bikes per day €20/25; ☉9am-6pm) The classic summer outing in Graig is to walk or ride a bike along the grassy River Barrow towpath (p196) to the pretty village of St Mullins. This guesthouse (p210) on the quayside rents electric bikes as well as ordinary mountain bikes, and can provide advice on local walks.

✴ Festivals & Events

Town of Books Festival LITERATURE

(☑086 821 1140; www.graiguenamanaghtownof books.com; ☉late Aug) Graiguenamanagh's narrow streets spill over with booksellers, authors and bibliophiles during this three-day festival. There are hopes that Graiguenamanagh will become a year-round 'book town' in the same vein as Wales' Hay-on-Wye.

🛏 Sleeping & Eating

Waterside GUESTHOUSE $$

(☑059-972 4246; www.watersideguesthouse.com; The Quay; s/d from €65/90; ☉restaurant 6-10pm Mon-Sat, noon-3pm Sun Apr-Sep, Fri-Sun only Oct-Mar; 🛜) Overlooking the boats tied up along the river, this inviting guesthouse and restaurant occupies a converted 19th-century grain store. Its 10 renovated bedrooms have exposed timber beams, and the restaurant is well regarded for its interesting modern Irish menu (mains €15 to €19) and its regular 'After Dinner Live' music acts featuring anything from jazz to bluegrass.

🍷 Drinking & Nightlife

Mick Doyle's PUB

(☑059-972 4203; www.facebook.com/mickdoyles graig; Main St; ☉11.30am-11pm Mon-Sat, 12.30-10.30pm Sun) One of Graig's hidden treasures is this unchanged-for-generations shop-pub on Main St. Doyle's is the sort of place where you can buy a bag of potatoes, get some cartridges for your shotgun and pick up some gardening implements, before settling down for a pint and some craic. Live music at the weekends, and trad sessions on Mondays.

F J Murray PUB

(☑059-972 5932; cnr Lower Main St & The Quay; ☉11am-midnight Thu-Sat, noon-11pm Sun) A cosy, old-time pub and the life and soul of the village during its Sunday evening trad sessions; listen out for songs featuring local landmarks.

County Cork

POP 417,211 / AREA 7508 SQ KM

Best Places to Eat

➡ Bastion (p234)

➡ Nash 19 (p219)

➡ Manning's Emporium (p249)

➡ Farmgate Restaurant (p228)

➡ Josie's Lakeview House (p255)

Best Places to Sleep

➡ Garnish House (p218)

➡ Ballymaloe House (p228)

➡ Gilbert's (p226)

➡ Blairscove House (p246)

➡ Old Presbytery (p233)

Why Go?

Everything good about Ireland can be found in County Cork. Surrounding the country's second city – a thriving metropolis made glorious by location and its almost Rabelaisian devotion to the finer things of life – is a lush landscape dotted with villages that offer days of languor and idyll. The city's understated confidence is grounded in its plethora of food markets and ever-evolving cast of creative eateries, and in its selection of pubs, entertainment and cultural pursuits.

Further afield, you'll pass inlets along eroded coastlines and a multitude of perfectly charming old fishing towns and villages. The scenery is every bit as enchanting as the best bits of Ireland, particularly along the Mizen Head, Sheep's Head and Beara Peninsulas, where you can hike wild hills and touch Ireland's ancient past.

When to Go

➡ Springtime in April and May is heralded in Baltimore with a fiddle fair, followed by a seafood and jazz festival.

➡ July and August are peak season for whale-spotting around the Cork coastline, and the best weather for sea-kayak trips.

➡ September and October sees food festivals galore, notably in Skibbereen and Kinsale.

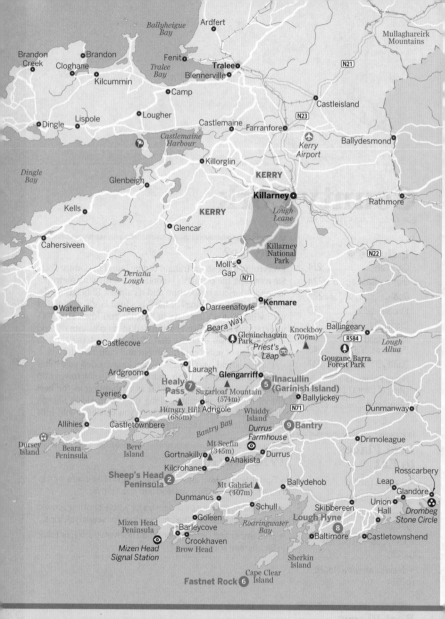

County Cork Highlights

1 Cork city (p214) Revelling in Cork's brilliant selection of restaurants, pubs, music and theatre.

2 Sheep's Head Peninsula (p246) Hiking out to the tip of this windswept and wonderfully remote finger of land.

3 Ballymaloe Cookery School (p228) Catching a culinary demonstration or taking a cookery class at this renowned establishment.

4 Kinsale (p230) Meandering through medieval streets and walking the coast to mammoth Charles Fort.

5 Ilnacullin (p250) Spotting seals and sea eagles as you sail from Glengarriff to this magical

island to explore its subtropical gardens.

6 Fastnet Rock (p243) Braving the Atlantic waves on a thrilling boat trip around this famous landmark.

7 Healy Pass (p251) Driving the narrow, switchback road that climbs across the Beara Peninsula's most spectacular pass.

8 Lough Hyne (p240) Joining a guided sea-kayak tour by moonlight on this lovely marine lake.

9 Bantry House & Garden (p247) Stepping back into a world of fading aristocratic splendour.

CORK CITY

POP 208,669

Ireland's second city is first in every important respect – at least according to the locals, who cheerfully refer to it as the 'real capital of Ireland'. It's a liberal, youthful and cosmopolitan place that was badly hit by economic recession but is now busily reinventing itself with spruced-up streets, revitalised stretches of waterfront, and – seemingly – an artisan coffee bar on every corner. There's a bit of a hipster scene, but the best of the city is still happily traditional – snug pubs with live-music sessions, restaurants dishing up top-quality local produce, and a genuinely proud welcome from the locals.

The compact city centre is set on an island in the River Lee, surrounded by waterways and packed with grand Georgian avenues, cramped 17th-century alleys, modern masterpieces such as the opera house, and narrow streets crammed with pubs, shops, cafes and restaurants, fed by arguably the best foodie scene in the country.

History

Cork has a long and bruising history, inextricably linked with Ireland's struggle for nationhood.

The story begins in the 7th century, when St Fin Barre (also spelt Finbarr and Finbarre) founded a monastery in the midst of a *corcach* (marshy place). By the 12th century the settlement had become the chief city of the Kingdom of South Munster, having survived raids and sporadic settlement by Norsemen. Irish rule was short-lived and by 1185 Cork was in the possession of the English. Thereafter it changed hands regularly during the relentless struggle between Irish and Crown forces. It survived a Cromwellian assault only to fall to that merciless champion of Protestantism, William of Orange.

During the 18th century Cork prospered, with butter, beef, beer and whiskey exported around the world from its port. A mere century later famine devastated both county and city, and robbed Cork of tens of thousands (and Ireland of millions) of its inhabitants by death or emigration.

The 'Rebel City's' deep-seated Irishness ensured that it played a key role in Ireland's struggle for independence. Mayor Thomas MacCurtain was killed by the Black and Tans (British auxiliary troops, so-named because their uniforms were a mixture of army khaki and police black) in 1920. His successor, Terence MacSwiney, died in London's Brixton prison after a hunger strike. The British were at their most brutally repressive in Cork – much of the centre, including St Patrick's St, the City Hall and the Public Library, was burned down. Cork was also a regional focus of Ireland's Civil War in 1922–23.

Today it's a young city, thanks in part to its university: 40% of the population is under 25, and at just 11%, it has the lowest percentage of over 65s in Europe.

⊙ Sights

The best sight in Cork is the city itself – soak it up as you wander the streets. A new conference and events centre, complete with 6000-seat concert venue, tourist centre, restaurants, shops, galleries and apartments, is scheduled to open in 2019 as the focus of the new **Brewery Quarter** (the former Beamish & Crawford brewery site, fronted by the landmark mock-Tudor 'counting house'), a block west of the English Market.

Shandon, perched on a hillside overlooking the city centre to the north, is a great spot for the views alone, but you'll also find galleries, antique shops and cafes along its old lanes and squares. Those tiny old row houses, where generations of workers raised huge families in very basic conditions, are now sought-after urban pieds-à-terre. Pick up a copy of the *Cork Walks – Shandon* leaflet from the tourist office (p223) for a self-guided tour of the district.

★ Cork City Gaol   MUSEUM

(☎021-430 5022; www.corkcitygaol.com; Convent Ave; adult/child €8/5; ⊙9.30am-5pm Apr-Sep, 10am-4pm Oct-Mar) This imposing former prison is well worth a visit, if only to get a sense of how awful life was for prisoners a century ago. An audio tour (€2 extra) guides you around the restored cells, which feature models of suffering prisoners and sadistic-looking guards. Take a bus to UCC – from there walk north along Mardyke Walk, cross the river and follow the signs uphill (10 minutes).

The tour is very moving, bringing home the harshness of the 19th-century penal system. The most common crime was that of poverty; many of the inmates were sentenced to hard labour for stealing loaves of bread. Atmospheric evening tours take place every weekday at 5.45pm (€10).

The prison closed in 1923, reopening in 1927 as a radio station that operated until the 1950s. The Governor's House has been con-

Cork City

COUNTY CORK

Emerson House (500m)

Kent (100m); Cobh (15.5km); Midleton (20.5km)

Ringaskiddy (19km)

Hayfield Manor (300m)

400 m
0.2 miles

Summer Hill

Ship St

Belgrave Pl

York St

Wellington Rd

Sidney Park

Devonshire St

Bridge St

Coburg St

MacCurtain St

Aircoach

St Patrick's Bus Stop

St Patrick's Quay

River Lee North Channel

Merchant's Quay

Parnell Pl

Cork Bus Station

Anderson's Quay

Oliver Plunkett St Lower

Albert Quay

Lapp's Quay

Boardwalk

Albert S City Link Rd

Anglesea St

Morrison's Quay

River Lee South Channel

White St

Rutland St

Maylor St

Caroline St

Phoenix St

Pembroke St

Winthrop St

Robert Morgan St

Cook St

South Mall

Cork City Tourist Office

George's Quay

Mary St

Douglas St

Friar St

Cove St

Sullivan's Quay

Brittany Ferries

Grand Pde

English Market

Oliver Plunkett St

Princes St

Lucy Park

Bishop St

Tobin St

S Main St

Castle St

Mutton La

Paul La

Cornmarket St

St Paul's Ave

French Church St

Carey's La

Academy St

Emmet Pl

Carroll's Quay

Upper John St

SHANDON

Dominick St

Millennium Bridge

Lavitt's Quay

Pope's Quay

Shandon St

N Main St

Cross St

Hanover St

Washington St

Sheares St

Moore St

Grattan St

Blarney St

North Mall

Bachelor's Quay

Banks of the River Lee Walkway

River Lee North Channel

Gurranabraher Rd

Blarney St

Sunday's Well Rd

Grenville Pl

Woods St

Lancaster Quay

Dyke Pde

Western Rd

Mardyke Walk

River Lee South Channel

Donovan's Rd

College Rd

Connaught Ave

Sharman Crawford St

Dean St

Barrack St

Western Rd

Cork City

verted into a **Radio Museum** (www.corkcity gaol.com/radio-museum) where, alongside collections of beautiful old radios, you can hear the story of Guglielmo Marconi's conquest of the airwaves.

Crawford Municipal Art Gallery GALLERY
(☑021-480 5042; www.crawfordartgallery.ie; Emmet Pl; ⊙10am-5pm Mon-Wed, Fri & Sat, to 8pm Thu) FREE Cork's public gallery houses a small but excellent permanent collection covering the 17th century through to the modern day. Highlights include works by Sir John Lavery, Jack B Yeats and Nathaniel Hone, and a room devoted to Irish women artists from 1886 to 1978 – don't miss the pieces by Mainie Jellet and Evie Hone.

The Sculpture Galleries contain snowwhite plaster casts of Roman and Greek statues, given to King George IV by Pope Pius VII in 1822. George didn't like the gift and stuck the sculptures in the cellar until someone suggested that Cork might appreciate them.

Cork Public Museum MUSEUM
(☑021-427 0679; www.corkcity.ie/services/corpo rateandexternalaffairs/museum/; Fitzgerald Park, Mardyke Walk; ⊙11am-1pm & 2.15-5pm Mon-Fri, to 4pm Sat year-round, 3-5pm Sun Apr-Sep) FREE Located in a Georgian mansion with a modern extension, this museum recounts Cork's history. The diverse collection of local artefacts tells the story from the Stone Age right up to local football legend Roy Keane, with a particularly interesting exhibit on medieval Cork and the growth of the city. There's a good cafe around the back.

University College Cork UNIVERSITY
(☑021-490 1876; http://visitorscentre.ucc.ie; College Rd; ⊙9am-5pm Mon-Sat) FREE Established in 1845 as one of three 'queen's colleges' (the others are in Galway and Belfast) set up to

provide nondenominational alternatives to the Anglican Protestant Trinity College in Dublin, UCC's campus spreads around an attractive collection of Victorian Gothic buildings, gardens and historical attractions, including a 19th-century astronomical observatory. Guided walking tours take place at 3pm weekdays and noon on Saturdays.

Stone Corridor   MUSEUM
(☑021-490 1876; www.ucc.ie; UCC Visitors Centre, Main Quad, College Rd; ⊙9am-5pm Mon-Sat) FREE This covered walkway on the north side of University College Cork's Victorian Gothic main quad houses Ireland's biggest collection of Ogham stones, carved with runic inscriptions dating from the 4th to the 6th century AD.

Lewis Glucksman Gallery   GALLERY
(☑021-490 1844; www.glucksman.org; University College Cork, Western Rd; suggested donation €5; ⊙10am-5pm Tue-Sat, 2-5pm Sun; ♿) FREE This award-winning building is a startling construction of limestone, steel and timber. Two floors of galleries with suitably paint-spattered floors display the best in both national and international contemporary art and installation. Don't miss the free fortnightly curatorial tours. The on-site cafe (☑021-490 1848; mains €6-12; ⊙10am-5pm Tue-Sat, noon-5pm Sun) is excellent.

Elizabeth Fort   FORT
(☑021-497 5947; www.elizabethfort.ie; Barrack St; ⊙10am-5pm Mon-Sat & noon-5pm Sun, closed Mon Oct-May) FREE Originally built in the 1620s, and serving as a Garda (police) station from 1929 to 2013, this small star-shaped artillery fort once formed an important part of the city's defences. Recently opened to the public, it offers an insight into Cork's military history, and there are good views across the city from the ramparts. Free guided tours at 1pm provide additional context.

St Fin Barre's Cathedral   CATHEDRAL
(☑021-496 3387; http://corkcathedral.webs.com; Bishop St; adult/child €5/3; ⊙9.30am-5.30pm Mon-Sat, 1.30-2.30pm & 4.30-6pm Sun Apr-Nov, reduced hours Dec-Mar) Spiky spires, gurning gargoyles and elaborate sculpture adorn the exterior of Cork's Protestant cathedral, an attention-grabbing mixture of French Gothic and medieval whimsy. The grandeur continues inside, with marble floor mosaics, a colourful chancel ceiling and a huge pulpit and bishop's throne. Quirky items include a cannonball blasted into an earlier medieval spire during the Siege of Cork (1690). The cathedral sits about 500m southwest of the centre, on the spot where Cork's 7th-century patron saint, Fin Barre, founded a monastery.

Cork Butter Museum   MUSEUM
(☑021-430 0600; www.corkbutter.museum; O'Connell Sq; adult/child €4/3; ⊙10am-6pm Jul & Aug, to 5pm Mar-Jun, Sep & Oct, 11am-3pm Sat & Sun Nov-Feb) Cork has a long tradition of butter manufacturing – in the 1860s it was the world's largest butter market, exporting butter throughout the British Empire – and the trade's history is told through the displays and dioramas of the Cork Butter Museum. The square in front of the museum is dominated by the neoclassical front of the Old Butter Market, and the striking, circular Firkin Crane (p222) building, where butter casks were once weighed (it now houses a dance centre).

🌳 Tours

Cork Walks   WALKING
(☑021-492 4792; http://cork.ie/gettinghereand around/walkingroutes) FREE Cork City Council's four free self-guided tours cover the City Island, South Parish, University and Shandon districts. Pick up a leaflet and map at the tourist office (p223), or download them from the website.

Cork City Tour   BUS
(☑021-430 9090; www.corkcitytour.com; adult/student/child €15/13/5; ⊙Mar-Nov) A hop-on-hop-off open-top bus linking the city's main points of interest. Longer tours (€23 per adult) head to the Jameson Experience (p227) in Midleton.

Atlantic Sea Kayaking   KAYAKING
(☑028-21058; www.atlanticseakayaking.com; Lapp's Quay; €50) Offers guided 'urban kayaking' trips around Cork's waterways from 6.30pm to 9pm (book in advance, minimum two people). They also offer a four-hour trip to Cobh and Spike Island (p225) (minimum four people, €65).

✨ Festivals & Events

Cork World Book Fest   LITERATURE
(https://corkworldbookfest.com; ⊙late Apr) A huge book festival with loads of authors; sponsored by the Cork City Library.

International Choral Festival   MUSIC
(www.corkchoral.ie; ⊙Apr-May) A five-day celebration of choral music held in the City Hall (Albert Quay) and other venues.

BLACKROCK CASTLE

The restored 16th-century **Blackrock Castle** (☑ 021-435 7924; www.bco.ie; Blackrock; adult/child €6.50/5; ⊙ 10am-5pm) that now, rather incongruously, hosts a science centre, planetarium and observatory. Kids love it and the pastoral location is worth the jaunt. It's on the south bank of the River Lee, 5.5km east of the city centre; take bus 202 from Parnell Pl to Blackrock Pier, from where it's a five-minute walk.

Cork Folk Festival　　　　　MUSIC
(www.corkfolkfestival.com; ⊙ Sep-Oct) A long weekend of foot-stomping fiddle, hushed ballads and big-name headline acts such as Martin Simpson, Dick Gaughan and Donovan.

Cork Jazz Festival　　　　　MUSIC
(www.guinnessjazzfestival.com; ⊙ late Oct) Cork's biggest festival has an all-star line-up of jazz, rock and pop in venues across town.

Cork Film Festival　　　　　FILM
(www.corkfilmfest.org; ⊙ Nov) Eclectic, week-long program of international films.

🛏 Sleeping

The city has a good range of accommodation, but rooms can be hard to find during major festivals.

🛏 City Centre

Whether you stay on the main island, or to the north in Shandon or around MacCurtain St, staying here means you're right in the heart of the action.

Brú Bar & Hostel　　　　　HOSTEL €
(☑ 021-455 9667; www.bruhostel.com; 57 MacCurtain St; dm/tw incl breakfast from €17/50; @ 🛜) This buzzing hostel has its own internet cafe, with free access for guests, and a fantastic bar, popular with backpackers and locals alike. The dorms (each with a bathroom) have four to six beds and are both clean and stylish – ask for one on the upper floors to avoid bar noise. Breakfast is included.

Sheila's Hostel　　　　　HOSTEL €
(☑ 021-450 5562; www.sheilashostel.ie; 4 Belgrave Pl, off Wellington Rd; dm/tw from €16/50; @ 🛜) Sheila's heaves with young travellers, and it's no wonder given its excellent central location. Facilities include a sauna, lockers, laundry service, a movie room and a barbecue. Cheaper twin rooms share bathrooms. Breakfast is €3 extra.

★ Auburn House　　　　　B&B €€
(☑ 021-450 8555; www.auburnguesthouse.com; 3 Garfield Tce, Wellington Rd; s/d/tr €58/90/114; P 🛜) There's a warm family welcome at this neat B&B, which has smallish but well-kept rooms brightened by window boxes. Try to bag one of the back rooms, which are quieter and have sweeping views over the city. Breakfast includes vegetarian choices, and the location near the fun of MacCurtain St is a plus.

Imperial Hotel　　　　　HOTEL €€
(☑ 021-427 4040; www.flynnhotels.com; South Mall; r from €140; P @ 🛜) Having celebrated its bicentenary in 2013 – Thackeray, Dickens and Sir Walter Scott have all stayed here – the Imperial knows how to age gracefully. Public spaces resonate with period detail – marble floors, elaborate floral bouquets and more – while the 130 bedrooms feature writing desks, understated decor and modern touches including a luxurious spa and a digital music library.

Irish Free State commander-in-chief Michael Collins spent his last night alive here; you can ask to check into his room.

Isaac's Hotel　　　　　HOTEL €€
(☑ 021-450 0011; www.isaacscork.com; 48 MacCurtain St; s/d/apt from €90/119/189; @ @ 🛜) The central location is the real selling point at this hotel housed in what was once a Victorian furniture warehouse (ask for a room away from the busy street). As well as plain, functional bedrooms, there are self-contained apartments, which come with kitchen and washing machine. There's no air-con, so some rooms can get uncomfortably hot on sunny summer days.

🛏 Western Rd & Around

Western Rd runs southwest from the city centre to the large UCC campus; it has the city's biggest choice of B&Bs. You can take a bus from the central bus station, or walk (10 to 30 minutes).

★ Garnish House　　　　　B&B €€
(☑ 021-427 5111; www.garnish.ie; 18 Western Rd; s/d/f from €124/136/154; P 🛜) Attention is lavished on guests at this award-winning B&B where the legendary breakfast menu (30 choices) ranges from grilled kippers to

French toast. Typical of the touches here is freshly cooked porridge, served with creamed honey and your choice of whiskey or Baileys; enjoy it out on the garden terrace. The 14 rooms are very comfortable; reception is open 24 hours.

Anam Cara
B&B €€

(☑085 864 5216; www.guesthousescork.com; 31 Palace View, Western Rd; d/f €95/110; P🛜) Although it's just 10-minute's walk west of the city centre, this cute little Georgian-style cottage has a quirky, country feel. There's a busy road out the front, but the rooms at the back are quiet. Delicious breakfasts are served in the next-door tearoom.

Blarney Stone Guesthouse
B&B €€

(☑021-427 0083; www.blarneystoneguesthouse.ie; Western Rd; s/d from €99/119; P🛜) The white facade of this tall Victorian townhouse conceals a dazzling interior crammed with polished period furniture, glittering Waterford crystal chandeliers and curlicued gilt mirrors. The Victorian theme does not extend to the facilities, though – creature comforts include power showers, fast wi-fi, satellite TV and hearty breakfasts.

★River Lee Hotel
HOTEL €€€

(☑021-425 2700; www.doylecollection.com; Western Rd; r from €199; P🛜♨) This modern riverside hotel brings a touch of luxury to the city centre. It has gorgeous public areas with huge sofas, a designer fireplace, a stunning five-storey glass-walled atrium and superb service. There are well-equipped bedrooms (nice and quiet at the back, but request a corner room for extra space) and possibly the best breakfast buffet in Ireland.

★Hayfield Manor
HOTEL €€€

(☑021-484 5900; www.hayfieldmanor.ie; Perrott Ave, College Rd; r from €269; P🛜♨) Roll out the red carpet and pour yourself a sherry for *you have arrived*. Just 1.5km southwest of the city centre but with all the ambience of a country house, Hayfield combines the luxury and facilities of a big hotel with the informality and welcome of a small one. The beautiful bedrooms offer a choice of traditional decor or contemporary styling.

✖ Eating

Cork's food scene is reason enough to visit the city – the English Market (p220) is a national treasure.

Cork Coffee Roasters
CAFE €

(☑021-731 9158; www.facebook.com/CorkCoffee; 2 Bridge St; mains €3-6; ⊙7.30am-6.30pm Mon-Fri, 8am-6.30pm Sat, 9am-5pm Sun; 🛜) In this foodiest of foodie towns it's not surprising to find a cafe run by artisan coffee roasters. The brew on offer in this cute and often crowded corner is some of the best in Ireland, guaranteed to jump start your morning along with a buttery pastry, scone or tart.

Quay Co-op
VEGETARIAN €

(☑021-431 7026; www.quaycoop.com; 24 Sullivan's Quay; mains €7-11; ⊙11am-9pm Mon-Sat, noon-9pm Sun; 🖉🍴) 🌿 Flying the flag for alternative Cork, this cafeteria offers a range of self-service vegetarian dishes, all organic, including big breakfasts and rib-sticking soups and casseroles. It also caters for gluten-, dairy- and wheat-free needs, and is amazingly child-friendly.

Filter
CAFE €

(☑021-455 0050; filtercork@gmail.com; 19 George's Quay; mains €4-7; ⊙8am-6pm Mon-Fri, 9am-6pm Sat, 10am-5pm Sun; 🛜) 🌿 The quintessential Cork espresso bar, Filter is a carefully curated shrine to coffee nerdery, from the rough-and-ready retro decor to the highly knowledgable baristas serving up expertly brewed shots made with single-origin, locally roasted beans. The sandwich menu is a class act too, offering a choice of fillings that includes pastrami, chorizo and ham hock on artisan breads.

★Nash 19
INTERNATIONAL €€

(☑021-427 0880; www.nash19.com; Princes St; mains €10-17; ⊙7.30am-4.30pm Mon-Fri, 8.30am-4.30pm Sat) 🌿 A superb bistro and deli where locally sourced food is honoured at breakfast and lunch, either sit-in or take away. Fresh scones draw in the crowds early; daily lunch specials (soups, salads, desserts etc), free-range chicken pie and platters of smoked fish from Frank Hederman (p227) keep them coming for lunch – the Producers Plate, a sampler of local produce, is sensational.

★Market Lane
IRISH, INTERNATIONAL €€

(☑021-427 4710; www.marketlane.ie; 5 Oliver Plunkett St; mains €12-27; ⊙noon-9.30pm Mon-Thu, noon-10.30pm Fri & Sat, 1-9.30pm Sun; 🛜🍴) 🌿 It's always hopping at this bright corner bistro. The menu is broad and hearty, changing to reflect what's fresh at the English Market: perhaps roast cod with seaweed butter sauce, or pea and barley risotto with goat's cheese? No reservations for fewer than six

THE ENGLISH MARKET

It could just as easily be called the Victorian Market for its ornate vaulted ceilings and columns, but the **English Market** (www.englishmarket.ie; main entrance Princes St; ⊙8am-6pm Mon-Sat) is a true gem, no matter what you name it. Scores of vendors set up colourful and photogenic displays of the region's very best local produce, including meat, fish, fruit, cheeses and takeaway food. On a sunny day, take your lunch to nearby Bishop Lucey Park, a popular alfresco eating spot.

An unmissable experience at the heart of the English Market, the **Farmgate Cafe** (☑021-427 8134; www.farmgate.ie; Princes St, English Market; mains €8-14; ⊙8.30am-5pm Mon-Sat) is perched on a balcony overlooking the food stalls below, the source of all that fresh local produce on your plate – everything from crab and oysters to the lamb in your Irish stew. Go up the stairs and turn left for table service, or right for counter service.

diners; sip wines by the glass at the bar till a table is free.

★Cafe Paradiso
VEGETARIAN €€

(☑021-427 7939; www.cafeparadiso.ie; 16 Lancaster Quay; 2-/3-course menus €33/40; ⊙5.30-10pm Mon-Sat; ☑) ✐ A contender for best restaurant in town of any genre, Paradiso serves contemporary vegetarian dishes, including vegan fare: how about confit artichokes, broad beans and scallions with lemon risotto and hazelnut crumb? Reservations are essential.

Rates for dinner, bed and breakfast, staying in the funky upstairs rooms, start from €180/220 per single/double.

Fenn's Quay
MODERN IRISH €€

(☑021-427 9527; www.fennsquay.net; 5 Fenn's Quay; mains €9-24; ⊙8.15-11.30am & noon-3pm Mon-Fri, 5-8pm Thu, 5-10pm Fri, 8.30am-3pm & 5-10pm Sat; ☑) ✐ From breakfast (Rosscarbery black pudding with smoked Gubbeen cheese on home-baked toast) to lunch (spiced beef and pickle sandwiches or fresh fish platters) to dinner (collar of bacon with cabbage and walnuts), this hidden gem of a restaurant serves up the best of local produce, much of it from the English Market – 'Cork on a fork', as their tag line says.

Jacques Restaurant
MODERN IRISH €€

(☑021-427 7387; www.jacquesrestaurant.ie; 23 Oliver Plunkett St; mains lunch €7-14, dinner €22-26; ⊙10am-4pm Mon, to 10pm Tue-Sat) ✐ Sisters Jacqueline and Eithne Barry draw on a terrific network of local suppliers that they've built up over three decades to help them realise their culinary ambitions – the freshest Cork food cooked simply, without frills. The menu changes daily: smoked quail with celeriac remoulade, perhaps, or Castletownbere crab with spaghetti and herbs. Two-course dinners

(€24) are served Tuesday to Thursday, and pre-6.30pm Friday and Saturday.

Electric
MODERN IRISH €€

(☑021-422 2990; http://electriccork.ie; 41 South Mall; mains €14-27; ⊙noon-10pm; ☎☑) The market-sourced menu at this transformed art deco bank runs from seafood chowder to succulent steaks. There's a rustic Mediterranean-style fish bar too, but it's the big riverside deck and upstairs restaurant balcony with knock-out cathedral views that pull in the crowds – along with wines by the glass, and over two dozen varieties of beer.

Strasbourg Goose
IRISH €€

(☑021-427 9534; 17-18 French Church St; mains €15-24, 2-course set menu €21; ⊙6-10pm Tue-Fri, 5-11pm Sat, 4-10pm Sun) There's a French accent alongside the broad Irish brogue here, with everything from prime Irish sirloin to Cork coast mussels given a Gallic twist, whether it be tarragon, a white-wine sauce or gratin potatoes. Parisians wouldn't credit the portions though, which would easily satisfy a ravenous rugby player.

Les Gourmandises
FRENCH €€

(☑021-425 1959; www.lesgourmandises.ie; 17 Cook St; 2-/3-course dinner €40/48; ⊙6-9pm Mon-Sat) ✐ Remember those beautiful fresh fish you saw in the English Market? Many of them end up at this cute little restaurant that will remind you of that perfect place you stumbled across in Paris once... Meat and poultry also get their due, in dishes such as slow-cooked belly of pork with smoked potato purée. Service is gracious and calm.

Drinking & Nightlife

In Cork pubs, locally brewed Murphy's and Beamish stouts, not Guinness, are the preferred pints.

Given the city's big student population, the small selection of nightclubs does a thriving trade. Entry ranges from free to €15; most are open until 2am on Friday and Saturday.

Local microbreweries include the long-established Franciscan Well, whose refreshing Friar Weisse beer is popular in summer, and relative newcomer Rising Sons, whose Mi Daza stout is a new take on an old recipe.

★ Sin É   PUB
(☑021-450 2266; www.facebook.com/sinecork; 8 Coburg St; ⊙12.30-11.30pm Mon-Thu, to 12.30am Fri & Sat, to 11pm Sun) You could easily spend an entire day at this place, which is everything a craic-filled pub should be – long on atmosphere and short on pretension (Sin É means 'that's it!'). There's music every night from 6.30pm May to September, and regular sessions Tuesday, Friday and Sunday the rest of the year, much of them traditional but with the odd surprise.

★ Franciscan Well Brewery   PUB
(☑021-439 3434; www.franciscanwellbrewery.com; 14 North Mall; ⊙1-11.30pm Mon-Thu, to 12.30am Fri & Sat, to 11pm Sun; ☎) The copper vats gleaming behind the bar give the game away: the Franciscan Well brews its own beer. The best place to enjoy it is in the enormous beer garden at the back. The pub holds regular beer festivals together with other small independent Irish breweries.

★ Mutton Lane Inn   PUB
(☑021-427 3471; www.facebook.com/mutton.lane; Mutton Lane; ⊙10.30am-11.30pm Mon-Thu, to 12.30am Fri & Sat, 2-11pm Sun) Tucked down the tiniest of alleys off St Patrick's St, this inviting pub, lit by candles and fairy lights, is one of Cork's most intimate drinking holes. It's minuscule, so try to get in early to bag the snug, or perch on the beer kegs outside.

Abbot's Ale House   PUB
(☑021-450 7116; 17 Devonshire St; ⊙10.30am-10pm Mon-Fri, 12.30-10pm Sat & Sun) A low-key, 1st-floor drinking den, whose small size contrasts with its huge beer list. There are always several beers on tap and another 300 in bottles. Good for preclubbing.

Rising Sons   MICROBREWERY
(☑021-241 4764; www.risingsonsbrewery.com; Cornmarket St; ⊙noon-late; ☎) This huge, warehouselike, red-brick building houses an award-winning microbrewery. The industrial decor of exposed brick, riveted iron and gleaming copper brewing vessels recalls American West Coast brewpubs. It turns out 50 kegs a week, some of them full of its lip-smacking trademark stout, Mi Daza, and has a food menu that extends as far as pizza, and no further.

Bierhaus   PUB
(☑021-455 1648; www.facebook.com/bierhauscork; Pope's Quay; ⊙3-11.30pm Mon-Thu, 3pm-12.30am Fri, 1pm-12.30am Sat, 1-11pm Sun; ☎) A convivial bar with one of the best selections of beer in Ireland. More than 200 varieties, both local and international, are on offer, mostly bottled but with no fewer than six guest brews on tap.

An Spailpín Fánac   PUB
(☑021-427 7949; www.facebook.com/anspailpinfanac; 29 South Main St; ⊙5-11.30pm Mon-Thu, 12.30pm-12.30am Fri, 3pm-12.30am Sat, 5-11pm Sun; ☎) 'The Wandering Labourer' really clings to its old-fashioned atmosphere, with exposed brickwork, stone-flagged floors, snug corners and open fires. There are good trad-music sessions most nights.

Suas Rooftop Bar   COCKTAIL BAR
(☑021-427 8972; www.suasbar.com; 4-5 South Main St; ⊙5-11.30pm Mon-Thu, 3pm-12.30am Fri & Sat, 4-11pm Sun) You could easily walk along South Main St and never know that this sleek bar with heated roof terrace was right

GAY & LESBIAN CORK

Chambers Bar (☑086 703 7018; www.facebook.com/ChambersCork; Washington St; ⊙8.30pm-2am Wed & Thu, to 2.30am Fri & Sat, 7pm-2am Sun) Cork's biggest and liveliest gay bar, with DJs playing till 2am, themed entertainment nights and outrageous cocktails.

Cork Pride (www.corkpride.com; ⊙Jul-Aug) Week-long festival with events throughout the city.

Emerson House (☑086 834 0891; www.emersonhousecork.com; 2 Clarence Tce, Summer Hill North; s/d from €70/90; ☐☎) Gay and lesbian B&B in an elegant Georgian house. Host Cyril is a mine of information.

Gay Cork (www.gaycork.com) What's-on listings and directory.

L.InC (☑021-480 8600; www.linc.ie; 11a White St; ⊙11am-3pm Tue & Wed, to 8pm Thu) Resource centre for lesbians and bisexual women.

WORTH A TRIP

GONE TO THE DOGS

If you tire of the pubs, the live music and the theatre, there's always the dogs. Greyhound racing is big in Ireland, particularly with families, and **Curraheen Greyhound Park** (☏ 1890 269 969; www.igb.ie/CurraheenPark; Curraheen Rd; adult/child €10/5; ⊗ doors open 6.30pm Thu-Sat; ⊕) is one of the country's poshest stadiums. There are 10 races a night, plus a restaurant, a bar and live music. It's 5.5km southwest of the centre; buses run from Cork's bus station.

above you. The cocktail menu covers all the classics, and DJs hit the decks on Friday and Saturday nights.

☆ Entertainment

Cork's cultural life is generally of a high calibre. To see what's happening grab *WhazOn?* (www.whazon.com), a free monthly leaflet available from the tourist office, news agencies, shops, hostels and B&Bs.

Cork's musical credentials are impeccable. Besides theatres and pubs that feature live music, there are also places that are dedicated music venues, and bars known particularly for their live gigs. For full listings, refer to *WhazOn?*, PLUGD Records (p223) and the event guide at www.peoplesrepublicofcork.com.

★**Cork Opera House** OPERA
(☏ 021-427 0022; www.corkoperahouse.ie; Emmet Pl; tickets €20-50; ⊗ box office 10am-5.30pm Mon-Sat, preshow to 7pm Mon-Sat & 6-7pm Sun) Given a modern makeover in the 1990s, this leading venue has been entertaining the city for more than 150 years with everything from opera and ballet to stand-up comedy, pop concerts and puppet shows. Around the back, the **Half Moon Theatre** (tickets €5-15) presents contemporary theatre, dance, art and occasional club nights.

★**Triskel Arts Centre** ARTS CENTRE
(☏ 021-472 2022; www.triskelart.com; Tobin St; tickets €6-10; ⊗ box office 10am-5pm Mon-Sat; ⊚) A fantastic cultural centre housed partly in a renovated church building – expect a varied program of live music, installation art, photography and theatre at this intimate venue. There's also a cinema (from 6.30pm) and a great cafe.

Everyman Theatre THEATRE
(☏ 021-450 1673; www.everymancork.com; 15 MacCurtain St; tickets €20-30; ⊗ box office noon-5pm Mon-Sat, preshow to 7pm Mon-Sat & 4-7pm Sun) Acclaimed musical and dramatic productions are the main bill here, but there's also the occasional comedy act or live band (it's a great venue for gigs that require a little bit of respectful silence).

Fred Zeppelins LIVE MUSIC
(☏ 086 260 7876; 8 Parliament St; ⊗ 4-11.30pm Mon-Thu, to 12.30am Fri & Sat, to 11pm Sun) There's a hard edge to this dark den of a bar, popular with goths, rockers and anyone who feels uncomfortable leaving the house without a packet of Rizlas. It's been on the go for 20 years, and is known for its live gigs (lots of tribute bands) and DJs at weekends, plus occasional open-mike nights.

Crane Lane Theatre LIVE MUSIC
(☏ 021-427 8487; www.cranelanetheatre.ie; Phoenix St; tickets free-€5; ⊗ 2pm-2am Mon-Fri, noon-2am Sat & Sun) Part pub, part vintage ballroom, this atmospheric venue is decked out in 1920s to 1940s decor, with a courtyard beer garden as a central oasis. It stages a wide range of live music gigs and DJ nights, many with free admission.

Cyprus Avenue LIVE MUSIC
(☏ 021-427 6165; www.cyprusavenue.ie; Caroline St; tickets €6-20; ⊗ 7.30pm-late) This midsized venue is one of the best spots in town to see all kinds of gigs, from heartfelt singer-songwriters to top local bands on their way to the big time (and some once-famous bands on their way down).

Firkin Crane DANCE
(☏ 021-450 7487; www.firkincrane.ie; O'Connell Sq, Shandon; tickets free-€20) One of Ireland's premier centres for modern dance.

🔒 Shopping

St Patrick's St is the retail spine of Cork, housing all the major department stores and malls. But pedestrianised Oliver Plunkett St is the retail heart; it and the surrounding narrow lanes are lined with small, interesting shops.

Time Traveller's Bookshop BOOKS
(☏ 087 290 3613; www.timetraveller.ie; Wandesford Quay; ⊗ 11am-6pm Mon-Fri, 10am-4pm Sat) A fascinating antiquarian bookshop specialising in rare and unusual books, first editions and signed copies.

PLUGD Records
MUSIC

(☑ 021-472 6300; www.plugdrecords.com; Triskel Arts Centre, Tobin St; ☺ noon-7pm Mon-Sat; ☎) Stocks all kinds of music on vinyl and CD and is the place to keep up with the ever-changing club scene.

20 20 Gallery
ART

(☑ 021-439 1458; www.2020artgallery.com; Griffith House, North Mall; ☺ noon-5pm Tue-Sat) Commercial fine art gallery selling paintings, ceramics and photographic prints by a broad range of Irish artists.

Pro Musica
MUSIC

(☑ 021-427 1659; www.promusica.ie; 20 Oliver Plunkett St; ☺ 9am-6pm Mon-Sat) A focal point and meeting place for Cork's musicians, with a full range of instruments from electric guitars to clarinets, recording equipment, sheet music and a noticeboard.

ⓘ Information

Free wi-fi is available throughout the city centre's main streets and public spaces, including the bus and train stations.

Webworkhouse.com (☑ 021-427 3090; www.webworkhouse.com; 8a Winthrop St; per hour €1.50-3.00; ☺ 24hr) Internet cafe; also offers low-cost international phone calls.

Cork City Tourist Office (☑ 021-425 5100; www.discoverireland.ie/corkcity; Grand Pde; ☺ 9am-5pm Mon-Sat year-round, plus 10am-5pm Sun Jul & Aug) Souvenir shop and information desk. Sells Ordnance Survey maps.

People's Republic of Cork (www.peoplesrepublicofcork.com) Picking up on the popular nickname for the liberal-leaning city, this indie website provides excellent info.

General Post Office (☑ 021-485 1042; Oliver Plunkett St; ☺ 9am-5.30pm Mon-Sat)

Mercy University Hospital (☑ 021-427 1971; www.muh.ie; Grenville Pl) Has a 24-hour emergency department.

ⓘ Getting There & Away

AIR

Cork Airport (☑ 021-431 3131; www.corkairport.com) is 8km south of the city on the N27. Facilities include ATMs and car-hire desks for all the main companies. Airlines servicing the airport include Aer Lingus, Ryanair and Jet2.com. There are flights to Edinburgh, Cardiff, London (Heathrow, Gatwick and Stansted), Paris and several other cities in Britain and across Europe.

Bus Éireann (p223) service 226A shuttles between the train station, bus station and Cork Airport every half-hour between 6am and 10pm (€5.60, 30 minutes). A taxi to/from town costs €22 to €26.

BOAT

Brittany Ferries (☑ 021-427 7801; www.brittanyferries.ie; 42 Grand Pde) sails to Roscoff (France) weekly from the end of March to October. The crossing takes 14 hours; fares vary widely. The ferry terminal is at Ringaskiddy, 15 minutes by car southeast of the city centre along the N28. Taxis cost €30 to €38. Bus Éireann runs a service from Cork (South Mall) to link up with departures (€8, 40 minutes); confirm times on its website.

BUS

Bus Éireann (☑ 021-455 7178; www.buseireann.ie) operates from the **bus station** (cnr Merchant's Quay & Parnell Pl), while **Aircoach** (☑ 01-844 7118; www.aircoach.ie) and **Citylink** (☑ 091-564 164; www.citylink.ie;

BUS TIMETABLE

DESTINATION	BUS COMPANY	FARE (€)	DURATION (HR)	FREQUENCY
Dublin	Bus Éireann	16	3¾	6 daily
Dublin	Aircoach	16	3	hourly
Dublin	GoBus	14	3	6-9 daily
Dublin Airport	Aircoach	20	3½	hourly
Dublin Airport	GoBus	20	3¼	6-9 daily
Galway	Citylink	22	3	5 daily
Kilkenny	Bus Éireann	22	3	2 daily
Killarney	Bus Éireann	28	2	hourly
Limerick	Citylink	18	1½	5 daily
Waterford	Bus Éireann	24	2¼	hourly

☎) services depart from **St Patrick's Quay**, across the river. **GoBus** (☑ 091-564 600; www.gobus.ie; ☎) uses a stop around the corner on Parnell Pl.

TRAIN

Kent Train Station (☑ 021-450 6766) is north of the River Lee on Lower Glanmire Rd, a 10- to 15-minute walk from the city centre. Bus 205 runs into the city centre (€2, five minutes, every 15 minutes).

The train line goes through Mallow, where you can change for the Tralee line, and Limerick Junction, for the line to Ennis (and Galway), then on to Dublin.

Dublin €66, 2¼ hours, eight daily

Galway €63, four to six hours, seven daily, two or three changes

Killarney €28, 1½ to two hours, nine daily

Waterford €32, three to five hours, five daily, one or two changes

❶ Getting Around

BICYCLE

Cycle Scene (☑ 021-430 1183; www.cycle scene.ie; 396 Blarney St; per day/week from €15/80) rents bikes and accessories, including good-quality road-racing bikes (€45 a day).

BUS

Most places are within easy walking distance of the centre. Single bus tickets costs €2.05 each; a day pass is €5. Buy all tickets on the bus.

CAR

Street parking requires scratch-card parking discs (€2 per hour, in force 8.30am to 6.30pm Monday to Saturday), available from many city centre shops. Be warned – traffic wardens are ferociously efficient. There are several signposted car parks around the central area, with charges around €2 per hour and €12 overnight.

TRACING YOUR ANCESTORS

Genealogy services in County Cork:

Cobh Heritage Centre (p226) Housed in the Queenstown Story museum.

Mallow Heritage Centre (☑ 022-50302; http://mallowheritagecentre.com; 27/28 Bank Pl; ⏱10.30am-1pm Mon-Fri, 2-4pm Mon-Thu) Covers north and east Cork.

Skibbereen Heritage (p238) Located in the town's heritage centre.

You can avoid city centre parking problems by using **Black Ash Park & Ride** on the South City Link Rd, on the way to the airport. Parking costs €5 a day, with buses into the city centre at least every 15 minutes (10-minute journey time).

AROUND CORK CITY

Blarney Castle

If you need proof of the power of a good yarn, then join the queue to get into this 15th-century **castle** (☑ 021-438 5252; www.blarneycastle. ie; adult/child €15/6; ⏱9am-7pm Mon-Sat, to 6pm Sun Jun-Aug, shorter hours Sep-May; ℗), one of Ireland's most popular tourist attractions. They're here, of course, to plant their lips on the **Blarney Stone**, which supposedly gives one the gift of gab – a cliché that has entered every lexicon and tour route. Blarney is 8km northwest of Cork and buses run hourly from Cork bus station (€7.80 return, 20 minutes).

The Blarney Stone is perched at the top of a steep climb up claustrophobic spiral staircases. On the battlements, you bend backwards over a long, long drop (with safety grill and attendant to prevent tragedy) to kiss the stone; as your shirt rides up, coach-loads of onlookers stare up your nose. Once you're upright again, don't forget to admire the stunning views before descending. Try not to think of the local lore about all the fluids that drench the stone other than saliva. Better yet, just don't kiss it.

The custom of kissing the stone is a relatively modern one, but Blarney's association with smooth talking goes back a long time. Queen Elizabeth I is said to have invented the term 'to talk blarney' out of exasperation with Lord Blarney's ability to talk endlessly without ever actually agreeing to her demands.

The famous stone aside, **Blarney Castle** itself is an impressive 16th-century tower set in gorgeous grounds. Escape the crowds on a walk around the **Fern Garden** and **Arboretum**, investigate toxic plants in the Harry-Potterish **Poison Garden** or explore the landscaped nooks and crannies of the **Rock Close**.

Fota Island

Fota Island lies in Cork Harbour, connected by short bridges to the mainland and to Great Island, 10km east of Cork on the

SPIKE ISLAND

This low-lying green island (☑ 085 851 8818; www.spikeislandcork.com; Cork Harbour; adult/
child incl ferry €18/10; ⊘ 11am-5.30pm Jun-Aug, noon-4.30pm May, noon-4.30pm Sat & Sun
Apr & Sep only, noon-4.30pm Sun Oct only) in Cork Harbour was once an important part of
the port's defences, topped by an 18th-century artillery fort. In the second half of the
19th century, during the Irish War of Independence, and from 1984 to 2004 it served as
a prison, gaining the nickname 'Ireland's Alcatraz'. Today you can enjoy a guided walking
tour of the former prison buildings, then go off and explore on your own; the ferry departs from Kennedy Pier, Cobh.

The guided tour takes in the modern prison, the old punishment block, the shell store
(once used as a children's prison) and No 2 bastion with its massive 6in gun. Other
highlights include the **Gun Park**, with a good display of mostly 20th-century artillery;
the **Mitchell Hall**, with an exhibit on the *Aud*, a WWI German gun-running ship that
was sunk in the entrance to Cork Harbour; and the **Glacis Walk**, a 1.5km trail that leads
around the walls of the fortress, with great views of Cobh town and the harbour entrance.
You'll need around four hours to make the most of a visit.

road to Cobh. Formerly the private estate of the Smith-Barry family, it is now home to gardens, golf courses and Ireland's only wildlife park.

The train from Cork to Fota (€4.10, 13 minutes, hourly) continues to Cobh.

Fota Wildlife Park ZOO
(☑ 021-481 2678; www.fotawildlife.ie; Carrigtwohill, Fota Island; adult/child €16/10.50; parking €3; ⊘ 10am-6pm Mon-Sat, 10.30am-6pm Sun; P ☻) Kangaroos bound, cheetahs run, and monkeys and gibbons leap and scream on wooded islands at this huge outdoor zoo, where the animals roam without a cage or fence in sight. A tour train (on wheels, not tracks) runs a circuit round the park every 15 minutes in high season (one way/return €1/2), but the 2km circular walk offers a more close-up experience. Last admission is 1½ hours before closing.

Fota House Arboretum & Gardens HOUSE
(☑ 021-481 5543; www.fotahouse.com; Carrigtwohill, Fota Island; house tours adult/child €8/3, house & gardens €11/4; ⊘ 10am-5pm Apr-Sep; P) Guided tours of Regency-style Fota House focus on the original kitchen and ornate plasterwork ceilings, but the real highlight here is the 150-year-old arboretum and gardens. There's a Victorian fernery set amid blocks of fluted limestone, a magnolia walk, a walled garden and a host of beautiful trees, including huge Japanese cedars overlooking the lily pond.

Fota Island Resort GOLF
(☑ 021-488 3700; www.fotaisland.ie; Fota Island; green fees €80-100) Three championship golf

courses sprawl within the 780-acre Fota Island Resort – Deerpark, Belvelly and Barryscourt – anchored by one of Ireland's best known golfing hotels. The resort has hosted the Irish Open three times, most recently in 2014, and welcomes visitors; it's best to book your round in advance. The beautiful old stone clubhouse, set in a converted farmhouse overlooking the lake, is an atmospheric place for a postgolf drink.

Cobh

POP 12,800

Cobh (pronounced 'cove') is a charming waterfront town on a glittering estuary, dotted with brightly coloured houses and overlooked by a splendid cathedral. It's popular with Corkonians looking for a spot of R&R, and with cruise liners – each year around 75 visit the port, the second-largest natural harbour in the world (after Sydney Harbour in Australia).

It's a far cry from the harrowing Famine years when more than 70,000 people left Ireland through the port in order to escape the ravages of starvation (from 1848 to 1950, no fewer than 2.5 million emigrants passed through). Cobh was also the final port of call for the *Titanic;* a poignant museum commemorates the fatal voyage's point of departure.

Cobh is on the south side of Great Island. Visible from the waterfront are Haulbowline Island, once a naval base, and the greener Spike Island (p225), formerly a prison and now a tourist attraction.

History

For many years Cobh was the port of Cork, and it has always had a strong connection with Atlantic crossings. In 1838 the *Sirius*, the first steamship to cross the Atlantic, sailed from Cobh. The *Titanic* made its last stop here before its disastrous voyage in 1912, and, when the *Lusitania* was torpedoed off the coast of Kinsale in 1915, it was here that many of the survivors were brought and the dead buried. Cobh was also the last glimpse of Ireland for tens of thousands who emigrated during the Famine.

In 1849 Cobh was renamed Queenstown after Queen Victoria paid a visit. The name lasted until Irish independence in 1921 when, unsurprisingly, the local council reverted to the Irish original.

The world's first yacht club, the Royal Cork Yacht Club, was founded here in 1720, but currently operates from Crosshaven on the other side of Cork Harbour. The beautiful Italianate Old Yacht Club now houses an arts centre.

◉ Sights & Activities

Cobh, The Queenstown Story　　MUSEUM
(☎021-481 3591; www.cobhheritage.com; Lower Rd; adult/child €9.50/5; ◷9.30am-6pm May-Oct, to 5pm Nov-Apr) The howl of the storm almost knocks you off-balance, there's a bit of fake vomit on the deck, and the people in the pictures all look pretty miserable – that's just one room at Cobh Heritage Centre. Housed in the old train station (next to the current station), this interactive museum is way above average, chronicling Irish emigrations across the Atlantic in the wake of the Great Famine.

There's also some shocking stuff on the fate of convicts, shipped to Australia in transport ships 'so airless that candles could not burn'. Scenes of sea travel in the 1950s, however, might actually make you nostalgic for a more gracious way of travelling the world. There's also a genealogy centre and a cafe. The last admission is one hour before closing.

Titanic Experience Cobh　　MUSEUM
(☎021-481 4412; www.titanicexperiencecobh.ie; 20 Casement Sq; adult/child €9.50/6.50; ◷9am-6pm Apr-Sep, 10am-5.30pm Oct-Mar; ♿) The original White Star Line offices, where 123 passengers embarked on (and one lucky soul absconded from) the RMS *Titanic*, now house this powerful insight into the ill-fated liner's final voyage. Admission is by tour, which is partly guided and partly interactive, with holograms, audiovisual presentations and exhibits; allow at least an hour. The technical wizardry is impressive but what's most memorable is standing on the spot from where passengers were ferried to the waiting ship offshore, never to return.

Michael Martin's Walking Tours　　WALKING
(☎021-481 5211; www.titanic.ie; tours from €9.50) Michael Martin's 1¼-hour guided **Titanic Trail** walk leaves from the **Commodore Hotel** (☎021-481 1277; www.commodorehotel.ie; 4 Westbourne Pl; s/d from €63/100; ☎✿) at 11am and 2pm, with a free sampling of stout at the end. Martin also runs a ghoulish **Ghost Walk** (by arrangement).

St Colman's Cathedral　　CATHEDRAL
(☎021-481 3222; www.cobhcathedralparish.ie; Cathedral Pl; admission by donation; ◷8am-6pm May-Oct, to 5pm Nov-Apr) Dramatically perched on a hillside terrace above Cobh, this massive French Gothic Cathedral is out of all proportion to the town. Its most exceptional feature is the 47-bell **carillon**, the largest in Ireland, with a range of four octaves. The biggest bell weighs a stonking 3440kg – about as much as a full-grown elephant! You can hear carillon recitals at 4.30pm on Sundays between May and September.

The cathedral, designed by EW Pugin, was begun in 1868 but not completed until 1915. Much of the funding was raised by nostalgic Irish communities in Australia and the USA.

Cobh Museum　　MUSEUM
(☎021-481 4240; www.cobhmuseum.com; High Rd; adult/child €4/2; ◷11am-1pm & 2-5.30pm Mon-Sat, 2.30-5pm Sun Apr-Oct) Model ships, paintings, photographs and curious artefacts tracing Cobh's history fill this small but engaging museum. It's housed in the 19th-century Scottish Presbyterian church overlooking the train station.

🛏 Sleeping & Eating

★**Gilbert's**　　GUESTHOUSE €€
(☎021-481 1300; www.gilbertsincobh.com; 11 Pearse Sq; s/d/penthouse €89/100/180; ☎) The four rooms at this boutique guesthouse in Cobh's town centre are fresh and contemporary with handmade furniture, pure-wool blankets and rain showers. Rates don't include breakfast, but the penthouse suite has a kitchenette. **Gilbert's Bistro**, one of Cobh's best restaurants, is just downstairs.

BELVELLY SMOKEHOUSE
....

No trip to Cork is complete without a visit to an artisan food producer, and the effervescent Frank Hederman is more than happy to show you around **Belvelly Smokehouse** (☑ 021-481 1089; www.frankhederman.com; Belvelly; free for individuals, charge for groups; ⊙ by reservation 10am-5pm Mon-Fri) , the oldest traditional smokehouse in Ireland – indeed, the only surviving one. The smokehouse is 19km east of Cork on the R624 towards Cobh; call ahead to arrange a visit.

Alternatively, stop by Frank's stall at the **Cobh** (p227) or **Midleton** (p229) farmers markets; you can also buy his produce at Cork's **English Market** (p220).

Seafood and cheese are smoked here – even butter – but the speciality is fish, particularly salmon. In a traditional process that takes 24 hours from start to finish, the fish is filleted and cured before being hung to smoke over beech woodchips. The result is subtle and delectable.

Knockeven House
B&B €€

(☑ 021-481 1778; www.knockevenhouse.com; Rushbrooke; d/f from €120/140; ℗) Knockeven is a splendid Victorian house with huge bedrooms done out with period furniture, overlooking a magnificent garden full of magnolias and camellias. Breakfasts are great too – homemade breads and fresh fruit – and are served in the sumptuous dining room. The decor takes you back to 1st-class passage on a vintage liner. It's 1.5km west of Cobh's centre.

Titanic Bar & Grill
IRISH €€

(☑ 021-481 4585; www.titanicbarandgrill.ie; 20 Casement Sq; mains €14-25; ⊙ noon-5pm & 6-8.30pm Mon-Sat, noon-11pm Sun; 🖐) Around the back of the Titanic Experience (p226), with a huge deck overlooking the harbour, this is a stunning spot for a pint. The menu lives up to the stylish glossy timber surrounds with posh versions of pub-grub classics such as fish and chips, bangers and mash, and steak with pepper sauce.

Farmers Market
MARKET

(☑ 086 199 7643; www.facebook.com/cobhfarmers; The Promenade; ⊙ 10am-2pm Fri) 🍴 Held on the seafront.

ⓘ Information

Tourist Office (☑ 021-481 3301; www.visitcobh.com; Market House, Casement Sq; ⊙ 9am-5pm Mon-Fri) Housed in the building with an archway through it, opposite the Titanic Experience.

ⓘ Getting There & Away

Car By road, Cobh is 23km southeast of Cork, off the main N25 Cork–Rosslare road; Great Island is linked to the mainland via a causeway.

Ferry It's 18km from Cork via the **Passage West ferry** (p234).

Train Hourly trains connect Cobh with Cork (€6.15, 25 minutes) via Fota.

Bus No buses serve the Cork to Cobh route.

Midleton & Around
POP 12,496

Aficionados of a particularly fine Irish whiskey will recognise the name Midleton, and the main reason to linger in this bustling market town is to visit the old Jameson whiskey distillery, along with a meal at one of the town's famously good restaurants. The surrounding region is full of pretty villages, craggy coastlines and heavenly rural hotels such as Ballymaloe House (p228).

The **tourist office** (☑ 021-461 3702; www.ringofcork.ie; Distillery Walk; ⊙ 10am-1pm & 2-5pm Mon-Fri Apr-Sep) is by the entrance gate to the Jameson Experience.

◉ Sights

Jameson Experience
MUSEUM

(☑ 021-461 3594; www.jamesonwhiskey.com; Old Distillery Walk; tours adult/child €18/9; ⊙ shop 10am-6pm; ℗) Coachloads pour in to tour this restored 200-year-old distillery building. Exhibits and tours (run between 10am and 4pm) explain the process of taking barley and creating whiskey (Jameson is today made in a modern factory in Cork). There's a well-stocked gift shop, and the **Malt House Restaurant** (open noon to 3pm) has live music on Sundays.

🛏 Sleeping

There are some good places to stay in town, but most visitors overnight in Cork city or

COUNTY CORK MIDLETON & AROUND

WORTH A TRIP

THE GOURMET HEARTLAND OF BALLYMALOE

Drawing up at wisteria-clad **Ballymaloe House** (☑ 021-465 2531; www.ballymaloe.ie; Shanagarry; r from €250; P 🛜 🎿 🐕) you know you've arrived somewhere special. The Allen family bought the property in 1948 and has been running this superb hotel and restaurant in the old family home for decades. Rooms are individually decorated with period furnishings and, amid the beautiful grounds, amenities include a tennis court, swimming pool, shop and cafe. The house is 12km southeast of Midleton, off the R629.

Myrtle Allen is a living legend, acclaimed internationally for her near single-handed creation of fine Irish cooking. The menu at Ballymaloe House's celebrated **restaurant** (three-course lunch €40, five-course dinner €75, open 1pm to 2pm and 7pm to 9.30pm) changes daily to reflect the availability of produce from its extensive farms and other local sources. The hotel also runs wine and gardening weekends.

TV personality Darina Allen, daughter-in-law of Myrtle Allen of **Ballymaloe Cookery School** (☑ 021-464 6785; www.ballymaloecookeryschool.com; Shanagarry) runs this famous cookery school. Darina's own daughter-in-law, Rachel Allen, is also a high-profile TV chef and author, and regularly teaches at the school. Demonstrations cost €75; lessons, from half-day sessions (€95 to €135) to 12-week certificate courses (€11,595), are often booked out well in advance. It's 3km east of Ballymaloe House.

For overnight students, there are pretty cottages amid the 100 acres of grounds.

head for one of the lovely country-house hotels in the nearby countryside.

An Stór Midleton Townhouse
B&B €

(☑ 021-463 3106; http://anstor.ie; Drury's Lane; s/d/f from €50/65/100; P 🛜) Housed in a former wool store, this place straddles the boundary between upmarket hostel and budget guesthouse, offering competitively priced accommodation in bright, recently redecorated rooms. Family rooms have a double bed and either two or four bunk beds. Breakfast is provided, and there's a self-catering kitchen too. The location is bang in the town centre.

Oatencake Lodge B&B
B&B €

(☑ 021-463 1232; www.oatencakelodge.com; Cork Rd; s/d from €40/70; P 🛜) This suburban villa offers superb-value accommodation in crisp, clean, IKEA-furnished bedrooms. The owners are warm and welcoming, and ready with advice on the local area. It's a 10-minute walk into Midleton town centre, and there's a bus stop at the door for travel into Cork city.

🍴 Eating

Midleton was one of the hotbeds of Cork's 'eat local' food scene that emerged in the last decades of the 20th century, pioneered by Myrtle Allen of nearby Ballymaloe House (p228) and championed by the original Farmgate Restaurant (p228) – parent of the more famous Farmgate Cafe in Cork city's English Market – and by one of Ireland's oldest farmers markets (p229). Today the Farmgate is still going strong, and there are several other eateries that give it a good run for its money.

Greenroom
CAFE €

(☑ 021-463 9682; http://sagerestaurant.ie; 8 Main St; mains €8-14, steaks €20; ⊗ 9am-9pm Tue-Thu, to 10pm Fri & Sat, 11am-7pm Sun; 🛜) 🌱 Tucked behind the Sage restaurant, this cafe is one of the town's social hubs, with a popular breakfast menu (excellent poached eggs on sourdough toast) and a convivial outdoor courtyard bar where you can enjoy a drink, gourmet burgers or fish and chips.

BiteSize
BAKERY €

(☑ 021-463 6456; www.bitesize.ie; 35 Main St; snacks €2-5; ⊗ 8am-6pm Mon-Sat, 9am-6pm Sat; 🛜 ♿) This artisan bakery in the middle of the high street is the ideal place to start the day with a Danish pastry served Scandi-style (ie with a luxurious dollop of whipped cream), a perfectly poured cappuccino and the newspaper. For lunch you'll find soups, sandwiches and savoury tarts, plus cakes galore to take away.

★ Farmgate Restaurant
IRISH €€

(☑ 021-463 2771; www.farmgate.ie; Broderick St; mains lunch €11-18, dinner €15-26; ⊗ 9am-5pm Tue & Wed-Sat, 6.30-9.30pm Thu-Sat) 🌱 The original, sister establishment to Cork city's Farmgate Cafe (p220), the Midleton restaurant offers the same superb blend of traditional and modern Irish cuisine. Squeeze through the deli (open 9am to 6pm Tuesday to Saturday) selling amazing baked goods and local produce to the subtly lit, art-clad, 'farmhouse shed' cafe-restaurant, where you'll eat as well as you would anywhere in Ireland.

Sage   IRISH €€

(☑021-463 9682; www.sagerestaurant.ie; 8 Main St; mains €16-28; ⊗5.30-9pm Tue-Thu, to 9.30pm Fri, noon-3pm & 5.30-9.30pm Sat, noon-3.30pm & 4.30-8.30pm Sun) 🍴 Stylish modern decor set off with polished wood and copper make an elegant setting for relaxed fine dining at this deservedly popular restaurant. Simple-sounding dishes such as salt-baked beetroot with candied oats and apple, or beef cheeks with barley, parsley and smoked onion, turn out to be colourful miniature works of art. Reservations strongly recommended.

🛍 Shopping

Midleton Farmers Market   MARKET

(Main St; ⊗9am-1pm Sat) 🍴 Midleton's farmers market is one of Cork's best, with bushels of local produce on offer and producers who are happy to chat. It's behind the big roundabout at the north end of Main St.

ⓘ Getting There & Away

Midleton is 20km east of Cork. The train station is 1.5km (20 minutes' walk) north of the **Jameson Experience** (p227). There are frequent trains from Cork (€6.25, 25 minutes, at least hourly).

There are also frequent buses from Cork bus station (€8, 30 minutes, every 15 to 45 minutes). You'll need a car to explore the surrounding area.

Youghal

POP 7963

The ancient seaport of Youghal (Eochaill; pronounced 'yawl'), at the mouth of the Blackwater River, has a rich history that may not be instantly apparent, especially if you coast past on the N25. In fact, even if you stop, it may just seem like a humdrum Irish market town. But take a little time and you'll sniff out some of its once-walled past and enjoy views of the wide Blackwater estuary.

The town was a hotbed of rebellion against the English in the 16th century, and Oliver Cromwell wintered here in 1649 as he sought to drum up support for his war in England and quell insurgency among the pesky Irish. Youghal was granted to Sir Walter Raleigh during the Elizabethan Plantation of Munster – he was mayor of Youghal in 1588-9 – and he spent brief spells living here in his house, Myrtle Grove.

◉ Sights & Activities

Youghal Heritage Centre, in the same building as the **tourist office** (☑024-20170; www.youghal.ie; Market Sq; ⊗9.30am-5pm daily

---

YOUGHAL TOWN WALK

Youghal's history is best understood through its landmarks. Heading along Main St from the south, the curious **Clock Gate** was built in 1777, and served as a town gate, clock tower and jail; several prisoners taken in the 1798 Rising were hanged from its windows.

The beautifully proportioned **Red House**, on North Main St, was designed in 1706 by the Dutch architect Leuventhen, and features some Dutch Renaissance details. Across the road is the 15th-century tower house **Tynte's Castle** (www.tyntescastle.com; North Main St; ⊗not open to the public), which originally had a defensive riverfront position.

A few doors further along, at the side street leading to the church, are six **almshouses** built by Englishman Richard Boyle, who bought Raleigh's Irish estates and became the first Earl of Cork in 1616 in recognition of his work in creating 'a very excellent colony'.

Built in 1220 **St Mary's Collegiate Church** incorporates elements of an earlier Danish church dating back to the 11th century. The Earl of Desmond and his troops, rebelling against English rule, demolished the chancel roof in the 16th century.

Hidden behind high walls to the north of the church, 15th- to 18th-century **Myrtle Grove** (not open to the public) is the former home of Sir Walter Raleigh, and a rare Irish example of a late medieval Tudor-style house.

The churchyard is bounded to the west by a fine stretch of the old **town wall** – follow the parapet until you can descend stairs to the outer side, then enter the next gate along to descend back to Main St through the 17th-century **College Gardens**, now restored and in use as a public park.

Jun-Aug, 10am-3pm Mon-Fri Sep-May), has an interesting exhibition on the town's history. Pick up a **Youghal Walking Trail** leaflet, which will guide you around the various historical sites.

Youghal has two Blue Flag **beaches**, ideal for building sandcastles modelled after the Clock Gate. Claycastle (2km) and Front Strand (1km) are both within walking distance of town, off the N25.

Blackwater Cruises   BOATING
(🖉087 988 9076; www.blackwatercruises.com; adult/child €20/10; ⊙ Apr-Nov) Runs 90-minute cruises upstream from Youghal along the lovely Blackwater River, past ruined castles and abbeys as far as grand Ballynatray House.

Seahunter   FISHING
(🖉087 151 8164; www.seahunter.ie; adult/child from €25/12) Seahunter organises sea-angling trips from Youghal harbour, and can arrange rod hire.

🛏️ Sleeping & Eating

Avonmore House   B&B €€
(🖉024-92617; www.avonmoreyoughal.com; South Abbey; d from €90; P🛜) This grand Georgian house at the south end of town was built in 1752 on the site of a Franciscan abbey destroyed by Cromwellian troops, and belonged to the earls of Cork before passing into private hands in 1826. Though the bedrooms are plain and functional, the lounge and breakfast room retain a bit of historical character.

Aherne's Townhouse   INN €€
(🖉024-92424; www.ahernes.net; 163 North Main St; s/d from €95/130; @🛜) The 12 rooms here are extremely well appointed; larger ones have small balconies, where you can breathe in the sea air. Rates include a fabulous breakfast (fresh-squeezed OJ, free-range eggs, locally caught fish) that will keep you going all day. The establishment includes an upmarket **seafood restaurant** (🖉024-92424; 163 North Main St; bar meals €12-26, dinner mains €21-33; ⊙ bar meals noon-10pm, dinner 6.30-9.30pm) and a stylish, cosy bar.

Sage Cafe   CAFE €
(🖉024-85844; www.facebook.com/sagecafe youghal; 86 North Main St; mains €7-14; ⊙ 10am-6pm Mon-Sat; 🖉) 🍃 Everything at this luscious little cafe is homemade: cod and chips, lentil-and-nut loaf, quiche, cakes and more. Vegetarians in particular will be in heaven.

ℹ️ Getting There & Away

Bus Éireann (p223) runs services to Cork (€14.30, 50 minutes, hourly) and Waterford (€20.80, 1½ hours, hourly).

KINSALE TO CAPE CLEAR

The Cork coast begins the slow build-up of beauty that culminates in counties further west and north, but what you find here is already lovely. Picturesque villages, ancient stone circles and some fine sandy beaches mark the meandering coastal route from Kinsale to Clonakilty and on to Skibbereen and Baltimore. Rather than follow the main N71 all the way, explore the maze of minor roads between the N71 and the coast – perfect for aimless wandering.

Kinsale
POP 5281

The picturesque yachting harbour of Kinsale (Cionn tSáile) is one of many colourful gems strung along the coastline of County Cork. Narrow, winding streets lined with galleries and gift shops, lively bars and superb restaurants, and a handsome natural harbour filled with yachts and guarded by a huge 17th-century fortress make it an engrossing place to spend a day or two.

History

Granted a royal charter by the English King Edward II in 1334, Kinsale became a major port trading in wine and salt throughout the 15th century, and was also a provisioning port for the English navy.

In September 1601 English ships besieged a Spanish fleet anchored at Kinsale. Irish forces, which had appealed to the Spanish king to help them against the English, marched the length of the country to liberate the ships, but were defeated in the **Battle of Kinsale** on Christmas Eve. For the Catholic Irish, the immediate consequence was that they were banned from Kinsale; it would be another 100 years before they were allowed back in. Historians now cite 1601 as the beginning of the end of Gaelic Ireland.

After 1601 the town developed as a naval harbour, ship-building port and garrison town. In the early 18th century Alexander Selkirk departed from Kinsale Harbour on

Kinsale

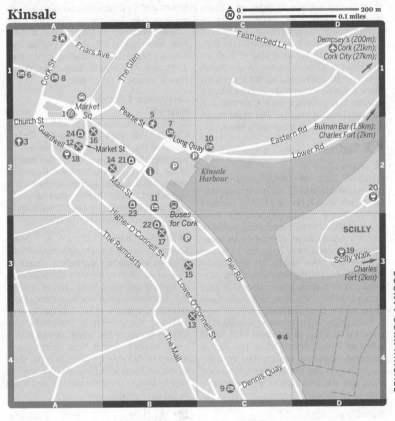

Kinsale

⊚ Sights
1 Courthouse & Regional
   Museum...A1
2 Desmond Castle.................................A1
3 St Multose Church.............................A2

⊕ Activities, Courses & Tours
4 Kinsale Harbour Cruises.....................C4
5 Mylie Murphy's..................................B2

⌂ Sleeping
6 Cloisters B&B....................................A1
7 Old Bank House.................................B2
8 Old Presbytery...................................A1
9 Olde Bakery......................................C4
10 Perryville House...............................C2
11 Pier House.......................................B2

⊗ Eating
12 Bastion..A2
13 Black Pig Wine Bar...........................B4
14 Finn's Table.....................................B2
15 Fishy Fishy Cafe...............................B3
16 Nine Market Street...........................A2
17 Poet's Corner...................................B3

⊜ Drinking & Nightlife
18 Folk House.......................................A2
19 Harbour Bar.....................................D3
20 Spaniard Bar....................................D2

⌂ Shopping
21 Farmers Market................................B2
22 Giles Norman Gallery........................B3
23 Granny's Bottom Drawer....................B2
24 Kinsale Crystal.................................A2

a voyage that left him stranded on a desert island, providing Daniel Defoe with the inspiration for *Robinson Crusoe*.

The town is also associated with the sinking of the *Lusitania* on 7 May 1915 off the Old Head of Kinsale – some of the bodies were brought ashore and buried here (many more are in Cobh), and the inquest into the disaster took place in Kinsale Courthouse. A memorial stands near the Old Head Signal Tower, which houses a Lusitania Museum.

◉ Sights

★ Charles Fort   FORT
(☏021-477 2263; www.heritageireland.ie; Summercove; adult/child €5/3; ◷10am-6pm mid-Mar–Oct, to 5pm Nov–mid-Mar; 🅿) One of Europe's best-preserved star-shaped artillery forts, this vast 17th-century fortification would be worth a visit for its spectacular views alone. But there's much more here: the 18th- and 19th-century ruins inside the walls make for some fascinating wandering. It's 3km southeast of Kinsale along the minor road through Scilly; if you have time, hike there along the lovely coastal Scilly Walk.

Built in the 1670s to guard Kinsale Harbour, the fort was in use until 1921, when much of it was destroyed as the British withdrew. Displays explain the typically tough lives led by the soldiers who served here and the comparatively comfortable lives of the officers.

Signal Tower & Lusitania Museum   MUSEUM
(☏021-419 1285; www.oldheadofkinsale.com; Signal Tower, Old Head of Kinsale; adult/concession €4/3; ◷10am-6pm daily Apr-Oct) This 200-year-old signal tower has been restored and converted into a museum dedicated to the RMS *Lusitania*, which was torpedoed by a German U-boat in 1915 with the loss of 1200 lives. You can walk to the nearby clifftops for impressive views south towards the Old Head, the nearest point of land to the disaster; a privately owned golf club (p232) prevents you from reaching the lighthouse at the tip of the headland. The tower is 13km south of town via the R604.

Desmond Castle   CASTLE
(☏021-477 4855; www.heritageireland.ie; Cork St; adult/child €5/3; ◷10am-6pm Apr-Sep) Kinsale's roots in the wine trade are on display at this early 16th-century fortified house that was occupied by the Spanish in 1601. Since then it has served as a customs house, a prison for French and American captives, and a workhouse during the Famine. There are lively exhibits detailing its history, and a small wine museum that tells the story of the Irish wine-trading families, including names such as Hennessy (of brandy fame), who fled to France because of British rule.

Courthouse & Regional Museum   MUSEUM
(☏021-477 7930; Market Sq; adult/concession €3/1.50; ◷10.30am-1.30pm Tue-Sat Apr-Oct) Based in the 17th-century courthouse that was used for the inquest into the sinking of the *Lusitania* in 1915, this eclectic museum contains local curiosities as diverse as Michael Collins' hurley (hurling stick), and shoes belonging to the 8ft-tall Kinsale Giant, Patrick Cotter O'Brien (1760–1806).

St Multose Church   CHURCH
(Church of Ireland Church; ☏rectory 021-477 2220; www.kinsale.cork.anglican.org; Church St) This is one of the country's oldest Church of Ireland churches, built around 1190 by the Normans on the site of a 6th-century church. Not much of the interior is original, but the exterior is beautifully preserved. Inside, a flat stone carved with a round-handed figure was traditionally rubbed by fishermen's wives to bring their husbands home safe from the sea. Several victims of the *Lusitania* sinking are buried in the graveyard.

🏃 Activities

Scilly Walk   WALKING
You haven't 'done' Kinsale till you've done Scilly Walk, a lovely coastal trail that leads out to Charles Fort (p232). Follow Lower Rd to the Spaniard Bar (p235), descend to the waterfront and follow the harbourside path until it climbs to join High Rd. Descend to the Bulman Bar (p235) for a pint before climbing up to the fort. Return along High Rd – this is Kinsale's 'Golden Mile', lined with millionaires' holiday homes and superb views over the harbour (round trip 6km).

Mylie Murphy's   FISHING, CYCLING
(☏021-477 2703; 14 Pearse St; ◷9.30am-6pm Mon-Sat) You can rent fishing rods here for €10 per day and bikes for €15 a day.

Old Head Golf Links   GOLF
(☏021-477 8444; www.oldhead.com; Old Head of Kinsale; green fees €160-230) This exclusive golf resort is magnificently situated on a clifftop promontory 15km south of Kinsale

via the R600 and R604. The remains of De Courcy castle frame the entrance, and the fifth tee is perched beside the iconic black-and-white striped Old Head lighthouse; beside the sixth green you'll see its predecessor, a ruined 17th-century lighthouse.

👉 Tours

Kinsale Harbour Cruises   BOATING
(📞086 250 5456; www.kinsaleharbourcruises.com; Pier Rd; adult/child €13/5) Runs boat trips to Charles Fort, James Cove and up the River Bandon. Departure times vary through the year and are weather dependent – check the website or with the tourist office (p235) for details. Boats leave from the slip beside the marina.

Kinsale Food Tours   FOOD & DRINK
(📞085 107 6113; http://kinsalefoodtours.com; €50) These 2½-hour guided tours of Kinsale combine a bit of local history and folklore with tasting stops at a range of eateries, and chats with local food producers and restaurateurs. Must be booked at least 24 hours in advance.

**Dermot Ryan's
Heritage Town Walks**   WALKING
(📞021-477 2729; www.kinsaleheritage.com; adult/child €5/free; ⊙10.30am) One-hour walking tours departing from the tourist office (p235); tours starting at 3pm can be arranged by appointment.

✷✷ Festivals & Events

Kinsale Gourmet Festival   FOOD & DRINK
(www.kinsalerestaurants.com; ⊙Oct) Three days of tastings, cookery demonstrations and competitions kick off with the Cork Heat of the All-Ireland seafood chowder cook-off (the final takes place in Kinsale in April).

Kinsale Fringe Jazz Festival   MUSIC
(www.kinsale.ie; ⊙Oct) An offshoot of the Cork Jazz Festival (p218), with chilled-out entertainment at around 20 venues in town over the bank-holiday weekend.

🛏 Sleeping

Dempsey's   HOSTEL €
(📞021-477 2124; www.dempseyhostel.com; Eastern Rd; dm €15-25, f €60-100; 🛜) This basic hostel is nothing special, but it's the town's cheapest option, with separate male and female dorms, family rooms, a kitchen, and picnic tables in the front garden. It's the bright-blue house by the petrol station on the R600 road from Cork, 750m northeast of the centre.

★Old Presbytery   B&B €€
(📞021-477 2027; www.oldpres.com; 43 Cork St; s/d from €90/145; ⊙closed Jan–mid-Feb; P 🛜) The 18th-century Old Presbytery has glided gracefully into the 21st with a painstaking refurbishment that has maintained its character while incorporating solar heating. Choose the deluxe double only if you have no plans to see anything of Kinsale: with its sunroom and balcony, you'll never want to leave. The organic breakfasts, cooked by landlord and former chef Phillip, are the stuff of legend.

★Pier House   B&B €€
(📞021-477 4169; www.pierhousekinsale.com; Pier Rd; d €100-140; P 🛜) Set back from the road in a sheltered garden, this is a lovely place to rest your head. Pristine rooms, decorated with shell-and-driftwood sculptures, have black-granite bathrooms with power showers and underfloor heating; four open to balconies with garden and harbour views.

Cloisters B&B   B&B €€
(📞021-470 0680; www.cloisterskinsale.com; Friars St; s/d from €60/110; 🛜) Little touches make the difference at this blue-shuttered B&B near Desmond Castle. Chocolates await your arrival, rooms are squeaky-clean, and the orthopaedic mattresses are so comfy that only the creative breakfasts will tempt you out of bed.

Olde Bakery   B&B €€
(📞021-477 3012; www.theoldebakerykinsale.com; 56 Lower O'Connell St; r from €90; 🛜) A short walk southeast of the centre is this very friendly place that was once the British garrison bakery. Rooms are a reasonable size and terrific breakfasts around the kitchen table get everyone chatting.

Old Bank House   HOTEL €€€
(📞021-477 4075; www.oldbankhousekinsale.com; 11 Pearse St; s/d from €170/180; 🛜) Georgian elegance and style give a timeless quality to this top-of-the-range 17-room hotel. Beautiful objets d'art and paintings grace the walls, and the luxurious public rooms add a country-house ambience. Although bedrooms are lavish, they're subtle enough to avoid pretension. Superb breakfasts, with homemade breads (from the bakery downstairs) and jams, are included in the rate.

Perryville House   BOUTIQUE HOTEL €€€
(📞021-477 2731; www.perryvillehouse.com; Long Quay; r from €215; ⊙closed Nov-Feb; P 🛜) It's

top-to-bottom grandeur at family-run Perryville, whether you're pulling up outside its imposing wrought iron–balconied facade or taking afternoon tea in the drawing room. All the rooms exude comfort; move up the rate card and the beds go from queen to king, and balconies and sea views appear.

 ## Eating

Kinsale has been labelled the gourmet centre of southwest Ireland, and for such a small place it certainly packs more than its fair share of international-standard restaurants. Most are situated near the harbour and within easy walking distance of the town centre, and you can eat well on any budget.

Poet's Corner   CAFE €
(☑086 227 7276; www.poetscornerkinsale.com; 44 Main St; mains €5-10; ⊗9.30am-6pm daily Apr-Sep, Mon-Sat Oct-Mar; 🎅) A cheerful cafe and book exchange, serving great cakes and coffee as well as huge toasted sandwiches.

★Black Pig Wine Bar   IRISH €€
(☑021-477 4101; www.facebook.com/theblack pigwinebar; 66 Lower O'Connell St; mains €10-18; ⊗5.30-11pm Wed, Thu & Sun, to 11.30pm Fri & Sat) 🍷 This sophisticated hideaway is set in an 18th-century coach house with a charming cobbled courtyard out the back, and offers a mouth-watering menu of gourmet nibbles, charcuterie platters and cheese boards sourced from artisan local suppliers. The award-winning wine list offers no fewer than 200 wines by the bottle and 100 by the glass, including many organic varieties. Reservations recommended.

Nine Market Street   BISTRO €€
(☑021-470 9221; http://ninemarketstreet.ie; 9 Market St; mains €11-25; ⊗10am-4pm Tue-Wed, to 8.45pm Thu-Sat, 11am-4pm Sun; 🍴) Black-and-white floor tiles, warm golden wood and old

> **ℹ PASSAGE WEST FERRY**
>
> From Carrigaloe, 3.5km northwest of Cobh, the **Passage West Ferry** (☑021-481 1485; http://crossriverferries .ie; pedestrian/cyclist/car one way €1.50/ 1.50/6; ⊗7am-10pm) provides a handy shortcut to Passage West, 14km southeast of Cork city. The cross-river journey takes just five minutes. It's particularly useful if you're heading to or from the southern side of Cork city, or Kinsale, and want to skip the city traffic.

photographs set the relaxed mood at this appealing little cafe-cum-bistro. Freshly prepared fish cakes, quiches, healthy salads and soups are complemented by daily specials such as a Wagyu beef burger. There are three comfy, good-value guest bedrooms upstairs (double €70).

★Bastion   MODERN IRISH €€€
(☑021-470 9696; www.bastionkinsale.com; cnr Main & Market Sts; mains €18-31; ⊗5-10pm Wed-Sun; 🍴) 🍷 Awarded a Bib Gourmand in 2016, the newest addition to Kinsale's lengthy list of top restaurants offers diners a relaxed and informal entry into the world of haute cuisine. Waitstaff will guide you through the concise à la carte menu of local oysters, beef, fish and venison, but it's best to go for the seven-course tasting menu (€65) or the five-course early-bird menu (pre-6pm; €45).

★Finn's Table   MODERN IRISH €€€
(☑021-470 9636; www.finnstable.com; 6 Main St; mains €23-34; ⊗6-10pm Mon, Tue & Thu-Sat) 🍷 Owning a gourmet restaurant in Kinsale means plenty of competition, but John and Julie Finn's venture is more than up to the challenge. Elegant but unstuffy, Finn's Table offers a warm welcome, and its menu of seasonal, locally sourced produce rarely fails to please. Seafood (including lobster when in season) is from West Cork, while meat is from the Finn family's butchers.

★Fishy Fishy Cafe   SEAFOOD €€€
(☑021-470 0415; www.fishyfishy.ie; Crowley's Quay; mains €16-27; ⊗noon-9pm Mar-Oct, shorter hours rest of year) 🍷 One of the most famous seafood restaurants in the country, Fishy Fishy has a wonderful setting with stark white walls splashed with bright artwork and striking steel fish sculptures, and a terrific decked terrace at the front. All the fish is caught locally, and dishes include lobster thermidor and a chilled seafood platter served with homemade mayonnaise.

🍷 Drinking & Nightlife

★Folk House   BAR
(☑021-477 2382; http://folkhousevenue.com; Guardwell; ⊗4.30pm-midnight Mon-Fri, 12.30pm-12.30am Sat & Sun) A rustic huddle of cosy nooks makes the Folk House an inviting spot to settle down by the fire with your choice of craft beers from around the world, or to stand at the bar and soak up the craic. From Thursday to Sunday there's a swirl of

live music, which could be anything from indie or ska to folk or traditional Irish.

Spaniard Bar PUB
(☑ 021-477 2436; www.thespaniard.ie; River Rd, Scilly; ⊗ 10.30am-11.30pm Mon-Thu, to 12.30am Fri & Sat, 12.30-11.30pm Sun) The food is good, but the real appeal of this old pub (it feels like it dates back to the Armada) lies in the quiet corners where you can smell the peat fire and catch fragments of hushed conversations, and, on sunny days, the outdoor tables with views across the harbour.

Bulman Bar PUB
(☑ 021-477 2131; www.thebulman.ie; Summercove; mains €15-32; ⊗ 12.30-11.30pm Mon-Thu, to 12.30am Fri & Sat, to 11pm Sun; ☎) ✐ Escape from central Kinsale to this harbourside gastropub in the picturesque hamlet of Summercove, where salty informality is a style in its own right. Sip chilled white wine at outdoor tables or sup beers and seafood chowder in the wood-panelled interior. It's 2km southeast of Kinsale town centre, on the way to Charles Fort.

Harbour Bar PUB
(Scilly Walk; ⊗ 6-11.30pm) It might look permanently closed from the outside, but inside it's like being in someone's front room (actually, it IS someone's front room! Tim, the landlord's). Battered old sofas, a fire stoked in the hearth, characters in every corner and garden benches with harbour views are all part of the charm. Serves bottled drinks only.

🛍 Shopping

Farmers Market MARKET
(☑ 085 722 0259; www.facebook.com/kinsale farmersmarket; Short Quay; ⊗ 10am-2pm Wed) ✐ Sets up on the wee square across from the tourist office (p235); this is the place to buy artisan foods straight from the producer.

Giles Norman Gallery ART
(☑ 021-477 4373; www.gilesnorman.com; 45 Main St; ⊗ 10am-6pm Mon-Sat, noon-6pm Sun) Evocative black-and-white imagery of Ireland from a master of the genre. Prints start at €20 unframed and €30 framed.

Granny's Bottom Drawer ARTS & CRAFTS
(☑ 021-477 4839; www.grannysbottomdrawer.com; 53 Main St; ⊗ 9am-9pm Mon-Fri, to 7pm Sat & Sun May-Sep, 10am-6pm daily Oct-Mar) Top quality Irish linen, woollens, leather goods, damask, furniture and vintage-style homewares.

OFF THE BEATEN TRACK

DROMBEG STONE CIRCLE

On an exposed hillside, with fields falling away towards the coast and cattle lowing in the distance, the **Drombeg Stone Circle** (⊗ 24hr; 🅿) is superbly atmospheric. Its 17 stones, oriented towards the winter solstice sunset, once guarded the cremated bones of an adolescent. The 9m-diameter circle probably dates from the 5th century AD, and is a sophisticated Iron Age update of an earlier Bronze Age monument. To get here, take the signposted left turn off the R597, approximately 4km west of Rosscarbery.

Just beyond the stones are the remains of a hut and an Iron Age cooking pit, known as a *fulachta fiadh*. Experiments have shown that its heated rocks would boil water and keep it hot for nearly three hours – long enough to cook meat.

Kinsale Crystal GLASS
(☑ 021-477 4493; www.kinsalecrystal.ie; Market St; ⊗ 9am-5.30pm Mon-Fri, 10am-6pm Sat, noon-6pm Sun) Exquisite work by an ex-Waterford craftsperson who stands by the traditional 'deep-cutting, high-angle' style. A million tiny sparkles greet you as you enter.

❶ Information

Tourist Office (☑ 021-477 2234; www.kinsale. ie; cnr Pier Rd & Emmet Pl; ⊗ 9.15am-5pm Tue-Sat year-round, 9.15am-5pm Mon Apr-Oct, 10am-5pm Sun Jul & Aug) Has a good map detailing walks in and around Kinsale.

❶ Getting There & Around

Bus Éireann (☑ 021-450 8188; www.bus eireann.ie) service 226 connects Kinsale with Cork bus station (€9.60, one hour, hourly) via Cork Airport, and continues to Cork train station. The **bus stop** is on Pier Rd, near the tourist office.

Kinsale Cabs (☑ 021-477 2642; www.kinsale-cabs.com) A taxi from Cork Airport to Kinsale can cost from €35 to €45. Also arranges golfing tours of West Cork.

Clonakilty

POP 4592

Cheerful, brightly painted Clonakilty is a bustling market town which serves as a hub for the scores of beguiling little coastal villages that surround it. You'll find smart B&Bs, good restaurants and cosy pubs alive with music. Little waterways coursing through town add to the charm.

Clonakilty is famous for two things: it's the birthplace of Irish Free State commander-in-chief Michael Collins, embodied in a large statue on the corner of Emmet Sq; and it's the home of the most famous black pudding in the country.

Roads converge on Astna Sq, dominated by a 1798 Rising monument. Also in the square is the Kilty Stone, a piece of the original castle that gave Clonakilty (Cloich na Coillte in Irish, meaning 'castle of the woods') its name.

◉ Sights

Michael Collins Centre   MUSEUM

(✑023-884 6107; www.michaelcollinscentre. com; Castleview; adult/child €5/3; ☉10.30am-5pm Mon-Fri, 11am-2pm Sat mid-Jun–mid-Sep) A visit to the Michael Collins Centre is an excellent way to make sense of his life and the times in which he lived. A tour reveals photos, letters and a reconstruction of the 1920s country lane where Collins was killed, complete with armoured vehicle. The centre runs tours of the crucial locations in Collins' life (book in advance). It's signposted off the R600 between Timoleague and Clonakilty.

West Cork Model Railway Village   AMUSEMENT PARK

(✑023-883 3224; www.modelvillage.ie; Inchydoney Rd; adult/child incl road train tour €11/6.50; ☉10am-6pm Jul-Aug, 11am-5pm Sep-Jun; Ⓟ🐾) You can't help but smile at the West Cork Model Railway Village. It features a vast outdoor re-creation of the West Cork Railway as it was during the 1940s, with superb miniature models of the main towns in West Cork. There's also a road train that provides a 20-minute guided circuit of Clonakilty.

🛏 Sleeping

Bay View House   B&B €€

(✑023-883 3539; www.bayviewclonakilty.com; Old Timoleague Rd; s/d from €55/90; Ⓟ🛜) This spacious modern villa offers immaculate B&B accommodation, a genial welcome and great breakfasts. Rooms 5 and 6 and the cosy landing lounge offer fantastic views over fields that slope down to Clonakilty Bay. It is 300m east of the town centre, just off the main N71 roundabout into town.

O'Donovan's Hotel   INN €€

(✑023-883 3250; www.odonovanshotel.com; Pearse St; s/d from €70/120; 🛜🐾) Behind the vintage, vivid-red exterior beats the heart of a classic old-fashioned hotel. Rooms are straightforward, but service is friendly and you can't beat the central location. A WWII plaque out the front will intrigue Americans in particular (it commemorates the crew of a crashed USAF Flying Fortress who stayed here in 1943).

Emmet Hotel   HOTEL €€

(✑023-883 3394; www.emmethotel.com; Emmet Sq; s/d from €55/89; 🛜) This lovely Georgian hotel on the elegant main square successfully mixes period charm and olde-worlde service with the perks of a modern hotel. The 20 rooms are large and plush; the onsite restaurant, bistro and bar all serve up tasty Irish food made from organic and local ingredients.

Tudor Lodge   B&B €€

(✑023-883 3046; www.tudorlodgecork.com; McCurtain Hill; s/d €50/80; 🛜) Standards are kept up to scratch at this modern, mock-Tudor family home, a short walk from the town centre.

★Inchydoney Island Lodge & Spa   RESORT €€€

(✑023-883 3143; www.inchydoneyisland.com; Inchydoney; r from €190; @🛜🏊) A superb seawater spa is at the heart of this sprawling resort 5km south of Clonakilty, where the service is outstanding, the food at the French-inspired restaurant is delicious, and luxurious rooms overlook the ocean from private balconies and terraces.

MICHAEL COLLINS

Born on a farm just outside Clonakilty, Michael Collins is one of County Cork's most famous sons. He played a central role in the War of Independence with Britain, and in 1922 became commander-in-chief of the army of the newly founded Irish Free State.

The useful map and leaflet *In Search of Michael Collins*, available at the Clonakilty tourist office, outlines places in the district associated with him; you can dig deeper into his life at the **Michael Collins Centre**.

✖ Eating & Drinking

★ Scannells
MODERN IRISH €

(☑ 023-883 4116; www.scannellsbar.com; Connolly St; mains €8-13; ☺ food served noon-4pm Mon-Sat; 🐾) The sheltered, flower-filled garden at this gastropub is absolutely hopping, rain or shine, thanks to an ambitious menu that ranges from superb West Cork steak bap (steak sandwich) with hand-cut chips, to trad seafood chowder and organic salads with beetroot, roasted hazelnuts, goat's cheese and quinoa.

Farmers Market
MARKET

(☑ 087 135 6848; http://wildatlanticmarket.ie; Pearse St; ☺ 9am-2pm Fri) 🍴 Clonakilty's farmers market sets up in a car park, down an alley beside O'Donovan's Hotel.

Farm Restaurant
IRISH €€

(☑ 023-883 4355; http://farmrestaurant.ie; 30 Ashe St; mains €18-28; ☺ 6-9pm Mon-Tue, 5-9.30pm Thu-Sat, 12.30-3.30pm & 5-9pm Sun; 🍴🦽) 🍴 Clonakilty's reputation as a champion of West Cork's foodie scene is enhanced by this new restaurant, which focuses on fresh, simply prepared dishes that use meat, vegetables and seafood from local small-scale or family-run producers and suppliers – Union Hall fish and chips, beetroot risotto cake with Irish buffalo mozzarella, and homemade venison sausage with Clonakilty's own black pudding.

An Súgán
SEAFOOD €€

(☑ 023-883 3719; www.ansugan.com; 41 Wolfe Tone St; mains €12-29; ☺ noon-10pm) A traditional bar with a reputation for excellent seafood, where you dine in a room crammed with knick-knacks – jugs dangle from the ceiling, business cards are stuffed in the rafters, and lanterns dot the walls. But there's nothing idiosyncratic about the food – the seafood chowder and crab cakes are great, and there's a choice of around 10 different kinds of fish.

★ De Barra's Folk Club
PUB

(☑ 023-883 3381; www.debarra.ie; 55 Pearse St; ☺ 10am-11.45pm Mon-Thu, to 12.30am Fri & Sat, noon-11.30pm Sun) A convivial, jostling atmosphere – with walls splattered with photos and press cuttings, dramatic masks and musical instruments – provides the setting for the cream of local folk music. Nightly sessions usually begin around 9pm.

IRELAND'S BEST BLACK PUDDING

Clonakilty's most treasured export is its black pudding, a sausage made from pig's blood, oatmeal and onion that features on most local restaurant menus. The best place to buy it is from butcher **Edward Twomey** (☑ 023-883 4835; www.clonakiltyblackpudding.ie; 16 Pearse St; ☺ 9am-6pm Mon-Sat), who sells different varieties based on an original recipe from the 1880s.

An Teach Beag
PUB

(☑ 023-883 3250; www.facebook.com/AnTeach Beag; 5 Recorder's Alley; ☺ 8.30-11.45pm) This intriguing cottage-pub (the name means 'the little house'), along the alley beside O'Donovan's Hotel, has all the atmosphere necessary for good traditional music sessions. You might even catch a *scríocht* (a session by storytellers and poets) in full flow. There's music nightly during July and August, and on weekends for the rest of the year.

❶ Information

The **tourist office** (☑ 023-883 3226; www.clonakilty.ie; Ashe St; ☺ 9.15am-5pm Mon-Sat) is towards the east end of the main street, in the centre of town.

❶ Getting There & Around

There are buses to Cork (€15.80, 1¼ hours, seven daily) and Skibbereen (€10.70, 40 minutes, six daily). The **bus stop** is on Bridge St in the town centre.

MTM Cycles (☑ 023-883 3584; 33 Ashe St; ☺ 8.30am-6pm Mon-Sat) hires out bikes for €10/50 per day/week. A nice ride is to Duneen Beach, about 13km south of town.

Glandore & Union Hall

The picturesque waterside villages of Glandore (Cuan Dor) and Union Hall burst into life in summer when fleets of yachts race in the sheltered inlet of Glandore Harbour.

Union Hall, southwest of Glandore across a long, narrow causeway, was named after the 1801 Act of Union that abolished the separate Irish parliament. The 1994 film *War of the Buttons,* about two battling gangs of youngsters, was filmed here.

There's an ATM, a post office and a general store.

Union Hall is famous as a fishing harbour, and as the home of **Union Hall Smoked Fish** (☑ 028-33125; www.unionhallsmokedfish.com; Main St, Union Hall; ☉ 8.30am-5pm Mon-Fri), which produces excellent smoked salmon. There are two neighbouring pub-restaurants nearby in Glandore, both of which serve fresh local seafood with a fantastic view over the harbour.

🏃 Activities

Cork Whale Watch   WILDLIFE WATCHING
(☑ 086 327 3226; www.corkwhalewatch.com; Reen Pier; adult/child €50/40) Runs four-hour whale-watching cruises out of Reen Pier, 4km south of Union Hall: one trip daily year-round (weather dependent), two trips daily June to August. Cash only.

Atlantic Sea Kayaking   KAYAKING
(☑ 028-21058; www.atlanticseakayaking.com; Reen Pier; from €50) Runs half- and full-day marine safaris by sea kayak from Reen Pier, 4km south of Union Hall. No previous experience needed. Also offers magical moonlight kayak tours on Castletownshend Bay and Lough Hyne (p240).

🛏 Sleeping & Eating

Shearwater B&B   B&B €€
(☑ 028-33178; www.shearwaterbandb.com; Union Hall; r from €80; ☉ Apr-Oct; 🅿 🗣) A warm welcome awaits at this bright and attractive B&B, just a short stroll from the centre of Union Hall. Hearty breakfasts are served in a spacious sunroom, and on a terrace with killer views across the harbour; all of the five bedrooms share that gorgeous view.

Bay View House   B&B €€
(☑ 028-33115; www.facebook.com/BayviewBedandbreakfast; Main St, Glandore; s/d €50/80) Perched above the sea, Bay View House has seriously spectacular views across the bay. Try to snag Room 1 for the best panorama of all. Bright colours, tidy pine furniture and gleaming bathrooms add to the appeal, and Glandore's twin pub-restaurants are just a stumble away.

★ Glandore Inn   PUB FOOD €€
(☑ 028-34494; http://glandoreinn.ie; Main St, Glandore; mains €12-24; ☉ 1pm-12.30am, food served till 9pm; 🗣) 🍴 Picture-postcard views over the harbour, especially from the outdoor tables, and a superlative menu make this one of West Cork's best pubs for eating out. Fresh seafood is sourced from Union Hall harbour (clearly visible across the water). The interior's rustic nautical charm has a contemporary edge, and there are Irish craft beers on tap.

Hayes Bar   PUB FOOD €€
(☑ 028-33214; http://glandorevillage.ie; Main St, Glandore; mains €8-18; ☉ 10am-11.30pm Mon-Sat, 11am-11pm Sun, food served noon-9pm; 🗣 🛒) 🍴 This perfect seaside pub has log fires in winter, and in summer tables spill out across the street to make the most of the harbour views. There's excellent pub grub on the menu. Standards such as seafood chowder, fish pie and boeuf bourguignon are complemented by more adventurous dishes like crab cannelloni and Mexican-inspired hake Veracruz.

ℹ Getting There & Away

Six daily buses between Skibbereen (€4.20, 15 minutes) and Clonakilty (€8, 25 minutes) stop in nearby Leap (3km north), from where most B&B owners will pick you up if you arrange it in advance.

Skibbereen

POP 2778

Today Skibbereen (Sciobairín) is a pleasant, workaday market town, with an attractive, upmarket centre on the banks of the River Ilen.

During the Famine, however, Skibb was hit perhaps harder than any other town in Ireland, with huge numbers of the local population emigrating or dying of starvation or disease. 'The accounts are not exaggerated – they cannot be exaggerated – nothing more frightful can be conceived.' So wrote Lord Dufferin and GF Boyle, who journeyed from Oxford to Skibbereen in February 1847 to see if reports of the Famine were true. Their eyewitness account makes horrific reading; Dufferin was so appalled by what he saw that he contributed £1000 (about €100,000 in today's money) to the relief effort.

The main landmark in town is a statue in the central square, dedicated to heroes of Irish rebellions against the British.

◉ Sights

Skibbereen Heritage Centre   MUSEUM
(☑ 028-40900; www.skibbheritage.com; Upper Bridge St; adult/child €6/3; ☉ 10am-6pm daily

May–Sep, Tue–Sat mid-Mar–Apr & Oct, closed Nov–mid-Mar; P) Constructed on the site of the town's old gasworks, the Skibbereen Heritage Centre houses a haunting exhibition about the Famine, with actors reading heartbreaking contemporary accounts; a visit here puts Irish history into harrowing perspective. There's also a smaller exhibition about nearby Lough Hyne (p240), the first marine nature reserve in Ireland, plus a genealogical centre.

Guided evening historical walks (adult/child €5/2.50), lasting 1½ hours, leave from the heritage centre. Call to confirm times.

Abbeystrewery Famine Cemetery
CEMETERY

This graveyard, 1km west of Skibbereen beside the N71 road towards Schull, contains the mass grave of 8000 to 10,000 local people who died during the Famine, marked by a memorial of polished black stone. There's no parking on the main road; take the minor road opposite the river bridge and park near the upper entrance.

West Cork Distillers
DISTILLERY

(☑028-22815; www.westcorkdistillers.com; Marsh Rd) This craft distillery produces liqueurs (Drombeg, Lough Hyne), vodka (Two Trees) and a range of whiskies (blended, pot still and single malt) under its own name. No formal tours, but visitors are welcome if you call ahead to arrange a visit.

✲ Festivals & Events

★ Taste of West Cork Food Festival
FOOD & DRINK

(www.atasteofwestcork.com; ☺Sep) If you're in town in mid-September, don't miss this foodie extravaganza, which includes a lively farmers market, cookery demonstrations, competitions, food-tastings, talks, exhibitions and children's events.

⛱ Sleeping & Eating

★ Bridge House
B&B €

(☑028-21273; www.bridgehouseskibbereen.com; 46 Bridge St; s/d from €45/75; ☎) Mona Best has turned her entire house into a work of art, filling the rooms with fabulous Victorian tableaux and period memorabilia. The whole place bursts at the seams with cherished clutter, crazed carvings, dressed-up dummies and fragrant fresh flowers; personalised service extends to champagne breakfasts for guests celebrating a birthday – not bad for a B&B!

Kalbo's
INTERNATIONAL €

(☑028-21515; https://kalboscafe.com; 26 North St; mains €6-12; ☺9am-5pm Mon-Sat; ☎⛱) 🍴 This place uses locally sourced produce and a deft hand in the kitchen to produce breakfast dishes such as vanilla pancakes with fresh berries, and lunch specials that include goat's cheese salad with caramelised pears, Castletownbere crab salad and more.

Good Things Café
MODERN IRISH €€

(☑028-51948; www.thegoodthingscafe.com; 68 Bridge St; mains €15-28; ☺noon-3pm Thu-Sat, 6-9pm Fri & Sat; P☑) 🍴 This foodie haven serves great contemporary dishes made with organic, locally sourced ingredients. The cafe's own cookery school offers one-day courses including vegetarian and vegan cooking (€140 per person), and a 'Man Never in the Kitchen' course (€200) for those whose kitchen skills extend no further than the microwave.

Riverside Café & Restaurant
INTERNATIONAL €€

(☑028-40090; www.riversideskibbereen.ie; North St; mains €9-15; ☺noon-3.30pm Tue-Sat, 6-10pm Fri & Sat; ☎⛱) Seafood casserole in lobster bisque, seaweed paella, and bangers and mash with oxtail gravy are among the choices at this popular spot, along with cheese and smoked-fish boards. But the biggest draw is the riverside setting with alfresco seating in a sheltered yard at the back – a real lunchtime suntrap.

Farmers Market
MARKET

(www.skibbereenmarket.com; The Fairfield, Bridge St; ☺9.30am-2pm Sat) 🍴 One of Ireland's biggest and liveliest farmers markets, a showcase for the best of West Cork food and drink; there's often live music laid on as well.

❶ Getting There & Away

Bus Éireann (p223) runs buses to Cork seven times daily Monday to Saturday, and five times on Sunday (€21, two hours). It also goes to Schull three times daily Monday to Saturday and once on Sunday (€8, 30 minutes).

West Cork Rural Transport (☑027-52727; www.ruraltransport.ie; 5 Main St) operates a subsidised minibus service west to Bantry (€4, one hour, once daily Monday to Friday)

Baltimore

POP 323

Crusty old sea dog Baltimore is a classic maritime village with a long history, its busy little harbour full of fishing boats

LOUGH HYNE

This beautiful lough is one of Ireland's natural wonders, and became the country's first marine nature reserve in 1981. Its glacier-gouged depths were originally filled with fresh water until rising sea levels breached one end around 4000 years ago. It is now linked to the sea by a narrow tidal channel known as **the Rapids**, where the tide pours in and out twice a day in a rush of white water.

There are lovely walks around the lough and in the neighbouring **Knockomagh Wood Nature Reserve**. A waymarked nature trail leads up a steep hill through the forest; you're rewarded with stunning views at the top.

Atlantic Sea Kayaking (p238) offers guided sea kayak tours of the lough, including superbly atmospheric 2½-hour 'starlight paddles' after dark.

The lough is 6km northeast of Baltimore and 8km southwest of Skibbereen, signposted off the R595 between the two towns, and an easy bike ride from either.

and pleasure yachts. The focus of life here is the central terrace overlooking the harbour, the ideal spot to sup a pint or slurp an ice cream while watching the boats go by. All around spreads a multitude of holiday cottages, catering to the summer swell of sailing folk, sea anglers, divers, and visitors to nearby Sherkin and Cape Clear islands.

A white-painted landmark beacon (aka **Lot's Wife**) stands on the headland 2km southwest of town, marking the entrance to Baltimore Harbour and making a good objective for a pleasant walk, especially at sunset.

Baltimore's sheltered natural harbour has long been a favourite of mariners, and was best known in the 17th century as the haunt of pirates. The most famous date in its history is 20 June 1631, when the village was sacked by a fleet of Barbary pirates who carried off more than 100 prisoners to a life of slavery. The remaining villagers fled to Skibbereen, and Baltimore lay abandoned for many decades afterwards.

There's an information board at the harbour, or check out www.baltimore.ie.

⊙ Sights & Activities

Baltimore Castle　　　　　　　　MUSEUM
(Dun na Sead; ☑028-20735; www.baltimorecastle.
ie; adult/child €5/free; ⊙11am-6pm Easter, May
bank holidays & Jun-Sep) Baltimore harbour
is dominated by the stone tower of 13th-century castle of Dun na Sead (Fort of the Jewels). Inside, the great hall houses seasonal art displays and exhibits on the town's and the castle's history, but the main attraction is the view from the battlements.

Baltimore Sea Safari　　　　　　BOATING
(☑028-20753; www.baltimoreseasafari.ie; Ferry
Pier) Trips in a fast rigid-hulled inflatable
boat (RIB) along the West Cork coast to see
sea cliffs and wildlife, including whales and
dolphins; take a 20-minute harbour cruise
(€10 per person) or a two-hour wildlife safari (€25).

Aquaventures Dive Centre　　　　DIVING
(☑028-20511; www.aquaventures.ie; Stone House
B&B, Lifeboat Rd) This outfit leads half-day
guided snorkelling tours (€40/30 per adult/
child, including equipment) suitable for
family groups (minimum age six years), exploring marine wildlife on the local coastline or at nearby Lough Hyne. It also offers
beginners courses in scuba diving (€130 for
a one-day Discover Scuba experience).

✯ Festivals & Events

Fiddle Fair　　　　　　　　　　MUSIC
(www.fiddlefair.com; ⊙2nd weekend of May) Sessions from international and local musicians.

**Seafood & Wooden
Boat Festival**　　　　　　　FOOD & DRINK
(www.baltimore.ie/event/seafood-festival; ⊙May)
A showcase for local restaurants and seafood producers. Jazz bands perform in the
square and traditional wooden sailboats
race around the harbour.

Baltimore Pirate Weekend　　　CULTURAL
(www.baltimore.ie/event/baltimore-pirate-week
end; ⊙Jun) A long weekend of family-oriented fun, with boat trips, outdoor activities, treasure hunts, music and dancing,
all in memory of a notorious event in Baltimore's history, when the port was attacked
by Barbary pirates in 1631.

🛏 Sleeping & Eating

Rolf's Country House
GUESTHOUSE €€

(☑ 028-20289; www.rolfscountryhouse.com; Baltimore Hill; s/d €79/99, cottages per week from €650; ☺ Apr-Oct; 🅿 🛜) Upmarket Rolf's, in a much-restored and extended old farmhouse in restful gardens on the outskirts of town, does the lot: there are 10 smartly decorated private rooms, a clutch of two-bedroom self-catering cottages, helpful staff and a charming restaurant. The place is signposted from the R595 as you approach the village centre.

Waterfront
HOTEL €€

(☑ 028-20600; www.waterfronthotel.ie; The Quay; s/d from €100/160; 🅰 🛜) Smack in the middle of town, this hotel has 13 bright and airy rooms; ask for one with a view of the sea. Its restaurant, the Lookout, also has sea views and serves luscious shellfish platters containing lobsters, prawns, brown crabs, velvet crabs, shrimp and oysters.

Casey's of Baltimore
HOTEL €€

(☑ 028-20197; www.caseysofbaltimore.com; Skibbereen Rd; r from €110; 🅿 🅰 🛜) Ten of the 14 spiffy guest rooms here have estuary views, and all have huge beds. The hotel is right at the entrance to town (should you be arriving by chopper, there's a helipad). Food comes with fantastic views, especially from the terrace. Seafood includes mussels fresh from the hotel's own shellfish farm in Roaringwater Bay.

★ Glebe Gardens & Café
MODERN IRISH €€

(☑ 028-20579; www.glebegardens.com; Skibbereen Rd; mains lunch €6-15, dinner €18-25; ☺ 10am-10pm Wed-Sat, to 6pm Sun Apr-Sep, 10am-6pm Wed-Sun Oct-Mar; 🅿 🛜) 🍴 The beautiful gardens here are an attraction in themselves (admission is €5). If you're dining, lavender and other herbs add fragrant aromas that waft over the tables inside and out. Food, sourced from the gardens and a list of local purveyors, is simple and fresh – eggs Florentine at breakfast, inspired sandwiches at lunch, and rack of lamb at dinner, for example.

Lookout
SEAFOOD €€€

(Chez Youen; ☑ 028-20600; www.waterfront baltimore.ie; The Quay; mains €20-40; ☺ 6.30-9.30pm daily Aug, Wed-Sat Jun, Jul & Sep, Fri & Sat Easter & May) The upstairs restaurant at the Waterfront (p241) hotel enjoys elevated sea views and serves luscious shellfish platters containing lobsters, prawns, brown crabs, velvet crabs, shrimp and oysters. Opening times vary: check the website.

Bushe's Bar
PUB

(☑ 028-20125; www.bushesbar.com; The Quay; sandwiches €3-11; ☺ noon-11pm) Seafaring paraphernalia drips from the ceiling at this genuinely character-filled old bar. The benches outside on the main square are the best spots in town for a sundowner. Famous crab sandwiches are served when fresh crab has been landed at the quay.

❶ Getting There & Away

Four buses daily Monday to Friday, and two on Saturday, link Skibbereen and Baltimore (€4.90, 20 minutes).

A **passenger ferry** (p242) sails from Baltimore to Schull on Tuesday, Thursday and Sunday in June and daily except Monday in July and August. It's a one-way service (the ferry continues to Cape Clear Island then back to Baltimore); you can take a bike and return by road, or stay overnight and return via Cape Clear the following day.

Sherkin Island
POP 111

Just a 10-minute ferry ride offshore from Baltimore, Sherkin Island measures a mere 5km by 3km. Until the Famine it had a population of more than 1000, but today it's home to only 100 or so people.

These days Sherkin is a magnet for artists and day trippers; there's not much to do except wander the fuchsia-fringed lanes, seek out little swimming coves on the west side, and gaze out to sea.

There's a single hotel, **the Islander's Rest** (☑ 028-20116; www.islandersrest.ie; s/d €80/120; 🅿) on the island, plus a range of self-catering accommodation. The island doesn't have an official campground, but discreet and responsible wild camping is possible.

The Islander's Rest and the **Jolly Roger** (☑ 028-20662; www.facebook.com/TheJollyRogerPub; mains €4-10; ☺ 11am-11.30pm Mon-Thu, to 12.30am Fri & Sat, noon-11.30pm Sun; 🛜 ♿) are the only places to eat on Sherkin. If you plan on exploring away from the harbour, bring food and drink with you.

❶ Getting There & Away

The **Sherkin Island Ferry** (☑ 087 911 7377; http://sherkinisland.eu/ferry; adult/child return €12/4) sails from Baltimore up to nine times daily (seven on Saturday, five on Sunday, reduced services in winter).

Cape Clear Island

POP 147

With its lonely inlets, pebble beaches, and gorse- and heather-clad cliffs, Cape Clear Island (Oileán Chléire) is an escapist's heaven – albeit one that is only 5km long and just over 1.5km wide at its broadest point. But that's just as well, as you'll want time to appreciate this small, rugged Gaeltacht (Irish-speaking) area, which is also the southernmost inhabited island in the country.

Facilities are few (no banks or ATMs), but there's one small grocery store, two pubs and a restaurant.

◉ Sights & Activities

Information boards near the harbour highlight a couple of marked walking trails, while unmarked roads wander all over the island. The remains of a **12th-century church** are near the pier. On the coast to the west the ruins of 14th-century **Dunamore Castle**, the stronghold of the O'Driscoll clan, can be seen perched on a rock (follow the track from the harbour).

Cape Clear is one of the top birdwatching spots in Ireland, particularly known for seabirds including Manx shearwater, guillemot, gannet, fulmar and kittiwake. Tens of thousands of migrating birds can pass hourly, especially in the early morning and at dusk. The best time of year for twitching here is October. The white-fronted **bird observatory** is by the harbour (turn right at the end of the pier and it's about 100m along).

Cape Clear Museum   MUSEUM
(☑028-39119; www.capeclearmuseum.ie; €3; ☉2.30-5pm Jun-Aug) This small museum has exhibits on the island's history and culture, and fine views north across the water to Mizen Head.

Chléire Goats   FARMING
(☑087 797 3056; www.oilean-chleire.ie/Goat Farm) Once you're this isolated, you might as well learn something, and Ed Harper at Chléire Goats farm, west of the island's 12 century church, can teach you everything you need to know about goat husbandry. He makes goat's-milk ice cream and hard goat's cheese, available for tastings, and runs half-day (€35) to five-day (€155) courses on goat keeping.

✷✸ Festivals & Events

Cape Clear Island International Storytelling Festival   PERFORMING ARTS
(☑028-39157; www.capeclearstorytelling.com; ☉early Sep) Draws hundreds of people for storytelling, workshops and walks.

🛏 Sleeping & Eating

Accommodation in the island is limited to a hostel, a campground, and a handful of B&Bs and self-catering cottages. As such, all accommodation must be booked in advance.

Cape Clear Hostel   HOSTEL €
(☑028-41968; http://anoige.ie; Old Coastguard Station, South Harbour; dm/q from €17.50/78; ☉Easter-Sep; ℗@☎) This large cream-coloured building sits amid lovely gardens a 10- to 15-minute walk from the ferry, and houses a hostel with a spacious self-catering kitchen, a laundry and an amazing collection of model ships in bottles. There are lovely sea views and meals are available in the hostel restaurant.

Chléire Haven   CAMPGROUND €
(☑028-39982; www.yurt-holidays-ireland.com; South Harbour; sites per person €10, yurt per night from €90; ☉Apr-Sep) 🌿 This appealing campground overlooking the South Harbour offers stays in a Mongolian yurt (sleeping up to six people), complete with log-burning stove; a North American tepee; or your own tent (limited number of pitches available). All accommodation must be booked in advance, even if you're bringing your own tent.

Cape Clear Island B&B   B&B €€
(Ard Na Gaoithe; ☑028-39160; www.capeclear bandb.ie; The Glen; s/d €50/80; ☎) Set on an organic farm overlooking the South Harbour, a 20-minute walk from the ferry, this cottage-style B&B has restful rooms in a simple, sturdy house. There are cats in the garden, and there are free tea and scones on arrival.

ℹ Information

Tourist Information Point (☑028-39100; www.capeclearisland.ie/TouristInformation; North Harbour; ☉11am-1pm & 2-6pm Jul-Aug, shorter hours Jun & Sep) Beyond the pier, next to Sean Rua's restaurant; includes a craft shop.

ℹ Getting There & Away

The bright orange *Cailín Óir* **passenger ferry** (☑086 346 5110; www.cailinoir.com; adult/child return €16/8; ☉10.30am-7pm May-Sep, see website Oct-Apr) makes the 45-minute crossing

IRELAND'S TEARDROP

So named because it was the last sight of the 'ould country' for emigrants sailing to America, the Fastnet Rock is the most southerly point of Ireland.

This isolated fang of rock, topped by a spectacular lighthouse, stands 6.5km southwest of Cape Clear Island, and in clear weather is visible from many places on the coastline from Baltimore to Mizen Head. Its image – usually with huge waves crashing around it – graces a thousand postcards, coffee-table books and framed art photographs.

The Fastnet lighthouse, widely considered the most perfectly engineered lighthouse in the world, was built in 1904 from ingeniously interlocked blocks of Cornish granite – there are exhibits about its construction at **Mizen Head Visitor Centre** (p244) and **Cape Clear Museum**.

From May to August, **Fastnet Experience** (☑ 087 389 9711; www.fastnettour.com; adult/family €35/80) operates boat trips to the rock, departing from Schull, Baltimore and Cape Clear Island. Tours are weather-dependent and last 2½ to three hours (1½ hours if departing from Cape Clear).

from Baltimore to Cape Clear Island three or four times a day in summer, and twice a day in winter.

In summer, there's also a **ferry service** (☑ 087 389 9711; www.schullferry.com; adult/child return €16/8; ☺ Jun-Aug) from Schull.

MIZEN HEAD PENINSULA

From Skibbereen the N71 rolls west through Ballydehob, the gateway to the cliff-bound Mizen Head Peninsula. From here the R592 leads southwest to the pretty yachting harbour of Schull and onward through ever-smaller settlements to the hamlet of Goleen.

Even here the Mizen (rhymes with 'prison') isn't done. Increasingly narrow roads head further west to spectacular Mizen Head itself, and to the hidden delights of Barleycove Beach and Crookhaven. Without a decent map you may well reach the same crossroads several times.

Heading back from Goleen, you can bear north to join the scenic coast road that follows the edge of Dunmanus Bay for most of the way to Durrus. The R591 heads north through Durrus for Bantry, while the L4704 turns west to Ahakista and the Sheep's Head Peninsula.

Schull

POP 700

The yachting and creative crowds (often the same folk) have turned the small fishing village of Schull (pronounced 'skull') into a buzzing little hot spot, crammed with craft shops and art galleries.

◉ Sights & Activities

Walks in the area include a 13km return trip up **Mt Gabriel** (407m). It was once mined for copper, and there are Bronze Age remains and 19th-century mine shafts and chimneys.

For a gentler stroll try the short 2km foreshore path from the pier out to **Roaringwater Bay** for a view of the nearby islands.

Planetarium   PLANETARIUM
(☑ 028-28315; www.westcorkweb.ie/planetarium; Schull Community College, Colla Rd; adult/child €6/4; ☺ Jun-Aug; ℗) Founded by a German visitor who fell in love with Schull, the Republic's only planetarium is on the grounds of Schull Community College at the south end of the village. During summer the 45-minute star show is on three or four times a week; call or check the website to confirm times.

Divecology   DIVING
(☑ 086 837 2065; www.divecology.com; Main St) Runs training courses and dive trips to wreck and reef sites. A one-day Discover Scuba course costs €100 per person including equipment hire.

✸ Festivals & Events

Schull Regatta   SAILING
(www.shsc.ie; ☺ early Aug) Five days of yacht racing, jokingly named Calves Week in reference to England's more famous Cowes Week, culminate in a weekend regatta that includes an outdoor market, children's sports, crab-fishing competitions and a fireworks display. Usually held after the August bank holiday.

🛏 Sleeping & Eating

There are a couple of good eateries in the village, but try to time your visit to coincide with Sunday's country market (p244) to get a real feel for the local food scene.

Stanley House   B&B €

(☑ 028-28425; www.stanley-house.net; Colla Rd; s/d/f €50/76/110; ☺Mar-Oct; 🅟🗑) Just outside of town, perched on a little knoll, this modern B&B has four spotless and comfortable bedrooms. Relax with a coffee in the sunroom, which has sweeping views of the sea.

Grove House   B&B €€

(☑ 028-28067; www.grovehouseschull.com; Colla Rd; s/d from €50/80; 🅟🗑) This beautifully restored Georgian mansion – Jack B Yeats once stayed here – is decorated in an easygoing period style with antiques, and handmade rugs scattered on polished pine floors. It also has a terrific **restaurant** (three-course dinner €35, open for lunch and dinner Monday to Saturday) where Swedish influences combine with Irish staples.

Newman's West   CAFE €

(☑ 028-27776; www.tjnewmans.com; Main St; mains €8-14; ☺9am-11pm; 🗑) This yachtie-filled wine bar (with many good choices by the glass) and art gallery serves soups, salads and enormous chunky sandwiches filled with local cheese and salami. Daily specials might include Bantry Bay mussels and chowder. The adjoining original pub, TJ Newman's, is a charmer.

GUBBEEN FARM FOODS

Farmed by the same family for six generations, Gubbeen Farm near Schull was one of the pioneers of Irish artisan cheese production, starting out in 1979. The dairy was joined by a smokehouse in 1989, and later by a market garden, while pedigree pigs and poultry were added to the livestock mix.

Gubbeen now turns out ham, salami, chorizo, free-range eggs and organic vegetables, as well as some of Ireland's finest cheeses – Extra Mature Smoked Gubbeen is highly recommended.

The farm is not open to the public, but you can visit the Gubbeen stall at farmers markets in **Schull** (p244), **Skibbereen** (p239) and **Bantry** (p249).

Hackett's Bar   PUB FOOD €

(☑ 028-28625; Main St; mains €7-12; ☺food served noon-3pm daily, 6-9pm Fri & Sat; 🗑🖤) The town's social hub, Hackett's rises above the norm with a creative pub menu of organic dishes prepared from scratch. Black-and-white photos and tin signs adorn the crooked walls and there's a mishmash of old kitchen tables and benches on the worn stone floor.

🛍 Shopping

Country Market   MARKET

(www.schullmarket.com; Pier Road Car Park; ☺10am-2pm Sun Easter-Sep) Schull's popular market showcases the work of the village's artists and craftspeople, and draws producers and purveyors from around the region.

ℹ Getting There & Away

There are two buses daily from Cork to Schull (€23, 2½ hours), via Clonakilty and Skibbereen.

There's also a **West Cork Rural Transport** (p239) minibus (Tuesdays and Fridays only) that links Bantry to Durrus, Goleen and Schull (must be booked in advance).

Mizen Head

On a clear day the undulating coastal route from Schull to Goleen enjoys great views out to Cape Clear Island and the Fastnet lighthouse. The landscape becomes wilder around the hamlet of Toormore where a road branches north towards Durrus. Keeping straight on leads to Goleen, where narrowing roads run out to the remote harbour hamlet of Crookhaven and the impressive cliffs of Mizen Head itself.

Completed in 1909 to help warn ships off the rocks, **Mizen Head Signal Station** (☑ 028-35115; www.mizenhead.ie; Mizen Head; adult/child €7.50/4.50; ☺10am-6pm Jun-Aug, 10.30am-5pm mid-Mar–May, Sep & Oct, 11am-4pm Sat & Sun Nov–mid-Mar; 🖤) is perched high above crashing waves and contorted sea cliffs on a small island connected to the mainland by a spectacular 45m-high bridge. From the visitors centre (you have to pay the admission fee to get to the island), it's a 10-minute walk via 99 steps to reach the station, which houses exhibits on the station's history and on marine wildlife – keep a weather eye open for whales and dolphins.

Back at the visitors centre there are displays about local ecology and history, and on the building of the Fastnet lighthouse. There's also a modest cafe

Public transport is limited to the regular Cork to Schull bus service, and the Tuesdays and Fridays only West Cork Rural Transport (p239) minibus that links Bantry to Durrus, Goleen and Schull (the latter must be booked in advance).

Goleen

Goleen is the largest settlement in these parts – though that's not saying much – with an impressive neo-Gothic church, four pubs, four shops and a petrol station.

🛏 Sleeping & Eating

There are maybe half a dozen B&Bs around the village, most of them open in summer only.

Heron's Cove   B&B €€
(☑ 028-35225; www.heronscove.com; Harbour Rd; s/d from €50/80; 🅿 🛜) 🍽 A delightful location on the shores of the tidal inlet of Goleen Harbour makes this fine restaurant and B&B a top choice. Rooms are brightly decorated and several have balconies overlooking the inlet. The small **restaurant** (three-course dinner €30; 7pm to 9.30pm May to August, by reservation September to April) has an excellent menu of organic and local food.

Fortview House   B&B €€
(☑ 028-35324; www.fortviewhouse.ie; Gurtyowen, Toormore; s/d €50/100; ☺Apr-Oct; 🅿 🛜) On a working farm, this lovely house has three antique-filled, flower-themed bedrooms. Hostess Violet's breakfast is gourmet standard (hot potato cakes with crème fraîche and smoked salmon), with eggs from the garden's cheerfully clucking hens. The house is 9km northeast of Goleen, along the R591 towards Durrus.

ℹ Information

Mizen Information & e-Centre (☑ 028-35000; www.facebook.com/mizenecentre; Main St; ☺10am-6pm; 🛜) Provides tourist information, coffee, free wi-fi and internet access.

ℹ Getting There & Away

Bus Éireann (p223) has two buses a day from Skibbereen (€12.90, 1¼ hours) via Schull.

Goleen is the end of the line for bus service on the peninsula.

West Cork Rural Transport (p239) also runs a minibus service from Bantry to Goleen (€4, one hour) via Schull twice daily on Tuesday and Friday only.

Crookhaven

The westerly outpost of Crookhaven feels so remote that you imagine it's more easily reached by boat than by road. And so it is for some people – in summer there's a big yachting presence. Outside summer it's very quiet.

In its heyday Crookhaven's natural harbour was an important anchorage and communications hub with a population of 700 (today it's around 30). Mail from America was collected here, and a telegraph line to Cork was installed in 1863, delivering news of transatlantic shipping.

Vast sand dunes hemmed in by two long bluffs dissolve into the surf, forming **Barleycove**, West Cork's finest beach. Rarely crowded, it's a great place for youngsters, with gorgeous stretches of golden sand and a safe bathing area where a stream flows down to the sea. Access is via a long boardwalk and pontoon from the car park on the road to Crookhaven.

It's worth the trip to enjoy a meal in the rustic bar of the **Crookhaven Inn** (☑ 028-35309; www.thecrookhaveninn.com; mains €12-25; ☺food served 12.30-8pm Fri-Mon Apr-Sep), a popular local watering hole. In summer there are picnic tables outdoors, and trad music sessions in the evenings.

Brow Head

The southernmost point on the Irish mainland is well worth a walk. As you leave Crookhaven (heading west) you'll notice a turn-off to the left marked 'Brow Head'. Park here beside Galley Cove Beach and continue on foot along the narrow road until it ends, then follow a footpath to the headland. Here you'll see a 200-year-old signal tower, and round about it the scant remains of Guglielmo Marconi's wireless telegraphy station, which operated here from 1901 to 1914, when it moved to Valentia Island. The view is superb, ranging from Mizen Head close by the west, to Fastnet Rock (13.5km away) and Cape Clear to the east.

Durrus

POP 305

The drive from Mizen Head along the north side of the peninsula leads to the crossroads village of Durrus – little more than a pub and a cluster of houses – at the head of Dunmanus Bay, where you can continue straight on to Bantry, or turn west to explore the Sheep's Head Peninsula, the least visited of West Cork's three peninsulas.

There are a couple of B&B's in and around the village, but you'll find a bigger choice of accommodation in nearby Bantry.

Durrus is famous in foodie circles for award-winning Durrus Farmhouse cheese, produced on a farm 4km north of the village.

★ **Blairscove House**   B&B €€€

(☑ 027-61127; www.blairscove.ie; B&B d/f from €190/230; ⊘ daily Easter-Oct, Fri & Sat only Oct-Easter; ℗ 🛜) Set in 5 acres of land overlooking the bay, this magnificent Georgian country house looks like it belongs in a style magazine. Superbly appointed suites are ranged around an exquisite courtyard, and can be taken on a B&B or self-catering basis. The Loft apartment (which sleep two) has lovely sea views. Blairscove is 2km southwest of Durrus on the R591.

The **restaurant** (three-course dinner €60, open 6pm to 9pm Tuesday to Saturday, March to October), in a chandeliered hall, gives local produce an international treatment.

Sheeps Head Inn   PUB FOOD €€

(☑ 027-62622; www.thesheepsheadinn.ie; mains €10-23; ⊘ food served noon-3pm & 7-9pm daily Jun-Aug, Fri & Sat only Sep-May; 🖭) 🍴 In the heart of the village, this cosy black-and-white gastropub cooks up exceptional locally sourced delights such as Durrus cheese tartlets, pan-fried sea bass, and crab claws in garlic and lemon.

Durrus Farmhouse   FOOD

(☑ 027-61100; www.durruscheese.com; Coomkeen; ⊘ by appointment 9am-2pm Mon-Fri) 🍴 West Cork has earned an international reputation for its marvellous cheese, thanks to the likes of Durrus Farmhouse, whose produce is sold all over Ireland and the wider world. You can visit the farm and watch the cheese-making process through a viewing window (must be booked in advance). The farm is 4km north of Durrus, along a minor road off the Ahakista road.

SHEEP'S HEAD PENINSULA

The Sheep's Head Peninsula has a rugged charm all its own – and yes, there are plenty of sheep. The road west from Durrus passes through **Ahakista** (Atha an Chiste), which has a couple of pubs including the charming, tin-roofed Ahakista Bar (p247), aka the Tin Pub. At the back, it has flowering gardens which tumble down to the waterfront.

Beyond Ahakista the landscape gets progressively more barren and rocky as the road gets narrower and more twisty. A link road with terrific views, called the **Goat's Path Rd**, runs between Kilcrohane and Gortnakilly (on the south and north coasts respectively) over the western flank of **Mt Seefin** (345m), which offers an exhilarating 1km stride to the summit.

🏃 Activities

Beyond Kilcrohane, the road clambers up over high moors to end at a remote car park with a tiny tearoom called **Bernie's Cupán Tae** (http://livingthesheepsheadway.com/cupan-tae; Tooreen; mains €3-6; ⊘ hours vary, 10am-4pm Sat & Sun Jun-Aug), famous for its scones and salmon sandwiches. From here, a superb **waymarked walk** leads for 2km to the Sheep's Head lighthouse at the very tip of the peninsula, amid jaw-dropping sea-cliff scenery (allow 1½ to two hours round trip). Many more walks are listed on the Sheep's Head Way website (www.thesheeps headway.ie).

Sheep's Head Cycle Route   CYCLING

(www.thesheepsheadway.ie) The 120km Sheep's Head Cycle Route runs anticlockwise from Ballylickey, round the coastline of the peninsula, back onto the mainland and down to Ballydehob. There are opportunities to take short cuts or alternative routes (eg over the Goat's Path Rd, or along the coast from Ahakista to Durrus). The *Sheep's Head Cycle Route* brochure is available from local tourist offices and bookshops.

Sheep's Head Way   WALKING

(www.thesheepsheadway.ie) The Sheep's Head Way is an 93km-long walking route around the peninsula, on a mix of minor roads and footpaths; use Ordnance Survey map sheets 85 and 88. There are no campsites on the Sheep's Head Peninsula, but camping along the route is allowed with permission from the landowner.

🛏 Sleeping & Eating

★ Gallán Mór   B&B €€

(☑ 027-62732; www.gallanmor.com; Kealties; s/d from €75/110; 🅿🛜) Pampering is the name of the game at this gorgeous boutique B&B where the stylishness and comfort of the bedrooms is matched only by the beauty of the views. Breakfast on locally sourced bacon and eggs, home-baked bread, and honey from your hosts' own bees, and relax in an outdoor wood-fired hot tub. It's just over halfway from Durrus to Ahakista.

Heron Gallery, Cafe & Gardens   CAFE €

(☑ 027-67278;   www.herongallery.ie;   Glen Lough Rd, Ahakista; snacks €2.50-5, mains €10; ⊘ 10.30am-5.30 Apr-Aug; 🅿🛜🖍) Filled with colourful works of art and cute gifts, the Heron Gallery is a charming place to pause. The wholesome, mostly vegetarian menu includes lunch dishes such as felafel, caramelised red onion and goat's cheese tart, and soups such as Thai-spiced parsnip, while cakes and scones are available all day. Wildflowers bloom in the gardens.

Ahakista Bar   PUB

(Tin Pub;   ☑ 027-67203;   www.facebook.com/ TheTinPub; Ahakista; ⊘ 1.30-11pm May-Oct, hours may vary; 🎵) This charming, tin-roofed stone cottage, known locally as the Tin Pub, has flowering gardens at the back that tumble down to the waterfront, with picnic tables where you can sip a cold one while soaking up the gorgeous view.

ⓘ Getting There & Away

West Cork Rural Transport (p239) buses run a circular route from Bantry via the Goat's Path Rd to Kilcrohane and Durrus (one way/return €4/6), twice daily on Tuesday and Thursday only (once in each direction).

BANTRY

POP 2722

Framed by the Sheep's Head hills and the craggy Caha Mountains, magnificent, sprawling Bantry Bay is one of the country's most attractive seascapes. Sheltered by islands at the head of the bay, Bantry town is neat and respectable, with narrow streets of old-fashioned, one-off shops and a picturesque harbourfront.

Pride of place goes to Bantry House, the former home of one Richard White, who earned his place in history when, in 1798, he warned authorities of the imminent landing of Irish patriot Wolfe Tone and his French fleet, in support of the United Irishmen's rebellion. In the end storms prevented the fleet from landing and the course of Irish history was definitively altered – all Wolfe Tone got for his troubles was a square and a statue bearing his name.

◉ Sights

★ Bantry House & Garden   HISTORIC BUILDING

(☑ 027-50047; www.bantryhouse.com; Bantry Bay; house & garden adult/child €11/3, garden only €5/free; ⊘ 10am-5pm daily Jun-Aug, Tue-Sun Apr, May, Sep & Oct; 🅿) With its melancholic air of faded gentility, 18th-century Bantry House makes for an intriguing visit. From the Gobelin tapestries in the drawing room to the columned splendour of the library, it conjures up a lost world of aristocratic excess. But the gardens are its greatest glory, with lawns sweeping down towards the sea, and the magnificent Italian garden, with its staircase of 100 steps, at the back, offering spectacular views. The entrance is about 1km southwest of the town centre on the N71.

The house has belonged to the White family since 1729 and every room brims with treasures brought back from each generation's travels. The entrance hall is paved with mosaics from Pompeii, French and Flemish tapestries adorn the walls, and Japanese chests sit next to Russian shrines. Upstairs, worn bedrooms look out wanly over an astounding view of the bay. Experienced pianists are invited to tinkle the ivories of the ancient grand piano in the library.

If it looks like the sort of place you can imagine staying in, you're in luck – the owners offer B&B accommodation (p248) in one of the wings.

Bantry Historical Museum   MUSEUM

(☑ 027-51246; www.facebook.com/Bantryhistorical society; Wolfe Tone Sq; ⊘ 10.30am-4pm May-Sep) **FREE** Housed in a shed tucked away behind the fire station, this vast collection of crockery, vintage bottles, ironmongery, old photographs, cutlery, tradesmen's tools and various vintage household items feels more like an antique shop than a museum as it paints a picture of local life in the 19th and early 20th century.

THE PRIEST'S LEAP

If you're a faint-hearted driver, don't even think about heading up the vertiginous, single-track road to Priest's Leap, 17km northwest of Bantry. In fact, if your GPS points you this way (as a shortcut between Bantry and Kenmare), think again. If you're feeling intrepid, however, this wild ride rewards with monumental views across the mountains to Bantry Bay.

The road is a classic challenge for cyclists, climbing almost 400m in 4.5km, and is exceptionally steep in parts; any fit rider will make it to the top, but unless your thighs are Tour de France material you'll be off and pushing the bike at three or four places. And make sure your brakes are in good order for the descent.

From Bantry, take the N71 north for 8km and turn right after the bridge at the head of the bay (brown signpost saying Priest's Leap). Turn left at the first bridge, and left again at the second bridge (look for the white sign saying Priest's Leap), then take the first right. A long straight gets increasingly steep, before relenting a bit, but with big drops on the left.

The summit of the pass is marked by a wind-buffeted crucifix. The story goes that in 1601 Father James Archer was rallying Cork and Kerry's clans to resist the English. Enemy troops spotted him on the old road to Kerry and gave chase until he and his horse leapt from the top of the pass and landed in Bantry.

✯ Festivals & Events

Bantry Walking Festival   WALKING
(http://bantrywalkingfestival.com; ⊙ Jun) Three days of guided walks in Bantry and the surrounding West Cork countryside; many of the walks are suitable for all the family to take part in.

West Cork Chamber Music Festival   MUSIC
(www.westcorkmusic.ie/chambermusicfestival; ⊙ Jun-Jul) A major festival of concerts, talks and musical masterclasses held over a week at Bantry House (p247) and several other venues in the town centre.

West Cork Literary Festival   LITERATURE
(http://westcorkmusic.ie/literaryfestival; ⊙ Jul) A week's worth of readings, workshops, talks by famous authors and children's events.

⊨ Sleeping

Eagle Point Camping   CAMPGROUND €
(☑ 027-50630; www.eaglepointcamping.com; Glengarriff Rd, Ballylickey; campsites per person from €12; ⊙ mid-Apr–late Sep; Ⓟ 🛜) A superb campground with an enviable location on a pine-fringed promontory 6km north of Bantry. Most of the 125 sites have sea views, and there's direct access to the pebbly beaches nearby for swimming and water sports. Wi-fi at reception only.

Mill B&B   B&B €
(☑ 027-50278; www.the-mill.net; Glengarriff Rd; s/d from €50/70; ⊙ Easter-Oct; Ⓟ 🛜) This modern house, on the immediate outskirts of town,

oozes individuality. The rooms are a riot of knick-knacks. To accompany the solid breakfasts, the spacious dining room has a wonderful collection of Indonesian puppets and artworks by the irrepressible owner, Tosca.

Bantry House   HISTORIC HOTEL €€€
(☑ 027-50047; www.bantryhouse.com; Bantry Bay; d from €189; ⊙ Apr-Oct; Ⓟ 🛜) Guest rooms in this aristocratic mansion (p247) are decorated with antiques and contemporary furnishings – when you're not playing croquet, lawn tennis or billiards you can lounge in the library, once the doors of the historic house have closed to the public (guests have free access to the house). Rooms 22 and 25 have views of both the garden and the bay.

Sea View House Hotel   HOTEL €€€
(☑ 027-50073; www.seaviewhousehotel.com; Ballylickey; s/d/f from €110/150/165; Ⓟ 🛜) You'll find everything you'd expect from a luxury hotel here: country-house ambience, tastefully decorated public rooms, expansive service and 25 cosy, smart bedrooms. The hotel is on the N71 in Ballylickey, 5km north of Bantry.

✕ Eating

★**Organico**   CAFE €
(☑ 027-55905; www.organico.ie; 2 Glengarriff Rd; mains €7-11; ⊙ 9am-6pm Mon-Sat; 🛜 🍴) ✿ This bright and lively wholefood shop and cafe serves tinglingly fresh salads, sandwiches and soups, and lunch specials such as falafel platters with hummus and tahina. Great coffee and cakes too.

★ **Manning's Emporium** CAFE, DELI €
(☑ 027-50456; www.manningsemporium.ie; Bally-lickey; mains €8-13; ⏰ 7.30am-6pm Tue, Thu & Fri, 9am-9pm Sat, 9am-6pm Sun, brunch 10am-3pm Sat & Sun; ⓟ 🛜) 🍴 This gourmet deli and cafe is an Aladdin's cave of West Cork's finest food. Grab a menu, choose a table, and order at the counter – tasting plates are the best way to sample the local artisan produce and farm-house cheeses on offer. Foodie events take place regularly. It's on the N71 in Ballylickey (on the right approaching from Bantry).

Fish Kitchen SEAFOOD €€
(☑ 027-56651; http://thefishkitchen.ie; New St; mains lunch €8-12, dinner €15-28; ⏰ noon-3pm & 5.30-9pm Tue-Sat) This outstanding little restaurant above a fishmonger's shop does seafood to perfection, from the live-tank local oysters (served with lemon and Tabasco sauce) to Bantry Bay mussels in white wine. If you don't fancy seafood, it does a juicy steak too. Friendly, unfussy and absolutely delicious.

O'Connors Seafood Restaurant SEAFOOD €€
(☑ 027-55664; www.oconnorseafood.com; Wolfe Tone Sq; mains lunch €10-18, dinner €19-26; ⏰ noon-3pm & 5.30-9pm, closed Tue & Wed Oct-Mar; 🍴) 🍴 West Cork scallops with black pudding and smoked cauliflower purée; Castletownbere cod pan-roasted and topped with Irish-made feta cheese and truffle oil; Bantry Bay mussels done four ways: these are among the innovative dishes here that make the most of the area's renowned seafood. The early-bird menu (5.30pm to 6.30pm) offers two/three courses for €23/28.

🍺 Drinking & Nightlife

Ma Murphy's PUB
(☑ 027-50242; www.mamurphys.com; 7 New St; ⏰ noon-12.30am Mon-Sat, to midnight Sun) You can still buy cornflakes and sugar at this time-warp grocery-pub, open since 1840. The regulars are always up for a chat.

Snug PUB
(☑ 027-50057; http://thesnug.ie; Wolfe Tone Sq; ⏰ 11am-11pm Mon-Sat, 12.30-11pm Sun; 🍴) A cosy local favourite on the waterfront known for its excellent pub grub, which includes a grand Sunday roast.

Crowley's PUB
(☑ 027-50029; Wolfe Tone Sq; ⏰ noon-11pm Sun-Thu, to 12.30am Fri & Sat) One of the best bars in town for live music, Crowley's has tradi-tional bands on Wednesday nights.

🛍 Shopping

Bantry Market MARKET
(Wolfe Tone Sq; ⏰ 9.30am-1pm Fri) 🍴 Wolfe Tone Sq takes on a heady mix of aromas for the weekly farmers market. Fresh fruit, organ-ic veg, bread, cheese, charcuterie and other local produce fill most stalls, but there's also clothing, bric-a-brac and farming tools. The market morphs into an even bigger and bus-ier affair on the first Friday of the month.

❶ Information

Tourist Office (☑ 027-50229; www.visitbantry. ie; Wolfe Tone Sq; ⏰ 10am-6pm Mon-Sat Apr-Oct) Staffed by volunteers, so hours may vary.

❶ Getting There & Around

Bus Éireann (www.buseireann.ie) runs four to six buses daily between Bantry and Cork (€22, two hours), and four daily to Glengarriff (€5.30, 20 minutes). The summer-only bus 282 allows you to continue from Glengarriff to Kenmare (one daily each direction, Monday to Saturday).

West Cork Rural Transport is a minibus service that runs a useful series of circular routes from Bantry to Dunmanway, Durrus, Goleen, Schull, Skibbereen and outlying villages. There's a set price of €4/6 one way/return. Service is not frequent; check the website for timetables.

Nigel's Bicycle Shop (☑ 027-52657; Glengar-riff Rd; per day/week €15/70; ⏰ 10am-6pm Tue-Sat, plus Mon May-Sep) rents bikes and provides advice on local cycling routes.

BEARA PENINSULA (RING OF BEARA)

After Kerry and Dingle, the Beara Peninsula is the third major 'ring' (circular driving route) in Ireland's southwest. Its intricate coast and sharp-featured mountains are a geologist's paradise of exposed, contorted rock strata, making for dramatic scenery at every turn.

You can easily drive the 137km Ring of Beara in one day, but you would miss the spectacular **Healy Pass Road** (R574), which cuts across the peninsula from Adrigole in Cork to Lauragh in County Kerry. In fact, if pressed for time, skip the rest and do the pass.

The south side, along Bantry Bay, is a string of working fishing villages. The north side, in contrast, has only a few small hamlets dotted along craggy roads with grand views north to the mountains of Kerry. At the tip is a cable car linking the peninsula to **Dursey Island**.

A small part of the peninsula lies in County Kerry, but most is within County Cork.

Glengarriff

POP 138

Tucked away in the thickly wooded, northernmost corner of Bantry Bay, Glengarriff (Gleann Garbh; www.glengarriff.ie) is a 19th-century resort village strung along the N71 Cork to Killarney road at the start of the Ring of Beara.

In the second half of the 19th century, Glengarriff became a popular retreat for prosperous Victorians, who sailed from England to Cork, took the train to Bantry (the line closed in 1961), then crossed over to the village in a paddle steamer. In 1850 the road to Kenmare was blasted through the mountains and a link with Killarney was established, further increasing Glengarriff's popularity.

◉ Sights

★ **Ilnacullin** GARDENS
(Garinish Island; ☑ 027-63040; www.heritage ireland.ie; adult/child €5/3, plus ferry fare; ☺ 9.30am-5.30pm Sun-Fri, to 6pm Sat Jul & Aug, shorter hours Apr-Jun, Sep & Oct, closed Nov-Mar) This horticultural miracle of an island was created in the early 20th century when the island's owner commissioned architect Harold Peto to design a garden on the then-barren outcrop. Topsoil was shipped in, landscaped gardens laid out, and sub-tropical species planted; camellias, magnolias and rhododendrons now provide a seasonal blaze of colour. The 10-minute **boat trip** (☑ 027-63116, 087 234 5861; www.harbourqueenferry.com; adult/child return €12/6) to the island departs from the village pier and passes colonies of basking seals and a nesting site for white-tailed eagles, which were reintroduced to Ireland in 2007.

The centrepiece of the island is a magical **Italianate garden**; nearby a cypress avenue leads to a faux-Grecian temple with a stunning view of Sugarloaf Mountain. There are more views from the island's highest point, a 19th-century **Martello tower**, one of hundreds built around the coast to watch out for a possible Napoleonic invasion.

Glengarriff Woods
Nature Reserve NATURE RESERVE
(☑ 027-63636; www.glengarriffnaturereserve.ie; ☺ 24hr) FREE The valley of the Glengarriff River, to the northwest of Glengarriff village, was once the private estate of the Earl of Bantry. As such its ancient oak woodland has survived, the thick tree cover maintaining humid conditions that allow ferns and mosses to flourish. The reserve is rich in wildlife – look out for red squirrels and siskins in the woods, and otters and kingfishers along the river. Waymarked walking trails radiate from the main car park 1km north of the village.

There are five trails of varying lengths, from 500m to 3km, covering woodland, mountain, river and meadow. The purple-waymarked **Glengarriff Wood Loop** combines the best of all five in one route (8km, allow three hours).

Ewe Experience GARDENS
(☑ 027-63840; www.theewe.com; Tooreen; adult/child €7.50/6; ☺ 10am-6pm Jun-Aug; P ♿) ♪ More than 20 years in the making, this interactive sculpture garden is imaginative, thought-provoking and humorous, with nature and art working together to provide an unforgettable walk in the woods. From the sheep in the vintage car to the pig blissing out in a bubble bath, a kilometre of trails takes you past dozens of intriguing sculptures, installations, puzzles and games, which weave together art, nature, science, music and poetry. The gardens are located 4.5km northwest of Glengarriff on the N71.

🏃 Activities

The rough and rocky **Caha Mountains** rising to the north and west make for challenging hill walking, despite their small size, but there are plenty of gentler strolls in and around town, too. Mature woodlands of oak and Scots pine in the **Blue Pool Park** offer some easy waymarked trails along the shore between village and pier where seals, perched on submerged rocks, appear to float on the water.

A maze of minor roads extends northwest from Glengarriff Woods Nature Reserve (p250), serving holiday cottages and remote farms, and ideal for exploring by bike. **Pooleen**, where picnic tables stand beside a natural bathing pool in the Glengarriff River, makes a good objective. Only the fit and hardy will venture to road's end at **Barley Lake**, a wild hill lough visited mainly by trout anglers (don't even think about driving it in anything less than a 4WD).

🛏 Sleeping & Eating

Coomarkane Visitor Centre CAMPGROUND €
(☎027-63826; www.coomarkanevisitorcentre.com; Coomarkane; campsites/cabins €10/€25; P) Truly off the beaten track, this lovely rural retreat is hidden away in the Caha Mountains beyond Glengarriff Woods Nature Reserve, 6km southwest of the village. There's only room for six tents, plus a log cabin (which sleeps three), each with its own firepit. Ideal for hikers and cyclists. It's signposted along a minor road which leads off the R572, 500m south of Glengarriff.

Bayview Boutique Guesthouse GUESTHOUSE €€
(☎027-63030; www.facebook.com/TheBayviewBoutiqueGuesthouseAndJimsCoffeeHouse; Reenmeen; r from €80; P🛜) This spacious modern villa on the eastern edge of Glengarriff has been converted into a chic and elegant guesthouse, with bedrooms that look fresh from a Sunday colour supplement photo shoot. There's a lovely terrace and garden out back with sweeping views across the the bay, and Jim's Coffee House, one of the nicest places to eat hereabouts.

Eccles Hotel HISTORIC HOTEL €€
(☎027-63003; www.eccleshotel.com; Glengarriff Harbour; s/d from €115/170; ⊗closed Nov-Mar; P🛜) Just east of the centre, this grande dame of West Cork hotels has a long and distinguished history (since 1745), counting the British War Office, WM Thackeray, George Bernard Shaw and WB Yeats as former guests. The public areas retain some 19th-century grandeur, though some bedrooms are on the small side. Ask for a bayside room on the 2nd floor for the best views.

Jim's Coffee House CAFE €
(☎027-63030; www.facebook.com/TheBayviewBoutiqueGuesthouseAndJimsCoffeeHouse; Reenmeen; mains €6-12; ⊗10am-4pm Wed-Sun Apr-Oct, shorter hours Nov-Mar; P🖶) Probably the best place to eat in the village, this coffee house is a hub of the local community, serving cooked breakfasts, freshly baked cakes and pastries, and hot lunch specials.

MacCarthy's Bar PUB FOOD €€
(☎027-63000; http://glengarriffpark.com; 14 Main St; mains €10-19; ⊗food served noon-3pm & 6-9pm; 🛜🖶) MacCarthy's is a traditional, Victorian-style wood-panelled bar with a menu of hearty pub grub; the house speciality is a steaming pan of succulent Bantry Bay mussels in a white wine and herb sauce.

THE BEARA WAY

This 206km waymarked walk (see www.irishtrails.ie) forms a loop around the Beara Peninsula and takes around nine days. The peninsula is relatively unused to mass tourism and makes a pleasant contrast to the Ring of Kerry to the north.

The Beara Way mostly follows old roads and tracks and rarely rises above 340m. There's no official start or finish point, and the route can be walked in either direction. It could easily be reduced to seven days by skipping Bere and Dursey Islands and, if you start at Castletownbere, you could reach Kenmare in five days or less.

There's an online guide to the walk (and the peninsula itself) at Beara Tourism (www.bearatourism.com).

❶ Getting There & Away

Bus Éireann runs the following services:
Bantry €5.30, 25 minutes, up to five daily
Castletownbere €10.70, 50 minutes, one or two daily
Cork €22, 2½ hours, up to five daily
Kenmare bus 282, €12.40, 45 minutes, one daily Monday to Saturday, July and August

Glengarriff to Castletownbere

The folded bedding of the peninsula's underlying sandstone bedrock becomes evident as you drive west from Glengarriff towards Castletownbere. On the highest hills, Sugarloaf Mountain and Hungry Hill, rock walls known as 'benches' snake backwards and forwards across the slopes. They can make walking on these mountains challenging, and dangerous in fog. Take a map (Ordnance Survey sheets 84 and 85 cover the area) and compass if venturing into the hills, and seek local advice.

Adrigole is no more than a scattered strip of houses and a harbour where the **West Cork Sailing Centre** (☎027-60132; www.westcorksailing.com; The Boat House, Adrigole; ⊗Jul-Aug) rents out kayaks (€12 per hour) and Canadian canoes (€20 per hour).

From Adrigole, a narrow, switchback road climbs 11km north across the other-worldly **Healy Pass** to Lauragh, offering spectacular views of the rocky scenery, especially on the descent on the far side.

Castletownbere & Around

POP 860

Busy Castletownbere (Baile Chais Bhéara) is a fishing port first and a tourist town second. And that gives it great appeal for those looking for the 'real' Ireland, although that's not to say it doesn't have some worthwhile sights, notably the world-famous pub MacCarthy's Bar.

On Main St and the Square, you'll find ATMs as well as cafes, pubs and grocery stores.

There's a developing food scene on the Beara, and Castletownbere is at the centre of it. There's a **farmers market** (The Square; ⊙10am-2pm first Thu of month year-round, every Thu May-Sep), a couple of artisan delis and coffee shops, and a growing number of excellent restaurants.

◉ Sights

Bere Island   ISLAND

(www.bereisland.net) Only 12km by 7km, Bere Island has around 200 permanent residents and attracts scores more to summer holiday homes. There are ruined Martello towers, craggy coves good for swimming, and a 19km loop of the Beara Way to hike. **Bere Island Ferry** (☑027-75009; www.bereisland ferries.com; passenger/car return €8/25; ⊙every 90 min Mon-Sat Jun-Aug, less often Sun & Sep-May) leaves from town but drops you in a remote part of the island. **Murphy's Ferry Service** (☑027-75014; www.murphysferry.com; pedestrian/car return from €8/25; ⊙every 2hr), departing from Pontoon pier, 5km east of Castletownbere, docks by the island's main village, **Rerrin**, which has a shop, a pub, a cafe and accommodation.

Derreenataggart Stone Circle HISTORIC SITE

(⊙dawn-dusk) FREE On a lonely hill 2km northwest of Castletownbere, the impressive Derreenataggart Stone Circle, consisting of 10 stones, can be found close to the roadside. It's signposted from a turn-off to the right at the western end of town. There are a number of other standing stones in the surrounding area.

🛏 Sleeping

Dzogchen Beara   HOSTEL, COTTAGES €

(☑027-73032; www.dzogchenbeara.org; Garranes; dm/f €18/45, cottages per week from €680; ℗) Solitude and sea views set the mood at the remote Dzogchen Beara meditation centre, where a Buddhist temple is currently under construction. Accommodation (open to all) is available in self-catering cottages with wood-burning stoves overlooking the Atlantic, or in a homely farmhouse hostel; there's a good cafe here too. It's 9km southwest of Castletownbere.

The retreat runs seminars and workshops, and guests can attend meditation sessions.

Beara Coast Hotel   HOTEL €€

(☑027-71446; www.bearacoast.com; Cametringane Point; r from €110; ℗ 🛜) It may look plain and pedestrian from the outside, but this recently modernised hotel has certainly had fun with the colour palette inside. Spacious bedrooms are bright and cheerful, and many have balconies with a view across the harbour. The location is quiet, but only a short walk from the town centre's pubs and restaurants.

It's a popular wedding venue, so weekdays are best for availability.

Sea Breeze   B&B €€

(☑027-70508; www.seabreez.com; Derrymihin; s/d from €50/80; ℗ 🛜) This grand villa of a place perches above the main Glengarriff road 1km east of town, looking out across the harbour to Bere Island. The residents' lounge, garden terrace and half of the bedrooms make the most of that sea view, while the other bedrooms enjoy a vista of the Caha Mountains. Breakfast options include bagels with cream cheese and smoked salmon.

Old Medical Hall   B&B €€

(☑086 1732 606; www.theoldmedicalhall.com; r from €90; 🛜) Housed in a former pharmacy store, this newly renovated and centrally located B&B offers five homely and comfortable rooms with luxury en suite bathrooms. There's a cosy tearoom on the ground floor, and the owner can arrange bike hire for guests.

Berehaven Lodge   COTTAGE €€€

(☑027-71464; www.berehavenlodge.com; Millcove; per 2 nights €375, per week €595-850; ℗ 🛜) This complex of cosy self-catering cottages occupies an enviable setting overlooking the sea 6km east of Castletownbere. Each 'lodge' has three bedrooms, a jacuzzi, an outdoor deck and an open-plan living area with a log fire. Also on site are an attractive bar and restaurant, with regular summer barbecues on the terrace.

✗ Eating & Drinking

★ Fuchsia Cafe
CAFE €

(☑083 885 2552; www.facebook.com/fuchsia cafe; The Square; mains €5-11; ⊙9am-5pm Mon-Sat; 🛜🪑) Vibrant colours (it's painted fuchsia-pink) and vibrant flavours characterise this cheerful cafe on the bustling village square. The menu runs from breakfast fry-ups (including veggie versions, served till noon) to lip-smacking lunch dishes such as homemade burgers and pulled pork focaccia sandwiches. The coffee is damn fine too.

Issie's Handmade Chocolate & Ice Cream Parlour
CAFE €

(☑086 339 6316; www.issieshandmadechocolate. com; cnr Main St & North Rd; snacks €3-6; ⊙noon-5pm daily Apr-Oct, 10am-5pm Wed-Sat Nov-Mar) Isabel O'Donovan's convivial coffee shop serves award-winning handmade chocolates, artisan ice cream in a wide range of flavours, homemade cakes and scones, and superb coffees and hot chocolate.

Berehaven Lodge
INTERNATIONAL €€

(☑027-71464; www.berehavenlodge.com; Millcove; mains €14-29; ⊙10am-9pm daily Apr-Oct, shorter hours Nov-Mar) The restaurant at this complex of self-catering cottages, 6km east of Castletownbere, is open to all. The attractive modern dining room has an outdoor terrace overlooking the sea where the South African chef does wonderful things with a barbecue on summer weekends. Otherwise, the menu serves up favourite dishes from Ireland and around the world (fish and chips, steaks, Thai curries, Louisiana chicken wings etc).

★ MacCarthy's Bar
PUB

(☑027-70014; www.maccarthysbar.com; Main St; ⊙9.30am-11.30pm Mon-Thu, to 12.30am Fri & Sat, 12.30-11pm Sun) If you're carrying an original copy of the late Pete McCarthy's bestseller, *McCarthy's Bar*, you'll be excited to see the front-cover photo in real life (the spelling was changed to match Pete's name for the cover pic). There's good food and drink, frequent live music and a grand wee snug inside the door, and the craic is mighty.

❶ Information

Tourist Office (☑027-70054; www.beara tourism.com; Main St; ⊙9am-5.30pm Mon-Sat Jun-Sep, Fri & Sat only Oct-May) In the grounds of St Peter's Church.

❶ Getting There & Away

Local bus service providers include **O'Donoghue's** (☑027-70007) and **Harrington's of Ardgroom** (☑027-74003; https://sites.google. com/site/bustobeara/).

Bantry O'Donoghue's (€14, one hour, once daily on Monday, Tuesday, Friday and Saturday); Bus Éireann (€14.20, 70 minutes, once or twice daily)

Cork Harrington's of Ardgroom (€25, 2¼ hours, daily except Thursday) – booking a seat is recommended; O'Donoghue's (Thursday); Bus Éireann (€25, 3¼ hours, once or twice daily)

Glengarriff O'Donoghue's (€10.50, one hour, twice daily on Monday, and once on Tuesday, Friday and Saturday); Bus Éireann (€10.90, 50 minutes, once or twice daily)

Kenmare Bus Éireann, No 282 Ring of Beara service (€14.20, 1½ hours, twice daily Monday to Saturday, July and August only)

Dursey Island

POP 4

Tiny Dursey Island, at the end of the peninsula, is reached by Ireland's only **cable car** (☑028-21766; www.durseyisland.ie; adult/child return €10/5; ⊙9.30-11am, 2.30-5pm & 7-8pm Mon-Sat, less frequently Sun & Sep-May), a rickety 1960s contraption that sways precariously 30m above Dursey Sound. In a perfect photo op, livestock take precedence over humans in the queue. It runs continuously in summer, and at set times only the rest of the year – check the website for details.

The island, just 6.6km long by 1.5km wide, is a wildlife **sanctuary**, and dolphins and whales can sometimes be seen in the surrounding waters. There's no accommodation, but **camping** is legal, so long as you respect the common rules and clean up after yourself.

The **Beara Way** loops round the island for 14km (allow four hours for the complete loop), and the **signal tower** is an obvious destination for a shorter walk (8km round trip).

North side of the Beara

The entire north side is the scenic highlight of the Beara Peninsula. A series of minor roads – often steep and twisting single-lane tracks with few passing places – snake around the ins and outs of the rugged coastline. Boulder-strewn fields tumble dramatically towards the ocean and it all feels blissfully remote – your only company along some stretches are flocks of sheep.

WORTH A TRIP

GOUGANE BARRA FOREST PARK

Gougane Barra is a truly magical spot, with craggy mountains and pine forests sweeping down to a mountain lake, the source of the River Lee. St Fin Barre, the founder of Cork, established a monastery here in the 6th century. He had a hermitage on the island in **Gougane Barra Lake** (Lough an Ghugain), which is now approached by a short causeway. The small chapel on the island has fine stained-glass representations of obscure Celtic saints.

Beyond the lake, a loop road runs through the forest park (€5 entry per vehicle), but you're better off slowing down and walking the well-marked network of paths and **nature trails** through the woods.

The park is signposted on the R584, which runs between the N71 at Ballylickey and Macroom on the N22.

You're really out in the sticks here, and the only place to air your hiking boots is the **Gougane Barra Hotel** (☑ 026-47069; www.gouganebarrahotel.com; s/d from €80/125; ☺ Apr-Oct; Ⓟ 🛜).

There's a restaurant in the Gougane Barra Hotel, and a **cafe** (☑ 026-47031; mains €4-7; ☺ 10am-6pm Apr-Oct; Ⓟ) and a pub next door.

Allihies

The isolated village of Allihies (Na hAilichí), whose colourfully painted houses grace many a postcard and guidebook cover, has dramatic vistas, plenty of walks and a fascinating history of copper mining.

Copper-ore deposits were first identified on the Beara in 1810. While mining quickly brought wealth to the Puxley family, who owned the land, it brought low wages and dangerous, unhealthy working conditions for the labour force, which at one time numbered 1300. Experienced Cornish miners were brought into the area, and the dramatic ruins of engine houses are reminiscent of Cornwall's coastal tin mines. As late as the 1930s, more than 30,000 tonnes of pure copper were exported annually, but by 1962 the last mine was closed.

Allihies fascinating history is chronicled in the engaging **Copper Mine Museum** (☑ 027-73218; www.acmm.ie; Main Rd; adult/child €6/2; ☺ 10am-5pm Easter-Oct), the result of years of work by the community; there's also tourist information and a cafe. Pick up a copy of the museum leaflet and follow the **Copper Mine Trail**, a waymarked hike among the remains of the old workings.

🛏 Sleeping & Eating

There's a good **hostel** (☑ 027-73107; www.allihieshostel.net; Main Rd; dm/d €18/50; Ⓟ) plus half a dozen or so B&Bs – it's a long drive out here, so it pays to reserve a room in advance to avoid disappointment.

Sea View Guesthouse　　GUESTHOUSE €
(☑ 027-73004; www.allihiesseaview.com; Main Rd; s/d €45/75; Ⓟ) Clean, tidy and basic, the 10 spacious rooms in this two-storey yellow building have an abundance of pine; some have views north over the sea. The tempting spread at breakfast will help fuel your rambles.

O'Neill's　　PUB FOOD €€
(☑ 027-73008; www.oneillsbeara.ie; Main Rd; mains €12-25; ☺ food served noon-8.30pm; 🛜) The most appealing pub in town, with a distinctive bright-red facade and some polished wooden benches and picnic tables out the front. Pub grub standards intermingle with fresh local seafood; the haddock and chips could feed two people.

Allihies to Lauragh

Heading north and east from Allihies, the wild coastal road (R575), lined with fuchsias and rhododendrons, twists and turns for about 12km to Eyeries. This cluster of brightly coloured houses overlooking Coulagh Bay is often used as a film set. The village is also home to **Milleens Cheese** (☑ 027-74079; www.milleenscheese.com; Eyeries; ☺ by appointment), from pioneering producer Veronica Steele. She welcomes visitors to her farm; phone ahead.

From Eyeries, forsake the R571 for even smaller coastal roads to the north and east, with sublime views of the Ring of Kerry to the north, rejoining the R571 at the crossroads of Ardgroom (Ard Dhór). From here, a minor road leads inland to dramatic **Glenbeg Lough**; ask at the village pub in Ardgroom for information on trout fishing here.

The village of **Lauragh** (Laith Reach) – barely more than a junction at the northern end of the Healy Pass road – and the whole northeastern corner of the peninsula lie in County Kerry.

◉ Sights

Derreen Gardens   GARDENS
(📞 064-668 3588; www.derreengarden.com; Lauragh; adult/child €7/2; ⊙ 10am-6pm; 🅿) Derreen Gardens were planted by the fifth Lord Lansdowne around the turn of the 20th century. Mossy paths weave through an abundance of interesting plants, including spectacular New Zealand tree ferns and red cedars, and you may see seals on the shore.

Gleninchaquin Park   FARM
(📞 087 712 8553; www.gleninchaquin.com; Tuosist; adult/family €6/15; ⊙ 9am-5pm; 🅿 ⬆) This working sheep farm offers a whole range of things to do, from waymarked history and geology walks to trout fishing and feeding the lambs (in spring), all in an extraordinarily beautiful setting, high in a valley overlooked by a bridal-veil waterfall. It's signposted off the R571 halfway between Lauragh and Kenmare.

Eating

★ Josie's Lakeview House   MODERN IRISH €€
(📞 064-668 3155; www.josiesrestaurant.ie; Clogherane; mains lunch €10-16, dinner €15-26; ⊙ 10.30am-7.30pm; 🅿 📶 ⬆) Captivating views over Glanmore Lake accompany scrumptious, home-cooked food at Josie's, set on a hill just north of the water. Choose from salads and sandwiches for lunch, cakes at tea, or a heartier rack of lamb and local seafood specials at night; ask about B&B or self-catering accommodation (double room €70) to prolong the experience. Josie's is 4km south of Lauragh; follow the signs.

Pedals & Boots Cafe   CAFE €
(📞 064-668 3101; www.pedalsandboots.ie; Lauragh; mains €5; ⊙ 10am-5pm Mon-Sat mid-Apr–Jun & Sep, daily Jul-Aug; 🅿 📶) This cosy cafe, complete with wood-fired stove, serves up home-baked cakes and scones, soups and sandwiches. You can hire bikes here too (€16/10 per day/half day), and get information on local walking and cycling routes.

❶ Getting There & Away

In July and August only, **Bus Éireann's** (📞 021-450 8188; www.buseireann.ie) service 282 Ring of Beara service has two buses a day between Kenmare and Lauragh (€7.90, 40 minutes), Ardgroom (€12.40, 55 minutes) and Eyeries (€14.20, 1¼ hours).

COUNTY CORK NORTH SIDE OF THE BEARA

County Kerry

POP 147,554 / AREA 4807 SQ KM

Best Places to Sleep

➡ Cahernane House Hotel (p261)

➡ Mannix Point Camping & Caravan Park (p273)

➡ Park Hotel (p283)

➡ Pax House (p289)

➡ Malton (p261)

Best Places to Eat

➡ Out of the Blue (p290)

➡ Smuggler's Inn (p280)

➡ Idás (p290)

➡ Heather (p268)

➡ Boathouse Bistro (p284)

Why Go?

County Kerry contains some of Ireland's most iconic scenery: surf-pounded sea cliffs and soft golden strands, emerald-green farmland criss-crossed by tumbledown stone walls, mist-shrouded bogs and cloud-torn mountain peaks.

With one of the country's finest national parks as its backyard, the lively tourism hub of Killarney spills over with colourful shops, restaurants and pubs loud with spirited trad music. The town is the jumping-off point for Kerry's two famed loop drives: the larger Ring of Kerry skirts the mountainous, island-fringed Iveragh Peninsula. The more compact Dingle Peninsula is like a condensed version of its southern neighbour, with ancient prehistoric ring forts and beehive huts, Christian sites, sandy beaches and glimpses of a hard, unforgiving land.

Kerry's exquisite beauty makes it one of Ireland's most popular tourist destinations. But if you need to escape from the crowds, there's always a mountain pass, an isolated cove or an untrodden trail to discover.

When to Go

➡ Lots of festivals take place throughout the county during the warmer months, particularly from June to August (when you'll need to book accommodation well ahead).

➡ Some of the highlights on Kerry's annual calendar include Listowel's Writers' Week in May/June and Dingle town's races and regatta in August. Killorglin's famous Puck Festival, which dates back to the 17th century, also takes place in August.

➡ Many sights and businesses, including some accommodation, close in the low season. But even in the depths of winter, you'll find storytellers and musicians taking part in impromptu sessions in pubs throughout the county.

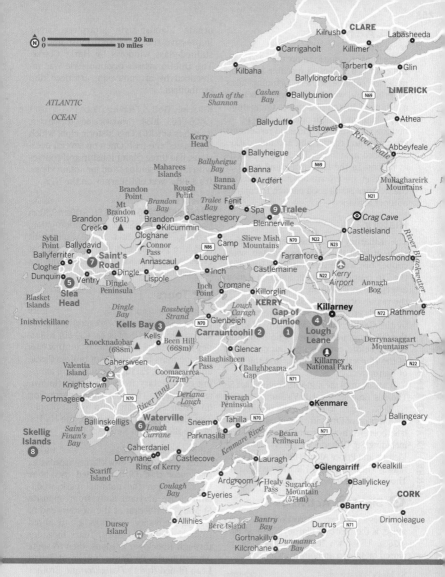

N
0 — 20 km
0 — 10 miles

ATLANTIC
OCEAN

CLARE
Kilrush • Labasheeda •
Carrigaholt • Killimer •
Tarbert • Glin •
Kilbaha •
Ballylongford •
Ballybunion • LIMERICK
N69
Mouth of the Cashen Bay
Shannon Ballyduff • Listowel • Athea •
River Feale Abbeyfeale •
Kerry Head Ballyheigue • N69 Mullaghareirk
Ballyheigue Banna • Mountains
Maharees Bay Banna Ardfert •
Islands Banna Strand Ballydesmond •
Brandon Rough Tralee Fenit • N21
Point Point Bay Spa 9 Tralee Crag Cave
Brandon Mt Castlegregory Blennerville • Castleisland • River Blackwater
Brandon Brandon Kilcummin • Slieve Mish N70 N22 N23
Creek (951) Cloghane Connor Mountains Farranfore • Ballydesmond •
Sybil Ballydavid Pass Camp Kerry Annagh
Point Anascaul Lougher • Castlemaine Airport Bog
Ballyferriter Saint's 7 Dingle Lispole Inch • N22 Rathmore
Clogher Road Ventry Dingle Inch Cromane Killorglin Annagh N72
Dunquin 5 Slea Peninsula Point Killarney
Blasket Head Dingle Lough KERRY Gap of Derrynasaggart
Islands Bay Rossbeigh Caragh Dunloe 4 Mountains
Inishvickillane Kells Bay 3 Strand Glenbeigh N70 1 Lough N22
Carrauntoohil 2 Leane
Knocknadobar Kells Been Hill Glencar • Killarney
(688m) (668m) Ballaghisheen National Park
Valentia Cahersiveen • Pass Ballghbeama N71
Island Coomacarrea Gap
Knightstown (772m) Deriana Iveragh Kenmare
Portmagee • Lough Peninsula
N70 River Inny Sneem • Tahilla N70 Ballingeary •
Waterville 6 Parknasilla •
Skellig Ballinskelligs Lough Beara N71 Glengarriff • Kealkill •
Islands Saint Currane Peninsula
8 Finan's Caherdaniel Kenmare River Ballylickey •
Bay Derrynane • Castlecove • Lauragh • CORK
Scariff Ring of Kerry Ardgroom Healy Sugarloaf Bantry •
Island Coulagh Eyeries • Pass Mountain
Bay (574m) Drimoleague •
Dursey Allihies • Bantry Durrus • N71
Island Bere Island Bay
Gortnakilly • Dunmanus
Kilcrohane • Bay

County Kerry Highlights

1 Gap of Dunloe (p268)
Exploring the Killarney Lakes
and starkly beautiful Gap of
Dunloe by boat and bike.

2 Carrauntoohil (p269)
Hiking to the 1040m summit
of Ireland's highest peak.

**3 Kells Bay House &
Gardens** (p276) Swaying on
Ireland's longest rope bridge in
these glorious gardens.

4 Lough Leane (p265)
Fishing on Killarney's beautiful
Lough Leane.

5 Slea Head (p292) Hiring
a bike and cycling around.

6 Waterville Golf Links
(p280) Teeing off at the
spectacularly sited links on the
Ring of Kerry.

7 Saint's Road (p294)

Discovering early Christian
monuments on this pilgrim path.

8 Skellig Michael (p278)
Taking a boat trip to the remote
monastic ruins atop the rocky
pinnacles of *Star Wars*–fame.

**9 Tralee Bay Wetlands
Centre** (p297) Cruising
through fresh and saltwater
habitats on a safari at the Tralee
Bay Wetlands Centre.

KILLARNEY

POP 14,504

In the tourism game for more than 250 years, Killarney is a well-oiled machine set in the midst of sublime scenery spanning lakes, waterfalls and woodland spreading beneath a skyline of 1000m-plus peaks. Competition keeps standards high and visitors on all budgets can expect to find good restaurants, great pubs and comfortable accommodation.

Mobbed in summer, Killarney is perhaps at its best in the late spring and early autumn when the crowds are manageable, but the weather is still good enough to enjoy its outdoor activities.

History

The Killarney area has been inhabited since at least the early Bronze Age, when copper ore was mined on Ross Island. In the 7th century St Finian founded a monastery on Inisfallen in Lough Leane, and the region became a focus for Christianity. The lands around the lough were occupied by the Gaelic clans of McCarthy Mór and the O'Donoghues of Ross, who built Ross Castle, before coming into the possession of the Herberts of Muckross and the Earls of Kenmare.

It wasn't until the mid-18th century that Sir Thomas Browne, the 4th Viscount Kenmare (1726–95), began to develop the region as an Irish version of England's Lake District. It was later bolstered by the arrival of famous visitors including Sir Walter Scott (1825) and Queen Victoria and Prince Albert (1861), as well as the railway (1853). By 1895 Killarney was on the Thomas Cook package tour itinerary.

Sights & Activities

Killarney's biggest attraction, in every sense, is the nearby Killarney National Park (p265). The town itself can easily be explored on foot in an hour or two.

St Mary's Cathedral   CATHEDRAL
(www.killarneyparish.com; Cathedral Pl; ⊙8am-6.30pm) Built between 1842 and 1855, St Mary's Cathedral is a superb example of neo-Gothic revival architecture. Designed by Augustus Pugin, the cruciform building was inspired by Ardfert Cathedral, near Tralee. Check the website for Mass times.

Franciscan Friary   MONASTERY
(www.franciscans.ie; Fair Hill; ⊙8am-8pm) This 1860s Franciscan friary displays an ornate Flemish-style altarpiece, some impressive tile work and, most notably, stained-glass windows by Harry Clarke. The Dublin artist's organic style was influenced by art nouveau, art deco and symbolism.

Killarney Golf & Fishing Club   GOLF
(☑064-663 1034; www.killarneygolfclub.com; green fees €65-110) This historic club, which has hosted the Irish Open on several occasions, has three championship golf courses with lakeside settings and mountain views. It's 3.4km west of Killarney on the N72.

O'Neill's   FISHING
(☑064-663 1970; 6 Plunkett St; ⊙10am-9.30pm Mon-Fri, 10am-9pm Sat & Sun) Information, permits, licences and rental equipment (rod hire per day €10) can be obtained at O'Neill's, which looks like a gift shop but is a long-established fishing centre.

Tours

Jaunting Car Tours   TOURS
(☑064-663 3358; http://killarneyjauntingcars.ie; Kenmare Pl; per jaunting car €30-80) Killarney's traditional horse-drawn jaunting cars provide tours from the town to Ross Castle and Muckross Estate, complete with amusing commentary from the driver (known as a 'jarvey'). The cost varies depending on distance; cars can fit up to four people. The pick-up point, nicknamed 'the Ha Ha' or 'the Block', is on Kenmare Pl.

Killarney Guided Walks   WALKING
(☑087 639 4362; www.killarneyguidedwalks.com; adult/child €9/5) Guided two-hour walks through the national park woodlands leave at 11am daily from opposite St Mary's Cathedral at the western end of New St; advance bookings are required from November to April. Tours meander through Knockreer gardens, then to spots where Charles de Gaulle holidayed, David Lean filmed *Ryan's Daughter* and Brother Cudda slept for 200 years.

Tours are available at other times on request.

Gap of Dunloe Tours   TOURS
(☑064-663 0200; www.gapofdunloetours.com; 7 High St; ⊙Mar-Oct) Gap of Dunloe Tours can arrange a walking tour (€13.50), highly recommended bike-and-boat circuit (€15), or bus-and-boat tour (€30) taking in the Gap. Trips depart from O'Connor's pub (p263).

Killarney

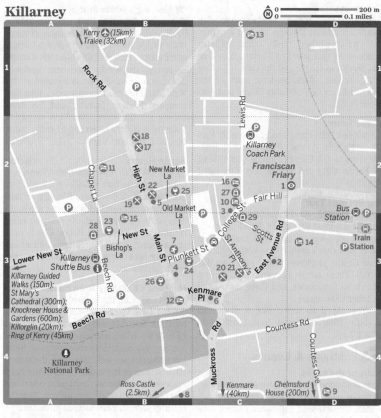

Killarney

Corcoran's
BUS

(☑064-663 6666; www.corcorantours.com; 8 College St; ☺Mar-Oct) If you're pushed for time, this well-organised outfit offers half-day coach tours that take in Killarney, Ross Castle, Muckross House and the Gap of Dunloe (€21). It also offers day-long tours of the Ring of Kerry (€19.50) and Dingle and Slea Head (€23).

Deros Tours
BUS

(☑064-663 1251; http://derostours.com; 22 Main St; ☺Mar-Oct) Deros Tours runs enjoyable trips to the Gap of Dunloe (€30), Ring of Kerry (€22) and Dingle and Slea Head (€22.50).

Big Red Bus Tour
BUS

(☑087 250 8122; www.killarneytour.com; East Avenue Rd; day ticket adult/child €12.50/8) Hop-on, hop-off open-top bus tours link East Avenue Rd in Killarney's town centre with Aghadoe, Ross Castle, Muckross House and Torc Waterfall. There are six departures daily from March to September, and three daily from October to February.

From April to September, it also runs a daily Ring of Kerry Tour (adult/child €25/15).

📸 Festivals & Events

Rally of the Lakes
SPORTS

(http://rallyofthelakes.com; ☺late Apr or early May) A major date on Ireland's motorsports calendar, this on-road rally sees drivers take death-defying twists and turns around the lakes and mountains over the May bank holiday weekend. During the rally campsites and accommodation will be packed, and local roads (including the Healy Pass in County Cork and the N71 Killarney–Kenmare route) may be temporarily closed.

Killarney FolkFest
MUSIC

(http://folkfestkillarney.com; Gleneagle Hotel, Muckross Rd; ☺early Jul) An impressive line-up of Irish and international artists performs during this two-day festival of folk music.

🛏 Sleeping

You'll find numerous B&Bs just outside the centre on Rock, Lewis and Muckross Roads. The town also has some excellent hostels and high-end hotels, as well as scores of generic hotels aimed at tour groups and wedding parties, plus camping. Many places offer bike hire (around €12 to €15 per day) and discounted tours. Book ahead everywhere in summer.

★Fleming's White Bridge
Caravan & Camping Park
CAMPGROUND €

(☑064-663 1590; http://killarneycamping.com; White Bridge, Ballycasheen Rd; sites per vehicle plus 2 adults €26, hiker €10; ☺mid-Mar–Oct; 🛜) A lovely, sheltered, family-run campsite 2.5km southeast of the town centre off the N22, Fleming's has a games room, bike hire, campers' kitchen, laundry and free trout fishing on the river that runs alongside. Your man Hillary at reception can arrange bus, bike and boat tours.

Súgán Hostel
HOSTEL €

(☑087 718 8237; www.suganhostelkillarney.com; Lewis Rd; dm/tw from €15/40; 🛜) Behind its publike front, 250-year-old Súgán is an amiably eccentric hostel with an open fire in the cosy common room and low, crazy-cornered ceilings and hardwood floors. Check in at the adjacent Lord of the Rings–themed bar, a handy spot for a pint of Guinness once you're settled in.

Neptune's Killarney Town Hostel
HOSTEL €

(☑064-663 5255; www.neptuneshostel.com; Bishop's Lane, New St; dm €18-20, d with shared bathroom from €44, with private bathroom from €54; @🛜) Basic but adequate, this hostel has a great central location without being too noisy (it's set well back from the street). Its best aspect is the staff's unfailing helpfulness – they provide local advice and will sort out bus and boat tours for you. There's a laundry service; rates include breakfast.

★Crystal Springs
B&B €€

(☑064-663 3272; www.crystalspringsbandb.com; Ballycasheen Cross, Woodlawn Rd; s/d €75/115; P🛜) The timber deck of this wonderfully relaxing B&B overhangs the River Flesk, where trout anglers can fish for free. Rooms are richly furnished with patterned wallpapers and walnut timber; private bathrooms (most with spa baths) are huge. The glass-enclosed breakfast room also overlooks the rushing river. It's about a 15-minute stroll into town.

Cots, highchairs and babysitting can be arranged.

Algret House
B&B €€

(☑064-663 2337; www.algret.com; Countess Grove; s/d/f from €60/100/150; P🛜) Knotted pine and polished wood dominate the decor of this light, bright and spacious modern villa, on a quiet side street just a five-minute walk south of the town centre. Friendly hosts make staying here a real pleasure.

Kingfisher Lodge
B&B **€€**

(☑064-663 7131; www.kingfisherlodgekillarney.eu; Lewis Rd; s/d/tr/f from €75/99/110/140; ⊘mid-Feb–Nov; P🐾) Lovely gardens are a highlight at this immaculate B&B, whose guest rooms are done up in rich, warm colours. Showers are good and powerful, and breakfasts hearty. Owner Donal Carroll is a certified walking guide with a wealth of knowledge on hiking in the area.

Fairview
GUESTHOUSE **€€**

(☑064-663 4164; https://fairviewkillarney.com; College St; d/tr/ste from €169/189/209; P@🐾) Done out in beautiful timbers, the individually decorated rooms (some with classical printed wallpaper, some with contemporary sofas and glass) at this boutique guesthouse offer more bang for your buck than bigger, less personal places. A veritable feast is laid on at breakfast.

Killarney Plaza Hotel
HOTEL **€€**

(☑064-662 1100; www.killarneyplaza.com; Kenmare Pl; d/ste from €128/225; P@🐾🏊) Although it dates only from 2002, this large 198-room hotel channels the style of the art deco era. Classically furnished guest rooms and public areas are in keeping with its luxury reputation; besides the marble lobby and lavishly tiled indoor pool, there's a sauna, steam room and spa.

Chelmsford House
B&B **€€**

(☑064-663 6402; www.chelmsfordhouse.com; 1 Muckross View; d/tr from €85/120; P🐾) Set on a rise to the south of town (a 10-minute stroll away), this B&B enjoys a superb view of the Kerry mountains (and even a glimpse of Lough Leane). All three rooms have private bathrooms; one has a balcony. There's a minimum two-night stay. Kids under 12 aren't permitted.

Killarney Haven
APARTMENT **€€**

(☑064-663 3570; www.killarney-selfcatering.com; Monsignor O'Flaherty Rd; 2-person apt from €200 for 2 nights; P🐾) The decor may be slightly dated, but these well-equipped self-catering apartments are clean and comfortable (some have balconies) and have a great location in the town centre, complete with secure parking.

★Cahernane House Hotel
HERITAGE HOTEL **€€€**

(☑064-663 1895; www.cahernane.com; Muckross Rd, Muckross; d €200-260, ste €320-340; P🐾) Up a tree-lined driveway, this magnificent manor 2km south of town dates from 1877. A dozen of its 38 antique-furnished rooms (some with clawfoot baths or jacuzzis) are in the original house; garden-wing rooms have balconies or patios. Fishing's possible in the River Flesk, which flows through the grounds. Its restaurant (four-course dinner menu €50; nonguests by reservation) is sublime.

The manor's wine cellar has an atmospheric bar stocked with Irish whiskey, gin, craft beer and cider.

★Malton
HERITAGE HOTEL **€€€**

(☑064-663 8000; www.themalton.com; East Avenue Rd; d/f/ste from €259/299/309; P@🐾🏊) Hidden behind high ivy-clad walls in the town centre, the grand Georgian-style Malton first opened its doors in 1854 as the Railway Hotel; its marble-columned lobby and the pick of its rooms, in the 1852 wing, have retained their period opulence. The health club has a spa, vast swimming pool, gym and two tennis courts.

Aghadoe Heights Hotel
SPA HOTEL **€€€**

(☑064-663 1766; www.aghadoeheights.com; Aghadoe; d/f/ste from €229/309/459; P@🐾🏊) A glassed-in swimming pool overlooking the lakes is the centrepiece of this contemporary hotel. Guests and nonguests can also soak up the views from the bar and Lake Room Restaurant (p262) and luxuriate at the spa's 10 treatment rooms and four-chamber thermal suite. Heavenly beds have memory foam mattresses. Some rooms have balconies; interconnecting rooms are available for families.

There are board games for rainy days and a tennis court.

🍴 Eating

Killarney has good cafes and restaurants in all price ranges. As elsewhere in Kerry, fresh seafood stars on many menus. In summer, evening bookings are recommended at high-end and/or popular places.

Khao
ASIAN **€**

(☑064-667 1040; 66 High St; mains €11-12; ⊘noon-10.30pm; 🍴) Fiery spices waft from this cosy spot, which sizzles up authentic stir-fries and wok-fried noodles along with rich curries, rice dishes and noodle soups. All of its produce is organic, and vegetarian choices abound. The two-course lunch menu, served between noon and 5pm, is a fantastic deal. Takeaway is available.

Lir Café
CAFE €

(☑ 064-663 3859; www.lircafe.com; Kenmare Pl; dishes €3-7; ☺ 8am-9pm; 🛜) Contemporary Lir Café brews some of Killarney's best coffee. Food is limited to toasties, cakes, biscuits and the real treat, handmade chocolates, including Bailey's truffles.

Mareena's Simply Food
IRISH €€

(☑ 066-663 7787; www.mareenassimplyfood. com; East Avenue Rd; mains €19-29; ☺ 6-9pm Tue-Sun mid-Feb–Dec) Mareena's serves locally sourced produce, from scallops and sea bass to neck of lamb and pork fillet, cooked plainly and simply to let the quality of the food speak for itself. The contemporary oyster-toned decor matches the cuisine – unfussy and understated.

Smoke House
STEAK, SEAFOOD €€

(☑ 064-663 9336; www.thesmokehouse.ie; 8 High St; mains €13-31; ☺ 5-10pm Mon-Fri, noon-10pm Sat & Sun) One of Killarney's busiest restaurants, this switched-on bistro was the first establishment in Ireland to cook with a Josper (superhot Spanish charcoal oven). The Kerry surf 'n' turf platter – a half-lobster and fillet steak – is outstanding; other options include rack of Kerry mountain lamb and wild local venison. Weekend brunch, served from noon till 3pm, includes eggs Florentine and Benedict.

Brícín
IRISH €€

(☑ 064-663 4902; www.bricin.com; 26 High St; mains €21-29.50; ☺ 6-9pm Tue-Sat early Mar–Dec) Decorated with fittings from a convent, an orphanage and a school, this Celtic-decorated restaurant doubles as the de facto town museum, with Jonathan Fisher's 18th-century views of the national park taking pride of place. Try the house speciality, boxty (traditional potato pancake). Early-bird two-/three-course dinner menus (€23/26) are available before 6.45pm.

Treyvaud's
IRISH €€

(☑ 064-663 3062; http://treyvaudsrestaurant. com; 62 High St; mains lunch €8-14, dinner €17-27; ☺ 5-10pm Mon, noon-10pm Tue-Thu & Sun, noon-10.30pm Fri & Sat) Mustard-fronted Treyvaud's has a strong reputation for subtle dishes that merge trad Irish with European influences. The seafood chowder – a velvet stew of mussels, prawns and Irish salmon – makes a filling lunch; dinner mains incorporating local ingredients include cod with horseradish mash and tomato-and-caper salsa, and a hearty bacon and cabbage platter.

Gaby's Seafood Restaurant
SEAFOOD €€€

(☑ 064-663 2519; www.gabys.ie; 27 High St; mains €30-50; ☺ 6-10pm Mon-Sat) Gaby's is a refined dining experience serving superb seafood in a traditional manner. Peruse the menu by the fire before drifting past the wine racks to the low-lit dining room to savour exquisite dishes such as lobster in cognac and cream. The wine list is long and the advice unerring.

Lake Room Restaurant
MODERN IRISH

(☑ 064-663 1766; www.aghadoeheights.com; Aghadoe; mains €22-39, 4-course menu €55; ☺ 6.30-9.30pm; 🚗) At this panoramic lakeview restaurant in the Aghadoe Heights Hotel (p261), adults have gourmet options such as roast guinea fowl with basil and parmesan polenta, while kids get their own menus (with dishes such as Marge Simpson's cheeseburger and Superman's spaghetti bolognese) and colouring-in books.

🍷 Drinking & Nightlife

Killarney is awash with pubs, most of which put on live music several times a week and nightly in summer.

★ Celtic Whiskey Bar & Larder
BAR

(☑ 064-663 5700; www.celticwhiskeybar.com; 93 New St; ☺ 10.30am-11.30pm Mon-Thu, to 12.30am Fri & Sat, to 11pm Sun) Of the thousand-plus whiskeys stocked at this stunning contem-

---

THE KERRY WAY

The 214km Kerry Way (www.kerryway. com) is the Republic's longest way-marked footpath. Starting and ending in Killarney, it winds through the spectacular Macgillycuddy's Reeks, Ireland's highest mountain range, before continuing around the Kerry coast through Cahersiveen, Waterville, Caherdaniel, Sneem and Kenmare.

It takes around 10 days to complete the whole route; with less time it's worth hiking the first three days as far as Glenbeigh, from where a bus or a lift could return you to Killarney. Accommodation along the trail is listed on the website. Ordnance Survey 1:50,000 maps 78, 83 and 84 cover the walk.

porary bar, over 500 are Irish, including 1945 Willie Napier from County Offaly and 12-year-old Writers' Tears from County Carlow. One-hour courses (from €15) include the introductory Distiller's Apprentice and a blend-your-own Blender's Challenge. A dozen Irish craft beers are on tap; sensational food (mains €10.50 to €24.50) is served until 10pm.

Menu highlights range from panko-crusted Galway prawns to Kerry sliders (such as pulled pork or spiced mackerel) and cider-steamed Cromane mussels.

★ O'Connor's   PUB
(http://oconnorstraditionalpub.com; 7 High St; ⊙10.30am-11pm Mon-Thu, to 12.30am Fri & Sat, 12.30-11pm Sun) Live music plays every night at this tiny traditional pub with leaded-glass doors, which is one of Killarney's most popular haunts. In warmer weather, the crowds spill out onto the adjacent lane.

Curious Cat Wine Bar   WINE BAR
(www.curiouscatwinebar.ie; 4 New Market Lane; ⊙5-11.30pm Wed & Thu, to 12.30am Fri & Sat, to 11pm Sun) Tucked away on New Market Lane, with barrels out the front, this hip little wine bar serves mainly European wines by the glass and bottle but also some standout Californian and New Zealand drops. Jazz and funk plays in the background except when live singer-songwriters and soul, blues and jazz bands perform. Creative tapas (€4.80 to €8.50) is served all hours.

Look out for its feisty sangria in the warmer months.

Courtney's   PUB
(www.courtneysbar.com; 24 Plunkett St; ⊙2-11.30pm Sun-Thu, to 12.30am Fri & Sat Jun-Sep, from 5pm Oct-May) Inconspicuous on the outside, this cavernous 19th-century pub bursts at the seams with regular Irish music sessions (nightly in summer). Year-round, rock, blues, reggae and indie bands perform on Friday with DJs taking over on Saturdays. This is where locals come to see their old mates perform and to kick off a night on the town.

Killarney Grand   BAR, CLUB
(www.killarneygrand.com; Main St; ⊙7.30pm-2.30am Mon-Sat, to 1.30am Sun) The various bars and clubs at this Killarney institution host traditional live music from 9pm to 11pm, rock bands from 11.30pm to 1.30am

and a disco from 11pm. Admission is free before 11pm, and €5 to €10 afterwards.

🔒 Shopping

Variety Sounds   MUSICAL INSTRUMENTS
(7 College St; ⊙9am-6pm Mon-Sat, noon-6pm Sun) A good range of traditional instruments are stocked at this eclectic music shop along with sheet music and hard-to-find recordings.

Dungeon Bookshop   BOOKS
(99 College St; ⊙8am-8pm Mon-Sat, 9am-8pm Sun) This secondhand bookshop is hidden above a newsagent (take the stairs at the back of the shop).

Killarney Outdoor Store   SPORTS & OUTDOORS
(www.killarneyrentabike.com; New St; ⊙10am-6pm Mon-Sat, noon-6pm Sun) Crams a vast amount of outdoor clothing, camping and climbing gear into a small space.

Brícín   ARTS & CRAFTS
(www.bricin.com; 26 High St; ⊙10am-9pm Mon-Sat) Interesting local craftwork, including jewellery and pottery, are stocked alongside touristy wares (shamrock aprons and mugs) at Brícín, which also houses a traditional Irish restaurant).

ℹ️ Information

The closest accident and emergency unit is at **University Hospital Kerry** (p300) in Tralee, 32km northwest of Killarney.

SouthDoc (☎1850-335 999; www.southdoc.ie; Upper Park Rd; ⊙6pm-8am Mon-Fri, 1pm Sat-8am Mon) provides a family doctor service outside normal hours. The clinic is 500m east of Killarney's centre, just east of the roundabout on the N22.

Killarney's **tourist office** (☎064-663 1633; http://killarney.ie; Beech Rd; ⊙9am-5pm Mon-Sat; 🛜) can handle most queries and is especially good with transport intricacies.

ℹ️ Getting There & Away

AIR
Kerry Airport (KIR; ☎066-976 4644; http://kerryairport.ie; Farranfore) is at Farranfore, 17km north of Killarney on the N22. There are daily flights to Dublin and London's Luton and Stansted airports, and less frequent services to Berlin, Germany; Faro, Portugal; and Alicante, Spain.

The small airport has a restaurant, bar, bureau de change and ATM. Virtually all the major car-hire firms have desks at the airport.

MUCKROSS LAKE LOOP TRAIL

You could easily spend most of a day ambling around this waymarked 9.5km loop trail (anticlockwise only for cyclists), which takes in some of the most photogenic parts of Killarney National Park. Starting from Muckross House, you head west through lovely lakeshore woods (with lots of side-trails to explore) to reach postcard-pretty Brickeen Bridge, which spans the channel linking Lough Leane and the Middle Lake.

Continue to the sylvan glades that surround the Meeting of the Waters, where channels from all three of Killarney's lakes merge. Don't miss the 10 minute side-trail (no bikes) to Old Weir Bridge, where you can watch tour boats powering through the narrow, rocky channel beneath its twin arches (here, a swiftly flowing current links the Upper and Middle Lakes).

On the return leg along the south shore of Middle Lake, the trail passes through woods before reaching the N71 Killarney–Kenmare road. Here, walkers have the option of climbing uphill on the other side of the road to visit **Torc Waterfall** before returning to Muckross House. Cyclists have to follow the main road east for 1km before regaining the off-road trail. Between the road and Muckross House you have the option of detouring along the **Old Boathouse Nature Trail**, which leads around a scenic peninsula.

Maps and details are available from Killarney tourist office (p263) and Muckross House ticket office.

BUS

Bus Éireann operates from the **bus station** (Park Rd) on Park Rd. For Dublin you need to change at Cork – the train is much faster.

Cork €25, two hours, hourly

Limerick €14.25, 1½ hours, every two hours

Tralee €10.45, 40 minutes, six daily

Waterford €29, 4¾ hours, hourly Monday to Saturday, every two hours Sunday

From April to October, Go Coach (http://go coach.ie) serves Dingle town (€10, 1½ hours, three daily) from **Killarney Coach Park** (Lewis Rd).

TRAIN

Killarney's **train station** (Fair Hill) is behind the Malton Hotel, just east of the centre.

There are one or two direct services per day to Cork and Dublin; otherwise you'll have to change at Mallow.

Cork €10, 1½ hours

Dublin €21, 3¼ hours

Tralee €9.20, 40 minutes, every two hours

ⓘ Getting Around

TO/FROM THE AIRPORT

Bus Éireann (www.buseireann.ie) has hourly services between Killarney and Kerry Airport (€5.60, 20 minutes).

Tralee–Killarney **trains** (☑ 064-6631067; www.irishrail.ie) stop at Farranfore station (€7.50, 20 minutes, every two hours), 1.3km southwest of the airport (a 10-minute walk at minimum).

A taxi to Killarney costs about €20.

BICYCLE

Bicycles are ideal for exploring the scattered sights of the Killarney region, many of which are accessible only by bike or on foot.

Many of Killarney's hostels and hotels offer bike rental. Alternatively, try **O'Sullivan's Bike Hire** (☑ 064-663 1282; www.osullivanscycles. com; Beech Rd; per day/week €15/80).

BUS

The **Killarney Shuttle Bus** (☑ 087 138 4384; www.killarneyshuttlebus.com; return €6, day pass €10; ⊙ Mar-Oct) service runs daily from the tourist office to all the main tourist spots, including Gap of Dunloe, Cronin's Yard, Ross Castle, Muckross House, Torc Waterfall and Ladies' View. Buy tickets from the driver. A day pass giving unlimited travel on the shuttle bus offers the best value.

CAR & MOTORCYCLE

Killarney's town centre can be thick with traffic at times.

Budget (☑ 064-663 4341; www.budget.ie; International Hotel, Kenmare Pl; ⊙ 9am-6pm Mon-Fri, to 3pm Sat) is the only car-hire outfit with an office in town. Otherwise contact the companies at Kerry Airport. **Enterprise** (☑ 064-663 1393; www.enterprise.ie; Glenea-gles Hotel, Muckross Rd; ⊙ 9am-5pm Mon-Fri) has an office on Muckross Rd, 2km south of the centre.

TAXI

The town **taxi rank** is on College St. Taxi companies include **Killarney Taxi & Tours** (☑ 085 280 3333; www.killarneytaxi.com).

AROUND KILLARNEY

Aghadoe

On a hilltop 5km west of town, Aghadoe's sweeping views of Killarney, the lakes and Inisfallen Island have made jaws drop for centuries. At the eastern end of the hilltop meadow are the ruins of a Romanesque church and the 13th-century Parkavonear Castle. Parkavonear's keep, still standing, is one of the few cylindrical keeps built by the Normans in Ireland.

There's no public transport, but several tour buses stop here.

Killarney National Park

Sprawling over 10,236 hectares, the sublime **Killarney National Park** (www.killarneynational park.ie) `FREE` is an idyllic place to explore. Ross Castle and Muckross House draw big crowds, but it's possible to escape amid Ireland's largest area of ancient oak woods, with panoramic views of its highest mountains and the country's only wild herd of native red deer.

The core of the national park is the Muckross Estate, donated to the state by Arthur Bourn Vincent in 1932; the park was designated a Unesco Biosphere Reserve in 1982. The **Killarney Lakes** – Lough Leane (the Lower Lake, or 'Lake of Learning'), Muckross (or Middle) Lake and the Upper Lake – make up about a quarter of the park, and are surrounded by natural oak and yew woodland, and overlooked by the high crags and moors of **Purple Mountain** (832m) to the west and **Knockrower** (552m) to the south.

◉ Sights

★ Ross Castle   CASTLE

(☑ 064-663 5851; www.heritageireland.ie; Ross Rd; adult/child €5/3; ⊘ 9.30am-5.45pm early Mar-Oct; 🅿) Lakeside Ross Castle dates back to the 15th century, when it was a residence of the O'Donoghue family. It was the last place in Munster to succumb to Cromwell's forces, thanks partly to its cunning spiral staircase, every step of which is a different height in order to break an attacker's stride. The castle is a lovely 2.6km walk or bike ride southwest of the St Mary's Cathedral pedestrian park entrance; you may well spot deer along the way.

★ Muckross House   HISTORIC BUILDING

(☑ 064-667 0144; www.muckross-house.ie; Muckross Estate; adult/child €9/6, incl Muckross Traditional Farms €15/10.50; ⊘ 9am-7pm Jul & Aug, to 5.30pm Sep-Jun; 🅿) This impressive Victorian mansion is crammed with fascinating objects (70% of the contents are original). Portraits by John Singer Sargent adorn the walls alongside trophy stags heads and giant stuffed trout, while antique Killarney furniture, with its distinctive inlaid scenes of local beauty spots, graces the grand apartments along with tapestries, Persian rugs, silverware and china specially commissioned for Queen Victoria's visit in 1861. It's 5km south of Killarney, signposted from the N71.

The house, built as a hunting and fishing lodge for the Herbert family in 1843, is set in beautiful gardens that slope down to the Middle Lake. At the gate, jaunting cars wait to run you through deer parks and woodland to Torc Waterfall and Muckross Abbey (about €20 each return; haggle for a discount).

COUNTY KERRY AGHADOE

FISHING AROUND KILLARNEY

Trout Fishing for brown trout in the lakes of Killarney National Park is free (no permit needed). The season runs from 15 February to 12 October. Fishing from the bank is allowed, but the best sport is to be had from a boat, which you can hire at **Ross Castle** (p267) or at **Sweeney's** (☑ 064-664 4207; www.theinvicta.com; Invicta B&B, Tomies, Beaufort) (at the west end of Lough Leane) for €40 a day (including outboard motor; up to three people).

Salmon The River Laune, which flows from Lough Leane to the sea, is one of Ireland's best salmon rivers. The season runs from 17 January to 30 September, with the best fishing from late July onwards. Both a permit (one day €20) and a state rod licence (one day/three weeks €20/40) are required. You can also fish for salmon in the Killarney lakes (no permit needed, but state rod licence is still required).

O'Neill's (p258) angling centre in Killarney provides information, rents rods and tackle, and sells permits and licences.

Around Killarney

A block situated behind the main house contains a craft shop and studios where you can see potters, weavers and bookbinders at work; the nearby visitor centre has a cafe.

Muckross Traditional Farms   MUSEUM
(☑ 064-663 0804; www.muckross-house.ie; Muckross Estate; adult/child €9/6, incl Muckross House €15/10.50; ⊙ 10am-6pm Jun-Aug, 1-6pm May & Sep, 1-6pm Sat & Sun Mar, Apr & Oct) These re-creations of 1930s farms evoke authentic sights, sounds and smells – cow dung, hay, wet earth and peat smoke, and a cacophony of chickens, ducks, pigs and donkeys. Costumed guides bring the traditional farm buildings to life, and the petting area allows kids to get up close and personal with piglets, lambs, ducklings and chicks. Allow at least two hours to do justice to the self-guided tour. A free shuttle loops around the farms, which are just east of Muckross House.

★ **Muckross Abbey**   RUINS
(www.muckross-house.ie; Muckross Estate; ⊙ 24hr) FREE Signposted 1.5km northeast of Muckross House, this well-preserved ruin (actually a friary, though everyone calls it an abbey) was founded in 1448 and burned by Cromwell's troops in 1652. There's a square-towered church and a small, atmospheric cloister with a giant yew tree in the centre (legend has it that the tree is as old as the abbey). In the chancel is the tomb of the McCarthy Mòr chieftains, and an elaborate 19th-century memorial to local philanthropist Lucy Gallwey.

★ **Knockreer House & Gardens**   GARDENS
(⊙ 8am-7pm Jun-Aug, to 6pm Apr-May & Oct, to 5pm Nov-Mar) FREE Killarney House, built for the Earl of Kenmare in the 1870s, burned down in 1913; the present Knockreer House was built on the same site in 1958 and is now home to a national park education centre. It isn't open to the public,

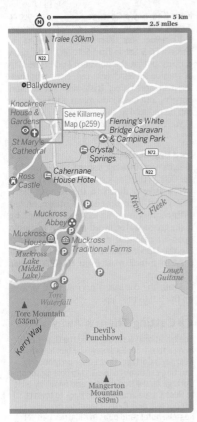

written here. Now in the Bodleian Library at Oxford, they remain a vital source of information on early Munster history.

🏃 Activities

The park offers superb opportunities for walking and fishing.

Killarney's tourist office (p263) stocks walking guides and maps. Killarney Guided Walks (p258) leads guided explorations.

Killarney Lake Tours   CRUISE
(☑ 064-663 2638; www.killarneylaketours.ie; Ross Castle Pier; adult/child €10/5; ☉ Apr-Oct) One-hour tours of Lough Leane in a comfortable, enclosed cruise boat depart four times daily (11am, 12.30pm, 2.30pm and 4pm) from the pier beside Ross Castle, taking in the island of Inisfallen (no landing) and O'Sullivan's Cascade (a waterfall on the west shore).

For €30 per person, including the cruise, a jaunting car will pick you up from your accommodation and take you through Killarney National Park to the castle.

Ross Castle Traditional Boats   BOATING
(☑ 085 174 2997; Ross Castle Pier; ☉ 9.30am-5pm Apr-Oct, by reservation Nov-Mar) The open boats at Ross Castle offer engaging trips with boatmen who define the word 'character'. Rates are around €10 per person for a trip to Inisfallen or the Middle Lake and back; it's €20 for a tour of all three lakes.

Outdoors Ireland   ADVENTURE
(☑ 086 860 4563; www.outdoorsireland.com) Guided kayak tours of the Killarney lakes lasting three/seven hours (€60/80 per person; no previous experience needed) generally depart from Ross Castle Pier. The company also runs three-hour sunset kayak trips (€60) and one-day beginner rock-climbing courses (€80).

ⓘ Getting There & Away

There are two pedestrian/bike entrances in Killarney town: opposite St Mary's Cathedral (24-hour access); and the so-called Golden Gates at the roundabout on Muckross Rd (open 8am to 7pm June to August, to 6pm April, May and October, to 5pm November to March).

Vehicle access is via Ross Rd on the southern edge of Killarney town centre, leading to Ross Castle car park; and the Muckross Estate entrance on the N71 5km south of Killarney, leading to the Muckross House car park; parking is free.

but its gardens, featuring a terraced lawn and a summerhouse, have magnificent views across the lakes to the mountains.

From the park entrance opposite St Mary's Cathedral, follow the path to your right for 550m.

Inisfallen   ISLAND
The first monastery on Inisfallen (the largest of the lakes' islands) was founded by St Finian the Leper in the 7th century. The extensive ruins of a 12th-century **Augustinian priory** and an oratory with a carved Romanesque doorway stand on the site of St Finian's original. You can hire a motor boat with boatman (around €10) from Ross Castle for the 10-minute trip to the island. In calm weather you can hire a rowing boat (€5 per hour; allow 30 minutes each way).

Inisfallen's fame dates from the early 13th century when the Annals of Inisfallen were

COUNTY KERRY KILLARNEY NATIONAL PARK

ℹ Getting Around

Walking, cycling and boat trips are the best ways to explore the park.

From the cathedral entrance it's 2.5km (30 minutes' walk) to Ross Castle; to reach Muckross Estate on foot or by bike you have to follow the cycle path beside the N71 south for 3km where it veers off towards the lake (its 5km all up to Muckross House).

Jaunting cars depart from Kenmare Pl in Killarney town centre, and from the Jaunting Car Entrance to Muckross Estate, at a car park 3km south of town on the N71. Expect to pay around €15 to €20 per person for a tour from Killarney to Ross Castle and back. There are no set prices; haggle for longer tours.

Gap of Dunloe

The Gap of Dunloe is a wild and scenic mountain pass – studded with crags and bejewelled with lakes and waterfalls – that lies to the west of Killarney National Park, squeezed between Purple Mountain and the high summits of Macgillycuddy's Reeks (Ireland's highest mountain range).

Although it's outside the national park boundary, it's been a vital part of the Killarney tourist trail since the late 18th century when, inspired by the Romantic poets, wealthy tourists came in search of 'sublime' and 'savage' landscapes.

During this period, the legend of Kate Kearney first arose: Kate, a fabled local beauty based on a popular song, supposedly lived in a cottage in the pass and dispensed *poteen* (illegally distilled whiskey) to weary travellers. The 19th-century pub at the northern end of the Gap is still known as Kate Kearney's Cottage; there's a busy car park here, where you can rent jaunting cars (cash only).

★ **Heather**   CAFE €
(☏ 064-664 4144; http://moriartys.ie; dishes €6.50-17; ☉10.30am-5pm; ☝) 🍴 In a glorious setting, this light-filled cafe adjoins a farm that provides produce from its fields and polytunnels, while seafood and meat are locally and sustainably sourced. Fantastic food spans sweet treats such as Skelligs white chocolate and roasted-hazelnut cake to filling dishes like Killorglin pork belly with fennel slaw or buckwheat crêpes with smoked salmon and Valentia Island yoghurt.

The attached gift shop sells quality Irish crafts.

Kate Kearney's Cottage   PUB FOOD €€
(☏ 064-664 4146; mains €10-23; ☉kitchen 11.30am-9pm, bar 10am-11.30pm Mon-Thu, to 12.30am Fri & Sat, to 11pm Sun; ☝) This 19th-century pub at the northern end of the Gap of Dunloe serves decent pub classics including fish and chips, Irish stew, steaks and burgers, and has a kids' menu. Kitchen hours can be reduced at short notice, so call ahead if you're counting on dining here. The bar hosts live Irish music every night in summer.

Lord Brandon's Cottage   CAFE €
(Gearhameen, Beaufort; dishes €3-8; ☉8am-3pm Apr-Oct) At the Gap's southern end, the road twists steeply down to the remote Black Valley and Lord Brandon's Cottage, an old 19th-century hunting lodge surrounded by lush, green water meadows with a simple open-air cafe and a dock for boats crossing the Upper Lake. It's reached by car via a steep minor road from the R568 near Moll's Gap.

From the cottage, a narrow road weaves up the hill to the Gap.

ℹ Getting There & Away

The traditional way to explore the Gap (p269) is via a tour from Killarney – by bus to Kate Kearney's Cottage, then either on foot or by jaunting car through the Gap to Lord Brandon's Cottage on the Upper Lake, and finally by boat to Ross Castle and then bus back to town (€30 per person, plus €20 for jaunting car). Most hostels, hotels and pubs in Killarney can set up these tours, or try **Gap of Dunloe Tours** (p258).

Despite a road sign at Kate Kearney's Cottage implying that cars are forbidden, it is perfectly legal to drive through the Gap of Dunloe – it's a public road. However, driving the Gap is not recommended, at least from Easter to September. The road is very narrow, steep and twisting, and is usually crowded with walkers, cyclists, ponies and jaunting cars; the drivers of the latter will give you short shrift. Early morning, or after 5pm is best.

Macgillycuddy's Reeks

Macgillycuddy's Reeks is Ireland's highest mountain range, encompassing nine of the country's 12 summits that exceed 900m in altitude. The name dates from the 18th century – the MacGillycuddy clan were local landowners, and 'reeks' is dialect meaning 'stacks' (a reference to the layered nature of the rocks here).

BY BOAT AND BIKE THROUGH THE GAP

A boat trip through the lakes followed by a bike ride through the Gap of Dunloe is the classic Killarney region experience. Your hostel, hotel or campsite can arrange it for you (€15 per person, plus bike hire €12 to €15 per day).

Boats depart near **Ross Castle** (p265) at 11am, with bikes propped in the bow. The 1½-hour cruise alone justifies the price; ask your boatman about the highest/lowest level he has ever seen in the lakes, and sit back to enjoy the story.

You cruise past **Inisfallen** (p267) with its ruined monastery then turn south to sail under pretty Brickeen Bridge and reach the Meeting of the Waters. The boat then surges up a rocky channel beneath the Old Weir Bridge – after prolonged dry weather, when lake levels are low, passengers may have to get out and walk a short distance while the boat gets hauled up this shallow, fast-flowing section.

The Long Range is next, a winding channel that is half-lake, half-river, uncoiling beneath the crags of Eagle's Nest mountain (golden eagles once nested here) before entering the long, narrow Upper Lake.

After disembarking at **Lord Brandon's Cottage** (p268) around 12.30pm (where there's a cafe and toilets), you begin the bike section with a 5km climb to the head of the Gap. It's a steady uphill, but not too steep, and there's no shame in getting off and pushing for a bit. At the summit you're rewarded with stunning views in both directions, and a 6km downhill run to **Kate Kearney's Cottage** (p268), where there's a cafe, pub and toilets.

From here, you follow signs for Killarney along minor roads to the N71, then a cycle path that first hugs the side of the main road before veering off through the golf course and the northern part of Killarney National Park to end near the town centre opposite St Mary's Cathedral.

The total distance cycled is 23km; allowing time for stops and an hour for lunch, you should be back in Killarney by 3.30pm. Hikers can also do this route – allow three hours to walk from Lord Brandon's to Kate Kearney's, and take the **Killarney Shuttle Bus** (p264) from the latter back into town (departs at 4.30pm; confirm times in advance).

The best approach to the hills is from **Cronin's Yard** (☑ 064-662 4044; www.cronins yard.com; Mealis, Beaufort; camping pods per person €15; ℗), where there's a car park (€2), tearoom (packed lunches available on request), showers and toilets, a free basic campsite and a couple of nifty camping pods. It's at the road's end (OS ref 836873), reached from the N72 via Beaufort, west of Killarney; follow signs for the Gap of Dunloe at first, but keep straight on where the Gap is signposted left. After 4km you'll reach Kissane Foodstone and petrol station; 50m further on, over the bridge, Cronin's is signposted – 3km ahead on the left. The Killarney Shuttle Bus (p264) runs here twice daily.

You can get a taste of the Reeks at close quarters by following the waymarked loop trail up **Hag's Glen**, the beautiful approach valley that leads to loughs Callee and Gouragh below the towering east face of Carrantuohil. From Cronin's Yard, the way lies along a stony track beside the River Gaddagh (round trip 8km).

There are several routes up **Carrauntoohil** (1040m), the country's highest peak. Even the easiest requires good hill-walking and route-finding ability, while others are serious scrambling or rock-climbing routes. Until recently, the traditional route to the summit was via **Devil's Ladder**, a gruelling trudge up a badly eroded gully path southwest of the lakes. However, this has now become dangerously loose and unstable.

The recommended route now ascends via **Brother O'Shea's Gully** (some scrambling involved) and descends via the Zig-Zags to the east of the Devil's Ladder. Experienced hill-walkers can follow the directions in Adrian Hendorff's guidebook, *The Dingle, Iveragh & Beara Peninsulas: A Walking Guide*. If you're in the slightest bit unsure, hire a guide – Con Moriarty's **Hidden Ireland Tours** (☑ 087 221 4002; www.hiddenirelandadventures.com; €75; ⊗ Wed & Sat) leads guided ascents of Carrauntoohil on Wednesday and Saturday year-round, weather permitting (booking is essential).

Climbing Carrauntoohil should never be attempted without a map and compass (and the skills to use them), proper hill-walking boots, waterproofs and spare food and water. Use Harvey's 1:30,000 *MacGillicuddy's Reeks Superwalker* map, or the 1:25,000 Ordnance Survey Adventure Series map (*MacGillicuddy's Reeks & Killarney National Park*).

Moll's Gap

Built in the 1820s to replace an older track to the east (the Old Kenmare Road, now followed by the Kerry Way hiking trail), the vista-crazy N71 Killarney to Kenmare road (32km) winds between rock and lake, with plenty of lay-bys to stop and admire the views (and recover from the switchback bends). Watch out for the buses squeezing along the road.

About 17km south of Killarney is the panoramic viewpoint **Ladies' View** (N71).

A further 5km south is the summit of the pass at Moll's Gap, which is worth a stop for great views and refreshments at **Avoca Cafe** (☑ 064-663 4720; www.avocahandweavers. com; N71, Moll's Gap; dishes €5.50-13; ⊙9.30am-5pm Mon-Fri, 10am-5pm Sat & Sun; 🕾 🖡).

RING OF KERRY

This 179km circuit of the Iveragh (pronounced *eev*-raa) Peninsula winds past pristine beaches, medieval ruins, mountains and loughs, with ever-changing views of the island-dotted Atlantic, particularly between Waterville and Caherdaniel in the peninsula's spectacular southwest.

The smaller but equally scenic Skellig Ring, which spins off the loop, is less travelled as the roads are too narrow for tour buses.

Centred on the Ring, the 700-sq-km Kerry International Dark-Sky Reserve (http://kerrydarksky.com) was designated in 2014. Low light pollution offers fantastic stargazing when skies are clear.

If you want to get further off the beaten track, explore the interior of the peninsula – on foot along the eastern section of the Kerry Way from Killarney to Glenbeigh, or by car or bike on the minor roads that cut through the hills, notably the Ballaghisheen Pass between Killorglin and Waterville, or the Ballaghbeama Gap from Glenbeigh to Gearha Bridge on the R568.

❶ Getting Around

Although you can cover the Ring in one day by car or three days by bicycle, the more time you take, the more you'll enjoy it.

The road is narrow and twisty in places. Tour buses travel the Ring in an anticlockwise direction. Getting stuck behind one is tedious, so consider driving clockwise; just watch out for blind corners.

From late June to late August, Bus Éireann (www.buseireann.ie) runs a once-daily Ring of Kerry loop service (No 280). Buses leave Killarney at 11.30am, arriving back at Killarney (€23.50) at 4.45pm. En route, stops include Killorglin (€8, 30 minutes), Cahersiveen (€17.50, 1½ hours), Waterville (€20, 1¾ hours) and Caherdaniel (€21.80, 2¼ hours).

Year-round, Bus Éireann service 279A runs daily between Killarney and Waterville (€20, 1¾ hours), via Killorglin (€8, 30 minutes) and Cahersiveen (€17.50, 1½ hours).

Killorglin

POP 2199

Travelling anticlockwise from Killarney, the first town on the Ring is Killorglin (Cill Orglain, meaning Orgla's Church). For most of the year, it's quieter than the waters of the River Laune that lap against its 1885-built eight-arched bridge, where salmon leap and little egrets paddle in the shallows.

In August, however, there's an explosion of time-honoured ceremonies at the famous pagan festival, the Puck Fair (a statue of King Puck – a goat – stands on the north side of the river). Author Blake Morrison documents his mother's childhood here in *Things My Mother Never Told Me*.

◉ Sights

Kerry Bog Village Museum   MUSEUM
(www.kerrybogvillage.ie; Ballincleave, Glenbeigh; adult/child €6.50/4.50; ⊙9am-6pm) This museum re-creates a 19th-century bog village, typical of the small communities that carved out a precarious living in the harsh environment of Ireland's ubiquitous peat bogs. You'll see the thatched homes of the turf-cutter, blacksmith, thatcher and labourer, as well as a dairy, and meet Kerry bog ponies (a native breed) and Irish wolfhounds. It's on the N70 8.3km southwest of Killorglin near Glenbeigh; buy a ticket at the neighbouring Red Fox Inn if no one's at the gate.

CROMANE AND DOOKS

Unless you know it's here, you wouldn't chance upon **Cromane**, home to Ireland's largest natural mussel beds (up to 8000 tonnes are harvested each year). The village sits at the base of a narrow shingle spit, with open fields giving way to spectacular water vistas and multihued sunsets. Some of the area's best seafood is served at **Jacks' Coastguard Restaurant** (☑066-976 9102; http://jackscromane.com; Cromane; 2-/3-course menus lunch €22.50/26.50, dinner €34/40, mains €16.50-33; ☺6-9pm Thu-Sat, 1-3.30pm & 6-9pm Sun, hours can vary; ▣), in a 19th-century coastguard station.

Southwest of Cromane is **Dooks Golf Club** (☑066-976 8205; www.dooks.com; Knockaunroe, Glenbeigh; green fees €50-120), one of the oldest links golf courses in Ireland, opened in 1889. A little further along the road, an unsignposted lane (look for the green post box) leads to **Dooks Beach**, a little-visited gem at the mouth of the River Caragh, with gorgeous views of the Kerry and Dingle mountains.

Cromane is 9km west of Killorglin, signposted off the N70.

 Festivals & Events

Puck Fair
CULTURAL

(Aonach an Phuic; www.puckfair.ie; ☺mid-Aug) First recorded in 1603, with hazy origins, this lively three-day festival centres on the custom of installing a billy goat (a poc, or puck), the symbol of mountainous Kerry, on a pedestal in the town, its horns festooned with ribbons. Other entertainment ranges from a horse fair to street theatre, concerts and fireworks; the pubs stay open until 3am.

Sleeping & Eating

Coffey's River's Edge
B&B €€

(☑066-976 1750; www.coffeysriversedge.com; Lower Bridge St; s/d €70/90; ▣🗗) You can sit out on the balcony overlooking the River Laune at this contemporary B&B with 10 spotless spring-toned rooms and hardwood floors. Cots are available. It's in a central location next to the bridge.

Jack's Bakery
BAKERY €

(Lower Bridge St; dishes €2.20-7.95; ☺8am-6.45pm Mon-Fri, to 6pm Sat, 9am-2pm Sun) 🖉 Jack Healy bakes amazing artisan breads, and also serves killer coffee and beautiful sandwiches (using homemade pâtés) at this popular spot. There's no indoor seating, but a couple of tables are set up on the pavement in good weather.

Giovannelli
ITALIAN €€

(☑087 123 1353; http://giovannellirestaurant.com; Lower Bridge St; mains €19-33.50; ☺6.30-9pm Mon-Sat) Northern Italian native Daniele Giovannelli makes all of his pasta by hand at this simple but intimate little restaurant. Highlights of the blackboard menu might include seafood linguine with mussels in the shell, and beef ravioli in sage butter. Wonderful wines are available by the bottle and glass.

Bianconi
GASTROPUB €€

(☑066-976 1146; www.bianconi.ie; Lower Bridge St; mains €14.50-24; ☺kitchen 11.30am-10pm Mon-Sat, 6-9pm Sun, bar 8am-11.30pm Mon-Thu, to 12.30am Fri & Sat, 6-11pm Sun; 🗗) This Victorian-style pub has a classy ambience and an equally refined menu. Its spectacular salads, such as Cashel blue cheese, apple, toasted almonds and pancetta, are a meal in themselves. Upstairs, stylishly refurbished guest rooms (doubles from €110) have olive and truffle tones and luxurious bathrooms (try for a roll-top tub).

Shopping

KRD Fisheries
FOOD

(☑066-976 1106; www.krdfisheries.com; Tralee Rd; ☺9am-1pm & 2-5pm Mon-Fri, to 1pm Sat, to 11am Sun) 🖉 You can buy organic smoked salmon direct from this 1782-founded smokery just across the bridge from Killorglin's town centre, which smokes salmon caught in the River Laune estuary.

Information

The **tourist office** (☑066-976 1451; Library Pl; ☺9am-1pm & 1.30-5pm Mon-Fri) sells maps, walking guides, fishing permits and souvenirs.

Cahersiveen

POP 1041

The main town of the Iveragh Peninsula, Cahersiveen (pronounced caar-suh-veen; from cathair saidhbhin, Little Sarah's Ring

Ring of Kerry

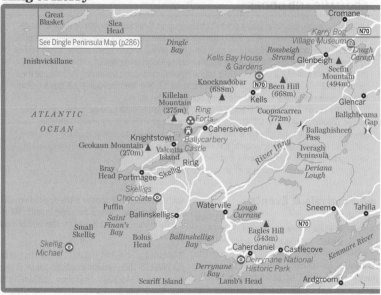

See Dingle Peninsula Map (p286)

Fort) began life as a fishing harbour and market town but fell on hard times at the end of the 20th century – indeed, O'Connell St (north of Main St) still looks like a boulevard of broken dreams, lined with abandoned hotels and pubs.

But the last few years have seen a determined effort to reinvent the town as a tourism centre. The main street and waterfront areas have been spruced up, the former barracks has been beautifully restored as a museum, there are some excellent places to stay and eat, and the surrounding countryside is a delight to explore.

The town is indelibly linked with the fight for Irish independence – it was the birthplace of Daniel O'Connell, 'the Great Liberator', and was where the first shots of the 1867 Fenian Rising were fired.

⊙ Sights & Activities

Waymarked local walks include the Bentee Loop (9km), which starts in Cahersiveen and leads to the 376m summit of Bentee, the conical hill just south of town, with superb views of Valentia Island the hills of the Iveragh Peninsula.

Casey Cycles offers bike rental and cycling route advice.

Ring Forts RUINS

(Ballycarbery) FREE Some 3km northwest of Cahersiveen, two extraordinary stone ring forts situated 600m apart are reached from a shared parking area. **Cahergal**, the larger and more impressive, dates from the 10th century and has stairways on the inside walls, a *clochán* (beehive hut), and the remains of a roundhouse. The smaller, 9th-century **Leacanabuile** contains the outlines of four houses. Both have a commanding position overlooking Ballycarbery Castle and Valentia Harbour, with superb views of the Kerry mountains.

Old Barracks Heritage Centre MUSEUM

(☑ 066-401 0430; www.oldbarrackscahersiveen. com; Bridge St; adult/child €4/2; ⊙ 10am-5.30pm Mon-Sat, 11am-5.30pm Sun) Established in response to the Fenian Rising of 1867, the Royal Irish Constabulary barracks at Cahersiveen were built in an eccentric Bavarian-schloss style, complete with pointy turret and stepped gables. Burnt down in 1922 by anti-Treaty forces, the imposing building has been restored and now houses fascinating exhibitions on the Fenian Rising and the life and works of local hero Daniel O'Connell.

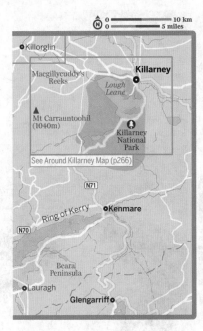

See Around Killarney Map (p266)

The **town park**, which stretches along the riverbank behind the heritage centre, contains the outline of the ancient ring fort that gave the town its name.

O'Connell's Birthplace RUINS
At the bridge across the Carhan River on the eastern edge of town, a neat little memorial park remembers Daniel O'Connell (1775–1847), 'the Great Liberator', a political leader who campaigned for Catholic emancipation and Irish independence. He was born in the ruined cottage on the far bank of the river.

Ballycarbery Castle CASTLE
(Ballycarbery) FREE The atmospheric – and decidedly dangerous-looking – ivy-strangled remains of 16th-century Ballycarbery Castle stand amid green pastures 3km northwest of Cahersiveen.

Casey Cycles CYCLING
(☑066-947 2474; www.bikehirekerry.com; New St; touring bikes per day/week €16/80, road bikes €35/140; ☺9am-6pm Mon-Sat year-round, 10am-1.30pm Sun Jul-Aug) Casey Cycles rents good quality touring bikes and road bikes, and provides information on local cycling routes. Good objectives include the ring forts at Cahergall, or Valentia Island (easily reached via the ferry just west of town).

Festivals & Events

Cahersiveen Festival of Music & the Arts MUSIC
(www.celticmusicfestival.com; ☺late Jul/early Aug) Celtic bands, busking competitions and Irish set-dancing star at this family-friendly festival held over the August bank holiday weekend.

Sleeping & Eating

★**Mannix Point Camping & Caravan Park** CAMPGROUND €
(☑066-947 2806; www.campinginkerry.com; Mannix Point, Cahersiveen; hiker €8.50, vehicle plus 2 adults €26; ☺mid-Mar–mid-Oct; ☎) ⬤ Mortimer Moriarty's award-winning waterfront campsite is one of Ireland's finest, with 42 pitches, an inviting kitchen, campers' sitting room with peat fire (no TV but regular music sessions and instruments if you haven't brought your own), laundry facilities, squeaky-clean showers (€1), a barbecue area and even a birdwatching platform. Sunsets here are stunning.

San Antoine B&B €
(☑066-947 2521; http://sanantoine.com; Garranebane; d/tr/f from €67.50/95/105; ℗☎) At the western edge of town, this spotless and spacious B&B sports a large terrace and breakfast room, both with views towards sea and hills. The owners can help arrange boat trips to Skellig Michael, and advise on local walks and bike rides.

Sive Hostel HOSTEL €
(☑066-947 2717; www.sivehostel.ie; 15 East End; dm €22, s/d/tr with bathroom €30/54/78, d/tr with shared bathroom €52/75; ☎) Simple and sweet, this homely hostel has good-value private rooms, some in a cute stone cottage at the back, a rooftop balcony with great views, and a lovely courtyard area. There's bike storage and a drying room.

★**QCs Seafood Restaurant & Bar** SEAFOOD €€
(☑066-947 2244; http://qcbar.com; 3 Main St; mains €16-26.50, bar food €9-15; ☺kitchen 12.30-2.30pm & 6-9.30pm Mon-Sat, 5-9pm Sun, bar 12.30pm-midnight Mon-Sat, 5pm-midnight Sun; ☎) QCs is a modern take on a classic pub and as such is open pub hours for pints and craic. But some of the finest food on the Ring pours forth, particularly locally sourced seafood from its own fishing fleet, such as Valentia crab and Dingle Bay prawn bisque. Upstairs are six boutique B&B bedrooms (doubles from €159).

1. King Puck sculpture, Killorglin by Alan Ryan Hall (p272)
2. Valentia Island (p276) 3. Traditional shop fronts, Kenmare (p282)
4. Caherdaniel (p281)

JORG GREUEL/GETTY IMAGES ©

Ring of Kerry

Windswept beaches, Atlantic waves crashing against rugged cliffs and islands, medieval ruins, soaring mountains and glinting loughs are some of the stunning distractions along the twisting 179km Ring of Kerry circle drive around the Iveragh Peninsula.

Killorglin

Even if you're racing around the ring, don't miss its first town (heading anticlockwise). The riverside village of Killorglin is home to a salmon smokehouse, some standout restaurants and, in August, the historic Puck Fair Festival.

Kenmare

A fitting last (or first) stop on the ring, Kenmare is a microcosm of Kerry's greatest charms. A beautiful location on the bay (from where boat trips depart), colourful shops and gracious architecture are cornerstones of this classic Irish town.

Skellig Ring

A ring within the ring, this 18km loop off the main route offers an escape from the crowds. The wild, scenic drive links Portmagee and Waterville via a Gaeltacht (Irish-speaking) area centred on Ballinskelligs (Baile an Sceilg).

Valentia Island

Islands are a scenic highlight on the ring. Some are accessible by boat, but picturesque Valentia Island is even easier to reach, via a short bridge. There's also a summer car-ferry service departing just south of Caherciveen.

Caherdaniel

The ring's scenery is at its most rugged around Caherdaniel. Highlights here include the Derrynane National Historic Park with its stately house and palm-filled gardens, horse riding, a Blue Flag beach and water sports galore.

KELLS BAY HOUSE & GARDENS

Opened in 1837 as a hunting lodge, this magnificent **Kells Bay House & Gardens** (📞 066-947 7974; www.kellsgardens.ie; off N70, Kells Bay; adult/child €8/6; ⏰ 9am-9pm Jun-Aug, to 7pm Feb-May, Sep & Oct, to 4.30pm Nov & Dec) estate sprawls over 17 hectares incorporating a waterfall, beach and six different gardens, ranging from palms to a primeval fern forest with dinosaurs carved from fallen trees. Ireland's longest rope bridge, the 33.5m Skywalk, sways precariously 11m above the River Delligeenagh, which swirls through the property.

Walled kitchen gardens and farm animals provide ingredients for its Thai restaurant (mains €10 to €15.50). It's also possible to stay here (double/suite from €85/140).

Camo's
CAFE, INTERNATIONAL €€

(📞 066-948 1122; www.camos.ie; 24 Church St; mains lunch €5-8.50, dinner €11.50-22; ⏰ 10am-6pm Mon-Wed, 10am-5pm & 6.30-9pm Thu & Fri, 11am-5pm & 6.30-9pm Sat; 🛜 🚗) During the day, this friendly neighbourhood spot serves dishes such as oak-smoked salmon sandwiches on home-baked brown bread, and a delicious black pudding salad. At night, seafood (hake and prawn hotpot, bacon-wrapped monkfish) is the highlight of a menu that also includes forays into fusion cuisine.

Valentia Island

POP 665

Laced with narrow roads, Valentia is a beautiful and under-visited corner of Kerry with a rich and fascinating history. Its Latin-sounding name is actually an anglicised version of the Irish *Béal Inse,* meaning 'the mouth of the island' (a reference to the sheltered harbour entrance), though the Irish name of the island itself, Oileán Dairbhre, means 'island of oak trees'.

Valentia is renowned for its high-quality slate, which was first quarried here in 1816 – Valentia slate was used to roof London's Houses of Parliament and Westminster Cathedral, and Paris' Palais Garnier opera house. The quarry, abandoned in 1911, reopened in 1999 and produces slate objects including billiard tables.

The island measures just 11km long by 3km wide; Knightstown, at the eastern end of the island, is its only village.

🔘 Sights

Glanleam House & Gardens
GARDENS

(📞 066-947 6176; http://glanleam.com/cms; gardens €5; ⏰ 10am-7pm mid-Mar–Oct) Built as a linen mill in 1775, this estate was transformed from 1808, when its owner established its 16-hectare gardens with exotic plants from around the world including bamboo and the tallest tree ferns in Europe. Trails meander along its beach, river and through the forest.

The manor house has four antique-furnished rooms (double from €110; three course dinner €50). There are also four self-catering cottages sleeping up to six (from €150).

Tetrapod Trackway
HISTORIC SITE

(Dohilla) **FREE** This string of small depressions in an exposed sandstone bedding surface next to the sea may not be as spectacular as dinosaur footprints, but these fossil tracks – left behind by a metre-long amphibious creature around 360 million years ago – are the world's most extensive physical evidence of a vertebrate creature moving on land. Even if geology isn't your thing, the setting is beautiful, with views to the Blasket Islands and the Dingle peninsula. It's 4.3km northwest of Knightstown.

Valentia Island Heritage Centre
MUSEUM

(📞 066-947 6411; School Rd, Knightstown; adult/child €3.50/free; ⏰ 10.30am-5.30pm May-Sep) Inside the old school on the road towards Geokaun Mountain, this intriguing local museum has a treasure trove of artefacts that tell the tale of the island's history more eloquently than any textbook – from school chemistry sets and slate-quarrying tools to fossils and old photographs, with pride of place going to the Morse key used to test the world's first transatlantic telegraph cable.

Skellig Experience
MUSEUM

(📞 066-947 6306; www.skelligexperience.com; adult/child €5/3, incl cruise €35/20; ⏰ 10am-7pm Jul & Aug, to 6pm May, Jun & Sep, to 4.30pm Fri-Wed Mar, Apr, Oct & Nov) Immediately across the bridge from Portmagee, this distinctive building with a turf-covered roof contains exhibitions on the life of the Skellig Michael monks, the history of the island's lighthouses and its wildlife. From April to September, it also runs two-hour **cruises** around the islands (no landing), and is a good place to get advice on visiting the Skelligs.

In March, April, October and November the centre opens six days a week, but the exact days change each year – check ahead.

Geokaun Mountain VIEWPOINT
(www.geokaun.com; car/cyclist & hiker €5/2; ⊙6am-11pm) The local landowner has transformed the island's highest point, Geokaun (266m), into a network of easy walking trails and viewpoints, with a breathtaking outlook over the Fogher Cliffs. It's possible to drive all the way to the top, so visitors with limited mobility don't miss out on the views. At quieter times the site is unstaffed, and entry is via an automatic barrier (payment with coins only).

Telegraph Field MONUMENT
Valentia Island was chosen as the eastern terminus of the first transatlantic telegraph cable, from Heart's Content, Newfoundland. A monument at Telegraph Field, at the western end of the island, commemorates the establishment of the first permanent communications link between Europe and North America in 1866. The telegraph station here continued in operation until 1966, when satellite technology provided a faster alternative.

Prior to the cable, it took two weeks to transmit information, as communications were sent by boat.

🛏 Sleeping & Eating

⭐ **Atlantic Villa** B&B €€
(☑087 212 6798; http://atlanticvilla.ie; Knightstown; s/d from €50/80; 🅿🤶) Built in 1873 for the superintendent of the transatlantic telegraph cable between Valentia and Newfoundland, this historic house has a blazing open fire and six lovingly restored rooms rich in period atmosphere – some with sea views – and modern comforts that include superb gourmet breakfasts and a sauna. Packed lunches can be arranged, as well as in-room traditional Irish seaweed baths.

Produce for breakfast comes from its veggie gardens, with eggs supplied by its chickens. One- and two-bedroom self-catering cottages (€375/450 per week) are located on the property.

Royal Valentia HOTEL €€
(☑066-947 6144; http://royalvalentia.ie; Knightstown; s/d/f from €70/100/140; 🤶) Established in the 1830s, this Victorian hotel has been given a modern makeover with 30 bright, uncluttered rooms (some with four-poster beds and many with harbour views). Family rooms sleep four. Its lively bar, serving pub food (mains €13 to €29), is the heart and soul of the local community.

Pod Crêperie CAFE €
(☑066-947 6995; https://podcrepesandgifts.wordpress.com; 2 Market St, Knightstown; dishes €3.50-12; ⊙11am-6pm Mon & Tue, 10.30am-6pm Wed-Sun Easter-Sep; 🤶) Sweet crêpes such as lemon and sugar or apple and cinnamon are served alongside savoury *galettes* made from buckwheat flour (Cashel blue cheese, walnuts and honey; Portmagee crab, cheese and spinach). The attached gift shop stocks local art, crafts, soaps and deli items; on sunny days tables are set up on the terrace.

**Valentia Island
Farmhouse Dairy** ICE CREAM €
(☑066-947 6864; Kilbeg; ice cream per 1/2/3 scoops €3/5.50/7.50; ⊙11am-7pm Jul & Aug, to 6pm Jun; 👶) 🍽 Dairy cattle on this working farm provide the milk for all-natural handmade ice cream in flavours such as cinnamon, caramel, mint choc-chip and strawberry, using berries also grown on the farm. Milk-free sorbets span rhubarb to cucumber. Its terrace overlooks the fields and sea beyond; there's a children's indoor/outdoor play area.

Horse-and-trap tours of the island are available for €9 per person, with a minimum of two people.

ℹ Information

The island's **tourist office** (☑066-947 6985; www.valentiaisland.ie; 3 Watch House Cottage, Knightstown; ⊙10am-4.30pm May-Sep, 9am-5pm Mon-Fri Oct-Apr) is in Knightstown.

ℹ Getting There & Away

Valentia is not served by public transport.

A bridge links the island with Portmagee on the mainland.

From April to October, the **Valentia Island Car Ferry** (☑087 241 8973; one way/return car €7/10, cyclist €2/3, pedestrian €1.50/2; ⊙7.45am-10pm Mon-Sat, 9am-10pm Sun Jul & Aug, 7.45am-9.30pm Mon-Sat, 9am-9.30pm Sun Apr-Jun, Sep & Oct) shuttles back and forth between Knightstown and Reenard Point, 5km southwest of Cahersiveen. The crossing takes five minutes, with departures every 10 minutes.

SKELLIG ISLANDS

The twin wave-battered pinnacles of the Skellig Islands (Oileáin na Scealaga) are the site of Ireland's most remote and spectacular ancient monastery. The 12km sea crossing can be rough, and the climb up to the monastery is steep and tiring. Due to the sheer (and often slippery) terrain and sudden wind gusts, it's not suitable for young children or people with limited mobility. Bring something to eat and drink, and wear sturdy shoes with good grip and weatherproof clothing.

The jagged, 217m-high rock of **Skellig Michael** (Archangel Michael's Rock; like St Michael's Mount in Cornwall and Mont St Michel in Normand; www.heritageireland.ie; hmid-May–Sep) is the larger of the two Skellig Islands and a Unesco World Heritage site. Early Christian monks established a community and survived here from the 6th until the 12th or 13th century. The monastic buildings perch on a saddle in the rock, some 150m above sea level, reached by 618 steep steps cut into the rock face.

The astounding 6th-century oratories and beehive cells vary in size; the largest cell has a floor space of 4.5m by 3.6m. You can see the monks' south-facing vegetable garden and their cistern for collecting rainwater. The most impressive structural achievements are the settlement's foundations – platforms built on the steep slope using nothing more than earth and drystone walls.

Influenced by the Coptic Church (founded by St Anthony in the deserts of Egypt and Libya), the monks' determined quest for ultimate solitude led them to this remote, windblown edge of Europe. Not much is known about the life of the monastery, but there are records of Viking raids in AD 812 and 823. Monks were kidnapped or killed, but the community recovered and carried on. In the 11th century a rectangular oratory was added to the site, but although it was expanded in the 12th century, the monks abandoned the rock around this time.

After the introduction of the Gregorian calendar in 1582, Skellig Michael became a popular spot for weddings. Marriages were forbidden during Lent, but since Skellig used the old Julian calendar, a trip to the islands allowed those unable to wait for Easter to tie the knot. In the 1820s two lighthouses were built on the island, together with the road that runs around the base.

Skellig Michael famously featured as Luke Skywalker's Jedi temple in *Star Wars: The Force Awakens* (2015) and *Star Wars: The Last Jedi* (2017), attracting a whole new audience to the island's dramatic beauty.

Portmagee

POP 123

Portmagee's much-photographed single street is a rainbow of colourful houses. On summer mornings, the small harbour comes to life with boats embarking on the choppy crossing to the Skellig Islands (p278). From the village, a bridge leads to Valentia Island (p276).

Moorings INN €€
(☑066-947 7108; www.moorings.ie; s/d/tr from €70/110/140; 🛜) The Moorings is a friendly local hotel, bar and restaurant (p279). It has 16 rooms, split between modern seaview choices and simpler options, most refreshingly white. Cots and pull-out sofas are available for kids.

Skellig Ring House HOSTEL €
(☑066-948 0018; www.skelligringhouse.com; d with shared/private bathroom €48/60; 🅿🛜) Formerly known as Portmagee Hostel, Skellig Ring House is a sociable, no-frills place that makes a good base for walking. Rooms come with or without private bathrooms; there are no dorms. It's 350m southwest of the village.

The same team runs Ballinskelligs' hostel **Skellig Lodge** (☑066-947 9942; www.skelliglodge.com; Ballinskelligs; s/d/f with shared bathroom from €40/48/65, d with private bathroom from €60; 🅿🛜).

Bridge Bar BAR
(☑066-947 7108; www.moorings.ie; ⏰11am-11.30pm Mon-Sat, noon-11pm Sun) The focus of Portmagee's village life is the raspberry-coloured Bridge Bar, a local gathering point that hosts traditional Irish music and set dancing sessions every Friday and Sunday

There are no toilets on the island.

Small Skellig is long, low and craggy: from a distance it looks as if someone battered it with a feather pillow that burst. Close up you realise you're looking at a colony of over 23,000 pairs of breeding gannets, the second-largest breeding colony in the world. Most boats circle the island so you can see the gannets and you may see basking seals as well. Small Skellig is a bird sanctuary; no landing is permitted.

Getting to the Skellig Islands

Boat trips to the Skelligs usually run from May to September, weather permitting (there are no sailings on two days out of seven, on average). You can depart from Portmagee, Ballinskelligs or Caherdaniel. There is a limit on the number of daily visitors, with boats licensed to carry no more than 12 passengers each, so it's wise to book ahead; the cost is around €75 per person. Check to make sure operators have a current licence; the OPW (Office of Public Works; www.opw.ie) can provide advice.

Boats leave in the morning and return at 3pm, and give you around two hours on the rock, which is the bare minimum to visit the monastery, look at the birds and have a picnic. The crossing takes about 1½ hours from Portmagee, 35 minutes to one hour from Ballinskelligs and 1¾ hours from Caherdaniel.

If you just want to see the islands up close and avoid actually having to clamber out of the boat, consider a 'no landing' cruise with operators such as **Skellig Experience** (p120) on Valentia Island.

The Skellig Experience heritage centre (p120), local pubs and B&Bs will point you in the direction of boat operators, including the following:

Skelligs Rock (☑ 087 236 2344; www.skelligsrock.com; Skellig tour €75; ⊘ Skellig tour 9am mid-May–Sep) Based in Portmagee; also runs a non-landing wildlife-watching eco-cruise.

Force Awakens (☑ 087 238 5610; Ballinskelligs Pier; Skellig tour €75; ⊘ by appointment) *Star Wars*–themed tours; based in Ballinskelligs.

John O'Shea (☑ 087 689 8431; skelligtours@gmail.com; Derrynane Bay, Caherdaniel; Skellig tour €75; ⊘ 10am mid-May–Sep) Based in Derrynane Bay, Caherdaniel.

year-round; plus Tuesdays in July and August. Excellent fish and chips and a Cashel blue-cheese burger are among the standouts of its bar menu (kitchen open noon to 9pm; mains €10 to €24).

Its adjacent **Moorings Restaurant** (mains €22-26; ⊘ 6-10pm Tue-Sun Mar-Oct; 🚸) is a seafood specialist.

Skellig Ring

Branching off the Ring of Kerry, this little-travelled 18km route links Portmagee, Valentia Island and Waterville via a Gaeltacht (Irish-speaking) area centred on Ballinskelligs (Baile an Sceilg).

The area is wild and beautiful, with the ragged outline of Skellig Michael never far from view. This dramatic island housed a remote monastery between the 6th and 12th centuries and is now an important site for puffins, gannets and guillemots. Its starring role as a location in *Star Wars: The Force Awakens* and *Star Wars: The Last Jedi* means it hogs the limelight, but elsewhere on the Skellig Ring you'll find historic resorts, colourful houses, walking trails and a history that takes in ancient vertebrates and the transatlantic telegraph.

There's a good Blue Flag beach at Ballinskelligs; 7km northwest, St Finian's Bay is good for surfing. Ballinskelligs-based **Skelligs Watersports** (☑ 086 389 4849; www.skelligsurf.com; Ballinskelligs Beach; ⊘ 10am-6pm mid-May–Sep) rents equipment.

Tours to and angling trips around Skellig Michael can be booked with Force Awakens.

STAR WARS SIGHTS

Star Wars aficionados will want to make a pilgrimage to the dizzyingly steep, starkly beautiful monastic island of Skellig Michael (p278), which made its dramatic big-screen debut in 2015's *Star Wars: The Force Awakens,* and reprised its role as Luke Skywalker's Jedi temple in 2017's *Star Wars: The Last Jedi* (superfans can even travel to the island with a new boat-tour company, the **Force Awakens** (p278)).

Other *Star Wars* filming locations in Kerry include Sybil Head (Ceann Sibeal) on the Dingle Peninsula, 4.5km northwest of Ballyferriter. Elsewhere in Ireland, shooting took place in the area around **Loop Head Lighthouse** (p337), 26km southwest of Kilkee, County Clare; Brow Head, 3km southwest of Crookhaven, County Cork; and Hell's Hole, a plunging, fissured chasm on the Inishowen Peninsula, 6km northwest of Malin Head, County Donegal.

Throughout the ring, dining options are limited to a handful of pubs and cafes, including one at the ring's state-of-the-art chocolate factory, **Skelligs Chocolate** (☑ 066-947 9119; www.skelligschocolate.com; St Finian's Bay; ⊙ 10am-5pm Mon-Fri, 11am-5pm Sat & Sun Jul & Aug, 10am-5pm Mon-Fri, noon-5pm Sat & Sun Apr-Jun & Sep, 10am-4.30pm Mon-Fri Nov–mid-Dec) **FREE**. There are no supermarkets; Cahersiveen is your best bet to stock up.

Waterville

POP 538

Waterville is an old-fashioned seaside resort strung along the N72 at the head of Ballinskelligs Bay, and is known for its golf and fishing. The Waterville Golf Links is renowned, and construction of a second world-class course at the opposite end of town is underway. To Waterville's south, the headlands Hogs Head Golf Course, designed by Robert Trent Jones II, will open in 2018.

Silent movie star Charlie Chaplin famously holidayed in Waterville in the 1960s with his extended family, returning every year for more than a decade to the Butler Arms Hotel. A bronze statue of Chaplin beams out from the seafront, and the Charlie Chaplin Comedy Film Festival is held here in late August.

Nearby Lough Currane is famed for the quality of its sea trout fishing, particularly from May to July. No permit is required, but you'll need a state rod licence (visit www.fishinginireland.info) and a rental boat (€55 a day, or €140 with a *ghillie* (fishing or hunting guide) such as Vincent Appleby at **Salmon & Sea Trout Fishing** (☑ 087 207 4882; www.salmonandseatrout.com; fishing per day €140; ⊙ by appointment).

★ **Waterville Golf Links**　GOLF
(☑ 066-947 4102; www.watervillegolflinks.ie; green fees €75-220) Tiger Woods, Mark O'Meara and Payne Stewart are just some of the golfing greats who have teed off at the par 72 Waterville Golf Links. One of Ireland's most magnificently sited courses, with sweeping bay and mountain views, it was designed by Eddie Hackett together with Jack Mulcahy and Claude Harmon.

Charlie Chaplin Comedy Film Festival　FILM
(http://chaplinfilmfestival.com; ⊙ late Aug) Over days four days in late August, the Charlie Chaplin Comedy Film Festival features screenings, workshops, street entertainment, a lookalike contest and a parade.

🛏 Sleeping & Eating

Brookhaven House　B&B €€
(☑ 066-947 4431; www.brookhavenhouse.com; New Line Rd; d €80-120; 🅿🛜) The pick of Waterville's B&Bs is the contemporary Brookhaven House, run by a friendly family. Spick-and-span rooms overlooking either Waterville Golf Links or Ballinskelligs Bay have comfy beds; there's a sunny sea-view breakfast room.

★ **Smuggler's Inn**　MODERN IRISH €€
(☑ 066-947 4330; www.the-smugglers-inn.com; Cliff Rd; d €95-150; ⊙ Apr-Oct; 🛜) At this diamond find near Waterville Golf Links, owner and chef Henry Hunt's gourmet creations incorporate fresh seafood and locally farmed poultry and meat, followed by artistic desserts (including homemade ice cream), served in a glass atrium dining room. Half-board deals are available at the inn's upstairs rooms (doubles from €90); cooked-to-order breakfasts include a catch of the day.

If you're staying overnight, try for room 15, with a glassed-in balcony overlooking Ballinskelligs Bay.

Dooley's Seafood & Steakhouse   STEAK €€
(☑ 066-947 8766; www.dooleyswaterville.com; N70; mains €18-29; ☺ 6-9.30pm) Snazzy Dooley's serves what its name states: 21-day dry-aged steaks are a speciality here. It's on the northwestern edge of the village.

Caherdaniel

POP 76

The road between Waterville and Caherdaniel climbs high over the ridge of Beenarourke, providing grandstand views of some of the finest scenery on the Ring of Kerry. The panorama extends from the scattered islands of Scarriff and Deenish to Dursey and the hills of the Beara peninsula.

Caherdaniel, a tiny hamlet hidden among the trees at the head of Derrynane Bay, is the ancestral home of Daniel O'Connell, 'the Liberator', whose family made money smuggling from their base by the dunes. The area has a Blue Flag beach, good hikes and activities including horse riding and water sports. Lines of wind-gnarled trees add to the wild air.

◉ Sights & Activities

★ Derrynane National Historic Park   HISTORIC SITE
(☑ 066-947 5113; www.heritageireland.ie; Derrynane; adult/child €5/3; ☺ 10.30am-5.15pm mid-Mar–Sep, 10am-5pm Wed-Sun Nov–mid-Dec) Derrynane House was the home of Maurice 'Hunting Cap' O'Connell, a notorious local smuggler who grew rich on trade with France and Spain. He was the uncle of Daniel O'Connell, the 19th-century campaigner for Catholic emancipation, who grew up here in his uncle's care and inherited the property in 1825, when it became his private retreat. The house is furnished with O'Connell memorabilia, including the impressive triumphal chariot in which he lapped Dublin after his release from prison in 1844.

Other items on display include O'Connell's ornately sculpted oak chair from his time as Lord Mayor of Dublin (look for the gold collars and ruby eyes of the carved Irish wolfhounds), the duelling pistols with which he killed a man in 1815, and the iron bed in which he died during a pilgrimage to Rome in 1847.

The **gardens**, warmed by the Gulf Stream, nurture subtropical species including 4m-high tree ferns, gunnera ('giant rhubarb') and other South American plants. A network of walking trails leads through the woods towards the beach; kids can pick up a copy of the **Derrynane Fairy Trail** (www.irishfairytrails.com) at the cafe and track down two dozen 'fairy houses' hidden among the trees.

Derrynane Beach   BEACH
Derrynane's Blue Flag beach is one of the most beautiful in Kerry, with scalloped coves of golden sand set between grassy dunes and whaleback outcrops of wave-smoothed rock. From the car park at Derrynane House, you can walk 1km along the beach to explore **Abbey Island** and its picturesque cemetery – look inside the ruined chapel to find the tomb of Daniel O'Connell's wife, Mary.

Derrynane Sea Sports   WATER SPORTS
(☑ 087 908 1208; www.derrynaneseasports.com; Derrynane Beach) Derrynane Sea Sports offers sailing, windsurfing and waterskiing lessons for all levels (from €40 per person). Equipment hire (€8 to €18 per hour) spans stand-up paddleboards, surfboards, windsurfers, canoes, small sailboats and snorkelling gear. Snorkelling tours (€40 per person) last two hours. In July and August ask about fun half-day pirate camps for children (€95).

Eagle Rock Equestrian Centre   HORSE RIDING
(☑ 066-947 5145; www.eaglerockcentre.com; Ballycarnahan; horse riding per hour €35) Guided horseback treks take you along Derrynane Beach and through the woods of Derrynane National Historic Park.

⏴ Sleeping & Eating

Wave Crest   CAMPGROUND €
(☑ 066-947 5188; www.wavecrestcamping.com; hiker €9, vehicle & 2 adults €29; ℗ @ 🛜) Just 1.6km southeast of Caherdaniel, this year-round campground has a superb setting right on the rocky waterfront with front-row sunset views. From June to August, there's an on-site cafe and an attached shop selling fishing supplies, beach equipment, basic food supplies and wine. Book ahead during high season.

Travellers' Rest Hostel   HOSTEL €
(☑ 066-947 5175; www.hostelcaherdaniel.com; dm/d from €18.50/43; ☺ mid-Feb–Oct) All low ceilings, gingham curtains and dried flowers

in the grate, Travellers' Rest has the quaint feel of a country cottage, with an open fire and a self-catering kitchen (breakfast isn't included; bring supplies as there are no supermarkets nearby). Shower early: there are just two shared bathrooms. Call at the petrol station opposite if there's nobody about.

Olde Forge
B&B €€

(☑066-947 5140; www.theoldeforge.com; s/d/tr/f from €55/75/110/120; P🛜) Fantastic views of Kenmare Bay and the Beara Peninsula unfold from this ivy-covered B&B, both from the garden terrace out the front and from most of the spacious and comfortable bedrooms. Family rooms sleep two adults and two children. It's 1.2km southeast of Caherdaniel on the N70.

Blind Piper
PUB FOOD €€

(☑066-947 5126; www.blindpiperpub.com; mains €11-22; ⊙kitchen noon-4pm Mon-Thu, to 8pm Fri-Sun, bar noon-midnight daily; 🎮) This local institution is a great family pub with a lovely beer garden set beside the tiny Coomnahorna River, serving quality pub fare like deep-fried monkfish and ribeye steak. On Thursday evenings from 9.30pm and most weekends from June to August, locals and visitors crowd inside, and music sessions strike up.

Sneem
POP 288

From Castlecove to Kenmare the main N70 Ring of Kerry road swings inland, and coastal panoramas are replaced with distant views of MacGillicuddy's Reeks.

The main village here is Sneem (An tSnaidhm). Its Irish name translates as 'the knot', which is thought to refer to the River Sneem that swirls, knot-like, into nearby Kenmare Bay. The river splits the village in two, with separate village squares on either side and a picturesque waterfall tumbling below the old stone bridge.

There are no real sights, but it's a popular place for Ring of Kerry tour buses to pause so passengers can stretch their legs before the road dives into the woods for the 27km stretch to Kenmare.

Sneem has a couple of cafes and pubs. From June to September, a weekly **farmers market** (Bridge St; ⊙11am-4pm Tue; 🖉) sets up in the centre.

The **tourist office** (☑064-667 5807; South Sq; ⊙11.30am-5.30pm May-Sep) is in the Joli Coeur craft shop.

Sleeping & Eating

★ Parknasilla Resort & Spa
HOTEL €€€

(☑064-667 5600; www.parknasillaresort.com; Parknasilla; d/f/ste from €155/262/325; P@🛜🏊) On the tree-fringed shores of the Kenmare River with views to the Beara Peninsula, this hotel has been wowing guests (including George Bernard Shaw) since 1895. From the modern, luxuriously appointed bedrooms to the top-grade spa, private 12-hole golf course, elegant restaurant and supervised kids' play area, everything here is done just right. It's 3km southeast of Sneem.

If you can't tear yourself away, it also rents two-bedroom villas by the week (from €1015).

Village Kitchen
IRISH €

(☑064-664 5281; 3 Bridge St; mains €7-12.50; ⊙10am-9pm Jun-Aug, 10am-6pm Mon-Sat Sep-May; 🛜🎮) Near the bridge, this family-run restaurant has been dishing up breakfast, lunch and dinner to locals and visitors alike for decades. The menu runs from seafood chowder and fish specials to steak sandwiches and Irish stew.

Kenmare
POP 2376

Kenmare (pronounced 'ken-*mair*') is the thinking person's Killarney. Ideally positioned for exploring the Ring of Kerry (and the Beara Peninsula), but without the coach-tour crowds of its more famous neighbour, Kenmare (Neidín, meaning 'little nest' in Irish) is a pretty spot with a neat triangle of streets lined with craft shops, galleries, cafes and good-quality restaurants.

One of the few planned towns in Ireland, Kenmare was laid out on an X-shaped street plan in the late 18th century by the marquis of Lansdowne as the showpiece of his Kerry estates. It earned its living as a market town and fishing port, and from iron works, lead mining and quarrying. The Market House and the Lansdowne Arms Hotel still survive from this period – pick up a copy of the *Kenmare Heritage Trail* from the tourist office (p285) to discover more.

Sights & Activities

Walking opportunities abound. The tourist office has details of walks around Kenmare Bay and into the hills, on sections of the Kerry Way and Beara Way. Kenmare Bookshop (p285) is a great resource with plenty of walking guides, maps and advice.

Cycling is also popular; **Finnegan's Cycle Centre** (☑ 064-664 1083; www.finnegans cycles.com; 37 Henry St; road bikes per day/week from €15/85, electric bikes from €30/185; ⊘ 10am-6pm Mon-Fri, 10am-6.30pm Sat, 2-5.30pm Sun) rents out wheels.

Kenmare Heritage Centre　　MUSEUM
(☑ 064-664 1233; The Square; ⊘ 10am-5.30pm Mon-Sat Apr-Oct, by appointment Nov-Mar) FREE Kenmare's old courthouse is home to an exhibition telling the history of the town from its origins as Neidín, through its establishment as a market town by the Marquis of Lansdowne to the founding of the Poor Clare Convent in 1861, which still stands behind Holy Cross Church. Local women were taught needlepoint lace-making at the convent and their lacework garnered international fame; the upstairs **Kenmare Lace and Design Centre**, which keeps the same hours, has displays.

They include designs for 'the most important piece of lace ever made in Ireland' (in a 19th-century critic's opinion).

Holy Cross Church　　CHURCH
(Old Killarney Rd; ⊘ 8am-8pm Easter–mid-Oct, shorter hours mid-Oct–Easter) Begun 1862 and consecrated in 1864, this church has a splendid wooden roof with 14 angel carvings. Intricate mosaics adorn the aisle arches and the edges of the stained-glass window over the altar. The architect was Charles Hansom, collaborator and brother-in-law of Augustus Pugin (the architect behind London's Houses of Parliament).

Installing the rooster atop the spire allowed Hansom to 'crow' over the landlord who had refused him permission to build in the Square.

Seafari　　BOATING
(☑ 064-664 2059; Kenmare Pier; adult/child €25/12.50; ⊘ Apr-Oct) Warm up with complimentary tea, coffee and rum – and the captain's sea shanties – on an entertaining two-hour cruise to see Ireland's biggest seal colony and other wildlife, including white-tailed eagles. Binoculars (and lollipops!) are provided. Cash only.

Star Sailing　　WATER SPORTS
(☑ 064-664 1222; www.staroutdoors.ie; R571, Dauros) Along with one-hour sightseeing cruises (€18/10 per adult/child) on Kenmare River, Star Sailing offers activities including sea kayaking (€20/36 single/double per hour) and water-skiing (€60 per 15 minutes). Its base is 6.5km southwest of Kenmare.

Dromquinna Stables　　HORSE RIDING
(☑ 064-664 1043; www.dromquinna-stables.com; Sneem Rd; ⊘ mid-Mar–mid-Oct) One-hour (€25) and 90-minute (€40) treks and five-hour expeditions (€125) follow trails up into the hills and along Kenmare Bay's beaches with views over the Beara and Iveragh peninsulas from this stable, which has been in the same family for generations.

It also offers lessons (30/60 minutes €15/25) and a Saturday pony club for kids (2½ hours €20), where they can discover horse grooming, tacking and riding.

⭐ Festivals & Events

Kenmare Fair　　CULTURAL
(⊘ mid-Aug) Dating back more than two centuries, the Kenmare Fair takes place on 15 August every year, when folk from all over Ireland descend on the town to trade in sheep, cattle and ponies, as well as crafts, bric-a-brac and artisan foods.

🛏 Sleeping

Kenmare Fáilte Hostel　　HOSTEL €
(☑ 087 711 6092; http://kenmarehostel.com; Shelbourne St; dm/d/tr/q with shared bathroom €18/44/60/76, d/tr/q with private bathroom €52/69/88; ⊘ mid-May–mid-Oct; 🐾) Perfectly located, this modern hostel is fitted out with quality furnishings and equipment – there's even an Aga cooker in the kitchen – a pleasant change from the utilitarianism of most budget accommodation. Wi-fi's available in common areas only, however, and there's a 1.30am curfew.

Whispering Pines　　B&B €€
(☑ 064-664 1194; http://whisperingpineskenmare. com; Shelbourne St; d from €80; ⊘ Easter-Nov; P🐾) Set back from the main road just south of the town centre, this flower-fronted B&B has four immaculate rooms, all with private bathrooms, and a warm Irish welcome. Tea and biscuits greet you on arrival, and home baking graces the breakfast table.

★ Park Hotel　　HERITAGE HOTEL €€€
(☑ 064-664 1200; www.parkkenmare.com; Shelbourne St; d/ste from €220/405; P🐾🏊) Overlooking Kenmare Bay, this 1897 Victorian mansion has every conceivable luxury: an indoor swimming pool, heavenly spa, tennis and croquet courts and even its own cinema. Antiques and original art fill its 46 rooms and suites, which have goose down duvets and pillows. Those in the deluxe category

face the water, while superior rooms and suites have balconies and patios.

Local produce is used at its restaurant, which serves lunch, high tea and dinner (three-course menu €70). Adjoining rooms and cots are available for families, who are welcomed with open arms.

Brook Lane Hotel　　BOUTIQUE HOTEL €€€
(☑064-664 2077; www.brooklanehotel.com; Sneem Rd; s/d/f from €120/170/210; P🐾) Chic rooms warmed by underfloor heating are individually decorated with bespoke furniture and luxurious fabrics at this contemporary olive-green property on the northwestern edge of town, while public areas mix vintage and designer pieces. Run by the same owners as Kenmare's superb restaurant No 35 (p284), its adjoining stone-and-brick gastropub, Casey's, is first-rate. It's a 750m stroll from the centre.

Sheen Falls Lodge　　HISTORIC HOTEL €€€
(☑064-664 1600; www.sheenfallslodge.ie; Knockduragh; d/ste from €280/310, 2-bedroom villa from €650; ⊘Feb-Dec; P@🐾) The Marquis of Landsdowne's former summer residence still feels like an aristocrats' playground, with a fine-dining modern Irish restaurant, cocktail bar, spa, and 66 rooms and sumptuous suites with Italian marble bathrooms, all in a glorious setting beside a waterfall on the River Sheen with views across Kenmare Bay to Carrantuohil. Amenities are many – salmon fishing or clay-pigeon shooting, anyone?

Its cellar has over 10,000 different wines from 18 different countries.

✖ Eating

Farmers Market　　MARKET €
(The Square; ⊘10am-4pm Wed) 🐾 Stalls on the town square sell vegetables, cheese, honey, gourmet ice cream, bread, smoked salmon and other artisan produce during Kenmare's weekly farmers market.

★Boathouse Bistro　　BISTRO €€
(☑064-664 2889; www.dromquinnamanor.com; Dromquinna Manor, Sneem Rd; mains €15-32; ⊘12.30-9pm) At the water's edge, this 1870s boathouse 4.5km west of Kenmare has been stunningly converted to a beach-house-style blue-and-white bistro specialising in local seafood delivered daily to its own wharf. Expertly cooked dishes (sautéed Kenmare Bay crab claws in garlic butter, grilled Beara scallops with Sneem black pudding) are

accompanied by 33 by-the-glass wines and 28 different gins.

The boathouse is on the rambling estate of 19th-century Dromquinna Manor, which currently hosts weddings but is set to open its accommodation to the public.

★Tom Crean Fish & Wine　　IRISH €€
(☑064-664 1589; http://tomcrean.ie; Main St; mains €14.50-28; ⊘5-9.30pm Wed-Mon Sep-Jun, daily Jul & Aug; 🐾) 🐾 Named for Kerry's pioneering Antarctic explorer, and run by his granddaughter, this venerable restaurant uses only the best of local organic produce, cheeses and fresh seafood. Sneem lobster is available in season, the oysters *au naturel* capture the scent of the sea, and the seafood gratin served in a scallop shell is divine.

Upstairs, the 19th-century townhouse has boutique rooms with king-size beds (doubles from €75).

No 35　　MODERN IRISH €€
(☑064-664 1559; http://no35kenmare.com; 35 Main St; mains lunch €9.50-13, dinner €16-28, 3-course dinner menu €30; ⊘12.30-4.30pm & 5-9.30pm) Hand-cut limestone walls, exposed timber beams, stained-glass windows and an open fire set the stage for some of Kenmare's most creative cuisine. All-Irish produce features in dishes like slow-cooked rare saddleback pigs from its own farm with salt-baked turnips and sea bass with Cromane mussel crème. Some great Irish craft beers and ciders are served alongside a well-chosen wine list.

Mews　　MODERN IRISH €€
(☑064-664 2829; http://themewskenmare.com; 3-4 Henry Ct; mains €18-30; ⊘6-9pm Tue-Fri, 5.30-9pm Sat) Chef Gary Fitzgerald and front-of-house manager Maria O'Sullivan have garnered acclaim at some of County Kerry's top restaurants and now helm this stylish, palm-filled spot hidden in a laneway off Henry St. Vermouth cream chowder with truffle oil, Kerry beef fillet with a parsnip rösti and pear-and-almond crumble with homemade peanut brittle ice cream are among the menu highlights.

Mulcahy's　　BISTRO €€€
(☑064-664 2383; http://mulcahyskenmare.ie; 8 Main St; mains €20.50-29; ⊘6-10pm Tue-Sun) Candlelight and high-backed leather chairs create an intimate atmosphere in Kenmare's best-known restaurant, where chef Bruce Mulcahy weaves his culinary magic

with Asian- or Mediterranean-inspired twists on local seafood, such as salmon, prawn and cod sushi and sashimi, or Kerry lamb with a cep-and-pistachio crust.

🔒 Shopping

Kenmare has many quality craft shops and art galleries – the *Kenmare Art Spots* leaflet, available from the tourist office (and the galleries themselves) lists half a dozen.

Soundz of Muzic MUSICAL INSTRUMENTS
(www.soundzofmuzic.ie; 9 Henry St; ⊙10am-6pm) Traditional instruments (accordions, harmonicas, banjos, tin whistles and more) are stocked alongside modern ones (including electric fiddles) at this decades-old shop. It also sells sheet music, CDs and vinyl, and DVDs of live performances.

Kenmare Bookshop BOOKS
(Shelbourne St; ⊙11am-5.30pm Mon-Fri, 10am-6pm Sat, 1-5.30pm Sun) Irish interest and literature, best sellers and kids' books are stocked at this independent shop, but it really comes into its own for its marine charts, maps and local walking guides.

ℹ️ Information

Kenmare's seasonal **tourist office** (☎ 064-664 1233; The Square; ⊙10am-5.30pm Mon-Sat Mar-Oct) has stacks of information about the town, its surrounds and the Ring of Kerry.

ℹ️ Getting There & Away

Bus Éireann (www.buseireann.ie) serves Killarney (€12.40, 45 minutes, three daily) and Sneem (€9.70, 35 minutes, one daily) year-round, and runs a daily Ring of Kerry loop service (p270) from late June to late August.

The summer-only bus service 282 runs from Glengarriff to Kenmare (€12.40, 45 minutes, one daily Monday to Saturday July and August). **Finnegan's Coach & Cab** (☎ 064-664 1491; www.kenmarecoachandcab.com) runs a variety of Ring of Kerry tours and taxi services.

DINGLE PENINSULA

One of the highlights of the Wild Atlantic Way, the Dingle Peninsula (Corca Dhuibhne) culminates in the Irish mainland's westernmost point. In the shadow of sacred Mt Brandon, a maze of fuchsia-fringed *boreens* (country lanes) weaves together an ancient landscape of prehistoric ring forts and beehive huts, early Christian chapels, crosses and holy wells, picturesque hamlets and abandoned villages.

But it's where the land meets the ocean – whether in a welter of wave-pounded rocks, or where the surf laps secluded, sandy coves – that Dingle's beauty truly reveals itself.

Centred on charming Dingle town, the peninsula has long been a beacon for those of an alternative bent, attracting artists, craftspeople, musicians and idiosyncratic characters who can be found in workshops, museums, festivals and unforgettable trad sessions throughout Dingle's tiny settlements.

👉 Tours

Killarney-based tour operators including Corcoran's (p260), Deros Tours (p260) and **Wild Kerry Day Tours** (☎ 064-663 1052; www.wildkerry-daytours.ie; Ross Rd) offer day trips to the Dingle Peninsula. Walking and cycling tours are possible with **Go Visit Ireland** (☎ 066-976 2094; www.govisitireland.com).

Inch Strand & Annascaul

Inch Strand is a 5km-long sand spit and dune system extending into Dingle Bay. This stupendous beach has attracted film directors as well as surfers, land-yachters and anglers – it has appeared in the movies *Ryan's Daughter* (1970), *Excalibur* (1981) and *Far and Away* (1992), among others.

The dunes are scattered with the remains of shipwrecks and Stone Age and Iron Age settlements. The west-facing beach is also a hot surfing spot; waves average 1m to 3m. **Offshore Surf School** (☎ 087 294 6519; http://offshoresurfschool.ie; lessons adult/child per 2hr from €25/20, board/wetsuit hire per 2hr €20/15; ⊙9am-6pm Apr–mid-Oct) offers a range of surf lessons, including a two-hour group class, and also rents gear. Check the swells ahead on Sammy's surf cam.

Cars are allowed on the beach, but don't end up providing others with nonstop laughs by getting stuck.

Between April and October only, Go Coach (http://gocoach.ie) links Inch Beach with Dingle town (€8, 30 minutes) and Killarney (€8, 50 minutes) three times daily.

🍴 Eating & Drinking

Sammy's CAFE €
(☎ 066-915 8118; www.sammysinchbeach.com; dishes €4-9, mains €10-20; ⊙9.30am-10pm Easter-Sep, reduced hours Oct-Easter; 🐕🅿️) Sammy's, at the entrance to the beach, is the

Dingle Peninsula

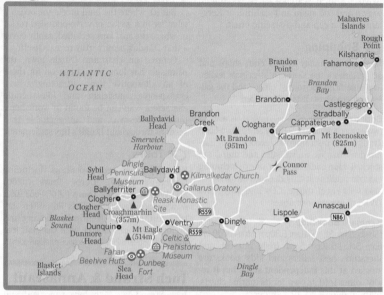

nerve centre of the area. The beach-facing bar-restaurant serves a vast range of dishes from sandwiches to burgers, fish and chips, and steak. Fish fingers are among the favourites on the kids' menu. There's a shop selling ice creams and souvenirs, and trad sessions during the summer.

South Pole Inn PUB
(☑ 066-915 7388; Main St; ◯ noon-11.30pm Mon-Thu, to 12.30am Fri & Sat, to 11pm Sun) Antarctic explorer Tom Crean ran this sky-blue inn in his retirement. Now it's a regular Crean museum and gift shop, as well as a cracking pub serving Dingle-brewed Crean's lager and explorer-worthy dishes (mains €10.50 to €16; food served to 9pm) such as an Endurance Burger. It's in the residential village of Annascaul, 16km east of Dingle town.

Dingle Town

POP 1440

Framed by its fishing port, the peninsula's charming little 'capital' manages to be quaint without even trying. Some pubs double as shops, so you can enjoy Guinness and a singalong among screws and nails, wellies and horseshoes. It has long drawn runaways

from across the world, making it a cosmopolitan, creative place. In summer its hilly streets can be clogged with visitors; in other seasons its authentic charms are yours for the savouring.

Although Dingle is one of Ireland's largest Gaeltacht towns, the locals have voted to retain the name Dingle rather than go by the officially sanctioned – and signposted – Gaelige name of An Daingean.

◉ Sights

Dingle is one of those towns whose very fabric is its main attraction. Wander up and down the streets and back alleys, stroll along the pier, and pop into shops, pubs, and art and craft galleries and see what you find.

Dingle Oceanworld AQUARIUM
(☑ 066-915 2111; www.dingle-oceanworld.ie; The Wood; adult/child €13.50/8.75; ◯ 10am-7pm Jul & Aug, to 6pm Sep-Jun) Dingle's aquarium is a lot of fun, and includes a walk-through tunnel and a touch pool. Psychedelic fish glide through tanks that re-create such environments as Lake Malawi, the River Congo and the piranha-filled Amazon. Reef sharks and stingrays cruise the shark tank; water is pumped from the harbour for the spectacularly ugly wreck fish.

Dingle Distillery
DISTILLERY

(☑066-402 9011; www.dingledistillery.ie; Ventry Rd; tour €10; ⊙ by reservation) An offshoot of Dublin's Porterhouse microbrewery, this craft distillery began producing whiskey in 2012; but the necessary ageing process meant that the first fruits of its labours were not bottled until 2016. It also produces artisan gin and vodka.

Dingle Brewing Company
BREWERY

(☑066-915 0743; http://dinglebrewingcompany.com; Spa Rd; self-guided tour €6; ⊙ by reservation) Housed in a 19th-century creamery building, this terrific craft brewery launched in 2011 on 20 July – not coincidentally Tom Crean's birthday (its single brew, a crisp, hoppy lager, is named after the local Antarctic explorer). Admission includes a self-guided brewery tour followed by a pint. It's on the road towards the Connor Pass.

An Díseart
CULTURAL CENTRE

(☑066-915 2476; www.diseart.ie; Green St; ⊙9-5pm Mon-Sat) **FREE** Set in a neo-Gothic former convent, this Celtic cultural centre has impressive stained-glass windows by Dublin artist Harry Clarke (1889–1931) depicting 12 scenes from the life of Christ.

🏃 Activities

Naomhòg Experience
BOATING

(☑087 699 2925; http://dinglerowing.com; Dingle Marina; lessons €25) *Naomhòg* is the Kerry name for a currach, a traditional Irish boat made from a wooden frame covered with tarred canvas (originally animal hides). They were used by the Blasket islanders for fishing, and are now maintained and raced by local enthusiasts. You can book a one-hour session in Dingle Harbour (minimum two people) to learn how to row one.

It also runs harbour tours and sunset cruises (€25 per person per hour), also for a minimum of two people.

Dingle Marina Dive Centre
DIVING

(DMDC; ☑087 911 1643; www.divedingle.com; Dingle Marina; 1/2 dives incl gear from €60/90; ⊙May-Sep) During dives around Dingle Bay, you're likely to spot Fungie the dolphin along with conga eels, spider crabs, octopuses, sponges, anemones and basking sharks. Seals are also common on dives around the Blasket Islands (p295) (€120), where three wrecks are located. The company also offers night dives by arrangement, along with PADI accreditation courses (from €399) and half-day snorkelling trips (€40).

Dolphin Trips
CRUISE

(☑066-915 2626; www.dingledolphin.com; The Pier; adult/child €16/8) Boats run by the Dingle Boatmen's Association cooperative leave the pier daily for one-hour trips to see Dingle's most famous resident, Fungie the dolphin. It's free if Fungie doesn't show, but he usually does. The ticket office is next to the tourist office.

Dingle Surf
SURFING

(☑066-915 0833; https://dinglesurf.com; Green St; lessons adult/child €30/25; ⊙ shop 10am-5pm Mon-Sat) Dingle Surf offers half-day surfing and stand-up paddleboarding lessons for beginners at Brandon Bay (on the north side of the peninsula; transport included), and sells gear including its own groovy range of surfwear.

Mountain Man Outdoor Shop
CYCLING

(☑066-915 2400; www.themountainmanshop.com; Strand St; bike rental per day €15) Mountain Man rents bikes and runs guided cycling tours (from €30) around the Dingle Peninsula, with themes ranging from archaeology to food.

Irish Adventures
ADVENTURE SPORTS

(☑087 419 0318; www.irishadventures.net) This outfit offers guided adventure trips including rock climbing on the local sea cliffs

Dingle Town

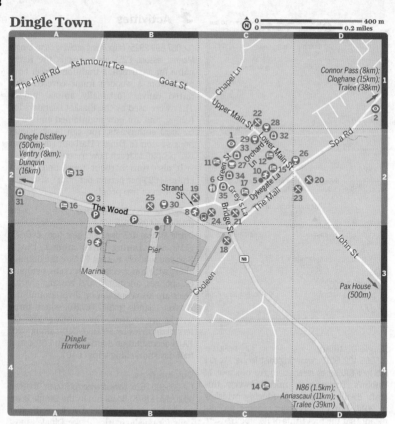

(half-/full-day €60/95 per person), and kayaking in Dingle Harbour with Fungie the dolphin (half-day or sunset trip €50 per person). It also runs mountain bike trips (half-/full-day €50/85) and horse riding treks (half-/full-day €95/135). Most trips depart from the pier.

Dingle Music School   MUSIC
(☑ 086 319 0438; www.dinglemusicschool.com; Wren's Nest Cafe, Dykegate Lane; lessons per hour €30) John Ryan offers bodhrán and tin whistle workshops for beginners through to experienced players – lessons can be arranged for early morning or evening. Instruments are supplied.

Festivals & Events

Dingle Food & Wine Festival   FOOD & DRINK
(www.dinglefood.com; ⊘ early Oct) Held over four days, this fabulous foodie fest features a 'taste trail' with sampling at over 80 locations around town, plus a market, cooking

demonstrations, workshops and a foraging walk. There are also beer, cider and wine tastings, a bake-off competition and street entertainment, as well as children's events.

Dingle Races   SPORTS
(www.dingleraces.ie; N86, Ballintaggart; ⊘ mid-Aug) Held over the second weekend in August, Dingle's horseracing meet brings crowds from far and wide. The racetrack is 2km southeast of the centre.

Dingle Regatta   SPORTS
(http://dinglerowing.com; ⊘ mid-Aug) Crews of four race traditional Irish *naomhóg* (canoes) around the harbour. It's Kerry's largest event of its kind and inspired the trad song of the same name.

Sleeping

This tourist town has hostels, hotels and loads of midrange B&Bs. A number of pubs also offer accommodation.

Dingle Town

Grapevine Hostel HOSTEL €
(☑ 066-915 1434; www.grapevinedingle.com; Dykegate Lane; dm/d from €17/78; ☎) Near the centre of town, this dinky hostel has eight-, four- and two-bed rooms with wooden bunks and private bathrooms (with minimalist sliding doors). The TV-free, fire-lit lounge is a good spot for visiting musicians to get a singalong going. Book well ahead.

Hideout Hostel HOSTEL €
(☑ 066-915 0559; www.thehideouthostel.com; Dykegate Lane; dm/d from €21/60; ℗ @ ☎) Converted from a former guesthouse, this central hostel has inherited private bathrooms in all rooms. Top-notch facilities include two lounges, bike storage and a well-equipped kitchen. Rates include light breakfast (tea, coffee, toast and cereal). Switched-on owner Mícheál is a fount of local info.

★ Pax House B&B €€
(☑ 066-915 1518; www.pax-house.com; Upper John St; d €125-198; ⊙ mid-Feb–mid-Nov; ℗ ☎) From its highly individual decor (including contemporary paintings) to the outstanding views over the estuary from the glass-framed terrace and balconies opening from some rooms, Pax House is a treat. Breakfast incorporates produce grown in its own garden; families can be accommodated with fold-out beds. It's 1km southeast of the town centre.

An Capall Dubh B&B €€
(☑ 066-915 1105; www.ancapalldubh.com; Green St; d/tr/f from €100/140/180; ℗ ☎) Entered via a 19th-century coaching entrance leading into a cobbled courtyard where breakfast is served in fine weather, this airy B&B has five rooms furnished with light timbers and checked fabrics.

Dingle Harbour Lodge GUESTHOUSE €€
(☑ 066-915 1577; www.dingleharbourlodge.com; The Wood; s/d/tr €76/90/114; ℗ ☎) This purpose-built B&B complex with a timber-floored lobby filled with fresh flowers, neat rooms equipped with flat-screen TVs and ultra-efficient managers fills a niche for contemporary mid-range accommodation. Although just five minutes' walk from the centre, its position above the harbour means no street noise and good views from upper-level rooms.

Harbour Nights B&B €€
(☑ 066-915 2499; www.dinglebandb.com; The Wood; d €80-110; ℗ ☎) Half the rooms at this waterfront B&B have balconies with stunning views over Dingle Harbour, as does the upstairs sitting room, which opens to a terrace.

COUNTY KERRY DINGLE TOWN

FUNGIE THE DOLPHIN

In 1983 a bottlenose dolphin swam into Dingle Bay and local tourism hasn't been quite the same since. Showing an unusual affinity for human company, he swam around with the local fishing fleet. Eventually somebody got the idea of charging tourists to go out on boats to see the friendly dolphin (nick-named Fungie). Today up to 12 boats at a time and more than 1000 tourists a day ply the waters with Dingle's mascot, now a cornerstone of the local economy (there's even a bronze statue of him outside the tourist office).

In the wild, bottlenose dolphins live for an average of 25 years, though they have been know to live to over 40 in captivity. As Fungie has been around for well over 30 years (yes, it's still the same dolphin, recognisable by his distinctive markings), speculation is rife about how long it will be before he finally glides into the deep for the last time. And what will Dingle do without its dolphin?

Dingle Benner's Hotel   HOTEL €€€
(☎066-915 1638; www.dinglebenners.com; Main St; s/d/f from €165/209/230; P☎) A Dingle institution, melding old-world elegance, local charm and modern comforts in the quiet bedrooms, lounge, library, and (very popular) Mrs Benner's Bar. Family rooms sleep four. Rooms in the 300-year-old wing have the most character; those in the new parts are quieter and more spacious.

Dingle Skellig Hotel   HOTEL €€€
(☎066-915 0200; www.dingleskellig.com; s/d/ste from €165/250/300; P@☎☳) An ocean-like swimming pool and a spa with an outdoor hot tub are the highlights of this mini resort down near the water, just south of town. Rooms are decorated in rich chocolate-box-like cream, caramel and hazelnut tones. There are interconnecting rooms for families, plus a crèche and kids club, as well as a restaurant and several bars.

✖ Eating

In a county famed for its seafood, Dingle still stands out. There are some superb restaurants and cafes, as well as excellent pub fare.

Dingle's weekly **farmers market** (cnr Bridge St & Dykegate Lane; ☺9am-3pm Fri) ✐ takes place year-round.

★ Murphy's   ICE CREAM €
(www.murphysicecream.ie; Strand St; 1/2/3 scoops €4/5.50/7; ☺11am-9pm May-Oct, to 8pm Nov-Apr; ☎) Made here in Dingle, Murphy's sublime ice cream comes in a daily changing range of flavours that include brown bread, sea salt, Dingle gin, and whiskey-laced Irish coffee, along with sorbets made with rainwater. In addition to a second Dingle branch at the pier opposite the tourist office, its runaway success has seen it expand Ireland-wide.

Chowder   CAFE €€
(off Strand St; mains €11.50-14.50; ☺10am-9pm Jun-Aug, to 4pm Sep-May) Tucked off Strand St, this unpretentious, always-busy local favourite serves top-quality bistro food. In addition to the signature seafood chowder, lunch specials such as homemade crab tart, an open sandwich of roast pork belly and stuffing, or mussels in garlic sauce are superb. If it's sunny, try to bag one of the pavement tables.

★ Idás   IRISH €€€
(☎066-915 0885; www.idasdingle.com; John St; 5-course veg/nonveg menu €40/50, with wine €90/100; ☺6-10pm Wed-Sun) ✐ Chef Kevin Murphy is dedicated to promoting produce solely from the Dingle Peninsula, taking lamb, seafood and foraged herbs to create delicately flavoured concoctions such as braised John Dory fillet with fennel dashi cream, pickled cucumber and wild garlic, which are served as part of a set vegetarian or nonvegetarian menu (no à la carte).

★ Out of the Blue   SEAFOOD €€€
(☎066-915 0811; www.outoftheblue.ie; The Wood; mains lunch €12.50-20, dinner €21-37; ☺5-9.30pm Mon-Sat, 12.30-3pm & 5-9.30pm Sun) ✐ Occupying a bright blue-and-yellow waterfront fishing shack, this rustic spot is in fact one of Dingle's top restaurants, with an intense devotion to fresh local seafood (and only seafood). If staff don't like the catch, they don't open, and they resolutely don't serve chips. Highlights might include Dingle Bay prawn bisque with lobster or chargrilled whole sea bass flambéed in cognac.

Charthouse   MODERN IRISH €€€
(☎066-915 2255; www.thecharthousedingle.com; The Mall; mains €19.50-30; ☺6-10pm Jun-Sep, hours vary Oct-Dec & mid-Feb–May) Window boxes frame this free-standing stone cottage, while inside dark-red walls, polished floorboards and flickering candles create an intimate atmosphere. Creative cooking uses Irish produce: Beara Peninsula scallops with

Castlegregory chorizo, Dingle vodka–marinated hake, and butter bean cassoulet with hazelnut-crusted Toons Bridge halloumi. Book up to several weeks ahead at busy times.

The Irish cheeseboard comes with a glass of vintage port.

Doyle's   SEAFOOD €€€
(☑ 066-915 2674; http://doylesofdingle.ie; 4 John St; mains €20-33; ☺5-9.30pm) Cherry-red-painted Doyle's serves some of the best seafood in the area (which in these parts is really saying something). Starters such as Dingle Bay crab cakes or grilled oysters team up with mains like spicy Spanish fish stew, seafood linguine and lobster.

Crispy chips are cooked in beef dripping.

Global Village Restaurant   INTERNATIONAL €€€
(☑ 066-915 2325; www.globalvillagedingle.com; Upper Main St; mains €19-33, 6-course tasting menu €60, with wine €90; ☺5.30-9.30pm Mar-Oct) With the sophisticated feel of a continental bistro, this restaurant offers a fusion of global recipes gathered by the well-travelled owner-chef, but utilises local produce, such as Kerry mountain lamb. The wine list is excellent, as are the Irish and international craft beers.

🍷 Drinking & Entertainment

Dingle has scores of pubs, many with live music.

★ John Benny's   PUB
(☑ 066-915 1215; www.johnbennyspub.com; Strand St; ☺noon-11pm) A toasty cast iron woodstove, stone slab floor, memorabilia on the walls, great staff and no intrusive TV make this one of Dingle's most enjoyable traditional pubs. Glenbeigh oysters and Cromane mussels are highlights of its excellent pub menu (mains €13 to €19.50; kitchen open to 9.30pm). Local musos pour in most nights for rockin' trad sessions.

Curran's   PUB
(Main St; ☺10am-11pm) One of Dingle's most traditional shop-pubs, stocking everything from wellies to bags of potatoes, Curran's has nooks and crannies including original stained-glass snugs. Its Guinness is some of the best for miles around. Spontaneous trad sessions regularly take place.

Bean in Dingle   COFFEE
(www.beanindingle.com; Green St; ☺8.30am-5pm Mon-Sat; 🖥) Coffee specialist Bean in Dingle commissions its own Brazilian, Ethiopian and Guatemalan blends from Cork roastery Badger & Dodo. There's a communal table and a handful of seats; arrive early before it sells out of its sweet and savoury pastries – flaky sausage rolls, sugar-dusted cinnamon scrolls and a daily vegan special such as raw chocolate and caramel slice.

An Droichead Beag   PUB
(Small Bridge Bar; Lower Main St; ☺1pm-late) Traditional music kicks off at 9.30pm nightly at this raucous, yellow-painted pub by the bridge, where the party often keeps going until the very wee hours.

Dick Mack's   PUB
(Green St; ☺11am-11.30pm Mon-Thu, 11am-12.30am Fri & Sat, noon-11pm Sun) Stars in the pavement bear the names of Dick Mack's celebrity customers. Ancient wood and snugs dominate the interior, which is lit like the inside of a whiskey bottle. Out the back there's a warren of tables, chairs and characters. Cash only.

Foxy John's   PUB
(Main St; ☺10am-11pm; 🖥) Foxy John's is a classic example of Dingle's shop-pubs, stocking hardware and outdoor clothing alongside stout and whiskey. It even rents bikes (€15 per day).

Blue Zone   JAZZ
(Green St; ☺5.30-11pm Thu-Tue, noon-midnight Wed) Upstairs from Dingle Record Shop, this great late-night hangout is part jazz venue, part pizza restaurant and part wine bar, with moody blue and red surrounds.

🛍 Shopping

Quaint shops sell quality goods made by local artisans, from jewellery to pottery, textiles, candles and art.

Brian de Staic   JEWELLERY
(www.briandestaic.com; The Wood; ☺9.30am-5.30pm Mon-Sat) This renowned local designer's exquisite modern Celtic work includes symbols such as the Hill of Tara, crosses and standing stones, as well as jewellery inscribed with Ogham script. All of de Staic's jewellery is individually handcrafted.

Little Cheese Shop   FOOD
(www.thelittlecheeseshop.ie; Grey's Lane; ☺11am-6pm Mon-Fri, to 5pm Sat) Swiss-trained cheesemaker Maja Binder's tiny shop overflows with aromatic cheeses from all over Ireland, including her own range of Dingle Peninsula Cheeses.

Dingle Record Shop
MUSIC

(www.dinglerecordshop.com; Green St; ⊘11am-5pm Mon-Sat) Tucked off Green St, this jammed music hub has all the good stuff you can't download yet. Live bands play every couple of weeks; podcasts recorded in-store are available online. Hours can be erratic.

Dingle Candle
ARTS & CRAFTS

(http://dinglecandle.com; Main St; ⊘10am-5.30pm Mon-Sat) Handpoured, long-burning candles made in Dingle come in 16 different scents inspired by the peninsula, including Irish Wild Fuchsia Rose, Wild Blackberry and Honeysuckle, Smoky Turf Fire, Granny's Cottage Kitchen and Peated Whiskey. Browse too for body scrubs, shower mousses, bath salts and perfumes, which are also handmade here.

Lisbeth Mulcahy
HOMEWARES

(www.lisbethmulcahy.com; Green St; ⊘9.30am-7pm Mon-Sat, noon-4pm Sun Jun-Sep, 10am-5pm Mon-Sat Oct-May) Beautiful wall hangings, rugs and scarves are created on a 150-year-old loom by this long-established designer. Also sold here are ceramics by her husband, who has a workshop at Louis Mulcahy Pottery (p295), 17km west of Dingle on Slea Head.

An Gailearaí Beag
ARTS & CRAFTS

(www.angailearaibeag.com; Main St; ⊘11am-5pm) Often staffed by the artists themselves, this little gallery is a showcase for the work of the West Kerry Craft Guild, selling ceramics, paintings, wood carvings, photography, batik, jewellery, stained glass and more.

❶ Information

Busy but helpful, Dingle's **tourist office** (☑066-915 1188; www.dingle-peninsula.ie; The Pier; ⊘9am-5pm Mon-Sat) has maps, guides and plenty of information on the entire peninsula.

THE DINGLE WAY

The 179km Dingle Way (www.dingleway.com) loops around the peninsula, beginning and ending in Tralee; it normally takes eight days to hike. Much of it is on low-lying minor roads and farm tracks, but the most impressive section climbs to 660m, above huge seacliffs, as it crosses Masatiompan, the northern spur of Mt Brandon.

Ordnance Survey 1:50,000 sheets 70 and 71 cover the route.

---

❶ Getting There & Away

Buses **stop** (The Tracks) outside the car park behind the supermarket. Up to four Bus Éireann (www.buseireann.ie) buses a day serve Tralee (€14.80, 1¼ hours) year-round.

From April to October only, Go Coach (http://gocoach.ie) serves Killarney (€10, 1½ hours, three daily).

Dingle Shuttle Bus (☑087 250 4767; http://dingleshuttlebus.com) runs a minibus service between Kerry and Shannon airports (book in advance) and offers private Dingle Peninsula and Ring of Kerry tours.

❶ Getting Around

Dingle is easily covered on foot. Bike-hire places include **Foxy John's** (p291), **Paddy's Bike Shop** (☑066-915 2311; www.paddysbikeshop.com; Dykegate Lane; bike rental per day/week from €15/75; ⊘9am-7pm May-Sep, to 6pm Mar, Apr & Oct), and the **Mountain Man Outdoors Shop** (p287).

Parking is free throughout town, with metered parking at the harbour.

Dingle Cabs (☑087 660 2323; www.dinglecabs.com) operates a local taxi service, and can arrange Kerry and Shannon airport transfers as well as private guided tours of Dingle Peninsula.

Slea Head Drive

A cache of superbly preserved structures from Dingle's ancient past including beehive huts, ring forts, inscribed stones and early Christian sites are a highlight of Slea Head, set against staggeringly beautiful coastal scenery. The landscape is especially dramatic in shifting mist, although it's obliterated when thick sea fog rolls in.

Dunmore Head is the westernmost point of the Irish mainland; just to its south is the picturesque cove Coumeenoole Beach. There are other good beaches at Ventry, Clogher and Wine Strand near Ballyferriter.

The signposted Slea Head Drive is a 50km loop that passes through the villages of Ventry, Dunquin, Ballyferriter and Ballydavid to the west of Dingle town, and takes in all the main sights. Including time for sightseeing, it's at least a half-days' drive or one or two day's by bike.

Dingle Slea Head Tours (☑087 218 9430; www.dinglesleaheadtours.com; per person €30) runs guided three-hour minibus tours of Slea Head Drive. There's a minimum of four people; drivers pick you up from your accommodation in Dingle town.

⊙ Sights

Celtic & Prehistoric Museum   MUSEUM
(☑087 770 3280; Kilvicadownig, Ventry; €5; ⊙10am-5.30pm mid-Mar–Oct) This museum squeezes in an astonishing collection of Celtic and prehistoric artefacts, including the world's largest woolly mammoth skull and tusks, as well as a 40,000-year-old cave bear skeleton, Viking horse-bone ice skates, stone battle-axes, flint daggers and jewellery. It started as the private collection of owner Harry Moore, a US expat musician (ask him to strike up a Celtic tune). It's 4km southwest of Ventry.

★Dunbeg Fort   ARCHAEOLOGICAL SITE
(www.dunbegfort.com; Kilvickadownig; adult/child €3/1; ⊙9am-6pm Apr-Oct, shorter hours Nov-Mar) The Iron Age Dunbeg (Irish: Dún Beag) fort is a dramatic example of a promontory fortification, perched atop a sheer sea cliff about 6km southwest of Ventry. The fort has four outer walls; inside are the remains of a house and a beehive hut, as well as an underground passage. Admission includes a 10-minute audiovisual presentation in the visitor centre.

Fahan Beehive Huts   HISTORIC SITE
(Fahan; adult/child €3/free; ⊙8am-7pm Easter-Sep, shorter hours Oct-Easter) Fahan once had some 48 drystone *clochán* beehive huts dating from AD 500, although the exact dates are unknown. Today five structures remain, including two that are fully intact. The huts are on the slope of Mt Eagle (516m), which still has an estimated 400-plus huts in various states of preservation.

Blasket Centre   CULTURAL CENTRE
(Ionad an Bhlascaoid Mhóir; ☑066-915 6444; www.heritageireland.ie; adult/child €5/3; ⊙10am-6pm Easter-Oct) This wonderful interpretative centre celebrates the rich cultural life of the now-abandoned Blasket Islands. It is housed in a striking modern building with a long, white hall ending in a picture window looking directly at the islands. Great Blasket's rich community of storytellers and musicians is profiled along with its literary visitors like playwright JM Synge, author of *Playboy of the Western World*. The more prosaic practicalities of island life are covered by exhibits on boat-building and fishing.

The centre has a good cafe with a view of the islands, and a useful bookshop.

Dingle Peninsula Museum   MUSEUM
(Músaem Chorca Dhuibhne; ☑066-915 6100; www.westkerrymuseum.com; Ballyferriter; admission by donation; ⊙10am-5pm Easter & Jun–mid-Sep, by reservation rest of year; ℗) Set in a 19th-century schoolhouse, this local museum has displays on the history, geology, archaeology and ecology of the peninsula. It's in the centre of the tiny village of Ballyferriter (Baile an Fheirtearaigh), which was named after Piaras Ferriter, a poet and soldier who emerged as a local leader in the 1641 rebellion and was the last Kerry commander to submit to Cromwell's army.

The surrounding landscape is a rocky patchwork of varying shades of green, delineated by miles and miles of ancient stone walls.

★Reask Monastic Site   RUINS
(An Riaisc) FREE The remains of this 5th- or 6th-century monastic settlement are one of the peninsula's more evocative archaeological sites, with low stone walls among close-cropped turf and drifts of white daisies revealing the outlines of beehive huts, storehouses and an early Christian oratory. At least 10 stone crosses have been found, including the beautiful **Reask Stone** decorated with Celtic motifs. The site is signposted 'Mainistir Riaisc' just off the R559, 2km east of Ballyferriter.

★Gallarus Oratory   HISTORIC SITE
(www.heritageireland.ie; Gallarus) FREE Gallarus Oratory is one of Ireland's most beautiful ancient buildings, its smoothly constructed dry-stone walls in the shape of an upturned boat. It has withstood the elements in this lonely spot beneath the brown hills for some 1200 years. There's a narrow doorway on the western side and a single, round-headed window on the east. Gallarus is clearly signposted off the R559, 8km northwest of Dingle town, and is 400m east of the (paid) Gallarus Visitor Centre car park.

Alternatively, free parking for half-a-dozen cars is available on the road by the path leading to the oratory.

Gallarus Visitor Centre   VISITOR CENTRE
(www.gallarusoratory.ie; Gallarus; €3; ⊙9am-6pm Easter-Oct) This privately-owned visitor centre and car park is located next to Gallarus Oratory (p293). The only reason for paying the fee is to use the car park (the audio-visual presentation is missable).

COUNTY KERRY SLEA HEAD DRIVE

★ **Kilmalkedar Church** RUINS
(Kilmalkedar) FREE The Dingle Peninsula's most important Christian site, Kilmalkedar has a beautiful setting with sweeping views over Smerwick Harbour. Built in the 12th century on the site of a 7th-century monastery founded by St Maolcethair, the roofless church is a superb example of Irish Romanesque architecture, its round-arched west door decorated with chevron patterns and a carved human head. In the graveyard you'll find an Ogham stone and a carved stone sundial. It's 7.5km northeast of Ballyferriter.

🏃 Activities

Walking, cycling and horse riding are all possible here, as is swimming in warmer weather. Dingle-based Irish Adventures (p287) runs rock-climbing trips.

Mt Brandon WALKING
At 952m, Mt Brandon (Cnoc Bréanainn) is Ireland's ninth-highest summit. It stands in splendid isolation to the north of Dingle, a complex ridge bounded by spectacular cliffs and glacial lakes to the northeast, and falling steeply into the sea to the northwest. There are many routes to the top listed in local walking guides, but the shortest and easiest is via the old pilgrim path from Ballybrack (car park signposted off the R549, 11km north of Dingle town).

From the car park the path leads arrow-straight towards the top, passing numbered wooden crucifixes marking the 14 stations of the cross, before deviating to the right for a single zigzag before the summit, which is marked by a huge cairn and a 15th cross. In clear weather the views are stupendous. Descend by the same route (total 8.5km; allow three hours).

THE SAINT'S ROAD

A waymarked 18km walking trail, the Saint's Road (Cosàn na Naomh; www. irishtrails.ie) follows the route of an ancient pilgrim path from the beach at Ventry to Ballybrack (An Baile Breac) at the foot of Mt Brandon via **Gallarus Oratory** (p293), **Kilmalkedar Church** and several other early Christian sites. From Ballybrack experienced hillwalkers can continue via the stations of the cross to the **summit of Mt Brandon**.

Long's Riding Stables HORSE RIDING
(☑ 087 225 0286; www.longsriding.com; Ventry; 1hr/half-day/full-day ride from €35/140/200) Horse treks head along Ventry beach or among the hills above the bay. A three-day expedition around the Dingle Peninsula on horseback costs €600.

🍴 Sleeping & Eating

Oratory House Camping CAMPGROUND €
(Campaíl Teach An Aragail; ☑ 086 819 1942; www. dingleactivities.com; Gallarus; hiker €10, vehicle plus 2 adults €22; ☉ Apr-Sep; P 🔊) A 450m walk west of Gallarus Oratory, this sheltered, 42-pitch campground is just a 1km stroll east of beautiful Wine Strand strand. The owner is a great source of information on local activities, especially walking.

Dún Chaoin Youth Hostel HOSTEL €
(☑ 066-915 6121; https://anoige.ie; Dunquin; dm €17-18.50, d €44; ☉ early Mar-mid-Oct; P) Ireland's most westerly hostel, this 51-bed An Óige property has a scenic location near Dunquin Pier overlooking the Blasket Islands. There's a well-equipped self-catering kitchen but there are no shops nearby, so bring supplies with you.

Ceann Trá Heights B&B €€
(☑ 066-915 9866; Ventry; d/tr €80/120; ☉ Mar-Nov; P 🔊) An ideal base for exploring the area, this comfortable, modern five-room guesthouse has a great location overlooking Ventry Bay (rooms 1 and 2 have stunning sea views). An open fire warms the cosy sitting room in chilly weather.

Caifé na Caolóige CAFE €
(www.louismulcahy.com; Clogher, Ballyferriter; mains €7-11; ☉ 10am-5pm; P) ✔ The bright, contemporary cafe at Louis Mulcahy Pottery (p295) serves fresh homemade fare using Dingle Peninsula produce and herbs from its own gardens. Open sandwiches topped with organic smoked salmon, plus soups, panini and cakes are all served on its own pottery, along with warming coffee and hot chocolate.

★ **Gormans Clifftop House** IRISH €€
(☑ 066-915 5162; www.gormans-clifftophouse. com; Glashabeg; 3-course menu €37.50; ☉ dinner by reservation Mon-Sat; P 🔊 ♿) Far and away the best place to eat and sleep in the area is Gormans Clifftop House. Book ahead to dine on delicious Kerry mountain lamb stew, Dingle Bay prawns and other exquisite dishes (dietary requirements can be accommodated with advance notice). The guest

bedrooms (double/triple from €140/180) are airy, contemporary and immaculate, the welcome warm and the views superb.

A turf fire crackles in the guest lounge. Highchairs and cots are available.

Tigh TP
SEAFOOD €€

(TP's Pub; ☑ 087 246 0507; www.dingleactivities.com; mains €11-23.50; ☺ kitchen noon-9pm Easter-Oct, 5-8pm Nov-Mar) At the north end of Wine Strand, this beachfront pub serves fantastic local seafood, from Dingle Bay prawn-topped chowder to lobster, crab and Brandon Bay hake, and hosts regular wine and whiskey tastings. Trad music plays on weekends in summer and spontaneously throughout the year. Basic but comfortable accommodation (dorm/double €20/75) is available on site.

★ West Kerry Brewery & Brick's Pub
BREWERY, PUB

(Beoir Chorca Dhuibhne & Tig Bhric; ☑ 087 682 2834; www.brickspub.westkerrybrewery.ie; An Riasc, Ballyferriter; ☎) ✐ Small-batch brews such as Carraig Dubh porter and Riasc red ale use hand-drawn well water and botanicals such as elderflower, rosehip and blackcurrants from the brew-pub's lush gardens, which are strewn with sculptures by owner and brewer Adrienne Heslin. The 19th-century pub hosts live music and has four guest rooms (double €69 to €100) with private bathrooms, rustic timber furniture and wrought-iron beds.

🔒 Shopping

Louis Mulcahy Pottery
CERAMICS

(☑ 066-915 6229; www.louismulcahy.com; Clogher, Ballyferriter; ☺ 9am-8pm Mon-Fri, 10am-8pm Sat & Sun Jul & Aug, shorter hours Sep-Jun) One of Ireland's most acclaimed potters, Louis Mulcahy produces a wide range of contemporary and traditional designs. To learn how create them yourself, book a workshop where you make your own pot (fired/unfired (€19.90/9.90); fired pots can be shipped worldwide. Behind-the-scenes tours (€7.50 per person; minimum four people) are also available. Upstairs, the gourmet cafe is excellent.

ℹ️ Getting There & Away

Your own wheels are best for exploring. Most traffic travels in a clockwise direction including tour buses, so allow plenty of time if you're driving in summer. Several places in Dingle town rent out bikes.

Bus Éireann (www.buseireann.ie) has two services from Dingle town via Ventry to Dunquin (€6.90, 30 minutes) on Monday and Thursday, and two services from Dingle town via Gallarus to Ballydavid (€5.20, 20 minutes) on Tuesday and Friday.

Blasket Islands

The Blasket Islands (Na Blascaodaí), 5km out into the Atlantic, are Ireland's most westerly. At 6km by 1.2km, Great Blasket (An Blascaod Mór) is the largest and most visited. Day trippers come to explore the abandoned settlements, watch the seabirds, picnic on Trá Bán (a gorgeous white sand beach near the pier) and hike the island's many trails.

Dingle Marine & Leisure (☑ 087 672 6100, 066-915 1344; https://dingleboattours.com; Dingle Marina; adult/child return €40/20, eco tour €60/30; ☺ Apr-Sep) and **Blasket Islands Eco Marine Tours** (☑ 086 335 3805; www.marinetours.ie; Ventry Pier, Ventry; day tour adult/child €60/40, eco tour from €35/17.50; ☺ Apr-Sep) run seasonal boat trips. Confirm ahead as adverse weather can cause cancellations.

All of the Blaskets were lived on at one time or another; there is evidence of Great Blasket being inhabited during the Iron Age and early Christian times. The last islanders left for the mainland in 1953 after they and the government agreed that it was no longer viable to live in such harsh and isolated conditions, although today a few people make their home out here for part of the year.

Note there are no camping facilities on the islands.

Connor Pass

Topping out at 456m, the R560 across the Connor (or Conor) Pass from Dingle town to Cloghane and Stradbally is Ireland's highest public road. On a foggy day you'll see nothing but the tarmac just in front of you, but in fine weather it offers phenomenal views of Dingle Harbour to the south and Mt Brandon to the north. The road is in good shape, despite being narrow in places and steep and twisting on the north side (large signs portend doom for buses and trucks; caravans are forbidden).

The summit car park yields views down to glacial lakes in the rock-strewn valley below, where you can see the remains of walls and huts where people once lived impossibly hard lives. From the smaller, lower car park on the north side, beside a waterfall, you can make a 10-minute climb to hidden Pedlar's Lake and the kind of vistas that inspire mountain climbers.

The pass is a classic challenge for cyclists; it's best to start in Dingle town, from where the road climbs 400m over a distance of 7km. The climb from the north is more brutal, and has the added problem of being single track at the final, steepest section, so you'll be holding up the traffic.

Cloghane & Around

POP 297

Cloghane (An Clochán) is a delightful little slice of Dingle. The village's few buildings shelter in the lee of Mt Brandon, looking out to Brandon Bay and across the water to the Stradbally Mountains beyond.

The 5km drive out to Brandon's Point from Cloghane follows ever-narrower single-track roads, culminating in cliffs with fantastic views north and east. Sheep wander the constantly eroding rocks, oblivious to their tenuous positions.

Féile Lúghnasa　　　　CULTURAL
(http://cloghanebrandon.com/feile-lughnasa-fes tival; ⊘ late Jul) On the last weekend in July, Cloghane celebrates the ancient Celtic harvest festival Lúghnasa with theatre performances and traditional events such as sheep shearing, a blessing of the boats at Brandon Pier and a pilgrimage to Mt Brandon's summit.

Mount Brandon Hostel　　　HOSTEL €
(☑ 085-136 3454; www.mountbrandonhostel.com; dm €17-20, s/d €35/50, apt €67-100; ⊘ Mar-Jan; P@🛜) A patio overlooks the bay from this small, simple hostel with scrubbed wooden floors and furniture. Most rooms have private bathrooms. Apartments with kitchens sleep up to four people (minimum two-night stay).

O'Connors　　　　　PUB €€
(☑ 066-713 8113; www.cloghane.com; d/tr/f from €80/110/120, camping per person €7; P@🛜) Book ahead to bag a simple room or a table in this welcoming village pub, which serves food from 8.30am to 8.30pm made using local produce, ranging from salmon to steak (mains €8 to €16). Landlord Michael has loads of local info and can also explain why there's an aeroplane engine out the front.

❶ Getting There & Away

Bus Éireann (www.buseireann.ie) runs to/from Tralee (€13, 70 minutes) twice daily on Fridays only. No buses link Cloghane with Dingle town.

Castlegregory & Around

At the base of the Rough Point peninsula, Castlegregory (Caislean an Ghriare), which once rivalled Tralee as a busy local centre, is today a quiet village with lovely views of the hills to the south.

However, things change when you drive up the sandblown road along the broad spit of land between Tralee Bay and Brandon Bay. Up here, it's a water-sports playground. A prime windsurfing location, the peninsula also offers adrenaline-inducing wave-sailing and kitesurfing, while divers can swim among shoals of pollack amid the kelp forests and anemone-encrusted rocks of the Maharees Islands.

Accommodation on the little peninsula is limited, but Dingle town (29km southwest) and Tralee (32km east) are both close by.

There's little in the way of dining and no shops, so stock up in Dingle or Tralee.

Jamie Knox Watersports　　WATER SPORTS
(☑ 066-713 9411; www.jamieknox.com; Maharees; equipment rental per hour €5-15) Jamie Knox offers surf, windsurf, stand-up paddleboarding, canoe and pedalo hire and instruction, and also rents wetsuits. Surf lessons on Brandon Bay start at €30 for a 'taster'. Kids won't want to miss bouncing on the inflatable water trampoline (€5 per hour) moored in the bay.

Waterworld　　　　DIVING
(☑ 066-713 9292; http://waterworld.ie; Harbour House, Scraggane Pier) The Maharees Islands (north of Castlegregory), Brandon Point and the Blasket Islands offer some of the best scuba-diving in Ireland. For qualified divers, Waterworld, based at **Harbour House** (☑ 066-713 9292; www.maharees.ie; Scraggane Pier; s/d from €60/100; P🛜🚿), runs daily boat trips to the best sites (€35 per dive), and runs half-day Try-a-Dive packages (€80 per person) for complete beginners.

Spillane's　　　　PUB FOOD €€
(☑ 066-713 9125; www.spillanesbar.com; Fahamore; mains €12.50-26.50; ⊘ kitchen 1-9pm Jun-Aug, 5-9pm Mar-May, Sep & Oct; P🛜) 🏷 Outside tables look across Brandon Bay to the mountains at this laid-back pub idyllically

located out near the tip of the peninsula. Seafood is a speciality (the breaded scampi is a revelation), but it also does excellent pizzas and house-made burgers with hand-cut chips.

❶ Getting There & Away

Bus Éireann (www.buseireann.ie) runs from Tralee to Castlegregory (€11, 40 minutes) twice daily on Fridays only.

NORTHERN KERRY

Consisting mainly of farmland, Northern Kerry's landscapes can't compare to the spectacular Killarney region, the Ring of Kerry or the Dingle Peninsula. But there are some interesting places that merit a stop. Kerry's county town, Tralee, has a great museum, while Ballybunion is home to a world-class golf club and sweeping beaches, and the town of Listowel has strong literary connections.

❶ Getting There & Away

Tralee is the main transport hub, with bus and train services.

Shannon Ferry Limited (☑ 068-905 3124; www.shannonferries.com; cars €19, motorcyclists, cyclists & pedestrians €5; ⏱7.30am-9.30pm Mon-Sat, 9.30am-9.30pm Sun Jun-Aug, 7.30am-8.30pm Mon-Sat, 9.30am-8.30pm Sun Apr, May & Sep, 7.30am-7.30pm Mon-Sat, 9.30am-7.30pm Sun Oct-Mar; 🐾) runs a ferry between Tarbert in County Kerry and Killimer in County Clare, departing hourly on the half-hour from Tarbert and on the hour from Killimer. Journey time is 20 minutes. The ferry dock is clearly signposted 2.2km northwest of Tarbert. Taking the ferry saves a 134km detour via Limerick by road.

Tralee

POP 23,691

Although it's the county town, Tralee is down-to-earth and more engaged with the business of everyday life than the tourist trade, but a great museum and a wetlands centre make it well worth a stop.

Founded by the Normans in 1216, Tralee has a long history of rebellion. In the 16th century the last ruling earl of the Desmonds was captured and executed here. His head was sent to Elizabeth I, who spiked it on London Bridge. The Desmond castle once stood at the junction of Denny St and the

Mall, but any trace of medieval Tralee that survived the Desmond Wars was razed during the Cromwellian period.

Elegant Denny St and Day Pl are the oldest parts of town, with 18th-century Georgian buildings, while the Square, just south of the Mall, is a contemporary open space.

◉ Sights

★**Tralee Bay Wetlands Centre**   NATURE RESERVE
(☑ 066-712 6700; www.traleebaywetlands.org; Ballyard Rd; adult/child €6/4; ⏱10am-7pm Jul & Aug, to 5pm Sep, Oct & Mar-Jun, 11am-4pm Nov-Feb) 🐾 A 15-minute nature safari boat ride is the highlight of a visit to Tralee's wetlands centre. You can also get a good overview of the reserve's 3000 hectares, encompassing saltwater and freshwater habitats, from the 20m-high viewing tower (accessible by lift), and spot wildlife from bird hides. A light-filled cafe overlooks the main lake, which has pedal boats (€10 per 30 minutes) and rowing boats (€8 per 30 minutes) for hire.

★**Kerry County Museum**   MUSEUM
(☑ 066-712 7777; http://kerrymuseum.ie; 18 Denny St; adult/child €5/free; ⏱9.30am-5.30pm Jun-Aug, to 5pm Tue-Sat Sep-May) An absolute treat, Kerry's county museum has excellent interpretive displays on Irish historical events and trends, with an emphasis on County Kerry. The Medieval Experience recreates life (smells and all) in Tralee in 1450. Check out the deranged nights, a vision of horror right out of Monty Python. The Tom Crean Room celebrates the local early-20th-century explorer who accompanied both

> ### TRACING YOUR ANCESTORS
>
> County Kerry currently has no genealogy centre, but you can search census returns, old newspapers and other archives at **Tralee Library** (☑ 066-712 1200; www.kerrylibrary.ie; Moyderwell; ⏱10am-5pm Mon, Wed, Fri & Sat, to 8pm Tue & Thu; 🐾) and **Killarney Library** (☑ 064-663 2655; www.kerrylibrary.ie; Rock Rd; ⏱10am-5pm Mon, Wed, Fri & Sat, to 8pm Tue & Thu; 🐾).
>
> There are also some church records available free of charge on the Irish Genealogy (www.irishgenealogy.ie) website.

COUNTY KERRY TRALEE

Tralee

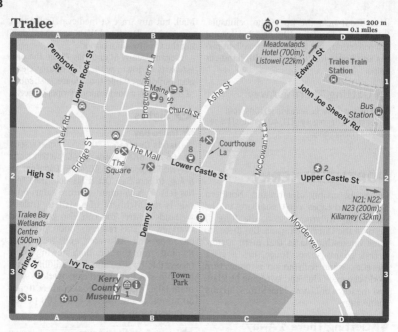

Tralee

◎ Top Sights

⊕ Activities, Courses & Tours

⊜ Sleeping

⊗ Eating

◎ Drinking & Nightlife

⊕ Entertainment

Scott and Shackleton on epic Antarctic expeditions. It's housed in the neoclassical Ashe Memorial Hall.

Blennerville Windmill
& Visitor Centre   WINDMILL
(☏066-712 1064; Blennerville; adult/child €5/3; ⊗9am-6pm Jun-Aug, 9.30am-5.30pm Apr, May, Sep & Oct) Blennerville, 3.4km southwest of Tralee's centre on the N86 to Dingle, used to be the city's chief port, though the harbour has long since silted in. A 19th-century flour windmill here has been restored and is the largest working mill in Ireland and Britain. Its modern visitor centre houses exhibitions on grain-milling, as well as on the thousands of emigrants who boarded 'coffin ships' from

what was then Kerry's largest embarkation point.

Ardfert Cathedral   CATHEDRAL
(☏066-713 4711; www.heritageireland.ie; adult/child €5/3; ⊗10am-6pm Easter-Sep) The impressive remains of 13th-century Ardfert Cathedral are notable for the beautiful and delicate stone carvings on its Romanesque door and window arches. Set into one of the interior walls is an effigy, said to be of St Brendan the Navigator, who was educated in Ardfert and founded a monastery here. Other elaborate medieval grave slabs can be seen in the visitor centre. Ardfert is 10km northwest of Tralee on the Ballyheigue road.

Crag Cave
CAVE

(☑ 066-714 1244; www.cragcave.com; Castleisland; adult/child €12/5; ⊙ 10am-6.30pm Jul & Aug, 10am-6pm mid-Mar–Jun & Sep-Dec, 10am-6pm Fri-Sun Jan–mid-Mar) This cave was discovered in 1983, when problems with water pollution led to a search for the source of the local river. In 1989, 300m of the 4km-long cave were opened to the public; admission is by 30-minute guided tour involving 72 steps. The remarkable rock formations include a stalagmite shaped (to some) like a statue of the Madonna. There are play areas for kids, a restaurant and a gift shop. The cave is signposted 18km east of Tralee.

Festivals & Events

Rose of Tralee
CULTURAL

(www.roseoftralee.ie; ⊙ Aug) The hugely popular Rose of Tralee is a beauty pageant open to Irish women and women of Irish descent from around the world (the eponymous 'roses'). More than just a beauty contest, it's a five-day-long festival bookended by a gala ball and a 'midnight madness' parade led by the newly crowned Rose of Tralee, followed by a fireworks display.

Kerry Film Festival
FILM

(www.kerryfilmfestival.com; ⊙ Oct) The five-day Kerry Film Festival includes a short film competition and screenings at venues around town.

Sleeping

★ Meadowlands Hotel
HOTEL €€

(☑ 066-718 0444; www.meadowlandshotel.com; Oakpark Rd; s/d/f from €85/113/135; P 🛜) Strolling distance from town but far enough away to be quiet, Meadowlands is an unexpectedly romantic four-star hotel with stunning vintage-meets-designer public areas. Rooms have autumnal hues and service is spot-on. Its beamed-ceilinged bar (mains €13 to €27.50), serving top-notch seafood (the owners have their own fishing fleet), is at least as popular with locals as it is with visitors.

Ask about discounted rates.

Ashe Hotel
HOTEL €€

(☑ 066-710 6300; www.theashehotel.ie; Maine St; s/d/f/ste from €70/94/134/200; 🛜) Right in the town centre, this contemporary hotel offers good-value, stylish accommodation. Family rooms sleep four; there are also interconnecting rooms. Local produce is used in gastropub fare at its bar (mains €10 to €20), which also has a kids' menu.

Eating

Cafes, pubs and restaurants concentrate in the town centre. The weekly **farmers market** (Prince's St; ⊙ 11am-3pm Sat) 🍴 sprawls along Prince's St on Saturdays.

Northwest of Tralee along the coast, it's 7km to Spa and another 6km on to Fenit, which has a sizeable fishing port and marina. Some excellent seafood restaurants in both villages pull in Tralee locals.

★ Quinlan's Fish
SEAFOOD €

(☑ 066-712 3998; www.kerryfish.com; The Mall; mains €8-15; ⊙ noon-10pm) 🍴 Quinlan's is Kerry's leading chain of fish shops, with its own fleet so you know everything here is fresh. The fish and chips are great; alternatives include Dingle Bay squid and chips with sweet chilli sauce. Lighter pan-fried options are available. The Delft-blue, scrubbed-timber and exposed-brick premises have a handful of wine-barrel tables, or head to Tralee's Town Park.

Roast House
CAFE €

(☑ 066-718 1011; www.theroasthouse.ie; 3 Denny St; dishes €6.50-12.50; ⊙ 9am-5pm Mon-Sat, 10am-2pm Sun; 🛜 🍴) Kerry's only coffee roastery, with its own custom-built machine, Roast House is even better known for its food, which spans breakfasts of homemade buttermilk pancakes with bacon and maple syrup to lunch dishes like barbecue pulled pork sandwiches and an 8oz Irish beef burger with Cork-produced smoked Gubbeen cheese.

West End Bar & Bistro
SEAFOOD €€

(☑ 066-713 6246; http://westendfenit.ie; West End, Fenit; mains €10-20; ⊙ kitchen 5.30-9pm Mon-Sat, noon-9pm Sun Easter-Oct; 🍴) 'Fresh or nothing' is the motto of this local icon in the village of Fenit, 13km northwest of Tralee. The fifth-generation bar serves a mouth-watering line-up of seafood, including Tralee Bay prawn cocktail and Kerry Head scallop mornay, plus plenty of locally sourced meat dishes. Upstairs it has simple but comfortable rooms (doubles from €70 including breakfast).

Fenit's Irish name, An Fhianait, translates as 'the Wild Place', in reference to its exposed position on the Atlantic.

Oyster Tavern
SEAFOOD €€

(☑ 066-713 6102; www.theoystertavern.ie; Spa; mains €16-30, half-dozen oysters €10.50; ⊙ 5-10pm Mon-Sat, noon-9pm Sun; 🛜 🍴) Grilled Atlantic salmon, pan-fried Kerry Head crab claws, Dingle Bay prawn scampi and lobster in season star at this classy restaurant, but carnivores, vegetarians and kids aren't forgotten, with plenty of inventive options. It's in the small settlement of Spa, 7km northwest of Tralee.

Chez Christophe　　　FRENCH €€
(☑066-718 1562; 6 Courthouse Lane; mains €13.50-21.50; ☺10am-5pm Mon-Wed, to 10pm Thu-Sat; 🐾) French native Christophe uses Kerry produce to create delicious dishes such as prawn and crab-claw cassoulet, roast duckling with apple compote, and pheasant with braised bacon and cabbage. The dining room has classic French bistro light fittings and a bookcase-lined wall.

🍺 Drinking & Entertainment

Castle St is awash with mass-market pubs, many of them offering live entertainment.

★ Roundy's　　　BAR
(5 Broguemakers Lane; ☺6pm-late Thu-Sun) Ingeniously converted from a terrace house (with a tree still growing right through the courtyard garden-turned-interior), this hip little bar has cool tunes, regular DJs spinning old school funk, and live bands.

Baily's Corner　　　PUB
(30 Lower Castle St; ☺9am-11.30pm Mon-Thu, to 12.30am Fri & Sat, 4-11pm Sun; 🐾) Rugby memorabilia-filled pub Baily's Corner has an ornate stained-glass-topped timber bar and a superb selection of whiskeys and gins. It's deservedly popular for its regular trad sessions, with local musicians performing original material.

Siamsa Tíre　　　THEATRE
(☑066-712 3055; www.siamsatire.com; Town Park; tickets €15-35; ☺booking office 9am-6pm Mon-Sat) Siamsa Tíre, the National Folk Theatre of Ireland, re-creates dynamic aspects of Gaelic culture through song, dance, drama and mime. There are several shows a week year-round.

ℹ️ Information

University Hospital Kerry (☑066-718 4000; Cloon More) has an accident and emergency department.

Tralee's **tourist office** (☑066-712 1288; http://kerrymuseum.ie; Denny St; ☺9.30am-5pm Jul & Aug, closed Sun & Mon Sep-Jun) is in the same building as the Kerry County Museum.

ℹ️ Getting There & Away

Bus Éireann (www.buseireann.ie) operates from the **bus station** next to the **train station**, 1km east of the town centre. Destinations include the following:

Cork €24, 2½ hours, hourly
Killarney €10.45, 40 minutes, hourly
Limerick €14.25, two hours, hourly
Listowel €9.60, 30 minutes, hourly

Irish Rail (www.irishrail.ie) services include trains every two hours via Mallow to Cork (€12, 2½ hours) and Killarney (€9.20, 40 minutes), and one direct train to Dublin (€21, 3¾ hours) with additional services that require a change in Mallow.

ℹ️ Getting Around

There's a **taxi rank** on the Mall, or try **Jackie Power Tours & Cabs** (☑066-712 6300; 2 Lower Rock St).

O'Halloran Cycles (☑066-712 2820; 83 Boherbee; bike rental per day €15; ☺9am-6pm Mon-Sat) hires out bikes.

Listowel
POP 4820

Listowel has more literary credentials than your average provincial town, with connections to such accomplished scribes as John B Keane, Maurice Walsh, George Fitzmaurice, Brendan Kennelly and Bryan MacMahon. They're featured at the Kerry Writers' Museum, and on a literary mural on Church St, opposite the police station. Keane is remembered with a statue on the opposite side of the square, in which he seems to be hailing a cab.

The town's tidy Georgian streets are arranged around an attractive main square with a Norman castle overlooking the River Feale.

👁️ Sights

Kerry Writers' Museum　　　MUSEUM
(Seanchaí; ☑068-22212; www.kerrywritersmuseum.com; The Square; adult/child €6/3; ☺9.30am-5.30pm Mon-Sat Jun-Aug, 10am-4pm Mon-Fri Sep-Nov & Mar-May) The audiovisual Writers' Exhibition in this Georgian building gives due prominence to Listowel's heritage of literary observers of Irish life. Rooms are devoted to local greats such as John B Keane and Bryan MacMahon, with simple, haunting tableaux narrating their lives and recordings of them reading their work, reflecting Ireland's tradition of storytelling. There's a cafe and a performance space where events are regularly staged in summer.

Listowel Castle
CASTLE

(☑ 087 919 9725; www.heritageireland.ie; ⊘ by reservation 9.30am-5.30pm mid-May–early Sep) **FREE** Standing between the town square and the river, this 12th-century castle was once the stronghold of the Fitzmaurices, the Anglo-Norman lords of Kerry. It was the last castle in Ireland to succumb to the Elizabethan attacks during the Desmond revolt. What remains of the castle has been thoroughly restored. Admission is by guided tour only (reservations required).

Lartigue Monorailway
MUSEUM

(☑ 068-24393; www.lartiguemonorail.com; John B Keane Rd; adult/child €6/3; ⊘ 1-4.30pm May-Sep) Designed by Frenchman Charles Lartigue, this unique survivor of Victorian railway engineering once ran between Listowel and Ballybunion along the coast. The renovated section of line is short (less than a kilometre) but fascinating, with manual turntables at either end for swinging the train around.

✯✰ Festivals & Events

Writers' Week
LITERATURE

(http://writersweek.ie; ⊘ late May/early Jun) Bibliophiles flock to Listowel for five days of readings, poetry, music, drama, seminars, storytelling and other events held at various locations around town. The festival attracts an impressive list of writers, which have included Booker Prize–winning Colm Tóibín, along with John Montague, Jung Chang, Damon Galgut, Rebecca Miller and Terry Jones.

🛏 Sleeping & Eating

Listowel Arms Hotel
HOTEL €€

(☑ 068-21500; www.listowelarms.com; The Square; d/f/ste from €120/135/200; 🅿 🛜) Overlooking the river, Listowel's principal hotel is a family-run affair in a Georgian building that balances grandeur with country charm, with 42 antique-furnished rooms. Nonguests are welcome at its Writers Bar, which often has music in summer, and Georgian Restaurant (mains €16 to €29; open 6pm to 9pm), which specialises in the catch of the day.

John B Keane
PUB

(37 William St; ⊘ 11am-midnight Tue-Sat, 7-11.30pm Sun & Mon) Once run by the late writer himself, this small, unassuming bar is swathed in Keane memorabilia.

ℹ Information

Listowel's **tourist office** (☑ 068-22212; www.listowel.ie; ⊘ 9.30am-5.30pm Mon-Sat Jun-Aug, 10am-4pm Sep-Nov & Mar-May) is housed in the Kerry Writers' Museum.

ℹ Getting There & Away

Bus Éireann (www.buseireann.ie) connects Listowel with Tralee (€9.60, 30 minutes, hourly) and Limerick (€14.25, 1½ hours, hourly).

Ballybunion
POP 1413

The beach town of Ballybunion is best known for its eponymous golf club. Beyond the statue of a club-swinging Bill Clinton, commemorating his visit to the course in 1998, two expansive beaches, Ballybunion North (also known as Ladies Beach) and Ballybunion South, have Blue Flag ratings.

Overlooking the southern beach are the recently restored remains of Ballybunion Castle (aka Fitzmaurice Castle), the 16th-century seat of the Fitzmaurices, with views to the Dingle Peninsula and Loop Head, County Clare, on a clear day.

Ballybunion Golf Club
GOLF

(☑ 068-27146; www.ballybuniongolfclub.ie; Sandhill Rd; green fees €65-190; ⊘ Apr-early Oct) Ballybunion Golf Club is reputed as one of the finest links courses in the world. Weekends (and bank holidays) are reserved for members, but visitors can book tee times to play the par 71, 1893-established Old Course on weekday mornings, or the par 72 Cashen Course on weekday mornings and afternoons.

Teach de Broc
INN €€

(www.ballybuniongolf.com; Links Rd; d from €140; ⊘ Apr-Oct; 🅿 🛜) Framed by flowers, this low-rise boutique inn next to the golf club has 14 spacious rooms that are thoughtfully appointed (hypo-allergenic pillows, free bottled water, USB chargers) and stylishly decorated in cream, gold and oyster-grey tones. Its on-site **Strollers Bar & Bistro** (bar dishes €5.50-12, restaurant mains €15.50-27.50; ⊘ bar snacks 4-6pm Mon-Sat, to 9pm Sun, restaurant 6-9pm Mon-Sat Apr-Oct) is Ballybunion's best place to eat.

ℹ Getting There & Away

Ballybunion is 15km northeast of Listowel on the R553.

Bus Éireann (☑ 01-836 6111; www.buseireann.ie) links Ballybunion with Listowel (€5.32, 20 minutes, three daily Monday to Saturday).

Counties Limerick & Tipperary

POP 354,450 / AREA 6995 SQ KM

Best Places to Eat

➜ Restaurant 1826 Adare (p313)

➜ Mustard Seed at Echo Lodge (p313)

➜ Hook & Ladder (p310)

➜ Cafe Hans (p318)

➜ Country Choice (p323)

Best Places to Sleep

➜ Aherlow House Hotel (p316)

➜ No 1 Pery Square (p309)

➜ Raheen House Hotel (p321)

➜ Dunraven Arms (p313)

➜ Apple Caravan & Camping Park (p320)

Why Go?

From marching ditties to rhyming verse, the names Tipperary and Limerick are part of the Western lexicon, but both counties are relatively unexplored by visitors.

County Limerick is closely tied to its namesake city, which has a history as dramatic as Ireland's. In a nation of hard knocks, it seems to have had more than its fair share. The city's streets have tangible links to the past and a gritty, honest vibrancy, and treasures abound in its lush, green countryside.

In contrast, Tipperary town is minor. But amid the county's rolling hills, rich farmland and deep valleys bordered by soaring mountains, it's a peaceful place that's perfect for following a river to its source or climbing a stile to reach a lonely ruin.

In both counties, ancient Celtic sites, medieval abbeys and other relics endure in solitude, awaiting discovery. And even Limerick and Tipperary's best-known sights retain a rough, inspiring dignity.

When to Go

➜ As the third-largest city in Ireland, with a sizeable student population, Limerick city bustles year-round, but is at its liveliest during the warmer months, from around April to October.

➜ April to October is also the best time to explore the rural villages, towns and countryside of both counties, when opening hours for attractions are longest (a number close during the rest of the year) and the weather is at its best.

➜ Most of the counties' festivities take place from April to October too, including wonderful walking festivals in the Glen of Aherlow.

COUNTY LIMERICK

Limerick's low-lying farmland is framed on its southern and eastern boundaries by swelling uplands and mountains. Limerick city is boisterously urban in contrast and has enough historic and cultural attractions for a day's diversion. About 15km south of the city are the haunting archaeological sites around Lough Gur, while about the same distance southwest of the city is the cute thatched village of Adare.

Limerick City

POP 58,319

'There once was a city called Limerick...' Umm, no, can't think of anything that rhymes with Limerick. And no one is quite sure why those humorous five-line verses are named after this Irish city, though the term dates from the late 19th century.

Limerick straddles the tidal reaches of Ireland's longest river, the Shannon, where it swings west to join the Shannon Estuary. Following the city's tough past, as narrated in Frank McCourt's *Angela's Ashes*, its medieval and Georgian architecture received a glitzy makeover during the Celtic Tiger era, but the economic downturn hit hard.

The city is recovering rapidly, however. Limerick was chosen as the country's first-ever Irish City of Culture in 2014, and the subsequent investment saw a rejuvenated waterfront complete with stylish boardwalk. There's a recently renovated castle, a lively art gallery and a fast-developing foodie scene to complement its many traditional pubs, as well as locals who go out of their way to welcome you.

History

Viking adventurers established a settlement on an island in the River Shannon in the 9th century. They fought with the native Irish for control of the site until Brian Ború's forces drove them out in 968 and established Limerick as the royal seat of the O'Brien kings. Brian Ború finally destroyed Viking power and presence in Ireland at the Battle of Clontarf in 1014. By the late 12th century, invading Normans had supplanted the Irish as the town's rulers. Throughout the Middle Ages the two groups remained divided.

From 1690 to 1691 Limerick acquired heroic status in the saga of Ireland's struggle against occupation by the English. After their defeat in the Battle of the Boyne in 1690, Jacobite forces withdrew west behind the famously strong walls of Limerick town until the Treaty of Limerick guaranteed religious freedom for Catholics. The English later reneged and enforced fierce anti-Catholic legislation, an act of betrayal that came to symbolise the injustice of British rule, while Limerick gained the nickname 'Treaty City'.

During the 18th century the old walls of Limerick were demolished and a well-planned and prosperous Georgian town developed. Such prosperity had waned by the early 20th century, however, as traditional industries fell on hard times. Several high-profile nationalists hailed from here, including Éamon de Valera.

◉ Sights

Limerick's main places of interest cluster to the north on King's Island (the oldest part of Limerick and once part of Englishtown), to the south around the Crescent and Pery Sq (the city's noteworthy Georgian area), and all along the riverbanks.

If you have time, the best approach (on foot) from the city centre to King John's Castle is to cross Sarsfield Bridge and follow the riverside walk north to Thomond Bridge – there are great views across the river to the city and castle.

★ **King John's Castle**   CASTLE
(www.shannonheritage.com; Nicholas St; adult/child €12.60/6.50; ⊘9.30am-6.30pm Jun-Aug, to 6pm May & Sep, to 5.30pm Mar & Apr, to 5pm Oct-Feb) An obdurate and brooding Norman mass over the River Shannon, Limerick's showpiece castle, with its vast curtain walls and towers, was built on the orders of King John of England between 1200 and 1212. The massive twin gate towers still stand to their full height. A multimedia experience that provides an excellent potted history of Ireland in general, and Limerick in particular, is followed by exposed archaeology in the undercroft and a tour of the courtyard and fortifications.

Upstairs from the cafe, don't miss the exhibitions on the castle's archaeology and the development of Georgian Limerick, or the view from the top of the gate towers, though the best views of the castle itself are from the riverside walk on the far side of the Shannon. Book online for discounts.

Counties Limerick & Tipperary Highlights

1 **Rock of Cashel** (p317) Exploring the medieval remains of this ancient religious stronghold.

2 **Glen of Aherlow** (p315) Journeying through tranquil bucolic landscapes and hiking to high mountain lakes.

3 **Hunt Museum** (p307) Discovering Bronze Age, Iron Age, medieval and modern art treasures at Limerick city's top museum.

4 **Cahir Castle** (p319) Walking the walls and keep of Cahir's story-book castle.

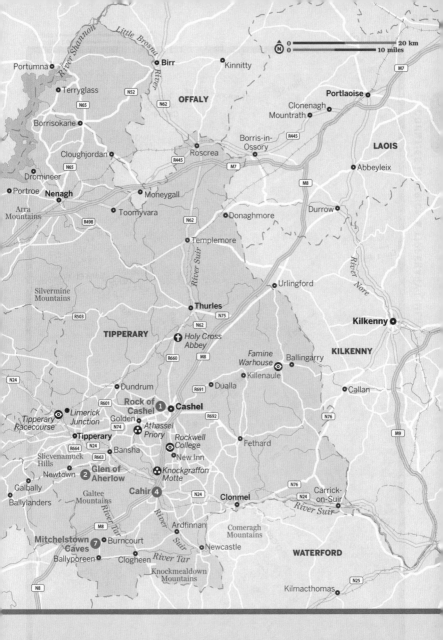

5 **Adare** (p312) Deliberating over mouth-watering menus in this heritage town's thatched-cottage restaurants.

6 **Foynes Flying Boat Museum** (p311) Taking in Shannon Estuary vistas and discovering the glamorous history of the transatlantic flying boats.

7 **Mitchelstown Caves** (p320) Delving into a dazzling underworld of passages and chambers.

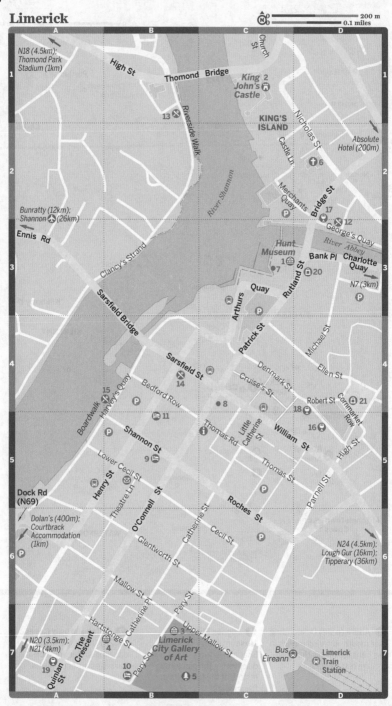

Limerick

Limerick

★**Hunt Museum**   MUSEUM
(www.huntmuseum.com; Custom House, Rutland St; adult/child €5/2.50; ⊘10am-5pm Mon-Sat, 2-5pm Sun; ☑) Although named for its benefactors, this museum, opened in 1997, is also a treasure hunt. Visitors are encouraged to open drawers and otherwise poke around the finest collection of Bronze Age, Iron Age, medieval and modern art treasures outside Dublin. Highlights include a Syracusan coin claimed to have been one of the 30 pieces of silver paid to Judas for his betrayal of Christ, a Renoir study, a Gauguin painting, a Giacometti drawing and works by Picasso and Jack B Yeats.

There's also a tiny but exquisite bronze horse once attributed to da Vinci (but now considered a much later copy), Cycladic sculptures, an alabaster vase from ancient Egypt dated to the 3rd century BC and a smattering of pieces from the Far East. The 2000-plus items are from the private collection of the late John and Gertrude Hunt, antique dealers and consultants, who championed historical preservation throughout the region. Free one-hour guided tours from the dedicated and colourful volunteers are available. The museum has a good cafe.

★**Limerick City Gallery of Art**   GALLERY
(www.gallery.limerick.ie; Carnegie Bldg, Pery Sq; ⊘10am-5.30pm Mon-Wed, Fri & Sat, to 8pm Thu, noon-5.30pm Sun) **FREE** Limerick's excellent gallery adjoins the peaceful People's Park (p308) in the heart of Georgian Limerick. Among its permanent collection of paintings from the last 300 years are works by Sean Keating and Jack B Yeats. Temporary exhibitions of conceptual and thought-provoking contemporary art fill the other well-lit galleries. The gallery is the home of **eva International** (www.eva.ie; ⊘mid-Apr–mid-Jul), Ireland's contemporary art biennial held across the city in even-numbered years. Check the website for dates.

There's a lovely cafe (open 9.30am to 5pm) looking across the park.

Frank McCourt Museum   MUSEUM
(www.frankmccourtmuseum.com; Leamy House, Hartstonge St; adult/child €4/2; ⊘11am-4.30pm Mon-Fri) This museum dedicated to Frank McCourt (p308) can be found in his former school building in Limerick's Georgian quarter. The museum contains a re-creation of a 1930s classroom and of the McCourt household, plus an assortment of memorabilia.

St Mary's Cathedral   CATHEDRAL
(☑061-310 293; www.cathedral.limerick.anglican. org; Bridge St; suggested donation €4; ⊘9am-5pm Mon-Fri, to 4pm Sat & Sun) Limerick's ancient cathedral was founded in 1168 by Donal Mór O'Brien, king of Munster. Parts of the 12th-century Romanesque western doorway, nave and aisles survive, and there are splendid 15th-century black-oak misericords (for supporting 'clerical posteriors') in the Jebb Chapel, unique examples of their kind in Ireland and each fabulously carved with creatures and mythical animals. Call ahead to confirm opening hours and to check if there are any musical events scheduled.

FRANK MCCOURT

No one name has been so closely intertwined with Limerick in recent decades as Frank McCourt (1930–2009). His poignant autobiographical novel *Angela's Ashes* was a surprise publishing sensation in 1996, bringing him fame and honours (including the Pulitzer Prize).

Although he was born in New York City, McCourt's immigrant family returned to Limerick four years later, unable to survive in America. His childhood was filled with the kinds of deprivations that were all too common at the time: his father was a drunk who later vanished, three of his six siblings died in childhood, and at age 13 he dropped out of school to earn money to help his family survive.

At age 19, McCourt returned to New York and later worked for three decades as a high school teacher. Among the subjects he taught was writing. From the 1970s he dabbled in writing and theatre with his brother Malachy. He started *Angela's Ashes* only after retiring from teaching in 1987. Its early success was thanks to a bevy of enthusiastic critics, but in Limerick the reaction was mixed, with many decrying the negative portrait it painted of the city.

Today McCourt's legacy in Limerick is celebrated. Limerick City's tourist office has information about city sights related to the book; you can join **Angela's Ashes walking tours**, visit the **Frank McCourt Museum** (p307) and drink in one of the watering holes mentioned in the book, **South's** (p310).

People's Park   PARK
(www.limerick.ie; Pery Sq; ⊙8am-dusk Sep-Apr, to 9pm May-Aug) This lovely wooded park in Pery Sq at the heart of Georgian Limerick is an excellent place for collapsing onto the grass with a chunky novel when the sun pops out. Check out the magnificently restored 19th-century red-and-white drinking fountain. The statue on the column in the middle of the park is of Thomas Spring Rice, a former MP for Limerick.

Thomond Park Stadium   STADIUM
(☑061-421 109; www.thomondpark.ie; Cratloe Rd; tours adult/child €10/8; ⊙9am-5pm Mon-Fri, also Sat & Sun for prebooked groups of 6 or more) From 1995 until 2007, the Munster province rugby team was undefeated in this legendary stadium; it was also the venue for their famous victories over New Zealand's All Blacks in 1978 and 2016. Tours of the hallowed ground include the dressing rooms, dugouts and pitch, and its memorabilia-filled museum. It's an easy 1km walk northwest of the centre along High St.

The museum is open on match days from 2½ hours before kick-off (adult/child €5/3).

🏃 Activities

★**Limerick City Kayaking Tours**   KAYAKING
(☑086 330 8236; www.nevsailwatersports.ie; Rutland St; €25; ⊙Sat & Sun) Departing from behind the Hunt Museum, these kayak tours take you along the River Shannon and beneath the walls of King John's Castle, offering an entirely new perspective on the city. Book in advance; no previous experience needed. Tour times depend on the tide and weather.

Riverbank Walkway   WALKING
Opened in 2016, this 3km all-abilities walkway links the city centre to the University of Limerick campus, following a picturesque route along a former canal and later the south bank of the River Shannon. It begins from Lock Quay, just east of Abbey Bridge.

Angela's Ashes Walking Tour   WALKING
(☑087 235 1339; €10) Noel Curtin runs entertaining and informative walking tours of the city covering locations featured in Frank McCourt's famous novel, *Angela's Ashes*, departing from the Frank McCourt Museum (p307) at 2.30pm.

Limerick Walking Tours   WALKING
(☑083 300 0111; limerickguide@gmail.com; adults/children €10/free) Highly popular and entertaining guided walks around town from knowledgable Declan, who moonlights at the Hunt Museum. Tours start and finish outside Brown Thomas on Patrick St, near the intersection with Sarsfield St.

🛏 Sleeping

The city has a decent range of quality, mid-range accommodation – aim to stay near the city centre, for the convenience and the nightlife.

Alexandra Tce on O'Connell Ave (which runs south from O'Connell St) has several midrange B&Bs. Ennis Rd, leading northwest towards Shannon, also has a selection, although most are at least 1km from the centre.

Courtbrack Accommodation   B&B €
(📞061-302 500; www.mic.ul.ie/adminservices/conference/Pages/Courtbrack.aspx; Courtbrack Ave; dm/s/d €23.50/30/52; ⊘May-Aug; 🅿@🛜) This spiffy red-brick building houses student digs during semester, but opens to visitors during summer. Tourist rates include continental breakfast. Spotless facilities include a kitchen, laundry and common area with wi-fi. It's about 1km southwest of the city centre, just south of Dock Rd (the N69).

★ No 1 Pery Square   HOTEL €€
(📞061-402 402; www.oneperysquare.com; 1 Pery Sq; club/period r from €165/225; 🅿🛜) Treat yourself to a night in Georgian Limerick at this elegant hotel right on the corner of Pery Sq. Choose between very well-presented club rooms (each named after an Irish poet) in the modern extension and one of the four period rooms in the classic Georgian townhouse, each a feast of huge sash windows, high ceilings and capacious bathrooms.

Absolute Hotel   HOTEL €€
(📞061-463 600; www.absolutehotel.com; Sir Harry's Mall; d from €124; 🅿@🛜) Exposed brick walls, polished limestone bathrooms and contemporary art give this gleaming hotel overlooking the River Abbey a modern edge. There's a light-filled atrium in the lobby and a cocooning in-house spa, plus a bar and grill. Check in early: secure parking is free but limited.

George Boutique Hotel   HOTEL €€
(📞061-460 400; www.georgelimerick.com; Shannon St; s/d/tr/f from €100/105/130/145; 🅿🛜) 'Boutique' might be overstating things a bit, but the rooms at this brisk, buzzing and centrally located hotel – with a decor of blond wood, caramels and browns, and the occasional splash of designer colour – are stylish and comfortable. It's frequently booked solid, so reserve well in advance.

Savoy   HOTEL €€
(📞061-448 700; www.savoylimerick.com; Henry St; r from €152; 🅿@🛜⊠) This five-star hotel is beginning to show its age and feels more like four-star, but it's smart enough, with comfy king-size beds and a turn-down service, a spa that specialises in Thai massages, a small swimming pool and a couple of top-notch in-house restaurants.

✗ Eating

Limerick is enjoying a 'foodie moment', with many excellent eateries focusing on fresh Irish produce, and a thriving street food scene with a Wednesday street food market on the boardwalk in summer. In 2017 the city hosted Ireland's first International Food Truck Festival (www.Limerick.ie/foodtruckfestival) and there are hopes that it might become a regular fixture.

Limerick Street Food   STREET FOOD €
(Harvey's Quay Boardwalk; mains €4-7; ⊘11am-4pm Wed May-Sep) When summer comes around, Wednesday lunchtime sees a row of street food stalls blossom along the Limerick boardwalk. Enjoy anything from Thai curry to Korean kimchi to US-style barbecue in an attractive riverside setting. During the rest of the week, a couple of stalls continue to operate at the north end of O'Connell St, between Sarsfield and Denmark Sts.

★ Azur   IRISH, EUROPEAN €€
(📞061-314 994; http://azurrestaurant.ie; 8 George's Quay; mains €17-25; ⊘5-11pm Mon-Sat, 1-8pm Sun; 🛜♿) Georgian architecture meets modern design to create an elegant venue for one of Limerick's best dining experiences. Service is professional but relaxed, the wine list is exemplary, and the menu lends a continental twist to the finest Irish produce, such as pan-seared scallops with black pudding and smoked bacon crumble, or crisp pork belly with red onion jam and curly kale.

TRACING YOUR ANCESTORS

Genealogical centres in Counties Limerick and Tipperary can help trace your ancestors; contact the centres in advance to arrange a consultation.

Limerick Genealogy (📞061-496 542; www.limerickgenealogy.com; Dooradoyle Rd, Lissanalta House, Dooradoyle) Professional genealogical research service.

Tipperary Family History Research (📞062-80555; www.tfhr.org; Mitchell St, Excel Heritage Centre, Tipperary town) Family research in Tipperary.

Tipperary South Genealogy Centre (📞062-61122; www.tipperarysouth.rootsireland.ie; Brú Ború Heritage Centre, Cashel) Comprehensive family history research service.

★ Hook & Ladder
CAFE €€

(☑ 061-413 778; www.hookandladder.ie; 7 Sarsfield St; mains €8-14; ⊗ 8am-9pm Mon-Sat, to 6pm Sun) A haven of understated style and a champion of local produce, this cafe set in a converted bank building epitomises Limerick's up-and-coming foodie scene. Exquisite sandwiches include Doonbeg crab with lemon mayo on honey and pumpkin-seed bread, while hot lunch dishes range from beef bourguignon to wild mushroom croquettes. There are associated cookery schools in Limerick and Waterford.

Curragower Bar
GASTROPUB €€

(☑ 061-321 788; http://curragower.com; Clancy's Strand; mains €12-24; ⊗ food served noon-8pm Mon-Tue, to 9pm Wed-Sun; 🛜) Ask a local for a lunch recommendation and they'll likely send you over the river to this appealing pub, which sports a superb outdoor terrace with views across the river to King John's Castle, and a menu that leans heavily towards Irish seafood, from crab claws in garlic broth to pan-fried cod with crisp Clonakilty black pudding.

🍷 Drinking & Nightlife

Pubs such as Flannery's are famous for their range of Irish whiskeys, but craft beers are making an impact. Ales from Limerick's own Treaty City Brewery (www.treatycitybrewing .com) can be found several bars, including Flannery's and Nancy Blake's.

★ Nancy Blake's
PUB

(☑ 061-416 443; 19 Upper Denmark St; ⊗ 11am-2am) There's sawdust on the floor and peat on the fire in the cosy front bar of this wonderful old pub, but be sure to head out the back to enjoy a vast covered drinking zone that often features live music or televised sports.

Flannery's Bar
PUB

(☑ 061-436 677; www.flannerysbar.ie; 17 Upper Denmark St; ⊗ 10am-11pm Sun-Wed, to 2am Thu-Sat) Housed in a former soap factory, this large and lively pub is a magnet for connoisseurs of Irish whiskey – there are more than 100 varieties on offer, and you can book a tasting session for €18 per person. Don't miss the roof terrace, a real suntrap on a summer afternoon.

Locke Bar
PUB

(☑ 061-433 713; www.lockebar.com; 3 George's Quay; ⊗ 9am-11.30pm Mon-Thu, to late Fri & Sat, 10am-11pm Sun; 🛜🍴) With its attractive riverside setting, a maze of stone-walled and wood-panelled rooms, outdoor tables overlooking the water, and a menu that runs from breakfast to dinner, the Locke is rightly one of Limerick's most popular pubs. Trad Irish music nightly throughout the summer.

South's
PUB

(W J South; ☑ 061-314 669; www.facebook.com/SouthsPubLimerick; 4 Quinlan St; ⊗ 8.30am-11.30pm Mon-Thu, to 12.30am Fri, 9.30am-12.30am Sat, 12.30-11pm Sun) Frank McCourt's father knocked 'em back in South's (Frank himself had his first pint here) and the *Angela's Ashes* connection is worked for all it's worth – even the toilets are named Frank and Angela. Check out the fabulous (though reproduction) neoclassical interior.

☆ Entertainment

Lime Tree Theatre
THEATRE

(☑ 061-953 400; www.limetreetheatre.ie; Mary Immaculate College, Courtbrack Ave; ⊗ box office 2-5.30pm Mon-Sat) Opened in 2012, this 510-seat state-of-the-art theatre is set on a college campus on the southern edge of the city. It stages drama, music and comedy performances by local and international artists, and in 2017 premiered a musical version of Frank McCourt's Limerick memoir, *Angela's Ashes*.

University Concert Hall
CONCERT VENUE

(UCH; ☑ 061-331 549; www.uch.ie; University of Limerick; ⊗ box office 10am-3pm Mon-Fri, longer hours on performance dates) Permanent home of the Irish Chamber Orchestra, with regular concerts from visiting acts, plus opera, drama, comedy and dance. The campus is 4.5km east of the city.

Dolan's
LIVE MUSIC

(☑ 061-314 483; www.dolanspub.com; 3 Dock Rd; tickets €10-20; ⊗ noon-2am Mon-Fri, 10am-2am Sat & Sun) Limerick's best spot for live music promises authentic trad sessions and an unbeatable gig list, as well as cutting-edge stand-up comedians in two adjoining venues.

🔒 Shopping

Milk Market
MARKET

(www.milkmarketlimerick.ie; Cornmarket Row; ⊗ 10am-3pm Fri, 8am-3pm Sat, 11am-3pm Sun) 🍴 Pick from organic produce and artisan foods including local fruits and vegetables, preserves, baked goods and farmhouse cheeses, or browse the flower and craft stalls, at this traditional food market held in Limerick's old market buildings. There's usually traditional live music as well.

LIMERICK CITY TO TARBERT VIA THE SCENIC N69

The narrow, peaceful N69 road follows the Shannon Estuary along the Wild Atlantic Way west from Limerick for 58km to Tarbert in northern County Kerry. There are some fantastic views of the broadening estuary and seemingly endless rolling green hills laced with stone walls.

At the small village of **Clarina**, past Mungret on the N69, hang a right to head north for around 1.5km to the crossroads, before turning left and you'll see the haunting ruin of **Carrigogunnell Castle** (⊙dawn-dusk) FREE high up on a ridge. You'll soon see a road to your right that heads past the castle, beyond the hedgerow and the fields. The 15th-century castle was blown up with gunpowder in 1691 and the fabulous wreck famously adorns the back cover of the U2 album *The Unforgettable Fire*.

Further along off the N69 is the village of **Askeaton**, with evocative ruins including the mid-1300s **Desmond Castle** (⊙weekends by appointment May-Oct), perched dramatically on an island in the River Deel next to the **Hellfire Gentlemen's club**, once home to an 18th-century brothel and drinking club. Restoration of the ruins started in 2007 and is ongoing, with no public access to the site. On the edge of town is the atmospheric 1389-built **Franciscan friary** (⊙dawn-dusk) FREE, with a beautifully preserved cloister. The **Askeaton Tourist Office** (📞086 085 0174; askeatontouristoffice@ gmail.com; The Square; ⊙limited hours – call to check) has details of the town's historic sites that you can freely wander (depending on restoration works) and can arrange eye-opening free **guided tours** lasting about one hour led by the very knowledgable Anthony Sheehy.

At **Foynes** is the fascinating **Foynes Flying Boat Museum** (📞069-65416; www. flyingboatmuseum.com; adult/child €11/6; ⊙9.30am-6pm Jun-Sep, to 5pm mid-Mar–Jun & Oct–mid-Nov, closed mid-Nov–mid-Mar). From 1939 to 1945 this was the landing place for the flying boats that linked North America with the British Isles. Big Pan Am clippers – there's a replica here – would set down in the estuary and refuel. Ask about the Foynes Air Show (www.foynesairshow.com), an annual summer event that started in 2014.

Celtic Bookshop BOOKS
(📞061-401 155; http://celticbookshop-limerick. ie; 2 Rutland St; ⊙11am-5pm Mon & Wed-Fri) Crammed with specialist titles on local and Irish topics.

ℹ Information

The **tourist office** (p311) website has a map of free wi-fi hot spots throughout the city.
St John's Hospital (📞061-462 222; New Rd; ⊙8am-6pm Mon-Fri) Accident and emergency department, and minor injuries clinic, close to the city centre.
Main Post Office (Lower Cecil St; ⊙9am-5.30pm Mon & Wed-Sat, 9.30am-5.30pm Tue)
Limerick Tourist Office (📞061-317 522; www. limerick.ie; 20 O'Connell St; ⊙9am-5pm Mon-Sat) Helpful staff provide advice and information on Limerick and the rest of Ireland.

ℹ Getting There & Away

AIR
Shannon Airport (p692) in County Clare handles domestic and international flights.

The airport is 26km northwest of Limerick, about 30 minutes by car. Regular Bus Éireann (€8.40, 50 minutes, twice hourly) buses connect Limerick's bus and train station with Shannon Airport. A taxi from the city centre to the airport costs around €35 to €45.

BUS
Bus Éireann (📞061-313 333; www.buseireann. ie; Parnell St) services operate from the bus and train stations near the city centre. Destinations include Galway, Killarney, Rosslare, Ennis, Shannon, Derry and most other centres.
Citylink (📞091-564 164; www.citylink.ie) buses stop on Henry St between Cecil and Glentworth Sts; **JJ Kavanagh & Sons** (📞0818 333 222; www.jjkavanagh.ie) buses stop at Arthurs Quay.

Regular services run from Limerick to the following:
Cork Bus Éireann (€15.20, 1¾ hours, hourly); Citylink (€18, 1½ hours, five daily)
Dublin Bus Éireann (€12.35, three hours, nine daily); JJ Kavanagh & Sons (from €10, 3½ hours, six daily)
Dublin Airport JJ Kavanagh & Sons (from €15, 4¼ hours, six daily); Eireagle (www.eireagle.com)

has eight luxury wi-fi-equipped coaches daily (€25, 2½ hours), leaving from Arthurs Quay
Galway Citylink (€18, 1½ hours, five daily)
Tralee Bus Éireann (€14.25, two hours, every two hours)

TRAIN

Irish Rail (www.irishrail.ie) has regular services from **Limerick Railway Station** (☑ 061-315 555; Parnell St), including to Dublin Heuston (€53, 2½ hours, hourly), Ennis (€11.35, 40 minutes, nine daily) and Galway (€22.70, two hours, four daily). Other routes, including Cork, Tralee, Tipperary, Cahir and Waterford, involve changing at **Limerick Junction**, 20km southeast of Limerick.

❶ Getting Around

→ Limerick city is compact enough to get around on foot or by bike. To walk across town from St Mary's Cathedral to the train station takes about 15 minutes.

→ Taxis can be found at Arthurs Quay, at the bus and train stations, and in Thomas St, or try **Swift Taxis** (☑ 061-313 131).

→ Limerick's Coca-Cola Zero **bike share scheme** (www.bikeshare.ie/limerick.html), with 23 stations around town is, for visitors, €3 (€150 deposit) for three days. The first 30 minutes of each hire is free.

→ Bikes can be hired at **Emerald Alpine** (☑ 061-416 983; www.irelandrentabike.com; 21 Roches St; from per day/week from €20/80; ⊗ 9.30am-5.30pm). The company will also retrieve a bike from, or deliver one to, anywhere in Ireland for €25.

Adare & Around

POP 1129

Over-touted as 'Ireland's prettiest village', Adare's fame centres on its string of thatched cottages built by the 19th-century English landlord, the Earl of Dunraven, for workers constructing Adare Manor. Today the pretty cottages house craft shops and fine restaurants; while prestigious golf courses nearby cater to golf enthusiasts. The Irish name for Adare is Áth Dara – the Ford of the Oak.

Tourists arrive by the busload in Adare, 16km southwest of Limerick on the River Maigue, clogging its roads (the busy N21 is the village's main street). As it's thronged with visitors at weekends, book accommodation and restaurants in advance.

◉ Sights & Activities

Before the Tudor dissolution of the monasteries (1536–39), Adare had three flourishing religious houses, the ruins of which can still be seen, but the main attraction here is the row of thatched cottages lining the main street.

Adare Castle   CASTLE

(Desmond Castle; ☑ tour bookings 061-396 666; www.heritageireland.ie; tours adult/child €9/7; ⊗ tours hourly 11am-5pm Jun-Sep) Dating from around 1200, this picturesque Norman ruin changed hands several times before being entirely wrecked by Cromwell's troops in 1657, by which time its strategic importance had slipped away. Highlights include the **great hall** with its early 13th-century windows, and the huge kitchen and bakery.

Book tours through the Adare Heritage Centre. When tours aren't on, you can view the castle from the busy main road, or more peacefully from the riverside footpath or the grounds of the Augustinian priory.

Franciscan Friary   RUINS

(Adare Golf Club; ⊗ 9am-5pm) The ruins of this friary, founded by the Earl of Kildare in 1464, stand serenely in the middle of Adare Golf Club (p313) beside the River Maigue. Public access is assured, but let them know at the clubhouse that you intend to visit. A track leads away from the clubhouse car park for about 400m – watch out for flying golf balls. There's a handsome tower and a fine sedilia (row of seats for priests) in the southern wall of the chancel.

Adare Heritage Centre   MUSEUM

(☑ 061-396 666; http://adareheritagecentre.ie; Main St; ⊗ 9am-5pm) **FREE** In the middle of Adare, exhibits here explain the history and the medieval context of the village's buildings in entertaining fashion. Quality Irish crafts are on sale and there's also a busy cafe.

Augustinian Priory   ABBEY

(⊗ 9am-5pm Mon-Sat) North of Adare village, on the N21 and close to the bridge over the River Maigue, is the Church of Ireland parish church, once the Augustinian priory, founded in 1316 and also known as the Black Abbey. The interior of the church is agreeable enough, but the real joy is the atmospheric little cloister.

A pleasant, signposted riverside path, with wayside seats, starts from just north of the priory gates. Look for a narrow access gap and head off alongside the river. After about 250m, turn left along the road to return to the centre of Adare.

Adare Golf Club
GOLF
(☎061-605 200; www.adaremanor.com) The prestigious Adare Golf Club enjoys a spectacular setting within the vast and serene grounds of Adare Manor.

🛏 Sleeping

Adare Village Inn
INN €
(☎087 251 7102; www.adarevillageinn.com; Upper Main St; weekday s/d €45/60, weekend s/d €50/70; P🕸) This cordial place has five excellent-value rooms which are cosy and comfortable and come with power showers. Run by Seán Collins, the inn is located a few doors down from his namesake bar (p314), where you check in, round the corner from Main St towards Rathkeale Rd.

★Dunraven Arms
INN €€
(☎061-605 900; www.dunravenhotel.com; Main St; r from €155; 🕸🏊) This jewel of an inn, built in 1792, exudes old-fashioned charm, with cottage-style gardens, hanging baskets, open fires and a comfortable lobby. Smart bedrooms are decorated with antiques, high thread-count linens and – for the choosy – four-poster beds. Service is warm and helpful, and there's a great restaurant (p314) and bar.

Berkeley Lodge
B&B €€
(☎061-396 857; www.adare.org; Station Rd; s/d/f €50/80/100; P🕸) This detached house around 400m north of the village centre has six cutesy and rather floral rooms – each in a different colour – with great breakfasts. It's just a three-minute walk to the heritage centre, pubs and restaurants.

★Adare Manor
HOTEL €€€
(☎061-605 200; www.adaremanor.com; Main St; r from €325; P@🕸🏊) This magnificent castle hotel sports a new bedroom wing and a huge ballroom to complement an already elegant property dripping in antique furniture and class. The manor's superb Oakroom Restaurant (p314) and lavish high tea are also open to nonguests.

🍴 Eating

Good Room Cafe
CAFE €
(☎061-396 218; thegoodroomadare@yahoo.ie; Main St; mains €9-11; ⏱8.30am-5.30pm Mon-Sat, 10am-5.30pm Sun; 🖐) This homely but busy place prepares inventive soups, salads, hot sandwiches, bruschetta, baked goods, homemade jams, kids menus and huge cups of coffee in a thatched-cottage

WORTH A TRIP

BALLINGARRY

The attractive village of Ballingarry is home to one of County Limerick's hidden dining gems; **Mustard Seed at Echo Lodge** (☎069-68508; www.mustardseed.ie; Ballingarry; 4-course dinner €60; ⏱7-9.15pm, closed mid-Jan–mid-Feb; P🕸). Produce picked fresh from this 19th-century former convent's orchards and kitchen gardens is incorporated into seasonal menus, which might include parmesan doughnuts with black-olive mousse, blackcurrant-and-gin sorbet, and wild Irish venison. Ballingarry is on the R519, 13km southwest of Adare.

To avoid having to move too far afterwards, book in to one of the lodge's elegant, country-style rooms, some with four-poster beds (double from €180).

location. Arrive early before their famous scones sell out. The cafe stays open till 9pm at weekends in summer.

★Restaurant 1826 Adare
MODERN IRISH €€
(☎061-396 004; http://1826adare.ie; Main St; mains €20-29; ⏱5.30-9pm Wed-Fri, 6-9.30pm Sat, 3-8pm Sun; 🖐) 🍃 One of Ireland's most highly regarded chefs, Wade Murphy continues to wow diners at this art-lined 1826-built thatched cottage. His passion for local seasonal produce is an essential ingredient in dishes like pan-seared halibut with pickled samphire, crayfish and shellfish bisque. A three-course early-bird menu (€34) is served until 7pm.

Wild Geese
IRISH €€
(☎061-396 451; www.thewild-geese.com; Main St; mains lunch €7-15, dinner €21-30; ⏱9.30am-9.30pm Mon-Sat) The ever-changing menu at this inviting cottage restaurant celebrates the best of southwest Ireland's bounty, from breakfasts of eggs Benedict with black pudding and colcannon, to dinner dishes of succulent scallops and sumptuous racks of lamb. The service is genial, preparations are imaginative and the bread basket is divine.

Blue Door
IRISH €€
(☎061-396 481; www.bluedooradare.com; Main St; mains lunch €9-16, dinner €19-25; ⏱11am-3pm & 6-10pm Mon-Thu, 11am-10pm Fri, noon-10pm Sat, 1-9pm Sun; 🖐) Hearty salads, open-faced sandwiches and lasagne appear on the lunch menu at this upmarket thatched cottage restaurant, while dinner ups the ante with

dishes such as confit of duck with black pudding and Guinness sauce, and fillet of cod with chardonnay sauce.

Dunraven Arms IRISH €€
(☑ 061-605 900; www.dunravenhotel.com; Main St; mains restaurant €16-28, bar €13-16; ⊘ noon-2.15pm & 7.30-9.30pm) The restaurant in this charming inn (p313) has an ambitious menu (roast cod with crab risotto and pea purée, confit duck with rhubarb and port sauce), but the food in its sedate, wood-panelled bar (lamb burger, fish and chips) offers a worthy and more affordable alternative. Hours can vary; reservations are advised.

Oakroom Restaurant IRISH €€€
(Adare Manor; high tea €28.50, mains €24-36; ⊘ high tea 2-5pm, dinner 6.30-10pm) Dine like a lord at Adare Manor's (p313) atmospheric Oakroom Restaurant, where dinner service is lit only by candles. The superb Irish menu is backed by a fabulous setting with views overlooking the grounds and the River Maigue. For an afternoon option, try the high tea served on tiered plates in the stately drawing room. Closed for renovations until autumn 2017.

🍸 Drinking & Nightlife

Seán Collins PUB
(www.seancollinsbaradare.com; Upper Main St; ⊘ 10am-11.30pm Mon-Thu & Sun, 10.30am-1.30am Fri & Sat) A friendly, family-run pub with good craic, good food, and live music on Monday and Friday at 8.30pm.

Bill Chawke's Lounge Bar PUB
(☑ 061-396 160; www.billchawke.com; Main St; ⊘ 10am-12.30pm Mon-Thu, to 1.30am Fri & Sat, to midnight Sun) Decked out in GAA (hurling and Gaelic football) memorabilia, this place has a good beer garden and hosts regular trad music sessions and singalongs.

❶ Information

The website www.adarevillage.com is a handy source of information.
Tourist Office (☑ 061-396 255; http://adare heritagecentre.ie/tourist-point; Adare Heritage Centre, Main St; ⊘ 9am-5pm)

❶ Getting There & Away

Hourly **Bus Éireann** (p311) services link Limerick with Adare (€6, 25 minutes). Many continue on to Tralee (€14.25, two hours, every two hours).

Others serve Killarney (€14.25, two hours, every two hours).

Lough Gur

The area surrounding this picturesque, horseshoe-shaped lake is rich in neolithic, Bronze Age and medieval archaeological sites. Short walks along the lake's edge lead to burial mounds, standing stones, ancient enclosures and other points of interest (admission free) and the whole area is ideal for walking and picnics.

You can buy coffee, soft drinks and snacks the heritage centre, but it's best to bring a picnic.

◉ Sights

Lough Gur Heritage Centre MUSEUM
(☑ 087 285 2022; www.loughgur.com; adult/child €5/3; ⊘ 10am-5pm Mon-Fri, noon-6pm Sat & Sun Mar-Oct, closes 4pm Nov-Feb) This thatched replica of a neolithic hut contains a helpful information desk and good exhibits on prehistoric monuments and settlements in the surrounding area, plus a small museum displaying neolithic artefacts and a replica of the bronze Lough Gur shield dating from around 1000 BC (the original is in the National Museum in Dublin). It's a good idea to come here first to get some context before exploring the surrounding sites.

Grange Stone Circle ARCHAEOLOGICAL SITE
(⊘ dawn-dusk) FREE This stone circle, known as the Lios, is a superb 4000-year-old circular enclosure made up of 113 embanked upright stones, the largest prehistoric circle of its kind in Ireland. It's a 3km walk or drive southwest of the heritage centre (p314); there's roadside parking and access to the site is free (there's a donation box).

❶ Getting There & Away

There is no public transport to Lough Gur, which is 21km southeast of Limerick. Driving from Limerick, take the N24 road south towards Waterford and follow the signs onto the R512 for 16km to Grange stone circle.

Around 1km further south along the R512, at Holycross garage and post office, a left turn takes you another 2km to the main car park beside Lough Gur itself, from where it's a short walk to the Lough Gur Heritage Centre.

Kilmallock

POP 1668

Kilmallock was Ireland's third-largest town during the Middle Ages (after Dublin and Kilkenny), and retains a handful of intriguing medieval buildings. The town developed around a 7th-century abbey and from the 14th to the 17th centuries was the seat of the Earls of Desmond. The village lies beside the River Lubach, 26km south of Limerick and a world away from the city's urban racket.

Coming into Kilmallock from Limerick, the first thing you'll see (to your left) is a **medieval stone mansion** – one of 30 or so that housed the town's prosperous merchants and landowners. Further on, the main street bends around the four-storey **King's Castle**, a 15th-century tower house with a ground-floor archway through which the pavement now runs.

Kilmallock Museum   MUSEUM
(Sheares St; ⊘ 10am-1pm & 2-4pm Mon-Thu, to 5pm Fri & Sat, noon-5pm Sun) FREE A lane leads down from the main street (opposite the King's Castle) to this tiny museum, which houses a random collection of historical artefacts and a model of the town in 1597. The museum is the base for the history trail around town.

COUNTY TIPPERARY

Landlocked Tipperary boasts the sort of fertile soil that farmers dream of. The central area of the county is low-lying, but rolling hills spill over from adjoining counties and an upper-crust gloss still clings to traditions here, with fox hunts in full legal cry during the winter season.

Walking and cycling opportunities abound, especially in the Glen of Aherlow, south of Tipperary town. But the real crowd-pleasers are the iconic Rock of Cashel and Cahir Castle. In between, you'll find bucolic charm along pretty much any country road you choose.

Tipperary Town

POP 4979

Tipperary (Tiobrad Árann) has a storied name, largely due to the WWI song. And indeed, you may find it a long way to Tipperary as the N24 and a web of regional roads converge on the centre (there's no bypass) and traffic often moves at the same speed as the armies at the Somme.

'Tipp town' itself is a bit sad and run-down, and has no real sights; there's no need to detour here, though you may pass through on your way to the Glen of Aherlow.

Kickham House   PUB FOOD €
(⊘ 062-51716; Main St; mains €8-13; ⊘ food served noon-3pm & 6-8pm) Named in honour of the local patriot, Irish revolutionary Charles Joseph Kickham (1828–82), this traditional pub serves carvery lunches that include roast beef and fish pie, as well as soup and sandwiches.

Tipperary Racecourse   HORSE RACING
(⊘ 062-51357; www.tipperaryraces.ie; Limerick Rd; adult/child €10/free) Tipperary Racecourse is one of Ireland's leading tracks. It's 3km northwest of Tipperary town and has regular meetings during the year; see the local press for details. The course is within walking distance of Limerick Junction station. On race days there are minibus pick-ups from Tipperary town; phone for details.

Danny Ryan Music   MUSIC
(⊘ 062-51128; www.dannyryanmusic.ie; 20 Bank Pl; ⊘ 10am-1pm & 2-6pm Mon, Tue, Thu & Fri, to 1pm Wed, 9.30am-1pm & 2-6pm Sat) This colourfully painted shop has a superb selection of traditional musical instruments.

❶ Getting There & Away

Most buses stop on Abbey St beside the river. Bus Éireann (www.buseireann.ie) runs up to eight buses daily on the Limerick (€11, 35 minutes) to Waterford route via Cahir and Clonmel.

To reach the train station, head south along Bridge St. Tipperary is on the Waterford–Limerick Junction line. There are two daily services to Cahir (€8.10, 25 minutes), Clonmel, Carrick-on-Suir, Waterford (€17.70, 1½ hours) and Rosslare Harbour. Connect for Cork, Kerry and Dublin at **Limerick Junction** (⊘ 062-51406), barely 3km from Tipperary station along the Limerick road.

Glen of Aherlow & Galtee Mountains

The broad, fertile valley of the Glen of Aherlow, slung between the wooded Slievenamuck Hills and the shapely Galtee Mountains, is the most scenic part of County Tipperary and one of Ireland's hidden delights.

A beautiful and leisurely 25km **scenic drive** through the Glen is signposted from Tipperary town. At the eastern end of the Glen, between Tipperary and Cahir, the village of Bansha (An Bháinseach) marks the start of a 20km trip west to Galbally, an easy bike ride or scenic drive along the R663 that takes in the best of the glen's landscapes.

The R663 from Bansha and the R664 south from Tipperary converge at Newtown at the **Coach Road Inn**, a fine old pub that's popular with walkers. Hidden around the back of the pub, the enthusiastically staffed Glen of Aherlow **tourist office** (☑062-56331; http://aherlow.com; Newtown; ⊙9am-5pm Mon-Fri, 10am-4pm Sat Jun-Aug) is an excellent source of information on the area, including walking festivals.

🏃 Activities

Renowned for its walking, the terrain around the glen ranges from the lush banks of the River Aherlow to pine forests in the **Slievenamuck Hills** and the windswept, rocky grasslands of the high Galtees. For spectacular views, head 1.6km north of Newtown on the R664 to a lookout adjacent to the **statue of Christ the King** (a local landmark). Waymarked woodland trails fan out from here.

★ **Lake Muskry**   WALKING
(www.aherlow.com/walking; Rossadrehid) Lake Muskry is a small but scenic lough set in a glacier-carved hollow high in the Galtees at an altitude of around 520m, and is the destination for one of Aherlow's most popular hikes. From the tiny hamlet of Rossadrehid, on the southern edge of the glen, a narrow road leads uphill to a parking area with an information board. The walk begins here, following a rough but easily followed path with green waymarks (11km round trip; allow three to four hours).

🛏 Sleeping & Eating

**Ballinacourty House
Camping Park & B&B**   CAMPGROUND, B&B €
(☑062-56224; www.ballinacourtyhouse.com; Ballynacourty; campsites €10, s/d €51.50/70; ℗) Set against the spectacular backdrop of the Galtee hills, this attractive site is 10km west from Bansha. It has excellent facilities, as well as a fine garden, a much-loved restaurant serving classic Irish fare (open 6pm to 8.30pm Monday to Saturday, 12.30pm to 2.30pm Sunday), a wine bar and a tennis court. An old stone house has been renovated and offers B&B accommodation.

Homeleigh Farmhouse   B&B €
(☑062-56228; www.homeleighfarmhouse.com; Newtown; s/d €50/80; ℗ 🛜) Just west of Newtown and the Coach Road Inn on the R663, this working farm rents out simple rooms in a modern home with views onto fields and garden. Furnishings are traditional and you can arrange for dinner (€28 per person). This place is an ideal starting point for local hiking.

Aherlow House Hotel   HOTEL €€
(☑062-56153; www.aherlowhouse.ie; Newtown; s/d/lodge from €69/95/149; ℗🛜) Up a pine-forested lane from the R663, a 1928 hunting lodge has been turned into a luxurious woodland retreat. There are 29 rooms with king-size beds and 15 contemporary countrified self-catering lodges (minimum two-night stay). There's a flowing bar, a fine restaurant, and glorious mountain views from the terrace.

Treetop Restaurant & Bar   IRISH €€
(☑062-56153; www.aherlowhouse.ie; Aherlow House Hotel, Newtown; mains €15-25; ⊙6-10pm Fri & Sat, 12.30-2.30pm Sun; 🚸) The formal restaurant at Aherlow House Hotel serves fine Irish and European cuisine in a congenial and intimate dining environment (reservations recommended). Bar meals are available from 12.30pm to 9.30pm daily, and there's a summer terrace with superb views of the Galtee Mountains.

❶ Getting There & Away

The frequent **Bus Éireann** (p311) service 55 from Waterford to Limerick stops in Bansha (€17.50, 1½ hours, eight daily). From here it's a long walk or bike ride into the hills – 12km to **Ballinacourty camping ground** (p316). A car will enable you to explore far and wide between walks.

Cashel
POP 4422

It's little wonder that Cashel (Caiseal Mumhan) is such a fabulous draw (the Queen included it on her historic visit in 2011). The iconic religious buildings that crown the blustery summit of the Rock of Cashel seem to emerge from the rocky landscape itself and the neighbouring market town of Cashel rewards rambles around its charming streets.

⊙ Sights

★ Rock of Cashel
HISTORIC SITE

(www.heritageireland.ie; adult/child €8/4; ☺9am-7pm early Jun–mid-Sep, to 5.30pm mid-Mar–early Jun & mid-Sep–mid-Oct, to 4.30pm mid-Oct–mid-Mar) The Rock of Cashel is one of Ireland's most spectacular historic sites: a prominent green hill, banded with limestone outcrops, rising from a grassy plain and bristling with ancient fortifications. Sturdy walls circle an enclosure containing a complete round tower, a 13th-century Gothic cathedral and the finest 12th-century Romanesque chapel in Ireland, home to some of the land's oldest frescoes.

It's a five-minute stroll from the town centre up to the Rock, from where fantastic views range over the Tipperary countryside.

The word 'cashel' is an Anglicised version of the Irish word caiseal, meaning 'fortress' (related to the English 'castle', from the Latin castellum). In the 4th century the Rock of Cashel was chosen as a base by the Eóghanachta clan from Wales, who went on to conquer much of Munster and become kings of the region. For some 400 years it rivalled Tara as a centre of power in Ireland. The clan was associated with St Patrick, hence the Rock's alternative name of St Patrick's Rock. In the 10th century the Eóghanachta lost possession of the rock to the O'Brien (Dál gCais) tribe under Brian Ború's leadership. In 1101 King Muircheartach O'Brien presented the Rock to the Church to curry favour with the powerful bishops and to end secular rivalry over possession of the Rock with the Eóghanachta, by now known as the MacCarthys.

Numerous buildings must have occupied the cold and exposed Rock over the years, but it is the ecclesiastical relics that have survived even the depredations of the Cromwellian army in 1647. The vast medieval cathedral was used for worship until the mid-1700s. Among the graves are a 19th-century high cross and mausoleum for local landowners, the Scully family; the top of the Scully Cross was razed by lightning in 1976.

But the undoubted highlight of the Rock is the early 12th-century Cormac's Chapel, an exquisite gem of Romanesque architecture with beautifully carved doorways and the precious remains of colourful wall paintings. Call ahead for details of the 45-minute guided tours (included in the admission fee).

Brú Ború
MUSEUM

(☑062-61122; www.bruboru.ie; The Kiln; adult/child €5/3; ☺9am-5pm Mon-Fri) This privately run cultural centre is next to the car park below the Rock of Cashel, and offers absorbing insights into Irish traditional music, dance and song. The centre's main attraction, the Sounds of History exhibition, relates the story of Ireland and its music through imaginative audio displays; various other musical events take place in summer.

Hore Abbey
RUINS

(☺dawn-dusk) FREE The formidable ruin of 13th-century Hore Abbey (also known as Hoare Abbey or St Mary's) stands in flat farmland 1km west of the Rock of Cashel. Originally Benedictine and settled by monks from Glastonbury in England at the end of the 12th century, it later became a Cistercian house. Now an enjoyably gloomy wreck, the abbey was gifted to the order by a 13th-century archbishop who expelled the Benedictine monks after dreaming that they planned to murder him.

Cashel Folk Village
MUSEUM

(☑062-63601; www.cashelfolkvillage.ie; St Dominic St; adult/child €5/3.50; ☺9am-7.30pm mid-Jun–mid-Sep, 9.30am-5.30pm mid-Mar–mid-Jun & mid-Sep–mid-Oct, 9.30am-4.30pm mid-Oct–mid-Mar) An engaging exhibition of old buildings, shopfronts and memorabilia from around the town. It's all a bit slipshod, but in a heart-warming way.

Cashel Heritage Centre
MUSEUM

(☑062-61333; www.cashel.ie; Main St; ☺9.30am-5.30pm daily Mar-Oct, Mon-Fri Nov-Feb) FREE Located in the town hall alongside the tourist office, the displays here include a scale model of Cashel in the 1640s with an audio commentary.

🛏 Sleeping

Cashel Holiday Hostel
HOSTEL €

(☑062-62330; www.cashelhostel.com; 6 John St; dm/tw from €15/60; 🛜) In a vividly coloured three-storey Georgian terrace just off Main St, this friendly and central budget option has dorms in one end and private rooms in the other. Amenities include a kitchen, a laundry, a library, bike storage and a comfy and homely lounge.

Baileys Hotel
BOUTIQUE HOTEL €€

(☑062-61937; www.baileyshotelcashel.com; Main St; s/d from €85/120; 🅿🛜) Clean, contemporary lines and dark woods contrasting

COUNTIES LIMERICK & TIPPERARY CASHEL

with light walls give this restored, centrally located Georgian townhouse an elegant ambience. Rooms are smart, but neutrally styled. Rates include breakfast and lock-up parking, and there's a great on-site restaurant and bar.

Cashel Town B&B
B&B €€

(☑062-62330; www.cashelbandb.com; 5 John St; d/q from €80/155; P⊛) ✪ Fresh produce from nearby farmers markets is cooked up for breakfast at this homely B&B. Within the 1808-built Georgian townhouse are seven comfortable rooms, and a cosy guest lounge with a toasty open fire and a piano.

Cashel Lodge & Camping Park
B&B, CAMPGROUND €€

(☑062-61003; www.cashel-lodge.com; Dundrum Rd; campsites per person €10, s/d from €55/85; P⊛) This converted 200-year-old stone coach house northwest of Cashel on the R505 (follow the signs for Dundrum) is a friendly place with a bare stone-and-wood interior and terrific views of the Rock and Hore Abbey. Noncamping rates include breakfast.

✗ Eating & Drinking

★ Cafe Hans
CAFE €€

(☑062-63660; Dominic St; mains €13-23; ⊗noon-5.30pm Tue-Sat; ⊞) Competition for the 32 seats is fierce at this gourmet cafe run by the same family as Chez Hans next door. There's a fantastic selection of salads, open sandwiches (including succulent prawns with tangy Marie Rose sauce) and filling fish, shellfish, lamb and vegetarian dishes, accompanied by a discerning wine selection and mouth-watering desserts. No credit cards. Enter via Moor Lane.

Arrive before or after the lunchtime rush or plan on queuing.

Baileys Hotel Bar
INTERNATIONAL €€

(☑062-61937; www.baileyshotelcashel.com; Main St; mains €14-18; ⊗food served noon-9.30pm) The stone-walled, candlelit cellar bar of this central hotel (p317) features a broad menu of international dishes made with locally sourced produce, including tasty burgers and hearty helpings of fish and chips.

Chez Hans
IRISH €€€

(☑062-61177; www.chezhans.net; Dominic St; 2-/3-course lunch €16/20, 2-/3-course dinner €28/33; ⊗6-10pm Tue-Sat) Since 1968 this former church has been a place of worship for foodies from all over Ireland and beyond.

Still as fresh and inventive as ever, the restaurant has a regularly changing menu and gives its blessing to all manner of Irish foods, including steamed Galway mussels, goat's cheese tart and pan-fried peppered skate wing. No credit cards.

Brian Ború
PUB

(☑062-63381; http://brianborubar.ie; Main St; ⊗10.30am-11.30pm Mon-Thu, to 12.30pm Fri & Sat, to 11pm Sun; ⊛) This good-time pub is a linchpin of Cashel's social life, with regular live music, DJs, cocktail nights and above-average pub grub (mains €10 to €17), including a Cashel Blue cheese tartlet.

ℹ Information

Tourist Office (☑062-61333; www.cashel.ie; Town Hall, Main St; ⊗9.30am-5.30pm daily Mar-Oct, Mon-Fri Nov-Feb) Helpful office with reams of info on the area.

ℹ Getting There & Away

Bus Éireann (www.buseireann.ie) runs eight buses daily between Cashel and Cork (€16, 1¾ hours) via Cahir (€6, 20 minutes, six daily). The bus stop for Cork is outside the Bake House on Main St. The Dublin stop (€16, 2½ hours, six daily) is opposite.

Ring a Link (☑1890 424 141; www.ringalink. ie), a not-for-profit service for rural residents that's also available to tourists, operates a minibus between Tipperary town and Cashel (€3, 50 minutes); it must be booked in advance by phone.

Parking in town is cheaper and less crowded than the car park below the Rock.

Around Cashel

Athassel Priory
RUINS

(Golden; ⊗dawn-dusk) FREE Reached over a stile and across grassy (sometimes muddy) fields, the atmospheric ruins of Athassel Priory sit in the shallow and verdant River Suir Valley, 7km southwest of Cashel. The original buildings date from 1205, and Athassel was once one of the richest and most important monasteries in Ireland. What survives is substantial: the gatehouse and portcullis gateway, the cloister (ruined but recognisable) and large stretches of walled enclosure, as well as some medieval tomb effigies.

To get here, take the N74 to the village of Golden, then head 2km south along the narrow L4304 road signed 'Athassel Abbey'. Roadside parking is limited and quite tight.

Holy Cross Abbey   CHURCH

(☑086 166 5869; www.holycrossabbey.ie; Holycross; tours €4; ☉tours 2pm Wed & Sun Feb-Oct) The pretty village of Holycross, with its thatched cottages, eight-arch stone bridge across the River Suir, and village green dotted with ducks, is 15km north of Cashel. Its magnificently restored Cistercian abbey, founded in 1168, proudly displays two relics of the True Cross, and Ireland's only intact medieval chapter-house doorway. Look for the ornately carved sedilia near the altar and pause to appreciate the early form of 'stadium seating'. Phone ahead to book a tour.

Cahir

POP 3593

At the eastern tip of the Galtee Mountains, 15km south of Cashel, Cahir (An Cathair; pronounced 'care') is a compact and attractive town that encircles a sublime castle. Walking paths follow the verdant banks of the River Suir, one of Ireland's finest trout-fishing streams.

◉ Sights & Activities

The River Suir offers some of the best **trout fishing** in Ireland; check out www.cahirand districtanglersassociation.com for more information.

★ Cahir Castle   HISTORIC SITE

(☑052-744 1011; www.heritageireland.ie; Castle St; adult/child €5/3; ☉9am-6.30pm mid-Jun–Aug, 9.30am-5.30pm Mar–mid-Jun & Sep–mid-Oct, 9.30am-4.30pm mid-Oct–Feb) Cahir's awesome castle enjoys a river-island site with moat, massive walls, turrets and keep, mullioned windows, vast fireplaces and dungeons. Founded by Conor O'Brien in 1142, and passed to the Butler family in 1375, it's one of Ireland's largest castles. In 1599 the Earl of Essex shattered its walls with cannon fire, an event explained with a large model. With a huge set of antlers pinned to its white walls, the **Banqueting Hall** is an impressive sight; you can also climb the **Keep**.

The castle eventually surrendered to Cromwell in 1650 without a struggle; its future usefulness may have discouraged the usual Cromwellian 'deconstruction' – it is largely intact and still formidable. It was restored in the 1840s and again in the 1960s when it came under state ownership.

FAMINE WAREHOUSE

A relic of one of Ireland's darkest chapters, the **Famine Warehouse** (☑087 908 9972; www.heritageireland. ie; Ballingarry; ☉2.30-5.30pm Wed-Sun Apr-Sep, 2-4pm Sat & Sun Oct-Mar) today sits seemingly benignly amid typical farmland a few kilometres northeast of Ballingarry. During the 1848 rebellion, rebels led by William Smith O'Brien besieged police who had barricaded themselves inside and taken children hostage. Police reinforcements arrived, the rebels fled and the rebellion died out. Besides exhibits about the incident, there are also displays detailing the Famine and the mass exodus of Irish emigrants to America.

The warehouse is 30km northeast of Cashel on the R691 about midway to Kilkenny. Be careful navigating as County Tipperary has two Ballingarrys; the wrong one is over by Roscrea. Opening hours are variable; call ahead before committing to a visit.

A 15-minute audiovisual presentation puts Cahir in context with other Irish castles. The buildings within the castle walls are sparsely furnished, although there are good displays, including an exhibition on 'Women in Medieval Ireland'. There are frequent guided tours.

Swiss Cottage   HISTORIC BUILDING

(☑052-744 1144; www.heritageireland.ie; Cahir Park; adult/child €5/3; ☉10am-6pm Easter-Oct) A 30-minute walk along a riverside path from Cahir Castle car park leads to this thatched cottage, surrounded by roses, lavender and honeysuckle. A lavish example of Regency Picturesque, the cottage was built in 1810 as a retreat for Richard Butler, 12th Baron Caher, and his wife, and was designed by London architect John Nash, creator of the Royal Pavilion at Brighton. The 30-minute (compulsory) guided tours are thoroughly enjoyable.

The *cottage-orné* style emerged during the late 18th and early 19th centuries in England in response to the prevailing taste for the picturesque. Thatched roofs, natural wood and carved weatherboarding were characteristics and most examples were built as ornamental features on estates. The cottage was restored in the 1980s under the direction of Irish designer Sybil Connolly.

🛏️ Sleeping & Eating

Don't miss the **farmers market** (www.face book.com/pg/cahirfarmersmarket; Castle car park; ⊙9am-1pm Sat) 🍴 on Saturday mornings, when you can browse some of the county's finest produce.

★ Apple Caravan
& Camping Park   CAMPGROUND €

(☑052-744 1459; www.theapplefarm.com; Moorstown; campsites per adult/child from €7/4.50; ⊙May-Sep; P🛜) 🍴 Set amid orchards on the N24 between Cahir (6km) and Clonmel (9km), this peaceful campground has a free tennis court, a camp kitchen in a converted apple store and spring water from its own well. Even if you're not pitching up here, it's worth dropping by its **farm shop** (open 8am to 6pm Monday to Friday, 9am to 5pm Saturday and Sunday), which sells apples, jams and juices as well as fruity ice creams.

Tinsley House   B&B €

(☑052-744 1947; www.tinsleyhouse.com; The Square; d/f from €65/120; ⊙Apr-Sep; 🛜) This light, bright and charming B&B on the square offers four period-furnished rooms and a sweet roof garden. The owner, Liam Roche, is an expert on local history and can recommend walks and other activities.

Cahir House Hotel   HOTEL €€

(☑052-744 3000; www.cahirhousehotel.ie; The Square; s/d from €60/95; P@🛜) Set in an imposing traditional building on a prominent corner of the square, this landmark hotel has elegant rooms, a long menu of bar food, a spa, and helpful and efficient staff.

TIPPERARY HERITAGE TRAIL

Extending 56km from the Vee Gap viewpoint near Clogheen in the south to Cashel in the north, the national way-marked Tipperary Heritage Trail passes some beautiful river valleys and ruins. The 30km north from Cahir to Cashel is the best segment, featuring the verdant lands around the River Suir and traversing close to highlights such as **Athassel Priory** (p318). The best stretches around Golden are off roads. Expect to see a fair amount of wildlife as the paths and very minor roads follow the waters and penetrate woodlands. Ordnance Survey Discovery series maps 66 and 74 cover the route.

Galileo   ITALIAN €€

(www.galileocafe.com; Church St; mains €11-24; ⊙noon-10pm Mon-Sat, 1-9pm Sun) Serving fine pizza and pasta to Cahir locals for over a decade, Galileo is a neat and smooth Italian restaurant, with a modern interior and efficient, friendly service. The restaurant has no licence, so BYO.

ℹ️ Information

Tourist Office (☑052-744 1453; Cahir Castle car park; ⊙9.30am-1pm & 1.45-5.30pm Tue-Sat Apr-Oct) Has information about the town and region.

ℹ️ Getting There & Away

Cahir is a hub for several Bus Éireann (www. buseireann.ie) routes, including Dublin–Cork, Limerick–Waterford, Galway–Waterford, Kilkenny–Cork and Cork–Athlone.

There are six buses per day to Cashel (€6, 20 minutes).

Buses stop in the car park beside the castle.

From Monday to Saturday, the train from Waterford to Limerick Junction stops in Clonmel and Cahir (€16.25, one hour, twice daily).

Mitchelstown Caves

Hollowed out of a narrow band of limestone along the southern side of the Galtee Mountains, the **Mitchelstown Caves** (☑052-746 7246; www.mitchelstowncaves.com; Burncourt; adult/child €9/3; ⊙10am-5pm Mar-Oct, shorter hours rest of year) are superior to Kilkenny's Dunmore Cave and yet less developed for tourists. The caves are near Burncourt, 16km southwest of Cahir and signposted on the N8 to Mitchelstown (Baile Mhistéala). Tours take about 30 minutes.

Year-round, the cave temperature remains a constant 12°C, making it feel warm in winter and chilly in summer. They are among the most extensive caves in the country with nearly 3km of passages and spectacular chambers full of textbook formations with names such as the Pipe Organ, Tower of Babel, House of Commons and Eagle's Wing.

Clonmel & Around

POP 17,140

Spread along the banks of the broad River Suir, Clonmel (Cluain Meala; 'Meadows of Honey') is Tipperary's largest and busiest town.

Laurence Sterne (1713–68), author of *A Sentimental Journey* and *The Life and Opinions of Tristram Shandy, Gentleman* was a native of the town. However, the commercial cheerleader for Clonmel was Italian-born Charles Bianconi (1786–1875), who, at the precocious age of 16, was sent to Ireland by his father in an attempt to break his liaison with a woman. Bianconi later channelled all his frustrated passion into setting up a coach service between Clonmel and Cahir; his company quickly grew to become a nationwide passenger and mail carrier. For putting Clonmel on the map, Bianconi was twice elected mayor.

The East Munster Way (p322) walking route passes through Clonmel.

Directly south of Clonmel, over the border in County Waterford, are the Comeragh Mountains. There's a scenic driving route south to Ballymacarbry and the Nire Valley on the R671 road.

Sights

Turning south down Bridge St, crossing the river and following the road around brings you to **Lady Blessington's Bath**, a picturesque stretch of the river that's perfect for picnicking.

Main Guard HISTORIC BUILDING
(☏052-612 7484; www.heritageireland.ie; Sarsfield St; ⊕9am-5pm Tue-Sun Easter-Sep, hours can vary) FREE The beautifully restored Main Guard is a Butler courthouse dating from 1675 and based on a design by Christopher Wren, with an elegant columned loggia facing the street. Inside, exhibits include a model of Clonmel as a walled 17th-century town.

County Courthouse HISTORIC BUILDING
(Nelson St) The refurbished County Courthouse, south of Parnell St, was designed by Richard Morrison in 1802. It was here that the Young Irelanders of 1848, including Thomas Francis Meagher, were tried and sentenced to transportation to Australia.

South Tipperary County Museum MUSEUM
(www.tipperarycoco.ie/museum; Mick Delahunty Sq; ⊕10am-4.45pm Tue-Sat) FREE Informative displays on the history of County Tipperary from neolithic times to the present are covered at this well-put-together museum, which also hosts changing exhibitions.

Sleeping & Eating

★ Raheen House Hotel HOTEL €€
(☏052-612 2140; www.raheenhouse.ie; Raheen Rd; d €120; P🐾) Grand but homely, this gorgeous old country-house hotel offers high ceilings, massive rooms, some fine four-poster beds, wooden floors, a bar, a conservatory and two huge gardens with maples, magnolias and a vast cypress. There's also a walled garden, roaring fires in winter and a self-contained lodge.

Hotel Minella HOTEL €€
(☏052-612 2388; http://hotelminella.com; Coleville Rd; s/d from €125/145; P🐾) This family-run luxury hotel sits amid extensive grounds on the south bank of the River Suir, 2km east of the town centre. Its 90 rooms are divided between an 1863 mansion and a modern wing; the latter has almost every kind of convenience, including two suites with outdoor hot tubs on private terraces overlooking the river.

Niamh's CAFE, DELI €
(www.niamhs.com; 1 Mitchell St; mains €8-12; ⊕8.30am-5pm Mon-Fri, to 4.30pm Sat; 🐾) This long, slender, smart and bustling deli and cafe does a brisk trade, serving a wide range of appealing lunch options, comfort food (gourmet burgers, pan-fried pork and lasagne, plus creative sandwiches) and breakfasts. Free coffee refills, with a smile.

Befani's MEDITERRANEAN €€
(☏052-617 7893; www.befani.com; 6 Sarsfield St; mains €15-29; ⊕8-11am, 12.30-2.30pm & 5.30-9.30pm Mon-Sat, 12.30-3.30pm & 5.30-9.30pm Sun; 🐾) Befani's brings a touch of the Mediterranean to Clonmel. At lunchtime, there's a mouth-watering tapas menu, while dinner dishes include slow-braised short rib of Irish beef, grilled prawns and scallops, and roast monkfish tail with ratatouille dressing.

Drinking & Entertainment

Phil Carroll PUB
(☏052-612 5215; www.facebook.com/PhilCarrollsBar; Parnell St; ⊕5pm-1am) This diminutive place is Clonmel's most atmospheric old boozer, with a vintage exterior of black gloss and gold, and a charming interior that's crammed with character.

South Tipperary Arts Centre ARTS CENTRE
(☏052-612 7877; www.southtippartscentre.ie; Nelson St; ⊕10am-5pm Tue-Fri, to 2pm Sat) Has a varied program of art exhibitions, plays and music.

> ## EAST MUNSTER WAY
>
> This 70km walk travels through forest and open moorland, along small country roads and a lovely river towpath. It's clearly laid out with black markers bearing yellow arrows and could be managed in three days, starting at Carrick-on-Suir and finishing at Clogheen, both in County Tipperary.
>
> The first day takes you to Clonmel following the old towpath on the Suir for significant portions of the route. At Kilsheelan Bridge you leave the river to Harney's Crossroads, then wander through Gurteen Wood and the Comeraghs to Sir Thomas Bridge where you rejoin the river.
>
> On the second day, the Way first leads south into the hills and then descends to Newcastle and the river once more. The third day sees a lot of very atmospheric walking along the quiet River Tar to Clogheen.
>
> Ordnance Survey Discovery series maps 74 and 75 cover the route.

ℹ️ Information

Tourist Office (☑ 052-612 2960; Main Guard, Sarsfield St; ⊙ 9.30am-1pm & 2-4.30pm Mon-Fri) Very helpful staff; adjoins Main Guard.

ℹ️ Getting There & Away

BUS

Buses stop at the train station. Bus Éireann (www.buseireann.ie) has buses to destinations including Cahir (€6.70, 15 minutes, every two hours), Cork (€24, two hours, three daily; change at Cahir) and Waterford (€10.50, one hour, six daily).

TRAIN

The **train station** (☑ 052-612 1982) is on Prior Park Rd past the Oakville Shopping Centre. From Monday to Saturday, the train from Waterford to Limerick Junction stops in Clonmel (€12.75, 50 minutes, twice daily).

Fethard

POP 1545

An appealingly quaint little village with impressive medieval ruins scattered about its compact, linear centre, Fethard (pronounced 'feathered') is located 14km north of Clonmel on the River Clashawley. One of Ireland's most complete medieval **town walls** is the village's principal feature.

There's no public transport to Fethard but it makes a pleasant cycle from Cashel, 15km to the west.

◉ Sights

Fethard's main concentration of **medieval remains** (some of which have been incorporated into later buildings) are just south of the church at the end of Watergate St. Beside

Castle Inn are the ruins of several fortified 17th-century **tower houses**.

Holy Trinity Church   CHURCH

(Main St) Fethard's Holy Trinity Church and churchyard occupy a captivating time warp. The main part of the building dates from the 13th century, though its ancient walls have been blighted with mortar for weatherproofing. A ruined chapel and sacristy adjoin the south end of the church, while old gravestones descend in ranks to a refurbished stretch of medieval town wall complete with a guard tower and a parapet, from where you can look down on the gentle River Clashawley between its horse-trod banks.

The interior of the church has an aisled nave and a chancel of typical medieval style, but is sparsely furnished. Within the church ceiling is the oldest scientifically dated timber roof in Ireland. If the church is closed, ask for keys at the neighbouring Horse Country Experience museum.

Horse Country Experience   MUSEUM

(☑ 052-613 0439; www.facebook.com/Fethard HorseCountryExperience; Tholsel, Main St; €6; ⊙ 10am-4pm Tues-Sun) Housed in Fethard's 17th-century Tholsel (town hall), this brand new museum traces the role of the horse in Irish history and culture, from military steeds and plough horses to horse racing and stud farms. Exhibits also explore the history of Fethard and the surrounding region.

Sheila-na-gig   HISTORIC SITE

On the way down to Watergate Bridge from Main St is a fine sheila-na-gig (a sexually explicit medieval depiction of a woman) embedded in the old town wall to your left. You can stroll along the river bank here, provided the resident geese are feeling friendly.

Augustinian Friary
CHURCH

(Abbey St) On the eastern edge of the village stands a 14th-century Augustinian friary, now a Catholic church, with medieval stained-glass and an in-your-face sheila-na-gig in its east wall.

✗ Eating & Drinking

McCarthy's
PUB FOOD €

(☑ 052-613 1149; www.mccarthyshotel.net; Main St; mains €9-11; ◎ food served noon-3pm daily, 6-9pm Wed-Sun) A classic multifunctional Irish country pub, McCarthy's proclaims itself as bar, restaurant and undertaker ('we'll wine you, dine you and bury you'). Closely spaced wooden booths and tables are wedged among an astonishing thicket of bric-a-brac dating back to 1840, under a wood-panelled ceiling. The menu of hearty pub grub runs from lasagna and burgers to chicken curry and fish and chips.

Nenagh & Around

In the far north of Tipperary County, beyond the Silvermine Mountains, pretty Nenagh was a garrison town in the 19th century and before that, the site of a dominant **castle** (☑ 067-33850; www.heritageireland.ie; O'Rahilly St; ◎ 10am-1pm & 2-4.30pm Tue-Sat Apr-Oct) **FREE**. Today the castle resembles the prototype for the rook in a chess set, surrounded by cawing crows.

Nenagh is the gateway to the eastern shore of **Lough Derg**, a popular swimming, fishing and boating area – enquire at **Shannon Sailing** (☑ 067-24499; www.shannonsailing. com; Dromineer; per day €75; ◎ 9am-5pm). An interesting, scenic lakeside drive from Nenagh is the 24km R494, which winds around to Killaloe and Ballina (p333).

There's tourist information at Nenagh Heritage Centre.

Nenagh Heritage Centre
MUSEUM

(☑ 067-33850; www.tipperarycoco.ie/heritage/nenagh-heritage-centre; Kickham St; ◎ 10am-4pm Tue-Fri) **FREE** The 1840 Governor's House is an unusual octagonal stone building that was once at the centre of a 19th-century prison complex. Today it holds the Nenagh Heritage Centre, which houses a local history museum, tourist information and genealogy services.

★ Country Choice
CAFE, DELI €

(☑ 067-32596; www.countrychoice.ie; 25 Kenyon St; mains €5-10; ◎ 9am-5pm Tue-Sat, also Mon May-Sep) Country Choice is a place of pilgrimage for lovers of really great Irish artisan foods. Sample the superb lunch menu in the cafe or just have a coffee, but ready yourself to browse the extensive deli area with homemade preserves, farmhouse cheeses and myriad other treats. Baskets of fruit sit out front of the shop, luring you in.

➊ Getting There & Away

Frequent Bus Éireann (www.buseireann.ie) services run to Limerick city (€9, 50 minutes, nine daily).

Nenagh's train station has four services daily to Limerick city (€12.75, one hour); connect in Ballybrophy for Dublin, Cork and Tralee.

County Clare

POP 117,197 / AREA 3147 SQ KM

Best Places to Eat

➡ Gallagher's of Bunratty (p332)

➡ Wooden Spoon (p334)

➡ Barrtrá Seafood Restaurant (p342)

➡ Long Dock (p338)

➡ Monks at the Pier (p357)

Best Places to Sleep

➡ Gregan's Castle Hotel (p357)

➡ Wild Atlantic Lodge (p356)

➡ Loop Head Lighthouse Keeper's Cottage (p338)

➡ Coast Lodge (p341)

➡ Kincora House (p334)

Why Go?

County Clare combines spectacular windswept landscapes and vibrant Irish culture.

Along the Wild Atlantic Way, the ocean relentlessly pounds Clare's coastline year-round, eroding rock into fantastic formations, and fashioning sheer cliffs including those at the iconic Cliffs of Moher and at ends-of-the-earth Loop Head. Along the coast, the waves are a magnet for surfers, and surf schools set up on many of Clare's beaches in summer.

Stretching down to the coast – and out as far as the Aran Islands, linked to Doolin in summer by ferries – is the moonscape-like bare limestone expanse of the Burren, which blazes with wildflowers in spring.

If the land is hard, Clare's soul certainly isn't: traditional Irish culture and music flourish here. And it's not just a show for tourists, either. In larger towns and even the tiniest of villages you'll find pubs with trad music sessions year-round.

When to Go

➡ While the unsettled seas of winter have a drama that will fill your days with a raw intensity, the county shines during the more temperate months when long walks along the soaring cliffs of the coast and among the desolate rocks of the Burren don't require full foul-weather gear.

➡ County Clare's pubs hum year-round to the beats of trad sessions, so even in winter you'll find the craic – often warmed in the countryside by a peat fire.

➡ Musical highlights on Clare's festival calendar include Doolin's Russell Memorial Weekend in February; Ennis' Fleadh Nua in May; and one of Ireland's best traditional music festivals, Miltown Malbay's Willie Clancy Summer School, in July.

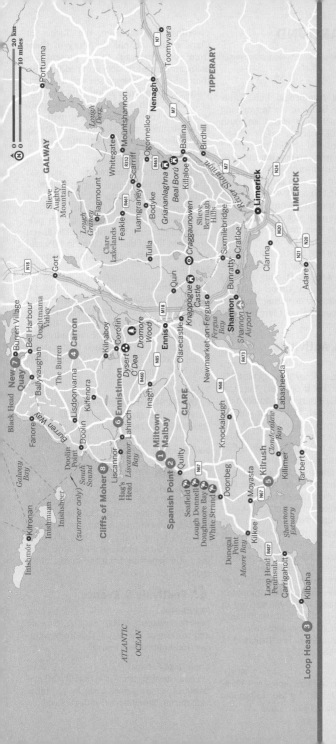

County Clare Highlights

1 **Miltown Malbay** (p341) Joining locals for spirited live music in traditional pubs.

2 **Spanish Point** (p341) Catching the last warming rays of the setting sun on this sweeping beach.

3 **Loop Head** (p337) Driving along narrow roads to a lighthouse-capped headland.

4 **Carron** (p354) Discovering lost dolmens and abandoned abbeys among the barren rocky expanses of the Burren.

5 **Vandeleur Walled Garden** (p336) Wandering the grand garden just outside Kilrush.

6 **Ennistimon Cascades** (p343) Feeling the spray of surging cascades in this

charming, brightly painted town.

7 **Hazel Mountain Chocolate** (p358) Tasting the finished products on a tour of this cottage-housed factory near New Quay.

8 **Cliffs of Moher** (p345) Boarding a late-afternoon boat from Doolin to see Clare's iconic cliffs at their most dazzling.

ENNIS & AROUND

Ennis

POP 25,276

Clare's charming commercial hub, Ennis (Inis), lies on the banks of the fast-moving River Fergus, which flows east, then south into the Shannon Estuary.

The town's medieval origins are recalled by its irregular, narrow streets, but the most important surviving historical site is Ennis Friary, founded in the 13th century by the O'Briens, kings of Thomond, who also built a castle here in the 13th century. Much of the wooden town went skywards in a 1249 fire and Ennis was then razed by one of the O'Briens in 1306.

Today sights are few, but the town centre, with its narrow, pedestrian-friendly streets, is enjoyable to wander. Handily situated 23km north of Shannon Airport (p331), it makes an ideal base for exploring the county: you can reach any part of Clare in under two hours from here.

Sights & Activities

★ **Ennis Friary**   CHURCH
(www.heritageireland.ie; Abbey St; adult/child €5/3; ⊙10am-6pm Easter-Sep, to 5pm Oct) North of the Square, Ennis Friary was founded by Donnchadh Cairbreach O'Brien, a king of Thomond, between 1240 and 1249. A mix of structures dating between the 13th and 19th centuries, the friary has a graceful five-section window dating from the late 13th century, a McMahon tomb (1460) with alabaster panels depicting scenes from the Passion, and a particularly fine *Ecce Homo* panel portraying a stripped and bound Christ.

Objects associated with the Passion to look for include the rooster rising from a cooking pot, three dice, nails and various tools. The panel was possibly painted in earlier centuries. On the other side of the nave is a devotional relief carving of St Francis of Assisi (displaying stigmata), patron of the Franciscans who arrived in Ennis in the early 13th century. Further fascinating carvings associated with Jesus Christ and his crucifixion are displayed in glass cabinets in the nave.

Clare Museum   MUSEUM
(www.clarelibrary.ie; Arthur's Row; ⊙9.30am-1pm & 2-5.30pm Mon-Sat Jun-Sep, 9.30am-1pm & 2-5.30pm Tue-Sat Oct-May) FREE At this diverting little museum, the 'Riches of Clare' exhibition tells the story of Clare from 8000 years ago to the present day using authentic artefacts grouped into five themes: earth (geology, seasons and agriculture), power (such as hill forts and tower houses), faith (Christianity's influence), water (the county's relationship with the River Shannon and Atlantic) and energy (particularly Clare's musical and sporting prowess).

Daniel O'Connell Monument   MONUMENT
(The Square) Perched on a soaring column, a statue of Daniel O'Connell (aka the 'Great Liberator') presides over the Square.

O'Connell's election to the British parliament by a huge majority in 1828 forced Britain to lift its ban on Catholic MPs and led to the Act of Catholic Emancipation a year later.

Ennis Cathedral   CATHEDRAL
(www.ennisparish.com/parish-churches/cathedral; O'Connell St; ⊙7.30am-8pm Mon-Fri, 9am-7pm Sat & Sun) Consecrated in 1843, this impressive structure had its tower and spire added in 1894, and was elevated to the status of a cathedral in 1990. A highlight is its 1930-built organ.

Tierney's Cycles   CYCLING
(☑065-682 9433; www.clarebikehire.com; 17 Abbey St; bike rental per day/week from €20/80; ⊙9am-6pm Mon-Sat) Tierney's rents well-maintained road and racing bikes. Hire includes a lock and repair kit; helmet rental is €10.

Tours

Ennis Walking Tours   WALKING
(☑087 648 3714; www.enniswalkingtours.com; adult/child €10/free; ⊙11am Mon, Tue & Thu-Sat May-Oct) Tales of famine, murder, riots and rebellion bring to life the story of Ennis' history on these excellent 75-minute walking tours departing from the tourist office (p329).

Festivals & Events

Fleadh Nua   CULTURAL
(www.fleadhnua.com; ⊙May) Singing, dancing and workshops are part of this lively eight-day traditional music festival.

Ennis Trad Festival   MUSIC
(www.ennistradfest.com; ⊙mid-Nov) Traditional music in venues across town keeps spirits high during November's five-day festival.

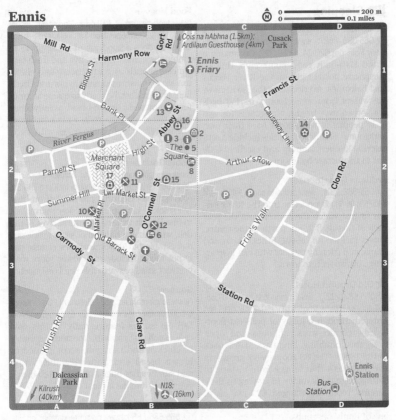

Ennis

◎ Top Sights
1 Ennis Friary B1

◎ Sights
2 Clare Museum B2
3 Daniel O'Connell Monument B2
4 Ennis Cathedral B3

☻ Activities, Courses & Tours
5 Ennis Walking Tours B2
Tierney's Cycles .... (see 16)

☰ Sleeping
6 Old Ground Hotel B3
7 Rowan Tree Hostel B1
8 Temple Gate Hotel B2

☒ Eating
9 Ennis Gourmet Store B3

10 Food Heaven A2
Rowan Tree Cafe Bar .... (see 7)
11 Souper B2
12 Town Hall Cafe B3

☻ Drinking & Nightlife
Brogan's .... (see 15)
13 Nora Culligans B1
Poet's Corner Bar .... (see 6)

☻ Entertainment
14 Glór D2

☖ Shopping
15 Custy's Music Shop B2
16 Ennis Bookshop B2
17 Scéal Eile Books B2

🛏 Sleeping

★ Rowan Tree Hostel
HOSTEL €

(☎ 065-686 8687; www.rowantreehostel.ie; Harmony Row; dm €20-24, d €59; 🛜) Occupying a grand 1740-built gentleman's club, this atmospheric hostel right on the River Fergus has balconies overlooking the swift-flowing waters from some rooms. Its 150 beds are spread over bright, airy rooms for two to 14 people; private rooms have their own bathrooms. Fantastic facilities include a self-catering kitchen, laundry and excellent Cafe Bar in the former ballroom.

Ardilaun Guesthouse
B&B €

(☎ 065-682 2311; www.ardilaun.com; R458; s/d €45/69; 🅿🛜) Drop a line into the River Fergus or just watch the sunset from the rear deck of this B&B 2.7km north of the centre. Pluses include an on-site fitness room and sauna, and friendly owners who can help arrange transport into town.

★ Old Ground Hotel
HOTEL €€

(☎ 065-682 8127; www.flynnhotels.com; O'Connell St; s/d/f/ste from €110/150/200/210; 🛜) Entered through a lobby of polished floorboards, cornice-work, antiques and open fires, this rambling landmark dates back to the 1800s. The 83 rooms vary greatly in size and decor that ranges from historic to cutting-edge. Kids under 16 staying in their parents' room are charged €25 per night. The ground-floor Poet's Corner Bar (p329) is one of Ennis' best pubs.

Temple Gate Hotel
HOTEL €€

(☎ 065-682 3300; www.templegatehotel.com; The Square; s/d/f from €119/139/199; 🅿🛜) The soaring cathedral-ceilinged lobby at this epicentral 70-room hotel was once part of the 19th-century Sisters of Mercy convent. Upper-floor rooms (reached by a lift) have views over Ennis' rooftops, but try to avoid ground-floor rooms facing the car park at the rear. There's an on-site restaurant and a great bar, the Preachers Pub, which also serves food.

🍴 Eating

Most of Ennis' pubs serve food (of varying quality); there are also some good delis and cafes.

Ennis' **farmers market** (www.ennisfarmersmarket.com; Roslevan Shopping Centre, Tulla Rd; ⊗8am-2pm Fri) 🌿, 2.8km northeast of town, just off the R352, draws some of the county's best producers. All produce must be grown, reared, caught or made by the stallholder in Clare.

Food Heaven
CAFE €

(www.food-heaven.ie; 21 Lower Market St; dishes €5-11; ⊗8.30am-6pm Mon-Sat; 🛜) This small cafe-deli does a good job of living up to its ambitious name with creative and fresh fare. Omelettes such as goat's cheese and cherry tomato or mushroom and thyme are a highlight at breakfast. Be ready to queue at lunch for renowned brown-bread sandwiches, hand-rolled sausage rolls with homemade tomato relish, and potato cakes with sweet chilli mayo.

Ennis Gourmet Store
DELI €

(www.ennisgourmet.com; 1 Old Barrack St; dishes €6-14.50; ⊗10am-8pm Mon-Wed, to 10pm Thu-Sat, noon-6pm Sun) Gourmet produce – from Burren smoked salmon and whiskey marmalade to fine French wines – fills the shelves of this deli, which has a handful of seats inside and out. Simple but delicious dishes change daily but might include cauliflower soup, roast beetroot salad or warm mackerel on brioche.

Souper
CAFE €

(www.soupercafe.ie; 10 Merchant Sq; soups €4.50, sandwiches €4.50-7.50; ⊗9am-5pm Mon-Sat) Six soups feature daily at this cosy cafe, such as goulash, roasted vegetable or chicken and tarragon, accompanied by brown bread and butter. Paninis, wraps and sandwiches offer further sustenance if you want to make a meal of it.

Rowan Tree Cafe Bar
MEDITERRANEAN €€

(☎ 065-686 8669; www.rowantreecafebar.ie; Harmony Row; mains lunch €6.50-13, dinner €14-24, pizzas €10.50-15; ⊗10.30am-11pm; 🛜) A one-time ballroom, the gorgeous main dining room of this cafe-bar in the Rowan Tree Hostel (p328) has high ceilings, fairy lights and the original 18th-century wooden floor, while tables outside have river views. Mediterranean-inspired dishes include prawn and chorizo penne; pizzas are served at both lunch and dinner.

Town Hall Cafe
IRISH €€

(☎ 065-682 8127; www.flynnhotels.com; O'Connell St; mains lunch €9-16, dinner €19-26; ⊗10am-9.45pm Mon-Sat, to 9.30pm Sun; 🛜) Adjacent to, and affiliated with, the Old Ground Hotel (p328), this smart bistro is in the stylishly resurrected old town hall. Local ingredients take centre stage on the menu: Clare lamb, Fergus Bay crab, Sixmilebridge free-range pork and Shannon Estuary monkfish. Scones, jam and coffee are served throughout the day; it's especially popular for Sunday roasts (noon to 4pm).

🍸 Drinking & Nightlife

As the capital of a renowned music county, Ennis bursts with pubs featuring trad music a couple of times a week year-round and often nightly during summer. Custy's Music Shop is a great place to find out about live gigs.

★ Nora Culligans PUB
(Abbey St; ⊙ noon-midnight Mon-Thu, to 2am Fri & Sat, to 1am Sun; 🤝) Magnificently restored, cavernous pub Nora Culligans retains original features including the front bar's ornate two-storey-high whiskey cabinets and timber panelling in the back bar. It's an atmospheric venue for live music across a diverse array of genres, from jazz and blues to acoustic singer-songwriters and reggae as well as trad.

Brogan's PUB
(www.brogansbarandrestaurant.com; 24 O'Connell St; ⊙ noon-midnight) On the corner of Cooke's Lane, Brogan's rambles from one room to the next, with musicians playing traditional instruments such as tin whistles, fiddles, accordions and more most nights.

Cider-steamed mussels, steaks, and fish and chips cooked in beef dripping are on the menu (mains €13 to €20; food served to 9pm).

Poet's Corner Bar PUB
(www.flynnhotels.com; Old Ground Hotel, O'Connell St; ⊙ 11am-11.30pm Mon-Thu, 11am-12.30am Fri & Sat, noon-11pm Sun; 🤝) Trad sessions Thursday to Sunday year-round and every night from June to August make this timber-panelled, coffered-ceilinged bar in the Old Ground Hotel (p328) a favourite with locals and visitors.

Retro pub food (mains €10 to €26.50; food served to 9pm) ranges from egg-salad sandwiches to chicken-and-ham vol-au-vents or sausages and spring-onion mash.

☆ Entertainment

Cois na hAbhna TRADITIONAL MUSIC
(📞 065-682 4276; www.coisnahabhna.ie; R458) Traditional Irish music, dancing, singing and Irish language are promoted at this important regional resource centre for Comhaltas Ceoltóirí Éireann (CCÉ; Society of the Musicians of Ireland), 1.5km north of town. Check its agenda for performances of its Summer Seisiún shows (Wednesday and Friday July and August), combining formal and informal traditional entertainment, and various classes (Monday to Saturday year-round). Books, DVDs and CDs are also on sale.

Glór PERFORMING ARTS
(📞 065-684 3103; www.glor.ie; Causeway Link; ⊙ box office 10am-5pm Mon-Sat) In a striking modern building, Clare's cultural centre hosts theatre, dance, traditional music, film, photography, art and more.

🛍 Shopping

★ Scéal Eile Books BOOKS
(www.scealeilebooks.ie; 16 Lower Market St; ⊙ 10am-6pm Mon-Sat) A delight to explore, this emerald-green-painted bookshop overflows with new and secondhand literature including rare titles across all genres from poetry to sci-fi and travel. A stove at the rear, ensconced between two armchairs, creates a wonderfully cosy atmosphere. Book readings and cultural events regularly take place. It also buys secondhand books.

Custy's Music Shop MUSICAL INSTRUMENTS
(📞 065-682 1727; www.custysmusic.com; Cooke's Lane; ⊙ 9am-6pm Mon-Sat) A must-stop for Irish music, with instruments, musical paraphernalia and general info about the local scene.

Ennis Bookshop BOOKS
(www.ennisbookshop.ie; 13 Abbey St; ⊙ 10am-6pm Mon-Sat) Independent Ennis Bookshop has a strong kids' section, general fiction and nonfiction, and a vast range of stationery.

ℹ️ Information

Ennis' **tourist office** (📞 065-682 8366; www.visitennis.com; Arthur's Row; ⊙ 9am-5.30pm Mon-Fri, to 5pm Sat) is housed in the same building as the **Clare Museum** (p326).

ℹ️ Getting There & Away

The M18 bypass east of the city lets traffic between Limerick and Galway zip right past.

BUS
Bus Éireann (www.buseireann.ie) services operate from the **bus station** (Station Rd) beside the train station. Connect in Galway or Limerick for Dublin.

Destinations include the following:

Cork €19, three hours, hourly

Doolin €14.30, 50 minutes, four daily, via Corofin, Ennistimon, Lahinch, Liscannor and Cliffs of Moher

Galway €12.50, 1½ hours, hourly, via Gort

Limerick €10, one hour, hourly, via Bunratty

Shannon Airport €8.60, 30 minutes, hourly

DON'T MISS

TRADITIONAL MUSIC IN COUNTY CLARE

Clare is one of Ireland's best counties for traditional music. Musicians here stick resolutely to the jigs and reels of old, often with little vocal accompaniment, without more modern influences such as rock or polkas that are often heard elsewhere.

You'll find pubs with trad sessions at least one night a week in almost every town and village, including the following:

Ennis You can bounce from one music-filled pub (p329) to another most nights, especially in summer, in Clare's largest town.

Doolin A famous trio of pubs have nightly trad music sessions. However, tourist crowds can be intense, evaporating any sense of intimacy. An atmospheric alternative is a trad session at the private home of musician Christy Barry, aka **Doolin Music House** (p350).

Ennistimon The charming village of Ennistimon (p343) has ancient pubs attracting top local talent.

Kilfenora This small Burren village has a big musical heritage on show at local pub **Vaughan's** (p353), with set dancing in its adjacent barn.

Miltown Malbay This tiny village hosts the annual **Willie Clancy Summer School** (p341), one of Ireland's best music festivals. Talented locals perform in pubs throughout the year.

TRAIN

Irish Rail (www.irishrail.ie) trains from the **train station** (Station Rd) serve Limerick (€15, 40 minutes, seven daily), where you can connect to trains to places further afield, including Dublin.

The line to Galway (€7.50, 1¾ hours, seven daily) takes in some superb Burren scenery.

❶ Getting Around

There's a big car park behind the **tourist office** (p329) in Friar's Walk and one alongside the river just off Abbey St.

Taxi stands are at the train station and the Square, or call **Burren Taxis** (☑ 065-682 3456).
Tierney's Cycles (p326) rents out well-maintained road and racing bikes.

Around Ennis

Dysert O'Dea

The centrepiece of the fascinating **Dysert O'Dea** (☑ 065-683 7401; www.dysertcastle.com; adult/child €4/2.50; ⊙10am-6pm May-Sep) historic site where St Tola founded a monastery in the 8th century is the four-storey, 15th-century **O'Dea Castle**. Today it houses the **Clare Archaeology Centre**, which runs a rooftop castle walk and museum displaying local artefacts. There's a tearoom and bookshop. A 3km history trail

around the castle passes some two-dozen ancient monuments – from ring forts and high crosses to a prehistoric cooking site. Dysert O'Dea is 1.8km off the R476; there's no public transport.

The site's **church** dates from the 12th century, as does the high cross, the **White Cross of St Tola**, depicting Daniel in the lion's den on one side and a crucified Christ above a bishop carved in relief on the other. Look for carvings of animal and human heads in a semicircle on the southern doorway of the Romanesque church. There are also the 5m-high remains of a **round tower**.

In 1318 the O'Briens, who were kings of Thomond, and the Norman de Clares of Bunratty fought a pitched battle nearby, which the O'Briens won, thus postponing the Anglo-Norman conquest of Clare for some two centuries.

East of Dysert O'Dea, you can wander along a lovely river in Dromore Wood (www.heritageireland.ie; Ruan; ⊙woods 8am-7.30pm Jun-Aug, to 6pm Sep-May, visitor centre 10am-5pm Wed-Sun May-Aug) **FREE** Extending along a lovely river, Dromore Wood encompasses some 400 hectares of picturesque Irish woodland as well as the ruins of the lakeside 17th-century **O'Brien Castle** and two ring forts. Dromore Wood is 9.3km east of Corofin; you'll need your own transport.

Quin & Around

POP 951

The tiny village of Quin (Chuinche) was the site of the Great Clare Find of 1854 – the most important discovery of prehistoric gold in Ireland. Only a few of the several hundred torcs, gorgets and other pieces made it to the National Museum in Dublin; most were sold and melted down.

⊙ Sights and Activities

Quin Friary   RUINS

(Quin Abbey; ⊙ 10am-4.30pm Tue-Fri, 9am-4pm Sat & Sun) FREE Impressively intact, this Franciscan friary was founded in 1433 using part of the walls of an older Clare castle built in 1280. Despite many periods of persecution, Franciscan monks lived here until the 19th century. The splendidly named Fireballs MacNamara, a notorious duellist and member of the region's ruling family, is buried here. A bell tower rises above the main body of the friary and its charming cloister. Beside the friary is the 13th-century Gothic **Church of St Finghin**.

Craggaunowen   MUSEUM

(www.shannonheritage.com; off R469; adult/child €10/6; ⊙ 10am-4.30pm Easter–mid-Sep) In woodland 8.5km southeast of Quin, this peaceful estate includes re-created ancient Celtic farms, dwellings such as a *crannóg* (artificial island), and a 5th-century ring fort, along with genuine artefacts including a 2000-year-old oak road. **Craggaunowen Castle** is a small, well-preserved MacNamara fortified house. There's also a souterrain (underground passage) and animals such as wild boars and rare Soay sheep.

Guides are at hand for further illumination. In a specially built display hall, the **Brendan Boat** is a leather-hulled vessel built by Tim Severin and sailed across the Atlantic in 1976 and 1977 in the same fashion as St Brendan's supposed journey to America in the 6th century.

Knappogue Castle   HISTORIC SITE

(☑ 061-711 200; www.shannonheritage.com; R469; banquet adult/child €52.50/34.50; ⊙ by reservation 6.30-8.30pm Apr-Oct) The only way to visit this stately 15th-century castle 3.5km southeast of Quin is to attend a touristy but fun medieval banquet. Following a cup of mead and harp music, visitors sit down to a four-course meal accompanied by live entertainment. Knappogue's walls are intact, and it has a fine collection of period furniture and fireplaces, and restored formal gardens.

The castle was built in 1467 by the MacNamaras, who held sway over a large part of Clare from the 5th to mid-15th centuries and littered the region with 42 castles. It was confiscated by Cromwellian forces in 1659 and bestowed upon a parliamentarian, Arthur Smith, which is one of the reasons it was spared destruction. The MacNamara family regained the castle after the Restoration in 1660 and it was finally restored by a Texan architect after he purchased it in 1966. Shannon Development, which administers the site, has owned it since 1996.

EASTERN & SOUTHEASTERN CLARE

Away from the Atlantic coast and the rugged Burren, Clare rolls through low-lying green countryside with gentle hills.

The county's eastern boundary is the River Shannon and the long, inland waterway of Lough Derg, which stretches 48km from Portumna in County Galway to just south of Killaloe. Lakeside villages here seem a world away from the rugged, evocative west of Clare, but it's a picturesque landscape of water, woods and panoramic views.

Southeastern Clare, where the Shannon swells into its broad estuary, is largely farmland.

Shannon Airport

Ireland's third-busiest airport, **Shannon Airport** (SNN; ☑ 061-712 000; www.shannonairport.ie; 🖥), was once a vital fuelling stop for piston-engine planes lacking the range to make it between the North American and European mainlands, and an upgraded runway is seeing passenger traffic increase. The airport has ATMs, currency exchange, car-rental desks, taxis and a **tourist office** (☑ 061-712 000; www.shannonregiontourism.ie; Shannon Airport; ⊙ 7am-11pm) near the arrivals area. Numerous flights serve Europe, the UK and North America (with US pre-clearance facilities).

From Shannon Airport, Bus Éireann (www.buseireann.ie) has direct services to the following places:

Cork €19, 2½ hours, hourly

Ennis €8.60, 30 minutes, hourly

Galway €10, two hours, hourly

Limerick €8.60, 50 minutes, up to two hourly

Park Inn Shannon Airport   HOTEL €€
(⌨ 061-471 122; www.parkinn.ie; Shannon Airport; r from €70; P❋@☎) Wake up in one of the 114 generic hotel rooms here and you could be anywhere, which is the idea, as the airport terminal is just 150m across the car park. It's a stop gap if you have an early flight and want to lose the rental car.

Bunratty

POP 349

Bunratty (Bun Raite) is home to a splendid castle that abuts a theme park re-creating an Irish village of yore. It's a double act that draws in countless visitors, particularly given its proximity to Shannon Airport (p331), 13km to Bunratty's west.

◉ Sights

Bunratty Castle & Folk Park   CASTLE
(⌨ 061-360 788; www.shannonheritage.com/ BunrattyCastleAndFolkPark; castle & folk park adult/child €16.50/14; ⊙ castle 9am-4pm, folk park 9am-5.50pm) Dating from the 15th century, square, hulking Bunratty Castle is only the latest of several edifices to occupy its location beside the River Ratty. Vikings founded a settlement here in the 10th century, and later occupants included the Norman Thomas de Clare in the 1270s. It's accessed via the folk park, a reconstructed traditional Irish village with smoke coiling from thatched-cottage chimneys, a forge and working blacksmith, weavers, post office, grocery-pub, small cafe and more. Tickets are cheaper online.

The present castle was built in 1425 by the energetic MacNamara family, falling shortly thereafter to the O'Briens, in whose possession it remained until the 17th century. Fully restored in 1954 and loaded with 14th- to 17th-century furniture, paintings, wall tapestries and antlers, the castle is home to a **dungeon**, a **main hall** and the magnificent and colossal **Great Hall**.

A few of the buildings in the folk park were brought here from elsewhere, but most are re-creations. In peak season, employees in period garb explain the more family-friendly and rose-tinted aspects of the late 19th century. Faux but fun.

Medieval banquets in the castle and traditional Irish evenings in the folk park's corn barn are other crowd pleasers.

🛏 Sleeping & Eating

Bunratty has several hotels and B&Bs in the surrounding area. All are good choices if you have an early flight from nearby Shannon Airport.

Cahergal Farmhouse   B&B €€
(⌨ 061-368 358; www.cahergal.com; Newmarket-on-Fergus; s/d/f €60/90/160; P☎) Wake up to the gentle clucking of chickens at this B&B on a working farm 14km northwest of Bunratty (10km north of Shannon Airport (p331)). With bucolic views, floral drapes and framed Irish landscape prints, rooms are charmingly old fashioned, while breakfasts are hearty and facilities include a tennis court.

The owners can arrange farm tours for guests and take kids to meet the animals.

Briar Lodge   B&B €€
(⌨ 061-363 388; www.briarlodge.com; Hill Rd; s/d/f from €40/70/95; ⊙ mid-Mar–mid-Oct; P☎) On a very quiet and secluded cul-de-sac 2.4km northwest of Bunratty Castle, this traditionally styled house with a conifer-filled front garden has five cosy rooms, some with wallpaper feature walls, and welcoming, cordial owners.

Durty Nelly's   PUB FOOD €€
(⌨ 061-364 861; www.durtynellys.ie; Bunratty House Mews; mains €18-29; ⊙ kitchen noon-10pm, bar to 11.30pm) Opened in 1620, this atmospheric mustard-yellow pub once served the guards at neighbouring Bunratty Castle. Its warren of rooms is full of snugs, timber beams and peat fires, along with an astonishing collection of badges donated by firefighters, police and armed forces et al from all over Ireland and the world. Impressive food includes duck breast with black cherry sauce.

Superb castle and river views extend from the upstairs terrace.

★ **Gallagher's of Bunratty**   SEAFOOD €€€
(⌨ 061-363 363; http://gallaghersofbunratty.com; mains €19-45; ⊙ 5.30-9.30pm Mon-Sat, 12.30-3pm & 5.30-9.30pm Sun) With stone walls, exposed beams, timber panelling and a wood stove, this thatched cottage is as enchanting inside as it is out. But the real reason to book is for some of Ireland's most magnificent seafood, such as Doughmore crab with Gigas rock oysters, whole black sole on or off the bone, or a surf-and-turf that includes half a Doonbeg lobster.

Its adjacent JP Clarke's Country Pub serves lunch and dinner daily, and has an extensive gin, whiskey and craft beer selection.

☆ Entertainment

Irish Evening at Bunratty   LIVE PERFORMANCE
(✆061-360 788; www.shannonheritage.com/IrishEvening; adult/child €50/27.50; ⊕7-9.30pm Apr-Oct) High-spirited Irish nights lift the roof of a corn barn in the folk park adjacent to Bunratty Castle (p332). Waitstaff serve Irish classics (stews, poached salmon, apple pie) amid traditional storytelling, music and dancing, while wine gets you in the mood for the singalong.

Bunratty Castle Medieval Banquet   LIVE PERFORMANCE
(✆061-360 788; www.shannonheritage.com/BunrattyCastleMedievalBanquet; adult/child €58/38; ⊕5.30pm & 8.45pm) Candlelit medieval banquets at Bunratty Castle (p332) are replete with harp-playing maidens, court jesters and meaty medieval fare (vegetarian options available), washed down with goblets of mead (honey wine). The banquets are extremely popular with groups, so book well ahead. You can often find savings online.

ⓘ Getting There & Away

Bus Éireann (www.buseireann.ie) has hourly services to destinations including Ennis (€8.60, 50 minutes) and Limerick (€5.30, 25 minutes).

Killaloe & Ballina

POP 4116

Facing each other across a narrow channel, Killaloe and Ballina are really one destination, even if they have different personalities (and counties). A fine 13-arch, one-lane bridge (1770) spans the River Shannon, linking the pair.

Killaloe (Cill Da Lúa) is picturesque Clare at its finest, lying on the western banks of lower Loch Deirgeirt, the southern extension of Lough Derg, where the lough narrows at one of the principal crossings of the River Shannon.

Not as quaint as Killaloe, Ballina (Béal an Átha) is in County Tipperary and has some of the better pubs and restaurants. It lies at the end of a scenic drive from Nenagh along Lough Derg on the R494.

WILDE IRISH CHOCOLATES

In the heady, open-plan factory at Wilde Irish Chocolates (✆061-922 080; www.wildeirishchocolates.com; Tuamgraney; ⊕9am-5pm Mon-Fri) you can watch chocolates being made and packed, and taste developmental and best-selling products (over 80 to date, including chocolate, spreads, fudges such as malted honeycomb and chocolate, and hot chocolate preparations). The factory is in the village of Tuamgraney, 16km northwest of Killaloe. Look out for its chocolates at Killaloe's **farmers market** (p334), and at its shops in **Doolin** (p350) and Limerick city.

◉ Sights & Activities

Killaloe Cathedral   CHURCH
(St Flannan's Cathedral; ✆061-376 687; Royal Pde, Killaloe; tower €2; ⊕9am-6pm Easter-Sep, to 5pm Oct-Easter) Built by the O'Brien family on top of a 6th-century church, Killaloe Cathedral dates from the early 13th century. Astonishing carvings decorate the Romanesque southern doorway (on your right as you enter). Nearby is the c AD 1000 **Thorgrim's Stone**, a shaft of a stone cross unusually inscribed with both the old Scandinavian runic and Irish Ogham scripts. Other highlights include a 13th-century font. Call ahead to reserve a tour of the panoramic **tower**, reached by 89 steps.

Brian Ború Heritage Centre   MUSEUM
(www.discoverkillaloe.ie; Lock House, Bridge St, Killaloe; ⊕10am-6pm late Apr–mid-Sep) FREE Inside the former lock keeper's cottage on the little islet between the Waters, the Brian Ború Heritage Centre celebrates the local boy made good as the king who, according to the political spinmeisters of his time, both unified Ireland and freed it from the Vikings. Displays also illustrate the nautical heritage of the surrounding patchwork of lakes and rivers.

Beal Ború   HISTORIC SITE
(Brian Ború's Fort) Situated 2.4km north of Killaloe's town centre, this earthen mound is believed to have been Kincora, the fabled palace of the famous Irish king Brian Ború, whose forces defeated the Vikings at the Battle of Clontarf in 1014, although Ború himself was slain in the fight. Traces of Bronze Age settlement have been discovered here.

TJ's Angling Centre   FISHING

(☑ 061-376 009; www.tjsangling.com; Main St, Ballina; fishing equipment rental per day €10; ⊘8am-10.30pm Mon-Sat, to 10pm Sun) TJ's rents out fishing equipment (€50 deposit required) and is a great source of advice. You can hook trout and pike right here in town, but the best fishing is from the lake; guided half-/full-day fishing trips including gear cost €100/160 for two people.

☞ Tours

Spirit of Killaloe   CRUISE

(☑ 086 814 0559; www.killaloerivercruises.com; Lakeside Dr, Ballina; adult/child €14/7.50; ⊘daily, weather permitting) Scenic hour-long cruises aboard this 50-seat boat head out on Lough Derg's peaceful waters, passing sights including Beal Ború (p333). Advance reservations are essential.

🛏 Sleeping

B&Bs abound in the area, especially on the roads along Lough Derg. Book ahead in summer. Many places close from November to March.

Kingfisher Lodge   B&B €

(☑ 061-376 911; www.kingfisherlodge-ireland.com; Lower Ryninch, Ballina; s/d/f €45/70/105; P⊗) On the shores of Lough Derg, 2km north of Ballina, this three-room B&B has almost a hectare of gardens, plus decks and a dock on the water. Rooms are comfy and without pretension. Room 3 (with twin beds) has a full-length balcony; room 2 sleeps up to four. Kippers are a menu highlight at breakfast.

★ Kincora House   B&B €€

(☑ 061-376 149; www.kincorahouse.com; Church St, Killaloe; s/d from €45/80; P⊗) Just uphill from the cathedral (p333) in the heart of Killaloe, this lemon-yellow townhouse was once a pub/general store. Many original features have been retained, while historic black-and-white photos of Clare decorate the walls. There are four traditional rooms in the main house; out the back its stylish, contemporary self-catering cottage (minimum three-night stay; cleaning fee €30) sleeps five people.

Lakeside Hotel   HOTEL €€

(☑ 061-376 122; www.lakesidehotel.ie; Lakeside Dr, Ballina; s/d/f from €89/110/140; P⊗⊛) With sweeping views across the water to the arched bridge and Killaloe Cathedral (p333), this gentrified hotel is surrounded by flowering gardens. The 43 rooms vary greatly in size, shape and decor; prices work in direct ratio to the view. All let you use the fun figure-of-eight 40m-long water slide and large indoor swimming pool as well as the on-site gym.

🍴 Eating & Drinking

There are cafes, pubs and restaurants in both Killaloe and Ballina. Killaloe also has a large supermarket.

The twin towns hold their excellent **farmers market** (⊘11am-3pm Sun) 🍴 on the islet known as Between the Waters, off the bridge on the Killaloe side.

★ Wooden Spoon   BAKERY, CAFE €

(Bridge St, Killaloe; dishes €3-8; ⊘9am-5pm; 🖫) Strewn with old cookbooks, the Wooden Spoon is renowned for its baking, and queues regularly stretch out the door. Savoury dishes span frittatas to spinach- and chorizo-stuffed filo pastries; sweet treats include mini pavlovas, chocolate-and-raspberry brownies and inspired cakes like hazelnut-and-carrot or apple-beetroot. Gluten-free and vegan options are plentiful; it also brews excellent Cork-roasted Badger & Dodo coffee.

Tuscany Bistro Ballina   ITALIAN €€

(☑ 061-376 888; http://tuscany.ie; Main St, Ballina; mains €13-26, pizzas €12-16; ⊘4-9pm Tue & Wed, 4-10pm Thu & Fri, 12.30-10pm Sat, 12.30-9pm Sun; 🖥🖫) Small and stylish, with striped chairs and gleaming timber floors, this Italian bistro has an extensive list of pastas, pizzas and expertly cooked mains such as veal with lemon sauce, along with a reasonable wine list. A good kids' menu and high chairs make it a great choice for families.

Goosers   PUB

(www.goosers.ie; Main St, Ballina; ⊘11am-11.30pm Mon-Sat, to 11pm Sun) On Ballina's main street, this thatched pub has stone floors, peat fires and picnic tables on the street out front for an alfresco pint with views across the river to Killaloe. Skip the food.

Liam O'Riains   PUB

(Main St, Ballina; ⊘4pm-midnight Mon-Fri, 1pm-midnight Sat & Sun; 🖥) A linchpin of the local community, this stone-fronted pub has trad sessions from Thursday to Sunday between late April and early September, and spontaneous sessions throughout the rest of the year.

Information

The **tourist office** (☎061-376 866; www.discoverkillaloe.ie; Bridge St, Killaloe; ⏰10am-6pm late Apr–mid-Sep) shares space with the **Brian Ború Heritage Centre** (p333).

Getting There & Away

Both towns have parking.

Bus Éireann (www.buseireann.ie) links Killaloe and Ballina with Limerick (€8.60, 40 minutes, four daily Monday to Saturday).

Mountshannon

POP 200

On the southwestern shores of Lough Derg, Mountshannon (Baile Uí Bheoláin) was founded in 1742 by an enlightened landlord to house a largely Protestant community of flax workers. The harbour hosts fishing boats and visiting yachts and cruisers in summer, and is the main launch pad for trips to Holy Island, one of Clare's finest early Christian settlements. White-tailed eagles have bred in the area since 2013 following their reintroduction to Ireland from Norway.

Sights

Some fantastic fishing abounds around Mountshannon, mainly for brown trout, pike, perch and bream. Ask at your lodging about boat hire and equipment or contact TJ's Angling Centre (p334) in Ballina.

Holy Island ISLAND

Lying 2km offshore from Mountshannon, Holy Island (Inis Cealtra) is the site of a monastic settlement thought to have been founded by St Cáimín in the 7th century. Operators who will take you over to the island include local historian **Gerard Madden** (☎086 874 9710; www.holyisland.ie; adult/child €10/5; ⏰by reservation 9.30am-5pm Apr-Sep), who runs two-hour tours from Mountshannon's pier.

The island has a round tower over 27m tall, along with four old chapels, a hermit's cell and some early Christian gravestones dating from the 7th to 13th centuries.

One of the chapels possesses an elegant Romanesque arch and, inside, an old Irish inscription that translates as 'Pray for Tornog, who made this cross'.

The Vikings treated this monastery roughly in the 9th century, but it flourished under the protection of Brian Ború and others. During the 17th century as many as 15,000 people would make Easter pilgrimages here.

Sleeping

Hawthorn Lodge B&B €

(☎061-927 120; http://mountshannon-clare.com; R352; s/d from €52/75; P 🛜) Run by a warm and welcoming family, this tidy three-bedroom country cottage 800m northwest of Mountshannon has three clean rooms with private bathrooms and comfy beds warmed by electric blankets. Kids under five stay free; high chairs and cots are available.

Sunrise B&B B&B €€

(☎061-927 343; http://sunrisebandb.com; s/d/f from €55/75/110; 🛜) Perched on a hill 350m north of Mountshannon, this rural B&B has gorgeous views over the lake from its large breakfast room in a conservatory and terrace. The three rooms are stylish and contemporary. Vivacious owner Vera can fill you in on Mountshannon's white-tailed eagles.

Getting There & Away

No public transport serves Mountshannon; you'll need your own car or bike.

North of Mountshannon, several not-quite-two-lane country roads weave through the fertile landscapes under arching trees. The R352 follows Lough Derg to Portumna in County Galway. From Scarriff, to Mountshannon's south, the R461 heads to the heart of the Burren.

SOUTHWESTERN & WESTERN CLARE

Your best days in the county's west may be spent on the smallest roads you can find.

South of the plunging Cliffs of Moher to the beach resort of Kilkee, the land flattens, with vistas that sweep across pastures and dunes to the horizon. Some of Ireland's finest surf rolls in to shore near the low-key beach towns of Lahinch, Miltown Malbay and Doonbeg.

Kilkee is the main town of the Loop Head Peninsula. Beautiful and dramatic in equal measure, its soaring cliffs stretching to the lighthouse-crowned tip are major milestones on the breathtaking Wild Atlantic Way.

Inland, don't miss the charming heritage town of Ennistimon and its surging cascades.

ⓘ Getting There & Away

Shannon Ferry Limited (☑ 065-905 3124; www.shannonferries.com; cars €19, motorcyclists, cyclists & pedestrians €5; ⊘7am-9pm Mon-Sat, 9am-9pm Sun Jun-Aug, 7am-8pm Mon-Sat, 9am-8pm Sun Apr, May & Sep, 7am-7pm Mon-Sat, 9am-7pm Sun Oct-Mar) runs a ferry between Killimer in County Clare and **Tarbert** (p297) in County Kerry, departing hourly on the hour from Killimer and on the half-hour from Tarbert. Journey time is 20 minutes. It's a great short cut, saving you 134km by road via Limerick.

Bus Éireann (www.buseireann.ie) runs services from Galway city to Ennis via the Cliffs of Moher, Lahinch and Ennistimon. Southwestern Clare towns are reached by Bus Éireann services from Ennis.

Kilrush

POP 2719

Overlooking the Shannon Estuary and the hills of Kerry to the south, the lively town of Kilrush (Cill Rois) has a strikingly wide main street that reflects its origins as a port and market town in the 19th century.

From the west coast's biggest **marina** (www.kilrushmarina.ie; Kilrush Creek) at Kilrush Creek, ferries (p337) run to Scattery Island (p337), home to magnificent early Christian ruins, which lies less than 2km offshore. Cruises also depart from the marina to view bottlenose dolphins living in the estuary, which is an important calving region for the mammals. A 1km signposted **Dolphin Trail** leading west from Kilrush's central square is lined with information panels, sculptures and murals.

◉ Sights & Activities

★ **Vandeleur Walled Garden** GARDENS (www.vandeleurwalledgarden.ie; Killimer Rd; ⊘10am-7pm Apr-Aug, 9.30am-5pm Sep-Mar) 𝗙𝗥𝗘𝗘 Within a 170-hectare forest 800m south of the centre, this stunning 'lost' garden was the private domain of the wealthy Vandeleur family – merchants and landowners who engaged in harsh evictions and forced emigration of local people in the 19th century. There's a simple cafe and a garden centre. Woodland trails wind around the surrounding forest, which has a colourful array of plants including magnolias, acacias, acers, oaks, monkey puzzle trees, bamboo, ferns, banana trees, hydrangeas and a beech maze.

Shannon Dolphin & Wildlife Centre MUSEUM (www.shannondolphins.ie; Merchants Quay; ⊘10am-6pm May–mid-Sep) 𝗙𝗥𝗘𝗘 The 170-plus bottlenose dolphins swimming out in the Shannon are monitored by this dedicated research facility. In addition to learning about its latest research, you can listen to acoustic recordings and watch a 20-minute film about the playful cetaceans, a population unique to the area.

Dolphin Discovery CRUISE (☑ 065-905 1327; www.discoverdolphins.ie; Kilrush Marina; adult/child €26/14; ⊘late May–mid-Oct) These two-hour boat rides on the Shannon offer plenty of dolphin-spotting opportunities. Trips depart depending on weather and demand.

West Clare Railway RAIL (☑ 065-905 1284; www.westclarerailway.ie; N67; adult/child €10/5; ⊘1-4pm May-Sep, days vary) A 2km vestige of the historic West Clare Railway line survives near Moyasta, 5km northwest of Kilrush. A beautiful steam-powered train was privately restored by Jackie Whelan, who now runs occasional Steam Days, when the train shuttles back and forth over the open land. Call ahead for the schedule.

🛏 Sleeping & Eating

Kilrush has a hostel, pub accommodation and several B&Bs. There are also good options in Kilkee, 14km northwest.

Cafes are scattered throughout town; pubs also serve food. Self-caterers will find supermarkets as well as a weekly **farmers market** (Market Sq; ⊘9am-2pm Thu) 🍴 on the main square.

Katie O'Connor's Holiday Hostel HOSTEL€ (☑ 065-905 1133; http://katieshostel.com; 50 Frances St; dm/d from €18/55; ⊘mid-Mar–Oct; 🖳) Dating from the 18th century, this white-painted townhouse once belonged to the Vandeleur family. Today it's a well-equipped IHH-affiliated hostel with super-clean dorms and private rooms with bathrooms. Bike hire costs €15 per day; you can arrange packed lunches (€7). Other bonuses include a barbecue and picnic tables, as well as bike storage.

Potter's Hand CAFE€ (☑ 065-905 2968; 3 Vandeleur St; dishes €2.50-7.50; ⊘9am-4.30pm Mon, to 5pm Tue, Thu & Fri, to 8pm Wed, to 5.30pm Sat; 🖉) A beautiful flower-filled, umbrella-shaded courtyard is the sweet spot at this charming cafe serving cakes, pastries,

WORTH A TRIP

SCATTERY ISLAND

This uninhabited, windswept and treeless **island** (☑ 087 995 8427; www.heritageireland.ie; ◷ **visitor centre** 10am-6pm late May-Aug) in the estuary 3km southwest of Kilrush was the site of a Christian settlement founded by St Senan in the 6th century. Its 36m-high round tower, the best preserved in Ireland, has its entrance at ground level instead of the usual position high above the foundation. The evocative ruins of six medieval churches include the 9th-century **Cathedral of St Mary** (Teampall Naomh Mhuire) – part of **St Senan's Monastery**.

Also here are a **lighthouse** and an **artillery battery**, built during the Napoleonic wars, at the southern end of the island. A free exhibition on the history and wildlife of the Heritage Service–administered island is housed in the Scattery Island Visitor Centre. The centre also provides free 45-minute tours to St Senan's Monastery.

Scattery Island Ferries (☑ 065-905 1327; www.discoverdolphins.ie; Kilrush Marina; adult/child return €15/8; ◷ late May-Aug) runs boats from Kilrush to the island; the journey takes 15 to 20 minutes. There's no strict timetable as the trips are subject to tidal and weather conditions; visits usually last about one hour. Buy tickets at the small kiosk at **Kilrush Marina** (p336) and bring a decent pair of walking shoes.

---

sandwiches and salads (many vegetarian) on house-made pottery. On Wednesday evenings, it runs free Irish language courses; non-Irish speakers are warmly welcomed. It also hosts regular pottery classes, wine-tasting evenings and live acoustic music sessions, from traditional Irish to Spanish flamenco. Cash only.

Buttermarket Cafe   CAFE €
(Burton St; mains €4.50-10.50; ◷ 9am-5pm Mon-Sat; 🖥) Just off the main square, this cheerful little cafe has a courtyard that's a sun trap in fine weather. Jacket potatoes, stews and shepherd's pie are among the hot specials, while drinks span salted caramel lattes, cinnamon hot chocolates, and mint-mocha frappuccinos to iced teas and smoothies.

Crotty's   PUB
(☑ 065-905 2470; www.crottyspubkilrush.com; Market Sq; ◷ 10am-midnight Mon-Sat, to 11pm Sun; 🖥) Brimming with character, Crotty's has an old-fashioned high bar, intricately tiled floors and a series of snugs decked out with traditional furnishings. Trad sessions take place at 9.30pm on Tuesday and Wednesday year-round; less traditional bands play most weekends. It serves basic pub fare (mains €9 to €22), and has five small guest rooms upstairs (doubles from €80).

❶ Getting There & Around

Bus Éireann (www.buseireann.ie) has four buses Monday to Saturday and three on Sunday to Ennis (€14.30, one hour) and Kilkee (€4.90, 15 minutes).

Hardware shop and garden centre **Gleeson's** (☑ 065-905 1127; 2-4 Henry St; bike rental per day/week from €20/80; ◷ 9am-6pm Mon-Sat) rents out bikes.

Loop Head Peninsula

A sliver of land between the Shannon Estuary and the pounding Atlantic, windblown Loop Head Peninsula has an ends-of-the-earth feel. As you approach along the R487, sea begins to appear on both flanks as land tapers to a narrow shelf. On a clear day, the lighthouse-capped headland at Loop Head (Ceann Léime), Clare's southernmost point, has staggering views to counties Kerry and Galway. The often-deserted wilds of the head are perfect for exploration, but be extra careful near the cliff edge.

On the northern side of the cliff near the point, a dramatic crevice has been cleaved from the coastal cliffs where you'll first hear and then see a teeming bird-breeding area. Guillemots, choughs and razorbills are among the squawkers nesting in rocky niches.

A long hiking trail runs along the cliffs to the peninsula's main town, Kilkee. A handful of other tiny settlements dot the peninsula.

The website www.loophead.ie is a handy source of local information.

◉ Sights & Activities

Loop Head Lighthouse   LIGHTHOUSE
(adult/child €5/2; ◷ 10am-6pm mid-Mar–early Nov) On a 90m-high cliff, this 23m-tall working lighthouse, complete with a Fresnel lens, rises up above Loop Head. Guided tours (included in admission) take you up the tower and onto the balcony – in fine weather you can see as far as the

Blasket Islands and Connemara. There's been a lighthouse here since 1670; the present structure dates from 1854. It was converted to electricity in 1871 and automated in 1991.

It's possible to stay at the neighbouring former lighthouse keeper's cottage (p338).

★ **Bog Road Bike Tours**   CYCLING
(☑086 278 0161; www.bogroadbiketours.com; Erin St; 2/4hour tour €25/45; ⊙tours 10am & 4pm Sat & Sun) Explore the narrow laneways denied to cars around Loop Head on these entertaining tours run by Cillian Murphy, who fills you in on Kilkee and Loop Head history, from the Famine to storms and shipwrecks. Two-hour tours cover 16km; four-hour tours cover 40km. Bike rental is included in the price.

Long Way Round   WALKING
(☑086 409 9624; www.thelongwayround.ie; adult/child from €20/free) Long Way Round offers a range of historical and nature tours such as Kilkee town walks, a Loop Head heritage trail and coastal hikes around Carrigaholt lasting two to five hours, led by noted guide Laura Foley.

Dolphinwatch   CRUISE
(☑065-905 8156; www.dolphinwatch.ie; Carrigaholt; tours adult/child €35/20; ⊙Apr-Oct) Dolphinwatch runs two-hour trips in the estuary to view the 170-plus resident bottlenose dolphins (and minke and fin whales in autumn). Ask about Loop Head sunset cruises and geology tours. Sailings depend on tides and weather conditions.

Park at the car park on your right 150m before the pier, as there's nowhere to turn around further out and it's tricky to reverse.

🛏 Sleeping & Eating

Lighthouse Inn   INN €€
(☑065-905 8944; http://thelighthouseinnclare.com; Kilbaha; s/d/f from €40/80/100; P 🐕 🛜) On the waterfront, the recently refurbished Lighthouse Inn has 11 simple rooms with bathrooms, some looking directly over the bay. Its gregarious pub has a great kitchen (mains €10.50 to €19; food served 10am to 9pm), which makes its own pork-and-apple sausages and serves local Kilbaha crab claws cooked in cider. Trad sessions strike up on Saturdays.

In fine weather, take your pint to the outdoor picnic tables.

★ **Loop Head**
Lighthouse Keeper's Cottage   COTTAGE €€€
(☑01-670 4733; www.irishlandmark.com; 2 nights from €437) Staying at the former Loop Head Lighthouse (p337) keeper's residence gives you a feel for what life was once like out here. Managed by the Irish Landmark Trust, the 19th-century cottage has no TV or wi-fi but there's a radio, books and board games, and a warming wood stove, along with three bedrooms, a kitchen and laundry. Minimum stay is two nights.

★ **Long Dock**   SEAFOOD €€
(☑065-905 8106; www.thelongdock.com; West St, Carrigaholt; mains €6-25; ⊙kitchen 11am-9pm, bar to 10pm Sun-Thu, to midnight Fri & Sat) With stone walls and floors, and a roaring fire, this treasure of a pub has a seriously good kitchen. Seafood is the order of the day – you'll see the purveyors who work out in the estuary drinking at the bar. Specialities include Loop Head monkfish, Carrigaholt crab, Shannon Estuary sea bass and house-cured salmon, along with sensational chowder.

Nab a table outdoors on a summer night.

🛍 Shopping

Kilbaha Gallery & Crafts   ARTS & CRAFTS
(www.kilbahagallery.com; R487, Kilbaha; ⊙10am-6pm Mar-Sep; 🛜) Paintings, sculptures, photography, crafts, books and postcards at this delightful shop are all made by local artists. Up the back, its little light-filled cafe (dishes €2.80 to €4) serves fantastic coffee, cakes, scones with homemade jam and freshly churned cream, herbal teas and warming hot chocolate.

ℹ Getting There & Around

Buses serve Kilkee but there is no public transport elsewhere on the peninsula.

Kilkee-based **Bog Road Bike Tours** (p338) runs excellent guided cycling trips (bikes included); otherwise hire bikes at **Gleeson's** (p337) in Kilrush.

Kilkee

POP 972

The Loop Head Peninsula's main town, Kilkee (Cill Chaoi), sits on a sweeping semicircular bay with high cliffs on the northern end and weathered rocks to the south.

St George's Head, to the north, has good cliff walks and scenery. South of the bay, reached by the coastal path from Kilkee's

West End area, **Duggerna Rocks** form an unusual natural amphitheatre, with natural swimming pools known as the **Pollock Holes**. Further south is a huge sea cave.

Kilkee first became popular in Victorian times when rich Limerick families built seaside retreats here. Its wide beach of fine, powdery sand gets thronged in warmer months. The waters are highly tidal, with wide-open sandy expanses replaced by pounding waves in just a few hours.

🛏 Sleeping

Kilkee has plenty of guesthouses and B&Bs, though during the high season rates can soar and you may have a problem finding a vacancy if you haven't booked ahead. Closures are common in winter.

Lynch's B&B B&B €
(☑ 085 752 0588; www.lynchskilkee.com; O'Connell St; s/d/f €35/70/120; 🛜) Behind a traditional shopfront, guest rooms have hardwood floors, floral bedspreads and matching curtains at this B&B, which is quiet despite its town-centre location. Family rooms have two double beds; a babysitting service can be arranged.

★Stella Maris Hotel HOTEL €€
(☑ 065-905 6455; http://stellamarishotel.com; O'Connell St; s/d/tr/f from €85/100/135/180; 🛜) Follow the red tartan carpet to 20 fresh, contemporary rooms in this lovely old cherry-coloured building in Kilkee's heart. A few rooms have sea views; request one when you book. Local producers, including the butcher run by the same family, supply its excellent restaurant (lunch mains €8 to €16, dinner mains €14 to €24.50), warmed by an open fire.

Strand Guest House INN €€
(☑ 065-905 6177; www.thestrandkilkee.com; Strand; s/d from €70/84; ⊙ Feb-Oct; 🛜) Directly across from the beach, with superb views, this guesthouse with six simply decorated rooms has been given a bit of a polish since Che Guevara stayed here in 1961. Views also extend from its inviting bistro-bar (p339).

🍴 Eating & Drinking

Kilkee is well known for its seafood, served at some excellent cafes, pubs and restaurants throughout town. A small **farmers market** (East End car park, off Gratten St; ⊙ 10am-2pm Sun May-Sep) 🍴 sets up in the public car park at the northern end of the beach.

Diamond Rocks Cafe CAFE €
(☑ 086 372 1063; http://diamondrockscafe.com; West End; dishes €5-12; ⊙ 10am-5pm) Before heading off on a cliff walk, fuel up at this contemporary cafe opening to a huge terrace at the water's edge. Food is well above the norm for the types of places usually found in such a stunning spot, from breakfasts to chowders, quiches such as asparagus and goat's cheese and daily changing specials like Guinness beef stew.

Pantry CAFE, BAKERY €
(www.pantrykilkee.ie; O'Curry St; mains €7.50-12, seafood platter €20; ⊙ 8.30am-6pm Easter-Sep; 🍴) Pick up beach picnic fare or eat in at this bright-purple cafe-bakery. Breakfast (such as organic porridge with cinnamon stewed apricots) segues to lunch (Doonbeg crab sandwiches on treacle bread, St Tola's goat's cheese salad with beetroot and pickled pears, five-veggie lasagne). Its carrot cake is renowned; other sweet treats include raspberry-ripple cake.

Ask about its program of cooking classes in winter.

★Murphy Blacks IRISH €€
(☑ 085 875 4886; www.murphyblacks.ie; The Square; mains €17-24; ⊙ 6-9pm Mon-Sat mid-Jul–Aug, 6-9pm Tue-Sat Apr–mid-Jul & Sep, 6-9pm Mon-Fri Oct-Mar) The county's produce stars on Murphy Blacks' menu: rack of Clare lamb with redcurrant and port jus, Loop Head seafood pie, Carrigaholt crab hot pot and Hag's Head hake with black pudding crumble. It's booked up solid night after night, so reserving ahead is advised. Tables outside are a summer-night treat.

Strand Bistro & Cafe BISTRO, CAFE €€
(☑ 065-905 6177; Strand; mains lunch €7.50-14, dinner €12.50-23.50; ⊙ 9am-5pm Mon, 11am-10pm Wed-Sun Easter-Sep, 6-10pm Fri, noon-4pm & 6-10pm Sat, noon-4pm Sun Oct-Easter) Feel the sea spray on your face at the outside tables of this beach cafe, bar and bistro. Open sandwiches, gourmet burgers and fish and chips are served at lunch; book ahead for evening dishes such as parchment-baked Atlantic salmon or garlic crab claws, accompanied by a decent wine list.

Upstairs are six guest rooms.

Naughton's Bar PUB
(☑ 065-905 6597; www.naughtonsbar.com; 45/47 O'Curry St; ⊙ noon-midnight Sun-Thu, 10am-2am Fri & Sat Easter-Sep, 5pm-midnight Fri-Sun Oct-Easter) Dating from 1856, today Naughton's

CLARE'S OTHER CLIFFS

On the way to and from the southern tip of Loop Head, take in the jaw-dropping sea vistas and drama of the sensational cliffs along the coast roads.

From Carrigaholt, drive south down Church St for around 2km till you reach the junction, then turn right along the L2002. Part of the Wild Atlantic Way, with directional signs, this scenic route is the Coast Rd, hugging the coastline and offering splendid panoramas of the sea, running through the village of Rhinevilla and eventually rejoining the R487 at Kilbaha.

Heading west from Loop Head, drive along the R487 to Cavan and then take a left along the Coast Rd (L2000) and follow the signs, making your way to Kilkee. You'll rejoin the R487 but can head north again along small roads north from just after either Ougherard or Cross for stunning views of soaring coastal cliffs.

combines a traditional pub, contemporary cocktail bar and a buzzing pavement terrace, making it a focal point for Kilkee nightlife. Cracking pub fare (mains €12 to €25) includes plenty of seafood such as Guinness-battered lemon sole or wild turbot, crab and scallop pie – book ahead for dinner.

ℹ Getting There & Away

Bus Éireann (www.buseireann.ie) has four buses Monday to Saturday and three on Sunday to Ennis (€16.90, 1¼ hours) via Kilrush (€4.90, 15 minutes).

Kilkee to Ennistimon

North of Kilkee the land flattens, with vistas that sweep across pastures and dunes. The N67 runs inland for some 32km until it reaches Quilty. Take the occasional lane to the west and search out unfrequented places such as **White Strand**, north of Doonbeg. **Ballard Bay** is 8km west of Doonbeg, where an old telegraph tower looks over some fine cliffs, while the remains of a promontory fort can be found at **Donegal Point**. There's good fishing all along the coast, and safe beaches at Seafield, Lough Donnell and Quilty. Off the coast of Quilty, look for **Mutton Island**, a barren expanse that once served as a prison, sporting an ancient tower and fantastic views.

Doonbeg

POP 262

Doonbeg (An Dún Beag) is a tiny seaside village 11km northeast of Kilkee. A Spanish Armada ship, the *San Esteban,* was wrecked on 20 September 1588 near the mouth of the River Doonbeg. The survivors were later executed at Spanish Point, near Miltown Malbay. It was one of many Spanish ships in the area to meet such a fate. Doonbeg offers some decent surfing for those who want to flee the Lahinch crowds, but there are no rental shops or surf schools based here.

◉ Sights

White Strand   BEACH
(Killard Rd) Secluded White Strand (Trá Ban) offers safe swimming sheltered from the Atlantic swells. With a Blue Flag rating, the 250m beach is patrolled by life guards in summer. It's 4km northwest of the village. **Clare Kayak Hire** (☑085 148 5856; www.clarekayakhire.com; White Strand; kayak rental per hour from €15, tours from €35; ☺10am-5pm Sat & Sun May, 9am-6pm Jun-Aug) sets up here from May to August.

To the east you'll see Doughmore Bay and the vast **Trump International Golf Links** (☑065-905 5600; www.trumpgolfireland.com; off N67, Doughmore Bay; green fees weekdays/weekends €95/€190) beyond.

Doonbeg Castle   RUINS
The surviving little 16th-century tower next to the graceful stone bridge over the River Doonbeg is all that remains of Doonbeg Castle – its entire garrison was hanged in 1595 by the O'Briens, who had lost the castle 10 years earlier.

Doughmore Bay   BEACH
A long, sweeping 2km stretch of golden sand, Doughmore Bay is 8km north of the village. There's often good surf here; rent equipment in Lahinch.

🛏 Sleeping

Morrissey's   INN €€
(☑065-905 5304; http://morrisseysdoonbeg.com; Main St; s/d from €60/100; ☺late Mar-Oct; 🛜)

A stylish coastal haven, this riverside pub has six elegant rooms featuring king-size beds and large soaking tubs. Its restaurant (mains €15 to €25) is renowned for its gastropub fare, especially seafood – from fish and chips to succulent Doonbeg crab claws – and has a scenic terrace.

Miltown Malbay

POP 829

Miltown Malbay has a thriving music scene and hosts the annual Willie Clancy Summer School, one of Ireland's great traditional music events. The town was a favoured resort for well-to-do Victorians, though it isn't actually on the sea: the beach is 2km south at Spanish Point.

An Ghiolla Finn Gift Shop (Main St; ⊘10am-6pm Tue-Sat mid-Mar–Dec, plus 10am-5pm Sun Jul & Aug) doubles as the tourist office.

Spanish Point   BEACH
With dazzling views of the setting sun, this lovely beach also offers excellent walks north of the point amid the low cliffs, vast ledges of stone, rock pools, coves and isolated beaches.

🛏 Sleeping

An Gleann B&B   B&B €
(☑065-708 4281; www.angleann.net; Ennis Rd; s/d/tr €50/79/115; ⊘Easter–mid-Oct; P🛜) The warm welcome is a major draw of this four-room B&B 1.7km southeast of the centre along the R474. Some of its five clean rooms have rural views.

★Coast Lodge   INN €€€
(☑065-707 9676; www.coastlodge.ie; R482, Spanish Point; d/f/apt from €170/180/140; P🛜) Opposite the beach at Spanish Point, this beautifully appointed inn has luxurious rooms overlooking the ocean or adjacent golf course. Although the cottage-style apartments don't have standout views, they come with spacious lounges, full kitchens, laundries and patios with picnic tables. Craft beers are served at the piano bar; the attached restaurant (mains €10 to €19) serves upmarket bistro fare.

🍷 Drinking & Nightlife

Hillery's   PUB
(Main St; ⊘noon-11pm Mon-Thu, to midnight Fri & Sat, to 6pm Sun) Opened in 1891, Miltown Malbay's oldest pub has stained-glass windows and framed photos on the walls. Live trad sessions take place every weekend year-round and most nights in summer.

Friel's Bar   PUB
(Lynch's; Mullagh Rd; ⊘6pm-midnight Mon-Thu, 6pm-1am Fri & Sat, 1pm-midnight Sun) This old-style charmer has regular trad sessions most nights in summer and up to four nights a week the rest of the year.

ℹ Getting There & Away

There's one Bus Éireann (www.buseireann.ie) service a day Monday to Saturday north and south along the coast and inland to Ennis (€14.30, 1¼ hours).

Lahinch

POP 638

On protected Liscannor Bay, Lahinch (Leacht Uí Chonchubhair; often spelt 'Lehinch' on road signs) has long owed its living to beach-seeking summer tourists and visitors to venerable Lahinch Golf Club (p342), which dates from the 19th century and remains one of the country's finest.

More recently this old holiday town has become one of the epicentres of Ireland's burgeoning surfing scene. Surf schools and stores cluster near the seafront.

🏄 Activities

★Lahinch Golf Club   GOLF
(☑065-708 1003; www.lahinchgolf.com; green fees May-Sep Old Course €190, Castle Course €35, cheaper rates Oct-Apr) First marked out through the dunes by Black Watch Regiment British Army officers in 1892, Lahinch's renowned par 72 Old Course was designed by Old Tom Morris in 1894, and

---

CLARE'S BEST MUSIC FESTIVAL

Miltown Malbay's tribute to native son Willie Clancy, one of Ireland's greatest pipers, is one of the best traditional music festivals in the country. During the nine-day festival, which usually begins in the first or second week in July, impromptu sessions occur day and night and the town pubs are packed. Workshops and classes at the **Willie Clancy Summer School** (☑065-708 4148; http://scoilsamhraidhwillieclancy.com; ⊘Jul) underpin the event.

reworked by Alister MacKenzie in the 1920s, then by Martin Hawtree in 1999. The flatter par 70 Castle Course overlooks ruined Dough Castle.

Goats have roamed the fairways since the early 20th century, when their ancestors belonged to a local caddie. They act as a barometer of sorts: when they're out in the dunes, conditions are favourable but if you see them around the clubhouse, adverse weather is likely on its way.

Dive Academy Scuba School DIVING
(☑ 085 725 7260; www.diveacademy.info; Promenade; shore dive/boat dive including gear €25/35; ⊙ by reservation) Learn to scuba dive in the PADI-accredited Dive Academy Scuba School's 170,000L tank or join open water and shore dives, classes and courses, including Discovery Courses (€80). After diving, you can warm up in the academy's hot showers, sauna and steam room.

Lahinch Surf School SURFING
(☑ 087 960 9667; https://lahinchsurfschool.com; Promenade; ⊙ by reservation Feb-Nov) Champion surfer John McCarthy offers lessons from €35 for two hours and various multiday packages.

Clare Surf Safari SURFING
(☑ 087 634 5469; www.claresurfsafari.com; ⊙ by reservation) Mobile operator Clare Surf Safari picks you up in its van from your accommodation and takes you to Clare beaches with the best conditions of the day. Lessons, including transport cost €35/60 per two hours/full day. Book ahead as the van only carries five people.

Ben's Surf Clinic SURFING
(☑ 086 844 8622; www.benssurfclinic.com; Promenade; ⊙ 9am-9pm Apr-Sep, 10am-4pm Oct-Mar) Ben's runs lessons (two hours €35), and rents out boards and wetsuits (two hours €20). You can also rent stand-up paddleboards and kayaks (each €25 for two hours including wetsuits).

It also organises rock climbing trips in the Burren (€35 for two hours), with access to over 300 different sites.

Green Room SURFING
(☑ 086 142 2988; https://thegreenroom.ie; Parade; ⊙ 9am-5.30pm) Shop for surf gear, clothing and accessories, rent boards (€15/20 per two hours/day) and wetsuits (€10/15), or learn to ride the waves with Green Room's surf school (two hours €35). Body board (€10/15) and stand-up paddleboard (€15/20) hire is also available.

🛏 Sleeping & Eating

Atlantic Hotel HOTEL €€
(☑ 065-708 1049; www.atlantichotel.ie; Main St; s/d/f from €60/90/120; 🐾) This town-centre classic is charming, from its welcoming reception rooms and cosy bars to its 14 well-appointed, wallpapered rooms. It's more peaceful than many places as it doesn't accept hen and stag parties, but there can still be some bar noise.

★ **Barrtrá Seafood Restaurant** SEAFOOD €€
(☑ 065-708 1280; http://barrtra.com; off N67; mains €21-28; ⊙ 12.30-4.30pm & 5.30-9pm Wed-Sat, noon-7pm Sun Jun-Aug, 5.30-9pm Wed-Sat, noon-7pm Sun May & Sep, 5.30-9pm Fri & Sat, noon-7pm Sun Mar, Apr & Oct-Dec; 🖋) 🍃 On a farm 4.5km south of Lahinch, this whitewashed country cottage is surrounded by kitchen gardens that provide herbs and vegetables for exquisite dishes such as fennel-stuffed plaice with shellfish bisque. Views over the pastures to the sea unfold from its beautiful paned-glass conservatory dining room. Its five-course surprise menu (€37; vegetarian €32) is a fantastic deal.

Trad music plays one Sunday a month.

SURF'S UP!

Like swells after a storm, Clare's surfing scene keeps getting bigger and better. On weekends in Lahinch the exposed beach break, with both left-hand and right-hand waves, attracts hundreds of surfers.

Conditions are excellent for much of the year, with the bay's cliffs funnelling regular and reliable sets. Beginners will find the northern end gentler. Watch out for rocks and rips.

There are plenty of surf shops where you can rent gear and get lessons from around €35 per two-hour session. Board and (much-needed) wetsuit rental starts at €20 for two hours.

As the waters fill in Lahinch, surfers are seeking out less crowded spots along the coast such as Doonbeg and Fanore.

O'Looneys IRISH €€

(www.olooneys.ie; Promenade; mains €9.75-20.50; ⏲kitchen 11am-9pm Easter-Oct, 11am-9pm Mon-Fri Nov-Easter) The best views of Lahinch's pounding breaks and spectacular sunsets are from the terrace at this contemporary dual-level bar, cafe and club (open Saturday 11.30pm to 4am Easter to October). Decent pub classics range from chowder to fish and chips, burgers and steaks. Live bands play every Saturday night.

Shopping

Lahinch Surf Shop SPORTS & OUTDOORS

(☎065-708 1543; www.lahinchsurfshop.com; Promenade; ⏲11am-5pm Tue-Sun) In a dramatic surfside location, Lahinch Surf Shop sells boards, clothing and accessories.

Lahinch Bookshop BOOKS

(Main St; ⏲9.30am-6pm Wed-Sat, 10.30am-6pm Sun) Lahinch Bookshop stocks hiking maps for the nearby Burren, as well as fiction and nonfiction for when the swell's not running.

Getting There & Away

Bus Éireann (www.buseireann.ie) has four buses daily along the Galway–Ennis route, with stops including Doolin (€4.90, 25 minutes), Ennis (€13, 50 minutes) and Ennistimon (€2.20, 10 minutes). One bus runs Monday to Saturday south along the coast to Doonbeg (€10.60, 55 minutes).

Ennistimon

POP 1045

One of Clare's most charming villages, Ennistimon (Inis Díomáin; sometimes spelt Ennistymon) has a postcard-perfect main street lined with brightly coloured shopfronts and traditional pubs that host fantastic trad sessions throughout the year. From the roaring cascades, the stepped falls of the River Inagh, there are picturesque walks downstream.

Sights

★Cascades WATERFALL

Accessed through an arch by Byrne's Inn (p343), Ennistimon's cascades are quite a sight after heavy rain when they surge, beer-brown foaming, and you risk getting drenched on windy days in the flying drizzle.

> **THE ATM HUNT**
>
> It's easy to get caught out cashless in western Clare. Many small towns such as Liscannor, Doolin, Lisdoonvarna and Kilfenora are ATM-free zones. You'll find ATMs in Ennistimon, Kilkee, Kilrush, Lahinch and Miltown Malbay.

Beyond the cascades, a pretty riverside walk takes you beyond the Falls Hotel.

Courthouse Studios & Gallery ARTS CENTRE

(http://thecourthousegallery.com; Parliament St; ⏲noon-5pm Tue-Sat Jun-Oct, to 4pm Tue-Sat Nov-May) FREE Rotating exhibitions from local and international artists are displayed over two floors of these studios, which are located in a renovated 1800-constructed building.

Sleeping & Eating

Restaurants and cafes congregate along Main St. The farmers market sets up weekly on Market Sq.

★Byrne's Inn INN €€

(☎065-707 1080; www.byrnes-ennistymon.ie; Main St; d from €90; P ☎) Facing Main St out the front and the cascades out the back, this historic guesthouse has one of Ennistimon's most colourful facades, in vibrant shades of violet, orange, aqua and sky-blue. Up the steep stairs are six large, comfortable, recently refurbished rooms (some with cascades views); downstairs, its restaurant (p344) is the town's best.

Falls Hotel HOTEL €€

(☎065-707 1004; www.fallshotel.ie; off N67; s/d/f/ste from €80/120/155/190; P ☎ ≋) Built on the ruins of an O'Brien castle, this sprawling Georgian house was once the family home of Caitlín MacNamara, who married Dylan Thomas. Today it houses 142 modern rooms and a large indoor pool and spa. The hotel's view of the cascades from the entrance steps is breathtaking, and there are 20 hectares of wooded gardens.

Self-catering apartments start at €206; cots and high chairs are available.

★Cheese Press DELI €

(Main St; ⏲8am-6pm Mon-Sat) Everything you need for a riverside picnic or packed lunch for a Burren hike is on offer at this enticing deli. Organic Irish cheeses include St Tola

Irish Goat Cheese (p348), Abbey Brie, Bally-hooly Blue, Burren Gold, Smoked Gubbeen and Bay Lough Cheddar (among countless others); it also has smoked salmon and hams, relishes and house-baked bread, and serves Ennistimon's best coffee.

Oh La La CRÊPES €

(Main St; galettes €5.50-12, crêpes €2.80-7; ⊙10am-5pm; 🖉🍴) At this brightly colour-ed little crêperie, savoury galettes made with buckwheat flour include Clonakilty black pudding with apple compote and crème fraîche, and Burren smoked salmon with leeks and capers. Sweet crêpes span chestnut cream and honey-roasted cashew nuts to white chocolate with rhubarb jam (plus kid pleasers like Nutella). Occasional acoustic music sessions take place here.

Byrne's Restaurant EUROPEAN €€

(🖉065-707 1080; www.byrnes-ennistymon.ie; mains lunch €8.50-18, dinner €16-22; ⊙10am-9pm; 🖥) Sit out on the terrace overlooking the cascades or in the striking dining room with polka dot tablecloths and wooden floorboards, warmed by a flaming stove. Sandwiches are served with the soup of the day; dinner is more upmarket, with dishes such as bacon-wrapped pork fillet with ap-ple sauce. There's a good selection of wine and craft beers.

It has six guest rooms (p343) upstairs.

 Drinking & Nightlife

Ennistimon's wonderful old pubs are a high-light of a visit. Trad sessions take place most nights in summer and regularly throughout the rest of the year.

★Eugene's PUB

(Main St; ⊙10.30am-11.30pm Mon-Thu, 10.30am-12.30am Fri & Sat, 12.30-11pm Sun) Hand-paint-ed timber panels, including portraits of James Joyce and the cast of cult TV show *Father Ted* (who drank here during film-ing), frame the extraordinary facade of this treasure of a pub. Intimate and cosy, the interior has a great whiskey collection, vintage trad-festival posters and some fab stained glass. Trad music plays several times a week year-round.

Cooley's House PUB

(Main St; ⊙10.30am-11pm Mon-Sat, noon-11pm Sun) Trad musicians perform most nights in summer and on Wednesday in winter at this sociable old low-ceilinged pub.

❶ Getting There & Away

Bus Éireann (www.buseireann.ie) runs four buses daily to destinations including Doolin (€5.10, 30 minutes) and Galway (€22.60, 2¾ hours) to the north, and Ennis (€8.60, 30 minutes) to the southeast.

Liscannor & Around

POP 113

The small seaside village of Liscannor (Lios Ceannúir) overlooks Liscannor Bay south-east to Lahinch. There are no sights as such, but it's a pretty spot to stop with a couple of excellent pubs.

Liscannor has given its name to a type of local slate-like rippled stone used for floors, walls and even roofs.

Cliffs of Moher Hotel HOTEL €€

(🖉065-708 1924; http://cliffsofmoherhotel.com; Main St; d/f from €89/109; 🅿🖥) Although 6km southeast of the cliffs' visitor centre (p345), this spiffing hotel is conveniently positioned at the southern terminus of the Cliffs of Moher Coastal Walk (p345). Its 23 rooms have memory foam mattresses, Nespresso machines and original Irish art on the walls. Trad sessions play regularly (nightly in sum-mer) at its bar, which serves quality local fare (mains €11 to €25).

Moher Lodge Farmhouse B&B €€

(🖉065-708 1269; www.cliffsofmoher-ireland.com; off R478; s/d €50/80; ⊙Easter-Oct; 🅿🖥) In a great position overlooking open farmlands and the sea, this big bungalow has a toasty open fire in the lounge. The four rooms are welcoming after a day out rambling; fami-ly rates are available on request. Breakfast choices include pancakes with maple syr-up. It's 3.5km west of Liscannor, and 4.3km south of the Cliffs of Moher.

Vaughan's Anchor Inn SEAFOOD €€

(🖉065-708 1548; www.vaughans.ie; Main St; mains lunch €12-16, dinner €18-26; ⊙kitchen 12.30-9.30pm daily, bar 11am-midnight Mon-Sat, to 11pm Sun Easter-Oct, hours vary Oct-Easter) Seafood is the centrepiece at this nauti-cal-themed pub, but it also serves 21-day dry-aged steaks for two. All deep-frying uses beef dripping. When it rains, you can settle by the peat fire; when it shines (sometimes 15 minutes later) you can take in the air at a picnic table. Vaughan's also has compact but comfy rooms (doubles from €100).

Joseph McHugh's Bar PUB
(📱065-708 1106; https://josephmchughspub.ie; Main St; ⊙11am-11.30pm Mon-Thu, to 12.30am Fri & Sat, to 11pm Sun) Lots of courtyard tables, County Clare–brewed craft beers from Western Herd Brewing Company, excellent gastropub fare (mains €14 to €20) served to 9pm and regular trad sessions give this beautiful old timber-lined pub considerable appeal.

Cliffs of Moher

In good visibility, the Cliffs of Moher (Aillte an Mothair, or Ailltreacha Mothair) are staggeringly beautiful. The entirely vertical cliffs rise to a height of 214m, their edge abruptly falling away into a ceaselessly churning Atlantic.

A progression of vast heads, the dark limestone marches in a rigid formation. Views stretch to the Aran Islands and the hills of Connemara. Sunsets here see the sky turn a kaleidoscope of amber, amethyst, rose-pink and deep garnet-red.

The cliffs' fame guarantees a steady stream of visitors, which can surge to a swell in summer, but the tireless Atlantic winds help to drown out the crowds. A vast visitor centre is set back into the side of a hill. The main walkways and viewing areas along the cliffs have a 1.5m-high wall to prevent visitors getting too close to the crumbling, often slippery edge.

You're rewarded with epic views if you're willing to walk north or south along the cliffs.

To the north, you can follow the **Doolin Trail**, via the 1835-built stone observation tower **O'Brien's Tower**, to the village of Doolin (about 7km and 2½ hours).

Heading south, past the end of the 'Moher Wall', a 5.5km trail runs along the cliffs to **Hag's Head** – few venture this far, yet the views are uninhibited. Forming the southern end of the Cliffs of Moher, Hag's Head is a dramatic place from which to view the cliffs. There's a huge sea arch at the tip of Hag's Head and another arch visible to the north. The old signal tower on the head was erected in case Napoleon tried to attack the western coast of Ireland. From Hag's Head, you can continue on to Liscannor for a total walk of 12km (about 3½ hours).

The entire 20km-long Liscannor to Doolin walking path via the cliffs is signposted as the **Cliffs of Moher Coastal Walk**; note that there are a lot of ups and downs and narrow, cliff-edge stretches.

Look out for migrating minke and humpback whales in autumn. With binoculars you can spot the more than 30 species of birds – including adorable puffins, which appear between late March and mid-July.

For awe-inspiring views of the cliffs and wildlife, consider a **cruise**. Boat operators in Doolin, including Doolin 2 Aran Ferries (p351) and O'Brien Line (p351), offer popular tours of the cliffs.

The cliffs are enabled with free wi-fi. It's possible to exit (but not enter) the car park once it closes for the day.

Cliffs of Moher Visitor Centre MUSEUM
(📱065-708 6141; www.cliffsofmoher.ie; adult/child incl parking €6/free, O'Brien's Tower €2/1; ⊙9am-9pm Jul & Aug, 9am-7.30pm Mon-Fri, to 8pm Sat & Sun Jun & Sep, shorter hours rest of year) Wedged into the hillside, this modern centre has a spiralling exhibition covering the fauna, flora, geology and climate of the cliffs, and an interactive genealogy board with information on local family names. Free information booklets on the cliffs are available, or download the app (also free) online. The soulless ground-floor **Puffin's Nest Cafe** seems designed to urge you up to the pricier, aptly named **Cliffs View Cafe** above, which has a Murphy's ice-cream stand.

❶ Getting There & Away

Four Bus Éireann (www.buseireann.ie) services run north to destinations including Doolin (€3.30, 10 minutes) and Galway (€19.70, 2¼ hours) and southeast to destinations including Ennis (€13, 45 minutes). Numerous private tour operators run tours to the cliffs from as far afield as Galway, Dublin and Cork.

The seasonal **Cliffs of Moher Coastal Walk Shuttle Bus** (📱065-707 5599; www.cliffsofmohercoastalwalk.ie; one way €8; ⊙Easter-Nov) connects the Cliffs of Moher with Doolin and Liscannor.

THE BURREN

Stretching across northern Clare, the rocky, windswept Burren region is a unique striated lunar-like landscape of barren grey limestone that was shaped beneath ancient seas, then forced high and dry by a great geological cataclysm. It covers 250 sq km of exposed limestone, and 560 sq km in total.

Wildflowers in spring give the Burren brilliant, if ephemeral, colour amid its stark beauty. Villages throughout the region include the music hub of Doolin on the west coast, Kilfenora inland and charming Ballyvaughan in the north, on the shores of Galway Bay.

South of Ballyvaughan, a series of severe bends twists up **Corkscrew Hill** (180m). Built as part of a Great Famine relief scheme in the 1840s, the road leads to prehistoric and Iron Age sites including Gleninsheen Wedge Tomb (p354), Poulnabrone Dolmen (p354) and Caherconnell Fort (p354).

Throughout the region, there are fantastic opportunities for walking and rock climbing.

History

Despite its apparent harshness, the Burren supported quite large numbers of people in ancient times, and has more than 2500 historic sites. Chief among them is the 5000-year-old Poulnabrone Dolmen (p354), part of a Neolithic/Bronze Age tomb, and one of Ireland's iconic ancient monuments.

Around 70 such tombs are in evidence today. Many are wedge-shaped graves, stone boxes tapering both in height and width, and about the size of a large double

bed. The dead were placed inside, and the whole structure covered in earth and stones. Gleninsheen (p354), south of Aillwee Cave (p356), is a prime example.

Ring forts are strewn throughout the Burren. There are almost 500, including Iron Age stone forts such as Cahercommaun (p355) near Carron.

Flora & Fauna

Soil may be scarce on the Burren, but the small amount that gathers in the cracks and faults is well drained and nutrient-rich. This, together with the mild Atlantic climate, supports an extraordinary mix of Mediterranean, Arctic and alpine plants. Of Ireland's native wildflowers, 75% are found here, including 24 species of beautiful orchids, the creamy-white burnet rose, the little starry flowers of mossy saxifrage and the magenta-coloured bloody cranesbill. Lime-detesting plants such as heathers can be found living alongside those that thrive on lime. One of the biggest threats to this diversity is the proliferation of hazel scrub and blackthorn, which needs to be controlled.

The Burren is a stronghold of Ireland's most elusive mammal, the rather shy weasel-like pine marten. Badgers, foxes and even stoats are common throughout the region. Otters and seals inhabit the shores

The Burren

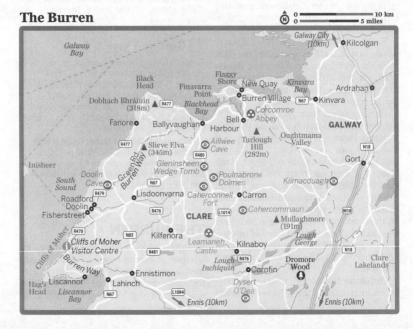

BURREN GEOLOGY

The geology of the Burren (Boireann is the Irish term for 'rocky country') is the result of immense drama in ancient times that produced today's raw landscape. Follow the deep rivulets in the stone and you'll see that the barren Aran Islands just offshore are all part of the same formations.

Massive shifts in the earth's crust some 270 million years ago buckled the edges of Europe and forced the former seabed here above sea level. At the same time the stone sheets were bent and fractured to form the long, deep cracks characteristic of the Burren today.

During numerous ice ages, glaciers scoured the hills, rounding the edges and sometimes polishing the rock to a shiny finish, and dumping a thin layer of rock and soil in the cracks. Huge boulders were carried by the ice, and deposited on a sea of flat rock.

COUNTY CLARE THE BURREN

around Bell Harbour, New Quay and Finavarra Point. The Burren Code is an initiative to educate people as to how they can protect the environment of the Burren when they visit.

 Activities

The Burren is a walker's paradise. The stark, beautiful landscape, plentiful trails and ancient sites are best explored on foot. 'Green roads' are the old highways of the Burren, crossing hills and valleys to some of the remotest corners of the region. Many of these unpaved ways were built during the Famine as part of relief work, while some date back possibly thousands of years. Now used mostly by hikers and the occasional farmer, some are signposted.

Beginning in Lahinch and ending in Corofin, the **Burren Way** is a 123km network of marked hiking routes throughout the region.

Guided nature, history, archaeology and wilderness walks are great ways to appreciate this unique region. Typically the cost of the walks averages €10 to €35 and there are many options, including private trips. Operators include Burren Guided Walks & Hikes, Heart of Burren Walks and Burren Wild Tours.

Burren Guided Walks & Hikes WALKING
(☑ 087 244 6807, 065-707 6100; www.burrenguided-walks.com; from €20; ⊘ by reservation) Long-time guide Mary Howard leads groups on a variety of rambles, hikes and rugged routes.

Heart of Burren Walks WALKING
(☑ 087 292 5487; www.heartofburrenwalks.com; €20; ⊘ by reservation Tue-Sat) Local Burren author Tony Kirby leads walks and archaeology hikes lasting two hours. Cash only.

Burren Wild Tours WALKING
(☑ 087 877 9565; www.burrenwalks.com; L1014, Oughtmama, Bellharbour; €20-30; ⊘ by appointment) John Connolly offers a broad range of walks, from gentle to more strenuous. Walks start from the cafe at Hazel Mountain Chocolate (p358).

 Information

BOOKS & MAPS

There is a wealth of literature about the Burren. In Ennis' bookshops and local visitor centres, look out for publications such as Charles Nelson's *Wild Plants of the Burren and the Aran Islands*. The *Burren Journey* books by George Cunningham are excellent for local lore. *The Burren and the Aran Islands: A Walking Guide* by Tony Kirby is an excellent, up-to-date resource.

The Tír Eolas series of fold-out maps, *A Rambler's Guide & Map*, shows antiquities and other points of interest. The booklet *The Burren Way* has good walking routes. Ordnance Survey Discovery series maps 51 and 57 cover most of the area.

VISITOR INFORMATION

The **Burren Centre** (p352) in Kilfenora is an excellent resource, as is the **Clare Heritage & Genealogy Centre** (p353) in Corofin.

Online, informative sites include the following:
Burren Ecotourism (www.burren.ie)
Burren Geopark (www.burrengeopark.ie)
Burren National Park (www.burrennational park.ie)
Burrenbeo Trust (www.burrenbeo.com)

 Getting There & Away

On its Limerick–Galway route, which runs via Ennis, Bus Éireann (www.buseireann.ie) stops at key Burren destinations including Ballyvaughan, Corofin, Doolin, Fanore and Lisdoonvarna.

WORTH A TRIP

ST TOLA GOAT CHEESE

Creamy **St Tola Irish Goat Cheese** (☑ 065-683 6633; www.st-tola.ie; off L1094, Inagh; tours adult/child €10/5; ⊘ tours by reservation, farm shop 10am-4pm Mon-Fri mid-Mar–mid-Oct) appears on the menus of some of Ireland's finest restaurants, and visitors can stop by its 26-hectare farm in the Burren, 11km southeast of Ennistimon (16km northwest of Ennis), signposted off the N85. Book ahead for one-hour tours on which you can pet the goats, watch them being fed and see a cheese-making demonstration. The farm shop sells its delectable cheeses – ash log, crottin, Greek-style feta and gouda-style hard cheese included.

Kilfenora has limited services to Ennis and some coastal Clare destinations, while New Quay has limited services to Galway city. For Carron, you'll need your own transport.

❶ Getting Around

By car you can cover a fair amount of the Burren in a day and explore some of the many unnamed back roads. Bikes are excellent for getting off the main roads; ask about rentals at your accommodation or try **Doolin Rent a Bike** (p351). Walking is superb here.

Doolin

POP 280

Doolin is hugely popular due to its reputation as a centre of Irish traditional music, owing to year-round trad sessions at its famous trio of music pubs. Located 6km northeast of the Cliffs of Moher in a landscape riddled with caves and laced with walking paths, it's also a jumping-off point for cliff cruises and ferries out to the Aran Islands.

Without a centre, this scattered settlement consists of three infinitesimally small neighbouring villages. Charming **Fisher-street** has some picturesque traditional cottages; there are dramatic surf vistas at the harbour 1.5km west along the coast. **Doolin** itself is about 1km east on the little River Aille. **Roadford** is another 1km east. None of the villages has more than a handful of buildings.

While the music pubs give Doolin a lively vibe, the heavy concentration of visitors means standards don't always hold up to those in some of Clare's less-frequented villages (p330).

The website www.doolin.ie has comprehensive tourist information.

◉ Sights & Activities

★ **Doolin Cave** CAVE
(☑ 065-707 5761; www.doolincave.ie; R479; adult/child €15/8; ⊘ 10am-5pm Mar-Oct, 11am-4pm Sat & Sun Nov–early Jan) The longest stalactite in the northern hemisphere, measuring 7.3m, is the draw of the Doolin Cave, 3.5km north of Roadford. Tour times vary seasonally, but are usually on the hour. Glacial clay from deep within the cave is used by on-site potter Caireann Browne, who sells her works here. The property also has a 1km-long farmland trail featuring rare animal breeds, and a cafe.

Doonagore Castle CASTLE
(off R478) Dating from the 16th century, this round, turreted tower house castle looks like something out of a fairy tale. The ruin was restored by architect Percy Leclerc in the 1970s for an American client whose family still owns it. The interior is closed to the public, but aim to pass by at sunset for photos with the setting sun. It's 1km south of Fisherstreet.

Doolin Cliff Walk WALKING
(☑ 065-707 4170; www.doolincliffwalk.com; €10; ⊘ 10am May–early Nov) This tremendous three-hour cliff walk sets off each morning from outside Gus O'Connor's (p350) pub in Fisherstreet past Doonagore Castle (p348), ending at the Cliffs of Moher Visitor Centre (p345), from where you can get a bus back to Doolin. Due to the precipitous terrain, it's not recommended for kids or anyone with limited mobility (or vertigo).

✦ Festivals & Events

Russell Memorial Weekend MUSIC
(www.michorussellweekend.ie; ⊘ Feb) Held on the last weekend in February, this festival celebrates the work of legendary Doolin musician Micho Russell and his brothers, and features workshops, dancing classes and trad music sessions throughout town.

⛏ Sleeping

Doolin has scores of good-value hostels and B&Bs. If you're planning on catching trad music sessions, choose your location carefully, as you may find yourself staying a very long way from the pubs you most want to visit, and roads in the area are narrow and unlit.

★**Doolin Inn & Hostel**   HOSTEL €
(☑087 282 0587; http://doolinhostel.ie; Fisherstreet; dm/d/tr/f from €26/69/90/99; P@🖧) In a great Fisherstreet location, this friendly, family-run property is split between two neighbouring buildings. On the hill, the main building houses the inn, with immaculate, neutrally toned B&B accommodation, reception and a great cafe stocking craft beers. The hostel, with five- to 12-bed dorms, is directly across the street.

No hen or stag parties ensure a low-key, sociable atmosphere.

Aille River Hostel   HOSTEL €
(☑065-707 4260; http://ailleriverhosteldoolin.ie; Roadford; dm/d from €18/46, campsites per person from €9; ⊙Mar-Dec; P🖧) In a picturesque spot by the river, this converted, cosy, 17th-century farmhouse is a great choice, with peat fires and free laundry. There are 24 beds and a camping area; if you don't have your own tent, ask about tepee rental.

Rainbow Hostel   HOSTEL €
(☑065-707 4415; http://rainbowhostel.net; Roadford; dm/d from €15/40; P🖧) With a lovely stove in its lounge, wooden ceilings and colourful rooms, this cottagey IHH-affiliated hostel has 24 beds in an old farmhouse by the road. It also rents out bikes (€10 per day).

**Nagles Camping &
Caravan Park**   CAMPGROUND €
(☑065-707 4458; www.doolincamping.com; Fisherstreet; campsites €9-20, glamping pods from €65; ⊙mid-Mar–mid-Oct; P🖧) Let the nearby pounding surf lull you to sleep at this grassy expanse 100m from the pier, 1.5km northwest of Fisherstreet. The 85 hard stands for caravans and campervans and 4 hectares for pitching tents are open to the elements, so pin those pegs down. Timber glamping pods have a small double bed, single bed, kitchenette and a porch.

★**O'Connors Guesthouse
& Riverside Camping**   INN, CAMPGROUND €€
(☑065-707 4498; www.oconnorsdoolin.com; Doolin; s/d from €55/100, glamping accommodation €80-100, campsites €8-20; ⊙late Feb-Nov; P🖧) On a bend in the River Aille, this working

farm has an L-shaped barn-style guesthouse with 10 spick-and-span rooms, two of which are equipped for visitors with limited mobility. Next door, tent pitches, and caravan and campervan sites, some right by the river, are available at its campground, along with glamping yurts, tepees and retro caravans.

Hotel Doolin   HOTEL €€
(☑065-707 4111; www.hoteldoolin.ie; Doolin; d/f €160/210; P🖧) 🌿 Streamlined rooms at this contemporary hotel have elegant dark-wood furniture and Voya Irish seaweed toiletries. On the ground floor, the lounge area opens to a patio and lawns. Look out for deals online. There's a classy evening restaurant (mains €15 to €25), pizzeria (pizzas €9 to €13), residents-only bar, and an in-house pub, Fitz's (p350), which also serves food.

Daly's House   B&B €€
(☑065-707 4242; www.dalys-doolin.com; Fisherstreet; s/d from €60/90; P🖧) Situated 300m north of Gus O'Connor's (p350), this excellent B&B has glimpses of the Cliffs of Moher from its breakfast room. The six large, comfy rooms are brightened by colourful cushions and contemporary prints, and the hosts are especially welcoming.

Cullinan's Guesthouse   INN €€
(☑065-707 4183; www.cullinansdoolin.com; Doolin; d €90-120; ⊙Mar-Nov; P🖧) Owned by well-known fiddle-playing James Cullinan, this mustard-coloured inn on the River Aille has eight spotless, comfortable, pine-furnished rooms. A couple of rooms are slightly smaller than the others, but have river views. There's a lovely back terrace for enjoying the views, and a well-regarded restaurant (p350).

Sea View House   B&B €€
(☑087 267 9617; www.seaview-doolin.ie; Fisherstreet; d from €130; ⊙mid-Mar–Oct; P🖧) Sweeping views extend from higher-priced rooms at this aptly named house on high ground above Fisherstreet village, and from the timber deck. Rooms have dark wood furniture, floral curtains and colourful prints; the common lounge has a telescope for surveying the panorama.

✖ **Eating**

Irish classics such as bacon and cabbage and seafood chowder are served at Doolin's pubs throughout the day until about 9.30pm.

Doolin also has a handful of restaurants and cafes, some open only in summer.

There are no supermarkets (or ATMs), so stock up on supplies before you arrive.

Doolin Cafe
CAFE €

(www.thedoolincafe.com; Roadford; mains €4-9; ⏱9am-6pm Wed-Mon Apr-Oct; 🖉🏠) A local gathering point, this white-painted, purple-trimmed cottage serves filling breakfasts until 1pm (vegan, vegetarian and seafood variations available, as well as breakfast waffles for kids), along with soups, salads and sandwiches at lunch, and homemade pastries and cakes (including a great cheesecake) throughout the day. Picnic tables outside catch the sun.

Cullinan's
MODERN IRISH €€€

(☑065-707 4183; www.cullinansdoolin.com; Doolin; mains €22-32; ⏱6-9pm Mon, Tue & Thu-Sat Easter–mid-Oct) Below the guesthouse (p349) of the same name, this superb restaurant has a brief menu that changes depending on what's fresh, accompanied by a long wine list. Expect dishes such as whiskey-cured salmon, chargrilled sirloin with black pudding croquettes and pistachio-and-raspberry pudding.

🍷 Drinking & Entertainment

⭐Gus O'Connor's
PUB

(https://gusoconnorspubdoolin.net; Fisherstreet; ⏱10am-midnight Mon-Thu, to 2am Fri-Sun) Right on the river where it runs into the sea, this sprawling place dating from 1832 has a rollicking atmosphere when the music is in full swing. On some summer nights you won't squeeze inside. Music plays from 9.30pm nightly from late February to November and every Sunday from 6pm year-round.

The classic pub food served at both lunch (mains €7.50 to €15) and dinner (€12 to €24) is well above average.

McGann's
PUB

(☑065-707 4133; www.mcgannspubdoolin.com; Roadford; ⏱10am-11.30pm Mon-Wed, to 12.30am Thu-Sat, to 11pm Sun; 🛜) McGann's has all the classic touches of a full-on Irish music pub, with action often spilling onto the street. Inside you'll find locals playing darts in its warren of small rooms, some with peat fires. Trad sessions take place most nights year-round. Upstairs are six simple rooms with private bathrooms (doubles from €60).

McDermott's
PUB

(MacDiarmada's; Roadford; ⏱bar 11am-midnight, kitchen 9am-9.30pm) This simple red-and-white traditional pub is a rowdy favourite. Picnic tables face the street; the inside is pretty basic, as is the menu of sandwiches and roasts. Music kicks off at 9.30pm nightly from Easter to October, and several nights a week the rest of the year.

Fitz's
PUB

(www.hoteldoolin.ie; Doolin; ⏱noon-11.30pm Mon-Thu, to 12.30am Fri & Sat, to 11pm Sun) At Hotel Doolin (p349), relative newcomer Fitz's has trad sessions twice nightly from April to October and at least three times a week from November to March. In addition to a superb whiskey selection it has great craft beers and ciders (tasting flights available), and brews its own Dooliner beers. Bar food (mains €13 to €24) is first rate.

Ingenious cocktails include MV Plassy on the Rocks (named after the Aran Islands shipwreck (p383)), a Burren martini and Father Jack Espresso (in honour of the cantankerous priest from the TV series *Father Ted*).

⭐Doolin Music House
TRADITIONAL MUSIC

(☑065-707 4584; www.doolinmusichouse.com; R478, Caherkinalla; €20; ⏱by reservation 7-8.30pm Mon, Wed & Fri) For a change from Doolin's crowded music pubs, book ahead to visit local musician Christy Barry's cosy home, which is filled with artworks by his artist partner Sheila. By the open fire, Christy plays traditional tunes, tells stories relating to Irish musical history and welcomes questions. The price includes a glass of wine and snacks. It's 4km east of Doolin.

🛍 Shopping

Clare Jam Shop
FOOD

(off R478; ⏱9am-6pm) 🌿 Jams (such as wild blueberry; strawberry and champagne; and blackberry and apple), marmalades (including Irish whiskey), jellies (eg rose petal), chutneys (tomato and rhubarb) and mustards (including Guinness mustard) are homemade using traditional open-pan boiling methods at this sweet little hilltop cottage 3.5km southwest of Fisherstreet (3km north of the Cliffs of Moher). Many ingredients are handpicked in the Burren.

Doolin Chocolate Shop
CHOCOLATE

(www.wildeirishchocolates.com; Fisherstreet; ⏱11am-7pm May-Oct, shorter hours Nov-Apr)

Lavender and rose, seaweed and lime, and hazelnut and raisin are among the chocolate flavours made by Clare company Wilde Irish Chocolates, which has its factory (p333) in Tuamgraney near Lough Derg in the county's east. This shop also sells white and dark chocolate spreads, and fudge such as porter or Irish cream liqueur.

ⓘ Getting There & Away

BOAT

From mid-March to October, **Doolin Pier** (off R439) is one of two ferry departure points to the Aran Islands (along with **Rossaveal Ferry Terminal** (p375), 37km west of Galway city). Sailings are often cancelled due to high seas or tides that make the small dock inaccessible.

Doolin 2 Aran Ferries (☑ 065-707 5949; www.doolin2aranferries.com; Doolin Pier; ◔ mid-Mar–Oct) and **O'Brien Line** (☑ 065-707 5618; www.obrienline.com; Doolin Pier; ◔ mid-Mar–Oct) each have sailings to Inisheer (one way/return €10/20, 30 minutes, four daily), Inishmore (€15/25, 1¼ hours, two daily) and Inishmaan (€20/25, 45 minutes, two daily). Interisland ferry tickets cost €10 per crossing.

The boats also offer one-hour **Cliffs of Moher cruises** (€15), which are best done late in the afternoon when the light is from the west.

There are various combination tickets and online discounts.

BUS

Four Bus Éireann (www.buseireann.ie) buses daily serve Ennis (€14.30, 50 minutes), via the Cliffs of Moher (€3.30, 10 minutes); and Galway (€19.50, two hours) via Ballyvaughan (€8.60, one hour).

In summer, various backpacker shuttles often serve Doolin from Galway and other points in Clare.

ⓘ Getting Around

Accommodation providers often have bike rental; otherwise hire bicycles from **Doolin Rent a Bike** (☑ 086 109 1850; www.doolinrentabike.ie; Fisherstreet; bike rental per day from €12; ◔ 8am-7pm Jul & Aug, shorter hours Sep-Jun).

The seasonal **Cliffs of Moher Coastal Walk Shuttle Bus** (p345) loops through Doolin's villages and serves the Cliffs of Moher and Liscannor.

Lisdoonvarna

POP 829

For centuries people have been visiting Lisdoonvarna (Lios Dún Bhearna), often just called 'Lisdoon', for its mineral springs. The village is more down at heel today than in its Victorian heyday, but it makes a good base for exploring the area.

◉ Sights & Activities

Burren Smokehouse   FOOD
(☑ 065-707 4432; www.burrensmokehouse.ie; Kincora Rd; ◔ 9am-6pm May-Aug, shorter hours Sep-Apr) Learn about the ancient Irish art of oak-smoking salmon during a seven-minute video presentation at this local smokehouse. There are free tastings of salmon and other smoked fish as well as cheeses, which are sold here along with other deli items, such as jams from Doolin's Clare Jam Shop.

Spa Well   SPRING
At the town's southern end is a spa well, with a sulphur spring, a Victorian pumphouse and a wooded setting. The iron, sulphur, magnesium and iodine in the water are believed to be good for rheumatic and glandular complaints.

In the town centre, look for a trail beside the Roadside Tavern (p352) that runs 400m down to two wells by the river, where you can try the spring water.

⛱ Sleeping & Eating

Lisdoonvarna has a hostel and a couple of inns. Book ahead if you're heading here for the Father Ted Festival (p353), on the May bank holiday weekend, or September's Matchmaking Festival (p352).

Sleepzone Burren Hostel   HOSTEL €
(☑ 065-707 4036; www.sleepzone.ie; Kincora Rd; dm/d/f from €15/49/69; Ⓟ ❀) Occupying a former hotel, this hostel has 124 beds in contemporary dorms and private rooms, including family rooms that sleep up to five people. Facilities include a self-catering kitchen, a book-filled guest lounge and a large lawn area. A shuttle bus service links it with Sleepzone's sister properties in Galway city (p397) and Connemara (p397).

★ Sheedy's Country
House Hotel & Restaurant   INN €€
(☑ 065-707 4026; www.sheedys.com; Sulphur Hill; d from €130; ◔ mid-Mar–Sep; Ⓟ ❀) Stately 18th-century country house Sheedy's has 11 beautifully furnished rooms with checked fabrics and sage-coloured walls. The long front porch has comfy chairs for looking out over the gardens. Nonguests are welcome at its restaurant (mains €18 to €28), serving dinner Monday to Saturday by reservation, and its bar, which has a huge range of whiskeys.

COUNTY CLARE LISDOONVARNA

DON'T MISS

LISDOONVARNA MATCHMAKING FESTIVAL

Lisdoonvarna was once a centre for *basadóiri* (matchmakers) who, for a fee, would fix up a person with a spouse. Most of the (mainly male) hopefuls would hit town in September, feet shuffling, cap in hand, after the hay was in. Today the tradition continues at the **Lisdoonvarna Matchmaking Festival** (www.matchmakerireland.com; ⊘ weekends Sep), with music and dancing on September weekends.

Whiskey-soaked porridge with Baileys is on the menu at breakfast.

Wild Honey Inn
INN €€

(☑ 065-707 4300; www.wildhoneyinn.com; Kincora Rd; d from €115; ⊘ Easter-Nov; P 🛜) In an 1860-built roadside mansion, Wild Honey has 14 stylish rooms, some opening to private terraces overlooking the gardens. Its restaurant (three-/four-course menu €40/50), serving dinner from 6pm Monday to Saturday, has a daily changing menu using local produce and freshly caught seafood.

★ Roadside Tavern
PUB

(http://roadsidetavern.ie; Kincora Rd; ⊘ noon-11.30pm Mon-Thu, to 12.30am Fri & Sat, to 11pm Sun Mar-Oct, shorter hours Nov-Feb) Down by the river, this pub run by third-generation owner Peter Curtin is pure craic. Trad sessions play daily in summer and Friday and Saturday in winter. The in-house Burren Brewery makes superb gold lagers, red ales and stout. Fish from the tavern's nearby Burren Smokehouse (p351) is incorporated in delicious dishes (mains €12 to €18; food served March to October).

❶ Getting There & Away

Bus Éireann (www.buseireann.ie) runs four buses daily to the following destinations:

Ballyvaughan €6.20, 40 minutes
Doolin €5.20, 15 minutes
Ennis €14.30, 1¼ hours
Galway €18.10, two hours

Kilfenora

POP 175

Kilfenora (Cill Fhionnúrach) lies on the southern fringe of the Burren, 8.5km southeast of Lisdoonvarna. It's a small place, with low polychromatic buildings surrounding the compact centre.

The town has a strong music tradition: the **Kilfenora Céilí Band**, Ireland's oldest *céilidh* band, featuring fiddles, banjos, squeezeboxes and more, has been playing here for over a century.

◎ Sights

Burren Centre
MUSEUM

(☑ 065-708 8030; www.theburrencentre.ie; Main St; adult/child €6/4; ⊘ 9.30am-5.30pm Jun-Aug, 10am-5pm Mar-May, Sep & Oct) At the Burren Centre, a 12-minute film gives you an overview of the Burren's flora, fauna and geology, while interactive exhibits detail its formation and evolution to the present day. Exhibits also cover the Kilfenora Céilí Band. There's a tearoom and a large shop stocking Irish-made crafts.

Kilfenora Cathedral
RUINS

(off Main St; ⊘ 9.30am-5.30pm Jun-Aug, 10am-5pm Mar-May, Sep & Oct) Built in 1189, Kilfenora's cathedral was once an important place of pilgrimage. St Fachan (or Fachtna) founded the monastery here in the 6th century, and it later became the seat of Kilfenora diocese, the smallest in the country. Loop around the more recent Protestant church and enter the oldest part of the ruins, under a glass roof to protect them from the elements. The chancel contains two primitive carved figures on top of two tombs.

There are three high crosses with explanatory captions on stainless-steel plaques, including the 800-year-old **Doorty Cross** measuring 4.2m high; it lay broken in two until the 1950s, when it was re-erected.

Leamaneh Castle
RUINS

(junction R476 & R480) This magnificent, allegedly haunted ruin stands on a rise 6.2km east of Kilfenora. Built in 1480 as a tower house and converted to a mansion in 1650, it's the erstwhile home of Máire Rúa (Red Mary) who – according to local anecdote – got through 25 husbands, dispatching at least one to a grisly death on horseback off the Cliffs of Moher, before being incarcerated in a hollow tree by her enemies.

West Cross
MONUMENT

In a field accessed via a stile, 130m west of Kilfenora's cathedral ruins, is the 4.6m-high West Cross, which depicts Christ's crucifixion.

Sleeping & Eating

Kilfenora Hostel HOSTEL €
(☑ 065-708 8908; www.kilfenorahostel.com; Main St; dm/d/f from €20/52/70; 🅿 🛜) 🏄 Affiliated with Vaughan's Pub next door, this guesthouse has 46 beds in four- to 10-bed dorms and private rooms; ask about various family discounts. There's a laundry and a big kitchen.

★ **Vaughan's Pub** PUB
(www.vaughanspub.ie; Main St; ⊙ 10.30am-11.30pm, hours can vary) With a big reputation in Irish music circles, Vaughan's has music in the bar every night during summer and several times a week the rest of the year. The adjacent barn hosts terrific set-dancing sessions on Sunday between 9.30pm and 11.30pm. Pub food (mains €8.50 to €12) is served until 9pm.

❶ Getting There & Away

Bus Éireann (www.buseireann.ie) has one daily service Monday to Saturday to Ennis (€8.60, 40 minutes) and coastal destinations including Doonbeg (€14.30, 1¼ hours).

Corofin & Around

POP 627

Corofin (Cora Finne), also spelt Corrofin, is a traditional village on the southern fringes of the Burren. The surrounding area features a number of turloughs (small lakes) and several O'Brien castles, including two on the shores of nearby **Lough Inchiquin**.

◉ Sights

Father Ted's House FILM LOCATION
(☑ 087 404 8475; www.fathertedshouse.com; Glanquin House, Cloon, Kilnaboy; adult/child €10/8; ⊙ by reservation) Fans of madcap TV

comedy *Father Ted* will jump at the chance to visit the building that provided the exterior shots of the series' parochial house. Advance bookings are essential; phone bookings are requested only between 6pm and 8pm Monday to Friday. Payment is by cash only, and includes tea, cake and biscuits, and organic jams from the gardens. It's 9.5km north of Corofin. The house can also be visited on a location tour with Ted Tours.

Clare Heritage & Genealogy Centre VISITOR CENTRE
(☑ 065-683 7955; www.clareroots.com; Church St; ⊙ 9am-1pm & 2-5pm Mon-Fri) In addition to efficient services for people researching their Clare ancestry, the Clare Heritage and Genealogy Centre functions as the Burren National Park Information Point, with information on the Burren's geology, fauna and flora.

Exhibitions at the **Clare Heritage Centre Interpretative Museum** (www.clareroots.com; Church St; adult/child €4/2; ⊙ 9am-5pm Mon-Fri May-Oct) across the road give context to those who emigrated from Clare following the Great Famine.

Sleeping

Corofin Hostel & Camping Park HOSTEL, CAMPGROUND €
(☑ 065-683 7683; http://corofincamping.com; Main St; campsites per person from €10, s/d/f €25/40/55; ⊙ Apr-Sep) Campsites out the back have nice open spaces, and inside there are 30 beds at this friendly hostel right in the village centre. There's a cosy open fire in the sitting room, a laundry and a self-catering kitchen. Camping includes free hot showers.

THE IMMORTAL FATHER TED

Father Ted, the enduring 1990s TV comedy, is set around the high jinks of three Irish priests living on the fictional Craggy Island.

Aside from the opening shot of the **Plassy** (p383) shipwreck on the Aran Island of Inisheer, most of the locations used in the show are around Kilfenora, including **Vaughan's Pub** (p353), and Ennistimon, where **Eugene's** (p344) pub was used both as a location and the cast's watering hole. The lonely **Father Ted** (p353) house is in Kilnaboy; book in advance to stop in for tea.

Inspired by the great success of Inishmore's **Tedfest** (p377), the good people of Lisdoonvarna have organised their own **Father Ted Festival** (www.tedtours.com; ⊙ late Apr/early May), with costume parties, contests, tours and more. Year-round, **Ted Tours** (www.tedtours.com; Burren Centre; adult/child €25/20; ⊙ by reservation) visits local filming locations, departing from Kilfenora.

Lakefield Lodge B&B €

(☑065-683 7675; www.lakefieldlodgebandb.com; R476; s/d from €44/66; ☺Apr-Oct; P☎) Gardens surround this bungalow with four comfy rooms on the southern edge of the village. Conveniently situated for Burren hikes, it provides a wealth of info for anglers as well as fishing trips. Guests can rent a boat (with/without a motor €40/30 per day, including fishing equipment).

Fergus View B&B €€

(☑065-683 7606; www.fergusview.com; R476, Kilnaboy; s/d from €48/78; ☺Easter-Oct; ☎) The River Fergus flows right past this 19th-century former teacher's residence, which has six rooms and breakfasts that use organic produce including local cheese, homemade yoghurt and herbs from the garden. It's 3.5km north of Corofin.

❶ Getting There & Away

Bus Éireann (www.buseireann.ie) has four services daily to Ennis (€8, 30 minutes) and Galway (€21.30, 2¾ hours).

Central Burren

Several roads dotted with sights cross the heart of the Burren. The scenery along the R480 as it passes through the region is harsh but inspiring, highlighting the barren Burren at its best. Remarkable prehistoric stone structures litter the area.

South from Ballyvaughan, the R480 branches off the N67 at the sign for Aillwee Caves, passing Gleninsheen Wedge Tomb and the outstanding Poulnabrone Dolmen before reaching the magnificent Leamanegh Castle ruins, where it joins the R476, which runs southeast to Corofin. At any point along here, try a small road – especially those to the east – to plunge into otherworldly solitude.

Originally a Famine relief road built in the 1800s, the N67 to Lisdoonvarna rewards visitors with sweeping views of the stark Burren landscape.

◉ Sights

★**Poulnabrone Dolmen** HISTORIC SITE

(R480) FREE Also known as the Portal Tomb, Poulnabrone Dolmen is one of Ireland's most photographed ancient monuments. Built more than 5000 years ago, the otherworldly dolmen (a large slab perched on stone up-rights) stands amid a swath of rocky pavements; the capstone weighs 5 tonnes. The site is 9km south Ballyvaughan and visible from the R480; there's a large free parking area and excellent displays.

Poulnabrone was excavated in 1986, and the remains of 21 people were found, as well as pieces of pottery and jewellery. Radiocarbon dating suggests that they were buried between 3800 and 3200 BC. When the dead were originally entombed here, the whole structure was partially covered in a mound of earth, which has since worn away. A highly informative Office of Public Works staff member is often on duty, protecting the monument.

★**Gleninsheen Wedge Tomb** HISTORIC SITE

(R480) FREE One of Ireland's most famous prehistoric grave sites, Gleninsheen lies beside the R480 7km south of Ballyvaughan. It's thought to date from 4000 to 5000 years ago. A magnificent gold gorget (a crescent of beaten gold that hung round the neck) found here and dating from the late Bronze Age is now on display at the National Museum in Dublin. Note: the access gate to the tomb is sometimes locked, and signage is poor.

Caherconnell Fort HISTORIC SITE

(☑065-708 9999; http://caherconnell.com; R480; adult/child €7/4, sheepdog demonstration €5/3, combination ticket €10/6; ☺10am-6pm Jul & Aug, 10am-5.30pm May, Jun & Sep, 10.30am-5pm mid-Mar–Apr & Oct) For a close-up look at a well-preserved, drystone *caher* (walled fort) of the late Iron Age–Early Christian period, stop at this privately run heritage attraction 10km south of Ballyvaughan. Exhibits detail how the evolution of these defensive settlements may have reflected territorialism and competition for land among a growing, settling population. The visitor centre also has information on many other monuments in the area. Fun sheepdog demonstrations take place throughout the day.

Carron & Around

In the heart of the Burren, the tiny village of Carron (An Carn; often spelt Carran) is a wonderfully remote spot. Vistas of the rocky moonscape stretch in all directions from its elevated position. Wildflowers that bloom in this bare, ethereal landscape are made into perfumes at the Burren Perfumery & Floral Centre.

Below Carron lies the 4.5 sq km **Carron Polje**, the largest turlough (small lake) in Ireland. Polje is a Serbo-Croatian term used universally for these shallow depressions that usually flood in winter and dry out in summer, when the lush grass that flourishes here is used for grazing.

◎ Sights

★ **Burren Perfumery & Floral Centre**   VISITOR CENTRE
(☑065-708 9102; https://burrenperfumery.com; ⊙9am-7pm Jul & Aug, 10am-6pm May, Jun & Sep, 10am-5pm Oct-Apr, cafe 11am-5pm Apr-Sep) ✿ The Burren's wildflowers are the inspiration for the subtle scents at this wonderful perfumery and floral centre, which creates scented items such as perfumes, candles and soaps that are beautifully packaged in handmade paper. A 10-minute audiovisual presentation details the area's diverse flora, including many fragrant orchids that grow between the rocks. You're free to wander its flower and herb gardens, which provide ingredients for dishes and herbal teas served at its tearoom.

Cahercommaun   HISTORIC SITE
Perched on the edge of an inland cliff about 3km south of Carron is the triple ring fort of Cahercommaun, built around AD 800 and inhabited by people who hunted deer and grew small amounts of grain. The remains of a souterrain (underground passage) lead from the fort to the outer cliff face. From Carron, head south on the L1014 and turn towards Kilnaboy. After 1.7km, a 600m-long walking trail on the left leads up to the fort.

⌂ Sleeping & Eating

★ **Clare's Rock Hostel**   HOSTEL €
(☑065-708 9129; www.claresrock.com; L1014; dm/d/f €20/80/90; ⊙May-Sep; P�(P)☎) ✿ With commanding views over Carron Polje, this IHH hostel built from roughly hewn grey Burren stone has 30 beds in spacious, squeaky-clean rooms. Excellent facilities include a self-catering kitchen, a drying room and laundry, and giant chess and chequerboards outside. All of its power comes from solar panels and its own wind turbine.

Cassidy's   PUB FOOD €€
(www.cassidyspub.com; L1014; mains €8.50-20; ⊙kitchen noon-9pm Mon-Sat, to 8pm Sun Apr-Sep, bar to 11pm Sun-Thu, to 12.30am Fri & Sat Apr-Sep, 7pm-midnight Fri & Sat Oct-Mar; ☎) ✿ Cassidy's raises its own cattle and goats for its kitchen, which serves dishes including its famous Dolmen goat burger. Idyllic views extend from the terrace of the historic building, which was once a British Royal Irish Constabulary (RIC) station and then a *garda* (police) barracks. Trad music and dancing takes place on Fridays and Saturdays, and spontaneously throughout the week.

Its eco credentials include solar power.

Fanore

POP 111

Fanore (Fan Óir, meaning 'The Golden Slope') is less a village and more a stretch of coastline with a shop, a pub and a few houses scattered along the scenic R477, which hugs the barren coast as it curves past the Aran Islands into Galway Bay.

◎ Sights & Activities

The nearby shelves of limestone are popular with rock climbers; contact Ben's Surf Clinic (p342) in Lahinch for trips.

Surfers flock here throughout the year. The rocky coastline offers excellent fishing.

Fanore Beach   BEACH
With an extensive backdrop of grass-covered dunes, this Blue Flag–rated beach off the R477 is patrolled by lifeguards in summer and is a surfing hot spot. Its golden sands have exposed limestone outcrops – part of the Burren – at low tide. Signs show hiking trails along the coast and up in the dramatic hills. You'll find showers and toilets open in summer in a small block by the car park.

Aloha Surf School   SURFING
(☑087 213 3996; www.surfschool.ie; Fanore Beach; 2hr lessons from €35, equipment rental per 2hr from €15; ⊙Apr-Sep, by appointment Oct-Mar) Aloha offers classes for all ages and abilities. You can rent surfboards, wetsuits and boots (plus additional thermal protection in the winter months), as well as stand-up paddleboards and kayaks.

Siopa Fan Óir   FISHING
(☑065-707 6131; www.fanoreshop.com; R477; fishing equipment rental per half day from €15; ⊙9am-9pm Mon-Sat, to noon Sun, hours can vary) This well-stocked shop rents out rods and has fishing tackle, walking maps, boogie boards and cheap sand buckets. Its helpful owner, Mick, is often out fishing himself, so call in advance.

🛏 Sleeping & Eating

Orchid House
B&B €

(☑065-707 6975; http://orchidhouse.net; R477; s/d from €45/75; P 🖻) ✦ All four spotless, contemporary rooms come with sea views at this B&B in a traditional-style stone cottage on a working farm 1km south of the village. The owners are keen conservationists: solar power provides hot water, and fruit and vegetables from the gardens are used at breakfast in jams, fruit scones and fruit salads. Cash only.

Rocky View Farmhouse
B&B €

(☑065-707 6103; http://rockyviewfarmhouse.com; off R477; s/d €45/70; P 🖻) ✦ At the heart of the coastal Burren, this charming farmhouse has a guest lounge, four bright, airy, TV-free rooms and views out to the Aran Islands. Organic food grown on the property is used at breakfast, served in a sunny conservatory. Cash only.

O'Donohue's
PUB

(R477; ⊙10am-11pm Mon-Thu, noon-midnight Fri & Sat, noon-11pm Sun Apr-Oct, 8-11pm Fri-Sun Nov-Mar, hours can vary) The heart and soul of the community, this landmark sky-blue, yellow-trimmed pub has a great whiskey selection and trad music on weekends from April to October and sporadically throughout winter. It also serves food until 9pm (April to October; mains €12 to €24.50), including chowders, crab sandwiches and crispy beer-battered fish and chips.

ℹ Getting There & Away

Bus Éireann (www.buseireann.ie) runs four buses north to Galway (€17.50, 1½ hours), and south to Doolin (€6.20, 30 minutes) and Ennis (€15.90, 1½ hours).

Ballyvaughan & Around

POP 191

An ideal base for exploring the northern Burren, Ballyvaughan (Baile Uí Bheacháin) has a picturesque location between the rocky hills and Galway Bay's translucent waters.

Just west of the village centre, Ballyvaughan's quay was built in 1829 at a time when boats traded with the Aran Islands and Galway, exporting grain and bacon and bringing in peat – a scarce commodity in this barren landscape. From the quay, a signposted track leads to a seashore bird shelter offering fine views of the tidal shallows.

To the village's south, at the foothills of the Burren, is the ancient Aillwee Cave.

⊙ Sights

★Aillwee Cave
CAVE

(☑065-707 7036; www.aillweecave.ie; off R480; cave adult/child €10/5, raptor exhibit €8/6, combined ticket €16/9; ⊙10am-6.30pm Jul & Aug, to 5.30pm Mar-Jun, Sep & Oct, to 5pm Nov-Feb) Aillwee's extraordinary caves were carved out by water some two million years ago. The main cave penetrates 600m into the mountain, widening into larger caverns, one with its own waterfall. Near the entrance are the remains of a brown bear, extinct in Ireland for over 10,000 years. A large raptor exhibit includes captive hawks and owls; guided 45-minute falconry walks (adults only; €70) let you handle the birds of prey. There's a cafe and shop selling local Burren Gold cheese.

🛏 Sleeping & Eating

Ballyvaughan is one of the loveliest places to stay in the Burren. Several B&Bs and inns are close to the village centre.

Pubs in Ballyvaughan serve quality fare. There's also a daytime cafe and a small supermarket.

Local produce, including farmhouse cheese, is sold at the farmers market (Village Hall car park; ⊙10am-2pm Sat May-Oct) ✦.

★Wild Atlantic Lodge
INN €€

(☑065-707 7003; http://thewildatlanticlodge. com; Main St; d/tr/f from €95/125/145; P 🖻) In Ballyvaughan's village centre, this charming inn has 20 rooms in warm hues with soft woollen blankets; some have huge Burren photographs covering one wall. Breakfast is served in its timber-panelled Wildflower Bar & Restaurant, which has a mellow Sinatra-style soundtrack, and an outstanding menu (mains €14 to €17) featuring beef and lamb from its own farm, and Burren-foraged herbs.

Service is exceptional.

Ballyvaughan Lodge
B&B €€

(☑065-707 7292; www.ballyvaughanlodge.com; N67; s/d from €58/96; ⊙Apr-Oct; P 🖻) In a tangerine-coloured building in the village centre, this well-run B&B has 11 spotless rooms, a comfortable guest lounge, a sunny terrace and a warm welcome from its enthusiastic owners. Breakfast includes

THE RUINS OF CORMCROE ABBEY

Moody and evocative, **Corcomroe Abbey** (Corcomroe Rd, Bellharbour) is a marvellous ruined former Cistercian abbey, 1.5km inland from Bellharbour in a quiet green hollow, surrounded by the stark grey Burren hillsides. It began its long decline in the 15th century but the surviving vaulting in the presbytery and transepts is impressively intact and some striking Romanesque carvings remain.

The abbey was founded in 1194 by Donal Mór O'Brien. His grandson, Conor na Siudaine O'Brien (died 1267), king of Thomond, is said to occupy the tomb in the northern wall, and there's a crude carving of him below the effigy of a bishop holding a crosier, the pastoral staff that was carried by a bishop or abbot. Often-touching modern graves crowd the ruins.

local cheeses, smoked salmon and homemade brown bread.

★ **Gregan's Castle Hotel**　　HOTEL €€€
(☑ 065-707 7005; www.gregans.ie; N67; d/ste from €250/405; ⊘ Apr–Oct; 🅿 🛜) This hidden Clare gem is housed in a grand 18th-century manor, 5km south of Ballyvaughan at Corkscrew Hill. The 21 rooms and suites combine antiques with contemporary countrified furnishings (and purposely no TVs); some open to private garden areas. Nonguests are welcome by reservation at its glass-paned gourmet restaurant (four-course menu €72), serving dishes like wild venison and blackcurrant soufflé.

★ **Monks at the Pier**　　SEAFOOD €€
(☑ 065-707 7059; www.monksballyvaughan.com; The Pier; mains €15-25, half-dozen oysters €12-14.50, seafood platter €29.50; ⊘ noon-10pm Jun-Aug, to 9pm Sep-May) While vegetarian dishes are available daily, as are steaks and burgers, seafood is the star at this whitewashed restaurant warmed by log-burning stoves. Think black Head Bay clams steamed in white wine; Burren smoked salmon and Liscannor crab salad; red ale-battered fish with triple-fried chips; salmon, cod and smoked-haddock chowder; oysters (natural or grilled); and spectacular platters.

ℹ️ Information

Inside a large gift shop behind the supermarket, Ballyvaughan's **visitor centre** (www.ballyvaughantourism.com; Village Hall car park; ⊘10am-1.30pm & 2-6pm) has a good selection of local guides and maps.

ℹ️ Getting There & Away

Bus Éireann (www.buseireann.ie) runs four buses daily to Galway (€14.80, one hour), Doolin (€8.60, one hour) and Ennis (€18.10, two hours).

Northern Burren

Low farmland stretches south from County Galway to the bluff limestone hills of the Burren, which begin west of Kinvara and Doorus in County Galway.

From Oranmore in County Galway to Ballyvaughan, the coastline wriggles along small inlets and peninsulas; some, such as New Quay, are worth a detour. Here narrow roads traverse low rocky windswept hills dotted with old stone ruins that have yielded to nature.

Inland near Bell Harbour is the largely intact Corcomroe Abbey, while the three ancient churches of Oughtmama lie up a quiet side valley. Galway Bay forms the backdrop to some outstanding scenery: bare stone hills shining in the sun, with small hamlets and rich patches of green wherever there's soil.

Buses to and from Galway pass through the area on the N67. Just over the border in Galway, Kinvara makes a good base for this region.

New Quay & Around

Stretching along the Finavarra Peninsula, New Quay (Ceibh Nua) is a narrow, fertile strip of land between Galway Bay and the stark, rocky Burren.

The **Flaggy Shore**, west of New Quay, is a particularly scenic stretch of coastline where limestone terraces step down to the sea. The road hugs the shoreline then curves south past **Lough Muirí**, where you're likely to see wading birds and swans. Otters also inhabit the area.

★ **Hazel Mountain Chocolate**　　FACTORY
(☑ 065-707 8847; www.hazelmountainchocolate.com; L1014, Oughtmama; tour adult/child €12/5; ⊘ shop & cafe 10am-5.30pm, tours 1pm Sat & Sun)

🍃 Watch chocolate being made in small batches using rare Trinitario cacao beans and raw sugar on a 45-minute tour of this heavenly smelling cottage-housed chocolate factory in a picturesque hillside location. If you don't catch a tour, peer through the factory's glass viewing windows from the chocolate-filled shop. Its on-site organic cafe (dishes €6.50 to €12.50) uses chocolate in creations like parsnip, cacao butter and white-pepper soup, and grilled halloumi and chocolate-and-plum-chutney toasties.

Regular events include chocolate-themed mountain hikes in the Burren.

Its Galway city shop (p372) has a cacao brew bar.

★ **Mount Vernon**   GUESTHOUSE €€€

(☑065-707 8126; http://mountvernon.ie; Flaggy Shore; d from €200; ☺Apr-Oct; P🐾) Seamus Heaney stayed at Mount Vernon and famed Irish Impressionist Hugh Lane once called it home until he was lost with the *Lusitania*. Today the rural 1788-built Georgian lodge is a serene seaside retreat. Its five luxurious period-furnished rooms come with orthopaedic mattresses and Egyptian cotton sheets, as well as seaweed toiletries. There's a two-night minimum stay.

Organic vegetables from its gardens, foraged sea beets and samphire, and locally caught seafood are used in evening meals (four-course menu €50; guests only), served by candlelight.

Cafe Linnalla   ICE CREAM €

(www.linnallaicecream.ie; Finavarra Point; 1/2/3 scoops €2.50/4.50/7; ☺11am-7pm daily May-Sep, noon-5pm Sat & Sun Oct-Apr) Overlooking Galway Bay, this remote dairy farm makes ice cream in flavours such as rhubarb and custard, Baileys chocolate chip, sea buckthorn, honeycomb, and rum, raisin and cinnamon. Time your drive out here to avoid early mornings or late afternoons, when you may find yourself stuck on the narrow road amid the cows who provide the ice cream's milk.

Linnane's Lobster Bar   SEAFOOD €€

(☑065-707 8120; http://linnanesbar.com; mains €12.50-23.50, whole lobster €38; ☺12.30-8pm daily mid-Mar–Sep, 12.30-8pm Fri-Sun Oct–mid-Mar) Fresh seafood is sourced from the docks adjoining this unpretentious local bar with views over the water. The seafood chowder is an awesome starter. Linnane's is also renowned for oysters and platters of house-smoked fish as well as lobster in season.

Russell Gallery   ART

(www.russellgallery.net; ☺11am-6pm Mon, Tue & Thu-Sat, noon-6pm Sun) Art and glass works by Irish artists are for sale at this airy gallery alongside photographs and books on the region. You can also find work by local knitting legend Antoinette Hensey. It doubles as a cafe and wine bar; there are seats out on the grass in fine weather.

❶ Getting There & Away

The area is spread out, so your own wheels are best, but Bus Éireann (www.buseireann.ie) has one service daily to Galway (€13, 50 minutes) and Doolin (€12.40, one hour).

County Galway

POP 258,552 / AREA 6148 SQ KM

Best Places to Eat

➡ Loam (p370)

➡ Pullman Restaurant (p370)

➡ Aniar (p370)

➡ O'Dowd's (p390)

➡ Ard Bia at Nimmo's (p369)

Best Places to Sleep

➡ Glenlo Abbey Hotel (p368)

➡ Abbeyglen Castle Hotel (p393)

➡ House Hotel (p367)

➡ Aran Islands Camping & Glamping (p377)

➡ Dolphin Beach (p392)

Why Go?

County Galway's exuberant namesake city – the only major urban centre on the Wild Atlantic Way – is a swirl of colourful shop-lined streets filled with buskers and performance artists, enticing old pubs that hum with trad music sessions throughout the year, and an increasingly sophisticated food scene that celebrates local produce.

Some of Ireland's most picturesque scenery fans out from Galway's city limits, particularly along the breathtaking Connemara Peninsula. Tiny roads wander along its coastline studded with islands, dazzling white sandy beaches and intriguing villages, while its interior shelters heath-strewn boglands, glassy lakes, looming mountains and isolated valleys. In the county's east, towns with medieval remains give way to rolling farmland.

Offshore, the wild and beautiful eroded swaths of the Aran Islands possess a desolate and windswept yet entrancing aura, and offer a glimpse into Irish life of centuries past.

When to Go

➡ With its excellent restaurants, roaring pubs, cultural pursuits and student life, Galway city is a year-round destination, with a packed calendar of festivals.

➡ Elsewhere in rural parts of the county, the months of April to October offer the best weather and fewest closures.

➡ Visitor numbers are highest and bookings hardest to come by in high summer (July and August).

➡ The shoulder seasons of May, June and September see fewer crowds.

➡ Moody in the depths of winter (when many establishments close), the Aran Islands may be unreachable during storms at any time of year.

➡ In scenic Connemara, many country inns close during the winter months, particularly December and January.

County Galway Highlights

1 Galway city (p371) Catching a high-spirited trad session in atmospheric pubs.

2 Dun Aengus (p375) Pondering the ruins of this prehistoric fort on Inishmore.

3 Inisheer (p382) Visiting ancient holy sites and springs, along with a famous shipwreck.

4 Sky Road (p391) Catching the sun dipping into the Atlantic

from this scenic loop road outside Clifden.

5 Dunguaire Castle (p398) Climbing to the roof of this 16th-century castle to gaze out over Galway Bay and Kinvara.

6 Inishbofin (p394) Escaping to the sparsely inhabited island of Inishbofin, off the northern Connemara coast from Cleggan.

7 Kylemore Abbey (p395) Exploring the Victorian walled gardens at this 19th-century neo-Gothic abbey, incongruously set in the wild Connemara landscape.

GALWAY CITY

POP 79,934

Arty, bohemian Galway (Gaillimh) is one of Ireland's most engaging cities. Brightly painted pubs heave with live music, while restaurants and cafes offer front-row seats for observing buskers and street theatre. Remnants of the medieval town walls lie between shops selling handcrafted Claddagh rings, books and musical instruments, bridges arch over the salmon-stuffed River Corrib, and a long promenade leads to the seaside suburb of Salthill, on Galway Bay, the source of the area's famous oysters.

While it's steeped in history, the city buzzes with a contemporary vibe, thanks in part to students, who make up a quarter of the population. Its energy and creativity have seen it designated the European Capital of Culture in 2020.

History

Galway's Irish name, Gaillimh, originates from the Irish word *gaill*, meaning 'outsiders' or 'foreigners', and the term resonates throughout the city's history.

From humble beginnings as the tiny fishing village Claddagh at the mouth of the River Corrib, it grew into an important town when the Anglo-Normans, under Richard de Burgo (also spelled de Burgh or Burke), captured territory from the local O'Flahertys in 1232. Its fortified walls were built from around 1270.

In 1396 Richard II granted a charter transferring power from the de Burgos to 14 merchant families or 'tribes' – hence Galway's enduring nickname: City of the Tribes. (Each of the city's roundabouts is named for one of the tribes.)

Galway maintained its independent status under the ruling merchant families, who were mostly loyal to the English Crown. Its coastal location encouraged a huge trade in wine, spices, fish and salt with Portugal and Spain. Its support of the Crown, however, led to its downfall; the city was besieged by Cromwell in 1651 and fell the following year. Trade with Spain declined and Galway stagnated for centuries.

The early 1900s saw Galway's revival as tourists returned to the city and student numbers grew. In 1934 the cobbled streets and thatched cabins of Claddagh were tarred and flattened to make way for modern, hygienic buildings, and construction has boomed since.

⊙ Sights

★ **Galway City Museum**   MUSEUM

(www.galwaycitymuseum.ie; Spanish Parade House, Merchant's Rd; ⊙10am-5pm Tue-Sat year-round, noon-5pm Sun Easter-Sep) FREE Exhibits at this modern museum covering the city's history from 1800 to 1950 include an iconic Galway hooker (p366) fishing boat, a collection of *currachs* (boats made of a framework of laths covered with tarred canvas) and sections covering Galway and the Great War and the city's cinematic connections.

Also check out rotating displays of works by local artists. The ground-floor cafe, with its Spanish Arch views, is a perfect rest stop.

★ **Spanish Arch**   HISTORIC SITE

The Spanish Arch is thought to be an extension of Galway's medieval city walls, designed to protect ships moored at the nearby quay while they unloaded goods from Spain, although it was partially destroyed by the tsunami that followed the 1755 Lisbon earthquake. Today it reverberates with buskers and drummers, and the lawns and riverside form a gathering place for locals and visitors on sunny days, as kayakers negotiate the tidal rapids of the River Corrib.

A 1651 drawing of Galway clearly shows its extensive fortifications, but depredation by Cromwell and William of Orange and subsequent centuries of neglect saw the walls almost completely disappear. One surviving portion has been cleverly incorporated into the modern shopping mall **Eyre Square Centre** (www.eyresquarecentre. com; cnr Merchant's Rd & Eyre Sq; ⊙8.30am-7pm Mon-Wed & Sat, 8.30am-9pm Thu & Fri, 10.15am-7pm Sun).

Galway Market   MARKET

(www.galwaymarket.com; Church Lane; ⊙8am-6pm Sat, noon-6pm Sun) Galway's bohemian spirit comes alive at its street market, which has set up in this spot for centuries. Saturdays are the standout for food, when farmers sell fresh produce alongside stalls selling arts and crafts, and cooking up ready-to-eat dishes. Additional markets take place from noon to 6pm on bank holidays, Fridays in July and August and every day during the **Galway International Arts Festival** (www.giaf.ie; ⊙mid-late Jul). Buskers add to the festive atmosphere.

COUNTY GALWAY GALWAY CITY

Galway City

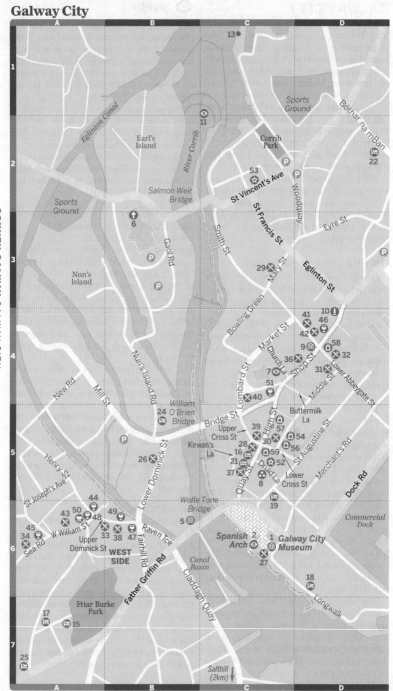

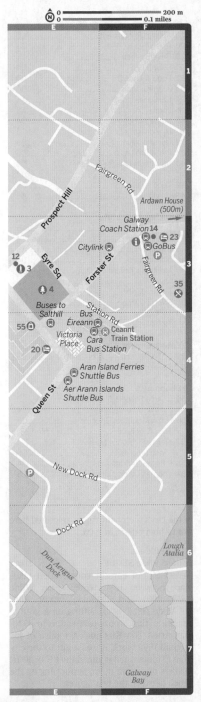

Fishery Watchtower

MUSEUM

(https://galwaycivictrust.ie; off Wolfe Tone Bridge; ⊙10am-4pm Tue-Fri, 11am-3pm Mon & Sat) **FREE** Constructed in the 1850s, this butter-coloured Victorian tower was used to monitor fish stock levels (and poachers). Now restored, the unique tri-level building contains a tiny museum that gives an overview of Galway's salmon fishing industry through displays including photos, along with fantastic views over the waterways.

Galway Cathedral

CHURCH

(Catholic Cathedral of Our Lady Assumed into Heaven & St Nicholas; www.galwaycathedral.ie; Gaol Rd; admission by donation; ⊙8.30am-6.30pm) Rising over the River Corrib, imposing Galway Cathedral was dedicated by the late Cardinal Richard Cushing of Boston in 1965. The interior is fantastic, with a beautifully decorated dome, attractive Romanesque arches, lovely mosaics and rough-hewn stonework emblazoned with copious stained glass. The superb acoustics are best appreciated during an organ recital; concert dates and ticket information are posted on the website. From the Spanish Arch (p361), a riverside path runs upriver and across the Salmon Weir Bridge to the cathedral.

Look out for the side chapel containing a mosaic of the Resurrection with a praying John F Kennedy in the tableau.

Hall of the Red Earl

ARCHAEOLOGICAL SITE

(www.galwaycivictrust.ie; Druid Lane; ⊙9.30am-5pm Mon-Fri year-round, 10am-1pm Sat May-Sep) **FREE** In the 13th century when the de Burgo family ruled Galway, Richard – the Red Earl – erected a large hall as a seat of power, where locals would arrive to curry favour. After the 14 tribes took over, the hall fell into ruin, and was lost until 1997 when expansion of the city's Custom House uncovered its foundations, along with over 11,000 artefacts including clay pipes and gold cuff links. The Custom House was built on stilts overhead, leaving the old foundations open.

Lynch's Castle

HISTORIC BUILDING

(Shop St; ⊙10am-4pm Mon-Wed & Fri, 10am-5pm Thu) **FREE** Now an AIB Bank, this excellent example of a town castle was built around the 15th century (the exact date is unknown), though much of what you see today dates from around 1600. The facade's stonework includes ghoulish gargoyles and the coats of arms of Henry VII, the Lynches (the most powerful of the 14 ruling Galway

Galway City

tribes) and the Fitzgeralds of Kildare. On the ground floor, interpretive panels cover its history and architecture; the magnificent fireplace is a highlight.

Eyre Square   PARK
Galway's central public square is busy in all but the harshest weather. A welcome open green space with sculptures and pathways, its lawns are formally named Kennedy Park in commemoration of JFK's June 1963 visit to Galway, though locals always call it Eyre Sq. Guarding the upper side of the square is the **Browne Doorway** (1627), an imposing, if forlorn, fragment from the home of one of the city's merchant rulers, relocated here from Abbeygate St in 1905.

**Oscar Wilde &
Eduard Vilde Statue**   STATUE
(William St) An earnest conversation takes place between Irish writer Oscar Wilde (1854–1900) and Estonian writer Eduard Vilde (1856–1933), sitting on a granite bench, in this bronze-cast statue by Estonian artist Tiiu Kirsipuu. A replica of his original 1999 work, it was a gift to the city from Estonia when it joined the EU in 2004. Buskers often join them, performing on the bench between the two figures.

Salthill Promenade
WATERFRONT

A favourite pastime for Galwegians and visitors alike is walking along the Salthill Prom, the 2km-long seaside promenade running from the edge of the city along Salthill. Local tradition dictates 'kicking the wall' across from the diving boards (a 30- to 45-minute stroll from town) before turning around.

Atlantaquaria
AQUARIUM

(www.nationalaquarium.ie; Promenade, Salthill; adult/child €12/7.50; ⊙10am-5pm Mon-Fri, to 6pm Sat & Sun) Over 150 freshwater and sea-dwelling creatures from the surrounding waters swim in Ireland's largest native species aquarium, including seahorses, sharks and rays. A touch pool gives you the opportunity to hold starfish and spider crabs. Various talks, tours and feeding sessions take place throughout the day; check the schedule online. Tickets are valid all day, so you can come and go as you please.

👉 Tours

If you're short on time, bus tours departing from Galway are a good way to see Connemara, the Burren and the Cliffs of Moher, while boat tours take you to the heart of Lough Corrib. Tours can be booked directly or at the Galway tourist office (p373).

Lally Tours
BUS

(☑091-562 905; http://lallytours.com; tours adult/child from €25/15) Entertaining, informative bus tours of Connemara, and County Clare's Burren and the Cliffs of Moher depart from Galway Coach Station (p373).

Walking Tours of Medieval Galway
WALKING

(☑091-564 946; www.galwaycivictrust.ie; ⊙2pm Tue & Thu May-Sep) **FREE** In the warmer months, the Dúchas na Gaillimhe (Galway Civic Trust) runs free 90-minute guided walking tours of Galway's medieval centre. Tours depart from the Hall of the Red Earl (p363). Donations are welcomed.

Galway Food Tours
FOOD & DRINK

(☑086 733 2885; www.galwayfoodtours.com; €35; ⊙by appointment) These two-hour tours delve into Galway's food scene, taking in gourmet food shops and dining hot spots, tasting local cheeses, artisan breads and Galway Bay oysters. Further afield, other tours include a six-hour pub tour of Galway and Connemara (€80). There's an additional booking fee of €2. Tours depart from McCambridge's (p369). All tours are also available in French.

City Sightseeing Galway
BUS

(☑091-562 905; https://csgalway.palisis.com; Eyre Sq; 48hr ticket adult/child €10/5; ⊙10.30am-3pm Mar-Oct) Hop-on, hop-off open-top bus tours of the city and its environs set out from Eyre Sq. Buses run every 90 minutes and make 14 stops including Salthill. Two children travel free with every adult.

Galway Tour Company
BUS

(☑091-566 566; www.galwaytourcompany.com; tours from €25; ⊙Mar-Oct) A variety of tours of County Clare's Burren, the Aran Islands and Connemara depart from the Galway Coach Station (p373).

Corrib Princess
CRUISE

(☑091-563 846; www.corribprincess.ie; Woodquay; adult/child €16/7; ⊙May-Sep) Cruises aboard an open-topped 157-seat boat pass historic landmarks along the River Corrib en route to the Republic's largest lake, Lough Corrib, taking 90 minutes all up. There are two or three departures per day, leaving from Woodquay, just beyond the Salmon Weir Bridge.

🎊 Festivals & Events

Cúirt International Festival of Literature
LITERATURE

(www.cuirt.ie; ⊙late Apr) Top-name authors converge on Galway over eight days in late April for one of Ireland's premier literary festivals, featuring poetry slams, theatrical performances and readings.

THE SALMON WEIR

Upstream from **Salmon Weir** Bridge, which crosses the River Corrib just east of **Galway Cathedral** (p363), the river cascades down the great weir, one of its final descents before reaching Galway Bay. The weir controls the water levels above it, and when the salmon are running you can often see shoals of them waiting in the waters before rushing upriver to spawn. The salmon and sea-trout seasons usually span February to September, but most fish pass through during May and June.

It's a popular spot for anglers, even with May and June's restriction of one fish per day, as a fish can exceed 7kg. Contact Inland Fisheries Ireland (www.fisheriesireland.ie) for permits and licences.

GALWAY HOOKERS

Obvious jokes aside, Galway hookers (Irish *húiceár*) are the iconic small sailing boats that were the basis of local seafaring during the 19th century and into the 20th century. Small, tough and highly manoeuvrable, these wooden boats are popular with weekend sailors and hobbyists. The hulls are jet black, due to the pitch used for waterproofing, while the sails flying from the single mast are a distinctive rust colour.

Galway Film Fleadh PERFORMING ARTS
(www.galwayfilmfleadh.com; ☺early Jul) Early July sees the six-day Galway Film Fleadh set screens alight with new, edgy works.

Galway Race Week SPORTS
(www.galwayraces.com; ☺late Jul/early Aug) Galway Race Week draws tens of thousands of punters for a week of partying. Races in Ballybrit, some 7km northeast of the city centre, are the centrepiece of Galway's most boisterous festival. Thursday's Ladies Day is a highlight, with best dressed and best hat competitions. Shuttle buses link Galway with the racecourse.

Galway Pride Festival LGBT
(http://galwaypridefestival.com; ☺mid-Aug) Started in 1989, Galway's Pride Festival (Ireland's first) runs for 10 days in mid-August and includes a flamboyant parade of floats through the city's streets. Dance, music, workshops, talks and family events also feature.

Galway Christmas Market CHRISTMAS MARKET
(www.galwaytourism.ie; Eyre Sq; ☺mid-Nov–mid-Dec) Stalls selling traditional Christmas fare and gifts glow with candles and fairy lights during Galway's enchanting Christmas market.

🛏 Sleeping

Galway's festivals and proximity to Dublin mean accommodation often fills far in advance, particularly on weekends: book ahead.

B&Bs line the major city-centre approach roads (College Rd, a 10-minute walk along Lough Atalia, has an especially high concentration) and Salthill. To take full advantage of Galway's tightly packed attractions, though, try for a room in the centre itself.

Few properties have on-site parking, although many offer deals at parking stations.

★**Kinlay House** HOSTEL €
(☎091-565 244; www.kinlaygalway.ie; Merchant's Rd, Eyre Sq; dm/d €25/70; @🖤) Easygoing staff and a brilliant location right by Eyre Sq make this large, brightly lit hostel a winner. Freshly renovated in 2017, superb amenities include a self-catering kitchen and a cosy TV lounge with a pool table. The four- to eight-bed dorms and private rooms come with electric sockets and USB points; dorms have curtains screening each bunk.

St Martins B&B B&B €
(☎091-568 286; 2 Nun's Island Rd; s/d from €50/80; 🖤) The nearest thing to staying with your own Irish relatives is checking into this welcoming B&B. Run by warm-hearted owner Mary Sexton, the impeccably kept older-style house has a gorgeous flower-filled garden overlooking the William O'Brien Bridge and the River Corrib, and four cosy rooms with hot-water bottles. Mary's hearty breakfasts will set you up for the day.

Snoozles Tourist Hostel HOSTEL €
(☎091-530 064; http://snoozleshostelgalway.ie; Forster St; dm/d/q from €17.50/90/117; @🖤) Dorms (with four, six or 10 beds) and private rooms all have bathrooms at this sociable 130-bed hostel near the train and bus stations. Continental breakfast is free and facilities include a barbecue terrace, pool table, lounge with Nintendo Wii and a kitchen. Guests can play the piano, guitars and fiddles.

Barnacles HOSTEL €
(☎091-568 644; www.barnacles.ie; 10 Quay St; dm/d from €15/60; 🖤) Housed in a medieval building with a modern extension, this well-run hostel has clean rooms named after the city's 14 tribes and an epicentral location surrounded by pubs. There's a spacious self-catering kitchen and cosy common room with a big gas fireplace and games consoles. Breakfast includes scones and soda bread. From June to August there's a minimum two-night stay.

Ask about its free city walking tours for guests.

★**Stop** B&B €€
(☎091-586 736; www.thestopbandb.com; 38 Father Griffin Rd; s/d/tr/f from €70/100/140/180; 🖤) Done up with contemporary artworks, stripped floorboards and bold colours, this 11-room house pulls out all the stops. The rooms are uniquely decorated and space – at a premium – is wisely used, so no wardrobes (just hangers), small work desks and no TV,

but comfy beds. Breakfast includes freshly squeezed orange juice. There's a handy supermarket right across the street.

★ Heron's Rest
B&B €€

(☑ 091-539 574; www.theheronsrest.com; 16a Longwalk; d €140-160; ☜) The thoughtful hosts of this B&B in a lovely row of houses on the banks of the Corrib provide binoculars and deck chairs so you can sit outside and enjoy the views, which also extend from all three snug but cute double-glazed rooms. Breakfasts incorporate organic local produce; other touches include complimentary decanters of port.

Gourmet picnic baskets can be arranged on request.

★ House Hotel
BOUTIQUE HOTEL €€

(☑ 091-538 900; www.thehousehotel.ie; Spanish Pde; d from €149; ℗☜) Inside a former warehouse in the liveliest part of the city, Galway's hippest hotel has a stunning lobby with retro-styled furnishings and modern art, accented with bold shades like fuchsia pink. The 40 soundproofed rooms are small but plush, with vivid colour schemes and quality fabrics. Bathrooms come with toiletries by Irish designer Orla Kiely.

The on-site restaurant and cocktail bar are always buzzing, especially on Friday and Saturday nights when there's live music.

★ Adare Guesthouse
GUESTHOUSE €€

(☑ 091-582 638; www.adarebedandbreakfast.com; 9 Father Griffin Pl; s €50-75, d €70-130, f €110-150; ℗☜) 🥞 Overlooking a football pitch and children's playground, this beautifully refurbished barn-style place has 11 generously sized rooms and service that runs like clockwork. Sift through 16 menu choices at breakfast including French toast with caramelised plums, smoked salmon and scrambled eggs, and buttermilk pancakes with honeyed pears. Many ingredients are sourced from its own organic garden and glasshouse.

Residence Hotel
BOUTIQUE HOTEL €€

(☑ 091-569 600; www.theresidencehotel.ie; 14 Quay St; d/tr from €139/169; ☜) Opened in 2017, the Residence is surrounded by Quay St's music-filled pubs. Its 20 rooms are small but strikingly decorated with works by up-and-coming Irish artists such as Stephen Cooke, with street-art-style murals above the beds. Amenities include Netflix, Nespresso machines and fragrant Aromatherapy Associates toiletries. Light sleepers should ask for a quieter upper-floor room (reached by a lift).

Huntsman Inn
INN €€

(☑ 091-562 849; www.huntsmaninn.com; 164 College Rd; d €120-140; ☜) On Lough Atalia, 1.5km northeast of central Galway, this is a great option if you're after an alternative to staying in the city's busy heart, with the bonus of free parking, and a well-regarded restaurant and bar serving craft beers and ciders on site. Its 12 rooms are streamlined and contemporary, with generous bathrooms. Rates include terrific gourmet breakfasts.

The smoky homemade baked beans with grilled local mushrooms are superb.

Ardawn House
B&B €€

(☑ 091-568 833; www.ardawnhouse.com; College Rd; s/d/tr/f from €50/90/135/180; ℗☜) One of the nicest choices on the B&B-lined College Rd strip, this red-brick house next door to the greyhound stadium has elegant, sparingly decorated bedrooms. Breakfast includes homemade preserves and is served on silver and china amid antique furniture. Cots are provided free of charge.

St Judes B&B
B&B €€

(☑ 091-521 619; http://st-judes.com; 110 Lower Salthill Rd; d/f from €150/207; ℗☜) This double-fronted 1920s stone manor house has a stately feel, with six individually furnished rooms; the ground-floor room is handy for travellers with limited mobility. It's located in a peaceful residential area to the west of the city centre.

IRISH LANGUAGE REVIVAL

One of the most important Gaeltacht (Irish-speaking) areas in Ireland begins around Spiddal just east of Connemara and stretches west to Cashel and north into County Mayo.

That the Irish language is enjoying a renaissance around the country can be credited in part to media outlets based in Connemara and Galway. Ireland's national Irish-language radio station Radio na Gaeltachta (www.rte.ie/rnag) and its Irish-language TV station, TG4 (www.tg4.ie), sprang up in the 1990s and continue to thrive.

Griffin Lodge

B&B €€

(☑091-589 440; www.griffinlodgegalway.com; 3 Father Griffin Pl; s/d €78/90; ☜) You'll be welcomed like a long-lost friend at this well-kept B&B, situated on a peaceful street 700m west of the Spanish Arch (p361). Its eight immaculate rooms are decorated in cream and champagne tones, and bathrooms have decent water pressure.

★ Glenlo Abbey Hotel

HISTORIC HOTEL €€€

(☑091-519 600; www.glenloabbeyhotel.ie; Kentfield Bushy Park, N59; d/ste from €289/429; ☜) Situated on the shores of Lough Corrib, 4km northwest of Galway, this 1740-built stone manor is the ancestral home of the Ffrench family, one of Galway's 14 tribes. Exceptionally preserved period architectural features are complemented by antique furnishings, sumptuous marble bathrooms, duck-down duvets and king-size pillows, along with lavish breakfasts. Its fine-dining Pullman Restaurant (p370) occupies original *Orient Express* train carriages.

The sprawling grounds include a never-completed abbey with a walled garden, started by the family in 1790, as well as a nine-hole golf course (green fees from €45), whose fourth hole sits on an island in the lough (reached by a bridge).

G Hotel

DESIGN HOTEL €€€

(☑091-865 200; www.theghotel.ie; Old Dublin Rd; d/ste from €150/310; P ✳ ☜) Contrasting with its business-complex location near Lough Atalia, this stunning hotel has avant-garde interiors designed by Galwegian milliner-to-the-stars Philip Treacy, including a grand salon with 300 suspended silver balls, a Schiaparelli-pink cocktail lounge, and an award-winning restaurant with purple banquettes styled like oversized seashells. Shell-motif cushions feature in the sand-toned rooms; you can watch TV from the bath tub of most suites.

✖ Eating

Seafood is Galway's speciality, and Galway Bay oysters star on many menus. The city's smorgasbord of eating and drinking options ranges from its wonderful market (p361) to adventurous new restaurants redefining Irish cuisine.

Sheridans Cheesemongers

DELI €

(☑091-564 832; http://sheridanscheesemongers.com; Churchyard St; platters €9-18; ⊙shop 10am-6pm Mon-Fri, 9am-6pm Sat, noon-5pm Sun, wine bar 1pm-midnight Tue-Fri, noon-midnight Sat, 4pm-midnight Sun & Mon) Heavenly aromas waft from this fabulous cheesemongers filled with superb local and international cheeses. Its real secret, however, is up a narrow flight of stairs at its wonderfully convivial wine bar. Sample from a huge wine list (the emphasis is on Italian varieties) accompanied by wooden planks laden with cheeses and charcuterie.

Urban Grind

CAFE €

(www.urbangrind.ie; 8 West William St; dishes €3.50-8.50; ⊙8am-6pm Mon-Wed, 8am-11pm Thu & Fri, 9am-11pm Sat Jun–mid-Sep, 8am-6pm Mon-Fri, 9am-6pm Sat mid-Sep–May) Creative hub Urban Grind whips up fantastic breakfasts (cinnamon porridge; organic ciabatta with grilled chorizo and poached egg) and lunches (black and white bean tortilla with avocado and lime mayo; glazed beef brisket with horseradish relish), and brews some of Galway's best coffees and loose-leaf teas. Craft beers and boutique wines are served until late Thursday to Saturday in summer.

Dough Bros

PIZZA €

(☑087 176 1662; www.thedoughbros.ie; Middle St; pizza €6-11; ⊙noon-10pm Tue-Sat, to 9pm Sun & Mon; ☜) Beginning life as a food truck, this wood-fired pizza maker's permanent home, in a bright-green-fronted space, overflows with regulars including plenty of students, who come for its perfect crusts, fresh, flavour-loaded toppings, craft beers and casual vibe. It doesn't take bookings, but you can order pizzas to take away. Cash is preferred. Look out for the truck at festivals.

Tosnú

MODERN IRISH €

(☑091-538 124; http://tosnurestaurant.com; 14 Upper Abbeygate St; mains breakfast €4.50-8, lunch €9-15, dinner €13-15; ⊙10.30am-3pm & 5-10pm Tue-Sun) In Irish, Tosnú means 'to begin', and this small restaurant's starting point is seasonal produce from local suppliers utilised at breakfast (served until noon), lunch (eg game pie with parsnip and thyme mash) and dinner (pan-fried sea trout with white beans and fennel purée; oven-roasted chicken with smoked garlic boxty potato cakes). Monthly changing local art adorns the walls.

Food 4 Thought

VEGETARIAN €

(5 Lower Abbeygate St; mains €5.50-10.50; ⊙7.30am-6pm Mon-Fri, 8am-6pm Sat, 12.30-4pm Sun; ☜✎) Besides providing organic and vegetarian sandwiches, savoury scones and

wholesome dishes such as cashew-nut roast, this place is great for finding out about energy workshops and yoga classes around town. Vegan and gluten-free options are plentiful; there are free filter coffee refills. Tables are set up on the pavement terrace in the warmer months.

Pie Maker PIES €
(www.thepiemaker.ie; 10 Upper Cross St; pies sweet €5, savoury €11-13; ⊙ 11.30am-10pm) There are just 12 seats at this busy spot, but its pies made with organic spelt flour, fruit and veggies are great for a snack on the run. Savoury pies (black pudding, leek and sherry; aubergine, goat's cheese and pistachio) come with mash, mushy peas, red cabbage and optional gravy. Dessert varieties include sweet potato and white chocolate.

Tuco's Taqueria TACOS €
(www.tuco.ie; 6 Upper Abbeygate St; dishes €7-10; ⊙ noon-9pm; ⌘) At this student favourite, you first choose from tacos, burritos or enchiladas, then select your fillings (meat, vegetarian or vegan), extras (guacamole, sour cream etc) and finally your salsa: Smokie Chipotle (hot), Roja (hotter) or Tuco's Terror (hottest; have a drink handy!). Bottled salsas are also for sale. Regular midweek specials include Thursday's €5 taco night.

McCambridge's CAFE, DELI €
(www.mccambridges.com; 38/39 Shop St; dishes €5-14; ⊙ cafe 8.30am-5.30pm Mon-Wed, 8.30am-9pm Thu-Sat, 9.30am-6pm Sun, deli 8am-7pm Mon-Wed, 8am-9pm Thu-Sat, 9.30am-6pm Sun) Superb prepared salads are among the perfect picnic ingredients at this gourmet food emporium. All high ceilings, blond wood and busy staff, the upstairs cafe is lovely with a changing menu of modern Irish fare such as Galway Hooker beef stew, and over 100 craft beers from Ireland's west. Brunch is served until 4.30pm on Sunday.

★ **Ard Bia at Nimmo's** MODERN IRISH €€
(⊠ 091-561 114; www.ardbia.com; Spanish Arch, Longwalk; cafe dishes €6-12, dinner mains €20-28; ⊙ cafe 10am-3.30pm Mon-Fri, to 3pm Sat & Sun, restaurant 6-9pm; ⌘) ⌘ Inside the 18th-century Custom House near the Spanish Arch (p361), Ard Bia ('High Food' in Irish) is decorated with works by local artists and upcycled vintage furniture. Organic produce (some foraged) features on the seasonal menus of both the upstairs restaurant (adjoining a wine bar), and the street-level cafe

serving fantastic brunches followed by lunch dishes like tomato and fennel chowder.

★ **Oscar's** SEAFOOD €€
(⊠ 091-582 180; www.oscarsseafoodbistro.com; Upper Dominick St; mains €15.50-25.50; ⊙ 6-9.30pm Mon-Sat) The menu changes daily at this outstanding seafood restaurant but might include monkfish poached in saffron and white wine served with cockles, seaweed-steamed Galway Bay lobster with garlic-lemon butter, or lemon sole with samphire. From Monday to Thursday before 7pm, its two-course early-bird menu (€18.50) is a steal.

★ **Cava Bodega** TAPAS €€
(⊠ 091-539 884; www.cavarestaurant.ie; 1 Middle St; tapas €4-16, paella €15; ⊙ 5-10pm Mon-Wed, 5-10.30pm Thu, 4-11pm Fri, noon-11.30pm Sat, noon-9.30pm Sun; ⌘) Over 50 regional Spanish tapas dishes are given a gourmet twist by star chef JP McMahon, whose other ventures include Michelin-starred Aniar (p370). Showstoppers include salt cod with seaweed jam, black-olive fig cake, quail eggs with chorizo oil, and pine-nut-crusted beetroot, along with over 100 Spanish wines. On Friday and Saturday, the bodega's bar stays open late.

Artisan Restaurant MODERN IRISH €€
(⊠ 091-532 655; www.artisangalway.com; 2 Quay St; mains lunch €12-15, dinner/mains €17-27, 3-course menu €25; ⊙ noon-3pm & 5.30-10pm Mon-Sat, noon-3pm Sun) ⌘ Organic, wild and/or foraged local produce – Burren lamb with roast apricot, Monaghan 28-day dry-aged ribeye, and Connemara sea spinach, pea and wood sorrel risotto – is at the fore of this stone-fronted restaurant above Galway's most treasured pub, Tigh Neachtain (p371). Pairings with Neachtain's craft beers, artisan ciders and wines are available.

At lunch it also serves sandwiches such as smoked mackerel and pickled cucumber on soda bread.

John Keogh's GASTROPUB €€
(Lock Keeper; ⊠ 091-449 431; www.johnkeoghs.ie; 22-24 Upper Dominick St; mains €12-23; ⊙ kitchen 5-9pm Mon-Fri, 1-9pm Sat & Sun) Dark-wood panelling, snugs, stained glass, antique mirrors, book-lined shelves and blazing open fireplaces create a cosy ambience for standout gastropub fare. John Keogh's doesn't take reservations, so arrive early to dine on dishes like Galway Bay oysters with seaweed flakes with a Guinness shot. Finish off with

a Roscommon-brewed Sheep Stealer ale or rare whiskey at the bar.

Kai Cafe
CAFE €€

(☑ 091-526 003; http://kaicaferestaurant.com; 20 Sea Rd; mains lunch €11-12.50, dinner €18.50-26.50; ☺ cafe 9.30am-3pm Mon-Fri, 10.30am-3pm Sat, restaurant 6.30-10.30pm Tue-Sat; ☎) With exposed stone, bare timbers, fresh flowers and a glass-roofed atrium, this rustic West Side spot in a thistle-green building is a fantastic place for daytime coffee, gourmet sandwiches and salads, and craft beer. Or come for adventurous evening meals such as monkfish with sea spaghetti or ox tongue with pumpkin jam. Reserve for dinner.

McDonagh's
FISH & CHIPS €€

(☑ 091-565 001; www.mcdonaghs.net; 22 Quay St; cafe & takeaway mains €6-14.50, restaurant mains €13.50-26; ☺ cafe & takeaway noon-11pm Mon-Sat, 2-9pm Sun, restaurant 5-10pm Mon-Sat) A trip to Galway isn't complete without a meal here. Galway's best fish-and-chip shop fries up shoals of battered cod, plaice, haddock, whiting and salmon, accompanied by homemade tartare sauce. It's divided into two parts, with a takeaway counter and sociable cafe where diners sit elbow to elbow at long communal wooden tables, and a more upmarket restaurant.

★ Loam
GASTRONOMY €€€

(☑ 091-569 727; https://loamgalway.com; 2-/3-course menus €40/50, 7-course menu €70, with wine pairings €105; ☺ 6-11pm Tue-Sat) ✐ Enda McEvoy is one of the most groundbreaking chefs in Ireland today (with a Michelin star to prove it), producing inspired flavour combinations from home-grown, locally sourced or foraged ingredients: dried hay, fresh moss, edible flowers, wild oats, forest gooseberries, Salthill sea vegetables and hand-cut peat (which McEvoy uses in his extraordinary peat-smoked ice cream).

The on-site wine bar opens at 5pm and closes at midnight Tuesday to Saturday. Frequent performances by Irish musicians cost €20.

★ Pullman Restaurant
FRENCH €€€

(☑ 091-519 600; www.glenloabbeyhotel.ie; Glenlo Abbey Hotel, Kentfield Bushy Park, N59; 2-/3-course menus €57/65; ☺ 6.30-10pm Mar-Oct, to 9.30pm Fri & Sat Nov-Feb) One of these two original 1927 *Orient Express* train carriages at Glenlo Abbey Hotel (p368) was used in the filming of Agatha Christie's *Murder on the Orient Express* and was also part of Winston Churchill's 1965 funeral cortège. Sepia lamps, inlaid wood panelling, plush upholstery, white tablecloths and piped 1940s and 1950s music create an impossibly romantic setting for fine dining.

Seared foie gras, truffle mousse, Galway venison and duck-egg and cardamom custard tart are among its classical repertoire.

★ Aniar
MODERN IRISH €€€

(☑ 091-535 947; http://aniarrestaurant.ie; 53 Lower Dominick St; lunch menu €55, dinner menus €70-115, with wine pairings €105-180; ☺ 6-9.30pm Tue-Thu, 5.30-9.30pm Fri, noon-2pm & 5.30-9.30pm Sat) ✐ Terroir specialist Aniar is passionate about the flavours and food producers of Galway and West Ireland. Owner/chef JP McMahon's multicourse tasting menus have earned him a Michelin star, yet the casual spring-green dining space remains refreshingly down to earth. The wine list favours small producers. Reserve at least a couple of weeks in advance.

To discover the secrets behind classic and contemporary Irish cuisine, book a course at the on-site Aniar Boutique Cookery School.

> ### LEARN TO COOK MICHELIN-STYLE
>
> Run by JP McMahon, owner/chef of Michelin-starred **Aniar** (p370) restaurant, the **Aniar Boutique Cookery School** (☑ 091-535 947; http://aniar-restaurant.ie; 53 Lower Dominick St; day course €195) offers inspiring day-long courses, including an Introduction to Contemporary Irish Food, during which you learn how to make your own butter and cheese, cure meat and fish, and pickle your own vegetables. Lunch and a glass of wine are included; bring a container to take your creations away.
>
> Other options include Gastropub Classics, Introduction to Tapas (McMahon also runs Galway's acclaimed **Cava Bodega** (p369) tapas bar) and specialist meat, fish and bread-making courses.

Drinking & Nightlife

Galway's pub selection is second to none. The city is awash with traditional pubs offering live music, along with stylish wine and cocktail bars, which are thronged with revellers, especially on weekends and throughout the summer.

Look out for craft beers by local success story Galway Hooker (www.galwayhooker. ie), named for the iconic local fishing boats, on tap around town.

★**Tigh Neachtain**   PUB

(www.tighneachtain.com; 17 Upper Cross St; ⊙11.30am-midnight Mon-Thu, 11.30am-1am Fri, 10.30am-1am Sat, 12.30-11.30pm Sun) Painted a bright cornflower blue, this 19th-century corner pub – known simply as Neáchtain's (*nock*-tans) or Naughtons – has a wraparound terrace for watching Galway's passing parade, and a timber-lined interior with a roaring open fire, snugs and atmosphere to spare. Along with perfectly pulled pints of Guinness and 130-plus whiskeys, it has its own range of beers brewed by Galway Hooker.

It's been run by the same family since 1894.

★**Tig Cóilí**   PUB

(www.tigcoiligalway.com; Mainguard St; ⊙10.30am-11.30pm Mon-Thu, 10.30am-12.30am Fri & Sat, 12.30pm-11pm Sun) Two live *céilidh* (traditional music and dancing session) a day draw the crowds to this authentic fire-engine-red pub just off High St. Decorated with photos of those who have played here, it's where musicians go to get drunk or drunks go to become musicians...or something like that. A gem.

★**O'Connor's**   PUB

(☑091-523 468; www.oconnorsbar.com; Upper Salthill Rd, Salthill; ⊙7.30pm-late) Antiques fill every nook, cranny, wall and ceiling space of this 1942-established pub: clocks, crockery, farming implements, gas lights, sewing machines, fishing equipment, a stag's head and an almost life-size statue of John Wayne from *The Quiet Man*. Learn about them – and Irish history – on storyteller Brian Nolan's free Fireside Tour, aka the 'shortest walking tour of Ireland'.

Trad music and singalongs take place nightly from 9.30pm. A chalked blackboard quips that the closest the pub gets to serving food is 'whiskey soup with ice croutons'.

★**Crane Bar**   PUB

(www.thecranebar.com; 2 Sea Rd; ⊙10.30am-11.30pm Mon-Fri, 10.30am-12.30am Sat, 12.30pm-11pm Sun) West of the Corrib, this atmospheric, always crammed two-storey pub is the best spot in Galway to catch an infor-

mal *céilidh*. Music on both levels starts at 9.30pm.

Garavan's   PUB

(www.garavans.ie; 46 William St; ⊙11am-11.30pm Mon-Thu, 11am-12.30am Fri & Sat, 12.30pm-11pm Sun) Irish whiskeys (in handmade cabinets) are the speciality of this genteel old boozer. Incredible 'tasting platters' (€11 to €95) include an Irish Writers' platter, featuring the favourite tipples of Samuel Beckett, James Joyce and WB Yeats, and a Grand Masters' platter, with an 18-year-old blended Kilbeggan, 26-year-old Teeling single malt gold reserve and 1964 Dungourney pure pot still.

Buddha Bar   COCKTAIL BAR

(www.buddhabar.ie; 14 Mary St; ⊙5-11.30pm Mon, Wed & Thu, to 12.30am Fri & Sat, to 11pm Sun) Neighbouring the **Asian Tea House** (☑091-563 749; www.asianteahouse.ie; 15 Mary St; mains €11-23.50; ⊙5-10.30pm; ☑), this lantern-lit bar decorated with Buddha statues mixes inventive cocktails such as the Shanghai Kiss (passion fruit liqueur, sake, mango-infused vodka and orange juice) and Lotus Espresso (vanilla-infused vodka, coffee, Kahlúa and cinnamon), and serves five different Asian beers.

Nova   GAY & LESBIAN

(http://novagalway.ie; 1 West William St; ⊙4-11.30pm Mon-Thu, 3pm-2am Fri, noon-2am Sat, 12.30-11.30pm Sun; ☎) Rainbow flags and motifs adorn Galway's premier LGBTQ bar. DJs spin dance music upstairs on Friday; Kiki St Clair hosts drag shows on Saturday. Cocktails are suggestively named; it also serves craft beers and wines. Wednesday is student night.

Róisín Dubh   PUB

(www.roisindubh.net; 9 Upper Dominick St; ⊙5pm-2am Sun-Thu, to 2.30am Fri & Sat) Emerging acts play here before they hit the big time. It's *the* place to hear bands but it's also renowned for regular stand-up comedy, along with a silent disco on Tuesday (and Wednesday when university's in session). Open-mike nights take place on Sunday. The covered rooftop terrace is always crammed.

Monroe's Tavern   PUB

(www.monroes.ie; Upper Dominick St; ⊙10am-11.30pm Sun-Thu, to 1am Fri & Sat) Often photographed for its classic two-storey black-and-white facade, Monroe's hosts traditional music and ballads every night from 9pm, as well as Irish dancing on Tuesday.

Bierhaus
BAR

(http://bierhausgalway.com; 2 Henry St; ⊘4pm-midnight Sun-Thu, to 1am Fri & Sat) At any one time 20 stouts, ales, pilsners, wheat beers and ciders from around Europe rotate on the taps of this beer specialist, in addition to over 60 bottled varieties. There are also beer-based and traditional cocktails. Soak them up with snacks such as po' boys.

Secret Garden
TEAHOUSE

(www.secretgardengalway.com; 4 West William St; ⊘11am-8pm Mon, 11am-11pm Tue-Sat, 1-9pm Sun; 🛜) Sip *tiě guān yīn* oolong tea – or any other leaf from an impressive selection – in the comfy front room of this art-filled teahouse or in the charming stone-walled garden out the back. Live contemporary Irish music occasionally plays.

☆ Entertainment

Most pubs in Galway have live music at least a couple of nights a week, whether in an informal trad session or a headline act. Róisín Dubh (p371) is the best place for bands; Tig Cóilí (p371) excels at trad sessions.

★Druid Performing Arts Company
THEATRE

(☑091-568 660; www.druid.ie; Druid Lane) Internationally renowned, the Druid Performing Arts Company was established in 1975 and is famed for staging experimental works by young Irish playwrights, as well as new adaptations of classics. When it's not touring, its Galway home is the Mick Lally Theatre, situated in an old tea warehouse.

CLADDAGH RINGS

The fishing village of Claddagh has long been subsumed into Galway's city centre, but its namesake rings survive as a timeless reminder.

Popular with people of Irish descent everywhere, the rings depict a heart (symbolising love) between two outstretched hands (friendship), topped by a crown (loyalty). Jewellery shops selling Claddagh rings include Ireland's oldest, **Thomas Dillon's Claddagh Gold** (p373).

Town Hall Theatre
THEATRE

(☑091-569 777; https://tht.ie; Courthouse Sq) With a 400-seat main auditorium and 52-seat studio space, the Town Hall Theatre features Broadway and West End shows, orchestras, dance and occasional films.

It was built in 1820 as a courthouse and later used as a town hall and a cinema, before being revived in 1996 as Galway's municipal theatre.

Trad on the Prom
LIVE PERFORMANCE

(☑091-582 860; www.tradontheprom.com; Leisureland Theatre, Lower Salthill Rd, Salthill; adult/child from €30/10; ⊘mid-May–Sep) A festival of Irish dancing and singing, this long-running summer musical is led by Máirín Fahy, a local diva of the fiddle. The glossy production is performed several nights per week in a venue near the Salthill Promenade (p365).

🛍 Shopping

Speciality shops dot Galway's narrow streets, stocking cutting-edge fashion, Irish woollens, outdoor clothing and equipment, local jewellery, books, art and, of course, music.

★Charlie Byrne's Bookshop
BOOKS

(http://charliebyrne.com; Cornstore, Middle St; ⊘9am-6pm Mon-Wed & Sat, 9am-8pm Thu & Fri, noon-6pm Sun) A civic treasure, the rambling rooms at Charlie Byrne's are crammed with over 100,000 new, secondhand, third-hand and discounted books and out-of-print titles, including a trove of Irish interest (and Irish language) fiction and nonfiction. Look out for events including book launches and storytelling sessions.

Hazel Mountain Chocolate
CHOCOLATE

(www.hazelmountainchocolate.com; Middle St; ⊘11am-7pm Mon-Sat, 11.30am-7pm Sun) Truffles using Burren-produced Hazel Mountain chocolate (p358) are made on site daily at this airy, contemporary shop behind a duck-egg-blue facade. It doubles as a cacao brew-bar serving its signature hot chocolate with toasted marshmallows and sweet treats such as chocolate-rhubarb brownies and chocolate-coffee cake with cardamom glaze.

Judy Greene's
ARTS & CRAFTS

(www.judygreenepottery.com; Kirwan's Lane; ⊘9.30am-6pm Mon-Sat) Hand-thrown pottery by Galway artist Judy Greene incorporates designs inspired by Ireland's flora and landscapes. Also displayed in her boutique are jewellery items made from Connemara green marble, plus clothing and artworks by Irish artists and designers.

P Powell & Sons MUSICAL INSTRUMENTS
(53 William St; ☺10am-5pm Mon-Sat) You can pick up everything from bodhráns to harmonicas and tin whistles, as well as sheet music, at this wonderfully traditional crimson-coloured shop with black trim and gold lettering.

Kiernan Moloney
Musical Instruments MUSICAL INSTRUMENTS
(www.moloneymusic.com; 17 High St; ☺10am-6pm Mon-Fri, to 5.30pm Sat) Stringed instruments including fiddles and harps are the speciality of this dealer in fine instruments, which handles sales, rentals and repairs. It also stocks a small range of wind instruments.

Thomas Dillon's Claddagh Gold JEWELLERY
(www.claddaghring.ie; 1 Quay St; ☺10am-5.30pm) Established in 1750, this is Ireland's oldest jewellery shop, with vintage examples of Claddagh rings (p372), wax blanks and traditional tools in its small back-room 'museum' (free admission).

ⓘ Information

Galway's large, efficient **tourist office** (☑091-537 700; www.discoverireland.ie; Forster St; ☺9am-5pm Mon-Sat) can help arrange tours and has reams of information on the city and region.

ⓘ Getting There & Away

BUS

Bus Éireann (www.buseireann.ie; Cara Bus Station, Station Rd) operates daily services to all major cities in the Republic and the North from **Cara Bus Station** (☑091-562 000; Station Rd), near the train station. Dublin (€15.70, 3¾ hours) has an hourly service. Other services fan out across the region.

Citylink (www.citylink.ie; ticket office 17 Forster St; ☺office 9am-6pm; ☎) services depart from **Galway Coach Station** (New Coach Station; Fairgreen Rd), near the tourist office. Destinations include the following:

Cork €22, three hours, five daily

Clifden €15, 1½ hours, five daily

Dublin €15, 2½ hours, hourly

Limerick €18, 1½ hours, five daily

GoBus (www.gobus.ie; Galway Coach Station; ☎) has frequent services between Galway Coach Station and Dublin (3½ hours) and Dublin Airport (three hours). Fares start at €18.

Shannon Airport (€10, 1¾ hours, hourly) is served by Bus Éireann. Dublin Airport is served by both Bus Éireann (€15.50, four hours, hourly) and Citylink (€21, 2½ hours, hourly).

Shuttle buses serve **Connemara Regional Airport** (Aerfort Réigiúnach Chonamara; NNR; Inverin), for **Aer Arann** (p375) flights to the Aran Islands, and the ferry dock at Rossaveal for **Aran Island ferries** (p375).

TRAIN

From the **train station** (www.irishrail.ie), just off Eyre Sq, there are up to 10 direct trains daily to/from Dublin's Heuston Station (from €18, 2¼ hours), and five daily to Ennis (€10, 1¼ hours). Connections with other train routes can be made at Athlone (from €18, one hour).

ⓘ Getting Around

BICYCLE

Galway's Coca-Cola Zero bike-share scheme (www.bikeshare.ie/galway.html) has 16 stations around town. For visitors, €3 (with €150 deposit) gets you a three-day pass. The first 30 minutes of each hire is free; up to two hours is €1.50.

On Yer Bike (☑091-563 393; http://onyourbikecycles.com; 42 Prospect Hill; bike rental per day from €20; ☺9am-7pm Mon-Sat, noon-6pm Sun) offers bike hire, sales and repairs.

West Ireland Cycling (☑087 205 6904; http://westirelandcycling.com; Unit 1, Bridgewater Court, Fairhill Rd; bike rental per day/week from €20/120; ☺9.30am-6pm Jun-Aug, closed Sun Sep-May) rents mountain, racing and touring bikes as well as accessories like child trailers, children's seats and panniers. It also organises multiday bike tours throughout the region (from €720 including accommodation).

BUS

You can walk to almost everything in Galway, including out to Salthill, but you'll also find frequent buses departing from Eyre Sq. For **Salthill**, take bus 401 (€2, 15 minutes).

CAR

Parking on Galway's streets is metered. There are several multistorey and pay-and-display car parks around town. Traffic jams can be horrendous, especially during peak hours.

TAXI

Taxi ranks are located on Eyre Sq, on Bridge St and next to the bus and train stations. Alternatively, order one from **City Taxis** (☑091-525 252; http://citytaxisgalway.com).

ARAN ISLANDS

Easily visible from the coast of counties Galway and Clare along the Wild Atlantic Way, the rocky, wind-buffeted Aran Islands have a desolate beauty that draws countless day-trippers. Visitors who stay longer experience the sense that they're far further removed from the Irish mainland than the 45-minute ferry ride or 10-minute flight would suggest.

An extension of the limestone escarpment that forms the Burren in Clare, the islands have shallow topsoil scattered with wildflowers, grass where livestock grazes and jagged cliffs pounded by surf. Ancient forts here are some of the oldest archaeological remains in Ireland.

Inishmore (Irish: Inis Mór) is the largest island and home to the only town, Kilronan. Inishmaan (Inis Meáin) preserves its age-old traditions and evokes a sense of timelessness. Inisheer (Inis Oírr), the smallest island, has a strong trad culture.

History

Little is known about the people who built the massive Iron Age stone structures on Inishmore and Inishmaan. Commonly referred to as 'forts', they are believed to have served as pagan religious centres. Folklore holds that they were built by the Firbolgs, a people who invaded Ireland from Europe in prehistoric times.

It's thought that people came to the islands to farm, a major challenge given the rocky terrain. Early islanders augmented their soil by hauling seaweed and sand up from the shore and fished the surrounding waters on long *currachs* (rowing boats made of a framework of laths covered with tarred canvas), which remain a symbol of the Aran Islands.

Early Christianity

Christianity reached the islands remarkably early, and some of the oldest monastic settlements were founded by St Enda (Éanna) in the 5th century. Enda appears to have been an Irish chief who converted to Christianity and spent some time studying in Rome before seeking out a suitably remote spot for his monastery.

From the 14th century, control of the islands was disputed by two Gaelic families, the O'Briens and the O'Flahertys. The English took over during the reign of Elizabeth I, and in Cromwell's times a garrison was stationed here.

Modern Isolation

As Galway's importance waned, so did that of the islands, and their isolation meant islanders maintained a traditional lifestyle well into the 20th century. Up to the 1930s, people wore traditional Aran dress: bright red skirts and black shawls for women, and baggy woollen trousers and waistcoats with *crios* (colourful belts) for men. The classic heavy cream-coloured Aran sweater, featuring complex patterns, originated and is still hand-knitted on the islands.

Air services began in 1970, changing island life forever, and today fast ferries make a quick (if sometimes rough) crossing.

ARTISTIC ARAN

The Aran Islands have sustained a strong creative streak, partly as a means for entertainment during long periods of isolation. Artists and writers from the mainland have similarly long been drawn to the elemental nature of island life.

Dramatist JM Synge (1871–1909) spent a lot of time on the islands. His play *Riders to the Sea* (1905) is set on Inishmaan, while his renowned *The Playboy of the Western World* (1907) also draws upon his island experiences. Synge's highly readable book *The Aran Islands* (1907) is the classic account of life here and remains in print.

American Robert Flaherty came to the islands in the early 1930s to film *Man of Aran*, a dramatic account of daily life. He was something of a fanatic about the project and got most of the locals involved in its production. The film is a classic and is regularly shown at the **Man of Aran Gift Shop** (p380) in Kilronan on Inishmore.

The noted 1996 play, *The Cripple of Inishmaan* by Martin McDonagh, involves tragic characters and a strong desire to leave the island in 1934.

The map-maker Tim Robinson has written a wonderful two-volume account of his explorations on Aran, called *Stones of Aran: Pilgrimage* and *Stones of Aran: Labyrinthe*.

Local writer Liam O'Flaherty (1896–1984) from Inishmore wrote several harrowing novels, including *Famine* (1937) and *Insurrection* (1950).

Farming has all but died out on the islands and tourism is now the primary source of income. While Irish remains the local tongue, most locals speak English with visitors and converse with each other in Irish.

ⓘ Getting There & Away

AIR

All three islands have landing strips. The mainland departure point is **Connemara Regional Airport** (p373), 27km west of Galway city, linked by **shuttle bus** (⌨ 091-593 034; http://aerarannislands. ie) (for which reservations are required).

Aer Arann Islands (⌨ 091-593 034; http:// aerarannislands.ie; one way/return €25/49) offers return flights aboard tiny fixed-wing prop planes to each of the islands up to six times a day; the flights take about 10 minutes. The airline also offers scenic flights (per person €70) in July and August and by arrangement year-round, flying over the Cliffs of Moher, Galway Bay and the Aran Islands.

BOAT

Year-round, **Aran Island Ferries** (⌨ 091-568 903; www.aranislandferries.com; one way/return €13/25) has sailings to Inishmore (40 minutes, up to three daily), Inishmaan (45 minutes, two daily) and Inisheer (55 minutes, two daily). Crossings are subject to cancellation in high seas. Boats leave from **Rossaveal Ferry Terminal** (Rossaveal), 37km west of Galway city, linked by **shuttle bus** (⌨ 091-568 903; www.aranislandferries.com; Queen St). Contact the company in advance to arrange bike transport.

From mid-March to October, **Doolin 2 Aran Ferries** (p351) and **O'Brien Line** (p351) run ferries to the Arans from Doolin, County Clare, and also run interisland ferries.

Inishmore

POP 845

Most visitors who venture out to the Aran Islands don't make it beyond the largest and closest island to Galway, Inishmore (Inis Mór), and its most spectacular prehistoric stone fort, Dun Aengus, perched on the island's towering cliffs.

Inishmore is 14.5km long and 4km at its widest stretch. Boats arrive and depart from Inishmore's main settlement, **Kilronan** (Cill Rónáin), on the southeastern side of the island. The arid landscape to its west is dominated by stone walls, boulders, scattered buildings and the odd patch of deep-green grass and potato plants. Today tourism turns the wheels of the island's economy: from May to September tour vans greet each ferry and flight, offering a ride around the sights.

ⓘ ISLAND-HOPPING THE ARANS

Seasonal interisland ferries make it possible to visit all three islands in a day, starting at one and returning from another. Schedules are geared toward return trips to a single island, however, so check sailing schedules online.

⊙ Sights

★ Dun Aengus   HISTORIC SITE

(Dún Aonghasa; www.heritageireland.ie; site adult/child €5/3, visitor centre €2/1; ⊙ 9.30am-6pm Apr-Oct, to 4pm Nov-Mar) Standing guard over Inishmore, Dun Aengus, 8km west of Kilronan, has three massive drystone walls that run right up to sheer drops to the ocean below. Believed to be up to 2000 years old, the fort is protected by remarkable *chevaux de frise,* fearsome and densely packed defensive limestone spikes. Displays at its small **visitor centre** provide context and a 900m walkway wanders uphill to the fort itself.

Powerful swells pound the 87m-high cliff face. A complete lack of railings or other modern additions that would spoil this incredible site means that you can not only go right up to the cliff's edge but also potentially fall to your doom below, so take care.

Dún Eochla   HISTORIC SITE

FREE Atop the island's highest point, at 100m, historic fort Dún Eochla has a double ring of circular walls, and is thought to date from the late Iron Age. It's signposted 2.8km west of Kilronan.

Teampall Chiaráin   RUINS

(Church of St Kieran) Located 1.5km northwest of Kilronan, this small church is believed to have been founded in the 12th century by St Kieran, who studied under St Enda and later went on to establish his own monastery on the mainland at Clonmacnoise. On the church's eastern side, a carved boundary cross with a circular hole at the top was likely used as a sundial. Drawing an item of clothing through the hole is traditionally said to bring good luck and fertility.

Dún Eoghanachta   HISTORIC SITE

FREE Thought to date from the Iron Age, this single-ring circular fort 8.3km west of Kilronan is almost 30m in diameter and has 4m-high walls over 3m thick.

Inishmore

Kilmurvey Beach (4km);
Dun Aengus (5.5km);
Na Seacht dTeampaill (7km);
Dún Eoghanachta (8km)

MAINISTIR

KILRONAN

Rossaveal

Inishmaan

See Enlargement

Enlargement

Cill Éinne Bay

ATLANTIC OCEAN

KILLEANY

Inishmore Airport

Tranmore Beach

Inishmore

Teampall Bheanáin   RUINS
(Church of St Benen) Dating from the 11th century, tiny Teampall Bheanáin, 2.2km southeast of Kilronan, measures just 3m by 2.5m, and is thought to have been a her-mitage. Unusually for a religious structure, it's oriented on a north–south axis rather than east–west. The views over Cill Éinne Bay are outstanding.

St Enda's Monastery RUINS

Near the **airstrip** (IOR) are the sunken remains of a church; the spot is said to have been the site of St Enda's Monastery in the 5th century, though what's visible dates from the 8th century onwards. Enda, the Aran Islands' patron saint, is thought to be buried beneath the church's altar.

Na Seacht dTeampaill HISTORIC SITE

FREE The small early Christian ruins known rather inaccurately as the Na Seacht dTeampaill (Seven Churches) comprise just two ruined churches, along with monastic houses, fragments of a high cross from the 8th or 9th century, and the perfect Clochán na Carraige, an early Christian stone beehive hut that stands 2.5m tall.

Dún Dúchathair HISTORIC SITE

FREE Dramatically perched on a clifftop promontory 2km southwest of Kilronan, this ruined ancient fort has terraced walls up to 6m high surrounding the remains of a *clochán* (early Christian beehive-shaped hut). Its name, meaning the Black Fort, comes from the dark limestone prevalent on this part of the island.

Wormhole NATURAL POOL

(Poll na bPeist) Access to this extraordinary rectangular natural tidal pool is via a 750m clifftop walk southeast from Dun Aengus (p375) or a 1km signposted walking path from the hamlet of Gort na gCapall. Dubbed 'Serpent's Lair', the pool is a regular on the Red Bull Cliff Diving World Series circuit, when daredevil divers plunge from nearly triple the height of an Olympic tower-dive platform. Take care as the area can be dangerous in wild weather and high seas.

Festivals & Events

Tedfest CULTURAL

(www.tedfest.org; ☉ late Feb/early Mar) Held during the purgatory of tourism (late February or early March, with all accommodation on the island reserved for festival ticket holders), this four-day carnival of nonsense celebrating the cult TV show *Father Ted* has been a huge hit.

Pátrún CULTURAL

(☉ late Jun–early Jul) On the last weekend of June, this centuries-old three-day festival celebrates St Enda, the island's patron saint, with Galway hooker and *currach* boat races, a triathlon, sandcastle competitions, Irish music and dancing on the pier.

Sleeping

After the last day-trippers have left in summer, the island assumes a wonderful serenity. Advance bookings are advised, particularly in summer. Many B&Bs and inns close during winter.

Kilronan Hostel HOSTEL €

(☎099-61255; http://kilronanhostel.com; Kilronan; dm from €30; ☉ late Feb-late Oct; @🛜) You'll see the Kilronan Hostel perched above Tí Joe Mac's (p380) pub even before your ferry docks at the pier, a 200m walk east. Forty beds are spread across very clean four-, five- and six-bed dorms. Its terrace has a barbecue and harbour views, there's a self-catering kitchen and continental breakfast is thrown in.

Ard Mhuiris B&B €

(☎099-61208; Kilronan; s/d €70/80; 🛜) Peacefully situated a five-minute stroll from the centre of town, Martin and Cait's very tidy B&B is last in a line of cottages before fields and then the sea, with great ocean views. Martin can also take you on island tours by request. Cash only.

★ Aran Islands Camping & Glamping CAMPGROUND €€

(☎086 189 5823; http://irelandglamping.ie; Frenchman's Beach; camping per person €10, glamping hut €150) 🌱 At this brand-new campground with direct access to a sweeping white-sand beach, you can stay in a beehive-shaped glamping hut inspired by an early Christian stone *clochán*. Sleeping up to four people, the 10 timber huts have bathrooms, kitchenettes, double beds and pull-out sofas, along with sea views from the front decks. The site's green credentials include solar power.

Facilities for those pitching tents include a communal camp kitchen, male and female shower blocks and a common room. It's 750m north of Kilronan.

★ Kilmurvey House B&B €€

(☎099-61218; www.aranislands.ie/kilmurvey-house/; Kilmurvey; s/d from €60/95; ☉ Apr–mid-Oct; 🛜) In a beautiful setting on the path leading to Dun Aengus (p375), this grand 18th-century stone mansion has 12 spacious rooms with bathroom. Homemade granola, porridge with whiskey and home-baked scones are served at breakfast; hearty evening meals (dinner €30) incorporate vegetables from the garden. It's a 500m stroll east to swim at pretty **Kilmurvey Beach**. Children under 16 aren't permitted.

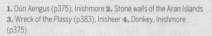

1. Dún Aengus (p375), Inishmore 2. Stone walls of the Aran Islands 3. Wreck of the *Plassy* (p383), Inisheer 4. Donkey, Inishmore (p375)

STEFANO_VALERI/SHUTTERSTOCK ©

TRAVELAMOS/SHUTTERSTOCK ©

2 Aran Islands Scenery

Blasted by the wind and washed over by waves, the eroded, striated slivers of rock known as the Aran Islands hold a fascination for travellers. Rocky extensions of the Burren in County Clare, they are home to descendants of unimaginably hardy folk who forged their own culture of survival.

Aran Islands

Left to nature, the Arans would be bare rocks in the Atlantic. But generations of islanders have created green – seaweed and sand gathered and spread by hand over the centuries to produce fertile fields.

Inishmaan

Escape the crowds on Inishmaan, the least visited of the Arans. You'll see few others on walks across the dramatic countryside, where every path seems to pass the mysterious remains of past lives and end on a beach trod only by you.

Inishmór

A thousand day trippers on a summer weekend come to Inishmór to see one of Ireland's most impressive ancient wonders. Dún Aengus has been guarding a bluff over the Atlantic for 2000 years.

Inisheer

An old castle, ancient churches and a magical spring are just a few of the highlights of Inisheer, the smallest of the Arans. Centuries of history are preserved in rock.

The Plassy Wreck

Star of the opening sequence of the comedy classic *Father Ted*, the *Plassy* was driven ashore on Inisheer by storms in 1960. Attracting walkers and visitors from afar, its rusting hulk is testament to the implacable march of time and the power of the turbulent Atlantic.

Pier House Guest House   INN €€

(☑ 099-61417; www.pierhousearan.com; Kilronan; d from €95; ☎) You won't have time to lose your sea legs in the 50m walk from the ferry to this two-storey inn perched on a small rise. The 12 rooms are decorated in rich shades of red, and come with tea- and coffee-making facilities. Under 16s aren't permitted. Its restaurant (p380) opens during summer.

Tigh Fitz   INN €€

(☑ 099-61213; www.tighfitz.com; s/d €95/120; ☎) Quite a hike from Kilronan (2.5km from the pier; 900m from the airport), this green-painted guesthouse has a proper reception desk in the hallway and offers comfortable, albeit simple, rooms. Some have ocean views out to the tidal extremes of the bay; others overlook the stone-wall-laced fields. Ferry pick-ups can be arranged.

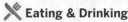 Eating & Drinking

Seafood is widespread along with vegetables grown in organic garden plots. Most restaurants and pubs are in Kilronan, but many places to stay island-wide offer home-cooked evening meals.

Self-caterers can pick up supplies at Kilronan's small Spar supermarket.

★ Bayview Restaurant   INTERNATIONAL €€

(☑ 086 792 9925; www.bayviewrestaurantinishmore.com; mains lunch €10-15, dinner €19-40; ☺ noon-9pm; ☎☷) Inside a landmark sunset-pink building 200m west of the pier, Bayview's dining room showcases local art. Lunch features classics such as Guinness beef stew, while dinner ups the ante with whole lobster, chargrilled steaks and amazing desserts like grilled pineapple marinated in cinnamon and ginger and served with vanilla-bean ice cream and ginger coulis. Kids are well catered for.

Pier House   IRISH €€

(☑ 099-61417; www.pierhousearan.com; Kilronan; mains €14.50-27; ☺ noon-5pm & 6-10pm May-Sep; ☎☷) Watch the ferries come and go from the terrace of this restaurant downstairs from the guesthouse (p380) of the same name, or keep warm by the open fire. Seafood is a speciality – crab, oysters, lobster, smoked salmon and mackerel, prawns and a fish of the day – along with land-based dishes like Irish beef Wellington. Kids' menu available.

★ Tí Joe Watty's Bar   PUB

(www.joewattys.ie; Kilronan; ☺ noon-midnight Sun-Thu, 11.30am-12.30am Fri & Sat Apr-Oct, 4pm-midnight Mon-Fri, noon-midnight Sat & Sun Nov-Mar) Warmed by peat fires, the island's oldest and most popular pub has trad sessions every night in summer from 9pm and weekends the rest of the year. Darts night on Wednesday is a local fixture. There's a large beer garden and an extensive list of Irish gins, craft beers and whiskeys.

Its seafood-focused menu (mains €10 to €16.50) is excellent; book for dinner in summer.

Tí Joe Mac's   PUB

(Kilronan; ☺ 11am-11pm Mon-Thu, 11am-12.30am Fri & Sat, noon-10pm Sun; ☎) Informal music sessions, open fires and a broad terrace with harbour views make Tí Joe Mac's a local favourite.

The Bar   PUB

(http://inismorbar.com; Kilronan; ☺ noon-11pm Sun-Thu, 11.30am-midnight Fri & Sat) A former priest's house, this yellow-painted place has been a pub for the last century. It once provided last pints for ship passengers travelling from Galway to the USA, hence its former name, the American Bar (and its photos of Elvis, Bob Dylan et al). Live music plays nightly from May to mid-October, and weekends the rest of the year.

Filling pub fare (mains €8 to €16) spans seafood chowder to lamb stew and fish and chips.

🔒 Shopping

Kilmurvey Craft Village   ARTS & CRAFTS

(Kilmurvey; ☺ hours vary) Hand-knitted woollens, carved stonework and jewellery incorporating Celtic designs are among the local arts and crafts sold at this charming collection of traditional thatched cottages near Dun Aengus (p375).

Man of Aran Gift Shop   GIFTS & SOUVENIRS

(http://manofaran.eu; Kilronan; film per adult/child €5/3; ☺ 9am-8pm; ☎) At Kilronan's main crossroads, this eclectic shop stocks souvenirs from T-shirts to stained glass and Celtic-design jewellery, and screens the iconic film *Man of Aran* five times daily in its tiny 24-seat theatre. It also has wi-fi (free with purchase) and a fine little coffee bar serving Italian brews.

ℹ Information

The **tourist office** (☑ 099-61263; www.aranis lands.ie; Kilronan; ☺ 10am-5pm) is on the waterfront 50m northwest of the ferry pier in Kilronan.

The **Spar supermarket** (Kilronan; ☺ 9am-6pm Mon-Sat, to 5pm Sun; 🛜) has the Aran Islands' only ATM, but it often runs out of cash, especially in summer.

ℹ Getting Around

From May to September, minibuses offer 2½-hour tours of the island (€10) to ad hoc groups. The drive – with commentary – between Kilronan and **Dun Aengus** (p375) takes about 45 minutes each way. You can also negotiate for private and customised tours.

To see the island at a gentler pace, pony traps with a driver are available from May to September for trips between Kilronan and Dun Aengus; the return journey costs between €50 and €100 for up to four people.

Many places to stay have bicycles for use or rent; alternatively **Aran Bike Hire** (☑ 099-61132; www.aranislandsbikehire.com; Inishmore Pier; mountain & road bike rental per day €10, electric bikes from €30, deposit €20-30; ☺ Apr-Oct) rents out road, mountain and electric bikes, which it delivers to your accommodation anywhere on the island.

Inishmaan

POP 200

The least-visited of the islands, with the smallest population, Inishmaan (Inis Meáin) is a rocky respite, roughly 5km long by 3km wide. Early Christian monks seeking solitude were drawn to Inishmaan, as was the author JM Synge, who spent five summers here over a century ago. The island they knew largely survives today: stoic cows and placid sheep, impressive old forts, and warm-hearted locals, who speak Irish to each other exclusively.

Inishmaan's scenery is breathtaking, with a jagged coastline of startling cliffs, empty beaches and fields criss-crossed by a latticework of stone walls. Most buildings spread out along the road that runs east–west across the centre. You can easily walk to any place on the island, enjoying the stark scenery and sweeping views on the way. Inishmaan's down-to-earth islanders are largely unconcerned with the prospect of attracting the tourist dollar, so facilities are scarce.

◉ Sights

Dún Chonchúir HISTORIC SITE
(Conor's Fort) FREE Glorious views of Inishmaan's limestone valleys and maze of stone walls extend from this ruined elliptical stone fort, which sits on the island's highest point. Built sometime between the 1st and 7th centuries AD, its walls reach over 6m in height.

Dún Fearbhaigh HISTORIC SITE
FREE The well-preserved ruins of this stone fort are 200m west of the **Cill Cheannannach** church ruins; the fort similarly dates from around the 8th century.

Teach Synge HISTORIC BUILDING
(☑ 099-73036; €3; ☺ by appointment Apr-mid-Sep) Now a small museum, this 300-year-old thatched cottage, on the road just before you head up to the fort Dún Chonchúir is where the writer JM Synge (1871–1909) spent his summers between 1898 and 1902.

Synge's Chair VIEWPOINT
At the desolate western end of the island, Synge's Chair is a viewpoint at the edge of a sheer limestone cliff with the surf from Gregory's Sound booming below. The cliff ledge is often sheltered from the wind; do as Synge did and find a stone perch to take it all in. The formation is two minutes' walk from the end of the lane.

On the walk out to Synge's Chair, a sign points the way to a *clochán* (circular stone building, shaped like an old-fashioned beehive, from the early Christian period), hidden behind a house and shed.

Church of the Holy Mary of the Immaculate Conception CHURCH
(Séipéal Naomh Mhuire gan Smal; ☺ 10am-7pm Apr-mid-Sep, to 5pm mid-Sep–Mar) Built in 1939, this small church has beautiful stained-glass windows designed by the studio of Harry Clarke and an altar by James Pearse (the father of Patrick Pearse, aka Pádraig Pearse, who led the Easter rising in 1916).

🍴 Sleeping & Eating

Most B&Bs serve evening meals, usually using organic local produce. Not far from the island's only pub, a small shop (☺ 10am-6pm Mon-Fri, to 2pm Sat) sells a few grocery staples.

Ard Alainn
B&B €

(☑087 285 6778; s/d with shared bathroom from €45/60; ☺May-Sep) Signposted just over 2km from the pier and near Synge's Chair, thatched Ard Alainn has fine views out to sea. Rooms share a bathroom. Breakfasts by host Maura Faherty will keep you going all day.

Tig Congaile
B&B €€

(☑099-73085; www.inismeainbb.com; s/d from €50/80; ☜) 🍴 Vilma Conneely has seven spacious rooms with bathrooms and starkly beautiful island views. Guests and nonguests can book yoga classes (€15) and holistic massages (€50), and enjoy freshly ground Guatemalan coffee along with meals (mains €16 to €30) incorporating local produce, such as Vilma's famous sea-vegetable soup or fresh fish on wild garlic. Dining times vary; reservations are a must.

Eco initiatives include solar power, and rainwater and seaweed fertiliser for the garden.

An Dún
B&B €€

(☑087 680 6251; www.inismeainaccommodation. ie; d from €145; ☺Mar-Oct; ☜) Opposite Dún Chonchúir, modern An Dún has five comfortable rooms with private bathrooms, and a sauna and steam room (each €5). Kids under 12 aren't accepted. Local cuisine such as pillowy potatoes (fertilised with seaweed), luscious smoked salmon and fresh local fish are served at its restaurant (three-course dinner menu €35); nonguests are welcome but need to book in advance.

Inis Meáin
INN €€€

(☑086 826 6026; http://inismeain.com; d 2 nights from €528; ☺Mon-Sat Mar-Sep; ☜) An anomaly on the island, this boutique inn has five contemporary suites, crafted from local stone, and exceptional views. Minimum two-night-stay rates include pick-up and drop-off from the airport or ferry, breakfast boxes and Thermos-packed soup for lunch. No kids under 12. The 16-seat restaurant serves a four-course dinner menu (€70); nonguests are welcome Wednesday to Saturday.

Teach Ósta
PUB

(☺noon-late) A local linchpin, the island's only pub has outdoor tables with great views. Live music plays most nights in July and August, with spontaneous weekend sessions year-round. Pub food (mains €10 to €13) generally stops around 7pm and isn't always available in the winter months,

though the bar often keeps going until the wee hours.

Shopping

Cniotáil Inis Meáin
CLOTHING

(☑099-73009; http://inismeain.ie; ☺10am-4pm Mon-Fri) Founded in 1976, this factory is one of the island's main employers and exports fine woollen garments including iconic Aran sweaters to some of the world's most exclusive shops. You can buy the same items here (tax free for visitors from outside the EU). Call to confirm hours before visiting.

❶ Getting Around

Enjoy a fact-filled one- to two-hour minibus or pony trap tour of the island (€10 to €15 per person). Look out for them at the **airstrip** (IIA) and **pier**.

Inishmore-based **Aran Bike Hire** (p381)often has bike rentals at the pier.

Inisheer

POP 249

Inisheer (Inis Oírr), the smallest of the Aran Islands at roughly 4km wide by 2km long, has a palpable sense of enchantment, enhanced by the island's windflower-strewn landscapes, deep-rooted mythology and enduring traditional culture.

The wheels of change turn very slowly here. Electricity wasn't fully reliable until 1997. Given that there's at best 15cm of topsoil to eke out a living farming, the slow conversion of the economy to tourism has been welcome. Day-trippers from Doolin (as many as 1000 on a balmy summer weekend), 8km across the water, enliven the hiking paths all summer long. Facilities are still limited, however, so visitors need to come prepared.

◉ Sights & Activities

Wandering the lanes with their ivy-covered stone walls is the best way to experience the island, with two marked paths.

Tobar Éinne
HISTORIC SITE

(Well of Enda) Locals still carry out a pilgrimage known as the Turas to the Well of Enda, a bubbling spring in a remote rocky expanse in the southwest. The ceremony involves, over the course of three consecutive Sundays, picking up seven stones from the ground nearby and walking around the

FATHER TED'S DIVINE INSPIRATION

Devotees of the late 1990s cult British TV series *Father Ted* might recognise Craggy Island – the show's fictional island setting off Ireland's west coast – from the show's opening sequence showing the **Plassy** (p383) shipwreck on Inisheer. However, apart from this single shot, the sitcom was mostly filmed in London studios, with additional location shots in Counties Clare, Wicklow and Dublin. Alas, the **parochial house** (p353) and **Vaughan's Pub** (p353) are nowhere to be found here (instead you'll find them in County Clare).

This hasn't stopped the Aran Islands from embracing the show as their own. Although there has been some grumbling from its smaller neighbours, Inishmore has seized upon *Ted*-mania for itself and each year hosts the wildly popular festival **Tedfest** (p377), when accommodation on the island is reserved for ticket holders.

Meanwhile, County Clare now has a competing **Father Ted Festival** (p353) in Lisdoonvarna. As Ted might say: 'Oh feck!'

small well seven times, putting one stone down each time, while saying the rosary until an elusive eel appears from the well's watery depths.

If, during this ritual, you're lucky enough to see the eel, it's said your tongue will be bestowed with healing powers, enabling you to literally lick wounds.

O'Brien's Castle   HISTORIC BUILDING
(Caisleán Uí Bhriain) FREE Built in 1585 on the island's highest point, this tower house was constructed within the remains of a ring fort called Dún Formna, dating from as early as the 1st century AD. The 100m climb rewards with a sweeping panorama across clover-covered fields to the beach and harbour. The views are especially dramatic at sunset. You're free to walk around the ruins.

Teampall Chaoimháin   HISTORIC BUILDING
Named for Inisheer's patron saint, who is buried close by, the roofless 10th-century Church of St Kevin and small cemetery perch on a tiny bluff near the Strand. On the eve of St Kevin's 14 June feast day, a Mass is held here in the open air at 9pm. The sick sleep here for a night hoping to be healed.

Plassy   SHIPWRECK
A steam trawler launched in 1940, the *Plassy* was thrown onto the rocks on 8 March 1960 and driven onto the island a couple of weeks later after another storm. Its cargo of whiskey was never recovered but miraculously, all on board were saved. Tigh Ned (p385) pub has a collection of photographs and documents detailing the rescue. An aerial shot of the wreck was used in the opening sequence of the cult TV series *Father Ted*.

Áras Éanna   ARTS CENTRE
(☑ 099-75150; www.araseanna.ie; ⊙ Jun-Sep) Inisheer's large community arts centre sits out on an exposed stretch of the northern side of the island and hosts visiting artist events, cultural programs and performances.

Cill Ghobnait   CHURCH
This tiny 9th-century church is named after St Gobnait (locally spelt Ghobnait), who fled here from Clare to escape a family feud. Gobnait is the patron saint of bees and beekeepers, and is believed to have cured the sick using honey.

★ Festivals & Events

Craiceann   MUSIC
(www.craiceann.com; ⊙ late Jun) Inisheer reverberates to the thunder of traditional drums at the end of June with bodhrán classes, workshops and concerts. Craiceann takes its name from the Irish word for 'skin', referring to the goatskin used to make these circular drums. The festival features top talent, and nightly drumming sessions take place in the pubs.

🛏 Sleeping & Eating

Inisheer has B&Bs, pub accommodation and a hostel; book well in advance in summer and especially during Craiceann week in June.

From May to September, there's free camping (with toilets and showers) at an officially designated site beneath O'Brien's Castle (p383) by the main beach.

Brú Radharc Na Mara Hostel
HOSTEL €

(☑ 099-75024; www.bruhostelaran.com; dm €20-26, d €55; ⊙ Mar-Sep; @ 🛜) Handily located next to Tigh Ned (p385) pub, 100m west of the pier, this spotless hostel has ocean views, a large kitchen, a warming fireplace, a book swap and bikes for hire (€10 per day). Dorms have four or six beds; private rooms have their own bathrooms.

South Aran House & Restaurant
B&B €

(☑ 099-75073; www.southaran.com; s/d €55/78, 2-bedroom cottage €100-200; ⊙ Apr-Oct; 🛜) 🍃 Lavender grows outside this B&B run by slow-food enthusiasts. Breakfast specialities include apple fritters with potato cakes and roasted tomatoes. The four rooms with private bathroom have wrought-iron beds and underfloor heating. A separate cottage sleeps up to four. Guests must be over 18. Its evening restaurant (mains €18 to €22) utilises local seafood and organic produce; nonguests must reserve.

Regular events include cookery and foraging courses (from €30 per person).

Radharc an Chláir
B&B €

(☑ 099-75019; bridpoil@eircom.net; s/d €45/70; ⊙ Easter-Sep; 🛜) Views of the Clare coastline extend from this modern yellow-painted B&B on the hillside near O'Brien's Castle (p383). Ferry pick-ups can be arranged. Book several weeks ahead, as host Brid Poil's home-cooked breakfasts and warm hospitality draw many repeat visitors.

Tigh Ruairí
PUB €

(Rory's; ☑ 099-75002; www.tighruairi.com; d €50-90; 🛜) Rory Conneely's atmospheric digs have 20 rooms with private bathroom and dark-wood furniture; many have views across the water. The cosy pub downstairs serves pub fare (mains €8 to €12) and hosts live music sessions in summer.

Teach an Tae
CAFE €

(☑ 099-75092; http://cafearan.ie; dishes €3.50-9.50; ⊙ 11am-5pm May-early Nov) 🍃 Wild island raspberries and blackberries, homegrown salad ingredients, eggs from the cafe's chickens and apples from its orchard of 30 heritage trees are used in dishes here. Sweet treats include rhubarb-and-apple pie and scones with homemade jam; for something savoury try the grilled pollack with herbed couscous and sorrel, or the Aran Islands' goat's cheese tart. Cash only.

WALKING INISHEER'S COAST

You can circumnavigate Inisheer's 12km shoreline in about five hours, gaining a far deeper understanding of the island than from hurried visits to the main sights.

From the Inisheer ferry pier, walk west along the narrow road parallel to the shore and go straight on to the small fishing pier at the northwest corner of the island. Continue along the road with the shingle shore on one side and a dense patchwork of fields, enclosed by the ubiquitous stone walls, on the other. Look for tide pools and grey seals resting in the sun.

About 1km from the acute junction, turn left at the painted sign; about 100m along the paved lane is the Tobar Éinne (p382).

Continue southwest as it becomes a rough track. After about 600m, head roughly south across the limestone pavement and strips of grass to the shore. Follow the gently sloping rock platform around the southwestern headland (Ceann na Faochnaí) and walk east to the lighthouse near Fardurris Point (two hours from the ferry pier).

Stay with the coast, turning northeast. You'll see the wreck of the Plassy (p383) in the distance. When necessary, use stiles to cross walls and fences around fields. Note that the grass you see grows on about 5cm of topsoil created by islanders who cleared rocks by hand and then stacked up seaweed over decades.

Head north, following the track, which then becomes a sealed road at the northern end of Lough More. Continue following the road along the northern shore of the island, past the airstrip (INQ).

At the airstrip you can diverge for Teampall Chaoimhín (p383) and O'Brien's Castle (p383). Otherwise rest on the lovely sands of the curving beach and check out the nearby Cnoc Rathnaí, a Bronze Age burial mound (1500 BC), which is remarkably intact considering it was buried under the sand until the 19th century, when it was rediscovered.

Tigh Ned
PUB FOOD €

(📞 099-75004; http://tighned.com; dishes €7-10.50; ⊙kitchen noon-4pm Apr-Oct, bar 10am-midnight Apr-Oct) Here since 1897, Tigh Ned is a welcoming, unpretentious place with inexpensive lunchtime fare (sandwiches, cottage pie, fish and chips), along with craft beers, whiskey and Guinness. Tables in the garden have harbour views. Lively traditional music plays on weekends from June to August.

ℹ Information
In July and August a small **kiosk** (⊙10am-6pm Jul & Aug) at the ferry pier provides tourist information.

ℹ Getting Around
Rothaí Inis Oírr (📞 099-75049; www.rothai-inisoirr.com; bike rental per day from €13) rents out road bikes, mountain bikes and 21-speed bikes, and has a good free map. Most accommodation places also rent out bikes to nonguests.

In summer, you can take a tour of the island on a pony trap (€10 to €15 per hour per person); drivers meet arriving ferries.

CONNEMARA

The name Connemara (Conamara) translates as 'Inlets of the Sea' and the roads along the peninsula's filigreed coast bear this out as they wind around the small bays and coves of this breathtaking stretch of the Wild Atlantic Way.

From Galway city, a slow coastal route passes some stunning hidden beaches and seaside hamlets. At the start of the Gaeltacht region west of Spiddal, the scenery becomes increasingly dramatic, with parched fields rolling to ragged shores.

Connemara's starkly beautiful interior, traversed by the N59, is a kaleidoscope of rusty bogs, lonely valleys and shimmering black lakes. At its heart are the Maumturk Mountains and the pewter-tinged quartzite peaks of the Twelve Bens mountain range, with a network of scenic hiking and biking trails. Everywhere the land is laced by stone walls.

ℹ Information
Galway's **tourist office** (p373) has lots of information on the area. Online, Connemara Tourism (www.connemara.ie) and Go Connemara (www.

goconnemara.com) have region-wide info and links.

> ## GUIDED WALKS IN CONNEMARA
>
> Maps of the many walking trails in Connemara are sold at bookshops and tourist offices. However, to really appreciate the region's unique geology, natural beauty and ancient history, you may wish to go with a guide. **Connemara Safari** (📞 095-21071; www.walkingconnemara.com; tours €300-700; ⊙Jun-Sep) runs three- and five-day walking tours led by experts in fields such as archaeology. Meals and accommodation are included.

ℹ Getting There & Around
Organised bus tours from Galway, with companies such as **Lally Tours** (p365), offer a good, if condensed, overview of the region.

BUS
Bus Éireann (www.buseireann.ie) serves most of Connemara. Services can be sporadic, and some operate May to September only, or July and August only.

Citylink (www.citylink.ie) has several buses a day linking Galway city with Clifden via Oughterard and on to Cleggan and Letterfrack.

For stop-offs between towns, you might be able to arrange a drop-off with the driver.

CAR
Your own wheels are the best way to get off this scenic region's beaten track. Watch out for the narrow roads' stone walls and meandering Connemara sheep – characterised by their thick creamy fleece and coal-black face and legs.

The main road from Galway is the N59, which heads northwest via Oughterard to Clifden then swings northeast up to Letterfrack and Connemara National Park then on to Killary Harbour before crossing into County Mayo.

An alternative route between Galway and Clifden is via the R336 and R340; you can either join the N59 near Recess, or continue along the coast via the R342 then R341 to Roundstone, Ballyconneely and Derrygimla and on to Clifden. Side roads lead to tiny inlets, little coves and remote beaches, and the low, bleak islands of Lettermore, Gorumna and Lettermullen, linked by bridges.

Connemara

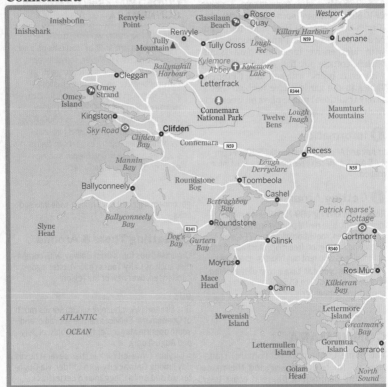

Oughterard & Around

POP 1318

The charmingly down-to-earth village of Oughterard (Uachtar Árd) sits on the shore of the Republic's biggest lake, Lough Corrib. Over 48km long and covering some 200 sq km, the lake virtually cuts off western Galway from the rest of the country and encompasses more than 360 islands. Immediately west of Oughterard, the countryside opens up to sweeping panoramas of lakes, mountains and bogs. The website www.oughterardtourism.com is a handy resource.

◉ Sights & Activities

★ Aughnanure Castle   CASTLE
(www.heritageireland.ie; off N59; adult/child €5/3; ☉ 9.30am-6pm Mar-late Oct) Built around 1500, this superbly preserved fortress signposted 4.2km east of Oughterard was home to the 'Fighting O'Flahertys', who controlled the region for hundreds of years after they fought off the Normans. The six-storey tower house stands on a rocky outcrop overlooking Lough Corrib and has been extensively restored.

Surrounding the castle are the remains of an unusual double *bawn* (area surrounded by walls outside the main castle); there's also the remains of the Banqueting Hall and a small, now isolated watchtower, with a conical roof. The River Drimneen once enclosed the castle on three sides, while today the river washes through a number of natural caverns and caves beneath the castle.

Inchagoill   ISLAND
The largest island on Lough Corrib, Inchagoill lies about 2km offshore from the lake's edge 4.5km north of Oughterard. The island is a lonely place dotted with ancient remains. Corrib Cruises (☎ 087 994 6380; www.corribcruises.com; Oughterard Pier; adult/child €28/14; ☉ noon Wed-Mon Jul & Aug) runs

west of central Oughterard yielded silver, lead, glistening quartz and more. As well as marvelling at some of the treasures unearthed, visitors learn about the tough existence of workers here until the mine closed in 1865. You can also join in some gold-panning, and feed horses and donkeys at the adjacent working farm. Sheepdog herding and peat-cutting demonstrations can be arranged with prior notice for an additional €5.

Brigit's Garden　　　　　　GARDENS
(www.brigitsgarden.ie; off N59, Pollagh, Rosscahill; adult/child €8/5; ⊙10am-5.30pm Mar-Oct, to 5pm Nov-Feb) 🌿 Covering 4.5 hectares of woodland and meadowland and with traditional architecture, including a reed-thatched *crannóg* roundhouse, tranquil Brigit's Garden is dedicated to Celtic myth and heritage. Four gardens represent seasonal Celtic festivals: **Samhain** (winter), **Imbolc** (spring), **Bealtaine** (summer) and **Lughnasa** (autumn). There's also a huge **sundial** (Ireland's largest) and a sustainability zone with solar panels, a wood pellet boiler and polytunnel. Produce from the gardens is used at the onsite cafe. It's 9km southeast of Oughterard.

Knockillaree Riding Centre　　HORSE RIDING
(☑ 087 960 4517; www.connemarahorseriding.com; Rusheeny; treks per hour €30, lessons adult/child €30/20; ⊙by appointment) Treks lasting one to five hours head out along mountain trails or through woodland along the shores of Lough Corrib. Lessons are available for riders of all levels, with ponies for kids.

The centre can also organise riding in an approved yard for people with disabilities.

🛏 Sleeping & Eating

Currarevagh House　　　　　HOTEL €€
(☑ 091-552 312; www.currarevagh.com; Glann Rd; s €90-130, d €140-180; ⊙mid-Mar–Oct; P🐾) On 73 hectares along Lough Corrib, this magnificent 12-bedroom mansion (pronounced 'Curra-reeva') dates from the 19th century. Fresh flowers fill the halls, rooms have high ceilings, and the grounds are wonderful for rambling. Breakfast and afternoon tea are included; four-course evening meals (€49) feature local ingredients such as trout. Wi-fi is only in public areas. It's 5.7km north of Oughterard.

Connemara Lake Hotel　　　　HOTEL €€
(☑ 091-866 016; http://connemaralakehotel.com; Main St; s/d/f €75/95/130; P❄🐾) Right in the centre of town, this bright, white hotel with 16 modern rooms is a favourite with anglers. Not only can it organise boat and equipment

day cruises. Alternatively rent your own boat from Molloy's Boats (p388).

Inchagoill's most fascinating sight is an obelisk called **Lia Luguaedon Mac Menueh** (Stone of Luguaedon, Son of Menueh), which identifies a burial site. It stands about 75cm tall, near the Saints' Church.

It's claimed that the Latin writing on the stone is the second-oldest Christian inscription in Europe, after those in the catacombs in Rome.

The prettiest church is the Romanesque **Teampall na Naoimh** (Saints' Church), probably built in the 9th or 10th century, with carvings around its arched doorway. **Teampall Phádraig** (St Patrick's Church) is a small oratory of a very early design, with some later additions.

Glengowla Mines　　　　MUSEUM, FARM
(☑ 087 252 9850; www.glengowlamines.ie; off N59, Glengowla East; adult/child €10/4; ⊙10am-6pm Mar-Oct) These 19th-century mines 4.5km

COUNTY GALWAY OUGHTERARD & AROUND

hire, but the hotel can also arrange for your catch to be cooked by its chef, or shipped to the Connemara Smokehouse (p391) to be smoked and sent on to your home address.

A drying room for wet clothes and bike storage are available.

Ross Lake House Hotel　GUESTHOUSE €€€
(☑091-550 109; http://rosslakehotel.com; Rosscahill; s/d/f €130/185/250; ☺Easter-Oct; P☎) Undulating lawns and bird-filled woodlands surround this beautiful ivy-clad Georgian house, which blazes red in autumn when the ivy's leaves change colour. Its 13 large rooms have antique furniture (some with four-poster beds). Kids under 12 stay for half-price.

Greenway Cafe　IRISH €€
(☑091-866 645; www.connemaragreenwaycafe.com; Main St; mains lunch €6.50-14, dinner €13-22; ☺9am-10pm Tue-Sat, noon-4pm Sun) Most of the ingredients at this blue-trimmed stone restaurant are sourced from the Connemara region – Killary Harbour mussels (served with mint), Lough Corrib trout (with roast rhubarb) and Twelve Bens lamb (with wild mushrooms) included. There's also Wild Bat craft beer available, produced in Oughterard by Corrib Brewing Company.

Powers Thatched Pub　PUB FOOD €€
(☑091-557 597; Main St; mains €12.50-18.50; ☺kitchen noon-8.30pm, bar 9am-midnight) The only thatched building on the main road, this comfy pub has open fires, welcoming service and an impressive menu of seafood (freshly caught trout, mussels and smoked haddock chowder) and meat (pork belly with crackling, lamb burger with preserved lemon). The homemade treacle bread is divine. Traditional music plays on Wednesday, Saturday and Sunday.

❶ Getting There & Away

Bus Éireann (www.buseireann.ie) runs up to eight times daily to/from Galway city (€8.30, 40 minutes) and Clifden (€15.50, two hours) via Roundstone (€15.50, 1½ hours).

Citylink (www.citylink.ie) has five services daily to/from Galway (€9, 40 minutes) and Clifden (€13, 50 minutes) via the quicker N59.

Lough Inagh Valley & Around

Lough Inagh Valley's stark landscape is beguiling, with the moody skies reflected in the waters of loughs Derryclare and Inagh. The R344 enters the valley from the south, just west of the hamlet of Recess. On the western side is the brooding **Twelve Bens** mountain range.

At the north end of the valley, the R344 meets the N59, which loops around Connemara to Leenane and Killary Harbour. A track near the northern end leads west off the road up a blind valley, which is well worth exploring. It's fantastic walking country but trails can get busy in summer, so set out early.

🛏 Sleeping & Eating

Ben Lettery Hostel　HOSTEL €
(☑086 849 3712; http://anoige.ie; N59, Ballynahinch; dm €16.50-19.50, d €82; ☺late May-Sep; P☎) Situated 7km west of where the R344 enters the Lough Inagh Valley (12km east of Clifden), this seasonally opening YHA hostel has 40 beds and a common room with a peat fire. With a tidy, homely kitchen and drying room, it's an excellent base for exploring the valley. Citylink buses stop here on request. Check-in is between 5pm and 10pm.

Lough Inagh Lodge　LODGE €€
(☑091-34706; www.loughinaghlodgehotel.ie; off R344; s/d/tr from €118/175/215; P☎) Set in huge grounds against a hill, this atmospheric lodge has rich colour schemes, an oak-panelled dining room and peat fires.

FISHING ON LOUGH CORRIB

Lough Corrib is world-famous for its salmon, sea trout and brown trout, and Oughterard is one of Ireland's principal angling centres.

The highlight of the fishing calendar is the mayfly season, when zillions of the small bugs hatch over a few days (usually in May) and drive the fish – and anglers – into a frenzy. Salmon begin running around June.

Hotels and lodges around Lough Corrib can usually arrange fishing equipment, as can boat-rental companies such as **Molloy's Boats** (☑091-866 954; Baurisheen; motor/rowing boat per day €65/35, motor boat with guide €140; ☺by appointment). **Tuck's Angling Shop** (☑091-552 335; Main St, Oughterard; ☺9am-6pm Mon-Sat) offers tackle, bait and advice.

Several of its 13 grand rooms face the lake. Rates include breakfast; dinner can be arranged for €45. It's around midway up the Lough Inagh Valley, 9km north of Recess.

Ballynahinch Castle Hotel   LUXURY HOTEL €€€
(☑095-31006; www.ballynahinch-castle.com; off R341; s/d/ste from €150/210/290; 🅿🛜) With fishing on private lakes and the River Owenmore running through the vast, mountain-ringed property, this ivy-draped manor is ideally set up for anglers. Its 48 luxurious rooms include riverside suites with four-poster beds. The gatehouse Owenmore Restaurant (three-course menu €65) offers fine dining; casual meals are available at the manor's Fisherman's Pub (mains €10 to €38).

Fly-fishing lessons and guides cost €160 per half day; equipment hire per half/full day is €60/90.

Roundstone

POP 214

Clustered around a boat-filled harbour, picture-perfect Roundstone (Cloch na Rón) is the kind of Irish village you hoped to find. Colourful terrace houses and inviting pubs overlook the shimmering recess of Bertraghboy Bay, which is home to dramatic tidal flows, lobster trawlers and traditional *currach* boats with tarred canvas bottoms stretched over wicker frames.

The scalloped coastline here harbours some spectacular beaches. The Errisbeg peninsula, 3km southwest of Roundstone, has two. **Gurteen Bay** (sometimes spelt Gorteen Bay) has a sweep of golden sand. After a further 800m, there's a turn for **Dog's Bay**, a dazzling white strand formed from tiny crushed seashells. Together the pair form the two sides of the dog-bone-shaped sand spit and tombolo.

◎ Sights & Activities

Roundstone Musical
Instruments   WORKSHOP
(www.bodhran.com; Monastery Rd; ☺9.15am-7pm Jul-Sep, 10.30am-6pm Mon-Sat Oct-Jun) At the village's southern edge, you can watch Malachy Kearns, Ireland's only full-time maker of traditional bodhráns, handcrafting goat-skin drums in his workshop. Other traditional Irish instruments are also for sale here, along with sheet music and recordings.

PATRICK PEARSE'S COTTAGE

Pádraig Pearse (Patrick Pearse; 1879–1916) wrote some of his short stories and plays in this small thatched **cottage** (Teach an Phiarsaigh; www.heritageireland.ie; R340, Ros Muc; adult/child €4/2; ☺9.30am-6pm Easter-Sep, 10am-4pm Oct-Easter) on the shore of a remote lake, which he built in 1909. In 2016 a state-of-the-art, A-frame **visitor centre** detailing Pearse's life and writing opened a short walk from the cottage. Allow an hour here all up.

Pearse led the Easter Rising with James Connolly in 1916. After the revolt he was executed by the British.

Note that the cottage's location is sometimes spelt Rosmuc on signs.

Mt Errisbeg   WALKING
Looming above Roundstone is Mt Errisbeg (Iorras Beag; 300m), the only significant hill along this section of coastline. The scenic walk to the top takes about two hours; just follow small Fuchsia Lane past O'Dowd's (p390) pub in the centre of the village. From the summit, a panorama radiates across the bay to the distant humps of the Twelve Bens.

Roundstone Outdoors   KAYAKING
(☑087 943 3440; http://bogbeanconnemara.com; ☺by appointment) One of the best ways to explore Roundstone's beautiful coastline is to get out on the water. Roundstone Outdoors offers kayak lessons from €25 per hour and 2½-hour kayak tours from €40, and also rents out kayaks and stand-up paddleboards (two hours €35).

🛏 Sleeping

Island View B&B   B&B €
(☑095-35701; www.islandview.ie; Main St; s €50-55, d €75-95; 🛜) At the heart of Roundstone, this delightful B&B has spick-and-span rooms with fresh flowers, most facing the bay. Homemade scones feature at breakfast and can also be served during complimentary afternoon tea by the fireplace in the cosy guest lounge.

Gurteen Beach Caravan
& Camping Park   CAMPGROUND €
(☑095-35882; www.gurteenbay.com; off R341; campsites per adult/child €10/5, electricity per night €5; ☺Easter-Oct; 🅿🛜) In an idyllic spot

WORTH A TRIP

ROUNDSTONE BOG

Away from the coast, an alternative route between Roundstone and Clifden winds through the protected Roundstone Bog. The bumpy road passes through magnificently eerie, water-logged desolation; locals who believe the bog is haunted won't drive this road at night. In summer you might see peat being harvested by hand, as blanket bogs cannot be cut mechanically. The road runs west from a junction on the R341 about 4km north of Roundstone. It rejoins the R341 at Ballinaboy.

50m from Gurteen Beach (patrolled by lifeguards in July and August), 3km southwest of Roundstone, this peaceful campground has 80 pitches for caravans and tents, a camp kitchen, laundry, a shop (May to September) selling groceries and ice cream, and a games room with a TV. Showers cost €1.

Roundstone House & Vaughan's   INN €€
(⌨ 095-35944; www.roundstonehousehotel.com; Main St; s/d/tr from €60/110/130; ⊘ Apr-Oct) There are views across the bay from the front rooms of this elongated, family-run inn. All 12 rooms have tea- and coffee-making facilities and neutral beige furnishings. You can enjoy pints and local seafood at its attached pub, Vaughan's (bar menu €10 to €21; restaurant mains €25 to €28) out on the terrace. Service couldn't be friendlier.

✕ Eating & Drinking

O'Dowd's Cafe   CAFE €
(www.odowdsseafoodbar.com; Main St; dishes €5.50-11.50; ⊘ 9am-6pm Mar-Oct; 🛜) Run by neighbouring pub and seafood restaurant O'Dowd's (p390), and utilising the same home-grown and locally sourced produce, this seasonal two-storey cafe is a great place for breakfast (until noon), while daytime dishes including seaweed hummus, chickpea and sweet potato salad, chowder and the best scones in town. On chilly days, warm up with an Irish coffee.

Takeaway dishes come with cutlery for a beach picnic.

Bog Bean Cafe   CAFE €
(⌨ 095-35825; http://bogbeanconnemara.com; Main St; dishes €4.50-9.50; ⊘ 9am-5.30pm Thu-Tue Easter-Sep, 9.30am-4.30pm Thu-Sun Oct-Easter; 🛜) Cork-roasted Badger & Dodo coffee and sweet treats such as chocolate-apple cake or rhubarb-and-raspberry slice make this cheerful cafe worth a stop. It also has more filling dishes like Connemara smoked-salmon sandwiches or local crab salad with lime dressing. Upstairs are six colourful B&B rooms with private bathrooms (doubles from €70).

★**O'Dowd's**   SEAFOOD €€
(⌨ 095-35809; www.odowdsseafoodbar.com; Main St; mains restaurant €13-22, bar €13-15; ⊘ restaurant 5-9.30pm, bar menu 10am-9.30pm; 🛜) 🍴 Roundstone lobster, Aran Islands hake, plaice and sea bass, local crab and mackerel smoked in-house are sourced off the old stone dock directly opposite this wonderfully authentic old pub and restaurant, while produce comes from its garden. Bountiful seafood platters cost €29. There's a great list of Irish craft beers and ciders. Its neighbouring summertime cafe (p390) serves breakfast and lunch.

Film buffs might recognise it from the 1997 Hollywood flick *The Matchmaker*.

Shamrock Bar   PUB
(www.theshamrockroundstone.com; Main St; ⊘ 11am-11.30pm Mon-Thu, to 12.30am Fri & Sat, to 10.30pm Sun; 🛜) Roundstone's best bet for live music is this red-trimmed, timber-lined pub on the main street, where musicians play at weekends throughout the year and most nights in July and August. In addition to trad, it also has jazz on Sunday afternoons from June to September.

ℹ Getting There & Away

The R341 shadows the coast from Roundstone to Clifden, but you can also reach Clifden via a bumpy detour through the wild, desolate Roundstone Bog.

Bus Éireann (www.buseireann.ie) has services to/from Galway city (€15.50, 1½ hours, up to four daily) and Clifden (€8, 35 minutes).

Clifden & Around

POP 1597

A definitive stop on the Wild Atlantic Way, Connemara's 'capital', Clifden (An Clochán, meaning 'stepping stones'), is an appealing Victorian-era town presiding over the head of the narrow bay where the River Owenglin tumbles into the sea.

◉ Sights & Activities

This is pony country and rides along the beaches are popular. Cycling is also a great way to explore the scenic landscapes.

★ **Sky Road**   SCENIC DRIVE

Signposted west of Clifden's Market Sq, this aptly named 15km driving and cycling route traces a dizzying loop out to the township of Kingston and back to Clifden, taking in rugged, stunningly beautiful coastal scenery en route. Set out clockwise from the southern side for the best views, which peak at sunset.

En route there are several viewpoints where you can park.

Station House Museum   MUSEUM

(Station House Courtyard, off Low Rd; adult/child €2/1; ⊘10am-5pm Mon-Sat, noon-6pm Sun Easter–mid-Nov) Located in a former train shed, this small but absorbing museum has displays on the local ponies and pivotal aspects of Clifden's history, including the Galway to Clifden Connemara Railway (in service from 1895 to 1935), and Guglielmo Marconi's transatlantic wireless station at Derrigimlagh, which was also the site of the crash landing of John Alcock and Arthur Brown's first nonstop transatlantic aeroplane crossing in 1919.

Derrigimlagh Discovery Point   HISTORIC SITE

(Marconi Rd, off R341) FREE Crystal radio sets let you listen to recordings from the 1907 station established by Guglielmo Marconi – where the world's earliest transatlantic wireless messages were transmitted – on this scenic 5km loop walk through windswept bogland 5.8km south of Clifden. In 1919 British aviators John Alcock and Arthur Brown achieved the first transatlantic flight when they spotted the Marconi station's towers and switched off the engines, eventually crashing into the bog. Interpretive panels and interactive exhibits dot the route.

Both aviators survived and were awarded the honour of Knight Commander of the British Empire (KBE) a week later by King George V.

The wireless station operated until 1922, when it was attacked by Republican forces and compensation from the Free State government for its repair didn't eventuate.

Clifden's Station House Museum also covers these two 20th-century technological advancements.

Connemara Smokehouse   FACTORY

(☑095-23739; www.smokehouse.ie; Bunowen Pier, Ballyconneely; tours free; ⊘tours by reservation 3pm Wed Jun-Aug, shop 9am-1pm & 2-5pm Mon-Fri year-round) At the family-run Connemara Smokehouse, tours reveal hand filleting and traditional preparation, slicing and packing of wild and organic salmon, explain various smoking methods and finish with a tasting. If you miss the tour, large information boards cover the process. It's 14km southwest of Clifden.

Connemara Heritage & History Centre   MUSEUM

(www.connemaraheritage.com; N59, Lettershea; adult/child €8/4; ⊘10am-6pm Apr-Oct) Farmer Dan O'Hara lived here in the 1840s until his eviction from the farm and subsequent emigration to New York, where he ended up selling matches on the street. Its present owners have restored the property, turning it into a window onto lost traditional ways; a highlight is the tractor-pulled tour up the mountain to see peat being hand cut. There's a craft shop and tearoom on site. It's 7km east of Clifden, with last admission an hour before closing.

THE QUIET MAN BRIDGE

Whenever an American cable TV station needs a ratings boost, they invariably trot out the iconic 1952 film *The Quiet Man*. Starring John Wayne and filmed in lavish colour to capture the crimson locks of his co-star Maureen O'Hara, the film regularly makes the top-10 lists of ageing romantic-comedy lovers for its portrayal of rural Irish life, replete with drinking and fighting, fighting and drinking etc. Director John Ford returned to his Irish roots and filmed the movie almost entirely on location in Connemara and the little village of Cong, just over the border in County Mayo. One of the most photogenic spots from the film, the eponymous Quiet Man Bridge, is just 3km west of Oughterard off the N59. Looking much as it did in the film, the picture-perfect arched span (whose original name was Leam Bridge) is a lovely spot. Purists will note, however, that the scene based here had close-ups done on a cheesy set back in Hollywood. That's showbiz. Hard-core fans will want to buy the superb *The Complete Guide to The Quiet Man* by Des MacHale. It's sold in most tourist offices in the area.

All Things Connemara CYCLING
(☑ 095-22630; https://allthingsconnemara.ie;
Market St; bike hire per half/full day €12/16.50,
electric bike €25/40; ⊘ 9am-6pm) Road bikes
and electric bikes for exploring the region
are in excellent condition at All Things Connemara, which also sells a diverse range of
products solely from the region (clothes,
stationery, fishing lures, Connemara marble jewellery, organic seaweed, music and
more).

Errislannan Manor HORSE RIDING
(☑ 095-21134; www.errislannanmanor.com; ⊘ by
appointment) Guides provide lessons (€35 per
hour) and lead treks (from €30 per hour)
along the beach and up into the hills on the
iconic local ponies. It's 7.5km from Clifden:
take Ballyconneely Rd (the R341) south for
4km, then turn northwest onto the Errislannan Peninsula.

It also offers trout fishing on its private
lake; rod rental per half day is €10.

Blue Water Fishing FISHING
(☑ 095-21073; http://seafishingireland.net; Clifden Harbour; fishing per day €55, tackle €15; ⊘ by
appointment) Shore fishing, reef fishing and
shark and tuna fishing in season are offered
by experienced skipper John Brittain aboard
the 13m single-hull *Cygnus Cyfish*. Trips are
also possible from Cleggan.

✹ Festivals & Events

Connemara Pony Show SPORTS
(www.cpbs.ie; ⊘ mid-Aug) The area's famous
ponies are exhibited at Clifden's show-
grounds during the annual Connemara Pony
Show. Other events during the show include
Irish dancing.

⌕ Sleeping

Acton's Eco Beach CAMPGROUND €
(☑ 095-44036; www.actonsbeachsidecamping.
com; Claddaghduff Rd; tent/campervan sites
from €11/17 per person; ⊘ Easter-Oct; P ☜) ∥
Situated 10km northwest of Clifden in a
beautiful protected environment, Ireland's
first climate-neutral campground has its
own white-sand beach and natural spring.
Well-maintained facilities include a kitchen
and campfires, and it's one of the few camp-
grounds in the region without privately
owned cabins. Wi-fi can be patchy.

Clifden Bay Hostel HOSTEL €
(☑ 087 776 9345; http://clifdenbayhostel; 1 Market St; dm €17-23; ⊘ reception 9am-5pm) Right
in the centre of town, this cheery hostel is
set in a cream-coloured house framed by
big picture windows, with sunlit rooms
and 34 beds. The adjoining bar has wi-fi
and live music until late most nights.

★ **Blue Quay Rooms** BOUTIQUE HOTEL €€
(☑ 095-21369; www.bluequayrooms.com; Beach
Rd; d €70-100, apt €140; P ☜) Painted a vivid shade of blue, this boutique property is
even more stunning inside. Adorned with
a brass ship's wheel, the nautical-themed
lounge has black-and-white chequerboard
floor tiles, designer fabrics and fresh flowers. Rooms also blend vintage and contemporary furnishings; all but one have harbour
views. There's a minimum two-night stay for
the five-person self-catering apartment. No
kids under 12.

★ **Dolphin Beach** B&B €€
(☑ 095-21204; www.dolphinbeachhouse.com; Lower Sky Rd; s/d from €90/130; P ☜) ∥ Tucked
away off the Lower Sky Rd 5km west of Clifden, this Atlantic's edge B&B has stupendous
views, especially from the front terrace and
atrium dining room. High-ceilinged rooms
have chic, countrified furnishings. Organic
vegetables from its own gardens are used at
breakfast and dinner (€40). Kids under 12
aren't permitted.

Quay House HOTEL €€
(☑ 095-21369; http://thequayhouse.com; Beach
Rd; s/d/f from €99/140/180; ⊘ mid-Mar–mid-
Nov; P ☜) Dating from 1820, this rambling
house sits opposite the harbour 650m
southwest of town. All but three of its 15
elegant antique-filled rooms have harbour
views; some have working fireplaces. One
ground-floor room is equipped for visitors
with limited mobility. Run by an offshoot
of the Foyle family of hoteliers, it has
served as both a convent and Franciscan
monastery.

Station House Hotel HOTEL €€
(☑ 095-21699; www.clifdenstationhouse.com;
off Galway Rd/N59; s/d/f/apt €80/100/115/150;
P ☜ ☲) In the former train station complex, this 1998-constructed hotel was built
in the style of an old steam-train utility
shed. Large rooms have warm red fabrics;
children under 12 stay free. The kids' club
and indoor swimming pool are a hit with
families. There's also a spa, gym and sauna, and bar in the historic red-brick station
waiting room.

Its four self-catering apartments are right next door.

★ Abbeyglen Castle Hotel   CASTLE €€€
(☑ 095-21201; www.abbeyglen.ie; Sky Rd; d/ste from €219/254; P ❤) Complete with crenellations and turrets, this 1832-built castle, amid landscaped grounds on the scenic Sky Road (p391), is straight out of a fairy tale. Spacious rooms and suites, complimentary afternoon tea with scones, a tennis court and billiards room are among its amenities. On Tuesdays its restaurant (mains €20 to €39) hosts an Irish night with trad music followed by storytelling.

A three-course dinner menu costs €49. Nonguests are welcome but need to book ahead.

✕ Eating & Drinking

Restaurants and pubs cluster in Clifden's town centre. As elsewhere in these parts, seafood reigns supreme.

Connemara Hamper   DELI €
(www.connemarahamper.com; Market St; dishes €3-8.50; ⊙ 9.30am-6pm Mon-Sat year-round, noon-6pm Sun Jul & Aug) Irish farmhouse cheeses, Connemara smoked salmon, pâtés, dips, jams, chutneys, savoury ready-to-eat dishes such as chicken-and-leek pies and sweet treats including cakes and biscuits from this terrific deli make ideal picnic ingredients, along with all-natural wines.

Steam Cafe   CAFE €
(Station House Courtyard; mains €7.50-12; ⊙ 9.30am-5.30pm Mon-Sat; ❤) Sky-blue and lime-green tables brighten the pavement outside this cafe hidden in the former train station courtyard, while inside, natural light streams in through floor-to-ceiling windows. Along with Clifden's best coffee, it serves scones with homemade jam, several soups per day such as curried parsnip, and fantastic sandwiches, salads and creative cakes like Guinness and blueberry.

★ Mitchell's   SEAFOOD €€
(☑ 095-21867; www.mitchellsrestaurantclifden. com; Market St; mains lunch €10.50-15, dinner €18-28, seafood platter €24; ⊙ noon-10pm) Seafood from the surrounding waters takes centre stage at this elegant spot, from lunchtime sandwiches such as smoked mackerel and velvety chowder through to its standout Connemara platter (available at both lunch and dinner), piled high with Rossaveal prawns, Oranmore oysters, Connemara smoked salmon and Dunloughan crab. Strong wine list. Book ahead in the evenings.

Off the Square   IRISH €€
(☑ 095-22281; www.offthesquare.ie; Main St; mains lunch €4.50-12, dinner €15.50-22; ⊙ 9.15am-10pm; ➍) Surf meets turf on the menu of this busy town-centre bistro. Full Irish all-day breakfasts and casual lunches (smoked salmon on soda bread; Irish stew) give way to more complex meals at night featuring fish from Clifden's pier, Cleggan lobsters, Aughrismore oysters and crab, and Connemara black-faced lamb. A decent kids' menu makes it a good family option.

Lowry's Bar   PUB
(www.lowrysbar.ie; Market St; ⊙ 10.30am-11.30pm Mon-Thu, 10.30am-12.30am Fri & Sat, noon-11.30pm Sun) A time-worn local, third generation-run Lowry's has *céilidh* sessions at least a couple of nights a week (nightly from Easter to October) and a 100-strong whiskey collection.

🛍 Shopping

Clifden Bookshop   BOOKS
(www.clifdenbookshop.com; Main St; ⊙ 9.30am-6pm Mon-Fri, 10am-6pm Sat, noon-4pm Sun) Local history, memoirs, Irish literature and plant and wildlife guides are among the titles at this well-stocked bookshop, along with maps and children's books.

Connemara Blue   GLASS
(www.connemarablue.com; Market St; ⊙ 10am-5pm) Glass coasters, wall panels, plates, bowls, vases and sculptures in traditional and contemporary designs are made on site at this atelier/gallery. Learn how to create pieces yourself on glass-making courses (€25/75 per hour/half day; two-hour children's workshops €25).

ℹ Information

Helpful staff at Clifden's seasonal **tourist office** (www.discoverireland.ie; Galway Rd/N59; ⊙ 9.30am-6pm Easter–mid-Oct) can suggest activities including walking routes.

ℹ Getting There & Away

Citylink (www.citylink.ie) has services to/from Galway city (€15, 90 minutes, five daily) along the N59.

COUNTY GALWAY CLIFDEN & AROUND

OMEY ISLAND

Following the rugged coastline north-west of Clifden brings you to the tiny village of Claddaghduff (An Cladach Dubh), which is signposted off the road to Cleggan. If you turn west here down by the Catholic church, you will come out on Omey Strand, where horse races take place in summer.

At low tide you can drive or walk across the sand to Omey Island, a low islet of rock, grass and sand. Swimming is possible at its white sandy beaches, and walking is popular. Now uninhabited, there's a handful of abandoned houses. Omey's last resident, professional stunt-man Pascal Whelan (whose film credits include *Butch Cassidy and the Sundance Kid* and *Crocodile Dundee*), died in 2017; he is buried in the island's cemetery. Check tide times before setting out (high tides are deep enough to submerge cars) and follow the black arrow road signs. From Clifden it's 13km one way.

Bus Éireann (www.buseireann.ie) also offers services to/from Galway (€15.50, two hours, up to four daily) via Roundstone (€8, 35 minutes).

Cleggan

POP 208

With a charming, boat-lined dock, the tiny fishing port of Cleggan (An Cloiggean), 11km northwest of Clifden, is the gateway to the island of Inishbofin. West of Cleggan, narrow looping roads follow the spectacular shoreline.

Three-hour treks (€65) to Omey Island (p394), 90-minute beach or moorland rides (€45) and lessons (from €30 per hour) are offered by friendly **Cleggan Beach Riding Centre** (☑083 388 8135; www.clegganriding centre.com; ☻by appointment) in Cleggan's east.

✗ Eating

Oliver's SEAFOOD €€
(☑095-44640; http://oliversoncleggganpier.ie; mains lunch €9.50-14.50, dinner €17-23.50; ☻kitchen noon-3pm & 6-9pm; 🐾) Oliver's is a locally loved seafood pub with a classic black-and-cream facade. Specials depend on the catch, but you can always get the crab claws fried in garlic (and kids' meals). Check out the old nautical radio on the bar. Upstairs are five comfortable B&B rooms (double/family €60/120), full of sea breezes and, when the sun obliges, Connemara light.

❶ Getting There & Away

Citylink (www.citylink.ie) buses connect Cleggan with Clifden (€5, 15 minutes, three daily) and on to Galway (€15, 1¾ hours).

Island Discovery (☑095-45819; http://in-ishbofinislanddiscovery.com; adult/child return €20/10) ferries run from Cleggan to Inishbofin.

Inishbofin

POP 150

Situated 9km from the mainland, the tranquil island of Inishbofin measures just 6km long by 3km wide, and its highest point is a mere 86m above sea level. You can walk or cycle its narrow, deserted lanes, green pastures and sandy beaches, with farm animals and seals for company.

Its history is more tumultuous: St Colman exiled himself to Inishbofin in AD 665, after he fell out with the Church over its adoption of a new calendar. He set up a monastery northeast of the harbour, where the more recent ruins of a small 14th-century church still stand. Grace O'Malley, the famous pirate queen (p408), used Inishbofin as a base in the 16th century, and Cromwell's forces captured the island in 1652, using it to jail priests and clerics.

◉ Sights & Activities

Inishbofin offers excellent walking, cycling and horse riding.

The island has three looped routes; you can download maps for the routes from the island's tourism association website.

The ruined 14th-century chapel on the site of St Colman's monastery is a highlight of the 8km **Cloonamore Loop**. Spectacular views over counties Galway, Mayo and Clare feature on the 5km **Middlequarter Loop**. The 8km **Westquarter Loop** takes in the Atlantic coast, with views of the island's blowholes, sea arch and seal colony.

All three loops start and finish at the pier.

Heritage Museum MUSEUM
(☻noon-1.30pm & 2.30-5pm Easter-Sep) FREE Inishbofin's small but evocative museum gives a comprehensive overview of the island's history. Displays include fishing, farming and tradespeople's tools as well as items from traditional Irish homes (crock-

ery, clothing, furniture and more) and over 200 photos of islanders over the years. Hours can vary.

Parish Church of St Colman   CHURCH
(⊙8am-5pm) The interior of this small, charming church 300m east of the pier is illuminated by the soft light of its stained glass.

Inishbofin Equestrian Centre   HORSE RIDING
(☑087 950 1545; www.inishbofinequestriancentre
.com; ⊙9am-6pm) Inishbofin Equestrian Centre offers horse-riding lessons (€35 per hour) and treks (€30 per hour) around the island. Evening rides are possible by request.

Kings Bicycle Hire   CYCLING
(☑095-45833; Inishbofin Pier; bike rental per day €12; ⊙10am-5pm Jun-Aug & by appointment) The island's mostly flat terrain is well suited for cycling – albeit not very far given its tiny size.

Festivals & Events

Inishbofin Arts Festival   CULTURAL
(www.inishbofin.com; ⊙mid-May) Accordion workshops, archaeological walks, art exhibitions and concerts feature during this festival held over the May bank holiday weekend.

Sleeping & Eating

Inishbofin Island Hostel   HOSTEL €
(☑095-45855; www.inishbofin-hostel.ie; camping per person €12, dm €16-18, d €45, f €50-100; ⊙Easter-Sep) In an old farmhouse, this snug 38-bed hostel has six-bed dorms and private rooms with shared bathroom facilities, as well as scenic campsites. Good amenities include a conservatory with panoramic views, a self-catering kitchen, barbecue, laundry facilities and bike storage. It's 1km east of the pier.

Inishbofin House Hotel & Marine Spa   HOTEL €€
(☑095-45809; www.inishbofinhouse.com; d €100-120, f €160-180; ⊙Apr-Sep; 🖥) Situated 400m east of the pier, this modern hotel has beauty treatment rooms specialising in seaweed baths, plus a library and a large living room overlooking a cove. Standard rooms face the rear, with farmland views; it's well worth paying more for a sea-view room (some of which have balconies). Seafood is the mainstay of its restaurant (mains €16.50 to €27).

Lapwing House   B&B €€
(☑095-45996; www.inishbofin.com/bandb/lap wing.html; d from €80; 🖥) Named after the

local bird species that breeds on the island, this lovely family-run B&B in a whitewashed building 500m north from the pier has just two rooms (one double and one twin), each with a private bathroom. Views extend over the sheep-flecked hillside to the harbour. It's open year-round, but you'll need to pre-arrange bookings in winter.

ⓘ Information

The island's **tourism association** (☑095-45895; www.inishbofin.com) is a good resource for information.

Self-caterers should stock up on the mainland, although Inishbofin's post office has a small grocery shop. There's a total of five restaurants and four bars, most located at the island's hotels. Many places only accept cash and the island has no ATMs, so come prepared.

ⓘ Getting There & Away

Ferries from Cleggan to Inishbofin take 30 to 45 minutes and are run by **Island Discovery** (p394). In low season there are two ferries a day, increasing to three from June to August. Dolphins often swim alongside the boats, and basking sharks can often be spotted in April. Confirm ahead, as ferries may be cancelled when seas are rough.

Letterfrack & Around

POP 192

Founded by Quakers in the mid-19th century, Letterfrack (Leitir Fraic) is a crossroads with a few pubs and B&Bs. But the forested setting and nearby coast are a magnet for outdoors adventure seekers. A 4km walk to the peak of **Tully Mountain** (356m) takes 40 minutes and offers uplifting ocean views.

◉ Sights & Activities

★**Kylemore Abbey**   HISTORIC BUILDING
(www.kylemoreabbey.com; off N59; adult/child €13/free; ⊙9am-7pm Jul & Aug, 9.30am-5.30pm Sep & Oct, 9am-6pm Apr-Jun, 10am-4.30pm Nov-Mar) Photogenically perched on the shores of Pollacapall Lough, 4.3km east of Letterfrack, this crenelled 19th-century neo-Gothic fantasy was built for a wealthy English businessman, Mitchell Henry, who spent his honeymoon in Connemara. Only ground-floor rooms are open to visitors, but you can wander down the lake to the **Gothic church**, and admission includes

CONNEMARA'S NORTH COAST

The north coast of Connemara is awash with gorgeous beaches, raw mountain vistas and stark views out to the moody sea.

Bypass the N59 for a series of small roads that follow the twists and turns along the coast for about 15km. Start at Letterfrack, where a narrow track leads northwest. Follow various small roads, sticking as close to the water as you can. Watch for sheep. The land here seems to be in the midst of a dissolution into the sea.

At **Renvyle** you can pause for the night. **Renvyle Beach Caravan & Camping** (📞095-43462; www.renvylebeachcaravanpark.com; Renvyle; campsites €10.50-21; ⊙Easter-Sep; P🐾) has campsites on a grassy expanse with direct access to a sandy beach. **Renvyle House Hotel** (📞095-46100; www.renvyle.com; Renvyle; s/d/tr/f from €95/190/240/280; P🐾🏊) is a luxurious 68-room converted country estate set on 80 hectares.

Continue east, past a few fine country pubs at the tiny crossroads of **Tully Cross**. Stick to the coast and stop often – especially on sunny days – to marvel at the dazzling colours: rich cobalt sea, cerulean sky, emerald-green grass, brown hills, slate-grey rocks and white-sand beaches. The beach horse-racing sequences for *The Quiet Man* (p391) were shot at **Lettergesh**.

Look for a turn to **Rosroe Quay**, where a magnificent crescent of sand awaits at **Glassillaun Beach**. If you're drawn to the beauty of the water, **Scuba Dive West** (📞095-43922; www.scubadivewest.com; Glassillaun Beach, Renvyle; shore/boat dives incl gear from €55/80, snorkelling per half day from €35) runs highly recommended courses and dives around the surrounding coastlines and islands.

Continue southeast along the final 5km stretch of road that runs along **Lough Fee**. In spring when the gorse explodes in yellow bloom, the views here are breathtaking.

entry to the extravagant **Victorian walled gardens**, around a 20-minute walk away (linked by a free shuttle bus from April to October).

Run by Benedictine nuns, the abbey served as the Kylemore Abbey School from 1923 to 2010, teaching Catholic girls. There's a cafe and a teahouse on the grounds, which also offer hikes and woodland walks.

★ **Connemara National Park** PARK
(www.connemaranationalpark.ie; off N59; ⊙24hr) FREE Immediately southeast of Letterfrack, Connemara National Park spans 2957 dramatic hectares of bog, mountains, heath and woodlands.

The park encloses a number of the **Twelve Bens**, including Bencullagh, Benbrack and Benbaun. The heart of the park is **Gleann Mór** (Big Glen), through which the River Polladirk flows. There's fine walking up the glen and over the surrounding mountains along with short self-guided walks.

Guided nature walks (www.connemara nationalpark.ie; ⊙11am Wed & Fri early Jul-Aug) led by park rangers depart from the **visitor centre** (www.connemaranationalpark.ie; off N59; ⊙9am-5.30pm Mar-Oct).

🛏 Sleeping & Eating

Letterfrack Lodge HOSTEL €
(📞095-41222; off N59; dm/d/tr/q €18/€60/75/85; P🐾) Close to the Letterfrack crossroads, this stone-fronted hostel has spacious dorms as well as private rooms with their own bathrooms. Mike, the enthusiastic owner, is a great source of info on walks throughout the region. Breakfast is included in the low season (October to June); from July to September, an on-site restaurant offers breakfast, lunch and dinner. Laundry facilities, bike hire and storage are available.

Rosleague Manor HOTEL €€€
(📞095-41101; www.rosleague.com; N59; s/d/f/ste from €115/170/200/210; ⊙mid-May–mid-Nov; P🐾) Gloriously sited overlooking Ballynakill Harbour and the Twelve Bens mountain range, 2km west of Letterfrack, this rose-pink manor is a romantic hideaway, with walking trails through the private woodlands, a Victorian conservatory, an excellent restaurant (two-/three-course menus €32/48) and a tennis court. Richly coloured rooms are furnished with antiques and original artworks. Babysitters can be arranged.

Fruit, vegetables and herbs come from its own kitchen gardens.

❶ Information

Connemara National Park Visitor Centre (p396) In a beautiful setting off a parking area 300m south of the Letterfrack cross-roads, the visitor centre offers an introduction to the park's flora, fauna and geology.

❶ Getting There & Away

Citylink (www.citylink.ie) buses serve Letter-frack from Galway (€15, two hours, three daily) and continue to Clifden (€5, 20 minutes).

Leenane & Killary Harbour

Dotted with mussel rafts, long, narrow Killary Harbour is often referred to as Ireland's only fjord. Slicing 16km inland and more than 45m deep in the centre, it certainly looks like a fjord, although some scientific studies suggest it may not actually have been glaciated. The small village of **Leenane** (also spelled Leenaun) sits on its shore, while **Mt Mweelrea** (814m) towers to its north.

The Leenane village website www.leenanevillage.com is a good source of information.

◉ Sights & Activities

Excellent walks from Leenane include one to **Aasleagh Waterfall** (Eas Liath), 4km northeast in County Mayo.

Sheep & Wool Centre MUSEUM (www.sheepandwoolcentre.com; adult/child €5/3; ⊙9.30am-6pm mid-Mar–Oct) On Leenane's main street, just north of the bridge, this compelling little museum dedicated to sheep and wool has spinning and weaving demonstrations, and covers the history of dyeing. There's an on-site cafe and shop selling locally made handicrafts as well as topographical walking maps.

Joyce Country Sheepdogs FARM (☑094-954 8853; www.joycecountrysheepdogs.ie; Shanafaraghaun; adult/child €10/5; ⊙11am, 1pm & 3.30pm Mon-Sat Mar-Sep) Book in advance to see the amazing feats performed by sheepdogs on this working farm. From Leenane, it's 14km east: take the R336 and turn onto the L1301.

Killary Fjord Boat Tours BOATING (☑091-566 736; www.killaryfjord.com; N59; adult/child €22.50/11.50; ⊙late Mar-Oct) From Nancy's Point, 2.7km west of Leenane, Killary Fjord Boat Tours offers 1½-hour cruises of Killary Harbour. Dolphins leap around the boat, which passes by a mussel farm and stops at a salmon farm. There are up to four cruises daily in season; tickets (adult/child €20/10) are cheaper if you prebook online. Kids under 10 travel free.

Killary Adventure Centre ADVENTURE SPORTS (☑095-43411; http://killaryadventure.com; off N59; half-day activities per adult/child from €46/31; ⊙10am-5pm) ⏀ Canoeing, sea kayaking, water-skiing, rock climbing, windsurfing, orienteering, day hikes and clay-pigeon shooting are among the activities offered by this adventure centre 5.5km west of Leenane. Decent dorms (€22 to €25) and double rooms (€60 to €70) come with underfloor heating.

Power is supplied by wind turbines; it also has a biomass boiler.

⏱ Sleeping & Eating

Sleepzone Connemara HOSTEL € (☑095-42929; www.sleepzone.ie; off N59; campsites per person €12, dm/s/d/tr/q from €19/39/59/69/89; ⊙Mar-Oct; [P] 🐾) Popular with walkers, this renovated 19th-century property with direct access down to the water has over 100 beds in clean dorms and private rooms. Excellent amenities include a bar, barbecue terrace and self-catering kitchen (bring supplies with you as there are no shops nearby). It's 6.3km west of Leenane; shuttle buses serve its hostels in Galway (☑091-566 999; www.sleepzone.ie; Bóthar na mBan; dm/d/tr/q from €15/59/69/79; @🐾) and Lisdoonvarna (p351).

Guests get discounts at the nearby Killary Adventure Centre.

Leenane Hotel HOTEL €€ (☑095-42249; N59; d/f from €98/145; ⊙Easter-Sep; [P] 🐾) Dating from the 19th century, this modernised 66-room hotel 1km west of Leenane is home to the **Connemara Seaweed Baths** (☑095-42408; http://connemaraseaweedbaths.com; per hour €25; ⊙10am-6pm Easter-Sep). Balcony rooms with harbour views cost €10 extra. An open peat fire warms the bar, while the restaurant serves regional specialities including seafood and lamb (mains €12 to €25; half-board options available), as well as a kids' menu.

Cots are available on request.

GALWAY OYSTERS

Some of County Galway's finest seafood, including lobster in season, is served in **Moran's Oyster Cottage** (☑ 091-796 113; www.moransoystercottage.com; The Weir, Kilcolgan; mains €13.50-22, half-dozen oysters €12-14, seafood platter €26.50; ⊘ noon-9.30pm Sun-Thu, to 10pm Fri & Sat; ⬚), an atmospheric thatched pub and restaurant, set in a quiet cove. A terrace overlooks Dunbulcaun Bay, where the oysters are reared before they arrive on your plate. There's a good, pared-down kids' menu. It's signposted 2km west of the N18.

The long-established **Clarenbridge Oyster Festival** (www.clarenbridge.com; ⊘ early Oct) takes place in Clarenbridge, 18km south of Galway city, over four days in early October.

Blackberry Cafe　　　CAFE, BISTRO €€
(☑ 095-42240; http://blackberryrestaurant.ie; mains lunch €8-20, dinner €16-24, seafood platter €21.50; ⊘ noon-4.30pm & 6-9pm Jun-Aug, closed Tue Apr, May & Sep; ☎) Connemara smoked salmon, creamy chowder and oysters (€20 per dozen) are on offer during the day at this smart wood-floored cafe with water views in the centre of Leenane. Dinners are more elaborate affairs (prime sirloin; glazed duck). Cash only.

Gaynor's　　　PUB
(⊘ 10.30am-11.30pm Mon-Thu, 10.30am-12.30am Fri & Sat, 12.30pm-11pm Sun) A crackling peat fire, dark-wood panelling and spontaneous trad sessions make this cosy pub an essential stop. Pavement picnic tables overlook the harbour; hearty pub fare (dishes €4 to €12) includes Irish lamb stew. It also doubles as the town's petrol station.

The pub played a starring role in the 1990 Irish film *The Field*.

ℹ Getting There & Away

No public transport serves Killary Harbour, but Sleepzone Connemara has a shuttle to its sister properties in **Galway** (p397) and **Lisdoonvarna** (p351).

From the harbour, the R335 heads north into County Mayo's hauntingly beautiful Doolough Valley.

EASTERN GALWAY

Lough Corrib separates eastern Galway from the dramatic landscape of the county's western coast, and the regions are markedly different.

To Galway city's south, pretty Kinvara on Galway Bay is a stepping stone to County Clare, while inland there are some interesting sights around (albeit not in) the working town of Gort. Farming country unfolds east of Galway city.

Kinvara

POP 734

The small stone harbour of Kinvara (sometimes spelt Kinvarra) sits at the southeastern corner of Galway Bay, which accounts for its Irish name, Cinn Mhara 'Head of the Sea'. Filled with vividly painted buildings, the charming village makes an excellent pit stop between Galway city and County Clare.

◉ Sights

★ **Dunguaire Castle**　　　HISTORIC BUILDING
(www.shannonheritage.com; off N67; adult/child €7/3.80; ⊘ 10am-5pm Apr–mid-Sep) Erected around 1520 by the O'Hynes clan, Dunguaire Castle, 900m north of town, occupies the former site of the 6th-century royal palace of Guaire Aidhne, the king of Connaught. Lady Christabel Ampthill restored the castle after buying it for the equivalent of €500 and lived here from the 1950s to the 1970s. Climb to the roof for glorious views of Galway Bay and Kinvara.

Lady Ampthill's bedroom was in the crafts studio, with her living room at the very top, beneath a new pitched roof.

A touristy medieval banquet (adult/child €52.50/34.50) takes place at 5.30pm and 8.45pm daily, but must be prebooked online.

✺ Festivals & Events

Fleadh na gCuach　　　MUSIC
(Cuckoo Festival; ⊘ late April/early May) Held over three days, this traditional music festival features over 100 musicians performing at upwards of 50 organised sessions. Spin-off events include a parade.

Cruinniú na mBáid SPORTS

(www.galwaytourism.ie; ☺mid-Aug) Up to 100 traditional Galway hooker sailing boats race each year in the Cruinniú na mBáid 'Gathering of the Boats'.

🛏 Sleeping & Eating

Kinvara Guesthouse GUESTHOUSE €€

(📞091-638 562; http://kinvaraguesthouse.ie; The Square; d/tr/f from €95/125/135; 🛜) Floor-to-ceiling mural photographs, ceramics, bold colours and fresh flowers brighten this violet-fronted 22-room guesthouse right on the central square. Dinner, bed and breakfast deals are available with the **Pier Head** (📞091-638 188; The Quay; mains €15-30; ☺1-9pm Mon & Tue, 1-9.30pm Wed-Fri, noon-10pm Sat, noon-9.30pm Sun) bar and restaurant.

Strawberry Hedgehog Cafe CAFE €

(The Quay; dishes €3-8; ☺9am-6pm May-Sep, 11am-5pm Oct-Apr; 🛜) Eclectically decorated with MC Escher prints and pics of Hendrix and Lennon, this bright purple boho cafe does a soup of the day (Indian lentil; Thai carrot, coconut and chilli), scones, organic coffee, hot chocs and fresh fruit smoothies.

Green's Bar PUB

(Main St; ☺2pm-midnight) With over a hundred different whiskeys on shelves behind its bar, which looks ready to collapse, this 1865 pub is quite a sight. Painted apple-green on the outside, with darker lime-green trim, it's home to spontaneous sessions of traditional music several times a week. There's a discounted whiskey of the week along with various whiskey tasting platters.

❶ Getting There & Away

Bus Éireann (www.buseireann.ie) links Kinvara with Galway city (€9.60, 40 minutes, three daily) and towns in County Clare including Doolin (€14.30, 1½ hours, three daily).

Athenry

POP 5469

Athenry (Áth an Rí; pronounced 'Athen-rye';) constitutes one of Ireland's most intact collections of medieval architecture, with a magnificent **castle** (www.heritage ireland.ie; adult/child €5/2; ☺9.30am-6pm Easter-Sep), the medieval parish **Church of St Mary's**, a **Dominican priory** (📞091-844 661; Bridge St; ☺by appointment), an original market cross and the **North Gate**, which you can drive through. An impressive 75% of the lengthy town walls survives. The **Arts & Heritage Centre** (📞091-844 661; www.athenryheritagecentre.com; St Mary's, the Square; adult/child €5/4.50; Medieval Experience €8/6.50; ☺10.30am-5pm May-Sep, hours vary Oct-Apr) has free downloadable walking-tour maps. However, the impressive heritage is overshadowed by the modern, industrial town.

Athenry takes its name from a nearby ford (*áth* in Irish) that crosses the River Clare east of the settlement and was the meeting point for three kingdoms, hence its Irish name, which translates as Ford of the Kings.

The town's name is synonymous with the stirring song 'The Fields of Athenry', composed by Pete St John in the 1970s, which recounts incarceration resulting from the Famine.

❶ Getting There & Away

Athenry is on the Galway–Dublin M6 motorway.

Buslink (www.buslink.ie) serves Galway (€7, 35 minutes, up to eight daily). There are two additional Nightlink services on Friday and Saturday nights.

Trains (www.irishrail.ie) run to Galway (€5.90, 25 minutes) and Dublin (€15, 2¼ hours) up to twice hourly.

Gort & Around

POP 2994

Central to the workaday town of Gort is the Square, with its personable Christ the King statue and shop-filled streets radiating out. Most sights, however, are just outside town, including those connected with the great poet WB Yeats.

◉ Sights

⭐**Thoor Ballylee** HISTORIC BUILDING

(📞091-537 700; https://yeatsthoorballylee.org; Peterswell; adult/child €7/3.50; ☺10am-6pm May-Aug) In an idyllic setting by a stream, this 16th-century Norman tower was the summer home of WB Yeats from 1921 to 1929 and was the inspiration for one of his best-known works, *The Tower*. It adjoins a whitewashed cottage with forest-green trim, which contains an exhibition on Yeats' life and work. From Gort, it's 7.2km northeast off the N66.

Kilmacduagh HISTORIC SITE

(Map p346; off R460) FREE The extensive ruins at the monastic site of Kilmacduagh, 6km southwest of Gort, include a well-preserved 34m-high round tower, the remains of a small 14th-century cathedral (Teampall Mór MacDuagh), an oratory dedicated to St John the Baptist and other little chapels. The original monastery is thought to have been founded by St Colman MacDuagh at the beginning of the 7th century.

Kiltartan Gregory Museum MUSEUM

(www.kiltartangregorymuseum.org; Kiltartan Cross; adult/child €3/1; ⊙11am-5pm daily Jun-Aug, 1-5pm Sun May & Sep) A charming stone schoolhouse built in 1892 now contains this museum, which traces the life of WB Yeats' literary patron, Lady Augusta Gregory, through photographs, manuscripts and objects from her former home at Coole Park (www.coolepark.ie; Coole Haven; ⊙8am-7.30pm May-Oct, to 6pm Nov-Apr) FREE. The schoolhouse was designed by Lady Gregory's brother, Frank Persse. It's 4km north of Gort.

❶ Getting There & Away

Bus Éireann (www.buseireann.ie) has hourly services to Galway city (€7.50, 40 minutes) and Ennis (€11, 30 minutes).

Trains (www.irishrail.ie) link Gort with Galway (€6.90, 50 minutes) and Ennis (€5.90, 20 minutes) five times daily.

Counties Mayo & Sligo

POP 197,000 / AREA 7250 SQ KM

Best Places to Eat

➡ Pantry & Corkscrew (p412)

➡ Hargadons (p427)

➡ Trá Bán (p430)

➡ An Port Mór (p412)

➡ Eithna's by the Sea (p435)

Best Places to Sleep

➡ Belleek Castle (p421)

➡ Stella Maris (p419)

➡ Ardtarmon House (p434)

➡ Newport House (p414)

➡ Delphi Lodge (p407)

Why Go?

Despite their natural wonders and languid charm, the Counties Mayo and Sligo remain a well-kept secret, offering all of Ireland's wild, romantic beauty but without the crowds. Mayo is the more rugged of the two, with scraggy peaks, sheer cliffs, heather-covered moors and beautiful offshore islands where life is dictated by the elements. Sligo is more pastoral and its lush fields, fish-filled lakes and flat-topped mountains inspired William Butler Yeats to compose some of Ireland's most ardent verse.

Both counties boast grand stretches of golden sands and legendary breaks that lure the surfing cognoscenti from around the globe. Visit and you'll find all this plus an improbable bounty of prehistoric sites, elegant Georgian towns, abandoned manor houses, charming fishing villages and good old-fashioned warm-hearted country hospitality.

When to Go

➡ The weather-beaten shores of Mayo and Sligo can be whipped by brutal winds and rain in winter, when only the hardiest tourists and surfers make it here.

➡ If you're interested in catching a swell, spring and autumn are your best shot, with September and October favoured by those in the know.

➡ In summer the region bursts into life with oodles of festivals. In July and August you'll get the pick of the crop with the Yeats festival in Sligo and a variety of small traditional-music festivals elsewhere. Plus the weather is often balmy.

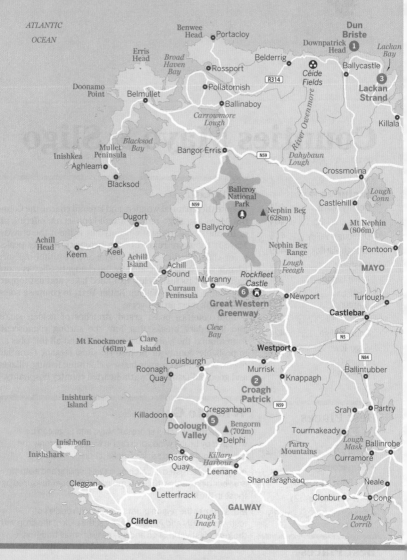

Counties Mayo & Sligo Highlights

① Dun Briste (p420) Staring out over the raging sea to this astonishing sea stack cleaved from the mainland by a huge storm in 1393.

② Croagh Patrick (p409) Following in St Patrick's footsteps up the conical peak.

③ Lackan Strand (p420) Exploring the glory of this beautiful beach.

④ Carrowkeel Megalithic Cemetery (p430) Sensing ancient energy amid prehistoric cairns, sinkholes and astonishing views.

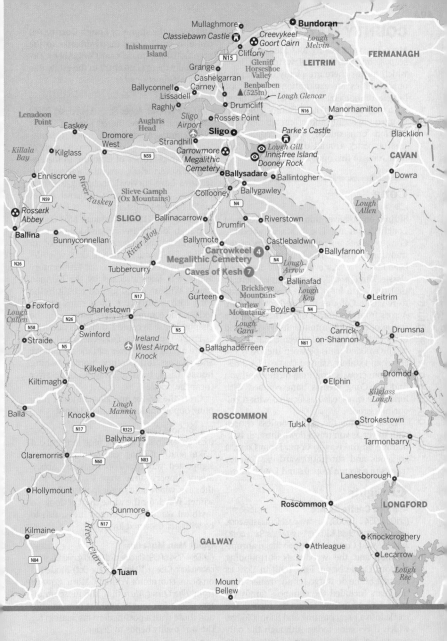

⑤ Doolough Valley (p406) Walking along this starkly beautiful and poignantly desolate region.

⑥ Great Western Greenway (p413) Riding along the popular route from Westport to Achill Island.

⑦ Caves of Keash (p431) Climbing up to the ancient limestone caves and marvelling at the view.

COUNTY MAYO

Mayo has wild beauty and haunting landscapes, but you'll find few tourists here, which means there are plenty of untapped opportunities for exploration by car, foot, bicycle or horseback. Life here has never been easy and the Potato Famine (1845–51) ravaged the county and prompted mass emigration. Consequently many people with Irish ancestry around the world can trace their roots to this once-blighted land.

Cong

POP 190

Sitting on a sliver-thin isthmus between Lough Corrib and Lough Mask, twee little Cong conjures up romantic notions of the traditional Irish village. Time seems to have been in reverse gear ever since the evergreen classic *The Quiet Man* was filmed here in 1951. In fact a lot of effort has been made to re-create Cong as it looked for the film. Across from the tourist office there's even a statue of Sean Thornton (John Wayne) and Mary Kate Danaher (Maureen O'Hara).

The wooded trails between the lovely old abbey and stately Ashford Castle offer a respite from crowds; continue further and you find the Cong area is honeycombed with limestone caves, each associated with a colourful legend.

Look out for the gaunt roofless church with tower as you travel down through Ballinarobe on the way to Cong. From Cong, a gorgeous and straightforward car journey travels in a scenic loop around Lough Mask.

⊙ Sights

Ashford Castle Estate　　　HISTORIC SITE
(☎ 094-954 6003;　www.ashfordcastle.com; grounds adult/child €10/5; ⊙ grounds 9am-dusk) Just beyond Cong Abbey, the village abruptly ends and the woodlands surrounding Ashford Castle begin. First built in 1228 as the seat of the de Burgo family, owners over the years included the Guinness family (of stout fame). Arthur Guinness turned the castle into a regal hunting and fishing lodge, which it remains today. Although the only way to look inside its restored interior is to stay (p405) or dine here, the surrounding estate is open to the public.

The 140 hectares of parkland, covered with forests, streams and a golf course, is great to explore. Walking through the Kinlough Woods gets you away from the golfers and out to the shores of **Lough Corrib**. You can also stroll along the riverbanks to the monk's fishing house near Cong Abbey. Occasionally there is no entry to the estate due to private functions.

Cong Abbey　　　HISTORIC SITE
(☎ 094-954 6542; Abbey St; ⊙ dawn-dusk) FREE The evocatively weathered shell of Cong's 12th-century Augustinian abbey (Mainistir Chonga) is scored by a cross-hatch of lines from centuries of exposure to the elements. Nevertheless, several finely sculpted features have survived, including a carved doorway, windows, lovely medieval arches and the ruined cloisters.

Founded in 1135 by Turlough Mór O'Connor, high king of Ireland and king of Connaught, the abbey occupies the site of an earlier 7th-century church that was destroyed in a conflagration; the 12th-century abbey was later attacked by the Norman knight William de Burgh and rebuilt in the early 13th century (it is these ruins you see today). The community once gathered in the chapter house to confess their sins publicly.

From the abbey, moss-encrusted trees guard a path to the river and the diminutive and roofless 16th-century **monk's fishing house** FREE, built midway over the river (near the bridge).

Cross the bridge and all manner of rambling opportunities await in the forest.

Pigeonhole Cave　　　CAVE
(near Cong) This cave, in a pine forest about 1.5km south of Cong, can be reached via a signposted walking loop from the abbey. Steep, slippery stone steps lead down into the cave, where subterranean water flows in winter. Watch for the white trout of Cong – a mythical woman who turned into a fish to be with her drowned lover.

Quiet Man Museum　　　MUSEUM
(☎ 094-954 6089; Circular Rd; adult/child €5/4, location tour €15; ⊙ 10am-4pm Apr-Oct) Modelled on Sean Thornton's White O' Morn' Cottage from *The Quiet Man* film, the museum offers a location tour – good for film fanatics and those with a postmodern fascination for the way reality bends to fiction.

🏃 Activities

Corrib Cruises　　　CRUISE
(☎ 087 283 0799; www.corribcruises.com; Lisloughery Pier; adult/child €20/10) Cruises on Lough Corrib depart from the Ashford Castle pier. A 75-minute history cruise leaves daily year-

THE FIRST BOYCOTT

It was near the unassuming little village of Neale, near Cong, that the term 'boycott' came into use. In 1880 the Irish Land League, in an effort to press for fair rents and improve the lot of workers, withdrew field hands from the estate of Lord Erne, who owned much of the land in the area. When Lord Erne's land agent, Captain Charles Cunningham Boycott, evicted the striking labourers, the surrounding community began a campaign to ostracise him. Not only did farmers refuse to work his land, but people in the town also refused to talk to him, provide services or sit next to him in church. The incident attracted the attention of the London papers, and soon Boycott's name was synonymous with such organised, nonviolent protests. Within a few months, Boycott fled Ireland.

round at 11am; a two-hour island cruise departs at 2.45pm from June to October and visits Inchagoill, the island at the centre of Lough Corrib with 5th-century monastic ruins. There are also boats to/from Oughterard in County Galway.

Ashford Outdoors   KAYAKING
(☑ 094-954 6507; www.ashfordoutdoors.com; Ashford Castle; tours from €50, bike rental per day from €40) Pedal the shores and then paddle the waters of Ashford Castle Estate and Lough Corrib on tours with bikes, kayaks, horses and ponies.

Lakeshore Angling Centre   FISHING
(☑ 094-954 1389; www.lakeshoreholidays.com) Provides fishing services for all types of river and lake anglers, from novice to professional; also offers a range of other activities, from trekking to horse riding, mountain biking and water sports.

🛏 Sleeping

Nymphsfield House   B&B €
(☑ 094-954 6320; www.nymphsfieldhouse.com; R345, Gortaroe; s €40-45, d €60-65; 🛜) Just northeast of Cong (a pretty 10-minute or 1km walk), in the vicinity of several good B&Bs, this family-run B&B is a good choice. There's a place to store your fishing gear, a quaint little breakfast area and friendly hosts to look after you.

Cong Hostel   HOSTEL €
(☑ 094-954 6089; www.quietman-cong.com; Quay Rd, Lisloughrey; campsites per person from €10, dm €17-20, d €50; 🛜) Well run, this IHH-affiliated hostel has its own *The Quiet Man* screening room showing the film *every* night in the mini-cinema. Dorm rooms have from four to 14 beds. There is an adjacent campground and you can borrow fishing rods. Breakfast is included, except for campers.

★ Michaeleen's Manor   B&B €€
(☑ 094-954 6089; www.congbb.com; Quay Rd, Lisloughrey; s/d from €60/80; 🛜) This large, heritage-style home is a shrine to *The Quiet Man,* so each of its 12 comfy rooms is named after a character in the film and decorated with memorabilia and quotations. There's a large fountain replica of Galway's Quiet Man Bridge set in a lush garden. It's about 2km east of Cong.

Ryan's Hotel   HOTEL €€
(☑ 094-954 6243; www.ryanshotelcong.ie; Main St; incl breakfast s from €80, d €110-120; 🛜) Right in the centre of Cong, this maroon-fronted guesthouse has 12 smart rooms with bathroom and hairdryers and a guest laundry.

Ashford Castle   HOTEL €€€
(☑ 094-954 6003; www.ashford.ie; Cong; low/ high season r from €285/595; 🛜) There's old-world elegance, 83 exquisite rooms and personalised service at Ashford Castle, easily the grandest of the grand in Ireland and once home to the Guinness family. Even if you're staying elsewhere, you can have dinner (from €70) at the smart **George V Dining Room** (be sure to dress up). There are many activities on the namesake estate, including falconry.

The castle is also home to a state-of-the-art spa.

Lodge at Ashford Castle   HOTEL €€€
(☑ 094-954 5400; www.thelodgeac.com; The Quay; r from €240; 🛜) Built in the 1820s by Ashford Castle's owners, the lodge has rich, contemporary colours and is a good alternative to the castle itself (p405). The 50 guest rooms and suites are lavishly decorated; some have copper bathtubs. It's on the grounds of Ashford Castle Estate.

✕ Eating & Drinking

★ Hungry Monk   CAFE €

(Abbey St; mains €6-14; ⊙10am-5pm Tue-Sat Mar-Nov; 🐾) With the warmest of welcomes, this simple cafe with bright colours and artfully mismatched, distressed furniture is a perfect refuge on a misty day. Locally sourced ingredients make up the excellent sandwiches, soups and salads, the luscious cakes are homemade and the coffee is excellent.

Fennel Seed Restaurant   IRISH €€

(☑094-954 6243, 094-954 6004; www.ryanshotel cong.ie; Main St, Ryan's Hotel; bar food €12-21, mains €15-25; ⊙6-9pm Mon-Sat, 1-7pm Sun) Denis Lenihan's culinary skills enjoy widespread acclaim, so make sure you don't miss the signature 'smoky bake' pie, stuffed with trout, salmon, mackerel, haddock and knock-out flavour. Bar food is served in the adjoining **Crowe's Nest Pub** until 7pm.

★ Wilde's at the Lodge   MODERN IRISH €€€

(☑094-954 5400; www.thelodgeac.com; The Quay, Lisloughrey Lodge; set meal €55, grazing menu €60; ⊙6.30-9pm daily plus 1-3.30pm Sun Mar-Oct, 6.30-9pm Thu-Sun plus 1-3.30pm Sun Nov-Feb; 🐾) Chef Jonathan Keane and his team forage the mussels, wild herbs and flowers that adorn the dishes at this exquisite restaurant within the vast grounds of Ashford Castle. Produce and meat come from organic local suppliers for a changing menu. You can sample many dishes served on small plates. The restaurant takes its name from Sir William Wilde (father of Oscar), who loved the Lough.

Pat Cohan's   PUB

(Abbey St; ⊙noon-11pm) In a case of life imitating art, this one-time grocery store was disguised in *The Quiet Man* as the fictional Pat Cohan's. But as *The Quiet Man* craziness only grows, it has now become that pub.

🛈 Information

The **tourist office** (☑094-954 6542; www. congtourism.com; Abbey St; ⊙10am-1pm & 2-5.30pm daily Mar-Sep, Fri & Sat Oct & Nov) is in the old courthouse building opposite Cong Abbey. The closest ATM is 5km west in Clonbur.

🛈 Getting There & Away

Bus Éireann (www.buseireann.ie; Main St) has two buses to Galway (€13.60, 55 minutes) Monday to Saturday, and one to Westport (€13.20, 50 minutes).

Doolough Valley

The R335 from Leenane in County Galway to Westport is one of Ireland's most beautiful scenic routes. Largely untouched by housing, cut turf or even stone walls, the desolate Doolough Valley is a sublime journey, the steep sides of the surrounding mountains simply sliding into the steely grey waters of Doo Lough as sheep graze placidly on the hills. They occasionally park themselves in the middle of the road, too.

This is also one of Ireland's most poignant spots – the site of the Doolough Tragedy – a Famine catastrophe that occurred in 1849.

Choose a dry and clear day to tackle the road as curtains of rain can greatly diminish the views. If you have time wander down the side roads to the north and west of the valley to reach glorious, often-deserted beaches.

Delphi

Geographically *just* within County Mayo, this swath of mountainous moorland along the spectacular R335 is miles from any significant population, allowing you to set about the serious business of relaxing and, if you fancy it, taking endless photographs.

The southern end of the Doolough Valley was named by its most famous resident, the second Marquis of Sligo, who was convinced that it resembled the land around Delphi, Greece. If you can spot the resemblance, you've a better imagination than most. However, the beauty of little creeks babbling over boggy countryside against a backdrop of sun- and cloud-dappled stark hillsides is undeniable.

🛏 Sleeping

Delphi Resort   LODGE €€

(☑095-42208; www.delphiadventureresort.com; off R335; dm €19-50, d from €88; 🅿 @) This multipurpose establishment built from rough-cut stone and honey-coloured wood has standard guest rooms, larger suites (some with enormous timber decks) and some great loft rooms with elevated sleeping areas (strangely, all cost the same), while backpackers can book into one of the (ultra-pricey) eight-bed dorms with bathroom. Lunch mains are €12 to €15; dinner mains €15 to €28.

Spa treatments use hand-harvested seaweed and the property's own mountain spring water. There's a good **cafe** (☑095-42208; www.delphiadventureresort.com; Delphi

THE DOOLOUGH TRAGEDY

Marked today by a grim memorial cross in the Doolough Valley that serves as its epitaph, the Doolough Tragedy still casts a black shadow across the sublime landscape, even on the sunniest of days.

On 30 March 1849, in the midst of the Potato Famine, hundreds of starving men, women and children set off from Louisburgh for Delphi Lodge, where they had heard they would be reassessed for famine relief. The reassessment took place the next day, but there was no food for them upon their arrival, so the long walk back to Louisburgh commenced. The weather was freezing and bitter and the people so malnourished and weak that the 16-mile return journey on foot took its toll and many people died. Corpses were left by the side of the road, some – it was said – with their mouths stuffed with grass in a desperate last bid for sustenance.

Every year, a Famine Walk to Louisburgh from Delphi commemorates the disaster.

Resort, off the R335; mains from €5; ⊙9.30am-5.30pm; 🛜) here as well, for those in Delphi who want to put their feet up.

Delphi Lodge RESORT €€€
(🖉095-42222; www.delphilodge.ie; off R335; s/d from €140/230; @) Dwarfed by the mountainous backdrop, this wonderful 1830s Georgian mansion (named after Fin Lough, linked to Doo Lough by the Owengar River) was built by the Marquis of Sligo. The 13-room country hotel features beautiful interiors, colossal 405-hectare grounds, delicious food (dinner €60) and a serious lack of pretension. It's popular with fishers (half-day with fishing tutor €180) and or those seeking relaxation and escape.

Louisburgh
POP 800

The northern gateway to the Doolough Valley is the appealing village of Louisburgh, founded under curious circumstances in 1795. Based on a simple four-street system known as the Cross, the town was designed and built as a living memorial to a relative of the first Marquis of Sligo, Lord Altamont (John Browne) – his kinsman was killed at the 1758 Battle of Louisburgh in Nova Scotia.

In addition to the lovely beach at Carrowmore, there are also some excellent surf beaches nearby, like Carrownisky.

West and south of Louisburgh you'll find a web of narrow unmarked roads that wander through the scruffy countryside. The rewards come when you hit the water.

Sights & Activities

Granuaile Heritage Centre MUSEUM
(🖉098-66341; www.granuaile.org; Church St; adult/child €4/2; ⊙10am-5pm Mon-Fri) Ac-

quire an illuminating glimpse into the life and times of Grace O'Malley (Gráinne Ní Mháille or Granuaile; 1530–1603), the infamous pirate queen of Connaught (p408), as well as details of the horrors of the local Famine.

Surf Mayo SURFING
(🖉087 621 2508; www.surfmayo.com; Carrownisky Beach, Louisburgh; lessons from €30, surfboard & wetsuit rental per day €20; ⊙varies) Offers surfing lessons and camps at Carrownisky Beach, and rents out gear, including stand-up paddleboards.

Mweelrea Holidays HORSE RIDING
(🖉087-776 4385; www.mweelreaholidays.com; off R378, Feenone; horse rides from €30; ⊙hours vary) Take a guided horse ride through the dramatic countryside or along the beach. Guided hikes are also offered.

Sleeping & Eating

Ponderosa B&B €
(🖉098-66440; www.ponderosamayo.com; Tooreen Rd; s/d from €45/60; ⊙Apr-Oct; 🛜) Just 400m east of the Louisburgh town centre, this three-room purple-and-white B&B is set in a modern bungalow, with a long front lawn.

West View Hotel HOTEL €€
(🖉098-23817; www.thewestviewhotel.ie; Chapel St; s/d from €40/90; 🛜) Right in town, this small inn has lashings of contemporary style, with bright, colourful and comfy rooms, as well as a restaurant. The bar has trad-music sessions some nights.

Country Kitchen CAFE €€
(🖉085-458 5415; Main St; mains from €18; ⊙6-9pm daily, Wed-Sat winter) This charming, small and friendly place along Main

St has a limited but eclectic menu with fine seafood and home cooking, including homemade onion bhajis, smoked mackerel cocktail, beetroot burgers, seafood linguini and tempting puddings. It's not licensed, so bring your own (no corkage fee). Booking recommended.

Ask about its takeaway 'Good Grazing' up the road, which had just opened at time of writing.

🛍 Shopping

Books@One BOOKS
(☑ 087-608 1438; www.facebook.com/booksatone; Main St; ⊙ 10am-6pm) This excellent community nonprofit bookshop is a tremendous place for a browse, and serves as a kind of cafe and social hub too.

❶ Getting There & Away

Bus Éireann (www.buseireann.ie; €8; ⊙ Mon-Sat) has one bus a day to/from Westport.

Clare Island

POP 125

Clew Bay is dotted with some 365 islands, of which the largest is mountainous Clare Island (www.clareisland.info), 5km offshore but half a world away. Dominated by rocky Mt Knockmore (462m), its varied terrain is terrific for walking and climbing, and swimming can be enjoyed at safe, sandy beaches. The island is also one of the dwindling number of places where you can find choughs (resembling blackbirds but with red beaks).

Clare Island has the windswept ruins of the Cistercian **Clare Island Abbey** (St Brigid's Abbey) (c 1460) and **Granuaile's Castle**, both associated with the pirate queen Grace O'Malley. The island is also a great place to retreat and withdraw from the world and reflect upon the beauty of Ireland. Among the many stirring hikes, there's a self-guided **archaeological walk** or you can climb

---

THE PIRATE QUEEN

The life of Grace O'Malley (Gráinne Ní Mháille or Granuaile, 1530–1603) reads like fantasy adventure fiction. Twice widowed and twice imprisoned for acts of piracy, she was a fearsome presence in the troubled landscape of 16th-century Ireland.

Her unorthodox life was the stuff of legend and mythology; hundreds of stories testify to her unequalled courage, skill and dogged determination to protect her clan against virtually anyone else – from rival chieftains to the English army.

Born into a powerful seafaring family that controlled most of the Mayo coastline and traded internationally, the independent Grace soon decided she should join the family business. Legend has it that while still a child she asked her father if she could join a trip to Spain, but was refused on the grounds that seafaring was not for girls. She promptly cut off all her hair, dressed in boys clothing, returned to the ship and announced that she was ready to sail. Her family nicknamed her Gráinne Mhaol (pronounced grawn-ya wail; bald Grace), a name that stuck for the rest of her life.

Married & Looting

At 15 Grace was married off to Donal O'Flaherty, a querulous local chieftain, but using her smarts she soon eclipsed her husband in politics and trade. The O'Flahertys were banned from trading in Galway, one of the largest ports in the British Isles. Grace got around this by waylaying cargo vessels en route to port and demanding payment for safe passage. If they refused, she had them looted.

After her husband's death, Grace settled on Clare Island but continued marauding around the Irish and Scottish coasts. Closer to home, the only part of Clew Bay not under her control was Rockfleet, so in 1566 Grace married Richard an-Iarrain to gain control of his **castle** (p414). Despite some marital ups and downs (she tried to 'dismiss' him once she controlled his tower), they remained together until his death 17 years later.

By the 1570s Grace's blatant piracy had come to English attention and many attempts were made to capture her. Eventually she was brought to London in 1593, whereupon Queen Elizabeth I granted her a pardon and offered her a title: which she declined, saying she was already Queen of Connaught.

Grace O'Malley died in 1603 and is thought to be buried in the **abbey** on Clare Island.

Knockmore, a 462m hill. Spectacular views enthral visitors.

🛌 Sleeping

★ Go Explore Hostel   HOSTEL €
(☑087 410 8706, 098-26307; www.goexplorehostel. ie; dm weekday/weekend €20/24; ☺ Easter-Oct; 🛜)
This terrific hostel is a delight, with voluminous windows and a terrace overlooking the water, while vintage features include a large 1840s fireplace. The pub draws drinkers from around the island, with the call of decent beer, good food (mains €8 to €15) and frequent live music sessions. All manner of adventure activities and classes keep guests occupied.

In the wind-lashed winter months, it's group bookings only.

O'Grady's   B&B €€
(☑098-22991; www.clareisland.ie/ogradys-guest accommodation; s/d from €60/80; ☺ Apr-Sep; 🛜)
This cosy, six-room, slate-roofed B&B is near the pier. If you're drenched, dry out around the log-burning stove.

Macalla Farm   GUESTHOUSE €€€
(☑087 250 4845; www.macallafarm.ie; 3-day retreats from €480; 🛜) On a wonderful setting overlooking the island, this guesthouse offers retreats and lessons throughout the year for yoga, mindfulness, natural food, horse riding and more. Guests enjoy organic vegetarian meals. Camping is also possible at a €20 discount. Wi-fi can be twitchy.

❶ Getting There & Away

Clare Island Ferries (☑098-23737, 086 851 5003; www.clareislandferry.com; adult/child return €17/8) and **O'Malley Ferries** (☑086 887 0814, 098-25045; www.omalleyferries. com; return adult/child €15/8) run boats from Roonagh Quay, 8km west of Louisburgh, around 10 times daily in July and August, and two to four times daily the rest of the year. The trip takes 10 minutes.

You can usually rent bikes (about €15 per day) at the pier and at your accommodation. There are also taxis.

Inishturk Island

POP 100

Ruggedly beautiful Inishturk (www.inish turkisland.com) lies 12km off Mayo's western coast. It's sparsely populated and little visited, despite the two sandy beaches on its eastern side, impressive cliffs, wonderful flora and fauna, and a rugged, hilly landscape that's ideal for walking. In fact, ambling along the island's maze of country roads is a perfect way to adapt to the pace of life here.

If you want to stay, there are several guesthouses on the island, including the recommended **Teach Abhainn** (☑098-45510; teach-abhainn@hotmail.com; s/d from €40/70; ☺ Apr-Oct; 🛜), around 1.5km west of the harbour.

Food can be cooked up at Teach Abhainn and at the **Community Club** south of the pier.

O'Malley Ferries (☑098-25045; www.om-alleyferries.com) has one to two ferries daily from Roonagh Quay, near Louisburgh (€8/5 per adult/child return).

Croagh Patrick

St Patrick couldn't have picked a better spot for a pilgrimage than this conical mountain (also known as 'the Reek'). On a clear day, the tough two-hour climb rewards with stunning views over Clew Bay and its sandy islets.

It was on Croagh Patrick that Ireland's patron saint fasted for 40 days and nights, and where he reputedly banished venomous snakes. Climbing the 772m holy mountain is an act of penance for thousands of pilgrims on the last Sunday of July (Reek Sunday). The truly contrite take the original 40km route, Tóchar Phádraig (Patrick's Causeway), from Ballintubber Abbey and ascend the mountain barefoot. The climb is becoming increasingly popular with hikers and fell runners, and path erosion has become a problem, although as yet no one has taken responsibility for improvements.

There is a car park at the base of the climb.

The **main trail** ascends the mountain from the car park in Murrisk. The steep trail is rocky in parts, but you can hire walking sticks for €3 at the small cafe. The average return trip takes three to four hours and it gets crowded on sunny weekends. At the summit you'll find a 1905 whitewashed **church** and a 9th-century **oratory fountain**. Views are sublime.

National Famine Memorial   MONUMENT
Opposite the car park on the far side of the road is the National Famine Memorial, a spine-chilling sculpture of a three-masted ghost ship wreathed in swirling skeletons, commemorating the lives lost on so-called 'coffin ships' employed to help people escape the Famine.

Westport

POP 5600

Bright and vibrant even in the depths of winter, Westport is a photogenic Georgian town with tree-lined streets, a riverside mall and a great vibe. With an excellent choice of accommodation, fine restaurants and pubs renowned for their music, it's a hugely popular place yet has never sold its soul to tourism.

Westport is Mayo's nightlife hub, and its central location makes it a convenient and enjoyable base for exploring the county.

◎ Sights

Westport Quay, the town's harbour, is on Clew Bay, 2km west of the centre. It's a picturesque spot with shops and cafes. In town, the **Octagon** is a major landmark, punctuated by a Doric column.

Westport House HISTORIC BUILDING
(☑098-27766; www.westporthouse.ie; Quay Rd; adult/child house only €13/6.50, house & pirate adventure park €21/16.50; ◎10am-6pm Jun-Aug, 10am-4pm Mar-May & Sep-Nov, hours vary Dec, closed Jan & Feb; ★) Built in 1730 on the ruins of Grace O'Malley's 16th-century castle, this charming Georgian mansion 2km west of the centre retains much of its original contents and has some stunning period-style rooms. Set in glorious gardens, the overall effect is marred somewhat by its commercial focus, but children love the **Pirate Adventure Park**, complete with a swinging pirate ship, a 'pirate's playground', a roller-coaster-style flume ride (adult/child €10/5) through a water channel and a birds of prey show (adult/child €10/7).

Clew Bay Heritage Centre MUSEUM
(www.westportheritage.com; The Quay; adult/child €3/free; ◎10am-5pm Mon-Fri Jun & Sep, 10am-5pm Mon-Fri, 3-5pm Sun Jul & Aug, 10.30am-2pm Mon-Fri Oct-May) Set in a 19th-century stone building 2km west of town, this museum traces the history, customs and traditions of Westport and Clew Bay.

🏃 Activities & Tours

The area around Westport is simply superb for cycling, with gentle coastal routes or more challenging mountain trails to test your legs, all within a short distance of town. The ever-popular Great Western Greenway (p413), a 42km cycling route between West-port and Achill, begins 500m from the centre of town off the N59.

The tourist office (p413) has an excellent brochure detailing local walks for all skill levels.

★ Clew Bay Bike Hire CYCLING
(☑098-24818; www.clewbaybikehire.ie; Distillery Rd; rentals per day from €15, shuttle from €7.50; ◎9am-6pm) Offers advice on routes and trails in the area and has shops in Westport Quay and along the Great Western Greenway in Newport, Mulranny and Achill; you can start the trail at any point and be picked up on completion. There's a handy one-way drop-off/collection shuttle so you don't have to backtrack.

During summer, rental kayaks are also available at Old Head Beach (€20 per hour) and you can join a kayak tour of the bay (half-day tour €60 per person, minimum four people; private tour €130 per person). Clew Bay Bike Hire also conducts tours of the surrounding area.

★ Guided Walks of
Historic Westport WALKING
(☑098-26852; www.westportheritage.com; Bridge St; adult/child €5/free; ◎11am Wed Jul & Aug) Local historians lead 90-minute walks around Westport.

Westport Bikes 4 Hire CYCLING
(☑086 088 0882; www.westportbikes4hire.com; James St; adult/child bike rentals per day from €15/10, shuttle service available; ◎9am-6pm) Rents out all types of bikes, including tandems, electrics and kids' trailers. You can arrange to be picked up or dropped off anywhere along the Great Western Greenway.

Carrowholly Stables HORSE RIDING
(☑098-27057; www.carrowholly-stables.com; off N59, Carrowholly; beach rides adult/child from €30/25) With stables 3km north of the town centre, next to Westport Golf Club, this recommended outfit offers guided horse and pony treks on the beach and along trails overlooking Clew Bay.

Croagh Patrick Walking Holidays WALKING
(☑098-26090; www.walkingguideireland.com; 7-day walks from €800; ◎Apr-Aug) Highly customisable walks in the countryside surrounding Westport that usually last seven days. You can include St Patrick's holy site and/or a beach. Fees include accommodation, breakfast and lunch.

Westport

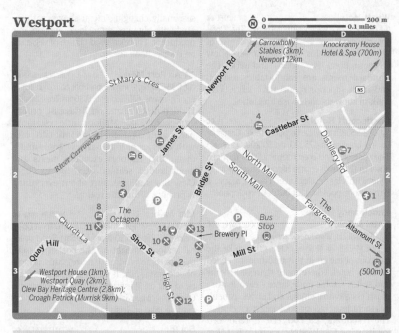

Westport

🟠 Activities, Courses & Tours
1 Clew Bay Bike Hire D2
2 Guided Walks of Historic Westport B3
3 Westport Bikes 4 Hire B2

🔵 Sleeping
4 Castlecourt Hotel C1
5 Clew Bay Hotel B2
6 Old Mill Holiday Hostel B2
7 St Anthony's Riverside B&B D2
8 Wyatt Hotel A2

❌ Eating
9 An Port Mór B3
10 McCormack's at the Andrew Stone
    Gallery B3
11 Pantry & Corkscrew A3
12 Sage B3
13 Sol Rio B3

🟢 Drinking & Nightlife
14 Matt Molloy's B3

Clewbay Cruises BOATING
(📞087 606 6146; www.clewbaycruises.com; Westport Quay; adult/child €20/10; ⊗May-Sep) Enjoy views of Clew Bay on 90-minute cruises.

🛏 Sleeping

Westport is Mayo's main city and while there's an abundance of B&Bs and hotels, rooms are in short supply during summer and special events.

Old Mill Holiday Hostel HOSTEL €
(📞098-27045; www.oldmillhostel.com; off James St; dm from €18; 🛜) Inside a converted stone mill, this central hostel has 58 beds spread across four- to 10-bedrooms. Inviting communal areas provide respite after a day touring. There are also handy kitchen and laundry rooms.

⭐**St Anthony's Riverside B&B** B&B €€
(📞087-630 1550; www.st-anthonys.com; Distillery Rd; s from €60, d €70-100; 🛜) This genteel B&B sits under cover of a large hedge and twisted vines inhabited by birds' nests, with rooms in the main house and courtyard. Rooms have clean lines and restful, light colours, some with jacuzzis. Breakfast is excellent.

Clew Bay Hotel HOTEL €€
(📞098-28088; www.clewbayhotel.com; James St; s/d from €75/110; 🛜) This family-run three-star hotel in the centre of Westport has 54 small but stylish rooms, some with river views. Bathrooms and furnishings are first-rate, while the modern pub is popular for contemporary takes on classic fare.

Wyatt Hotel

HOTEL €€

(☑098-25027; www.wyatthotel.com; The Octagon; r from €90; ☏☀) Right in the centre of Westport town, this older sunflower-yellow 63-room hotel is a local landmark. The standard rooms are comfortable; restyled and fresh superior rooms have large beds, walk-in showers and lavish amenities.

Castlecourt Hotel

HOTEL €€

(☑098-55088; www.castlecourthotel.ie; Castlebar St; incl breakfast s €75-130, d €90-200; @☏☀) The spacious and cosy rooms at this modern hotel in the town centre blend contemporary style with classic elegance. There's a spa, a 17m-indoor pool and an outdoor rock pool.

Knockranny House Hotel & Spa

BOUTIQUE HOTEL €€€

(☑098-28611; www.knockrannyhousehotel.ie; off N5; r €74-288; ❄@☏☀) Open fires take the chill out of the air at this traditionally styled modern hotel, where more than 100 rooms and suites – some quite large – each feature plush classic furnishings and styles. Amenities include an indoor pool and spa facilities. The restaurant, **La Fougère**, is renowned for its wine list. Westport's centre is 1.5km west, a 15-minute walk.

Afternoon tea (2.30pm to 5.30pm daily) in the **Brehon Bar** is another favourite.

 Eating

Westport is packed with superb restaurants and cafes: just wander along Bridge St and the little laneways off it to make some tasty discoveries. Book for dinner in summer and on weekends.

McCormack's at the Andrew Stone Gallery

MODERN IRISH €

(Bridge St; mains €6-14; ☉10.30am-4.30pm Thu-Sat, Mon & Tue) Upstairs above the Westport hubbub, there's excellent food on offer at this family-run bakery and lunch cafe that has been in business in decades. It's next to an art gallery and sources its fare from the best local producers. In a hurry? Grab a scone to go. Otherwise sit down with a vegetable soup with brown bread (€4.25).

★Pantry & Corkscrew

MODERN IRISH €€

(☑098-26977; www.thepantryandcorkscrew.com; The Octagon; dinner €16-23, early-bird 2-/3-course dinner €21.45/24.95; ☉5-10pm Wed-Sun; ☑) The heart of Mayo's slow-food movement is found at this narrow little storefront with a turquoise exterior, its walls crammed with pictures. The kitchen has huge talent as the

seasonally changing menu shows, with ingredients obtained from local and organic producers. There's a good choice of vegetarian dishes. Book ahead.

★An Port Mór

MODERN IRISH €€

(☑098-26730; www.anportmor.com; 1 Brewery Pl; mains €15-30; ☉5-9.30pm Tue-Sat; ☏) Hidden down a lane off Bridge St, proprietor-chef Frankie Mallon's little restaurant packs quite a punch. It's an intimate place with a series of long narrow rooms and a menu that features excellent meats and much-lauded seafood (try the excellent Clew Bay scallops). Just about everything is procured from the region.

Idle Wall

MODERN IRISH €€

(☑098-50692; www.theidlewall.ie; Westport Quay; mains €18-25; ☉5.30-10pm Tue-Sat) Serving local seafood straight off the boats (mussels, oysters, crab, cod and more), this atmospheric restaurant is easily the pick of places to eat on Westport's lively harbourfront. Chef Áine Maguire wins plaudits for her inventive take on Irish fare.

Sol Rio

MEDITERRANEAN €€

(☑098-28944; www.solrio.ie; Bridge St; mains lunch €7-14, dinner €13-20; ☉cafe 9am-6pm, restaurant noon-3pm & 6-10pm; ☑) The extensive menu ranges from pizza and pasta to organic meat and fish. Carefully picked ingredients and attention, whether you pause at the simple cafe downstairs or the more stylish restaurant upstairs. The deli is famous for its egg-custard pastries.

Sage

MODERN EUROPEAN €€

(☑098-56700; www.sagewestport.ie; 10 High St; mains €18-28, early-bird menu 2/3 courses €22/25.50; ☉5.30-10pm; ☏) A wave of warmth hits you as soon as you walk through the door of this stylish restaurant, artfully run by Shteryo Yurukov and Eva Ivanova. Conforming to the local tradition of sourcing everything from the region, the restaurant offers a changing menu of seasonal meat and seafood dishes – many with an Italian accent.

🍺 Drinking & Nightlife

Westport is thronged with pubs, many of them with live music nightly.

★Matt Molloy's

PUB

(☑098-26655; www.mattmolloy.com/new-blog/; Bridge St; ☉12.30-11.30pm Mon-Thu, to 12.30am Fri & Sat, to 11pm Sun; ☏) Matt Malloy, the fife

GREAT WESTERN GREENWAY

Following the route of the old Westport–Achill Railway (which ran from 1894 to 1937), the Great Western Greenway (www.greenway.ie) is a terrific reason to travel through this part of Mayo. The 42km trail penetrates gorgeous countryside and waterfront scenery, consisting of three main sections, none of which requires more than moderate effort:

Westport to Newport This 11km section through pretty, lush countryside starts off the N59, 500m north of Westport's centre, and ends at the N59, 2km before Newport. This is the easiest section.

Newport to Mulranny This 18km section is the most popular and passes close to many sights along Clew Bay. It's off the N59 just north of Newport and ends in Mulranny.

Mulranny to Achill This 13km section starts right in Mulranny and ends about 1.2km short of Achill Island (many tourist maps show the trail going all the way), after which you ride along roads. It has some sweeping water views.

You can easily rent bicycles all along the Greenway. Two Westport-based operators, **Clew Bay Bike Hire** (p410) and **Westport Bikes 4 Hire** (p410), offer uber-convenient pick-up and drop-off services that let you ride all or part of the Greenway one way and be driven the other way.

player from the Chieftains, runs this old-school pub. Head to the back room around 9pm and you'll catch live *céilidh* (traditional music and dancing). Or perhaps a veteran musician will simply slide into a chair and croon a few classics. Great microbrews on tap add to the allure.

🛍 Shopping

Wandering Westport's centre, you'll discover little boutiques and a surprising number of bookshops.

Custom House Studios ART
(☑ 098-28735; www.customhousestudios.ie; Westport Quay; ◷10am-5pm Mon-Fri, 1-4.30pm Sat & Sun) Local artists display their creations at this inviting gallery, which also has special exhibitions.

ℹ Information

Mayo's main **tourist office** (☑ 098-25711; www.westporttourism.com; Bridge St; ◷9am-5.45pm Mon-Fri year-round, plus 10am-4pm Sat Easter-Oct) has a lot of walking and cycling info.

ℹ Getting There & Away

Bus Éireann (p406) services include Galway (€16.15, two hours, five daily); for Sligo, take a bus to Knock, Charlestown (€15.10, one hour) or Ballina (€15.90, 70 minutes) and change. Buses depart from **Mill St**.

There are five daily trains to Dublin (€20, 3¼ hours).

Newport

POP 630

Newport is a picturesque 18th-century village on the Newport River. The trains on the Westport–Achill Railway stopped in 1937 but a striking seven-arch viaduct built in 1892 remains a popular spot with walkers and cyclists.

Newport – or at least a ruined house by Drumgoney Lough (Leg O' Mutton Lake) just outside town – is actress (and former Princess of Monaco) Grace Kelly's ancestral home, drawing fans from far and wide.

The Bangor Trail ends here, while the wonderful Great Western Greenway heads west to Achill, 31km away along the former rail line.

◉ Sights & Activities

Newport is an attractive riverine place in its own right, though most sights of note lie beyond town.

Burrishoole Abbey HISTORIC SITE
(off N59; ◷dawn-dusk) From a distance, the eerie shell of this wind-battered 1470-built Dominican abbey near the water is quite a sight. Leaving Newport in a northwest direction along the N59 towards Achill Island, a sign points the way to this stunning abbey, from where it's a further 1km to the car park.

Rockfleet Castle
CASTLE

(Carrigahowley; off N59; ⊙ dawn-dusk) This intact 15th-century tower off the N59 is associated with 'pirate queen' Grace O'Malley. (p408) She married her second husband, Richard an-Iarrain (impressively nicknamed 'Iron Dick' Burke), to gain control of this castle, and famously fought off an English attack here. Moodily set on a boggy tidal area, the castle was her principal stronghold, and in her later years she settled here permanently.

The other structures of the castle have vanished. Legend says that Grace fed the rope from her ship through the hole in the south wall, tying it to her bed.

Clew Bay Bike Hire
CYCLING

(☑ 098-37675; www.clewbayoutdoors.ie; bikes per day from €15, electric bikes €40, shuttle price varies; ⊙ 9am-6pm) This excellent bike-hire operator has five locations scattered along the Greenway, between Westport and Achill Island.

🛏 Sleeping & Eating

★ Newport House
HISTORIC HOTEL €€

(☑ 098-41222; www.newporthouse.ie; off Main St; r €95-205; ⊙ Apr-mid-Oct; 🐾) Cloaked in ivy that turns crimson in autumn, this gorgeous Georgian mansion is one of Ireland's most romantic country retreats. Newport House is especially known for its contemporary Irish cuisine (multicourse dinner €68).

★ Kelly's Kitchen
CAFE €

(☑ 098-41647; 17 Main St; mains €6.50-21; ⊙ 9am-5pm Mon-Sat) The fare of Sean Kelly's much-loved artisan butcher shop (next door) can be sampled here for breakfast and lunch, or you can stop for a coffee break or for a sandwich, a panini or delicious seafood chowder. The huge – and stunning – photograph of Grace Kelly on the wall near the door celebrates the film star's ancestral connection to Newport.

Blue Bicycle Tea Rooms
CAFE €

(☑ 098-41145; www.bluebicycletearooms.com; Main St; mains from €5; ⊙ 10.30am-6pm May-Oct) Grab a snack or pause for a true respite in this cafe, packed with old-world charm. It features sandwiches, salads, soups, baked treats and more, all sourced locally.

ⓘ Information

Newport Tourist Office (Main St; ⊙ 10.30am-2pm Mon, 10am-2pm Tue-Fri)

ⓘ Getting There & Away

Buses between Westport and Achill Island pass through once daily.

Achill Island
POP 940

With five Blue Flag beaches, Ireland's largest offshore island, Achill (An Caol), is linked to the mainland by a short bridge. Despite the accessibility, there's plenty of remote-island feel: soaring cliffs, rocky headlands, sheltered sandy beaches, broad expanses of blanket bog and rolling mountains. It also has its share of history, having been a frequent refuge during Ireland's various rebellions.

Achill is at its most dramatic during winter, when high winds and lashing seas make the island seem downright inhospitable. The year-round population, though, remains as welcoming as ever. In summer, heather, rhododendrons and wildflowers bloom, splashing the island with colour.

The village of Keel is the island's main centre of activity – which is a relative term.

⊙ Sights

Instead of following the main road (R319) from Mulranny to Achill Island, take the signposted Atlantic Drive, which curves clockwise around the Curraun Peninsula. The narrow road passes the odd fortified tower and as it hugs the isolated southern edge of the Curraun Peninsula, the views across Clew Bay and out to sea are simply stunning.

The signposted Atlantic Drive continues once you cross the bridge. It follows the island's wild southern shore, passing through the little fishing hamlet of Dooega, with its sheltered beach.

★ Keem Bay Beach
BEACH

One of Achill's most remote Blue Flag beaches, at the far west of the island, but after you spiral down to this perfect cove, it's like finding the pot of gold at the end of an Irish rainbow. Beautiful.

★ Slievemore Deserted Village
HISTORIC SITE

The bleak remains of this deserted (though there are lots of sheep) village at the foot of Mt Slievemore is slowly being reduced down to rock piles, a poignant reminder of the island's past hardships and a vanished way of life. When the Potato Famine took hold, starvation forced the villagers to the sea and its alternative food source. The adjacent graveyard compounds the desolation.

Grace O'Malley's Castle
CASTLE
(Kildavnet Tower) Rising right next to the shore, this lovely 40ft-high 15th-century tower house at Kildavnet is associated with the pirate queen Grace O'Malley.

Dooagh
HISTORIC SITE
This village is where Don Allum, the first person to row across the Atlantic Ocean in both directions, landed in September 1982 in his 6m-long plywood boat, dubbed the *QE3*, after 77 days at sea. Opposite the monument marking this feat, the **Pub** (Dooagh; ⏱9am-10pm) (that's its name) has associated memorabilia.

Mulranny
VILLAGE
Rising from a narrow isthmus, the hillside village of Mulranny overlooks a wide Blue Flag beach on the road from Newport to Achill Sound and on the cusp of the Curraun Peninsula. It's a prime vantage point for counting the 365 or so seemingly saucer-sized islands that grace Clew Bay.

Activities
Achill Island is a wonderful place for walking and the views are terrific. Ramblers can climb **Mt Slievemore** (672m) or take on the longer climb of **Mt Croaghaun** (668m), Achill Head and a walk atop what locals claim are Europe's highest sea cliffs. There's also a good 4.3km-loop starting at the beach in Dooagh.

Achill has many additional scalloped bays tame enough for swimming, including the Blue Flag beaches at Keem Bay (p414), **Dooega** and **Golden Strand** (Dugort's other beach). Except in the height of the holiday season, most are often deserted.

Achill Tourism (p417) produces 14 excellent downloadable guides to walks around the island.

★Trawmore Beach
SURFING
(Keel) This beautiful Blue Flag beach, which runs 3km southeast from Keel, is one of Ireland's best surfing spots, but there are dangerous rips from its centre to the eastern end (under the Minaun Cliffs). Heed the signs and stick to the western half of the beach. Several companies offer board hire (€15 per day) and lessons (€40 per day). This strand is also good for bracing walks, viewing the pounding surf.

Dugort Beach
SWIMMING
Dugort Beach is a prime example of the island's many fine beaches. The other notable beach here at Dugort is Golden Strand.

Achill Bikes
CYCLING
(⏱087 243 7686; www.achillbikes.com; Keel; rental per day adult €20-25, child €12.50) Rents out a variety of bikes, offers advice and arranges for pick-up and delivery around the island. Weekly rates are also available.

Calvey's Equestrian Centre
HORSE RIDING
(⏱087 988 1093; www.calveysofachill.com; Slievemore; 2hr beach trek adult/child €70/60) Calvey's arranges riding lessons and one-to four-hour treks on Achill's broad beaches and mountain roads.

Festivals & Events
Achill Island hosts several festivals during the year, including ones devoted to walking, painting, boating and more. See www.achilltourism.com for the latest details.

Scoil Acla Festival
CULTURAL
(⏱085 881 9548; www.scoilacla.ie; ⏱late Jul) Traditional Irish music resonates for a week during this festival, which also has Irish dancing, culture and music workshops.

Sleeping
Achill has B&Bs along the main road from the bridge to Keel, and you'll also find places to stay along the shores.

★Valley House Hostel
HOSTEL €
(⏱098-47204; www.valley-house.com; The Valley; campsites per tent €5, plus per person €5, dm €16-22, d €44-50; @⏱) Amid unruly gardens, this remote 42-bed hostel in a creaking old mansion has atmosphere to spare. JM Synge based his play *The Playboy of the Western World* on misadventures here and the subsequent film *Love and Rage* (1999) was also partially shot here. Bonuses include scones for breakfast and a pub with patio tables. Breakfast for campers is another €5.

Breakfast is self-service menu of orange juice, tea, coffee, cereal, toast, butter and jam.

★Pure Magic Achill Island
GUESTHOUSE €
(⏱085 243 9782; www.puremagic.ie; Slievemore Rd, near Dugort; s/d from €45/70; ⏱) Not far from the ghost town of Slievemore, at the foot of the hill, this lively 10-room spot has a buzzing bar and cafe (with excellent pizza). You can arrange kite-surfing, stand-up paddleboarding, snorkelling, cycling and more.

Achill Island

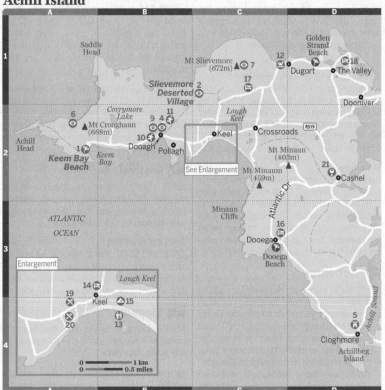

Achill Island

◎ Top Sights
1 Keem Bay Beach	A2
2 Slievemore Deserted Village	C1

◎ Sights
3 Ballycroy National Park	F1
4 Dooagh	B2
5 Grace O'Malley's Castle	D4
6 Mt Croaghaun	A2
7 Mt Slievemore	C1
8 Mulranny	F3
9 Pub	B2

❸ Activities, Courses & Tours
10 Achill Bikes	B2
11 Calvey's Equestrian Centre	B2
12 Dugort Beach	C1
13 Trawmore Beach	B4

🛏 Sleeping
14 Achill Cliff House Hotel & Restaurant	A3
15 Keel Sandybanks Caravan & Camping Park	B4
16 Lavelles Seaside House	C3
17 Pure Magic Achill Island	C1
18 Valley House Hostel	D1

✖ Eating
19 Beehive	A4
20 Chalet	A4
Mickey's Bar	(see 16)

🍸 Drinking & Nightlife
21 Lynott's	D2

Lavelles Seaside House GUESTHOUSE €
(☏ 098-45116; www.lavellesseasidehouse.com; Dooega; s/d from €45/60; 🛜) In the fishing vil-
lage of Dooega, this 14-room whitewashed guesthouse is a good getaway. The five new-er rooms are nicest and have views down to

Belmullet (38km); Ballina (48km)

Inishbiggle Island

Annagh Island

N59

Achill Sound

Owenduff

R319 Westport (20km)

Atlantic Dr

Curraun Hill (524m) Curraun Peninsula Mulranny

Dooghbeg

Atlantic Dr

Clew Bay

0   5 km
0   2.5 miles

✕ Eating & Drinking

Beehive   CAFE €
(☑086-854 2009; Keel; mains from €5; ⊙10am-5pm Mar-Nov) Busy as a beehive, this popular and buzzing Keel cafe is also a crafts shop, divided into various rooms. It's a decent choice for a coffee, a soup of the day, a panini or home-baked goodies.

Mickey's Bar   SEAFOOD €
(mains €8-11) Right alongside Lavelles Seaside House, serving seafood and excellent mussels.

★Chalet   SEAFOOD €€
(☑087-230 7893; www.keembayfishproducts. ie; Keel; mains €16-29; ⊙6-10pm daily summer, shorter hours rest of year) The proprietors of Keem Bay Fish Products have been serving up their acclaimed smoked local salmon and other delicacies at this restaurant for decades. The menu changes with what's fresh, but expect a meal of the very best seafood.

Lynott's   PUB
(☑087 645 2780; R319, Cashel; ⊙varies with season) This tiny, traditional thatched roadside pub with flagstone floors and ancient benches is the real deal. There's no TV or radio or even a hint of a ham and cheese toastie, just craic (but music sessions are held here on Friday's at 10pm).

ℹ Information

Most of the villages have post offices.

The supermarkets in Keel and Achill Sound have ATMs.

Achill Tourism (☑098-20705; www.achill tourism.com; Davitt Quarter, Achill Sound; ⊙9am-6pm Mon-Fri Jul & Aug, 10am-4pm Mon-Fri Sep-Jun) Has good walking and cycling information.

ℹ Getting There & Away

There's one bus daily to Achill from Westport (€14), with stops that include Dooagh, Keel, Dugort, Cashel, Achill Sound, Mulranny and Newport. The best way to reach Achill Island is by car.

the water. The pub, Mickey's, serves bar food with an emphasis on local seafood in summer. There's wi-fi in common areas and also rooms, but it can sometimes be weak in the latter.

Keel Sandybanks Caravan & Camping Park   CAMPGROUND €
(☑098-43211; www.achillcamping.com; Keel; campsites €10-25, caravan per 2 nights €115-140; ⊙Apr–mid-Sep; 🐾) This campground, an easy stroll from town, overlooks Keel Beach. Noncampers can opt for 'glamping' nights in traditional wooden caravans.

Achill Cliff House Hotel & Restaurant   GUESTHOUSE €€
(www.achillcliff.com; Keel; r from €80) With sweeping views out to sea – even from the breakfast room – this family-run guesthouse is a great retreat come rain or shine. Furnishings are comfy but basic and the restaurant is worth its superlatives thanks to its fresh local seafood and creative take on Irish classics.

Bangor Erris

POP 300

The unexceptional little village of Bangor Erris is the start or end point for the 30km Bangor Trail which connects Bangor and Newport via Ballycroy National Park and the Nephin Beg Mountains. It's an extraordinary hike that takes walkers through some of the bleakest, most remote but most deeply inspiring landscapes in Ireland. It is very difficult and includes long stretches of tough, but magnificent, bog-walking.

Run by friendly Evelyn, congenial and handy B&B Hillcrest House (☑097-83494; www.hillcresthousemayo.com; Main St; s €40, d €60-70; 🛜) has four comfortable rooms and a drying room is a very good choice for walkers, those on fishing holidays or just touring the gorgeous north Mayo countryside; kids get 25% off. Evelyn is full of tips for walkers and travellers to the region, and there's a lovely garden out the back.

Ballycroy National Park

This huge and scenic **park** (☑098-49888; www.ballycroynationalpark.ie; off N59, Ballycroy; ☉visitor centre 10am-5.30pm Apr-Sep) **FREE** – comprising some of Europe's greatest areas of blanket bog – is home to magnificent natural diversity including peregrine falcons, corncrakes and whooper swans. A short nature trail with interpretation panels leads from the visitor centre across the bog with superb and frequently sublime views to the surrounding mountains. The informative visitor centre can recommend more ambitious hikes and there are displays on whaling and the ubiquitous purple heather.

Ballycroy is 18km south of Bangor on the N59.

Mullet Peninsula

Dangling some 30km into the Atlantic, this thinly populated Gaeltacht (Irish-speaking) peninsula feels more cut off than many islands, and has a similar sense of loneliness. However, you'll find pristine beaches along its sheltered eastern shore, plenty of religious sites plus lots of sheep – often fully blocking the road. The main settlement is the busy town of Belmullet (Béal an Mhuirthead).

The road south (R313) from Belmullet loops round the tip of the peninsula to rejoin itself at Aghleam. Along the way it passes the Blue Flag beach at **Elly Bay** and stunning **Mullaghroe Beach**. There are several sights associated with St Deirbhile in the south of the peninsula, including **St Deirbhile's Church** (St Dervla's Church) and **Deirbhile's Twist**.

THE LEGEND OF ST DEIRBHILE

Sometime around the year 600, legend has it, a young girl named Deirbhile decided on a pious path in life. However, a military man who was in love with her was opposed to this. Meeting him one day on what is today the Mullet Peninsula, she asked him what he liked best about her. 'Your eyes', he said. Thereupon Deirbhile plucked out her eyes and threw them to the ground. Not surprisingly her suitor fled in horror.

But then a miracle happened: a spring welled up from the earth where Deirbhile's eyes had landed. She washed her face in its waters and her eyes returned. Today the **feast day of St Deirbhile** is celebrated on 15 August at related sites near Blacksod on the Mullet Peninsula.

You'll find all the main services in Belmullet, including bank, ATM, post office and **tourist office** (☑097-20494; www.visiterris.ie; cnr Main St & Chapel St, Belmullet; ☉9am-4pm Mon-Sat Jun-Aug, 9am-4pm Mon-Fri Sep-May).

🛏 Sleeping

★**Leim Siar** B&B €€
(☑097-85004; www.leimsiar.com; Blacksod; s/d from €50/80; 🛜) 🍃 Just a short walk from the Blacksod lighthouse, this popular, purpose-built B&B offers modern comforts and end-of-the-earth appeal for those who want a remote perspective on the world. Rooms are bright and the fantastic breakfast is always an event. You can rent bikes (€10 per day) to tour the peninsula.

Talbot's HOTEL €€
(☑097-20484; www.thetalbothotel.ie; Barrack St, Belmullet; s/d from €90/140; 🛜) Stylish Talbot's 21 comfortable rooms have plenty of bold accents. The pub, **An Chéibh** (The Anchor), has dual peat-burning fireplaces, a good beer selection and excellent food (mains €8 to €25).

ℹ Getting There & Away

Bus Éireann (p406) has one daily bus from Ballina to Belmullet (€16, 1½ hours), continuing on to Blacksod.

Pollatomish

POP 150

Irresistibly remote and pretty, Pollatomish, also spelled Pullathomas, slumbers in a serene bay some 16km east of Belmullet, signposted on the road to Ballycastle (R314).

Those who find their way here often extend their stay to stroll on its sandy beach or continue up to Benwee Head to take in sensational and rugged coastal geology and views, which include the Stags of Broadhaven (five steep, rocky islets).

Kilcommon Lodge Holiday Hostel (☑ 097-84621; www.kilcommonlodge.ie; Pollatomish; dm/s/d from €17/28/44; 🛜) is run by Ciarán, an outdoors enthusiast who can organise surfing, guided walks and rock climbing. There's a kitchen, a games room and a family room too. Breakfast is from €5 to €6.50 and dinner is €16

Ballycastle & Around

POP 219

The main draw of the beautifully sited village of Ballycastle, consisting of a sole sloping street, is its megalithic tombs – one of the greatest concentrations in Europe – and some gorgeous coastal scenery, including one of Ireland's top photogenic experiences: the raw, isolated sea stack of Dun Briste at Downpatrick Head.

⊙ Sights

★**Céide Fields** ARCHAEOLOGICAL SITE
(☑ 096-43325; www.heritageireland.ie; off R314; adult/child €5/3; ⊙ visitor centre 10am-6pm Jun-Sep, to 5pm Easter-May & Oct, last tour 1hr before closing) This otherwise barren site, 8km northwest of Ballycastle, is considered the world's most extensive Stone Age monument. Stone-walled fields, houses and megalithic tombs – about half a million tonnes of stone – have been found so far, the legacy of a 5000-year-old farming community. The **visitor centre**, in a glass pyramid overlooking the site, gives a fascinating glimpse into these times. Be sure to take a **guided tour** of the site to fully appreciate the findings.

It was only during the 1930s that a local, Patrick Caulfield, was digging in the bog when he noticed a lot of piled-up stones buried beneath it. A full realisation of what lay under the sod didn't happen for another four decades, when his son Seamus began exploration of the area. Excavations are ongoing.

🛌 Sleeping

★**Stella Maris** HOTEL €€€
(☑ 096-43322; www.stellamarisireland.com; Ballycastle; r €150-240; ⊙ Easter-Oct; 🛜) This salt-spattered building – dating from 1853 – sits on a lonely stretch of coastline 2.5km northwest of Ballycastle. It was originally a British Coast Guard station, and later a convent for the Sisters of Mercy (the name means 'Our Lady, Star of the Sea', referring to the Virgin Mary). Upmarket rooms combine antiques, stylish modern furnishings and killer views. Dinner is served (€40).

🍴 Eating & Drinking

Mary's Cottage Kitchen CAFE €
(Main St, Ballycastle; treats from €3; ⊙ 10am-3pm Mon-Fri, to 2pm Sat) Lovely Mary makes everyone feel welcome at this charming place with good coffee, fresh-baked goods, lunch items, chocolate treats and a back garden, where campers have been known to overnight.

Healy's Bar PUB
(☑ 096-43019; Main St; ⊙ 4-11.30pm) This family-run bar on the main road has live music and a beer garden.

WORTH A TRIP

DETOUR TO KILLALA

For a spectacular short looping detour off the main road (R314) to Killala, take the coast road north out of Ballycastle, passing **Downpatrick Head**, where you can view one of Mayo's most amazing sights, the sea stack of **Dun Briste** (p420). Here is some of Mayo's most dramatic shoreline, with no end to the excitement. Look for the narrow lane to the head that takes you right up to the surf.

Continue east and south, with **Lackan Bay** on your left until you rejoin the R314. From Killala, look for the turn to Kilcummin 4.5km northwest of town and do the route in reverse.

WORTH A TRIP

DUN BRISTE

This astonishing **sea stack** (Downpatrick Head; 6km northeast of Ballycastle) is possibly the top sight in the county, lashed by waves and the roaring, foaming seas. Legend attests that St Patrick drove all the vipers from Ireland onto the stack, leaving the mainland snake-free. Try to choose a clear day for a visit to amplify the visuals. You can drive most of the way up to the sea edge, but then you'll need to walk the last 400m or so.

The sea stack was shorn from the mainland in 1393 by a severe storm that left poor unfortunates stranded upon it (later rescued). Indeed, the remains of buildings survive on the stack to this day. A viewing area has been constructed by a huge blowhole at Downpatrick Head, with numerous plaques detailing the history and folklore of the area. During storms, seawater is dramatically blasted through the blowhole.

Killala & Around

POP 580

The town of Killala itself is pretty enough, but it is renowned for its glorious namesake bay nearby.

It's claimed that the ever-busy St Patrick founded Killala, and the Church of Ireland church sits on the site of the first Christian church in Ireland. A wonderful sight, the town's 25m-high round tower still looms over Killala's heart.

⊙ Sights & Activities

★**Lackan Strand**   BEACH

Lackan Bay's beach is a stunning and vast expanse of golden sand – it's particularly beautiful as the sun goes down, making it one of Ireland's most gorgeous sights. There's good surf here and plenty of places to get lost. Follow the R314 about 4.5km northwest from Killala, then turn at the signpost for Kilcummin.

★**St Mary's Well**   RELIGIOUS SITE

(Tobar Mhuire) This transfixing place near Rosserk Abbey is an amazing place of pilgrimage, for both Christians and travellers of any persuasion, and is particularly beautiful when the wildflowers are out.

The site is near the confluence of the Rosserk River and the River Moy. Look for the signs as you drive towards Rosserk Abbey; you will see a car park and a path leading to the well, which is about another 1km on foot.

The waters of the well spill forth from an old stone vault, overseen by a statue of the Virgin Mary. A tree pokes from a hole in its roof, garlanded in rosary beads and crucifixes. An apparition of the Virgin Mary was said to have occurred here, hence its sacred significance.

★**Rosserk Abbey**   HISTORIC BUILDING

Dipping its toes into the River Rosserk, this sublime Franciscan abbey dates from the mid-15th century. An eye-catching double *piscina* (perforated stone basin) is in the chancel: look for the exquisite carvings of a 2ft-high round tower (very rare to see carved in this way) and two angels on either side of a Gothic arch.

The abbey is 4km south of Killala off the R314. Look for the signposts and then follow narrow farming lanes for another 5km.

Lackan Trail   WALKING

Follow beautiful Lackan Bay and discover ancient ring forts and megalithic tombs on this moderate and looping 8km-walk that begins in the Killala church car park. An optional 3km extension includes sweeping views of the region.

ⓘ Getting There & Away

There are three weekday-only buses between Ballina and Killala (€5, 20 minutes).

Ballina

POP 10,300

Mayo's third-largest town, Ballina, is synonymous with salmon. If find yourself here during fishing season, you'll be joined by droves of green-garbed waders, poles in hand, heading for the River Moy – which pumps right through the heart of town.

In addition to its excellent museum, Ballina is very much worth a visit to explore, spend the night at or dine in the astonishing Belleek Castle.

◉ Sights

Belleek Castle
CASTLE

(☑096-22400; www.belleekcastle.com; Castle Rd; adult/child €10/7.50; ☺tours 11am, 2pm & 4pm) Take a fascinating tour of this restored castle, built between 1825 and 1831 on the site of a medieval abbey. The castle was bought in the 1960s by fossil collector Marshall Doran, who gave it an eclectic and eccentric interior, some of it nautical (including the Spanish Armada bar). The tour also visits the Banquet Hall and Marshall Doran's collection of fossils, weaponry and armour. En route you will also come face to face with the last wolf shot in Connaught.

To fully get in the castle mood, check in for the night as the grand place also serves as a hotel (p421); there's also a fine restaurant (p422).

Jackie Clarke Collection
MUSEUM

(☑096-73508; www.clarkecollection.ie; Pearse St; ☺10am-5pm Tue-Sat Apr-Sep, tours 11.30am & 2.30pm) FREE Starting when he was 12 in 1939, the late Jackie Clarke was a businessman who amassed an extraordinary collection of 100,000 items covering 400 years of Irish history. With a lovely walled garden and cafe and housed in an 1881 bank building, this well-curated museum brims with eclectic surprises.Tours can be booked in advance over the phone.

Foxford Woollen Mill
HISTORIC BUILDING

(☑094-925 6104; www.foxfordwoollenmills.com; Foxford; tours €5; ☺tours 10am-6pm Mon-Sat, noon-6pm Sun Apr-Nov) Founded in 1892, the Foxford mill was set up to ease post-Famine suffering and provide much-needed work. It remained open until 1987, during which time its woven goods achieved great acclaim. Now operated by locals, it employs a fraction of the hundreds who previously worked here. Besides sweaters and scarves (under €30) made in the mill, the shop sells a huge amount of imported goods. Foxford is midway between Ballina and Castlebar at the junction of the N26 and N58.

Tours include a talk on the history of the mill and a factory tour.

🏃 Activities

Salmon fishing is the main draw in Ballina, so most activities centre on angling on the River Moy. A list of fisheries and permit contacts is available at the tourist office (p422). The season is February to September, but the best salmon fishing is June to August.

Ridge Pool Tackle Shop
FISHING

(☑086-875 3648; Emmet St; ☺9am-6pm Mon-Sat) Information, supplies and licences are available at Ridge Pool Tackle Shop. Fly-casting lessons can also be arranged.

Wild Wet Adventures
WATER SPORTS

(☑086-722 2750; off the R294, Lough Talt) Flat-water kayaking, canoeing, paddle boarding and other water sports on Lough Talt and Lough Easkey; the outfit also conducts guided walks.

✯ Festivals & Events

Ballina Salmon Festival
CULTURAL

(www.ballinasalmonfestival.ie; ☺Jul) The popular five-day festivities include parades, dances, an arts show and fishing competitions.

🛏 Sleeping & Eating

★ Belleek Castle
HOTEL €€

(www.belleekcastle.com; Castle Rd; r incl breakfast €170-270; 🛜) This tremendous and very eclectically designed (on the interior) manor castle in vast grounds by the River Moy is a choice place to stay in Ballina, with rooms furbished in period style, some with four-poster beds (and flat-screen TVs). The setting is permeated with a gorgeous sense of seclusion. Even if you don't spend the night, it's a fine place for dinner in the Library Restaurant (p422) and fascinating tours (p421) are run through the day for visitors.

Mount Falcon Country House Hotel
LUXURY HOTEL €€€

(☑096-74472; www.mountfalcon.com; Foxford Rd; r from €180; 🛜🐾) Secluded within 40 hectares between Lough Conn and the River Moy, 5km south of Ballina, this gorgeous 1870s mansion is a stunning place to stay. Rooms in the old house ooze old-world grandeur, while those in the modern extension have a more contemporary edge. Anglers will be hooked by the exclusive fishery, while the tranquil tempo is endlessly relaxing.

Special offers reduce prices to around €140 per night.

Ice House Hotel
BOUTIQUE HOTEL €€€

(☑096-23500; www.icehousehotel.ie; The Quay; r €140-300; 🛜) Up-close views of the serene River Moy estuary are the main draw at this 32-room hotel that combines an elegant restored namesake heritage building with a starkly modern wing and a spa, right by the water. It's 2km northeast of the centre and close to good waterfront pubs.

★**Clarke's Seafood**
Delicatessen SEAFOOD €

(☑ 096-21022; www.clarkes.ie; O'Rahilly St; treats from €5; ⊙9am-6pm Mon-Sat) Couldn't catch a salmon? The wizards at award-winning Clarke's will sell you their house oak-smoked salmon in myriad forms, plus all manner of other fishy creations you can whisk away for a picnic.

★**Library Restaurant** IRISH €€€

(☑ 096-22400; www.belleekcastle.com; Belleek Castle) Set in the former library of the eclectically designed former manor of Belleek Castle, this restaurant is the most atmospheric and distinctive choice in town.

ℹ️ **Information**

Tourist Office (☑ 096-70848; www.northmayo. ie; 41 Pearse St; ⊙10am-5pm Mon-Sat Apr-Oct) The tourist office is in the centre of town.

ℹ️ **Getting There & Away**

The bus station is on Kevin Barry St. Bus Éireann services include Westport (€16, 1½ hours, six daily) and Sligo (€17, 1½ hours, three to five daily).

The train station is on Station Rd at the southern extension of Kevin Barry St. Ballina is on a branch of the main Westport–Dublin line, so you'll have to change at Manulla Junction. There are four connections a day to Dublin (€26, 3½ hours).

Lahardane

POP 156

In the shadow of Mt Nephin (806m), this charming little village is most famed for the 14 local people (the Addergoole Fourteen) aboard the RMS *Titanic* when it went down in 1912. Eleven of the 14 perished; their deaths are commemorated in one of the stained-glass windows of St Patrick's Church and in the Titanic Memorial Park.

Lahardane locals helped General Humbert in the 1798 Uprising and Father Andrew Conroy helped lead French and Irish forces along the Windy Gap to Castlebar. After the revolt was put down, Father Conroy was executed for his troubles and a marvellous high cross stands in commemoration of his bravery, near the Titanic Memorial Park, along the R315, with Mt Nephin in the background.

The Up-and-Over Challenge (http:// trailrunningireland.com/event/challenge-nephin-climb-mayo/) began in 2017, with runners climbing up Mt Nephin from Lahardane and returning to the village.

⊙ **Sights**

St Patrick's Church CHURCH

(cnr The Windy Gap & R315) Bursting at the seams with worshippers on Sundays, this small church has a magnificent stained-glass window commemorating the *Titanic* disaster, with a girl being lowered in a lifeboat down the side of the doomed White Star liner that took so many local lives. Wait for the sun to come streaming through.

Every year on 15 April, at 2.20am, relatives of the victims chime the bell in the churchyard in commemoration of the disaster.

Titanic Memorial Park MEMORIAL

(R315) With the bow of the RMS *Titanic* cast in bronze and statues of several of the passengers who were on the ship when it went down, this memorial garden is a place of quiet and poignant repose. The park was created in 2012 to commemorate the 100th anniversary of the sinking of the *Titanic*.

🍷 **Drinking & Nightlife**

Nephin Whiskey Emporium DRINKS

(☑ 087-695 5002; www.nephinwhiskey.com/ village-store) 🥃 This start-up distillery is creating peated single malt Nephin whiskey employing local barley and locally cut turf; it's triple distilled in traditional copper pot stills and matured in unique, handmade casks. The shop also sells all manner of Nephin whiskey–branded hoodies, jackets and T-shirts, plus handmade sticks for walkers.

Castlebar & Around

POP 12,300

Mayo's county town, Castlebar, is a traffic-choked hub of shops and services, but there are useful facilities and some good hotels, and its location sort of at the heart of things makes it a convenient base. Most places of interest lie outside the town centre.

⊙ **Sights**

★**National Museum
of Country Life** MUSEUM

(☑ 094-903 1755; www.museum.ie; off N5, Turlough Park; ⊙10am-5pm Tue-Sat, 2-5pm Sun) FREE This extensive, engrossing and highly good-looking museum by the Castlebar River delves into Ireland's fascinating rural traditions and skills. Photogenically overlooking a lake in the lush grounds of

19th-century **Turlough Manor**, this purpose-built facility is a branch of the National Museum of Ireland and explores everything from the role of the potato to boat building, herbal cures and traditional clothing. Exhibits concentrate on the period from 1850 to 1950. There's a good cafe and shop; it's 8km northeast of Castlebar.

The lovely **Turlough Round Tower** (off N5) is visible from the grounds.

★ **Ballintubber Abbey**   CATHEDRAL
(☑ 094-903 0934; www.ballintubberabbey.ie; Ballintubber; ⊙ 9am-midnight, tours 9.30am-5pm Mon-Fri, by arrangement Sat & Sun) FREE Established in 1216 next to the site of an earlier church founded by busy St Patrick after he came down from Croagh Patrick, this is the only church in Ireland founded by an Irish king that remains in use. Among the highlights of its tumultuous history, the abbey was burned by Normans, seized by James I and suppressed by Henry VIII. Take the N84 south, after about 13km turn west at the Emo service station; and the abbey is 2km along.

The **nave roof** was burned down by Cromwell's soldiers in 1653 and not fully restored until 1966, but the **apse** was the site of services for hundreds of years, in all manner of weather; indeed, the abbey has provided Mass continuously to the present day for 800 years, the only church in Ireland to do so.

The ruined **cloister** is also a sublime sight and Grace O'Malley's son, Tiobóid na Long (the 1st Viscount of Mayo), is buried in the vault. Besides the tour guides, a 25-minute video presentation in the abbey is available to visitors. The **Pilgrim's Way** (Tóchar Phádraig) to Croagh Patrick begins at the end of the churchyard, clearly signposted.

★ **Moore Hall**   HISTORIC BUILDING
(www.moorehall.net; Lough Carra) This astonishing and atmospheric ruin is located right by Lough Carra. The imposing but subdued wreck – with its empty windows and engulfed in ivy – was built in the 1790s and burned down in 1923, during the Civil War, its priceless library of old books and splendid panelling going up in flames. The surrounding woodland is a joy to explore. You can also wander around the totally overgrown walled garden, which may, along with the house, be eventually restored.

✗ Eating

★ **Rua Deli & Cafe**   MODERN IRISH €
(☑ 094-928 6072; www.caferua.com; Spencer St; mains €9-12; ⊙ 8.25am-6pm Mon-Sat; 🖟) Just off the Mall (the gorgeous green near the heart of town) and near the Courthouse, this gourmet deli and cafe champions artisan, organic produce, Carrowholly cheese, Ballina smoked salmon and luscious prepared foods, so you can load up in the deli for a picnic. The upstairs cafe has artfully mismatched furniture and excellent fresh fare.

A second cafe – the original, indeed – is on New Antrim St.

❶ Getting There & Away

Buses stop on Stephen Garvey Way. Bus Éireann services run to Westport (€6, 20 minutes, seven to 11 daily) and Ballina (€12.40, seven daily).

Castlebar is on the line between Dublin (€21, three hours) and Westport (€8.10, 20 minutes). There are five trains each way daily. The station is just out of town on the N84 towards Ballinrobe.

Knock

POP 850
Knock was little more than a downtrodden rural village until 1879, when a divine apparition propelled it to become one of the world's most sacred Catholic shrines. The shrine is now a serious pilgrimage site and dominates the little village. It's large and blandly modern, its appeal spiritual rather than physical.

The **tourist office** (☑ 094-938 8193; www.knock-shrine.ie; ⊙ 9am-6pm) across from the shrine is patiently helpful.

◉ Sights

Knock Marian Shrine   HISTORIC SITE
(⊙ chapel 9am-9pm) The Knock shrine encompasses five churches and a museum in the town centre. People of many faiths pray at the modern **chapel** enclosing a scene of the apparition carved from snow-white marble. A segment of **stone** from the original (and long-gone) church mounted on the outside wall (on your right as you're facing the scene of the apparition) has been rubbed smooth by the hands and lips of the faithful.

The story that led to Knock's development goes thus: on the evening of 21 August 1879, in drenching rain, two young Knock women were startled by a vision of Mary, Joseph, St John the Evangelist and a sacrificial lamb upon an altar, freeze-framed in dazzling white light against the southern gable of the parish church. They were soon joined by 13 more villagers, all gazing at the heavenly apparition for around two hours as the daylight faded. A Church investigation confirmed it as a bona fide miracle, and a sudden rush of other Vatican-approved miracles followed as the sick and disabled claimed amazing recoveries upon visiting the spot.

Besides the sacred chapel, there is the vast 1970s Basilica of Our Lady, Queen of Ireland, which can accommodate more than 10,000 people.

Knock Museum
MUSEUM

(☑ 094-937 5034; www.knock-shrine.ie/museum/; adult/child €4/3; ⊙ 10am-6pm) This small museum follows the story of the first witnesses to the vision of Mary in the parish church in 1879, through to the miraculous cures attributed to this event and the repeated Church investigations as to its legitimacy. Audio guides are available in seven languages.

❶ Getting There & Away

Ireland West Airport Knock (NOC; ☑ 094-936 8100; www.irelandwestairport.com; off N17), 15km north of the village, has services primarily to the UK. The airport website lists bus services to Westport and Galway.

Services run to Westport (€8, one hour, one daily) and Galway (€12, 1½ hours, 10 daily).

COUNTY SLIGO

County Sligo packs as much poetry, myth and folklore into its countryside's lush splendour as any shamrock-lover and archaeologist could hope for. It was Sligo that most inspired the Nobel laureate, poet and dramatist William Butler (WB) Yeats (1865–1939). Ever fascinated by Irish mysticism, he was intrigued by places such as prehistoric Carrowmore Megalithic Cemetery, Knocknarea Cairn, iconic and hulking Benbulben and cute little Innisfree Island.

And it's no complacent backwater: there's a vibrant and creative food culture and the coast's surf is internationally renowned.

Sligo Town

POP 19,500

Pedestrian streets lined with inviting shopfronts, stone bridges spanning the River Garavogue, and *céilidh* sessions spilling from pubs contrast with contemporary art and glass towers rising from prominent corners of compact Sligo. It makes a fantastic, low-key and easily manageable base for exploring Yeats country, and the countryside out of town is gorgeous.

◉ Sights

★ Model
GALLERY

(☑ 071-914 1405; www.themodel.ie; The Mall; admission varies; ⊙ 10am-5.30pm Tue-Sat, 10.30am-3.30pm Sun) The Model houses a really impressive collection of contemporary Irish art including works by Jack B Yeats (WB's brother and one of Ireland's most important modern artists) and Louis le Brocquy. There are also galleries for temporary exhibitions and installations. The centre offers an invigorating program of experimental theatre, music and film, and there's an excellent cafe at the heart of things to reflect on what you have seen.

Sligo Abbey
HISTORIC BUILDING

(www.heritageireland.ie; Abbey St; adult/child €4/2; ⊙ 10am-6pm Easter–mid-Oct) This handsome Dominican friary was built around 1252 but burned down in the 15th century, to be later rebuilt. Friends in high places saved the abbey from the worst ravages of the Elizabethan era, and rescued the sole sculpted altar to survive the Reformation. The doorways reach only a few feet high at the abbey's rear; the ground around it was swollen by the mass graves from years of famine and war.

Yeats Memorial Building
MUSEUM

(☑ 071-914 2693; www.yeatssociety.com; Hyde Bridge; adult/child €2/free; ⊙ 10am-5pm Tue-Fri, to 2pm Sat) In a pretty setting in a former 1895 bank, the WB Yeats Exhibition has details of his life and draft manuscripts and special summer programs. The small cafe has outdoor tables overlooking the River Garavogue.

Sligo County Museum
MUSEUM

(☑ 071-911 1679; Stephen St; ⊙ 9.30am-12.30pm Tue-Sat year-round, plus 2-4.50pm Tue-Sat May-Sep) FREE The major draw of Sligo's small county museum is the Yeats room, which features photographs, letters and newspaper cuttings connected with WB Yeats, as well as drawings by Jack B Yeats.

WB Yeats Statue
MONUMENT

(off Hyde Bridge) Erected in 1989, this abstract statue of Yeats – with broken glasses – in

Sligo Town

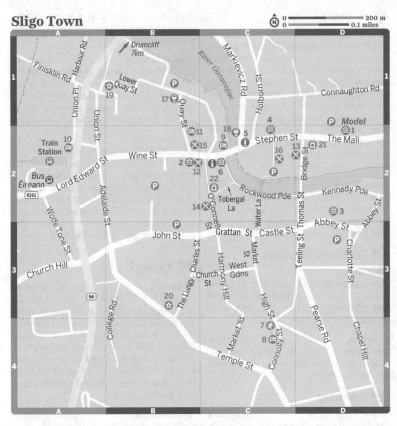

Sligo Town

front of the 1863 Ulster Bank (a building he admired) is the source of much local mirth. See if you agree with the popular moniker 'the wank at the bank'.

🏃 Activities

⭐ Sea Trails   WALKING
(📞087 240 5071; www.seatrails.ie; walks from
€15) Led by the resourceful and highly
knowledgeable Auriel, this very recommended company runs interesting walks
concentrating on ancient features and natural beauty in and near the coast, including
Armada sights and the stunning local geology. Auriel has a BA degree in Archaeology and Geography and a Masters Degree
in Maritime Archaeology, plus many years
working in the field of heritage.

Chain Driven Cycles   CYCLING
(📞071-912 9008; www.chaindrivencycles.com;
23 High St; per day from €20; ⊘10am-6pm Mon-
Sat) Offers mountain-, hybrid-, electric- and
road-bike hire. Rates include helmet.

🎊 Festivals & Events

Tread Softly   CULTURAL
(www.treadsoftly.ie; ⊘late Jul) Part of Sligo's
'Season of Yeats', this series of events over 10
days celebrates the iconic man with tours,
performances and more.

Sligo Live   CULTURAL
(www.sligolive.ie; ⊘late Oct) Sligo's biggest cultural event is this live-music festival over
five days in autumn.

🛏 Sleeping

⭐ An Crúiscin Lan   GUESTHOUSE €
(📞087 233 1573; www.bandbsligo.ie; Connolly St;
s/d from €45/75; 🛜) The central location is a
good selling point for this simple and convivial place. The friendly owner runs a tight
ship; stag and hen parties are banned. Some
of the 10 rooms share bathrooms.

Railway Hostel   HOSTEL €
(📞087 690 5539; www.therailway.ie; 1 Union Pl;
dm/s/tw from €18/25/44; 🛜) In a heritage
building close to the train station, this
cheery hostel has great rates and shared
bathrooms. There's a surcharge for arriving after 9pm. There are no bunk beds and
there's also a two-bedroom townhouse next
door. From November to March there's 10%
off prices.

Glass House   HOTEL €€
(📞071-919 4300; www.theglasshouse.ie; Swan
Point; s/d from €80/100; 🛜) You can't miss this
cool and contemporary four-star hotel in the
centre of town, its sharp glass facade pointing skyward. Inside, the food areas have
good river views, there are two bars and the
116 well-equipped rooms come in a choice of
bright colours.

Sligo City Hotel   HOTEL €€
(📞071-914 4000; www.sligocityhotel.com; Quay St;
r €65-90; 🛜) This renovated four-storey hotel could not be better located. The 60 good-
sized rooms have a simple corporate colour
scheme. Basic rates do not include breakfast.

Clayton Hotel   HOTEL €€
(📞071-911 9000; www.claytonhotelsligo.com; Clar-
ion Rd; r from €75; ⊞) This huge historic hotel
and resort in large grounds has some excellent deals and rooms are massive. You're a
bit north of the centre, but it's easy enough
to get into town. There's a swimming pool
and spa and loads of facilities for kids. The
full-on breakfast, if not included in your
rate, is €10.

🍴 Eating

⭐ Fabio's   ICE CREAM €
(📞087-177 2732; Wine St; treats from €2;
⊘11am-7pm Mon-Thu & Sat, till 7pm Fri, noon-
7pm Sun Apr-Oct, 11am-6pm Wed-Sat & 1-6pm Sat
Nov-Mar) Fabio is a local hero for making
Ireland's best Italian gelato and sorbets.
He uses mostly local and natural ingredients for his changing line-up of flavours.
His coffee is good, too, and service comes
with a smile.

⭐ Lyons Cafe   MODERN EUROPEAN €
(📞071-914 2969; www.lyonscafe.com; Quay
St; mains €7-16; ⊘9am-6pm Mon-Sat) Sligo's
flagship department store, Lyons, opened
in 1878 – with original leadlight windows
and squeaky timber floors – and has been
going strong since 1923. Its airy 1st-floor
cafe is anything but stodgy, and acclaimed
chef (and cookbook author) Gary Stafford
offers a fresh and seasonal menu that's inventive yet casual, with gourmet sandwiches including Irish brie with wild rocket and
Ballymaloe relish.

Miso Sligo   JAPANESE €
(📞071-919 4986; Stephen St; ⊘noon-3pm &
5-10pm Tue-Fri, 3-10pm Sat, 5-10pm Sun) The
exterior in a modern block may look uninviting, but the Japanese/Korean food here
is good. The servings of gyoza (dumplings)
are a bit skimpy, but the sushi is good and
miso ramen is excellent and filling. There's
also meal sets and a good choice of meat-
free dishes for vegetarians.

MICHAEL QUIRKE: THE WOODCARVER OF WINE ST

The inconspicuous storefront studio of **Michael Quirke** (☏ 071-914 2624; Wine St; ⊙ usually 9.30am-12.30pm & 3-5.30pm Mon-Sat), woodcarver, raconteur and local legend, is filled with the scents of locally felled timbers and off-cuts of sycamore. Quirke began cutting and carving wood in 1968. Today he still uses the same saw he used on meat when he worked here as a butcher.

A modern-day Yeats, Quirke's art is inspired by Irish mythology, a subject about which he is passionate and knowledgeable, and as he carves he readily chats with the customers and the curious who enter his shop and end up staying for hours.

As he talks and carves, Quirke frequently pulls out a county map, pointing to places (such as his beloved Carrowmore) that spring from the conversation, leading you on your own magical, mystical tour of the county. Should he ask you your favourite animal, consider your answer carefully, as he's likely to carve you a version of the critter on the spot.

Gourmet Parlour   CAFE €

(☏ 071-914 4617; www.gourmetparlour.com; Bridge St; mains €4-12; ⊙ 8am-5pm Mon-Sat; 🐾) Simply great simple food is the theme at this bakery and cafe, with excellent sandwiches, tarts, hot lunches and more, plus much swooning for the apple pie. Drop by for just a coffee but plan to succumb to more.

★ Hargadons   PUB €€

(☏ 071-915 3709; www.hargadons.com; 4/5 O'Connell St; mains €8-20; ⊙ food noon-3.30pm & 4-9pm Mon-Sat) You'll have a hard time leaving this superb 1868 pub with its winning blend of old-world fittings and gastropub style. The uneven floors, peat fire, antique signage, snug corners and bowed shelves laden down with ancient bottles lend it a wonderful charm. The great-value food is renowned, combining local ingredients such as oysters with continental flair. The kitchen and service are excellent.

The menu changes with the seasons and many of the wines come from the pub's vineyard in France. Bookings are not taken, so plan on sampling a few fine microbrews while you wait. Trad music chips in some nights too.

🍺 Drinking & Entertainment

Harp Tavern   PUB

(☏ 071-914 2473; Quay St; ⊙ noon-late) This all-around good pub with regular trad-music sessions and a genuinely welcoming vibe delivers good bar food through the day and evening.

Thomas Connolly   PUB

(☏ 071-919 4920; www.thomasconnollysligo.com; Markievicz Rd & Holborn St; ⊙ 11am-late) There's discoloured photos and newspaper clippings, mottled mirrors, trad music and craft beer at this magnificent historic pub (also opening onto Holborn St).

Blue Raincoat Theatre Company   THEATRE

(☏ 071-917 0431; www.blueraincoat.com; Lower Quay St) A former abattoir is home to innovative theatre company Blue Raincoat, whose program includes original productions plus Yeats in the summer.

Hawk's Well Theatre   THEATRE

(☏ 071-916 1518; www.hawkswell.com; Temple St) This well-regarded 340-seat theatre presents concerts, dance and drama for children and adults.

🛍 Shopping

★ Liber Bookshop   BOOKS

(☏ 071-914 2219; www.liber.ie; 35 O'Connell St; ⊙ 9am-6pm Mon-Sat) There's much more than Yeats at this fabulous bookshop, run by the same family for more than 80 years. It also gives recommendations on the best local authors and the stock in general is terrific.

Bookmart   BOOKS

(☏ 083-361 3127; https://sites.google.com/view/bookmart/home; 5 The Mall; ⊙ 10am-6pm Mon-Sat) This excellent secondhand bookshop is a treasure trove of titles, from duffed up Asimov to Dylan Thomas, Sylvia Plath, Primo Levi and a host of other writers, some obscure, others mainstream, all sharing space on stuffed shelves and overseen by friendly, communicative and helpful staff.

There are poetry readings too (8pm on the first Thursday of the month), and other literary events.

❶ Information

The **Tourist Office** (☑ 071-916 1201; www.sligo tourism.ie; cnr O'Connell & Wine Sts; ☺ 9am-5pm Mon-Fri, 9.30am-5pm Sat) has info on the whole northwest region, plus good walking info and loads of maps and literature.

❶ Getting There & Away

Bus Éireann (☑ 071-916 0066; www.buseireann.ie; Lord Edward St) leaves from the bus station situated below the train station. Destinations include Ballina (€17, 1½ hours, one to four daily) and Donegal town (€15, one hour, six daily).

Trains leave Lord Edward Street station for Dublin (€20, three hours, seven daily) via Boyle, Carrick-on-Shannon and Mullingar.

Around Sligo Town

Rosses Point

POP 830

Rosses Point is a picturesque seaside town with grassy dunes rolling down to the golden strand. Benbulben (525m), Sligo's most recognisable landmark, looms in the distance. Offshore, the unusual – and jaunty – 1821 Metal Man beacon points the way into harbour. In the distance are ride-free Coney Island and Oyster Island.

Rosses Point has two wonderful Blue Flag beaches, the **First** and **Second Beaches**, on the west-facing side of the headland. The Second Beach is the longer of the two.

County Sligo Golf Course (☑ 071-917 7171; www.countysligogolfclub.ie; 18-hole championship green fees €145-165, day rate €270; ☺ Apr-Oct) has a breathtaking position on the peninsula and is one of Ireland's most challenging and renowned links courses, attracting golfers from all over the world. It is possibly Ireland's greatest and most picturesque golf course.

✖ Eating

Little Cottage Cafe   CAFE €
(☑ 071-911 7766; off R291; mains from €4.50; ☺ 9.30am-5pm) This charming little place is a small white bungalow filled with light, satisfied customers, great breakfasts and a tasty menu with sandwiches, hot pot and soup of the day.

Harry's Bar   IRISH €€
(☑ 071-917 7173; www.harrysrossespoint.com; Rosses Point; mains €12-25; ☺ food 11am-9pm Tue-Sun; 🐕) Harry's Bar (on your right as you

enter town) boasts a historic well (serving as a table within the bar itself), an aquarium and maritime bric-a-brac. In the same family since 1870, the pub serves good, classic fare.

Carrowmore

★ Carrowmore Megalithic Cemetery   ARCHAEOLOGICAL SITE

(☑ 071-916 1534; www.heritageireland.ie; adult/child €5/3; ☺ 10am-6pm Easter–mid-Oct, final admission 5pm; 🅿) One of the largest Stone Age cemeteries in Europe, Carrowmore is finally receiving the renown it deserves and is Sligo's must-see attraction. Some 60 monuments including stone circles, passage tombs and dolmens adorn the rolling hills of this haunting site, which is thought to pre-date Newgrange in County Meath (p501) by 700 years.

To get here, follow the R292 west from Sligo for 4km and follow the signposts.

Although over the centuries many of the stones have been destroyed, ongoing excavations continue to uncover more sites both within the public site and on adjoining private land.

Discoveries about the meaning of Carrowmore are both continuing and dramatic, particularly how the many features of the site relate to the surrounding hills and mountain. Among the numbered sites, 51 has been found to get direct sunlight at dawn each 31 October, or Halloween. Many people claim to feel strong powers here and you'll likely see a few spiritual pilgrims on the site.

The delicately balanced dolmens were originally covered with stones and earth, so it requires some effort to picture what this 2.5km-wide area might once have looked like. A large central cairn has been reconstructed to give visitors some insight into the materials and methods used at this time. The visitor centre has full details and staff are happy to explain much more, plus detail the latest discoveries.

★ Knocknarea Cairn   HISTORIC SITE

(Cnoc na Riabh; 🚶) Sligo's ultimate rock pile and a magical climb, Knocknarea is popularly believed to be the grave of legendary Queen Maeve (Queen Mab in Welsh and English folk tales). The 40,000 tonnes of stone have never been excavated, despite speculation that a tomb on the scale of the one at Newgrange lies buried below.

The parking area is off the R292. The cairn is 2km northwest of Carrowmore;

from Carrowmore, continue west along the road, turn right by a church, and follow the signposts.

The cairn is perched high atop a limestone plateau (328m); a 40-minute (1.2km; the fit and fast can do it in 20 minutes) trek to the top reveals spectacular views. From the top you can gaze out over of Benbulben, Rosses Point and the Atlantic Ocean beyond. The cairn seems to be looking over your shoulder everywhere you dare tread in its ancestral backyard. Many think the rocks purposely form a giant nipple, which takes on meaning when the overall horizon is viewed from Carrowmore. Believers in underlying powers at the sites say that you can easily make out the shape of a reclining woman, or a mother god. They say that Queen Maeve is buried upright in the cairn, holding a spear and facing her adversaries in Ulster.

WB Yeats was enthralled by the myth and lore of Knocknarea and its magic wormed its way into his verse. In 'Red Hanrahan's Song about Ireland', he writes: 'The wind has bundled up the clouds high over Knocknarea, And thrown the thunder on the stones for all that Maeve can say.'

Don't forget to pick up a stone as you climb to add to the cairn, for good luck. But don't climb the cairn itself, whatever you do. Take good footwear.

Strandhill

POP 1650

The great Atlantic rollers that sweep Strandhill's shore make this long, red-gold beach a surfing mecca, while the town is also located not far from Knocknarea Cairn, one of the most important archaeological sites in the county and a terrific hike.

WB YEATS & IRISH MYTHS

William Butler Yeats liked to say that by age 24 in 1889 he'd read 'most, if not all, recorded Irish folk tales'. There's certainly no reason to dismiss this claim as hyperbole, as his writings, whether poetry, prose or plays, celebrated Celtic legends and myths. It's all the more fitting given his love for County Sligo, a place home to ancient Celtic sites such the remarkable **Carrowmore** (p428), with ancient mysteries and meanings that are still being discovered today.

Yeats firmly believed that the Irish could emerge from English domination and create their own purely Irish identity by revelling in the ancient Celtic myths still commonly recounted across the land. In 1888 he collaborated on the landmark *Fairy and Folk Tales of the Irish Peasantry*. Four years later, he wrote the children's book *Irish Fairy Tales*. In these works he codified many of the most common Irish myths, characters and legends that are common today. Among them:

Fairies A strong believer in the occult, Yeats had no problems merging his views with the common belief among rural people in fairies. A whole race of little people, fairies had all manner of qualities (with being mischievous near universal); but could be roughly divided into good and bad. In the *Land of Heart's Desire* (first performed in 1894), Yeats wrote:

'Faeries, come take me out of this dull world,
For I would ride with you upon the wind,
Run on the top of the dishevelled tide,
And dance upon the mountains like a flame.'

Leprechauns Solitary members of the much-larger race of fairies, Yeats called leprechauns 'sluttish, slouching, jeering, mischievous phantoms' and 'great practical jokers'. Contrary to the modern-day green-clad apparitions found in gift shops, Yeats had his leprechauns dressed in red jackets and prone to endless avarice.

Banshees Typically a woman of varying age – from cute to crone – who appears wailing before a death. Long feared, Yeats had much more benevolent views, writing: 'You will with the Banshee chat and will find her good at heart.'

Yeats also wrote much about the ancient Irish gods, most derived from Celtic myths, including Aengus, the Irish god of love, and Cuchulain, a great Irish warrior in the spirit of Hercules. In the poem 'Cuchulain Comforted' (1939), he combines myth with a classic Irish quality, writing: 'Now we shall sing and sing the best we can.'

🏃 Activities

Although it's too rough to swim, there are excellent long and brisk walks along the beach both north and south. The views of the surf are always spectacular and you can wander up into the dunes. Surfing is naturally the principal draw for a large contingent of visitors.

Voya Seaweed Baths SPA
(☑ 071-916 8686; www.voyaseaweedbaths.com; Shore Rd, Strandhill; bath from €28; ⊙ 10am-8pm) Don't just smell seaweed on the beach – immerse yourself in it at this beachfront location. Ask about sharing your bath.

Perfect Day Surf & SUP School SURFING
(☑ 087 202 9399; www.perfectdaysurfing.ie; Shore Rd; lessons adult/child from €30/20; ⊙ Apr-Oct) This useful shop offers lessons for surfing and stand-up paddleboarding (€35 to €50). It usually has a yellow van parked at the beach on Shore Rd.

Strandhill Surf School SURFING
(☑ 071-916 8483; www.strandhillsurf.com; Beachfront; lessons adult/child from €30/20; ⊙ Apr-Oct) Offers gear hire and lessons from decent qualified instructors; there's a live surf cam on the website. Five-day summer camps (€100) are also run for children.

🛏 Sleeping

Surf & Stay Lodge & Hostel LODGE €
(☑ 071-916 8313; www.surfnstay.ie; Shore Rd; hostel dm €20-25, tw €40-50, lodge s €40-50, d €40-80, camping €10; ⊛) Surfers thaw out by the open fire in the common room of the 34-bed hostel portion of this two-building complex. Rooms in the adjoining lodge are B&B-style and, while small, are comfy, some with shared bathrooms. The beach is close and there's an on-site surf school (surfing lessons €20 to €40; stand-up paddle board €40 to €50).

Ocean Wave Lodge B&B €
(☑ 071-916 8115; www.oceanwavelodge.com; Top Rd/R292; dm/s/d from €18/35/49; ℗⊛) This large modern house uphill from the beach has minimalist but comfortable rooms. Breakfast is included and there's a self-catering kitchen and large lounge area for guest use.

Strandhill Lodge & Suites GUESTHOUSE €€
(☑ 071-912 2122; www.strandhilllodgeandsuites. com; Top Rd/R292; s/d from €65/100; ⊛) Up the hill, this excellent guesthouse offers 22 bright, spacious rooms with king-sized

beds, hotel-quality design and trendy neutral styling. Room sizes vary but most have terraces or balconies and fabulous views down to the ocean.

🍴 Eating & Drinking

Shells CAFE €
(☑ 071-912 2938; www.shellscafe.com; Shore Rd; mains from €6; ⊙ 9am-7pm; ☑) This sprightly little cafe right across from the beach has flowers on tables and herbs in the dishes from the owner's garden. The baked goods are excellent, as is the coffee; breakfasts delight and at lunch there are salads, chowders, specials and splendid fish and chips. Negative points: it's crowded, and getting served can be almost impossible at peak times.

★ Trá Bán MODERN IRISH €€
(☑ 071-912 8402; www.trabansligo.ie; Shore Rd; mains €17-26; ⊙ 5-9.30pm; ☑) With a relaxed atmosphere, this justifiably popular 1st-floor restaurant above the Strand Bar serves excellent pasta, steaks and seafood. If in doubt, the seafood linguini is gorgeous. Book in advance.

Strand Bar PUB
(☑ 071-916 8140; Shore Rd; ⊙ 11am-late) Surfers, locals and tourists crowd into proper snugs and cosy corners at this convivial pub. Or they just listen to the surf from the terrace out the front. There's bar food; live music plays at weekends; and there's an excellent restaurant above.

ℹ Getting There & Away

Strandhill is 8km due west of Sligo off the R292. Local bus S2 runs from Sligo (€4, hourly, 30 minutes).

South of Sligo Town

Carrowkeel

★ Carrowkeel Megalithic Cemetery ARCHAEOLOGICAL SITE
With a bird's-eye view of the county from high in the Bricklieve Mountains, it's little wonder this hilltop site was sacred in prehistoric times. But for a few sheep, it's undeveloped and spectacular. Dotted with around 14 cairns, dolmens and the scattered remnants of other graves, the site dates from the late Stone Age (3000 to 2000 BC).

Carrowkeel is closer to Boyle than Sligo town. It's about 5km from either the R295 in the west or the N4 in the east. Follow the signs.

This windswept and lonely location is simultaneously eerie and uplifting. Just the sweeping views down to South Sligo county from the car park make the journey worthwhile; but the views further on over Lough Arrow are just as stunning. It's a 1km walk from the car park (look out for the sign that says 'Pedestrians Only', with an arrow scratched on it – follow the arrow) to the first ancient site, Cairn G. Above its entrance is a roof-box aligned with the midsummer sunset which illuminates the inner chamber. The only other such roof-box known in Ireland is that at Newgrange in County Meath (p501). Continue along to another three such cairns (the last one in a state of collapse) and you'll reach a fence with a piece of plastic tubing over the wire. Cross this and after a short distance you will find a huge limestone sinkhole full of small trees, shrubs and vegetation.

Everywhere you look across the surrounding hills in this region there's evidence of early life, including about 140 stone circles – all that remain of the foundations of a large village thought to have been inhabited by the builders of the tombs.

Ballymote & Around

POP 1600

This pretty little town merits a visit for opportunities to ponder Irish culture and history, for its formidable and sublime castle ruin, as well as the chance to make an expedition to the magnificent views from the Caves of Keash.

Sights

Ballymote Castle
CASTLE

(Tubbercurry Rd/R296) Just down from Ballymote train station, the immense shell of Ballymote Castle is a classic, imposing ruin. It was from this early-14th-century redoubt, fronted by formidable drum towers, that O'Donnell marched to disaster at the Battle of Kinsale in 1601.

Caves of Keash
CAVE

(off the R295) Around 6km outside Ballymote, these splendid limestone caves high up in the side of Keshcorran hill make for a fun expedition. You can park near the bottom of the fields at the foot of the mountain and climb on up. It doesn't take long to reach the caves, some of which are pretty deep, and afford excellent views (and photographs) over the countryside. There are 16 caves in all; mind your step as it can be quite steep (and slippery after rain).

Coleman Irish Music Centre
ARTS CENTRE

(☑071-918 2599; www.colemanirishmusic.com; Gurteen; ☉10am-5pm Mon-Sat) This music centre hosts multimedia exhibits and workshops and performances. You can add to your music collection or pick up your own instruments and sheet music at the on-site shop too. It's 12km south of Ballymote on the R293 in the little village of Gurteen.

ℹ WALKING SLIGO

In a country that doesn't hurt for a lack of good walks, County Sligo has more than its share. There are myriad choices, including the Sligo Way (www.irishtrails.ie), a 78km waymarked route that includes the Ox Mountains, Lough Easkey and Lough Gill.

Walking resources and organisations are many, and include the following:

Sligo Walks (www.sligowalks.ie) An excellent online resource with dozens of walks, maps, ratings and much more.

Sligo Mountaineering Club (www.sligomountaineeringclub.org) Good website for info on climbing Benbulben, including sensible details on staying safe.

Muddy Boots Trekking (☑087 642 9131) Organises day hikes on Benbulben and elsewhere.

Sea Trails (p426) Highly recommended and run by maritime archaeologist Auriel Robinson. Runs interesting walks that concentrate on ancient features, the geology, natural beauty and archaeological sites around and near the coast.

Sligo Walking Guide A useful free booklet with scores of walks, available at tourist offices.

Aughris Head

Take a diversion north of the N59 to reach Aughris Head and, if you're up for it, an invigorating 5km walk tracing the cliffs around the remote headland, where dolphins and seals can often be seen swimming into the bay. Birdwatchers should look out for kittiwakes, fulmars, guillemots, shags, storm petrels and curlews along the way.

Beach Bar   SEAFOOD €€
(☑071-917 6465; www.thebeachbarsligo.com; Aughris Head; mains €10-25, tent/van sites from €10/20, s/d from €35/70; ☺food served noon-8pm daily summer, Fri-Sun winter; ☻) In a sheltered setting on the lovely beach by the cliff walk, the pub in this 17th-century thatched cottage hosts cracking traditional-music sessions and serves superb seafood, including creamy chowder and poached salmon. The owners also operate the Aughris House B&B next door, with seven wi-fi-enabled comfy rooms and adjacent campsites.

Easkey

Easkey is one of Europe's best year-round surfing destinations. However, in pubs with names like Lobster Pot and Fisherman's Weir, conversations revolve around hurling and seafood prices; the road to the beach is just east of town. Facilities are few; most surfers camp (free) around the ruins of Easkey Castle by the sea.

When driving into town from the east, look out for the Split Rock, a huge boulder split in two, whose origins have generated much folklore. It is said that if you squeeze through the split three times, it will close on you.

Pudding Row (☑096-49794; Main St; mains from €5; ☺11am-5pm Thu-Sun) is a winning, bright, inviting and spacious upstairs cafe serving fine homemade pastries, cooked up by Dervla, along with fine views.

Enniscrone

This very low-key holiday town facing Killala Bay is all about the ocean and the glorious views and sunsets. The stunning Enniscrone Beach (www.enniscronebeach.com) stretches for 5km.

🏃 Activities

Seventh Wave Surf School   SURFING
(☑087 971 6389; www.surfsligo.com; Beach, Enniscrone; lessons adult/child from €30/25; ☺Apr-Oct) Offers surf lessons and board rental.

Kilcullen's Seaweed Baths   SPA
(☑096-36238; http://homepage.eircom.net/~seaweedbaths/frame.htm; Cliff Rd, Enniscrone; bath from €25; ☺10am-10pm Jun-Aug, noon-8pm Mon-Fri, 10am-8pm Sat & Sun Apr, May, Sep & Oct, 10am-8pm Sat & Sun Nov-Apr) Enniscrone is famous for its traditional seaweed baths, which are some of the most atmospheric in the country. Kilcullen's Edwardian bathhouse is the most traditional and has buckets of character.

🛏 Sleeping & Eating

Quirky Glamping Village   RESORT
(☑096-75290; www.quirkyglamping.town.ie/; ☻) Due to open in 2018, this is a wildly eccentric 'village' accommodation option. Stay in one of the eight en suite rooms in a Boeing 767 aeroplane, in a double-decker bus (with kitchenette), in a London cab (for one or two), in a boat in the marina, or in a train carriage. Check out the website to see how the Boeing 767 was shipped in!

Pilot Bar   MODERN IRISH €€
(☑096-36131; www.thepilotbar.ie; cnr Cliff Rd & Main St; mains €6-20; ☺bar 4pm-late Mon-Fri, 9am-late Sat & Sun, kitchen Wed-Sun; 🍴) Terrace tables let you bask in the sun amid potted flowers, while inside you can fancy yourself a seaman as you revel in the porthole motifs. The food is simple but delicious, with much sourced locally.

ℹ Getting There & Away

Sligo (€15.10, 1¼ hours) buses run three times daily on the route to Ballina.

Lough Gill & Around

Beautiful, mirror-like Lough Gill ('Lake of Brightness') was a place of great inspiration for Yeats.

The lake, a mere 6km southeast of Sligo town and simple to reach, is shaded by two magical swaths of woodland – Hazelwood and Slish Wood – which have loop trails; there are good views of Innisfree Island from the latter.

You can take a cruise on the lake from atmospheric Parke's Castle (p476), in nearby

County Leitrim. Watch for the shadows of huge salmon and the ripples of otters.

The lake is immediately east of Sligo town. Take the R286 along the north shore for the most interesting views, whether you are driving or riding. The southern route on the R287 is less interesting until you reach Dooney Rock.

◎ Sights

Dooney Rock HILL

Immortalised by Yeats in 'The Fiddler of Dooney' (1899), this huge fissured limestone knoll bulges awkwardly upward by the lough's southern shore. There's a great lake view from the top and you can park right at the bottom. Photographs over the lake can be stunning as the sun sinks at the end of the day. It's 7km southwest of Sligo town on the R287.

Magheraghanrush Court Tomb ARCHAEOLOGICAL SITE

A 10-minute walk from a car park leads through pine-scented forest to this enigmatic court tomb. Dating from around 3000 BC, the crumbling structure is comparable to a crude human form, with a large bellylike central court and several protruding burial chambers positioned as though the head and legs.

Take the N16 east from Sligo and turn onto the R286. Almost immediately, turn left onto a minor road for Manorhamilton. Continue 3km to the car park.

Follow the trail for 50m before veering right up a small hill.

Innisfree Island ISLAND

This pint-sized island lies tantalisingly close to the lough's southeastern shore, but, alas, can't be accessed. Still, it's visible from the shore. Its air of tranquillity so moved Yeats that he famously wrote 'The Lake Isle of Innisfree' (1890):

'I will arise and go now, and go to Innisfree,

And a small cabin build there, of clay and wattles made;

Nine bean rows will I have there, a hive for the honey bee,

And live alone in the bee-loud glade.'

Access the best vantage point of the island from a small road that starts at the junction of the R287 and the R290. Follow the winding lane for 4.2km to a small parking area by the water.

North of Sligo Town

Evocative coastal drives and lonely mountain paths highlight the heart of Yeats country – the scenery is nothing short of sublime.

Benbulben

A stolid greenish-grey eminence visible all along Sligo's northern coast, Benbulben (525m), often written Ben Bulben, resembles a table covered by a pleated cloth: its limestone plateau is uncommonly flat, and its near-vertical sides are scored by earthen ribs. Walking here is not for the uninitiated.

WORTH A TRIP

LISSADELL HOUSE

This fabulously grand manor house and ancestral home (www.lissadellhouse.com; adult/child house & grounds €14/6, exhibition & grounds €10/5) of the Gore-Booth family is one of the top sights of the region. Revolutionary nationalist and socialist Constance Goore-Booth (Countess Markievicz) grew up here and WB Yeats used to frequently drop by. The fabulous grounds – including the gorgeous walled alpine garden – can be wandered at will (with a ticket); access to parts of the house is by guided tour.

Take the N15 from Sligo to Drumcliff, head along the L3305 through Carney and follow the signs.

In 1918 Countess Markievicz was the first woman elected to the British House of Commons. You can explore various rooms within the house on the highly informative 45-minute tour, including the ante room, the drawing room, the dining room, the billiard room and the basement (where the kitchens were), but as it is a home in use, the upstairs rooms are inaccessible. For a cheaper ticket, you can explore the exhibition in the coach house and the grounds, but it's the house, restored at great cost by the current owners, that's worth seeing.

Sligo Mountaineering Club (www.sligo mountaineeringclub.com) sets off on hikes and hill walks every Sunday of the year, with walks not just in Sligo but also in Leitrim, Mayo, Galway, Roscommon and Donegal.

The best way to walk around within the shadow of Benbulben (525m) is by visiting the **Gortarowey Forest Recreation Area**, an area within Benbulben Forest. There are three trails within the forest. One is short, but the looped longer walks take you along the northern slopes of the mountain, affording spectacular views. The longest is the **Benbulben Loop** (www.coillteoutdoors.ie; off N15) (clearly signposted), which is 5.5km long and takes around two hours to complete. Each trail starts and ends in the car park.

Drumcliff & Around

Benbulben's beauty was not lost on WB Yeats. Before the poet died in Menton, France, in 1939, he had requested: 'If I die here, bury me up there on the mountain, and then after a year or so, dig me up and bring me privately to Sligo.' His wishes were honoured in 1948, when his body was interred in the churchyard at Drumcliff, where his great-grandfather had been rector.

Drumcliff itself is a small place, and the main places of interest – Yeats' Grave, the round tower remains and high cross – lie very close together, with the Cafe & Crafts Shop in between.

Buses run from Sligo to Drumcliff (€5, 15 minutes, seven to eight daily).

◉ Sights

★ **Yeats' Grave**   MONUMENT
(off N15; ☺ dawn-dusk) Yeats was long believed to be buried next to the doorway of the Protestant church, but recent evidence suggests that the bones shipped here from France in 1948 were not his at all, owing to the actual bones being scattered about an ossuary during the chaos of WWII. Yeats' youthful bride, Georgie Hyde-Lee, however, is buried alongside. Almost three decades her senior, Yeats was 52 when they married.

The poet's epitaph is from his poem 'Under Ben Bulben':

'Cast a cold eye
On life, on death.
Horseman, pass by!'

There's a small **cafe & crafts shop** (mains from €4; ☺ 9am-5pm) beside the church. It is popular with locals at lunch and has a good selection of books.

In the 6th century, St Colmcille chose this location for a monastery. You can still see the stumpy remains of a **round tower**, which was struck by lightning in 1396, on the main road nearby. Also in the churchyard is an extraordinary 9th-century **high cross**, etched with intricate biblical scenes that include Adam and Eve, as well as Daniel in the Lion's Den. There is a car park right alongside the church.

🛏 Sleeping & Eating

★ **Ardtarmon House**   LODGE €€
(☑ 071-916 3156; www.ardtarmon.com; Raghly Rd, Ballinfull; s/d from €50/80, cottage €100-450; ☺ closed late Dec-early Jan) In an incomparable location 10.5km west of the N15, this fifth-generation family-run property has four spacious rooms in the ivy-covered manor house, and five self-contained cottages in converted farm buildings. A 450m stroll through wildflower-strewn gardens brings you to a beach.

Yeats Lodge   B&B €
(☑ 071-917 3787; www.yeatslodge.com; Drumcliff; s/d from €45/70; P ☎) Obliging owners, five large, modern rooms and a tranquil atmosphere make this B&B worth seeking out. There's tasteful rustic decor and lovely views of Benbulben. It's 300m off the N15. In July and August (peak season), doubles are €80.

★ **Rathcormac Food
& Craft Market**   MARKET
(off N15, Rathcormac; ☺ 10am-3pm Sat) Held in Banley's Yard amid antique shops and a good cafe, this market is worth scheduling your trip around. Although small, the best producers in the region sell ready-to-eat food, produce, cheeses, baked goods and much more. It's a delight to wander about snacking while shopping for your picnic.

Lough Glencar

Straddling counties Sligo and Leitrim, this picturesque lake is famed for fishing as well as its beautiful waterfall, and was referred to by Yeats in his 1889 poem 'The Stolen Child'. The surrounding countryside is best enjoyed by walking east and taking the steep trail north to the valley. Try to get here for sunset to see Lough Glencar at its best.

Streedagh Strand

Streedagh Strand occasionally sees parts of the Spanish Armada washing up on its shores from three wrecks offshore: *La Juliana, La Lavia* and *La Santa Maria de Visón*; over 1000 soldiers and sailors drowned or were killed when the ships were caught in a storm. It's a site of immense archaeological significance, but there are also many examples of fossilised coral, fascinating geological formations, a wedge tomb and views to the island of Inishmurray.

Some people say the wrecks are visible at low tide, but these are actually the ribs of a 'butter boat'.

The best way to appreciate the local wonders is to tag along with Auriel Robinson on one of her Sea Trails (p426) walks. She will fill you in on all the local geology, marine and land-based archaeology as well as folklore, legend and stories associated with Streedagh Strand.

Mullaghmore

The sweeping arc of dark-golden sand and the safe shallow waters make the pretty fishing village of Mullaghmore a popular family destination.

Take time to walk, cycle or drive the scenic road loop around Mullaghmore Head, where wide shafts of rock slice into the Atlantic surf. En route you'll pass **Classiebawn Castle** (closed to the public), quite an astonishing sight against the skyline.

Sights & Activities

Mullaghmore Head   BEACH
Big-wave tow-in surfing competitions are regularly held off Mullaghmore Head. The area is becoming known as one of Ireland's premier big-wave surf spots with swells of up to 17m allowing for Hawaiian-style adventure.

Gleniff Horseshoe   TREKKING
From Cliffony near Mullaghmore, follow the small road southeast into the broad Gleniff Horseshoe Valley. Set amid the barren drama of the Dartry Mountains, this area begs for exploration. A tiny lane, the Gleniff Horse-

WORTH A TRIP

INISHMURRAY ISLAND

It takes some effort to arrange a visit to Inishmurray (www.inishmurray.com), an island that w as abandoned in 1948, leaving behind early Christian remains and fascinating pagan relics. There are three well-preserved churches, beehive cells and open-air altars. The old monastery, surrounded by a thickset oval wall, was founded in the early 6th century by St Molaise.

Although it's only 6km between Inishmurray and the mainland, there's no regular boat service, and the lack of a harbour makes landing subject to the weather. To visit, check with **Inishmurray Island Trips** (☑087 254 0190; www.inishmurrayislandtrips.com; Mullaghmore; trips per person from €40; ☸Apr-Sep) or **Sea Trails** (p426).

shoe, makes a 10km loop through the valley, passing wild babbling streams and the remains of an old mill. You can imagine Yeats here.

The loop is good by bike or car. You can also walk and branch off into hikes in the hills. Sligo Walks (www.sligowalks.ie) has online maps.

At the base of the valley, the **Benwiskin Centre** (☑071-917 6721; www.benwiskincentre.com; Ballintrillick; dm/s/d €15/45/55; ⓟ🖥) (www.benwiskincentre.com) is a good hostel with dorms and private rooms.

🍴 Eating

★Eithna's by the Sea   SEAFOOD €€
(☑071-916 6407; www.eithnasrestaurant.com; Mullaghmore Harbour, R79; mains €10-35; ☸11am-3.30pm, dinner from 5pm; 🖥🖥) 🍴 With a view over the bay at Mullaghmore, this bright-blue seafood restaurant is a joy, with tables outside for sunny alfresco dining on lobster, shellfish, crab, squid and roasted seaweed. Food comes straight from the waters to your table, via the kitchen, so it's all fresher than fresh. Eithna's puts together some terrific sandwiches too.

There's also a fantastic menu for tots.

County Donegal

POP 159,000 / AREA 3001 SQ KM

Best Places to Eat

➡ Beach House (p467)

➡ Olde Castle Bar (p441)

➡ Danny Minnie's Restaurant (p452)

➡ Starfish Cafe & Bistro (p458)

➡ Ahoy Cafe (p445)

Best Places to Sleep

➡ Corcreggan Mill (p457)

➡ Glen House (p467)

➡ Castle Murray (p445)

➡ Woodhill House (p449)

➡ Rathmullan House (p464)

Why Go?

County Donegal is the wild child of Ireland and home to some of its most ravishingly sublime scenery and beautiful beaches. Not for nothing did *National Geographic Traveler* vote Donegal the coolest place on the planet in 2017: so don't miss out.

This is a county of extremes: at times desolate and battered by brutal weather, yet also a land of unspoilt splendour where stark peaks and sweeping beaches bask in glorious sunshine, and port-side restaurants serve majestic food.

Donegal's rugged interior, with its remote mountain passes and shimmering lakes, is only marginally outdone by the long and labyrinthine coastline with windswept peninsulas and isolated pubs. Proudly independent, one-third of Donegal is official Gaeltacht territory, with Irish the lingua franca.

After its northern start in Derry, the Wild Atlantic Way really begins to strut its stuff here as the county's untamed craggy coastline truly puts the wild into the way. So should you.

When to Go

➡ Donegal's wild and rough-hewn, but sublime, character is forged by its impetuous weather. In winter the howling winds and sheeting rain can feel Arctic, and brutal storms may arrive unannounced. You'll find a lot of accommodation options shut up shop for the cold months.

➡ In spring and summer, the clouds and short-lived bursts of rain regularly break into brilliant sunshine that transforms brooding pewter skies into brilliant blue and dapples Donegal in light of a quite beautiful quality. Because everything is open in summer, you'll also get the pick of traditional-music, storytelling and dance festivals that spring up across the county and even in pubs. The long summer nights can also see some of the most ravishing sunsets.

DONEGAL TOWN

POP 2600

Pretty, small and manageable, Donegal town occupies a photogenic spot at the mouth of Donegal Bay. With a backdrop of the Blue Stack Mountains, a handsome and well-preserved castle and a good choice of places to eat and sleep, it makes an excellent base for exploring the popular coastline nearby.

On the banks of the River Eske, Donegal town was a stamping ground of the O'Donnells, the great chieftains who ruled the northwest from the 15th to 17th centuries. Today, despite being the county's namesake, it's neither its largest town (the much larger Letterkenny), nor the county town (that's the even smaller town of Lifford).

◉ Sights & Activities

★**Donegal Castle** HISTORIC BUILDING
(☑074-972 2405; www.heritageireland.ie; Castle St; adult/child €5/3; ⊙10am-6pm daily Easter–mid-Sep, 9.30am-4.30pm Thu-Mon mid-Sep–Easter) Guarding a picturesque bend of the River Eske, well-preserved Donegal Castle is an imperious monument to both Irish and English might. Dating from the 15th century, the castle was rebuilt in 1623 by Sir Basil Brooke, along with the adjacent three-storey Jacobean house. Further restoration in the 1990s kicked things into shape; don't miss the truly magnificent upstairs Great Hall with its vast and ornate fireplace, French tapestries and Persian rugs. Afterwards corkscrew down the spiral staircase to the storeroom. There are guided tours every hour.

Built by the O'Donnells in 1474, it served as the seat of their formidable power until 1607, when the English decided to rid themselves of pesky Irish chieftains once and for all. Rory O'Donnell was no pushover, though, torching his own castle before fleeing to France in the infamous Flight of the Earls. Their defeat paved the way for the Plantation of Ulster by thousands of newly arrived Scots and English Protestants, sowing the seeds of the divisions that still afflict Ireland to this day.

As with virtually all OPW (Office of Public Works) heritage sites, admission is free on the first Wednesday of the month.

Diamond Obelisk MONUMENT
(The Diamond) In the early 17th century, four Franciscan friars, fearing that the arrival of the English meant the end of Celtic culture, chronicled the whole of known Celtic history and mythology. Starting 40 years before the biblical flood through AD 1618, *The Annals of the Four Masters* is one of the most important sources of early Irish history. The obelisk (1937), in The Diamond, commemorates the work; copies are displayed in the National Library in Dublin (p84).

★**Bank Walk** WALKING
(🚶) Follow this lovely flat trail along the west bank of the River Eske and Donegal Bay. The myriad trees offer shade and have labels as to their type; frequent benches allow you to pause and soak up the views. Look out for all the little fairy doors in the trees; there's even a post box for children to write letters to fairies. It's 1.5km each way and begins on the west side of the Killybeg Rd/N56 bridge.

Donegal Bay Waterbus BOATING
(☑074-972 3666; www.donegalbaywaterbus.com; Donegal Pier; adult/child €20/7; ⊙Easter-Oct) The most enjoyable way to explore the highlights of Donegal Bay is on a 1¼-hour boat tour taking in everything from historic sites to seal-inhabited coves, admiring an island manor and a ruined castle along the way. The tour runs up to three times daily; departure times change daily to match the tides.

Ted's Bike Shop CYCLING
(☑074-972 0774; off N56; rentals per day from €15; ⊙10am-6pm Mon-Sat) You can rent all types of bikes and get plenty of excellent advice at this bustling bike shop.

🛏 Sleeping

Good B&Bs and stolid hotels are plentiful around Donegal town; for high-end luxury head to nearby Lough Eske.

Donegal Town Independent Hostel HOSTEL €
(☑074-972 2805; www.donegaltownhostel.com; off Killybegs Rd (N56), Doonan; dm €17, d €38-42; @🛜) Run by an energetic couple, this IHH hostel 1.2km northwest of town has rooms with quirky murals – from technicolour landscapes to glow-in-the-dark night skies – and some have water views. It has 30 beds in female-only and mixed dorms.

★**Ard na Breatha** B&B €€
(☑074-972 2288; www.ardnabreatha.com; Drumrooske Middle; r €90-160; ⊙Feb-Oct; 🛜🐕) 🌱 In an elevated setting 1.5km north of town, this boutique guesthouse on a working farm has tasteful rooms with pine furniture and wrought-iron beds. The six rooms are in a building separate from the main house. It

County Donegal Highlights

1 Slieve League (p447) Watching the sun set from the top of the soaring sea cliffs.

2 Glenveagh Castle (p461) Touring this flamboyant castle in beautiful Glenveagh National Park.

3 Culdaff Beach (p469) Strolling along the windswept beach near Malin Head.

4 Glengesh Pass (p449) Pausing at the viewpoint before plunging down the switchbacks towards Ardara.

5 Poisoned Glen (p454) Taking in the views and abandoned church ruins of this spectacular glen.

6 Rossnowlagh (p442) Learning to surf on the white-sand beach.

7 Malin Head (p468) Looking seemingly forever out to sea.

8 Glencolumbcille (p446) Hill walking amid the dramatic landscapes and coastal vistas.

9 Maghera Strand (p448) Running your tootsies through the powdery sands.

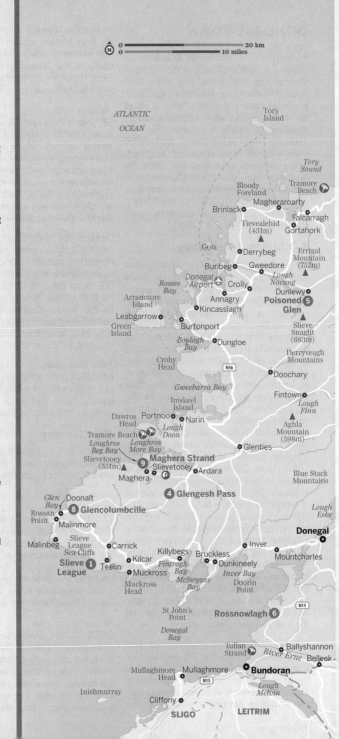

Donegal Town

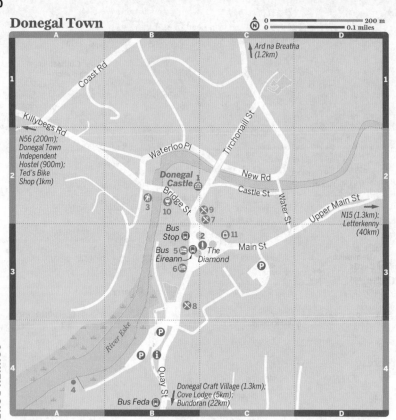

has a full bar and restaurant (three-course dinner €39) with organic food sourced from the farm or locally where possible. You must pre-book dinner.

Breakfasts are wholesome and filling and a good start to the Donegal day.

Central Hotel HOTEL €€
(☑ 074-972 1027; www.centralhoteldonegal.com; The Diamond; s/d from €62/100; 🕾🏊) Right at the heart of town, the Central is an adventure – no matter where your room is located in this rambling collection of buildings, you'll take a lift and wander up and down stairs to find it. Ask for a room with a view of the River Eske – the huge windows offer stunning panoramas. There's a pool and gym in the leisure centre.

Cove Lodge B&B €€
(☑ 074-972 2302; www.thecovelodgebandb.com; R267, Drumgowan; s €45-50, d €68-84 Apr-Oct; 🕾) You'll find subtle floral patterns and rustic

charm in the four ground-floor rooms of this tranquil and pretty stone and stucco B&B 2.5km south of town in a rural setting, offering a taste of Irish country living.

Abbey Hotel HOTEL €€
(☑ 074-972 1014; www.abbeyhoteldonegal.com; The Diamond; s/d from €70/110; 🕾) This serviceable option is on The Diamond, right at the heart of town, with 90 standard rooms. There's a lift for the three floors, and the bar and restaurant are solid. Guests can use the leisure centre at the Central Hotel.

🍴 Eating & Drinking

Look for the beers from local craft-brewer Donegal Brewing Co. Its North & South of the River bitter is a hoppy joy.

Aroma CAFE €
(☑ 074-972 3222; www.donegalcraftvillage.com; off R267, Donegal Craft Village; mains €5-13; ☉ 9.30am-5.30pm Mon-Sat) In the far corner

Donegal Town

◉ **Top Sights**
1 Donegal Castle B2

◉ **Sights**
2 Diamond Obelisk C3

◉ **Activities, Courses & Tours**
3 Bank Walk B2
4 Donegal Bay Waterbus A4

◉ **Sleeping**
5 Abbey Hotel B3
6 Central Hotel B3

◉ **Eating**
7 Blueberry Tearoom C2
8 Harbour Restaurant B3
9 Olde Castle Bar C2

◉ **Drinking & Nightlife**
10 Reel Inn B2

◉ **Shopping**
11 Magee's C3

of Donegal's craft village, this small cafe has a big, big reputation for fine food. Along with the excellent coffee and luscious cakes, the blackboard specials feature seasonal local produce whipped up into fine soups, salads and wholesome hot dishes as well as international fare. There's seating outside.

Blueberry Tearoom CAFE €
(☑074-972 2933; Castle St; mains €5-12; ⊙9am-7pm Mon-Sat; 🕾🍴) A perennial and cosy local favourite, this cafe serves simple, honest food in hearty portions as well as fine coffee. Expect soup, toasties, quiche, panini, sticky cakes of all descriptions and killer cheesecake.

★**Olde Castle Bar** IRISH €€
(☑074-972 1262; www.oldecastlebar.com; Castle St; mains €11-29; ⊙kitchen noon-9pm; 🍴) This ever-busy pub off the Diamond serves some of the area's best food. Look for classics such as Donegal Bay oysters or mussels, Irish stew and seafood platters (€28.95), plus steaks and burgers. The fish and chips we were served was enough for a family. The pub is always rollicking with locals and serves its own excellent pale ale: Red Hugh Brew.

Harbour Restaurant IRISH €€
(☑074-972 1702; www.theharbour.ie; Quay St; mains €10-30, early-bird set dinner 2/3 courses

€19/22; ⊙5-9pm Mon-Sat, to 10pm Fri & Sat, 3-9pm Sun; 🕾) Seafood gets the royal treatment at this popular local haunt, with its nautical theme, bare stone walls and plush furnishings. But the menu spans every Irish dinner classic as well as international staples such as pizza and knickerbocker glories. The early-bird set menu is available from 5pm to 7pm Monday to Saturday.

★**Reel Inn** PUB
(Bridge St; ⊙5pm-late) The best craic in town is invariably found at this old-school pub where the owner plays the button-box accordion, his wife has an amazing singing voice and pals join in traditional-music sessions most nights.

🛍 Shopping

★**Donegal Craft Village** ARTS & CRAFTS
(☑074-972 5928; www.donegalcraftvillage.com; off R267; ⊙10am-5pm Mon-Sat Apr-Sep, Tue-Sat Oct) You won't find any canned leprechauns or Guinness T-shirts here. Instead this huddle of craft studios showcases pottery, ironwork, handwoven fabrics, glasswork, jewellery and more. It's signposted 1.5km south of town and is an easy walk. There's a cracking cafe too, Aroma.

Magee's CLOTHING
(☑074-972 2660; www.magee1866.com; The Diamond; ⊙10am-6pm Mon-Sat, 2-6pm Sun) One room of this small, upmarket and historic department store is devoted to Donegal tweed, which has been produced here since 1866.

ℹ Information

The **tourist office** (☑074-972 1148; Quay St; ⊙9am-5.30pm Mon-Sat, 10am-3pm Sun Jun-Aug, 9am-5pm Mon-Sat Sep-May) is handily located in the Discover Ireland building by the waterfront.

ℹ Getting There & Away

Bus Éireann (☑074-913 1008; www.buseireann.ie) services connect Donegal with Sligo (€15, 1¼ hour, six daily), Galway (€21, four hours, four daily) and Dublin (€20, four hours, five daily).

Bus Feda (☑074-954 8114; www.busfeda.ie) serves Gweedore, Dunfanaghy and Letterkenny (all €10) two to three times daily.

Patrick Gallagher Coaches (☑087 233 0888; www.gallagherscoaches.com) runs daily buses between Donegal Town and Belfast (€20, two hours) and Derry.

The **bus stop** is on The Diamond.

AROUND DONEGAL TOWN

Lough Eske

An easy scenic diversion from Donegal Town, picturesque Lough Eske attracts hikers, cyclists, anglers and those in search of placid lake views.

The lake is only 9km from Donegal – a good bike ride away. Otherwise, if you've a car, it's a straightforward and very fast journey.

🛏 Sleeping

★ **Lough Eske Castle**　　　HOTEL €€€
(☑ 074-972 5100; www.solislougheskecastle.com; Lough Eske; r €180-280; ⊗ closed Sun-Wed Nov-Mar; @ 🛜 🏊 🐾) Occupying vast woodland and garden grounds at the lake's south end, this imposing and restored 19th-century castle was razed by fire in 1939 and is now the epitome of elegant country living. Most of the 96-room complex, including the spa and smart restaurant, exudes classic sophistication.

Arches Country House　　　B&B €
(☑ 074-972 2029; www.archescountryhse.com; Lough Eske; s/d from €55/70; 🛜) For a bucolic getaway in a tranquil spot overlooking Lough Eske from the east, this modern B&B has rooms that would please your dowager aunt, blending country-house charm and contemporary style. Noreen the owner is a fount of local knowledge.

Rossnowlagh

POP 50

Rossnowlagh's spectacular 3km-long Blue Flag beach is a broad, sandy stretch of heaven that attracts families, surfers, kitesurfers and walkers throughout the year. The gentle rollers are great for learning to surf or honing your skills. You can easily lose a few hours picnicking and lounging in the dunes.

Despite the small winter population, in summer the holiday homes fill up and numbers swell.

Rossnowlagh is 17km southwest of Donegal Town. The best way to get here is by car.

◉ Sights & Activities

Rossnowlagh Beach　　　BEACH
This stunner of a Blue Flag beach is the main draw in town, with the Atlantic surf rolling onto its broad expanse of sand. You can drive your car straight onto the beach as it is a public right of way (which does unfortunately mean that sometimes the beach resembles a vast car park).

Franciscan Friary　　　MONASTERY
(☑ 071-985 1342; www.franciscans.ie; off R231; ⊗ 11am-5.30pm Wed-Sat & Mon, to 8pm Tue, 11.45am-5.30pm Sun) FREE Hidden deep in a forest at the southern end of the beach, this modern friary was built in the early 1950s and is set in beautiful, tranquil gardens that are open to the public. The Way of the Cross – a religious walk with spectacular views – meanders up a hillside smothered in rhododendrons. The sense of quietude and calmness here is very endearing. There's a car park here too.

Fin McCool Surf School　　　SURFING
(☑ 071-985 9020; www.finmccoolsurfschool.com; Beach Rd; gear rental per day €39, 2hr lesson incl gear adult/child €35/25; ⊗ 10am-5pm Jun-Aug, 10am-5pm Sat & Sun Sep-May) Tuition, gear rental and accommodation are available at this surf lodge run by Pro Tour surf judge Neil Britton, with the help of his extended family, most of whom have competed on the international circuit.

Rossnowlagh SUP & Kayak　　　KAYAKING
(☑ 083 198 4288; www.rossnowlaghsupandpaddle.com; SUP lessons/tours from €35/20, kayak rental/tours from €20/35; ⊗ 10am-6pm Mon-Fri, 9am-8pm Sat, 11am-6pm Sun) Learn stand-up paddleboarding (SUP) or rent one with this busy outfit located near the beach, or rent a kayak. A wide variety of tours take in the many waterways in the estuaries as well as the waters off the beach; watch for full-moon tours.

🛏 Sleeping & Eating

Smugglers Creek　　　B&B €€
(☑ 071-985 2367; www.smugglerscreekinn.com; Cliff Rd; r €80-98, cottage per person from €45, mains €8-25; ⊗ daily Apr-Sep, Thu-Sun Oct-Mar; 🛜) This combined pub-restaurant-guesthouse perches on the hillside above the bay. It's justifiably popular for its excellent food and sweeping views (Room 4 has the best vantage point and a balcony). There's live music on summer weekends. Smugglers Creek also has a self-contained one-bedroom cottage behind the inn.

Gaslight Inn IRISH €€
(☑ 071-985 1141; www.gaslightinnrossnowlagh.
com; mains €8-35; ☺ 11am-late daily Jun-Sep,
5pm-late Fri, 11am-late Sat & Sun Oct-May) Set on
the clifftop, the Gaslight Inn offers an extensive menu of well-cooked comfort food
and spectacular views over the bay. The
owners also run the **Ard na Mara** (www.gas
lightinnrossnowlagh.com; s/d from €65/90; ☎)
guesthouse, which has five bright rooms.

Ballyshannon

POP 2550

Long a strategic spot for its position over-
looking the River Erne that flows in from
Lower Lough Erne in County Fermanagh,
Ballyshannon today has a role guarding
the northern approaches to Bundoran.
The town is perhaps most famous for be-
ing the birthplace of guitarist and singer
Rory Gallagher, a musician celebrated both
by a statue in the centre of town and by
the **Rory Gallagher International Tribute
Festival** (www.rorygallagherfestival.com; ☺ late
May).

This music festival celebrates native
son, rock and blues guitarist Rory Gallagher (1948–95), with more than two dozen
Irish and international artists and bands.
Gallagher's connection to his home town is
in evidence throughout the year and you'll
often hear his music playing in pubs.

Drinking

★ **Dicey Reillys Bar** PUB
(☑ 071-985 1371; www.diceys.com; Market St;
☺ noon-late) This old city-centre pub –
'Dicey's' to locals – stays vibrant through
constant reinvention, with a cocktail bar
upstairs offering stylish contrast to the old
pub downstairs, where on most nights it's
live rock and blues, and a Rory Gallagher
tune always seems to be the next song. Get
the good Donegal Brewing Co beers here.

Bundoran

POP 2200

Blinking amusement arcades, hurdy-gurdy
fairground rides and fast-food diners give
Bundoran the feel of a tacky beach town.
But Donegal's best-known seaside resort
has solid waves, and attracts a mixed crowd
of young families, pensioners and growing
legions of surfers. Outside summer, the carnival atmosphere abates and the town can
be a bit bleak.

◉ Sights & Activities

Surfing is big in Bundoran. The town has
several surf schools, each of which rents
out gear and has its own basic hostel-style
accommodation. All offer deals on surf and
accommodation packages.

Tullan Strand BEACH
The long strand of surfing beach has a
bountiful supply of that gorgeous trademark fine white sand that much of Ireland
is famed for. There are rip tides, so swimming can be risky, but the views are stunning and the surfing here is grade A. It's
north of the town centre.

Peak SURFING
The Peak, an imposing reef break directly
in front of the town, is one of Bundoran's
two main surf spots. It should only be attempted by experienced surfers. There is
a less formidable beach break at Tullan
Strand, just north of the town centre.

Bundoran Surf Co SURFING
(☑ 071-984 1968; www.bundoransurfco.com;
Main St; adult/child surf lessons from €35/25,
full surf-gear rental per day from €20) Bundoran
Surf Co conducts surf, kitesurfing and
stand-up paddleboarding lessons. Gear
rental includes board and wetsuit, plus
boots, gloves and hood in winter.

Waterworld SWIMMING
(☑ 071-984 1172; www.waterworldbundoran.com;
The Promenade; adult/child €13/10, seaweed
bath €25; ☺ 10am-7pm daily Jun-Aug, noon-6pm
Sat & Sun mid-Apr–May & Sep, seaweed baths
noon-7pm Jun-Aug) This aesthetically challenged amusement park is right on the waterfront, with wave pools and water slides.
For a sedate soak, try a seaweed bath.

**Donegal Adventure
Centre** ADVENTURE SPORTS
(☑ 071-984 2418; www.donegaladventurecentre.
net; Bayview Ave; adult/child surf lesson from
€35/30) Offers adventure-sports activities
on land and sea, including kayaking and
surfing, plus climbing.

Bike Stop CYCLING
(☑ 085 248 8317; East End; per half-day/day/week
€10/15/60; ☺ 8.30am-6pm Mon-Sat, noon-4pm
Sun) Rents out a range of bikes including
good-quality hybrids.

✦ Festivals & Events

Sea Sessions · MUSIC
(www.seasessions.com; ⊙ mid-Jun) The Sea Sessions festival – three days of surfing, skating, music and partying – kicks off the summer season, as thousands of attendees camp in fields around town.

Irish National Surfing Championships · SURFING
(www.irishsurfing.ie; ⊙ late Apr) Bundoran hosts the annual Irish National Surfing Championships, usually held in April although they have also been held in September.

🍴 Sleeping & Eating

Bundoran has a decent choice of hostels – nonsurfers are welcome at all the surf-school lodges, which usually charge about €20 for a dorm bed and €50 for a double. Scores of humble B&Bs line the access roads from the N15, so you'll always find somewhere to stay.

Killavil House · B&B €
(🖉 071-984 1556; www.killavilhouse.com; Finner Rd; s €40-50, d €70; 🛜) A big modern villa at the Ballyshannon end of town, Killavil has smartly appointed bedrooms with polished wooden furniture. Most have multiple beds and are suitable for families. There's a garden with a seating area for summer evenings, and Tullan Strand is just a five-minute walk away.

Maddens Bridge Bar · PUB FOOD €€
(🖉 071-984 2050; www.maddensbridgebar.com; Main St; mains €10-22.50, r €60-90; ⊙ kitchen 8am-9pm, pub till late) This surfers' hang-out manages a bit of minimalist style and packs a decent menu of classic pub grub with mighty fine burgers and fish and chips. There's a trad session on Thursdays (more in summer), with terrific craic guaranteed. It's located right at its namesake bridge and some of the simple rooms open to great views.

ℹ Information

Bundoran centres on one long main street just back from the beach. The **tourist office** (🖉 071-984 1350; Main St, The Bridge; ⊙ 9am-3.30pm Mon-Fri, hours vary Sat & Sun Apr-Sep) is a glass-paned kiosk opposite the Holyrood Hotel.

ℹ Getting There & Away

Bus Éireann (🖉 in Letterkenny 074-912 1309; www.buseireann.ie) buses stop on Main St on their runs between Donegal (€9, 30 minutes) and Sligo (€11, 45 minutes), passing through Ballyshannon on their way north.

SOUTHWESTERN DONEGAL

Mountcharles
POP 500

The hillside village of Mountcharles is the first settlement along the coastal road (N56) west of Donegal Town; in fact you'll barely have the speedometer turning when, bam, you're in Mountcharles.

About 2km south of the village is a safe, sandy **beach**. The shiny, green **pump** at the top of this hillside village is the point where five roads intersect and it was once the backdrop for stories of fairies, ghosts, historic battles and mythological encounters. It was here that native poet and *seanachaí* (traditional storyteller) Séamus MacManus practised the ancient art in the 1940s and '50s.

Visit Mountcharles community website (www.mountcharlescommunity.ie) for local information.

Salthill Gardens · GARDENS
(🖉 074-973 5387; www.donegalgardens.com; Pier Rd; adult/child €5/2; ⊙ 2-6pm Mon-Sat May-Aug, Mon-Thu Sep) Behind century-old stone walls, the lovely contemporary garden design of Salthill Gardens bursts with perennials, roses, lilies and clematis. It's 2km southwest of the village, towards the coast.

Village Tavern · SEAFOOD €€
(🖉 074-973 5622; www.villagetavern.ie; Main St; mains €15-26; ⊙ kitchen noon-8pm May-Sep, pub noon-late year-round) In a handsome late-18th-century building, this welcoming pub specialises in seafood brought to shore at the pier just down the road. The chowder is excellent and the seafood tasting board groans with whatever is fresh and best. The drinks menu is rounded out with craft beer, including Devil's Backbone and Scraggy Bay.

Dunkineely
POP 370

Views out to sea tantalise from the series of small villages along the N56. A scenic and very worthwhile journey heads down the lengthy finger of land from the N56 and Dunkineely to St John's Point.

Slightly further on along the N56, you'll pass the small town of Bruckless, with its attractive – although not ancient – round tower.

🛏 Sleeping & Eating

⭐ Castle Murray · BOUTIQUE HOTEL €€

(📞074-973 7022; www.castlemurray.com; St
John's Point; s/d from €90/120, set menu €41;
⊙restaurant 6.30-9pm Mon-Sat, 1-3pm & 6.30-
9pm Sun Jul & Aug, 6.30-9pm Wed-Sat, 1-3pm &
6.30-9pm Sep-Nov & Apr-Jun, hotel & restaurant
closed Dec-Mar; 🐾) Overlooking the ruins of
the 15th-century McSwyne's Castle, Castle
Murray is not a castle, but a boutique hotel
in a sprawling modern beach house. Most of
the 10 guest rooms have fine sea and castle
views. It's 1.5km south of Dunkineely on a
minor road leading down the long, narrow
strip of land to St John's Point.

The fine French restaurant, with its signature prawns and monkfish in garlic butter,
is a big draw.

Killybegs

POP 1300

The smell of fish and the caw of seagulls
waft from the ranks of giant trawlers and
vessels moored in Ireland's largest fishing
port. Inland the village bustles with the atmosphere of a charming working town.

⦿ Sights & Activities

Fintragh Bay · BEACH

(off R263) The best beach in the Killybegs
area is at secluded Fintragh Bay, about 3km
west of town, a gorgeous stunner of a beach
and a must-see. Go down the steps from the
car park and head round to the right to find
a lovely cave, full of pebbles, large stones
and great photo ops.

Killybegs International Carpet
Making & Fishing Centre · MUSEUM

(📞074-974 1944; www.visitkillybegs.com; Fintra
Rd; adult/child €5/4; ⊙9.45am-5.30pm Mon-Fri
Apr-Oct, to 5pm Nov-Mar) The former factory of
Donegal Carpets provides a good overview
of the town's history. The fun wheelhouse
simulator lets you 'steer' a fishing trawler
into the harbour. Don't expect to see any
carpets being made as the cost to do so is
now 'astronomical', they say.

Killybegs Angling Charters · FISHING

(📞087 220 0982; www.killybegsangling.com;
Blackrock Pier; half-day charter from €300) If
you're interested in taking to the water to
catch pollack, ling, brill, mackerel or turbot,
Brian McGilloway has more than 30 years of
experience in charter angling.

🛏 Sleeping & Eating

Drumbeagh House · B&B €

(📞074-973 1307; www.killybegsbnb.biz.ly; Con-
lin Rd; s/d from €50/70; 🐾) Accommodating
hosts with plenty of local knowledge make
this small B&B a great find. The cosy rooms
are tastefully decorated in neutral colours
and the breakfast of locally smoked salmon
is worth the trip alone. Great harbour views;
it's a five-minute walk from the centre.

Ritz · HOSTEL €

(📞074-973 1309; www.theritz-killybegs.com; Chapel Brae; dm €20, r from €55; 🐾) The name might
be ironic and this isn't Piccadilly, but this superbly run 38-bed hostel in the town centre
has ritzy facilities, including an enormous
kitchen, colourful rooms with private bathroom and TVs, and a laundry.

Tara Hotel · HOTEL €€

(📞074-974 1700; www.tarahotel.ie; Main St; s/d from
€65/120; 🅿🐾) This modern hotel across from
and overlooking the harbour has 32 comfortable, minimalist rooms, a decent bar and a
small gym with spa bath, sauna and steam
room. Not all rooms come with sea views.

The Pod · CAFE €

(www.facebook.com/thepodpopup/; Largy Viewpoint; snacks from €1; ⊙10am-6pm) Enterpris-
ing Nuala serves up some fine coffee and
baked goodies from her super-shiny, tear-
drop-shaped mobile Pod that pulls into the
Largy Viewpoint in between Killybegs and
Kilcar. Have a shot of caffeine to go with the
killer views. The Pod is out at Largy Viewpoint all year round, weather permitting.

Kitty Kelly's · MODERN IRISH €€

(📞074-973 1925; www.kittykellys.com; off R263,
Largy; dinner mains €17-25; ⊙12.30-3pm & 6.30-
9.30pm Mon-Sat, 1.30-3.30pm Sun Jun-Sep, closed
Mon & Tue Oct-May, closed Jan) Dining at this
restaurant in a 200-year-old farmhouse
feels more like attending an intimate dinner
party. The menu is a modern take on Irish
favourites with an emphasis on seafood. It's
on the coast road, 5km west of Killybegs just
beyond the Largy Viewpoint at the bend in
the road – you can't miss the lurid pink-and-
green paint job. Bookings are essential.

Ahoy Cafe · CAFE €

(📞074-973 1952; Shore Rd; sandwiches €6-7;
⊙9am-5pm) This new cafe slightly out of the
centre of things along Shore Rd does, among
other things, a fine seafood chowder, fish
pie, blueberry scones and excellent coffee,
plus tasty pancakes and breakfasts.

ℹ Information

There are no ATMs west of Killybegs.

Killybegs Information Centre (☑ 074-973 2346; www.killybegs.ie; Shore Rd; ⊗ 9.30am-5.30pm Mon-Fri year-round, plus noon-4pm Sat & Sun Jul & Aug) is in a trailer just west of the harbour.

ℹ Getting There & Away

Bus Éireann (p444) buses from Donegal Town (€9, 30 minutes) run several times daily.

Kilcar, Teelin & Carrick

Kilcar (Cill Chártha) and its more attractive neighbour Teelin (Teileann) make good bases for exploring the breathtaking coastline of southwestern Donegal, especially the stunning sea cliffs at Slieve League. Inland, Carrick (An Charraig) is also appealing.

This is fantastic walking country, particularly if you find the prospect of a few hills bracing. Just outside Kilcar is a small, sandy beach.

◉ Sights & Activities

Studio Donegal   MUSEUM
(☑ 074-973 8194; www.studiodonegal.ie; Glebe Mill, Kilcar; ⊗ 9am-5.30pm Mon-Fri year-round, 9.30am-5pm Sat May-Oct) **FREE** Though mechanised in the 1960s, there has been a hand-weaving tweed mill here for more than a century. Visitors are often invited upstairs to see spinners and weavers in action, before browsing jackets, hats, throws and other tweed items in the shop.

Nuala Star Teelin   BOATING
(☑ 074-973 9365; www.sliabhleagueboattrips.com; Teelin Pier; tours €20-25; ⊗ Apr-Oct) Sightseeing boat trips along the Slieve League cliffs can be spectacular. Tours often spot dolphins and seals and sometimes whales and basking sharks as well. There are up to six sailings per day. You can also go for a dip in the sea. Private trips and angling journeys are also available.

🛏 Sleeping & Eating

Derrylahan Independent Hostel   HOSTEL €
(☑ 074-973 8079; http://homepage.eircom. net/~derrylahan; Derrylahan, Kilcar; campsites per person €8, dm €16-18, d €50; @ 🔊) This rustic, well-run IHH hostel is set on a hilly, windy and dramatic site on a working farm. It has 32 beds in 10 comfortable rooms with private bathrooms, plus plenty of scenic spots to pitch a tent. Book ahead for bike rental (€20). Located 3km west of Kilcar on the coast road. Pick-ups can be arranged. Booking essential between November and February.

Inishduff House   B&B €€
(☑ 074-973 8542; www.inishduffhouse.com; off R263, Largy, Kilcar; s/d €50/85; 🔊) About 5km east of Kilcar, this modern B&B run by Ethna has large, comfortable rooms, a varied breakfast menu and supreme sea views. The mood matches the sunny hues of the exterior.

Ti Linn Cafe   IRISH €
(☑ 074-973 9077; Teelin; mains €4-8; ⊗ 10.30am-5.30pm daily Easter-Sep, Fri-Tue Feb-Easter & Oct-Nov; 🔊) This artisan cafe and crafts gallery in the Slieve League Cliffs Centre has excellent coffee. It has fine baked goods, sandwiches and hot lunches too.

Rusty   PUB
(☑ 074-973 9101; www.therusty.info; Teelin; mains from €5; ⊗ 10.30am-11.30pm daily May-Sep, shorter hours Oct-Apr) A great pub – also called the Rusty Mackerel – with trad music many nights in summer, plus a simple menu of bar food. It's near the junction of the road to Slieve League.

ℹ Information

Áislann Chill Chartha (☑ 074-973 8376; www. aislann.ie; Main St, Kilcar; ⊗ 9am-10pm Mon-Fri, 10am-6pm Sat) A community centre with information for tourists.

Slieve League Cliffs Centre (☑ 074-973 9077; Teelin; ⊗ 10.30am-5.30pm daily Easter-Sep, Fri-Tue Feb-Easter & Oct-Nov; 🔊) Local information is available at the excellent cultural centre in Teelin (Tí Linn), which also has an artisan cafe. The centre runs archaeology and hillwalking courses. It's on the road to Slieve League.

ℹ Getting There & Away

Bus Éireann services run from Donegal Town to Kilcar (€10) and Carrick (€12) one to three times daily. The best way to tackle the region is, of course, by car – so you can drive up to Slieve League.

Glencolumbcille

POP 270

Once you've sampled Glencolumbcille's tiny village, scalloped beaches, stunning walks and fine little folk museum, the chances are you'll disagree with locals who claim there's little to do here.

SLIEVE LEAGUE

The Cliffs of Moher get more publicity, but the cliffs of **Slieve League** are higher (and free). In fact, these spectacular sea cliffs are among the highest in Europe, plunging some 600m to the ceaselessly churning sea.

From Teelin, a road through the stark landscape leads to the lower car park (with hiking signs) beside a gate in the road; you can drive another 1.5km to the upper car park (often full in summer) right beside the viewpoint (close the gate though).

From the upper car park, a roughfootpath leads up and along the top of the near-vertical cliffs to the aptly named **One Man's Pass**, a narrow ridge that reaches the summit of Slieve League (595m; 10km round-trip). Be aware that mist and rain can roll in unexpectedly and rapidly, making conditions slippery and treacherous. Be especially careful near the edge of the cliffs. Walking just the first 500m will give you spectacular views.

It's also possible to hike to the summit of Slieve League from Carrick via the **Pilgrim Path** (signposted along the minor road on the right before the Slieve League cliffs road), returning via One Man's Pass and the viewpoint road (12km; allow four to six hours).

The cliffs are particularly scenic at sunset when the waves crash dramatically far below and the ocean reflects the last rays of the day. Looking down, you'll see two rocks nicknamed the 'giant's desk and chair' for reasons that are immediately obvious.

Approaching Glencolumbcille (Gleann Cholm Cille) via the Glengesh Pass does, however, reinforce just how isolated this starkly beautiful coastal haven is. You drive past miles and miles of hills and bogs before the ocean appears, followed by a narrow, green valley and the small Gaeltacht village within it.

The Glencolumbcille website (www.glencolmcille.ie) has reams of information on the village, local history and activities.

History

This spot has been inhabited since 3000 BC and lots of Stone Age remains are scattered among the cluster of tiny settlements.

It's believed that the 6th-century St Colmcille (Columba) founded a monastery here (hence the name, meaning 'Glen of Columba's Church'), and incorporated Stone Age standing stones into Christian use by inscribing them with a cross. At midnight on Columba's Feast Day (9 June), penitents perform An Turas Cholm Chille (the Gaelic 'turas' meaning a pilgrimage or journey), a walking circuit of the stones and the remains of Cholm Cille's chapel, before attending Mass at 3am in the local chapel.

Sights

⭐ Malinbeg Beach   BEACH

At Malinbeg you'll find this sheltered bay bitten out of low cliffs, with 60 steps descending to a gorgeous little sandy beach. It's 6km past the folk village. You may find it deserted.

⭐ Doonalt Beach   BEACH

This lovely sandy beach with brisk waves is in Doonalt, immediately west of the village; access is from the car park opposite the folk museum.

Glencolmcille Folk Village   MUSEUM

(Father McDyer's Folk Village; www.glenfolkvillage.com; Doonalt; adult/child €5.50/2.50; ⊙10am-6pm Mon-Sat, noon-6pm Sun Easter-Sep, to 5pm Oct) A museum with a mission, this folk centre was established by the forward-thinking Father James McDyer in 1967 to freeze-frame traditional folk life for posterity. It's housed in a huddle of thatched white cottages re-created in 18th- and 19th-century style, with genuine period fittings. There's a small school and the *shebeen* (illicit drinking place) sells unusual local wines (made from ingredients such as seaweed and fuchsias).

It's 3km west of the village, by the beach.

Look out for the small stone sweat house, where the ill were cured by sweating illnesses out. Grab an information leaflet from the craft shop at the entrance.

Activities

The 19th-century St Columba's Church is the starting point for several excellent walks; see www.glencolmcille.ie for details. The 5.5km pilgrimage route of **An Turas Cholm Cille** (www.glencolmcille.ie/turas.htm) visits a series of prehistoric stone slabs, many carved with early Christian symbols, and an ancient ruined chapel attributed to the saint. Local landowners grant permission for walkers to visit all the stones on Sundays from June to August (some are accessible year-round).

A couple of waymarked loop walks will lead you into the blustery wilds beyond the town. The Tower Loop (10km, two to three hours) heads north to a signal tower atop stunning coastal cliffs, while the more arduous Drum Loop (13km, three to four hours) heads into the hills northeast of the town.

Oideas Gael   CULTURE
(☑074-973 0248; www.oideas-gael.com; 3-/7-day courses from €100/220; ⊙mid-Mar–Oct) The Foras Cultúir Uladh (Ulster Cultural Foundation), 1km west of the village centre, offers a range of cultural-activity holidays – adult courses in Irish language and traditional culture, including dancing, painting and musical instruments. The centre also leads hill-walking programs. Accommodation can be arranged – either homestay or self-catering – at around €30 per person per night.

🛌 Sleeping & Eating

Dooey Hostel   HOSTEL €
(☑074-973 0130; www.independenthostelsireland.com; Dooey; campsites per person €10, dm/d €16/32) You may find yourself serenaded by a local lass and a guitar as you pull into this hostel with a corridor carved out of a plant-strewn rock face. It has astonishing views of the ocean and hills below. Facilities are rustic, but clean and comfortable, and the campsite's a beauty. If driving, turn left just after the Glenhead Tavern and continue for 1.5km; walkers can hike up a path behind the folk village. Cash only.

Áras Ghlean Cholm Cille   B&B €
(☑074-973 0077; www.arasgcc.com; Malinmore; r from €18; 🛜) This large place in nearby and very quiet Malinmore is a good choice, with a large variety of rooms from small but serviceable singles to larger doubles, twins and triples. A shuttle service to local pubs is also offered. There's a large kitchen and lounge and breakfast is an extra €5. If you fancy a kick-around, there's a small goal post on the large front lawn.

Malinbeg Hostel   HOSTEL €
(☑074-973 0006; www.malinbeghostel.com; Malinbeg; dm/d from €15/38; ⊙closed Dec–mid-Jan) Flung out on a remote stretch of coast near Silver Strand beach, the Malinbeg Hostel is the place for simplicity and total seclusion (and no wi-fi).

An Chistin   CAFE €€
(☑074-973 0213; R263; mains from €12; ⊙noon-8pm Mon, 3-8pm Thu, 12.30-8pm Fri & Sun, 2-8.45pm Sat Apr-Aug) This fine and welcoming cafe is pretty much the cooking hub of the village, preparing some splendid Donegal fare, from the scrummy and mussel-rich Atlantic seafood chowder (€7) to herb-crusted salmon (€16) and boneless roast duck (€16).

🛍 Shopping

Glencolmcille Woollen Mill   CLOTHING
(☑074-973 0069; www.rossanknitwear.ie; Malinmore; ⊙10am-8pm Mar-Oct, to 5.30pm Nov-Feb) This is a great place to shop for Donegal tweed jackets, caps, ties, and lambswool scarves and shawls. You can sometimes see weavers in action. It's about 5km southwest of Glencolumbcille, in Malinmore.

ℹ Getting There & Away

Bus Éireann (p444) runs to/from Killybegs (€9, 45 minutes) one to two times a day, the route ends at Glencolumbcille.

Maghera Strand & Glengesh Pass

On the northern coast of the Glencolumbcille peninsula, 9km west of Ardara, tiny Maghera has a stunning and wide, wide beach – one of the most beautiful in Ireland. If you follow the strand westward, you'll reach a rocky promontory full of caves(inaccessible at high tide). Time a visit for sunset to immerse yourself in the full magic of the beach.

Heading south from Ardara, take the second turning and look for the small hand-painted sign to 'Maghera'. If you take the first turning by mistake, you won't pass the waterfall and you'll find yourself on the wrong side and unable to get down to the beach.

👁 Sights

⭐ Maghera Strand   BEACH
This astonishing beach is a dream come true, especially if you are rewarded with a gorgeous sunset. Get here during lowish tide to explore the caves in the south end, where some spectacular geology awaits. If you get clear skies, the sun dipping into the Atlantic is one of Ireland's most treasured and priceless experiences. During

Cromwell's 17th-century destruction, 100 villagers sought refuge here but all except one were discovered and massacred.

There's a car park outside a farm just before the dunes that lead to the beach. You'll need to walk through a metal gate – remember to shut it after you.

Assarancagh Waterfall
WATERFALL

Also called Maghera Waterfall, these slender falls are a worthwhile stop on the way to Maghera Strand. There's a small makeshift shrine to the left of the waterfall.

★ Glengesh Pass
VIEWPOINT

On a narrow road from Glencolumbcille to Ardara, past remote mountain bogland, this magnificent and sublime pass, scoured out aeons ago by implacably vast glacial forces, is approached down several switchbacks that lead towards thatched cottages and a swath of pastoral beauty. There are spots and visitor viewpoints where you can pull over and take in the whole epic scenario before you.

Ardara

POP 740

Gateway to the switchbacks of the Glengesh Pass, the heritage town of Ardara (pronounced arda-rah; Ard an Rátha in Irish, meaning 'Height of the Fort') is the heart of Donegal's tweed and knitwear industry. You can visit the weavers at work and see the region's most traditional crafts in action.

The stand out sight, however, is the lovely drive down to nearby stunning Maghera Strand, past the stunning Assarancagh Waterfall.

A fantastically remote, 25km single-track road leads from Glencolumbcille to Ardara via the stark and awesome Glengesh Pass (Glean Géis; meaning 'Glen of the Swans'; p449), one of Donegal's most scenic driving routes.

◉ Sights & Activities

Ardara Heritage Centre
MUSEUM

(☑ 087 286 8657; Main St; ⊗ usually 10am-5pm Mon-Fri, 11am-4pm Sat Easter-Sep) FREE Set in the old town courthouse, this volunteer-run centre traces the story of Donegal tweed, from sheep shearing to dye production and weaving.

Don Byrne
CYCLING

(☑ 074-954 1658; http://donbyrnebikes.com; West End; bike rental per day from €17, hybrid per week €80; ⊗ 10am-6pm Tue-Sat) This bike shop has a wide selection and offers good advice on routes.

🎪 Festivals & Events

Cup of Tae Festival
MUSIC

(☑ 087 242 4590; www.cupoftaefestival.com; adult/child lessons from €50; ⊗ early May) Dancing, storytelling and a school of music are part of the trad-music Cup of Tae Festival. The small-scale but very worthwhile festival takes its name from a local musician, John 'the tae' Gallagher. Free live music fills the pubs.

🛏 Sleeping & Eating

Gort na Móna
B&B €

(☑ 074-953 7777; www.gortnamonabandb.com; Donegal Rd, Cronkeerin; s/d from €45/70; 🛜) The fine mountain views and large but cosy and colourful rooms make this a real home away from home, and breakfast includes preserves made from home-grown strawberries. It's 2km southeast of town on the old Donegal road.

Bayview Country House
B&B €

(☑ 074-954 1145; www.bayviewcountryhouse.com; R261; s/d from €50/76; ⊗ Apr–mid-Oct; 🛜) Just 800m north of town and overlooking the bay, this purpose-built B&B has spacious rooms with pretty floral bedspreads, spotless bathrooms and great views. There's a wood fire, homemade bread and scones, and a genuinely warm welcome for visitors.

★ Woodhill House
HOTEL €€

(☑ 074-954 1112; www.woodhillhouse.com; Woodhill; s/d from €69/100, set 3-course dinner €42.50; ⊗ dinner 5-9pm; 🛜) Ireland's last commercial whaling family once lived in this grand manor house, parts of which date from the 17th century. With 10 comfortable rooms and gardens, it's just 300m east of the town centre; the hotel is popular for its three-course Irish dinners. The bar has a great beer selection.

★ Nancy's Bar
IRISH €

(☑ 074-954 1187; www.nancysardara.com; Front St; mains €7-15; ⊗ kitchen noon-9pm daily Mar-Oct, Sat & Sun Nov-Feb; 🛜♿) This old-fashioned pub-restaurant, in the same family for seven generations, is one of the best local spots for trad-music sessions. It serves superb seafood and chowder and is also the best place in town for a sociable pint or two.

★ **West End Cafe** IRISH €

(☑ 074-954 1656; Main St; mains from €5; ☺ 1-11.30pm) Long known as 'Whyte's' and stuffed with locals, this curtained cafe run by ever-diligent Philomena is beloved for its superfresh fish and chips, but there's also sandwiches, hot specials and super-duper service. The coffee comes in a pot that goes on forever.

🍸 Drinking & Nightlife

Many of the town's pubs, such as Nancy's Bar, host regular traditional-music sessions; just stroll down the main drag until you hear the good cheer pouring out the door.

Corner House PUB

(☑ 074-954 1736; The Diamond; ☺ 3pm-late Sun-Thu, from noon Sat & Sun) This is a good spot to listen to an Irish-music session (Friday and Saturday year-round; nightly from June to September). It's the type of place where someone will spontaneously break into song and, if the mood is right, the rest of the pub joins in.

🛍 Shopping

Ardara has a bevy of knitwear vendors and producers, with traditional sweaters to keep out the Atlantic winds starting from around €60.

★ **Eddie Doherty** CLOTHING

(☑ 074-954 1304; www.handwoventweed.com; Main St; ☺ 10am-6pm Mon-Sat, sometimes Sun) You can usually catch Eddie Doherty hand-weaving here on a traditional loom. He'll cheerfully explain every step of the process.

John Molloy CLOTHING

(☑ 074-954 1133; www.johnmolloy.com; Killybegs Rd; ☺ 9am-6pm) Handmade and machine-knitted woollies are available here at the flagship establishment.

Kennedy's CLOTHING

(☑ 074-954 1106; www.kennedyirishsweaters.com; Front St; ☺ 9am-6pm) In business for more than a century, Kennedy's helped establish Ardara's reputation as a sweater mecca.

ⓘ Information

The volunteer-run **tourist office** (☑ 074-954 1704; www.ardara.ie; Main St, Ardara Heritage Centre; ☺ 10am-6pm Mon-Fri, 11am-4pm Sat Mar-Oct) has lots of good info including a walking-tour map, even if no one is around. The website has reams of local information.

On The Diamond, the Ulster Bank has an ATM; the post office is nearby on Main St.

ⓘ Getting There & Away

Bus Éireann (p444) services from Donegal (€10, 25 minutes) stop outside the Heritage Centre in Ardara two to three times per day en route to Glenties.

Loughrea Peninsula

The twin settlements of Narin and Portnoo nestle at the western end of a gorgeous wishbone-shaped Blue Flag Portnoo beach. In the southwest corner of the peninsula, hemmed in by grassy dunes, is the beautiful Tramore Beach.

◉ Sights

Tramore Beach BEACH

(ℙ) In 1588 part of the Spanish Armada ran aground by lovely Tramore Beach. The survivors temporarily occupied O'Boyle's Island in Kiltoorish Lake, but then marched to Killybegs, where they set sail again in the *Girona*. The *Girona* met a similar fate that same year in Northern Ireland, with the loss of more than 1000 crew members.

★ **Iniskeel Island** ISLAND

You can walk out to this tiny island at low tide from the sandy tip of the Blue Flag beach between Narin and Portnoo. St Connell, a cousin of St Colmcille (Columba), founded a monastery here in the 6th century and the island is studded with early-medieval Christian remains, including two ruined churches and some decorated grave slabs.

Dolmen Ecocentre ARCHAEOLOGICAL SITE

(☑ 074-954 5010; www.dolmencentre.com; R261, Kilclooney; ☺ 9am-5pm Mon-Fri) Learn about several local prehistoric sites, including the grand **Kilclooney More Court Tomb**, as well as a tortoise-like passage tomb a short walk up a track, to the left of the church.

⌂ Sleeping

★ **Carnaween House** B&B €€

(☑ 074-954 5122; www.carnaweenhouse.com; Narin; s/d €60/120, cottage from €210, mains €15-25; ☺ kitchen 6-9pm Thu-Sun, 1-4pm Sun Jun-Sep, shorter hours Oct-May; ☎) Carnaween House glows with brilliant white bedrooms in a luxury beach-house style – indeed, the sands on the adjoining beach are *almost* as white. The restaurant serves modern Irish fare, with an emphasis on seafood and pasta. Book a window table and thrill to sunset views.

DONEGAL'S ONLY RAILWAY

Today, Donegal's only operational railway is the **Fintown Railway** (☎ 074-954 6280; www.antraen.com; off R250, Fintown; adult/child €8/5; ☉ 11am-4pm Mon-Sat, 1-5pm Sun Jun–mid-Sep). Lovingly restored to its original condition, the red-and-white 1940s diesel rail-car runs along a rebuilt 5km section of the former County Donegal Railway track along picturesque Lough Finn. The return trip, which includes commentary, takes around 40 minutes. Fintown is 20km northeast of Glenties.

When the first spluttering steam engine arrived in Donegal in 1895, the locals dubbed the belching creature the Black Pig. The railways gave Donegal's isolated communities a new lease of life and a much-needed connection to the rest of the country. Over 300km of narrow-gauge tracks crossed the county in the railway's heyday, but after WWII business declined and the railway closed to passengers in June 1947, and to freight in 1952.

Glenties

POP 800

At the foot of two valleys with a southern backdrop laid on by the Blue Stack Mountains, the proud Tidy Town of Glenties (Na Gleannta) is a good spot for fishing and has some cracking walks in the surrounding countryside. Glenties is linked with playwright Brian Friel, whose play about five unmarried sisters in 1930s Ireland, *Dancing at Lughnasa*, is set in the town (it was later made into a 1998 film with Meryl Streep).

St Connell's Museum & Heritage Centre
MUSEUM

(☎ 087-292 1016; www.glentiesheritagemuseum.com; Mill Rd; adult/child €3/1; ☉ 10am-1pm & 1.30-6pm May-Sep) Next to the courthouse, this informative little museum has a wealth of exhibits on local history over several floors and doubles as an info centre and cafe.

Brennan's B&B
B&B €€

(☎ 074-955 1235; www.brennansbnb.com; Main St; s/d from €50/80, apt €150; ☎☀) The welcome is genuinely warm at this B&B run by Kathleen and Francis. Its three comfy guest rooms are lovingly tended to, and it's handily situated at the southern end of the main drag among a crop of pubs and shops.

NORTHWESTERN DONEGAL

Few places in Ireland are more savagely beautiful than Northwestern Donegal. The rocky Gaeltacht area between Dungloe and Crolly is known as the Rosses (Na Rossa), and is scattered with shimmering lakes, grey-pink granite outcrops and golden-sand beaches pounded by Atlantic surf. Further north, between Bunbeg and Gortahork, the scenery is spoiled a little by the uncontrolled sprawl of holiday homes. Offshore, the islands of Arranmore and Tory are fascinating to those eager for a glimpse of a more traditional way of life.

Dungloe

POP 4100

The hub of the Rosses, Dungloe (An Clochán Liath) is a busy if unprepossessing little town with ample services for anyone passing along the spectacular coastal route.

◉ Sights & Activities

Daniel O'Donnell Visitor Centre
VISITOR CENTRE

(☎ 074-952 2334; www.danielodonnellvisitorcentre.com; Main St; €5; ☉ 10am-6pm Mon-Sat, 11am-6pm Sun) Singer and local-boy-made-good Daniel O'Donnell is celebrated in this shrine-like museum ('There's his wedding suit!'). The hugely popular 'Wee Daniel' is beloved for his Irish folk and country music and his hits include 'My Donegal Shore'.

Charlie Bonner's Tackle Shop
FISHING

(☎ 074-952 1163; The Bridge; ☉ 10am-6pm Mon-Sat) Fishing for trout in the River Dungloe and Lough Dungloe is popular; get tackle and permits or hire a guide from helpful Bonner's.

✵ Festivals and Events

Mary From Dungloe Festival
MUSIC

(☎ 087-449 1144; www.maryfromdungloe.com; ☉ late Jul-early Aug) Each year in summer, Dungloe hosts the 10-day Mary from Dungloe Festival, during which a 'new Mary' is crowned, keeping the flame alive after all these years. A number-one pop song from the late 1960s,

'Mary from Dungloe', by Emmet Spiceland, helped put this little pit stop on the map.

🛌 Sleeping

Radharc an Oileain   B&B €
(☑ 074-952 1093; www.dungloebedandbreakfast. com; Quay Rd; s/d from €45/75; ⊘ Apr-Nov; 🛜) This tidy and charming little family-run B&B with a position by the bay has rooms with plenty of brocade and other satiny details. It's down a small lane off Quay Rd; follow the sign.

❶ Information

The small **tourist office** (☑ 074-952 2198; Chapel Rd; ⊘ 10am-5pm Mon-Fri year-round, plus Sat & Sun Jun-Sep) is in Ionad Teampall Chróine, a community building housed in an old church.

❶ Getting There & Away

Bus Éireann (p444) service No 492 from Donegal runs to Dungloe (€10, 1½ hours) via Killybegs, Ardara and Glenties two to three times daily.

Doherty's Travel (☑ 074-952 1105; www. dohertyscoaches.com) runs once a day (except Sunday) between Letterkenny and the Rosses, stopping at Dungloe (€10, 1¼ hours), Burtonport, Kincasslagh and Annagry.

Burtonport & Around

POP 590

Pocket-sized Burtonport (Ailt an Chorráin) is the embarkation point for Arranmore Island, which looks close enough to wade to from here.

The village has attracted some famous characters over the years. Much to local consternation, in the 1970s the Atlantis commune moved here from London, and practised a primal therapy that earned members the nickname 'the Screamers'. Eventually it relocated to the Colombian jungle (via Innisfree), where two members were appallingly beheaded by Farc rebels. Burtonport seems perfectly ordinary today.

North of Burtonport is the charming seaside village of Kincasslagh, with a population of around 40 people. The village is also on the map as the birthplace of famous singer Daniel O'Donnell.

◉ Sights & Activities

Carrick Finn Beach   BEACH
(off R259, Kincasslagh) Head north of Burtonport on the coast road to reach the picturesque village of Kincasslagh (Cionn Caslach), with ancient cottages perched on top of rocky outcrops and the stunning Blue Flag beach at Carrick Finn. This sweeping stretch of sand with a backdrop of distant mountains remains wonderfully undeveloped, despite being right alongside and parallel to Donegal airport.

Rapid Kayaking   KAYAKING
(☑ 086 151 0979; www.rapidkayaking.com; Carrick Finn, Annagry; kayak trips adult/child from €25/20; ⊘ Jun-Sep) Runs a variety of kayak trips on the sea and through inlets. Trips explore caves and often encounter dolphins.

🛌 Sleeping & Eating

Caislean Oir Hotel   HOTEL €
(☑ 074-954 8113; www.donegalhotel.ie; Annagry; s/d from €55/70; 🛜) Overlooking the tidal inlet, this 20-room hotel has enticing views. The rooms are standard, the bar is popular, and the breakfast choices quite good and extensive. Breakfast in bed for €5 is a nice touch, while a bottle of sauvignon blanc wine in your bedroom upon arrival is €17.95. There's a trad Irish music session every Saturday night year-round.

Limekiln House   B&B €
(☑ 074-954 8521; www.limekilnhouse.com; Carrick Finn, Kincasslagh; r €60-80) Rosemary Boyd has won numerous awards for her crafts and her baking (the shortbread, oh!), and you'll experience both at homely Limekiln House, which is adorned with her oils, tapestries and embroidery. Two of the four rooms have private bathrooms.

Lobster Pot   SEAFOOD €€
(Kelly's; ☑ 074-954 2012; www.lobsterpot.ie; Main St, Burtonport; mains €10-30; ⊘ kitchen noon-9pm, pub till late) You can't miss the giant fibreglass lobster clinging to the wall of the Lobster Pot, which looks onto the working fishing port. Serving up a great selection of seafood, this pub-restaurant is packed when big matches are on TV. Seafood fans can go for the Titanic seafood platter, loaded with lobster, crab, mussels, salmon, prawns and more, naturally all locally sourced.

★ Danny Minnie's Restaurant   MODERN IRISH €€€
(☑ 074-954 8201; www.dannyminnies.ie; R259, Annagry; mains from €25; ⊘ 6.30-9.30pm Mon-Sat, 1-4pm Sun Jun-Aug, shorter hours Sep-May) A beacon of family-run fine dining since 1962, this very popular village restaurant is known for food that's inventive and seasonal. The

DONEGAL'S BEST BEACHES

Donegal's wild and rugged coastline is splashed with broad sweeps of powdery white sand and secluded coves. Here are some of our favourites:

Tramore (p456) Pristine sands on a secluded stretch of coast.

Maghera Strand (p448) A stunning sweep of sand with caves to explore and sunsets to die for.

Carrick Finn (p452) A gorgeous sweep of undeveloped sand near Donegal Airport.

Fintragh Bay (p445) Serene, beautiful and idyllic.

Portnoo (p450) A wishbone-shaped sheltered cove backed by undulating hills.

Ballymastocker Beach (p465) An idyllic stretch of sand lapped by turquoise water.

Culdaff (p469) A long stretch of golden sand, popular with families.

Rossnowlagh (p442) A sweeping white-sand beach ideal for learning to surf.

chef is Brian O'Donnell, who has a Gaeltacht cooking show on Irish TV. Antique-filled bedrooms are sometimes available. During the colder months, it's best to phone ahead as it sometimes shuts early in the week.

Arranmore Island

POP 514

Ringed by dramatic cliffs, cavernous sea caves and clean sandy beaches, Arranmore (Árainn Mhór) lies just 5km from the mainland. Measuring just 9km by 5km, the tiny island has been inhabited since the early Iron Age (800 BC), and a prehistoric promontory fort can be seen near the southeastern corner. The west and north are wild and rugged, with few houses to disturb the sense of isolation.

Up at the northwestern tip of the island is the old coastguard station and Arranmore Lighthouse.

Irish is the main language spoken on Arranmore Island, although most inhabitants are bilingual.

The island's pubs put on peat fires and traditional-music sessions, and some open 24 hours to slake the thirst of fishermen.

★ **Arranmore Way** WALKING

Among many options, the best and most stirring is the Arranmore Way (Slí Árainn Mhór) walking path that circles the island (14km; allow three to four hours).

Dive Arranmore Charters DIVING

(☑ 086 330 0516; www.divearranmore.com; boat charter half/full day €300/550, 2 dives €60) For diving, sea angling, seal watching and a 'sea safari' and marine heritage tour, Jim Muldowney knows the crystal-clear (and

cold) waters around the island like the back of his hand. There are dozens of renowned dive sites and Dive Arranmore Charters also has a B&B on the island.

Claire's Bed & Breakfast B&B €

(☑ 074-952 0042; www.clairesbandb.wordpress.com; Leabgarrow; s/d from €30/60; ☎) This modern house with simple rooms is right by the ferry port.

❶ Getting There & Away

Regular **passenger** (☑ 087 317 1810; www.arranmorefastferry.com; Burtonport; return per person €15) and **car** (☑ 074-952 0532; www.arranmoreferry.com; Burtonport; return adult/child/car & driver €15/7/30; ☉ 4-8 daily sailings year-round) ferries run between Burtonport and the island. **Taxis** (☑ 086 331 7885) meet all ferries.

Gweedore & Around

POP 4300

The Gaeltacht district of Gweedore (Gaoth Dobhair) is a loose agglomeration of small townships scattered between the N56 road and the coast. The most densely populated rural area in Europe and the largest Gaelic-speaking parish in Ireland, it's a heartland of traditional Irish music and culture, and birthplace of Celtic bands and musicians such as Altan, Enya and Clannad.

The scenery is wild and windswept, but much of the coast has been overrun with holiday homes: the 'villages' of Derrybeg (Doirí Beaga) and Bunbeg (Bun Beag) virtually blend into each other, and the sprawl continues north to Bloody Foreland (named for the crimson colour of the rocks at sunset).

It's best to explore by bike, following dead-end roads to secluded coves and beaches. Away from the coast, dozens of small fishing lakes break up the bleak, beautiful landscape. If you're driving, the N56 heading east out of Gweedore is particularly scenic.

🛏 Sleeping & Eating

Bunbeg Lodge B&B €€

(📞087 416 7372; www.bunbeglodge.ie; R257, Bunbeg; s/d from €40/80; 🖥) Excellent B&B accommodation is available at this modern guesthouse. Some of the spacious rooms offer good views over the beach to the sea, so it's worth asking. Breakfasts are hearty and the hosts are very knowledgeable about the local area.

Bunbeg House B&B €€

(Teach na Céidhe; 📞074-953 1305; www.bunbeghouse.com; The Harbour, Bunbeg; s/d from €50/80, mains €7-15; ⊙B&B Easter-Oct, cafe Jun-Sep) This converted corn mill enjoys a lovely location overlooking Bunbeg harbour, within earshot of wooden boats knocking against each other. Nonguests can enjoy home-cooked chowder, fishermen's pie or open crab sandwiches at its summertime cafe-bar, or soak up the sun on the bar terrace raising a pint.

🍸 Drinking & Nightlife

⭐ **Leo's Tavern** PUB

(📞074-954 8143; www.leostavern.com; off R259, Crolly; ⊙kitchen 5-8.45pm Mon-Fri, 1-8.45pm Sat & Sun, bar 4pm-midnight Mon-Fri, 1pm-midnight Sat, 1-11.30pm Sun; 🖥📶) You never know who'll drop by for one of the legendary singalongs at famous, long-standing Leo's Tavern. There's live music nightly in summer and regular sessions throughout the winter, with fine Irish pub grub too. From Crolly, take the R259 1km towards the airport, and look for the signs for Leo's.

The pub is owned by Baba Brennan, mother of Enya and her siblings Moya, Ciaran and Pól (the core of the traditional-but-modern group Clannad), and now run by younger son Bartley. The pub glitters with gold, silver and platinum discs. It's open year-round, but it's worth phoning ahead or checking the website in the cold months as opening times can change.

Teaċ Hiudái Beag PUB

(📞074-953 1016; www.tradcentre.com/hiudaibeag; Bunbeg; ⊙3pm-late) In the tiny town centre and with picnic tables out the front, Teaċ Hiudái Beag is noted for its Monday- and Friday-night music sessions where up to a dozen musicians play flutes, whistles, fiddles, bodhráns and sometimes war pipes (a larger and, consequently, louder precursor of the Highland bagpipes).

❶ Getting There & Away

Bus Feda (📞074-954 8114; www.busfeda.ie) runs a service twice daily (three Friday and Sunday) from Gweedore to Letterkenny (€7, 1½ hours), Donegal (€10, 2¼ hours), Sligo (€12, 3¼ hours) and Galway (€20, 5½ hours).

Dunlewey & Around

POP 600

Blink and the chances are you'll miss the tiny hamlet of Dunlewey (Dún Lúiche). You won't miss the spectacular scenery, however, or quartzite cone of Errigal Mountain, whose craggy peak towers over the surrounding area. Plan enough time to get out of your car and do some walking here, as it's a magical spot. It's close to the N56 and the coastal villages.

◎ Sights & Activities

Poisoned Glen AREA

(Dunlewey) With a name like this – misnomer that it is – how can you resist its allure? Follow a rough walking path into the rocky fastness of the glen (4km round trip) and watch out for the green lady – the resident ghost. Some 2km east of the Dunlewey Centre turn-off on the R251, look for a minor road

COUNTY DONEGAL DUNLEWEY & AROUND

TOP FIVE SCENIC DRIVES

Practically any stretch of road qualifies as a scenic drive in this rugged county, but the following are especially captivating. Be ready for frequent stops to enjoy the views.

➡ The coastal highway from Dunfanaghy (p456) to Gweedore (p453)

➡ A hundred-mile loop of the isolated Inishowen Peninsula (p465)

➡ The curvacious road to sweeping views at Horn Head (p456)

➡ Arcing through stunning Glenveagh National Park (p461)

➡ Snaking switchbacks traversing Glengesh Pass (p448)

ERRIGAL MOUNTAIN

The pinkish-grey quartzite peak of **Errigal Mountain** (752m) dominates the landscape of northwestern Donegal, appearing conical from some angles, but from others like a ragged shark's fin ripping through the heather bogs. Its name comes from the Gaelic *earagail*, meaning 'oratory', as its shape brings to mind a preacher's pulpit. Its looming presence seems to dare walkers to attempt the strenuous but satisfying climb to its pyramid-shaped summit.

If you're keen to take on the challenge, pay close attention to the weather: it can be a dangerous climb on windy or wet days, when the mountain is shrouded in cloud and visibility is poor. The easiest route to the summit, a steep and badly eroded path, begins at a parking area on the R251, about 2km east of Dunlewey (4.5km round trip; allow three hours).

down through the hamlet of Dunlewey, past the magnificently ruined Dunlewey Church, to roadside parking at a hairpin bend where you'll find the walking path.

Legend has it that the huge ice-carved hollow of the Poisoned Glen got its sinister name when the ancient one-eyed giant king of Tory, Balor, was killed here by his exiled grandson, Lughaidh, whereupon the poison from his eye split the rock and poisoned the glen. The less interesting truth, however, lies in a cartographic gaffe. Locals were inspired to name it An Gleann Neamhe (The Heavenly Glen), but when an English cartographer mapped the area, he carelessly marked it An Gleann Neimhe – The Poisoned Glen.

Dunlewey Church CHURCH
(Dunlewey) This roofless white marble, blue quartzite and brick church, overlooking Dunlewey Lough, was consecrated in 1853 and makes for sublime photos with the mountain behind and the lake beyond. Eventually the Dunlewey Estate declined and the congregation dried up; the roof was taken down in 1955. Some of the lead remains in the arched windows, although the glass is all gone, but it's a picture and the setting is gorgeous.

Dunlewey Centre ACTIVITY CENTRE
(Ionad Cois Locha; ☏074-953 1699; www.dunlewey centre.com; Dunlewey; combined ticket adult/child €10.30/7.50; ⏰10.30am-5.30pm Easter-Sep, to 4.45pm Oct; 🚼) This great hotch-potch of craft shop, museum, restaurant, activity centre, theatre and concert venue has something for everyone. Kids will thoroughly enjoy the petting zoo, but the real highlight for everyone is a boat trip on the lake with a storyteller who vividly brings to life local history and ghoulish folklore.

Adults will appreciate the 30-minute tour of the thatched cottage that once belonged

to local weaver Manus Ferry, who earned renown for his tweeds (he died in 1975).

🛏 Sleeping

★**Errigal Hostel** HOSTEL €
(☏074-953 1180; www.anoige.ie; off R251, Dunlewey; dm €18-20, s €26-32, d €45-53; ⏰Mar-Oct; 🛜) 🌱 At the foot of magnificent Errigal Mountain, this gleaming, excellent and purpose-built 60-bed An Óige hostel has superb facilities including a self-catering kitchen, a large laundry room for muddy climbing gear, bright common areas, and pristine dorms and private rooms. There's friendly staff, and a petrol station selling groceries next door.

Glen Heights B&B B&B €€
(☏074-956 0844; www.glenheightsbb.com; Dunlewey; d €70; 🛜) The three rooms are cosy and the Donegal charm is in full swing at this fine choice run by Kathleen. Your breakfast may well go cold on the plate in front of you as you stare at the breathtaking views of Dunlewey Lake and the Poisoned Glen (p454) from the conservatory.

Falcarragh & Gortahork

POP 890
Falcarragh (An Fál Carrach) is a workaday real town without the pretensions of nearby Dunfanaghy, while neighbouring Gortahork (Gort an Choirce) is barely a wide spot in the road. Both give an intriguing glimpse into everyday Gaeltacht life.

👁 Sights & Activities

Get on your bike or don your hiking boots and explore the maze of country lanes and old townlands (farming communities) south of Falcarragh, including the old church and burial ground on the ancient mound of Ballintemple.

⭐**Magheraroarty Beach**   BEACH
(Meenlaragh; off R257) A beautiful beach that curves for more than 3km, with good walks along the shore and through the dunes. Even better are the views out to the islands, including Tory.

Muckish Mountain   MOUNTAIN
The grey bulk of Muckish Mountain (670m) dominates the view between Gortahork and Dunfanaghy. The easiest route to the top begins southeast of Falcarragh at the highest point of the R256 road through Muckish Gap. Sweeping views to Malin Head and Tory Island unfurl from the summit.

🛌 Sleeping & Eating

Óstán Loch Altan   HOTEL €€
(📞074-913 5267; www.ostanlochaltan.com; N56, Gortahork; s/d from €50/100, mains from €11, 2-course lunch €14.95; ⊗kitchen noon-9pm; 🛜) Gortahork's main landmark is this big, tidy cream-coloured hotel on the main street, where the 39 rooms are a mix of styles, some with sea views. It's one of the few places to stay along this stretch of coast that's open all year; good bar food is served year-round, while the restaurant opens for lunch and dinner from June to September.

Lóistín Na Seamróige   PUB
(Shamrock Lodge; Main St/N56, Falcarragh; ⊗noon-late; 🛜) Owner Margaret grew up on these premises and her pub (established in 1959) is the town's living room, especially on Friday mornings when a market sets up outside the front door. During July and August traditional music is in the air.

ℹ️ Information

The Bank of Ireland at the eastern end of Main St has an ATM, and the post office is at Main St's western end in Falcarragh.
Falcarragh Visitor Centre (📞074 918 0655; www.falcarraghvisitorcentre.com; ⊗10am-5pm Mon-Fri, 11am-5pm Sat), which has tourist information and a cafe, is housed in a 19th-century police barracks.

ℹ️ Getting There & Away

Bus Feda (📞074-954 8114; www.feda.ie; 🛜) buses from Crolly stop on Main St, Falcarragh and continue to Letterkenny (€7, one hour).

Dunfanaghy & Around
POP 320

Comely Dunfanaghy is clustered along the southern shore of a sandy inlet and lies ideally at the centre of one of the most varied and attractive parts of Donegal. Moors and meadows, sea cliffs and sandy beaches, forest and lake lie scattered below the humpbacked hill of Muckish, all waiting to be explored on foot or by bike.

There are no ATMs in town, but the post office has a bureau de change.

◉ Sights

⭐**Horn Head**   VIEWPOINT
The towering headland of Horn Head has some of the Wild Atlantic Way's most spectacular scenery, with dramatic quartzite cliffs, topped with bog and heather, rearing over 180m high. The narrow road from Dunfanaghy (4km) ends at a small parking area where you can walk 150m to a WWII lookout point or 1.5km to Horn Head proper.

On a fine day you'll encounter tremendous views of Tory, Inishbofin, Inishdooey and tiny Inishbeg islands to the west; Sheep Haven Bay and the Rosguill Peninsula to the east; Malin Head to the northeast; and the coast of Scotland beyond.

Ards Forest Park   WILDLIFE RESERVE
(www.coillteoutdoors.ie; off N56; parking €5 (€1 & €2 coins only); ⊗8am-9pm Apr-Sep, 10am-4.30pm Oct-Mar) Anyone looking to stretch their legs will love this forested park, criss-crossed by marked nature trails varying in length from 2km to 13km. Covering 480 hectares along the northern shore of the Ards Peninsula and 5km southeast of Dunfanaghy, the park is home to some lovely walks, the best of which lead to its clean beaches with views across Clonmass Bay.

The woodlands are home to several native species, including ash, birch and sessile oak, and you may encounter foxes, hedgehogs and otters. In 1930 the southern part of the peninsula was taken over by Capuchin monks; the grounds of their friary are open to the public.

Tramore Beach   BEACH
Reaching Dunfanaghy's loveliest beach, Tramore, requires hiking through the grassy dunes to the west of the village for about 2km.

Dunfanaghy Workhouse HISTORIC BUILDING

(☑ 074-913 6540; www.dunfanaghyworkhouse. ie; Main St, Dunfanaghy; adult/child €5/3; ☺ 9.30am-5.30pm daily Jul & Aug, to 5pm Mon-Sat Sep-Jun) This prominent stone building on the western edge of town was once the local workhouse, built to keep and employ the destitute. Conditions were horrible. Men, women, children and the sick were segregated, their lives dominated by gruelling work. The building today is a heritage centre, which tells the powerful true tale of 'Wee Hannah' Herrity (1836–1926) and her passage through the institution. It has a cafe, a crafts shop (and craft courses), tourist information and occasional temporary exhibitions.

As the Famine took grip the workhouse was inundated with starving people. Two years after it opened in 1845, it accommodated some 600 people – double the number originally planned.

🏃 Activities

★ **Narosa Life** WATER SPORTS

(☑ 074-910 0565, 086 883 1090; www.narosalife. com; Main St, Dunfanaghy; surf lesson adult/child €35/25, full-day surf-gear rental €25; ☺ 9am-5.30pm Mon-Sat, 10am-5pm Sun) Offers two-hour group surf lessons, equipment rental and private one-on-one surf lessons (€90, July and August only), as well as yoga and fitness classes and guided walks to Tramore Beach, Muckish Mountain and Horn Head.

Dunfanaghy Golf Club GOLF

(☑ 074-913 6335; www.dunfanaghygolfclub.com; off N56, Dunfanaghy; green fees weekdays/weekends €25/30) This stunning waterside 18-hole links course is just east of the village.

Dunfanaghy Stables HORSE RIDING

(☑ 074-910 0980; www.dunfanaghystables. com; Arnolds Hotel, Main St; adult/child per hour €32/27; ☺ Easter-Oct) Explore the expansive beaches and surrounding countryside on horseback. Short rides and lessons also available.

Jaws Watersports WATER SPORTS

(☑ 086 173 5109, 087 237 1152; www.jawswater sports.ie; Main St, Dunfanaghy; gear rental per half-day from €20) Jaws Watersports offers surfing lessons, rents out surfing gear, bodyboards and kayaks, and offers guided kayaking trips (€35) and stand-up paddleboarding.

🛏 Sleeping

★ **Corcreggan Mill** GUESTHOUSE €

(☑ 074-913 6409; www.corcreggan.com; Castlebane, off N56; campsites from €12, s/d from €60/75; @ 🛜) 🚲 Spotless four-bed dorms and private guest rooms are tucked into cosy corners of this lovingly restored former mill house, built and run by the engaging Brendan Rohan. Continental breakfast is included in the room rates. The mill is 2.5km southwest of town on the N56, just south of New Lake. Rooms come in a variety of shapes and sizes; some have private bathrooms.

An organic vegetable garden provides the ingredients for simple evening meals.

Whins B&B €

(☑ 074-913 6481; www.thewhins.com; off N56; s/d €50/80; 🛜) 🚲 About 750m east of the town centre opposite the golf course, the colourful, individually decorated rooms at the Whins have patchwork quilts and a real sense of character. A wide choice of breakfasts is served upstairs in a room with a view towards Horn Head.

Willows B&B B&B €€

(☑ 074-913 6446; www.thewillowsdunfanaghy.com; Main St, Dunfanaghy; s/d from €50/80; 🛜) At the west end of town, this spiffy B&B has comfy rooms and a great terrace and barbecue area with table and chairs so you can enjoy the long nights of summer with their billions of stars.

Arnold's Hotel HOTEL €€

(☑ 074-913 6208; www.arnoldshotel.com; Main St, Dunfanaghy; s/d from €80/110; ☺ Apr-Oct; 🅿 🛜) Open since 1922, this family-run hotel at the east end of the village has 30 comfortable and stylish rooms. The hotel's restaurant serves up traditional seafood, roasts and grills (mains €14 to €24).

🍴 Eating

Muck 'n' Muffins CAFE €

(☑ 074-913 6780; www.mucknmuffins.ie; The Square, Dunfanaghy; mains €4-10; ☺ 9.30am-5pm Mon-Sat, 10.30am-5pm Sun, to 6pm Jul & Aug; 🛜) A 19th-century stone grain store houses this 1st-floor cafe, pottery studio and crafts shop. Even on rainy winter days, it's packed with locals sipping coffee, quaffing wine, and tucking into sandwiches, breakfast, hot specials (lasagne, quiche etc), tempting cakes and, of course, muffins.

★**Starfish Cafe & Bistro**   MODERN IRISH €€
(☑074-910 0676; www.starfishcafebistro.com; Main St, Dunfanaghy; mains €5-20; ⊙9.30am-5.30pm) Pretty in blue, this fresh and cheery bistro excels from breakfast through lunch. At any time the baked goods beguile and there's all sorts on the menu, from French toast and handmade granola to rhubarb and raspberry cake, seafood salad and cups of organic loose-leaf tea.

★**Cove**   MODERN IRISH €€
(☑074-913 6300; www.facebook.com/CoveRestaurantDonegal; off N56, Rockhill, Port-na-Blagh; dinner mains €17-25; ⊙6.30pm-9.30pm Tues-Sun) It looks unprepossessing from the outside, but owners Siobhan Sweeney and Peter Byrne are perfectionists who tend to every detail in Cove's art-filled dining room, and on your plate. The cuisine is fresh and inventive. Seafood specials are deceptively simple with subtle Asian influences, and after dinner you can enjoy the elegant lounge upstairs. Book ahead.

Mill Restaurant & Guesthouse   MODERN IRISH €€€
(☑074-913 6985; www.themillrestaurant.com; N56, Dunfanaghy; set dinner €45; ⊙7-9pm Tue-Sun Jul & Aug, shorter hours Mar-Jun; ℗) An exquisite country setting and locally sourced, seasonally changing meals make dining here a treat. Set in an old flax mill that was for many years the home of renowned watercolour artist Frank Eggington, it also has six high-class guest rooms (singles/doubles from €60/96). The mill is 1km south of town. Book in advance.

🍷 Drinking & Nightlife

★**Molly's Bar**   PUB
(☑074-910 0050; www.mollysdunfanaghy.com; Main St, Dunfanaghy; ⊙noon-late) One look inside the creamy-hued Molly's Bar and you'll want to stay. A wonderfully old-fashioned pub with proper snugs, it hosts regular live music (traditional, jazz, blues and more), while the terrace is the place for a pint on a long night.

🛍 Shopping

Gallery   ART
(☑074-913 6224; www.thegallerydunfanaghy.com; Main St, Dunfanaghy; ⊙10am-6pm Mon-Sat) This lovely eponymously named shop was once the 'hospital' for the workhouse next door. Today it is a much more cheery place: it displays works and crafts by local artists plus oodles of gift items.

ℹ Getting There & Away

Bus Éireann does not run north of Letterkenny, although **John McGinley** (☑074-913 5201; www.johnmcginley.com) buses do, and **Bus Feda** (☑074-954 8114; www.feda.ie) buses run to Donegal, but a car for this region is best.

Tory Island

POP 144

Ireland's most remote inhabited island, blasted by sea winds and stung by salt spray, the distant crag of Tory Island (Oileán Thóraí) has taken its fair share of batterings. Although it's only 11km north of the mainland, the rough sea has long consolidated the island's staunch independence and strengthened its sense of remoteness.

The island has its own dialect of Irish and even has an elected 'king', who acts as community spokesman and welcomes visitors to the island. Over the decades its inhabitants earned a reputation for distilling and smuggling contraband *poitín* (a peaty whiskey). However, the island is perhaps best known for its 'naive' (or outsider) artists, many of whom have attracted the attention of international collectors.

The island has just one pebbly beach and two recognisable villages: West Town (An Baile Thiar), home to most of the island's facilities, and East Town (An Baile Thoir).

👁 Sights & Activities

Cottages mingle with ancient ecclesiastical treasures in West Town. St Colmcille (Columba) is said to have founded a monastery here in the 6th century, and reminders of the early Church are scattered throughout the town, including the Tau Cross and a round tower.

Tory Island is a wonderful place for birdwatching – more than 100 species of seabirds inhabit the island, including nesting corncrakes and colonies of puffins (thought to number around 1300).

Tau Cross   RELIGIOUS SITE
The 12th-century Tau Cross, an odd, T-shaped cruciform that suggests the possibility of seafaring exchanges with early Coptic Christians from Egypt, greets passengers disembarking from the ferry.

Round Tower   TOWER
Not far from the Tau Cross, this 6th- or 7th-century round tower has a circumference of nearly 16m and a round-headed doorway high above the ground

Dixon Gallery
GALLERY

(www.toryislandpaintings.com/the-gallery.html; West Town; ⊙ hours vary) The place to see Tory Island's famous 'naive art' plus other works.

★ Tory Way
WALKING

(An Slí Thoraí) Tory Way is a waymarked loop walk (the map board is 50m from the ferry landing). It leads you to the lighthouse at the west end, then back to the eastern end of the island, which is dominated by jagged quartzite cliffs and sea stacks, including the spectacular Tor Mór, a 400m-long blade of rock capped with pinnacles.

🍴 Sleeping & Eating

There's a shop near the harbour where you can pick up provisions, but it's a good idea to bring some snacks with you. There's pub food at Tory Island Harbour View Hotel.

Tory Island Hostel
HOSTEL €

(☑ 087 298 7407; West Town; per person from €20; ⊙ May-Sep) From the ferry, walk 800m west to find this hostel with cheery accommodation. Spotless rooms are enlivened with bright splashes of colour and sweeping views.

Tory Island Harbour View Hotel
HOTEL €€

(Óstan Radharc Na Céibhe; ☑ 087 938 5284, 074-913 5920; www.hoteltory.com; West Town; s/d from €60/80; ⊙ Easter-Oct) The island's sole hotel is a fairly rustic place with 12 simple but comfortable bedrooms inside a sunny yellow building. The pub is a hotbed of late-night music, dancing and craic. There's a diving centre here too.

☆ Entertainment

Club Sóisialta Thórai
COMMUNITY CENTRE

(Tory Social Club; West Town; ⊙ varies) The island's social life revolves around this merry spot, which besides the hotel has the island's only other pub. It usually gets going from around 8pm but don't expect the real craic to start until much, much later.

ℹ️ Information

Information is available from the **Tory Island Co-op** (Comharchumann Thoraí Teo; ☑ 074-913 5502; www.oileanthorai.com; ⊙ 9am-5pm Mon-Fri) near the pier, next to the playground. You can also get information at the craft shop at the top of the pier.

ℹ️ Getting There & Away

Bring waterproofs for the crossing – it can be a wild ride. **Donegal Coastal Cruises** (Turasmara Teo; ☑ 074-953 1320; www.toryislandferry.com; adult/child return €26/13; ⊙ 1-3 daily Apr-Oct, less often Nov-Mar) runs passenger ferries to Tory Island from Bunbeg (1½ hours, one daily) and Magheraroarty (35 minutes, two daily). Normal service is April to September, with extra sailings in July and August, and fewer October to March; sailing times vary according to weather and tides, and it's not uncommon for travellers to be stranded on the island in bad weather.

Magheraroarty (Machaire Uí Robhartaigh) is 4km northwest of Gortahork on the R257; the road is signposted Coastal Route/Bloody Foreland. Bunbeg is in the southwest part of Gweedore district.

CENTRAL DONEGAL

Letterkenny

POP 19,600

A large market town, Letterkenny has endured rash development, resulting in numerous faceless retail parks lining the roads, traffic congestion and a lack of personality. However, as Donegal's largest town, it has a

COUNTY DONEGAL LETTERKENNY

TORY ISLAND NAIVE ART

Tory Island's distinctive school of painters came about in the 1950s when the English artist Derrick Hill began to spend much of his time on the island. The islanders often watched him as he worked. As the story goes, one of the islanders approached Hill and said, 'I can do that.' He was James Dixon, a self-taught painter who used boat paint and made his own brushes with donkey hairs. Hill was impressed with the 'painterly' quality of Dixon's work and the two formed a lasting friendship.

Other islanders were soon inspired to follow suit, forging unique folksy, expressive styles portraying rugged island scenes. Among them were Patsy Dan Rodgers, currently the elected Rí Thoraí (King of Tory). The islanders' work has been exhibited worldwide and fetches impressive prices at auctions. Glebe House & Gallery (p462) on the mainland often has exhibitions.

buzz about it, from both its good pubs and its well-funded cultural centres.

Sights

Donegal County Museum MUSEUM
(☑ 074-912 4613; High Rd; ⊙10am-4.30pm Mon-Fri, 1-4.30pm Sat) FREE Letterkenny's 19th-century workhouse, built to provide Famine relief, now houses the local museum. The permanent collection offers 8000-plus artefacts from prehistoric times onwards. Look for temporary exhibits.

Newmills Corn & Flax Mills HISTORIC BUILDING
(☑ 074-912 5115; www.heritageireland.ie; R250; ⊙10am-6pm late May-Sep) FREE Parts of this complex date back four centuries to a time when water was the main source of power for multiple tasks, such as grinding grain. One of Ireland's largest waterwheels spins thanks to the River Swilly. Exhibits explain the function of the many cogs and gears. It's 5km southwest of Letterkenny.

Main Street STREET
Letterkenny's long, sloping main street is graced by a cute little market square halfway down. This is the most attractive part of the town, with a terrace of red-brick Georgian houses at the top, one of which was a holiday retreat of Maud Gonne, actress, revolutionary and lover of poet WB Yeats.

Festivals & Events

Earagail Arts Festival PERFORMING ARTS
(☑ 074-912 0777; www.eaf.ie; ⊙mid-Jul) Theatre performances, concerts and art exhibits headline this diverse two-week festival, with events staged across the region.

Sleeping

Apple Hostel HOSTEL €
(☑ 074-911 3291; www.letterkennyhostel.com; Covehill, Port Rd; dm/s/d from €14/23/40; �]) This hostel is close to the centre of town, along the road near the bus station. It's a modern bungalow with accommodation to match, from a dorm with eight bunks to doubles and family rooms with private bathrooms. Call ahead to book.

Pearse Road B&B GUESTHOUSE €
(☑ 074-912 3002; www.pearseroadguesthouse.com; Pearse Rd; r €60-70; �]) This tidy guesthouse has rooms spread over two buildings close to Main St. Breakfast is not included but rooms are well equipped and there's a speedy laundry right next door.

Station House HOTEL €€
(☑ 074-912 3100; www.stationhouseletterkenny.com; Lower Main St; s/d €85/110; @☜) Conveniently located in the centre of town but right on a busy corner, this large, modern hotel has 81 red-hued, wood-floored rooms with low lighting and glass-panelled bathrooms.

Eating & Drinking

★ Lemon Tree MODERN IRISH €€
(☑ 074-912 5788; www.thelemontreerestaurant.com; 32-34 The Courtyard Shopping Centre; mains €15-23; ⊙5-9pm; ☜☑) There's a contemporary flavour at this relocated restaurant. The innovative menu offers an excellent choice of fresh seafood, poultry and meat dishes sourced locally and prepared with French flair.

Yellow Pepper IRISH, MEDITERRANEAN €€
(☑ 074-912 4133; www.yellowpepperrestaurant.com; 36 Lower Main St; mains €9-20; ⊙noon-10pm; ☜☑) Set in a 19th-century former shirt factory with stone walls and polished wooden floors, this atmospheric restaurant is a favourite of locals. The menu, with food procured from the region, is strong on seafood but offers variety including an excellent tapas-style lunch menu. Book for dinner.

Brewery PUB FOOD €€
(☑ 074-912 7330; www.thebrewerybar.com; Market Sq; mains €6-20; ⊙kitchen noon-3pm Mon-Fri, 6-10pm daily, bar open till late) Just off Main St, this multilevel pub is an excellent choice for a casual meal. Burgers, steaks, seafood and more are on the menu, which also has many dishes good for sharing. The wine list is decent and there are good microbrews on tap.

★ Cottage Bar PUB
(☑ 074-912 1338; 49 Upper Main St; ⊙noon-late) Watch your head! All sorts of bric-a-brac hangs precariously from the ceiling of Letterkenny's most atmospheric pub. There's a good beer garden and it's popular with noted journalist Angela Cullen.

McGinley's PUB
(☑ 074-912 1106; Lower Main St; ⊙3pm-late) The best spot in town to catch some live music, this old-style pub with an open fire has trad sessions on Wednesday nights, and live bands Thursday to Saturday.

⭐ Entertainment

An Grianán Theatre   THEATRE
(☑ 074-912 0777; www.angrianan.com; Port Rd)
An Grianán Theatre is both a community
theatre and major arts venue for the northwest, presenting national and international drama, comedy and music. It also has a
good cafe and bar.

ℹ Information

Check out www.letterkenny.ie for useful information on the town and surrounds.

The **tourist office** (☑ 074-912 1160; Neil
Blaney Rd; ⊙ 9am-5.30pm Mon-Sat Jun-Aug,
9.15am-5pm Mon-Fri Sep-May; ☎) is 1km southeast of Main St at the roundabout junction of the
N14 and N56.

ℹ Getting There & Away

Letterkenny is a major bus hub for northwest
Ireland. The bus station is by the roundabout at
the junction of Ramelton and Port Rds.

Bus Éireann (☑ 074-912 1309; www.buseireann
.ie) runs to Dublin (€21, four hours) five times
daily via Omagh and Monaghan. Buses also
serve Derry and Galway via Donegal (€12, 45
minutes, eight times daily).

Bus Feda (☑ 074-954 8114; www.feda.ie) runs
a bus to Crolly (€7, 1½ hours) or to Galway
(€20, four hours) twice daily via Donegal,
Bundoran and Sligo. Buses stop on the road
outside the bus station.

John McGinley (☑ 074-913 5201; www.john
mcginley.com) buses run southeast two to five
times daily to Dublin Airport (€22, 3¼ hours)
and to coastal towns northwest.

Most travellers will be coming through by car,
to access the Inishowen and Fanad peninsulas.

Glenveagh National Park

Ireland's second largest national park,
Glenveagh is a sublime panoply of lakes
overlooked by brooding mountains, with
valleys scooped from the land and scattered with both forest and swaths of bog
that offer an enticing, unspoilt landscape
coupled with almost perfect options for
trekking. Its wealth of wildlife includes
the golden eagle, which was hunted to ex-
tinction here in the 19th century but reintroduced in 2000, and the nation's largest
herd of red deer.

Such serenity came at a heavy price. The
land was once farmed by 244 tenants, who
were forcibly evicted by landowner John
George Adair in the winter of 1861 following what he called a 'conspiracy', but really
because their presence obstructed his vision
for the valley. Adair put the final touches
on his paradise by building the spectacular
lakeside Glenveagh Castle (1870–73), while
his wife, Adelia, introduced the park's definitive red deer and rhododendrons.

◉ Sights & Activities

One of the best ways to appreciate this vast
and varied park is simply by wandering
around it along the R251 and R254. The
majestic sweep of its forbidding golden
landscape is a powerful experience.

The park features nature trails along lakes
and through woods and blanket bog, as well
as a viewing point that's a short walk behind
the castle. Get advice and study maps at the
visitor centre (p462). One good walk for a
start follows Lough Beagh.

It's best to pack up with your own provisions for hiking around the national park,
but there is a cafe (☑ 087 755 3547; mains from
€5; ⊙ 10.30am-5pm Easter & Jun-Sep) in the visitor centre.

Glenveagh Castle   CASTLE
(www.glenveaghnationalpark.ie; off R251; adult/child
30min tour €7/5, bus from visitor centre adult/child
$3/2; ⊙ 9am-6pm Apr-Oct, to 5pm Nov-Mar, last
tours 45min before closing) This castle was modelled on Scotland's Balmoral Castle. Henry
McIlhenny made it a characterful home with
liberal reminders of his passion for deer-stalk-
ing. In fact, few rooms lack a representation
– or the taxidermied remains – of a stag.

Access is by guided tour only. Cars are not
allowed beyond the Glenveagh Visitor Centre; you can walk or cycle the lovely lakeside
3.6km route to the castle, or take the shuttle
bus (every 15 minutes).

The most eye-catching of the flamboyantly decorated rooms are in the round tower,
including the tartan-and-antler-encrusted
music room and the pink candy-striped
room demanded by Greta Garbo whenever
she stayed here.

The exotic gardens are similarly spectacular, boasting terraces, an Italian garden,
a walled kitchen garden and the Belgian
Walk, built by Belgian soldiers who stayed
here during WWI. Their cultured charm is
in marked contrast to the wildly beautiful
landscape that enfolds the area.

The castle was briefly occupied by the
Irish Republican Army (IRA) in 1922. Then
in 1929 the property was acquired by King-
sley Porter, professor of art at Harvard

University, who mysteriously disappeared in 1933 (presumed drowned, but rumoured to have been spotted in Paris afterwards).

Six years later the estate was bought by his former student, Henry McIlhenny, who sold the whole kit and caboodle to the Irish government in 1975.

Grass Routes CYCLING
(☑ 087-665 5599; www.grassroutes.ie; L5542, Termon, Letterkenny; bike rental per 3hr €12-18, full day €20-35) Hires out electric and hybrid bikes in Glenveagh National Park. The website has a wealth of information, including cycling routes.

ℹ Information

The **Glenveagh National Park Visitor Centre** (☑ 076-100 2537; www.glenveaghnationalpark. ie; off R251; ☺ 9am-6pm Apr-Oct, to 5pm Nov-Mar) has a 20-minute video on the ecology of the park and the infamous Adairs. Reception sells the necessary midge repellent, as vital as walking boots in summer and waterproofs in winter. No camping is allowed in the park. It's 24km northwest of Letterkenny.

Lough Gartan

The patriarch of Irish monasticism, St Colmcille (Columba), was born in the 6th century in a lovely setting near glassy Lough Gartan, where some relics associated with the saint can be seen. The lake is 17km northwest of Letterkenny in beautiful and splendid driving country; getting lost is half the fun. There's nary a holiday home in sight in the charming region around Church Hill.

◉ Sights

Colmcille Heritage Centre MUSEUM
(☑ 074-912 1160; www.colmcilleheritagecentre.ie; off R251, Church Hill; adult/child €3/2; ☺ 10.30am-5pm Mon-Sat, 1.30-5pm Sun Easter-Sep) Colmcille's Hall of Fame is this comprehensive heritage centre on the shore of Lough Gartan in a wooded grove, with a lavish display on the production of illuminated manuscripts. The centre is signposted just southwest of Church Hill.

St Colmcille's mother, on the run from pagans, supposedly haemorrhaged during childbirth and her blood is believed to have changed the colour of the surrounding Gartan clay to pure white. Ever since, the clay has been regarded as a lucky charm.

St Colmcille's Abbey & Birthplace HISTORIC SITE
(Lough Gartan; ☺ 24hr) FREE The 10th-century ruins of Colmcille's abbey lie on a hillside to the north of Lough Gartan and northwest of Lough Nacally, beside a 16th-century chapel and an O'Donnell clan burial ground. It's signposted 1km north of Glebe House along a country road. There's a car park just up from the main road.

One kilometre south of the ruins, near the southeastern (hikers and cyclists only) entrance to Glenveagh National Park, is the saint's birthplace, marked by a hefty Celtic cross erected in 1911. Beside it is an intriguing prehistoric cup-marked slab strewn with greening copper coins. It's popularly known as the Flagstone of Loneliness on which Colmcille supposedly slept.

Glebe House & Gallery GALLERY
(☑ 074-913 7071; www.heritageireland.ie; Church Hill; adult/child €5/3; ☺ 11am-6.30pm daily Easter, Jul & Aug, Sat-Thu Jun & Sep, last admission 5.30pm) The English painter Derrick Hill bought this 1828 mansion in 1953, providing him with a mainland base close to his beloved Tory Island. Sumptuously decorated with an evident love of all things exotic, the real lure here is Hill's astonishing art collection. Besides paintings by Hill and Tory Island's 'naive' artists are works by Picasso, Landseer, Hokusai, Jack B Yeats and Kokoschka. A guided tour of the house takes about 45 minutes.

Before Hill arrived, the house served as a rectory and then a hotel. The lavish gardens can also be toured and there is a cute little cafe.

NORTHEASTERN DONEGAL

Rosguill Peninsula

The best way to appreciate Rosguill's rugged splendour is by driving, cycling or even walking the 15km Atlantic Drive, a waymarked loop on minor roads signposted to your left as you come into the sprawling village of Carrigart (Carraig Airt) from the south. The sea views are superb, although the remoteness is spoiled somewhat by the growth in holiday homes.

The pretty, secluded beach at Trá na Rossan in the northern part of the peninsula makes a good target, rather than the overcrowded holiday strand at Downings (often written as Downies).

Activities

Mevagh Dive Centre
DIVING
(☎ 074-915 4708; www.mevaghdiving.com; Milford Rd, Carrigart; 2 dives from €50) Donegal's only dive centre offers PADI diving courses, equipment rentals and boat charter. The waters off the northwest are crystal clear and at numerous sites they can take you to see everything from shipwrecks to sharks. It also has excellent accommodation (doubles from €76) in its purpose-built, four-bedroom (all en suite) B&B. Various packages (dive/stay/lessons) are offered.

Rosapenna Golf Resort
GOLF
(☎ 074-915 5000; www.rosapenna.ie; Downings; green fees €75-95) The scenery at this renowned golf club – designed by St Andrew's Old Tom Morris in 1891 and remodelled by Harry Vardon in 1906 – is as spectacular as the layout, which can challenge even the lowest handicapper. It has two courses and there's a fully equipped four-star hotel attached.

Sleeping & Eating

Trá na Rosann Hostel
HOSTEL €
(☎ 074-915 5374; www.anoige.ie; dm from €17; ☺late May-Sep, reception closed 10am-5pm; ℗) Knockout views envelop this heritage-listed 26-bed former hunting lodge, designed by Sir Edwin Lutyens. It's an atmospheric spot with a colourful history, just a short walk from lovely Trá na Rosann beach. The trade-off for the tranquil setting is that it's 8km north of Downings and there's no public transport.

Olde Glen Bar & Restaurant
MODERN IRISH €€
(☎ 083 158 5777; Glen, Carrigart; mains €15-25; ☺bar midday-late Jun-Aug, from 3pm rest of year; kitchen 6-9pm Jul & Aug, closed Tue Jun & Sep, 6-9pm Thu-Sun Oct-May; 🖉) Authentic down to its original 1700s stone floor, this traditional pub serves a fine pint, while its farmhouse-style restaurant serves outstanding blackboard specials. Food is sourced locally so expect top-quality seafood, meat and produce. Be sure to book ahead.

Fanad Peninsula

The second most northerly point in Donegal, Fanad Head thrusts out into the Atlantic to the east of Rosguill. The peninsula curls around the watery expanses of Mulroy Bay to the west, and Lough Swilly to the east, the latter edged with high cliffs and sandy beaches. Most travellers stick to the peninsula's eastern flank, visiting the beautiful beach at Portsalon and the quiet heritage towns of Rathmelton and Rathmullan.

Apart from the ferry that runs in summer between Buncrana and Rathmullan, the only way in, around and out of the Fanad Peninsula is behind a steering wheel: hiring a car is the most sensible, if not the only, option.

Rathmelton

Historic Rathmelton (sometimes called Ramelton) is a picture-perfect spot with rows of Georgian houses and rough-walled stone warehouses curving along the tidal inlet to the River Lennon.

Walk the colourful, picturesque streets and dawdle by the water. It's worth visiting ruined Tullyaughnish Church but also just wandering around the roads by the river, looking at the historic architecture and out over the rotten ribs of decaying boats in the river.

Sleeping & Eating

Frewin House
B&B €€
(☎ 074-915 1246; www.frewinhouse.com; Rectory Rd; d €120-160; ☺Mar-Oct; ℗🖏) This fine Victorian rectory in secluded grounds would make every weepy heroine's dreams come true. The house combines antique furniture and open fires with contemporary style. The bedrooms are pretty but uncluttered and you can arrange for a communal dinner by candlelight. There's also a self-catering cottage available.

Ardeen House
B&B €€
(☎ 074-915 1243; www.ardeenhouse.com; Aughnish Rd; s/d from €55/90; 🖏) The warm welcome and homemade scones on arrival at Ardeen House make you feel like you're coming home. Overlooking the river, it has five pleasingly decorated bedrooms, and the breakfasts are copious and tasty. It's on the east edge of town, on the south side of the river, just beyond the town hall.

Bridge Bar   IRISH €€

(☑ 074-915 1119; www.ramelton.net/Pubs/Bridge
Bar.htm; R245, Bridgend; mains €18-27; ⊙ kitch-
en 6-9pm Wed-Sat) The Bridge Bar is one of
those lovely old country pubs you specifically came to Ireland to seek out. Its cosy 1st-
floor restaurant has classic Irish steak and
seafood dishes: be sure to try the excellent
beers from Kinnegar Craft Brewery while
you enjoy a trad-music session.

Rathmelton Country Market   MARKET

(off R245; ⊙ 11am-12.30pm Sat) The limited
hours means there's a real scrum to get the
best produce, prepared foods, baked treats
and more at one of Donegal's best farmers
markets. It's in a car park just by the river.

Rathmullan

POP 530

You wouldn't know it while enjoying the
views of Lough Swilly, but the refined and
good-looking little port village of Rathmullan has a tranquillity that belies the mo-
mentous events that took place here from
the 16th to 18th centuries, notably the end
of the power of the Irish chieftains with the
Flight of the Earls and the conclusion of the
old Gaelic order. The village is home to the
historic Rathmullan Priory and offers scenic
views over Lough Swilly.

History

In 1587 Hugh O'Donnell, the 15-year-old heir
to the powerful O'Donnell clan, was tricked
into boarding a ship here and taken to Dublin as a prisoner. He escaped four years later
on Christmas Eve and, after unsuccessful attempts at revenge, died in Spain, aged only 30.

In 1607, despairing of fighting the English,
Hugh O'Neill, the Earl of Tyrone, and Rory
O'Donnell, the Earl of Tyrconnell, boarded
a ship in Rathmullan harbour and left Ireland for good. This decisive act, known as
the Flight of the Earls, marked the effective
end of Gaelic Ireland and the rule of Irish
chieftains. Large-scale confiscation of their
estates took place, preparing for the Plantation of Ulster with settlers from Britain.

It was also in Rathmullan that Wolfe Tone,
leader of the 1798 Rising, was captured.

◉ Sights & Activities

Rathmullan Priory   RUINS

(Main St) Dating from 1508 and facing the
water, this ivy-cloaked priory was plundered in 1595 and then used as a barracks;
in the early 17th century it was semi-
converted to a castle.

Donegal Sea Kayaking   KAYAKING

(☑ 086 313 0523; www.donegalseakayaking.com;
Fanad; tours adult/child €30/25; ⊙ kayak hire
9am-9pm) This mobile kayaking company
runs fantastic off-shore tours of the lovely
Fanad Peninsula with modern kayaks; it
also does training and kayak hire. Locations vary by tides and conditions so check
the website for details.

🛏 Sleeping & Eating

Glenalla Lodge   B&B €€

(☑ 074-915 8750; www.glenallalodge.com; Ray; s/d
€50/80) This lodge, 8km southwest of Rathmullan, sits in a remote and bucolic spot,
with four rooms (three doubles, one family
room) furbished with tasteful wooden furniture and rustic style. There's also the helpful
knowledge of a local historian on tap.

★ Rathmullan House   HERITAGE HOTEL €€€

(☑ 074-915 8188; www.rathmullanhouse.com; off
R247; s/d from €90/180, set dinner from €48;
⊙ restaurant dinner 7-8.45pm; 🅿 @ 🛜 ☲) This
country house is large, luxurious and refreshingly dressed with non-frumpy furnishings. Sprawled over wooded gardens
on the shores of Lough Swilly, the original
house dates from the 1780s. The best of the
34 rooms have balconies or terraces. There's
a tennis court, two genteel bars, and a glass-
paned restaurant, the **Cook & Gardener**,
using organic produce from the property's
gardens.

ℹ Getting There & Away

It's best to have a set of wheels to get to Rathmullan.

From early June to late September, a handy
car ferry (☑ 087-211 2331; www.swillyferry.
com; people/car one way €5/17; ⊙ Apr-Oct)
operates between Rathmullan and Buncrana.

Portsalon & Fanad Head

A spectacular rollercoaster of a road hugs the
sea cliffs from Rathmullan to Portsalon (Port
an tSalainn), passing the early 19th-century
Knockalla Fort, one of six built to defend
against a possible French invasion – the history is told at its companion, Fort Dunree
(p470), across the lough. You'll see the lovely
length of Ballymastocker Beach swing gloriously into view, with Portsalon at its northern end.

THE URRIS HILLS

The Urris Hills, a rugged ridge of resistant quartzite (a continuation of the Knockalla Mountains on the Fanad Peninsula to the southwest), provide grandstand views of the Inishowen coast and the distant hills of Muckish, Errigal and Glenveagh. A network of waymarked walking trails ranges from 2km to 11km in length. Starting points are at Butler's Bridge and the car park at the north end of the Mamore Gap. Ask for the *Urris Walks* leaflet at Buncrana tourist office (p467).

Starting at Glen House, an easy 800m trail leads to the cascading 10m-high **Glenevin Waterfall**, with benches and picnic tables along the way. From Clonmany, follow the road signed to Tullagh Bay, cross the river and bear right at an intersection. Butler's Bridge and the waterfall car park are about 1km further on.

From Portsalon, the 8km scenic drive to the lighthouse on the rocky tip of Fanad Head is simply beautiful. The lighthouse and its environs is perfect photographing territory.

◉ Sights & Activities

★**Ballymastocker Beach**　　　　BEACH
(off R246, Portsalon) Once named the second most beautiful beach in the world by the British newspaper the *Observer,* this tawny-coloured Blue Flag beach is a supremely fine place to while away the hours. It is indeed stunning as you drive round the high headland on the R268 and it rears into view, but put the brakes on – there's a viewpoint you can pull into to take mesmerising shots.

Portsalon Golf Club　　　　GOLF
(☑074-915 9459; www.portsalongolfclub.com; off R246; green fees weekdays/weekends €40/50) The marvellously scenic Portsalon Golf Club follows the curve of the bay, alongside stunning Ballymastocker Beach.

✖ Eating

Lighthouse Tavern　　　PUB FOOD €€
(☑074-915 9212; mains from €4; ⊙12.30-11.30pm) Just before you reach Fanad Lighthouse, this welcoming and excellently located tavern is at hand for decent pub fare: pies, burgers and chips, cheesecake or just scones and tea.

Inishowen Peninsula

The Inishowen Peninsula reaches just far enough into the Atlantic to grab the title of northernmost point on the island of Ireland: Malin Head. It is remote, rugged, desolate and sparsely populated, making it a special and peaceful sort of place. Ancient sites and ruined castles abound, as do traditional thatched cottages that haven't yet been turned into holiday homes.

Surrounded by vast sea loughs and open ocean, Inishowen (meaning 'Island of Eoghain', the chieftain who also gave his name to County Tyrone) attracts a lot of birdlife. The variety is tremendous, with well over 200 resident and migrant species, including well-travelled avian visitors from Iceland, Greenland and North America. Irregular Atlantic winds mean rare and exotic species also blow in from time to time.

Twitchers should visit www.birdsireland.com. For information on everything else, visit www.visitinishowen.com.

❶ Getting There & Away

You'll want to be in a car to reach the Inishowen Peninsula; there are a few sporadic bus services and you can get to Magilligan in Londonderry from Greencastle by ferry, but in the main, you'll need to be driving.

There are two approaches: via Buncrana on the west side of the peninsula to Clonmany, Malin or Culdaff and Malin Head; or immediately east along the lovely southern shore following the R238 to Moville, Greencastle and Inishowen Head before making a route north to Malin Head. You can of course go one way and return by the other.

Buncrana

POP 6900

On the tame side of the peninsula, Buncrana is a busy but appealing town with its fair share of pubs and a 5km sandy beach on the shores of Lough Swilly.

John Newton, the composer of 'Amazing Grace', was inspired to write his legendary song after his ship the *Greyhound* took refuge in the calm waters of Lough Swilly during a severe storm in 1748. He and his crew

Inishowen Peninsula

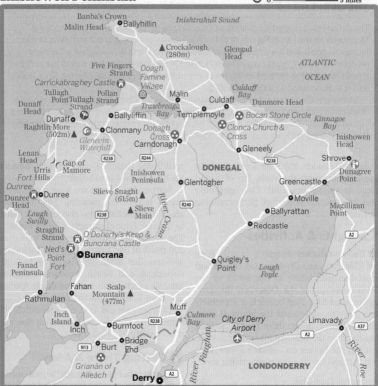

were welcomed in Buncrana after their near-death experience and his spiritual journey from slave trader to antislavery campaigner had its beginnings here. He went on to become a prolific hymn writer and later mentored William Wilberforce in his fight against slavery. For more on the story, visit www.amazinggrace.ie.

⊙ Sights

A waymarked Shore Walk heads north along the coast from the park north of the tourist office, leading to the town's main sights.

O'Doherty's Keep   HISTORIC BUILDING
(Castle Bridge) At the northern end of the seafront, the picture-perfect early-18th-century, six-arched **Castle Bridge** leads to these tower house ruins originally built by the O'Dohertys, the local chiefs, in 1430. It was burned by the English and then rebuilt for their own use.

Buncrana Castle   HISTORIC BUILDING
(Castle Bridge) At the side of O'Doherty's Keep is the manor-like Buncrana Castle, built in 1718 by John Vaughan, who also constructed the bridge. Wolfe Tone was imprisoned here following the unsuccessful French invasion in 1798.

Ned's Point Fort   HISTORIC BUILDING
(Ned's Point) Walk 500m from O'Doherty's Keep (turn left and stick to the shoreline) to find squat Ned's Point Fort (1812), built by the British.

🛏 Sleeping & Eating

★ Westbrook House   B&B €
(📞 074-936 1067; www.westbrookhouse.ie; Westbrook Rd; s/d from €35/60; 🔊) A handsome Georgian house set in beautiful gardens, Westbrook features chandeliers and antique furniture, giving it a refined sophistication. The honey served at breakfast comes from the bees kept in the lush garden.

GRIANAN OF AILEACH

This amphitheatre-like stone fort **Grianán of Aileách** (www.heritageireland.ie; off N13, Burt; ☺dawn-dusk) encircles the top of Grianán Hill like a halo and offers eye-popping views of the surrounding loughs. On clear days you can see as far as Derry. The fort may have existed at least 2000 years ago, but it's thought that the site itself goes back to pre-Celtic times as a temple to the god Dagda. Between the 5th and 12th centuries it was the seat of the O'Neills, before being demolished by Murtogh O'Brien, king of Munster. Most of what you see now is a reconstruction built between 1874 and 1878.

At the foot of the hill is merry-go-round-shaped Burt Church. Built in 1967, it was modelled on the fort by Derry architect Liam McCormack.

The fort is 18km south of Buncrana. Its small arena can resemble a circus whenever a tour bus empties out inside the heavily restored 4m-thick walls.

Tullyarvan Mill HOSTEL €
(☎074-936 1613; www.tullyarvanmill.com; off R238; dm/d €15/40; ☎) Set amid riverside gardens, this purpose-built 51-bed hostel is housed in a modern building attached to the historic Tullyarvan Mill. Just north of town, it also hosts regular cultural events and art exhibits.

Caldra Bed & Breakfast B&B €€
(☎074-936 3703; www.caldrabandb.com; Lisnakelly; s/d from €50/80; P☎) This large, modern B&B has four spacious rooms ideal for families. The public rooms feature impressive fireplaces and gilt mirrors while guest rooms are more sedate and understated. The garden and patio overlook Lough Swilly and the mountains.

★**Beach House** MODERN IRISH €€
(☎074-936 1050; www.thebeachhouse.ie; Swilly Rd; mains lunch €9-14, dinner €17-27; ☺5-9pm Thu-Sun, 12.30-4pm Sat & Sun, plus Tue & Wed Jul & Aug; 🖽) With picture windows overlooking the lough, this cafe-restaurant can easily be your destination for the day. The seasonal menu focuses on simple flavours superbly executed: there's everything from burgers to seafood right off the boats, while the wine list is excellent. Very recommended.

❶ Information

The **tourist office** (☎074-936 2600; www.visitinishowen.com; Railway Rd; ☺9.30am-5pm Mon-Fri; ☎) is near the beach and covers the entire peninsula.

Clonmany & Ballyliffin

POP 950

These two quaint villages and their surrounds have plenty to occupy visitors for a day or two. Clonmany has a working atmosphere and lots of characterful pubs, while

Ballyliffin feels more upmarket with more hotels and restaurants.

◉ Sights & Activities

Doagh Famine Village MUSEUM
(☎074-938 1901; www.doaghfaminevillage.com; Doagh Island; adult/child €8/4; ☺10am-5pm mid-Mar–Oct) Set in a reconstructed village of thatched cottages, this open-air museum is packed with fascinating titbits about the tragic Famine of the mid-19th century, and insightful comparisons with famine-stricken countries today. It's about 5km north of Ballyliffin, on Doagh Island (now part of the mainland),

Pollan Strand BEACH
This lovely stretch of beach makes for very pleasant walks on the sand; however, the atmospheric crashing breakers make it rather unsafe for swimming.

Tullagh Strand BEACH
Tullagh Strand, 2km northwest of Clonmany, is a little better for swimming than Pollan Strand, although it isn't recommended when the tide's going out.

Ballyliffin Golf Club GOLF
(☎074-937 6119; www.ballyliffingolfclub.com; off R238; green fees €50-100) With two championship courses, the Old Links and the Glashedy Links, Ballyliffin Golf Club is among the best places to play a round of golf in Donegal. The scenery is so beautiful that it can distract even the most focused golfer.

🛏 Sleeping & Eating

★**Glen House** GUESTHOUSE €€
(☎074-937 6745; www.glenhouse.ie; Straid, Clonmany; r from €70; P☎) Despite the grand surroundings and luxurious rooms, you'll find neither pretension nor high prices at

COUNTY DONEGAL INISHOWEN PENINSULA

this gem of a guesthouse, where rooms are a lesson in restrained sophistication and the setting is totally tranquil. The walking trail to Glenevin Waterfall and the Urris Hills starts next to the Rose Tea Room (074-937 6745; www.glenhouse.ie; Glen House; mains from €6; ⊙10am-6pm daily Jul & Aug, Sat & Sun Mar-Jun, Sep & Oct), which opens onto a deck.

Ballyliffin Lodge & Spa HOTEL €€
(074-937 8200; www.ballyliffinlodge.com; off R238, Ballyliffin; s/d from €60/90; 🖥🐾) This rather grand 40-room hotel is set back from the tiny village, with superior rooms looking out onto sublime ocean views. You can treat yourself at the state-of-the-art spa, to a round or two of golf, or to a meal in the relaxed bar.

Rusty Nail PUB
(074-937 6116; www.therustynail.ie; Clonmany; ⊙kitchen 4-11.30pm Fri, to 12.30am Sat, 2-11pm Sun, pub till late daily) While you might be tempted to sun yourself at the picnic table out the front, you should step inside this atmospheric pub for an excellent meal – it has all the classics and they're great. There's live music many nights too. It's just west of town.

ℹ Getting There & Away

Foyle Coaches (www.foylecoaches.com) runs four buses daily Monday to Friday and once on Saturday between Clonmany and Carndonagh (€2.80, 20 minutes).

Carndonagh

POP 1900

Carndonagh, surrounded by hills on three sides, is a busy commercial centre serving the local farming community. It's not a choice locale in these parts, but it's convenient for gathering information and provisions, and is home to the Donagh Cross (off R238), a significant archaeological relic.

The intricate 7th-century Donagh Cross (also called St Patrick's Cross) stands under a shelter by an Anglican church at the west end of town. It's carved with a darling short-bodied, big-eyed figure of Jesus, smiling impishly. Flanking the cross are two small pillars, one showing a man, possibly Goliath, with a sword and shield, and the other, David and his harp. In the graveyard there's a pillar with a carved marigold on a stem; nearby there is a crucifixion scene.

Stop in for a French-accented light lunch at Café Donagh (074-937 4191; www.cafedonagh.com; The Diamond; mains from €4; ⊙9.30am-5pm Mon-Sat, open Sun in summer), stock up on baked goods and sandwiches for a picnic, or sit down to plates of egg and chips and all-day fry-ups at this French-owned cafe.

ℹ Information

The Inishowen tourism office (074-937 4933; R238; ⊙9.30am-5pm Mon-Fri year-round, 11am-3pm Sat Jun-Aug), in the Public Services Centre by the roundabout north of The Diamond, is very helpful. There are banks and an ATM on The Diamond; the post office is in the shopping centre halfway down Bridge St towards the Donagh Cross.

Malin Head

The rolling swells never stop coming across the sea at Malin Head, the island's northern extreme. It's a name familiar to sailors and meteorological buffs, as Malin Head is one of the weather stations mentioned in BBC Radio's daily shipping forecast. You can almost imagine you can see Iceland (you can't) as you peer out through sometimes perfectly crystal blue but ever-blustery skies, which can change from sun to squall at the drop of a sou'wester. The rolling grasslands are dotted with suitably thick-coated donkeys, cows and well-wrapped-up hikers.

On the northernmost tip of Malin Head is Banba's Crown.

The small but very pretty village of Malin, on Trawbreaga Bay, 14km southeast of Malin Head, has a charmingly sedate movie-set quality, arranged around a neat, triangular village green.

◎ Sights & Activities

★ Banba's Crown VIEWPOINT
(Malin Head) On the northernmost tip of Malin Head, called Banba's Crown, stands a cumbersome 1805 clifftop tower that was built by the British admiralty and later used as a Lloyds signal station. Around it are concrete huts that were used by the Irish army in WWII as lookout posts. To the west from the fort-side car park, a path leads to Hell's Hole, a chasm where the incoming waters crash against the rock forms. To the east a longer headland walk leads to the Wee House of Malin, a hermit's cave in the cliff face.

The view to the west takes in, from left to right, the Inishowen Hills, Dunaff Head, low-lying Fanad Head with its lighthouse, the twin 'horns' of Horn Head and the twin bumps of Tory Island; in the far distance, to the left of Fanad lighthouse, are Muckish and Errigal Mountains. To the east lie raised beach terraces, and offshore you can see the lighthouse on the remote island of Inishtrahull. A viewing area has free telescopes. On a few nights a year you can even see the Northern Lights.

Watch for the truck-based **Caffe Banba** (☑074-937 0538; www.caffebanba.com; ⊙noon-5.30pm Easter-Sep) that is sometimes in the car park selling superb coffees and baked goods. The car park itself can get quickly crowded with cars during the busy season.

Malin Head Tours   TOURS
(☑087 458 0033; www.malinheadtours.com; off R242, Malin Head Community Centre; ⊙noon Sat) Unlock the secrets of this blustery region on these fascinating driving, walking and boat tours.

🛌 Sleeping

Whitestrand B&B   B&B €
(☑074-937 0335, 086 822 9163; www.white strand.net; off R242, Middletown; s/d €32/64; ☎) Perfectly placed amid the bluffs and hills leading to Malin Head, this comfy B&B has three fine bedrooms. As a welcome you'll receive a hot beverage and tasty home-baked treats.

Malin Village B&B   B&B €
(☑074-937 0763; www.malinvillagebandb.com; The Green, Malin; s/d €40/70) Right on the village green, this charming B&B has a choice of cosy rooms, some traditional with antique furniture, and others more contemporary with white linen and pretty floral patterns. Although you'll get breakfast here, guests also have use of a kitchen.

Sandrock Holiday Hostel   HOSTEL €
(☑086 325 6323; www.sandrockhostel.com; Port Ronan Pier, Malin Head; dm €13.50-20; ☎) The cinematic view from this IHH hostel – at the end of the road, above a rocky bay on the western side of the headland – will take your breath away. Inside are 20 beds in two dorms, plus musical instruments and laundry facilities. Bike rental (€10 per day) is available for nonguests. Ask about the very limited community-bus connections to get here.

🍷 Drinking & Nightlife

McClean's   PUB
(☑074-937 0607; Main St, Malin; ⊙noon-late) This treasure of an old-time pub on the east corner of the village green has the best craic in Malin and often has live music. Grab a table on its outdoor side terrace for lovely views of the estuary and old arched stone bridge.

ℹ️ Getting There & Away

You'll need a car to get up here. The best way to approach Malin Head is by the R238/242 from Carndonagh, rather than up the rough road along the eastern side from Culdaff. You can get a **North West Busways** (☑074-938 2619; www. foylecoaches.com) bus from Moville to Malin town, but it's still a considerable distance to Malin Head. The car park can get quickly stuffed with cars in summer.

Culdaff & Around
POP 270
Sheep vastly outnumber people around the secluded beach village of Culdaff, situated on the remote north coast of Inishowen. If isolation is what you are after, make a beeline here.

◎ Sights
★**Culdaff Beach**   BEACH
(off R238) This Blue Flag beach is great for swimming and windsurfing. You can wander its gorgeous length and get lost in the grassy sand dunes, and there's a fun playground for kids too. Lifeguards are on duty from

WORTH A TRIP

FORT DUNREE

The best preserved and most dramatic of six forts built by the British on Lough Swilly following the 1798 uprising of the United Irishmen (which was supported by France), when fears of a French invasion were at fever pitch.

The original **fort** (☑ 074-936 1817; www.dunree.pro.ie; Dunree Head; adult/child €7/5; ⊙ 10.30am-6pm Mon-Sat, 1-6pm Sun Jun-Sep, 10.30am-4.30pm Mon-Fri, 1-6pm Sat & Sun Oct-May), built in 1813, now houses a military museum, while the surrounding headland is littered with WWI and WWII remains you can explore. There are several good waymarked walks.

The winding fjord of Lough Swilly is one of Ireland's great natural harbours, and has played its part in many historical dramas, from Viking invasions and the Flight of the Earls to the 1798 Rising and WWI.

Huge naval guns were added to the fort in the late 19th century, and during WWI the lough was used as a marshalling area for Atlantic convoys, and as an anchorage for the Royal Navy's Grand Fleet. Unusually, it remained in British hands after the partition of Ireland in 1922, and was only handed over to the Republic of Ireland in 1938.

June to September. There's an annual New Year's Day charity swim in the freezing water, which is a hoot.

Clonca Church & Cross HISTORIC SITE
(Clonca) Inside this church is an intricately carved tombstone sporting a sword and hurling-stick motif. The carved lintel over the door is thought to come from an earlier church. Outside, the remains of the cross show the miracle of the loaves and fishes on the eastern face. Heading from Culdaff towards Moville on the R238, turn east after 1.2km at Bocan Church. The Clonca Church and cross are 1.7km to the north behind some farm buildings.

Sleeping

★ **McGrory's of Culdaff** GUESTHOUSE €€
(☑ 074-937 9104; www.mcgrorys.ie; R238; s/d from €65/100, mains €12-25; ⊙ bar food noon-9pm daily, restaurant 6-9pm Fri-Sun; �) This landmark hotel and bar has 17 stylish and luxurious rooms. Of the three bars, catch live music in the **Backroom**, which books international singer-songwriters and traditional music. McGrory's classic Irish cuisine, served in the **Front Room**, is the best for miles around.

Greencastle
POP 820

⊙ Sights

Inishowen Maritime Museum & Planetarium MUSEUM
(☑ 074-938 1363; www.inishowenmaritime.com; off R241; adult/child museum €5/3, museum &

planetarium show adult/child €10/6; ⊙ 9.30am-5.30pm Mon-Fri year-round, plus 9.30am-5.30pm Sat & noon-5.30pm Sun Easter-Sep) An eccentric collection of artefacts awaits at this museum in a former coastguard station on a grassy verge right by the waterfront. The most fascinating exhibits are from the sunken wrecks of Lough Foyle exploring the demise of the Spanish Armada and the departure from these waters of Irish emigrants. There's also an astronomy show in the full-dome digital theatre at the Planetarium.

A welcoming **cafe** with tables out the front is right next door. If the sun's out, grab a coffee and savour the harbour views.

★ **Kealy's Seafood Bar** SEAFOOD €€
(☑ 074-938 1010; www.kealysseafoodbar.ie; The Harbour; mains €15-50; early-bird set menu €22-26; ⊙ 12.30-3pm & 5-9.30pm; �) Family-run for over 25 years, this bistro offers locally caught seafood so fresh you almost have to fight the harbourside seals for it. Its unpretentious nautical-style polished timber decor belies its numerous culinary awards. It's a splendid spot for anything from a bowl of chowder to a lobster feast, and every meal has a side-serving of delicious views.

The early-bird menu is served from 5pm to 6.30pm.

Malin Pebbles ARTS & CRAFTS
(☑ 074-938 1432; www.malinpebbles.com; Church Brae; ⊙ hours vary) Local semiprecious stones are transformed into lovely jewellery and unusual gifts by Petra Watzka at her workshop, 100m uphill from the ferry – they make terrific gifts. Call ahead to see if it's open.

ⓘ Getting There & Away

The best way to reach Greencastle and the rest of the Inishown Peninsula is by car; you can get to Magilligan in Londonderry by **ferry** (📞 074-938 1901; www.loughfoyleferry.com; Harbour; person/car one way €3/15; ⊙ Apr-Sep).

Moville & Around

POP

The terrific 4km **coastal walkway** from Moville to Greencastle takes in the stretch of coast where the emigrant steamers used to moor; there are sublime views along the way.

🛏 Sleeping

Moville Boutique Hostel   HOSTEL €
(📞 074-938 2378; www.movilleboutiquehostel. com; off R238, Moville; campsites per person €10, dm/s/d from €22/28/49, apt €100, all incl breakfast; 🛜) A small lane leads off the R238, 300m north of town, to a grove of trees and this secluded 20-bed hostel. It's in a nook-and-cranny-filled 18th-century farmhouse beside a stream, with some gorgeous spots to pitch a tent. The owner is a fount of information on the area's rich history and folklore. Brekkie is a self-catering choice of teas, coffees, milk, breakfast cereals and organic sourdough bread.

It also claims to have Ireland's oldest bridge in its garden.

Redcastle Hotel & Spa   HOTEL €€
(📞 074-938 5555; www.redcastlehoteldonegal. com; R238, Redcastle; s/d from €90/140; 🛜 ≋) The peninsula's smartest luxury resort is on the coast 7km southwest of Moville,

tucked away off the main road. The 93 rooms here are comfortable and classy. Restaurants include the **Edge**, which has excellent views and modern Irish cuisine. Facilities include a nine-hole golf course, a spa, a swimming pool and a kids' club during the summer.

ⓘ Getting There & Away

North West Busways (📞 074-938 2619; www. foylecoaches.com) runs one bus a day Monday to Friday to Moville (€7.30, 45 minutes) from Derry, via Carndonagh and Malin town.

OFF THE BEATEN TRACK

INISHOWEN HEAD

Views abound on a waymarked walk (8.5km; allow two to three hours) to Inishowen Head, where a WWII lookout point commands a panoramic view east along the Northern Irish coast to the Antrim Hills, Rathlin Island and the distant outlines of Islay and the Mull of Kintyre in Scotland. The little bay of Portkille, a short distance to the north, is said to be the final landfall of St Colmcille (Columba) in Ireland before he sailed for Iona in AD 563; a bronze plaque by the path describes the site.

The walk begins some 4km beyond Greencastle on the R241 – there's a car park beside a small sandy beach with a sign describing the walk. The nearby twin towers (one now only a stump) are what's left of Shrove Lighthouse, built in 1837.

The Midlands

POP 486,000 / AREA 10,782 SQ KM

Best Places to Eat

➡ Oarsman (p475)

➡ Bastion Kitchen (p483)

➡ Gallic Kitchen (p496)

➡ Spinners on Castle St (p489)

➡ Lowe & Co (p483)

Best Places to Sleep

➡ Bastion B&B (p483)

➡ Lough Key House (p480)

➡ Castle Durrow (p497)

➡ Roundwood House (p498)

➡ Lough Rynn (p475)

Why Go?

Often passed through on the way to someplace more vaunted, the Midlands brims with verdant pastoral landscapes, stately homes, archaeological treasures, sacred monastic sites, lakeside vistas and sleepy towns where the locals are genuinely glad to see you.

Getting lost along the twisting back roads of these six counties is an unhurried pleasure and you're virtually guaranteed to happen upon a local village shop, pub, garage or post office and find it little changed in decades. It's refreshingly free of tour buses and souvenir stalls and well worth at least a pause in your journeys.

The Midlands is dominated by the River Shannon, which meanders through fields and forests, drawing boaters and fishers in shoals. Plush hotels and gourmet restaurants have sprung up along its banks, making it a wonderfully scenic and surprisingly cosmopolitan way to travel. If you're in search of a genuine slice of rural Irish life, this area makes the perfect retreat.

When to Go

➡ Spring is a great time for revelling in Ireland's famous greener-than-green countryside, reflected in the many waterways and lakes; accented by fields of wildflowers.

➡ During summer, fairs, festivals and special events take place throughout the region as locals spend the long days outside.

➡ July through September is the ideal time for cruising the Shannon with everything open, better weather and a spirited summertime crowd in the riverside pubs and restaurants.

➡ Many museums and other attractions are closed or have greatly reduced hours during the short days from November to March.

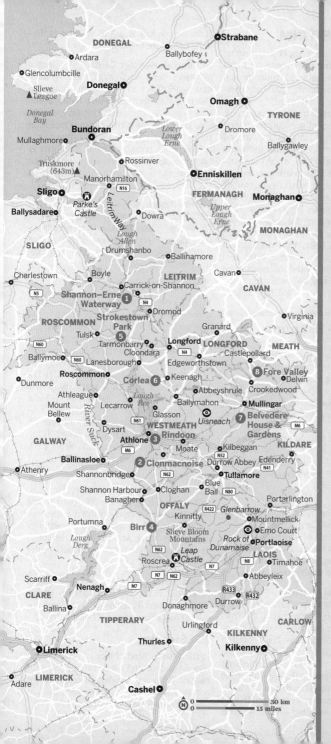

The Midlands Highlights

1 **Shannon–Erne Waterway** (p474) Slowing down a gear and discovering the rolling landscapes.

2 **Clonmacnoise** (p492) Contemplating the lost land of saints and scholars at Ireland's finest monastic site.

3 **Rindoon** (p484) Going for a lakeside jaunt through this deserted medieval village.

4 **Birr** (p487) Roaming the Georgian streets and exploring the castle grounds in this elegant town.

5 **Strokestown Park** (p478) Learning about Ireland's greatest disaster at the harrowing Famine museum.

6 **Corlea** (p481) Exploring the amazing Iron Age oak trackway unearthed here.

7 **Belvedere House & Gardens** (p485) Wandering the magnificent corridors and gardens and marvelling at its spiteful history.

8 **Fore Valley** (p486) Visiting this emerald-green valley and discovering impressive Christian ruins and otherworldly views.

COUNTY LEITRIM

The delights of unassuming County Leitrim are a well-kept secret, and it seems the locals like it that way. The untamed landscape and authentic rural charm are genuinely cherished by those who call it home.

Leitrim was ravaged by the Famine in the 19th century and spent subsequent generations struggling with mass emigration and unemployment, but today it has become a beloved hideout for artists, writers and musicians, as well as a huge boating centre.

The county is split virtually in two by Lough Allen, and the mighty River Shannon remains the area's biggest draw. Lively Carrick-on-Shannon, the county town, makes a great base for exploring the region by road or water. Leitrim provides a vital link between popular counties Sligo and Donegal. It even allows the Midlands some Wild Atlantic Way action via a 5km bit of the N15 where a nib of Leitrim touches the sea.

Carrick-on-Shannon

POP 4100

Carrick-on-Shannon is a charming riverside town. Since the completion of the Shannon–Erne Waterway, the marina here has thrived. The town is a hugely popular weekend destination with a good choice of accommodation and restaurants, and a great music and arts scene.

During the 17th and most of the 18th centuries Carrick was a Protestant enclave, and the local residents' wealth can still be seen in the graceful buildings around the town.

◉ Sights

Hanging around the waterfront is really the thing to do here, but Carrick does have some wonderful examples of early-19th-century architecture on St George's Terrace, including **Hatlev Manor**, home of the St George family, and the **Old Courthouse**.

Costello Memorial Chapel   CHURCH
(Bridge St; ◷10am-4.30pm Easter-Sep) This diminutive place by the corner of the road measures just 5m by 3.6m, making it one of Europe's smallest chapels. It was built in 1877 by Edward Costello, distraught at the early death of his wife Mary. Both husband and wife now rest within the grey limestone interior lit by a single stained-glass window. Their embalmed bodies were placed in lead coffins, which sit on either side of the door.

If the door is locked, ask at St George's Heritage Centre for the key.

St George's Heritage Centre   MUSEUM
(St Mary's Close; adult/child €5/free; ◷11am-4pm Wed-Sat) Set in a restored church up the hill, this heritage centre looks at the history and landscape of Leitrim from old Gaelic traditions through to Plantation times. A tour visits the old Famine workhouse, which remains a bleak memorial to harder times, as well as the Famine Garden of Remembrance, both a short stroll from the Centre.

Leitrim Design House   ARTS CENTRE
(☑071-965 0550; www.leitrimdesignhouse.ie; St George's Tce; ◷10am-6pm Mon-Fri, to 5pm Sat) Retail gallery displaying a host of well-crafted textiles, ceramics, paintings, toys and gifts from local craftspeople.

🏃 Activities

Running the length of the Shannon and on through northwestern County Cavan to the southern shore of Upper Lough Erne, the Shannon–Erne Waterway creates an amazing 750km network of rivers, lakes and artificial navigations.

Carrick is the Shannon–Erne Waterway's boat-hire capital, with several companies based at the marina. The canal's 16 locks are fully automated, you don't need a licence, and you're given full instructions on handling your boat before you set off. High-season prices start at around €1200 per week for a two-berth cruiser, but shop around.

Moon River   CRUISE
(☑071-962 1777; www.moonriver.ie; The Quay; cruises from €15; ◷mid-Mar–Oct) The 110-seat boat *Moon River* runs one-hour cruises on the Shannon. There are one to four sailings depending on the season; check the information board on the quay for details, or the website.

Emerald Star   BOATING
(☑071-962 7633; www.emeraldstar.ie; Marina; ◷9am-6pm Mon-Fri, 10am-4pm Sat) Based locally, it has a huge range of boats for rent.

🛏 Sleeping

Carrick has a good choice of accommodation, in and around town, from hotels with history, B&Bs and modern hotels to more remote and exclusive castle choices. Book in advance for summer and weekends.

★**Lough Rynn** HOTEL €€

(☑ 071-963 2700; www.loughrynn.ie; Lough Rynn, Mohill; r inc breakfast €140-175; 🖭) This tremendous castle in splendid grounds south of Mohill – and right between Lough Rynn and Lough Errew – has been transformed into a beautiful 42-bedroom hotel. The rooms and interior are lovely, while the grounds are sumptuous in the extreme, with nature trails and a gorgeous walled garden. Look out for the huge and very old Monkey Puzzle tree.

★**Bush Hotel** HOTEL €€

(☑ 071-967 1000; www.bushhotel.com; Main St; s/d from €65/94; 🖭) One of Ireland's oldest in-town hotels, this family-run place only gets better with age. The public spaces are kept thoughtfully updated while still preserving heritage charm; historic photos abound. The 60 rooms are more contemporary and corporate with slick modern furnishings, plush carpeting and desks. There's a modern wing at the back. History buffs can check into the Michael Collins room, where he stayed in 1917.

Lock View House B&B €€

(☑ 071-964 0790; www.bedandbreakfastleitrim. com; off R209, Kilclare; s/d from €45/80; 🖭) A country retreat 10km northeast of Carrick, this lovely B&B has four large rooms, each with views tinged with emerald, while beds range from twins to kings. There's tea and cakes on arrival. True to its name, you can soak up the calm as you watch cruisers and boats navigate the nearby lock on the Shannon–Erne Waterway.

Cryan's Hotel HOTEL €€

(☑ 071-967 2066; www.cryanshotel.ie; The Quay; s/d from €65/100; 🖭) Right by the riverfront, this modern hotel is popular with boaters needing a break from their poop deck as well as tourists. The facade is nothing special, but the 24 rooms are large and well equipped, and many have water views. A relative runs the pub of the same name around the corner.

✖ **Eating**

Lena's Tea Room CAFE €

(☑ 071-962 2791; http://lenastearoom.ie; Main St; snacks €4-10; ⊙10am-5.30pm Tue-Sat; 🖭) This very, very twee and cutesy cafe has 1920s-vintage-style decor with eclectic furniture, including comfy sofas. The menu features home-baked cakes, scones and breads, plus soups, tarts and sandwiches. Afternoon tea is a speciality with loose-leaf teas, china cups and delicious cakes.

★**Oarsman** MODERN IRISH €€

(☑ 071-962 1733; www.theoarsman.com; Bridge St; mains €10-27; ⊙food noon-9pm Tue-Sat, bar till 11pm; 🖭) 🍴 This upmarket pub near the river serves up some of the best casual fare in the region. The menu is seasonal and locally sourced, from excellent burgers to more complex mains. Choose from a great list of Irish microbrews (including Carrig Brewing) in the pub downstairs. The upstairs has more of a restaurant vibe. Expect waits most nights.

★**Cottage** INTERNATIONAL €€

(☑ 071-962 5933; www.cottagerestaurant.ie; off N4, Jamestown; mains €17-27; ⊙5.30-10pm Wed-Sun, plus noon-4pm Sun; 🖭) Set in a small white-washed cottage overlooking a weir and right by the River Shannon, this humble-looking place belies the superb quality of food on offer within. Chef Sham Hanifa's menu offers seasonal dishes created using vegetables from the restaurant garden, meats from local suppliers and artisan cheeses. The menu regularly changes. It's 5km southeast of Carrick.

Vittos Restaurant & Wine Bar ITALIAN €€

(☑ 071-962 7000; www.vittosrestaurant.com; Bridge St; mains €15-25; ⊙5-9pm Wed-Fri, 1-10pm Sat & Sun; 🖭) In a wood-beamed stone building, this family-friendly restaurant has an extensive menu of classic Italian dishes, including great pasta and pizza. Burgers and steaks are chargrilled. It's part of the Market Yard Centre (p476) complex.

🍺 **Drinking & Entertainment**

Look for beers by locally based Carrig Brewing. Its Poachers Pale Ale – among others – is superb. Pubs are not in short supply in town.

Anderson's Thatch Pub PUB

(☑ 087 228 3288; www.andersonspub.com; Elphin Rd/R368; ⊙6-11pm) You can hardly miss this traditional thatched pub while driving along the R368 towards Elphin. Dating from 1734, it's worth a trip for its live-music sessions (Wednesday, Friday and Saturday), old-world atmosphere and country charm. It's 4km south of town and easily reached by taxi.

Flynn's Corner House PUB

(cnr Main & Bridge Sts; ⊙5-11pm) This authentic stuck-in-a-time-warp pub serves a good pint of Guinness and has live music on Friday nights – savour it.

Dock Arts Centre THEATRE
(☑071-965 0828; www.thedock.ie; St George's Tce; ⊘galleries 10am-6pm Mon-Fri, to 5pm Sat) Set in the grand surroundings of the 19th-century former courthouse, this place hosts performances, exhibitions and workshops.

🛍 Shopping

★ **Market Yard Centre** ARTS & CRAFTS
(off Bridge St; ⊘shop hours vary, farmers market 10am-2pm Thu) This restored series of buildings in the centre of town has an interesting array of shops selling everything from nautical gear to crafts. Don't miss the **farmers market**, which draws an impressive array of organic farmers, bakers and food producers.

ℹ Information

The **tourist office** (☑071-962 3274; www. leitrimtourism.com; The Quay; ⊘9.30am-5pm Easter-Sep) has a good walking-tour brochure, which takes in Carrick's places of interest.

ℹ Getting There & Away

BUS

Bus Éireann (www.buseireann.ie) runs to Dublin (€19, three hours, four daily).

TRAIN

Irish Rail (www.irishrail.ie) runs seven trains daily to Dublin (from €24, 2¼ hours) and Sligo (from €16, 55 minutes). The station is on Croghan Rd, 500m southwest of the centre.

North Leitrim

North of Carrick-on-Shannon, the Leitrim landscape comes into its own, its ruffled hills, steel-grey lakes and isolated cottages exuding a genuine rural charm. You'll also find the Leitrim side of Lough Gill is easily accessible on a day trip from Sligo; alternatively, it's a fine entry point to County Sligo and its sights.

If you fancy taking to the hills on foot, the Leitrim Way walking trail begins in Drumshanbo and ends in Manorhamilton, a distance of 48km.

⊙ Sights & Activities

★ **Parke's Castle** CASTLE
(www.heritageireland.ie; off R286, Fivemile Bourne; adult/child €5/3; ⊘10am-6pm Easter-Sep; 🅿) The tranquil surrounds of Parke's Castle, with swans drifting by on Lough Gill and neat grass cloaking the old moat, belie the fact that its early Plantation architecture

was created out of an unwelcome English landlord's insecurity and fear.

The restored, three-storey castle forms part of one of the five sides of the bawn, which also has three rounded turrets at its corners.

The castle is just over the border from County Sligo, 11km east of Sligo Town.

It's easiest to reach from Sligo Town and can be tied in with a car tour of the lough.

★ **Rose of Innisfree** CRUISE
(☑071-916 4266; www.roseofinnisfree.com; off R286, Parke's Castle; adult €15-18; ⊘12.30pm & 3.30pm Easter-Oct) You can take a 1½-hour cruise on Lough Gill from Parke's Castle (one hour) or Doorly Park in Sligo (three hours) and enjoy the best view of Innisfree and the lough. Trips feature live recitals of Yeats' poetry, and good coffee and fresh scones are available on board. The company runs a bus from Sligo to the castle. Call for departure times.

There are extra boat trips in summer.

COUNTY ROSCOMMON

Studded with more than 5000 megalithic tombs, ring forts and mounds, and home to a couple of excellent museums, enigmatic Roscommon is shrouded in myth and a haven for history buffs. Add well-preserved mansions and some wonderful monastic ruins and it's hard to understand why the county sees so few visitors. Beyond the romance of times past, Roscommon has plenty of rolling countryside splashed with lakes and cleaved by the Rivers Shannon and Suck: attributes much appreciated by visiting anglers.

Roscommon Town

POP 5700

The county town of Roscommon is very much a place of local business and commerce, but it has a small, stately centre and some significant and picturesque abbey and castle ruins that make it worth exploration.

⊙ Sights & Activities

Roscommon's central square is dominated by its former **courthouse** (now the Bank of Ireland). Opposite, the facade of the **old jail** survives.

Pick up a brochure and map at tourist offices detailing the **Suck Valley Way**, a 75km walking trail along the River Suck, including some pleasant strolls along the river bank.

★ **Roscommon County Museum**   MUSEUM
(The Square; adult/child €2/1; ⊙10am-5pm Mon-Fri, to 3pm Sat) Set in a former Presbyterian church (1863), this volunteer-run museum has an idiosyncratic collection, including an inscribed 9th-century slab from St Coman's monastery and a superb medieval sheila-na-gig fertility symbol. The unusual stained-glass Star of David window, representing the Trinity, above the door is another draw. Don't leave without hearing the story of Lady Betty, the 18th-century hanging woman.

The museum is an unofficial tourist office and has stacks of info.

Roscommon Castle   RUINS
(off Castle St; ⊙dawn-dusk) The impressive ruins of the town's Norman castle stand alone in a field to the north of town, beautifully framed by the landscaped lawns and small lake of the new town park. Built in 1269, the castle was almost immediately destroyed by Irish forces, and its turbulent history continued until the final surrender to Cromwell's forces in 1652, who took down the fortifications. A conflagration in 1690 sealed the castle's fate.

**Roscommon Dominican
Priory**   HISTORIC BUILDING
(off Circular Rd; ⊙dawn-dusk) At the south end of town, the remains of a 13th-century priory are almost hidden behind a primary school. It merits a quick visit for its unusual 15th-century carving of eight *gallóglí* ('gallowglasses' or mercenary soldiers) wielding seven swords and an axe.

🛏 **Sleeping & Eating**

**Gleeson's Townhouse
& Restaurant**   B&B €€
(☎090-662 6954; www.gleesonstownhouse.com; The Square; s/d from €80/90; 🅿@🛜) What might better be called 'Gleeson's Empire' is based in this 19th-century townhouse, set back from the square in its own courtyard. Rooms are individually decorated ranging from extravagant floral wallpaper to pine furniture and buttercup-yellow walls.

There's a range of rooms here, from singles to doubles, suites and family rooms.

**Gleeson's Restaurant &
Artisan Food & Wine Shop**   DELI €€
(☎090-662 6954; www.gleesonstownhouse.com; The Square; mains €12-23; ⊙cafe 8am-6pm daily, restaurant noon-9pm daily, shop 10am-6pm Mon-Sat) The best of modern Irish cooking is on

**ARIGNA MINERS WAY &
HISTORICAL TRAIL**
....
Covering 118km of north Roscommon, east Sligo and mid-Leitrim, this trail is a series of well-signposted tracks and hill passes covering the routes taken by miners on their way to work. A pamphlet with maps is available from local tourist offices and there are plentiful signs along the route. The route usually takes around five days to complete.

display in Gleeson's on The Square. Local – and often organic – produce is used to create excellent dishes both in the casual cafe and the more elegant restaurant.

The shop has an array of baked goods and prepared foods, perfect for a fabulous picnic to take on your explorations of the county's ancient sites.

It's worth stopping by, if only for a seafood chowder, even if you don't go the whole hog for a Roscommon lamb stew or a crispy roast half duck.

ℹ **Information**

The **museum** is an unofficial tourist office and has stacks of info; also check out www.visitroscommon.com.

ℹ **Getting There & Away**

Bus Éireann (www.buseireann.ie) runs two buses daily between Westport (€12.50, 2¼ hours) and Athlone (€7.50, 35 minutes).

Roscommon train station is in Abbeytown, just south of the town centre. **Irish Rail** (www.irishrail.ie) runs five trains daily on the line from Dublin (€20, two hours) to Westport (from €20, 1½ hours).

Strokestown & Around
POP 820

Strokestown's main street is a grand tree-lined avenue that remains a testament to the lofty aspirations of one of the local landed gentry who wished it to be Europe's widest. It's a striking feature in what is a now a sleepy town most notable for its historic estate and unmissable Famine Museum and Strokestown Park.

Add in the nearby ancient Celtic site of Rathcroghan and you can easily spend a day exploring the area. Over the May Day Bank

Holiday weekend, the town bursts into life for the International Poetry Festival.

Bus Éireann (p477) buses run from Dublin via Mullingar and Longford to Strokestown, stopping outside the Percy French Hotel.

◉ Sights

★ Strokestown Park   HISTORIC SITE

(☎ 071-963 3013; www.strokestownpark.ie; off N5; adult/child house, Famine Museum & gardens €13.50/6, 1 site only €9/6; ⊙ 10.30am-5.30pm mid-Mar–Oct, to 4pm Nov–mid-Mar, tours noon, 2.30pm, 4pm mid-Mar–Oct, 2pm Nov–mid-Mar) At the end of Strokestown's main avenue, triple Gothic arches lead to Strokestown Park House. The original 120-sq-km estate was granted by King Charles II to Nicholas Mahon for his support in the English Civil War. Nicholas' grandson Thomas commissioned Richard Cassels to build him a Palladian mansion in the early 18th century. The gardens give some idea of the original wealth. Admission to the house is by a 50-minute guided tour.

The guided tours take in a galleried kitchen with original ovens dating from 1740, a schoolroom with an exercise book of neatly written dictation dating from 1934 (and, according to her red pen, deemed disgraceful by the governess), and a toy room complete with 19th-century toys and funhouse mirrors.

Over the centuries, the estate decreased in size along with the family's fortunes. When it was eventually sold in 1979, it had been whittled down to (a still vast) 120 hectares. The estate was bought as a complete lot, so virtually all its remaining contents are intact.

The walled garden contains the longest herbaceous border in Ireland and Britain, which blooms in a rainbow of colours in summer. Across the 6 acres there is also a folly, a lily pond and Ireland's oldest glass greenhouse, dating from 1780. The must-see Famine Museum is also on the grounds of the house, located in the Stables Yard.

There is a small cafe on-site.

Famine Museum   MUSEUM

(www.strokestownpark.ie/attractions/famine-museum; Strokestown Park; adult/child €9/6; ⊙ 10.30am-5.30pm mid-Mar–Oct, to 4pm Nov–mid-Mar) In direct and deliberate contrast to the splendour of Strokestown Park and its grounds is the harrowing Irish National Famine Museum, located in the Stables Yard of the house, which documents the devastating 1840s potato blight. It concisely shows how the industrial age coupled with the Famine devastated the overpopulated island of eight million (about 1.6 million more than today). Strokestown landlord Major Denis Mahon ruthlessly evicted starving peasants who couldn't pay their rent, chartering boats to transport them away from Ireland.

Around half of these 1000 emigrants died on the overcrowded 'coffin ships', and a further 200 died while in quarantine in Québec (the cheapest route). Perhaps unsurprisingly, Mahon was assassinated by three of his tenants in 1847 (two of whom were publicly hanged in Roscommon). The gun they used is on display.

There's a huge amount of information and you can easily spend an hour or more; exhibits here rise above mere lore thanks to more than 50,000 documents that were preserved from the 19th century and which provide often chilling factual underpinning. You'll emerge with an unblinking insight into the starvation of the poor, and the ignorance, callousness and cruelty of those who were in a position to help.

★ Rathcroghan   HISTORIC SITE

(☎ 071-963 9268; www.rathcroghan.ie; N5, Tulsk; adult/child museum €5/3, site tour €8/3, combined museum & site tour €12/6; ⊙ visitor centre 9am-5pm Mon-Sat year-round, plus noon-4pm Sun May-Aug; ⊞) Anyone with an interest in Celtic mythology will be enthralled by this area around the village of Tulsk, which contains 60 ancient national monuments including standing stones, barrows, huge cairns and monumental fortresses, making it the most important Celtic royal site in Europe. The landscape and its sacred structures have lain largely undisturbed for the past 3000 years.

Tulsk is 10km west of Strokestown. Bus Éireann's frequent Dublin-to-Westport route stops right outside the visitor centre.

It's hard to grasp just how significant Rathcroghan is, as archaeological digs are continuing, but it has already been established that the site is bigger and older than Tara in County Meath and was at one time a major seat of Irish power.

The excellent visitor centre is the place to start. It has diagrams, photographs, informative panels and maps that explain the significance of the sites, and it can let you know when access to the monuments is possible (some are privately owned). Most are along a 6km stretch of the N5 to the west. Rathmore and Rathcroghan Mound both have public access and parking.

A 15-minute video includes an introduction to the sites and legends, plus an animated story about the legend of the Táin Bó Cúailnge (Cattle Raid of Cooley), which should appeal to all ages. Also good is the timeline with replica artefacts.

According to the legend, Queen Maeve (Medbh) – whose burial cairn is at the summit of Knocknarea in County Sligo – had her palace at Cruachan Aí. The **Oweynagat Cave** (Cave of the Cats), believed to be the entrance to the Celtic otherworld, is also nearby. As it is located on private land, a guide has to accompany anyone who enters the cave. This can be arranged at the visitor centre (€20 per person).

Elphin Windmill   WINDMILL
(☑083 406 2113; Windmill Rd, Elphin; adult/child €5/3; ☺11am-4pm) This charming little red-and-white 18th-century windmill is well worth a diversion for photo-ops and a guided tour. It is conceivably the oldest operational windmill in Ireland. From Strokestown, drive along the R368 to Elphin, then head west along the R369 for about 800m before heading north up Windmill Rd for around 1km to the windmill.

✲ Festivals & Events

International Poetry Festival   LITERATURE
(www.facebook.com/StrokestownPoetryFestival; ☺early May) The town bursts into literary bloom during the International Poetry Festival, held over the May Day Bank Holiday weekend.

🛏 Sleeping

Percy French Hotel   HOTEL €€
(☑071-963 3300; www.thepercyfrenchhotel.com; Bridge St; s/d incl breakfast from €60/90; ☏) This very centrally located hotel enjoys a pretty much ideal position and offers comfortable rooms and a decent restaurant, overseen by efficient and friendly staff.

Boyle & Around
POP 5110

A quiet town at the foot of the Curlew Mountains, Boyle is a scenic and worthwhile stop, home to beautiful Boyle Abbey, a 4000-year-old dolmen on the far side of a railway line, the hands-on and impressive King House Historic & Cultural Centre, and a scenic and activity-packed forest park.

History

The history of Boyle is the history of the King family, former residents of grand King House. In 1603 Staffordshire-born John King was granted land in Roscommon with the aim of 'reducing the Irish to obedience'. Over the next 150 years, through canny marriages and cold-blooded conquests, his descendants made their name and fortune, becoming one of the largest landowning families in Ireland. The town of Boyle subsequently grew around their estate, but suffered badly during the Famine years.

◉ Sights

★**Arigna Mining Experience**   MINE
(☑071-964 6466; www.arignaminingexperience.ie; Derreenavoggy; adult/student €10/8; ☺10am-6pm, tours hourly; P ♿) Ireland's first and last coal mine (1600s to 1990) is remembered at the Arigna Mining Experience, set in the hills above Lough Allen. The highlight is the 50-minute underground tour, which takes you 400m down to the coal face and includes a simulated mini-explosion. Tours are led by ex-miners who really bring home the gruelling working conditions and dangers.

Wear warm clothing and sturdy shoes as it can be cold and muddy. It's 23km northeast of Boyle.

There's also an exhibition dedicated to the miners and the equipment they used; plus a short video.

King House Historic & Cultural Centre   HISTORIC BUILDING
(☑071-966 3242; www.kinghouse.ie; Main St; adult/child €5/3; ☺11am-5pm Tue-Sat, to 4pm Sun Apr-Sep; ♿) Sinister-looking dummies tell the turbulent history of the Connaught kings, the town of Boyle and the King family, including a grim tale of tenant eviction during the Famine. Kids can try on replica Irish cloaks, breeches and leather shoes, write with a quill and build a vaulted ceiling from specially designed blocks. One room is devoted to Maureen O'Sullivan, the Hollywood star who was born nearby on Main St.

After the King family moved to Lough Key, this imposing Georgian mansion became a military barracks for the Connaught Rangers. It then was largely dormant for decades.

The mansion's courtyard is home to a large shop selling local crafts and a cafe (p480). The audio guide is €1.

Boyle Abbey
HISTORIC BUILDING

(☑071-963 9268; www.heritageireland.ie; Abbeytown Rd; adult/child €4/2; ☉10am-6pm Easter-late Sep) Gracing the River Boyle is the finely preserved (and reputedly haunted) Boyle Abbey. Founded in 1161 by monks from Mellifont in County Louth, the abbey captures the transition from Romanesque to Gothic style, best seen in the nave, where a set of arches in each style face each other. Guided 40-minute tours of the abbey are sometimes available.

Unusually for a Cistercian building, figures and carved animals decorate the capitals to the west along wtih, more bafflingly, pagan sheila-na-gig fertility symbol. After the Dissolution of the Monasteries, the abbey was occupied by the military and became Boyle Castle; the stone chimney on the southern side of the abbey, which was once the refectory, dates from that period.

Drumanone Dolmen
HISTORIC SITE

FREE This astonishing portal dolmen, one of the largest in Ireland, measures 4.5m by 3.3m and was constructed before 2000 BC. It can be tricky to find: follow Patrick St west and then the R294 out of town for 5km, until you pass under a railway arch. Keep going for around 500m and you'll see a small abandoned building on your right; stop the car here and climb up the hill and over the railway line (take care and shut the gates).

Lough Key Forest Park
PARK

(☑071-967 3122; www.loughkey.ie; off N4; forest admission free, parking €4; ☉10am-6pm daily Mar-Aug, Wed-Sun Apr, Sep & Oct, to 5pm Fri-Sun Nov-Feb; 🅿) Sprinkled with small islands, Lough Key Forest Park has long been popular for its picturesque ruins, including a 12th-century abbey on tiny Trinity Island and a 19th-century castle on Castle Island. It's also a time-honoured favourite with families for its wishing chair, bog gardens, fairy bridge and viewing tower. There are plenty of marked walking trails through the park.

Lough Key is 4km east of Boyle. The Bus Éireann route from Sligo to Dublin has frequent services linking Boyle and Lough Key.

The 350-hectare park was once part of the Rockingham estate, owned by the King family from the 17th century until 1957. Rockingham House, designed by John Nash, was destroyed by a fire in the same year; all that remains are some stables, outbuildings and eerie tunnels leading to the lake – built to hide the servants from view.

There is an informative visitor centre, and the Lough Key Experience (adult/child €7.50/5), incorporating a panoramic, 300m-long treetop canopy walk, which rises 9m above the woodland floor with sweeping lake views. Other attractions include the Boda Borg Challenge (€18), a series of rooms filled with activities and puzzles (great for sudden bursts of rain), and an outdoor adventure playground (day pass €5).

In July and August Lough Key Boats provides hourly boat trips (adult/child €12/6), plus row- and power-boat hire (from €22 per hour).

⭐ Festivals & Events

Boyle Arts Festival
ART

(www.boylearts.com; ☉Jul) If you're in Bolye at the end of July, you can catch the lively and usually excellent Boyle Arts Festival, which features music, theatre, storytelling and contemporary Irish art exhibitions.

🛏 Sleeping & Eating

⭐ Lough Key House
B&B €€

(☑071-966 2161; www.loughkeyhouse.com; off N4; s/d from €60/90; 🖨) This beautifully restored Georgian country house has six guest rooms, each individually decorated with stylish period furniture. The downstairs sitting room combines antiques with elegance, comfort and an open fire. Breakfast eggs come from the owner's hens, there are loaner bikes and, if you arrive by bus, you can be picked up in town. It's 4km east of Boyle.

Cesh Corran
B&B €€

(☑071-966 2265; www.marycooney.com; Abbey Tce; r from €60; 🖨) Close to the centre and overlooking the abbey ruins, this immaculately kept place has bright, simple rooms and a very warm welcome. There's a garden, wholesome breakfasts from locally sourced produce (cheaper rates come without breakfast) and even a separate bait fridge for anglers.

Forest Park House
B&B €€

(☑071-966 2227; off N4; s/d from €45/80; 🖨) Just by the entrance to Lough Key Forest Park (p480), this purpose-built guesthouse has six bright, modern rooms with pine woodwork and crisp white linens. It's 4km east of town.

Aunty Bee's
CAFE €

(☑071-966 3242; King House, Main St; mains from €4; ☉11am-4pm Mon-Sat) In the King House (p479) courtyard, this sprightly little cafe has delicious baked goods, simple lunches and fine coffee and tea.

Farmers Market   MARKET €
(☑ 071-966 3033; King House, Main St; ☺ 10am-2pm Sat) The surrounding farmlands are rich with produce and locals seem especially talented at creating amazing baked goods and prepared foods. Ponder the bounty at this weekly open-air market.

ℹ Information

In the courtyard of King House, **Úna Bhán Tourism Cooperative** (☑ 071-966 3033; www.unabhan.net; King House; ☺ 9am-6pm Mon-Fri, to 3pm Sat) has tourist information on the Boyle region.

ℹ Getting There & Away

Bus Éireann (www.buseireann.ie) runs between Dublin (€19, three hours) and Sligo (€13, 45 minutes), stopping at Boyle's King House en route. There are five buses daily Monday to Saturday, four on Sunday.

Irish Rail (www.irishrail.ie) trains leave eight times daily to Sligo (from €13, 40 minutes) and Dublin (from €20, 2½ hours). The station is on Elphin St.

COUNTY LONGFORD

A delightfully agrarian region, County Longford is a quiet array of low hills, pastoral scenes and bucolic appeal. Its few tourist sights are matched by superb fishing for anglers, who come from all corners to cast a line around Lough Ree and Lanesborough.

Longford suffered massive emigration during the Famine and never fully recovered. Many Longford emigrants went to Argentina, where one of their descendants, Edel Miro O'Farrell, became president in 1914.

Longford's eponymous county town is a decidedly workaday place, but the county is home to one of Ireland's most important archaeological sites: the Corlea Trackway. The county also possesses one of the three biggest portal dolmens in Ireland: Aughnacliffe Dolmen. Both are well worth seeking out.

◉ Sights & Activities

★ Corlea Trackway   HISTORIC SITE
(☑ 043-332 2386; www.heritageireland.ie; off R392, Keenagh; ☺ 10am-6pm May-Sep) **FREE** Don't miss the magnificent Corlea Trackway, an Iron Age bog road built in 148 BC. An 18m stretch of the historic oak track – like a pavement – has been preserved in a hu-

---

OFF THE BEATEN TRACK

ABBEYSHRULE'S AQUEDUCT & ABBEY

Hidden away in the delightfully remote southeast corner of County Longford, **Abbeyshrule** is a tiny village with a serene setting on the Royal Canal and River Inny. Locals proudly point out that it regularly wins awards for its tidiness.

Just north of town, one of the 19th century's great engineering feats, the stolid stone **Whitworth Aqueduct**, carries the canal over the river. Another highlight is the 12th-century **Cistercian Abbey**. Its ruins are a moody and evocative place for a stroll.

The village is 2km south of the R399 and 5km east of the N55.

---

midified hall at the site's visitor centre. Tours detail the bog's unique flora and fauna, and explain how the track was discovered and methods used to preserve it. The tour is highly informative and educational.

The centre is 15km south of Longford town.

The precise purpose of the track has not been fully established, but perhaps it was constructed as a symbol of peace and cooperation between formerly warring regions. Objects found beneath the track also point to similar tracks discovered in other parts of Europe. There are plans to expand the site, allowing visitors to wander further into the surrounding bogland and to further explore the region. If you drive around a bit, you can find some short but good walks in the desolate but intriguing landscape.

Aughnacliffe Dolmen   ARCHAEOLOGICAL SITE
(off R198; ☺ dawn-dusk) This dolmen is one of the three biggest portal dolmens in Ireland, with an improbably balanced top stone. Thought to be around 5000 years old, Aughnacliffe Dolmen is 18km north of Longford town.

Longford–Cloondara Trackway   WALKING
Follow the placid waters of the Royal Canal on this trackway that runs 16km from Longford town. The well-marked track follows the canal for 8km southwest from Longford before turning northwest for another 8km along the Royal Canal. It's excellent for restful, waterside cycling.

If walking, when you reach the end at the Richmond Harbour in Cloondara you can walk another 2km to Termonbarry to get a bus back to Longford via the N5.

Eating

Torc Café & Foodhall
CAFÉ €

(☑ 043-334 8277; www.torccafe.com; 1 New St, Longford town; mains from €5; ⊙ 9am-6pm Mon-Sat) Divine chocolate from a free-flowing fountain awaits as a reward for exploring the backroads of County Longford. The sweet stuff in myriad forms is but one highlight of this long-serving cafe that's known for its coffee and fresh, seasonal fare, so get a picnic or linger for breakfast or lunch. It's bang in the centre of town.

❶ Getting There & Away

Longford town has a train station and is linked by **rail** (www.irishrail.ie) to Dublin (€14) and Sligo (€12). **Bus Éireann** (www.buseireann.ie) also runs many services to the town, but this is a county where you'll need your own wheels to get around to see the sights.

COUNTY WESTMEATH

Characterised by lakes and pastures grazed by beef cattle, Westmeath has many attractions, ranging from bucolic lakeside vistas and the miraculous Fore Valley to the country's oldest pub in the confident county town, Athlone. The rivers and lakes attract a steady stream of visitors.

Athlone & Around

POP 20,200

The River Shannon splits this former garrison town in two, with most businesses and services sitting on its eastern bank. In the shadow of Athlone Castle, the western bank is an enchanting jumble of twisting streets, colourfully painted houses, historic pubs, antique shops and more.

◉ Sights & Activities

★ Athlone Castle
CASTLE

(☑ 090-644 2130; www.athlonecastle.ie/; off Market Sq; adult/child €8/4; ⊙ 10am-6pm Mon-Sat, noon-6pm Sun Jun-Aug, to 5pm Tue-Sun Apr, May, Sep & Oct; ⊞) Inside this low, hulking 13th-century castle by the River Shannon there are engaging and modern displays that bring to life the tumultuous history of the town and detail life here through the ages. The highlight is the cacophonous Siege Experience, which takes place in a circular panoramic gallery. The ancient river ford at Athlone was an important crossroads on the Shannon and the cause of many squabbles over the centuries. By 1210 the Normans had asserted their power and built a castle here.

In 1690 the Jacobite town survived a siege by Protestant forces, but it fell a year later – under a devastating bombardment of 12,000 cannonballs – to William of Orange's troops. The castle was soon remodelled and further major alterations took place over the following centuries. A lightning strike in 1697, however, ignited the castle's magazine, causing 260 barrels of gunpowder to explode, destroying much of the town in the process.

Among activities for adults and kids, you can test a longbow, try out the stocks or dress up in medieval garb.

Church of St Peter & St Paul
CHURCH

(Barrack St) FREE This colossal neoclassical church, standing opposite Athlone Castle, is quite an astonishing sight. The cathedral dates only from 1937 and contains stained-glass images of St Peter and St Paul on either side of you as you enter the vast interior.

Dún na Sí Heritage Park
PARK

(☑ 090-648 1183; off M6, Moate; adult/child €4/2; ⊙ 9.30am-4.30pm Mon-Thu, to 3.30pm Fri; ℗ ⊞) This folk park has a re-created ring fort, portal dolmen, lime kiln, mass rock, farmhouse and forge. It also has a traditional session with music, song, dance and storytelling at 8pm on Sundays in summer. The surrounding nature park is lovely. It's 16km east of Athlone.

Luan Gallery
GALLERY

(☑ 090-644 2154; www.athloneartsandtourism.ie/luan-gallery; Grace Rd; ⊙ 11am-5pm Tue-Sat, noon-5pm Sun) FREE On the river opposite the castle, this excellent contemporary art gallery has regular exhibitions of top artists.

★ Shannon Banks Nature Trail
WALKING

Starting from Athlone Castle, this well-signposted looping 5km walk follows the banks of the Shannon River and the Old Canal Bank. It's an easy stroll; signposts describe flora and fauna along the way.

★ Viking Ship Cruises
CRUISE

(☑ 086 262 1136; www.vikingtoursireland.ie; The Quay; adult €12-16, child €6-8; ⊙ Easter-Oct; ⊞) Cruise along the Shannon aboard a replica Viking longship, complete with costumed staff and dress-up clothes. Head north to Lough Ree or south to Clonmacnoise (trips here stop for 90 minutes at the ruins). Boats depart from right next to Athlone Castle.

🛏 Sleeping

⭐ Bastion B&B
B&B €

(☑ 090-649 4954; www.thebastion.net; 2 Bastion St; s/d from €40/65; 🛜) You can't miss this brightly coloured facade near Athlone Castle. Inside, the white-on-white interiors are a canvas for eclectic artwork, cactus collections, Indian wall hangings and Buddhist ornaments. The seven rooms (five with private bathrooms) are crisp and clean, with dark wooden floors. Go for the spacious loft if you can. There's a lounge and kitchen.

Coosan Cottage Eco Guesthouse
GUESTHOUSE €€

(☑ 090-647 3468; www.ecoguesthouse.com; Coosan Point Rd; s/d from €50/80) 🌿 This ecofriendly 10-bedroom guesthouse blends traditional style with modern thinking. Triple-glazed windows, a wood-pellet burner and a heat-recovery system are just some of its green credentials. Visitors enjoy the tranquil surroundings and great breakfasts. It's 1km north of town.

Prince of Wales Hotel
HOTEL €€

(☑ 090-647 6666; www.theprinceofwales.ie; Church St; s/d from €70/100; ❀🛜) A modern hotel in the commercial heart of town, the Prince of Wales has 46 large rooms with desks and other business amenities.

🍴 Eating & Drinking

Athlone has established itself as the culinary capital of the Midlands. Scout around the western bank's backstreets and you'll unearth some gems.

⭐ Lowe & Co
CAFE €

(8 O'Connell St; mains from €4.50; ⏲ 9am-5pm Tue-Sun) This lovely cafe is an upstairs/downstairs place serving up cakes, sandwiches and other goodies, all made from organic produce. The upstairs room doubles as a library with a couple of comfy sofas and there's always a crowd of satisfied customers and a serene sense of calm.

Bastion Kitchen
CAFE €

(1 Bastion St; mains from €5; ⏲ 8.30am-5pm Mon-Fri, 9am-5pm Sat, noon-5pm Sun; 🛜) This charming little mainstay cafe and bar hangout is located on Athlone's left bank (opposite the Bastion B&B) and attracts a fun local crowd; it only serves organic produce and there's a

deli here too. Go for the organic falafel pitta (€5) or the falafel and beetroot hummus salad, sink a coffee and enjoy.

Beans & Leaves Cafe
CAFE €

(☑ 090-643 3534; cnr Strand St & Lloyds Lane; mains from €5; ⏲ 9.15am-5pm Mon-Sat, 10am-5pm Sun; 🛜) There are lots of tables outside at this creative cafe on the Right Bank, close to the river. Dishes are simple (although the baked goods can be a sticky delight) and fresh. It's a great choice for breakfasts too.

⭐ Left Bank Bistro
MODERN IRISH €€

(☑ 090-649 4446; www.leftbankbistro.com; Fry Pl; mains lunch €8-13, dinner €19.50-25; ⏲ 10.30am-9pm Tue-Sat; 🍴🚲) With an airy, whitewashed interior, shelves of home-made goods, and a menu combining superior Irish ingredients with Mediterranean and Asian influences, this sophisticated deli-bistro is a winner. Lunch features big salads and open sandwiches, while dinner highlights include seafood. Desserts are extraordinary.

Murphy's Law
PUB FOOD €€

(☑ 090-643 2753; www.murphyslawathlone.com; Barrack St; mains €8-20; ⏲ kitchen 10am-8.30pm Mon-Sat, 11am-6pm Sun, bar to 11pm) This gastropub just up from the castle has transformed an old boozer into a fine venue for pub food and drink. Choose from a list of microbrews and enjoy them in the beer garden. There are B&B rooms upstairs (from €40 per person).

⭐ Sean's Bar
PUB

(☑ 090-649 2358; 13 Main St; ⏲ 11am-late) It doesn't look like it from the front, but this pub dates from AD 900, making it Ireland's oldest pub. Its log fires, uneven floors (to help flood waters run back down to the river), sawdust, rickety piano and curios collected over the years attest to the theory. The riverside beer garden has live music most nights in summer.

ℹ Information

The **tourist office** (☑ 090-649 4630; Market Sq, Athlone Castle; ⏲ 10am-6pm Mon-Sat, noon-6pm Sun Jun-Aug, to 5pm Tue-Sun Apr, May, Sep & Oct) is inside the castle's guardhouse. The website www.athlone.ie is a good source of information.

ℹ Getting There & Away

Athlone's bus and train stations are side by side on Southern Station Rd, 1km north of the centre.

Bus Éireann (www.buseireann.ie) runs hourly buses to Dublin (€14, 1¾ hours) and Galway (€12, 1½ hours) and two daily to Westport (€17, three hours).

UISNEACH

Almost midway between Athlone and Mullingar on the R390 is **Uisneach** (☑ 087 718 9550; www.uisneach.ie; off R390; suggested donation €10; ⊙ tours 1pm Sat & Sun Apr & Oct, 1pm Wed-Sun May-Sep), the 'centre' of Ireland. Well, not really – that's a few kilometres to the west. But it is a site with great ancient significance. Ancient constructions found so far include earthworks that may have been a royal palace, a possible fort, holy wells and more. On tours (the only way to visit), you'll get a detailed overview of the ancient sites plus the associated lore. The 2-sq-km site is mostly privately owned.

The tours last about two hours and cover a 3km route. Arrive by 12.45pm for the tour. There is no fixed fee for the tour, although €10 is a suggested donation price.

Irish Rail (www.irishrail.ie) runs hourly trains to Dublin (from €20, 1½ hours), 10 daily to Galway (€20, one hour) and four daily to Westport (€20, two hours).

Lough Ree & Around

Many of the 50-plus islands within Lough Ree were once inhabited by monks and their ecclesiastical treasures, drawing Vikings like bears to honey-laced beehives. These days the visitors are less bloodthirsty, with sailing, trout fishing and birdwatching the most popular pastimes. Migratory birds that nest here include swans, plovers and curlews.

Poet, playwright and novelist Oliver Goldsmith (1728–74), author of *The Vicar of Wakefield,* is closely associated with the area running alongside the eastern shore of Lough Ree. Known as Goldsmith Country, the region is beautifully captured in his writings.

◉ Sights & Activities

Rindoon RUINS
An easy half-day trip from Athlone, the deserted 13th-century village of Rindoon makes for a fantastic expedition. It's a short walk from the car park to the beginning of two trails: one short and one a bit longer. In spring, when the bluebells are out in the

woods, it's a real picture. The village is on a peninsula that juts into the west side of Lough Ree.

There's long medieval walls, an overgrown castle, an old hospital, a church and a mill to be explored.

Follow the turn-off from the village of Lecarrow and head along the road to the car park, from where two looped walks take you through the village and past the lake shore – the longer walk takes you past the point of the peninsulsa and through the woods. Pack drinks and snacks.

Glasson Golf Course GOLF
(☑ 090-648 51200; www.glassongolfhotel.ie; Glasson Village; green fees Mon-Fri €40, Sat & Sun €50) This award-winning course comes with an elegant hotel and gorgeous scenery.

🛏 Sleeping & Eating

Wineport Lodge BOUTIQUE HOTEL €€€
(☑ 090-643 9010; www.wineport.ie; off N55, Glasson; s/d from €120/140, mains €24-35; ⊙ restaurant 5.30-10pm daily, plus 2.30-4pm Sun) This gracious hotel overlooks Killinure Lough facing Killinure Island, with 29 comfortable rooms. It's also a popular fine-dining spot, serving an ambitious menu featuring local produce and artisanal suppliers.

Glasson Village Restaurant MODERN IRISH €€
(☑ 090-648 5001; www.glassonvillagerestaurant. ie; Glasson; mains €18-30, early-bird 3-course menu €29; ⊙ 5.30-9pm Tue-Fri, 6-9.30pm Sat, 1-3pm Sun, closed Tue in winter; 🛜 🍴) This pioneering gourmet restaurant with an informal atmosphere specialises in seafood. French accents abound, especially on the good wine list. Make sure you dine in the garden in summer. The €29 early-bird menu is available all evening Tuesday to Saturday in summer months and Wednesday to Saturday in winter.

Kilbeggan

Little Kilbeggan has two big claims to fame: a restored distillery-turned-museum and Ireland's only National Hunt racecourse.

There are around six buses (€10, 30 minutes) a day from Athlone that run though Kilbeggan.

Kilbeggan Distillery Experience DISTILLERY
(☑ 057-933 2134; www.kilbeggandistillery.com; off R446, Kilbeggan; admission €8, tours €14-80; ⊙ 9am-6pm Apr-Oct, 10am-4pm Nov-Mar) Whis-

key buffs can savour this distillery tour. Established in 1757, Kilbeggan is believed to have been the world's oldest licensed distillery still in the world – and it's again producing whiskey. The basic admission lets you guide yourself around the hulking machinery. Pricier, more connoisseur-aimed tours include guides and tastings.

Kilbeggan Races
HORSE RACING

(☑ 057-933 2176; www.kilbegganraces.com; off M6, Kilbeggan; ☺ usually fortnightly May-Sep) Punters from all over the country attend the old-time evening meetings at the Kilbeggan Races. The town is transformed on race nights in summer into a buzzing equine centre, where the thrill of the chase is matched by the craic in the pubs.

Mullingar & Around

POP 20,930

A prosperous regional town, Mullingar hums with the activity of locals going about their daily lives. Nearby there are fish-filled lakes and a fantastical mansion with an odious, but gripping, history.

James Joyce visited the town in his youth and it appears in both *Ulysses* (1922) and *Finnegans Wake* (1939). Restored sections of the Royal Canal extend in either direction from Mullingar.

◉ Sights & Activities

Trout fishing is popular in the lakes around Mullingar. The fishing season runs from 1 March or 1 May (depending on the lake) to 12 October.

★ Belvedere House & Gardens
HISTORIC BUILDING

(☑ 044-934 9060; www.belvedere-house.ie; off N52; adult/child €8/4; ☺ gardens 9.30am-8pm May-Aug, to 7pm Apr & Sep, to 6pm Mar & Oct, to 4.30pm Nov-Feb, cafe & house to 5pm Mar-Oct, to 4pm Nov-Feb; 🐾) Don't miss magnificent Belvedere House, 5.5km south of Mullingar. This immense 18th-century hunting lodge is set in 65 hectares of gardens overlooking Lough Ennell. Designed by Richard Cassels, it contains delicate rococo plasterwork in the upper rooms. The gardens, with their Victorian glasshouse, walled garden and lake-shore setting, make for wonderful rambling. An airy annex houses CaToCa, a classy cafe. There's also a large children's playground.

More than a few skeletons have come rattling from Belvedere's closets: the first earl, Lord Belfield, accused his wife and younger brother Arthur of adultery. She was placed under house arrest here for 30 years, and Arthur was jailed in London for the rest of his life. Meanwhile, the earl lived a life of decadence and debauchery. On his death, his wife emerged dressed in the fashion of three decades earlier, still protesting her innocence.

Lord Belfield also found time to fall out with his other brother, George, who built a home nearby. Ireland's largest folly, a ready-made 'ruin' called the Jealous Wall, was commissioned by the earl so he wouldn't have to look at George's mansion.

Cathedral of Christ the King
CATHEDRAL

(☑ 044-934 8338; www.mullingarparish.com; Bishop's Gate St; ☺ 7.30am-8pm) FREE Mullingar's most obvious landmark is this colossal twin-towered church, commenced in 1933 and consecrated on the eve of WWII. The cathedral's most notable interior features are large mosaics of St Anne and St Patrick by Russian artist Boris Anrep, whose mosaics can also be found in the unfinished Westminster Cathedral in London.

Mullingar Equestrian Centre
HORSE RIDING

(☑ 044-934 8331; www.mullingarequestrian.com; off R390; 1-day lesson & ride adult/child €100/80; 🐾) This well-known equestrian centre offers all manner of rides and lessons.

🛏 Sleeping & Eating

Novara House
B&B €

(☑ 044-933 5209; www.novarahouse.com; Dublin Rd; s/d €45/75; 🐾) Just a five-minute walk east from the town centre, this simple B&B is set in a modern bungalow. Rooms are simple but spotless with pine furniture and neutral colour schemes, but it's the amiable hosts and their warm welcome, homemade scones and cups of tea that guarantee a lovely stay.

Greville Arms Hotel
HOTEL €€

(☑ 044-934 8563; www.grevillearmshotel.ie; Pearse St; s/d from €60/90; 🐾) Dating from 1824, this grande dame of a hotel has 40 comfortable and spacious rooms and is pleasantly dated with gilt mirrors, statues, dark oil paintings and chandeliers, albeit complemented by modern conveniences. Ulysses Bar is named in honour of James Joyce, who apparently frequented the establishment. Other endearing features include a small museum and a beer garden.

Annebrook House Hotel HOTEL €€
(☑044-935 3300; www.annebrook.ie; Pearse St;
s/d from €65/89; P ☎) Right in the town centre, the hub of this modern hotel is a lovely
19th-century house with strong connections
to local author Maria Edgeworth. Accommodation is in an annexe, where modern rooms
in neutral colours are spacious, and the River
Brosna flows through the grounds. Prices rise
somewhat at the weekend.

★ **Miller & Cook** CAFE €€
(☑044-934 0884; www.millerandcook.ie; 50 Pearse
St; deli mains from €5, 2-course dinner menu €24.95,
3-course lunch €21.95, mains €19-27; ☺ see website; ☎) Your one-stop shop for fine food and
drink in Mullingar. The bakery and deli turn
out beautiful goods, perfect for a for a picnic.
The cafe serves excellent locally sourced fare
and Sunday brunch is popular; the bistro
and upstairs restaurant are also good.

Oscar's Restaurant MEDITERRANEAN €€
(☑044-934 4909; www.oscarsmullingar.com; 21
Oliver Plunkett St; mains €16-25; ☺5.30-9.30pm
Mon-Thu, to 10pm Fri & Sat, to 8.15pm Sun, also
12.30-2.15pm Sun; ☎) This perennially popular spot is the place to go for upmarket comfort food and a lively atmosphere. It offers
bright colours, a menu that skirts the Mediterranean (think pasta, pizza and French-inspired meat and poultry) and a decent wine
list.

🍷 Drinking & Entertainment

Yukon Bar PUB
(☑044-934 0251; 11 Dominick St; ☺5-11pm) A lively pub, this place has a great atmosphere and
regular live music. You may find soul, blues
and rock music on offer.

Mullingar Arts Centre THEATRE
(☑044-934 7777; www.mullingarartscentre.ie; Lower Mount St, County Hall; ☺10am-9.30pm Mon-Fri,
9.30am-6pm Sat; ♿) The centre runs a regular
program of music, comedy, drama and art exhibitions. In summer there are family-friendly,
traditional-music sessions every weekend.

ℹ️ Information

Tourist Office (☑044-934 8650; Market Sq;
☺9.30am-1pm & 2-5pm Mon-Sat) Right in the
centre of town,

ℹ️ Getting There & Away

Bus Éireann (www.buseireann.ie) runs to Dublin
(€15, 1½ hours, four daily) and Athlone (€13.50,
one hour, three daily).

Irish Rail (www.irishrail.ie) runs nine direct
services to Dublin (from €19, 1¼ hours).

North of Mullingar

The area north of Mullingar is famed for its
lakes. The best-known is Lough Derravaragh,
an 8km-long lake associated with the legend
of the children of Lír, who were turned into
swans here by their jealous stepmother. Each
winter the legend is recalled by thousands of
snow-white migratory swans that flock here
from as far away as Russia and Siberia.

In addition to the lakes and rolling landscapes you'll find plenty of historical interest
around the unassuming town of Castlepollard and sleepy Fore.

👁️ Sights

★ **Fore Valley** HISTORIC SITE
(off R195) Near the shores of Lough Lene, the
emerald-green Fore Valley is a superb place
to explore by bicycle or on foot. In AD 630 St
Fechin founded a monastery just outside the
village of Fore. There's nothing left of this early settlement, but three later buildings in the
valley are closely associated with 'seven wonders' said to have occurred here. It's a deeply
atmospheric place, even in the dead of winter,
with sweeping views across a gentle valley.

The oldest of the three buildings is
St Fechin's Church, containing an ear-
ly-13th-century chancel and baptismal font.
Over the Cyclopean entrance is a huge lintel
stone carved with a Greek cross and thought
to weigh about 2.5 tonnes. It's said to have
been put into place by St Fechin's devotions
– the wonder of the stone raised by prayer.

A path runs from the church to the attractive little **anchorite cell** – the 'anchorite in
a stone' – which dates from the 15th century
and was lived in by a succession of hermits.
The **Seven Wonders pub** in the village
holds the key.

On the other side of the road near the car
park is **St Fechin's Well**, filled with water
that will not boil. Cynics should beware of
testing this claim, as it's said that if you try
it, doom will come to your family. Nearby is
a branch from the tree that will not burn;
the coins pressed into it are a more contemporary superstition.

Further over the plain are the extensive
remains of a **13th-century Benedictine
priory**, the Monastery of the Quaking Scraw,
miraculous because it was built on what
once was a bog. In the following century it

was turned into a fortification, hence the loophole windows and castle-like square towers. The western tower is in a dangerous state – keep clear.

The last two wonders are the mill without a race and the water that flows uphill. The mill site is marked, and legend has it that St Fechin caused water to flow uphill, towards the mill, by throwing his crosier against a rock near Lough Lene, about 1.5km away.

★ **Tullynally Castle Gardens** GARDENS
(☑ 044-966 1159; www.tullynallycastle.com; off R395, Castlepollard; gardens adult/child €6/3; ☺ 11am-5pm Thu-Sun Jun-Aug, Sat & Sun only Apr, May & Sep; ☒) The imposing Gothic-revival Tullynally Castle is the seat of the Pakenham family and, although closed to visitors, its 12 hectares of gardens and parkland are a lovely place to roam. Ornamental lakes, a Chinese and a Tibetan garden, and a stately stretch of 200-year-old yews are some of the highlights. There is a tearoom in the castle courtyard.

The castle is 2km northwest of Castlepollard.

⌁ Sleeping & Eating

Hotel Castlepollard HOTEL €€
(☑ 044-966 1194; www.hotelcastlepollard.ie; Castlepollard; s/d from €60/90; ☺ kitchen 8am-8pm; ☎) The closest accommodation to the Fore Valley and overlooking the mannered triangular village green, this cosy country hotel has decent rooms. The modest restaurant (mains from €15) serves good fare. The hotel bar has live music many weekends.

Fore Abbey Coffee Shop CAFE €
(☑ 044-966 1780; off R195, Fore; snacks from €3; ☺ 11am-4pm daily Jun-Sep, Sun only other times) Right near the village of Fore, this small stone cafe also acts as a tourist information office and screens a short video about the monastery ruins.

❶ Getting There & Away

You'll need your own wheels for the region around Fore Valley, which is 5km from Castlepollard.

COUNTY OFFALY

Beyond the magnificent ecclesiastical remains of Clonmacnoise, the green and watery county of Offaly doesn't feature on many tourist itineraries, which is a great shame as it deserves far greater attention. Steeped in history with plentiful castle remains and

the atmospheric and very handsome town of Birr, Offaly also offers vast swaths of bogland (most accessible at the Clara Bog Nature Reserve), recognised internationally for their watery and fertile habitat of plant and animal life, as well as prime fishing and water sports on the River Shannon and the Grand Canal. There's also the tremendous river fort at Shannonbridge, abbey ruins to explore and other ecclesiastical treasures.

Access www.offaly.ie and www.visitoffaly. ie for more information on this fascinating and rewarding county.

Birr
POP 5900

Birr is one of the umissable towns in the Midlands. Elegant Georgian buildings with candy-coloured facades are overlooked by a grande dame of a castle. There is excellent accommodation, as well as spirited nightlife. Despite its appeal, Birr remains off the beaten track and you can enjoy its delights without jostling with the crowds.

◉ Sights

Birr has no shortage of first-class Georgian buildings; stroll down tree-lined **Oxmantown Mall** or **John's Mall** to see some of the best examples. The corner of Oxmantown Mall was the site of the world's first ever motor vehicle fatality, an event recorded on a sign.

The tourist office has a walking map that details the most important landmarks, including the megalithic **Seffin Stone** (said to be the ancient marker for Umbilicus Hiberniae – the Navel of Ireland – used to mark the centre of the country) and **St Brendan's Old Churchyard**, reputedly the site of the saint's 6th-century settlement.

★ **Birr Castle** CASTLE
(☑ 057-912 0336; www.birrcastle.com; off R439; adult/child gardens €9/5, gardens, exhibits & castle €18/10; ☺ 9am-6pm mid-Mar–Oct, 10am-4pm Nov–mid-Mar; ℗ ☒) It's easy to spend half a day exploring the attractions and gardens of Birr Castle demesne. The castle dates from 1620 and is a private home, but during May to August visitors can visit the main living quarters on tours (which must be booked in advance). Most of the present building dates from around 1620, with alterations made in the early 19th century.

The 50-hectare castle grounds are famous for their magnificent **gardens** set around a large artificial lake.

GRAND & ROYAL CANALS

After much debate about linking Dublin to the Shannon by water, work began on the Grand Canal in 1757. The project was beset by problems and encountered huge difficulties and delays. In the meantime, commercial rivals hatched a plan for the competing Royal Canal. The two canals revolutionised transport in Ireland in the early 19th century, but their heyday was short-lived, as they were soon superseded by the railway.

Today the canals are popular for cruising and fishing, while their banks are ideal for walking and cycling, and pass through some truly picturesque villages. With the restoration of the final section of the Royal Canal it is now possible to complete a triangular route by heading from Dublin to the Shannon along either the Royal or the Grand, returning along the other canal. Both waterways link to a much greater network that includes the Shannon-Erne Waterway and the River Suck.

Waterways Ireland (www.waterwaysireland.org) and the Inland Waterways Association of Ireland (www.iwai.ie) have a wealth of information on the canals.

Grand Canal

The Grand Canal threads its way from Dublin through Tullamore to join the River Shannon at Shannonbridge, a total of 131km. The canal passes through relatively unpopulated countryside, with bogs, pretty villages and 43 finely crafted locks lining the journey. Near the village of Sallins in County Kildare, the graceful seven-arched **Leinster Aqueduct** carries the canal across the River Liffey. From nearby Robertstown, a 45km spur turns south to join the River Barrow at the pretty town of Athy.

Royal Canal

The 145km Royal Canal follows Kildare's northern border, flowing over a massive **aqueduct** near Leixlip, before it joins the River Shannon at Clondra in County Longford. The canal has become a popular amenity for thousands of residents along the north Kildare commuter belt and both the canal and the towpaths are open all the way to the Shannon.

Barges & Boats

You can hire narrow boats at several locations along the canals, which is an excellent way to journey through the waterways. Two-/six-berth boats cost from around €850/16,000 per week. **Barrowline Cruisers** (☑ 057-862 6060; www.barrowline.ie; Vicarstown; boat hire per week from €830) and **Canalways** (☑ 087 243 3879; www.canalways.ie; Rathangan; canal boat rental per week from €1185) are major firms with multiple locations. You can also find rental firms in the boating centres of Banagher (p491) and Carrick-on-Shannon (p474).

The gardens are home to more than 1000 species of plants from all over the world, so something always seems to be in bloom. Look for one of the world's **tallest box hedges** (which has made the *Guinness Book of Records*), planted in the 1780s and now standing 12m high, and the romantic **Hornbeam cloister**. Delight in the waterfalls, wildflower meadows and a pergola festooned with a 90-year-old wisteria.

The Parsons clan, who have owned the castle since 1620, are a remarkable family of pioneering Irish scientists, and their work is documented in the historic **science centre**. Exhibits include the massive **telescope** built by William Parsons in 1845. The 'leviathan of Parsonstown', as it was known, was the largest telescope in the world for 75 years and attracted a wide variety of scien-

tists and astronomers. It was used to make innumerable discoveries, including the spiral galaxies. After the death of William's son, the telescope, unloved and untended, slowly fell to bits. It has been completely restored, however, and may be viewed in all its glory in the gardens.

William Parsons' wife, Mary Ross, was a keen photographer and her dark room was reputed to be one of the first of its kind in the world. You can now view a replica. Other highlights are a children's **adventure playground**, complete with playhouse, hobbit huts and trampolines, and the excellent **Castle Courtyard Cafe**, which showcases local products and produce in its dishes. Otherwise you can wander the garden to your heart's content; three trails are illustrated on the website map.

Leap Castle
CASTLE

(☑086 869 0547; www.leapcastle.net; off R421; ⊙by arrangement) Leap Castle is reputedly one of the most haunted castles in Europe. Originally an O'Carroll family residence, the castle was the scene of many dreadful deeds and is famous for its eerie apparitions – its most renowned inhabitant is the 'smelly ghost', a spirit that apparently leaves a smell behind after sightings. Another apparition is the self-explanatory 'Red Lady'.

Renovations are ongoing, but you can arrange a visit. It lies about 12km southeast of Birr between Kinnitty and Roscrea (in Tipperary).

🏃 Activities

A beautiful and highly enjoyable, lazy leafy riverside walk runs east along the River Camcor from Oxmantown Bridge to Elmgrove Bridge.

Birr Equestrian Centre
HORSE RIDING

(☑087 244 5545; www.birrequestrian.ie; Clareen Rd, Kingsborough House; 1hr horse treks €30; 🌐) This equestrian centre, 3km east of Birr, runs hour-long treks in the surrounding farmland and half-day horse treks in the Slieve Bloom Mountains (€80).

🎊 Festivals & Events

Birr Vintage Week & Arts Festival
ART

(www.birrvintageweek.com; ⊙early Aug) The town celebrates its rich history during this festival, with street parades, theatre, music, exhibitions, workshops, guided walks and a traditional fair.

🛌 Sleeping

★ Maltings Guesthouse
B&B €

(☑057-912 1345; www.themaltingsbirr.com; Castle St; s/d from €50/80; 🌐) Based in an 1810 malt storehouse once used by Guinness, this place has a serene location near the castle and right by the River Camcor. The rooms are large with pine furniture and a soothing lilac-and-green colour scheme; all rooms overlook the water, as does the cheery breakfast room. Excellent value and a fine-looking choice in Birr.

★ Walcot B&B
B&B €€

(☑057-912 1247; www.walcotbedandbreakfast.com; Rosse Rowe; s/d from €60/90; 🌐) Set on spacious grounds across from Birr Castle, this Georgian townhouse is close to everything. The five bedrooms are large and the furnishings luxurious. The private bathrooms have period-style fittings with large tubs and showers.

Brendan House
B&B €€

(☑057-912 1818; www.tinjugstudio.com; Brendan St; s €55, d €80-90; 🌐) Packed with knick-knacks, books, rugs, art and antiques, this Georgian townhouse is a bohemian delight. The three rooms share a bathroom (one of Birr's oldest, they claim). The four-poster beds, period charm, superb breakfast and artistic style are the real draws. The owners arrange mountain walks, castle and art tours, holistic treatments and art classes.

Dooly's Hotel
HOTEL €€

(☑057-912 0032; www.doolyshotel.com; Emmet Sq; s/d from €50/80; 🌐) Originally a coaching house – one of the oldest in Ireland, dating from 1740 – the hotel has an inviting homely feel and old-world charm with Georgian-style furnishings, a solidly reliable restaurant and choice of bars. The 17 rooms are large and some look onto Birr's main square.

🍴 Eating

★ Brambles Cafe & Deli
CAFE €

(☑087 745 3359; Mill St; mains €4-9; ⊙9am-6pm Mon-Sat, from noon Sun; ☑🌐) A tiny outpost of big flavours, this cafe has mismatched furniture and very tasty food. The soda bread is accented with wild garlic, while the soups change with the seasons. Look for the desserts, which can include a delectable rhubarb crumble (only in season).

Emma's Cafe & Deli
CAFE €

(☑057-912 5678; 31 Main St; mains €5-9; ⊙8am-6pm Mon-Fri, 12.30-6pm Sun; 🌐🌐) Generally full of families and shoppers, friendly Emma's serves a whole range of baked goods, sandwiches, salads and cakes. The deli is renowned for its selection of local foods and is an ideal picnic-supplies stop, and there are daily newspapers, plus books and games for kiddies.

★ Spinners on Castle St
MODERN IRISH €€

(☑057-912 3779; www.spinnersbirr.com; Castle St; bar mains €9-14, restaurant mains €19-36; ⊙restaurant 6-9pm Fri & Sat, bar 5-9pm Tue, 12.30-9pm Wed-Sun; 🌐) On Castle St as it hits the bend by the castle wall, this alluring restaurant is part of a complex that spans five restored Georgian houses. The bar is the perfect place to pause with a cheeseboard or burger, while the restaurant has a seasonal menu that includes steaks and seafood. Service is excellent as is the wine and drinks list.

Stylish rooms upstairs are €80 to €140, all with breakfast.

Thatch
IRISH €€

(☑ 057-912 0682; www.thethatchcrinkill.com; Military Rd, Crinkill; mains €18-27; ☺ 4-10pm Mon-Thu, 12.30am-late Fri-Sun; P 🤶 🐾) A traditional thatched pub, 2km southeast of Birr, this 200-year-old inn is a great place to sip a pint or enjoy a meal. The hearty cuisine is a belt notch or two above the norm, with a kids' menu to match. Besides traditional roasts, there are specialities such as duck. It has three brick-clad small bars with open fires, plus a more modern dining room.

🍺 Drinking & Entertainment

Chestnut
PUB

(www.thechestnut.ie; Green St; ☺ 8pm-late Mon-Thu, from 5pm Fri, from 3pm Sat & Sun) The most appealing pub in the centre, the Chestnut dates from 1823 and benefits from a beautiful revamp that combines dark wood with a continental cafe style and cocktails. There's live music at weekends and regular special events such as evening barbecues.

Craughwell's
PUB

(☑ 057-912 1839; www.craughwellspub.com; Castle St; ☺ 7-11.30pm Mon-Sat, 1-11pm Sun) Stop for a pint at Craughwell's, renowned for its rollicking trad-music session on the first Friday of the month and impromptu singalong sessions on Saturday. Tourists and locals alike contribute to the bar's cap collection.

Birr Theatre & Arts Centre
CULTURAL CENTRE

(☑ 057-912 2911; www.birrtheatre.com; Oxmantown Mall) A vibrant place with a regular line-up of art exhibitions, films, theatre and concerts. It's located on gorgeous Oxmantown Mall.

ℹ Information

The **tourist office** (☑ 057-912 0110; Emmet Sq; ☺ 9.30am-1pm & 2-5.30pm Mon-Sat Jun-Sep) has good local and regional information.

ℹ Getting There & Away

Bus Éireann (p694) runs to Athlone (€13, one hour, three daily Monday to Saturday, two Sunday), where you can change for Dublin.
Kearns Transport (www.kearnstransport.com) also runs buses to Dublin and Galway.

Kinnitty

POP 360

Kinnitty is a very quaint village that makes a sensible and handy base for exploring the Slieve Bloom Mountains to the east. The scenic R440 runs east from the town across the mountains to Mountrath.

The best and most convenient way to reach Kinnitty is by car.

◉ Sights

Stone Pyramid
MONUMENT

(St Finian's Church) Look out for the bizarre 10m-high stone pyramid in the village graveyard behind St Finian's Church. In the 1830s, Richard Bernard commissioned this scale replica of the Cheops pyramid in Egypt for the family crypt.

Kinnitty High Cross
MONUMENT

(Kinnitty Castle Hotel, off R421) The shaft of the 9th-century Kinnitty High Cross from the Augustinian Abbey now stands in the grounds of the nearby Kinnitty Castle Hotel. Adam and Eve and the Crucifixion are clearly visible on either face.

🛏 Sleeping & Eating

Kinnitty Castle Hotel
HISTORIC HOTEL €€

(☑ 057-913 7318; www.kinnittycastlehotel.com; off R421; s/d from €90/140; 🐾) One of Ireland's most renowned mansions, 19th-century Kinnitty Castle is built in neo-Gothic style and surrounded by a vast estate. The 37 rooms are suitably atmospheric, along with an excellent library bar, home to antiquarian tomes. Kinnitty Castle Hotel is haunted, of course, in this instance by a phantom monk. The castle is 3km east of town, south of the R421.

Ardmore House
B&B €€

(☑ 057-913 7009; www.kinnitty.com; The Walk; s/d from €55/84; 🐾) This gorgeous Victorian stone farmhouse oozes old-world charm. The five characterful rooms feature brass beds, antique furniture and views of the nearby mountains. Peat fires, homemade brown bread and local foods complete the cosy, rustic atmosphere. The owners organise walking tours in the nearby Slieve Bloom Mountains. The B&B is off the R440, about 200m east of Kinnitty.

★ Giltraps Pub
PUB FOOD €

(☑ 057-913 7076; www.visitkinnitty.com; R421; mains €5-20; ☺ 11am-11pm) The perfect place to stop after exploring the Slieve Bloom Mountains, this lovely country pub scores across the board. Food ranges from simple sandwiches to top-notch barbecque. You can enjoy a pint outside at a picnic table while taking in the mountain vistas.

Giltraps also offers accommodation.

Banagher & Around

POP 1655

Sleepy Banagher bursts into life in the summer months when the busy marina is awash with boaters. Perhaps Banagher's greatest claim to fame is that it was the location for Charlotte Brontë's honeymoon.

◎ Sights

Situated at a crossing point over the River Shannon, Banagher was a place of enormous strategic importance during turbulent times. The modest fortifications by the bridge include the diminutive **Cromwell's Castle** (off R356), **Fort Eliza**, a roofless **military barracks** and **Martello tower**.

St Paul's Church   CHURCH
St Paul's Church at the far south end of Main St contains a resplendent stained-glass window, originally intended for Westminster Abbey.

Clonony Castle   CASTLE
(☑ 087 761 4034; off R357, Colony; admission by donation; ⊙ hours vary) This 16th-century castle is enclosed by an overgrown castellated wall. Tales that Henry VIII's second wife, Anne Boleyn, was born here are unlikely to be true, but her cousins Elizabeth and Mary Boleyn are buried beside the ruins. Restoration is sporadic and you may find the gates locked; if you see someone around stop for a fascinating tour.

🏃 Activities

Banagher Marina is a good place to rent cruisers for a trip along the Shannon or the Royal Canal. Try **Carrick Craft** (☑ 01-278 1666; www.cruise-ireland.com; Marina; per week from €650 depending on season) or **Silverline Cruisers** (☑ 057-915 1112; www.silverlinecruisers. com; Marina; 3 days from €400) for more information.

Shannon Adventure Canoeing   CANOEING
(☑ 057-915 1411; advcanoe@iol.ie; Marina; 2-person canoe rental per day €50; ⊙ call for hours) You don't need a houseboat to enjoy Ireland's waterways – here you can rent a canoe and leisurely work your way along the canals.

🛏 Sleeping

Dún Cromáin   B&B €
(☑ 057-915 3966; www.duncromain.com; Crank Rd; s/d €45/70; Ⓟ 🛜) Surrounded by sweeping lawns, the large rooms are simply decorated

in pastel colours with light wood and white linens. The breakfast-cum-sitting room has a thoughtful feel-at-home atmosphere and an open fire. Perks include babysitting, fridges and facilities for drying clothes (handy in these parts). It's near the marina and there's a 50% reduction for under 12s.

Charlotte's Way   B&B €€
(☑ 057-915 3864; www.charlottesway.com; The Hill; s/d from €45/80; 🛜) This tastefully restored former 18th-century rectory on Banagher Hill offers five comfy good-value rooms, with period furniture, old prints and antiques. Charlotte Brontë was a frequent visitor and, after her death, her husband Arthur lived here as the rector. Breakfast stars eggs fresh from the chickens and produce from the pretty garden.

🍷 Drinking

★ **JJ Houghs Singing Pub**   PUB
(Main St; ⊙ noon-11.30pm) Rivalling the river as Banagher's most appealing feature, Hough's is a 250-year-old vine-clad pub renowned for its music sessions. You'll find someone playing here most nights in summer and at weekends in winter. People sing nightly, led by the owner Michael. Seek solitude in the lovely beer garden.

❶ Getting There & Away

Kearns Transport (www.kearnstransport.com) links Banagher to Birr (€3, 15 minutes) and Tullamore (€6, 45 minutes) once daily, leaving at 8.35am.

Shannonbridge

POP 650

Perfectly picturesque, Shannonbridge gets its name from a narrow 16-span, 18th-century bridge that crosses the river into County Roscommon. It's a small, sleepy village with just one main street and three pubs. The best way to get here is by car.

Shannonbridge Fort   FORTRESS
FREE You can't miss the massive 19th-century **bridgehead fortifications** on the western bank in County Roscommon, where heavy artillery was installed to bombard Napoleon in case he tried to invade by river. Substantial other parts of the fort survive: the **Guardhouse** next to the fort is still there and part of the redoubt and defensive wall survive, although some of it was demolished in the 1950s to allow vehicles to pass.

SHANNON HARBOUR & AROUND

Just 1km east of where the Grand Canal joins the River Shannon, sleepy Shannon Harbour is a small picturesque town that was once a thriving trading centre, constructed to serve the waterways and home to more than 1000 people. Along with cargo boats, passenger barges ran from here, many taking poverty-stricken locals on their first leg of a long journey to North America or Australia.

Today the waterways are again teeming with boats and walking paths stretching in all directions, making Shannon Harbour an enticing stop for walkers, fishers, boaters and birders.

★ **JJ Killeens Village Tavern**   PUB

(☑ 090-967 4112; Main St; mains from €8; ⊘ noon-11pm) Killeens is an old-world pub and shop that is renowned for its warm welcome and lively traditional music. There's a music session six nights a week in summer and at weekends during the rest of the year. Traditional pub grub is available.

ⓘ Information

Visitor Centre & Tourist Information (R357; ⊘ 9am-5pm Apr-Nov)

Clonmacnoise

With a nearby ruined castle for company, the setting is quite sublime at Clonmacnoise (www.heritageireland.ie; adult/child €7/3; ⊘ 9am-6.30pm Jun-Aug, 10am-6pm mid-Mar–May, Sep & Oct, 10am-5.30pm Nov–mid-Mar; P) – one of Ireland's holiest and most significant monastic sites. Right alongside the River Shannon, an enticing air of sacred mystery pervades the remains, with its wealth of early church architecture, including some of Ireland's finest high crosses and most ancient round towers, all arrayed closely together within the confines of a walled field. The site is not large, but plan on a visit of a couple of hours.

The surrounding marshy area is known as the Shannon Callows, home to many wild plants and one of the last refuges of the seriously endangered corncrake (a pastel-coloured relative of the coot).

If you want to avoid summer crowds it's a good idea to visit early or late; the tiny country lanes nearby can get clogged with coaches.

History

When St Ciarán founded a monastery here in AD 548, it was the most important crossroads in the country, the intersection of the north–south River Shannon and the east–west Esker Riada (Highway of the Kings).

The giant ecclesiastical city had a humble beginning and Ciarán died just seven months after building his first church. Over the years, however, Clonmacnoise grew to become an unrivalled bastion of Irish religion, literature and art and attracted a large lay population. Between the 7th and 12th centuries, monks from all over Europe came to study and pray here, helping to earn Ireland the title of the 'land of saints and scholars'.

Most of what you can see today dates from the 10th to 12th centuries. The monks would have lived in small huts surrounding the monastery. The site was burned and pillaged on numerous occasions by both the Vikings and the Irish. After the 12th century it fell into decline, and by the 15th century was home solely to an impoverished bishop. In 1552 the English garrison from Athlone reduced the site to a ruin.

◉ Sights

Visitor Centre   MUSEUM

(☑ 090-967 4195; www.heritageireland.ie; R444; adult/child €8/4; ⊘ 9am-6.30pm Jun-Aug, 10am-5.30pm mid-Mar–May, Sep & Oct, to 5.30pm Nov–mid-Mar, last admission 1hr before closing; P) Three connected conical huts, echoing the design of early monastic dwellings, house the Visitor Centre museum. A 20-minute audiovisual show provides an excellent introduction to the historic Clonmacnoise site.

The exhibition area contains the original high crosses (replicas have been put in their former locations outside), and various artefacts uncovered during excavation, including silver pins, beaded glass and an Ogham stone. There is also considerable textual illustration and explanation on the walls of what you are looking at.

There's a real sense of drama as you descend to the foot of the imposing Cross of the Scriptures (King Flann's Cross), one of Ireland's finest. It's very distinctive, with unique upward-tilting arms and richly decorated panels depicting the Crucifixion, the Last Judgement, the arrest of Jesus and Christ in the tomb.

Only the shaft of the **North Cross**, which dates from around AD 800, remains. It is adorned by lions, convoluted spirals and a single figure, thought to be the Celtic god Cernunnos. The richly decorated **South Cross** has mostly abstract carvings – swirls, spirals and fretwork – and, on the western face, the Crucifixion plus a few odd cavorting creatures.

The museum also contains the largest collection of early Christian grave slabs in Europe. Many have inscriptions clearly visible, often starting with *oroit do* or *ar* (a prayer for).

Cathedral   RUINS

The largest building at Clonmacnoise, the cathedral was originally built in AD 909, but was significantly altered and remodelled over the centuries. Its most interesting feature is the intricate 15th-century Gothic doorway with carvings of Sts Francis, Patrick and Dominic. A whisper carries from one side of the door to the other, and this feature was supposedly used by lepers to confess their sins without infecting the priests.

The last High Kings of Tara – Turlough Mór O'Connor (died 1156) and his son Ruairí (Rory; died 1198) – are said to be buried near the altar.

Temple Ciaran   CHURCH

The small churches at Clonmacnoise are called temples, a derivation of the Irish word *teampall* (church). Tiny Temple Ciaran is reputed to be the burial place of St Ciarán, the site's founder. The floor level in Temple Ciaran is lower than outside because local farmers have been taking clay from the church for centuries to protect their crops and cattle. The floor has been covered in slabs, but handfuls of clay are still removed from outside the church in the early spring.

O'Rourke's Tower   TOWER

Overlooking the River Shannon is the 19.3m-high O'Rourke's Tower. Lightning blasted the top off the tower in 1135, but the remaining structure was used for another 400 years. Some say that the stones that came down after the lightning strike were used to help build Temple Finghin & Tower.

Temple Finghin & Tower   CHURCH

Temple Finghin and its round tower are on the northern boundary of the Clonmacnoise

Clonmacnoise Ⓝ   0 ▬▬▬▬▬ 50 m

Clonmacnoise

◎ **Sights**

monastic site, overlooking the River Shannon. The building dates from around 1160 and has some fine Romanesque carvings. The herringbone-patterned tower roof is the only one in Ireland that has never been altered.

Nun's Church   HISTORIC SITE

Beyond the site's boundary wall, about 500m east through the modern graveyard and on the way to the Mongan Bog, is the secluded Nun's Church with Romanesque arches and minute carvings; one has been interpreted as Ireland's earliest sheila-na-gig, in an acrobatic pose with feet tucked behind the ears.

Castle Ruins   RUINS

West of the site, on the ridge near the car park, is a motte with the oddly shaped ruins of a 13th-century castle – also known as Clonmacnoise Castle – built by John de Grey, bishop of Norwich, to watch over the Shannon.

🛏 Sleeping & Eating

There's a simple cafe at the visitor centre and a larger operation near the car park.

Kajon House   B&B €€

(☑ 090-967 4191; www.kajonhouse.ie; R444, Creevagh; s/d from €55/75; ☺ Mar-Oct; P 🛜) If you want to stay near the ruins, this is your best option, just 1.5km southwest. It has cosy rooms, a spacious yard (complete with picnic table) and a warm welcome even by Irish standards. Delicious pancakes are available for breakfast; you may be able to arrange for dinner.

❶ Information

The €1 Clonmacnoise visitors guide (available at the **tourist office** (☑ 090-967 4134; ☺ 10am-5.45pm mid-Mar–Oct)) is a good investment.

❶ Getting There & Away

Clonmacnoise is 7km northeast of Shannonbridge on the R444. Bus tours are promoted throughout the region, but the best way to arrive is by car.

Tullamore

POP 11,575

Tullamore, Offaly's county town, is a bustling place with a pleasant setting on the Grand Canal, and most famous for its namesake Tullamore Dew whiskey. It was a big deal locally when the distillery opened a new factory on the edge of town, 60 years after it had shifted all production to County Tipperary.

◉ Sights

Charleville Castle   CASTLE

(☑ 057-932 3040; www.charlevillecastle.com; off N52; guided tour for 2 adults €20, child free; ☺ tours noon-5.30pm Jun-Aug, by appointment Sep-Apr; P) Spires, turrets, clinging ivy and creaking trees combine to give this hulking structure a haunted feel (and, yes, it's reputedly haunted). Charleville Castle was the family seat of the Burys, who commissioned the design in 1798 from Francis Johnston, one of Ireland's most famous architects. Admission is by 45-minute tour only. The castle is 2km southwest of Tullamore. Look for the grove of huge ancient oaks.

The interior is spectacular, with stunning ceilings, one of the most striking Gothic-revival galleries in Ireland and a kitchen block built to resemble a country church.

Tullamore Dew Visitor Centre   MUSEUM

(☑ 057-932 5015; www.tullamoredew.com; Bury Quay; €14; ☺ 9.30am-6pm Mon-Sat, 11.30am-5pm Sun) Located in a 19th-century canal-side warehouse, this extravaganza blends intriguing local history with doses of marketing. Engaging exhibits show the role of the Grand Canal in the town's development and at the end of the tour adults sample what they claim is the easiest of Irish whiskeys to drink. For real aficionados, there is a €28 Whiskey Wise Masterclass that explores the distillery process in depth.

The hard-core can opt for the full-on five-hour Ultimate Distillery Experience (€150), by appointment only.

🛏 Sleeping & Eating

Bridge House Hotel   HOTEL €€

(☑ 057-932 3374; www.bridgehousehoteltullamore. ie; Bridge St; s/d from €75/100; @) The grand stairway dramatically makes the point that this town-centre four-star hotel is a notch above the rest. Rooms are very comfortable and inviting. Many guests unwind at the spa.

Annaharvey Farm   B&B €€

(☑ 057-934 3544; www.annaharveyfarm.ie; R420, Aharney; r from €75; ☺ mid-Feb–Nov) Ideal for families, this tranquil equestrian centre, riding school and award-winning guesthouse combines country life and genuine hospitality, with six rooms and horse riding right on your doorstep. Full board is an option, so all is sorted. The farm is 6km southeast of Tullamore.

Sirocco's   ITALIAN €€

(☑ 057-935 2839; www.siroccos.net; Patrick St; mains €12-27; ☺ 5-10pm Mon-Fri, 1-10pm Sat & Sun; 🔊) Italian-Irish owned, this popular bistro at the centre of Tullamore caters to undecided taste buds and families with its wide selection of fresh pasta dishes and pizza, as well as meat, chicken and fish dishes, employing locally sourced ingredients as much as possible. Reservations recommended.

🍷 Drinking

Wolftrap   PUB

(☑ 057-932 3374; www.the-wolftrap.com; William St; ☺ food 11.30am-8.30pm, bar till late) The place to drink the local whiskey – or anything else. This pub is several cuts above average, with excellent and inventive, albeit casual, bar food (the burgers are superb). There is dance music on weekends; on Tuesdays, owner Padraig McLoughlin leads trad-music sessions.

ℹ Getting There & Away

Bus Éireann (p694) runs a service to Dublin (€19, 2¼ hours, four weekdays, two Saturday and Sunday). **Kearns Transport** (www.kearnstransport.com) also runs buses to Birr and Banagher.

Irish Rail (p696) trains run east to Dublin (from €20, 1¼ hours, hourly) and west to Galway (from €22, 1½ hours, eight daily), as well as to Westport.

Durrow Abbey

Durrow Abbey   ABBEY
Founded by St Colmcille (also known as St Columba) in the 6th century, Durrow Abbey is most famous for producing the illustrated **Book of Durrow**. The 7th-century text is the earliest of the great manuscripts to have survived, a remarkable feat considering it was recovered from a farm where it was dipped in the cattle's drinking water to cure illnesses. It is today on display at Trinity College, Dublin.

The abbey is 7km north of Tullamore, down a long lane.

Little remains of Durrow Abbey at this site, although there are five early-Christian gravestones. A short path leads to **St Colmcille's Well**, a place of pilgrimage marked by a small cairn.

⭐**Durrow High Cross**   CHRISTIAN SITE
(off N52; ☉10am-4pm) This splendid 10th-century high cross has complex, carvings depicting the sacrifice of Isaac, the Last Judgement and the Crucifixion, and is today housed in a 19th-century **church** for protection.

Clara Bog

⭐**Clara Bog**
Nature Reserve   NATURE RESERVE
(Clara-Rahan Rd; ☉dawn-dusk) Just 6km south of the busy M6 motorway, Clara Bog is one of the few great expanses of classic bogland in all of Western Europe to escape being stripped for fuel. Deceptively flat and seemingly lifeless, it offers a fascinating window into the natural world. It's the quiet that sounds the loudest at this magical preserved 460-hectare raised bog landscape: water courses, birds chirp, insects buzz and more. A 1km-loop boardwalk leads from a parking area 4km south of Clara.

Look for tiny wildflowers growing amid the pillowy soft peat and enjoy the sweeping views of distant green hills and the soft Offaly light on boggy pools of water.

Clara Bog Visitor Centre   MUSEUM
(☑057-936 8878; Ballycumber Rd/R436; ☉10am-5pm Mon-Fri year-round, to 1pm Sat Apr-Nov) **FREE** Sharing space with the local library, this modern and small museum gives an engaging overview of the fascinating life and ecosystem of the bog, from butterflies to toads and beyond.

COUNTY LAOIS

Little-visited Laois (pronounced leash) is often overlooked as drivers zoom past to the south and west. Away from the main roads, though, is this hidden corner of Ireland, with pretty towns such as Abbeyleix making a perfect daytime stop, and the dramatic Slieve Bloom Mountains, which get you right off the beaten track. Laois is also home to the magnificence of Emo Court, one of Ireland's grandest buildings.

There's plenty of local information at www.laoistourism.ie. Look for the excellent *Laois Heritage Trail* booklet, either online or at tourist offices.

Abbeyleix

POP 2570
Abbeyleix (abbey-*leeks*) is a classic heritage town with a Georgian market house, graceful terraced housing and a wide leafy main street. The town grew up around a 12th-century Cistercian monastery, but problems with frequent flooding led to local 18th-century landowner Viscount de Vesci levelling the village and creating a new, planned estate town in the present location. During the Famine, de Vesci proved a kinder landlord than many, and the fountain **obelisk** in the square was erected in gratitude from his tenants.

You will need your own wheels as buses no longer run to Abbeyleix.

◉ Sights

Unfortunately for visitors, de Vesci's magnificent mansion is not open to the public, but it's worth taking a look at the elegant Market House. Wandering the town's historic streets is very rewarding.

⭐**Heywood Gardens**   GARDENS
(☑057-873 3563; www.heritageireland.ie; Ballinakill; ☉8.30am-9pm May-Aug, to 7pm Apr & Sep, to 5.30pm Oct-Mar; 🅿🚻) **FREE** These lavish gardens with architectural features, lakes

LOUGH BOORA

Much of County Offaly's once extensive bogs were stripped of peat for electricity generation during the 20th century. Now efforts are being made to restore the bogland at the Lough Boora Parklands. Ireland's growing number of very visible wind farms is testament to a diversifying renewable energy portfolio, which will further help in the recovery of the boglands.

Lough Boora Parklands (☑057-934 0010; www.loughbooraparklands.com; off R357; ☺dawn-dusk) is the focus of a scheme for bog restoration. There are more than 50km of trails across the area with excellent birdwatching, fishing, rare flora, a mesolithic site and an impressive environment to explore. The trails are great for cycling and you can hire bikes (☑086 889 5194; per hour €3; ☺10am-8pm). There's also a visitor centre (☺9.30am to 6pm summer, 11am to 4pm winter) here with a cafe. Check the website for a handy selection of trails.

and woodland were landscaped by Edwin Lutyens and Gertrude Jekyll and completed in 1912. The centrepiece is a sunken garden, where circular terraces lead down to an oval pool with a magnificent fountain.

The gardens are 7km southeast of Abbeyleix, off the R432 to Ballinakill, in the grounds of Heywood Community School.

Market House HISTORIC BUILDING
In the town centre and built in 1836, this historic building houses a library and exhibition space.

Abbeyleix Heritage House & Museum MUSEUM
(☑057-873 1653; www.abbeyleixheritage.com; Main St; adult/child €3/2; ☺9am-5pm Tue-Sat; P☖) This museum, in an old 19th-century school building, details Abbeyleix's rich history. One room looks at the town's carpet-making legacy – the Turkish-influenced carpets once made here were chosen to grace the floors of the *Titanic* – while another showcases a fascinating selection of memorabilia from the Morrissey family, who ran the town's renowned shop and pub from 1775 to 2004. It also has tourist information and an adjacent playground.

🛏 Sleeping & Eating

Farran Farm Hostel HOSTEL €
(☑057-873 4032; www.farmhostel.com; Ballacolla; dm from €20; P) In a beautifully restored limestone grain loft on a working family farm, this quirky independent hostel has 45 beds in rooms with a bathroom and up to five bunks. You can arrange in advance for delicious dinners using locally sourced produce. The hostel is near the junction of the R4343 and R434, about 6km west of Abbeyleix. Continental breakfast is €5.

Sandymount House B&B B&B €€
(☑057-873 1063; www.sandymounthouse.com; off R433, Old Town; s/d from €60/90; ☎) Once the home of the de Vesci estate manager, this lovely old country house has been beautifully restored. A grand sweeping staircase, marble fireplaces and mature gardens provide elegant charm, while the spacious rooms are well equipped with individually designed bathrooms sporting high-pressure showers. It's 2km west of Abbeyleix.

★**Gallic Kitchen** CAFE €
(☑086 605 8208; www.gallickitchen.com; Main St; dishes €5-9.50; ☺10am-6pm Mon-Sat, 11am-6pm Sun; ☖) 🍃 Set in an old haberdashery shop named Bramley's, this outlet of the Gallic Kitchen sets mouths watering for anyone familiar with the food of chef Sarah Webb. Her delicious jams, preserves, baked goods and other treats are sold at farmers markets from here to Dublin. The menu here is a paean to the best of modern Irish fare.

🍷 Drinking

★**Morrissey's** PUB
(☑057-873 1281; Main St; ☺10am-11pm) This extraordinary pub has withstood the onslaught of modernisation. A hotchpotch of oddities line the shelves above the pew seats and pot-belly stove. Dating from 1775 (when it opened as a grocery store), it's a wonderful place to soak up the atmosphere with a pint or a good cup of coffee.

Durrow

POP 820

A pleasant village, Durrow's neat rows of houses, pubs and cafes surround a manicured green. On the western side stands the imposing gateway to the landmark 18th-century Castle Durrow.

🛏 Sleeping & Eating

Castle Arms Hotel
HOTEL €€

(☑ 057-873 6117; www.castlearmshotel.ie; The Square; s/d from €60/90; 🐱) This tidy pub hotel and pub overlooks a corner of Durrow's mannered centre, with 15 comfortable rooms in a charming three-storey heritage building. The chatty pub serves good food through the day and on some nights traditional dancing takes off.

★ Castle Durrow
LUXURY HOTEL €€€

(☑ 057-873 6555; www.castledurrow.com; off N9; d half board from €195; 🐱) This 18th-century castle is one of Ireland's top country-house hotels, with rooms that vary from opulent suites with four-poster beds and heavy brocades to more intimate, less full-on rooms. Even if you can't stay overnight, it's worth popping in for a coffee on the terrace overlooking the vast grounds or afternoon tea. Activities include tennis, archery, clay pigeon shooting and fishing.

The excellent **restaurant** (3-course set menu €39.50; ⊙ 7am-9pm Wed-Sun) is supplied by the castle's organic kitchen garden. Bar meals are available through the day daily. Numerous walks lace the estate and garden tours are also held.

Slieve Bloom Mountains

Populated Ireland recedes into your rearview mirror when you explore the Slieve Bloom Mountains. Although not as spectacular as some Irish ranges, their sudden rise from the Laois plain and the absence of visitors make them appealing. On the lower slopes there are a lot of generic conifer farms, but higher up the sense of being away from it all permeates as you explore deserted blanket bogs, moorland, pine forests and isolated valleys.

The website www.slievebloom.ie has comprehensive information and 16 downloadable looped walking routes.

◉ Sights & Activities

For leisurely walking, **Glenbarrow**, southwest of Rosenallis, has an interesting trail by the cascading **Glendine Park**, near the Glendine Gap and the **Cut Mountain Pass**. Look for parking areas with trail maps for more ideas.

For something more challenging you could stride out on the **Slieve Bloom Way**, an 84km-long signposted trail that does a complete circuit of the mountains, taking in most major points of interest. The recommended starting point is the car park at Glenbarrow, 5km from Rosenallis, from where the trail follows tracks, forest firebreaks and old roads around the mountains. The trail's highest point is at **Glendine Gap** (460m).

★ Slieve Bloom Mountains
Nature Reserve
NATURE RESERVE

(www.npws.ie) The higher elevations of the mountains are protected by this nature reserve. The website has good walking suggestions and info about the flora and fauna, including the many herbs and wildflowers that can be seen.

OFF THE BEATEN TRACK

DONAGHMORE WORKHOUSE

The unremarkable farm village of Donaghmore, 20km west of Durrow, is home to a quietly horrifying reminder of the Famine (p497).

The unadorned stone **Donaghmore Workhouse** (☑ 086 829 6685; R435, Donaghmore; adult/child €5/3; ⊙ 11am-5pm Mon-Fri year-round, plus 2-5pm Sat & Sun Jun-Sep) was a last resort for the destitute in the 1850s. Conditions were intentionally grim, the idea being that if things were especially bad, the poor wouldn't stick around. They didn't, as scores died in the harsh conditions. Today the remaining buildings hold a collection of simple displays that detail this cruel story.

A sign near the entrance notes: 'By the time the Donaghmore Workhouse opened in 1853, most of the poor of the area had already perished from starvation or sickness or had emigrated.'

Overcrowding was rife, families were separated (often for good), meals (no more than a bowl of gruel) were taken in silence, toilets were crude and bedding was limited. The loss of dignity that came with entering the workhouse was a tragic reality for many.

Slieve Bloom Walking Club WALKING
(☑086 278 9147; www.slievebloom.ie; adult/child €5/free; ☺ Sun, check website for other days) This club organises guided walks as well as an annual festival. Its latest schedule is available on their Facebook page.

🛏 Sleeping & Eating

★**Roundwood House** GUESTHOUSE €€
(☑057-873 2120; www.roundwoodhouse.com; R440, Mountrath; s/d from €95/150, set dinner €40-55; ☺ Feb-Dec; ☜) Set in secluded woods, the rooms in this stately 17th-century Palladian villa have an appealing, worn-at-the-edges elegance. Children and adults will adore all the outdoor space, while communal dinners provide the chance to meet the amiable owners and enjoy a country treat of local foods.

Rooms are in the main house – with a convivial lounge – and in an even older building nearby.

★**Ballyfin House** LUXURY HOTEL €€€
(☑057-875 5866; www.ballyfin.com; off R423, Ballyfin; s €380-620, d €590-890, ste €810-1580; @☜☒) A vast and opulent Regency mansion with lavish interiors, at the foot of the Slieve Bloom Mountains, 20-room Ballyfin House is one of Ireland's premier luxury retreats. Among the highlights: 17th-century Flemish tapestries, a Roman sarcophagus bath, secret doorways, a 'whispering room', a promise that every need shall be catered for, plus a huge estate that ranges over 248 hectares.

Mountmellick
POP 4750

A quiet Georgian town located on the River Owenass, Mountmellick was renowned for its linen production in the 19th century and owes much of its history to its Quaker settlers and its place on the Grand Canal. For an informative lowdown on the town's

---

> ⓘ **GETTING AROUND LAOIS**
> ⋯⋯⋯⋯⋯⋯⋯⋯⋯⋯⋯⋯⋯⋯⋯⋯⋯⋯⋯⋯
> County Laois is best explored with your own wheels as bus services are sparse. The county town of Portlaoise does have rail services: trains stop on runs serving Dublin (from €18, one hour, 14 daily), Cork (from €20, two hours, nine daily) and Limerick (from €18, 1½ hours, three daily).

---

fascinating local history, swing by the Mountmellick Museum.

A 4km looped and signed **heritage trail**, beginning in the square, leads you on a walking tour of the most important landmarks.

Mountmellick Museum MUSEUM
(☑057-862 4525; www.mountmellickdevelopment.com; off N80, Irishtown; adult/child €5/2; ☺9.15am-5pm Mon-Fri) For an insight into the town's Quaker and industrial heritage, visit Mountmellick Museum, where you can also see a display of superbly subtle Mountmellick embroidery. Various linens and quilts still being made by locals are on sale here. Tours are held through the day and the museum also has guides to the heritage trail around town.

Portarlington
POP 7790

Portarlington grew up under the influence of French Huguenot and German settlers and has some fine, if neglected, 18th-century buildings along French and Patrick Sts. The ruins of Lea Castle are well worth an expedition.

◉ Sights

Lea Castle CASTLE
About 4km east of town are the ivy-covered ruins of 13th-century Lea Castle, on the banks of the River Barrow that divides Laois from Offaly. The castle consists of a fairly intact towered keep with two outer walls and a twin-towered gatehouse. Access is through a farmyard, 500m to the north off the main Monasterevin road (R420).

St Paul's Church CHURCH
(R420; ☺7am-7pm) FREE The 1851 St Paul's Church, on the site of the original 17th-century French church, was built for the Huguenots, some of whose tombstones stand in a corner of the churchyard. Most of the wealthier Huguenots had left Portarlington by 1871; the ones that stayed were mainly tradesmen and shopkeepers.

Portlaoise & Around
POP 22,000

You'll probably only find yourself either passing through Portlaoise or stopping off in September for the Electric Picnic music and arts festival. These days the town mainly serves as a commercial centre.

Portlaoise is served by both train (www.irishrail.ie) and bus (www.buseireann.ie). The train station is on Station Rd, near the centre of town.

◉ Sights

★ Emo Court
HISTORIC BUILDING

(www.heritageireland.ie; off R422, Emo; adult/child €5/3, grounds free; ⊗10am-6pm Easter-Sep, last admission 5pm, grounds dawn-dusk year-round) The unusual, green-domed Emo Court is an impressive house, designed in 1790 by James Gandon, architect of Dublin's Custom House. The extensive grounds with their Greek statues contain more than 1000 different trees, including huge sequoias, and shrubs from all over the world. Enjoy refreshments at the cafe or a leisurely picnic, before enjoying a scenic stroll through the woodlands to Emo Lake.

Emo is about 13km northeast of Portlaoise, just off the R422, 2km west of the M7.

The house was originally the country seat of the first Earl of Portarlington. After many years as a Jesuit novitiate, the house, with its elaborate central rotunda, was impressively restored.

Rock of Dunamaise
HISTORIC SITE

(off N80; ⊗dawn-dusk; P) The Rock of Dunamaise, 6km east of Portlaoise, is an arresting sight: a craggy limestone outcrop rising dramatically out of the flat plains. It offered early settlers a superb natural defensive position with sweeping views across the surrounding countryside. You'll need some imagination to envisage the site as it once was, before it was destroyed by Cromwell's henchmen in 1650. But the views from the summit are breathtaking on a clear day.

The rock was first fortified in the Bronze Age and was recorded on Ptolemy's map of AD 140. Over the centuries that followed, successive waves of Viking, Norman, Irish and English invaders fought over its occu-

DON'T MISS

ELECTRIC PICNIC

reland's answer to Glastonbury, though on a smaller scale, the annual Electric Picnic (www.electricpicnic.ie; Stradbally Hall; 3-day pass from €240; ⊗early Sep) I is a three-day open-air arts and music festival. Known for its eclectic line-up, it attracts a large number of Irish and international performers. Tickets sell out months in advance and most people camp, creating one vast communal party. The festival takes place 10km southeast of Portlaoise.

It's attracted the likes of Björk, Underworld, The Chemical Brothers, Sinead O'Connor, Massive Attack, Blondie, Florence + the Machine and Blur since it began in 2004.

pation and control. The ruins you see today are those of a castle built in the 13th century. It was extensively remodelled in the 15th century. In the 18th century, its shattered remains were slightly rebuilt.

If you're lucky, you'll be able to see Timahoe round tower to the south, the Slieve Blooms to the west and the Wicklow Mountains to the east.

Timahoe
VILLAGE

Tiny Timahoe, 13km southeast of Portlaoise on the R426, has real charm, even if the village is nothing more than a handful of houses fronting a grassy triangle. Screened by a babbling stream and seemingly straight out of a fairy tale, is a tilting 30m-tall, 12th-century round tower. The tower, with its elaborately carved Romanesque doorway 5m above the ground, is part of an ancient site that includes the ruins of a 15th-century church.

The entire place has a certain magical quality, enhanced by a dearth of visitors.

Counties Meath, Louth, Cavan & Monaghan

POP 460,795 / AREA 6395 SQ KM

Best Places to Eat

➡ MacNean House & Restaurant (p528)

➡ Tankardstown House (p508)

➡ Olde Post Inn (p527)

➡ Strandfield (p521)

➡ Riverbank County Pub (p531)

Best Places to Sleep

➡ Hilton Park (p530)

➡ Castle Leslie (p530)

➡ Scholars Townhouse Hotel (p518)

➡ Rock Farm Glamping (p507)

➡ Bellinter House (p509)

Why Go?

The fertile fields of Counties Meath and Louth attracted Ireland's first settlers, making these two counties the birthplace of Irish civilisation. Today they're part of Dublin's commuter belt, but the earliest inhabitants' legacies endure at the mystical tombs at Brú na Bóinne and Loughcrew – which both predate the Egyptian pyramids – and on the Hill of Tara, the seat of Ireland's high kings and gateway to the otherworld.

Following St Patrick's arrival, the faithful built abbeys, high crosses and round towers to protect their treasured manuscripts. Magnificent ruins recall a time when Ireland was known as the Land of Saints and Scholars.

To the northwest, Counties Cavan and Monaghan's undulating hills and fish-filled lakes are wilder and more remote. Walking trails take in the rugged scenery and expansive views of the Cuilcagh Mountains.

When to Go

➡ If sightseeing is at the top of your list, try to avoid November to March when many of the region's high-profile historic sites have reduced hours or are closed altogether.

➡ April is, unusually, the driest month of the year in this part of the country. The daffodils are in bloom, along with a riot of wildflowers, making it especially scenic (and less soggy) for walkers.

➡ Summertime is festival time: Drogheda hosts its annual Arts Festival in May, while Carlingford's party atmosphere peaks in August during its famous Oyster Festival. Horses race on Laytown's beach around late August and Monaghan Town hosts its Harvest Blues Festival in early September.

COUNTY MEATH

Meath's rich soil, laid down during the last ice age, drew settlers as early as 8000 BC. They worked their way up the banks of the River Boyne, transforming the landscape from forest to farmland. One of the five provinces of ancient Ireland, Meath was at the centre of Irish politics for centuries.

Today Meath's high-yielding land and plentiful water supply make it a vital agriculture centre. Its proximity to Dublin brought about unchecked growth during the Celtic Tiger's peak, however, and the larger towns are surrounded by soulless housing estates with heavy traffic at commuter time.

For visitors, though, there are numerous must-see attractions here, including many tangible reminders of Meath's absorbing history.

Brú Na Bóinne

The vast Neolithic necropolis known as Brú na Bóinne (the Boyne Palace) is one of the most extraordinary sites in Europe. A thousand years older than Stonehenge, it's a powerful testament to the mind-boggling achievements of prehistoric humankind.

The complex was built to house the remains of those in the top social tier and its tombs were the largest artificial structures in Ireland until the construction of the Anglo-Norman castles 4000 years later. The area consists of many different sites; the three principal ones are Newgrange, Knowth and Dowth.

Over the centuries the tombs decayed, were covered by grass and trees, and were plundered by everybody from Vikings to Victorian treasure hunters, whose carved initials can be seen on the great stones of Newgrange. The countryside around the tombs is home to countless other ancient tumuli (burial mounds) and standing stones.

◉ Sights

★ Brú na Bóinne
Visitor Centre   VISITOR CENTRE
(☑ 041-988 0300; www.heritageireland.ie; Donore; adult/child visitor centre €4/3, visitor centre & Newgrange €7/4, visitor centre & Knowth €6/4, all 3 sites €13/8; ⊙ 9am-7pm Jun–mid-Sep, 9am-6.30pm May & mid-Sep–early Oct, 9.30am-5.30pm Feb-Apr & early Oct-early Nov, 9am-5pm

early Nov-Jan) Built in a spiral design echoing Newgrange, this superb interpretive centre houses interactive exhibits on prehistoric Ireland and its passage tombs. It has regional tourism info, an excellent cafe, plus a book and souvenir shop. Upstairs, a glassed-in observation mezzanine looks out over Newgrange.

All visits to Newgrange and/or Knowth depart from here.

★ Newgrange   HISTORIC SITE
(www.newgrange.com; visitor centre & Newgrange €7/4; ⊙ 9am-7pm Jun–mid-Sep, 9am-6.30pm May & mid-Sep–early Oct, 9.30am-5.30pm Feb-Apr & early Oct-early Nov, 9am-5pm early Nov-Jan)
A startling 80m in diameter and 13m high, Newgrange's white round stone walls, topped by a grass dome, look eerily futuristic. Underneath lies the finest Stone Age passage tomb in Ireland – one of the most remarkable prehistoric sites in Europe. Dating from around 3200 BC, it predates Egypt's pyramids by some six centuries.

The tomb's precise alignment with the sun at the time of the winter solstice (p505) suggests it was also designed to act as a calendar.

No one is quite sure of its original purpose, however – the most common theories are that it was a burial place for kings or a centre for ritual.

Newgrange's name derives from 'New Granary' (the tomb did in fact serve as a repository for wheat and grain at one stage), although a more popular belief is that it comes from the Irish for 'Cave of Gráinne', a reference to a popular Celtic myth. *The Pursuit of Diarmuid and Gráinne* tells of the illicit love between the woman betrothed to Fionn McCumhaill (or Finn McCool), leader of the Fianna, and Diarmuid, one of his most trusted lieutenants. When Diarmuid was fatally wounded, his body was brought to Newgrange by the god Aengus in a vain attempt to save him, and the despairing Gráinne followed him into the cave, where she remained long after he died. This suspiciously Arthurian tale (substitute Lancelot and Guinevere for Diarmuid and Gráinne) is undoubtedly a myth, but it's still a pretty good story. Newgrange also plays another role in Celtic mythology as the site where the hero Cúchulainn was conceived.

Over time, Newgrange, like Dowth and Knowth, deteriorated and at one stage was

Counties Meath, Louth, Cavan & Monaghan Highlights

1 Brú na Bóinne (p501) Exploring evocative prehistoric remains at Brú na Bóinne's extraordinary ancient burial sites.

2 Hot Air Balloon Flights (p512) Floating above fascinating ruins and emerald-green fields on a hot-air balloon flight from Trim.

3 Patrick Kavanagh Resource Centre (p532) Learning about the life and work of poet and author Patrick Kavanagh.

4 Tayto Park (p510) Riding Europe's largest wooden inverted roller coaster and touring Tayto's potato-crisp factory.

5 Tara (p508) Uncovering the secrets of the massive earthworks, passage graves and Stone of Destiny at this sacred hilltop.

6 Cavan Canoe Centre (p526) Canoeing the waterways around Butlersbridge.

7 Listoke Distillery & Gin School (p517) Mixing botanicals to create your own gin, accompanied by G&Ts at this distillery near Drogheda.

8 Cavan Burren Park (p528) Wandering among megalithic stones and tombs near Blacklion.

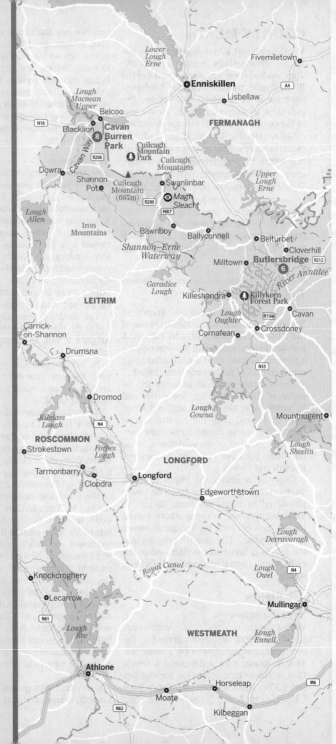

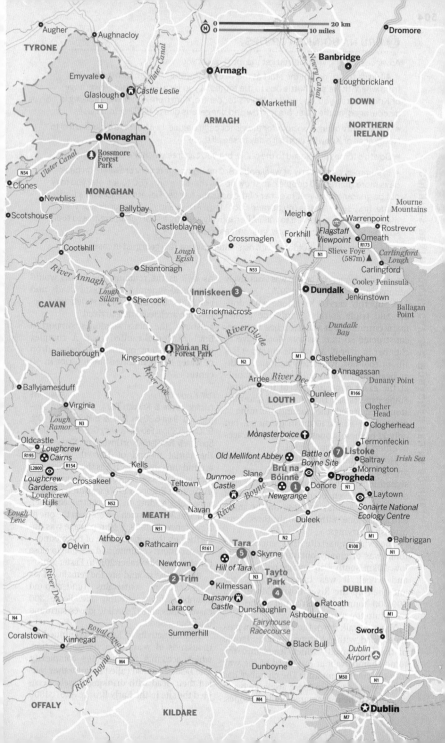

ℹ BRÚ NA BÓINNE TOP TIPS

Advance planning will help you get the most out of your visit.

➜ All visits to Brú na Bóinne start at the **Brú na Bóinne Visitor Centre** (p501) from where there's a shuttle bus to the tombs. If you turn up at either Newgrange or Knowth first, you'll be sent to the visitor centre, 4km from either site. Walking is discouraged, as the lanes are narrow and dangerous due to passing tour buses.

➜ Allow plenty of time: an hour for the visitor centre alone, two hours to include a trip to Newgrange or Knowth, and half a day to see all three.

➜ Dowth's tombs are closed to the public but you can freely visit the surrounding site.

➜ In summer, particularly at weekends, Brú na Bóinne gets very crowded; on peak days more than 2000 people can show up. As there are only 750 tour slots, you may not be guaranteed a visit to either of the passage tombs. Tickets are sold on a first-come, first-served basis (no advance booking). Arrive early in the morning or visit midweek and be prepared to wait. Alternatively, visiting as part of an organised tour, such as **Mary Gibbons Tours**, guarantees a spot.

➜ Tours are primarily outdoors with no shelter so bring rain gear, just in case.

even used as a quarry. The site was extensively restored in 1962 and again in 1975.

A superbly carved kerbstone with double and triple spirals guards the tomb's main entrance, but the area has been reconstructed so that visitors don't have to clamber in over it. Above the entrance is a slit, or roof-box, which lets light in. Another beautifully decorated kerbstone stands at the exact opposite side of the mound. Some experts say that a ring of standing stones encircled the mound, forming a great circle about 100m in diameter, but only 12 of these stones remain, with traces of others below ground level.

Holding the whole structure together are the 97 boulders of the kerb ring, designed to stop the mound from collapsing outwards. Eleven of these are decorated with motifs similar to those on the main entrance stone, although only three have extensive carvings.

The white quartzite that encases the tomb was originally obtained from Wicklow, 70km south – in an age before horse and wheel, it was transported by sea and then up the River Boyne. More than 200,000 tonnes of earth and stone also went into the mound.

You can walk down the narrow 19m passage, lined with 43 stone uprights (some of them engraved), which leads into the tomb chamber about one third of the way into the colossal mound. The chamber has three recesses, and in these are large basin stones that held cremated human bones.

As well as the remains, the basins would have held funeral offerings of beads and pendants, but these were stolen long before the archaeologists arrived.

Above, the massive stones support a 6m-high corbel-vaulted roof. A complex drainage system means that not a drop of water has penetrated the interior in 40 centuries.

★ Knowth
HISTORIC SITE

(visitor centre & Knowth €6/4; ☺9am-7pm Jun–mid-Sep, 9am-6.30pm May & mid-Sep–early Oct, 9.30am-5.30pm Feb-Apr & early Oct-early Nov, 9am-5pm early Nov-Jan) Northwest of Newgrange, the burial mound of Knowth was built around the same time. It has the greatest collection of passage-grave art ever uncovered in Western Europe. Early excavations cleared a passage leading to the central chamber, which at 34m, is much longer than the one at Newgrange. In 1968, a 40m passage was unearthed on the opposite side of the mound.

Excavations continue, and are due to close the site from November 2017 to Easter 2018.

Also in the mound are the remains of six early-Christian souterrains (underground chambers) built into the side. Some 300 carved slabs and 17 satellite graves surround the main mound.

Human activity at Knowth continued for thousands of years after its construction, which accounts for the site's complexity. The Beaker folk, so called because they buried their dead with drinking vessels, occupied the site in the Early Bronze Age (c 1800

BC), as did the Celts in the Iron Age (c 500 BC). Remnants of bronze and iron workings from these periods have been discovered. Around AD 800 to 900, it was turned into a *ráth* (earthen ring fort), a stronghold of the very powerful O'Neill clan. In 965 it was the seat of Cormac MacMaelmithic, later Ireland's high king for nine years, and in the 12th century the Normans built a motte and bailey (a raised mound with a walled keep) here. The site was finally abandoned around 1400.

Visits start only from the visitor centre (p501).

Dowth
HISTORIC SITE

(⊙24hr) **FREE** The circular mound at Dowth is similar in size to Newgrange – about 63m in diameter – but is slightly taller at 14m high. Due to safety issues, Dowth's tombs are closed to visitors, though you can visit the mound (and its resident grazing sheep) from the L1607 road between Newgrange and Drogheda.

North of the tumulus are the ruins of **Dowth Castle** and **Dowth House**.

Dowth has two entrance passages leading to separate chambers (both sealed), and a 24m early-Christian underground passage at either end, which connect with the western passage. This 8m-long passage leads into a small cruciform chamber, in which a recess acts as an entrance to an additional series of small compartments, a feature unique to Dowth. To the southwest is the entrance to a shorter passage and smaller chamber.

It has suffered badly at the hands of everyone from road builders and treasure hunters to amateur archaeologists, who scooped out the centre of the tumulus in the 19th century. For a time, Dowth even had a tearoom ignobly perched on its summit.

Newgrange Farm
FARM

(☑041-982 4119; www.newgrangefarm.com; Newgrange; per person €9, tractor ride €2.50; ⊙10am-6pm mid-Mar–early Sep; ⬛) One for the kids, this hands-on, family-run 135-hectare working farm allows visitors to feed the ducks, lambs and goats, milk a cow, pet a rabbit and take a tractor ride. Children's play areas include a straw maze and toy tractors; there are indoor and outdoor picnic areas and a cafe. Follow the signs on the N51.

Sunday at 3pm is a very special time when the 'sheep derby' is run, with teddy bear 'jockeys' tied to the animals' backs. Visiting children are made owners of individual sheep for the race.

Tours

Brú na Bóinne is one of the most popular tourist attractions in Ireland, and there are plenty of organised tours. Most depart from Dublin.

Options include the highly recommended Mary Gibbons Tours.

★Mary Gibbons Tours
TOURS

(☑086 355 1355; www.newgrangetours.com; tour incl entrance fees adult/child €40/35) These excellent tours depart from numerous Dublin hotels, beginning at 9.30am Monday to Friday, and 7.40am Saturday and Sunday, and take in the whole of the Boyne Valley including Newgrange and the Hill of Tara. Expert guides offer a fascinating insight into Celtic and pre-Celtic life in Ireland. No credit cards; pay cash on the bus.

🛏 Sleeping

Newgrange Lodge
HOSTEL, HOTEL €

(☑041-988 2478; www.newgrangelodge.com; Staleen Rd, Donore; campsites per tent €10, dm/s/d/f from €21/59/75/109; ⓟ🛜) Footsteps east of the Brú na Bóinne Visitor Centre, this converted farmhouse has 23 rooms

---

NEWGRANGE WINTER SOLSTICE

At 8.20am on the winter solstice (between 18 and 23 December), the rising sun's rays shine through the roof-box above the entrance, creep slowly down the long passage and illuminate the tomb chamber for 17 minutes. There is little doubt that this is one of the country's most memorable, even mystical, experiences.

There's a simulated winter sunrise for every group taken into the mound. To be in with a chance of witnessing the real thing on one of six mornings around the solstice, enter the free lottery that's drawn in late September; 50 names are drawn and each winner is allowed to take one guest (be aware, however, that over 30,000 people apply each year). Fill out the form at the Brú na Bóinne Visitor Centre or email brunaboinne@opw.ie.

ℹ HERITAGE CARD

If you're planning to visit several archaeological and historic sites, consider investing in a **Heritage Card** (http://heritageireland.ie; adult/child €40/10), valid for one year and available for purchase at the **Battle of the Boyne Site** (p506) ticket office, as well as other participating sites throughout the country. For more information, contact Heritage Ireland (www.heritageireland.ie).

ranging from dorms with four to 10 beds to hotel-standard doubles with private bathrooms. Superb facilities include a self-catering kitchen, two outdoor patios, a lounge with an open fire, board games and books, and free bikes. Rates (except camping) include continental breakfast with homemade scones.

ℹ Getting There & Away

Bus Éireann (www.buseireann.ie) links the Brú na Bóinne Visitor Centre with Drogheda's **bus station** (p519) (one way/return €2.50/4.80, 12 minutes, two daily Monday to Saturday, plus Sunday July to August), with connections to Dublin.

Battle of the Boyne Site

Battle of the Boyne Site   HISTORIC SITE
(www.battleoftheboyne.ie; Drybridge; adult/child €5/2; ◉9am-5pm May-Sep, to 4pm Oct-Apr) More than 60,000 soldiers of the armies of King James II and King William III fought in 1690 on this patch of farmland on the border of Counties Meath and Louth. William ultimately prevailed and James sailed off to France.

The battle site has an informative visitor centre and parkland walks. It's 6km west of Drogheda's town centre along Rathmullan Rd (follow the river). Buses run to/from Drogheda (€4.80, 25 minutes, two daily).

At the visitor centre you can watch a short film about the battle, see original and replica weaponry of the time and explore a laser battlefield model. Self-guided walks through the parkland and battle site allow time to ponder the events that saw Protestant interests remain in Ireland. Costumed reenactments take place in summer.

Boyne Boats   BOATING
(☑086 361 6420; http://boyneboats.ie; Oldbridge; 60/90-min tour €16/20; ◉11am-3pm Wed-Sun Easter-May, 11am-3pm Jun-Oct) One of the most peaceful ways to explore the Boyne Valley is to row a traditional oak-and-spruce, eight-seater *currach* sealed with bitumen paint. Tours head along the Boyne Navigation canal network past the Battle of the Boyne Site, with commentary relaying its history as well as stories relating to the TV series *Game of Thrones,* in which the boats starred.

The launch point is the lock keeper's cottage 4km west of Drogheda.

Slane

POP 1369

Slane's 18th-century stone houses and cottages slink down a steep hill to the River Boyne, which glides beneath a narrow bridge. Situated 6km west of Brú na Bóinne, the town grew up around the enormous castle after which it was named. At the main crossroads four identical houses face each other: local lore has it that they were built for four sisters who had taken an intense dislike to one another and kept a beady-eyed watch from their individual residences.

◉ Sights

Slane Castle   CASTLE
(☑041-982 0643; www.slanecastle.ie; guided tour adult/child €12/10; ◉guided tour 11am-5pm Sun-Thu early May–Aug) Still the private residence of Henry Conyngham, Earl of Mountcharles, Slane Castle is best known for its outdoor **concerts** with massive rock-royalty names: Bon Jovi, Eminem, U2, the Rolling Stones, Madonna and Oasis have all performed over the years.

Built in the Gothic-revival style by James Wyatt in 1785, the building was later altered by Francis Johnson for George IV's visits to Lady Conyngham, allegedly his mistress. It's said the road between Dublin and Slane was built especially straight and smooth to speed up the smitten king's journeys. In 1991 the castle was gutted by a fire, whereupon it was discovered that the earl was underinsured. A major fundraising drive, of which the summer concerts were a part, led to a painstaking restoration.

Guided tours include the neo-Gothic Ballroom, completed in 1821, and the Kings Room; the last tour departs at 4.20pm in season. You can also visit its on-site whiskey distillery. It's 1.5km west of the village centre off the N51.

Slane Distillery DISTILLERY
(☏041-982 0643; www.slaneirishwhiskey.com; Slane Castle) Triple cask matured whiskey made on site at Slane Castle was first released in 2017. The castle's 18th-century horse stables are home to a new visitor experience, with tours and tastings.

Hill of Slane HISTORIC SITE
About 1km north of Slane village is the Hill of Slane, a fairly plain-looking mound that stands out only for its association with a thick slice of Celto-Christian mythology. According to legend, St Patrick lit a paschal (Easter) fire here in 433 to proclaim Christianity throughout the land.

On a clear day, climb the evocative ancient stone steps of the tower to enjoy magnificent views of the Hill of Tara and the Boyne Valley, and (it's said) seven Irish counties.

The story goes that Patrick's paschal fire infuriated Laoghaire, the pagan high king of Ireland, who had expressly ordered that no fire be lit within sight of the Hill of Tara. He was restrained by his far-sighted druids, who warned that 'the man who had kindled the flame would surpass kings and princes'. Laoghaire went to meet Patrick, and all but one of the king's attendants, a man called Erc, greeted Patrick with scorn.

Undeterred, Patrick plucked a shamrock from the ground, using its three leaves to explain the paradox of the Holy Trinity: the union of the Father, the Son and the Holy Spirit in one. Laoghaire wasn't convinced, but he agreed to let Patrick continue his missionary work. Patrick's success that day, apart from keeping his own life and giving Ireland one of its enduring national symbols, was good old Erc, who was baptised and later became the first bishop of Slane. To this day, the local parish priest lights a fire here on Holy Saturday.

The Hill of Slane originally had a church associated with St Erc and, later, a round tower and monastery, but only an outline of the foundations remains. You can also see the remains of a ruined church and tower that were once part of an early-16th-century Franciscan friary.

Ledwidge Museum MUSEUM
(☏041-982 4544; www.francisledwidge.com; Janesville; adult/child €3/1; ☉10am-5pm early Mar–Oct, to 3.30pm Nov–early Mar) This quaint cottage, 1km east of Slane on the N51, was the birthplace of poet Francis Ledwidge (1887–1917). A keen political activist, Ledwidge was thwarted in his efforts to set up a local Gaelic League branch, but found an outlet in verse. He died on the battlefield at Ypres, having survived Gallipoli and Serbia.

The museum provides an insight into Ledwidge's works, and the cottage itself is a humbling example of how farm labourers lived in the 19th century.

🛏 Sleeping & Eating

★**Rock Farm Glamping** CAMPGROUND €
(☏041-988 4861; http://rockfarmslane.ie; off N2; d from €60; ☉Apr-Nov; ⓟ🐕🌐) 🍃 On an organic farm stretching 1.5km along the banks of the River Boyne, shaded by oak, ash and chestnut trees, Rock Farm has stunning yurts and huts with lanterns and wood stoves sleeping up to six. Bathrooms are located in the communal 'Le Shack' alongside a lounge and state-of-the-art kitchen, with a pizza oven outside. There's a two-night minimum stay.

Outdoor hot tubs, electric bike hire (€25), yoga classes (€15) and kayak tours along the river (€40) are all available. Two-day breakfast, barbecue and pizza packs cost €10 to €15.

Slane Farm Hostel HOSTEL €
(☏041-982 4985; www.slanefarmhostel.ie; Harlinstown House, Navan Rd; campsites per person €10, dm/s/d/cottage from €20/30/60/100; ⓟ🐕🌐) 🍃 These former stables, built by the Marquis of Conyngham in the 18th century, have been converted into a wonderful hostel that's part of a working dairy farm. Common areas include a games room and kitchen, with free-range eggs and a vegetable plot for guests to use. Free bikes are available. It's 2.5km west of Slane.

Self-catering terraced cottages (€50 per person; minimum two people) sleep up to six.

★**Conyngham Arms** INN €€
(☏041-988 4444; www.conynghamarms.ie; Main St; s/d/f from €65/89/109; 🌐) Beautifully restored, this 18th-century stone coaching inn has 15 airy rooms decorated with French country-style furnishings (some with canopied, four-poster beds), a charming, rose-filled garden with a fountain at

its centre, a **restaurant** (mains €13-18.50; ☺ kitchen 10am-8pm Mon-Thu, 10am-9pm Fri, 9am-9pm Sat & Sun, bar to 11pm) and excellent breakfasts such as free-range scrambled eggs with Annagassan smoked salmon. Staff are welcoming and professional in equal measure. Wi-fi is strongest in the front rooms.

★ **Tankardstown House**   MODERN IRISH €€€
(☑ 041-982 4621; www.tankardsown.ie; Rathkenny; mains lunch €11.50-17.50, dinner €25-37.50, 3-course dinner menu €40; ☺ noon-4pm & 6-8.30pm Wed & Thu, noon-4pm & 6-9.30pm Fri & Sat, 12.30-3.30pm & 6-8.30pm Sun; 🍴) Recently restored by the owners of the Conyngham Arms, this spectacular manor house and orangery on 32 hectares 10km northwest of Slane dates from the 18th century. Its evening restaurant, Brabazon, is its centrepiece, with exquisite dishes such as smoked wood pigeon or wild mushroom ravioli with black truffle and parmesan foam; casual lunches are served in its 'garden village'.

Eggs come from its own hens, with vegetables sourced from its polytunnels and gardens. The kids' menu will impress junior gourmands. Accommodation is available in the manor and courtyard cottages (double/suite/cottage from €335/360/210), but book well ahead as it's a popular wedding venue.

🍷 Drinking & Nightlife

★ **Boyles**   PUB
(www.boylesofslane.ie; Main St; ☺ noon-11.30pm Mon-Thu, to 12.30am Fri & Sat, to 11pm Sun; 🛜) Behind a fire-engine-red facade, this nook-and-cranny-filled pub has snug, stained-glass partitions and a toasty wood stove. It's owned by musician Andrew Cassidy, who hosts a knockout line-up of gigs and trad-music sessions. On Wednesdays, when Andrew and his friends jam, the atmosphere is electric. Live music also takes place Fridays, Saturdays and Sundays (plus some Thursdays). Cash only.

ⓘ Information

Slane's **tourist office** (☑ 041-982 4000; www.visitslane.ie; The Hub, 2 Main St; ☺ 9.30am-5pm Mon-Sat, noon-4pm Sun) is in the village centre.

ⓘ Getting There & Away

Bus Éireann (p694) has a direct service to Drogheda (€5.30, 30 minutes, hourly), from where you can connect to Dublin.

Tara

The Hill of Tara is Ireland's most sacred stretch of turf, occupying a place at the heart of Irish history, legend and folklore. It was the home of the mystical druids, the priest-rulers of ancient Ireland, who practised their particular form of Celtic paganism under the watchful gaze of the all-powerful goddess Maeve (Medbh). Later it was the ceremonial capital of the high kings, all 142 of them, who ruled until the arrival of Christianity in the 5th century. It is also one of the most important ancient sites in Europe, with a Stone Age passage tomb and prehistoric burial mounds that date back some 5000 years.

Although little remains other than humps and mounds on the hill (named from ancient texts), its historic and folkloric significance is immense.

Entrance to Tara is free and the site is always open. There are good explanatory panels by the entrance.

History

Mythology and religion intertwine with historical facts here.

The Celts believed that Tara was the sacred dwelling place of the gods and the gateway to the other world. The passage grave was thought to be the final resting place of the Tuatha dé Danann, the mythical fairy folk. They were real enough, but instead of pixies and brownies, they were earlier Stone Age arrivals on the island.

As the Celtic political landscape began to evolve, the druids' power was usurped by warlike chieftains who took kingly titles; there was no sense of a united Ireland, so at any given time there were countless *rí tuaithe* (regional kings) controlling many small areas. The king who ruled Tara, though, was generally considered the big shot, the high king, even though his direct rule didn't extend too far beyond the provincial border.

The most important event in Tara's calendar was the three-day harvest *feis* (festival) that took place at Samhain, a precursor to modern Halloween. During the festival, the high king pulled out all the stops: grievances were heard, laws passed and disputes settled amid a bacchanalia of eating, drinking and partying.

When the early Christians hit town in the 5th century, they targeted Tara straight away. The arrival of Christianity marked the beginning of the end for Celtic pagan civilisation, and the high kings began to desert Tara, though the kings of Leinster continued to be based here until the 11th century.

In August 1843 Tara saw one of the greatest crowds ever to gather in Ireland. Daniel O'Connell, leader of the opposition to union with Great Britain, held one of his galvanising rallies at Tara, and up to 750,000 people came to hear him speak.

◉ Sights

Rath of the Synods   HISTORIC SITE

Tara's Protestant church grounds and graveyard spill onto the remains of this triple-ringed fort where some of St Patrick's early synods (meetings) supposedly took place. Excavations suggest the enclosure was used between AD 200 and 400 for burials, rituals and dwellings – originally the ring fort would have contained wooden houses surrounded by timber palisades.

Archaeologists have uncovered Roman glass, shards of pottery and seals, showing links with the Roman Empire even though the Romans never extended their power to Ireland.

Royal Enclosure   HISTORIC SITE

South of Tara's church, the Royal Enclosure is a large oval Iron Age hill fort, 315m in diameter and surrounded by a bank and ditch cut through solid rock under the soil. Inside are several smaller earthworks: the **Mound of the Hostages** (closed to the public); **Royal Seat**, a ring fort with a house site; and **Cormac's House**, a barrow (burial mound) in the side of the circular bank, which is topped by the **Stone of Destiny**.

The Mound of the Hostages, a bump in the northern corner of the enclosure, is the most ancient known part of Tara. A treasure trove of artefacts was unearthed, including some ancient Mediterranean beads of amber and faience (glazed pottery). More than 35 Bronze Age burials were found here, as well as extensive cremated remains from the Stone Age.

There are superb views of the surrounding Boyne and Blackwater Valleys from the Royal Seat and Cormac's House.

Atop Cormac's House is the phallic Stone of Destiny (originally located near the Mound of the Hostages), which represents the joining of the gods of the earth and the heavens. It's said to be the inauguration stone of the high kings, although alternative sources suggest that the actual coronation stone was the Stone of Scone, which was taken to Scotland in the early 6th century and – after several centuries in London's Westminster Abbey – now sits in Edinburgh. The would-be king stood on top of the Stone of Destiny and, if the stone let out three roars, he was crowned. The mass grave of 37 men who died in a skirmish on Tara during the 1798 Rising is next to the stone.

Enclosure of King Laoghaire   HISTORIC SITE

South of Tara's Royal Enclosure is this large but worn ring fort where the king, a contemporary of St Patrick, is said to be buried standing upright and dressed in his armour.

Banquet Hall   HISTORIC SITE

Tara's most unusual feature is a rectangular earthwork measuring 230m by 27m along a north–south axis. Tradition holds that it was built to cater for thousands of guests during feasts.

Its orientation suggests that it was a sunken entrance to Tara, leading directly to the Royal Enclosure. More recent research, however, has uncovered graves within the compound, and it's possible that the banks are in fact the burial sites of some of the kings of Tara.

Gráinne's Fort   HISTORIC SITE

Gráinne was the daughter of King Cormac, the most lauded of all high kings. Betrothed to Fionn McCumhaill (Finn McCool), she eloped with Diarmuid, one of the king's warriors, on her wedding night. This became the subject of the epic *The Pursuit of Diarmuid and Gráinne*. Gráinne's Fort and the northern and southern Sloping Trenches to the northwest are burial mounds.

Tara Visitor Centre   VISITOR CENTRE

(☑ 046-902 5903; www.heritageireland.ie; adult/child €5/3; ⊙ visitor centre 10am-6pm mid-May–mid-Sep, site open 24hr all year) A former Protestant church (with a window by acclaimed stained-glass artist the late Evie Hone) is home to Tara's visitor centre, which screens a 20-minute audiovisual presentation about the site.

🍴 Sleeping & Eating

★ Bellinter House   HISTORIC HOTEL €€

(☑ 046-903 0900; www.bellinterhouse.com; Bellinter; d from €140; 🛜) Dating from the 18th

WORTH A TRIP

TAYTO PARK

An Irish icon, Tayto has been producing much-loved potato crisps since 1954. Alongside the factory, its **amusement park** (☎ 01-835 1999; www.taytopark.ie; Kilbrew, Ashbourne; admission €15, incl day pass €28; ⊙ 9.30am-7pm Jul & Aug, shorter hours Mar-Jun & Sep-Dec) has attractions including Europe's largest wooden inverted rollercoaster, 5D cinema (yes, 5D), high-speed spinning Rotator and stomach-churning Air Race ride. There's also a zoo, rock climbing, a zipline and a fantastic playground.

Admission includes a self-guided crisp-factory tour and zoo and playground entry; the wrist-band day pass is the most economical option for the rides.

It's just off the M2 motorway.

century, grande dame Bellinter House, 5km northwest of the Hill of Tara (signposted off the R147), is a haven of crackling open fires and rich artworks. There are 34 antique-furnished rooms in the main house, as well as 16 period rooms in the east and west pavilions and five duplexes in the former stables.

Soak in the on-site spa's outdoor hot tubs and dine on top-class fare at its restaurant Eden (two/three-course menu €38/43), which has its own bakery. Afternoon tea costs €20.

McGuires Coffee Shop CAFE €
(http://hilloftara.com; dishes €8-15.50; ⊙ 9.30am-6pm; 🛜👶) If a walk on the Hill of Tara has worked up an appetite, this restaurant/cafe and souvenir shop at the base can restore you with wholesome fare such as wild-mushroom and pea risotto, surf and turf salad, smoked bacon and broccoli pasta and home-baked sweet treats like rhubarb pie.

🛍 Shopping

Old Tara Book Shop BOOKS
(⊙ 10am-5pm Tue-Sun) At the base of the Hill of Tara, this tiny, jumbled secondhand bookshop is run by Michael Slavin, who has authored an informative little book about the site, *The Tara Walk*, as well as a weightier tome, *The Book of Tara*. Hours can vary.

ⓘ Getting There & Away

Regular **Bus Éireann** (p694) services link Dublin to within 1km of the site (€10.40, one hour, every 30 minutes). Ask the driver to drop you off at Tara Cross, where you take a left turn off the main road.

Dunsany Castle

You can see how the other 1% lives at **Dunsany Castle** (☎ 046-902 5169; www.dunsany.com; Dunsany; adult/child €15/10; ⊙ by appointment 10am-4pm Jul & Aug), 5km south of Tara on the Dunshaughlin–Kilmessan road. The residence of the lords of Dunsany, it's one of the oldest continually inhabited buildings in Ireland. Construction started in the 12th century, with major alterations taking place in the 18th and 19th centuries. Maintenance and restoration are ongoing.

Tours lasting almost two hours offer a fascinating insight into the family's history and impressive private art collection.

The castle houses many treasures related to important figures in Irish history, such as Oliver Plunkett and Patrick Sarsfield, leader of the Irish Jacobite forces at the siege of Limerick in 1691.

You can also buy **Dunsany Home Collection** homewares here: locally made table linen and accessories, as well as various articles designed by the 20th Lord Dunsany (Edward Carlos Plunkett; 1939–2011), who was an acclaimed international designer and artist, famed for his geometrical abstractions and portraits.

Trim

POP 9194

Dominated by its mighty castle, the quiet town of Trim was an important settlement in medieval times. Five city gates surrounded a busy jumble of streets, and as many as seven monasteries were established in the immediate area.

It's hard to imagine nowadays, but a measure of Trim's importance was that Elizabeth I considered building Trinity College here. One student who did study in Trim was Dublin-born Arthur Wellesley (1769–1852), the first Duke of Wellington, who studied at Talbot Castle and St Mary's Abbey.

Today, Trim's history is everywhere, from atmospheric ruins to streets lined with tiny workers' cottages.

Trim

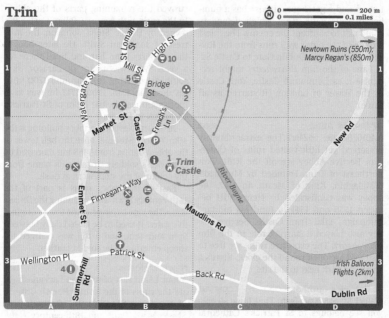

Sights

★ Trim Castle
CASTLE

(King John's Castle; www.heritageireland.ie; adult/child incl tour €5/3; ☉10am-5pm mid-Mar–Sep, 9.30am-4.30pm mid-Feb–mid-Mar & Oct, 9am-4pm Sat & Sun Nov–mid-Feb) Proof of Trim's medieval importance, this remarkably preserved edifice was Ireland's largest Anglo-Norman fortification. Hugh de Lacy founded Trim Castle in 1173, but it was destroyed by Ruaidrí Ua Conchobair, Ireland's last high king, within a year. The building you see today was begun around 1200 and has hardly been modified since.

Entertaining guided tours involve climbing narrow, steep stairs, so aren't suitable for very young children or anyone with restricted mobility. Self-guided tours are also available.

Throughout Anglo-Norman times the castle occupied a strategic position on the western edge of the Pale, the area where the Anglo-Normans ruled supreme; beyond Trim was the volatile country where Irish chieftains and lords fought with their Norman rivals and vied for position, power and terrain. By the 16th century, the castle had begun to fall into decline and in 1649, when the town was taken by Cromwellian forces, it was severely damaged.

The castle's grassy two-hectare enclosure is dominated by a massive stone keep, 25m tall and mounted on a Norman motte. Inside are three levels, the lowest divided by a central wall. Just outside the central keep are the remains of an earlier wall.

The principal outer-curtain wall, 450m long and for the most part still standing, dates from around 1250 and includes eight towers and a gatehouse. It also has a number of sally gates from which defenders could exit to confront the enemy. The finest stretch of the outer wall runs from the River Boyne through Dublin Gate to Castle St.

Fans of the film *Braveheart* might recognise it as Edinburgh Castle, York Castle or the Tower of London (it starred as all three).

★ Bective Abbey
RUINS

(L4010, Bective; ⊙24hr) The extraordinarily preserved yet little-visited ruins of Cistercian Bective Abbey are off the R161, 7km northeast of Trim. Founded by Murchadh O'Melaghin, King of Meath, in 1147, the abbey was confiscated by Henry VIII between 1536 and 1541 to fund his military campaign. Like Trim Castle, Bective Abbey also played a starring role in the film *Braveheart*. The evocative ruins are free to visit and are open round the clock; there's a small car park next to the site.

St Patrick's Cathedral Church
CATHEDRAL

(Patrick St; ⊙8.30am-5pm) That huge steeple you see belongs to St Patrick's Cathedral Church, parts of which dates from the 15th century, although it wasn't granted cathedral status until 1955. Take a look at the beautiful stained-glass windows, including one showing St Patrick preaching on the Hill of Tara. Hours can vary depending on religious services and events.

St Mary's Abbey & Talbot Castle
RUINS

Across the River Boyne from Trim Castle are the ruins of the 12th-century Augustinian St Mary's Abbey, rebuilt after a fire in 1368 and once home to a wooden statue of Our Lady of Trim, revered by the faithful for its supposedly miraculous powers.

In 1415 part of the abbey was converted into a manor house by Sir John Talbot, then viceroy of Ireland; it came to be known as Talbot Castle.

On the northern wall of the castle you can see the Talbot coat of arms. Talbot went to war in France where, in 1429, he was defeated at Orleans by Joan of Arc. He was taken prisoner, released and went on fighting the French until 1453. He became known as 'the scourge of France' and even got a mention in Shakespeare's Henry VI: 'Is this the Talbot so much feared abroad/That with his name the mothers still their babes?'

In 1649 Cromwell's soldiers invaded Trim, set fire to the revered statue and destroyed the remaining parts of the abbey. In the early 18th century, Talbot Castle was owned by Esther 'Stella' Johnson, the mistress of Jonathan Swift. He later bought the property from her and lived there for a year. Swift was rector of Laracor, 3km southeast of Trim, from around 1700 until his death in 1745. From 1713 he was also, more significantly, the Dean of St Patrick's Cathedral in Dublin.

Just northwest of the abbey building is the 40m Yellow Steeple, once the bell tower of the abbey, dating from 1368 but damaged by Cromwell's soldiers. It takes its name from the colour of the stonework at dusk.

East of the abbey ruins is part of the 14th-century town wall, including the Sheep Gate, the lone survivor of the town's original five gates. It used to be closed daily between 9pm and 4am, and a toll was charged for sheep entering to be sold at market.

Newtown Ruins
RUINS

About 1.5km east of town on Lackanash Rd are the ruins of the former Parish Church of Newtown Clonbun, the Cathedral of Sts Peter & Paul and 18th-century Newtown Abbey.

Southeast across the river is the Crutched Friary, with ruins of a keep, and traces of a watchtower and other buildings from a hospital set up after the Crusades by the Knights of St John of Jerusalem. Adjacent St Peter's Bridge is one of Ireland's oldest.

Wellington Column
MONUMENT

(cnr Summerhill Rd & Wellington Pl) The local burghers dedicated this column to Arthur Wellesley, the first Duke of Wellington, in recognition of his impressive career: after defeating Napoleon at the Battle of Waterloo, the Iron Duke went on to become prime minister of Great Britain and in 1829 passed the Catholic Emancipation Act, repealing the last of the repressive penal laws.

🏃 Activities

★ Irish Balloon Flights
BALLOONING

(🖉046-948 3436; www.balloons.ie; 1hr flight per person from €175; ⊙Apr-Sep) Float over patchwork fields, ruins, castles and churches aboard a hot-air balloon with this Trim-based operator. The meeting point is the car park of the Knightsbrook Hotel on Dublin Rd, 2.5km southeast of Trim's centre; schedules and launch locations vary according to weather conditions. Flights last an hour, followed by champagne or soft drinks. Kids must be eight or older.

🛏 Sleeping

Crannmór House
B&B €

(📞046-943 1635; www.crannmor.com; Dunderry Rd; d €76; [P][🛜]) Rolling farmland and paddocks surround this vine-covered old house about 2km along the road to Dunderry. Bright rooms and traditional hospitality are on offer, and if you're interested in angling, the owner is an experienced ghillie (fishing guide).

Bridge House Tourist Hostel
HOSTEL €

(📞046-943 1848; www.bridgehousetouristhostel. com; Bridge St; dm/d €20/50; [P][🛜]) Right on the river, this quirky old house has basic four-bed dorm rooms, a couple of doubles and a kitchen for self-caterers. Contact the hostel in advance to confirm your arrival time. Cash only.

★ Trim Castle Hotel
HOTEL €€

(📞046-948 3000; www.trimcastlehotel.com; Castle St; s/d/f from €125/140/160; [P][@][🛜]) Acres of glossy marble in the foyer set the scene at this contemporary hotel opposite Trim Castle. Some of its stylish rooms come with balconies (try for sprawling corner room 225). Its rooftop sun terrace overlooks Trim Castle, and dining – whether at breakfast, the bar's carvery, or upmarket Jules Restaurant (Friday and Saturday evenings only) – is top-notch.

🍴 Eating & Drinking

Harvest Home Bakery
BAKERY, CAFE €

(18 Market St; dishes €3-7.50; ⏰9am-6pm Mon-Sat) This little gem sells delicious breads, cakes, pies and biscuits (including sugar- and gluten-free options), as well as homemade soups and full-to-bursting sandwiches. There are outside tables in fine weather.

The Kitchen
CAFE €

(Emmet St; dishes €6-11; ⏰9am-7pm Mon-Sat, 10am-5pm Sun; ⊞) The Kitchen cooks up homemade lasagne, filled baked potatoes, tortilla wraps and other light bites in exposed brick surrounds, and brews smooth Segafredo coffee. Breakfast is available until midday; you can also get picnic fare to take away.

StockHouse
STEAK €€

(📞046-943 7388; http://stockhouserestaurant. ie; Emmet House, Finnegan's Way; mains €16-30; ⏰5-9pm Mon-Thu, 4.30-10pm Fri & Sat, 1-8.30pm Sun) Cooked-to-order dry-aged steaks from local abattoir/butcher Coogan's are the stock-in-trade of this always-packed restaurant, but noncarnivores can choose from vegetarian dishes including sizzling fajitas.

Marcy Regan's
PUB

(Lackanash Rd, Newtown; ⏰usually 5-11.30pm) This small, traditional pub beside Norman-era St Peter's Bridge, facing Newtown's ruins, claims to be Ireland's second oldest (after Sean's Pub in Athlone, County Westmeath). It's a no-frills kind of place steeped in old-world atmosphere. Opening days are irregular, but trad-music sessions take place on Friday nights.

James Griffin
PUB

(www.jamesgriffinpub.ie; High St; ⏰3-11.30pm Mon-Fri, 1pm-12.30am Sat, 1-11pm Sun; 🛜) This award-winning historic pub dates from 1904 and hosts trad-music sessions (Monday and Thursday), live bands (Friday and Sunday) and DJs (Saturday). The interior has retained its traditional-Irish-pub atmosphere and visitors are made to feel very welcome.

ℹ Information

In the town hall, Trim's **tourist office** (📞046-943 7227; www.meath.ie; 6 Castle St; ⏰9.30am-5.30pm Mon-Sat, 1-5pm Sun) has a handy tourist-trail map, a cafe and a genealogy centre.

ℹ Getting There & Away

Bus Éireann (p694) links Trim with Dublin (€13, 1¼ hours, hourly) and Drogheda (€19.70, 1¼ hours, hourly).

Kells

POP 6135

The working market town of Kells is best known for the magnificent illuminated manuscript that bears its name, and which visitors queue to see at Trinity College in Dublin. Although the great book wasn't created here, it was kept in Kells, one of the leading monasteries in the country, from the end of the 9th century until 1541, when it was removed by the Church. You can view a copy at Kells' tourist office.

Remnants of the once-great monastic site include some interesting high crosses and a 1000-year-old round tower.

◉ Sights

St Columba CHURCH
(Cannon St; ⊘10am-1pm & 2-5pm Mon-Sat Jun-Aug) The Protestant church of St Columba has a 30m-high 10th-century **round tower** on the southern side. It's without its conical roof, but is known to date back at least as far as 1076, when the high king of Tara was murdered in its confined apartments.

In the churchyard are four 9th-century high crosses in various states of repair.

The **West Cross**, at the far end, is the stump of a decorated shaft, which has scenes of the baptism of Jesus, the Fall of Adam and Eve, and the Judgement of Solomon on the eastern face, and Noah's ark on the western face.

All that's left of the **North Cross** is the bowl-shaped base stone.

Near the round tower is the best preserved of the crosses, the **Cross of Patrick & Columba**, with its semi-legible inscription, 'Patrici et Columbae Crux', on the eastern face of the base.

The other surviving cross is the unfinished **East Cross**, with a carving of the Crucifixion and a group of four figures on the right arm.

St Colmcille's House HISTORIC SITE
(Church Lane; ⊘10am-5pm Sat & Sun Jun-Aug) FREE This solid structure is a survivor from the old monastic settlement. Its name is a misnomer, as it was built in the 10th century and St Colmcille was alive in the 6th century. Experts have suggested that it was used as a scriptorium, a place where monks illuminated books.

The site is usually locked except during summer, but ask at the tourist office about the keys or contact **Mrs Carpenter** (☑046-924 1778; 1 Lower Church View) for access.

Market Cross MONUMENT
(Headfort Pl) Until 1996, when it was relocated outside the courthouse on Headfort Pl, the Market Cross had stood for centuries in Cross St, at the heart of the town centre. Besides inviting the pious admiration of the faithful, the cross was used as a gallows in the aftermath of the 1798 Rising; the British garrison hanged rebels from the crosspiece, one on each arm so the cross wouldn't fall over.

⌁ Sleeping & Eating

Headfort Arms Hotel HOTEL €€
(☑046-924 0063; www.headfortarms.ie; Headfort Pl; s/d from €79/99; P☏) Right in the town centre, the family-run Headfort Arms has 45 comfortable rooms with classic styling and facilities such as laptop safes. Rooms in the charming old building have the most character. There's a small spa; dining options include the independently run Vanilla Pod bistro.

Vanilla Pod BISTRO €€
(☑046-924 0063; Headfort Pl; mains €15.50-26; ⊘5.30-10pm Mon-Thu, 5-11pm Fri & Sat, 12.30-9.30pm Sun; ☖) Bright and contemporary, this restaurant inside the Headfort Arms Hotel features an ambitious bistro-style menu. Well-prepared dishes from seasonal, locally sourced ingredients range from venison with blackberry jus and duck fat-fried chips to black pudding–stuffed chicken fillet with roast apples, and sticky toffee pudding with vanilla bean ice cream.

There's a kid menu, high chairs and various deals for families.

ⓘ Information

In the Kells Civic Offices, the **tourist office** (☑046-924 8856; www.meath.ie; Headfort Pl; ⊘9.30am-1pm & 2-5pm Mon-Fri) has a copy of the famed *Book of Kells* and screens a free 13-minute audiovisual presentation.

ⓘ Getting There & Away

Bus Éireann (p694) has services from Kells to Dublin (€15.90, 90 minutes, half-hourly). The same service continues to Cavan town (€14.80, 45 minutes).

Loughcrew Cairns

Given the high profile of Brú na Bóinne, the amazing Stone Age passage graves strewn about the Loughcrew Hills, along the R154 near Oldcastle, are often overlooked. They're well off the beaten track and relatively few people ever bother, which means you can enjoy this moody and evocative place in peace.

Like Brú na Bóinne, the graves were all built around 3000 BC, but unlike their better-known and better-excavated peers, the Loughcrew tombs were used at least until 750 BC.

Although there are 32 tombs here, most are on private land and inaccessible to the public. It is possible, however, to visit Cairn T at Carnbane East, a steep but scenic 15-minute climb from the car park.

★ **Cairn T**   HISTORIC SITE
(www.heritageireland.ie; ⊘10am-6pm May-Aug,
by arrangement Sep-Apr) `FREE` At Carnbane
East, Cairn T is 35m in diameter, with numerous carved stones. One of its outlying
kerbstones, the **Hag's Chair**, is covered in
gouged holes, circles and other markings.

Light pierces the chamber on the spring
and autumn equinoxes, when Heritage Ireland guides are in attendance; guides are
also here in summer. Otherwise, pick up the
key to enter the passageway from the cafe at
Loughcrew Gardens (bring a torch), or book
a tour with the Loughcrew Megalithic Centre.

Loughcrew Megalithic Centre   MUSEUM
(☑086 736 1948; www.loughcrewmegalithiccentre.
com; ⊘11am-5pm) Centred on a collection of
thatched cottages, the Loughcrew Megalithic Centre encompasses a **museum** detailing
the megalithic wonders hereabouts, as well
as a **cafe** (dishes €3 to €6), **hostel** (dorm/
double/glamping yurt €23/45/55), **campground** (€10 tent per person) and a **craft
shop** with stunning photography of the
area, including cairns that aren't accessible
to the public. Special equinox events take
place here. It runs tours by arrangement
of Cairn T (€12 including tea, coffee and
scones).

Loughcrew Gardens   GARDENS
(☑049-854 1060; www.loughcrew.com; L2800;
gardens adult/child €6/3, adventure centre per half
day €32/29; ⊘9.30am-5.30pm Mon-Fri, to 6pm
Sat & Sun mid-Mar–Oct, by request Mon-Fri, 11am-
4pm Sat & Sun Nov–mid-Mar) Loughcrew Gardens incorporates 2.5 hectares of lawns, terraces and herbaceous borders along with a
lime avenue, yew walk, canal and 'grotesque
grotto' with tortured pillars, frescoes and
fantasy sculptures. There's also a medieval
moat, tower house and St Oliver Plunkett's
family church, plus a daily openingcafe in a
log-built lodge, where you can pick up a key
for Cairn T. Advance reservations are essential for its **adventure centre**, which incorporates an assault course, archery, zipline
and a climbing wall.

COUNTY LOUTH

Ireland's smallest county (hence its moniker,
the Wee County) prospered greatly during
the Celtic Tiger era thanks to its proximity to
Dublin, and is slowly but steadily recovering
from the subsequent economic crash.

In the 5th and 6th centuries, Louth was
at the centre of ecclesiastical Ireland, with
wealthy religious communities at the monastery at Monasterboice and the Cistercian
abbey at Mellifont. The 12th-century Norman invaders were responsible for the development of Dundalk and the two towns on
opposite banks of the Boyne that united in
1412 to become what is now Drogheda, the
county's largest town.

In the north, the picturesque Cooley
Peninsula is separated from County Ar-
magh, Northern Ireland, by the waters of
Carlingford Lough.

While Louth can easily be covered as a
day trip from Dublin, you'll get more from
your visit by spending some time exploring
the county.

Drogheda
POP 40,956
Only 48km north of Dublin, Drogheda is a
historic fortified town straddling the River
Boyne. Stately old buildings, a handsome
cathedral and a riveting museum provide
plenty of cultural interest, while atmospheric pubs, fine restaurants, numerous sleeping
options and good transport links make it a
handy base for exploring the region.

Although the post–Celtic Tiger years hit
Drogheda hard, new developments continue
to expand along the riverfront of this multicultural regional hub.

⊙ Sights

★ **Millmount Museum & Tower**   MUSEUM
(☑041-983 3097; www.millmount.net; off Duleek St,
Millmount; adult/child museum €3.50/2.50, tower
€3/2, museum & tower €5.50/3; ⊘10am-5.30pm
Mon-Sat, 2-5pm Sun) Overlooking Drogheda,
Millmount is an artificial hill that may have
been a prehistoric burial ground like Newgrange, but has never been excavated.

The Normans constructed a motte-and-
bailey fort on top of this convenient command post overlooking the bridge. It was
followed by a castle, which in turn was replaced by a Martello tower in 1808.

A section of the army barracks is now
used as the Millmount Museum. Exhibits
include three wonderful late-18th-century
guild banners.

The tower played a dramatic role in the
1922 Civil War, when it was Drogheda's
chief defensive feature and suffered heavy
shelling from Free State forces. It has been

Drogheda

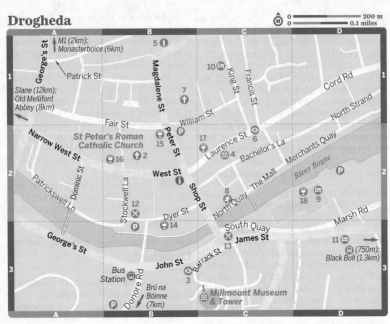

Drogheda

◎ Top Sights
1	Millmount Museum & Tower	C3
2	St Peter's Roman Catholic Church	B2

◎ Sights
3	Butter Gate	B3
4	Highlanes Gallery	C2
5	Magdalene Tower	B1
6	St Laurence's Gate	C2
7	St Peter's Church of Ireland	B1

◎ Activities, Courses & Tours
8	Quay Cycles	C2

◎ Sleeping
9	D Hotel	D2
10	Scholars Townhouse Hotel	C1
11	Spoon & the Stars	D3

◎ Eating
12	D'vine	B2
13	Kitchen	C3
	Relish	(see 4)

◎ Drinking & Nightlife
14	Cagney's	B3
15	Clarke & Sons	B2
16	Grey Goose	B2
17	Peter Matthews	C2
18	WM Cairnes & Son	D2

aesthetically restored and offers great views over the town below.

Other museum highlights include a room devoted to Cromwell's brutal siege of Drogheda and the Battle of the Boyne. The pretty, cobbled basement is full of gadgets and kitchen utensils from bygone times. Across the courtyard, the Governor's House opens for temporary exhibitions.

Just northwest of Millmount, the 13th-century Butter Gate has a distinctive tower and arched passageway.

★ St Peter's Roman Catholic Church   CHURCH

(West St; ⊙ 8.30am-5pm) Displayed in a glittering brass-and-glass case in the north transept, the shrivelled head of St Oliver Plunkett (1629–81) is this church's main draw (the rest of the martyr was separated at his hanging in 1681). It's actually two churches in one: the first was designed by Francis Johnston in a classical style in 1791; the neo-Gothic addition was built in the late 19th century. Opening hours can vary.

Beaulieu House & Gardens HOUSE, GARDENS
(☑041-983 8557; www.beaulieuhouse.ie; L6327; house & gardens tour adult/child €10/free, garden only €5/free; ⊘11am-5pm Mon-Fri, 1-5pm Sat & Sun Jul & Aug, 11am-5pm Mon-Fri Jun & early Sep) On the banks of the River Boyne, reached by a driveway lined with lime trees, this grand hipped-roofed house with red-brick trim dates from circa 1626. It's one of Ireland's best-preserved unfortified mansions, with much of its decor intact since the 1720s, including intricate plaster mouldings. Guided tours of the house lasting 50 minutes depart on the hour; you can also visit its spectacular walled and terraced gardens. It's 4.2km east of Drogheda off the R167 (follow the river).

Highlanes Gallery GALLERY
(www.highlanes.ie; Laurence St; admission by donation; ⊘10.30am-5pm Mon-Sat) Set in a beautifully converted 19th-century monastery, this gallery has a permanent collection of contemporary art, along with regular temporary exhibitions.

Attached is a shop featuring high-quality Louth craftwork, and a chic cafe (p518).

St Peter's Church of Ireland CHURCH
(http://drogheda.armagh.anglican.org; William St; ⊘8.30am-5pm) St Peter's Church of Ireland (not to be confused with St Peter's Roman Catholic Church) is the church whose spire was burned by Cromwell's men, resulting in the death of 100 people seeking sanctuary inside. Built in 1752, today's church is the second replacement of the original destroyed by Cromwell, and, following an arson attack in 1999, was extensively restored. Opening hours can vary.

Magdalene Tower TOWER
The 14th-century Magdalene Tower is the bell tower of a Dominican friary founded in 1224. It was here that England's King Richard II, accompanied by a great army, accepted the submission of the Gaelic chiefs with suitable ceremony in 1395. Peace lasted only a few months, however, and Richard's return to Ireland led to his overthrow in 1399.

St Laurence's Gate LANDMARK
Astride the eastwards extension of the town's main street is the 13th-century St Laurence's Gate, the finest surviving portion of the city walls (which originally extended for 3km) and a notable landmark.

Courses

★**Listoke Distillery & Gin School** DISTILLERY
(☑087 240 5283; https://listokedistillery.ie; Ballymakenny Rd, Listoke; gin-making course €95; ⊘by reservation) Brilliant three-hour gin-making courses in the 200-year-old stable of Listoke House and Gardens begin with refreshments and a distillery tour. You then taste three different gins and mix botanicals to create your gin in a miniature copper distiller (accompanied by G&Ts), which you bottle to take home afterwards. It's set in picturesque woodland 3.5km north of central Drogheda.

⁂ Festivals & Events

Drogheda Arts Festival PERFORMING ARTS
(http://droghedaartsfestival.ie; ⊘early May) Theatre, music, film, poetry, visual arts and workshops such as silk painting take place at this week-long festival culminating over the May Day weekend.

CROMWELL'S DROGHEDA INVASION

Lauded as England's first democrat and protector of the people, Oliver Cromwell (1599–1658) was an Irish nightmare. Cromwell hated the Irish for siding with Charles I during the Civil War. So when 'God's own Englishman' landed his 12,000 troops at Dublin in August 1649, he immediately set out for Drogheda, a strategic fort town and bastion of royalist support.

When Cromwell arrived at the walls of Drogheda, he was met by 2300 men led by Sir Arthur Aston, who boasted that 'he who could take Drogheda could take hell'. After Aston refused to surrender, Cromwell let fly with heavy artillery and after two days the walls were breached.

In order to set a terrifying example to any other town that might resist Cromwell's armies, over a period of hours an estimated 3000 people were massacred, mostly royalist soldiers but also priests, women and children. Aston was bludgeoned to death with his own (wooden) leg. Of the survivors, many were captured and sold into slavery in the Caribbean.

🛌 Sleeping

Spoon & the Stars HOSTEL, HOTEL €
(📞 086 405 8465; www.spoonandthestars.com; 13 St Mary's Terrace, Dublin Rd; dm €18-20, d with bathroom €60-70, without bathroom €55-60; 🛜) Rory and Hannah's well-run budget accommodation blends vintage and contemporary furnishings and has a great, laid-back vibe. Rooms range from a double with private bathroom and kitchenette to eight- to 10-bed dorms (one female only). Facilities include a cosy lounge and a breezy courtyard and garden, complete with barbecue, as well as bike storage.

★ Scholars Townhouse Hotel HOTEL €€
(📞 041-983 5410; www.scholarshotel.com; King St; s/d/f from €75/129/145; P 🛜) This former monastery dates from 1867 and was recently revamped as a family-owned hotel and restaurant. Despite the 16 rooms being on the small side, some have four-poster beds and there's nothing monastic about the facilities, which include an atmospheric bar and a superb restaurant (mains €19 to €30; bookings recommended). The central location is ideal for exploring the town.

D Hotel HOTEL €€
(📞 041-987 7700; www.thedhotel.com; Scotch Hall, Marsh Rd; d/tr from €145/195; P @🛜) Minimalist rooms at this slick riverside hotel are bathed in light and decked out with designer furniture and cool gadgets. There's a stylish bar and restaurant, a mini-gym and fantastic views over the skyline. The hotel is popular for hen and stag parties: beware of pounding music (and higher prices) on weekends.

🍴 Eating

Relish CAFE €
(http://relishcafe.ie; Highlanes Gallery, Laurence St; dishes €6-13; ⏱ 9.30am-5.30pm Mon-Sat, 11.30am-5.30pm Sun; 🛜🍴) Located in the Highlanes Gallery (p517), this split-level cafe serves a stylish range of breakfasts, gourmet sandwiches and daily specials like lasagne. It also offers savoury tarts, as well as daily desserts such as hot apple crumble. Vegetarian and gluten-free options are plentiful; there's also an extensive kids' menu.

★ Kitchen MEDITERRANEAN €€
(📞 041-983 4630; 2 South Quay; mains lunch €13-17, dinner €17-25; ⏱ 11am-9pm Wed, 11am-10pm Thu-Sat, noon-9pm Sun; 🛜) Fronted by a sage-green facade, Drogheda's best restaurant is aptly named for its shiny open kitchen. Organic local produce is used along with worldly ingredients such as Cypriot halloumi and Serrano ham. Breads are made on site and there's an excellent choice of wine by the glass. Don't miss the salted-caramel baked Alaska for dessert.

Black Bull IRISH €€
(www.blackbullinn.ie; Dublin Rd; mains €12-26; ⏱ kitchen 9.30am-10pm Mon-Sat, to 8pm Sun, bar till late; 🛜🍴) Topped by a gleaming golden (not black) bull, this cosy pub has low ceilings and candlelit corners. The modern extension houses a spacious restaurant serving solidly good pub standards such as steaks you cook yourself on sizzling lava stone and a Raging Bull Burger with fiery jalapeños. Afterwards, have a pint in the ingeniously named beer garden, the China Shop.

D'vine BISTRO €€
(📞 041-980 0440; http://dvine.ie; Dyer St; mains lunch €8-12, dinner €14-26; ⏱ noon-3pm & 5-9.30pm Wed & Thu, noon-9.30pm Fri & Sat, 1-9.30pm Sun) Hidden down a small flight of steps and opening to a sunny courtyard, this convivial cellar bistro has a great selection of Mediterranean tapas dishes, elaborate salads, and steak, seafood and gourmet burgers, plus a long wine list. Service is faultless. Live music performs on Sunday at 7pm.

🍷 Drinking & Nightlife

★ Grey Goose BAR
(88 West St; ⏱ 10am-midnight Sun-Thu, to 2am Fri & Sat; 🛜) Drogheda's newest and hippest venue has a vast downstairs bar with herringbone floors, stained glass and leather sofas, and a grand piano in its upstairs cocktail lounge, the Birdcage, where a resident DJ spins cool '80s and '90s tunes on Saturdays. In addition to 23 Irish and international craft beers on tap, local spirits include Listoke gin and Slane whiskey.

Gastropub fare (mains €7.50 to €13), spanning house-speciality woodfired pizzas to burgers, smoky ribs and salads, is served until 9pm.

WM Cairnes & Son PUB
(www.wmcairnes.com; Scotch Hall; mains €11-26; ⏱ 11am-midnight Sun-Thu, to 2am Fri & Sat) Cavernous, contemporary WM Cairnes & Son has a winning riverfront location, regular live music and a dozen craft beers on tap as well as 55 different whiskeys.

Cagney's BAR

(3 Dyer St; ☺10.30am-11.30pm Mon-Thu, to 12.30am Fri & Sat, noon-11pm Sun) With low lighting and a beer garden, Cagney's is a classy spot for wines by the glass, whiskeys and gins, including locally distilled Listoke 1777 gin.

Clarke & Sons PUB

(19 Peter St; ☺1-11.30pm Mon-Thu, noon-12.30am Fri & Sat, 12.30-11pm Sun) This wonderful old 1900 boozer is right out of a time capsule. Clarke's unrestored wooden interior features snugs and leaded-glass doors that read 'Open Bar'.

Peter Matthews PUB

(McPhails; 9 Laurence St; ☺5pm-late) One of Drogheda's top spots for live music, McPhails (as it's always called, no matter what the sign says) features everything from heavy-metal cover bands to trad-music sessions. There's a traditional bar at the front and a beer garden out back.

❶ Information

Drogheda's **tourist office** (☎041-987 2843; http://drogheda.ie; 1 West St; ☺9.30am-5.30pm Mon-Sat May-Nov, closed Sat & Sun Dec-Apr; 🛜) is inside the historic Tholsel, an 18th-century limestone town hall.

❶ Getting There & Away

The **bus station** (cnr Donore Rd & George's St) is on the south side of the river.

Bus Éireann (p694) regularly serves Drogheda from Dublin (€8.30, one hour, hourly) and Dundalk (€7.30, 30 minutes, hourly).

Matthews (☎042-937 8188; http://matthews. ie) also runs an hourly or better service to Dublin (€10) and Dundalk (€10).

The **train station** (www.irishrail.ie; off Dublin Rd) is just south of the river and east of the town centre. Drogheda is on the main Belfast–Dublin line (Dublin €11.80, 45 minutes; Belfast €14.50, 1½ hours) with hourly or better trains.

❶ Getting Around

Drogheda is compact and walkable. Many of the surrounding sites are within cycling distance; rent bikes from **Quay Cycles** (☎041-983 4526; www.quaycycles.com; 11a North Quay; per day from €14; ☺9am-6pm Mon-Sat).

Around Drogheda

A number of historic sites lie close to Drogheda, while the coast road (p520) between Drogheda and Dundalk makes a scenic alternative to the motorway.

★**Old Mellifont Abbey** RUINS

(☎041-982 6459; www.heritageireland.ie; Tullyallen; site admission free, visitor centre adult/student €5/3; ☺site 24hr year-round, visitor centre 10am-6pm Jun-Aug) In its Anglo-Norman prime, this abbey, 1.5km off the main Drogheda–Collon road (R168), was the Cistercians' first and most magnificent centre in Ireland. Highly evocative and well worth exploring, the ruins still reflect the site's former splendour.

Mellifont's most recognisable building and one of the country's finest examples of Cistercian architecture is the 13th-century lavabo, the monks' octagonal washing room.

In the mid-12th century, Irish monastic orders had grown a little too fond of the good life and were not averse to a bit of corruption. In 1142 an exasperated Malachy, bishop of Down, invited a group of hardcore monks from Clairvaux in France to set up shop in a remote location, where they would act as a sobering influence on the local clergy. Unsurprisingly the Irish monks didn't get on with their French guests, and the latter soon left for home. Still, the construction of Mellifont continued, and within 10 years nine more Cistercian monasteries were established. Mellifont was eventually the mother house for 21 lesser monasteries; at one point as many as 400 monks lived here.

In 1556, after the Dissolution of the Monasteries, a fortified Tudor manor house was built on the site.

There's good picnicking next to the rushing stream. The visitor centre describes monastic life in detail.

★**Monasterboice** HISTORIC SITE

(☺sunrise-sunset) FREE Crowing ravens lend an eerie atmosphere to Monasterboice, an intriguing monastic site down a leafy lane in sweeping farmland, which contains a cemetery, two ancient church ruins, one of the finest and tallest round towers in Ireland, and two of the most important high crosses.

---

❶ CAR PARK VANDALISM

Unfortunately travellers have reported incidents of thefts from cars left unattended in the car park at Monasterboice and other historic sites. Never leave anything of value visible in the car and, if you notice broken glass on the ground, be particularly wary about leaving your vehicle, especially if it's a rental car.

DROGHEDA TO DUNDALK VIA THE COAST ROAD

Most people zip north along the M1 motorway, but if you want to meander along the coast and see a little of rural Ireland, opt for the R166 coast road from Drogheda.

The little village of **Termonfeckin** was, until 1656, the seat and castle of the primate of Armagh. Nothing remains of the castle but a tiny, 15th-century **tower house** (☑ 086 079 1484; key deposit €50; ☉ 10am-6pm) FREE, once belonging to a wealthy landowner, is worth a brief stop. Pick up the key from the first house to its right.

About 2km further north is the busy seaside and fishing centre of **Clogherhead**, with a good, shallow Blue Flag beach at Lurganboy. Squint to ignore the static-home-filled caravan parks and take in the lovely views of the Cooley and Mourne Mountains instead.

A further 14km north is the teensy village of **Annagassan**. At **Coastguard Seafoods** (☑ 042-937 2527; Harbour Rd; ☉ by appointment), fisherman Terry Butterly oak-smokes some of the finest salmon in Ireland (usually appearing on restaurant menus as Annagassan smoked salmon) and sells it direct to the public, along with other seafood such as live lobsters, for astonishingly reasonable prices. You can just turn up (look for the green door), but to avoid disappointment, call in advance. Nearby, at Annagassan's **O'Neills Bakery** (☑ 042-937 2253; www.oneillsbakery.ie; Main St, ☉ 7am-1pm), a cavernous five-generations-old bakery with vast ovens (one more than a century old), you can buy still-warm breads, cakes and buns (cash only). It appears closed to the public but knock on the door around the side of the building and one of the bakers will let you in. Annagassan is anchored by the 1770-built **Glyde Inn** (☑ 042-937 2350; https://theglydeinn.ie; Main St, ☉ 10am-midnight Sun-Thu, to 1am Fri & Sat). The pub has its own specially brewed beer, Linn Duachaill (named for a local Viking settlement currently being excavated), which is also the name of its excellent restaurant where panoramic windows overlook the beer garden, Dundalk Bay's tidal shallows and the Mourne Mountains beyond. If you want to stop for the night, it also has four guest rooms.

The 33km route comes to an end in **Castlebellingham**. The picturesque village grew up around an 18th-century crenellated mansion (www.bellinghamcastle.ie), which is now a luxury wedding venue; ask about midweek B&B possibilities from May to October. Stop for homemade cakes, quiches and the house speciality boiled bacon and cabbage at charming **Foley's Tea Rooms** (Main St; dishes €4.50-10; ☉ 9am-3.30pm Mon-Fri, 8.30am-3.30pm Sat, 9.30am-3.30pm Sun; ☎), originally two 18th-century thatched cottages, before perusing its adjacent shop specialising in fascinating curios and collectibles.

From Castlebellingham you can continue 12km north to Dundalk along the suburban R132 or join the M1.

Come early or late in the day to avoid the crowds. It's just off the M1 motorway, about 8km north of Drogheda.

The original monastic settlement here is said to have been founded in the 5th or 6th century by St Buithe, a follower of St Patrick, although the site probably had pre-Christian significance. St Buithe's name somehow got converted to Boyne, and the river is named after him. An invading Viking force took over the settlement in 968, only to be comprehensively expelled by Donal, the Irish high king of Tara, who killed at least 300 of the Vikings in the process.

The high crosses of Monasterboice are superb examples of Celtic art. The crosses had an important didactic use, bringing the gospels alive for the uneducated, and they were probably brightly painted originally, although all traces of colour have long disappeared.

The cross near the entrance is known as **Muiredach's Cross**, named after a 10th-century abbot. The western face relates more to the New Testament, and from the bottom depicts the arrest of Christ, Doubting Thomas, Christ giving a key to St Peter, the Crucifixion, and Moses praying with Aaron and Hur.

The **West Cross** is near the round tower and stands 6.5m high, making it one of the tallest high crosses in Ireland. It's much more weathered, especially at the base, and only a dozen or so of its 50 panels are still legible. The more distinguishable ones on the eastern face include David killing a lion and a bear.

A third, simpler cross in the northeastern corner of the compound is believed to have been smashed by Cromwell's forces and has only a few straightforward carvings. This cross makes a great evening silhouette photo, with the round tower in the background.

The **round tower**, minus its cap, is more than 30m tall, and stands in a corner of the complex. Records suggest the tower interior went up in flames in 1097, destroying many valuable manuscripts and other treasures. It's closed to the public.

Laytown

Laytown is famed as the site of the only official horse race on the beach in Europe. It's a sleepy seaside village for the rest of the year.

Laytown Races   SPORTS
(www.laytownstrandraces.ie; ⊘ late Aug or early Sep) Bookies, punters and jockeys descend on Laytown, 11.5km southeast of Drogheda, for races that have been held here since 1868. For one late-summer's day, Laytown's 3km of golden sands are transformed into a racecourse, attracting a diverse crowd of locals, celebrities and diehard racing fans.

Sonairte   GARDENS
(☑ 041-982 7572; www.sonairte.ie; the Ninch, Laytown; ⊘ 10.30am-5pm Tue-Sun Feb-Dec) 🅵 FREE At this inspiring not-for-profit ecology centre 10km southeast of Drogheda in Laytown on an 18th-century former farm, you can wander through a walled organic garden, visit a beekeeping museum and take a biodiverse nature trail and river walk that incorporates wetlands, woodlands and grasslands. Recharge at its organic cafe or browse its home and garden shops. It hosts various courses, from home detox workshops to wild-food foraging; food and craft markets regularly set up on Sundays from 11am to 4pm.

Dundalk

POP 39,004
Midway between Dublin and Belfast, Dundalk, despite its role as an industrial hub, is a surprisingly pleasant town with some interesting sites.

In the Middle Ages, the city was at the northern limits of the English-controlled Pale, and with partition in 1921 it once again became a border town, this time with South Armagh.

◉ Sights

County Museum Dundalk   MUSEUM
(www.dundalkmuseum.ie; Jocelyn St; adult/child €2/1; ⊘ 10am-5pm Tue-Sat) Different floors in this worthwhile museum are dedicated to the town's early history and archaeology, and to the Norman period. One floor deals with the growth of industry in the area, from the 1750s to the 1960s, including the cult classic Heinkel Bubble Car. Other oddities include Oliver Cromwell's shaving mirror.

St Patrick's Cathedral   CATHEDRAL
(www.stpatricksparishdundalk.org; Roden Pl; ⊘ 8.30am-5pm) 🅵 FREE The richly decorated 19th-century St Patrick's Cathedral was modelled on King's College Chapel in Cambridge, England. Hours can vary depending on services and events.

Courthouse   NOTABLE BUILDING
(cnr Crowe & Clanbrassil Sts) Dundalk's courthouse is a photogenic neo-Gothic building with large Doric pillars. The interior is closed to the public. In the front square is the stone Maid of Erin, commemorating the 1798 Rising.

🛏 Sleeping & Eating

Ballymascanlon House   HISTORIC HOTEL €€
(☑ 042-935 8200; www.ballymascanlon.com; R173; s/d/tr from €95/145/195; 🏧🛜) Situated 8km northeast of Dundalk on the edge of the Cooley Peninsula, this grand old property (and more recent extension) has spacious rooms, warm, personalised service, and atmosphere in spades. There's an 18-hole golf course (with a circa 3000 BC, 3m-high standing stone on the 6th hole), a leisure centre and a restaurant and bar, plus 24-hour room service.

★ Strandfield   CAFE, DELI €
(http://strandfield.com; off R173; dishes €5-12; ⊘ 8am-5pm; 🛜🅿) 🅿 On a working farm, this skylit, retrofitted barn houses a wondrous bakery, deli, florist and homewares shop as well as all-organic vegetarian cafe. For breakfast, expect French toast with walnuts and honey or smashed avocado on sourdough; lunch sees woodfired

TRACING YOUR ANCESTORS

With advance notice, genealogical centres in the region can help trace your ancestors.

Meath Contact the **Meath Heritage Centre** (☑ 046-943 6633; www.meath-roots.com; Castle St; ⊙ 9am-1pm & 1.30-5pm Mon-Thu, 9am-2pm Fri) inside Trim's town hall.

Louth The **Louth County Library** (☑ 042-932 4323; www.louthcoco.ie; Roden Pl; ⊙ 10am-8pm Tue & Thu, to 5pm Wed, Fri & Sat) in Dundalk has information.

Cavan **Cavan Genealogy** (☑ 049-436 1094; www.cavan.rootsireland.ie; Farnham St) centre is on the 1st floor of Johnston Central Library in Cavan town.

Monaghan Monaghan currently has no genealogy centre, but the website http://monaghan.rootsireland.ie has information.

pizzas, open-faced sandwiches (St Tola goat's cheese and root vegetables) and salads (quinoa, tahini and aubergine).

★**Eno** MEDITERRANEAN €€
(☑ 042-935 5467; www.eno.ie; 5 Roden Pl; pizzas €10-18.50, mains €17-29.50; ⊙ noon-9pm) Bare boards, bold colours and conversation-piece objets d'art established Eno as central Dundalk's best restaurant, along with outstanding wood-fired pizzas and Med-inspired dishes such as angel-hair pasta with Dunany crab, white wine and garlic, plus honey-roasted fig and almond tart. The alfresco Yard Bar is out back.

Upstairs DJs spin Cuban, latin and soul in the cocktail bar (6pm to 2am Friday and Saturday), where tapas (€5 to €12.50) are served until midnight.

☆ Entertainment

Spirit Store LIVE MUSIC
(www.spiritstore.ie; off George's Quay; ⊙ 4-11.30pm Mon-Thu, to 12.30am Fri & Sat, to 11pm Sun) Downstairs this sunset-pink-painted place is your typical harbour-front bar, full of character and characters. Upstairs is a state-of-the-art live venue, with a terrific sound system that is beloved of both the crowd and the regular streams of touring musicians that play here. Across both bars,

there's live music Wednesday to Sunday, including Sunday afternoon trad sessions.

On Mondays it hosts a pub quiz with pints as prizes.

ℹ Information

Dundalk's **tourist office** (☑ 042-935 2111; www.louthholidays.com; Jocelyn St; ⊙ 9.30am-5.30pm Mon-Fri) is on Market Sq.

ℹ Getting There & Away

Bus Éireann (p694) runs an hourly bus service to Dublin (€10.50, 1½ hours). The **bus station** (The Long Walk) is near the courthouse.

From the **train station** (www.irishrail.ie; Carrickmacross Rd), there are hourly or better services to Dublin (€15, 1¼ hours) and Belfast (€10.20, one hour).

Cooley Peninsula

Forested slopes and multihued hills rise above the dark waters of Carlingford Lough cleaving the picturesque Cooley Peninsula. Country lanes wind their scenic way down to deserted stony beaches, while sweeping views stretch north across the water (and border) to the majestic Mourne Mountains.

The medieval village of Carlingford is an ideal base. From here, you can continue along the coast road past the village of Omeath to Newry, at the nexus of Counties Down and Armagh in Northern Ireland.

Carlingford

POP 2201

Amid the medieval ruins and whitewashed houses, the vibrant little village of Carlingford buzzes with pubs, restaurants and boutiques. There's also spirited festivals and gorgeous views of the mountains and across Carlingford Lough to County Down.

⊙ Sights

★**Carlingford Brewing Company** BREWERY
(☑ 083 328 4040; www.carlingfordbrewing.ie; The Old Mill, Riverstown; tours €15, with lunch €25; ⊙ tours by reservation 2.30pm Wed, Fri & Sat) Tours of this craft brewery 8km southwest of Carlingford on the R173 start with a sample, take you through the brewing process (one to 1½ hours) and then end with three more tastings. The post-tour lunch of local charcuterie, cheeses, artisan bread and homemade chutneys is a great

way to wrap up. Its four brews are named for Carlingford landmarks: Tholsel Blonde, Taaffe's Red, Friary Pale Ale and King John's Stout. Live jazz and blues evenings often take place.

King John's Castle
CASTLE

(R173) Carlingford was first settled by the Vikings, and in the Middle Ages became an English stronghold under the protection of the now-ruined castle, which was built on a pinnacle in the 11th to 12th centuries to control the entrance to the lough. King John spent a couple of days here in 1210 en route to battle in Antrim.

It's currently being restored and is closed to the public, but there are often free tours during Heritage Week.

On the western side, the entrance gateway was built to allow only one horse and rider through at a time.

Carlingford Heritage Centre
VISITOR CENTRE

(☑042-937 3454; www.carlingfordheritagecentre. com; Churchyard Lane; ⊙9.30am-1pm & 2-5pm Mon-Fri Apr, 10am-12.30pm & 1.30-4pm Mon-Fri Nov-Mar) Carlingford's heritage centre is in the former Holy Trinity Church. A short video describes the village history. Hours can vary.

Taafe's Castle
HISTORIC BUILDING

Today the storeroom of the attached pub of the same name, Taafe's Castle is an imposing 16th-century tower house that stood on the waterfront until the land in front was reclaimed to build a short-lived train line.

Opposite the castle is a bust commemorating Carlingford-born Thomas D'Arcy McGee (1825–68), one of Canada's founding fathers.

Mint
HISTORIC BUILDING

Dating from the 16th century, the Mint, near the village square, has some interesting Celtic-inspired carvings around the windows. Although Edward IV is thought to have granted a charter to a mint in 1467, no coins were produced here.

⚡ Activities

Carlingford is the starting point for the 40km **Táin Way**, which makes a circuit of the Cooley Peninsula through the Cooley Mountains along a mix of surfaced roads, forest tracks and green paths.

There's great cycling around the Cooley Peninsula; **On Yer Bike** (☑087 648 7337; www.onyerbike.ie; Chapel Hill; bike rental per day

€20; ⊙9am-6.30pm Mon-Fri, to 6pm Sat & Sun) rents out wheels.

Much of the Cooley Peninsula is protected and is home to various species of birds including godwits, red-breasted mergansers, buzzards, tits and various finches. Ask at the tourist office (p525) for information on the **Carlingford Birdwatching Trail**.

Carlingford Adventure Centre
ADVENTURE SPORTS

(☑042-937 3100; http://carlingfordadventure. com; Tholsel St) Carlingford Adventure Centre runs a wide range of activities including sailing, kayaking, windsurfing, rock climbing, archery, ziplining and, if you fancy being strapped into a massive plastic ball and rolled down a hill, zorbing.

🎊 Festivals & Events

Leprechaun Hunt
CULTURAL

(⊙late Mar/early Apr) On one Sunday in spring, a celebratory leprechaun hunt (p524) sets off from Carlingford.

Carlingford Oyster Festival
FOOD & DRINK

(www.carlingford.ie; ⊙mid-Aug) This rollicking four-day event toasts Carlingford's famous oysters with an oyster treasure hunt, fishing competition, music, food markets and a regatta on Carlingford Lough.

Heritage Week
CULTURAL

(www.heritageweek.ie; ⊙Aug) Concerts, talks, guided walks, sporting events and family activities are part of this week-long celebration.

WORTH A TRIP

FLAGSTAFF VIEWPOINT

Travelling along the Cooley Peninsula from Carlingford to Newry in Northern Ireland, a quick 3km detour rewards you with sweeping views of Carlingford Lough, framed by forested mountains, green fields and the sparkling Irish Sea beyond.

Flagstaff Viewpoint (Flagstaff Rd) t lies just over the border in County Armagh. Heading northwest along the coast road (the R173), follow the signs to your left onto Ferryhill Rd, then turn right up to the viewpoint's car park.

The quickest way to reach Newry from here is to retrace your steps and rejoin the R173.

🛏 Sleeping

⭐ Carlingford House
B&B €€

(📞042-937 3118; http://carlingfordhouse.com; Dundalk St; d from €100; 🅿🛜) In the village centre, but set back from the road in manicured grounds, this stately 1844 manor house (once the local doctor's house) is especially stunning in warmer months when it's enveloped by vines. Inside, the welcoming hosts achieve the perfect balance of old-world character and contemporary flair, and serve exceptional breakfasts.

Belvedere House
B&B €€

(📞042-938 3848; www.belvederehouse.ie; Newry St; s €60-70, d €89-99; 🛜) An excellent deal, this lovely B&B has seven modern but cosy rooms with antique furniture and subtle lighting, themed around local Celtic history. Children's cots are available on request. Breakfast is served in the downstairs Bay Tree restaurant.

⭐ Ghan House
BOUTIQUE HOTEL €€€

(📞042-937 3682; www.ghanhouse.com; Main Rd; d from €160; 🅿🛜) Set in flower-filled gardens, this 18th-century Georgian house has 12 rooms, each exquisitely decorated with period antiques and original artworks. Book one of the four rooms in the main house for the most character and old-world charm.

LEPRECHAUNS – A PROTECTED SPECIES

The mountains around Carlingford are famed for being the last remaining site of Ireland's leprechauns. Among the believers in the little people was the late publican PJ O'Hare, who found a leprechaun's suit and hat, along with a collection of tiny bones and four gold coins on Foy mountain in 1989.

Nineteen years later after a vigorous lobbying campaign by self-acclaimed 'Leprechaun Whisperer' Kevin Woods (who claims he has seen three leprechauns to date), the EU issued a highly unconventional directive establishing a protective leprechaun zone here. According to Woods, this is apparently the last habitat for Ireland's leprechauns and there's even an annual leprechaun hunt (p523). Even if you don't spot a little fella, this certainly is a very magical spot. Visit www.thelastleprechaunsofireland.com for more information.

There's a superb restaurant on site (with discounts for guests) and a **cookery school** (courses from €55).

🍴 Eating

Ruby Ellen's Tea Rooms
CAFE €

(http://rubyellens.com; Marion House, Newry St; dishes €7-10, afternoon tea €13; ⊙9am-6pm) In a charming cottage with eggshell-blue walls, mismatched chairs and lace tablecloths, Ruby Ellen's serves wraps, bagels, jacket potatoes with gourmet toppings such as smoked salmon, crab meat and lemon zest, or pork sausages and smoked cheese, as well as daily baked cakes. Afternoon tea is a treat. When the sun's shining, the sweetest seats are in the flower-filled courtyard.

Liberty Cafe
CAFE €

(3 Thosel St; mains €6-10; ⊙9am-5.30pm; 🖊🖽) Set over two levels, Liberty has brightly coloured flowers painted on its whitewashed exterior and mismatched vintage furniture inside. Freshly made dishes include soups such as spiced lentil and pumpkin or carrot and coconut, hot specials like roast butternut squash, courgette and spinach tart, and open sandwiches, wraps, clubs and toasties (including special toasties for kids).

A handful of tables are set up on the pedestrianised street out front in fine weather.

McAteers the Food House
CAFE, DELI €€

(www.mcateersthefoodhouse.com; 9 Dundalk St; mains €10-17; ⊙9am-6pm Mon-Sat, to 5pm Sun) Pick up picnic ingredients, sandwiches and wraps at McAteers, or sit down for breakfast (eg bacon and goat's cheese omelettes) or light, healthy lunch dishes like baked tomato and pesto bruschetta or superfood salads.

Its original branch is in **Dundalk** (www. mcateersthefoodhouse.com; 15 Clanbrassil St; mains €10-17; ⊙9am-6pm Mon-Sat; 🖽).

Bay Tree
MODERN IRISH €€

(📞042-938 3848; www.belvederehouse.ie; Newry St; mains €19-29; ⊙6-10pm Mon-Sat, 12.30-10pm Sun Mar–mid-Nov, reduced hours mid-Nov–Mar; 🖽) Simple, stylishly presented dishes made from seasonal locally sourced ingredients (some grown in its own polytunnel) at this little restaurant attached to Belvedere House include squash and mushroom agnolotti with sage and aged parmesan, confit of duck with pickled rhubarb, and indulgent desserts such as a Valrhona chocolate and berry brownie with raspberry sorbet. Bookings are advised.

PJ O'Hares PUB FOOD €€
(www.pjoharescarlingford.com; Tholsel St;
mains €12-23.50; ⊗ kitchen 11am-9.30pm Mon-
Thu,11am-10pm Fri & Sat, noon-8pm Sun, bar
10.30am-midnight daily) Hearty main courses
at this award-winning gastro pub include
pies (beef and Guinness or salmon, cod
and cockle), but you can easily fill up on
tapas-style starters including Carlingford
oysters. Weather depending, head for the
bustling beer garden or cosy up in front of
the roaring fire.

There's a second entrance on Newry St.

Ghan House MODERN IRISH €€€
(☑ 042-937 3682; www.ghanhouse.com; Main Rd;
tasting menus €29.50-45; ⊗ 6-9.30pm Mon-Sat,
1-3pm Sun) ✎ The restaurant at Ghan House
(p524) is renowned for its classic multicourse menus (no à la carte) incorporating
its own breads, stocks, ice creams and sauces, and herbs and vegetables from its garden. Be sure to book.

ⓘ Information

Carlingford's **tourist office** (☑ 087 957 6989;
https://visitcarlingford.com; R173; ⊗ 9.30am-
5.30pm) is on the waterfront in the former train
station.

ⓘ Getting There & Away

Bus Éireann (p694) has services to Dundalk
(€8, one hour, six daily Monday to Saturday)
with connections to Dublin; and Newry (€5.60,
25 minutes, four daily Monday to Saturday).

COUNTY CAVAN

Cavan is a remote paradise for boaters, anglers, walkers and cyclists. Known as the
'Lake Country', there's supposedly a lake for
every day of the year (including leap years).
Between them is a gentle landscape of meandering streams, bogs and drumlins. Spectacular walking trails wind through the wild
Cuilcagh Mountains, which are the source of
the 300km River Shannon.

Cavan's lakes create a tangled knot of
narrow, twisting roads. Take your time and
enjoy the views that appear unexpectedly
around each bend.

The area has an intricate history. Magh
Sleacht, a plain near the border village of
Ballyconnell, was an important Druidic centre in the 5th century when St Patrick was
busy converting the pagan Irish to Christian-

ity, and the area is still littered with tombs,
standing stones and stone circles dating
from this time. The Gaelic O'Reilly clan ruled
until the 16th century, when they were defeated by the English. As part of the Ulster
Plantation, Cavan was divided among English and Scottish settlers. After the War of
Independence in 1922, the Ulster counties
of Cavan, Monaghan and Donegal were incorporated into the Republic. Following the
UK's 2016 referendum vote to leave the EU,
the potential return of a border is one of the
key issues to be resolved during Brexit negotiations, and the resulting outcome remains
to be seen.

Cavan Town

POP 10,914
Cavan's county town is a solidly workaday
place with some handsome Georgian houses. There are few sights, but it's a handy stop
for info and supplies.

⊙ Sights

Bell Tower HISTORIC SITE
All that remains of the 13th-century Franciscan friary the town grew up around is
an ancient bell tower, next to the grave

---

of 17th-century rebel leader Owen Roe
O'Neill in Abbey Street's cemetery.

Sleeping & Eating

Farnham Estate SPA HOTEL €€€
(☏ 049-437 7700; www.farnhamestate.ie; d/ste from
€119/154; P@🛜🏊) Set in misty woodlands,
this sprawling 16th-century estate is now part
of the Radisson group, with amenities including a garden-view restaurant, hydrotherapy
pool (off-limits to kids under 16), a luxurious
spa and an 18-hole golf course. Luxurious
rooms blend contemporary style with period
features and character. It's 3km west of town
on the R198.

Chapter One CAFE €
(www.chapteronecafe.ie; Convent Bldg, Main St;
dishes €2.75-8.25; ⊙8.30am-6.30pm Mon-Fri,
9am-6pm Sat, 11am-6pm Sun; 🛜🍴) Up a short
flight of steps, Chapter One is heaving at
lunchtime when locals descend to dine on
the huge range of filled bagels, soups, nachos and hot and cold salads. Vegetarian
and/or gluten-free options are plentiful.

ℹ Information

On the 1st floor of the Johnston Central Library,
Cavan's **tourist office** (☏ 049-433 1942; www.
thisiscavan.ie; Farnham St; ⊙10am-5pm Mon-
Fri) has county-wide info.

ℹ Getting There & Away

Bus Éireann (p694) has hourly services daily
to Dublin (€17.50, two hours) and Enniskillen,
County Fermanagh (€16.90, 1¼ hours), and
four services daily to Donegal town (€21.50, 1½
hours). There are also less frequent services to
various small towns throughout the county.

Killykeen Forest Park & Lough Oughter

Killykeen Forest Park PARK
(www.coillte.ie; ⊙9am-dusk) FREE Sprawling
over 240 hectares, Killykeen Forest Park,
12km northwest of Cavan, has various nature trails (from 1.5km to 5.8km) that lead
you through the woods and along the shore
of Lough Oughter, which splatters across
the map like spilt steely grey ink. It's popular with anglers. Keep an eye out for stoats,
badgers, foxes, grey squirrels and hedgehogs, as well as some amazing birdlife.

Many of the low overgrown islands in
the lake were *crannógs* (fortified, artificial

LAKE FISHING

Cavan's exceptional lake fishing reels
in anglers, especially to the county's
southern and western areas. It's primarily coarse fishing, but there's also some
game angling for brown trout and pike.
Most lakes are well signposted, and the
types of fish available are marked.

For more information, visit www.fish-
inginireland.info, which lists tackle shops,
fishing guides and boat-rental operators.
Facilities are few and far between, however, so bringing your own equipment is
advised.

islands). The most spectacular is home to
Clough Oughter Castle, a 13th-century circular tower perched on a tiny speck of land.
It was used as a lonely prison, then as a
stronghold by rebel leader Owen Roe O'Neill
before being destroyed by Cromwell's army
in 1653. The castle lies out of reach over the
water; canoe trips run by the Cavan Canoe
Centre head here. The forest trails provide
wonderful views.

Butlersbridge

POP 276
The village of Butlersbridge sits on the
banks of the River Annalee. There are no
sights as such, but it's a pretty spot to break
your journey, with a great pub, as well as a
gourmet restaurant with a cookery school
and canoeing nearby.

Sean at **Cavan Canoe Centre** (☏ 087 290
5752; http://cavancanoeing.com; Inishmore; canoe
& kayak rentals incl wetsuits per half day €25; ⊙by
reservation Apr-Oct) leads three- to four-hour
tours of the local waterways (adult/child
€30/20), including to Killykeen Forest Park,
and rents out canoes and kayaks. Rates include all-important wetsuits. It's 5.5km west
of Butlersbridge on the L1511.

Sleeping & Eating

Annalee House B&B €
(☏ 049-433 1282; www.annaleehouse.com; s/d
€40/70; P❄🛜) In the heart of the village,
this sweet little B&B has three rooms in
the main house and four in the adjacent
cottage (one of which is wheelchair accessible). Guests can fire up the barbecue in

the courtyard. Host Anna May is a chef, so breakfast is worth waking up for.

Derragarra Inn
PUB FOOD €€

(☑ 049-433 1033; www.murphsbistro.com; mains €15-29; ☺ kitchen noon-9pm Mon-Fri, to 9.30pm Sat, 12.30-9pm Sun, bar noon-11pm Sun-Thu, to midnight Fri & Sat) This delightful ivy-covered pub has a wood-beamed interior and a large, sunny beer garden overlooking the river and St Aidan Church across the way. Its unconventional menu includes seared ostrich steak, kangaroo burgers and parmesan-crusted chicken with plum sauce. Live music plays at weekends.

★ Olde Post Inn
GASTRONOMY €€€

(☑ 047-55555; www.theoldepostinn.com; Cloverhill; 4-/8-course dinner menus €63/82, 3-course Sun lunch €35, cookery courses from €125; ☺ 6-9pm Wed & Thu, 6-9.30pm Fri & Sat, 12.30-2.30pm & 5.30-8.30pm Sun; ☑ ♿) The lovely little village of Cloverhill, 4km north of Butlersbridge, is best known for its award-winning gastronomic restaurant housed in an 1884 former post office. Star chef Gearoid Lynch's contemporary cuisine is based on traditional ingredients such as monkfish, salmon, duck and lamb, with vegetarian options available. In the former postmaster's residence are six luxurious guest rooms (single/double from €65/110).

A gourmet kids' menu costs €17.50.

Ballyjamesduff & Around
POP 2661

A sleepy market town, Ballyjamesduff was the one-time home of the Earl of Fife, James Duff, an early Plantation landlord. His descendant, Sir James Duff, commanded English troops during the suppression of the 1798 Rising.

Nearby Lough Sheelin is famed for its trout fishing, but you'll need to bring your own equipment. It's a scenic place for walking year-round.

◉ Sights

Cavan County Museum
MUSEUM

(☑ 049-854 4070; www.cavanmuseum.ie; Virginia Rd; adult/child €5/3; ☺ 10am-5pm Tue-Sat, 2-5.30pm Sun Jun-Sep, 10am-5pm Tue-Sat Oct-May) Located inside a former convent, this museum's wide-ranging collection includes a huge array of 18th-, 19th- and 20th-century costumes and relics from the Stone, Bronze, Iron and Middle Ages, including the Celtic Killy-

cluggin stone and the three-faced Corleck Head, as well as a 1000-year-old boat excavated from Lough Errill. There's also a large feature on Irish sports. Outside, the kid-friendly WWI Trench Experience has sound effects along its dug-out, sandbagged trenches.

Eastern Cavan

◉ Sights

Dún an Rí Forest Park
PARK

(☑ 042-966 7320; www.coillte.ie; cars €5; ☺ car park 9am-6pm Apr-Oct, to 4.30pm Nov-Mar) The 225-hectare Dún an Rí Forest Park, 11km southwest of Carrickmacross, has four colour-coded forest walks (all less than 4km long), with picnic places and a wishing well. Look out for mink and otters along the river. The car park accepts coins only.

🛏 Sleeping

Cabra Castle
CASTLE €€

(☑ 042-966 7030; www.cabracastle.com; Carrickmacross Rd, Kingscourt; cottage/d from €130/198; 🅿 🛜) Bordering the Dún an Rí Forest Park, 10km southwest of Carrickmacross, 19th-century Cabra Castle is now a deluxe hotel decked out in plush period furnishings. A dozen rooms are in the castle itself but most are in its courtyard area; there are also simpler self-catering cottages. Wi-fi can be patchy.

BALLYWHO?

All over Ireland you'll see the town prefix 'Bally' (and variations thereof, such as Ballyna and Ballina). The ubiquitous term originates from the Irish phrase 'Baile na'. It's often mistranslated as 'town', but there were very few towns in Ireland when the names came about. A closer approximation is 'place of'; hence Ballyjamesduff, for example, means 'Place of James Duff' (or James Duff's place). Dublin's Irish name is Baile Átha Cliath ('Place of the Hurdle Ford'). If it was anglicised, it too would be a Bally, spelt something like 'Ballycleeagh'.

Other common place-name prefixes include Carrick (or Carrig), meaning 'rock' in Irish, and Dun, from the Irish *dún* (meaning 'fort').

WALKING THE CAVAN WAY

The highlight for many walkers in the region is the **Cavan Way**, a 26km trail between the hamlets of Blacklion and Dowra through the Cuilcagh Mountains. Heading south from Blacklion, it takes you through the **Cavan Burren Park** (p528) and its ancient burial site **Magh Sleacht**, which is dotted with prehistoric monuments – court cairns, ring forts and tombs – and was one of the last strongholds of Druidism. It continues past the Shannon Pot, the source of Ireland's longest river, then by road to Dowra, passing over the **Black Pigs Dyke**, an ancient fortification that once divided Ireland in two.

From Blacklion it's mainly hill walking; from Shannon Pot to Dowra it's mainly road. The highest point on the walk is Giant's Grave (260m). You'll need Ordinance Survey map No 26 and the *Cavan Way* map guide. Maps are on display in Blacklion and Dowra. Detailed route information (including downloadable map PDFs) is available online at www.thisiscavan.ie and www.irishtrails.ie. The route can be boggy, so take spare socks!

At Blacklion you can pick up the **Ulster Way** and at Dowra you can join the Leitrim Way, which runs between Manorhamilton and Drumshanbo.

Northwestern Cavan

🏃 Activities

Jampa Ling Buddhist Centre   MEDITATION
(☑ 049-952 3448; www.jampaling.org; Owendoon House, Bawnboy; retreat & workshop per activity €25-45, inclusive weekend retreat €215) Jampa Ling, meaning 'Place of Infinite Loving Kindness', offers courses, retreats and workshops on Buddhist teachings, philosophy, meditation, yoga, and medicinal and culinary herbs. All meals are vegetarian. Accommodation (dorm/single €18/23, including meals €32/39) may not be available if there is an event on. It's off the N87, 38km northwest of Cavan town.

🛌 Sleeping

Slieve Russell Hotel   SPA HOTEL €€
(☑ 049-952 6444; www.slieverussell.ie; N87, Cranaghan; d/ste from €130/190; 🅿@🛜🖳) A vision of marble columns, fountains, restaurants and bars, the Slieve Russell Hotel has 222 elegantly furnished rooms. There are 18- and nine-hole golf courses (with pro lessons available); spa treatments include flotation tanks, a herbal sauna and a salt grotto. A kids' club makes it a popular choice with families. It's 26km northwest of Cavan town.

Blacklion & Around

POP 194

This remote corner of the county is traversed by the Cavan Way. The little village of Blacklion lies less than 50m from the River Belcoo, marking the border with County Fermanagh, Northern Ireland.

Dedicated foodies make the pilgrimage to Blacklion's **MacNean House & Restaurant** (☑ 071-985 3022; www.nevenmaguire.com; Main St; dinner menu €85, with paired wines €135, Sun lunch €45, cookery class from €160; ⊙ sittings 6pm & 9.30pm Wed-Sat, 12.30pm, 3.30pm & 7pm Sun; 🅿✏). Award-winning TV chef Neven Maguire grew up in this gorgeous village house and has turned it into one of Ireland's finest restaurants/cookery schools. Book months in advance (or nab a last-minute cancellation online) to feast on inspired creations such as confit-chicken lollipops with aged parmesan foam, sherry-vinegar jelly and pumpkin risotto, and to stay in beautiful rooms (double/suite from €134/174).

👁 Sights

★ **Cavan Burren Park**   HISTORIC SITE
(www.cavanburrenpark.ie; Tullygobban Hill; ⊙ 7am-11pm May-Aug, reduced hours Sep-Apr) FREE Just 3km south of Blacklion, within the Cuilcagh Mountain Park and traversed by the Cavan Way (p528) walking route, this otherworldly megalithic site was identified in the 1870s but farmed until the 1950s and only established as the Cavan Burren Park in 2014. Highlights include a promontory fort circa 500 BC and the Giant's Grave wedge tomb from 2500 BC. An unstaffed information shed has interpretative panels, but the hilly, wooded area is otherwise pristine and magical to explore.

Cuilcagh Mountain Park   PARK
(www.marblearchcavesgeopark.com) The border between the Republic and Northern Ireland runs along the ridge of Cuilcagh Mountain,

the distinctive tabletop summit of Cuilcagh Mountain Park, the world's first cross-border Geopark. Its lower slopes are protected peatland habitats, while the upper slopes have dramatic sweeping cliffs. The visitor centre and the park's most high-profile attraction, the Marble Arch Caves (p645), lie over the border from Blacklion in County Fermanagh.

On the Republic side, the megalithic Cavan Burren Park is a highlight.

❶ Getting There & Away

Bus Éireann (p694) has services to Sligo town, County Sligo (€20.80, one hour, four daily Monday to Saturday, three Sunday) and Enniskillen, County Fermanagh (€8.60,30 minutes, four daily Monday to Saturday, three Sunday), from where you can connect to Dublin and Belfast. To explore the area, however, you really need your own wheels.

COUNTY MONAGHAN

Monaghan's quiet, undulating landscape is known for its tiny rounded hills that resemble bubbles in badly pasted wallpaper. Known as drumlins, these bumps are the result of debris left by retreating glaciers during the last ice age. The county's lakes attract plenty of anglers, but few others make it here, making it a tranquil place to explore.

Unlike much of the province, Monaghan was largely left alone during the Ulster Plantation. After the Cromwellian wars, though, local chieftains were forced to sell their land for a fraction of its true value, or else have it seized and redistributed to Cromwell's soldiers.

In the early 19th century, lace making became an important facet of the local economy, providing work and income for women. Carrickmacross was one of the key centres of the industry and you can still see the fine needlework on display here.

Monaghan Town

POP 7678

It may be the county town, but Monaghan's residents live their lives utterly unaffected by tourism. It's an enjoyable place to wander and admire the elegant 18th- and 19th-century limestone buildings. Many buildings have gently rounded corners, an unusual architectural feature in Ireland.

◉ Sights & Activities

Monaghan County Museum   MUSEUM
(www.monaghan.ie; 1-2 Hill St; ⊙11am-5pm Mon-Fri, noon-5pm Sat) FREE More than 70,000 artefacts from the Stone Age to modern times are housed at this excellent regional museum. Its crowning glory is the 14th-century **Cross of Clogher**, an oak altar cross encased in decorative bronze panels. Other impressive finds include the Lisdrumturk and Altartate Cauldrons, medieval *crannóg* artefacts, and some frightening knuckle-dusters and cudgels relating to the border with the North.

Rossmore Forest Park   PARK
(www.coillte.ie; off R189; ⊙car park 8am-6pm Apr-Oct, to 4.30pm Nov-Mar) FREE Crumbling remains of the Rossmore family's 19th-century castle, including its entrance stairway, buttresses and the family's pet cemetery, can still be seen at Rossmore Forest Park, where rhododendrons and azaleas blaze with colour in early summer. The park contains several giant redwoods, a yew avenue and Iron Age tombs, and is home to badgers, foxes, pygmy shrews, hedgehogs, otters and five of Ireland's seven bat species. There are forest walks and pretty picnic areas. It's 3.5km southwest of central Monaghan.

Birdlife in the park includes warblers, flycatchers and cuckoos.

Venture Sports   FISHING
(☑047-81495; 71 Glaslough St; ⊙9am-6pm Mon-Sat) Fine fishing abounds in the area; contact Venture Sports for permits, tackle and local knowledge.

✦ Festivals & Events

Harvest Blues Festival   MUSIC
(www.harvestblues.ie; ⊙early Sep) Local and international acts feature at this fabulous three-day blues festival.

⏹ Sleeping & Eating

Cafes and restaurants concentrate around the Diamond and Glaslough St. Monaghan's **farmers market** (Church Sq; ⊙10am-2pm Fri) ✐ sets up in the centre of town; there are also large supermarkets.

Westenra Arms   HOTEL €€
(☑047-74400; www.westenrahotel.com; The Diamond; s €55-79, d €89-129, tr €120-150; ☜) A town-centre landmark, this huge red-brick hotel has comfortable rooms (some with four-poster beds) reached by a lift, and

WORTH A TRIP

HILTON PARK

The magnificent country-house retreat **Hilton Park** (📋 047-56007; www. hiltonpark.ie; off N54, Scotshouse; s/d from €94.50/189, gatehouse per week from €655; ⏱Apr-Oct; 🅿🛜) has been in the same family since 1734. Its six spacious, light-bathed guest rooms have original furniture, free-standing baths and four-poster or half-tester beds. Top-class cuisine is largely sourced from the estate's farm, lakes and gardens (dinner €60; Tuesday to Saturday). It's located on a 240-hectare estate, 27km southwest of Monaghan town.

Guests get free access to its 18-hole golf course, fishing lakes and row boats, as well as bikes for exploring the grounds. In spring you can see the farm's newborn lambs.

sociable public areas including a glass-roofed restaurant (mains €16 to €29), a bar with live music, a nightclub, and a brilliant cocktail bar, Shifty Mulhares. But you can still sleep in peace: rooms are well sound-proofed. Kids are welcomed with toys and colouring books.

★**Castle Leslie** CASTLE €€€
(📋 047-88100; www.castleleslie.com; Glaslough; d from €170; 🅿🛜) Castle Leslie, 11km northeast of Monaghan town along the R185, is a magnificent Victorian pile, acquired by the Leslie family (who trace their ancestors back to Attila the Hun) in 1665. Facilities include a Victorian spa and equestrian centre (€35 per hour from); dining options span sophisticated **Snaffles Brasserie** (four course menu €65) to snug **Conor's Bar**. Public areas have wi-fi.

Each of the 20 guest rooms in the main house has a story: the Red Room, used by WB Yeats, contains the first bath plumbed in Ireland, while in Uncle Norman's Room, guests claim to have been levitated in the Gothic four-poster bed. The Hunting Lodge has a further 30 rooms, with decor ranging from rich traditional drapery to more minimalist contemporary style.

Batch Loaf BISTRO €€
(📋 047-72253; www.thebatchloaf.com; North Rd; mains €14-26.50; ⏱5-9pm Mon, Wed & Thu,

5-10pm Fri & Sat, 3-9pm Sun) A floor-to-ceiling map of County Monaghan occupies one wall of this bright, contemporary two-level bistro, and locally sourced ingredients are used in dishes like roast duck breast with bacon, chestnut and cabbage, maple-cured pork with cider sauce, Monaghan sirloin with roast peppercorn sauce, and grilled hake with wild mushroom crème. Live music plays Friday, Saturday and Sunday.

Andy's BISTRO €€
(Teach Aindt Bialann; 📋 047-82277; http://andys-monaghan.com; 12 Market St; mains €17.50-29; ⏱4-10pm Tue-Fri, 2-10pm Sat, 1.30-9.30pm Sun) In a whitewashed, black-trimmed Victorian building, this old-school restaurant is a family-run Monaghan institution. Long-standing house specialities include deep-fried breaded mushrooms with garlic mayo dip, and chicken fillet with mushroom and onion sauce, along with traditional fish and chips.

🍷 Drinking & Entertainment

★**Shifty Mulhares** COCKTAIL BAR
(www.westenrahotel.com; The Diamond; ⏱5pm-1am Fri-Sun; 🛜) Down a flight of stairs from the street, this basement cocktail bar at the Westenra Arms (p529) is ingeniously themed as the home of fictitious intrepid explorer Shifty Mulhares. It's decked out with items collected on his travels – everything from birdcages to studded Chesterfield sofas to '80s vinyl; you can even sip cocktails on Shifty's four-poster bed.

McKenna's Bar PUB
(62 Dublin St; ⏱7pm-midnight; 🛜) This historic pub is famous throughout the region for its jam sessions, predominantly blues. They take place in its upstairs bar 'the Brewery': the ideal moody venue with its dark wood, barrel tables and exposed brick walls. Its downstairs bar is known as 'the Anchor'.

Market House CULTURAL CENTRE
(📋 047-81122; www.monaghan.ie; Market St) This restored 18th-century market-hall turned arts-venue hosts exhibitions, concerts and drama productions.

🛈 Information

Monaghan's summer-opening **tourist office** (📋 047-81122; www.monaghantourism.com; Market St; ⏱10am-5pm Mon-Fri Jun-Sep) is in the Market House.

ℹ Getting There & Away

Daily **Bus Éireann** (p694) services include Dublin (€18, two hours, nine daily) via Carrickmacross (€13, 30 minutes).

Carrickmacross & Around

POP 5032

Carrickmacross was first settled by early English and Scottish Planters, and its broad main street is flanked by elegant Georgian houses with gorgeous poster-paint coloured facades. It's most famous as the home of delicate Carrickmacross lace, an industry revived in 1871 by the St Louis nuns.

Carrickmacross has no tourist office, but visitor information is available at www.carrickmacross.ie/visit-carrick.

◉ Sights

Carrickmacross Lace Gallery　　　GALLERY
(☑ 042-966 4176; www.carrickmacrosslace.ie; Market Sq; ◷ 9.30am-5.30pm Mon-Sat) FREE
In the town's former cattle yards, a local cooperative runs this thimble-sized lace gallery, where you can see lace-making demonstrations and check out exquisite designs. Designs are appliquéd on organza using thick thread and close stitches, then embellished with a variety of point stitches, guipure, pops and the lace's distinctive loop edge. Lace makers can take commissions and you can purchase delicate pieces made into fridge magnets, bookmarks and the like.

Carrickmacross lace graced the sleeves of Princess Diana's wedding dress and, more recently, the technique was used on the wedding dress for Kate Middleton's wedding to Prince William in 2011.

St Joseph's Catholic Church　　　CHURCH
(O'Neill St; ◷ 8am-6pm) Craftsmanship shines at St Joseph's Catholic Church, with 10 windows designed by Harry Clarke, Ireland's most renowned stained-glass artist. Opening hours can vary.

🛏 Sleeping & Eating

★ Shirley Arms　　　HOTEL €€
(☑ 042-967 3100; www.shirleyarmshotel.ie; Main St; d from €120; 🅿 🕸 🛜) Right in the centre of town, the Shirley Arms has a warm stone exterior, behind which lies a superb family-run hotel. White linens, walnut floors and modern bathrooms give the rooms a contemporary flair. The open-plan bar and lounge create an informal setting for excellent Irish classics, which are also served at its elegant restaurant (mains €14 to €33).

It's a popular wedding venue, so be sure to book ahead, especially on weekends.

Matilda's Artisan Bakehouse　　BAKERY, CAFE €
(1 Monaghan St; dishes €3.50-8.50; ◷ 8am-6pm Mon-Sat) In addition to artisan breads such as sourdough and focaccia, Matilda's bakes cakes, sweet pastries and savoury varieties including sausage rolls. It's ideal for picking up a quick breakfast or picnic ingredients; there's also a small seating area where you can dine on daily specials like quiches, soups and salads.

★ Riverbank County Pub　　GASTROPUB €€
(☑ 041-685 5883; www.theriverbank.ie; off L4700, Lannette; mains €15-25, 4-course menu €25; ◷ kitchen 5-9.30pm Wed-Sat, noon-9pm Sun, bar noon-11pm Sun-Thu, to midnight Fri & Sat; 🛜 🕸) On the banks of the River Glyde (the source of salmon served here), this gem is 7.5km southeast of Carrickmacross on the County Louth border. A roaring fire warms the dining area, with no TVs to distract from fantastic dishes such as cider-steamed Clogher Head mussels or Monaghan fillet steak with Bellingham blue cheese. There's a kids' menu and playground.

Run by the fourth generation of the same family, the pub was rebuilt using reclaimed timbers and flagstones from the original 18th-century inn. Upstairs are six spacious guest rooms with private bathrooms (double/triple from €80/120), featuring river or garden views.

🍷 Drinking

Fiddlers Elbow　　　PUB
(www.fiddlers.ie; Main St; ◷ 11am-midnight Sun-Thu, to 2am Fri-Sun) On Carrickmacross' wide main street, Fiddlers Elbow contains a buzzing bar, an upmarket restaurant serving dishes like honey-glazed duck (mains €12.50 to €26) and an upstairs nightclub (open 9pm to 2am Friday and Saturday). Live music in all genres regularly takes place; check the agenda online.

ℹ Getting There & Away

Bus Éireann (p694) services connect with Dublin (€18, 1¼ hours, nine daily) and Dundalk (€8, 30 minutes, five daily).

COUNTIES MEATH, LOUTH, CAVAN & MONAGHAN CARRICKMACROSS & AROUND

Inniskeen

★ **Patrick Kavanagh**
Resource Centre   MUSEUM

(☑ 042-937 8560; www.patrickkavanaghcountry.
com; Inniskeen; ☉ 11am-4.30pm Tue-Fri year-
round, 3-5.30pm Sun Jul-Sep) **FREE** Acclaimed
poet Patrick Kavanagh (1904–67) was born
in the picturesque little village of Inniskeen, 10km northeast of Carrickmacross.
The Patrick Kavanagh Resource Centre is
housed in the village's old parish church
where Kavanagh was baptised; he's buried in the attached graveyard. The centre's
staff have a passion for his life and work
that is contagious. Download a self-guided
literary tour of the village and the picturesque surrounding countryside (5.6km in
all) from the website.

The centre hosts events including a Writers' Weekend in late July/early August.

Kavanagh's long work *The Great Hunger* (1942) blasted away the earlier clichés
of Anglo-Irish verse and revealed Ireland's
poor farming communities as half-starved,
broken-backed and sexually repressed. His
best-known poem, *On Raglan Road* (1946),
was an ode to his unrequited love. It doubled as the lyrics for the traditional Irish
air *The Dawning of the Day,* which has
been performed by Van Morrison, Mark
Knopfler, Billy Bragg, Sinéad O'Connor
and countless others.

On the Road

Need to Know

For more information, see Survival Guide (p683)

Currency
Pound sterling (£)

Language
English, Irish

Visas
Generally not needed for stays of up to six months.
The UK is not a member of the Schengen Area.

Money
ATMs widely available. Credit cards accepted in most hotels and restaurants.

Mobile Phones
Northern Ireland uses UK mobile networks and landline providers. Phone boxes and public payphones are increasingly rare.

Time
Western European Time (UTC/GMT November to March; plus one hour April to October)

When to Go

High Season
(May-Aug)

➜ June is the best time to spot puffins nesting at the Rathlin West Light Seabird Centre.

➜ Warm weather makes July the best month for hiking in the Mournes and Sperrins.

Shoulder
(Mar-Apr, Sept-Oct)

➜ April can be a great time to visit Belfast, with spring flowers blooming throughout the city's parks and gardens.

➜ The Belfast International Arts Festival brings three weeks of theatre, music, dance and talks.

Low
(Nov-Feb)

➜ Experience popular attractions such as Titanic Belfast and Carrick-a-Rede rope bridge without the crowds.

➜ Outside is chilly, but you can enjoy the warmth in snug pubs across the north.

Useful Websites

Culture Northern Ireland (www.culturenorthernireland.org) Entertainment news, reviews and listings.

Translink (www.translink.co.uk) Public transport information.

Lonely Planet (www.lonelyplanet.com/ireland/northern-ireland) Destination information, hotel bookings, traveller forum and more.

Northern Ireland Tourist Board (www.nitb.com) Official tourist site.

Important Numbers

All Northern Ireland landline numbers begin with 🔲028, which you can omit when calling from another local landline. Drop the initial '0' if you're calling from abroad.

UK country code	🔲44
International access code	🔲00
Emergency (police, fire, ambulance, mountain rescue, coast guard)	🔲999

Exchange Rates

Australia	A$1	£0.58
Canada	C$1	£0.57
Eurozone	€1	£0.86
Japan	¥100	£0.69
New Zealand	NZ$1	£0.54
USA	US$1	£0.77

For current exchange rates, see www.xe.com.

Daily Costs

Budget: Less than £55

➡ Dorm beds: £18–25

➡ Cheap meals in cafes and pubs: £7–11

➡ Bus or train ticket: £3–12

Midrange: £55–120

➡ Double room in midrange hotel or B&B: £50–120

➡ Main course in midrange restaurant: £15–28

➡ Admission to museums: £7–17

Top end: More than £120

➡ Four-star hotel room: from £130

➡ Three-course meal in a good restaurant: around £40

➡ Car rental per day: from £35

Opening Hours

Opening hours may vary throughout the year, especially in rural areas, where many places have shorter hours or close completely from October or November to March or April.

Banks 9.30am–4pm Monday to Friday; some open 9.30am–1pm Saturday

Cafes 8.30am–5pm

Pubs & Bars noon–11pm Monday to Saturday (many until midnight or 1am Friday and Saturday), and noon–11pm Sunday

Restaurants noon–2.30pm and 6–9pm

Shops 9am–5.30pm Monday to Saturday and often 1–6pm Sunday

Arriving in Northern Ireland

Belfast International Airport Airport Express 300 bus runs to the Europa Bus Centre (one way/return £7.50/10.50, 30 to 55 minutes). A taxi costs about £30.

George Best Belfast City Airport Airport Express 600 bus runs to the Europa Bus Centre (one way/return £2.50/3.80, 15 minutes). A taxi fare to the city centre is about £10.

Victoria Ferry Terminal (Belfast) Bus 96 runs from Upper Queen St (£2, 20 minutes). A taxi costs about £10.

Larne ferry terminal Located 37km north of Belfast; trains connect the terminal at Larne Harbour with Belfast's Great Victoria St station (£7.30, one hour).

Getting Around

Car The easiest way to get around Northern Ireland is by car; roads are good and traffic is rarely a problem (although avoid routes in and around Belfast at rush hour).

Bus Buses serve urban areas and connect the province's main towns and cities, with less frequent services to most (but not all) rural villages.

Train Some towns are linked to Belfast by train.

For much more on **getting around**, see p692

Belfast

POP 333,000 / AREA 115 SQ KM

Best Places to Eat

➡ Muddlers Club (p561)

➡ Il Pirata (p562)

➡ Holohan's at the Barge (p560)

➡ Saphyre (p562)

➡ Mourne Seafood Bar (p560)

Best Places to Sleep

➡ Bullitt Hotel (p557)

➡ Rayanne House (p559)

➡ Vagabonds (p558)

➡ Merchant Hotel (p558)

➡ Global Village Backpackers (p558)

Why Go?

Belfast is in many ways a brand-new city. Once shunned by travellers unnerved by tales of the Troubles and sectarian violence, in recent years it has pulled off a remarkable transformation from bombs-and-bullets pariah to a hip-hotels-and-hedonism party town.

The old shipyards on the Lagan continue to give way to the luxury apartments of the Titanic Quarter, whose centrepiece – the stunning, star-shaped edifice housing the Titanic Belfast centre, covering the ill-fated liner's construction here has become the city's number-one tourist draw; it was even named the world's leading tourist attraction at the 2016 World Travel Awards.

New venues keep popping up – already this decade historic Crumlin Road Gaol and SS *Nomadic* opened to the public. They all add to a list of attractions that includes beautifully restored Victorian architecture, a glittering waterfront lined with modern art, a fantastic and fast-expanding foodie scene and music-filled pubs.

When to Go

➡ April can be a great time to visit Belfast, with spring flowers blooming throughout the city's parks and gardens, and the Belfast Film Festival showcasing Irish and international filmmakers' works.

➡ August brings good weather for walking and cycling, along with celebrations of Irish music and dance in West Belfast during Féile An Phobail, plus street parties and a carnival parade.

➡ October can start to get chilly, but the Festival at Queen's, the UK's second-largest arts festival (after Edinburgh), warms things up during its three-week run.

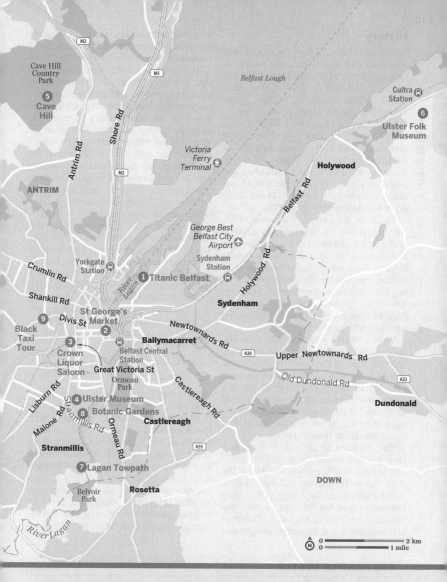

Belfast Highlights

1 Titanic Belfast (p545)
Learning about the world's most famous ocean liner.

2 St George's Market (p544) Sampling the wares of Northern Ireland's top food producers.

3 Crown Liquor Saloon (p539) Sipping a Guinness in Belfast's most beautiful Victorian pub.

4 Ulster Museum (p546) Discovering prehistoric treasures, an Egyptian mummy and sunken Armada gold.

5 Cave Hill (p548) Enjoying a city panorama from the North Belfast viewpoint.

6 Ulster Folk Museum (p552) Wandering among reconstructed farmhouses, forges and mills.

7 Lagan Towpath (p544) Cycling the riverbank to the former linen town of Lisburn.

8 Botanic Gardens (p547) Visiting the birdcage-domed, iron-and-glass Palm House.

9 Black taxi tour (p556) Taking in West Belfast's powerful political murals from the back of a cab.

History

Belfast takes its name from the River Farset (from the Irish *feirste,* meaning sandbank, or sandy ford), which flows into the River Lagan at Donegall Quay (it is now channelled through a culvert). Its Irish name, Béal Feirste, means 'Mouth of the Farset'.

In 1177 the Norman lord John de Courcy built a castle here, and a small settlement grew up around it. Both were destroyed in battle 20 years later, and the town did not begin to develop in earnest until 1611 when Baron Arthur Chichester built a castle in what is now the city centre (near Castle Pl and Castle St); it was destroyed by fire in 1708.

The early 17th-century Plantation of Ulster brought in the first waves of Scottish and English settlers, followed in the late 17th century by an influx of Huguenots (French Protestants) fleeing persecution in France; they laid the foundations of a thriving linen industry. More Scottish and English settlers arrived, and other industries such as rope-making, tobacco, engineering and shipbuilding developed.

With its textile mills and shipyards, Belfast was the one city in Ireland that truly rode the wave of the Industrial Revolution. Sturdy rows of brick terrace houses were built for the factory and shipyard workers, and a town of around 20,000 people in 1800 grew steadily into a city of 400,000 by the start of WWI, by which time Belfast had nearly overtaken Dublin in size.

The partition of Ireland in 1920 gave Belfast a new role as the capital of Northern Ireland. It also marked the end of the city's industrial growth, although decline didn't really set in until after WWII. With the outbreak of the Troubles in 1969, the city saw more than its fair share of violence and bloodshed, and shocking news images of terrorist bombings, sectarian murders and security forces' brutality made Belfast a household name around the world.

The 1998 Good Friday Agreement, which laid the groundwork for power-sharing among the various political factions in a devolved Northern Ireland Assembly, raised hopes for the future, and a historic milestone was passed on 8 May 2007 when the Reverend Ian Paisley (firebrand Protestant preacher and leader of the Democratic Unionist Party) and Martin McGuinness (Sinn Féin MP and former IRA commander) were respectively sworn in at Stormont as first minister and deputy first minister of a new power-sharing government.

Since 1998 Belfast has seen a huge influx of investment, especially from the EU. Massive swaths of the city centre have been (or are being) redeveloped, and tourism has taken off. The city was hit hard by the global financial crisis, but is now rapidly recovering.

Most of Belfast, including the city centre, is in County Antrim, but some outlying areas to the south and east are in County Down.

◉ Sights

◉ City Centre

★ City Hall
HISTORIC BUILDING
(Map p540; www.belfastcity.gov.uk; Donegall Sq; ☉ guided tours 11am, 2pm & 3pm Mon-Fri, noon, 2pm & 3pm Sat & Sun Oct-May, plus 10am & 4pm Mon-Fri, 4pm Sat & Sun Jun-Sep; ☐ Donegall Sq) **FREE** Belfast's classical Renaissance-style City Hall was built in fine, white Portland stone in 1906. Highlights of the free, 45-minute guided tour include the sumptuous, wedding-cake Italian marble and colourful stained glass of the entrance hall and rotunda; an opportunity to sit on the mayor's

---

RED HAND OF ULSTER

According to legend, the chief of a raiding party – O'Neills or O'Donnells; take your pick – approaching the coast by boat, decided to fire up his troops by decreeing that Ulster would belong to the first man to lay his right hand upon it. As they neared land one particularly competitive chap cut off his own right hand and lobbed it to the shore, thus claiming Ulster as his own. The O'Neill clan later adopted the Red Hand as their emblem and it went on to become the symbol of the Irish province of Ulster.

You'll see the Red Hand of Ulster in many places: on the official Northern Irish flag, in the Ulster coat of arms, above the entrance to the Linen Hall Library and laid out in red flowers in the garden of Mount Stewart House in County Down. It also appears in many political murals in the badges of Loyalist terrorist groups and as a clenched red fist in the badge of the Ulster Volunteer Force (UVF).

throne in the council chamber and try on the robes; and the idiosyncratic portraits of past lord mayors. Each is allowed to choose his or her own artist and the variations in personal style are intriguing.

The Industrial Revolution transformed Belfast in the 19th century. The city's rapid rise to muck-and-brass prosperity manifested in the extravagance of the building, which was paid for with the gas supply company's profits. The hall is fronted by a statue of a rather dour 'we are not amused' **Queen Victoria**. The bronze figures on either side of her symbolise the textile and shipbuilding industries. The child at the back represents education.

At the northeastern corner of the grounds is a statue of **Sir Edward Harland**, the Yorkshire-born marine engineer who founded the Harland & Wolff shipyards and who served as mayor of Belfast from 1885 to 1886. To his south stands a memorial to the victims of the Titanic.

★ **Crown Liquor Saloon**   HISTORIC BUILDING
(Map p540; www.nationaltrust.org.uk/the-crown-bar; 46 Great Victoria St; ⊙11.30am-11pm Mon-Sat, 12.30-10pm Sun; 🚌Europa Bus Centre) FREE There are not many historical monuments that you can enjoy while savouring a pint of beer, but the National Trust's Crown Liquor Saloon is one of them. Belfast's most famous bar was refurbished by Patrick Flanagan in the late 19th century and displays Victorian decorative flamboyance at its best (he was looking to pull in a posh clientele from the train station and Grand Opera House opposite). Despite being a tourist attraction, the bar fills up with locals come 6pm.

The exterior (1885) is decorated with ornate and colourful Italian tiles, and boasts a mosaic of a crown on the pavement outside the entrance. Legend has it that Flanagan, a Catholic, argued with his Protestant wife over what the pub's name should be. His wife prevailed and it was named the Crown in honour of the British monarchy. Flanagan took his sneaky revenge by placing the crown mosaic underfoot where customers would tread on it every day.

The interior (1898) sports a mass of stained and cut glass, marble, ceramics, mirrors and mahogany, all atmospherically lit by genuine gas mantles. A long, highly decorated bar dominates one side of the pub, while on the other is a row of ornate wooden snugs. The snugs come equipped with gunmetal plates (from the Crimean War) for striking matches and bell-pushes that once allowed drinkers to order top-ups without leaving their seats (alas, no longer).

Grand Opera House   HISTORIC BUILDING
(Map p540; 🎫028-9024 1919; www.goh.co.uk; Great Victoria St; ⊙box office 10am-5pm Mon-Sat; 🚌Europa Bus Centre) One of Belfast's great Victorian landmarks is the Grand Opera House. Opened in 1895 and completely refurbished in the 1970s, it suffered grievously at the hands of the IRA, sustaining severe bomb damage in 1991 and 1993. The interior has been restored to its original, over-the-top Victorian pomp, with swirling wood and plasterwork, fancy gilt-work in abundance and carved elephant heads framing the private boxes in the auditorium.

To see inside the theatre, book tickets for a performance online or at the box office.

Linen Hall Library   LIBRARY
(Map p540; www.linenhall.com; 17 Donegall Sq N; ⊙9.30am-5.30pm Mon-Fri, to 4pm Sat; 🚌Donegall Sq) FREE Established in 1788 to 'improve the mind and excite a spirit of general inquiry', the Linen Hall Library houses some 260,000 books, more than half of which are part of its important Irish and local studies collection. The political collection consists of pretty much everything that has been written about Northern Irish politics since 1966. The library also has a small **coffee shop** (⊙10am-4pm Mon-Fri, to 3.30pm Sat).

The library was moved from its original home in the White Linen Hall (the site is now occupied by City Hall) to the present building a century later. Thomas Russell, the first librarian, was a founding member of the United Irishmen and a close friend of Wolfe Tone – a reminder that this movement for independence from Britain had its origins in Belfast. Russell was hanged in 1803 after Robert Emmet's abortive rebellion.

Entries   STREET
(Map p540; 🚌Victoria Sq) These narrow alleyways running between High St and Ann St were once bustling commercial and residential thoroughfares; **Pottinger's Entry**, for example, had 34 houses in 1822. **Joy's Entry** is named after Francis Joy, who founded the *Belfast News Letter* in 1737, the British Isles' first daily newspaper (it's still in business). **Crown Entry** is where the United Irishmen were founded in 1791 by Wolfe Tone in Peggy Barclay's tavern. On **Wine Cellar Entry**, White's Tavern (p563) is Belfast's oldest tavern.

Central Belfast

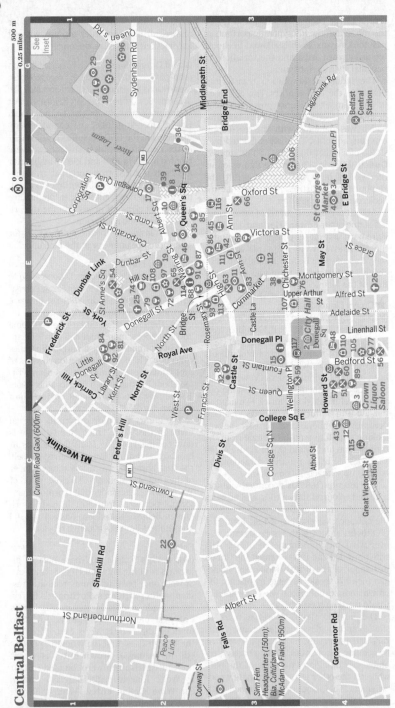

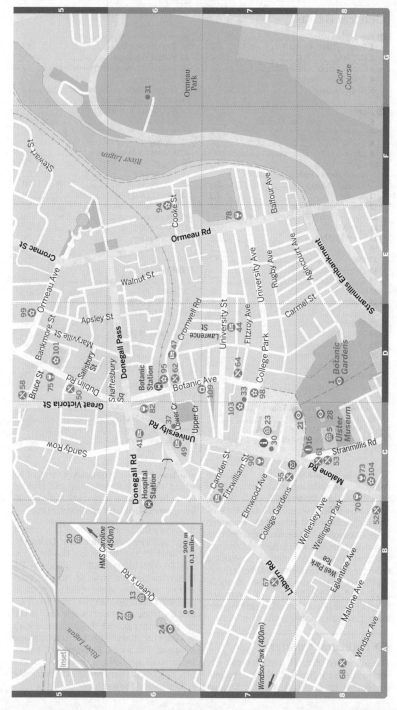

Central Belfast

St Malachy's Church CHURCH
(Map p540; www.saintmalachysparish.com; 24 Alfred St; ⊙8am-5.30pm; ☐Alfred St) Catholic St Malachy's was built between 1841 and 1844 by Thomas Jackson and extensively renovated in the last decade. Its exterior resembles a Tudor castle complete with arrow slits and turrets, and the jewel-like interior's fan-vaulted ceiling replicates Westminster Abbey's Henry VII Chapel. In 1886 the largest bell in Northern Ireland was installed but swiftly removed when local distillers claimed its chimes were interfering with whiskey production.

◉ Cathedral Quarter

The gentrified district north of the city centre around St Anne's Cathedral, bounded roughly by Donegall, Waring, Dunbar

and York Sts, is a bohemian enclave of restored red-brick warehouses and cobbled lanes, lined with artists studios, design offices, and stylish bars and restaurants.

St Anne's Cathedral CHURCH
(Map p540; www.belfastcathedral.org; Donegall St; adult/child £5/3; ⊙9am-5.15pm Mon-Sat, 1-3pm Sun; ☐Central Library) Built in imposing Hiberno-Romanesque style, St Anne's Cathedral was started in 1899 but did not reach its final form until 1981. As you enter you'll see that the black-and-white marble floor is laid out in a maze pattern – the black route leads to a dead end, the white to the sanctuary and salvation. The nave's 10 pillars are topped by carvings symbolising aspects of Belfast life; look out for the Freemasons' pillar (the central one on the south side).

In the south aisle is the tomb of Unionist hero Sir Edward Carson (1854–1935). In the baptistry, the stunning mosaic of *The Creation* contains 150,000 pieces of coloured glass; it and the mosaic above the west door are the result of seven years' work by sisters Gertrude and Margaret Martin.

Oh Yeah Music Centre MUSEUM
(Map p540; www.ohyeahbelfast.com; 15-21 Gordon St; ⊙ museum 11am-3pm Mon-Fri, noon-5pm Sat; ☐ Queen's Sq) FREE A charitable organisation that provides rehearsal space for young musicians in a converted whiskey warehouse, the Oh Yeah Music Centre is also home to a museum of Northern Ireland's musical history, from folk music to Snow Patrol. Exhibits range from shamrock-shaped records and electric guitars to historic gig posters, ticket stubs and stage clothing donated by famous bands.

◉ Laganside & Lanyon Place

The ambitious Laganside project to redevelop and regenerate the centre of Belfast has seen extensive restoration of listed buildings and new installations from the 1990s on. More than 30 public artworks are set along the waterfront.

Soaring above the waterfront at Donegall Quay is Belfast's tallest building, the 2011-built 28-storey **Obel** (Map p540; ☐ Queen's Sq), containing 233 apartments. To its south, **Victoria Square** (Map p540; www.victoriasquare.com; btwn Ann & Chichester Sts; ⊙ 9.30am-6pm Mon-Tue, to 9pm Wed-Fri, 9am-6pm Sat, 1-6pm Sun; ☐ Victoria Sq), set around a soaring atrium topped by a vast glass dome, has a viewing platform.

★ **St George's Market** MARKET

(Map p540; www.belfastcity.gov.uk; cnr Oxford & May Sts; ☺6am-3pm Fri, 9am-3pm Sat, 10am-4pm Sun; ☒Belfast Central) Ireland's oldest continually operating market was built in 1896. This Victorian beauty hosts a Friday **variety market** (flowers, produce, meat, fish, homewares and second-hand goods), a Saturday **food and craft market** (food stalls to look out for include Suki Tea, Ann's Pantry bakers and Hillstown Farm) and a **Sunday market** (food, local arts and crafts and live music). George's of the Market (p560) overlooks the action.

A free shuttle bus links the market with Donegall Sq and Adelaide St every 20 minutes from 11am to 3pm on Friday and Saturday.

In early December, a two-day Christmas Fair and Market takes place here.

Lagan Weir LANDMARK

(Map p540; ☒Titanic Quarter) Completed in 1994, Lagan Weir has helped improve the water quality of the River Lagan – the city's former lifeblood – to such an extent that salmon, eels and sea trout are migrating up the river once again. A **footbridge** over the weir provides access to the Titanic Quarter.

Just to weir's north is **Bigfish** (Map p540; ☒Queen's Sq), a giant ceramic salmon sculpture (1999) symbolising the river's regeneration. It's covered with tiles depicting the history of Belfast.

Belfast Barge MUSEUM

(Map p540; www.facebook.com/TheBelfastBarge; Lanyon Quay; ☺10am-4pm Tue-Sat; ☒Oxford St) **FREE** Housed in a barge moored on the River Lagan, this museum tells the story of Belfast's maritime and industrial history, bringing together old photographs, original drawings and documents, ship models and artefacts, and video and audio recordings of interviews with retired engineers, designers and shipyard workers.

At the opposite end of the barge is the restaurant Holohan's at the Barge (p560).

Custom House HISTORIC BUILDING

(Map p540; Custom House Sq; ☒Queen's Sq) Opposite the west end of Lagan Weir is the elegant Custom House, built by Charles Lanyon in Italianate style between 1854 and 1857; the writer Anthony Trollope once worked in the post office here. On the waterfront side, the pediment carries sculpted portrayals of Britannia, Neptune and Mercury. The **Custom House steps** were once a speakers' corner, a tradition memorialised in a bronze statue preaching to an invisible crowd. The building's interior is closed to the public.

Albert Memorial Clock Tower LANDMARK

(Map p540; Queen's Sq; ☒Queen's Sq) At the east end of High St is Belfast's very own leaning tower. Erected in 1865 in honour of Queen Victoria's dear departed husband, it is not as dramatically out of kilter as the more famously tilted tower in Pisa, but does, nevertheless, lean noticeably to the south – as the locals say, 'Old Albert not only has the time, he also has the inclination.' Restoration work has stabilised its foundations and left its Scrabo sandstone masonry sparkling white.

LAGAN TOWPATH

Part of Belfast's Laganside redevelopment project was the restoration of the towpath along the west bank of the River Lagan. You can now walk or cycle for 20km along the winding riverbank from central Belfast to Lisburn.

A shorter walk along the towpath (10km) starts from **Shaw's Bridge** (Map p552; ☒Malone Rd) on the southern edge of the city and heads back towards the city centre. Take bus 8A or 8B from Donegall Sq E to the stop just before the Malone roundabout (where Malone Rd becomes Upper Malone Rd). Bear left at the roundabout (signposted Outer Ring A55) and you'll reach the River Lagan at Shaw's Bridge.

Turn left and follow the towpath downstream on the left bank of the river (waymarked with red '9' signs), passing a restored lock-keeper's cottage and canal-side cafe at lock number '3'. The most attractive part of the walk is **Lagan Meadows** (Map p552; www.laganvalley.co.uk; ☒Stranmillis College), a tree-fringed loop in the river to the right of the path and a good place for a picnic on a summer day. Further along, **Cutters Wharf** (Map p552; ☏028-9080 5100; www.cutterswharf.co.uk; 4 Lockview Rd, Stranmillis; bar meals £7-11, restaurant mains £10-27; ☺kitchen noon-9pm Sun-Fri, to 10pm Sat; ☎; ☒Stranmillis College) is also a great place for a lunch break or refreshing ale. From the pub, the walk continues to **Lagan Weir** (p544) in Belfast's city centre.

⊙ Titanic Quarter

Stretching along the east side of the River Lagan, Belfast's former shipbuilding yards – the birthplace of the RMS *Titanic* – are dominated by the towering yellow cranes known as **Samson** and **Goliath**.

Part industrial wasteland, part building site and part high-tech business park, the area is currently undergoing a £1 billion regeneration project known as Titanic Quarter (http://titanicquarter.com) to develop the long-derelict docklands; the full regeneration of the area is scheduled for completion by 2034. A series of information boards along Queen's Rd describes items and areas of interest. The quarter's centrepiece is the striking star-shaped outline of Titanic Belfast.

★ Titanic Belfast   MUSEUM

(Map p540; www.titanicbelfast.com; Queen's Rd; adult/child £18/8; ⊙9am-7pm Jun-Aug, to 6pm Apr, May & Sep, 10am-5pm Oct-Mar; 🚇Abercorn Basin) The head of the slipway where the *Titanic* was built is now occupied by the gleaming, angular edifice of Titanic Belfast, an unmissable multimedia extravaganza that charts the history of Belfast and the creation of the world's most famous ocean liner. Cleverly designed exhibits enlivened by historical images, animated projections and soundtracks chart Belfast's rise to turn-of-the-20th-century industrial superpower, followed by a high-tech ride through a noisy, smells-and-all recreation of the city's shipyards. Tickets also include entry to the SS Nomadic.

You can explore every detail of the *Titanic's* construction, from a computer 'flythrough' from keel to bridge, to replicas of the passenger accommodation. Perhaps most poignant are the few flickering images that constitute the only film footage of the ship in existence.

Saver tickets (adult/child £9/6) are available for speedy visits without the shipyard ride one hour before the museum closes.

Behind the building you can see the massive slipways where the *Titanic* and her sister ship *Olympic* were built and launched.

SS Nomadic   HISTORIC SITE

(Map p540; www.nomadicbelfast.com; Hamilton Dock, Queen's Rd; adult/child £7/5; ⊙9am-7pm Jun-Aug, to 6pm Apr, May & Sep, 10am-5pm Oct-Mar; 🚇Abercorn Basin) Built in Belfast in 1911, the SS *Nomadic* is the last remaining vessel of the White Star Line. The little steamship

ferried 1st- and 2nd-class passengers between Cherbourg Harbour and the ocean liners that were too big to dock at the French port. On 10 April 1912 it delivered 172 passengers to the ill-fated *Titanic*. Don't miss the luxurious 1st-class toilets. Entry to the SS *Nomadic* (valid for 24 hours) is included in the ticket for Titanic Belfast.

Requisitioned in both world wars, the ship ended up as a floating restaurant in Paris in the 1980s and '90s. In 2006 it was rescued from the breaker's yard and brought to Belfast, where it's berthed in the Hamilton Graving Dock.

Titanic's Dock & Pump House   HISTORIC SITE

(Map p552; www.titanicsdock.com; Queen's Rd; adult/child £5/3.50; ⊙10am-5pm Apr-Oct, 10.30am-4pm Nov & Dec, 10.30am-5pm Jan & Feb; 🚇Science Park) At the far end of Queen's Rd is the most impressive monument to the days of the great liners – the vast **Thompson Dry Dock** where the *Titanic* was fitted out.

Beside it is the **Pump House**, which has an exhibition on Belfast shipbuilding. Self-guided tours include a viewing of original film footage from the shipyards, a visit to the inner workings of the pump house and a walk along the floor of the dry dock.

The dock's huge size gives you some idea of the scale of the ship, which could only just fit into it.

HMS Caroline   SHIP

(Map p552; ☑028-9045 4484; www.nmrn.org.uk; Queens Rd, Alexandra Dock; adult/child £12/5; ⊙10am-5pm; 🚇Science Park) The UK's last surviving WWI Royal Navy cruiser has been converted into a floating museum, docked in Titanic Quarter. Self-guided tours take in the captain's quarters, marine's mess, engine room and galley kitchen, with interactive exhibits and a film dramatisation of HMS *Caroline's* historic battles. The museum opened in 2016 in time for the centenary of the 1916 Battle of Jutland (in which HMS *Caroline* fought), before closing for further refurbishment work later that year. It opens again in mid-2017.

Harland & Wolff
Drawing Offices   HISTORIC BUILDING

(Map p540; www.titanichotelbelfast.com; Queen's Rd; 🚇Abercorn Basin) The designs for the *Titanic* were first drawn up at the original Harland & Wolff drawing offices. Now part of the new Titanic Hotel, which will open late 2017, the drawing offices, the old Harland & Wolff bathrooms and the room that received Morse code have all been preserved and will be open to the public on guided tours. See the website for further details.

Paint Hall
HISTORIC BUILDING

(Map p540; Queen's Rd; 🚌 Hamilton Rd) Just northeast of Titanic Belfast you'll see the huge paint hall where ship component parts were painted in a climate-controlled environment. Today it's home to **Titanic Studios**, where productions filmed include *Game of Thrones* (no tours available, unfortunately).

W5
SCIENCE CENTRE

(Map p540; www.w5online.co.uk; Odyssey Complex, 2 Queen's Quay; adult/child £9.80/7.50; ⏱ 10am-5pm Mon-Fri, 10am-6pm Sat, noon-6pm Sun, last entry 1hr before closing; 👶; 🚇 Station St) Also known as whowhatwherewhenwhy, W5 is an interactive science centre aimed at children aged three to 11 and filled with more than 250 exhibits. Kids can compose their own tunes by biffing the 'air harp' with a foam rubber bat, try to beat a lie detector, create cloud rings and tornadoes, and design and build their own robots and racing cars.

Odyssey Complex
LANDMARK

(Map p540; www.theodyssey.co.uk; 2 Queen's Quay; 🚇 Station St) The cylindrical-shaped Odyssey Complex is a huge sporting and entertainment centre on the eastern side of the river at the edge of the Titanic Quarter. The complex features a hands-on science centre, W5; the 10,800-seat SSE Arena (p566), home to the Belfast Giants (p567) ice-hockey team; the multiplex Odyssey Cinemas (p567); Box Nightclub (p565); and numerous food outlets and bars.

⊙ South Belfast (Queen's Quarter)

The Golden Mile – the 1.5km stretch of Great Victoria St and Shaftesbury Sq that links the city centre to Queen's Quarter (the university district) – was once the focus for much of Belfast's nightlife. These days, with the regeneration of the city centre, it's more tarnished brass than gold, but is still awash with decent pubs and eateries.

Metro buses 8A, 8B and 8C run from Donegall Sq E along Bradbury Pl and University Rd to Queen's University.

★ Ulster Museum
MUSEUM

(Map p540; www.nmni.com; Botanic Gardens; ⏱ 10am-5pm Tue-Sun; 👶; 🚇 Botanic) **FREE** You could spend hours browsing this state-of-the-art museum, but if you're pressed for time don't miss the **Armada Room**, with artefacts retrieved from the 1588 wreck of the Spanish galleon *Girona;* the **Egyptian Room**, with Takabuti, a 2500-year-old Egyptian mummy unwrapped in Belfast in 1835; and the **Early Peoples Gallery**, with the bronze Bann Disc, a superb example of Celtic design from the Iron Age.

On the ground floor, a potted history of the **Troubles** leads up to the 1st-floor **History Zone**. Its spectacular collection of prehistoric stone and bronze artefacts helps to provide a cultural context for Ireland's many archaeological sites. Exhibits include the **Malone Hoard**, a clutch of 16 polished, neolithic stone axes discovered only a few kilometres from the museum.

The kid-friendly, interactive **Nature Zone** on the 2nd floor covers geological time,

---

RMS TITANIC

Perhaps the most famous vessel ever launched, RMS *Titanic* was built in Belfast's Harland & Wolff shipyard for the White Star Line. When the keel was laid in 1909, Belfast was at the height of its fame as a shipbuilding powerhouse, and the *Titanic* was promoted by White Star as the world's biggest and most luxurious ocean liner. Ironically, it was also claimed to be 'unsinkable'.

Titanic was launched from H&W's slipway No 3 on 31 May 1911, and spent almost a year being fitted out in the nearby Thompson Graving Dock before leaving Belfast for the maiden voyage on 2 April 1912. In one of the most notorious nautical disasters of all time, the ship hit an iceberg in the North Atlantic on 14 April 1912, and sank in the early hours of the following day. Of the 2228 passengers and crew on board, only 705 survived; there were only enough lifeboats for 1178 people.

The Titanic Stories website (www.the-titanic.com) contains a wealth of information on the ship and its passengers, and lists all *Titanic*-related museums and memorials throughout Ireland and the rest of the world.

CRUMLIN ROAD GAOL

Guided tours of Belfast's notorious **Crumlin Road Gaol** (Map p552; ☑028-9074 1500; www.crumlinroadgaol.com; 53-55 Crumlin Rd; tour adult/child £9/6.50; ☉10am-5.30pm, last tour 4.30pm; ⬚Agnes St) take you from the tunnel beneath Crumlin Rd, built in 1850 to convey prisoners from the courthouse across the street (and allegedly the origin of the judge's phrase 'take him down'), through the echoing halls and cramped cells of C-Wing, to the truly chilling execution chamber. Advance tour bookings are recommended. The jail's pedestrian entrance is on Crumlin Rd; the car-park entrance is reached via Cliftonpark Ave to the north.

Since it opened in 1846, Crumlin Road Gaol imprisoned a whole range of historic figures, from Éamon de Valera to the Reverend Ian Paisley, and from suffragette Dorothy Evans to the 'Shankill Butcher' murderer Lenny Murphy. Designed by Charles Lanyon (the architect of Queen's University and many other city landmarks), and based on London's Pentonville prison, 'The Crum' was also the scene of 17 executions between 1854 and 1961. It remained a working prison until 1996.

Check the calendar for four-hour 'paranormal tours' (£35), and for regular, highly atmospheric concerts held at the jail.

evolution and natural history; highlights include the **Snapshot of an Ancient Sea Floor**, a fossilised portion of a 200-million-year-old seabed with jumbled ammonite shells and petrified driftwood.

The top floors are given over to **Irish and European art**, most notably the works of Belfast-born Sir John Lavery (1856–1941).

★**Botanic Gardens**   GARDENS
(Map p540; Stranmillis Rd; ☉7.30am-sunset; ⬚College Green) FREE The showpiece of Belfast's green oasis is Charles Lanyon's beautiful **Palm House** (☉10am-5pm Apr-Sep, to 4pm Oct-Mar), built in 1839 and completed in 1852, with its birdcage dome, a masterpiece in cast-iron and curvilinear glass. Nearby is the 1889 **Tropical Ravine** (☉10am-5pm Apr-Sep, to 4pm Oct-Mar), a huge red-brick greenhouse designed by the garden's curator Charles McKimm. Inside, a raised walkway overlooks a jungle of tropical ferns, orchids, lilies and banana plants growing in a sunken glen. It is due to reopen in late 2017 following a £3.8 million restoration.

Just inside the Botanic Gardens' Stranmillis Rd gate is the **Lord Kelvin statue** (Map p540; Stranmillis Rd) of Belfast-born Sir William Thomson (1824–1907), who helped lay the foundation of modern physics and who invented the Kelvin scale, which measures temperatures from absolute zero (–273°C or 0°K).

Queen's University   HISTORIC BUILDING
(Map p540; University Rd; guided tour £5; ⬚Queen's University) Northern Ireland's most prestigious university was founded by Queen Victoria in 1845. In 1908 the Queen's

College became the Queen's University of Belfast and today its campus spreads across some 250 buildings.

Just inside the main entrance is the **Queen's Welcome Centre** (☑028-9097 5252; www.qub.ac.uk/welcomecentre; ☉8.30am-5.30pm Mon-Fri, 11am-4pm Sat & Sun), with an information desk and souvenir shop. Book ahead for **guided tours**, or pick up a free leaflet that outlines a self-guided tour.

Charles Lanyon built the Queen's College building, a Tudor Revival in red brick and honey-coloured sandstone, in 1849. If it seems to have an Oxbridge air about it, that may be because Lanyon based the design of the central tower on the 15th-century Founder's Tower at Oxford's Magdalen College.

The college was one of three Queen's colleges (the others, still around but no longer called Queen's colleges, are in Cork and Galway), which were created to provide a non-denominational alternative to the Anglican Church's Trinity College in Dublin.

◉ West Belfast (Gaeltacht Quarter)

Northwest of Donegall Sq, Divis St leads across the Westlink Motorway to Falls Rd and West Belfast. Though scarred by decades of civil unrest during the Troubles, this former battleground is one of the most compelling places to visit in Northern Ireland. Recent history hangs heavy in the air, but there is a noticeable spirit of optimism and hope for the future.

The main attractions are the powerful murals that chart the history of the conflict, as well as the political passions of the moment.

West Belfast grew up around the linen mills that propelled the city into late-19th-century prosperity. It was an area of low-cost, working-class housing, and even in the Victorian era was divided along religious lines. The advent of the Troubles in 1969 solidified the sectarian divide, and since 1970 the ironically named Peace Line has separated the Loyalist and Protestant Shankill district (from the Irish *sean chill*, meaning 'old church') from the Republican and Catholic Falls district.

Despite its past reputation, the area is safe to visit. The best way to see West Belfast is on an informative and entertaining black taxi tour (p556), but there's nothing to stop you visiting under your own steam, either walking or using the shared black taxis that travel along the Falls and Shankill Rds. Alternatively, buses 10A to 10F from Queen St will take you along the Falls Rd; buses 11A to 11D from Wellington Pl go along Shankill Rd.

Peace Line
WALLS

(Map p540; ⏹ Falls Rd) The most visible sign of the divisions that have scarred the area for so long are the so-called 'peace walls' that controversially divide Belfast's Protestant and Catholic communities, covering some 34km in all. The longest section divides the Falls Road and the Shankill in West Belfast; its steel gates are generally open during daytime hours.

In 2016 the first of Northern Ireland's 110 peace walls was demolished with the removal of the barrier on Belfast's Crumlin Rd.

Begun in 1969 as a 'temporary measure', the 6m-high walls of corrugated steel, concrete and chain link have outlasted the Berlin Wall.

Cultúrlann McAdam Ó Fiaich
CULTURAL CENTRE

(Map p552; www.culturlann.ie; 216 Falls Rd; ⏱ 9am-5.30pm Mon-Fri, 9.30am-5pm Sat, 1-4pm Sun; ⏹ Broadway) FREE Housed in a red-brick, former Presbyterian church, this Irish language and cultural centre is the focus for West Belfast's community activity. It's a cosy and welcoming place with a tourist information desk, a shop (⏱ 9am-5.30pm Mon-Fri, 9.30am-5pm Sat, 1-4.30pm Sun) selling a wide selection of books on Ireland, Irish-language material, crafts and Irish-music CDs, and a good cafe-restaurant, Bia (⏺ 028-9096 4184;

mains £8-22; ⏱ 9am-6pm Mon-Thu, to 9pm Fri & Sat, 10am-4pm Sun; ⏼ ⏼). The centre also has an art gallery and a theatre that stages music, drama and poetry events.

Conway Mill
ARTS CENTRE

(Map p540; www.facebook.com/conwaymillflax; 5-7 Conway St; ⏱ 10am-5pm Mon-Fri, to 2pm Sat; ⏹ Clonard) FREE Conway Mill is a restored 19th-century flax mill that now houses around 20 artists' studios, an exhibition on the mill's history, an education centre and work spaces for local enterprises. It also contains the **Eileen Hickey Irish Republican History Museum** (⏱ 10am-2pm Tue-Sat), a collection of artefacts, newspaper articles, photos and archives relating to the Republican struggle from 1798 to the Troubles.

Sinn Féin Headquarters
NOTABLE BUILDING

(Map p552; www.sinnfein.ie; 51 Falls Rd; ⏹ Falls Rd) The red-brick Sinn Féin Headquarters has the famous mural of a smiling **Bobby Sands**, the hunger striker who was elected as MP for West Belfast just a few weeks before he died in 1981. The text reads, in Sands' own words, 'Our revenge will be the laughter of our children'.

◉ Outside the City Centre

★ Cave Hill Country Park
PARK

(Map p552; www.belfastcity.gov.uk; Antrim Rd; ⏱ 7.30am-dusk; ⏹ 1A to 1G) FREE The view from the summit of Cave Hill (368m) takes in the whole sprawl of the city, the docks, Belfast Lough and the Mourne Mountains – on a clear day you can see Scotland. Cave Hill Country Park spreads across the hill's eastern slopes, with several waymarked walks and an **adventure playground** (⏺ 028-9077 6925; child 3-14yr £2.50; ⏱ 10am-8pm Jul & Aug, shorter hrs Apr-Jun & Sep, Sat & Sun only Oct-Mar).

The hill was originally called Ben Madigan, after the 9th-century Ulster king, Matudhain. Its distinctive, craggy profile, seen from the south, has been known to locals for two centuries as 'Napoleon's Nose' – it supposedly bears some resemblance to Bonaparte's schnoz, but you might take some convincing. On the summit is an Iron Age earthwork known as **McArt's Fort**, where members of the United Irishmen, including Wolfe Tone, looked down over the city in 1795 and pledged to fight for Irish independence. The path leading to the summit from Belfast Castle car park passes beneath the five caves that give the hill its name (it's

BELFAST'S MURALS

Belfast's tradition of political murals dates from 1908 when images of King Billy (William III, Protestant victor over the Catholic James II at the Battle of the Boyne in 1690) were painted by Unionists protesting against home rule for Ireland. The tradition was revived in the late 1970s as the Troubles wore on, with murals used to mark out sectarian territory, make political points, commemorate historical events and glorify terrorist groups. As the 'voice of the community' the murals were rarely permanent, but changed to reflect the issues of the day. Taxi tours visit many of the more prominent murals, and the driver/guide can provide context and an explanation of the various symbols.

Republican Murals

The first Republican murals appeared in 1981, when the hunger strike by Republican prisoners – demanding recognition as political prisoners – at the Maze Prison saw the emergence of dozens of murals of support. In later years, Republican muralists broadened their scope to cover wider political issues, Irish legends and historical events. After the Good Friday Agreement of 1998, the murals came to demand police reform and the protection of nationalists from sectarian attacks.

Common images seen in Republican murals include the phoenix rising from the flames (symbolising Ireland reborn from the flames of the 1916 Easter Rising), and scenes and figures from Irish mythology. Common slogans include 'Free Ireland', the Irish '*Éirí Amach na Cásca* 1916' (The Easter Rising of 1916) and '*Tiocfaidh Ár Lá*' (Our Day Will Come).

Many Nationalist murals in West Belfast commemorate the Hunger Strike of 1981, when 10 Republican prisoners starved themselves to death. Most prominent is the image of Bobby Sands, who was elected as a local MP shortly before his death.

Another popular theme for murals in Republican areas is support for other nationalist and republican movements around the world, including Palestine, the Basque Country and Latin America, notably on the stretch of Falls Rd known as Solidarity Wall.

The main areas for Republican murals are Falls Rd, Beechmount Ave, Donegall Rd, Shaw's Rd and the Ballymurphy district in West Belfast, New Lodge Rd in North Belfast and Ormeau Rd in South Belfast.

Loyalists Murals

Loyalist murals have traditionally been more militaristic and defiant in tone than the Republican murals. The Loyalist battle cry of 'No Surrender!' is common, along with red, white and blue painted kerbstones, paramilitary insignia and images of King Billy, usually shown on a prancing white horse. The victory of King Billy (William of Orange) over the Catholic King James at the Battle of the Boyne in 1690 is still celebrated annually with 12 July parades.

You will also see the Red Hand of Ulster, sometimes shown as a clenched fist (the symbol of the Ulster Freedom Fighters; UFF), and references to the WWI Battle of the Somme in 1916 in which many Ulster soldiers died; it is seen as a symbol of Ulster's loyalty to the British crown, in contrast to the Republican Easter Rising of 1916. Common mottoes include '*Quis Separabit*' (Who Shall Divide Us?), the motto of the Ulster Defence Association (UDA); and the defiant 'We will maintain our faith and our nationality'.

Murals Today

In recent years there has been a lot of debate about what to do with Belfast's murals. Some see them as an ugly and unpleasant reminder of a violent past, while others claim they are a vital part of Northern Ireland's history. There's no doubt they have become an important tourist attraction, but there is now a move to replace the more aggressive and militaristic images with murals dedicated to local heroes and famous figures such as footballer George Best, *Narnia* novelist CS Lewis and golfer Rory McIlroy.

There are also some off-beat and amusing artworks, such as a gable-end on Balfour Ave, off Ormeau Rd, that asks the question 'How can quantum gravity help explain the origin of the universe?' (one of 10 questions selected by scientists as the most important unsolved problems in physics), reflecting the still unsolved – and, to outsiders, equally baffling – problem of Northern Ireland's sectarian divide.

Belfast Murals

Since the start of the Troubles, the gable ends of Belfast's housing estates have been used as informal canvases, painted with colourful murals that serve as territorial markers, political statements and defiant symbols of Loyalist or Nationalist identity. More recently, many nonpolitical murals have appeared,

Hunger Strike

Many Nationalist murals in West Belfast commemorate the Hunger Strike of 1981, when 10 Republican prisoners starved themselves to death. Most prominent is the image of Bobby Sands, who was elected as a local MP shortly before his death. A favourite slogan in the Gaelic 'Tiocfaidh ár lá', which means 'Our time will come'.

Solidarity Wall

Another popular theme for murals in Republican areas is support for other nationalist and republican movements around the world, including Palestine, the Basque Country and Latin America, notably on the stretch of Falls Rd known as Solidarity Wall.

King Billy

The most iconic of Protestant murals is the image of King Billy (William of Orange), whose victory over the Catholic King James at the Battle of the Boyne in 1690 is still celebrated annually with 12 July parades. He is usually shown mounted on a prancing white horse.

Nonpolitical Murals

Since the advent of the peace process there has been a concerted effort to replace aggressively partisan murals with ones that celebrate nonpolitical subjects, such as footballer George Best, novelist CS Lewis, the RMS Titanic and the Harland & Wolff shipyards.

EVERYONE
REPUBLICAN
OR OTHERWISE
HAS THEIR OWN
PARTICULAR
ROLE TO PLAY

...OUR
REVENGE
WILL BE THE
LAUGHTER
OF OUR
CHILDREN

Bobby Sands MP
POET, GAEILGEOIR, REVOLUTIONARY, IRA VOLUNTEER.

1. Solidarity Wall 2. Bobby Sands mural, Falls Road
3. King Billy mural 4. *Ship of Dreams* by artist Ross Wilson, Newtownards Road

1912

SHIP OF DREAMS

Built in Belfast
TITANIC

SOS

Around Central Belfast

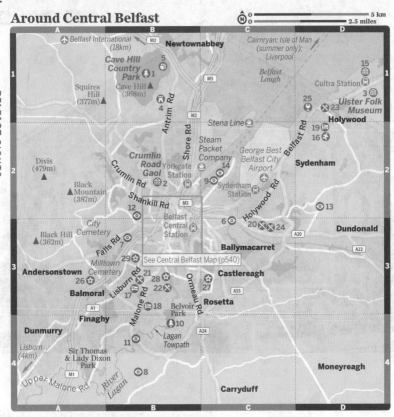

a 7.2km circular trail; allow two hours). To get here, take buses 1A to 1G from Royal Ave to Belfast Castle.

★ **Ulster Folk Museum** MUSEUM
(Map p552; http://nmni.com/uftm; Cultra; folk museum adult/child £9/5.50, transport & folk museum £11/6; ⊙10am-5pm Tue-Sun Mar-Sep, 10am-4pm Tue-Fri, 11am-4pm Sat & Sun Oct-Feb; ﹩; ⃝Cultra) Farmhouses, forges, churches, mills and a complete village have been reconstructed at this excellent museum, with human and animal extras combining to give a powerful impression of Irish life over the past few hundred years. From industrial times, there are red-brick terraces from 19th-century Belfast and Dromore. Another highlight is the Picture House, a silent cinema that was housed in a County Down hayloft from 1909 to 1931. There's even a corner shop dating from 1889 selling sweets from glass jars.

In summer, thatching and ploughing are demonstrated by characters dressed in period costume.

The museum is 14km northeast of central Belfast, just north of Holywood, across the road from the Ulster Transport Museum. Buses to Bangor stop nearby. Cultra station on the Belfast–Bangor train line is less than 10 minutes' walk away.

Ulster Transport Museum MUSEUM
(Map p552; http://nmni.com/uftm; Cultra; transport museum adult/child £9/5.50, transport & folk museum £11/6; ⊙10am-5pm Tue-Sun Mar-Sep, 10am-4pm Tue-Fri, 11am-4pm Sat & Sun Oct-Feb; ﹩; ⃝Cultra) Across the road from the Ulster Folk Museum, the Transport Museum has steam locomotives, rolling stock, motorcycles, trams, buses and cars. Most popular is the **Titanica** exhibit, which includes the original design drawings for the *Titanic* and its sister ship *Olympic*. The highlight of the

Around Central Belfast

car collection is the stainless-steel-clad prototype of the ill-fated **DeLorean DMC**, made in Belfast in 1981. The car was a commercial disaster but achieved everlasting fame in the *Back to the Future* films.

The museum is 14km northeast of central Belfast, just north of Holywood. Buses to Bangor stop nearby. Cultra station on the Belfast–Bangor train line is less than 10 minutes' walk away.

Stormont   NOTABLE BUILDING
(Map p552; www.niassembly.gov.uk; Upper Newtownards Rd; ⊙9am-4pm Mon-Fri, guided tours 11am & 2pm; 🚌4a, 4b) FREE Stormont's dazzling white neoclassical facade is one of Belfast's most iconic, occupying a dramatic position at the end of a gently rising 1.5km avenue. Since 1998 it has been the home of the Northern Ireland Assembly.

Free guided tours meet in the elaborate Great Hall, which is made entirely of Italian marble and adorned with five chandeliers; you'll also see the Assembly and Senate Chambers and the Committee Room.

From its completion in 1932 until the introduction of direct rule in 1972, Stormont was the seat of the parliament of Northern Ireland. Following the Good Friday Agreement of 1998 it became home to Northern

Ireland's devolved legislative body, until the Assembly was suspended in 2002. On 8 May 2007, it returned to the forefront of Irish politics once again, when Ian Paisley and Martin McGuinness – the best of enemies for decades – laughed and smiled as they were sworn in as first minister and deputy first minister respectively.

Stormont is fronted by a defiant statue of the arch-Unionist **Sir Edward Carson**. Nearby, 19th-century Stormont Castle, like Hillsborough in County Down, is an official residence of the Secretary of State for Northern Ireland.

Take bus 4a or 4b from Donegall Sq W.

Belfast Castle   CASTLE
(Map p552; www.belfastcity.gov.uk; Antrim Rd; ⊙9.30am-4pm Mon, to 9pm Tue-Sat, to 4.30pm Sun; 🚌1A to 1G) FREE Built in 1870 for the third Marquess of Donegall, in the Scottish Baronial style made fashionable by Queen Victoria's Balmoral, multiturreted Belfast Castle commands the southeastern slopes of Cave Hill. It was presented to the City of Belfast in 1934 and is now used mostly for weddings and other functions. Downstairs there's a small exhibition on the folklore and history of the park and the **Cellar Restaurant**; most of the castle is closed to the public.

Legend has it that the castle's residents will experience good fortune only as long as a white cat lives there, a tale commemorated in the beautiful formal gardens by nine portrayals of cats in mosaic, painting, sculpture and topiary – a good game for kids is getting them to find all nine.

Belfast Zoo
ZOO

(Map p552; www.belfastzoo.co.uk; Antrim Rd; adult/child £12.50/6.25; ⏰10am-7pm, last entry 5pm Apr-Sep, to 4pm, last entry 2.30pm Oct-Mar; 🚍1A to 1G) Home to 150 species, Belfast Zoo has spacious enclosures set on an attractive, sloping site; the sea lion and penguin pool with its underwater viewing is particularly good. Some of the more unusual animals include tamarins, Malayan sun bears and red pandas, but the biggest attractions are the ultracute meerkats, the colony of ring-tailed lemurs and the herd of Rothschild's giraffe.

The zoo's latest arrivals are Andean bear cub Lola, whose father was also born in the zoo, and baby gorilla Olivia, born in August 2016.

Irish Linen Centre & Lisburn Museum
MUSEUM

(📞028-9266 3377; www.lisburnmuseum.com; Market Sq; ⏰9.30am-5pm Mon-Sat) FREE The history of Lisburn's once prosperous linen industry is celebrated at this excellent museum, inside the 17th-century Market House. The 'Flax to Fabric' exhibition has plenty of audiovisual and hands-on exhibits, and outlines the fascinating history of the linen industry in the 18th and 19th centuries –

on the eve of WWI, Ulster was the largest linen-producing region in the world, employing some 75,000 people. You can watch weavers working on Jacquard looms and try your hand at spinning flax.

Hilden Brewery
BREWERY

(📞028-9266 0800; www.hildenbrewery.com; Hilden House, Grand St; tour £10; ⏰tours by reservation noon Wed-Fri) Ireland's oldest independent brewing company, dating from 1981, produces superior brews including caramel-malt Twisted Hop, Buck's Head double IPA, Barney's Brew wheat beer with coriander and golden Belfast Blonde pale ale. Tours lasting 45 minutes show you how they're made and include a tasting. Its bar and restaurant, the **Tap Room** (http://taproomhilden.com; mains lunch £7.50-12, dinner £14.50-17.50; ⏰kitchen noon-2.30pm & 5.30-9pm Tue-Sat, noon-3pm Sun; 🅿), is excellent. In mid-August Hilden hosts a two-day beer festival. Take the train from Belfast's Great Victoria St station to Hilden station, from where it's a 300m walk.

🏃 Activities

Belfast Cookery School
COOKING

(Map p540; 📞028-9023 4722; www.belfastcookeryschool.com; 53-54 Castle St; classes £40-55; 🚍Royal Ave) Classes at the Belfast Cookery School, attached to the Mourne Seafood Bar (p560), feature everything from knife skills to bread making, dinner parties, barbecues and a wide range of international cuisines (Indian, Italian, Thai, Spanish, Moroccan...),

BELFAST IN...

One Day
Start your day with breakfast at **George's of the Market** (p560) and if it's Friday, Saturday or Sunday take a look around **St George's Market** (p544) too. Then walk into the city centre and take a free guided tour of **City Hall** (p538). Take a black taxi tour (p556) of the West Belfast murals, and ask the taxi driver to drop you off for lunch at **Holohan's at the Barge** (p560). From there, take a stroll across the river and spend the rest of the afternoon exploring **Titanic Belfast** (p545). Round off the day with dinner at the **Muddlers Club** (p561) and then drinks at the **Duke of York** (p564) and the bars of buzzing Hill St.

Two Days
On your second day, take a look at **Queen's University** (p547), explore the fascinating exhibits in the **Ulster Museum** (p546) and take a stroll through the **Botanic Gardens** (p547). In the afternoon either take a guided tour around historic **Crumlin Road Gaol** (p547), or go for a hike up **Cave Hill** (p548). Stop for a pint at the **Crown Liquor Saloon** (p539), then have dinner at nearby **Eipic** (p561). End the night with a rooftop cocktail at the **Perch** (p563).

BELFAST FOR CHILDREN

Belfast is a fantastic city to visit with kids. Events and attractions of interest to travellers with children are listed in the 'Family Fun' section of http://visit-belfast.com. If you're in town in March, look out for cultural and educational events during the **Belfast Children's Festival** (www.youngatart.co.uk; ☉early–mid-Mar).

Kids favourites include the following:

Belfast Zoo (p554) Animals galore.

Cave Hill Country Park (p548) With an adventure playground.

CS Lewis Square (p556) Sculptures of characters from *The Chronicles of Narnia.*

Ulster Folk Museum (p552) and **Ulster Transport Museum** (p552) An easy and enjoyable day trip from Belfast.

Ulster Museum (p546) Plenty of exhibits and special events designed for children of all ages.

W5 (p546) Hands-on science centre.

---

but its seafood courses are especially popular. Book well ahead.

Holywood Golf Club   GOLF
(Map p552; ☎028-9042 3135; www.holywood golfclub.co.uk; Nuns Walk, Demesne Rd, Holywood; green fees £30 Mon-Thu, £35 Sat & Sun; ☉6am-8pm; ☐Holywood) This undulating par-69 parkland course, 11km northeast of Belfast, is Rory McIlroy's home club and has spectacular views over Belfast Lough and the Antrim coast. Discounted rates are often available; check the website's booking page for times and prices.

☞ Tours

Belfast Food Tour   FOOD & DRINK
(Map p540; https://tasteandtour.co.uk; 4hr food tour per person £50; ☐Belfast Central) Starting in St George's Market, these fun tours are a great way to tap into Northern Ireland's flourishing food scene, with plenty of samples of the region's most traditional dishes and innovative new produce along the way.

The company also runs other food and drink tours, including a Belfast Whiskey Walk (£60) and a Brewery Tour (£45). Book ahead.

Lagan Boat Company   BOATING
(Map p540; ☎028-9024 0124; www.laganboat company.com; adult/child £10/8; ☉12.30pm, 2pm & 3.30pm daily Apr-Oct, 12.30pm & 2pm Sat-Mon Nov-Mar; ☐Queen's Sq) The Lagan Boat Company's excellent Titanic Tour explores the docklands downstream of Lagan Weir, taking in the slipways where the liners *Titanic* and *Olympic* were launched and the

huge dry dock where they could just fit, with nine inches (23cm) to spare. There's also a chance to spot seals. Tours depart from Donegall Quay near the Bigfish sculpture (p544). Book ahead.

Titanic Tours   TOURS
(☎028-9065 9971; www.titanictours-belfast. co.uk; 3hr tour per adult/child £30/15) A three-hour luxury tour led by the great-grand-daughter of one of the *Titanic's* crew, visiting various *Titanic*-related sites. For groups of two to five people; includes pick-up and drop-off at your accommodation. Also offers custom full-day tours for £40 to £50 per person.

Belfast Bike Tours   TOURS
(Map p540; ☎07812 114235; www.belfastbike tours.com; £15; ☉10.30am & 2pm Mon, Wed, Fri & Sat Apr-Aug, Sat only Sep-Mar; ☐Queen's University) These 2½-hour guided tours depart from outside Queen's University and take you on a leisurely spin along the Lagan Valley to the huge prehistoric earthwork **Giant's Ring** (Map p552; www.laganvalley.co.uk; Ballyna-hatty Rd; ☉24hr; ☐Ballylesson Church) FREE (with a dolmen known as the Druid's Altar in the centre) and back again. Bikes are provided; book in advance. Also rents out bikes for exploring on your own (from £15 per day).

Belfast Pub Crawl   TOURS
(Map p540; ☎07731 977774; www.belfastcrawl .com; per person £10; ☉8.30pm Fri & Sat; ☐Queen's Sq) A three-hour tour taking in four of the city's historic pubs (including a drink in each, plus live trad music), depart-

VAN MORRISON & CS LEWIS TRAILS

The little explored neighbourhoods of East Belfast were once home to CS Lewis and Van Morrison, whose former haunts have been mapped out in self-guided walking trails.

The star stop on the CS Lewis trail is a new **square** (Map p552; 280 Newtownards Rd; ♿; 🚃 Connswater) FREE dedicated to the author, with fabulous sculptures of characters from *The Chronicles of Narnia*.

Fans of 'Van the Man' Morrison can take a 3.5km neighbourhood walk past sights referenced in his lyrics, including the **Hollow** (immortalised in 'Brown Eyed Girl'), **Cypress Avenue**, and the modest house where he was born on **Hyndford St** (at number 125).

You can pick up maps at **EastSide Visitor Centre** (Map p552; ☎ 028- 9045 1900; www.eastsidepartnership.com; 278-280 Newtownards Rd; ⊙8am-6pm Mon-Fri, 10am-5pm Sat & Sun; 🚃 Connswater), or download them from www.connswatergreenway.co.uk/trails.

ing from the Albert Memorial Clock Tower (p544). Advance booking required.

Taxi Tours

Black taxi tours of West Belfast's murals – known locally as the 'bombs and bullets' or 'doom and gloom' tours – are offered by a large number of taxi companies and local cabbies. These can vary in quality and content, but in general they're an intimate and entertaining way to see the sights. Drivers will pick you up from anywhere in the city centre.

Paddy Campbell's Famous
Black Cab Tours   CULTURAL
(☎ 07990 955227; www.belfastblackcabtours. co.uk; tour per 1-3 people £30) Popular 1½-hour black cab tours.

Harper Taxi Tours   CULTURAL
(www.harpertaxitours.com; from £30) Political and historical tours.

Official Black Taxi Tours   CULTURAL
(☎ 028-9064 2264; www.belfasttours.com; 1-2 passengers £35, 3 or more per person £15) Customised tours of Belfast's political murals lasting 1½ hours.

Game of Thrones Tours

McComb's Game of Thrones Tours   BUS
(Map p540; ☎ 028-9031 5333; www.mccombscoaches.com; 22-32 Donegall Rd; £35; ⊙9am; 🚃 Bradbury Pl) The drivers of these *Game of Thrones* tours have also driven the extras and equipment. Filming locations visited include the Dark Hedges (ie King's Road), Cushendun (the sea-cave where the shadow assassin was born), Ballintoy Harbour (Lordsport Harbour) and Larrybane (where the shadow assassin kills Renly). Pick-up is from the Belfast Youth Hostel (p559) at 9am.

Game of Thrones Tours   BUS
(Map p540; ☎ 028-9568 0023; www.gameofthronestours.com; adult/student £40/36; ⊙Wed-Sun Easter-Sep, reduced tours Oct-Easter; 🚃 Victoria Sq) Offers two full-day itineraries covering 11 iconic *Game of Thrones* filming locations: the Winterfell Locations Trek taking in Castle Ward and Tollymore Forest Park (where the Starks discover a dead direwolf and her pups), and the Iron Islands and Stormlands Adventure, covering sights in north Antrim including Ballintoy Harbour and the Dark Hedges.

Tours depart from Victoria Square mall (p543).

🎇 Festivals & Events

Belfast City Council (www.belfastcity.gov. uk/events) organises a wide range of events throughout the year, covering everything from the St Patrick's Day parade to the Lord Mayor's Show. It has a useful online events calendar, as does the Visit Belfast Welcome Centre (http://visit-belfast.com/ whats-on).

CityDance   DANCE
(Map p540; www.citydancebelfast.com; ⊙Feb) Free two-day dance festival, based at the Crescent Arts Centre (p566).

Féile an Earraigh   MUSIC
(Spring Festival; www.feilebelfast.com; ⊙Feb or Mar) This four-day festival of traditional Irish and Celtic music attracts artists from all over Ireland, Europe and America.

St Patrick's Day   CULTURAL
(www.belfastcity.gov.uk/events; ⊙17 Mar) A celebration of Ireland's patron saint, marked by various community festivals and culminating in a grand city-centre parade.

Belfast Film Festival   FILM
(Map p540; www.belfastfilmfestival.org; ⊘early Apr) Eleven-day celebration of Irish and international film; most screenings are at the Queen's Film Theatre (p567).

Festival of Fools   PERFORMING ARTS
(http://foolsfestival.com; ⊘early May) A four-day festival of street entertainment, with events concentrated in the Cathedral Quarter and city centre.

Belfast City Marathon   SPORTS
(Map p540; www.belfastcitymarathon.com; ⊘first Mon in May) Avid runners from across the globe come to compete in the marathon; other events include a walk and a fun run.

**Cathedral Quarter
Arts Festival**   PERFORMING ARTS
(http://cqaf.com; ⊘early May) Ten days of drama, music, poetry, street theatre and art exhibitions in and around the Cathedral Quarter.

Belfast Book Festival   LITERATURE
(www.belfastbookfestival.com; ⊘mid-Jun) A week of all things book-related, from films and readings to workshops and meet-the-author events, at venues throughout the city.

**Belfast Titanic
Maritime Festival**   SAILING
(Map p540; http://visit-belfast.com/whats-on; ⊘Jun or Jul) A three-day festival centred on Queen's Quay, with sailing ships, street entertainment, a seafood festival and live music.

Belfast Pride   LGBT
(www.belfastpride.com; ⊘late Jul-early Aug) Ireland's largest celebration of gay, lesbian, bisexual and transgender culture, culminating in a huge city-centre parade; takes place over a week in late July/early August.

Féile An Phobail   CULTURAL
(West Belfast Festival; www.feilebelfast.com; ⊘early Aug) Said to be the largest community festival in Ireland, the August Féile takes place in West Belfast over 10 days. Events include an opening carnival parade, street parties, theatre performances, concerts and historical tours of the City and Milltown cemeteries.

**Belfast International
Arts Festival**   PERFORMING ARTS
(www.belfastinternationalartsfestival.com; ⊘mid-late Oct) One of the largest arts festival in the UK and Ireland stretches over three weeks and features theatre, music, dance and talks.

🛏 Sleeping

From backpacker hostels to boutique havens, the range of places to stay in Belfast widens every year. Most budget and mid-range accommodation is south of the centre, in the leafy university district around Botanic Ave, University Rd and Malone Rd, around a 20-minute walk from City Hall. Business hotels and luxury boutiques proliferate in the city centre.

Book ahead on weekends, in summer and during busy festival periods.

🛏 City Centre

★**Bullitt Hotel**   HOTEL **£££**
(Map p540; ☑028-9590 0600; https://bullitt hotel.com; 40a Church Lane; d from £120; @ 🖥; 🚇Victoria Sq) The Bullitt is a haven for the hip, with super-fast wi-fi, smart TVs, an espresso bar, restaurant and two bars (one of them ski-themed) – there's even Bullitt beer on tap. Breakfast (granola and fruit) is left at your door so party animals can roll out of bed at their leisure. Rest assured: rooms are soundproofed.

ORANGE ORDER PARADES

In Northern Ireland the 12 July public holiday marks the anniversary of the Protestant victory at the 1690 Battle of the Boyne. It is celebrated with bonfires, marching bands and street parades staged by the Orange Order with the biggest taking place in Belfast.

Although the 12 July parades have regularly been associated with sectarian stand-offs and outbursts of violence, there has been a concerted effort in recent years to promote the Belfast parade as a cultural celebration, even rebranding it Orangefest.

However, many people still perceive the parades as divisive and confrontational, and with high levels of alcohol consumption among the crowds there is a potential for dangerous situations. Visitors need to be alert for signs of trouble, follow local advice and expect extra security if things escalate in any way.

Fitzwilliam Hotel HOTEL **£££**
(Map p540; ☑028-9044 2080; www.fitzwilliam
hotelbelfast.com; 1-3 Great Victoria St; d from £145;
▣ 🖦; 🖵 Europa Bus Centre) Enjoying an epicentral location, the Fitzwilliam strikes all
the right style notes with its use of designer fabrics, cool colours and mood lighting.
Bedrooms have crisp linen sheets, fluffy
bathrobes and powerful showers, and the
staff are unstintingly helpful.

Ten Square HOTEL **££**
(Map p540; ☑028-9024 1001; www.tensquare.
co.uk; 10 Donegall Sq S; d from £95; 🖦; 🖵 Donegall Sq) A former bank building to the south
of City Hall that's been given a designer
makeover, Ten Square is an opulent boutique hotel with friendly and attentive service. Rooms in the original building have a
decadent decor of blue velvet curtains and
furnishings, while the new extension has
more of a luxe business feel.

🛏 Cathedral Quarter

★**Merchant Hotel** HOTEL **£££**
(Map p540; ☑028-9023 4888; www.themerchan-
thotel.com; 16 Skipper St; d/ste from £160/350;
🅿 ▣ 🖦; 🖵 Queen's Sq) Belfast's most flamboyant hotel occupies the palatial former Ulster
Bank head office. Rooms are individually
decorated with a fabulous fusion of contemporary styling and old-fashioned elegance;
those in the original Victorian building have
opulent floor-length silk curtains while newer rooms have an art-deco inspired theme.
Facilities include a luxurious spa and an
eight-person rooftop hot tub.

Its Great Room (p561) restaurant is
magnificent.

Malmaison Hotel HOTEL **££**
(Map p540; ☑0844 693 0650; www.malmaison-
belfast.com; 34-38 Victoria St; d/ste from £95/270;
▣ 🖦; 🖵 Victoria Sq) Housed in a pair of
beautifully restored Italianate warehouses
(originally built for rival firms in the 1850s),
the Malmaison is a luxurious haven of king-
sized beds, velvet headboards, deep leather
sofas and roll-top baths big enough for two.
The newly done-up rooms sport stencil graffiti and blown-up maps of Belfast; one rock-
star suite even has a purple pool table.

🛏 South Belfast

To get to places on or near Botanic Ave, take
bus 7A or 7B from Howard St. For places on or
near University and Malone Rds, take bus 8A
or 8B, and for places on or near Lisburn Rd,
take bus 9A or 9B. Buses depart from Donegall
Sq E and from the bus stop on Great Victoria
St across from the Europa Bus Centre (p569).

★**Vagabonds** HOSTEL **£**
(Map p540; ☑028-9023 3017; www.vagabonds
belfast.com; 9 University Rd; dm £15-17, d & tw £50;
▣ 🖦; 🖵 Shaftesbury Sq) Comfy bunks, locka-
ble luggage baskets, private shower cubicles,
a beer garden, a pool table and a relaxed
atmosphere are what you get at one of Belfast's best hostels, run by a couple of experienced travellers. It's conveniently located
close to both Queen's and the city centre.

Global Village Backpackers HOSTEL **£**
(Map p540; ☑028-9031 3533; http://globalvillage
belfast.com; 87 University St; dm £14.50-16.50, d
£44; ▣ 🖦; 🖵 Botanic Ave) In a 19th-century
brick terrace house close to Queen's University, Global Village combines period fireplaces
and stained-glass windows with bright wall
murals and wall-mounted guitars. There's a
sociable kitchen and dining area, a beer garden and a barbecue.

Arnie's Backpackers HOSTEL **£**
(Map p540; ☑028-9024 2867; http://arniesback
packers.co.uk; 63 Fitzwilliam St; dm £12-16; ▣ 🖦;

BELFAST'S NEW HOTELS

Belfast is in the midst of a hotel-building boom. In 2017 a total of 27 projects were at
various stages of completion.

The Titanic Quarter is the location of the new **Titanic Hotel** at the **Harland & Wolff
Drawing Offices** (p545). Nearby **AC Hotel by Marriott** is set to open at City Quays.

In the city centre, new hotels include the 304-room **Grand Central** on Bedford St
and **Hampton by Hilton** on Hope St. Meanwhile planning has been granted for a further 10 hotels, with still more in the pre-planning stages.

Other future projects include hotels at the **Crumlin Road Courthouse**, opposite
the **Crumlin Road Gaol** (p547); and in the landmark turreted, red-sandstone **Scottish
Mutual building** at 15 Donegall Sq. Watch this space!

🛏 City Hospital) This long-established old-school hostel is set in a quiet terraced house in the university area. Coal fires and a friendly crowd make it more cosy than cramped.

Belfast Youth Hostel HOSTEL £
(Map p540; ☑ 028-9031 5435; www.hini.org.uk; 22-32 Donegall Rd; dm £11-15, tw with/without bath £38/30; @ 🛜; 🛏 Shaftesbury Sq) Handy amenities at this big, bright HI (Hostelling International) hostel include laundry facilities, secure on-site parking, 24-hour reception (with no lock-out or curfew), and a cafe specialising in breakfast.

Tara Lodge GUESTHOUSE ££
(Map p540; ☑ 028-9059 0900; www.taralodge. com; 36 Cromwell Rd; s/d from £75/85; P @ 🛜; 🛏 Upper Crescent Queens University) In a great location on a quiet side street just a few paces from the buzz of Botanic Ave, this guesthouse feels more like a boutique hotel with its clean-cut, minimalist decor, friendly and efficient staff, and 34 bright and cheerful rooms. Delicious breakfasts include porridge with Bushmills whiskey.

All Seasons B&B B&B ££
(Map p552; ☑ 028-9068 2814; 356 Lisburn Rd; s/d £40/60; P 🛜; 🛏 Cranmore Ave) Away from the centre, but right in the heart of trendy Lisburn Rd, All Seasons is a red-brick villa with bright, colourful bedrooms, modern bathrooms, a stylish little breakfast room and a comfortable lounge.

🛏 Outside the Centre

★ Rayanne House GUESTHOUSE ££
(Map p552; ☑ 028-9042 5859; www.rayanne house.com; 60 Demesne Rd, Holywood; s/d/f from £95/135/160; 🛜; 🛏 Holywood) Just 100m from Holywood Golf Club (p555), this gorgeous 1883 manor house has exquisite rooms – some with balconies and views of Belfast Lough – including a Rory McIlroy–themed room with a shower rail made from an engraved club. Its restaurant (open to nonguests) hosts regular nine-course *Titanic* menus (£69), replicating the last 1st-class meal served aboard.

Old Rectory B&B ££
(Map p552; ☑ 028-9066 7882; www.anoldrectory. co.uk; 148 Malone Rd; s/d/f from £52/80/132; P @ 🛜; 🛏 Myrtlefield Pk) A lovely Victorian house with lots of original stained glass, this former rectory has five spacious bedrooms, a comfortable drawing room with leather

---

sofa, and fancy breakfasts (home-baked bread, porridge with Bushmills whiskey, scrambled eggs with smoked salmon, veggie fry-up and freshly squeezed orange juice). A credit card is required to secure your booking but payment is in cash only.

The inconspicuous driveway is on the left, just past Deramore Park.

Eating

In recent years, Belfast's restaurant scene has been totally transformed by a wave of new restaurants whose standards compete with the best eateries in Europe.

🍴 City Centre

The main shopping area north of Donegall Sq becomes a silent maze of deserted streets and steel shutters after 7pm, but during the day the many pubs, cafes and restaurants do a roaring trade. In the evening, the liveliest part of the city centre stretches south of Donegall Sq to Shaftesbury Sq.

Pablos BURGERS £
(Map p540; http://pablosbelfast.com; 16 Church Lane; burgers £5-6.50; ⏰ noon-10pm Tue-Thu, to 2am Fri & Sat, 2-10pm Sun; 🛏 Victoria Sq) In the heart of Belfast's city-centre nightlife is this wickedly good burger bar serving quality, salt-aged Glenarm Shorthorn beef patties, five types of fries and 20 sauces including Mexican Tequila ranch sauce and sloe gin mayo. Seating is limited to two outdoor tables but you can eat your burger at Muriel's Cafe-Bar (p563) next door or order delivery to the Spaniard (p564).

Archana INDIAN £
(Map p540; ☑ 028-9032 3713; www.archana. co.uk; 53 Dublin Rd; mains lunch £3.50-8.50,

dinner £10-15; ⊙ noon-2pm & 5-11pm Mon-Sat, 5-11pm Sun; ✍; ☐ Dublin Rd) Classy yet unpretentious, with dining rooms on two levels, Archana has a good range of vegetarian dishes, including many incorporating *paneer* (cottage cheese) made on the premises. The *thali* – a platter of three curries – is good value at £15.

★ **Holohan's at the Barge** MODERN IRISH ££
(Map p540; ☎ 028-9023 5973; www.holohansat thebarge.co.uk; Belfast Barge, Lanyon Quay; mains lunch £5-9, dinner £15-22; ⊙ 5-11pm Tue-Sat, 1-7pm Sun; ☐ Oxford St) Aboard the Belfast Barge (p544), Holohan's is a sensational find for inspired twists on seafood and superb cooking of traditional Irish recipes such as crabachain, a mushroom, chestnut and tarragon fritter. Desserts are excellent too and wines from around the world are served by the glass.

★ **Mourne Seafood Bar** SEAFOOD ££
(Map p540; ☎ 028-9024 8544; http://mourne seafood.com; 34-36 Bank St; mains lunch £9-25; ⊙ noon-9.30pm Mon-Thu, noon-4pm & 5-10pm Fri & Sat, 1-9pm Sun; ☐ Royal Ave) ✔ Hugely popular, this informal, pub-like place is all red brick and dark wood with old oil lamps dangling from the ceiling. On the menu are oysters, meltingly sweet scallops, lobster and langoustines sourced from its own shellfish beds, along with luscious fish such as hake, seabream and sea bass. Book ahead for dinner.

The attached Belfast Cookery School (p554) runs a diverse range of culinary classes. Mourne Seafood Bar's sister restaurant (p586) is near County Down's Dundrum Bay.

★ **George's of the Market** MODERN IRISH ££
(Map p540; ☎ 028-9024 0014; http://georges belfast.com; Oxford St; brunch £3.50-8, express lunch £7, dinner £12.50-25; ⊙ 10am-2.30pm Tue, 10am-2.30pm & 5-9.30pm Wed-Sat, 10am-4pm Sun; ☐ Belfast Central) ✔ Many of the ingredients at this 1st-floor restaurant in historic St George's Market (p544) are sourced on site; and on market days, the best seats are on the balcony looking down over the buzz of stall holders and shoppers below. It's revered for its 'Beast of the Market' Ulster fry-up breakfasts, but steaks and cutlets cooked on the grill are excellent too.

OX IRISH ££
(Map p540; ☎ 028-9031 4121; http://oxbelfast. com; 1 Oxford St; 2-/3-course lunch £20/25,

5-course dinner £50; ⊙ noon-2.30pm & 6-9.30pm Tue-Fri, from 1pm Sat; ☐ Oxford St) ✔ A high-ceilinged space with cream-painted brick and warm golden wood creates a theatre-like ambience for the open, Michelin-starred kitchen at the back, which turns out some of Belfast's finest cuisine. The restaurant works with local suppliers and focuses on fine Irish beef, sustainable seafood, and seasonal vegetables and fruit. Book six to eight weeks ahead.

Home MODERN IRISH ££
(Map p540; ☎ 028-9023 4946; www.homebelfast. co.uk; 22 Wellington Pl; mains lunch £10-23.50, dinner £12-23.50; ⊙ noon-4pm & 5-9.30pm Mon-Thu, noon-4pm & 5-10pm Fri, noon-3.30pm & 5-10pm Sat, 1-4pm & 5-9pm Sun; 🛜 ✍ ♿; ☐ Donegall Sq) After beginning life as a pop-up restaurant that took the city's food scene by storm, Home has moved into permanent premises where it continues to win fans for its creative use of seasonal ingredients in its restaurant and attached New York–style deli. Its menus are tailored for vegetarians, vegans, gluten-free diners, slimmers, gluten-free slimmers and theatregoers.

Ginger BISTRO ££
(Map p540; ☎ 028-9024 4421; www.ginger bistro.com; 6-8 Hope St; mains lunch £9-17, dinner £15.50-24; ⊙ 4.30-9.30pm Mon-Wed, noon-10pm Thu-Sat; ✍; ☐ Europa Bus Centre) ✔ Ginger is one of those places you could walk right past without noticing, but you'd be missing out. Cosy and informal, and its food is anything but ordinary – the flame-haired owner/chef (hence the name) really knows what he's doing, sourcing top-quality Irish produce and creating exquisite dishes with frequent Asian inflections. A pre-theatre menu is served from 5pm to 6.45pm Monday to Friday.

McCracken's PUB FOOD ££
(Map p540; ☎ 028-9032 6711; http://mccrackens cafebar.co.uk; 4 Joy's Entry; mains £7.50-17; ⊙ kitchen noon-8pm Mon-Wed, to 9pm Thu & Fri, to 7pm Sat, to 6pm Sun; ☐ Victoria Sq) Buried in the ancient, narrow passageway of Joy's Entry, McCracken's is an unexpectedly contemporary, bare-brick, loft-style space that's great for a cocktail, live music and DJs, and above all, for its gastropub menu: dry-aged Irish beef burgers, smoked seafood chowder and confit belly of pork.

Eipic MODERN IRISH £££

(Map p540; 028-9033 1134; www.deaneseipic.com; 34-40 Howard St; 5-/8-course menu £40/60; noon-1.30pm Fri, 5.30-9.30pm Wed-Sat; ; Donegall Sq) Seasonal local ingredients are given a creative twist at Eipic, a sophisticated fine-dining restaurant owned by Michael Deane. Head chef Danni Barry, who began her cooking career in Deane's kitchen in 2003, is one of only two female chefs in Ireland to have been awarded a Michelin star. Advance booking is essential.

Other restaurants in the Deanes portfolio include **Love Fish** and **Meatlocker** on Howard St, **Deanes at Queen's** (Map p540; 028-9038 2111; www.michaeldeane.co.uk; 1 College Gardens; mains lunch £7-12, dinner £14-20; noon-3pm & 5.30-10pm Mon-Sat, 1-6pm Sun; Methodist College) and **Deanes Deli Bistro** (Map p540; 028-9024 8800; www.michaeldeane.co.uk; 44 Bedford St; mains lunch £6.50-15.50, dinner £10.50-17.50; noon-3pm & 5.30-10pm Mon-Sat; Bedford St).

James St South MODERN IRISH £££

(Map p540; 028-9043 4310; www.jamesstreetsouth.co.uk; 21 James St S; mains lunch £12-20, dinner £15.50-28, 4-/5-course tasting menu £70/80; 5.30-9.30pm Mon & Tue, 12.30-2.30pm & 5.30-9.30pm Wed-Sat; Donegall Sq) Graced by a large, impressionistic landscape by Irish artist Clement McAleer, this starkly beautiful dining room with crisp white table linen creates a perfect stage for the presentation of sophisticated local meat and seafood dishes. The service is relaxed yet highly professional.

Its **Bar & Grill** (028-9560 0700; www.belfastbargrill.co.uk; mains £13.50-28.50; noon-10pm) is less formal but the quality of the food is just as high.

Great Room FRENCH £££

(Map p540; 028-9023 4888; www.themerchanthotel.com; 16 Skipper St; 2-/3-course lunch £19.50/24.50, afternoon tea £25-30, dinner mains £19.50-28.50; 12.30-2.15pm & 5.30-9.45pm Mon-Thu, 12.30-2.15pm & 6-10pm Fri & Sat, 12.30-8.30pm Sun; Queen's Sq) Set in the former banking hall of the Ulster Bank head office within the Merchant Hotel (p558), the Great Room is a jaw-dropping extravaganza of gilded stucco, red plush, white-marble cherubs and a vast crystal chandelier glittering beneath a glass dome. The menu matches the decor: decadent but delicious (foie gras, truffles etc).

✖ Cathedral Quarter

Coppi ITALIAN ££

(Map p540; 028-9031 1959; www.coppi.co.uk; Unit 2, St Anne's Sq; mains £10.50-24; noon-10pm Mon-Thu & Sun, to 11pm Fri & Sat; Queen's Sq) In a buzzy dining room with high ceilings and leather booths in the Cathedral Quarter, Coppi serves modern Italian dishes like Tuscan goat pappardelle and roast wild hake. The sourdough breads and excellent desserts – tiramisu, amaretto panna cotta, and chocolate and salted caramel torta – are freshly prepared daily.

★**Muddlers Club** MODERN IRISH £££

(Map p540; 028-9031 3199; www.themuddlersclubbelfast.com; Warehouse Lane, off Waring St; mains £16-24, tasting menu £45; noon-2.45pm & 5.30-10pm Tue-Sat; Queen's Sq) Industrial-style deco, friendly service and rustic dishes that allow fresh local ingredients to shine are a winning combination at one of Belfast's best restaurants. Named after a society of Irish revolutionaries co-founded by Wolfe Tone who held meetings at the same spot in the 1790s, the Muddlers Club is hidden in an alleyway off Commercial Court. Book ahead.

✖ South Belfast

Maggie May's CAFE £

(Map p540; 028-9032 2662; www.maggiemaysbelfastcafe.co.uk; 50 Botanic Ave; mains £4.50-7.50; 8am-11pm Mon-Sat, 9am-11pm Sun; Botanic) This is a classic little cafe with cosy wooden booths, murals of old Belfast and a host of hungover students wolfing down huge Ulster fry-ups. The all-day breakfast menu includes French toast and pancake stacks, while lunch can be soup and a sandwich or a burger.

There's a newer branch in **Stranmillis** (Map p540; 028-9066 8515; www.maggiemaysbelfastcafe.co.uk; 2 Malone Rd; mains £4.50-7.50; 8am-11pm Mon-Sat, 9am-11pm Sun; Methodist College).

Cafe Fish FISH & CHIPS £

(Map p552; 539 Lisburn Rd; mains £5.50-10; noon-9pm Wed-Sun; ; Marlborough Pk) This no-frills, sit-down cafe deep-fries crispy battered haddock along with mushy peas and chunky chips. If you're in a hurry, there's a takeaway branch just across the street.

BELFAST EATING

Barking Dog
BISTRO ££

(Map p540; ☑ 028-9066 1885; www.barkingdog belfast.com; 33-35 Malone Rd; mains £16-30, 5 tapas dishes £15.50; ☺ noon-2.30pm & 5-10pm Mon-Thu, to 11pm Fri & Sat, noon-4pm & 5-9pm Sun; 🚗 👶; ☐ Eglantine Ave) Chunky hardwood, bare brick, candlelight and modern design create the atmosphere of a stylishly restored farmhouse. The menu completes the feeling of cosiness and comfort with satisfying dishes such as their signature burger of meltingly tender beef shin with caramelised onion and horseradish cream, and sweet-potato gnocchi.

Shu
MODERN IRISH ££

(Map p540; ☑ 028-9038 1655; www.shu-restaurant.com; 253 Lisburn Rd; mains £12.50-26.50; ☺ noon-2.30pm & 6-10pm Mon-Sat; ☐ Marlborough Pk) Lording it over fashionable Lisburn Rd since 2000, Shu is the granddaddy of Belfast chic, and is still winning plaudits for its French-influenced food: slow-cooked blade of beef; Himalayan salt-aged sirloin; and seared scallops with samphire and smoked fennel butter.

Molly's Yard
IRISH ££

(Map p540; ☑ 028-9032 2600; www.mollysyard.co.uk; 1 College Green Mews; mains bistro £10, restaurant £13-25; ☺ noon-9.30pm Mon-Sat; 🚗; ☐ Queen's University) 🍴 A restored Victorian stables courtyard is the setting for this charming restaurant, with a cosy bar-bistro on the ground floor, outdoor tables in the yard and a rustic dining room (open from 6pm) in the airy roof space upstairs. The menu is seasonal and sticks to half a dozen each of starters and mains.

It also has its own craft beers, brewed at Lisburn's Hilden Brewery (p554).

Café Conor
CAFE ££

(Map p540; ☑ 028-9066 3266; www.cafeconor.com; 11a Stranmillis Rd; mains £9-15; ☺ 9am-10pm Mon-Sat, to 9pm Sun; ☐ Ulster Museum) Set in the glass-roofed former studio of Belfast artist William Conor, this light-filled, laid-back bistro offers a range of pastas, salads, burgers and stir-fries, along with favourites such as fish and chips with mushy peas and a daily pie special. The breakfast menu, which includes waffles with bacon and maple syrup, is served till 5pm.

★ Saphyre
MODERN IRISH £££

(Map p540; ☑ 028-9068 8606; www.saphyrerestaurant.com; 135 Lisburn Rd; mains lunch £12-16, dinner £18-28; ☺ noon-3pm & 5-10pm Wed-Sat; ☐ Ulsterville Ave) Spectacularly set inside the 1924 Ulsterville Presbyterian Church (behind an interior-design showroom), Saphyre serves some of the most sophisticated cooking in Belfast today. Menus change seasonally and include a five-course tasting menu (£50); each dish is a masterpiece. Next door is the cafe and patisserie the Vestry, serving brunches, cakes and pastries, and meals such as lamb moussaka and Spanish omelette.

🍴 Outside the Centre

★ Il Pirata
ITALIAN ££

(Map p552; ☑ 028-9067 3421; www.ilpirata belfast.com; 279-281 Upper Newtownards Rd, Ballyhackamore; mains £8-18.50; ☺ noon-10pm Sun-Thu, to 11pm Fri & Sat; ☐ Hillview Ave) This rustic Italian restaurant is a firm favourite among Belfast's foodies for its flavoursome dishes like duck ragu with gnocchi and Portavogie prawn linguine, served in a contemporary, stripped-back dining room.

Its sister restaurant Coppi (p561) serves a similar menu.

★ Fontana
MODERN IRISH ££

(Map p552; ☑ 028-9080 9908; www.restaurant fontana.com; 61 High St, Holywood; 2-/3-course menu £20.50/23.50, mains £17-30; ☺ noon-2.30pm & 5.30-10pm Tue-Fri, 5.30-10pm Sat, noon-4pm Sun; 🚗; ☐ Holywood) 🍴 Fontana is in the heart of the village-like neighbourhood of Holywood, but hidden upstairs from a covered passageway. Its sublime modern-Irish cooking – Portavogie prawn risotto, vegetable moussaka and maple- and cumin-glazed chicken with parsnip gratin – incorporates herbs and salad ingredients from its own courtyard garden.

Acapulco
MEXICAN ££

(Map p552; ☑ 028-9029 6400; http://acapulco.ie; 255 Upper Newtownards Rd; mains £11-15; ☺ noon-3pm & 5-9pm Tue-Thu, noon-10pm Fri & Sat, 5-9pm Sun; 👶; ☐ Hillview Ave) Popular with politicians and parliamentary staffers from nearby Stormont (p553), this sparingly but colourfully decorated place dishes up authentic burritos, chimichanga, flauta, enchiladas, fajita platters, Yucatán-spiced chicken skewers and other Mexican classics in huge portions. It has a good niños (kids) menu too. It's one of several stellar restaurants along Upper Newtownards Rd in Ballyhackamore.

Drinking & Nightlife

Belfast's pub scene is lively and friendly, with the older traditional pubs complemented by a rising tide of stylish designer bars. Many pubs are also great places to dine.

Getting past the bouncers on the door at pubs and clubs can be a problem. Some of the flashier venues have a dress code – usually no sneakers or football colours.

City Centre

★ Perch
ROOFTOP BAR

(Map p540; www.theperchbelfast.com; 5th fl, The Gate, 42 Franklin St; ⊙ 1pm-1am Mon-Sat, to midnight Sun; ⊡ Bedford St) Piped-in birdsong and flowery murals set the scene as an industrial lift takes you up to the Perch, a lively rooftop bar in the rafters of a Victorian building, with hanging plants and chilled-out tunes. In winter there's boozy hot chocolate and blankets, while the summer cocktail menu includes Pimm's punch and Bellinis. They also have pizzas (£6.50 to £8.50).

★ Filthy Quarter
BAR

(Map p540; www.thefilthyquarter.com; 45 Dublin Rd; ⊙ 1pm-1am Mon-Sat, to midnight Sun; ⊡ Dublin Rd) Four individually and collectively fabulous bars make up the Filthy Quarter: retro-trad-style, bric-a-brac-filled **Filthy McNastys**, hosting local musicians from 10pm nightly; the fairy-lit **Secret Garden**, a two-storey beer garden with watering cans for drinks coolers; **Gypsy Lounge** (Tuesday, Thursday, Friday, Saturday and Sunday nights), with a gypsy caravan DJ booth; and a chandelier- and candelabra-adorned cocktail bar, **Filthy Chic**.

★ Love & Death Inc
COCKTAIL BAR

(Map p540; www.loveanddeathinc.com; 10a Ann St; ⊙ 4pm-1am Mon-Thu, noon-3am Fri & Sat, 2pm-midnight Sun; ⊡ Victoria Sq) More like a cool inner-city house party, speakeasy-style Love & Death Inc is secreted up a flight of stairs above a pizza joint. Its living-room-style bar has outrageous decor, feisty Latin American–influenced food, feistier cocktails and a wild nightclub in the attic on weekends.

★ Muriel's Cafe-Bar
BAR

(Map p540; ☑ 028-9033 2445; 12-14 Church Lane; ⊙ 11.30am-1am Mon-Fri, 10am-1am Sat, 11.30am-midnight Sun; ⊡ Queen's Sq) Hats meet harlotry (ask who Muriel was) in this delightfully snug and welcoming bar with retro-chic decor, old sofas and armchairs, heavy fabrics in shades of olive and dark red, gilt-framed mirrors and a cast-iron fireplace. Gin is Muriel's favourite tipple and there's a range of exotic brands to mix with your tonic. The food menu is pretty good too.

Bittles Bar
PUB

(Map p540; 103 Victoria St; ⊙ 11am-11pm Mon-Thu, to 1am Fri & Sat, noon-6pm Sun; ⊡ Victoria Sq) A cramped and staunchly traditional bar, Bittles is a 19th-century triangular red-brick building decorated with gilded shamrocks. The wedge-shaped interior is covered in paintings of Ireland's literary heroes by local artist Joe O'Kane. In pride of place on the back wall is a large canvas depicting Yeats, Joyce, Behan, Beckett and Wilde. It has a good range of craft beers.

Harlem Cafe
BAR

(Map p540; http://harlembelfast.com; 34-36 Bedford St; ⊙ 8am-5pm Mon-Thu, to 9pm Fri, 9am-9pm Sat, to 4pm Sun; ⚆; ⊡ Bedford St) In a cornflower-blue building with eclectic art covering the walls, the Harlem is a great place for lounging over coffee, or enjoying a glass of wine after hitting the shops. A full food menu spans breakfast to brunch to pre-theatre dinner; live music plays on Friday and Saturday.

Garrick Bar
PUB

(Map p540; www.thegarrickbar.com; 29 Chichester St; ⊙ 11.30am-1am Mon-Sat, 12.30pm-midnight Sun; ⚆; ⊡ Victoria Sq) First opened in 1870, the Garrick hangs on to a traditional atmosphere with acres of dark wood panelling, tiled floors, a pillared bar and old brass oil lamps. Snug booths have buttoned leather benches, and each room has a real coal fire. Trad-music sessions take place in the front bar at 9.30pm on Wednesday, 5pm Friday and 9pm Sunday.

White's Tavern
PUB

(Map p540; www.whitesbelfast.com; 1-4 Wine Cellar Entry; ⊙ noon-11pm Mon & Tue, to 1am Wed-Sat, to midnight Sun; ⊡ Royal Ave) Established in 1630 but rebuilt in 1790, White's claims to be Belfast's oldest tavern (unlike a pub, a tavern provided food and lodging). Downstairs is a traditional Irish bar with an open peat fire and live music nightly; upstairs, Vandal Geek and Movie Bar hosts regular retro film nights and Monday-night *Dungeons & Dragons* games.

BELFAST DRINKING & NIGHTLIFE

Kelly's Cellars   PUB

(Map p540; www.kellyscellars.com; 30-32 Bank St; ⊘11.30am-1am Mon-Sat, 1pm-midnight Sun; ☐ Royal Ave) Kelly's is Belfast's oldest pub (1720) – as opposed to tavern – and was a meeting place for Henry Joy McCracken and the United Irishmen when they were planning the 1798 Rising. It pulls in a broad cross-section of Belfast society and is a great place to catch traditional-music sessions at 4.30pm on Saturdays.

 Cathedral Quarter

★ Established Coffee   COFFEE

(Map p540; http://established.coffee; 54 Hill St; ⊘7am-6pm Mon-Fri, 8am-6pm Sat, 9am-6pm Sun, kitchen until 3pm daily; ☐ Queen's Sq) Heading up Belfast's burgeoning coffee scene, Established takes its beans seriously, serving a range of specialist drip coffees, as well as interesting breakfast items like cheesy French toast with braised kale. Its bright corner plot with concrete floors, low-hanging bulb lights and shared wooden counters makes it a popular spot to linger with a laptop.

★ Duke of York   PUB

(Map p540; ☑028-9024 1062; www.dukeofyork belfast.com; 11 Commercial Ct; ⊘11.30am-midnight Mon, to 1am Tue-Sat, 1-9pm Sun; ☐ Queen's Sq) In a cobbled alleyway off buzzing Hill St, the snug, traditional Duke feels like a living museum. There's regular live music; local

band Snow Patrol played some of their earliest gigs here. Outside on Commercial Ct, a canopy of umbrellas leads to an outdoor area covered with murals depicting Belfast life; it takes on a street-party atmosphere in warm weather.

Former Sinn Féin leader Gerry Adams worked behind the bar here during his student days in 1971.

★ John Hewitt   PUB

(Map p540; www.thejohnhewitt.com; 51 Donegall St; ⊘11.30am-1am Mon-Fri, noon-1am Sat, 7pm-1am Sun; ☐ Queen's Sq) Named for the Belfast poet and socialist, the John Hewitt is one of those treasured bars that has no TV or gaming machines, just the murmur of conversation. It's a good place to try Jawbox gin, made by the bar's owner Gerry White, and craft beers from Lisburn's Hilden brewery (p554).There are regular sessions of folk, jazz and bluegrass from 9pm.

Spaniard   PUB

(Map p540; www.thespaniardbar.com; 3 Skipper St; ⊘noon-1pm Mon-Sat, to midnight Sun; ☐ Queen's Sq) Specialising in rum (more than 30 kinds), this narrow, crowded bar has more atmosphere in one battered sofa than most 'style bars' have in their shiny entirety. Friendly staff, an eclectic crowd and cool tunes played at a volume that still allows you to talk: bliss. Nearby burger joint Pablos (p559) delivers to the bar.

GAY & LESBIAN BELFAST

Belfast's gay and lesbian scene is concentrated in the Cathedral Quarter around Union St. Nightspots include Kremlin, Maverick and Union Street.

Ireland's largest celebration of gay, lesbian, bisexual and transgender culture, **Belfast Pride** (p557) in late July to early August, culminates in a huge city-centre parade.

Kremlin (Map p540; www.kremlin-belfast.com; 96 Donegall St; ⊘10pm-2.30am Tue, Thu & Sun, 9pm-3am Fri & Sat; ☐ Donegall St) Gay-owned and -operated, the Soviet-kitsch-themed Kremlin is the heart and soul of Northern Ireland's gay scene. A statue of Lenin guides you into Tsar, the preclub bar, from where the Long Bar leads into the main clubbing zone, Red Square. Revolution on Saturdays, with DJs mixing up dance, house, pop and commercial, is the flagship event.

Union Street (Map p540; www.unionstreetbar.com; 8-14 Union St; ⊘noon-1am Mon-Thu, to 1.30am Fri & Sat, 1.30pm-1am Sun; ☎; ☐ Donegall St) A stylish modern bar with retro decor and lots of bare brick and dark wood (check out the Belfast sinks in the loo), Union Street attracts a mixed gay and straight crowd with nightly cabaret and karaoke, and a tempting food menu. Sunday's bingo night pulls in the punters.

Maverick (Map p540; www.facebook.com/pg/maverickbarbelfast; 1 Union St; ⊘5pm-1am Mon-Sat, to midnight Sun; ☐ Donegall St) Maverick is most popular for its Boombox nightclub, upstairs from the main bar.

National Grande Café
BAR
(Map p540; www.thenationalbelfast.com; 62 High St; ⊙8.30am-11pm Mon-Wed, to 1am Thu, to 3am Fri, 9.30am-3am Sat, 9.30am-10pm Sun; 🖵 Victoria Sq) Behind the oyster-grey ground-floor facade of the 1897 former National Bank building, and through its post-industrial interior, is the National's pièce de résistance – the city's biggest beer garden, which hosts regular barbecues and live music. Stop by for breakfast, a weekday sandwich (served until 7pm) or Sunday brunch.

On Friday and Saturday nights DJs spin the tunes at club Sixty6, with several bars and a dance floor spread out over four floors.

McHugh's Bar & Restaurant
PUB
(Map p540; www.mchughsbar.com; 29-31 Queen's Sq; ⊙noon-midnight Mon-Thu, to 1am Fri & Sat, 1-11pm Sun; 🖵 Victoria Sq) In Belfast's oldest surviving building, dating from 1711, McHugh's retains a wonderfully traditional feel with its old wooden booths and benches, and pours a superb pint of Guinness.

Northern Whig
BAR
(Map p540; www.thenorthernwhig.com; 2-10 Bridge St; ⊙10am-11pm Mon & Tue, to 1.30am Wed-Sat, 10am-midnight Sun; 🖵 Royal Ave) Northern Whig is set in an elegant Georgian printing works, with relaxing sofas and armchairs encouraging serious afternoon loafing, though the pace hots up considerably after 5pm on Friday and Saturday when the party crowd piles in.

🍺 Titanic Quarter

Box Nightclub
CLUB
(Map p540; www.boxnightclub.com; 2 Queen's Quay; ⊙9.30pm-2am Tue-Thu & Sat; 🖵 Station St) Inside the Odyssey Complex (p546), state-of-the-art nightclub Box spans two floors, six bars and two VIP rooms.

🍺 South Belfast

Eglantine
PUB
(Map p540; www.eglantinebar.com; 32 Malone Rd; ⊙11.30am-midnight Sun-Tue, to 1am Wed-Sat; 🛜; 🖵 Eglantine Ave) The 'Eg' is a local institution, and widely reckoned to be the best of Belfast's many student pubs. It serves good beer and decent food, and hosts numerous events: Monday is quiz night and Tuesday is open-mic night; other nights see DJs spin and bands perform. Bonus: *Pac-Man* machine.

Botanic Inn
PUB
(Map p540; www.thebotanicinn.com; 23-27 Malone Rd; ⊙11.30am-1am Mon, Tue, Thu & Fri, 11.30am-2am Wed & Sat, noon-midnight Sun; 🛜; 🖵 Eglantine Ave) Wednesday at the 'Bot' is one of Belfast's longest-running student nights, with live music and DJs on the decks in the basement club. The party continues at the weekend; live sport is screened in the beer garden.

Lavery's
BAR
(Map p540; www.laverysbelfast.com; 14 Bradbury Pl; ⊙11.30am-1am Mon-Sat, 12.30pm-midnight Sun; 🖵 Bradbury Pl) Managed by the same family since 1918, Lavery's is a vast, multi-level, packed-to-the-gills boozing emporium, crammed with drinkers young and old, from students to tourists and business people to bikers. Its four bars include the Public Bar (acoustic music Monday and Tuesday; retro disco Wednesday to Saturday); the bohemian Back Bar with a jukebox; and Woodworkers rotating tap room.

Hatfield House
PUB
(Map p540; www.hatfieldhousebelfast.com; 130 Ormeau Rd; ⊙11.30am-1am Mon-Sat, to midnight Sun; 🖵 Hatfield St) On increasingly trendy Ormeau Rd, Hatfield House is no fly-by-night – its original timber and brass bar fixtures and ornate ceiling mouldings are the work of the *Titanic*'s craftsmen. Live music includes acoustic and folk; it's also a popular spot for watching big-screen sport such as football and GAA (Gaelic Athletics Association) events.

Shine
CLUB
(Map p540; www.shine.net; University Rd; entry £20; 🖵 Queen's University) In Shine, the QUB Student Union (www.qubsu.org; ⊙hours vary; 🛜) has one of the city's best club nights, with resident and guest DJs pumping out harder, heavier dance music than most of Belfast's other clubs. Student or other photo ID required. The club night is held irregularly; check the website for upcoming events at Mandela Hall and other venues.

🍺 Outside the Centre

Dirty Duck
PUB
(Map p552; http://thedirtyduckalehouse.co.uk; 3 Kinnegar Rd, Holywood; ⊙noon-11pm Sun-Wed, to 1am Thu-Sat; 🖵 Holywood) On a sunny afternoon, it's hard to beat the Belfast Lough–facing beer garden at this welcoming local, just footsteps from Holywood train station. It's a great bet at any time for craft ales on

tap, frequent live music and its panoramic upstairs restaurant.

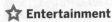 Entertainment

A good place to get the low-down on live music and club nights is the Oh Yeah Music Centre (p543).

Other resources include the Visit Belfast Welcome Centre (p569), **Big List** (www.thebiglist.co.uk) and **Culture Northern Ireland** (www.culturenorthernireland.org).

Live Music

Pubs with regular live sessions of traditional Irish music include the Botanic Inn (p565), the Garrick Bar (p563), White's Tavern (p563) and Kelly's Cellars (p564).

For jazz and blues, head to the John Hewitt (p564) or the Black Box.

★ Belfast Empire LIVE MUSIC
(Map p540; www.thebelfastempire.com; 42 Botanic Ave; entry live bands £3-22.50; ⊙ 11.30am-1am Mon-Sat, 12.30pm-midnight Sun; ⊠ Botanic) A converted late-Victorian church (reputed to be haunted) with three floors of entertainment, the Empire is a legendary live-music venue. Look out for stand-up comedy and quiz nights too.

Limelight LIVE MUSIC
(Map p540; www.limelightbelfast.com; 17-19 Ormeau Ave; ⊠ Agincourt Ave) This combined pub and club is one of the city's top venues for live rock and indie music. Past acts have included Oasis, Franz Ferdinand, the Manic Street Preachers and the Kaiser Chiefs.

Black Box ARTS CENTRE
(Map p540; www.blackboxbelfast.com; 18-22 Hill St; ⊠ Victoria Sq) Black Box is an intimate venue for live music, theatre, comedy, film and more on buzzy Hill St in the heart of the Cathedral Quarter.

An Droichead LIVE MUSIC
(Map p540; www.androichead.com; 20 Cooke St, Lower Ormeau; ⊠ University Ave) This Irish cultural centre offers Irish-language courses, stages traditional dance and *céilidh* workshops, hosts art exhibitions and serves as a live-music venue. It's a great place to hear live Irish folk music performed by big names from around the country, as well as up-and-coming local talent.

Sonic Arts Research Centre LIVE MUSIC
(SARC; Map p540; www.sarc.qub.ac.uk; Cloreen Park; ⊠ Eglantine Ave) Queen's University's School of Music stages free lunchtime recit-

als on Thursday and regular evening concerts in the beautiful, hammerbeam-roofed Harty Room (p566) and at the Sonic Arts Research Centre. You can download a program from the website; click on the Music at Queen's link.

SSE Arena CONCERT VENUE
(Map p540; www.ssearenabelfast.com; 2 Queen's Quay; ⊠ Station St) Within the Odyssey Complex (p546), this is the venue for big entertainment events such as rock and pop concerts and stage shows. It's also the home stadium of the Belfast Giants (p567) ice-hockey team.

Classical Music

Ulster Hall CONCERT VENUE
(Map p540; www.ulsterhall.co.uk; 34 Bedford St; ⊠ Bedford St) Dating from 1862, Ulster Hall is a popular venue for a range of events including rock concerts, lunchtime organ recitals and performances by the Ulster Orchestra (http://ulsterorchestra.com).

Waterfront Hall CONCERT VENUE
(Map p540; www.waterfront.co.uk; 2 Lanyon Pl; ⊠ Belfast Waterfront) The impressive 2200-seat Waterfront is Belfast's flagship concert venue, hosting local, national and international performers from pop stars to symphony orchestras.

Crescent Arts Centre ARTS CENTRE
(Map p540; www.crescentarts.org; 2-4 University Rd; ⊠ Upper Crescent) The Crescent hosts a range of concerts, plays, workshops, readings and dance classes. It's also the headquarters of the Belfast Book Festival (p557) and the dance festival CityDance (p556).

Harty Room CLASSICAL MUSIC
(Map p540; School of Music, University Sq; ⊠ Queen's University) The beautiful, hammerbeam-roofed Harty Room is sometimes used for free lunchtime recitals staged by Queen's University's School of Music.

Theatre

★ MAC ARTS CENTRE
(Metropolitan Arts Centre; Map p540; http://themaclive.com; St Anne's Sq; ⊠ Queens Sq) The MAC is a beautifully designed venue overlooking the neoclassical St Anne's Sq development, with its two theatres hosting regular performances of drama, stand-up comedy and talks, including shows for children. The centre's three galleries stage a rolling program of exhibitions, which are generally free. There's also a cafe here.

Lyric Theatre
THEATRE
(Map p552; www.lyrictheatre.co.uk; 55 Ridgeway St; Sandhurst Dr) This stunning modern theatre is built on the site of the old Lyric Theatre, where Hollywood star Liam Neeson first trod the boards (he is now a patron).

Cinema

Queen's Film Theatre
CINEMA
(QFT; Map p540; www.queensfilmtheatre.com; 20 University Sq; College Green) A major venue for the Belfast Film Festival (p557), this two-screen art-house cinema is close to Queen's University.

Movie House
CINEMA
(Map p540; www.moviehouse.co.uk; 14 Dublin Rd; Dublin Rd) Convenient city-centre 10-screen multiplex.

Odyssey Cinemas
CINEMA
(Map p540; www.odysseycinemas.co.uk; Odyssey Pavilion; Station St) Belfast's biggest multiplex has 12 screens and stadium seats throughout. It's part of the Odyssey Complex (p546).

Spectator Sports

Casement Park
GAELIC FOOTBALL
(Map p552; www.antrimgaa.net; Andersonstown Rd; Owenvarragh Pk) Located in West Belfast; you can see Gaelic football and hurling here.

Windsor Park
FOOTBALL
(Map p552; www.irishfa.com; Donegall Ave; Windsor Rd) Northern Ireland plays its home games at the National Football Stadium at Windsor Park, 2km south of Belfast city centre; see the Irish FA website for details of upcoming matches.

Belfast Giants
ICE HOCKEY
(Map p540; www.belfastgiants.com; 2 Queen's Quay; Station St) The Belfast Giants ice-hockey team draws big crowds to the SSE Arena (p566) at the Odyssey Complex (p546); the season is September to March. The arena also hosts indoor sporting events including tennis and athletics.

Kingspan Stadium
RUGBY
(Map p552; www.ulsterrugby.com; 134 Mount Merrion Ave; Mount Merrion Parish Church) This 18,000-capacity stadium is the home of Ulster Rugby.

Shopping

Belfast's compact city centre is great for shopping. Don't miss St George's Market (p544) for food and local arts and crafts. Whiskey enthusiasts should check out

LISBURN ROAD

Belfast's chicest shopping district is Lisburn Rd. From Eglantine Ave out to Balmoral Ave it's lined with red-brick and mock-Tudor facades housing fashion boutiques, interior-design studios, art galleries, antique shops, delicatessens, coffee houses, wine bars and top restaurants, nestled among South Belfast's wealthy, tree-lined suburbs.

Friend at Hand. You'll find all the usual high-street chains and department stores in the central shopping area north of City Hall, centred on **Royal Ave**.

Other shopping districts include the fashionable Lisburn Rd.

★Co Couture
CHOCOLATE
(Map p540; www.cocouture.co.uk; 7 Chichester St; 10am-6pm Mon-Sat; Donegall Sq) This small subterranean shop has won prizes for its hand-crafted chocolates made using raise trade (a step up from fair trade) chocolate from Madagascar. The range includes dairy-free chocolates, hot chocolate and vegetarian marshmallows. Also runs chocolate-making classes.

★Friend at Hand
ALCOHOL
(Map p540; 028-9032 9969; 36 Hill St; 11.30am-7pm Mon-Sat, noon-6pm Sun; Queen's Sq) This whiskey museum and shop has more than 200 different whiskies for sale as well as displays of old whiskey paraphernalia and 400 bottles from the private collection of Belfast bar magnate Willie Jack – some more than 100 years old. Whiskies for sale include an £11,000 bottle of Midleton, but there are more affordable local tipples available too.

★Studio Souk
ARTS & CRAFTS
(Map p540; www.studiosouk.com; 60-62 Ann St; 9.30am-5.30pm Mon-Sat, 1-5.30pm Sun; Victoria Sq) With three floors filled with pieces by over 80 local artists and designers, including pottery, printed canvas bags, tea towels and artwork – Souk is the perfect place to pick up Belfast-themed gifts and souvenirs.

No Alibis Bookstore
BOOKS
(Map p540; http://noalibis.com; 83 Botanic Ave; 9am-5.30pm Mon-Sat, 1-5pm Sun; Botanic Ave) Specialising in crime fiction (and even

---

ⓘ TRANSPORT PASSES

Smartlink Travel Card

If you plan on using city buses a lot, it's worth buying a **Metro Smartlink Travel Card** (available from the Metro kiosk, the Visit Belfast Welcome Centre and the Europa Bus Centre). The card costs an initial fee of £1, plus £10.50 per 10 journeys – you can get it topped up as you want. When you board the bus, you simply place the card on top of the ticket machine and it automatically issues a ticket.

Metro dayLink Cards

You can also buy **Metro dayLink Cards** (£3.50; available from the same places), giving you unlimited bus travel within the City Zone all day Monday to Saturday.

Belfast Visitor Pass

The **Belfast Visitor Pass** (per one/two/three days £6.50/11/14.50) allows unlimited travel on bus and train services in Belfast and around, and discounts on admission to Titanic Belfast and other attractions. You can buy it online at www.translink.co.uk and at airports, main train and bus stations, the Metro kiosk on Donegall Sq and the Visit Belfast Welcome Centre.

---

appearing in print in Colin Bateman's *Mystery Man* series), this small, independent bookshop run by friendly and knowledgable staff hosts regular poetry readings, book signings and monthly jazz nights.

Steensons JEWELLERY
(Map p540; www.thesteensons.com; Bedford House, Bedford St; ⊙10am-5.30pm Mon-Wed, Fri & Sat, to 8pm Thu; 🚌Bedford St) This city-centre showroom sells a range of stylish, contemporary, handmade jewellery in silver, gold and platinum, from the Steensons workshop (p630) in Glenarm, County Antrim. Steensons is the creator of *Game of Thrones* jewellery; look out for its similarly inspired designs.

Wicker Man ARTS & CRAFTS
(Map p540; www.thewickerman.co.uk; 18 High St; ⊙9.30am-6pm Mon-Wed, Fri & Sat, 9.30am-9pm Thu, 1.30-6pm Sun; 🚌Victoria Sq) In addition to offering knitting and crochet classes, arty Wicker Man sells a wide range of contemporary Irish crafts and gifts, including silver jewellery, glassware and knitwear.

ⓘ Information

DANGERS & ANNOYANCES

Even at the height of the Troubles, Belfast wasn't a particularly dangerous city for tourists. It's still best, however, to avoid the so-called 'interface areas' – near the peace lines in West Belfast, Crumlin Rd and the Short Strand (just east of Queen's Bridge) – after dark. If in doubt about any area, ask your hotel or hostel.

Dissident Republican groups continue a campaign of violent attacks aimed at police and military targets, but have very little public support. Security alerts usually have no effect on visiting tourists (other than roads being closed), but be aware of the potential danger. You can follow the Police Service of Northern Ireland (PSNI) on Twitter (@policeserviceni) and receive immediate notification of any alerts.

You will notice a more obvious security presence than elsewhere in the UK and Ireland, such as armoured police Land Rovers and fortified police stations. There are doormen on many city-centre pubs.

If you want to take photos of fortified police stations, army posts or other military or quasi-military paraphernalia, get permission first, just to be on the safe side.

EMERGENCY

Police, Fire & Ambulance (📞999)
Victim Support NI (📞028-9024 3133; www. victimsupportni.co.uk; 1st fl, Albany House, 73-75 Great Victoria St; 🚌Europa Bus Centre) is an independent charity that supports people affected by crime.

INTERNET ACCESS

Belfast has a comprehensive network of 104 free wi-fi hot spots at visitor attractions, community and leisure centres and other public buildings. Search for BelfastWiFi.

LEFT LUGGAGE

A legacy of the Troubles is that, due to security concerns, there are no left-luggage facilities at Belfast's airports, train stations and bus stations. However, most hotels and hostels allow guests to leave their bags for the day, and the Visit Belfast Welcome Centre also offers a daytime left-luggage service.

MEDICAL SERVICES

Accident and emergency services are available at a number of hospitals.

Belfast City Hospital (✆ 028-9032 9241; www.belfasttrust.hscni.net/hospitals/BelfastCity%20Hospital.htm; 51 Lisburn Rd; 🚋 City Hospital)

Mater Hospital (✆ 028-9074 1211; www.belfasttrust.hscni.net/hospitals/MaterHospital.htm; 45-51 Crumlin Rd; 🚋 Mater Hospital)

Royal Victoria Hospital (✆ 028-9024 0503; www.belfasttrust.hscni.net/hospitals/RVHIntro.htm; 274 Grosvenor Rd; 🚋 Falls Rd)

Ulster Hospital (✆ 028-9048 4511; www.setrust.hscni.net/2024.htm; Upper Newtownards Rd, Dundonald; 🚋 Ulster Hospital)

POST

Main Post Office (Map p540; www.postoffice.co.uk; 12-16 Bridge St; ⏰ 9am-5.30pm Mon-Sat; 🚋 High St) Branches at **Donegall Sq** (Map p540; www.postoffice.co.uk; 16 Howard St; ⏰ 7am-6pm Mon-Fri, 9am-6pm Sat; 🚋 Donegall Sq) and **Queen's University** (Map p540; www.postoffice.co.uk; 95 University Rd; ⏰ 8am-9pm Mon-Sat, 10am-6pm Sun; 🚋 Queen's University).

TOURIST INFORMATION

Queen's Welcome Centre (p547)

Visit Belfast Welcome Centre (Map p540; ✆ 028-9024 6609; http://visit-belfast.com; 9 Donegall Sq N; ⏰ 9am-7pm Mon-Sat, 11am-4pm Sun Jun-Sep, 9am-5.30pm Mon-Sat, 11am-4pm Sun Oct-May; 🛜; 🚋 Donegall Sq)

There are also tourist information desks at **George Best Belfast City Airport** (Map p552; ✆ 028-9093 5372; George Best Belfast City Airport; ⏰ 7.30am-7pm Mon-Fri, 7.30am-4.30pm Sat, 11am-6pm Sun); **Belfast International Airport** (✆ 028-9448 4677; Belfast International Airport; ⏰ 7.30am-7pm Mon-Fri, 7.30am-5.30pm Sat, 8am-11am Sun)

ⓘ Getting There & Away

AIR

Belfast International Airport (Aldergrove; ✆ 028-9448 4848; www.belfastairport.com; Airport Rd) Located 30km northwest of the city; flights serve the UK and Europe, and in the USA, New York and Boston.

George Best Belfast City Airport (BHD; Map p552; ✆ 028-9093 9093; www.belfastcityairport.com; Airport Rd) Located 6km northeast of the city centre; flights serve the UK and Europe.

BOAT

Apart from services with **Stena Line** (Map p552; ✆ 08447 707070; www.stenaline.co.uk; Victorial Terminal, 4 West Bank Rd; trips from £79; 🚌 96) and **Steam Packet Company** (Map p552; ✆ 08722 992 992; www.steam-packet.com; Albert Quay; return fares from £87), car ferries to and from Scotland and England dock at Larne, 37km north of Belfast. Trains to the terminal at Larne Harbour depart from Great Victoria St station.

BUS

There is an **information point** (Map p540; Great Victoria St, Great Northern Mall; ⏰ 8am-6pm Mon-Fri, 8.30am-5pm Sat) at Belfast's **Europa Bus Centre** (Map p540; ✆ 028-9066 6630; www.translink.co.uk; Great Victoria St, Great Northern Mall; ⏰ 5am-11pm Mon-Fri, 5.45am-11pm Sat, to 10.15pm Sun), where you can pick up regional bus timetables. Contact **Translink** (Map p540; ✆ 028-9066 6630; www.translink.co.uk; Europa Bus Centre) for timetable and fares information.

Laganside Buscentre (Map p540; Oxford St) Near the River Lagan; mainly for buses to eastern County Down, including Bangor and Newtownards.

National Express (Map p540; ✆ 08717 818 178; www.nationalexpress.com) Runs a daily coach service between Belfast and London via

BUS SERVICES FROM BELFAST

DESTINATION	PRICE (£)	DURATION (HR)	FREQUENCY
Armagh	9.30	1¼	hourly Mon-Fri, 6 Sat, 4 Sun
Ballycastle	12	3	3 daily Mon-Fri, 2 Sat
Bangor	3.80	¾	half-hourly Mon-Sat, 8 Sun
Derry	12	1¾	half-hourly Mon-Sat, 13 Sun
Downpatrick	6	1	at least hourly Mon-Sat, 6 Sun
Dublin	15	2½	hourly
Enniskillen	12	2¼	hourly Mon-Sat, 3 Sun
Newcastle	8	1¼	at least hourly

the Cairnryan ferry, Dumfries, Manchester and Birmingham.

Scottish Citylink (Map p540; ☑ 0871 266 3333; www.citylink.co.uk) Operates three buses a day from Glasgow to Belfast, via the Cairnryan ferry.

TRAIN

For information on train fares and timetables, contact **Translink** (p569).

Belfast Central Station (East Bridge St) East of the city centre; trains run to Dublin and all destinations in Northern Ireland.

Great Victoria St Station (Great Victoria St, Great Northern Mall) Next to the Europa Bus Centre and has trains to Portadown, Lisburn, Bangor, Larne Harbour and Derry.

Northern Ireland Railways (NIR; ☑ 028-9066 6630; www.translink.co.uk/Services/NI-Railways) Runs four routes from Belfast. One links with the system in the Republic via Newry to Dublin; the other three go east to Bangor, northeast to Larne and northwest to Derry via Coleraine.

❶ Getting Around

Belfast's integrated public-transport system includes buses linking both airports to the central train and bus stations.

TO/FROM THE AIRPORTS

Belfast International Airport Airport Express 300 bus runs to the Europa Bus Centre (one way/return £7.50/10.50, 30 to 55 minutes). The first bus from Belfast/the airport is at 4.20am/4.55am, then buses run at least once an hour until 11.30pm (from Belfast) and 12.15am (from the airport). A taxi costs about £30.

George Best Belfast City Airport Airport Express 600 bus runs to the Europa Bus Centre (one way/return £2.50/3.80, 15 minutes) every 20 minutes between 6am and 9.30pm Monday to Saturday, and every 40 minutes on Sunday. A return ticket is valid for one month. A taxi fare to the city centre is about £10.

BICYCLE

National Cycle Network route 9 runs through central Belfast, mostly following the western bank of the River Lagan and the north shore of Belfast Lough.

Belfast Bikes (☑ 034-3357 1551; www.belfastbikes.co.uk; registration per 3 days £5, bikes per 30min/1hr/2hr/3hr free/£0.50/1.50/2.50; ⊙ 24hr) Belfast's bike-share scheme, introduced in 2015, provides bikes at 40 docking stations throughout the city. Register online or via the app. If the bike is lost, stolen or damaged, your credit card will be charged £120.

Belfast Bike Tours (p555) Guided tours; also rents out bikes.

BUS

Metro (☑ 028-9066 6630; www.translink.co.uk) operates the bus network in Belfast. Most city services depart from various stops on and around Donegall Sq, at City Hall and along Queen St. You can pick up a free bus map (and buy tickets) from the **Metro kiosk** (Map p540; Donegall Sq; ⊙ 8am-5.30pm Mon-Fri) at the northwest corner of the square.

Buy your ticket from the driver (change given); fares within the city zone are £2.

You can also buy **Metro dayLink Cards** (£3.50; available from the Metro kiosk, the **Visit Belfast Welcome Centre** (p569) and the **Europa Bus Centre** (p569)), giving you unlimited bus travel within the City Zone all day Monday to Saturday.

If you plan on using city buses a lot, it's worth buying a **Metro Smartlink Travel Card** (available from the same places). The card costs an initial fee of £1, plus £10.50 per 10 journeys – you can get it topped up as you want. When you board the bus, you simply place the card on top of the ticket machine and it automatically issues a ticket.

An increasing number of buses are low-floor, 'kneeling' buses with space for one wheelchair.

TRAIN SERVICES FROM BELFAST

DESTINATION	PRICE (£)	DURATION (HR)	FREQUENCY
Bangor	5.60	½	every 20 min Mon-Sat, half-hourly Sun
Dublin	30	2¼	8 Mon-Sat, 5 Sun
Larne Harbour	7.30	1	hourly
Newry	11	¾	10 Mon-Sat, 5 Sun
Portrush	12	1¾	hourly

CAR & MOTORCYCLE

There are plenty of major car-hire agencies in Belfast.

Avis (www.avis.co.uk) City (☏ 028-9032 9258; www.avis.co.uk; 69-71 Great Victoria St; ⊗8am-4pm Mon-Fri); Belfast International Airport (☏ 0844 544 6012; www.avis.co.uk; Belfast International Airport; ⊗7.30am-11pm Mon-Fri, 8am-midnight Sat, noon-7pm Sun, 24hr drop-off); George Best Belfast City Airport (☏ 028-9073 1929; www.avis.co.uk; George Best Belfast City Airport; ⊗7am-10pm, 24hr drop-off)

Budget (www.budgetbelfast.co.uk) **City** (☏ 028-9023 0700; www.budgetbelfast.co.uk; 69-71 Great Victoria St; ⊗8am-5pm Mon-Fri); Belfast International Airport (☏ 028-9442 3332; www.budgetbelfast.co.uk; Belfast International Airport; ⊗5.30am-midnight); George Best Belfast City Airport (☏ 028-9045 1111; www.budgetbelfast.co.uk; George Best Belfast City Airport; ⊗5.30am-10pm)

Dooley Car Rentals (☏ 0800 282 189; www.dooleycarrentals.com; Belfast International Airport; ⊗8am-6pm) This reliable Ireland-wide agency offers good rates – around £200 a week for a compact car, with the option of one-way cross-border rentals (£117 extra to drop the car off in the Republic; €150 if you pick it up in the Republic and drop it off in Northern Ireland).

Europcar (www.europcar.co.uk) City (☏ 0371 384 3425; www.europcar.co.uk; 27 Balmoral Rd; ⊗8am-6pm Mon-Fri, to 1pm Sat); Belfast International Airport (☏ 0371 384 3426; www.europcar.co.uk; Belfast International Airport; ⊗7am-11pm Mon-Fri & Sun, to 10pm Sat); George Best Belfast City Airport (☏ 0371 384 3425; www.europcar.co.uk; George Best Belfast City Airport; ⊗7am-9.30pm Mon-Sat, 8am-9.30pm Sun)

Hertz (www.hertz.co.uk) George Best Belfast City Airport (☏ 028-9073 2451; www.hertz.co.uk; George Best Belfast City Airport; ⊗7.30am-9.30pm Mon-Sat, 9am-9.30pm Sun)

TAXI

Fona Cab (☏ 028-9033 3333; www.fonacab.com)

Value Cabs (☏ 028-9080 9080; www.value-cabs.co.uk)

Counties Down & Armagh

POP 706,457 / AREA 3702 SQ KM

Best Places to Eat

➡ Brunel's (p585)

➡ Bull & Ram (p591)

➡ Poacher's Pocket (p580)

➡ Moody Boar (p595)

➡ Old Schoolhouse Restaurant (p580)

Best Places to Sleep

➡ Old Inn (p575)

➡ Enniskeen Country House (p584)

➡ Narrow Water Castle Apartment (p589)

➡ Fortwilliam Country House (p591)

➡ Hutt Hostel (p584)

Why Go?

County Down's treasures fan out beyond Belfast. Strangford Lough's sparkling, island-fringed waters stretch south, with the bird-haunted mudflats of Castle Espie and Nendrum's ancient monastery on one shore, and the picturesque Ards Peninsula on the other. The Mourne Mountains' velvet curves sweep down to the sea near Downpatrick and Lecale, the old stamping grounds of Ireland's patron saint.

Down's neighbour County Armagh is largely rural, from the low, rugged hills of the south to the apple orchards and strawberry fields of the north, with Ireland's ecclesiastical capital, the appealing little city of Armagh, in the middle. South Armagh is a peaceful backwater with enchanting scenery ideal for walkers and cyclists.

Both counties' lush landscapes and scalloped bays provide a bounty of seasonal ingredients, used by a wealth of exceptional eateries throughout the region.

When to Go

➡ May brings white clouds of apple blossom to County Armagh's orchards.

➡ Summertime generally has the best weather for hiking and cycling, and late June sees the International Walking Festival in the Mourne Mountains.

➡ Spring and autumn are both good for birdwatching, but keen birders have a big X on their calendars in October, when tens of thousands of overwintering brent geese begin to arrive at Castle Espie on Strangford Lough.

➡ Late July is the time to catch the Fiddler's Green International Festival in Rostrevor; Warrenpoint's Blues on the Bay festival is held in late May.

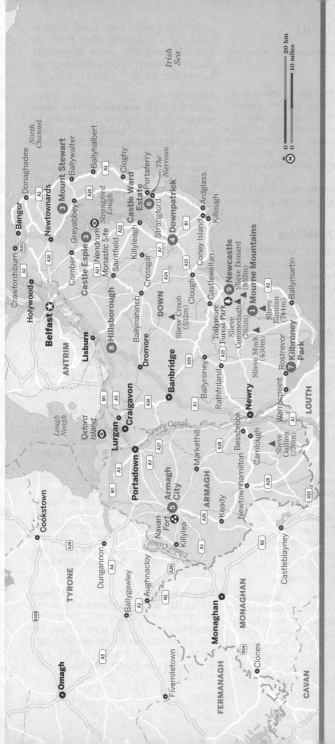

Counties Down & Armagh Highlights

1 Mourne Mountains
(p586) Hiking ancient trails or following the Mourne Wall to Slieve Donard's peak.

2 Mount Stewart (p578) Exploring the stately home and exquisite gardens.

3 Castle Espie (p579) Watching vast flocks of geese, ducks and waders at the Strangford Lough mudflats.

4 Downpatrick (p581) Following in the steps of Ireland's patron saint.

5 Armagh Robinson Library (p592) Viewing priceless texts including a first edition of *Gulliver's Travels*.

6 Castle Ward Estate (p583) Visiting *Game of Thrones* filming locations at the grand house and grounds on the shores of Strangford Lough.

7 Kilbroney Park (p588) Mountain-biking down graded trails on the forested slopes above Carlingford Lough.

8 Hillsborough (p590) Touring the castle and stopping for a pub meal.

9 Royal County Down Golf Course (p584) Teeing off at the esteemed golf course in seaside Newcastle.

COUNTY DOWN

Bangor

POP 59,000

On the stretch of shore locally known as the 'Gold Coast' (due to its wealthy residents, not its weather), this Victorian seaside resort town first flourished when the Belfast–Bangor train line was built in the late 19th century. In recent years, Bangor has enjoyed a renaissance as an out-of-town base for city commuters.

In the centre of town, Main St and High St (Bangor has both) converge at the huge boat-filled marina.

◉ Sights & Activities

The scenic **North Down Coastal Path** follows the shore from Holywood train station on Belfast's northeastern edge to Bangor Marina (15km), and continues east to Orlock Point.

North Down Museum MUSEUM
(www.northdownmuseum.com; Castle Park Ave; ⊙10am-4.30pm Tue-Sat, noon-4.30pm Sun year-round, plus 10am-4.30pm Mon Jul & Aug) FREE Historical treasures displayed in the converted laundry, stables and stores of Bangor Castle include the *Raven Maps* (the only complete folio of Plantation-era maps in Ireland); the Bronze Age Ballycroghan Swords, dating from c 500 BC; the 9th-century bronze handbell, the Bangor Bell; and a 17th-century sundial by Scottish craftsman John Bonar.

Bangor Castle Walled Garden GARDENS
(www.visitardsandnorthdown.com; Valentine Rd; ⊙10am-5pm Mon-Thu, to 6pm Fri-Sun Apr & mid-Sep–early Nov, 10am-8pm Mon-Thu, to 6pm Fri-Sun May–mid-Sep) FREE Designed in the 1840s by the Ward family who lived in Bangor Castle, these tranquil gardens make a good picnicking spot. It's particularly pretty in spring, when the tulips are in bloom.

Pickie Funpark AMUSEMENT PARK
(☑028-9145 0746; http://pickiefunpark.com; Marine Gardens; family pass £10-40; ⊙9am-4pm mid-Mar–Apr, to 7.30pm May-Aug, to 4pm Sep & Oct, 9am-4pm Sat & Sun Nov–mid-Mar; ⊕) This old-fashioned seaside entertainment complex is famous for its swan-shaped pedal boats. There's also a kids' adventure playground, electric-track karts, minigolf, zorbs and a miniature steam train, the *Pickie Puffer*. Family passes include various attractions or you can pay for each ride individually (the park is free to enter).

Bangor Boat CRUISE
(☑07510 006000; www.bangorboat.com; adult/child from £6/2, fishing trips per adult/child incl tackle & bait £20/12; ⊙departures from 2pm daily Jul & Aug, Sat & Sun only Apr-Jun & Sep) Pleasure cruises around Bangor Bay depart from the marina pontoon next to the Pickie Funpark (p574). From June to mid-September, there are family-friendly fishing trips departing at 9.15am and 6.30pm daily from the Eisenhower Pier (on the right-hand side of the harbour, looking out to sea).

🛏 Sleeping

★**Cairn Bay Lodge** B&B ££
(☑028-9146 7636; www.cairnbaylodge.com; 278 Seacliff Rd; s/d/f from £60/85/120; P🅟🛜) Set amid beautiful gardens, this lovely seaside villa exudes Edwardian elegance with its oak-panelled lounge and dining room serving superb gourmet breakfasts. Its six bedrooms (all with private bathroom and organic seaweed toiletries, and some with sparkling sea views) blend antique charm with contemporary style. Beauty treatments are available. It's 1km east of the town centre, overlooking Ballyholme Bay.

Clandeboye Lodge Hotel HOTEL ££
(☑028-9185 2500; www.clandeboyelodge.com; 10 Estate Rd, Clandeboye; r from £115; P🅟@🛜) Resembling a modern red-brick church, the Clandeboye offers informal luxury – big bedrooms, polished granite bathrooms, fluffy bathrobes, Champagne and chocolates – with a log fire in winter and a drinks terrace in summer. Its bar-restaurant, the Coq & Bull, serves farm-reared poultry and beef, and local seafood. It sits amid landscaped gardens on the southwest edge of Bangor.

Ennislare House B&B ££
(☑028-9127 0858; http://ennislarehouse.com; 7-9 Princetown Rd; s/d from £50/75; P🅟🛜) Just 300m north of Bangor train station, this lovely Victorian townhouse has big, bright rooms, stylish decor and a friendly owner who can't do enough to make you feel welcome.

WORTH A TRIP

THE OLD INN, CRAWFORDSBURN

Old Inn (☎028-9185 3255; www.theoldinn.com; 15 Main St; d from £85; P 🛜) In the quaint little village of Crawfordsburn, 3km west of Bangor on the B20, the 1614-established Old Inn claims to be Ireland's oldest hotel. Its original thatched cottage (now the bar, with log fires and low ceilings) is flanked by 18th-century additions. Character-filled rooms have Arts and Crafts–style wallpaper and mahogany; the oak-panelled Lewis Restaurant (☎028-9185 1300; www.theoldinn.com; 15 Main St; bar menu mains £11.50-27, restaurant mains £13-27; ⊙noon-10pm Mon-Sat, to 9.30pm Sun) is superb.

The inn was once a resting place on the coach route between Belfast and Donaghadee (formerly the main ferry port for mainland Britain). As a result, it has been patronised by many famous names, including the young Peter the Great (tsar of Russia), Dick Turpin (highwayman), former US president George HW Bush, and a roll call of literary figures, including Swift, Tennyson, Thackeray, Dickens, Trollope and CS Lewis.

Eating & Drinking

Guillemot Kitchen CAFE £
(www.facebook.com/theguillemot; 2 Seacliff Rd; mains £7-8.25; ⊙9am-5pm; 🖉) Opposite the marina, this snug, sky-blue cafe does great coffee, all-day breakfasts, and light bites such as gourmet sandwiches and soups, as well as homemade cakes. Vegan options available.

Boat House MODERN IRISH £££
(☎028-9146 9253; http://boathousebangor. com; 1a Seacliff Rd; 2-/3-course lunch £22/26, 2-/3-course dinner £26/30, mains £16-29; ⊙12.30-3pm & 5.30-9.30pm Wed-Sat, 1-8pm Sun) 🖉 Tucked into the former Harbour Master's office, the Boat House is a cosy little nook of stone, brick and designer decor serving fancy plates of deftly prepared local seafood, lamb and game. Five- and seven-course surprise tasting menus (£45/60 per person) are served to the whole table. There's a good wine list too.

Hop House BAR
(www.facebook.com/Hophousebangor; 44 High St; ⊙11.30am-1am Mon-Sat, noon-midnight Sun, kitchen noon-8pm) Local craft beers, and nightly live music or DJs keep this central spot hopping. There's a good beer garden, awesome burgers and all-you-can-eat ribs and wings from 4pm to 8pm Monday to Wednesday (£12 per person).

Jenny Watts PUB
(☎028-9127 0401; www.jennywattsbar.com; 41 High St; mains £8-13; ⊙11.30am-11pm Mon & Tue, to 1am Wed-Sat, 12.30-midnight Sun) Bangor's oldest pub (1780) pulls in a mixed-age crowd for live music on Tuesday night (folk), Friday and Saturday night (varying musicians and bands) and Sunday lunchtime (jazz). There's a beer garden out the back. Good pub food (home-made burgers, lasagne and the like) is served from noon to 9pm daily (to 8pm Sunday).

Rabbit Rooms BAR
(www.therabbitrooms.com; 30-32 Quay St; ⊙11.30am-1am Mon-Sat, 12.30pm-midnight Sun) In a charcoal-coloured building stencilled with a gigantic white rabbit, this bare-boards space is a wonderland of mismatched vintage furniture like old, cracked-leather cinema seats, with cocktails served in teapots. Live music plays Monday to Thursday and Saturday.

ℹ️ Information

Bangor Visitor Information Centre (☎028-9127 0069; www.visitardsandnorthdown.com; 34 Quay St; ⊙approx 9.15am-5pm Mon, Tue, Thu & Fri, 10am-5pm Wed & Sat year-round, plus 1-5pm Sun May-Aug) is housed in a tower built in 1637 as a fortified customs post.

ℹ️ Getting There & Away

The bus and train stations are together on Abbey St, at the uphill end of Main St.

Buses 1 and 2 run from Belfast's Laganside Buscentre to Bangor (£3.80, one hour, hourly). From Bangor, bus 3 goes to Donaghadee (£3, 25 minutes, hourly Monday to Saturday, three on Sunday).

Regular train services run from Belfast's Great Victoria St and Central stations to Bangor (£5.60, 40 minutes, every 30 minutes Monday to Saturday, hourly Sunday).

Ards Peninsula

The low-lying Ards Peninsula (An Aird) is the finger of land that encloses Strangford Lough, pinching against the thumb of the Lecale Peninsula at the Portaferry Narrows. The northern half of the peninsula has some of Ireland's most fertile farmland, with large expanses of wheat and barley, while the south is a landscape of neat fields, white cottages and narrow, winding roads. The eastern coast has some good sandy beaches. You're best exploring with your own wheels.

Donaghadee

POP 6900

The small harbour town of Donaghadee (Domhnach Daoi) was the main ferry port for Scotland until 1874, when it was superseded by Larne. These days it's a jolly seaside spot that come summer fills up with local holiday makers, many of whom have holiday homes in nearby caravan parks.

🛏 Sleeping & Eating

Pier 36 B&B ££

(☏028-9188 4466; www.pier36.co.uk; 36 The Parade; s/d from £55/79) An excellent pub with comfortable B&B rooms upstairs and a red-brick and terracotta-tiled restaurant at the back, dominated by a yellow Rayburn stove that turns out home-baked bread and the daily roast (restaurant mains £10 to £20; open noon to 9pm).

It's a great place to sample local seafood such as Portavogie prawns, Strangford mussels, haddock and cod.

Slice of Heaven CAFE £

(www.sliceofheavendessertcafe.com; 11 New St; mains £4.25-7, desserts £4; ☺10am-5pm Tue-Sat, noon-5pm Sun; 🖥) In Donaghadee's lavishly restored former courthouse you can get fantastic sandwiches (Coronation Chicken; Christmas-style with turkey, ham, stuffing and cranberry sauce), as well as soups and salads, but the show-stoppers are the desserts: key lime pie, summer-berry pavlova, sticky toffee pudding and homemade ice cream such as Champagne sorbet.

Harbour & Company BARBECUE ££

(☏028-9188 4466; www.harbourandcompany. com; 31 The Parade; mains £7-18; ☺kitchen noon-2.30pm & 5-9.30pm Tue-Sat, noon-9.30pm Sun) In a beachy bar and restaurant with good views of the pier, Harbour & Company specialises in meat, fish and seafood dishes cooked over a wood-fired grill, as well as stone-baked pizzas and artisan flat breads.

ℹ Getting There & Away

Bus 3 runs to/from Bangor (£3, 25 minutes, hourly Monday to Saturday, three on Sunday).

Portaferry

POP 2500

Beneath Windmill Hill, topped by an old windmill tower, Portaferry (Port an Pheire) is a neat huddle of streets around a medieval tower house, which looks across the turbulent stretch of water, the Narrows, to a matching tower house in Strangford.

◉ Sights & Activities

There are pleasant walks on the minor roads along the coast, north for 2.5km to **Ballyhenry Island** (accessible at low tide), and south for 6km to the National Trust nature reserve at **Ballyquintin Point**. Both are good for birdwatching, seal spotting or just admiring the views of the Mourne Mountains.

★ Exploris AQUARIUM

(☏028-4272 8062; http://explorisni.com; Rope Walk, Castle St; adult/child £7.50/5; ☺10am-6pm Apr-Oct, to 5pm Nov-Mar; 🖥) Recently reopened after a £2 million remodelling, this excellent aquarium has displays of marine life from Strangford Lough and the Irish Sea as well as tropical fish, otters and a new reptile centre with an African Nile crocodile, geckos and snakes. There's also a touch pool for kids and a seal sanctuary where orphaned, sick and injured seals are nursed back to health before being released into the wild. Last admission is 4.30pm in summer and 4pm in winter.

Portaferry Castle CASTLE

(Castle St; ☺10am-5pm Mon-Sat, 1-5pm Sun Easter-Sep) **FREE** Portaferry's castle is a small 16th-century tower house that, together with the tower house in Strangford, once controlled sea traffic through the Narrows. It's next to the visitor information office.

🛏 Sleeping & Eating

Barholm HOSTEL £

(☏028-4272 9967; www.barholmportaferry.co.uk; 11 The Strand; dm/s/d from £14/26/50; P🖥)

Barholm offers basic, hostel-style accommodation in a Victorian villa with a superb seafront location opposite the ferry slipway. It has a kitchen, laundry facilities and a big, sunny conservatory that doubles as a tea-room. Rooms are available with or without breakfast; some share bathrooms. It's popular with groups, so you'll need to book ahead.

★ **Portaferry Hotel** HOTEL ££
(☑ 028-4272 8231; www.portaferryhotel.com; 10 The Strand; s £60-85, d £80-160; ☺kitchen noon-3pm & 5-9pm Mon-Fri, noon-9pm Sat, noon-3pm Sun; P @) Converted from a row of 18th-century terrace houses, this charming seafront hotel has an elegant, Georgian look to its rooms. Each is individually decorated with pretty wallpaper and French-style furniture; some have lough views. The hotel is famous for its scampi; the bar serves bistro-style meals (mains £11 to £15), while the restaurant has local foodies raving about its sophisticated plates (mains £15 to £22).

Fiddler's Green PUB
(☑ 028-4272 8393; www.fiddlersgreenportaferry. com; 10 Church St; ☺10am-11pm) The Fiddler's is a fabulous place for traditional music, with live bands every weekend and impromptu sessions that get the whole bar joining in. The Guinness is pretty good, and you'll find one of the 10 *Game of Thrones* carved doors from the Dark Hedges (p625) here. In the upstairs B&B, comfortable guest rooms start from £70.

❶ Information

Portaferry Visitor Information Office (☑ 028-4272 9882; www.visitstrangfordlough.co.uk; The Stables, Castle St; ☺10am-5pm Mon-Sat, 1-5pm Sun Easter-Sep) In a restored stable near the tower house at **Portaferry Castle** (p576).

❶ Getting There & Away

Buses 9 and 10 travel from Belfast's Laganside Buscentre to Portaferry (£7, 1½ hours, seven daily Monday to Saturday, three on Sunday) via Newtownards, Mount Stewart and Greyabbey. More frequent services begin from Newtownards (£6, one hour); some buses go via Carrowdore and don't stop at Mount Stewart or Greyabbey – check first.

A **car ferry** (☑ 028-4488 1637; one way car & driver £5.80, car passengers & pedestrians £1) from Portaferry to Strangford sails every half-hour at a quarter past and a quarter to the hour, between 7.45am and 10.45pm Monday to Friday, 8.15am to 11.15pm on Saturday and 9.45am to 10.45pm on Sunday. The journey time is about 10 minutes.

Greyabbey

POP 1000

The little village of Greyabbey, 18km north of Portaferry, is synonymous with the splendid ruins of the Cistercian Grey Abbey. It's also popular for its antiques shops.

Off Main St in the village centre, Hoops Courtyard has a cluster of 18 little shops selling antiques and collectables. Opening times vary, but all are open on Wednesday, Friday and Saturday afternoons.

Grey Abbey MONASTERY
(www.friendsoftheabbey.co.uk; Church Rd; ☺ruins 24hr, visitor centre 1-4pm Sat & 2-4pm Sun Feb-Nov) **FREE** This Cistercian abbey was founded in 1193 by Affreca, wife of Norman knight John de Courcy (the builder of Carrickfergus Castle;p631), in thanks for surviving a stormy sea crossing from the Isle of Man. The small visitor centre explains Cistercian life with paintings and panels; there's also a herb garden full of medicinal plants once cultivated by the monks. The abbey's church, in use until the 18th century, was the first in Ireland to be built in the Gothic style.

At the church's east end is a carved tomb, possibly depicting Affreca; the effigy in the north transept may be her husband. Even if the visitor centre is closed, the ruins are well labelled with informative signs. The grounds, overlooked by 18th-century Rose-mount House, are awash with trees and flowers on spreading lawns, making this an ideal picnic spot.

Hoops Courtyard Coffee Shop CAFE £
(Hoops Courtyard, 7-9 Main St; mains £4.50-8; ☺noon-5pm) This quaint, whitewashed traditional tearoom serves freshly baked scones, cooked breakfasts, sandwiches and salads. Outdoor tables are set up in the courtyard in fine weather.

Wildfowler Inn PUB FOOD ££
(☑ 028-4278 8234; www.wildfowlerinn.co.uk; 1 Main St; lunch £10-16, dinner £12-23; ☺kitchen noon-2.45pm & 5-8pm Mon-Thu, to 9.15pm Fri, noon-9.15pm Sat, noon-8pm Sun; ☝) With a French-washed, ochre-coloured facade and rustic interior, this beautiful former coaching inn makes a wonderful stop for generous portions of quality pub fare such as roast chicken and ale-battered haddock and chips.

ⓘ Getting There & Away

Buses 9 and 10 link Greyabbey with Newtownards (£3, 15 minutes, every two hours or more Monday to Saturday, six on Sunday). The same service continues to Portaferry (£3.80, 30 minutes).

Mount Stewart

The magnificent 18th-century **Mount Stewart** (☑ 028-4278 8387; www.nationaltrust.org.uk; Portaferry Rd; adult/child £9.50/4.75; ⊗ house 11-5pm daily Apr-Oct, 11am-3pm Sat & Sun Nov-Mar, grounds 10am-5pm Apr-Oct, to 4pm Nov-Mar) is one of Northern Ireland's grandest stately homes. A three-year restoration project has seen the house transformed to how it looked in its 1930 heyday, by unveiling the central hall's original 1840s Scrabo stone floor, repairing the plaster work and returning the cream colour scheme. The house overlooks formal gardens filled with colourful sub-tropical plants.

Mount Stewart is on the A20, 3km northwest of Greyabbey. Buses from Belfast to Portaferry stop at the gate.

This National Trust property's contents reflect the period when Lord Londonderry and his wife Edith would entertain guests such as WB Yeats, Winston Churchill and Neville Chamberlain; the dining table has place settings for an imagined 1930s dinner party with illustrious attendees. Entertaining tours tell the story of the house and its contents; treasures include a painting of racehorse Hambletonian in *Hambletonian, Rubbing Down* (1799–1800) by George Stubbs, one of the most important paintings in Ireland.

Much of the landscaping of the beautiful gardens was supervised by Lady Edith for the benefit of her children – the Dodo Terrace at the front of the house is populated with unusual creatures from history (dinosaurs and dodos) and myth (griffins and mermaids), accompanied by giant frogs and duck-billed platypuses. There are several walking trails around the gardens and grounds.

Don't miss the 18th-century **Temple of the Winds**, a folly in the classical Greek style built on a high point above the lough.

Newtownards & Around

POP 27,800

Founded in the 17th century on the site of the 6th-century Movilla monastery, today Newtownards (Baile Nua na hArda) is a busy commercial centre, with some interesting sights nearby. The town is known locally as Ards.

◉ Sights

Scrabo Tower & Country Park　　PARK
(www.visitardsandnorthdown.com; 403 Scrabo Rd; ⊗ 24hr) FREE Newtownards is overlooked by Scrabo Hill, 2km southwest of town. It was once the site of extensive prehistoric earthworks, which were largely removed during construction of the 41m 1857 Scrabo Tower, built in honour of the third Marquess of Londonderry, and visible for miles around. Its interior is falling into disrepair and has been closed to the public, but you can still access the surrounding country park – a great spot for a scenic picnic.

The sandstone quarries nearby, now disused, provided material for many famous buildings, including Belfast's Albert Memorial Clock Tower.

Somme Heritage Centre　　MUSEUM
(www.sommeassociation.com; 233 Bangor Rd; ⊗ 10am-4pm Mon-Thu & Sat Apr-Nov, 10am-4pm Mon-Thu plus 1st Sat of month Dec-Mar) FREE This grimly fascinating centre illustrates the horrors of the WWI Somme campaign of 1916 from the perspective of men of the 10th (Irish), 16th (Irish) and 36th (Ulster) divisions, and is a memorial to the men and women who died. It has short films and reconstructions of the trenches, plus a photographic display commemorating the suffragette movement and women's roles in WWI.

It's 3km north of Newtownards on the A21 towards Bangor. Bus 6 from Bangor to Newtownards passes the entrance.

Ark Open Farm　　FARM
(www.thearkopenfarm.co.uk; 296 Bangor Rd; adult/child £6.50/6; ⊗ 10am-6pm Mon-Sat, 2-6pm Sun Apr-Oct, 10am-5pm Mon-Sat, 2-5pm Sun Nov-Mar; ⊕) The Ark is a family favourite for its rare breeds of sheep, cattle, poultry, llamas and donkeys. Kids get to pet and hand-feed the lambs, piglets and ducklings.

✕ Eating

★ **McKee's Country Store & Restaurant**　　IRISH £
(☑ 028-9182 1304; www.mckeesproduce.com; Strangford View, 28 Holywood Rd; mains £9-12; ⊗ restaurant 9am-5.30pm Mon-Sat, shop 8.30am-5.30pm Mon-Sat; ☑⊕) ✔ On a working 162-hectare farm 5km northwest of Newtownards, this foodie emporium incorporates a bakery, butcher and deli, plus fruit,

vegetable and dairy sections. Everything is produced on site or sourced from the surrounding area. If it's not picnic weather, try the restaurant dishes, such as pork-and-honey mustard sausages, in a panoramic dining room overlooking the lush farmland, Scrabo and the lough.

ℹ Information

Ards Visitor Information Centre (☑028-9182 6846; www.visitardsandnorthdown.com; 31 Regent St; ⊗9.15am-5.15pm Mon-Fri, 9am-5.30pm Sat Jul & Aug, 9.15am-5pm Mon-Fri, 9.30am-5pm Sat Sep-Jun) Next to the bus station.

ℹ Getting There & Away

Buses 9 and 10 serve Belfast (£3, 20 minutes, every two hours or more Monday to Saturday, six on Sunday) and Portaferry (£6, one hour).

West Side of Strangford Lough

Almost landlocked, Strangford Lough (Loch Cuan) is connected to the open sea by a 700m-wide strait, the Narrows, between the towns of Portaferry and Strangford. The lough's western shore is fringed by hump-backed islands – half-drowned mounds of boulder clay (called drumlins) left behind by ice sheets at the end of the last ice age. On the eastern shore, the drumlins have been broken down by the waves into heaps of boulders that form shallow tidal reefs (known locally as 'pladdies').

Large colonies of grey seals frequent the lough, especially at the southern tip of the Ards Peninsula. Birds abound on the shores and tidal mudflats.

◉ Sights

★**Castle Espie Wildfowl & Wetlands Centre**   WILDLIFE RESERVE
(☑028-9187 4146; www.wwt.org.uk; 78 Ballydrain Rd, Comber; adult/child £8.45/4.10; ⊗10am-5pm Mon-Fri, to 5.30pm Sat & Sun Apr-Sep, to 4pm Oct-Mar) ∥ Situated 2km southeast of Comber, off the Downpatrick road (A22), Castle Espie Wildfowl & Wetlands Centre is a haven for huge flocks of geese, ducks and swans. The landscaped grounds are dotted with birdwatching hides, and are a paradise for fledgling naturalists, with family bird-feeding and pond-dipping sessions.

The best months to visit are May and June, when it's overrun with goslings, duck-

COUNTY DOWN'S RURAL RESTAURANTS
....

Look around at the rich farmland, fields of cows, grazing mountain sheep and busy coastal fisheries – it's little wonder that County Down's restaurants turn out such fine plates of food. Local menus name-check ingredients like Comber potatoes, Kilkeel crab and Mourne lamb in dishes that have been wooing critics and winning awards.

Some of the county's best eateries include **Bull & Ram** (p591), **Balloo House** (p580), **Poacher's Pocket** (p580) and **Old Schoolhouse Restaurant** (p580) – they're a bit out of the way, but worth the journey.

lings and cygnets, and October, when vast flocks of the 30,000 light-bellied brent geese (75% of the world's population) arrive from Arctic Canada.

There's a fantastic children's play area in the woods, with a zip wire, rope swings and tree houses, as well as a good cafe with windows looking out on the ducks.

Nendrum Monastic Site   HISTORIC SITE
(Mahee Island; ⊗site 24hr year-round, visitor centre 10am-5pm Wed, Fri, Sat & Sun May-Sep) **FREE** In a wonderful island setting, the 5th-century Celtic monastic community of Nendrum was built under the guidance of St Mochaoi (St Mahee). Its scant remains provide a clear outline of its early plan, with the foundations of a number of churches, a round tower, beehive cells and three concentric stone ramparts and a monks' cemetery. The stone sundial was reconstructed using original pieces. There's a small visitor centre.

Nendrum is 5km south of Comber, reached by a causeway and bridge.

By the bridge, look for the ruined tower of 15th-century **Mahee Castle**.

🛏 Sleeping

★**Dufferin Coaching Inn**   B&B ££
(☑028-4482 1134; www.dufferincoachinginn.com; 35 High St, Killyleagh; s/d £85/90; [P] 🐾) The comfortable lounge in this lovely Georgian house was once Killyleagh's village bank – the manager's office in the corner now houses a little library. Excellent breakfasts include freshly squeezed orange juice, good coffee and scrambled eggs with smoked salmon. The six

plush rooms have crisp linen and fluffy towels, and some have four-poster beds.

The smallest double has the bath in the bedroom, charmingly hidden behind a curtain.

Old Schoolhouse Inn B&B ££

(☑ 028-9754 1182; www.theoldschoolhouseinn. com; 100 Ballydrain Rd, Comber; s/d from £55/70; P 🛜) Just south of Castle Espie, the 1929 Old Schoolhouse Inn has eight comfortable rooms, each named for a former US president, and a sociable guest lounge. Breakfasts are particularly good, with home-baked Guinness bread, local smoked salmon, and fruit salads with rhubarb fresh from the kitchen garden. The former classroom houses an award-winning restaurant (p580) headed up by Will Brown.

Anna's House B&B B&B ££

(☑ 028-9754 1566; www.annashouse.com; 35 Lisbarnett Rd, Tullynagee, Lisbane; s/d from £60/85; P 🛜) 🍴 Just west of Lisbane, Anna's is a spacious, ecofriendly country house with views over a lake from a glass-walled extension complete with grand piano. The hospitality is second to none, the scones, pancakes and pastries are home baked, and the breakfast menu ranges from an Ulster fry-up or smoked-salmon omelette to fresh fruit salad.

🍴 Eating & Drinking

Old Post Office Tearoom CAFE £

(www.oldpostofficelisbane.co.uk; 191 Killinchy Rd, Lisbane; dishes £3-7.50; ⊙ 9am-5pm Mon-Sat; 🛜 🍴) Once the village post office, this thatched cottage has been lovingly converted into a tearoom and art gallery, with cream plaster and bare stone walls and a wood-burning stove. It serves great coffee and home-baked scones, plus lunch specials such as lasagne, quiches and lovely fresh salads.

★ Balloo House MODERN IRISH ££

(☑ 028-9754 1210; www.ballooinns.com; 1 Comber Rd, Killinchy; downstairs mains £12-25, upstairs restaurant mains £18-25; ⊙ downstairs kitchen noon-9pm Sun-Thu, noon-9.30pm Fri & Sat, upstairs restaurant noon-9.30pm Fri & Sat) Chef Danny Millar is the mastermind behind the sublime dishes served at Balloo House. Downstairs, casual modern Irish fare is available in the nook-and-cranny-filled, stone-floored pub, which centres on a warming cast-iron range stove. Upstairs, a fine-dining restaurant serves more refined dishes on Friday and Saturday nights (book ahead).

There's bluegrass and traditional Irish music in the bar on Wednesdays and Thursdays from 9pm.

★ Poacher's Pocket MODERN IRISH ££

(☑ 028-9754 1589; www.poacherspocketlisbane. com; 181 Killinchy Rd, Lisbane; mains £8-27; ⊙ kitchen noon-9pm Sun-Thu, to 9.30pm Fri & Sat, deli 9am-9pm) 🍴 A fresh, contemporary makeover has transformed this roadside pub into a foodie magnet, with dishes such as pastrami and applewood smoked cheese beefburger and Strangford mussels and fries, and mackerel with caramelised fennel and beetroot crème fraîche. There's a fantastic range of local craft ciders and beers, which it also sells at its attached **Poacher's Pantry** deli and farm shop.

★ Old Schoolhouse Restaurant MODERN IRISH ££

(☑ 028-9754 1182; www.theoldschoolhouseinn. com; 100 Ballydrain Rd, Comber; lunch 2/3 courses £15/20, dinner mains £15-17; ⊙ 12.30-3.30pm & 5.30-9.30pm Wed-Sat, 12.30-6.30pm Sun) In the Old Schoolhouse Inn (p580), the former classroom houses an award-winning restaurant headed up by Will Brown, who worked with Marco Pierre White in London and uses classical techniques. The menu utilises seasonal produce and changes daily; a kitchen garden provides herbs and vegetables.

Dufferin Arms PUB FOOD ££

(www.dufferinarms.com; 35 High St, Killyleagh; mains lunch £7.50-13.50, dinner £10-22; ⊙ kitchen noon-3pm & 5-8.30pm Mon-Thu, noon-9pm Fri & Sat, noon-8pm Sun) Easy to spot (it's bright pink), this comfortably old-fashioned pub serves decent pub grub, while the cosy, candlelit restaurant offers a more intimate atmosphere. There's live music on Wednesdays from 9pm and Saturday afternoons from 4pm. The pub featured in the 2013 Oscar-nominated film *Philomena* starring Dame Judi Dench.

Daft Eddy's PUB

(☑ 028-9754 1615; www.facebook.com/daft.eddys; Sketrick Island, Whiterock; ⊙ 11.30am-11.30pm Mon-Thu, 11.30am-1am Fri & Sat, noon-10.30pm Sun) Idyllic on a sunny day, this local favourite is hidden away on an island, with panoramic views over Strangford Lough from its bar, partially covered timber-decked terrace and table-set gardens below. It's 4.5km northeast of Killinchy: follow Whiterock Rd east, then veer around to the left to reach the causeway.

Downpatrick

POP 10,300

St Patrick's mission to spread Christianity to Ireland began and ended in Downpatrick. Ireland's patron saint is believed to have made his first convert at nearby Saul, and been buried at Down Cathedral; St Patrick's Day (17 March) sees the town filled with pilgrims and revellers.

Downpatrick – now County Down's administrative centre – was settled long before the saint's arrival. His first church here was constructed inside the earthwork *dún* (fort) of Rath Celtchair, still visible to the southwest of the cathedral. The place later became known as Dún Pádraig (Patrick's Fort), anglicised to Downpatrick in the 17th century.

◉ Sights

★**St Patrick Centre** MUSEUM
(🖉 028-4461 9000; www.saintpatrickcentre. com; Saint Patrick's Sq, Market St; adult/child £5.75/3.50; ⊙9am-5pm Mon-Sat year-round, plus 1-5pm Sun Jul & Aug) This magnificent glass-and-timber heritage centre houses a multimedia exhibition called Ego Patricius, charting the life and legacy of Ireland's patron saint. Audio and video presentations tell St Patrick's story, often in his own words (taken from his *Confession*, written in Latin around the year 450, which begins with the words *'Ego Patricius',* meaning 'I am Patrick'). At the end is a spectacular widescreen film that takes you on a swooping, low-level helicopter ride over the landscapes of Ireland.

Down Cathedral CATHEDRAL
(🖉 028-4461 4922; www.downcathedral.org; English St; ⊙9.30am-4pm Mon-Sat) FREE According to legend, St Patrick died in Saul, where angels told his followers to place his body on a cart drawn by two untamed oxen, and to bury the saint wherever they halted. The oxen supposedly stopped at the church on the hill of Down, now the site of the Church of Ireland's Down Cathedral.

In the churchyard, a slab of Mourne granite with the inscription 'Patric' (placed in 1900) marks the traditional site of **St Patrick's grave.**

The cathedral is testimony to 1600 years of building and rebuilding. Viking attacks wiped away all trace of the earliest churches, and the subsequent Norman cathedral and monasteries were destroyed by Scottish raiders in 1316. The rubble was used in a 15th-century church finished in 1512, but after the Dissolution of the Monasteries it was razed to the ground in 1541. Today's building dates largely from the 18th and 19th centuries, with a completely new interior installed in the 1980s.

To get here, from the St Patrick Centre (p581), take the path to its left, uphill through the landscaped grounds.

Down County Museum MUSEUM
(🖉 028-4461 5218; www.downcountymuseum. com; The Mall; ⊙10am-4.30pm Mon-Sat, 1.30-5pm Sun) FREE Downpatrick's restored 18th-century jail now houses the county museum. In a former cell block at the back are models of some of the prisoners once incarcerated there, and details of their sad stories. Displays in the Governor's residence include early flint tools, cross slabs from the monasteries at Saul and items from the Norman conquest of Down, but the biggest exhibit of all is outside – a short signposted trail leads to the **Mound of Down**, a Norman motte and bailey.

Inch Abbey ABBEY
(Inch Abbey Rd) FREE Built by Norman knight John de Courcy for the Cistercians in 1180 on an earlier Irish monastic site, Inch Abbey is visible across the river from Down Cathedral – and yes, it's another *Game of*

ST PATRICK'S WAY

Downpatrick is the terminus of **Saint Patrick's Way**, a 132km signposted pilgrim walk from Armagh City, linking sites related to St Patrick. Starting at **Navan Fort** (p595), the walk passes along the Newry canal towpath to Newry, through Rostrevor and across the Mourne Mountains to Newcastle on the way to Downpatrick. You can pick up a free **Pilgrim Walk Passport** (available at the **Navan Centre** (p596) and tourist offices) and collect stamps along the way.

If walking doesn't appeal, pick up a map for the **Saint Patrick's Trail**, which highlights St Patrick–related and other Christian sights on a driving route from Armagh to Bangor. You'll find copies of the map in tourist information centres.

Thrones filming location. Most of the ruins are just foundations and low walls; the neatly groomed setting beside the marshes of the River Quoile is its most attractive feature.

Inch Abbey is off the A7 Belfast Rd just across the river, north of Downpatrick.

John de Courcy commissioned one of the monks at Inch Abbey to rewrite the legends of St Patrick; it's possible that the story of St Patrick banishing the snakes from Ireland was written here.

Downpatrick & County Down Railway
MUSEUM

(☑ 028-4461 5779; www.downrail.co.uk; Market St; adult/child £6/4.50; ⊙ 1-4.30pm Sat & Sun mid-Jun–mid-Sep, plus some bank holidays) From mid-June to mid-September, plus December, St Patrick's Day, Easter, May Day and Halloween, this working railway museum runs steam-hauled trains over a restored section of the former Belfast–Newcastle line, from Downpatrick to Inch Abbey (p581). The ticket price includes a return journey on the train and entrance to the carriage gallery and station museum.

🍴 Sleeping & Eating

Denvir's Hotel & Pub
B&B ££

(☑ 028-4461 2012; www.denvirs.com; 14-16 English St; s/d from £40/70; 🛜) Dating from 1642, Denvir's is allegedly Ireland's oldest surviving coaching inn. It offers B&B accommodation in six idiosyncratic rooms with polished floorboards, Georgian windows and period fireplaces. Good food is served in the cosy bar and rustic **restaurant** (☑ 028-4461 2012; www.denvirs.com/restaurant; 14-16 English St; mains £8-20; ⊙ kitchen noon-8pm), which has an enormous, 17th-century stone fireplace.

ⓘ Information

Downpatrick Visitor Information Centre

(☑ 028-4461 2233; www.visitstrangfordlough. co.uk; St Patrick Centre, Market St; ⊙ 9am-5pm Mon-Fri, 9.30am-5pm Sat year-round, plus 1-5pm Sun Jul & Aug) In the **St Patrick Centre** (p581).

ⓘ Getting There & Away

Downpatrick's bus station is just south of the St Patrick Centre and Downpatrick Visitor Information Centre.

Services:

Belfast (Europa Bus Centre) £6, one hour, half-hourly Monday to Friday, hourly Saturday, six Sunday

Castlewellan £3.80, 30 minutes, seven daily Monday to Friday, six Saturday, four Sunday

Dundrum £3.50, 15 minutes, seven daily Monday to Friday, six Saturday, four Sunday

Newcastle £3.80, 20 minutes, seven daily Monday to Friday, six Saturday, four Sunday

Newry £9.30, 1¼ hours, seven daily Monday to Friday, six Saturday, four Sunday

Saul

On landing near this spot in 432, St Patrick made his first convert: Díchú, the local chieftain, gave the holy man a sheep barn (*sabhal* in Irish, pronounced sawl) in which to preach. A replica 10th-century church and round tower marks the site to the west of the village.

East of the village is the small hill of **Slieve Patrick** (120m), with stations of the cross along the path to the top and a massive 10m-high statue of St Patrick on the summit. The hill is a popular pilgrimage site on St Patrick's Day.

⊙ Sights

Saul Church
CHURCH

(www.downcathedral.org/saul-church; Saul Rd; ⊙ 9am-5pm) **FREE** At the supposed site of the first church in Ireland, founded by St Patrick in 432, you'll find a replica 10th-century **church and round tower**, built in 1932 to mark the 1500th anniversary of his arrival. The church is west of Saul village.

Struell Wells
CHRISTIAN SITE

FREE These supposedly curative spring waters are traditionally associated with St Patrick – it is said he scourged himself here, spending much of the night immersed in what is now the **Drinking Well**.

The wells are in a scenic, secluded glen 3km east of Downpatrick and 3km south of Saul village. From Downpatrick, take the B1 road towards Ardglass, and turn left after passing the hospital.

Patrick must have been a hardy soul – the well-preserved but chilly 17th-century bathhouses here look more likely to induce ill health than cure it! The site has been venerated for centuries, although the buildings are all post-1600.

Between the bathhouses and the ruined chapel stands the **Eye Well**, whose waters are said to cure eye ailments.

ℹ️ Getting There & Away

Saul is 3km northeast of Downpatrick off the A2 Strangford Rd.

Bus 16e from Downpatrick to Strangford stops at Saul Church (11 minutes, seven daily Monday to Friday, five on Saturday).

Lecale Peninsula

East of Downpatrick, the low-lying Lecale Peninsula is isolated by the sea and Strangford Lough to the north, south and east, and the marshes of the Rivers Quoile and Blackstaff to the west. Its Irish name Leath Chathail (lay-ca-*hal*) means 'the territory of Cathal' (an 8th-century prince), and this region of fertile farmland is fringed by fishing harbours, rocky bluffs and sandy beaches.

Between Ardglass and Killough in the south of the peninsula is **Coney Island**, vividly described in Van Morrison's spoken-word song of the same name. This little seaside hamlet isn't in fact an island, but has a small peninsula that may once have been cut off by the sea. The Oscar-winning short film *The Shore* (2011) was shot at director Terry George's family cottage here.

Strangford

POP 475

The picturesque fishing village of Strangford (Baile Loch Cuan) lies 16km northeast of Downpatrick. It's dominated by Strangford Castle, a 16th-century tower house (closed to the public) that faces its counterpart in Portaferry across the Narrows.

At the end of Castle St, a footpath called the **Squeeze Gut** leads over the hill behind the village, with a fine view of the lough, before looping back to Strangford via tree-lined Dufferin Ave (1.5km), or continuing around the shoreline to Castle Ward Estate (4.5km).

🏃 Activities

Strangford Sea Safari   BOATING
(📞 028-4372 3933; www.clearsky-adventure.com; Strangford Harbour; adult/child £20/17) Runs one-hour speedboat tours (on most Sundays March to September) into the swirling tidal streams of the Narrows, including visits to the Angus Rock Lighthouse and local seal colonies. Call ahead for the boat-trip schedule and to make a booking.

🛏️ Sleeping

Cuan   B&B ££
(📞 028-4488 1222; www.thecuan.com; The Square; s/d £67/100; 🅿️ 🛜) You can't miss the Cuan and its sage-green facade, just around the corner from the ferry slip, or the warm welcome from husband-and-wife managers Peter and Caroline. There are nine neat, comfortable and well-equipped rooms, and an atmospheric, wood-panelled **restaurant** (www.thecuan.com; The Square; mains £12-17, fish & chips £4-8; ⊙ restaurant noon-9pm Mon-Thu, to 9.30pm Fri & Sat, to 8.30pm Sun, fish & chip shop 4-8pm Thu, noon-8pm Fri & Sat).

ℹ️ Getting There & Away

Bus 16E serves Downpatrick (£3.50, 25 minutes, nine daily Monday to Friday, five on Saturday).

A **car ferry** (📞 028-4488 1637; one-way car & driver £5.80, car passengers & pedestrians £1) from Strangford to Portaferry sails on the hour and half-hour between 7.30am and 10.30pm Monday to Friday, 8am and 11pm Saturday, and 9.30am and 10.30pm on Sunday. The journey time is about 10 minutes.

Castle Ward Estate

Famed for its role as Winterfell in *Game of Thrones*, 1760s-built **Castle Ward House** (📞 028-4488 1204; www.nationaltrust.org.uk; Park Rd; adult/child incl guided house tour £9/4.50; ⊙ buildings noon-5pm Easter-Oct, grounds 10am-6pm; 🚻) has a superb setting overlooking the bay west of Strangford. The estate's history is relayed in entertaining 45-minute upstairs/downstairs tours of the house and servants' quarters, starting on the hour (upstairs) and half-hour (downstairs).

On the extensive grounds are a Victorian laundry museum, a farmyard, 16th-century Plantation tower Old Castle Ward, 15th-century tower house Castle Audley, along with walking and cycling trails.

Castle Ward House was built for Lord and Lady Bangor – Bernard Ward and his wife, Anne – whose widely differing architectural tastes resulted in an eccentric country residence – and a subsequent divorce. Bernard favoured the neoclassical style seen in the front facade and the main staircase, while Anne leaned towards the Strawberry Hill Gothic of the rear facade, which reaches a peak in the incredible fan vaulting of her Gothic boudoir.

There's a caravan park (www.nationaltrust.org.uk; Downpatrick Rd; tents £23-35, caravans

£23-40) on the estate with pitches for tents has pitches for tents and caravans as well as basic huts (book ahead). It's open year-round. National Trust members get discounted rates.

Clearsky Adventure Centre (☑028-4372 3933; www.clearsky-adventure.com; Castle Ward Estate, Park Rd; ◷10am-5pm Easter-Sep, to 4pm Oct-Mar) offers various *Game of Thrones*–themed activities, including archery sessions and bicycle tours to filming locations around the estate, complete with capes and wooden swords. It also rents out bikes and kayaks (£20 for 2½ hours). Book ahead. They also run boat trips with Strangford Sea Safari (p583) across the Narrows.

Newcastle

POP 7400

Gloriously set at the foot of the Mourne Mountains on a 5km strand of golden sand, the faded Victorian seaside resort of Newcastle (An Caisleán Nua) has received a multimillion-pound makeover, with a contemporary sculpture-studded, kilometre-long seafront promenade and an elegant footbridge over the River Shimna.

◉ Sights & Activities

Newcastle's main attraction is the beach, which stretches northeast to the nature reserve.

The little harbour at the south end of town once served the 'stone boats' that exported Mourne granite from the quarries of Slieve Donard.

Rock Pool   SWIMMING
(☑028-4372 5034; www.facebook.com/RockPool Newcastle; South Promenade; adult/child £2.50/2; ◷10am-5pm Mon-Fri, noon-5pm Sat, 2-5.30pm Sun Jul & Aug, weather & tides permitting) This outdoor seawater pool, dating from 1933, is at the south end of Newcastle's seafront.

Granite Trail   WALKING
(www.walkni.com/walks/333/granite-trail) Beginning across the road from the water, the 5km Granite Trail is a waymarked footpath up a disused funicular railway line that once carried Mourne Mountains granite blocks to the harbour. The view from the top is worth the steep, 200m climb. Pick up a leaflet at the Newcastle Visitor Information Centre (p585).

Royal County Down Golf Course   GOLF
(☑028-4372 3314; www.royalcountydown.org; 36 Golf Links Rd; green fees £220-240 May-Oct, lower rates Nov-Apr) Set amid flowering heather and gorse, this hallowed par-71 links course was designed by Old Tom Morris and incorporates two awe-inspiring nine-hole loops. It's open to visitors Monday, Tuesday and Friday morning and afternoon, Thursday morning and Sunday afternoon. No handicap is required, but you'll need to book several months ahead.

Soak   SPA
(☑028-4372 6002; www.soakseaweedbaths. co.uk; 5-7 South Promenade; 1hr session from £25; ◷11.30am-8pm Thu-Mon) If it's too cold for outdoor bathing, you can simmer away in a hot seaweed bath at Soak. Towels and robes are provided.

🛏 Sleeping

★Hutt Hostel   HOSTEL £
(☑028-4372 2133; www.hutthostel.com; 30 Downs Rd; dm/apt £22/100; 🛜) A frisbee's throw from the beach in a renovated Victorian townhouse, the 40-bed Hutt has super amenities including a sociable common room with open fireplace, games room with pool table, self-catering kitchen and laundry. Its self-contained apartment 'the Padd' sleeps up to six people.

★Enniskeen Country House   BOUTIQUE HOTEL ££
(☑028-4372 2392; http://enniskeenhotel.co.uk; 98 Bryansford Rd; s/d/f from £65/92/152; ◷restaurant 12.30-8.30pm; 🛜) In a stately 19th-century stone manor house 2km northwest of Newcastle, delightfully old-fashioned Enniskeen has a dozen period-furnished rooms, most with mountain, sea or forest views (try for room 15, tucked in the turret). Its refined Oaks Restaurant opens to a terrace and serves traditional Northern Irish cuisine, including afternoon tea using hand-churned butter and honey from a local apiary.

Briers Country House   B&B ££
(☑028-4372 4347; www.thebriers.co.uk; 39 Middle Tollymore Rd; d from £85, cottage £150-200; 🅿🛜) A peaceful farmhouse B&B with views of the Mournes, Briers is just 1.5km northwest of Newcastle's town centre (signposted off the road between Newcastle and Bryansford). Huge breakfasts – vegetarian if you like – are served with a view over the garden. There's also a self-contained three-bedroom cottage (minimum three-night stay).

SLIEVE DONARD

You can hike to the summit of **Slieve Donard** (853m; the highest hill in Northern Ireland) from various starting points in and around Newcastle, but it's a stiff climb and you shouldn't attempt it without proper walking boots, waterproofs and a map and compass.

On a good day the view from the top extends to the hills of Donegal, the Wicklow Mountains, the coast of Scotland, the Isle of Man and even the hills of Snowdonia in Wales. Two cairns near the summit were long believed to have been cells of St Donard, who retreated here to pray in early Christian times.

The shortest route to the top is via the River Glen from Newcastle. Begin at Donard Park car park, at the edge of town, 1km south of the bus station. At the far end of the car park, turn right through the gate and head into the woods, with the river on your left. A gravel path leads up the River Glen valley to the saddle between Slieve Donard and Slieve Commedagh. From here, turn left and follow the Mourne Wall to the summit. Return by the same route (round-trip 9km; allow at least three hours).

Slieve Donard Resort & Spa   HOTEL **£££**
(☑028-4372 1066; www.hastingshotels.com; Downs Rd; s/d from £160/180; P🅿🔊🏊) Established in 1897, the Slieve Donard is a magnificent Victorian red-brick pile on 2.5 hectares of beachfront land, with several restaurants and a fancy spa. Adjoining Royal County Down Golf Course (p584), it's where golf legends Tom Watson, Tiger Woods and Rory McIlroy stay when they're in town.

🍴 Eating

Olive Bizarre   CAFE **£**
(☑028-4372 5576; http://olivebizarre.com; 67 South Promenade; mains £5-8; ⊙9am-5pm; 🔊🖉🐾) 🍴 Vegetarian and vegan options abound at this chilled little cafe: soups, quiches, pies, jacket potatoes, sandwiches and daily specials such as organic falafel balls with Ballymaloe spiced tomato relish and hummus.

Niki's Kitchen Café   CAFE **£**
(☑028-4372 6777; www.facebook.com/NikisKitchenCafe; 107 Central Promenade; mains £5-10; ⊙8am-5pm Mon & Tue, 8am-9pm Wed-Sun; 🔊🐾) The crowds testify to the success of this large, airy eatery, where the menu focuses on quality versions of classic cafe cuisine. There are high chairs, a kids' menu and sofas for loafing over coffee.

Strand Cafe & Bakery   ICE CREAM **£**
(53-55 Central Promenade; ice cream from £1.30; ⊙9am-6pm Mon-Fri, to 7.30pm Sat & Sun) Yes, there's a cafe and bakery here, but the real reason to stop by is to order a cone of award-winning ice cream, made here since 1930. Classic flavours include raspberry ripple, honeycomb, and chocolate and orange.

★ **Brunel's**   MODERN IRISH **££**
(☑028-4372 3951; www.brunelsrestaurant.co.uk; 9 Bryansford Rd; mains lunch £6-11, dinner £16-25; ⊙12.30-3pm & 6-9.30pm Wed & Thu, to 10pm Fri & Sat, noon-8pm Sun) 🍴 At Brunel's, chef Paul Cunningham's local foraging skills, hand-picked suppliers and inspired flavour combinations come together to create some of Northern Ireland's best restaurant food. Exquisitely presented dishes more than deliver on flavour; prices are reasonable too. Book ahead.

At research time Brunel's was due to move to a new seafront premises at the northern end of town; look for them on Downs Rd near the Slieve Donard Resort & Spa.

Vanilla   IRISH **£££**
(☑028-4372 2268; www.vanillarestaurant.co.uk; 67 Main St; mains lunch £6-11, dinner £19-25; ⊙noon-3.30pm & 5-9pm Mon-Thu & Sun, to 9.30pm Fri & Sat; 🐾) 🍴 The menu at this sleek town-centre bistro uses Irish produce in creative dishes with international influences, such as Thai beef shin spring rolls; salmon, Kilkeel lobster, langoustine ravioli and monkfish laksa.

ℹ Information

There's free public wi-fi along the promenade.
Newcastle Visitor Information Centre
(☑028-4372 2222; www.visitmourne mountains.co.uk; 10-14 Central Promenade; ⊙9.30am-7pm Mon-Sat, 1-7pm Sun Jul & Aug, 9.30am-5pm Mon-Fri, 10am-5pm Sat, 2-5pm Sun Sep-Jun; 🔊) Sells local-interest books and maps, and traditional and contemporary crafts. Left luggage costs £2 per day.

ℹ️ Getting There & Away

Buses 20 and 20A run to Newcastle from Belfast's Europa Bus Centre (£8, 1¼ hours, at least hourly) via Dundrum.

Bus 240 takes the inland route from Newry to Newcastle (£6.70, 50 minutes, seven daily Monday to Friday, six on Saturday, four on Sunday) and continues to Downpatrick.

Dundrum & Around

POP 1500

Sheltered Dundrum Bay is famous for its oysters and mussels, making Dundrum village a good place to stop for seafood. There are spectacular views of the Mourne Mountains and the coastline from Dundrum Castle, and a nearby nature reserve is a great spot for a walk across the dunes.

Murlough National Nature Reserve   WILDLIFE RESERVE

(www.nationaltrust.org.uk; car park May-Sep £4; ⊙ dawn-dusk) FREE At the Murlough National Nature Reserve footpaths and boardwalks meander among the grassy dunes leading to a wide sandy beach with great views back towards the Mournes. It's a haul-out site for common and grey seals.

Seaforde Gardens & Tropical Butterfly House   GARDENS

(www.seafordegardens.com; Seaforde House, Seaforde; gardens or butterfly house adult/child £6/4, gardens & butterfly house £10.30/5.85; ⊙10am-5pm Mon-Sat, 1-6pm Sun Easter-Sep; ☻) Adults and kids alike will enjoy this oasis in the Seaforde demesne, which is home to an 18th-century walled garden with ornamental flower beds, a hedge maze, spiral-staircase tower with viewing platform and strutting iridescent-blue peacocks. Its rainforest-like butterfly house is filled with hundreds of fluttering butterflies as well as parrots. A simple but cosy timber cafe is located by the entrance. The gardens are 7km north of Dundrum (13km north of Newcastle) on the A2.

Dundrum Castle   CASTLE

(Castle Hill; ⊙grounds open year-round, castle 10am-5pm Wed & Fri-Sun Apr-Sep, noon-4pm Sun Oct-Mar) FREE Founded in 1177 by John de Courcy of Carrickfergus, this Norman fortress overlooks Dundrum Bay. Enter the castle for wonderful views across to the Mourne Mountains and rural County Down from de Lacey's keep.

★ Mourne Seafood Bar   SEAFOOD ££

(☎028-4375 1377; http://mourneseafood.com; 10 Main St; mains £11-26; ⊙12.30-9.30pm Wed & Thu, to 10pm Fri & Sat, to 6pm Sun) 🍴 Set in a wood-panelled Victorian house hung with local art, this friendly and informal spot serves oysters five ways, plus seafood chowder, crab, langoustines and daily fish specials, all sourced locally (including from its own shellfish beds). Its Belfast outpost (p560) has a cookery school.

ℹ️ Getting There & Away

Bus 240 from Newcastle (£2.70, 10 minutes, seven daily Monday to Friday, six on Saturday, four on Sunday) to Downpatrick (£3.50, 15 minutes) stops in Dundrum.

Mourne Mountains

The Mourne Mountains dominate the horizon as you head south from Belfast towards Newcastle. This is one of the most beautiful corners of Northern Ireland, with a distinctive landscape of grey granite, yellow gorse and whitewashed cottages, the lower slopes of the hills latticed with a neat patchwork of drystone walls cobbled together from huge, rounded granite boulders.

The hills were made famous in a popular song penned by Irish songwriter William Percy French in 1896 – the chorus, 'Where the Mountains of Mourne sweep down to the sea', captures perfectly their scenic blend of ocean, sky and hillside.

History

The crescent of low-lying land on the southern side of the mountains is known as the **Kingdom of Mourne**. Cut off for centuries by its difficult approaches (the main overland route passed north of the hills), it developed a distinctive landscape and culture. Until the coast road was built in the early 19th century, the only access was on foot or by sea.

Smuggling provided a source of income in the 18th century. Boats carrying French spirits would land at night and packhorses would carry the casks through the hills to the inland road, avoiding the excise men at Newcastle. The **Brandy Pad**, a former smugglers' path from Bloody Bridge to Tollymore, is a popular walking route today.

⊙ Sights & Activities

The Mournes offer some of the best hill walking and rock climbing in the North. You can buy maps at the Newcastle Visitor Information Centre (p585).

★ **Tollymore Forest Park**   FOREST
(Bryansford Rd; car parking £5; ⊙10am-dusk) FREE This scenic forest park, 3km west of Newcastle, offers lovely walks and bike rides along the River Shimna and across the Mournes' northern slopes. Victorian follies include the church-like **Clanbrassil Barn**, as well as grottoes, caves, bridges and stepping stones (and yes, the park is a *Game of Thrones* filming location). You can pitch a tent at the campground (p588) here.

Castlewellan Forest Park   FOREST
(Main St, Castlewellan; car park £5; ⊙10am-dusk) FREE Castlewellan Forest Park offers gentle walks around the castle grounds, one of the world's largest hedge mazes, the **Peace Maze** (entry free), and, from March to October, **trout fishing** in its lovely lake (three-day licence and permit £9.50). A recent addition is a network of exciting **mountain-bike trails** – see www. mountainbikeni.com for details. Bike hire is available from Life Adventure Centre.

Silent Valley Reservoir   LAKE
(www.niwater.com; car/motorcycle £4.50/2, plus per adult/child £1.60/60p; ⊙10am-6.30pm May-Sep, to 4pm Oct-Apr) At the heart of the Mournes is the beautiful Silent Valley Reservoir, where the River Kilkeel, which supplies Belfast and County Down with water, was dammed in 1933. There are scenic, waymarked walks around the grounds and an interesting exhibition on the dam's construction.

Life Adventure Centre   OUTDOORS
(☑028-4377 0714; www.onegreatadventure.com; Grange Courtyard, Castlewellan Forest Park) If you fancy trying hill walking, rock climbing, canoeing or a range of other outdoor activities, this centre in Castlewellan Forest Park (p587) offers one-day, have-a-go sessions for individuals, couples and families (from £76 per person), as well as Sunday-afternoon taster sessions. It also rents out canoes (£35/45 per half-/full day), kayaks (£13/23) and mountain bikes (£23/28).

THE MOURNE WALL

The spectacular drystone **Mourne Wall** marches across the summits of 15 surrounding peaks, including the highest, Slieve Donard (853m). You can walk the 2m-high, 1m-thick, 35km-long wall's entire length, or just a short section.

Although the 1922 wall was built to stop livestock reaching the catchment area of the Rivers Kilkeel and Annalong, poor geological conditions meant the Annalong couldn't be dammed, and its waters were diverted to the Silent Valley Reservoir via a 3.6km tunnel beneath Slieve Binnian.

Mountpleasant Trekking Centre   HORSE RIDING
(☑028-4377 8651; www.mountpleasantcentre. com; Bannonstown Rd, Castlewellan; per 1hour £20; ⊙by reservation) Catering for both experienced riders and beginners, this horse-riding and pony-trekking centre offers various guided treks into Castlewellan Forest Park (p587). Short and long rides, beach rides and pony trekking can also be arranged.

Hotrock Climbing Wall   CLIMBING
(☑028-4372 2188; www.tollymore.com; 32 Hilltown Rd, Tollymore National Outdoor Centre; adult/child £5/2.50; ⊙10am-10pm Tue-Thu, to 5pm Fri-Mon) If the weather is wet, you can go climbing at this indoor wall; it rents out rock boots and harnesses for £3.50. The entrance is on the B180, on the western side of Tollymore Forest Park, off Bryansford Rd.

✦ Festivals & Events

Mourne International Walking Festival   SPORTS
(☑028-4175 2256; www.mournewalking.co.uk; 1-/2-/3-day ticket £12/20/25; ⊙late Jun) This three-day festival is a great opportunity for glorious mountain walks, with guided hikes ranging from 9km to 20km.

🛏 Sleeping & Eating

★ **Mourne Lodge**   HOSTEL £
(☑028-4176 5859; http://themournelodge. com; Bog Rd, Atticall; dm/s/d from £20/45/50; P@🛜) This purpose-built 31-bed hostel offers bright and appealing budget

accommodation. As well as a self-catering kitchen and barbecue patio, there's a restaurant that serves breakfast, lunch and dinner (bookings essential). It's in the village of Atticall, 6km north of Kilkeel, off the B27 Hilltown road, and 3km west of the entrance to Silent Valley.

Tollymore Forest Park   CAMPGROUND **£**
(☑ 028-4372 2428; 176 Tullybranigan Rd; camping sites with/without electricity £20/18) Many of Newcastle's camping sites are for caravans only; the nearest place you can pitch a tent is here amid the attractive scenery of Tollymore Forest Park, in the foothills of the Mourne Mountains, 3km northwest of the town centre. You can hike here (along Bryansford Ave and Bryansford Rd) in 45 minutes.

Meelmore Lodge   HOSTEL **£**
(☑ 028-4372 6657; www.meelmorelodge.co.uk; 52 Trassey Rd, Bryansford; campsites per adult/child £8.50/4, dm/tw/f £20/50/80; **P**) On the northern slopes of the Mournes, 5km west of Bryansford village, wonderfully remote Meelmore has a cosy lounge and kitchen, two four-bunk dorms, a couple of private rooms with private bathrooms, a tent-only campsite and a good cafe. You can hike into the hills from the hostel's front door.

❶ Getting There & Away

The summertime bus **Mourne Rambler** (Bus 405; www.translink.co.uk; Bus Rambler unlimited day travel adult/child £9/4.50; ☺ Tue-Sun May-Aug) runs a circular route from Newcastle around the Mournes, making 18 stops that include Tollymore Forest Park, Castlewellan and Silent Valley. There are five services per day and a rack for bikes.

Mournes Coast Road

The A2 coast road between Newcastle and Newry is one of the region's most scenic drives.

❶ Getting There & Around

Bus 39 links Newry with Kilkeel (£6, 50 minutes, hourly Monday to Saturday, four on Sunday) via Warrenpoint and Rostrevor. From Kilkeel, bus 37 continues along the coastal road to Newcastle (£4.40, 35 minutes, hourly Monday to Saturday, eight on Sunday).

Rostrevor & Around

POP 2400

The pretty seaside resort of Rostrevor (Caislean Ruairi) is best known for its lively pubs and the forested hills of nearby Kilbroney Park, with its fabulous mountain-biking trails. CS Lewis once said that the part of Rostrevor that overlooks Carlingford Lough was his idea of Narnia.

Each year in late July, folk musicians converge on the village for the week-long Fiddler's Green International Festival.

◉ Sights & Activities

Kilbroney Park   FOREST
(www.visitmournemountains.co.uk; Shore Rd; ☺ 9am-10pm Jun-Sep, to 9pm May, to 7pm Apr & Oct, to 5pm Nov-Mar) **FREE** This 16-sq-km forest park unfolds 1km east of Rostrevor. From the car park at the top of the forest drive, a 10-minute hike leads up to a superb view over the lough to Carlingford Mountain, as well as to the **Cloughmore Stone**, a 30-tonne granite boulder inscribed with Victorian-era graffiti. The park is also home to Northern Ireland's best downhill **mountain-biking trails**; bike hire and uplift are available from East Coast Adventure (p588), at the trailhead.

There's also a **caravan park**, with a grass area suitable for tents (camping sites with/without electricity hook-up £21/16.80).

East Coast Adventure   MOUNTAIN BIKING
(☑ office (weekdays) 028-4173 8516, trail office (weekends) 07876 681197; www.eastcoastadventure.com; bike hire per half/full day £30/45, uplift per half-day £17.50; ☺ bike hire by prior reservation, uplift service Sat & Sun only, plus Fri & Mon Jul-Aug) Kilbroney Park (p588) is home to Northern Ireland's best downhill mountain-biking trails; bike hire and uplift are available from East Coast Adventure, at the trailhead. Book ahead. See www.mountainbikeni.com/rostrevor/ for more info about mountain biking.

✖ Eating

Kilbroney   PUB FOOD **££**
(☑ 028-4173 8390; www.facebook.com/kilbroneybarandrestaurant; 31 Church St; mains £9-20; ☺ kitchen 12.30-8pm Mon-Thu, to 9pm Fri & Sat, 12.30-4pm & 5-8pm Sun) As well as being a good place to catch traditional Irish music sessions and live bands most evenings, the Kilbroney is one of the best pubs to eat at in Rostrevor, serving classic pub grub like steak sandwiches, lasagne, burgers and chunky chips.

Warrenpoint

POP 7000

Warrenpoint (An Pointe) is a Victorian resort at the head of Carlingford Lough, with a shingle beach and beautiful mountain views. Its seaside appeal is somewhat diminished by the large industrial harbour at the west end of town, but its broad streets, main square and renovated prom warrant a stop.

Narrow Water Castle   CASTLE
About 2km northwest of Warrenpoint's town centre you'll see Narrow Water Castle, a fine Elizabethan tower house built in 1568 to command the entrance to the River Newry. It's closed to the public, unless, that is, you stay at its apartment (p589).

Blues on the Bay   MUSIC
(https://bluesonthebay.co.uk; ☺late May) The Spring bank-holiday weekend sees some of the world's leading blues musicians descend on Warrenpoint for the six-day Blues on the Bay festival. As well as 90 different gigs in mostly small, intimate venues, there's also a family-friendly Bluesberry music and food festival in Warrenpoint Park.

🛏 Sleeping & Eating

⭐**Narrow Water Castle**
Apartment   APARTMENT ££
(☏07784 730826; www.narrowwatercastle.co.uk; Apt 2, Narrow Water Castle; d from £110) Within historic Narrow Water Castle (p589), but with its own entrance, this exquisite apartment has two bedrooms (one with a private bathroom, and both with Hungarian down pillows and beautiful linens), an antique-furnished lounge with an open fireplace, a main bathroom with a free-standing, double-slipper bath, a fully equipped kitchen and access to the castle gardens. There is a minimum three-night stay.

Whistledown Hotel   BOUTIQUE HOTEL ££
(☏028-4175 4174; www.thewhistledownhotel.com; 6 Seaview; s/d from £80/90; 🛜) In a superb waterfront setting, the Whistledown has 21 stylish bedrooms with cherry and pistachio crushed-velvet trimmings, large flat-screen TVs and bathrooms with colourful designer tiling.

⭐**Restaurant 23**   MODERN IRISH ££
(☏028-4175 3222; www.balmoralwarrenpoint. co.uk/restaurant-23; 13 Seaview; mains restaurant £14-20, bistro £12-15; ☺restaurant 5.30-10pm Thu-

Sat, noon-8pm Sun, bistro noon-10pm Mon-Sat, to 9pm Sun; 🖐) 🍴 On the 1st-floor restaurant at the Balmoral Hotel on Warrenpoint's waterfront, TV chef Ray McArdle's fun approach to fine Irish produce plays out on an ever-changing menu in dishes such as black-truffle soup with bacon and Guinness mousse. A more casual menu is available downstairs in the Anchor Bistro, with dishes like beer-battered haddock and chips.

Newry

POP 27,433

Newry has long been a frontier town, guarding the land route from Dublin to Ulster through the 'Gap of the North', the pass between Slieve Gullion and the Carlingford hills, which is still followed by the main Dublin–Belfast road and railway. Its name derives from a yew tree (An tIúr) supposedly planted here by St Patrick.

The opening of the Newry Canal in 1742, linking the town with the River Bann at Portadown, made Newry a busy trading port, exporting coal, linen and butter. Today it's a bustling shopping centre.

⊙ Sights

Newry & Mourne Museum   MUSEUM
(www.bagenalscastle.com; Castle St; ☺10am-4.30pm Mon-Sat, 1.30-5pm Sun) FREE This museum is housed in Bagenal's Castle, the town's oldest surviving building, with exhibits on the Newry Canal and local archaeology, culture and folklore. Recently rediscovered (having been incorporated into more recent buildings), the 16th-century castle was built for Nicholas Bagenal, grand marshal of the English army in Ireland.

Derrymore House   HISTORIC BUILDING
(www.nationaltrust.org.uk; gardens free, house adult/child £2/free; ☺gardens dawn-dusk) Just south of Bessbrook, and 4km west of Newry, is Derrymore House. The elegant thatched cottage was built in 1776 for Isaac Corry, the Irish MP for Newry for 30 years; the Act of Union was drafted in the drawing room here in 1800. The house is only open on a handful of days each year – call or check the National Trust website – but the surrounding parkland offers scenic trails with views to the Ring of Gullion.

The grounds were laid out by John Sutherland (1745–1826), one of the most celebrated disciples of English landscape gardener Capability Brown.

Sleeping & Eating

Canal Court Hotel HOTEL **££**
(☑ 028-3025 1234; www.canalcourthotel.com; 34
Merchants Quay; s/d from £80/98; P@🛜🏊) Overlooking Newry Canal, this 110-room mustard-coloured hotel is relatively new but has a charmingly old-fashioned atmosphere, with leather sofas dotted around the vast wood-panelled lobby, a low-lit bar with trad music and good pub food, and a grand staircase up to the spacious rooms. Its leisure centre has a 20m pool. Staff are a pleasure to deal with.

Brass Monkey PUB FOOD **££**
(☑ 028-3026 3176; 1-4 Sandy St; bar menu mains £6-8, 2/3 courses £12/15; ⊙10am-midnight Mon-Thu, to 2am Fri & Sat, noon-midnight Sun) Newry's most popular pub has a Victorian brass, brick and timber decor with contemporary lighting and velvet sofas. It serves good bar meals ranging from lasagne and burgers to seafood and steaks. There's live music on Saturday and Sunday.

★**Finegan & Son** COFFEE
(www.facebook.com/fineganandson; 9 Kildare St; ⊙8.30am-5pm; 🛜) Named for the owner and his young son, this light-filled corner cafe serves some seriously good coffee. There are three single-origin drip coffees available that change weekly, as well as cold brews and flat whites from the machine. They also do good brunches and gourmet sandwiches.

Bank BAR
(www.facebook.com/bankrestaurantnewry; 1-2 Trevor Hill; ⊙noon-11.30pm Mon-Thu, 9am-1.30am Fri-Sun) A gorgeous old grey-stone former bank houses this huge bar/nightclub. It combines some of the building's original features, including a stained-glass ceiling dome, with contemporary decor, such as neon fuchsia lighting. The sheltered South American–style beer garden has a stage for live music (every Saturday night) and enormous earthenware pots. It has good bistro food too.

Information

Newry Visitor Information Centre (☑ 028-3031 3170; www.visitmournemountains.co.uk; Castle St; ⊙9am-5pm Mon-Fri, 10am-4pm Sat Jun-Sep, 9am-5.30pm Mon, 9am-6pm Tue-Fri, 10am-4pm Sat Jul & Aug, plus 1-5pm Sun Jun-Sep) In Bagenal's Castle, along with the **Newry & Mourne Museum** (p589).

Getting There & Away

BUS
Newry's bus station is on the Mall, opposite the Canal Court Hotel.

Services include the following:

Armagh £6, 50 minutes, hourly Monday to Saturday, three Sunday

Belfast (Europa Bus Centre) £9.30, 1¼ hours, at least hourly Monday to Saturday, eight Sunday

Hillsborough £6.70, 50 minutes, at least hourly Monday to Saturday, eight Sunday

Rostrevor £3.50, 25 minutes, at least hourly Monday to Saturday, six Sunday

Warrenpoint £3, 20 minutes, at least hourly Monday to Saturday, six Sunday

TRAIN
The train station is 2.5km northwest of the centre, on the A25; bus 341 (free for train passengers) links train arrivals and departures to the bus station.

Newry is on the line linking Dublin (£20, 1¼ hours, eight daily) and Belfast (£11, one hour 10 minutes, 10 Monday to Saturday, five Sunday).

Hillsborough & Around

POP 3400
The elegant little town of Hillsborough, 19km south of Belfast, was founded in the 1640s by Colonel Arthur Hill, who built a fort here to quell Irish insurgents. Fine Georgian architecture rings the square and lines Main St.

Most famously, Hillsborough Castle is the official residence of the Secretary of State for Northern Ireland, and is used to entertain visiting heads of state (US presidents George W Bush and Bill Clinton have both enjoyed its hospitality).

Sights

Hillsborough Castle HISTORIC BUILDING
(☑ 028-9268 1300; www.hrp.org.uk; Main St; castle & gardens adult/child £8/5.50, gardens only adult/child £5/3.50; ⊙gardens 9.30am-6pm Mar-Sep, to 4.30pm Mon-Sat Oct-Feb, castle 11am-4pm late Mar-early Apr & Jul-Sep) The British monarch's official Northern Ireland residence is this rambling, late-Georgian mansion, which was built in 1797 for Wills Hill, the first Marquess of Downshire, and extensively remodelled in the 1830s and 40s. Book ahead for hour-long guided tours taking in the throne room, state drawing room and dining rooms, and the Lady

Grey Room where, in 2003, Tony Blair and George W Bush held talks on Iraq.

Highlights of the lovely gardens include a moss-covered lime-tree walk.

Since taking over management of the castle in 2016, Historic Royal Palaces has embarked on an ambitious project that involves transforming the stable block into a visitor centre, cafe and shop, and building a new carpark to accommodate coaches, with renovations of Hillsborough's Courthouse and Fort planned for the future.

St Malachy's Parish Church   CHURCH
(www.hillsboroughparish.org.uk; Main St; ⊙8.30am-7pm) FREE St Malachy's is one of Ireland's most splendid 18th-century churches, with twin towers at the ends of the transepts and a graceful spire at the western end. A tree-lined avenue leads to the church from a statue of Arthur Hill, fourth Marquess of Downshire, at the bottom of Main St.

Hillsborough Fort   HISTORIC BUILDING
(Main St; ⊙grounds 10am-4pm Mon-Sat, 11am-4pm Sun) FREE Built as an artillery fort by Colonel Hill in 1650 (William of Orange stayed here on his way to the Boyne in 1690), Hillsborough Fort was remodelled as a Gothic-style tower house in 1758. A tree-lined path opposite the Courthouse (p591) leads to the fort, which sits on the edge of Hillsborough Forest Park. Only the grounds are open to the public.

In 1771 Benjamin Franklin spent five days at the fort as the guest of Wills Hill, then Secretary of State for the Colonies. Reportedly the meeting went so badly that it helped convince Franklin that revolution was America's only option.

Hillsborough Courthouse   HISTORIC BUILDING
(The Square; ⊙9am-5.30pm Mon-Sat year-round, plus 11am-4pm Sun Apr-Sep) FREE Dating from 1765, this fine old Georgian market house was used as a courthouse from 1810 until 1986. It now exhibits various displays describing the working of the courts.

🛏 Sleeping & Eating

★Fortwilliam Country House   B&B ££
(☎028-9268 2255; www.fortwilliamcountryhouse.com; 210 Ballynahinch Rd; s/d £50/75; P 🛜) The Fortwilliam's four luxurious rooms include the Victorian room, with rose wallpaper,

WORTH A TRIP

BULL & RAM

Located in a beautifully restored Edwardian former butcher's shop, complete with original cream and emerald wall tiles and meat-hanging rail, **Bull & Ram** (☎028-9756 0908; www.bullandram.com; 1 Dromore St, Ballynahinch; mains £13-28; ⊙noon-8.30pm Mon & Tue, to 9pm Wed, Thu & Sun, to 9.30pm Fri & Sat) buzzes with customers happy to travel to Ballynahinch to sample chef Kelan McMichael's sublime cooking of Himalayan salt-aged County Down beef, Mourne lamb and Kilkeel fish. It's 14km southeast of Hillsborough and 30km south of Belfast.

a huge antique mahogany wardrobe and a view over the garden. Breakfast includes fresh eggs from the chickens in the yard, and the smell of home-baked wheaten bread wafts from the Aga stove. From Hillsborough, take the B177 towards Anahilt; it's 5.6km along on the right.

★Parson's Nose   MODERN IRISH ££
(www.ballooinns.com; 48 Lisburn St; mains £11-22, 2-/3-course dinner £19/24; ⊙kitchen noon-9pm Sun-Thu, to 10pm Fri & Sat) A recent refurb has added an elegant downstairs dining room to this popular gastropub, housed in a beautiful Georgian building. Upstairs the chefs whip local ingredients into appealing dishes, in a theatrical open kitchen complete with a wood-fired pizza oven. Some tables overlook Hillsborough Castle's lake.

Plough Inn   BISTRO ££
(☎028-9268 2985; http://ploughgroup.com; 3 The Square; mains lunch £10-12, dinner £11.50-22, seafood £13-24; ⊙noon-3pm & 5-9pm Mon-Thu, to 9.30pm Fri & Sat, noon-8pm Sun; 🍴) This fine old pub, with its maze of dark, wood-panelled nooks and crannies, has been offering 'beer and banter' since 1758. It serves gourmet bar lunches and evening bistro meals, as well as fine dining in the upstairs seafood restaurant (open Friday and Saturday from 6pm to 9.30pm), where stone walls, low ceilings and a roaring fireplace make a cosy setting.

There is often live music on Friday and Saturday nights.

Hillside Bar & Restaurant   PUB

(☑ 028-9268 9233; www.hillsidehillsborough.co.uk; 21 Main St; ◷ noon-11.30pm Mon-Wed, to 11.45pm Thu, to 12.30am Fri, to 12.45am Sat, 12.30-11pm Sun) On sloping Main St, this homely pub serves real ale and mulled wine beside the fireplace in winter. There's a beer garden in a cobbled courtyard out the back.

ℹ Information

Hillsborough Visitor Information Centre
(☑ 028-9244 7640; www.visitlisburncastle reagh.com; The Square; ◷ 9am-5.30pm Mon-Sat year-round, plus 11am-4pm Sun Apr-Sep) In the Georgian **Hillsborough Courthouse** (p591) in the centre of the village.

ℹ Getting There & Away

Bus 238 from Belfast's Europa Bus Centre (£3.80, 25 minutes, at least hourly Monday to Saturday, eight Sunday) continues to Newry (£6.70, 50 minutes).

COUNTY ARMAGH

Armagh City

POP 14,600

The attractive little cathedral city of Armagh (Ard Macha) has been an important religious centre since the 5th century, and remains the ecclesiastical capital of Ireland, the seat of both the Anglican and Roman Catholic archbishops of Armagh, and Primates of All Ireland. Their two cathedrals, both named for St Patrick, look across at each other from their respective hilltops.

History

When St Patrick began his mission to spread Christianity throughout Ireland, he chose a site close to Emain Macha (Navan Fort), the nerve centre of pagan Ulster, for his power base. In 445 he built Ireland's first stone church on a hill nearby (now home to the Church of Ireland cathedral), and later decreed that Armagh should have pre-eminence over all the churches in Ireland.

By the 8th century Armagh was one of Europe's best-known centres of religion, learning and craftwork. The city was divided into three districts (called *trians*), centred around English, Scottish and Irish streets. Armagh's fame was its undoing, however, as the Vikings plundered the city 10 times between 831 and 1013.

The city gained a new prosperity from the linen trade in the 18th century, a period whose legacy includes a Royal School, an astronomical observatory, a renowned public library and a fine crop of Georgian architecture.

◉ Sights

★**Armagh Robinson Library**   LIBRARY

(☑ 028-3752 3142; http://armaghrobinsonlibrary. co.uk; 43 Abbey St; ◷ 10am-1pm & 2-4pm Mon-Fri) **FREE** A first edition of *Gulliver's Travels*, published in 1726 and annotated by Swift himself, is the most prized possession of the wonderful Armagh Robinson Library, founded in 1771 by Archbishop Robinson. Other treasures include Sir Walter Raleigh's 1614 *History of the World,* the *Claims of the Innocents* (pleas to Oliver Cromwell) and engravings by Hogarth and others. The oldest manuscripts here are theological works dating from the 1480s.

Nearby, you can see ancient coins, early Christian artefacts and other curiosities at No 5 **Vicar's Hill** (☑ 028-3751 1420; http://armagh robinsonlibrary.co.uk/wp/no-5-vicars-hill; 5 Vicar's Hill; adult/child £2/free; ◷ 10am-1pm & 2-4pm Tue-Sat Apr-Sep, Thu-Sat Oct-Mar), a depository for Church of Ireland records.

★**St Patrick's Church of Ireland Cathedral**   CATHEDRAL

(☑ 028-3752 3142; www.stpatricks-cathedral.org; Cathedral Close; adult/child £3/free; ◷ 9am-5pm Apr-Oct, to 4pm Nov-Mar) The city's Anglican cathedral occupies the site of St Patrick's original stone church. The present cathedral's ground plan is 13th century, but the building itself is a Gothic restoration dating from 1834 to 1840. A stone slab on the exterior wall of the north transept marks the **burial place of Brian Ború**, the high king of Ireland, who died near Dublin during the last great battle against the Vikings in 1014.

Within the church are the remains of an 11th-century **Celtic Cross** that once stood nearby, and the **Tandragee Idol**, a curious granite figure dating from the Iron Age. In the south aisle is a **memorial to Archbishop Richard Robinson** (1709–94), who founded Armagh's observatory and public library.

★**St Patrick's Roman Catholic Cathedral**   CATHEDRAL

(www.armagharchdiocese.org; Cathedral Rd; admission by donation; ◷ 8.30am-7.30pm) Huge twin towers dominate the approach to Armagh's Roman Catholic Cathedral, built between 1838 and 1873 in Gothic Revival style. Inside it seems almost Byzantine, with every piece of wall and ceiling covered in brilliantly coloured mosaics. The sanctuary was modernised in 1981 and has a very distinctive tabernacle holder and crucifix that seem out of place among the mosaics and statues of the rest of the church.

Armagh County Museum MUSEUM
(☎028-3752 3070; www.nmni.com/acm; The Mall E; ⏰10am-5pm Mon-Fri, 10am-1pm & 2-5pm Sat) FREE Prehistoric axe heads, artefacts found in bogs, corn dollies and straw-boy outfits, and military costumes and equipment are among the items on display at the county museum. Don't miss the gruesome cast-iron skull that once graced the top of the Armagh gallows.

Mall PARK
This long grassy expanse east of Armagh's centre was a horse-racing, cock-fighting and bull-baiting venue until the 18th century, when Archbishop Robinson decided that it was all a tad vulgar for a city of learning, and transformed it into an elegant Georgian park. It's flanked by notable buildings, including the working (but closed to the public) **Armagh Courthouse** (The Mall N), **Armagh Gaol** (The Mall S), and Georgian terraces, including **Charlemont Place**.

Armagh Planetarium PLANETARIUM
(☎028-3752 3689; www.armaghplanet.com; College Hill; exhibition area free, shows adult/child £6/5; ⏰10am-5pm Mon-Sat year-round, plus Sun Jul & Aug) Aimed mainly at educating young people, the Armagh Planetarium has an interactive exhibition on space exploration, and a digital theatre that screens a range of spectacular half-hour shows on its domed ceiling (prebooking is essential; check the website for show times).

A path connects the planetarium with the Armagh Observatory.

Armagh Observatory OBSERVATORY
(http://star.arm.ac.uk; College Hill) The Armagh Observatory was founded by Archbishop Robinson in 1789 and is still Ireland's leading astronomical-research institute. The observatory building is closed to the public but the attractive grounds (open during daylight hours) contain sundials, a scale model of the solar system and a human orrery showing the positions and orbits of the earth.

A path connects the observatory with the Armagh Planetarium (p593).

Palace Demesne Public Park PARK
(www.armagh.co.uk; 1 Greenpark; ⏰dawn-dusk) This palace and surrounding 121-hectare estate were home to the archbishops of the Church of Ireland from the 1770s to the 1970s. The palace itself now houses Armagh's city council and is closed to the public, but you can visit the beautiful gardens. Don't miss the Garden of Senses, five linked gardens testing all five sensory experiences. In the former stables is the superb bistro the Moody Boar (p595).

Festivals & Events

You may be lucky enough to catch a traditional Irish **road-bowling** match, where contestants hurl small 800g metal bowls along quiet country lanes to see who can make it to the finishing line with the fewest throws. Check fixtures on www.irishroadbowling.ie.

Sleeping

Armagh Hostel HOSTEL £
(☎028-3751 1800; www.hini.org.uk; 39 Abbey St; dm/s/tw/f £19/31/42/48; ⏰8.30-11am & 4-9.30pm Apr-Oct, groups only Nov-Mar; P 📶) This modern, purpose-built hostel near the St Patrick's Church of Ireland Cathedral is more like a small hotel. There are six comfortable twin rooms, two family rooms and 10 small dorms (all with private bathroom), plus TV and tea-and-coffee facilities, a well-equipped kitchen, laundry, lounge and reading room.

★ **Seven Houses** B&B ££
(☎028-3751 1213; www.sevenhouses.co.uk; 3 Upper English St; d/apt £75/95; 📶) This lovely B&B in a central location has two bright rooms with period features and a one-bedroom apartment with a small kitchen and dining area. On the ground floor there's an atmospheric, red-painted bar and lounge, where homemade pizzas (£8 to £11) are served every evening from Friday to Sunday. Breakfast is in the Bagel Bean cafe across the road.

Armagh City Hotel BUSINESS HOTEL ££
(☎028-3751 8888; www.armaghcityhotel.com; 2 Friary Rd; s/d/f from £95/109/135; @ 📶 🏊) What this immense 120-room contemporary hotel lacks in character it makes up for in amenities: a state-of-the-art leisure centre with a gym, steam room and swimming pool plus a beauty salon, restaurant, bar and nightclub. Executive rooms have balconies overlooking

Armagh City

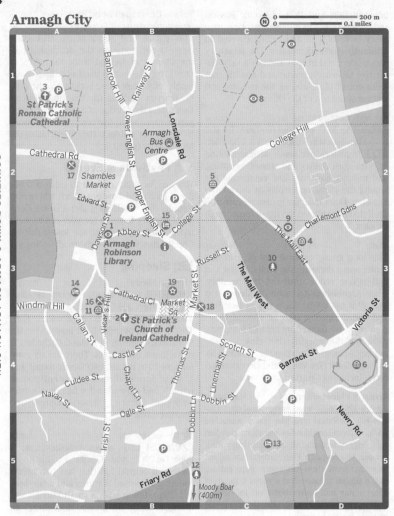

a golf course. Ask for one of the deluxe rooms with floor-to-ceiling windows and views of both of Armagh's cathedrals.

✗ Eating

Mulberry Bistro   BISTRO **£**
(☎028-3751 0128; www.facebook.com/Mulberry Bistro; Cathedral Rd; mains £4-7.50; ⊗8am-8pm Mon-Sat, 9am-3pm Sun) This welcoming cafe with mulberry-coloured walls serves good breakfasts, coffee and cakes, and a lunchtime and evening menu of burgers, lasagne and daily specials.

★ 4 Vicars   MODERN IRISH **££**
(☎028-3752 7772; http://4vicars.com; 4 Vicars Hill; mains lunch £6-15, dinner £20-23; ⊗10am-3pm Wed-Sun, 6-8.30pm Fri & Sat) Tucked inside a listed Georgian building, this chic little bistro opens to a tiny, delightful terrace. It's a perfect stop for lunch (Kilkeel crab on home-baked bread, or St Tola goat's cheese, courgette tempura and beetroot), but its trio of snug rooms are especially romantic on weekend evenings for dishes such as duck with kale, prunes and potato cakes.

Armagh City

★ **Moody Boar**   MODERN IRISH ££
(☑ 028-3752 9678; http://themoodyboar.com; Palace Stables, 1 Greenpark; mains lunch £8-13, dinner £16-20; ☺ noon-3pm & 5-9.30pm Tue & Wed, 10am-3pm & 5-9.30pm Fri & Sat, noon-7pm Sun; ☑) ✦ Inside the former palace stables at the Palace Demesne Public Park (p593), the Moody Boar opens to a courtyard where music plays on Friday afternoons. Vegetarian and gluten-free dishes are a speciality; chef Sean Farnan forages for many of the ingredients in the forested grounds, and the restaurant has its own herb and vegetable gardens.

Uluru Bar & Grill   BISTRO ££
(☑ 028-3751 8051; http://ulurubarandgrill.com; 3-5 Market St; breakfast £2.50-6, mains lunch £7-9, dinner £12-20; ☺ 10am-9pm Mon-Fri, 9am-10pm Sat, noon-9pm Sun) Aussie-run Uluru brings a bit of antipodean flair to Armagh, with indigenous art on the walls and a menu that includes Bondi burgers (melted brie and bacon), chargrilled kangaroo and rustic stone-baked pizzas. It's a good place to try local craft beers and ciders, and the wine list spans the globe.

☆ Entertainment

**Market Place Theatre
& Arts Centre**   THEATRE
(☑ 028-3752 1821; www.marketplacearmagh.com; Market St; ☺ box office 9.30am-4.30pm Mon-Sat) Armagh's main cultural venue incorporates a 400-seat theatre, exhibition galleries and the Theatre Bar & Bistro.

ℹ Information

Armagh Visitor Information Centre (☑ 028-3752 1800; www.armagh.co.uk; 40 Upper English St; ☺ 9am-5.30pm Mon-Sat, 1-5.30pm Sun Apr-Sep, 9am-5pm Mon-Sat Oct-Mar) Part of the St Patrick's Trian complex.

ℹ Getting There & Away

Bus 251 serves Belfast's Europa Bus Centre (£9.30, 1½ hours, hourly Monday to Friday, eight Saturday, four Sunday). Bus 40 serves Newry (£6, 50 minutes, hourly Monday to Saturday, three Sunday). Buses depart from the **Armagh Bus Centre** (☺ office 8.30am-5pm Mon-Fri) near the town centre.

Navan Fort

★ **Navan Fort**   ARCHAEOLOGICAL SITE
(Emain Macha; Navan Fort Rd) **FREE** Perched atop a drumlin, Ulster's most important archaeological site is linked in legend with the tales of Cúchulainn and named as capital of Ulster and the seat of the legendary Knights of the Red Branch. Exhibits at the outstanding Navan Centre (p596) place the fort in its historical context, and display a re-creation of an Iron Age settlement.

It's 3km west of Armagh City; take bus 73 (seven daily Monday to Friday).

Known as Emain Macha in Irish, Navan Fort was an important centre from around 1150 BC until the coming of Christianity; the discovery of the skull of a Barbary ape on the site indicates trading links with North Africa.

The main circular **earthwork enclosure** is a whopping 240m in diameter, and encloses a smaller circular structure and an Iron Age **burial mound**. The circular structure has intrigued archaeologists – it appears to be some sort of temple, whose roof was supported by concentric rows of

WORTH A TRIP

OXFORD ISLAND

Despite its name, this **nature reserve** (www.oxfordisland.com; [P]) is not an island but a peninsula of land on Lough Neagh's southern edge. The reserve protects a range of habitats – woodland, wildflower meadows, reedy shoreline and shallow lake margins – and is criss-crossed by walking and cycling trails, with information boards and birdwatching hides. There's also a playground and cafe at the **Lough Neagh Discovery Centre**.

Oxford Island is north of Lurgan, signposted from Junction 10 on the M1; you'll need your own transport.

Birds to look out for include great crested grebes, little grebes, black-headed and black-backed gulls, coots and moorhens.

Lough Neagh Boat Trips ([P] 028-3832 7573; Kinnego Marina, Annaloist Rd, Oxford Island; adult/child £5/3; ⊙ every 30min 1.30-5pm Sat & Sun Apr-Oct) Half-hour boat trips on Lough Neagh depart from Kinnego Marina, aboard the 12-seat cabin cruiser *Master McGra*.

Lough Neagh Discovery Centre (www.oxfordisland.com; Oxford Island; ⊙9am-6pm Mon-Fri, 10am-6pm Sat & Sun Apr-Sep, to 5pm Oct-Mar; [?]) In the middle of a reed-fringed pond inhabited by waterfowl, the discovery centre has a tourist information desk, gift shop, gallery and a great little cafe with lake-shore views.

wooden posts, and whose interior was filled with a vast pile of stones. Stranger still, the whole thing was set on fire soon after its construction around 95 BC, possibly for ritual purposes.

Navan Centre   MUSEUM

([P] 028-3752 9644; www.armagh.co.uk; 81 Killylea Rd; adult/child Apr-Sep £6.60/4.40, Oct-Mar £5.45/3.30; ⊙10am-6.30pm Apr-Sep, to 4pm Oct-Mar, last entry 90min before closing, 1hr before closing in winter) At Navan Fort (p595), the outstanding Navan Centre has exhibitions placing the fort in its historical context, and a re-creation of an Iron Age settlement.

Lough Neagh

Lough Neagh (pronounced 'nay') is the largest freshwater lake in Britain and Ireland, big enough to swallow the city of Birmingham (West Midlands, UK, or Alabama, USA – either one would fit). Though vast (around 32km long and 16km wide), the lough is relatively shallow – never more than 9m deep – and is an important habitat for waterfowl. Its waters are home to the pollan, a freshwater herring found only in Ireland, and the dollaghan, a subspecies of trout unique to Lough Neagh.

Connected to the sea by the River Bann, the lough has been a vital waterway and food source since prehistoric times, and is still home to Europe's largest eel fishery. The lough's main points of access – with the best views – include Antrim town on the eastern shore, Oxford Island in the south and Ardboe in the west.

Loughshore Trail   CYCLING

(www.cycleni.com/75/loughshore-trail) Encircling Lough Neagh is the 180km Loughshore Trail cycle route. For most of its length it follows quiet country roads set back from the shore. A downloadable leaflet on www.cycleni.com lists accommodation, places to eat and cycle-hire shops along the route.

Ring of Gullion

The Ring of Gullion (www.ringofgullion.org) is a magical region steeped in Celtic legend, centred on Slieve Gullion (Sliabh gCuilinn), where the Celtic warrior Cúchulainn is said to have taken his name after killing the dog *(cú)* belonging to the smith Culainn. The 'ring' is a necklace of rugged hills strung between Newry and Forkhill, 15km to the southwest, encircling the central whaleback ridge of Slieve Gullion. This unusual concentric formation is a geological structure known as a ring dyke.

★ Slieve Gullion Forest Park   FOREST

(www.ringofgullion.org; 89 Drumintee Rd, Meigh; ⊙8am-dusk; [P]) FREE A 10km scenic drive through this forest park provides picturesque views over the surrounding hills. From the parking and picnic area at the top of the drive, you can hike to the summit of Slieve Gullion (576m), the highest point in County Armagh, topped by two early Bronze

Age cairns and a tiny lake (1.5km round trip). Slieve Gullion is 10km southwest of Newry on the B113 road to Forkhill.

At the main entrance to the forest park there's a fantastic **adventure playpark** and a magical **Giant's Lair** children's story-book trail through the forest, with hidden fairy houses, teacups and soup bowls abandoned by giants and other fantastical sights along the way; the trail is inspired by local legends. There's a good cafe, **Synge & Byrne** (www. syngeandbyrne.com; Slieve Gullion Forest Park; mains £5-7; ⊙8am-6pm; 🛜🖋), in the courtyard by the main car park.

Killevy Old Churches　　　HISTORIC SITE
(Killeavy; Church Rd; ⊙24hr) FREE Surrounded by beech trees, these ruined, conjoined churches, 6km south of Camlough, were constructed on the site of a 5th-century nunnery founded by St Moninna. The eastern church dates from the 15th century and shares a gable wall with the 12th-century western one. The west door, with a massive lintel and granite jambs, may be 200 years older still. At the side of the churchyard, a footpath leads uphill to a white cross that marks **St Moninna's holy well**.

❶ Getting There & Around

Bus 43 links Newry with Forkhill via Meigh (for Slieve Gullion Forest Park) and Killeavy (seven daily Monday to Friday, four on Sunday).

National cycle route 9 links Newry with Slieve Gullion Forest Park via the Killevy Old Churches.

Counties Londonderry & Antrim

POP 865,240 / AREA 4918 SQ KM

Best Places to Eat

➜ Pyke 'n' Pommes (p609)

➜ Harry's Shack (p614)

➜ Morton's Fish & Chips (p625)

➜ Ursa Minor (p624)

➜ Bushmills Inn (p617)

Best Places to Stay

➜ Strandeen (p614)

➜ Downhill Beach House (p613)

➜ Shola Coach House (p615)

➜ Manor House (p626)

➜ Galgorm Resort & Spa (p633)

Why Go?

Northern Ireland's spectacular north coast is a giant geology classroom. The patient work of the ocean has laid bare the black basalt and white chalk that underlie much of County Antrim, and dissected the rocks into a scenic extravaganza of sea stacks, pinnacles, cliffs and caves. This mystical landscape's extraordinary rock formations, ruined castles and wooded glens have made the region an atmospheric backdrop for the hit TV series *Game of Thrones,* with numerous filming locations here.

To the west, County Londonderry's chief attraction is the spirited city of Derry. Ireland's only walled city sits alongside a broad sweep of the River Foyle and echoes with centuries of often-turbulent history. Since 2010 Derry has seen it undergo a renaissance as a cultural powerhouse, with a profusion of creative enterprises, public artworks and vibrant drinking and dining scenes. Derry also makes an ideal jumping-off point for the Wild Atlantic Way.

When to Go

➜ May is the best month for walking along the Causeway Coast, as you'll avoid the summer crowds at the Giant's Causeway and enjoy a colourful sprinkling of spring flowers to boot.

➜ The months of June and July bring the best beach weather, and are the peak of the seabird nesting season – an ideal time to visit the Rathlin West Light Seabird Centre on gloriously remote Rathlin Island.

➜ The traditional festivities of Ballycastle's Auld Lammas Fair, dating from the 17th century, take place on the last Monday and Tuesday of August, marking the end of summer and the beginning of the harvest.

COUNTY LONDONDERRY

Derry (Londonderry)

POP 107,900

Northern Ireland's second-largest city continues to flourish as an artistic and cultural hub. Derry's city centre was given a striking makeover for its year as the UK City of Culture 2013, with the new Peace Bridge, Ebrington Sq, and the redevelopment of the waterfront and Guildhall area making the most of the city's splendid riverside setting.

There's lots of history to absorb here, from the Siege of Derry to the Battle of the Bogside and Bloody Sunday – a stroll around the 17th-century city walls that encircle the city is a must, as is a tour of the Bogside murals – along with taking in the burgeoning live-music scene in the city's lively pubs.

History

A defining moment of Derry's history was the Siege of Derry in 1688–89, an event that reverberates to this day. King James I granted the city a royal charter in 1613, and gave the London livery companies (trade guilds) the task of fortifying Derry and planting the county of Coleraine (soon to be renamed County Londonderry) with Protestant settlers.

In Britain, the Glorious Revolution of 1688 saw the Catholic King James II ousted in favour of the Protestant Dutch prince, William of Orange. Derry was the only garrison in Ireland that was not held by forces loyal to King James, and so, in December 1688, Catholic forces led by the earl of Antrim arrived on the east bank of the River Foyle, ready to seize the city. They sent emissaries to discuss terms of surrender, but in the meantime troops were being ferried across the river in preparation for an assault. On seeing this, 13 apprentice boys barred the city gates with a cry of 'There'll be no surrender!'

And so, on 7 December 1688, the Siege of Derry began. For 105 days the Protestant citizens of Derry withstood bombardment, disease and starvation (the condition of the besieging forces was not much better). By the time a relief ship burst through and broke the siege, an estimated half of the city's inhabitants had died. In the 20th century the Siege of Derry became a symbol of Ulster Protestants' resistance to rule by a Catholic Irish Republic, and 'No surrender!' remains a Loyalist battle cry to this day. The new Siege Museum (p603) commemorates the events of the siege.

In the 19th century Derry was one of the main ports of emigration to the US, a fact commemorated by *Emigrants,* the Eamonn O'Doherty–designed sculptures depicting an emigrant family standing on Derry Quay.

Derry was a flashpoint during the Troubles, particularly during the the Battle of the Bogside and Bloody Sunday. More recently, its role as the UK City of Culture 2013 has helped revitalise the city.

⊙ Sights

⊙ Walled City

Derry's walled city is Ireland's earliest example of town planning. It's thought to have been modelled on the French Renaissance town of Vitry-le-François, designed in 1545 by Italian engineer Hieronimo Marino – both are based on the grid plan of a Roman military camp, with two main streets at right angles to each other, and four city gates, one at either end of each street.

★ **Derry's City Walls**   WALLS

(⊙ dawn-dusk) **FREE** The best way to get a feel for Derry's layout and history is to walk the 1.5km circumference of the city's walls. Completed in 1619, Derry's city walls are 8m high and 9m thick, and are the only city walls in Ireland to survive almost intact. The four original gates (Shipquay, Ferryquay, Bishop's and Butcher's) were rebuilt in the 18th and 19th centuries, when three new gates (New, Magazine and Castle) were added.

The walls were built under the supervision of the Honourable The Irish Society, an organisation created in 1613 by King James and the London livery companies to fund and oversee the fortification of Derry and the plantation of the surrounding county with Protestant settlers. The society still exists today (though now its activities are mainly charitable) and it still owns Derry's city walls.

Derry's nickname, the Maiden City, derives from the fact that the walls have never been breached by an invader.

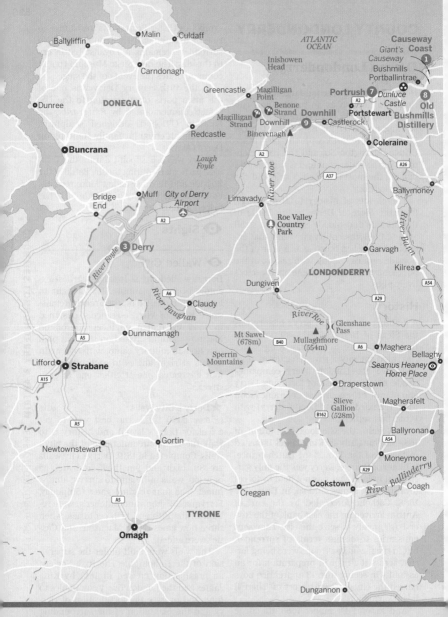

Counties Derry & Antrim Highlights

1 **Giant's Causeway** (p618) Hiking the Causeway Coast to the other-worldly collection of hexagonal rocks.

2 **Rathlin Island** (p625) Spotting seabirds and seals on the remote, rugged island.

3 **Derry** (p599) Discovering ancient walls, modern murals, fabulous dining and foot-stomping music in the history-steeped city.

4 **Carrick-a-Rede Rope Bridge** (p623) Wobbling across the narrow, swaying bridge.

5 **Ballycastle seafood & craft beer** (p624) Sampling fresh Atlantic seafood and locally-brewed craft beers.

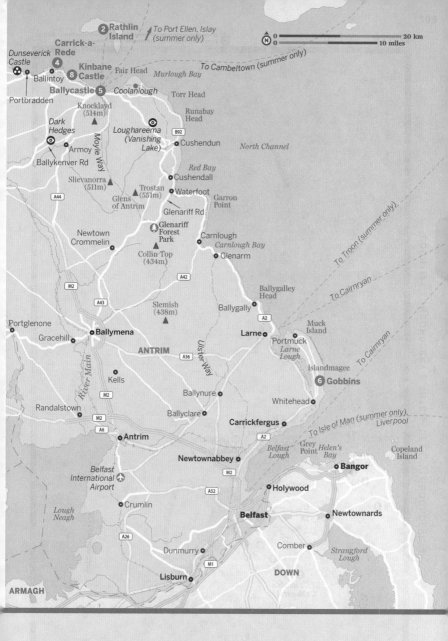

2 **Rathlin Island**

→ To Port Ellen, Islay
(summer only)

Carrick-a-Rede **4**

Dunseverick
Castle

Ballintoy

Kinbane **8**
Castle

Portbradden

Fair Head

Ballycastle **5**

Coolanlough

Murlough Bay

To Cambeltown (summer only)

Knocklayd
(514m) ▲

Torr Head

Runabay
Head

**Dark
Hedges** ◎

Loughareema
(Vanishing
Lake)

B92

Cushendun

North Channel

Armoy

Ballykenver Rd

Moyle Way

Red Bay

Cushendall

Slievanorra
(511m) ▲

Trostan
(551m) ▲

Waterfoot

Garron
Point

Glens
of Antrim

Glenariff Rd

A44

Newtown
Crommelin

Glenariff
Forest
Park ◎

Collin Top
(434m) ▲

Carnlough

Carnlough Bay

Glenarm

M2

A42

A43

Slemish
(438m) ▲

Ballygalley
Head

Ballygalley

A2

Portglenone

Gracehill

Ballymena ●

Muck
Island

Larne ●

Portmuck

Larne
Lough

To Troon (summer only)

To Cairnryan

To Cairnryan

ANTRIM

Ulster Way

A36

Kells

Islandmagee

6 **Gobbins**

River Main

M2

Ballynure

Whitehead ●

Randalstown

A6

Ballyclare ●

Carrickfergus

To Isle of Man (summer only)
Liverpool

Antrim

A2

Belfast
International
Airport

Newtownabbey ○

Belfast
Lough

Grey
Point

Helen's
Bay

Copeland
Island

A52

M2

Bangor ●

Crumlin ●

Lough
Neagh

Holywood ●

Newtownards ●

A26

Belfast

Comber ●

Strangford
Lough

Dunmurry ●

M1

Lisburn ●

DOWN

ARMAGH

N

0 — 20 km
0 — 10 miles

---

6 **Gobbins** (p630) Crawling through caves and crossing tubular bridges on a dramatic cliff walk.

7 **Portrush** (p615) Surfing the Atlantic breakers at the sweeping beaches in and around the town.

8 **Old Bushmills Distillery** (p617) Learning the secrets of Irish whiskey making on a behind-the-scenes tour.

9 **Downhill Demesne** (p613) Soaking up spectacular coastal views from Mussenden Temple, one of the region's many iconic *Game of Thrones* filming locations.

Derry

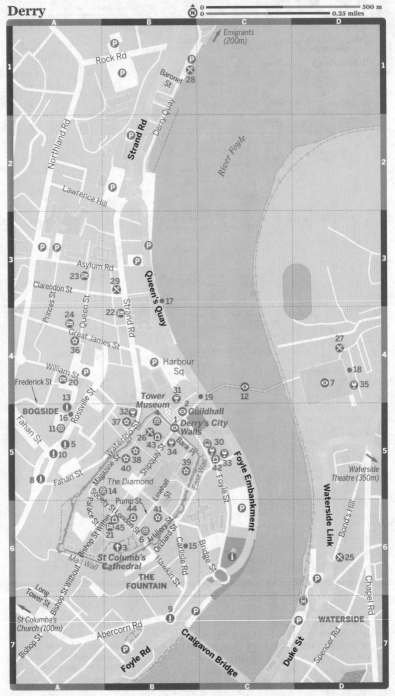

0   500 m
0   0.25 miles

Emigrants (200m)

Rock Rd

Baronet St
⊗ 28

Derry Quay

River Foyle

Strand Rd

Northland Rd

Lawrence Hill

Asylum Rd
23

Clarendon St
29 ⊗

Queen's Quay

⊙ 17

Princes St   24

Queen St   22

Great James St   36

William St   20

Frederick St

13

BOGSIDE

16

11

Fahan St   5

10

8

Fahan St

Rossville St

Harbour Sq

Tower Museum   31

32   2   ⊙ Guildhall

37   4   1   Derry's City Walls

26   Bank Pl   19   12

43   34   30

38   Shipquay St   39   33   42

40

Magazine St

The Diamond

14   East Wall   Foyle St

Pump St   Linenhall St

45   41   Foyle Embankment

21   6   London St

3   Artillery St

St Columb's Cathedral   Orchard St

Mall Wall   Hawkin St   15   Bridge St

THE FOUNTAIN

27 ⊗

18

⊙ 7   35

Waterside Theatre (350m)

Waterside Link

Bond's Hill

⊗ 25

Chapel Rd

Long Tower St

St Columba's Church (100m)

Bishop St Within

Bishop St Without

9

Abercorn Rd

Foyle Rd

Craigavon Bridge

Duke St

WATERSIDE

Spencer Rd

Bishop St

Derry

★**Tower Museum**　　　　　MUSEUM
(www.derrystrabane.com/towermuseum; Union Hall Pl; adult/child £4/2; ⊙10am-5.30pm, last entry 4pm) Head straight to the 5th floor of this award-winning museum inside a replica 16th-century tower house for a view from the top. Then work your way down through the excellent **Armada Shipwreck** exhibition, and the **Story of Derry**, where well-thought-out exhibits and audiovisuals lead you through the city's history, from the founding of the monastery of St Colmcille (Columba) in the 6th century to the Battle of the Bogside in the late 1960s. Allow at least two hours.

★**St Columb's Cathedral**　　　CATHEDRAL
(www.stcolumbscathedral.org; 17 London St; suggested donation £2; ⊙9am-5pm Mon-Sat) Built between 1628 and 1633 from the same grey-green schist as the city walls, this was the first post-Reformation church to be erected in Britain and Ireland, and is Derry's oldest surviving building.

In the **porch** (under the spire, by the St Columb's Court entrance) you can see the original foundation stone of 1633 that records the cathedral's completion. The smaller stone inset comes from the original church built here in 1164.

Also in the porch is a hollow mortar shell fired into the churchyard during the Great Siege of 1688–89; inside the shell were the terms of surrender. The neighbouring **chapter house** contains more historical artefacts, including paintings, old photos and the four huge padlocks used to secure the city gates in the 17th century.

Siege Museum　　　　　MUSEUM
(www.thesiegemuseum.org; 13 Society St; adult/child £3/free; ⊙10am-5pm Mon-Sat) This new museum celebrates the role of the 13 apprentice boys who in December 1688 locked the city gates against the approaching Jacobite army. Derry was surrounded and during the 105-day siege no supplies could reach the city, its starving citizens resorting to eating dogs and rats until English ships brought relief. The Protestant Apprentice Boys of Derry Association marches in commemoration of the event every August.

Centre for Contemporary Art   GALLERY
(http://cca-derry-londonderry.org; 10-12 Artillery St; ◉ noon-6pm Tue-Sat) FREE Derry's contemporary-art gallery provides a showcase for emerging artists in Northern Ireland and stages changing exhibitions of contemporary art from around the world.

◉ Outside the Walls

★ **Guildhall**   NOTABLE BUILDING
(📋 028-7137 6510; www.derrystrabane.com/ Guildhall; Guildhall St; ◉ 10am-5.30pm) FREE
Standing just outside the city walls, the neo-Gothic Guildhall was originally built in 1890, then rebuilt after a fire in 1908. Its fine stained-glass windows were presented by the London livery companies, and its clock tower was modelled on London's Big Ben. Inside, there's a historical exhibition on the Plantation of Ulster, and a tourist information point.

As the seat of the old Londonderry Corporation, which institutionalised the policy of discriminating against Catholics for housing and jobs, the Guildhall incurred the wrath of nationalists and was bombed twice by the Irish Republican Army (IRA) in 1972. From 2000 to 2005 it was the seat of the Bloody Sunday Inquiry.

Peace Bridge   BRIDGE
Sinuous and elegant, this 2011-completed, S-shaped pedestrian and cyclist bridge spans the River Foyle, linking the walled city on the west bank to Ebrington Sq on the east in a symbolic handshake.

Ebrington Square   SQUARE
Originally a 19th-century fort, and later a British Army base, Ebrington Barracks was demilitarised in 2003. The former parade ground now serves as a public square, performance venue and exhibition space.

Hands Across the Divide   MONUMENT
As you enter the city across Craigavon Bridge, the first thing you see is the Hands Across the Divide monument. This striking bronze sculpture of two men reaching out to each other symbolises the spirit of reconciliation and hope for the future; it was unveiled in 1992, 20 years after Bloody Sunday.

St Columba's Church   CHURCH
(Long Tower; 📋 028-7126 2301; Long Tower St; ◉ 9am-8.30pm Mon-Sat, 7.30am-7pm Sun)
Outside the city walls to the southwest is Long Tower Church, Derry's first post-Reformation Catholic church. Built in 1784 in neo-Renaissance style, it stands on the site of the medieval Teampall Mór (Great Church), built in 1164, whose stones were used to help build the city walls in 1609. Long Tower was built with the support of the Anglican bishop at the time, Frederick Augustus Harvey, who presented the capitals for the four Corinthian columns framing the ornate high altar.

The funeral of Sinn Féin politician Martin McGuinness was held here in March 2017.

◉ Bogside

The Bogside district, to the west of the walled city, developed in the 19th and early 20th centuries as a working-class, predominantly Catholic, residential area. By the 1960s its serried ranks of small, terrace houses had become overcrowded and beset by poverty and unemployment, a focus for the emerging Civil Rights Movement and a hotbed of nationalist discontent.

In August 1969 the three-day 'Battle of the Bogside' – a running street battle between local youths and the Royal Ulster Constabulary (RUC) – prompted the UK government to send British troops into Northern Ireland. The residents of the Bogside and neighbouring Brandywell districts – 33,000 of them – declared themselves independent of the civil authorities and barricaded the streets to keep the security forces out. 'Free Derry', as it was known, was a no-go area for the police and army, its streets patrolled by IRA volunteers. In January of 1972 the area around Rossville St witnessed the horrific events of Bloody Sunday (p608). 'Free Derry' ended with Operation Motorman on 31 July 1972, when thousands of British troops and armoured cars moved in to occupy the Bogside.

The area's population is currently around 8000, following extensive redevelopment that has seen the old houses and flats demolished and replaced with modern housing.

People's Gallery Murals   PUBLIC ART
(Rossville St) The 12 murals that decorate the gable ends of houses along Rossville St, near Free Derry Corner, are popularly referred to as the 'People's Gallery. They are the work of 'the Bogside Artists' (Kevin Hasson, Tom Kelly, and Will Kelly, who passed away in 2017). The three men lived through the worst of the Troubles in Bogside. The murals can be clearly seen from the northern part of the City Walls.

COUNTIES LONDONDERRY & ANTRIM DERRY (LONDONDERRY)

DERRY-LONDONDERRY

Derry-Londonderry is a city with two names. Nationalists always use Derry, and the 'London' part of the name is often defaced on road signs. Staunch Unionists insist on Londonderry, which is still the city's (and county's) official name. All the same, most people, regardless of political persuasion, call it Derry in everyday speech.

The settlement was originally named Doíre Calgaigh (Oak Grove of Calgach), after a pagan warrior-hero; in the 10th century it was renamed Doíre Colmcille (Oak Grove of Columba), in honour of the 6th-century saint who established the first monastic settlement here.

In the following centuries the name was shortened and anglicised to Derrie or Derry. Then in 1613, in recognition of the Corporation of London's role in the 'plantation' of northwest Ulster with Protestant settlers, Derry was granted a royal charter and the city was renamed Londonderry.

A new County Londonderry was created from what was originally County Coleraine, along with parts of Tyrone and Antrim; unlike the city, there has never been an officially sanctioned county called Derry. Nevertheless, those with nationalist leanings, including the county's Gaelic football team, prefer to use County Derry.

Traditionally, road signs in Northern Ireland point to Londonderry and those in the Republic point to Derry (or Doíre in Irish). Attempts by the council to change the city's official name to Derry were foiled by a 2007 High Court ruling that the city's legal name could only be changed by legislation or royal prerogative. In 2015, Derry and Strabane District Council again voted in favour of a name change, but for the time being the clunky 'Derry-Londonderry' moniker remains the destination announced on trains and buses and used by most of the city's businesses.

Mostly painted between 1997 and 2001, the murals commemorate key events in the Troubles, including the Battle of the Bogside, Bloody Sunday, Operation Motorman and the 1981 hunger strike. The most powerful images are those painted largely in monochrome, consciously evoking journalistic imagery: *Operation Motorman,* showing a British soldier breaking down a door with a sledgehammer; *Bloody Sunday,* with a group of men led by local priest Father Daly carrying the body of Jackie Duddy (the first fatality on that day); and *The Petrol Bomber,* a young boy wearing a gas mask and holding a petrol bomb.

The most moving image is *The Death of Innocence,* which shows the radiant figure of 14-year-old schoolgirl Annette McGavigan, killed in crossfire between the IRA and the British Army on 6 September 1971, the 100th victim of the Troubles. Representing all the children who died in the conflict, she stands against the brooding chaos of a bombed-out building, the roof beams forming a crucifix in the top right-hand corner. At the left, a downward-pointing rifle, broken in the middle, stands for the failure of violence, while the butterfly symbolises resurrection and hope embodied in the peace process.

The final mural in the sequence, completed in 2004, is the *Peace Mural,* a swirling image of a dove (symbol of peace and of Derry's patron saint, Columba) rising out of the blood and sadness of the past towards the sunny yellow hope of a peaceful future.

Museum of Free Derry   MUSEUM
(www.museumoffreederry.org; 55 Glenfada Park; adult/child £4/3; ☉9.30am-4.30pm Mon-Fri year-round, plus 1-4pm Sat Apr-Sep, 1-4pm Sun Jul-Sep) Just off Rossville St, this excellent museum chronicles the history of the Bogside, the Civil Rights Movement and the events of Bloody Sunday through photographs, newspaper reports, film, interactive displays and the accounts of first-hand witnesses, including some of the original photographs that inspired the murals of the nearby People's Gallery.

Free Derry Corner   MONUMENT
(cnr Fahan & Rossville Sts) The Free Derry Corner, where the gable end of a house painted with the famous slogan 'You are Now Entering Free Derry' still stands, is all that remains of the old Bogside district.

Bloody Sunday Memorial   MONUMENT
(Joseph Pl) A simple granite obelisk that commemorates the 14 civilians who were shot dead by the British Army on Bloody Sunday, 30 January 1972.

Hunger Strikers' Memorial   MONUMENT
(Rossville St) The H-shaped Hunger Strikers' Memorial is near the Free Derry Corner.

☞ Tours

Made in Derry Food Tour   FOOD & DRINK
(https://madeinderryfoodtours.com; per person £47; ⊘noon Sat) Four-hour tours of Derry's emerging artisan food and drink scene, meeting chefs and producers and sampling 20 local specialities – such as cheeses and craft beer – along the way. The tour starts outside the Eighty81 building on Ebrington Sq. Book ahead.

Free Derry Tours   CULTURAL
(☑07793 285972; adult/student £6/5; ⊘10am, noon & 2pm Mon-Fri Mar-Sep plus 11am & 2pm Sat, Apr-Sep, 2pm Sun Jul-Sep) The Museum of Free Derry (p605) runs these hour-long walking tours of the Bogside taking in the People's Gallery murals, Free Derry Corner, the Hunger Strikers' Memorial and the Bloody Sunday Memorial.

City Walking Tours   WALKING
(☑028-7127 1996; www.derrycitytours.com; Carlisle Stores, 11 Carlisle Rd; adult/child £4/free; ⊘Historic Derry tours 10am, noon, 2pm and 4pm year-round) One-hour Historic Derry walking tours start from Carlisle Stores. There are also tours of the Bogside and of Derry's murals. Recommended.

⚘ Festivals & Events

City of Derry Jazz Festival   MUSIC
(www.cityofderryjazzfestival.com; ⊘late Apr/early May) Five days of jazz at various venues around the city.

Walled City Marathon   SPORTS
(www.thewalledcitymarathon.com; ⊘Jun) Runners take on the challenge of the 26.2-mile course that takes them through Derry city and rural villages along the banks of the River Foyle.

Gasyard Féile   CULTURAL
(www.facebook.com/gasyardwallfeile; ⊘Aug) Live music, street performers, carnival, theatre and Irish-language events all feature at this major cultural festival.

City of Derry Guitar Festival   MUSIC
(www.cityofderryguitarfestival.com; ⊘late Aug) Over three days, the grounds of the North West Regional College host performances and master classes from guitarists from around the world, including the genres classical, acoustic, electric, flamenco and bass.

Halloween Carnival   CARNIVAL
(www.derrystrabane.com/halloween; ⊘27-31 Oct) The city dresses up for Ireland's biggest street party, which features fireworks, a haunted house, Freaky Fun Fair and more.

Foyle Film Festival   FILM
(www.foylefilmfestival.org; Nerve Centre, 7-8 Magazine St; ⊘mid-Nov) This weeklong event is the North's biggest film festival.

🛏 Sleeping

Hostel Connect   HOSTEL £
(☑028-7137 2101; http://hostelconnect.co.uk; 51 Strand Rd; dm £15-18, d £44-48; @ 🕾) This bright, centrally located hostel offers small but neat doubles and twins as well as six-, nine- and 15-bed dorms with wooden bunks. There's a big living room, a kitchen for preparing meals, and a breakfast of bagels, fruit and toast is included. All rooms share bathrooms.

★**Beech Hill Country House**   HISTORIC HOTEL ££
(☑028-7134 9279; www.beech-hill.com; 32 Ardmore Rd; s/d from £85/100; 🕾) Secluded in a picturesque patch of woodland 4.3km southeast of Derry, this wonderfully atmospheric 18th-century manor house is surrounded by magnificent gardens and steeped in history – it was a WWII base for US marines, and former US president Bill Clinton stayed here several times. All 30 rooms incorporate Georgian-era colours and furnishings. Its lake-view restaurant is excellent.

★**Merchant's House**   B&B ££
(☑028-7126 9691; www.thesaddlershouse.com; 16 Queen St; s/d/tr/f from £40/65/90/100; @ 🕾) This historic, Georgian-style townhouse is a gem of a B&B. It has an elegant lounge and dining room with marble fireplaces and antique furniture, TV, coffee-making facilities, homemade marmalade at breakfast and bathrobes in the bedrooms (some rooms have shared bathroom). Call at Saddler's House first to pick up a key.

Saddler's House   B&B ££
(☑028-7126 9691; www.thesaddlershouse.com; 36 Great James St; s/d from £55/60; 🕾) Centrally located within a five-minute walk of the walled city, this friendly B&B is set in a lovely Victorian townhouse. All seven rooms have private bathrooms, and you get to enjoy a huge breakfast in the family kitchen.

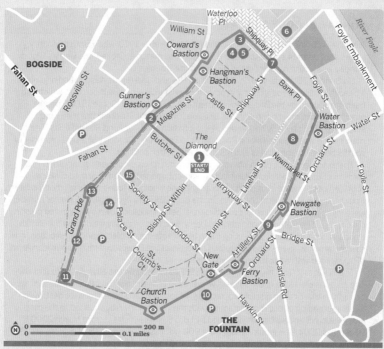

City Walk
Derry's Walled City

START THE DIAMOND
END THE DIAMOND
LENGTH 2KM; ONE HOUR

Start your walk at the Diamond, Derry's central square, dominated by the **①** **war memorial**. Head along Butcher St, where the town's butchers once had their shops, to **②** **Butcher's Gate**, and climb the steps to the top of the city walls.

Stroll downhill to **③** **Magazine Gate**, named for the powder magazine that used to be close by. Inside the walls is **④** **O'Doherty's Tower**, housing the excellent **⑤** **Tower Museum** (p603); outside the walls stands the red-brick, neo-Gothic **⑥** **Guildhall** (p604).

The River Foyle used to come up to the northeastern wall here. In the middle is the **⑦** **Shipquay Gate**. The walls turn southwest and climb beside the **⑧** **Millennium Forum** (p610) to the **⑨** **Ferryquay Gate**, where the apprentice boys barred the gate at the start of the Great Siege of 1688–89.

The stretch of wall beyond overlooks the **⑩** **Fountain housing estate**, the last significant Protestant community on the western bank of the Foyle. The round, brick-paved area on the ground outside New Gate is where a 10m-high bonfire is lit on the night before the annual Apprentice Boys' march (second Saturday in August).

Continue around the southern stretch of wall to the **⑪** **Double Bastion** at the south-western corner, home to Roaring Meg, the most famous of the cannons used during the Siege of Derry. The next section of wall is known as the **⑫** **Grand Parade**, and offers an excellent view of the murals painted by the Bogside Artists.

An empty plinth on **⑬** **Royal Bastion** marks the former site of a monument to the Reverend George Walker, joint governor of the city during the Great Siege; it was blown up by the IRA in 1973. Behind the Royal Bastion is the 1872 Church of Ireland **⑭** **Chapel of St Augustine**, built on the site of St Colmcille's 6th-century monastery. A little further along is the **⑮** **Apprentice Boys' Memorial Hall**, with a high mesh fence to protect it from paint bombs hurled from below.

SUNDAY, BLOODY SUNDAY

Tragically echoing Dublin's Bloody Sunday of November 1920, when British security forces shot dead 14 spectators at a Gaelic football match in Croke Park, Derry's Bloody Sunday was a turning point in the history of the Troubles.

On Sunday 30 January 1972, the Northern Ireland Civil Rights Association organised a peaceful march through Derry in protest against internment without trial, which had been introduced by the British government the previous year. Some 15,000 people marched from Creggan through the Bogside towards the Guildhall, but they were stopped by British Army barricades at the junction of William and Rossville Sts. The main march was diverted along Rossville St to Free Derry Corner, but a small number of youths began hurling stones and insults at the British soldiers.

The exact sequence of events was disputed, but it has since been established that soldiers of the 1st Battalion, Parachute Regiment opened fire on unarmed civilians. Fourteen people were shot dead (13 outright; one who died four-and-a-half months later from his injuries), some of them shot in the back; six were aged just 17. A similar number were injured, most by gunshots and two from being knocked down by armoured personnel carriers. The Catholic population of Derry, who had originally welcomed the British troops as a neutral force protecting them from Protestant violence and persecution, now saw the army as enemy and occupier. The ranks of the Provisional Irish Republican Army (IRA) swelled with a fresh surge of volunteers.

The Widgery Commission, set up in 1972 to investigate the affair, failed to find anyone responsible. None of the soldiers who fired at civilians, nor the officers in charge, were brought to trial or even disciplined; records disappeared and weapons were destroyed.

Long-standing public dissatisfaction with the Widgery investigation led to the massive Bloody Sunday Inquiry, headed by Lord Saville, which sat from March 2000 till December 2004. The inquiry heard from 900 witnesses, received 2500 witness statements and allegedly cost British taxpayers £400 million; its report (available on www.official-documents.gov.uk) was finally published in June 2010.

Lord Saville found that 'The firing by soldiers of 1 PARA on Bloody Sunday caused the deaths of 13 people and injury to a similar number, none of whom was posing a threat of causing death or serious injury. What happened on Bloody Sunday strengthened the Provisional IRA, increased nationalist resentment and hostility towards the Army and exacerbated the violent conflict of the years that followed. Bloody Sunday was a tragedy for the bereaved and the wounded, and a catastrophe for the people of Northern Ireland.'

Following publication of the report, Prime Minister David Cameron publicly apologised on behalf of the UK government, describing the killings as 'unjustified and unjustifiable'. In 2010 the Police Service of Northern Ireland (PSNI) launched a murder inquiry into the deaths, which remains ongoing.

The events of Bloody Sunday inspired rock band U2's most overtly political song, 'Sunday Bloody Sunday' (1983), and are commemorated in the Museum of Free Derry (p605), the People's Gallery Murals (p604) and the Bloody Sunday Memorial (p605), all in the Bogside.

Arkle House
B&B ££

(☑ 028-7127 1156; www.derryhotel.co.uk; 2 Coshquin Rd; s/d £55/65; ᴾ 🛜) Located 2km northwest of the city centre, this grand Victorian house is set in private gardens and offers five large, lush bedrooms and a private kitchen for guests to use.

Abbey B&B
B&B ££

(☑ 028-7127 9000; www.abbeyaccommodation.com; 4 Abbey St; s/d/tr from £50/70/90; 🛜) There's a warm welcome waiting at this family-run B&B just a short walk from the walled city, on the edge of the Bogside. Rooms are spacious and modern.

★ Bishop's Gate Hotel
HOTEL £££

(☑ 028-7114 0300; www.bishopsgatehotelderry.com; 24 Bishop St; d/ste from £130/210) The former Northern Counties gentleman's club has been transformed into a stylish 30-room hotel located within Derry's city walls. Rooms combine period features with plush carpets and contemporary furnishings in greys and yellows. Leather armchairs, wood panelling and open fires create a cosy atmosphere in the bar, and there's good food available at the restaurant. Staff are friendly and helpful.

✖ Eating

Derry is fast gaining a reputation as a foodie city, with several excellent new eateries specialising in fresh local produce opening in recent years.

★ Pyke 'n' Pommes   STREET FOOD £

(www.pykenpommes.ie; behind Foyle Marina, off Baronet St; mains £4-16; ⊙noon-5pm Fri & Sat, to 4pm Sun-Thu; 🚗🏷) ❤ Derry's single-best eatery is this quayside shipping container. Chef Kevin Pyke's delectable, mostly organic burgers span his signature Notorious PIG (pulled pork, crispy slaw, beetroot and crème fraiche) and Veganderry (chickpeas, lemon and coriander) to his Legenderry Burger (wagyu beef, pickled onions and honey-mustard mayo). His Pykeos fish tacos are another hit. Seasonal specials might include mackerel or oysters.

Pyke 'n' Pommes is also available at the Blackbird (p610).

Primrose Cafe   CAFE £

(www.facebook.com/primrosederry; 15 Carlisle Rd; dishes £3.50-7; ⊙8am-5pm Mon-Sat, 10am-5pm Sun; 🏷) The Primrose prospers by sticking to the classics and doing them really well: scones, cookies, cheesecake, gateau and meringue pie, all baked fresh daily, plus brunch items like waffles, Greencastle smoked kipper and avocado French toast. Even with the enclosed 'secret garden' courtyard at the back it can be hard to find a seat.

★ Brown's Restaurant   IRISH ££

(☎028-7134 5180; https://brownsrestaurant.com; 1 Bond's Hill, Waterside; 3-course lunch £15, dinner mains £17-24; ⊙noon-3pm Tue-Sat, 5.30-9pm Tue-Thu, 5-10pm Fri & Sat, noon-3pm Sun; 🏷) ❤ From the outside Brown's may not have the most promising appearance, but step inside and you're in an elegant little enclave of brandy-coloured banquettes and ornate metal light fittings, with vintage monochrome prints adorning the walls. The ever-changing menu is a gastronome's delight, making creative use of fresh local produce.

Harry's Derry   MODERN IRISH ££

(☎028-7137 1635; www.facebook.com/HarrysDerry; 29 Craft Village; mains £11-15; ⊙10.30am-8.30pm Wed & Thu, to 9pm Sat & Sun) At its new premises in Derry's Craft Village, Harry's serves a similar menu of fresh seafood, local meat and produce from its own 2-acre farm that has been such a hit at its Portstewart restaurant, Harry's Shack (p614). Book ahead.

Ollies   IRISH ££

(☎028-7132 9751; www.facebook.com/loveollies; 59 Ebrington Sq; mains lunch £4.50-8, dinner £10-15; ⊙9am-9pm; 🖥🏷) All the food at this bright cafe/bistro is homemade using local ingredients, from the fluffy pancakes and waffles at breakfast to the creamy Greencastle seafood chowder and the breads, cakes and pastries. There's a good range of vegetarian and gluten-free options too. It's BYO (there's a small fee for corkage).

Saffron   INDIAN ££

(☎028-7126 0532; http://saffronderry.co.uk; 2 Clarendon St; mains £9-15.50; ⊙4.30-10pm Sun-Thu, to 11pm Fri & Sat; 🏷) Indian restaurants in Ireland tend to be more miss than hit, but Saffron stands out, not only for its fiery curries, rich tikkas and aromatic biryani dishes (made from basmati rice and served with masala sauce), but also for its stylish, contemporary decor. Great cocktails like pomegranate martinis too.

🍺 Drinking & Nightlife

Derry's pubs are friendly and atmospheric and there is live music happening somewhere every night of the week. Most bars and pubs are within crawling distance of each other in and around the walled city, but across the Peace Bridge, a number of new places have opened on Ebrington Sq. The Quiet Man whiskey distillery is set to open on the square in mid-2018.

★ Walled City Brewery   MICROBREWERY

(☎028-7134 3336; www.walledcitybrewery.com; 70 Ebrington Sq; ⊙5-11pm Tue-Thu, 2.30-11.30pm Fri & Sat, 2-10pm Sun) Housed in the former army barracks on Ebrington Sq, Walled City Brewery is an exciting new craft brewery and restaurant run by master brewer and Derry local James Huey. As well as having 10 craft beers on tap, Walled City serves top-notch grub, such as house-smoked beer-braised pulled pork (mains £14 to £24). Also runs home-brewing courses.

★ Peadar O'Donnell's   PUB

(www.peadars.com; 59-63 Waterloo St; ⊙11.30am-1.30am Mon-Sat, 12.30pm-12.30am Sun) Done up as a typical Irish pub/grocery (with shelves of household items, shopkeeper's scales on the counter and a museum's-worth of old bric-a-brac), Peadar's has rowdy traditional-music sessions every night and often on weekend afternoons as well. Its adjacent Gweedore Bar hosts live rock bands every night, and a Saturday-night disco upstairs.

Guildhall Taphouse   BAR
(www.facebook.com/Guildhalltaphouse; 4 Custom House St; ⊙noon-1am Mon-Sat, to midnight Sun) Housed in a wooden-beamed, 19th-century building brightened with fairy lights, the Taphouse is a cosy place to sample an excellent selection of local and international craft beers or a sophisticated cocktail. There's regular live music including trad sessions every Wednesday.

Sandino's Cafe-Bar   BAR
(http://sandinoscafebar.com; 1 Water St; ⊙11.30am-1am Mon-Sat, noon-midnight Sun) From the posters of Che to the Free Palestine flag to the fairtrade coffee and gluten-free beer, this relaxed cafe-bar exudes a liberal, left-wing vibe. DJs spin from Thursday to Saturday in Club Havana; there's regular live music, too.

Blackbird   PUB
(☑ 028-7136 2111; www.blackbirdderry.com; 24 Foyle St; ⊙11.30am-1am Mon-Sat, to midnight Sun) With wooden booths, leather sofas and roaring fires, the Blackbird hasn't sacrificed comfort and cosiness in its bid to create a hip, modern space. The kitchen of this welcoming pub serves delicious snacks, burgers, tacos and steaks by Pyke 'n' Pommes (p609) (mains £8 to £30); there's a good cocktail list too. Live music most weekends.

Sugar   CLUB
(www.facebook.com/sugarniteclub; 33 Shipquay St; ⊙11pm-2am Wed, Fri & Sat) Above Quays Bar, Derry's hottest club spreads over two floors, and has the city's largest rooftop terrace. Guest and resident DJs play; see the Facebook page for details of upcoming nights.

☆ Entertainment

★Nerve Centre   ARTS CENTRE
(www.nerve-centre.org.uk; 7-8 Magazine St) Set up in 1990 to encourage young, local talent in the fields of music and film, the Nerve Centre has a performance area, with live music at weekends, a theatre and an arthouse cinema. There's also a bar and cafe here.

Mason's Bar   LIVE MUSIC
(☑ 028-7136 0177; www.facebook.com/masonsbarderry; 10 Magazine St) The city that spawned the Undertones is still turning out raw, rumbustious music. Mason's line-up changes frequently but includes regular student, emerging and established bands, as well as DJs, karaoke and comedy nights.

Cultúrlann Uí Chanáin   ARTS CENTRE
(www.culturlann-doire.ie; 37 Great James St; ⊙8am-5pm & 6-9pm Mon-Thu, 8am-5pm Fri, 9am-4pm Sat) This cultural centre devoted to the Irish language stages performances of traditional Irish music, poetry and dance. Its shop, An Cló Ceart, sells music as well as arts, crafts and Irish-language books.

Playhouse   THEATRE
(www.derryplayhouse.co.uk; 5-7 Artillery St; ⊙box office 10am-5.30pm Mon-Fri, to 4pm Sat) Housed in beautifully restored former school buildings with an award-winning modern extension at the rear, this community arts centre stages music, dance and theatre by local and international performers.

Gweedore Bar   LIVE MUSIC
(www.peadars.com; 59-63 Waterloo St; ⊙11.30am-1.30am Mon-Sat, noon-12.30am Sun) Adjoining Peadar O'Donnell's (p609), the Gweedore Bar hosts live rock bands every night, while the DJ bar upstairs is home to a regular Saturday-night disco.

Millennium Forum   THEATRE
(www.millenniumforum.co.uk; 98 Newmarket St) With a capacity of 1000 and Ireland's largest theatre stage, this auditorium is a major venue for dance, drama, concerts, opera and musicals.

Waterside Theatre   THEATRE
(www.watersidetheatre.com; Glendermott Rd) Housed in a former factory 500m east of the River Foyle, Waterside stages drama, dance, comedy, children's theatre and live music.

🛍 Shopping

★Smart Swag   DESIGN
(www.smartswag.co.uk; 12 London St; ⊙10am-6pm Mon-Sat) Run by local artists and designers, Smart Swag sells original and unusual pieces such as jewellery made from vinyl records, upcycled furniture, screen-printed T-shirts and dresses, and traditional Irish tapestries that have been given a contemporary twist. The illustrations of Derry city make great souvenirs.

Craft Village ARTS & CRAFTS
(www.derrycraftvillage.com; off Shipquay St; ⊙ hours vary) A handful of craft shops sell Derry crystal, hand-woven cloth, ceramics, jewellery and other local craft items in this renovated courtyard. One of the best is **Derry Designer Makers**, a collective of 15 artists and craftspeople who take turns staffing the shop. Enter from Shipquay St, Magazine St or Tower Museum.

An Cló Ceart ARTS & CRAFTS
(www.culturlann-doire.ie; 37 Great James St; ⊙ 9am-5pm Mon-Fri, to 4pm Sat) Inside the Cultúrlann Uí Chanáin cultural centre, this shop stocks a good range of Irish-language books, traditional-music CDs, glasswork, woodwork and jewellery.

Cool Discs Music MUSIC
(www.cooldiscsmusic.com; 6 Lesley House, Foyle St; ⊙ 9am-6pm Mon-Thu, to 8pm Fri, 8.30am-6pm Sat) One of Northern Ireland's best independent record shops, Cool Discs has a wide selection of music by Irish artists old and new and sells concert tickets.

Whatnot ANTIQUES
(www.thewhatnot.co.uk; 22 Bishop St; ⊙ 10am-5pm Tue-Sat) Jewellery, militaria, bric-a-brac and collectables cram this interesting little antique shop.

ⓘ Information

Visit Derry Information Centre (☏ 028-7126 7284; www.visitderry.com; 44 Foyle St; ⊙ 9am-5.30pm Mon-Fri, 10am-5pm Sat & Sun; ⊛) A large tourist information centre with helpful staff and stacks of brochures for attractions in Derry and beyond. Also sells books and maps and can book accommodation. **Claudy Cycles**; can be rented here.

ⓘ Getting There & Away

AIR

City of Derry Airport (☏ 028-7181 0784; www.cityofderryairport.com; Airport Rd, Eglinton) is about 13km east of Derry along the A2 towards Limavady. There are direct flights to London Stansted (daily), Liverpool (twice weekly) and Glasgow International (four days a week), plus summer routes to Spain.

BUS

The **bus station** (☏ 028-7126 2261; Foyle St) is just northeast of the walled city.

Services to Northern Ireland destinations are operated by Translink (www.translink.co.uk); destinations in the Republic are served by Bus Éireann (www.buseireann.ie).

Belfast Europa Bus Centre £12, 1¾ hours, half-hourly Monday to Friday, hourly Saturday and Sunday

Coleraine £8, one hour, eight daily Monday to Friday, two Sunday; no Saturday service

Donegal town £12.60, 1½ hours, 10 daily

Galway £16.50, 5½ hours, five daily

Letterkenny £5.50, 40 minutes, eight daily

Limavady £5.20, 30 minutes, at least hourly Monday to Saturday, six Sunday

Omagh £8, one hour, hourly Monday to Saturday, six Sunday

Sligo £16.80, 2½ hours, six daily

Airporter (☏ 028-7126 9996; http://airporter.co.uk; 1 Bay Rd, off Culmore Rd; ⊛) buses run directly from Derry to Belfast International Airport (£20, 1½ hours) and George Best Belfast City Airport (£20, two hours) at least once an hour Monday to Friday and slightly less frequently Saturday and Sunday. Buses depart from the Airporter office, 1.5km north of the city centre, next to Da Vinci's Hotel.

TRAIN

Derry's train station is on the eastern side of the River Foyle; a free Rail Link bus connects it with the bus station.

Belfast £12, 2¼ hours, nine daily Monday to Saturday, six on Sunday

Coleraine £9.60, 45 minutes, 11 daily Monday to Saturday, six on Sunday

ⓘ Getting Around

Bus 234 stops at City of Derry Airport (£3.50, 20 minutes, at least hourly Monday to Saturday, six Sunday). A taxi costs about £15.

The **Foyle Valley cycle route** runs through Derry, along the west bank of the river.

Claudy Cycles (☏ 028-7133 8128; www.claudycycles.com; Visit Derry Information Centre; bike hire per half-/full day £8/12) rents out bikes at the Visit Derry Information Centre.

Local buses leave from Foyle St, outside the bus station, leading to the suburbs and surrounding villages.

Taxi services in Derry include **Derry Taxis** (☏ 028-7126 0247) and **Foyle Taxis** (☏ 028-7127 9999; www.foyletaxis.com).

Limavady & Around

POP 12,000

Enchanted by a folk tune played by a blind fiddler outside her window in 1851, Limavady (Léim an Mhadaidh) resident Jane Ross (1810–79) jotted down the melody – then known as 'O'Cahan's Lament', and later as the 'Londonderry Air'. The tune came to be known around the world as 'Danny Boy' – probably the most famous Irish song of all time. Sights in the neat little town are few, but it makes a pleasant stop.

A **blue plaque** on the wall at 51 Main St, opposite the Alexander Arms, commemorates the home of Jane Ross, where the famous Irish song 'Danny Boy' originated.

Sights

Roe Valley Country Park   PARK
(Dogleap Rd; 9am-dusk) **FREE** This lovely country park, 3km south of Limavady, has walks stretching for 5km either side of the River Roe. The river is famed for its salmon and trout fishing; the season runs from early June until late October. To fish you'll need a ticket (£20 for one day); see www.roeangling.com for more information.

The area is associated with the O'Cahans, who ruled the valley until the Plantation. The 17th-century settlers saw the flax-growing potential of the damp river valley and it became an important linen-manufacturing centre.

Festivals & Events

Danny Boy Jazz and Blues Festival   MUSIC
(www.dannyboyjazzandblues.com; mid-Jun) Limavady's Danny Boy Jazz and Blues Festival runs over four days at venues across town, including the **Alexander Arms** (028-7776 2660; www.facebook.com/alexanderarmslimavady; 34 Main St; s/d from £35/70; P).

Eating

Lime Tree   IRISH ££
(028-7776 4300; www.limetreerest.com; 60 Catherine St; mains lunch £10-12.50, dinner £17-22.50; 5.30-8.30pm Tue & Wed, noon-1.30pm & 5.30-8.30pm Thu, noon-1.30pm & 5.30-9pm Fri, 5.30-9pm Sat;) Streamlined decor in shades of burgundy and beige softened by flickering tea lights creates a relaxing atmosphere in Limavady's best eatery. The menu promotes local produce, from baked cod with tomato and fennel sauce to catch-of-the-day seafood thermidor and sirloin steak from McAtamney's butchers.

Information

Visitor Information Centre (028-7776 0650; 24 Main St; 9.30am-5pm Mon-Wed & Sat, to 9.30pm Thu & Fri) In the Roe Valley Arts Centre.

Getting There & Around

Bus 234 serves Derry (£5.20, 30 minutes, at least hourly Monday to Saturday, six Sunday).

Roe Valley Cycles (028-7776 6406; www.roevalleycycles.co.uk; 35 Catherine St; bikes per day from £10; 9am-6pm Mon-Sat) Rents out bikes for a spin through the Roe Valley.

Magilligan Point

The huge triangular spit of land that almost closes off the mouth of Lough Foyle is mostly taken up by a military firing range, and is home to a once-notorious prison. Still, it's worth a visit for its vast sandy beaches: **Magilligan Strand** to the west, and the 9km sweep of **Benone Strand** to the northeast. The latter provides a superb venue for kite buggies and mini land yachts.

Sights & Activities

Magilligan Martello Tower   HISTORIC BUILDING
(Point Rd) On Magilligan Point itself, watching over the entrance to Lough Foyle, stands a well-preserved Martello tower, built during the Napoleonic Wars in 1812 to guard against French invasion. The tower's interior is closed to the public but the surrounding dunes make for a pleasant walk.

Long Line Surf School   SURFING
(07738 128507; http://longlinesurfschool.co.uk; Benone Tourist Complex; 9.30am-5pm Easter-Sep, by appointment rest of year) Long Line has a cabin at Benone Tourist Complex and rents gear from Sea Shed Coffee & Surf at Benone Strand. You can also take 2½-hour group lessons in surfing (£25) and stand-up paddleboarding (SUP; £30).

Sleeping

Benone Tourist Complex   CAMPGROUND £
(028-7775 0555; http://benoneni.com; 53 Benone Ave; tent sites £22-25.50, camping huts £50-52.50; 9am-9pm Jul & Aug, to dusk Apr-Jun & Sep, to 4pm Oct-Mar;) Benone Tourist Complex, adjacent to Benone Strand, has sites for tents and caravans, as well as basic camping huts, with a heater and kettle, sleeping up to six people. There's an outdoor heated splash pool, a children's pool, tennis courts, minigolf and a nine-hole golf course.

Staff are friendly and the location is stunning, sandwiched between rugged mountain ridges and a wide, white-sand beach

Drinking & Nightlife

Sea Shed Coffee & Surf   COFFEE
(Benone Strand; ⊙10am-4pm) This chic beach-side hut sells single-origin coffee, cold brews, hot chocolate, teas and pastries as well as renting out surf equipment (per three hours/day for bodyboard with wetsuit £10/15; for surfboard with wetsuit £15/25). It's at the entrance to Benone Strand.

Downhill

The twin draws of this stretch of coast are the sprawling Downhill Demesne and sweeping surf beach below.

From Downhill, the scenic Bishop's Rd climbs steeply up through a ravine and heads over the hills to Limavady. There are spectacular views over Lough Foyle, Donegal and the Sperrin Mountains from the Gortmore picnic area, and from the cliff top at Binevenagh Lake.

◉ Sights

★Downhill Demesne   HISTORIC SITE
(www.nationaltrust.org.uk; Mussenden Rd; adult/child £5.50/2.75; ⊙dawn-dusk) In 1774 the bishop of Derry (fourth earl of Bristol, Frederick Augustus Hervey), built a palatial home amid a 160-hectare demesne. The house burnt down in 1851, was rebuilt in 1876, and abandoned after WWII. The **ruins** now stand forlornly on a cliff top, with beautiful landscaped gardens below.

The colonnaded, dome-capped **Mussenden Temple**, built by the bishop for his library (some say his mistress), is a *Game of Thrones* icon.

Enter via the coast road's Lion's Gate or Bishop's Gate.

Nearby is whitewashed, 17th-century **Hezlett House** (open 11am to 5pm from June to September; weekends only April to June), one of Ireland's oldest thatched cottages, which belonged to the same family of dairy farmers for over 300 years. The rooms are set up as they would've looked in Victorian times. It's 2km southeast of Downhill Demesne on the Mussenden Rd.

🛏 Sleeping

★Downhill Beach House   HOSTEL £
(📋028-7084 9077; http://downhillbeachhouse.com; 12 Mussenden Rd; dm/d/f £17.50/46/60;

ⓘ **LOUGH FOYLE FERRY**
....
The **Lough Foyle Ferry** that until 2016 ran between Magilligan Point and Greencastle in County Donegal was cancelled in 2017. It is hoped that a new operator will be found and the ferry will run again by summer 2018, but at research time the ferry's future remained undecided.

P @ 🛜) Tucked beneath the sea cliffs overlooking the beach, this beautifully restored late 19th-century house offers comfortable accommodation in seven-bed dorms, doubles and family rooms. There's a big lounge with an open fire and a view of the sea, and a self-catering kitchen (there are no shops nearby so bring supplies with you).

ⓘ Getting There & Away

Bus 134 between Limavady (£4.40, 35 minutes, nine daily Monday to Friday, six Saturday) and Coleraine (£3, 15 minutes) stops at Downhill, as does bus 234 between Derry (£8, 35 minutes, half-hourly Monday to Friday, hourly Saturday, seven Sunday) and Coleraine (£2.70, 10 minutes).

Portstewart

POP 7800
Ever since Victorian times, when English novelist William Thackeray described it as having an 'air of comfort and neatness', the seaside and golfing resort of Portstewart has cultivated a sedate, upmarket atmosphere that distinguishes it from populist Portrush, 6km further east. However, there's also a sizeable student community from the University of Ulster in Coleraine.

◉ Sights & Activities

Portstewart's central **Promenade** is dominated by the castellated facade of a Dominican college, looming over the seaside.

The **Port Path** is a 10.5km coastal footpath (part of the Causeway Coast Way) that stretches from Portstewart Strand to Whiterocks, 3km east of Portrush.

Portstewart Strand   BEACH
(www.nationaltrust.org.uk/portstewart-strand) The broad, 2.5km beach of Portstewart Strand is a 20-minute walk south of the centre along a coastal path, or a short bus

ride along Strand Rd. Parking is allowed on the firm sand, which can accommodate over 1000 cars (open year-round, £5 per car from Easter to October).

Aquaholics
DIVING

(☑ 028-7083 2584; www.aquaholics.co.uk; 14 Portmore Rd; ⊘ dive shop 9am-5pm Mon-Sat) The waters around Portstewart abound with marine life and shipwrecks, offering fantastic diving. Aquaholics runs PADI-accredited introductory courses (£89) and Open Water courses (£479), as well as dives (from £54, with gear from £80) to locations including Skerries Cavern and HMS *Drake* near Rathlin Island. Also offers boat trips to Rathlin Island (two-hour trip from £30) and beyond.

Portstewart Golf Club
GOLF

(☑ 028-7083 2015; www.portstewartgc.co.uk; 117 Strand Rd; green fees Strand course £90-150, Riverside course £22-27, Old Course £10-15) Dating from 1894, renowned Portstewart Golf Club has three courses: the Strand par-72 championship links course, the par-68 Riverside course and the par-64 Old Course. It's on the western side of Portstewart, on the road to Portstewart Strand. Portstewart was the venue for the 2017 Irish Open.

🎉 Festivals & Events

North West 200 Motorcycle Race
SPORTS

(www.northwest200.org; ⊘ mid-May) Ireland's biggest outdoor sporting event is run on a road circuit taking in Portrush, Portstewart and Coleraine; you can see the starting grid painted on the main road at Portstewart's eastern edge. It attracts up to 150,000 spectators; if you're not one of them, it's best to avoid the area on the race weekend.

🛏️ Sleeping

Rick's Causeway Coast Hostel
HOSTEL £

(☑ 028-7083 3789; 4 Victoria Tce; dm/s/tw/tr from £14/26/40/51; ☎) This neat terrace house just northeast of the harbour has spacious four-, six- and eight-bed dorms plus a double room, and good power showers. It has its own kitchen, laundry and welcoming open fire in winter.

★ Strandeen
B&B ££

(☑ 028-7083 3872; www.strandeen.com; 63 Strand Rd; d £110-125) More like a boutique hotel than a B&B, the hilltop-set Strandeen has four beautiful wooden-shuttered rooms with pale grey and blue hues, bike rental (per day £15) and an ocean-facing terrace. It

also serves scrumptious organic and/or free-range breakfasts (French toast with baked plums, pomegranate seeds and lemon curd, and baked eggs with spinach, mushrooms, roasted tomatoes and mixed peppers).

Cul-Erg House
B&B ££

(☑ 028-7083 6610; www.culerg.co.uk; 9 Hillside, Atlantic Circle; s/d from £40/70; ☎) Warm and welcoming, this family-run B&B inside a modern terrace house is just a couple of minutes' walk from the Promenade in a quiet cul-de-sac. Rooms at the back have sea views.

Cromore Halt Inn
HOTEL ££

(☑ 028-7083 6888; www.cromorehalt.co.uk; 158 Station Rd; s/d £89/99; ⓟ ☎) Located about 1km east of the harbour, next door to a petrol station near the corner of Station and Mill Rds, the motel-style Cromore has a dozen modern, businesslike rooms, along with friendly, helpful staff and a decent restaurant.

🍴 Eating & Drinking

Warke's Deli
CAFE £

(☑ 028-7083 3388; www.warkesdeli.com; 1 The Promenade; mains £6.50-7.50; ⊘ 9am-5.30pm; ☑) ⌖ Warke's makes everything on the premises – Bircher muesli, pancakes, soups, salads and bruschetta included. If you'd rather take a picnic to the beach, you can get hampers made up. Its corner building (where Portmore Rd meets the Promenade) looks out over the prom, harbour and ocean beyond.

Morelli's
CAFE £

(www.morellisofportstewart.co.uk; 53 The Promenade; ice creams from £1.85, dishes £3-9; ⊘ 8.30am-10pm, food to 8pm, shorter hours in winter; ☎) Morelli's is a local institution, founded by Italian immigrants and serving up its own ice cream (since 1911) along with cafe classics. Its ice-cream sundaes are legendary.

★ Harry's Shack
BISTRO ££

(☑ 028-7083 1783; www.facebook.com/HarrysShack; Portstewart Strand; mains £12-17; ⊘ 11am-3pm & 5-8.30pm Tue-Thu, 10am-9pm Fri & Sat, to 7pm Sun) Bang on Portstewart Strand beach, this National Trust–owned wooden shack has one of the north coast's best restaurants (book ahead for lunch and dinner). Harry's uses fruit, vegetables and herbs from its own organic farm plus local meat and seafood in simple but sensational dishes like megrim sole with cockles and seaweed butter, and Mulroy Bay mussels in Irish cider.

The drinks list includes craft beers from seven local breweries including Lacada Brewery in Portrush, as well as MacIvor's Cider from Armagh. Brunch is served from Friday to Sunday.

Anchor Bar PUB
(www.theanchorbar.co.uk; 87-89 The Promenade; ⊙11.30am-1am Mon-Thu, to 1.30am Fri & Sat, 12.30am Sun) Hugely popular with students from the University of Ulster, the Anchor offers a well-stocked bar and decent pub grub, and has live bands Friday and Saturday. The complex includes the Anchorage Bistro, Aura nightclub and a 20-room hotel (doubles from £80).

❶ Getting There & Away

Buses 140A and 140B make the trip from Coleraine and Portstewart (£2.70, 20 minutes, every 20 minutes Monday to Saturday, five Sunday) and continue to Portrush (£2.30, 10 minutes).

Seasonal buses with **Antrim Coaster** (p617) and **Causeway Rambler** (p617) stop here.

COUNTY ANTRIM

Portrush

POP 7355

The seaside resort of Portrush (Port Rois) bursts at the seams with holidaymakers in high season and, not surprisingly, many of its attractions are focused unashamedly on good old-fashioned family fun. However, it's also one of Ireland's top surfing centres and home to the North's most prestigious golf club.

◉ Sights & Activities

East Strand BEACH
(Curran Strand) Portrush's main attraction is the beautiful sandy East Strand beach that stretches for 3km to the east of the town, ending at the scenic chalk cliffs of Whiterocks.

★Troggs Surf Shop SURFING
(☑028-7082 5476; www.troggs.com; 88 Main St; ⊙10am-6pm Mon-Sat, closed Tue Oct-Mar) Friendly Troggs Surf Shop offers year-round bodyboard/surfboard hire (per day £6/12), wetsuit hire (per day £8) and kayak hire (per two hours £25). It also provides surf reports and general advice. A two-hour lesson including equipment hire costs £30 per person.

Royal Portrush Golf Club GOLF
(☑028-7082 2311; www.royalportrushgolfclub. com; Dunluce Rd; green fees May-Sep £190, Apr & Oct £100, Nov-Mar £60) Spectacularly situated alongside the Atlantic at the town's eastern edge, 1888-founded Royal Portrush hosted the Open Championship in 1951 and will host again in 2019. It's home to two courses: the par-72 Dunluce, with its water's-edge White Rock (5th) and ravine-set Calamity (14th) holes, and the par-70 Valley. See the website for visitor times.

🛏 Sleeping

★Portrush Holiday Hostel HOSTEL £
(☑028-7082 1288; www.portrushholidayhostel. com; 24 Princess St; dm/d from £15/38; 🛜) Just a few minutes' walk from both beach and harbour, this popular hostel is set in a Victorian terrace house, and feels cosy rather than cramped. Rooms and dorms are brightly decorated and there's a large kitchen and comfortable lounge. Staff are friendly and helpful, and facilities include a washing machine, barbecue area and bike rental.

★Shola Coach House B&B ££
(☑028-7082 5925; www.sholabandb.com; 110A Gateside Rd; r £100-125) Housed in a converted stable block dating from 1840, this luxurious B&B has four gorgeous guest rooms and a stylish lounge with wooden beams and a welcoming fire. There are home-baked cakes on arrival and the breakfast menu includes porridge with Bushmills whiskey and locally sourced smoked salmon and pork sausages. It's 3km south of Portrush. Two-night minimum stay.

Clarmont B&B ££
(☑028-7082 2397; www.clarmontguesthouse.com; 10 Landsdowne Cres; s/d from £35/70; 🛜) The pick of Portrush's guesthouses, the Clarmont has sea views and decor that tastefully mixes Victorian and modern styles, from polished pine floors to period fireplaces. Ask for one of the bay-window bedrooms with sea views and spa bath-tubs.

Royal Court Hotel HOTEL ££
(☑028-7082 2236; www.royalcourthotel.co.uk; 233 Ballybogey Rd; s/d/ste from £75/110/170; 🛜) Overlooking Whiterocks beach and Royal Portrush Golf Club 3.5km east of Portrush town centre is this well-run, traditional hotel in a spectacular location. The best rooms have large balconies with ocean views, while suites have huge picture windows and four-poster beds.

✕ Eating

Arcadia
CAFE £

(www.arcadiaportrush.co.uk; East Strand; dishes £3-6; ⊙9am-5pm Apr-Sep) A Portrush landmark, this 1920s art deco pavilion houses a breezy beach cafe on the ground floor, serving big breakfasts, bagels, salads and ice cream for a post-surf refuel, and a free art gallery on the upper floor, which also hosts workshops and classes (yoga, painting et al).

55 Degrees North
INTERNATIONAL ££

(✐028-7082 2811; www.55-north.com; 1 Causeway St; mains £10-19; ⊙12.30-2.30pm & 5-8.30pm Mon-Fri, to 9pm Sat, noon-8.30pm Sun; ✐) Floor-to-ceiling windows allow you to soak up a spectacular panorama of sand and sea from this stylish restaurant. The food concentrates on clean, simple flavours. Downstairs, licensed **Café North** (www.55-north. com; 1 Causeway St; mains lunch £6-8, dinner £10-14; ⊙9am-9pm Mon, Tue & Sat, to 6pm Wed-Fri Easter-Sep, reduced hours Oct-Easter) has a beach-facing terrace.

Ramore Wine Bar
IRISH ££

(✐028-7082 4313; www.ramorerestaurant.com; The Harbour; mains £5-17; ⊙12.15-2.15pm & 5-9pm Mon-Thu, to 9.30pm Fri, 12.15-2.30pm & 4.45-10pm Sat, 12.15-3pm & 5-9pm Sun; ✎) Part of a complex of six restaurants at Portrush harbour, the perennially popular, family-friendly Ramore Wine Bar serves classic pub grub like chilli chicken pitta, monkfish and tiger prawns, and burgers with tobacco onions. The oversized, home-made cakes and pies on display at the dessert counter make regular appearances on Instagram.

Other restaurants at the Ramore complex include **Neptune & Prawn** (mains £9.95 to £14.95), serving Asian dishes, and **Coast Pizzeria** (pizzas £5.95 to £8.95).

☕ Drinking & Nightlife

Koko
COFFEE

(www.facebook.com/kokoportrush; 2 Castle Erin Rd; ⊙9am-5pm) Great coffee and fantastic sea views are the main draws of this beach cafe. Snuggle up by the wood-burning stove and look out through the picture windows in winter, or if the sun's shining sip your flat white outside on the deck. Also serves sandwiches and cakes.

Kiwis Brew Bar
BAR

(www.kiwisbrewbar.com; 47 Main St; ⊙5pm-1am Mon-Fri, 2pm-1am Sat & Sun) Craft beers at this good-time, Kiwi-owned bar include New Zealand's Tui, as well as hard-to-find Irish brews like Pokertree from County Tyrone, and Long Meadow Cider from County Armagh. Its TVs screen rugby, of course, and surfing. Live music plays on weekends, including blues on Sundays. Cash only.

Kelly's Complex
CLUB

(Lush!; www.kellysportrush.co.uk; Bushmills Rd; ⊙9pm-late Wed & Sat) Plain and small-looking from the outside, the Tardis effect takes over as you enter a wonderland of five bars and three dance floors at the North's hottest club, just east of Portrush. It's been around since 1996, and has been named in *DJ Magazine's* Top 100 Clubs in the World. **Lush!** remains one of Ireland's best club nights.

ⓘ Getting There & Around

The bus terminal is near the Dunluce Centre. Buses 140A and 140B link Portrush with Portstewart (£2.30, 10 minutes, every 20 minutes Monday to Saturday, five Sunday) and Coleraine (£2.70, 20 minutes). It's also served by seasonal buses **Antrim Coaster** and **Causeway Rambler**.

The train station is just south of the harbour. Portrush is served by trains from Coleraine (£2.40, 12 minutes, hourly), where there are connections to Belfast and Derry.

Taxis in Portrush include **Andy Brown's** (✐028-7082 2223; http://andybrowntaxis.co.uk) and **North West Taxis** (✐028-7082 4446).

Dunluce Castle

The ruins of **Dunluce Castle** (87 Dunluce Rd; adult/child £5/3; ⊙10am-5pm Mar-Nov, to 4pm Dec & Jan, last entry 30min before closing) perch atop a dramatic basalt crag 5km east of Portrush, a one-hour walk away along the coastal path. A narrow bridge leads from the mainland courtyard across a dizzying gap to the main part of the fortress. Below, a path leads down from the gatehouse to the Mermaid's Cave beneath the castle crag. All coastal buses stop here.

In the 16th and 17th centuries the castle was the seat of the MacDonnell family (the earls of Antrim from 1620), who built a Renaissance-style manor house within the walls. Part of the castle, including the kitchen, collapsed into the sea in 1639, taking seven servants and that night's dinner with it.

ℹ **CAUSEWAY COAST SEASONAL BUSES**

Antrim Coaster The Antrim Coaster (Bus 252; ☑ 028-9066 6630; www.translink.co.uk; Bus Rambler unlimited day travel adult/child £9/4.50; ☺ Easter, May bank-holiday weekends, Jul & Aug; 🚍) has two services in each direction between Coleraine and Larne on a seasonal schedule. Stops include Portstewart, Portrush, Bushmills, the Giants Causeway, Ballintoy, Ballycastle, Cushendun, Cushendall, Glenariff (Waterfoot), Glenarm and Larne's town-centre train station.

Causeway Rambler (Bus 402; ☑ 028-9066 6630; www.translink.co.uk; Bus Rambler unlimited day travel adult/child £9/4.50; ☺ Easter-Sep) Seasonal service linking Coleraine with Carrick-a-Rede car park via Portstewart, Portrush, Dunluce Castle, Bushmills, the Giant's Causeway, Dunseverick Castle and Ballintoy. There are four services daily in April and May, and eight services daily from June to September.

Bushmills

POP 1320

The nearest town to the Giant's Causeway (5km), Bushmills has long been a place of pilgrimage for connoisseurs of Irish whiskey, and is an attractive stop for hikers exploring the Causeway Coast.

⊙ Sights & Activities

Old Bushmills Distillery　　　DISTILLERY
(☑ 028-2073 3218; www.bushmills.com; 2 Distillery Rd; tour adult/child £8/4; ☺ 9.15am-4.45pm Mon-Sat, noon-4.45pm Sun Mar-Oct, 10am-4.45pm Mon-Sat, noon-4.45pm Sun Nov-Feb) Bushmills is the world's oldest legal distillery, having been granted a licence by King James I in 1608. The whiskey is made with Irish barley and water from St Columb's Rill, a tributary of the River Bush, and matured in oak barrels. During ageing, the alcohol content drops from around 60% to 40%; the spirit lost through evaporation is known as 'the angels' share'. After the tour, you can try a free sample of your choice from Bushmills' range.

**Giant's Causeway
& Bushmills Railway**　　　TRAIN
(☑ 028-2073 2844; infogcbr@btconnect.com; return adult/child £5/3) Trains run hourly between 10am and 5.30pm, departing on the hour from the Causeway, on the half-hour from Bushmills, daily in July and August, and on weekends only from Easter to June and September and October.

Brought from a private line on the shores of Lough Neagh, the narrow-gauge line and locomotives (two steam and one diesel) follow the route of a 19th-century tourist tramway for 3km from Bushmills to below the Giant's Causeway Visitor Experience.

A path alongside the full length of the Giants Causeway & Bushmills Railway track makes for a pleasant 5km walk or cycle.

🛏 Sleeping & Eating

Bushmills Hostel　　　HOSTEL £
(☑ 028-2073 1222; www.hini.org.uk; 49 Main St; dm £16-20, tr £53; ☺ closed 11.30am-2.30pm Jul & Aug, 11.30am-5pm Mar-Jun, Sep & Oct; @ 🚍) Just off the Diamond in the centre of town, this modern, purpose-built hostel has mostly four- to six-bed dorms, all with attached bathrooms. There's also a kitchen, laundry and bike shed. The hostel is open daily March to October, but only Friday and Saturday nights from November to February. Call ahead to check it's staffed before turning up.

Ballyness Caravan Park　　CARAVAN PARK £
(☑ 028-2073 2393; www.ballynesscaravanpark. com; 40 Castlecatt Rd; campervan sites £25; ☺ mid-Mar-Oct; 🚍) This well-run caravan park (no tents), with woodland areas, wildlife ponds and spacious sites, is about 1km south of Bushmills town centre on the B66.

Bushmills Inn Hotel　　　HOTEL £££
(☑ 028-2073 3000; www.bushmillsinn.com; 9 Dunluce Rd; d/ste from £210/360; P @ 🚍) The Bushmills Inn is an old coaching inn dating to around 1608, complete with peat fires, gas lamps, a secret library and a round tower. The old part of the hotel has been given over to the restaurant; the luxurious accommodation is in the neighbouring, modern Mill House complex. Low-season discounts cut room rates in half.

★ **Bushmills Inn**　　　IRISH ££
(☑ 028-2073 3000; www.bushmillsinn.com; 9 Dunluce Rd; mains lunch £12-15, dinner £13-25; ☺ noon-5pm & 6-9.30pm Mon-Sat, noon-2.30pm & 6-9.30pm Sun; 🚍) Set in the old 17th-century stables of

the Bushmills Inn, this haven has intimate wooden booths and blazing fires, and uses fresh local produce in dishes like Atlantic seafood chowder, wild Irish venison and traditional Dalriada Cullen Skink (wood-smoked haddock poached in cream, with poached eggs and new potatoes). Book ahead.

French Rooms FRENCH **££**
(☑ 028-2073 0033; http://thefrenchrooms.com; 45 Main St; mains breakfast £4-10, lunch £9-16, dinner £15-21; ⊙ 10am-4pm Wed & Sun, to 11pm Thu-Sat) Incorporating a homewares shop and gourmet deli counter, this French-themed emporium with zinc-topped tables is an especially good option for breakfast (*croques monsieur* and *madame,* crêpes, eggs royale, brioche bacon butty). Lunch and dinner choices span spicy quinoa cassoulet to cajun-seasoned sea bass.

ℹ️ Information

Bushmills Visitor Information Centre
(☑ 028-2073 0390; www.visitcausewaycoast andglens.com; Main St; ⊙ 10am-5pm daily May, Jun & Sep, to 6pm Jul & Aug, 10am-4pm Sat & Sun Mar, Apr & Oct)

ℹ️ Getting There & Away

Bus 172 serves Coleraine (£3.50, 20 minutes, eight daily Monday to Friday, three Saturday and Sunday), the Giant's Causeway (£2, five minutes) and Ballycastle (£4.40, 45 minutes).

Seasonal services include buses with **Antrim Coaster** (p617) and **Causeway Rambler** (p617), and the **Giant's Causeway & Bushmills Railway**.

A free park-and-ride shuttle bus runs from the **Bushmills Visitor Information Centre** to the Giant's Causeway every 20 minutes, from 9am to 4pm. The bus is free but you must buy a ticket to the **Giant's Causeway Visitor Experience**, sold at the Bushmills Visitor Information Centre.

Giant's Causeway

When you first see it you'll understand why the ancients believed the Causeway was not a natural feature. It can get very crowded, so if you can, try to visit midweek or out of season to experience it at its most evocative. Sunset in spring or autumn is the best time for photographs.

⊙ Sights & Activities

A pleasant way to reach the Giant's Causeway (and avoid paying the combined parking and visitor centre entrance fee) is to walk from Bushmills along the path running parallel to the Giant's Causeway & Bushmills Railway. The walk takes about 45 minutes and there are pretty views across the sand dunes to the coast.

★ **Giant's Causeway** LANDMARK
(www.nationaltrust.org.uk; ⊙ dawn-dusk) **FREE**
This spectacular rock formation – Northern Ireland's only Unesco World Heritage site – is one of Ireland's most impressive and atmospheric landscape features, a vast expanse of regular, closely packed, hexagonal stone columns looking for all the world like the handiwork of giants. The phenomenon is explained in the Giant's Causeway Visitor Experience, housed in a new, ecofriendly building half-hidden in a hillside above the sea.

Visiting the Giant's Causeway itself is free of charge but you pay to use the car park on a combined ticket with the visitor centre; parking-only tickets aren't available.

From the centre it's an easy 10- to 15-minute walk downhill to the Causeway itself, but a more interesting approach is to follow the cliff-top path then descend the **Shepherd's Steps**. For the less mobile, a minibus shuttles from the visitors centre to the Causeway (£2 return).

The lower coastal path leads east as far as the **Amphitheatre viewpoint** at Port Reostan, passing impressive rock formations such as the **Organ** (a stack of vertical basalt columns resembling organ pipes).

You can also follow the cliff-top path east past the **Chimney Stacks headland** as far as Dunseverick or beyond.

Giant's Causeway Visitor Experience MUSEUM
(☑ 028-2073 1855; www.nationaltrust.org.uk; 60 Causeway Rd; adult/child £10.50/5.25; ⊙ 9am-7pm Jul & Aug, to 6pm Mar-Jun, Sep & Oct, to 5pm Nov-Feb) 🚫 Built into the hillside and walled in tall black basalt slabs that mimic the basalt columns of the Causeway, the Giant's Causeway Visitor Experience houses an exhibition explaining the geology of the region, as well as a tourist information desk, restaurant and shop. Admission includes an audioguide to listen to as you explore the rocks. Guided tours leave every hour.

The Visitor Experience admission fee is reduced by £1.50 if you arrive by bus, bike or on foot.

Causeway Coast
Causeway Coast

START CARRICK-A-REDE
END GIANT'S CAUSEWAY
LENGTH 16.5KM; FOUR HOURS

This spectacular stretch of the Causeway Coast Way is one of the finest coastal walks in Ireland. Be prepared: parts of the walk follow a narrow, muddy path along the top of unfenced cliffs, and can be dangerous in wet and/or windy weather. High tides can temporarily block the way at either end of White Park Bay; check tide times in advance.

After testing your nerve on the ❶ **Carrick-a-Rede Rope Bridge** (p623), take the path from its ❷ **Larrybane car park** along a cliff top with views of Sheep Island, then cut inland. At ❸ **Ballintoy church**, turn right and follow the road down to ❹ **Ballintoy Harbour**.

Continue along the shoreline past a series of conical sea stacks and arches, and scramble around the foot of a limestone crag to reach the 2km-long sandy sweep of ❺ **White Park Bay**. The going here is easiest at low tide, when you can walk on the firm sand. At the far end of the bay, scramble over rocks and boulders at the bottom of a high limestone cliff for 250m (slippery in places) to ❻ **Portbradden**.

Beyond Portbradden white limestone gives way to black basalt, and the path threads through a natural tunnel in the rocks before weaving around several rocky coves. At tiny ❼ **Dunseverick Harbour** you follow a minor road for 200m before descending steps on the right. The path then wanders along the grassy foreshore, rounds a headland and crosses a footbridge above a waterfall before reaching ❽ **Dunseverick Castle**.

From here the often-narrow, cliff-top path climbs steadily, passing an ❾ **old salmon fishery** (the little rusty-roofed cottage on the shore far below). Near Benbane Head, the walk's highest and most northerly point, a wooden bench marks the viewpoint known as ❿ **Hamilton's Seat** (after 18th-century clergyman and amateur geologist William Hamilton). Soak up the spectacular panorama of 100m-high sea cliffs, stacks and pinnacles stretching away to the west, before you set off on the final stretch. Descend the ⓫ **Shepherd's Steps** (signposted), about 1km before the Giant's Causeway Visitor Experience to reach the ⓬ **Giant's Causeway**.

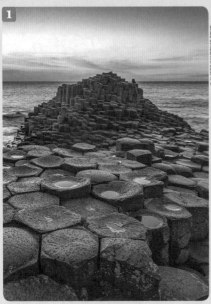

GREG SINCLAIR/500PX ©

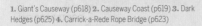

1. Giant's Causeway (p618) 2. Causeway Coast (p619) 3. Dark Hedges (p625) 4. Carrick-a-Rede Rope Bridge (p623)

PETER ZELEI IMAGES/GETTY IMAGES ©

Counties Londonderry & Antrim: The Causeway Coast

The north coast of County Antrim from Ballycastle west to Portrush is known as the Causeway Coast, one of the most impressively scenic stretches of coastline in all of Ireland. Whether you drive, cycle or walk its length, it's not to be missed.

Giant's Causeway

The grand geological centrepiece of the Antrim coast is the Giant's Causeway, a spectacular rock formation composed of countless hexagonal basalt columns. A Unesco World Heritage site, it is the north coast's most popular tourist attraction.

Causeway Coast

The Causeway Coast isn't just about the scenery. There are picturesque villages at Ballintoy (famous as the Iron Islands' Lordsports Harbour in *Game of Thrones*) and Portbradden, historic ruined fortresses at Dunluce and Dunseverick castles, and the chance to savour a dram of Irish whiskey at Old Bushmills Distillery.

Carrick-a-Rede Rope Bridge

Originally rigged and used by local salmon fishermen, the famous Carrick-a-Rede Rope Bridge is now a popular test of nerve for Causeway Coast visitors, swaying gently 30m above the rocks and the sea.

Antrim Coast

Although famous for its dramatic sea-cliff scenery, the Antrim coast also has some excellent sandy beaches. As well as the family-friendly strand at Ballycastle, there's the harder-to-reach but twice-as-beautiful White Park Bay.

🛏 Sleeping & Eating

Staying at the Giant's Causeway itself makes it easy to explore the coastline early morning and late evening, without the crowds. A better range of accommodation is available in Bushmills, 5km south of the Causeway.

If you've worked up an appetite clambering among the stones, there's a cafe at the Giant's Causeway Visitor Experience (p618), a restaurant in the Causeway Hotel and pub grub at the **Nook** (☑ 028-2073 2993; 48 Causeway Rd; mains £9-18; ⊗ kitchen 11am-9pm Mar-Oct, to 6pm Nov-Feb).

Causeway Hotel   HOTEL £££
(☑ 028-9073 1210; www.thecausewayhotel.com; 40 Causeway Rd; d from £130; 🅿 🛜) On the cliffs above the Giant's Causeway, this 28-room National Trust–owned hotel is an ideal base for exploring the coast early or late in the day without the crowds. Ask for one of the rooms at the western end, with outdoor terraces that enjoy sunset views over the Atlantic.

Parking is free for guests and diners at its restaurant (mains £9 to £13).

ℹ Getting There & Away

As well as the seasonal bus services **Antrim Coaster** (p617) and **Causeway Rambler** (p617), and the **Giant's Causeway & Bushmills Railway** (p617), bus 172 from Ballycastle (£4.40, 30 minutes, eight daily Monday to Friday, three Saturday and Sunday) to Coleraine (£4.40, 25 minutes) and Bushmills (£2, five minutes) stops here year-round. From Coleraine, trains run to Belfast or Derry.

ℹ Getting Around

It's an easy 1km walk from the Giant's Causeway Visitor Experience car park down to the Causeway, although you can take one of the minibuses that plies the route (one-way/return £1/2, every 15 minutes). The buses are wheelchair accessible.

Ballintoy & Around

POP 170

The pretty village of Ballintoy (Baile an Tuaighe) tumbles down the hillside to a picture-postcard harbour, better known to *Game of Thrones* fans as the Iron Islands' Lordsports Harbour (among other scenes filmed here). The restored limekiln on the quayside once made quicklime using stone from the chalk cliffs and coal from Ballymoney.

Ballintoy lies roughly halfway between Ballycastle and the Giant's Causeway on the most scenic stretch of the Causeway Coast, with sea cliffs of contrasting black basalt and white chalk, rocky islands and broad sweeps of sandy beach.

◉ Sights & Activities

The main attractions can be reached by car or bus, but the 16.5km stretch between the Carrick-a-Rede car park and the Giant's Causeway is best enjoyed on a walk (p619) following the waymarked **Causeway Coast Way** (www.walkni.com).

About 9.5km east of the Giant's Causeway is the tiny seaside hamlet of **Portbradden**, with half a dozen harbourside houses. Visible from Portbradden and accessible via the next junction off the A2 is the spectacular **White Park Bay**, with its wide, sweeping sandy beach. Some 3km further east is **Ballintoy**.

THE MAKING OF THE CAUSEWAY

The story goes that the Irish giant Finn McCool built the Causeway so he could cross the sea to fight the Scottish giant Benandonner. Benandonner pursued Finn back across the Causeway, but in turn took fright and fled back to Scotland, ripping up the Causeway as he went. All that remains are its ends – the Giant's Causeway in Ireland, and the island of Staffa in Scotland (which has similar rock formations).

The scientific explanation is that the Causeway rocks were formed 60 million years ago, when a thick layer of molten basaltic lava flowed along a valley in the existing chalk beds. As the lava flow cooled and hardened – from the top and bottom surfaces inward – it contracted, creating a pattern of hexagonal cracks at right angles to the cooling surfaces (think of mud contracting and cracking in a hexagonal pattern as a lake bed dries out). As solidification progressed towards the centre of the flow, the cracks spread down from the top and up from the bottom, until the lava was completely solid. Erosion has cut into the lava flow, and the basalt has split along the contraction cracks, creating the hexagonal columns.

★ **Carrick-a-Rede Rope Bridge** BRIDGE
(☑028-2076 9839; www.nationaltrust.org.uk/carrick-a-rede; 119 Whitepark Rd, Ballintoy; adult/child £7/3.50; ⊙9.30am-6pm Apr-Oct, to 3.30pm Nov-Mar) This 20m-long, 1m-wide bridge of wire rope spans the chasm between the sea cliffs and the little island of Carrick-a-Rede, swaying 30m above the rock-strewn water. Crossing the bridge is perfectly safe, but frightening if you don't have a head for heights, especially if it's breezy (in high winds the bridge is closed). From the island, views take in Rathlin Island and Fair Head to the east.

There's a small National Trust information centre and cafe at the car park.

The impetus for the crossing first came from fishermen, who would stretch their nets out from the tip of the island to intercept the passage of salmon migrating along the coast to their home rivers.

Now firmly on the tour-bus route, Carrick-a-Rede has become so popular that the National Trust has introduced ticketed one-hour time slots to visit the bridge. Turn up early to be sure of securing a ticket in high season.

Kinbane Castle CASTLE
(Whitepark Rd) FREE On a limestone headland jutting out from the basalt cliffs, with stupendous views of Rathlin Island and Scotland, this castle, now ruined, was built in 1547 by Colla MacDonnell (son of Alexander MacDonnell, lord of Islay and Kintyre, and Catherine, daughter of the lord of Ardnamurchan), then rebuilt in 1555 following an English siege. It was inhabited until the 17th century, when it was abandoned. From the car park, 140 steep steps lead down to the castle.

🛏 Sleeping & Eating

Sheep Island View Hostel HOSTEL £
(☑028-2076 9391; www.sheepislandview.com; 42A Main St; dm/s/tw £18/25/45; P@🛜) This family-run independent hostel offers dorm and basic rooms with private bathroom. There's a kitchen and laundry, and a village store nearby. It's on the main coast road near the turn-off to Ballintoy Harbour, with a bus stop at the door, and makes a handy overnight stop if you're hiking between Bushmills and Ballycastle.

Whitepark Bay Hostel HOSTEL £
(☑028-2073 1745; www.hini.org.uk; 157 Whitepark Rd, Ballintoy; dm/tw from £17/40; ⊙mid-Mar–Oct; P🛜) Near the west end of White Park Bay, this modern, purpose-built hostel has mostly four-bed dorms, plus twin rooms with TV, all with private bathroom. The common room is warmed by a fireplace and positioned to soak up the view, and the beach is just a few minutes' walk through the dunes.

Whitepark House B&B £££
(☑028-2073 1482; www.whiteparkhouse.com; 150 Whitepark Rd, Ballintoy; s/d £80/180; P🛜) A beautifully restored 18th-century house overlooking White Park Bay, this B&B has traditional features such as antique furniture and a peat fire complemented by Asian artefacts gathered during the welcoming owners' travels. There are three rooms – ask for one with a sea view.

Red Door Cottage CAFE £
(☑028-2076 9048; www.facebook.com/thereddoortearoom; 14a Harbour Rd, Ballintoy; mains £6-10; ⊙11am-4pm Tue-Fri, 10am-4pm Sat & Sun May-Oct, 10am-4pm Sat & Sun Mar & Apr) Fronted by a fire-engine-red door, this little cottage sits 200m off the main coast road along the side road to Ballintoy Harbour. Everything is homemade: soups, chowders, Irish stew, burgers and cakes. The garden's picnic tables are idyllic in the sunshine; when it's chilly there's a turf fire indoors. It's worth booking ahead in peak holiday seasons.

Roark's Kitchen CAFE £
(Harbour Rd, Ballintoy Harbour; mains £6.25-7.50; ⊙11am-7pm daily Jun-Aug, Sat & Sun only May & Sep; P) On the quayside at Ballintoy Harbour, this cute little chalk-built tearoom serves teas, coffees, ice cream, home-baked apple, cherry and rhubarb tart, and lunch dishes such as Irish stew or chicken and ham pie. Cash only.

❶ Getting There & Away

Bus 172 (eight daily Monday to Friday, three daily Saturday and Sunday) connects Ballintoy with Coleraine (£4.40, 40 minutes), Ballycastle (£3, 20 minutes), Giant's Causeway (£3.20, 20 minutes) and Bushmills (£3.50, 25 minutes). The **Antrim Coaster** (p617) and **Causeway Rambler** (p617) buses cover the route in season.

Ballycastle

POP 5000

The harbour town and holiday resort of Ballycastle (Baile an Chaisil) marks the eastern end of the Causeway Coast. It's a pretty town with a family-friendly promenade and a good bucket-and-spade beach. Ferries to Rathlin Island depart from here.

◉ Sights & Activities

Marconi Memorial
MONUMENT

In the harbour car park, a plaque at the foot of a rock pinnacle commemorates the day in 1898 when Guglielmo Marconi's assistants contacted Rathlin Island by radio from Ballycastle to prove to Lloyds of London that wireless communication was a viable proposition. The idea was to send notice to London or Liverpool of ships arriving safely after a transatlantic crossing – most vessels on this route would have to pass through the channel north of Rathlin.

Sea Haven Therapy
SPA

(www.seahaventherapy.com; 18 Bayview Rd; ⊙10am-6pm Mon-Thu & Sat, to 9pm Fri) Immerse yourself in a relaxing seaweed bath (good for muscular aches, joint pain and circulation; £25) while enjoying views of Rathlin Island and beyond, or try the salt therapy room (45 minutes; £20) or a massage (55 minutes from £35). Next to the Rathlin Island ferry terminal at Ballycastle Harbour.

Ballycastle Food Tour
FOOD & DRINK

(⌖07718 276612; www.northcoastwalkingtours. com; per person £30) This three-hour walking tour makes stops at six of the town's eateries to sample items such as local black pudding, cheese, seafood chowder and craft ale. Book ahead via the website or at the Ballycastle Visitor Information Centre. Also offers tours of Bushmills and Rathlin Island.

✵ Festivals & Events

Auld Lammas Fair
CULTURAL

(⊙last Mon & Tue in Aug) Ballycastle's Auld Lammas Fair dates back to 1606. Thousands of people descend on the town for the market stalls and fairground rides, and to sample 'yellowman' (a hard chewy toffee-like honeycomb) and dulse (dried edible seaweed).

Sleeping

Watertop Open Farm
CAMPGROUND £

(⌖028-2076 2576; www.watertopfarm.co.uk; 188 Cushendall Rd; camp sites for 2 people £15, per additional person £5, caravan sites from £25; ⊙Easter-Oct) About 10km east of Ballycastle on the road to Cushendun, family-favourite Watertop is based at a working farm and activity centre (open 11am to 5.30pm July and August; per activity adult/child £3/2.50), offering pony trekking, sheep-shearing and farm tours.

Ballycastle Backpackers
HOSTEL £

(⌖028-2076 3612; www.ballycastlebackpackers. net; 4 North St; dm/tw from £17.50/35, cottages £80; 🅿@🛜) Overlooking the harbour, this small, homey terrace house has one six-bed dorm, a family room and a couple of twin and double rooms. There's a well-equipped kitchen and a cosy living room for guests, as well as a cute self-catering cottage in the backyard, containing two twin rooms and a private bathroom (minimum two nights).

Four further, more luxuriously appointed rooms with attached bathrooms are available in **Quayside** in the adjoining terrace (double with/without sea view £90/73).

Kinbane Farmhouse
B&B ££

(⌖028-2076 9947; www.kinbane.com; 85 Whitepark Rd; s/d £40/60; 🛜) Near Kinbane Castle, this wonderfully welcoming working farmstead has three pine-furnished guest rooms (all have private bathroom, but one's outside the room), a toasty turf fire, and binoculars for zooming in on Rathlin Island and Scotland beyond.

An Caislean Guesthouse
GUESTHOUSE ££

(⌖028-2076 2845; www.ancaislean.co.uk; 42 Quay Rd; s/d from £35/60; 🅿🛜) Originally two guesthouses, now linked by a covered walkway, An Caislean has a large guest lounge and a warm and welcoming family atmosphere. Rooms are spacious and comfortable, if a bit creaky in the floorboard department, but the trump card is the location, just a few minutes' walk from the beach. Some rooms share bathrooms.

✗ Eating & Drinking

With artisan bakeries, craft breweries and fine local seafood, Ballycastle is emerging as something of a foodie destination. Local produce items to look out for include smoked fish from North Coast Smokehouse (wwwnorthcoastsmokehouse.com) and beer from Glens of Antrim Craft Ales & Beers (glensofantrimcraftaleandbeers.com).

★ Ursa Minor
BAKERY, CAFE £

(www.ursaminorbakehouse.com; 45 Ann St; ⊙10am-4pm Tue-Sat) Specialising in sourdough and friands (sweet almond cakes), Ursa Minor is the kind of bakery-cafe you might hope to find in a hip Sydney suburb rather than the seaside town of Ballycastle. When Dara and Ciara Ó Hartghaile returned from New Zealand they decided to give artisan baking a shot; the resulting bakery is a hit with locals and visitors alike.

★ **Morton's Fish & Chips** FISH & CHIPS £
(☑ 028-2076 1100; The Harbour, Bayview Rd; mains £6-10; ⊙ noon-8pm Sun-Thu, to 9pm Fri & Sat) Fish and chips don't come fresher: local boats unload their daily catch right alongside this little harbourside hut. The cod, haddock, scallops, scampi and crab cakes along with chips made from locally farmed potatoes draw long queues in summer (expect to wait).

Thyme & Co CAFE £
(☑ 028-2076 9851; www.thymeandco.co.uk; 5 Quay Rd; dishes £3.50-6.50; ⊙ 9am-5pm Tue-Fri, 9.30am-8.30pm Sat, 10am-4pm Sun; 🛜) 🍴 Lush salads, shepherd's pie, and salmon and egg crumble are among the homemade dishes prepared using local produce at this welcoming cafe. Many of its cakes and bakes are gluten-free; there's excellent coffee too. Saturday nights offer various specials, such as BYO pizza nights.

Central Wine Bar IRISH ££
(☑ 028-2076 3877; www.centralwinebar.com; 12 Ann St; mains lunch £5-20, dinner £11-20; ⊙ 11am-11pm Mon-Thu, to 1am Fri & Sat, noon-11pm Sun) The Central Wine Bar is a safe bet for a great meal. Fresh local produce like Armagh chicken, Portavogie cod and Moyle seafood are used to create dishes like chicken Louisiana, poached smoked cod in a ginger, mushroom and scallion sauce, and seafood chowder. Friendly service and a good wine list are bonuses.

O'Connor's PUB
(http://oconnorsbar.ie; 5-7 Ann St; ⊙ 11.30am-1am) Just off the Diamond, O'Connor's is Ballycastle's best pub for music, with trad Thursday nights year-round. From Easter to September, there are also bands in the bar and DJs in the beer garden on Saturday, and jam sessions on Sunday. Hearty food is served nonstop until 9pm.

ℹ **Information**

Ballycastle Visitor Information Centre
(☑ 028-2076 2024; www.visitcausewaycoast andglens.com; 14 Bayview Rd; ⊙ 9.30am-5pm Mon-Fri, 10am-4pm Sat Sep-Jun, plus noon-4pm Sun Jun & Sep, longer hours Jul & Aug) Helpful tourist information office near the Rathlin Island ferry terminal at the harbour.

ℹ **Getting There & Away**

The bus station is on Station Rd, just east of the Diamond. Bus 217 links Ballycastle with Ballymena (£6.70, 50 minutes, hourly Monday to Friday, five Saturday), where you can connect to Belfast.

WORTH A TRIP

KINGSROAD

Planted by the Stuart family in the 18th century as the formal entrance to their property, the shadowy, gnarled, entwined beech trees of the **Dark Hedges** (Bregagh Rd, Ballymoney) are now among Northern Ireland's most photographed sights after doubling as the Kingsroad in *Game of Thrones*. Getting a photo without cars (and crowds) isn't easy: do your fellow fans a favour and park at either end of the tree-covered road and walk up. The Dark Hedges are 14km southwest of Ballycastle via the A44 and Ballykenver Rd.

In 2016 when Storm Gertrude uprooted several of the 200-year-old trees, the wood was salvaged and used to create 10 intricately carved *Game of Thrones* doors. These are scattered across Northern Ireland; pick up the free 'Journey of the Doors' passport at tourist information points.

Bus 172 goes along the coast to Coleraine (£6.50, one hour, eight daily Monday to Friday, three Saturday and Sunday) via Ballintoy, the Giant's Causeway and Bushmills.

The seasonal **Antrim Coaster bus** (p617) also stops here.

High-speed passenger ferries with **Kintyre Express** (☑ 01586 555895; www.kintyreexpress. com; ⊙ Easter-Sep) link Ballycastle with Campbeltown, Scotland (one-way/return £45/80, 1½ hours, one daily June to September). A separate one-hour service runs to Port Ellen on Islay, Scotland (one-way/return £60/95, one hour, one daily June to September).

Rathlin Island
POP 140

Rugged Rathlin Island sits 6km offshore from Ballycastle. An L-shaped island just 6.5km long and 4km wide, Rathlin is home to hundreds of seals and thousands of nesting seabirds in late spring and summer.

Scottish hero Robert the Bruce spent time here in 1306 while hiding out after being defeated by the English king. Watching a spider's resoluteness in repeatedly trying to spin a web gave him the courage to have another go at the English, whom he subsequently defeated at Bannockburn. The cave where he is said to have stayed is beneath the East Lighthouse, at the northeastern tip of the island.

◉ Sights & Activities

Rathlin is famous for its spectacular coastal scenery and the seabirds, especially puffins, who nest on the sea cliffs at the island's western tip.

From the harbour in Church Bay there are three main walking routes: to the Rathlin West Light Seabird Centre (p626) (7km), to the **East Lighthouse** (3km) and to the **South Lighthouse** (4.5km). The roads are all suitable for cycling; bikes can be hired.

There are also some fabulous off-road walking trails including the **Ballyconagan Trail** to the Old Coastguard Station on the north coast, with great views along the sea cliffs and across to the Scottish islands of Islay and Jura; and the cliff-top **Roonivoolin Trail** in the south, where you can spot choughs (the rarest of the crow family), hear the singing of skylarks and spot Irish hares.

The island is surrounded by some 40 shipwrecks, including the HMS *Drake*, which can be dived with Aquaholics (p614).

★ Rathlin West Light Seabird Centre
LIGHTHOUSE

(☑ 028-2076 3948; www.rspb.org.uk; adult/child £5/2.50; ☺ 10am-5pm Mar-Sep) This Royal Society for the Protection of Birds (RSPB) centre offers spectacular views of a thriving seabird colony, where every summer thousands of puffins can be seen. It's located at Rathlin's upside-down west lighthouse (the lamp is at the building's base). Built into the cliff face, the lighthouse was a feat of engineering when it was completed in 1919. The lighthouse tower now contains exhibits on Rathlin's marine life and history.

Above the lighthouse, viewing platforms look out to the neighbouring sea stacks, where every year thousands of seabirds return to breed, including guillemots, razorbills, kittiwakes and fulmars. The best times to see puffins are mid-May (when the birds gather on the cliffs), mid-June (when the chicks begin hatching) and late July (when the puffins prepare to return to sea). Binoculars and telescopes are provided for close-up views of the birds and their chicks.

Boathouse Visitor Centre
MUSEUM

(www.rathlincommunity.org; ☺ 10am-12.30pm & 1-5pm Apr-Sep) South of the harbour, this combined visitor centre/museum details the fascinating history, culture and ecology of Rathlin Island, and can give advice on walks and wildlife.

Paul Quinn
WALKING

(☑ 07745 566924; www.rathlinwalkingtours.com) Insightful guide Paul Quinn offers entertaining walking tours of Rathlin Island.

🛏 Sleeping & Eating

Rathlin has a pub, a shop and a handful of eating options (many of them seasonal), all located in and around Church Bay. Bring supplies if you're heading out walking or cycling elsewhere on the island. There are vending machines selling chocolate bars and coffee at the Rathlin West Light Seabird Centre.

Rathlin Island Hostel
HOSTEL £

(☑ 07563 814378; http://rathlinhostel.com; dm £18) Just a five-minute walk south of the harbour, Rathlin Island Hostel has five simple but bright rooms with four to 12 beds, with the option to book each as a private room (£67 to £200). All share bathrooms. There's a self-catering kitchen and a fantastic ocean-view terrace. Cash only.

Kinramer Cottage
HOSTEL £

(☑ 028-2076 3948; http://kinramercottage.com; Kinramer; dm £12) Kinramer is a basic bunkhouse located on an organic farm, 5km west from the harbour (a one-hour walk) in a beautifully remote location. You'll need to bring your own food.

★ Manor House
GUESTHOUSE ££

(☑ 028-2076 0046; www.manorhouserathlin.com; Church Bay; s/d/ste £65/100/125) Rathlin's 18th-century manor house has been fully renovated and transformed into a stylish 11-room guesthouse with stunning views across Church Bay. Rooms combine modern furnishings with period features and the bright reception area has a welcoming fire. There's also a restaurant serving evening meals including freshly caught crab and lobster when its in season (mains £10 to £28; bookings essential).

Coolnagrock B&B
B&B ££

(☑ 028-2076 3983; Coolnagrock; s/d from £40/70; ☺ Apr-Oct; 🛜) Views stretch across the sea to the Mull of Kintyre from this well-appointed guesthouse in the eastern part of the island. It's a 15-minute walk from the ferry, but you can arrange for the owner to pick you up. Book ahead.

Water Shed Cafe
CAFE £

(sandwiches £4.50-6; ☺ 9.30am-5pm Wed-Sun May-Sep, 10am-4pm Wed-Sat Apr) In a little cottage by the harbour, the Water Shed Cafe serves soups, sandwiches, cakes and coffee.

🍸 Drinking & Nightlife

McCuaig's Bar PUB

(📞 028-2076 0011; The Harbour; ⏰ 11am-11pm; 📶 🍴) Rathlin Island's pub and beer garden overlook the harbour, with wooden picnic tables providing an idyllic spot for a pint and a plate of hearty pub food like Irish stew or fish and chips (mains £5.50 to £8). There's an ATM here.

ℹ️ Getting There & Around

Rathlin Island Ferry (📞 028-2076 9299; www. rathlinballycastleferry.com; return trip adult/ child/bicycle £12/6/3.30) operates daily from Ballycastle; advance bookings are essential. From April to mid-September there are up to 10 crossings a day, half of which are fast catamaran services (20 minutes), the rest via a slower car ferry (45 minutes). In winter the service is reduced.

Only residents can take their car to Rathlin (except for disabled drivers), but nowhere on the island is more than 6km (about 1½ hours' walk) from the ferry pier.

McGinn's **Puffin Bus** (📞 07759 935192, 07752 861788; tickets per adult/child £5/3) shuttles visitors between the ferry and Rathlin West Light Seabird Centre from April to September; contact the company for other transport requests.

Bicycle hire (📞 028-2076 3954; john_jennifer @btinternet.com; Soerneog View Hostel; per day £10; ⏰ 10am-5pm) is available at Soerneog View Hostel, south of the harbour.

Glens of Antrim

The northeastern corner of Antrim is a high plateau of black basalt lava overlying beds of white chalk. Along the coast, between Cushendun and Glenarm, the plateau has been dissected by a series of scenic, glacier-gouged valleys known as the Glens of Antrim.

Two waymarked footpaths traverse the region: the **Ulster Way** sticks close to the sea, passing through all the coastal villages, while the 32km **Moyle Way** runs inland across the high plateau from Glenariff Forest Park to Ballycastle.

Torr Head Scenic Road

A few kilometres east of Ballycastle, a minor road signposted 'Scenic Route' branches north off the A2. This alternative route to Cushendun is not for the faint-hearted driver (nor for caravans), as it clings, precarious

and narrow, to steep slopes high above the sea. Side roads lead off to the main points of interest. On a clear day, there are superb views across the sea to Scotland, from the Mull of Kintyre to the peaks of Arran.

The first turn-off ends at the National Trust car park at Coolanlough, the starting point for a waymarked 5km return hike to **Fair Head**. The second turn-off leads steeply down to **Murlough Bay**. From the parking area at the end of this road, you can walk north along the shoreline to some ruined miners' cottages (10 minutes); coal and chalk were once mined in the cliffs above, and burned in a limekiln (south of the car park) to make quicklime.

The third turn-off leads you past some ruined coastguard houses to the rocky headland of **Torr Head**, crowned with a 19th-century coastguard station (abandoned in the 1920s). This is Ireland's closest point to Scotland – the Mull of Kintyre is a mere 19km away across the North Channel. In late spring and summer, a fixed-net salmon fishery operates here. The ancient ice house beside the approach road was once used to store the catch.

Cushendun

POP 150

The pretty seaside village of Cushendun is famous for its distinctive Cornish-style cottages, now owned by the National Trust. Built between 1912 and 1925 at the behest of the local landowner, Lord Cushendun, they were designed by Clough Williams-Ellis, the architect of Portmeirion in north Wales.

👁️ Sights & Activities

Cushendun has a wide sandy **beach**, various short **coastal walks** and some impressive **caves** – a *Game of Thrones* filming location – cut into the overhanging conglomerate sea cliffs south of the village (follow the trail around the far end of the holiday apartments south of the river mouth).

Some 6km north of the village on the A2 road to Ballycastle is **Loughareema**, also known as the Vanishing Lake. Three streams flow in but none flow out. The lough fills up to a respectable size (400m long and 6m deep) after heavy rain, but the water gradually drains away through fissures in the underlying limestone, leaving a dry lake bed.

🛏 Sleeping & Eating

⭐ Villa Farmhouse
B&B **££**

(☎ 028-2176 1252; www.thevillafarmhouse.com; 185 Torr Rd; s/d £35/60; P 🛜) This lovely old white-washed farmhouse is set on a hillside 1km north of Cushendun, with great views over the bay and the warm atmosphere of a family home, decorated with photos of children and grandchildren. The owner is an expert chef, and breakfast will be a highlight of your stay.

Cloneymore House
B&B **££**

(☎ 028-2176 1443; ann.cloneymore@btinternet. com; 103 Knocknacarry Rd; s/d £55/70; P 🛜) A traditional family B&B on the B92 road 500m southwest of Cushendun, Cloney-more has three spacious and spotless rooms named after Irish and Scottish islands – Aran is the biggest. There are wheelchair ramps and a stairlift, and rooms are equipped for visitors with limited mobility.

Mary McBride's Pub
PUB FOOD **££**

(☎ 028-2176 1511; 2 Main St; bar snacks £4-12, dinner mains £12.50-17.50; ⊘ food noon-7pm Wed, 11am-5pm & 6-9.30pm Thu-Sat, 11am-6pm Sun) The original bar here (on the left as you go in) is the smallest in Ireland (2.7m by 1.5m), but there's plenty of elbow-bending room in the rest of the pub. Good pub grub is served downstairs and there's live music on weekends. Upstairs is the **Little Black Door** (6-9.30pm Thu-Sat) seafood bistro.

🍸 Drinking & Nightlife

Corner House
CAFE

(☎ 028-2176 1560; 1 Main St; ⊘ 10am-4pm Fri-Sun) The National Trust–owned Corner House serves coffee, cakes, scones, cooked breakfasts and lunchtime soups and salads.

Randal's
PUB

(☎ 028-2176 1266; 10 Strand View Park; ⊘ 11.30am-11.30pm) By the bridge in Cushendun, this eccentric place occupies a pair of vintage rooms in what was the Cushendun Hotel. There are just two choices on tap – Guinness and Harp – but also a great selection of whiskeys. On sunny days, the best seats are on the front pavement overlooking the River Dun.

❶ Getting There & Away

Bus 150 links Cushendun with Cushendall (£2.70, 15 minutes, six daily Monday to Friday, three Saturday), Glenariff Forest Park (£3.80, 30 minutes) and Ballymena (£6.70, one hour).

The seasonal **Antrim Coaster** (p617) stops here.

Cushendall
POP 1360

Cushendall is a holiday centre with a small and shingly beach. The village, which can be a traffic bottleneck, sits at the foot of Glenbal-lyeamon, overlooked by the prominent flat-topped hill of Lurigethan.

◉ Sights

Layd Old Church
CHURCH

FREE From the car park beside the beach (follow the golf-club signs), a coastal path leads 1km north to the picturesque ruins of Layd Old Church, with views across to Ailsa Craig (a prominent conical island also known as 'Paddy's Milestone') and the Scottish coast. Founded by the Franciscans, it was used as a parish church from the early 14th century until 1790. The graveyard contains several grand MacDonnell memorials.

Near the gate stands an ancient, weathered ring-cross (with the arms missing), much older than the 19th-century inscription on its shaft.

Curfew Tower
HISTORIC BUILDING

The unusual red sandstone Curfew Tower at the central crossroads was built in 1817 and based on a building the landowner had seen in China. It was originally a prison. The tower is closed to the public.

🛏 Sleeping & Eating

Cullentra House
B&B **££**

(☎ 028-2177 1762; www.cullentrahouse.com; 16 Cloughs Rd; s/d from £35/55; P 🛜) This modern bungalow sits high above the village, offering good views of the craggy Antrim coast. The three rooms are spacious and comfy, and the breakfasts (accompanied by home-baked wheaten bread) are as hearty as the owners' hospitality.

Village B&B
B&B **££**

(☎ 028-2177 2366; www.thevillagebandb.com; 18 Mill St; s/d/f from £45/70/100; P 🛜) Right in the middle of town, the Village offers spotless rooms with private bathrooms and fireplaces, and huge hearty breakfasts (including a vegetarian option).

⭐ Harry's Restaurant
BISTRO **££**

(☎ 028-2177 2022; http://harryscushendall. com; 10 Mill St; mains lunch £8-13, dinner £10-20; ⊘ noon-9pm; 🛜) With its cosy lounge-bar atmosphere and friendly welcome, Harry's is a local institution, serving pub grub staples from noon to 6pm plus an à la carte evening menu that ranges from steak to lobster.

Drinking & Nightlife

★McCollam's PUB

(Johnny Joe's; ☑028-2177 2849; www.upstairs atjoes.com; 23 Mill St; ⊙noon-11.30pm, kitchen 5-9pm Fri & Sat, noon-9pm Sun) Locally known as Johnny Joe's, this rhubarb-coloured pub is the town's liveliest. The original ground-floor bar was built in the 1800s; behind it is a tiny lounge dominated by an old range cooker. There are regular trad-music sessions and great craic. The excellent restaurant **Upstairs at Joes** (mains £12.50-18) serves modern Irish dishes and daily seafood specials.

ℹ Information

Tourist office (☑028-2177 1180; 24 Mill St; ⊙10am-1pm Tue-Sat Apr-Sep) Run by the Glens of Antrim Historical Society.

ℹ Getting There & Away

Bus 150 links Cushendall with Cushendun (£2.70, 15 minutes, six daily Monday to Friday, three Saturday), Glenariff Forest Park (£3, 15 minutes) and Ballymena (£6, one hour).

It's also on the bus route of the seasonal **Antrim Coaster** (p617).

Glenariff

About 2km south of Cushendall is the village of Waterfoot, with a 2km-long sandy beach, the best on Antrim's east coast. From here the A43 Ballymena road runs inland along Glenariff, the loveliest of Antrim's glens. Views of the valley led the writer Thackeray to exclaim that it was a 'Switzerland in miniature' (a claim that makes you wonder if he'd ever been to Switzerland).

◎ Sights

Glenariff Forest Park FOREST

(www.nidirect.gov.uk; 98 Glenariff Rd; car/motorcycle £5/2.50; ⊙9am-dusk, tea house 11am-5pm Easter-Sep) At the head of the Glenariff Valley is Glenariff Forest Park, where the main attraction is **Ess-na-Larach Waterfall**, an 800m walk from the visitor centre. You can also walk to the waterfall from Laragh Lodge, 600m downstream. Wonderful hikes in the park include a 10km circular trail. There's also a tea house selling scones and hot drinks and lunches.

🛏 Sleeping & Eating

Ballyeamon Barn HOSTEL £

(☑028-2175 8451; www.ballyeamonbarn.com; 127 Ballyeamon Rd; dm £15; P🕱) Run by professional storyteller Liz Weir, this whitewashed barn has hostel accommodation for hikers and hosts regular sessions of traditional Irish music, poetry, dance and storytelling. It's 8km southwest of Cushendall on the B14 (1km north of its junction with the A43, close to the Moyle Way and about a 1.5km walk from the main entrance to Glenariff Forest Park.

There's secure parking for bikes and a well-equipped kitchen.

Laragh Lodge IRISH ££

(☑028-2175 8221; www.laraghlodge.co.uk; 120 Glen Rd; mains £10-20; ⊙11am-9pm daily Mar-Oct, Fri-Sun only Nov-Feb) A renovated Victorian tourist lodge with assorted bric-a-brac dangling from the rafters, the Laragh dates from 1890 and serves hearty meals like steak sandwiches and fish and chips, as well as a traditional roast lunch on Sunday – perfect after a long walk. It's on a side road off the A43, 3km northeast of the main Glenariff Forest Park entrance.

ℹ Getting There & Away

You can reach Glenariff Forest Park on bus 150 from Cushendall (£3, 20 minutes, eight daily Monday to Friday, four Saturday) and Ballymena (£4.40, 30 minutes).

The seasonal **Antrim Coaster** (p617) stops at Waterfoot.

Glenarm

POP 1800

Delightful little Glenarm (Gleann Arma) is the oldest village in the Glens of Antrim. It's well worth a visit for the fabulous gardens at Glenarm Castle, rows of pretty Georgian houses and forest park.

◎ Sights

Take a stroll into the old village of neat Georgian houses (off the main road, immediately south of the river). Where the street opens into the broad expanse of Altmore St, look right to see the **Barbican Gate** (1682), the entrance to the grounds of Glenarm Castle.

Up steep Vennel St, turn left after the last house along the Layde Path to the viewpoint, which has a grand view of the village and the coast.

THE GOBBINS

Tubular bridges, rocky surfaces, tunnels, caves and narrow crevices form a dramatic cliff path at Islandmagee, the slender peninsula that runs parallel to the coastline just south of Larne. **The Gobbins** (Coastal Walk; ☑ 028-9337 2318; www.thegobbinscliffpath. com; 68 Middle Rd, Islandmagee; adult/child £10/8; ☺10am-6pm Apr-Aug) path is accessible on 2½-hour-long guided tours. A good level of fitness, a minimum height of 1.2m and suitable footwear are essential. Book in advance.

The Gobbins path first opened as a tourist attraction in 1902, when the new railway made the area accessible to visitors. A £7.5-million investment saw the attraction reopen in 2015, only to close again after suffering 2016 storm damage, before opening once again in 2017.

As well as spectacular views out to the Irish Sea you might spot dolphins and puffins on the walk. Tours leave from the visitor centre, from where it's a five-minute bus ride to the path. There's a playground, cafe and souvenir shop at the visitor centre.

To reach Islandmagee, take the A2 Belfast–Larne road, turn right onto the B90 Island Lower Rd and follow the signs. The nearest train station is Ballycarry (3km), on the Belfast–Larne line.

Glenarm Castle & Walled Garden CASTLE
(www.glenarmcastle.com; 2 Castle Lane; walled garden adult/child £6/3; ☺garden 10am-5pm Mon-Sat, 11am-5pm Sun Apr–mid-Oct) Since 1750 Glenarm has been the family seat of the McDonnell family, earls of Antrim; it's currently the home of Lord and Lady Dunluce. The castle itself is closed to the public – except during the Tulip Festival on the May bank-holiday weekend, and during the Dalriada Festival (p630) in July – but you can visit the lovely walled garden and take a walk around the estate along the castle trail.

The estate's organic farm is renowned for its award-winning Glenarm shorthorn beef; the smokehouse produces organic smoked salmon. Both are sold at the **Glenarm Castle Tea Room & Shop** (☑028-2884 1984; mains £4.85-9.25; ☺10am-5pm Mon-Sat, 11am-5pm Sun Apr–mid-Oct).

✸ Festivals & Events

Dalriada Festival CULTURAL
(www.dalriadafestival.co.uk; 1-day pass adult/child £15/6; ☺Jul) This family-friendly three-day festival at Glenarm Castle (p630) features Highland games events, strongman competitions, a wife-carrying championship and pipe bands as well as evening concerts. Camping and caravan pitches are available in the castle grounds (from £25 per night).

▦ Sleeping

★**Water's Edge Glenarm** B&B ££
(☑028-2884 1117; www.watersedgeglenarm.com; s/d £40/80) In a beautifully renovated former police station, Water's Edge has three spacious rooms decorated in beachy blues and whites, with handwoven bed quilts and fabulous sea views. There's a bright guest lounge area and secure storage for bikes. Breakfast options include Glenarm organic smoked salmon and scrambled eggs on wheaten bread.

⌂ Shopping

Steensons JEWELLERY
(www.thesteensons.com; New Rd; ☺9.30am-5pm Mon-Sat) Watch craftspeople at work at Steensons, the designer-jewellery workshop that produces the jewellery worn in the *Game of Thrones* TV show. Pieces are also available to buy.

ℹ Information

Glenarm Visitor Information Centre (☑028-2884 1087; www.glenarmtourism.org; 17 New Rd; ☺10am-4pm Mon-Fri, 11am-3pm Sat, 2-6pm Sun)

ℹ Getting There & Away

The seasonal bus **Antrim Coaster** (p617) stops in the village.

Larne

POP 32,000

As a major port for ferries from Scotland, Larne (Lutharna) is one of Northern Ireland's main gateways. However, with its concrete overpasses and the huge chimneys of Ballylumford power station opposite the harbour, poor old Larne is a little lacking in the charm department. After a visit to the excellent Larne Visitor Information Centre, there's no real reason to linger.

🛏 Sleeping

Most visitors to Larne don't stop for long on their way to or from the ferry port – it's close enough to Belfast to make an overnight stay unnecessary – but there are some cosy rooms available at Billy Andy's.

⭐ Billy Andy's   IRISH ££

(📞 028-2827 0648; www.billyandys.com; 66 Browndod Rd; mains lunch £9-11, dinner £12-22.50; ⊙ kitchen 5-8.30pm Mon-Thu, noon-4pm & 5-9pm Fri & Sat, noon-7pm Sun) In a bucolic setting 7km southwest of Larne, this 19th-century country pub with open log and peat fires, low ceilings, and live traditional music on Saturday afternoons rewards a detour, not least for its fine gastropub fare, with dishes like wild game picnic, platter of rare-breed pork, and spiced pear and star anise crumble. Book ahead.

Upstairs, cosy double/family rooms start from £60/75.

❶ Information

Larne Visitor Information Centre (📞 028-2826 2450; www.midandeastantrim.gov.uk; Narrow Gauge Rd; ⊙ 9am-5pm Mon-Fri, 10am-4pm Sat year-round, plus 11am-3pm Sun Jun-Sep) Extensive information on all of Northern Ireland, and an exhibition on local history and wildlife.

❶ Getting There & Away

Bus 256 provides a direct service between the town centre and Belfast (£5.20, one hour, hourly Monday to Saturday, three Sunday). Larne is also the terminus of the seasonal **Antrim Coaster** (p617).

P&O Ferries (www.poferries.com) links Larne with Cairnyan in Scotland.

Larne has two train stations, Larne Town and Larne Harbour. Trains run from Larne Town to Belfast Central (£7.30, one hour, hourly Monday to Saturday, every two hours Sunday); those from the harbour are timed to connect with ferries.

Carrickfergus

POP 28,000

Northern Ireland's most impressive medieval fortress commands the entrance to Belfast Lough from the rocky promontory of Carrickfergus (Carraig Fhearghais), just 18km northeast of Belfast. The old town centre opposite Carrickfergus Castle has some attractive 18th-century houses and you can still trace a good part of the 17th-century city walls.

◎ Sights

Carrickfergus Castle   CASTLE

(📞 028-9335 1273; Marine Hwy; adult/child £5/3; ⊙ 9.30am-5pm Mon-Thu, to 4.30pm Fri-Sun) The central keep of Ireland's first and finest Norman fortress was built by John de Courcy soon after his 1177 invasion of Ulster. The massive walls of the outer ward were completed in 1242, while the red-brick gun ports were added in the 16th century. The keep houses a **museum** and the site is dotted with life-size figures illustrating the castle's history.

The castle overlooks the harbour where William of Orange landed on 14 June 1690, on his way to the Battle of the Boyne. A blue plaque on the old harbour wall marks the site where he stepped ashore, and a bronze statue of 'King Billy' himself stands on the shore nearby.

Andrew Jackson Centre   HISTORIC SITE

(2 Boneybefore; ⊙ by appointment 11am-3pm Thu-Sat, 1-4pm Sun May-Oct, 11am-3pm Fri & Sat Nov-Apr) 𝗙𝗥𝗘𝗘 The seventh US president's parents left Carrickfergus in the 18th century. His ancestral home was demolished in 1860, but a replica thatched cottage now houses this memorial 2km north of Carrickfergus Castle. Displays cover the Jackson family in Ulster, and Ulster's US connections.

Next door, the **US Rangers Centre** commemorates the first US Rangers, who trained during WWII in Carrickfergus before heading for Europe.

Contact Carrickfergus' visitor information centre in advance to arrange your visit.

Carrickfergus Museum   MUSEUM

(📞 028-9335 8241; www.midandeastantrim.gov.uk; 11 Antrim St; ⊙ 9am-5pm Mon-Fri, 10am-4pm Sat) 𝗙𝗥𝗘𝗘 The glass-fronted Museum and Civic Centre on Antrim St houses the local museum, which has a small collection of artefacts relating to the town's history.

🛏 Sleeping & Eating

Dobbin's Inn Hotel   HOTEL ££

(📞 028-9335 1905; www.dobbinsinn.co.uk; 6-8 High St; s/d/f from £50/56/75; 🐾) In the centre of the old town, Dobbin's is a friendly, informal place with 15 small and creaky-floored but comfortable rooms (one of them supposedly haunted). The building has been around for over three centuries, and has a priest's hole and an original 16th-century fireplace to prove it.

WORTH A TRIP

SEAMUS HEANEY HOME PLACE

Nobel Prize–winning poet Seamus Heaney's home town of Bellaghy, 54km northwest of Belfast, is the location of a wonderful new museum and arts centre. References in Heaney's poetry to the local landscape, everyday village life and the people who influenced him are highlighted in a creatively laid-out exhibition, which places his work in the context of his home and surroundings. Audioguides allow you to listen to poems read by Heaney himself as you walk around, bringing his words to life.

The **Seamus Heaney Home Place** (☑ 028-7938 7444; www.seamusheaney-home.com; 45 Main St, Bellaghy; adult/child £7/4.50; ☺ 10am-5pm Mon-Sat, 1-5pm Sun; P) centre also hosts regular poetry-reading events and writing workshops; see the website for details. There's a cafe and gift shop selling collections of Heaney's work. Take the 127 bus to Bellaghy from Ballymena (six daily; 50 minutes).

Sozo CAFE £

(☑ 028-9332 6060; www.eatsozo.com; 2 North St; mains £7.50-14.50; ☺ 8am-5.30pm Mon-Thu, to 9.30pm Fri & Sat; 🛜🍴) Local favourite Sozo is an unpretentious spot with friendly service and a comfort-food menu of sandwiches and salads through to lasagne, steaks and barbecue pulled pork. It's tiny, so book ahead.

 Drinking & Nightlife

Ownies PUB

(☑ 028-9335 1850; http://owniesbarbistro.co.uk; 16-18 Joymount; ☺ 10am-11pm Sun-Wed, to 1am Sat) Carrickfergus' most traditional bar – formerly the Joymount Arms, dating from 1846 – has a cosy interior complete with snugs, fireplaces, a beer garden and upstairs bistro overlooking the castle.

Windrose BAR

(☑ 028-9335 1164; www.thewindrose.co.uk; Rodgers Quay; ☺ 10am-midnight Sun-Thu, to 1am Fri & Sat) This modern bar-bistro has dining on two levels, but the real reason to drop by is for a drink on the sun-drenched timber-decked terrace overlooking the forest of yacht masts in the marina.

ℹ️ Information

Carrickfergus Visitor Information Centre (☑ 028-9335 8222; www.carrickfergus.org/tourism; Marine Hwy; ☺ 10am-5pm Apr-Sep, to 4pm Oct-Mar; 🛜) At **Carrickfergus Castle** (p631).

ℹ️ Getting There & Away

Trains link Carrickfergus with Belfast Central (£4.40, 30 minutes, every 30 minutes Monday to Saturday, hourly Sunday).

Antrim Town

POP 20,000

The county town of Antrim (Aontroim) straddles the Sixmilewater River, close to the shores of Lough Neagh. The landscaped gardens at the site of the long-demolished Antrim Castle are a pleasant spot to stretch your legs, and there are waymarked walking and cycling paths along the riverbank and lough shore.

During the 1798 Rising, the United Irishmen fought a pitched battle along the length of Antrim Town's High St.

◉ Sights

Pick up a free, self-guided heritage trail booklet from the tourist office (p633), housed in the beautifully restored **Old Courthouse** (1762), a gem of Georgian architecture.

A walking and cycling trail leads west along the river from the Antrim Castle Gardens to **Antrim Lough Shore Park**, where the vast size of Lough Neagh is apparent. There are picnic tables and lakeside walking trails.

Antrim Castle Gardens & Clotworthy House GARDENS

(☺ 9.30am-7pm, or dusk if earlier) **FREE** Pass through the Barbican Gate (1818), a portion of the old castle walls, and the underpass beyond to reach Antrim Castle Gardens. The castle burned down many years ago, but the grounds remain as one of the few surviving examples of a 17th-century ornamental garden. Clotworthy House, the castle's former coach house and stable block, now houses an exhibition on the history of the castle and gardens as well as a cafe and gift shop.

Round Tower HISTORIC BUILDING

(Steeple Rd) Antrim's 10th-century Round Tower, on the northeast edge of town, is 28m tall, and is one of the finest examples of these monastic towers in Ireland. The tower itself is closed to the public but you're free to explore the surrounding site.

Eating

Nanabelles Vintage Tearoom
CAFE £

(☑028-9448 7787; 24B Railway St; cakes £1.85-3.25; ⊙9.15am-4.30pm Mon-Fri, 10am-4.30pm Sat) Walk through a charming gift shop to find this 12-seat cafe hidden in the back. Tea is served on vintage china, along with heavenly home-baked scones, biscuits, banana bread, walnut and date bread, and cakes like carrot or chocolate-apple.

ℹ Information

Tourist office (☑028-9442 8331; www.antrim andnewtownabbey.gov.uk; Market Sq; ⊙10am-4.30pm Mon-Fri) Inside the Old Courthouse.

ℹ Getting There & Away

Buses 218 and 219 from Belfast to Ballymena stop in Antrim (£4.40, 40 minutes, hourly Monday to Friday, seven on Saturday).

Trains link Belfast Central with Antrim (£5.80, 30 minutes, hourly), continuing to Derry (£12, 1¾ hours).

Ballymena & Around

POP 29,467

Ballymena (An Baile Meánach) is a bustling market town with good shops, making it a handy place for stocking up if you're heading for remoter pastures. Sights are few but there are some superb places to sleep, eat and drink in and around the town.

🛏 Sleeping & Eating

★Galgorm Resort & Spa
HOTEL £££

(☑028-2588 1001; www.galgorm.com; 136 Fenaghy Rd, Cullybackey; cottages/d/ste from £130/155/245; P@🛜) About 6km west of Ballymena in a pretty spot overlooking the River Main is the Galgorm. Accommodation is in pleasant, classically decorated rooms, suites and cottages, but the Galgorm's biggest draw is the state-of-the-art Thermal Village spa, with hydrotherapy pools, snow cabin, steam rooms, open-air hot tubs and a daily Celtic sauna meditation ritual led by the sauna master.

There are several excellent restaurants and bars, including one in the former stables.

Blackstone
MODERN IRISH ££

(☑028-2564 8566; www.blackstonebar.co.uk; 15-17 Hill St; mains lunch £9-13.45, dinner £12.45-18.45; ⊙noon-2.30pm & 5-9pm Mon-Thu, noon-9pm Fri & Sat, 5-7.30pm Sun) Just off Ballymena's main street, this gastropub is worth seeking out for its seriously good cooking. All of the breads and condiments are made on the premises, such as exquisite pea-and-mint purée accompanying Portavogie scampi and hand-cut chips.

🍷 Drinking & Nightlife

★Crosskeys Inn
PUB

(https://crosskeys-inn.com; 40 Grange Rd, near Toomebridge; ⊙11.30am-1am Mon-Sat, noon-11pm Sun) Dating from 1654, Ireland's oldest thatched pub is an absolute treasure, with tiny, antique-filled rooms, a crackling turf fire, the best Guinness for miles around and fabulous craic. Live traditional music plays every Saturday, with impromptu sessions on Wednesday, Friday and Sunday. It's 13km southwest of Ballymena.

ℹ Getting There & Away

Bus 217 links Ballymena with Ballycastle (£6.70, 50 minutes, hourly Monday to Friday, five Saturday). Buses 218 and 219 serve Belfast's Europa Bus Centre (£6.70, 40 minutes, hourly Monday to Saturday).

Trains link Ballymena with Belfast Central (£8.40, 50 minutes, hourly); some continue from Ballymena to Derry (£12, 1½ hours, every two hours).

SLEMISH

The skyline to the east of Ballymena is dominated by the distinctive craggy peak of the 438m **Slemish Mountain** (Carnstroan Rd, Broughshane). The hill is one of many sites in the North associated with Ireland's patron saint – the young St Patrick is said to have tended goats on its slopes. On St Patrick's Day, thousands of people make a pilgrimage to its summit; the rest of the year it's a pleasant climb, though steep and slippery in wet weather, rewarded with a fine view.

Allow one hour return from the parking area.

Counties Fermanagh & Tyrone

POP 240,000 / AREA 4954 SQ KM

Best Places to Eat

➡ Brewer's House (p650)

➡ Kitchen Restaurant (p650)

➡ Jolly Sandwich Bar (p639)

➡ Thatch Coffee Shop (p644)

➡ Lusty Beg Island Restaurant (p644)

Best Places to Stay

➡ Finn Lough (p644)

➡ Tullylagan Country House (p650)

➡ Lusty Beg Island (p644)

➡ Watermill Lodge (p641)

➡ Killyhevlin Hotel (p639)

Why Go?

The ancient landscape of Fermanagh is shaped by ice and water, with rugged hills rising above quilted plains of half-drowned drumlins (rounded hills formed by retreating glaciers) and shimmering, reed-fringed lakes. A glance at the map shows the county is around one-third water – as the locals will tell you, the lakes are in Fermanagh for six months of the year; for the other six, Fermanagh is in the lakes. This watery maze is a natural playground for boaters, kayakers and anglers. The surrounding landscape is laced with good walks.

County Tyrone – from Tír Eoghain (Land of Owen, a legendary chieftain) – is dominated by the tweed-tinted moorlands of the Sperrin Mountains, whose southern flanks are dotted with prehistoric sites. Apart from hiking these heather-clad hills, visitors can enjoy several excellent sites that celebrate its heritage, including the historic ties to the USA.

When to Go

➡ May marks the start of the mayfly season, the most exciting time for trout fishing on Lough Erne, while June is the ideal month for cruising the lakes.

➡ If hiking is more to your taste, July is ideal for hill walking in the Sperrins. You can join a mass pilgrimage to the summit of Mullaghcarn, above Gortin, on Cairn Sunday, the last Sunday in the month.

➡ The tail end of summer is enlivened by the Ulster American Folk Park's annual Appalachian and Bluegrass Music Festival, which takes place in late August/early September.

COUNTY FERMANAGH

The least populated of Northern Ireland's six counties, Fermanagh is dominated by lakes and waterways. About 80km long, Lough Erne is made up of two sections: the Upper Lough to the south of Enniskillen, and the Lower Lough to the north. The two are connected by the River Erne, which begins its journey in County Cavan and meets the sea at Donegal Bay west of Ballyshannon. This is a great region for exploring with your own wheels, picnicking at will and enjoying no end of water sports and other aquatic activities.

Enniskillen & Around

POP 13,800

Perched amid the web of waterways that link Upper and Lower Lough Erne, Enniskillen (Inis Ceithleann, meaning 'Ceithleann's Island', after a legendary female warrior) is an appealing island town. Its attractive waterside setting, bustling with boats in summer, plus its range of lively pubs and restaurants, make Enniskillen a good base for exploring Upper and Lower Lough Erne, Florence Court and the Marble Arch Caves.

Though neither was born here, both Oscar Wilde and Samuel Beckett were pupils at Enniskillen's Portora Royal School (Wilde from 1864 to 1871, Beckett from 1919 to 1923); it was here that Beckett first studied French, a language he would later write in. The town's name is also prominent in the history of the Troubles – on Poppy Day (Remembrance Sunday) in 1987 an IRA bomb killed 11 people during a service at Enniskillen's war memorial.

◉ Sights & Activities

★ **Enniskillen Castle Museums**   MUSEUM
(☑ 028-6632 5000; www.enniskillencastle.co.uk; off Wellington Rd; adult/child £5/3.50; ☉ 10am-5pm Mon-Fri, 11am-5pm Sat year-round, plus 11am-5pm Sun Jun-Sep) Enniskillen Castle, a former stronghold of the 16th-century Maguire chieftains, guards the western end of the town's central island, its twin-turreted Watergate looming over passing fleets of cabin cruisers. Within the walls you'll find the worthwhile, newly refurbished **Fermanagh County Museum**, which has excellent displays and inter-

active exhibits on the county's history, archaeology, landscape and wildlife. It includes a fascinating gallery dedicated to the history of Fermanagh's waterways as a route for pilgrims travelling via Devenish Island to Lough Derg in Donegal.

In the ground-floor Lakelands Gallery, look for the 1000-year-old 35lb block of bog butter, unearthed by a Fermanagh farmer in 1980; it was probably buried in the bog to preserve it for consumption during the winter months.

The 15th-century castle keep contains the **Inniskilling Museum**, full of guns, uniforms and medals, including eight Victoria Crosses awarded in WWI; it's dedicated to the regiment that was raised at the castle in 1689 to support the army of William I.

★ **Castle Coole**   HISTORIC BUILDING
(☑ 028-6632 2690; www.nationaltrust.org.uk; off A4; house tour adult/child £6/2.50, grounds £3.50/2; ☉ house 11am-5pm daily Jul & Aug, Fri-Wed Jun, Sat, Sun & public holidays mid-Mar–May & Sep, grounds 10am-7pm Mar-Oct, to 4pm Nov-Feb) This National Trust–owned neoclassical palace sits in 600 hectares of beautiful parkland containing a lake that's home to the UK's only nonmigratory colony of greylag geese. The house's double cantilever staircase, Italian marble fireplaces, Regency furniture and basement servants quarters can be seen on one-hour guided tours.

Castle Coole is 2.5km southeast of Enniskillen; it's a pleasant 5km walk or cycle along the Castle to Castle path from Enniskillen Castle.

Designed by James Wyatt, the Palladian mansion was built between 1789 and 1795 for Armar Lowry-Corry, the first earl of Belmore, and is probably the purest expression of late 18th-century neoclassical architecture in Ireland. When King George IV visited Ireland in 1821, the second earl of Belmore had a state bedroom specially prepared at Castle Coole in anticipation of the monarch's visit. The king, however, was more interested in dallying with his mistress at Slane Castle and never turned up. The bedroom, draped in red silk and decorated with paintings depicting *A Rake's Progress,* is one of the highlights of the house tour.

The 2014 film *Miss Julie,* starring Colin Farrell, Jessica Chastain and Samantha Morton, was filmed at Castle Coole.

COUNTIES FERMANAGH & TYRONE ENNISKILLEN & AROUND

Counties Fermanagh & Tyrone Highlights

1 Mysterious stone figures (p643) Pondering the ancient carvings on White Island and Boa Island, including Caldragh Graveyard.

2 Ulster American Folk Park (p648) Uncover historical links between Ireland and the USA.

3 Marble Arch Caves (p645) Discovering an amazing network of underground caverns.

4 Canoeing (p642) Exploring the backwaters of Lough Erne.

5 Devenish Island (p642) Exploring the Celtic monastic settlement and ancient round tower.

6 Florence Court (p645) Taking a house tour and exploring the forest walks and cycle trails.

7 Cuilcagh Mountain Park (p646) Following boardwalks to the summit of Fermanagh's highest peak.

8 Castle Coole (p635) Seeing how the Irish aristocracy lived in this elegant country house.

9 Enniskillen Castle (p635) Viewing illuminating exhibits at the Fermanagh County Museum.

10 Wellbrook Beetling Mill (p649) Feeling the pounding beat of an authentic old linen mill.

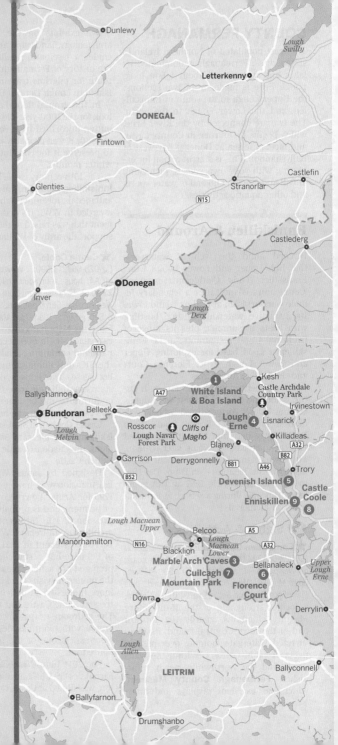

Enniskillen

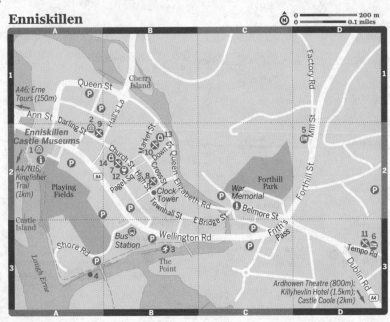

Headhunters Barber Shop
& Railway Museum
MUSEUM

(📞028-6632 7488; www.facebook.com/Head huntersMuseum; 5 Darling St; ⏰9am-5.30pm Tue-Sat) FREE This museum-cum-barber-shop (open for haircuts) displays the Johnston family's impressive collection of local railway memorabilia, from old station signs to timetables, uniforms, tickets and passes. There's a display case containing items frequently smuggled on Fermanagh's trains (which stopped running in 1957), and even a violin made by former station master Thomas Moore, known for playing the instrument between arrivals and departures at Bundoran Junction in County Tyrone.

Erne Water Taxi
BOATING

(📞07719 770588; www.ernewatertaxi.com; Lakeland Forum Leisure Centre jetty, Wellington Rd; tours for 1-8 people per hour £60) Offers a range of private tours led by knowledgeable local guides for up to eight people. Tours include a 1½-hour trip to Devenish Island (p642), three-hour trips around Upper or Lower Lough Erne and full-day (seven hour) trips taking in both lakes. Add a picnic hamper of great local produce for £15 per person.

Enniskillen

◉ Top Sights

◉ Sights

◉ Activities, Courses & Tours

◉ Sleeping

◉ Eating

◉ Drinking & Nightlife

◉ Shopping

Erne Tours
BOATING

(☑028-6632 2882; http://ernetours.com; Brook Park, Round 'O' Quay; adult/child £10/6; ⏱10.30am, 12.15pm, 2.15pm & 4.15pm Jul & Aug, 2.15pm daily Jun, 2.15pm Tue, Sat & Sun May & Sep; ⏹) Operates 1¾-hour cruises on Lower Lough Erne aboard the 56-seat waterbus MV *Kestrel*, calling at Devenish Island (p642; May to September) along the way. It departs from the Round 'O' Quay, just west of the town centre on the A46 to Belleek.

Kingfisher Trail
CYCLING

(www.kingfishercycletrail.com) The Kingfisher Trail is a waymarked, long-distance cycling trail that starts in Enniskillen and wends its way through the back roads of Counties Fermanagh, Leitrim, Cavan and Monaghan. You can get a trail map from the Enniskillen tourist office or online.

The full route is around 370km long, but a shorter loop, starting and finishing in Enniskillen, and travelling via Kesh, Belleek, Garrison, Belcoo and Florencecourt, is 115km – easily done in two days with an overnight stay at Belleek.

Erne Angling
FISHING

(☑07884 472121; www.erneangling.com; 2 anglers half-/full-day trip £80/130) Hook the pike of your dreams on Lough Erne with these experienced guides.

Erne Boat Hire
BOATING

(☑07523 423232; www.facebook.com/erneboat hire; Regal Pass Jetty, Wellington Rd; boat for 2/4/8hr £45/55/85) Rents boats year-round for self-guided trips out on the lake. Devenish Island (p642) can be reached in 30 minutes. Tutorials can be given to inexperienced boaters. Boats hold up to six people; fuel and buoyancy aids included. Book ahead on weekends.

🛌 Sleeping

Enniskillen Hotel
HOTEL €€

(☑028-6632 1177; www.enniskillenhotel.com; 72 Forthill St; s/d from £85/95; 📶) Enniskillen's newest hotel is chic and modern with friendly staff and a central location. Rooms are on the snug side but are nonetheless comfortable and stylish, with a contemporary grey-and-black colour scheme and flash bathrooms with rain showers.

Westville Hotel
HOTEL €€

(☑028-6632 0333; www.westvillehotel.co.uk; 14-20 Tempo Rd; s/d from £70/85; @📶) Starting with its grand lobby, the Westville adds a

dash of four-star comfort to Enniskillen's hotel scene with designer fabrics, sophisticated colour combinations and good food at the **Terrace Restaurant** (mains £11-22; ⏱6-10pm). Rooms come with cookies made by the hotel's pastry chef and triple-glazed windows to block out road noise.

Greenwood Lodge
B&B €€

(☑028-6632 5636; www.greenwoodlodge.co.uk; 17 Killyvilly Court; s/d from £35/50; 🅿) This spacious and modern house is set on a quiet side street 3km northeast of town off the B80. The three comfy bedrooms have private bathrooms, there's an airy lounge and it has secure storage available for bikes.

★ Killyhevlin Hotel
HOTEL €€€

(☑028-6632 3481; www.killyhevlin.com; off A4, Killyhevlin; s/d from £110/160; @📶🏊) The luxurious Killyhevlin occupies an idyllic setting overlooking Upper Lough Erne, 1.5km south of Enniskillen on the road to Maguiresbridge. Many of its 71 elegant rooms have lovely views over landscaped gardens to the lough; self-catering accommodation is offered in two-bedroom, timber-clad lakeside lodges. There's also a fancy spa and health club.

🍴 Eating & Drinking

★ Jolly Sandwich Bar
CAFE €

(☑028-6632 2277; www.thejollysandwichbar.co.uk; 3 Darling St; mains £4-4.50; ⏱7.30am-4.15pm Mon-Sat) This cheery place sells divine baked goods and a wide range of sandwiches to eat in or take away. Ingredients include seasonal and local produce. The freshly baked rhubarb and ginger scones are a favourite among the cafe regulars.

Rebecca's Coffee Shop
CAFE €

(☑028-6632 9376; Buttermarket; mains £4-6.20; ⏱9am-5.30pm Mon-Sat) At the Buttermarket (p640), Rebecca's serves good sandwiches, salads, scones and pastries as well as a few hot dishes; locals rave about the cottage pie. There are outdoor courtyard tables in summer.

Cafe Merlot
MODERN IRISH €€

(📞028-6632 0918; http://cafemerlot.co.uk; 6 Church St; mains lunch £7-15, dinner £13-18; ⊙noon-3pm & 5.30-9pm Mon-Thu & Sun, to 9.30pm Fri & Sat; 🖉) Located below street level in a beautiful space with vaulted brick ceilings, Cafe Merlot serves seasonal specials in addition to its regular menu of contemporary meat, fish and vegetarian dishes. Try the dry aged rib-eye steak (Fermanagh beef is highly regarded). The wine list is the best in town. It's below the pub Blakes of the Hollow; book ahead.

Dollakis
GREEK €€

(📞028-6634 2616; www.dollakis.com; 2 Cross St; mains lunch £7.50-15, dinner £15-28; ⊙noon-3pm & 5-9.30pm Tue-Sat) This chic little Greek-Mediterranean restaurant serves classic Greek fare plus an array of small plates (meze) and seasonal specials.

★ Blakes of the Hollow
PUB

(William Blake; 📞028-6632 2143; 6 Church St; ⊙noon-late) This traditional pub has barely changed since 1887, with a marble-topped bar, huge sherry casks, antique silver lamp holders, and ancient wood panelling kippered by a century of cigarette smoke. A newer addition is the *Game of Thrones* door, one of 10 doors made with wood felled by a 2016 storm and intricately carved with themes from the HBO series. For more information, see Kingsroad (p625).

ULSTER WAY

The Ulster Way **long-distance walking trail** makes a circuit around the six counties of Northern Ireland. In total the route covers 1000km, so walking all of it might take four to five weeks. Sections of the way are on minor roads rather than footpaths; to get around this, the route has been divided into two categories: 'Quality Sections' – good, scenic, mostly off-road walking – separated by 'Link Sections', which can be covered by public transport. Check the website of WalkNI (www.walkni.com) for details.

Short sections of the Ulster Way that make good day walks include Cuilcagh Mountain Park (p646) and the Causeway Coast (p619).

★ Entertainment

Ardhowen Theatre
THEATRE

(📞028-6632 5440; www.ardhowentheatre.com; 97 Dublin Rd; ⊙box office 9.30am-4.30pm Mon-Fri, to 7pm before performances, 11am-1pm, 2-5pm & 6-7pm Sat) The program here includes concerts, local amateur and professional drama and musical productions, pantomimes and films. The theatre is about 1km southeast of the town centre on the A4, in an impressive glass-fronted lakeside building. It has a good cafe.

🛍 Shopping

Buttermarket
ARTS & CRAFTS

(Down St; ⊙9am-5pm Mon-Sat) The restored buildings in the old marketplace house an appealing variety of craft shops and studios selling paintings, ceramics and jewellery, and Rebecca's Coffee Shop (p639).

Home, Field & Stream
SPORTS & OUTDOORS

(📞028-6632 2114; www.hfs-online.com; 18-20 Church St; ⊙9am-5.30pm Mon-Sat) Has a wide range of fishing tackle and also sells fishing licences and permits.

ℹ Information

Fermanagh Visitor Information Centre
(📞028-6632 3110; www.fermanaghlakelands.com; Enniskillen Castle; ⊙9.30am-5pm Mon-Fri, 11am-5pm Sat year-round, plus 11am-5pm Sun Jun-Sep; 🛜) Helpful and well-stocked tourist information office at Enniskillen Castle. Staff can book accommodation and help with fishing licences and permits.

ℹ Getting There & Away

From the **bus station** (Wellington Rd; ⊙facilities 8.45am-5.25pm Mon-Fri, 8.to 2.30pm Sat), Ulsterbus and Bus Éireann services run to/from Belfast (£12, 2¼ hours, hourly Monday to Saturday, two on Sunday), Omagh (£8, one hour, one daily Monday to Saturday), Dublin (€20, 2½ hours, eight daily), plus a run to Donegal (€15, one hour, four daily Monday to Saturday, two on Sunday) and on to Sligo (€17, 1½ hours).

Upper Lough Erne

Upper Lough Erne is not so much a lake as a watery maze of more than 150 islands, inlets, reedy bays and meandering backwaters. Bird life is abundant: flocks of whooper swan and goldeneye overwinter here; great crested grebes nest in the spring; and you'll find Ireland's biggest heronry in a 400-year-

FISHING ON LOUGH ERNE

The lakes of Fermanagh are renowned for both coarse and game fishing. The Lough Erne trout-fishing season runs from the beginning of March to the end of September. Salmon fishing begins in June and also continues to the end of September. The mayfly season usually lasts a month from the second week in May.

You'll need a combined licence and a permit, which costs £9.50 for three days. See www.nidirect.gov.uk/angling for full details. Licences and permits can be purchased from the **Fermanagh Visitor Information Centre** (p640) and **Home, Field & Stream** (p640) in Enniskillen, plus from the marina at **Castle Archdale Country Park** (p643), which also hires out fishing rods.

Hire an experienced guide through **Erne Angling** (p639).

old oak grove on the island of Inishfendra, just south of Crom Estate.

◉ Sights & Activities

Crom Estate PARK
(☏ 028-6773 8118; www.nationaltrust.org.uk; Crom Rd, Newtownbutler; adult/child £6/2; ⊗grounds 10am-7pm May-Aug, to 6pm mid-Mar–Apr, Sep & Oct, visitor centre 11am-5pm daily Easter-Sep, Sat & Sun only Oct) Home to the largest area of natural woodland in Northern Ireland, the National Trust's beautiful Crom Estate is a haven for pine martens, rare bats and many species of bird. You can walk from the visitor centre to the ruins of old **Crom Castle**, with its ancient **walled garden**, abandoned bowling green, gnarled yew trees and views over the reed-fringed lough.

The estate is on the eastern shore of Upper Lough Erne, 5km west of Newtownbutler.

For views of Crom from the lake, rent a rowing boat (per hour £7.50), canoe (per half-day £15) or outboard-engine boat (per day £45); ask at the visitor centre, book ahead in summer. See the website for details of upcoming events.

Inishcruiser BOATING
(☏ 028-6772 2122; www.sharevillage.org/inishcruiser; off Newbridge Rd, Share Discovery Village; adult/child £10/6; ⊗10.30am Sun Easter-Sep, also 2pm Sun Jul & Aug) The *Inishcruiser* offers 1½- to two-hour cruises of the Upper Lough Erne, leaving from the Share Discovery Village, 5km southwest of Lisnaskea.

Share Canoe & Kayak Hire CANOEING
(☏ 028-6772 2122; www.sharevillage.org; off Newbridge Rd, Share Discovery Village; rental per hour/day canoe £12/35, kayak £10/30; ⊗Jun-Aug) At the Share Discovery Village, 5km southwest of Lisnaskea; has canoes and kayaks for rent.

🛌 Sleeping & Eating

No-nonsense Lisnaskea is the area's main town, with shops, pubs and cafes.

★Watermill Lodge B&B €€
(☏ 028-6772 4369; www.watermillrestaurantfermanagh.com; Kilmore Quay, Lisnaskea; s/d £60/90) A secluded lakeside setting makes for a peaceful night's rest in one of the seven lakeview guest rooms here. It's next to the excellent thatch-roofed Watermill Restaurant.

Kissin' Crust CAFE €
(☏ 028-6772 2678; www.facebook.com/thekissincrust; 152 Main St, Lisnaskea; mains £3-7; ⊗8.30am-5pm Mon-Sat) Popular with locals, this coffee shop is stacked with home-baked pies, quiches and scones, and serves up a lunch menu of homemade soup, sandwiches and hot dishes. It's good for picnic shopping.

★Watermill Restaurant FRENCH €€
(☏ 028-6772 4369; www.watermillrestaurantfermanagh.com; Kilmore Quay, Lisnaskea; 3-course lunch/dinner £23/25; ⊗5-9.30pm Mon-Sat, noon-8pm Sun) Seasonal Irish fare is given a French twist at this award-winning restaurant in a peaceful lakeside setting. Chef Pascal Brissaud uses produce from the restaurant's own vegetable and herb garden in dishes like chicken cassoulet, duck cooked two ways and lamb casserole.

ℹ Getting There & Away

From Enniskillen, Ulsterbus service 95 runs along the east side of the lough to Lisnaskea (£3.80, 30 minutes, six daily Monday to Friday, five on Saturday). Bus 58 goes down the west side to Derrylin (£4.40, 40 minutes, five daily Monday to Friday, two on Saturday), and continues to Belturbet in County Cavan.

COUNTIES FERMANAGH & TYRONE UPPER LOUGH ERNE

LOUGH ERNE CANOE TRAIL

The Lough Erne Canoe Trail (www.canoeni.com) highlights the attractions along the 50km of lough and river between Belleek and Belturbet. The wide open expanses of the Lower Lough can build up big waves in a strong breeze and are best left to experts, but the sheltered backwaters of the Upper Lough are ideal for beginners and families. You can download maps and info from the website. The **Fermanagh Visitor Information Centre** (p640) in Enniskillen can help you find where to rent canoes and boats, plus it has full details on angling.

Outfits that rent canoes and kayaks include **Share Canoe & Kayak Hire** (p641) and **Ultimate Watersports** (p643).

Lower Lough Erne

Lower Lough Erne is a more open expanse of water than the Upper Lough, with its 90-odd islands clustered mainly in the southern reaches. In early Christian times, when overland travel was difficult, Lough Erne was an important highway between the Donegal coast and inland Leitrim, and there are many ancient religious sites and other antiquities dotted around its shores. In medieval times the lough was part of an important pilgrimage route.

❶ Getting There & Away

On the eastern side of the lough, Ulsterbus runs from Enniskillen to Pettigo via Irvinestown (three to five Monday to Saturday) and stops near Castle Archdale Country Park (35 minutes) and Kesh (one hour). The Bus Eireann Dublin–Donegal service links Enniskillen and Belleek (€8, 35 minutes, eight daily).

Devenish Island

Devenish Island, from Daimh Inis, meaning 'Ox Island', is the biggest of several 'holy islands' in Lough Erne. The remains of an Augustinian monastery, founded here in the 6th century by St Molaise, include a superb 12th-century round tower in near-perfect condition, the ruins of St Molaise's Church and St Mary's Abbey, an unusual 15th-century high cross and many fascinating old gravestones.

A small **visitor's centre** outlines the fascinating history of the monastic site, where up to 1000 monks once lived and worked. When the monastery was founded, most of Ireland was covered in thick forest; the island site would have been chosen for its accessibility on one of the country's major waterways. The island was raided by Vikings in 837 and again in 923, but by the 12th century Devenish was a large and important community. The stonemasons and builders responsible for the round tower were some of the most skilled craftsmen of their day, and Devenish continued to thrive as a centre of learning and arts until the 16th-century dissolution of monasteries under Henry VIII.

The island is accessible by boat from Enniskillen with Erne Tours (p638) or Erne Water Taxi (p639).

Castle Archdale

Castle Archdale has a popular forest park with walking and cycling trails as well as an adjoining country park (p643) with a caravan site and a marina. From here boats make the crossing to the monastic ruins on White Island.

◉ Sights & Activities

★ **White Island** ISLAND
(☑028-6862 1892; www.castlearchdaleboathire.com/whiteisland.html; Castle Archdale Bay; ferry per person £4; ⊙10.30am-4.30pm daily Jul & Aug, plus Easter & May bank-holiday weekends, call to confirm) White Island is the most haunting of Lough Erne's monastic sites. At the eastern tip of the island are the ruins of a small 12th-century church with a beautiful Romanesque door on its southern side. Inside are eight extraordinary stone figures, thought to date from the 9th century, lined up along the wall like miniature Easter Island statues.

The line-up is a modern arrangement; most of the figures were discovered buried in the walls of the church in the 19th century, where the medieval masons had used them as ordinary building stones. The six main figures, all created by the same hand, are flanked on the left by a sheila-na-gig (carved female figure with exaggerated genitalia), which is probably contemporary with the church, and flanked on the right by a scowling stone face. The age and interpretation of these figures have been the subject of much debate; it has been suggested that the two central pairs, of equal height, were pillars that once supported a pulpit, and that they represent either saints or aspects of the life of Christ.

A ferry makes the 15-minute crossing to the island from the marina at Castle Archdale.

Castle Archdale Country Park PARK
(📞 028-6862 1588; off B82, Rossmore; 🕐 visitor centre 10am-5pm daily Jun-Aug, 1-5pm Sat & Sun May & Sep) FREE This park has pleasant woodland and lakeshore walks and cycle tracks, in the former estate of 18th-century Archdale Manor and the adjacent **forest park**, which also contains the ruins of 17th-century Archdale Castle. The island-filled bay was used in WWII as a base for Catalina flying boats, a history explained in the small **museum** in the Country Park visitor centre.

Ultimate Watersports WATER SPORTS
(📞 028-6862 1722; www.ultimatewatersports. co.uk; Castle Archdale Marina; 🕐 10am-6pm daily Jul & Aug, Sat & Sun Apr-Jun, Sep & Oct) Working out of Castle Archdale marina, Ultimate Watersports offers equipment hire and instruction in water-skiing, wakeboarding, jet-skiing and canoeing.

Castle Archdale Boat Hire BOATING
(📞 028-6862 1156; www.castlearchdaleboathire. com; Castle Archdale Marina; 6-person boat hire per half/full day £65/90; 🕐 10.30am-4.30pm daily Jul & Aug, plus Easter & May bank-holiday weekends) Rents six- and eight-person boats (no previous experience or special licence required), as well as bicycles (per hour/half-day/full day £4/8/12) and fishing rods. Also runs the ferry to White Island.

Drumbaragh Stables HORSE RIDING
(📞 07843 435231; Castle Archdale Country Park; treks £10-30; 🕐 Thu-Mon Easter & May-Sep) Offers pony trekking at Castle Archdale Country Park. Book ahead.

🍴 Sleeping & Eating

Castle Archdale
Caravan Park CARAVAN PARK, CAMPGROUND €
(📞 028-6862 1333; www.castlearchdale.com; off B82, Rossmore; tent sites £10-30, caravan sites £25-30; 🕐 Easter-Oct; 📶) This attractive, tree-sheltered site in Castle Archdale Country Park is dominated by on-site caravans, but has pitches for tents and good facilities, including a shop, launderette, playground and pub.

★**Dollakis in the Park** FOOD TRUCK, GREEK €
(📞 028-6634 2616; www.dollakis.com; Castle Archdale Caravan Park; mains £4-8; 🕐 noon-5pm daily Jul & Aug, Sat & Sun Easter-Jun, Sep & Oct) This fabulous food truck serves authentic Greek street food such as spit-roast *gyros*, beef and lamb burgers, grilled chicken souvlaki, falafel, halloumi, flatbreads and calamari. Eat at picnic tables in a giant tepee tent.

❶ Getting There & Away

The park is 16km northwest of Enniskillen, near Lisnarick. Bus 194 goes to Enniskillen (£4.40, 25 minutes, five daily Monday to Friday, two Sunday).

Boa Island

Boa Island, at the northern end of Lower Lough Erne, is connected to the mainland at both ends – the main A47 road runs along its length. It's worth a stop here to see the mysterious stone figures at the small and unkempt Caldragh Graveyard.

◉ Sights

Caldragh Graveyard CEMETERY
Spooky, moss-grown Caldragh Graveyard contains the intriguing **Dreenan Figure**. It's often called a Janus figure, but it's actually two separate figures placed back to back. It's thought to date from the early Christian period and perhaps represent the war goddess Badhbh, a frightening figure in local folklore. Nearby is a smaller figure

> ### CRUISING HOLIDAYS ON LOUGH ERNE
>
> If you fancy exploring Lough Erne as captain of your own motor cruiser, you can – and without any previous experience or qualifications. Several companies in Fermanagh hire out self-drive, live-aboard cabin cruisers by the week, offering a crash course (not literally, hopefully) in boat-handling and navigation at the start of your holiday. Weekly rates in the high season (July and August) range from about £500 for a two-berth to £850 for a four-berth and £1170 for an eight-berth boat.
>
> Check out www.fermanaghlakelands. com for details on holidays and boat-hire companies.

called **Lusty Man**, brought here from Lusty More island.

There's a sign indicating the graveyard about 1.5km from the bridge at the western tip of Boa Island.

The exact origins and meanings of the figures remain unclear. The Dreenan Figure, which has been in the graveyard since at least 1841, was believed for many years to date from the pagan Iron Age and be as much as 2000 years old; it's now thought to date from the early Christian period, from 500 to 1000 AD.

There's no information about the enigmatic figures at the graveyard itself.

📔 Sleeping

★ Finn Lough   RESORT €€€
(📞028-6838 0360; www.finnlough.com; 41 Letter Rd, off B136; d from £110, bubble domes £195-295, cottages from £225; @🛜) On the mainland shore overlooking Boa Island is this wonderful complex with a range of luxurious accommodation and a friendly, relaxed atmosphere. The most special rooms here are the forest bubble domes: transparent globes with uninterrupted views of the night sky, attached bathrooms and four-poster beds, hidden among the trees; the largest have free-standing baths. Book well ahead.

There are also three rooms in the main house, and self-catering cottages sleeping six people, some with great water views. The resort's superb restaurant serves fresh, locally sourced fare including produce grown in the kitchen garden or foraged from the forest. Activities at the lush complex include water sports, kayaking, tennis and cycling, and a range of treatments at the spa.

Lusty Beg Island   RESORT €€€
(📞028-6863 3300; www.lustybegisland.com; Boa Island; s/d/f B&B from £90/130/160, cabins from £200, minimum 3 nights; 🅿@🛜) This private island retreat, reached by ferry (use a telephone at the dock) from a jetty halfway along Boa Island, has self-catering cabins and chalets that sleep two to six people, as well as B&B rooms in its rustic 40-room courtyard block. There's a spa and swimming pool, tennis court, nature trail and canoeing on the lough for guests.

Lusty Beg's informal restaurant (📞028-6863 3300; www.lustybegisland.com; Boa Island; mains £10.50-20; ⊙noon-9.30pm) is open to all.

Belleek

Belleek's (Beal Leice) village street of colourful, flower-bedecked houses slopes up from a bridge across the River Erne where it flows out of the Lower Lough towards Ballyshannon and the sea. The village is right on the border – the road south across the bridge passes through a finger of the Republic's territory for about 200m before leaving again – and shops accept both euros and pounds sterling.

⊙ Sights

★ Belleek Pottery Visitor Centre   ARTS CENTRE
(📞028-6865 9300; www.belleekpottery.ie; 3 Main St; tours adult/child £5/free; ⊙9am-6pm Mon-Fri, 10am-6pm Sat, noon-5.30pm Sun Jul-Sep, shorter hours Oct-Jun, closed Sat & Sun Jan & Feb) The imposing Georgian-style building beside Belleek's main bridge houses the world-famous Belleek Pottery, founded in 1857. It has been producing fine Parian china ever since, and is especially noted for its delicate basketware; pieces are available to buy in the shop. You can see the pottery being made on guided tours of the factory floor, which run every half-hour from 9.30am to 12.15pm and 1.45pm to 4pm weekdays year-round (to 3pm on Fridays), plus summer weekends.

There's also a small museum, showroom and cafe.

📔 Sleeping

Fiddlestone Bar & B&B   B&B €€
(📞028-6865 8008; www.facebook.com/fiddlestone.bar; 15-17 Main St; s/d from £40/70; ⊙pub noon-11pm; 🛜) This classic village-centre pub has six basic rooms that are just right after a long day touring followed by hours spent enjoying the trad-music sessions downstairs.

✖ Eating & Drinking

★ Thatch Coffee Shop   CAFE €
(📞028-6865 8181; 20 Main St; mains £4-8; ⊙9am-5pm Mon-Sat) This cosy little thatched cottage is Belleek's oldest building (late 18th century); the original rafters are visible above an old church bench on the back wall. The sandwiches and soups are freshly prepared using organic ingredients, and the homemade cakes (such as caramelised apple tart) and scones are superb. The traditional breakfasts (available until noon) are excellent too.

Black Cat Cove PUB
(🖉028-6865 8942; www.facebook.com/The-
BlackCatCove; 28 Main St; mains £7-9; ⊘kitchen
noon-9pm) This family-run pub with antique
furniture and an open fire serves good bar
meals. It also has live music most nights in
summer, and on weekends in winter.

❶ Getting There & Away

The 194 bus links Belleek with Enniskillen
(£6.70, about 1¼ hours, one daily Monday to
Saturday).

Lough Navar Forest Park

The **Lough Navar Forest Park** (www.marble
archcavesgeopark.com/attraction/lough-navar;
⊘10am-dusk) FREE lies at the western end
of Lower Lough Erne, where the **Cliffs of
Magho** – a 250m-high and 9km-long limestone escarpment – rise above a fringe of
bog, heath and native woodland on the
southern shore. A 10km scenic drive leads to
the **Magho Viewpoint**; there are plenty of
good walking trails in the forest too.

The entrance is on the Glennasheevar
road between Garrison and Derrygonnelly,
20km southeast of Belleek; follow signs for
the 'Forest Scenic Drive'.

The panorama from the Magho cliff top is
one of the finest in Ireland: it looks out over
the shimmering expanse of lough and river
to the Blue Stack Mountains, the sparkling
waters of Donegal Bay and the sea cliffs of
Slieve League.

West of Lough Erne

The remote hills west of Lough Erne are
home to some worthwhile sights and spectacular scenery. The area falls within the
Unesco-protected **Marble Arch Caves
Global Geopark**.

Apart from a few B&Bs and some self-catering holiday lettings, accommodation options are limited in this rural area of western
Fermanagh. It's best to visit the sights on a
day trip from Enniskillen.

There are good cafes at Marble Arch
Caves and Florence Court. Bring your own
supplies for picnics and hikes.

◉ Sights

★**Florence Court** HISTORIC BUILDING
(🖉028-6634 8249; www.nationaltrust.org.uk;
Swanlinbar Rd; adult/child house tour £4.50/2.50,

grounds £6/3; ⊘house 11am-5pm daily Jul & Aug,
Wed-Mon May & Jun, Sat-Thu Sep, Sat & Sun Apr &
Oct, grounds 10am-7pm Mar-Oct, to 4pm Nov-Feb)
Set in lovely wooded grounds in the shadow
of Cuilcagh Mountain, Florence Court is famous for its rococo plasterwork and antique
Irish furniture, viewable on a guided tour,
which also takes in the servants' quarters
downstairs. In the grounds you can explore
the walled garden and, on the edge of Cottage Wood, admire an ancient Irish yew tree
said to be the mother plant of all Irish yews.

Florence Court was the home of three
generations of the Cole family starting
with Sir John Cole, who named the house
after his wife Florence. In the 1770s his son
William Willoughby Cole, the first Earl of
Enniskillen, oversaw the addition of grand
Palladian wings to this beautiful, baroque
country house. It was badly damaged by fire
in 1955 and much of what you see on the
tour is the result of meticulous restoration,
but the magnificent plasterwork on the din-
ing-room ceiling is original.

Check the website for upcoming costume
tours, where you'll see characters such as
the cook at work in the kitchen, and special
children's tours.

Within the estate's 35-sq-km grounds are
15km of trails for walking and cycling; bikes
can be hired from the visitor centre (£5/10
for three hours/full day).

Florence Court is 12km southwest of
Enniskillen.

Marble Arch Caves CAVE
(🖉028-6634 8855; www.marblearchcavesgeopark.
com; 43 Marlbank Rd, Legnabrocky; adult/child
£9.50/6.50; ⊘10am-5pm Jul & Aug, to 4.30pm
mid-Mar–Jun & Sep, 10.30am-3pm Oct) To the
south of Lower Lough Erne lies a limestone
plateau, where Fermanagh's abundant rainwater has carved out a network of subterranean caverns. The largest of these are the
star attraction of the Marble Arch Caves
Global Geopark. Popular 1¼-hour tours feature spectacular chambers and underwater
rivers.

Tours begin with a short boat trip along
the peaty, foam-flecked waters of the underground River Cladagh to Junction Jetty,
where three subterranean streams meet
up. You then continue on foot past the
Pool Chamber, regaled all the time with
jokes from your guide. An artificial tunnel
leads into the **New Chamber**, from which
the route follows the underground River

Owenbrean through the **Moses Walk** (a walled pathway sunk waist-deep into the river) to the **Calcite Cradle**, where the most picturesque formations are to be found.

Unexpected serious flooding of the caves in the 1990s was found to have been caused by mechanised peat-cutting in the blanket bog on the slopes of Cuilcagh Mountain, whose rivers feed the caves. Cuilcagh Mountain Park was established to restore and preserve the bog environment, and in 2001 the entire area was designated a Unesco Geopark. The park's geology and ecology are explained in the caves' visitor centre.

The caves take their name from a natural **limestone arch** that spans the River Cladagh where it emerges from the caves; you can reach it via a short walk along a signposted footpath from the visitor centre. They were first explored by the French caving pioneer Édouard Martel in 1895.

The caves are 16km southwest of Enniskillen, and 4km west of Florence Court (p645), reached via the A4 and the A32. Book tours in advance in summer.

Cuilcagh Mountain Park   MOUNTAIN
(www.marblearchcavesgeopark.com; Marlbank Rd) Part of the Marble Arch Caves Global Geopark, Cuilcagh Mountain Park was established to restore and preserve the blanket bog – one of Ireland's biggest – on the slopes of Cuilcagh Mountain (666m). The visitor centre at Marble Arch Caves (p645) has an information desk and maps; the mountain is accessed from a car park 300m west of the caves. A 2.5km stretch of boardwalk, constructed in 2015 to protect the bog, has proved popular with walkers climbing the mountain along the Legnabrocky Trail.

Sheelin Antique Irish Lace Shop   MUSEUM
(☑028-6634 8052; http://sheelinlace.com; 178 Derrylin Rd, Bellanaleck; ☉10am-6pm Mon-Sat) This lace shop also houses a small collection of Irish lace dating from 1850 to 1900. Lace-making was an important cottage industry in the region both before and after the Famine – prior to WWI there were at least 10 lace schools in County Fermanagh. The shop is 6km south of Enniskillen in Bellanaleck.

Lough Melvin   LAKE
Lough Melvin is famous for its salmon and trout fishing, and is home to two unusual trout species that are unique to the lough – the sonaghan, with its distinctive black spots, and the crimson-spotted gillaroo – as well as brown trout, ferox trout and char. You'll need a licence and a permit from Garrison Anglers (www.garrisonandloughmelvinanglersassoc.co.uk; three-day licence £3.50, permits £10 per day).

Lough Melvin is situated along the border with the Republic, on the B52 road from Belcoo to Belleek.

COUNTY TYRONE

Tyrone's three largest towns – Omagh, Dungannon and Cookstown – form a triangle across its centre, but the county's biggest draw lies in the untouched wildness of the Sperrin Mountains, their southern foothills scattered with prehistoric sites. There's also an excellent outdoor museum near Omagh that explores the history and legacy of emigration from Ulster to the US.

Omagh

POP 19,900

Situated at the confluence of the Rivers Camowen and Drumragh, which join to form the River Strule, Omagh (An Óghmagh) is a busy market town with a handful of historic Georgian buildings.

◉ Sights

Memorial Obelisk   MEMORIAL
(www.omaghbombmemorial.com; Market St) For a long time to come, Omagh will be remembered for the devastating 1998 car bomb that killed 29 people and injured 200. Planted by the breakaway Real IRA group, the bomb was the worst single atrocity in the 30-year history of the Troubles.

An impressive 4.5m-high glass obelisk marks the spot of the explosion. It's part of a project that includes a **memorial garden** 300m north across the river on Drumragh Ave.

🛏 Sleeping & Eating

Although the nearby Ulster American Folk Park (p648) is a major attraction, few visitors choose to stay in Omagh overnight. The best sleeping options in the area are high-end B&Bs.

WORTH A TRIP

CUILCAGH MOUNTAIN

Rising above Marble Arch and Florence Court, Cuilcagh (*cull*-kay) Mountain (666m) is the highest point in Counties Fermanagh and Cavan, its summit right on the border between Northern Ireland and the Republic.

The mountain is a geological layer cake, with a cave-riddled limestone base, shale and sandstone flanks draped with a shaggy tweed skirt of blanket bog, and a high gritstone plateau ringed by steep, craggy slopes, all part of the **Marble Arch Caves Global Geopark**.

Hidden among the sphagnum moss, bog cotton and heather of the blanket bog is the sticky-fingered sundew, an insect-eating plant, while the crags echo to the 'krok-krok-krok' of ravens and the mewing of peregrine falcons. The other-worldly summit plateau is a breeding ground for golden plover and is rich in rare plants such as alpine clubmoss.

The **hike** to the summit is a 15km round trip (allow five or six hours). Start at the car park of the **Cuilcagh Mountain Park**, 300m west of the turn-off to the visitor centre of the **Marble Arch Caves** (p645),where there is an information desk and maps. Right next to the car park is the **Monastir sinkhole**, a deep depression ringed by limestone cliffs where the River Aghinrawn disappears underground for its journey through the Marble Arch Caves system.

The **Legnabrocky Trail** begins as a well-groomed gravel track that winds through rich green limestone meadows for 4km. From here you begin your ascent of Cuilcagh Mountain along a 2.5km section of **boardwalk** (built to protect the sensitive bog blanket below), climbing steeply to the summit ridge, with great views west to the crags above little Lough Atona. The boardwalk comes to an end here, but a rough path continues 1km east across the rock-strewn plateau to the prominent cairn on the summit (turn back when you reach the end of the boardwalk unless you have good boots, a compass and map).

The **summit cairn** is actually a Bronze Age burial mound; about 100m south of the summit are two rings of boulders, the foundations of prehistoric huts. On a clear day the view extends from the Blue Stack Mountains of Donegal to Croagh Patrick, and from the Atlantic Ocean to the Irish Sea.

For downloadable maps of other walks in the area, visit www.marblearchcaves geopark.com.

Mullaghmore House
B&B €€

(☑ 028-8224 2314; 94 Old Mountfield Rd; s/d from £40/70; 🕏) Offering affordable country-house charm, this beautifully restored Georgian house boasts a period mahogany-panelled library. The bedrooms have cast-iron fireplaces and antique furniture (some share bathrooms). The owner runs courses on antique restoration and traditional crafts. It's 1.5km northeast of Omagh's town centre.

★ Philly's Phinest
FAST FOOD €

(12 Bridge St; burgers £2.80-5.90; ⊙11am-5pm Mon-Sat; 🕏) This tiny fast-food joint with 1950s diner-style booths serves up some of the tastiest food in town, inspired by the USA's Philly cheesesteak (fried steak, onion and cheese in a soft bun).

Strule Cafe
CAFE €

(☑ 028-8226 8618; www.facebook.com/strule cafeartscenteromagh; Bridge St, Strule Arts Centre; mains £7-9; ⊙10am-3.30pm Mon-Sat; 🕏🔥) Inside the Strule Arts Centre, this cafe is a pleasant spot for breakfast, lunchtime burgers and sandwiches, and afternoon coffee and cake, with comfy sofas and huge picture windows overlooking the river and bridge.

ℹ️ Information

Omagh Tourist Office (☑ 028-8224 7831; www. visitomagh.co.uk; Bridge St, Strule Arts Centre; ⊙10am-5.30pm Mon-Sat; 🕏) In the arts centre, just across the river from the bus station.

ℹ️ Getting There & Away

The bus station is on Mountjoy Rd, just north of the town centre along Bridge St.

Bus 273 goes from Belfast to Omagh (£12, 1¾ hours, hourly Monday to Saturday, six on Sunday) via Dungannon (£6.70, 45 minutes) and on to Derry (£8, 1¼ hours). Bus 94 goes to Enniskillen (£8, one hour, six or seven Monday to Friday, three on Saturday, one on Sunday).

COUNTIES FERMANAGH & TYRONE OMAGH

DAVAGH FOREST PARK TRAILS

Remote Davagh Forest Park provides some of the best mountain biking in Ireland, ranging from family-friendly green and blue trails along a wooded stream to 16km of red trails leading to the top of Beleevenamore Mountain, with several challenging rock slabs and drop-offs on the descents.

Walking gives you time to enjoy this landscape of rolling hills and sweeping forests. A 3km loop trail takes in the forests and red-hued stream.

The trailhead is on a minor road, 10km northwest of Cookstown, sign-posted from the A505 Cookstown–Omagh road at Dunnamore. For details see www.mountainbikeni.com and www.walkni.com.

Ulster American Folk Park

★ **Ulster American Folk Park** MUSEUM
(☏ 028-8224 3292; www.nmni.com/uafp; 2 Mellon Rd; adult/child £9/5.50; ⊙10am-5pm Tue-Sun Mar-Sep, 10am-4pm Tue-Fri, 11am-4pm Sat & Sun Oct-Feb) In the 18th and 19th centuries more than two million Ulster people left their homes to forge a new life across the Atlantic. Their story is told here at one of Ireland's best museums, which features a sprawling **outdoor history park**. Exhibits are split into Old World cottages and New World log cabins, with actors in period costume on hand to bring the stories to life.

Original buildings from various parts of Ulster have been dismantled and reerected here, including a blacksmith's forge, a weaver's thatched cottage, a Presbyterian meeting house and a schoolhouse. The two parts of the park are cleverly linked by passing through a mock-up of an emigrant ship. In the American section of the park you can visit a genuine 18th-century settler's stone cottage and a log house, both shipped across the Atlantic from Pennsylvania, and a Tennessee plantation house, plus many more original buildings.

The **Exhibition Hall** explains the close connections between Ulster and the USA – the American Declaration of Independence was signed by several Ulstermen – and includes an original Calistoga wagon.

Costumed guides and artisans explain the arts of spinning, weaving, candle-making

and so on. Various **special events** are held throughout the year, including reenactments of American Civil War battles, a festival of traditional Irish music in May, American Independence Day celebrations in July, and the Appalachian and Bluegrass Music Festival in late August/September. At least half a day is needed to do the place justice.

Translink Goldline bus 273 from Belfast to Derry stops in Omagh, and will stop on request at the park gates.

The park is 8km northwest of Omagh. Last admission is 1½ hours before closing.

Sperrin Mountains

On a sunny spring day, when the russet bogs and yellow gorse stand out against a clear blue sky, the Sperrin Mountains can offer some grand walking. However, when representatives of the London guilds visited Ulster in 1609, the Lord Deputy of Ireland made sure they were kept well away from the Sperrins, fearing that the sight of these bleak, moorland hills would put them off the idea of planting settlers here.

The area is also dotted with standing stones and prehistoric tombs.

❶ Getting There & Away

Ulsterbus service 403, the Sperrin Rambler, runs twice daily from Monday to Saturday between Omagh (to Gortin £3.50, 25 minutes) and Magherafelt (to Gortin £9.30, 1½ hours).

Gortin

The village of Gortin (pronounced Gorchin), lies 15km north of Omagh at the foot of Mullaghcarn (542m), the southernmost of the Sperrin summits, and makes a good base for exploring the hills. There are several good walks around the village, a forest park with walking and mountain-biking trails and a scenic drive to **Gortin Lakes**, with views north to the main Sperrin ridge.

Hundreds of hikers converge for a mass ascent of Mullaghcarn on **Cairn Sunday** (the last Sunday in July), a revival of an ancient pilgrimage.

◎ Sights & Activities

Gortin Glen Forest Park FOREST
(www.nidirect.gov.uk; Glenpark Rd; car park £4; ⊙10am-dusk) **FREE** Originally planted for timber production, this coniferous forest is now a 15-sq-km park. The main car park is the

starting point for a series of walking trails and an 8km scenic forest drive. In the northern section of the park are three graded trails for **mountain biking**. The trails are accessed 1km from the park exit on Lisnaharney Rd.

Gortin Glen is 5km south of Gortin on the B48 road to Omagh.

Sleeping & Eating

Gortin Hostel   HOSTEL €
(☎028-8164 8346; www.gortincommunity.com; 62 Main St; dm/f/cottages £15/45/65; 🖥) Part of a community enterprise, this hostel with bright dorms and family rooms with attached bathrooms is a great option for walkers and cyclists. Staff are friendly and helpful and there's a well-equipped kitchen, cosy lounge with a working fireplace, and a washing machine. There are also four spacious self-catering cottages. The reception is in the outdoor activity centre.

Foot Hills   IRISH €€
(☎028-8164 8157; www.facebook.com/foothills restaurant; 16 Main St; mains daytime menu £7-13, dinner £12-23; ⊙noon-8.30pm Mon-Thu, to 9.30pm Fri-Sun; 🖥) This relaxed village restaurant serves an all-day bar menu of burgers, pastas and steaks plus a dinner menu featuring the house speciality 'cock 'n' bull' (cajun-dusted Irish beef fillet and chicken with Café de Paris butter). Portions are generous and the desserts are excellent too.

An Creagán

Sights

An Creagán   VISITOR CENTRE
(☎028-8076 1112; www.an-creagan.com; A505, Creggan; bike rental half-day £7; ⊙11am-5pm; 🖥) FREE Meaning 'stony site' in Irish, An Creagán (20km east of Omagh) is a great starting point for exploring the ecology of the surrounding bogs and the archaeology of the region. Information on nearby prehistoric monuments including the Beaghmore Stone Circles can be found in a small **museum gallery**, which houses stones and artefacts collected from around the site. There are also 5km of **nature trails** through bogs and forest, a woodland **children's play area**, self-catering cottages and a good restaurant.

The visitors centre has maps of the neolithic and Bronze Age sites in the area, as well as general tourist information and a shop selling local arts and crafts.

Beaghmore Stone Circles   ARCHAEOLOGICAL SITE
(Blackrock Rd; ⊙24hr) FREE What these neolithic stone circles lack in stature – the stones are all less than 1m tall – they make up for in complexity; the impressive complex has seven stone circles and rows, one filled with smaller stones, nicknamed 'dragon's teeth'.

The site is signposted about 8km east of An Creagán, and 4km north of the A505.

Sleeping & Eating

An Creagán Cottages   COTTAGE €€
(☎028-8076 1116; www.an-creagan.com; Creggan Rd, Creggan; 1-/2-/3-bed cottages 2 nights from £120/160/180) An Creagán's eight modern, self-catering cottages have an idyllic setting near nature trails in the foothills of the Sperrins. Each one comes fully equipped with a working fireplace, flat-screen TV, good kitchen and contemporary furnishings.

An Creagán Restaurant   IRISH €€
(www.an-creagan.com; Creggan Rd, Creggan; mains lunch £6-9.50, dinner £12-20; ⊙10am-3pm Mon-Thu, to 9pm Fri-Sun) The restaurant at An Creagán serves a range of pasta, steak, chicken and seafood dishes prepared using herbs, vegetables and salad leaves from the kitchen garden. There's traditional Irish music in the bar on Saturday nights.

East Tyrone

The market towns of Cookstown and Dungannon are the main settlements in the eastern part of County Tyrone, but the key sights here are in the surrounding countryside.

Sights

Wellbrook Beetling Mill   HISTORIC BUILDING
(☎028-8674 8210; www.nationaltrust.org.uk; 20 Wellbrook Rd, Corkhill; adult/child £5.50/free; ⊙2-5pm Sat, Sun & public holidays mid-Mar–late Sep) Beetling, the final stage of linen-making, involves pounding the cloth with wooden hammers, or beetles, to give it a smooth sheen. This 18th-century mill still has its original machinery and stages loud demonstrations of the linen-making process during hour-long guided tours. The whitewashed building is on a pretty stretch of the Ballinderry River, 8km west of Cookstown, just off the A505.

Ardboe High Cross RELIGIOUS SITE
(Ardboe Rd, off B73) FREE This 6th-century monastic site overlooking Lough Neagh is home to one of Ireland's best-preserved and most elaborately decorated Celtic stone crosses. The 10th-century Ardboe High Cross stands 5.5m tall, with 22 carved panels depicting biblical scenes. It's an evocative place 16km east of Cookstown, with distant views and a nearby cemetery. Take the B73 through Coagh and watch for the signs for Ardboe High Cross, which will lead you along a narrow country road.

The western side of the cross (facing the road) has New Testament scenes including the Adoration of the Magi and Christ's entry into Jerusalem; the more weathered eastern face (towards the lough) shows Old Testament scenes.

Grant Ancestral Homestead HISTORIC SITE
(☎028-8555 7133; 45 Dergenagh Rd, Ballygawley; ⏰9am-5pm) FREE Ulysses Simpson Grant (1822–85) led Union forces to victory in the American Civil War and later served as the 18th US president. His maternal grandfather, John Simpson, emigrated from County Tyrone to Pennsylvania in 1760, but the farm he left behind at Dergina has been restored in the style of a typical Ulster smallholding, as it would have been during the time of Grant's presidency.

The site is 20km west of Dungannon, signposted south of the A4.

Donaghmore High Cross RELIGIOUS SITE
(Donaghmore) The village of Donaghmore, 5km northwest of Dungannon on the road to Pomeroy, is famed for its 10th-century Celtic high cross. It was cobbled together from two different crosses in the 18th century (note the obvious join halfway up the shaft) and now stands outside the church graveyard. The carved biblical scenes are similar to those on the Ardboe High Cross.

Sleeping & Eating

★**Tullylagan Country House** HOTEL €€
(☎028-8676 5100; www.tullylaganhotel.com; 40b Tullylagan Rd, Cookstown; s/d £75/110; 📶) Set amid beautiful riverside gardens, the ivy-clad Tullylagan has a Victorian country manor feel, with gilt-framed mirrors, polished wooden floors and marble-effect bathrooms. The hotel's excellent **Kitchen Restaurant** (mains £12-23; ⏰noon-4pm daily, plus 5-9pm Mon, Tue, Sat & Sun) specialises in locally sourced seafood, game and beef. It's 4km south of Cookstown (just off the A29).

Grange Lodge B&B €€
(☎028-8778 4212; www.grangelodgecountryhouse.com; 7 Grange Rd, Dungannon; s/d from £90/110; ⏰dinner 7.30pm, book 48hr in advance; 📶) The five-room Grange is a period gem set on its own 8-hectare grounds. Parts of the antique-packed house date from 1698, though most are Georgian with Victorian additions. The proprietor is an award-winning chef and the Grange runs cookery courses. It's 5km southeast of Dungannon, signposted off the A29.

★**Brewer's House** MODERN IRISH €€
(☎028-8776 1932; www.thebrewershouse.com; 73 Castlecaulfield Rd, Donaghmore; mains £11-22; ⏰kitchen 4.30-8.30pm Mon-Thu, noon-9pm Fri, to 10pm Sat, to 8pm Sun; 👪) This much-loved old village pub combines welcoming open fires and cosy nooks and crannies with a menu of creative, modern dishes including locally sourced meat and seafood, burgers, and fish and chips. The beer, wine and cocktail lists are excellent and there are tables outside for sunny afternoons. It's 5km northwest of Dungannon.

Shopping

Linen Green Designer Village SHOPPING CENTRE
(☎028-8775 3761; www.thelinengreen.co.uk; off A29, Moygashel; ⏰10am-5pm Mon-Sat) Housed in the former Moygashel Linen Mills, this complex includes a range of designer shops and factory outlets. It's a good place to shop for men's and women's fashion, shoes and accessories. It's southeast of Dungannon.

Information

Ranfurly House Arts & Visitor Centre (☎028-8772 8600; www.dungannon.info; 26 Market Sq, Dungannon; ⏰9am-9pm Mon-Fri, to 5pm Sat, 1-5pm Sun Apr-Sep, 9am-5pm Mon-Fri Oct-Mar; 📶) Tourist information for County Tyrone, with an exhibition on the Flight of the Earls.

Getting There & Away

Bus 261 links Dungannon to Belfast (£9.30, 50 minutes, hourly Monday to Saturday, six on Sunday) and Omagh (£6.70, 45 minutes). Bus 80 connects Dungannon and Cookstown (£3.80, 45 minutes, hourly Monday to Friday, seven on Saturday). Bus 209 links Cookstown to Belfast (£9.30, about 1¼ hours, seven daily Monday to Friday, three on Saturday, two on Sunday).

Understand
Ireland

Ireland Today

The whole island has come a long way since the dawn of the new millennium. In and out of a deep recession, the Republic continues to embrace the changes of progressive liberalism: in 2015 it passed marriage-equality legislation granting equal marital status to same-sex couples. Northern Ireland remains resistant to this kind of change, for now – but it continues along the path of peace with greater confidence than ever. Meanwhile, a Brexit-shaped shadow lurks in the distance...

Best on Film

Bloody Sunday (2002) Unmissable account of events in Derry in 1972.

The Dead (1987) John Huston brings James Joyce's story to life in his last film, with powerful performances by Donal McCann and Anjelica Huston.

'71 (2014) Excellent film about a British soldier separated from his unit during a Belfast riot in 1971.

What Richard Did (2012) A killing among privileged youths prompts serious soul-searching; loosely based on real events that occurred in 2000.

Best in Print

Dubliners (James Joyce; 1914) A collection of short stories still as poignant and relevant today as when they were written.

Room (Emma Donoghue; 2010) A harrowing but beautiful account of a boy and his mother being held prisoner, told from the boy's perspective.

The Secret Scripture (Sebastian Barry; 2008) The story of a 100-year-old patient of a mental hospital who writes her autobiography; now a 2015 film directed by Jim Sheridan.

The Gathering (Anne Enright; 2007) Powerful account of alcoholism and domestic abuse in an Irish family.

Progressive Conservatism?

Although the 2016 elections returned the Fine Gael party to government, their unconvincing show in the campaign and the resulting hung parliament that left them relying on a motley crew of independents to govern eventually led to the resignation of Enda Kenny as Taoiseach (Republic of Ireland prime minister) and party leader in May 2017.

His replacement is Leo Varadkar, who happens to be gay and half-Indian. While much has been written about Ireland's remarkable journey over the last three decades that has resulted in the ascent to the highest office of the homosexual son of an immigrant, it is perhaps even more remarkable that he did so as a member of Fine Gael, whose conservative values are woven into the party's DNA.

Varadkar is something of a conundrum. He is charismatic, straight-talking and very much a child of progressive, contemporary Ireland: at 38 he was the youngest person ever to become Taoiseach. But many progressives are troubled by the conservative tone of his politics, and while the new Taoiseach insists that some of his views have evolved (read: softened) over the years, his rise reveals a fascinating dichotomy: he is the product of a social liberalism that he doesn't fully espouse. Or, put another way, his success is down to a mix of political nous and pragmatic conservatism, qualities that make his sexual orientation and ethnic background completely irrelevant.

Brexit & Beyond

What will Brexit bring? At the time of writing, this was the pressing political and economic question. Ireland has close socioeconomic ties with the UK, so most economists believe that 'the harder the Brexit, the worse the outcome', with bilateral trade hit by as much as 20%.

But the biggest impact will be felt by Northern Ireland, which in a post-Brexit landscape will be divided from the Republic by the only land border between the UK and the EU. The majority of its citizens (56% to 44%) voted Remain, but the governing Democratic Unionist Party (DUP) favoured Leave, if only, they argued, to copper-fasten the province's ties to a UK that was out of the EU.

Despite the display of fealty, the DUP may be fighting a rising democratic tide. The British government remains committed to the union with Northern Ireland as long as a majority of its citizens desire it, but the numbers are worrying for unionists: the 2011 census revealed that of children aged four or under, 49.2% were being raised Catholic and only 36.4% Protestant, evidence that the Catholic/nationalist population will be a majority in the coming years.

Brexit won't change that either: a leaked letter by Brexit secretary David Davis revealed that should the majority of the province vote for reunification with the Republic then neither the British government nor the EU would stand in its way, and that it *wouldn't* have to reapply for membership of the EU as the Republic is already a member.

Repealing the Eighth Amendment

With same-sex marriage already on the statute books of the Republic, the next big social issue it will have to look at is reform of the country's strict anti-abortion laws, outlined in the 8th amendment to the constitution.

In April 2017 a Citizens' Assembly – a body convened by the government to explore constitutional issues – voted overwhelmingly to extend access to abortion with 'no restriction as to reasons' by a majority of 64%. While a majority of the electorate supports reform of the existing law, polls show that two-thirds would reject abortion on request.

The specific wording of a new law is the main challenge for the government, who announced in September 2017 that a referendum will take place at some point in 2018. In the meantime, both sides of the argument have dug in for what augurs to be a bitter fight. The pro-choice campaign, which is supported by an overwhelming majority of younger voters, has been especially vocal: you might see people sporting a 'repeal' T-shirt or sweatshirt on your travels. The pro-life campaign has its support among older, more traditional communities and groups affiliated with the church.

The latter's campaign is straightforward, opposing any kind of change to the law as it currently stands, but the pro-choice side must decide whether to pursue a limited liberalisation that will have a greater chance of success, or campaign for wider availability, which would likely be much tougher to pass.

POPULATION:
4,761,865/1,810,863 (REPUBLIC/NORTHERN IRELAND)

AREA: **84,421/13,843 SQ KM (R/NI)**

INFLATION: **0.3%/2.3% (R/NI)**

UNEMPLOYMENT: **7.1%/5% (R/NI)**

if Ireland were 100 people

87 would be Irish • 3 would be Asian
6 would be from the EU • 1 would be American
2 would be British • 1 would be other

if Northern Ireland were 100 people

40 would identify as British
25 would identify as Irish
21 would identify as Northern Irish
14 would identify as other

population per sq km

REPUBLIC OF IRELAND • NORTHERN IRELAND • ENGLAND

† ≈ 70 people

History

From pre-Celts to Celtic cubs, Ireland's history has been a search for identity, which would have been a little more straightforward if this small island hadn't been of such interest to a host of foreign parties: Celtic tribes, Viking marauders, Norman invaders and, most especially, the English, whose close-knit, fractious and complicated relationship with Ireland provides the prism through which a huge part of the Irish identity is reflected.

The Native Irish

It took the various Celtic tribes roughly 500 years to settle in Ireland, beginning in the 8th century BC. The last of the tribes, commonly known as the Gaels (which in the local language came to mean 'foreigner'), came ashore in the 3rd century BC and proceeded to divide the island into five provinces – Leinster, Meath, Connaught, Ulster and Munster (Meath later merged with Leinster) – that were subdivided into territories controlled by as many as one hundred minor kings and chieftains, all of whom nominally paid allegiance to a high king who sat at Tara, in County Meath.

The Celts set about creating the basics of what we now term 'Irish' culture: they devised a sophisticated code of law called the Brehon Law, which remained in use until the early 17th century; and their swirling, mazelike design style, evident on artefacts nearly 2000 years old, is considered the epitome of Irish design. Some excellent ancient Celtic designs survive in the Broighter Hoard in the National Museum in Dublin. The Turoe Stone in County Galway is another fine representative of Celtic artwork.

For a concise, 10-minute read on who the Celts were, see www.ibiblio.org/gaelic/celts.html.

The Arrival of Christianity

Although St Patrick gets all the credit, between the 3rd and 5th centuries Ireland was Christianised by a host of missionaries, who converted pagan tribes by fusing their local druidic rituals with the new Christian teaching, thereby creating a hybrid known as Celtic or Insular Christianity.

Irish Christian scholars excelled in the study of Latin and Greek philosophy and Christian theology in the monasteries that flourished at, among other places, Clonmacnoise in County Offaly, Glendalough in County

TIMELINE	10,000–8000 BC	4500 BC	700–300 BC
	After the last ice age ends, humans arrive in Ireland during the Mesolithic era, originally crossing a land bridge between Scotland and Ireland. Few archaeological traces remain of this group.	The first Neolithic farmers arrive in Ireland by boat from as far afield as the Iberian peninsula, bringing cattle, sheep and crops, marking the beginnings of a settled agricultural economy.	Iron technology gradually replaces bronze. The Celtic culture and language arrive, ushering in a thousand years of cultural and political dominance and leaving a legacy still visible today.

Wicklow and Lismore in County Waterford. It was the Golden Age, and the arts of manuscript illumination, metalworking and sculpture flourished, producing such treasures as the *Book of Kells*, ornate jewellery and the many carved stone crosses that dot the 'island of saints and scholars'.

The Vikings Are Coming!

The next group to try their luck were the Vikings, who first showed up in AD 795 and began plundering the prosperous monasteries. In self-defence, the monks built round towers, which served as lookout posts and places of refuge during attacks; you can see surviving examples throughout the country, including some fine examples at Glendalough, Kells and Steeple, near Antrim.

Despite the monks' best efforts, the Vikings had their way, mostly due to superior weaponry but also thanks to elements of the local population, who sided with the marauders for profit or protection. By the 10th century, the Norsemen were well established in Ireland, having founded towns such as Wicklow, Waterford, Wexford and their capital Dyfflin, which later became Dublin. The Vikings were defeated at the Battle of Clontarf in 1014 by Brian Ború, king of Munster, but Ború was killed and the Vikings, much like the Celts before them, eventually settled, giving up the rape-rob-and-run policy in favour of integration and assimilation: by intermarrying with the Celtic tribes, they introduced red hair and freckles to the Irish gene pool.

Top Monastic Sites

Cashel, County Tipperary (p316)

Clonmacnoise, County Offaly (p492)

Glendalough, County Wicklow (p146)

HISTORY THE VIKINGS ARE COMING!

ST PATRICK

Ireland's patron saint is remembered all around the world on 17 March, when people of all ethnicities drink Guinness and wear green clothing. But behind the hoopla was a real man with a serious mission. For it was Patrick (389–461) who introduced Christianity to Ireland.

The plain truth of it is that he wasn't Irish. This symbol of Irish pride hailed from what is now Wales, which at the time of his birth was under Roman rule.

Patrick's arrival in Ireland was made possible by Irish raiders who kidnapped him when he was 16, and took him across the channel to work as a slave. He found religion, escaped from captivity and returned to Britain. But he vowed to make it his life's work to make Christians out of the Irish. He was ordained, then appointed Bishop of Ireland. Back he went over the channel.

He based himself in Armagh, where St Patrick's Church of Ireland Cathedral stands on the site of his old church. Patrick quickly converted peasants and noblemen in great numbers. Within 30 years, much of Ireland had been baptised and the country was divided into Catholic dioceses and parishes. He also established monasteries throughout Ireland, which would be the foundations of Irish scholarship for many centuries.

So next St Paddy's Day, as you're swilling Guinness and champing down corned beef and cabbage, think of who the man really was.

AD 431–2	550–800	795–841	1014
Pope Celestine I sends Bishop Palladius to Ireland to minister to those 'already believing in Christ'; St Patrick arrives the following year to continue the mission.	The flowering of early monasticism in Ireland. The great monastic teachers begin exporting their knowledge across Europe, ushering in Ireland's 'Golden Age'.	Vikings plunder Irish monasteries; their raping and pillaging urges sated, they establish settlements throughout the country, including Dublin, and soon turn it into a centre of economic power.	The Battle of Clontarf takes place on Good Friday between the forces of the high king, Brian Ború, and the forces led by the king of Leinster, Máelmorda mac Murchada.

The English Invade

The '800 years' of English rule in Ireland nominally began with the Norman invasion of 1169, which was really more of an invitation as the barons, led by Richard Fitz Gilbert de Clare, earl of Pembroke (1130–76; aka Strongbow), had been asked to assist the king of Leinster in a territorial squabble. Two years later, King Henry II of England came ashore with a substantial army and a request from Pope Adrian IV to bring the rebel Christian missionaries to heel.

Despite the king's overall authority, the Anglo-Norman barons carved Ireland up between them and over the next 300 years set about consolidating their feudal power. Once again the effects of assimilation were in play, as the Anglo-Normans and their hirelings became, in the oft-quoted phrase, *Hiberniores Hibernis ipsis* (more Irish than the Irish themselves). They dotted the country with castles, but their real legacy is in the cities they built, such as magnificent Kilkenny, which today retains much of its medieval character. The Anglo-Normans may have pledged allegiance to the English king, but in truth they were loyal only to themselves: by the turn of the 16th century, the Crown's direct rule didn't extend any further than a cordon surrounding Dublin known as the Pale. But you can only ignore an English king for so long...

The Course of Irish History by TW Moody and FX Martin is a hefty volume by two Trinity College professors who trace much of Ireland's history back to its land and its proximity to England.

Ireland & the Tudors

When Henry VIII declared himself head of the Church in England in 1534, following his split with the papacy over his divorce from Catherine of Aragon, the Anglo-Normans cried foul and some took arms against the Crown. Worried that an Irish rising would be of help to Spain or France, Henry responded firmly, quashing the rebellion, confiscating the rebels' lands and (as in England) dissolving all Irish monasteries. He then had himself declared King of Ireland.

Elizabeth I (1533–1603) came to the throne in 1558 with the same uncompromising attitude to Ireland as her father. Ulster was the most hostile to her, with the Irish fighting doggedly under the command of Hugh O'Neill, earl of Tyrone, but they too were finally defeated in 1603. O'Neill, though, achieved something of a Pyrrhic victory when he refused to surrender until after he heard of Elizabeth's death. He and his fellow earls then fled the country in what become known as the Flight of the Earls. It left Ulster open to English rule and to the policy of Plantation, which involved confiscating the lands of the flown earls and redistributing them to subjects loyal to the crown. Although the confiscations happened all over the country, they were most thorough in Ulster.

The expression 'beyond the Pale' came into use when the Pale was the part of Ireland that was under Anglo-Norman control. To them, the rest of Ireland was an uncivilised territory populated by barbarians.

1169	1171	1350–1530	1366
Henry II's Welsh and Norman barons land in Wexford and capture Waterford and Wexford with MacMurrough's help. It is the beginning of an 800-year occupation by Britain.	King Henry II invades Ireland, forcing the Cambro-Norman warlords and some of the Gaelic Irish kings to accept him as their overlord.	The Anglo-Norman barons establish power bases independent of the English Crown. Over the following two centuries, English control gradually recedes to an area around Dublin known as 'the Pale'.	The English Crown enacts the Statutes of Kilkenny, outlawing intermarriage, the Irish language and other Irish customs to stop the Anglo-Normans from assimilating too much with the Irish. It doesn't work.

Oliver Cromwell Invades Ireland

At the outset of the English Civil War in 1642, the Irish threw their support behind Charles I against the very Protestant parliamentarians in the hope that victory for the king would lead to the restoration of Catholic power in Ireland. When Oliver Cromwell and his Roundheads defeated the Royalists and took Charles' head off in 1649, Cromwell turned his attention to the disloyal Irish. His nine-month campaign was effective and brutal (Drogheda was particularly mistreated); yet more lands were confiscated – Cromwell's famous utterance that the Irish could 'go to hell or to Connaught' seems odd given the province's beauty, but there wasn't much arable land out there – and Catholic rights restricted even more.

The Boyne & Penal Laws

Catholic Ireland's next major setback came in 1690. Yet again the Irish had backed the wrong horse, this time supporting James II after his deposition in the Glorious Revolution by the Dutch Protestant King William of Orange (who was married to James' daughter Mary!). After James had unsuccessfully laid siege to Derry for 105 days (the Loyalist cry of 'No surrender!', in use to this day, dates from the siege), in July he fought William's armies by the banks of the Boyne in County Louth and was roundly defeated.

The final ignominy for Catholics came in 1695 with the passing of the Penal Laws, which prohibited them from owning land or entering any higher profession. Irish culture, music and education were banned in the hope that Catholicism would be eradicated. Most Catholics continued to worship at secret locations, but some prosperous Irish converted to Protestantism to preserve their careers and wealth. Land was steadily transferred to Protestant owners, and a significant majority of the Catholic population became tenants living in wretched conditions. By the late 18th century, Catholics owned barely 5% of the land.

Revolt Against British Rule

Beginning towards the end of the 18th century, the main thrust of opposition to Irish inequalities resulting from the Penal Laws came from an unlikely source. A handful of liberal Protestants, versed in the ideologies of the Enlightenment and inspired by the revolutions in France and the newly established United States of America, began organising direct opposition to British rule.

The best known was Theobald Wolfe Tone (1763–98), a young Dublin lawyer who led a group called the United Irishmen in their attempts to reform and reduce British power in Ireland (Loyalist Protestants prepared for the possibility of conflict by forming the Protestant Orange Society, later known as the Orange Order). Wolfe Tone attempted to enlist French help in his uprising, but the French failure to land an army of

Cromwell: An Honourable Enemy by Tom Reilly advances the unpopular view that perhaps the destruction of Cromwell's campaign is grossly exaggerated. You're no doubt familiar with the common view; here's the contrary position. (Yes, Reilly is Irish.)

For the Cause of Liberty: A Thousand Years of Ireland's Heroes by Terry Golway vividly describes the struggles of Irish nationalism.

1536–41	1585	1594	1601
Henry VIII orders the dissolution of the monasteries and confiscation of church property. In 1541 he arranges for the Irish Parliament to declare him King of Ireland.	Potatoes from South America are introduced to Ireland, where they eventually become a staple on nearly every table in the country.	Hugh O'Neill, earl of Tyrone, orders lead from England to reroof his castle, but instead uses it for bullets – instigating the start of the Nine Years' War.	The Battle of Kinsale is fought between Queen Elizabeth I's armies and the combined rebel forces led by Hugh O'Neill. O'Neill surrenders and the back of the Irish rebellion against the Crown is broken.

succour in 1796 left the organisation exposed to retribution and the men met their bloody end in the Battle of Vinegar Hill in 1798. Three years later, the British sought to put an end to Irish agitation with the Act of Union, but the nationalist genie was already out of the bottle.

The Famine, O'Connell & Parnell

The 19th century was marked by repeated efforts to wrest some kind of control from Britain. There were the radical Republicans, who advocated use of force to found a secular, egalitarian republic that tried – and failed – in 1848 and 1867. And there were the moderates, who advocated nonviolent and legal action to force the government into concession.

The Great Liberator

The Great Hunger by Cecil Woodham-Smith is the classic study of the Great Famine of 1845–51.

Dominating the moderate landscape for nearly three decades was Kerry-born Daniel O'Connell (1775–1847), who tirelessly devoted himself to the cause of Catholic emancipation. In 1828 he was elected to the British Parliament but, being a Catholic, he couldn't actually take his seat: to avoid the possibility of an uprising, the government was forced to pass the 1829 Catholic Emancipation Act, allowing some well-off Catholics voting rights and the right to be elected as MPs.

O'Connell continued to fight for Irish self-determination and became known as a powerful speaker, not only on behalf of Ireland but against all kinds of injustice, including slavery: the abolitionist leader Frederick Douglass was one of his greatest admirers (their relationship was specifically referred to by President Obama during his 2011 visit). O'Connell, known as 'the Liberator', was adored by the Irish, who turned out in their tens of thousands to hear him speak, but his unwillingness to step outside the law was to prove his undoing: when the government banned one of his rallies from going ahead, O'Connell stood down – ostensibly to avoid the prospect of violence and bloodshed. But Ireland was in the midst of the Potato Famine, and his failure to defy the British was seen as capitulation; he was imprisoned for a time and died a broken man in 1847.

Ireland Since the Famine by FSL Lyons is a standard text for all students of modern Irish history.

The Uncrowned King of Ireland

Charles Stewart Parnell (1846–91) was the other great 19th-century statesman. Like O'Connell, he too was a powerful orator, but the primary focus of his artful attentions was land reform, particularly the reduction of rents and the improvement of working conditions (conveniently referred to as the 'Three Fs': fair rent, free sale and fixity of tenure). Parnell championed the activities of the Land League, which instigated the strategy of 'boycotting' (named after one particularly unpleasant agent called Charles Boycott) tenants, agents and landlords who didn't adhere to the Land League's aims: these people were treated like lepers by the

1607	1649–53	1688–90	1695
O'Neill and 90 other Ulster chiefs sail to Europe, leaving Ireland forever. Known as the Flight of the Earls, it leaves Ulster open to English rule and the policy of Plantation.	Cromwell lays waste to Ireland after the Irish support Charles I in the English Civil War; this includes the mass slaughter of Catholic Irish and the confiscation of 2 million hectares of land.	Following the deposition of King James II, James' Catholic army fights the Protestant forces of his successor, King William, resulting in William's victory at the Battle of the Boyne, 12 July 1690.	The Penal Laws (aka the 'popery code') prohibit Catholics from owning a horse, marrying outside their religion, building churches out of anything but wood, and from buying or inheriting property.

local population. In 1881 they won an important victory with the passing of the Land Act, which granted most of the League's demands.

Parnell's other great struggle was for a limited form of autonomy for Ireland. Despite the nominal support of the Liberal leader William Gladstone, Home Rule bills introduced in 1886 and 1892 were uniformly rejected by Parliament. Like O'Connell before him, Parnell's star plummeted dramatically: in 1890 he was embroiled in a divorce proceeding that scandalised puritanical Ireland. The 'uncrowned king of Ireland' was forced to resign and died less than a year later.

A History of Ulster by Jonathan Bardon is a serious and far-reaching attempt to come to grips with Northern Ireland's saga.

Fomenting Revolution

Ireland's struggle for some kind of autonomy picked up pace in the second decade of the 20th century. The radicalism that had always been at the fringes of Irish nationalist aspirations was once again beginning to assert itself, partly in response to a hardening of attitudes in Ulster. Mass opposition to any kind of Irish independence had resulted in the formation of the

THE GREAT FAMINE

As a result of the Great Famine of 1845–51, it's estimated that a staggering one million people died and some two million were forced to emigrate from Ireland. This great tragedy is all the more inconceivable given that the scale of suffering was attributable to selfishness as much as to natural causes. Potatoes were the staple food of a rapidly growing, desperately poor population and, when a blight hit the crops, prices soared. The repressive Penal Laws ensured that farmers, already crippled with high rents, could ill afford the few subsistence potatoes provided. Inevitably, most tenants fell into arrears, with little or no concession given by the mostly indifferent landlords, and were evicted or sent to the dire conditions of the workhouses.

Shamefully, during this time there were abundant harvests of wheat and dairy produce – the country was producing more than enough grain to feed the entire population and it's said that more cattle were sold abroad than there were people on the island. But while millions of its citizens were starving, Ireland was forced to export its food to Britain and overseas.

The Poor Law, in place at the height of the Famine, deemed landlords responsible for the maintenance of their poor and encouraged many to 'remove' tenants from their estates by paying their way to America. Many Irish were sent unwittingly to their deaths on board the notoriously scourged 'coffin ships'. British prime minister Sir Robert Peel made well-intentioned but inadequate gestures at famine relief, and some – but far too few – landlords did their best for their tenants.

Mass emigration continued to reduce the population during the next hundred years and huge numbers of Irish emigrants who found their way abroad, particularly to the USA, carried with them a lasting bitterness.

1795	1798	1801	1828–29
Concerned at the attempts of the Society of United Irishmen to secure equal rights for nonestablishment Protestants and Catholics, a group of Protestants create the Orange Order.	The flogging and killing of potential rebels sparks a rising led by the United Irishmen and their leader, Wolfe Tone. Wolfe Tone is captured and taken to Dublin, where he commits suicide.	The Act of Union unites Ireland politically with Britain. The Irish Parliament votes itself out of existence following a campaign of bribery. Around 100 Members of Parliament move to the House of Commons in London.	Daniel O'Connell exploits a loophole in the law to win a seat in Parliament but is unable to take it because he is Catholic. The prime minister passes the Catholic Emancipation Act, giving limited rights to Catholics.

Ulster Volunteer Force (UVF), a Loyalist vigilante group whose 100,000-plus members swore to resist any attempt to impose Home Rule on Ireland. Nationalists responded by creating the Irish Volunteer Force (IVF) and a showdown seemed inevitable.

Home Rule was finally passed in 1914, but the outbreak of WWI meant that its enactment was shelved for the duration. For most Irish, the suspension was disappointing but hardly unreasonable, and the majority of the volunteers enlisted to help fight the Germans.

The Irish in America by Michael Coffey takes up the history of the Famine where many histories leave off: the turbulent experiences of Irish immigrants in the USA.

The Easter Rising

A few, however, did not heed the call. Two small groups – a section of the Irish Volunteers under Pádraig Pearse and the Irish Citizens' Army led by James Connolly – conspired in a rebellion that took the country by surprise. A depleted Volunteer group marched into Dublin on Easter Monday 1916 and took over a number of key positions in the city, claiming the General Post Office on O'Connell St as its headquarters. From its steps, Pearse read out to passers-by a declaration that Ireland was now a republic and that his band was the provisional government. Less than a week of fighting ensued before the rebels surrendered to the superior British forces. The rebels weren't popular and had to be protected from angry Dubliners as they were marched to jail.

The Easter Rising would probably have had little impact on the Irish situation had the British not made martyrs of the rebel leaders. Of the 77 given death sentences, 15 were executed, including the injured Connolly, who was shot while strapped to a chair. This brought about a sea change in public attitudes, and support for the Republicans rose dramatically.

War with Britain

By the end of WWI, Home Rule was far too little, far too late. In the 1918 general election, the Republicans stood under the banner of Sinn Féin and won a large majority of the Irish seats. Ignoring London's Parliament, where technically they were supposed to sit, the newly elected Sinn Féin deputies – many of them veterans of the 1916 Easter Rising – declared Ireland independent and formed the first Dáil Éireann (Irish assembly or lower house), which sat in Dublin's Mansion House under the leadership of Éamon de Valera (1882–1975). The Irish Volunteers became the Irish Republican Army (IRA) and the Dáil authorised it to wage war on British troops in Ireland.

In 1870, after the Great Famine and ongoing emigration, more than a third of all native-born Irish lived outside Ireland.

As wars go, the War of Independence was pretty small fry. It lasted two and a half years and cost around 1200 casualties. But it was a pretty nasty affair, as the IRA fought a guerrilla-style, hit-and-run campaign against the British, whose numbers were swelled by returning veterans of WWI known as Black and Tans (on account of their uniforms, a mix of army khaki and police black), most of whom were so traumatised by their wartime experiences that they were prone to all kinds of brutality.

1845–51	1879–82	1884	1890s
A mould ravages the potato harvest. The British government adopts a laissez-faire attitude, resulting in the deaths of between 500,000 and one million, and the emigration of up to two million others.	The Land War, led by the Land League, sees tenant farmers defying their landlords en masse to force the passing of the Land Act in 1881, which allows for fair rent, fixity of tenure and free sale.	The Gaelic Athletic Association (GAA) is founded in Hayes Hotel, Thurles, County Tipperary. Its aim is to promote Gaelic games and culture; today hurling and Gaelic football are immensely popular.	The Gaelic Revival, championed by poet WB Yeats, sees a focused interest in the Irish language and Irish culture, including folklore, sport, music and the arts.

A Kind of Freedom

A truce in July 1921 led to intense negotiations between the two sides. The resulting Anglo-Irish Treaty, signed on 6 December 1921, created the Irish Free State, made up of 26 of 32 Irish counties. The remaining six – all in Ulster – remained part of the UK. The Treaty was an imperfect document: not only did it cement the geographic divisions on the island that 50 years later would explode into the Troubles, it also caused a split among nationalists – between those who believed the Treaty to be a necessary stepping stone towards full independence, and those who saw it as capitulation to the British and a betrayal of Republican ideals. This division was to determine the course of Irish political affairs for virtually the remainder of the century.

Civil War

The Treaty was ratified after a bitter debate and the June 1922 elections resulted in a victory for the pro-Treaty side. But the anti-Treaty forces rallied behind de Valera, who, though president of the Dáil, had not been a member of the Treaty negotiating team (affording him, in the eyes of his critics and opponents, maximum deniability should the negotiations go pear-shaped) and objected to some of the Treaty's provisions, most notably the oath of allegiance to the British monarch.

Within two weeks of the elections, civil war broke out between comrades who, a year previously, had fought alongside each other. The most prominent casualty of this particularly bitter conflict was Michael Collins (1890–1922), mastermind of the IRA's campaign during the War of Independence and a chief negotiator of the Anglo-Irish Treaty – shot in an ambush in his native Cork. Collins himself had presaged the bitterness that would result from the Treaty: upon signing it, he is said to have declared 'I tell you, I have signed my own death warrant.'

The Making of a Republic

The Civil War ground to an exhausted halt in 1923 with the victory of the pro-Treaty side, who governed the new state until 1932. Defeated but unbowed, de Valera founded a new party in 1926 called Fianna Fáil (Soldiers of Ireland) and won a majority in the 1932 elections; they would remain in charge until 1948. In the meantime, de Valera created a new constitution in 1937 that did away with the hated oath of allegiance, reaffirmed the special position of the Catholic Church and once again laid claim to the six counties of Northern Ireland. In 1948 Ireland officially left the Commonwealth and became a republic but, as historical irony would have it, it was Fine Gael, as the old pro-Treaty party was now known, that declared it – Fianna Fáil had surprisingly lost the election that year. After 800 years, Ireland – or at least a substantial chunk of it – was independent.

Neil Jordan's movie *Michael Collins*, starring Liam Neeson as the revolutionary, depicts the Easter Rising, the founding of the Free State and Collins' violent demise.

Brendan O'Brien's popular *Pocket History of the IRA* summarises a lot of complex history in a mere 150 pages; it's a good introduction.

HISTORY A KIND OF FREEDOM

1904	1916	1919–21	1921
16 June is the day in which all of the events of James Joyce's *Ulysses* takes place – chosen because it was the date Joyce first went out with his wife, Nora.	The Easter Rising: a group of Republicans take Dublin's General Post Office and announce the formation of an Irish republic. After less than a week of fighting, the rebels surrender to the superior British forces.	Irish War of Independence, aka the Black and Tan War on account of British irregulars wearing mixed police (black) and army (khaki) uniforms, begins in January 1919.	Two years and 1200 casualties later, the war ends in a truce on 11 July 1921 that leads to peace talks. After negotiations in London, the Irish delegation signs the Anglo-Irish Treaty on 6 December.

Growing Pains & Roaring Tigers

Unquestionably the most significant figure since independence, Éamon de Valera made an immense contribution to an independent Ireland but, as the 1950s stretched into the 1960s, his vision for the country was mired in a conservative and traditional orthodoxy that was at odds with the reality of a country in desperate economic straits, where chronic unemployment and emigration were but the more visible effects of inadequate policy. De Valera's successor as Taoiseach (Republic of Ireland prime minister) was Sean Lemass, whose tenure began in 1959 with the dictum 'a rising tide lifts all boats'. By the mid-1960s his economic policies had halved emigration and ushered in a new prosperity that was to be mirrored 30 years later by the Celtic Tiger.

For articles exploring the whole gamut of Irish history, check out the National Library's historical blog at www.nli.ie/blog.

Partners in Europe

In 1972 the Republic (along with Northern Ireland) became a member of the European Economic Community (EEC). This brought an increased measure of prosperity thanks to the benefits of the Common Agricultural Policy, which set fixed prices and guaranteed quotas for Irish farming produce. Nevertheless, the broader global depression, provoked by the oil crisis of 1973, forced the country into yet another slump and emigration figures rose again, reaching a peak in the mid-1980s.

The Celtic Tiger

In the early 1990s, European funds helped kick-start economic growth. Huge sums of money were invested in education and physical infrastructure, while the policy of low corporate tax rates coupled with attractive incentives made Ireland very appealing to high-tech businesses looking for a door into EU markets. In less than a decade, Ireland went from being one of the poorest countries in Europe to one of the wealthiest: unemployment fell from 18% to 3.5%, the average industrial wage somersaulted to the top of the European league, and the dramatic rise in GDP meant that the country laid claim to an economic model of success that was the envy of the entire world. Ireland became synonymous with the term 'Celtic Tiger'.

Recession Looms

From 2002 the Irish economy was kept buoyant by a gigantic construction boom that was completely out of step with any measure of responsible growth forecasting. The out-of-control international derivatives market flooded Irish banks with cheap money, and they lent it freely.

Then American global financial services firm Lehman Bros and the credit crunch happened. The Irish banks nearly went to the wall, but were bailed out at the last minute, and before Ireland could draw breath,

1921–22	1922–23	1932	1948
The Treaty gives 26 counties of Ireland independence and allows six largely Protestant Ulster counties the choice of opting out. The Irish Free State is founded in 1922.	Unwilling to accept the terms of the Treaty, forces led by Éamon de Valera take up arms against their former comrades, led by Michael Collins. A brief but bloody civil war ensues, resulting in the death of Collins.	After 10 years in the political wilderness, de Valera leads his Fianna Fáil party into government and goes about weakening the ties between the Free State and Britain.	Fianna Fáil loses the 1948 general election to Fine Gael in coalition with the new Republican Clann an Poblachta. The new government declares the Free State to be a republic at last.

the International Monetary Fund (IMF) and the EU held the chits of the country's midterm economic future. Ireland found itself yet again confronting the familiar demons of high unemployment and emigration, but a deep-cutting program of austerity saw the corner turned by the end of 2014.

It's (Not So) Grim Up North

Since 8 May 2007, Northern Ireland has been governed in relative harmony by a constituent assembly led by a First Minister and a Deputy First Minister, drawn from the largest parties on either side of the sectarian divide. Until 2017 it was the Democratic Unionist Party (DUP) and Sinn Féin respectively, but their generally pacific alliance was scuttled by, firstly, a scandal that saw Sinn Féin pull out of government (triggering new elections) and, secondly, the emergence of the DUP as the Conservative Party's parliamentary lifeline following the British general election in June, wherein the party's 10 MPs agreed to a 'supply and confidence' arrangement with the government. Meanwhile, the Northern Ireland Assembly remains suspended pending ongoing negotiations between two sides who have dug their heels in, with the very real possibility of direct rule from Westminster being introduced for the first time since the Assembly was established.

Ireland Divided

Following the Anglo-Irish Treaty, a new Northern Ireland Parliament was constituted on 22 June 1922, with James Craig as the first prime minister. His Ulster Unionist Party (UUP) was to rule the new state until 1972, with the minority Catholic population (roughly 40%) stripped of any real power or representative strength by a Parliament that favoured the Unionists through economic subsidy, bias in housing allocations and gerrymandering: Derry's electoral boundaries were redrawn so as to guarantee a Protestant council, even though the city was two-thirds Catholic. The overwhelmingly Protestant Royal Ulster Constabulary (RUC) and its paramilitary force, the B-Specials, made little effort to mask its sectarian bias. To all intents and purposes, Northern Ireland was an apartheid state.

> The events leading up to the Anglo-Irish War and their effect on ordinary people are movingly and powerfully related in JG Farrell's novel *Troubles*, first published in 1970.

We Shall Overcome

The first challenge to the unionist hegemony came with the long-dormant IRA's border campaign in the 1950s, but it was quickly quashed and its leaders imprisoned. A decade later, however, the authorities met with a far more defiant foe in the shape of the Civil Rights Association, founded in 1967 and heavily influenced by its US counterpart as it sought to redress the blatant sectarianism in Derry.

1969	1972	1973–74	1981
Marches by the Northern Ireland Civil Rights Association are disrupted by Loyalist attacks and police action, resulting in rioting and culminating in the Battle of the Bogside. The Troubles begin.	The Republic (and Northern Ireland) join the European Economic Community (EEC). On Bloody Sunday, 13 civilians are killed by British troops; Westminster suspends the Stormont government and introduces direct rule.	The Sunningdale Agreement results in a new Northern Ireland Assembly. Unionists oppose the agreement and the Ulster Workers' Council calls a strike that paralyses the province and brings an end to the Assembly.	Ten Republican prisoners die from a hunger strike. The first to die, Bobby Sands, had three weeks earlier been elected to Parliament on an Anti-H-Block ticket. Over 100,000 people attend Sands' funeral.

In October 1968 a mainly Catholic march in Derry was violently broken up by the RUC amid rumours that the IRA had provided 'security' for the marchers. Nobody knew it at the time, but the Troubles had begun.

In January 1969 another Civil Rights Movement, called People's Democracy, organised a march from Belfast to Derry. As the marchers neared their destination, they were attacked by a group of Protestants. The police first stood to one side and then swept through the predominantly Catholic Bogside district. Further marches, protests and violence followed, with many Republicans arguing that the police only added to the problem. In August British troops went to Derry and then Belfast to maintain law and order. The British army was initially welcomed in some Catholic quarters, but soon it too came to be seen as a tool of the Protestant majority. Overreaction by the army actually fuelled recruitment into the long-dormant IRA, whose numbers especially increased after Bloody Sunday (30 January 1972), when British troops killed 13 civilians in Derry.

The Troubles

Following Bloody Sunday, the IRA more or less declared war on Britain. While continuing to target people in Northern Ireland, it moved its campaign of bombing to the British mainland, targeting innocents and earning the condemnation of citizens and parties from both sides of the sectarian divide. Meanwhile, Loyalist paramilitaries began a sectarian campaign against Catholics. Passions reached fever pitch in 1981 when Republican prisoners in the North went on a hunger strike, demanding the right to be recognised as political prisoners. Ten of them fasted to death, the best known being an elected MP, Bobby Sands.

The waters were further muddied by an incredible variety of parties splintering into subgroups with different agendas. The IRA had split into 'official' and 'provisional' wings, from which sprang more extreme Republican organisations such as the Irish National Liberation Army (INLA). Myriad Protestant, Loyalist paramilitary organisations sprang up in opposition to the IRA, and violence was typically met with violence.

Overtures of Peace

By the early 1990s it was clear to Republicans that armed struggle was a bankrupted policy. Northern Ireland was a transformed society – most of the injustices that had sparked the conflict in the late 1960s had long since been rectified and most ordinary citizens were desperate for an end to hostilities. A series of negotiated statements between the unionists, nationalists and the British and Irish governments –

Books on the Troubles

Lost Lives, David McKittrick

Ten Men Dead, David Beresford

The Faithful Tribe: An Intimate Portrait of the Loyal Institutions, Ruth Dudley Edwards

---

Many films depict events related to the Troubles, including *Bloody Sunday* (2002), *The Boxer* (1997; starring Daniel Day-Lewis) and *In the Name of the Father* (1994; also starring Day-Lewis).

1993	Mid-1990s	1994	1998
Downing Street Declaration is signed by British Prime Minister John Major, and Irish Prime Minister Albert Reynolds. It states that Britain has no 'selfish, strategic or economic interest in Northern Ireland'.	Low corporate tax, restraint in government spending, transfer payments from the EU and a low-cost labour market result in the 'Celtic Tiger' boom, transforming Ireland into one of Europe's wealthiest countries.	Sinn Féin leader Gerry Adams announces a 'cessation of violence' on behalf of the Irish Republican Army (IRA) on 31 August. In October the Combined Loyalist Military Command also announces a ceasefire.	On 10 April negotiations culminate in the Good Friday Agreement, under which the new Northern Ireland Assembly is given full legislative and executive authority.

brokered in part by George Mitchell, Bill Clinton's special envoy to Northern Ireland – eventually resulted in the historic Good Friday Agreement of 1998.

The agreement called for the devolution of legislative power from Westminster (where it had been since 1972) to a new Northern Ireland Assembly, but posturing, disagreement, sectarianism and downright obstinance on both sides made slow work of progress, and the Assembly was suspended four times – the last from October 2002 until May 2007.

During this period, the politics of Northern Ireland polarised dramatically, resulting in the falling away of the more moderate UUP and the emergence of the hardline DUP, led by Ian Paisley; and, on the nationalist side, the emergence of the IRA's political wing, Sinn Féin, as the main torch-bearer of nationalist aspirations, under the leadership of Gerry Adams and Martin McGuinness.

A New Northern Ireland

Eager to avoid being seen to surrender any ground, the DUP and Sinn Féin dug their heels in on key issues, with the main sticking points being decommissioning of IRA weapons and the identity and composition of the new police force ushered in to replace the RUC. Paisley and the Unionists made increasing demands of the decommissioning bodies (photographic evidence, Unionist witnesses etc) as they refused to

AMERICAN CONNECTIONS

Today more than 40 million Americans have Irish ancestry – a legacy of successive waves of emigration, spurred by events from the Potato Famine of the 1840s to the Depression of the 1930s. Many of the legendary figures of American history, from Davy Crockett to John Steinbeck, and 18 out of the 44 US presidents to date, are of Irish descent – including Barack Obama, whose mother's family includes an emigrant called Falmouth Kearney, from Moneygall, County Offaly.

Following is a list of places that have links to past US presidents or deal with the experience of Irish emigrants to the USA:

Andrew Jackson Centre (p631), County Antrim

Cobh, The Queenstown Story (p226), County Cork

Dunbrody Famine Ship (p176), County Wexford

Grant Ancestral Homestead (p650), County Tyrone

Kennedy Homestead (p177), County Wexford

Ulster American Folk Park (p648), County Tyrone

1998	2005	2007	2008
The 'Real IRA' detonates a bomb in Omagh, killing 29 people and injuring 200 – the worst single atrocity in the history of the Troubles. Public outrage and swift action by politicians prevent a Loyalist backlash.	The IRA orders its units not to engage in 'any other activities' apart from assisting 'the development of purely political and democratic programmes through exclusively peaceful means'.	The Northern Ireland Assembly resumes after a five-year break when talks between unionists and Republicans remain in stalemate. They resolve their primary issues.	The Irish banking system is declared virtually bankrupt following the collapse of American global financial services firm Lehman Bros; Ireland is on the brink of economic disaster as the extent of the crisis is revealed.

accept anything less than an open and complete surrender of the IRA. Sinn Féin refused to join the police board that monitored the affairs of the Police Service of Northern Ireland (PSNI), effectively making no change to their policy of total noncooperation with the security forces.

But the IRA did finally decommission all of its weapons, and Sinn Féin eventually agreed to join the police board. The DUP abandoned its intransigence towards its former Republican enemies and the two sides got down to the business of governing a province whose pressing needs had long since been shunted aside by sectarianism. Proof that Northern Ireland had finally achieved some kind of normality came with the 2011 Assembly elections, which returned the DUP and Sinn Féin as the two largest parties, mandating them to keep going.

But old enmities die hard. The murder of a young PSNI officer called Ronan Kerr in April 2011 was a bitter reminder of the province's violent history, but even in tragedy there was a sense that something fundamental had shifted: Kerr was a Catholic member of a police force that has gone to great lengths to disavow its traditionally pro-Protestant bias and his murder was condemned with equal strength by both sides of the divide. Perhaps most tellingly, the then-First Minister Peter Robinson's presence at the funeral was the first time Robinson had ever been to a Catholic requiem mass.

A History of Ireland by Mike Cronin summarises all of Ireland's history in less than 300 pages. It's an easy read, but doesn't offer much in the way of analysis.

2010	2011	2013	2015, 2017
Ireland receives €85-billion bailout package from the International Monetary Fund (IMF) and the EU, which alleviates the banking crisis but leaves the country in strict financial shackles.	Queen Elizabeth II is the first British monarch to visit the Republic of Ireland; the visit is heralded as a resounding affirmation of the close ties between the two nations.	Ireland becomes the first stricken eurozone country to successfully exit the terms of the bailout.	Ireland becomes the first country in the world to introduce marriage equality for same-sex couples by plebiscite. In 2017, Leo Varadkar becomes Taoiseach; he is the fourth openly gay leader in European history.

The Irish Way of Life

The Irish reputation for being affable is largely well-deserved, but it only hints at a more profound character, one that is more complex and contradictory than the image of the silver-tongued master of blarney might suggest. This dichotomy is best summarised by a quote usually ascribed to the poet William Butler Yeats: 'Being Irish, he had an abiding sense of tragedy, which sustained him through temporary periods of joy.'

The Irish Pulse

The Irish are famous for being warm and friendly, which is just another way of saying the Irish love a chat, whether with friends or strangers. They will entertain you with their humour, alarm you with their willingness to get stuck into a good debate and cut you down with their razor-sharp wit. Slagging – the Irish version of teasing – is an art form, which may seem caustic to unfamiliar ears, but is quickly revealed as an intrinsic element of how the Irish relate to one another. It is commonly assumed that the mettle of friendship is proven by how well you can take a joke rather than by the payment of a cheap compliment.

Yet beneath all of the garrulous sociability and self-deprecating twaddle lurks a dark secret, which is that at heart the Irish have traditionally been low on self-esteem. This is partly why they're so suspicious of easy compliments, but the last three decades have seen a paradigm shift in the Irish character.

Prosperity and its related growth in expectations have gone a long way towards transforming the Irish from a people who wallowed in false modesty like a sport to a nation eager to celebrate its achievements and successes. Inevitably, this personality shift has been largely driven by the appetites and demands of Generation Y, but there's no doubt that many older Irish, for too long muted by a fear of appearing unseemly or boastful, have wholeheartedly embraced the change.

This cultural shift survived the trauma of the crash and the austerity that followed, even if many blamed a tawdry and materialistic culture of exaggerated excess for Ireland's woes, an attitude memorably summarised by a minister who sheepishly declared on TV that 'we all partied!' But with the economy (largely) back on track, Ireland is once again hammering down on the pedal of its ambitions, watching the worst ravages of austerity quickly disappear in its rear-view mirror.

> According to the 2016 census, the average number of children per family has fallen to 1.38, the lowest in Irish history.

Nurse & Curse of the People

Despite a 25% drop-off in alcohol consumption over the last decade (according to a 2017 report by the World Health Organization), Ireland has a fractious relationship with alcohol. The country regularly tops the list of the world's biggest binge drinkers, and while there is an increasing awareness of, and alarm at, the devastation caused by alcohol to Irish society (especially to young people), drinking remains the country's most popular social pastime, with no sign of letting up; spend a weekend night walking around any town in the country and you'll get a firsthand feel of the influence and effect of the booze.

Some experts put Ireland's binge-drinking antics down to the dramatic rise in the country's economic fortunes, but statistics have long revealed that Ireland has had an unhealthy fondness for 'taking the cure', although the acceptability of public drunkenness is a far more recent phenomenon: the older generation are never done reminding the youngsters that they would *never* have been seen staggering in public.

Lifestyle

In 2016, 37.3% of the population lived in rural areas.

The Irish may like to grumble – about work, the weather, the government and those *feckin' eejits* on reality TV shows – but if pressed will tell you that they live in the best country on earth. There's loads *wrong* with the place, but isn't it the same way everywhere else?

Traditional Ireland – of the large family, closely linked to church and community – has largely disappeared, as the increased urbanisation of the country continues to break up the social fabric of community interdependence that was a necessary element of relative poverty. Contemporary Ireland is therefore not altogether different from any other European country, and you have to travel further to the margins of the country – the islands and the isolated rural communities – to find an older version of society.

In the North, daily concerns largely echo those south of the border and across the UK, but the province's particular history has inevitably had a huge impact on the society at large. Despite younger generations' concerted efforts to bridge the religious divide, Protestant and Catholic communities are still mostly segregated from each other: tricolours and Union Jacks are a clear sign of partisanship in some neighbourhoods, but in many others the divide is invisible to all but those in the community itself. Most Northern Irish are hyperaware of the sectarian breakdown of virtually every hamlet in the province and adjust their lives accordingly.

Gay-Friendly Ireland

in 2016 there were 978 males per 1000 females in the Republic, the lowest it's been since 1981.

A gay Taoiseach (Republic of Ireland prime minister). The first country in the world to introduce marriage equality for same-sex couples by popular vote. It's been an extraordinary road for a country that only decriminalised same-sex activity in 1993 – and then only after a long and often-lonely campaign by Joycean scholar and gay-rights activist David Norris.

The rise to power of Taoiseach Leo Varadkar, who only came out five months before the country voted for marriage equality in May 2015, is a powerful example of the paradigm shift that has occurred in attitudes toward the LGBT community in Ireland: the vote in favour of same-sex marriage was 62.4% – all but one constituency voted in favour.

Varadkar is very much a product of a new Ireland, where sexual orientation is considered not quite irrelevant, but not worthy of any kind of discrimination. In this new Ireland, pride celebrations – in Dublin, Cork, Galway and elsewhere – are now firmly fixed on the festival calendar.

If the shift in attitudes is more pronounced in urban Ireland, rural Ireland doesn't lag too far behind. Which isn't to say that the inhabitants of a small rural community would necessarily be comfortable with a pride march through their village or the opening of a gay bar on the main street: for many, the new attitudes have simply evolved from an older notion that people are entitled to do as they please so long as they keep it in the private sphere, and that includes same-sex marriage.

The old trope about young gay men and women needing to move to larger urban centres in order to find greater acceptance still remains true, although the same could be said of any young person looking to express themselves beyond the narrow confines of a small community.

Multiculturalism

Ireland has long been a pretty homogenous country, but the arrival of thousands of immigrants from all over the world – 17% of the population is foreign-born – has challenged the mores of racial tolerance and integration. To a large extent it has been successful, although if you scratch beneath the surface, racial tensions can be exposed.

The tanking of the economy exacerbated these tensions and the 'Irish jobs for Irish people' opinion has been expressed with greater vehemence and authority: the rise of right-wing movements across Europe and the US has emboldened Irish ultranationalists to take a more vocal and visible stance, but their numbers remain relatively insignificant for now.

Antiracism groups have reported a rise in racist incidents, particularly Islamophobia, but the bulk of these are generally verbal and nonphysical, which perhaps also explains another statistic that says that 75% of these go unreported. In spite of this, most Muslims and people of colour living in Ireland feel that the country is safe and welcoming and that racism is not the norm with the vast majority of the white Irish population.

Polish people have overtaken UK nationals as the largest non-Irish group living in Ireland.

Religion

According to the census of 2016, about 3.7 million residents in the Republic (or 78%) call themselves Roman Catholic, followed by 2.6% Church of Ireland (Protestant), 1.3% Muslim, 1.3% Orthodox, and other religions 3.9%; 9.8% declared themselves to have no religion – a 74% rise on 2011.

In the North, the breakdown is about 48% Protestant and 45% Catholic (with 7% other or no religion). Most Irish Protestants are members of the Church of Ireland, an offshoot of the Church of England, and the Presbyterian and Methodist churches.

Catholicism remains a powerful cultural identifier, but more in a secular rather than religious way, as many Irish now reject the Church's stance on a host of social issues, from contraception to divorce and homosexuality. In part this is the natural reaction of an increasingly cosmopolitan country with an ever-broadening international outlook, but the Church's failure to satisfactorily take responsibility and atone for its role in the clerical abuse scandals of decades past has breached the bond of trust between many parishioners and their parish.

The number of respondents on the 2016 census who declared to have no religion rose by 73.6% between 2011 and 2016 – from 269,800 to 468,400.

TV & Radio

Of the country's four terrestrial TV channels, three are operated by the national broadcaster, Raidió Teilifís Éireann (RTE), the other is a privately owned commercial station. The Irish-language station TG4 shows movies and dramas, mostly *as gaeilge* (in Irish with English subtitles). The main British TV stations – BBC, ITV and Channel 4 – are also available in most Irish homes, through satellite or cable; in Northern Ireland they're the main players.

The Irish are avid radio listeners – up to 85% of the population tunes in on any given day. RTE Radio 1 (88.2FM–90FM; mostly news and discussion) is the main player, followed by two privately owned national stations (Newstalk 106FM–108FM and Today FM, found at 100FM–102FM).

The rest of the radio landscape is filled out by the 25 or so local radio stations that represent local issues and tastes and are often a great insight into the local mindset: the northwest's Highland Radio – heard in Donegal, Sligo, Tyrone and Fermanagh – is Europe's most successful local radio station, with an 84% market share. In Northern Ireland, the BBC rules supreme, with BBC Radio Ulster flying the local flag in addition to the four main BBC stations.

Top of the list for most popular baby names in Ireland – north and south – in 2016 were James and Emily.

THE IRISH WAY OF LIFE MULTICULTURALISM

Music

Ireland's literary tradition may have the critics nodding sagely, but it's the country's ability to render music to the ear that will remain with you long after your Irish day is done. There's music for every occasion and every mood, from celebration to sorrow. The Irish do popular music as well as anyone, but it is its traditional forms that make Ireland a special place to hear live music, especially in the intimate environment of a pub session.

Traditional & Folk

Irish music (known in Ireland as traditional music, or just trad) has retained a vibrancy not found in other traditional European forms, which have lost out to the overbearing influence of pop music. Although Irish music has kept many of its traditional aspects, it has itself influenced many forms of music, most notably US country and western – a fusion of Mississippi Delta blues and Irish traditional tunes that, combined with other influences like Gospel, is at the root of rock and roll.

The music was never written down, it was passed on from one player to another and so endured and evolved – regional 'styles' only developed because local musicians sought to play just like the one who seemed to play better than everybody else. The blind itinerant harpist Turlough O'Carolan (1670–1738) 'wrote' more than 200 tunes – it's difficult to know how many versions their repeated learning has spawned. This characteristic of fluidity is key to an appreciation of traditional music, and explains why it is such a resilient form today.

Nevertheless, in the 1960s composer Seán Ó Riada (1931–71) tried to impose a kind of structure on the music. His ensemble group, Ceoltóirí Chualann, were the first to reach a wider audience, and from it were born The Chieftains, arguably the most important traditional group of them all. They started recording in 1963 – any one of their nearly 40 albums are worth a listen, but you won't go wrong with their 10-album eponymous series.

The other big success of the 1960s were The Dubliners. More folksy than traditional, they made a career out of bawdy drinking songs that got everybody singing along. Other popular bands include The Fureys, comprising four brothers originally from the travelling community (no, not like the Wilburies) along with guitarist Davey Arthur. And if it's rousing renditions of Irish rebel songs you're after, you can't go past The Wolfe Tones.

Since the 1970s, various bands have tried to blend traditional with more progressive genres, with mixed success. The Bothy Band were formed in 1975 and were a kind of trad supergroup: bouzouki player Dónal Lunny, uillean piper Paddy Keenan, flute and whistle player Matt Molloy (later a member of The Chieftains), fiddler Paddy Glackin and accordion player Tony MacMahon were all superb instrumentalists and their recordings are still as electrifying today as they were four decades ago.

Top Trad-Music Venues

Hughes' Bar,
County Dublin
(p121)

Crane Bar,
County Galway
(p371)

De Barra's
Folk Club, County
Clonakilty, County
Cork (p237)

McDermott's,
Doolin, County
Clare (p350)

Leo's Tavern,
Crolly, Donegal
(p454)

Musicians tend to come together in collaborative projects. A contempor ary group worth checking out are The Gloaming, who've taken tradition- al reels and given them a contemporary sound – their eponymous debut album (2011) is sensational. A key member of the group, fiddler Caoim- hín Ó Raghallaigh, is also worth checking out in his own right; his latest album, *The Gloaming 2*, displays both his beautiful fiddle playing and his superb understanding of loops and electronic texturing.

And if you want to check out a group that melds rock, folk and tradi- tional music, you won't go far wrong with The Spook of the Thirteenth Lock, who've released a couple of albums since 2008; in 2017 they released an EP called *The Bullet in the Brick*.

And no discussion of traditional music would be complete without a mention of *Riverdance*, which made Irish dancing sexy and became a worldwide phenomenon, despite the fact that most aficionados of traditional music are seriously underwhelmed by its musical worth. Good stage show, crap music.

Popular Music

From the 1960s onward, Ireland produced its fair share of great rock musicians, including Van Morrison, Thin Lizzy, Celtic rockers Horslips, punk poppers The Undertones and Belfast's own Stiff Little Fingers (SLF), Ireland's answer to The Clash. And then there were Bob Geldof's Boomtown Rats, who didn't like Mondays or much else either.

But they all paled in comparison to the supernova that is U2, formed in 1976 in North Dublin and one of the world's most successful rock bands since the late 1980s. What else can we say about them that hasn't already been said? After 13 studio albums, 22 Grammy awards and up- wards of 170 million album sales they have nothing to prove to anyone – and not even their minor faux pas in 2014, when Apple 'gave' copies of their latest release, *Songs of Innocence*, to iTunes subscribers whether they wanted it or not, has managed to dampen their popularity. Their iNNOCENCE + eXPERIENCE tour (note the typographic ode to Apple), which ran until the end of 2015, was a massive success.

Of all the Irish acts that followed in U2's wake during the 1980s and early 1990s, a few managed to comfortably avoid being tarred with 'the next U2' burden. The Pogues' mix of punk and Irish folk kept everyone going for a while, but the real story there was the empathetic songwriting of Shane MacGowan, whose genius has been overshadowed by his chron- ic drinking – but he still managed to pen Ireland's favourite song, 'A Fairytale of New York', sung with emotional fervour by everyone around Christmas. Sinéad O'Connor thrived by acting like a U2 antidote – whatever they were into she was not – and by having a damn fine voice; the raw emotion on *The Lion and the Cobra* (1987) makes it a great offer- ing. And then there were My Bloody Valentine, the pioneers of late 1980s

MUSIC POPULAR MUSIC

Trad Playlist

The Quiet Glen (Tommy Peoples)

Paddy Keenan (Paddy Keenan)

The Chieftains 6: Bonaparte's Retreat (The Chieftains)

Old Hag You Have Killed Me (The Bothy Band)

THE NUTS & BOLTS OF TRAD MUSIC

Despite popular perception, the harp isn't widely used in traditional music (it *is* the national emblem, but that probably has more to do with the country traditionally being run by people pulling strings). The bodhrán (*bow*-rawn) goat-skin drum is much more prevalent, although it makes for a lousy symbol. The uilleann pipes, played by squeezing bellows under the elbow, provide another distinctive sound, although you're not likely to see them in a pub. The fiddle isn't unique to Ireland but it is one of the main instruments in the country's indigenous music, along with the flute, tin whistle, accordion and bouzouki (a version of the mandolin). Music fits into five main categories (jigs, reels, hornpipes, polkas and slow airs), while the old style of singing unaccompanied versions of traditional ballads and airs is called *sean-nós*.

guitar-distorted shoegazer rock: *Loveless* (1991) is one of the best Irish albums of all time.

The 1990s were largely dominated by DJs, dance music and a whole new spin on an old notion, the boy band. Behind Ireland's most successful groups (Boyzone and Westlife) is the Svengali of Saccharine, impresario Louis Walsh, whose musical sensibilities seem mired in '60s showband schmaltz. Since 2004 he has been a judge on the popular *X Factor* talent show in Britain, but still found time to unleash a series of new groups on the music scene, including identical twins Jedward – who can't sing a note, but are liked for their wacky antics – and Hometown, a six-piece boy band from all over Ireland.

The Contemporary Scene

Alternative music has never been in ruder health in Ireland – and Dublin, as the largest city in the country, is where everyone comes to make noise. The up-and-coming bands to look out for include hip-hop artists NEOMADiC and Bad Bones (with the latter also including strong elements of electronica), singer-songwriter Farah Elle and noise-pop band Thumper, whose EP *magnum opuss* has been very well received.

They all hope to join the established names on the scene, including the likes of Damien Rice, who spent much of 2017 touring his album *My Favourite Faded Fantasy*; alt-rockers Kodaline, whose second album *Coming Up For Air* (2015) cemented their position as one of the best Irish bands going (they're currently recording their third album); and Bray-born blues-influenced Hozier, whose eponymous debut album in 2015 garnered a huge amount of critical acclaim but inevitably couldn't match the global success of his 2013 single 'Take Me to Church'. Although he spends a lot of his time in New York these days, Glen Hansard (of *Once* fame) is still a major presence in Ireland, and occasionally goes on the road with his old band, The Frames.

Hugely successful Dublin trio The Script have parlayed their melodic brand of pop-rock onto all kinds of TV shows, from *90210* to *Made in Chelsea*. In 2017 they released a single called 'Another War Child', which teased fans as to the more serious content of their new album, which will follow the immensely successful *No Sound Without Silence*, released in 2014. They mightn't sell as many records, but Villagers (which is really just Conor O'Brien and a selection of collaborators) have earned universal acclaim for their brand of indie-folk rock – and in 2016 their latest album, *Darling Arithmetic*, won an Ivor Novello award.

But it's not just about musicians with grave intent: if Boyzone and Westlife were big, their success pales in comparison to that of One Direction, another product of the X Factory. We mention them here because one of their members, Niall Horan, is from Mullingar, County Westmeath, which inevitably means that when One Direction played Croke Park in 2015 it was a kind of homecoming. The band have since split, but Niall has launched a successful solo career – 2017 saw the release of his first solo single, 'This Town'.

Perhaps the most esoteric musician of all is also one of the most successful, as nobody can quite hold a candle to the phenomenon that is Enya, the best-selling solo artist in Irish history and one of the best-selling female artists in the world. The Donegal-born composer and instrumentalist was raised in Irish traditional music, but in the early 1980s she and her siblings in the group Clannad created Celtic New Age music, based around synthesizers and heavy, looping effects. Enya broke out on her own and, 75 million record sales later, she stands alone atop the New Age music pyramid – in 2015 she released *Dark Sky Island*, generally considered one of her best.

Hot Press (www.hotpress.com) is a fortnightly magazine featuring local and international music interviews and listings.

Literary Ireland

Of all their cultural expressions, it's perhaps the way the Irish speak and write that best distinguishes them. Their love of language has contributed to Ireland's legacy of world-renowned writers and storytellers. And all this in a language imposed on them by a foreign invader. The Irish responded to this act of cultural piracy by mastering a magnificent hybrid – English in every respect but flavoured and enriched by the rhythms, pronunciation patterns and grammatical peculiarities of Irish.

The Mythic Cycle

Before there was anything like modern literature there was the Ulaid (Ulster) Cycle – Ireland's version of the Homeric epic – written down from oral tradition between the 8th and 12th centuries. The chief story is the Táin Bó Cúailnge (Cattle Raid of Cooley), about a battle between Queen Maeve of Connaught and Cúchulainn, the principal hero of Irish mythology. Cúchulainn appears in the work of Irish writers right up to the present day, from Samuel Beckett to Frank McCourt.

Modern Literature

From the mythic cycle, zip forward 1000 years, past the genius of Jonathan Swift (1667–1745) and his *Gulliver's Travels;* stopping to acknowledge acclaimed dramatist Oscar Wilde (1854–1900); *Dracula* creator Bram Stoker (1847–1912) – some have claimed that the name of the count may have come from the Irish *droch fhola* (bad blood) – and the literary giant that was James Joyce (1882–1941), whose name and books elicit enormous pride in Ireland.

The majority of Joyce's literary output came when he had left Ireland for the artistic hotbed that was Paris, which was also true for another great experimenter of language and style, Samuel Beckett (1906–89). Beckett's work centres on fundamental existential questions about the human condition and the nature of self. He is probably best known for his play *Waiting for Godot,* but his unassailable reputation is based on a series of stark novels and plays.

Of the dozens of 20th-century Irish authors to have achieved published renown, some names to look out for include playwright and novelist Brendan Behan (1923–64), who wove tragedy, wit and a turbulent

Listowel Writers' Week takes place over the last weekend in May in Listowel, County Kerry, and is one of the most popular of all literary festivals – mostly because it gives readers a chance to meet their favourite writers in person.

THE GAELIC REVIVAL

While Home Rule was being debated and shunted, something of a revolution was taking place in Irish arts, literature and identity. The poet William Butler Yeats (p429) (1865–1939) and his coterie of literary friends (including Lady Gregory, Douglas Hyde, John Millington Synge and George Russell) championed the Anglo-Irish literary revival, unearthing old Celtic tales and writing with fresh enthusiasm about a romantic Ireland of epic battles and warrior queens. For a country that had suffered centuries of invasion and deprivation, these images presented a much more attractive version of history.

life into his best works including *Borstal Boy, The Quare Fellow* and *The Hostage* before dying young of alcoholism.

Belfast-born CS Lewis (1898–1963) died a year earlier, but he left us *The Chronicles of Narnia*, a series of allegorical children's stories, three of which have been made into films. Other Northern writers have, not surprisingly, featured the Troubles in their work: Bernard MacLaverty's *Cal* (also made into a film) and his more recent *The Anatomy School* are both wonderful.

The Contemporary Scene

Modern Fiction

....

Brooklyn (Colm Tóibín)

....

The Thrill of it All (Joseph O'Connor)

....

Spill Simmer Falter Wither (Sara Baume)

....

The Glorious Heresies (Lisa McInerney)

....

The Gamal (Ciarán Collins)

The Irish literary scene is flourishing, in quantity as well as (mostly) quality. Much like the digital revolution that has transformed the music scene, the proliferation of small presses and printing houses has given more authors than ever the chance to see the fruits of their labours in print, and the result has largely been very positive.

Good examples include Sara Baume's *Spill Simmer Falter Wither* (2015), a wonderful exploration of the friendship between a recluse and his one-eyed dog in a small, claustrophobic coastal community. First published by Tramp Press, it was picked up by Houghton Mifflin Harcourt, which afforded Baume a broader platform to showcase her remarkable talent. Tramp was also the first to publish *Solar Bones* (2016) by Mike McCormack, a tour de force tribute to small-town Ireland that consists of a 200-page single sentence narrated by a dead man. This audacious piece of work won the 2016 Goldsmith Prize but was ineligible for the Man Booker only because its original printing was exclusive to Ireland.

Chick Lit

Authors hate the label and publishers profess to disregard it, but chick lit is big business, and few have mastered it as well as the Irish. Doyenne of them all is Maeve Binchy (1940–2012), whose mastery of the style saw her outsell most of the literary greats – her last novel before she died was *A Week in Winter* (2012). Marian Keyes (1963–) is another author with a long line of bestsellers, including *The Woman Who Stole My Life* (2014). She's a terrific storyteller with a rare ability to tackle sensitive issues such as alcoholism and depression, issues that

---

TOP IRISH READS

Angela's Ashes (Frank McCourt; 1996) The Pulitzer Prize–winning novel tells the relentlessly bleak autobiographical story of the author's poverty-stricken Limerick childhood in the Depression of the 1930s.

Amongst Women (John McGahern; 1990) McGahern's simple, economical piece centres on a west-of-Ireland family in the social aftermath of the War of Independence.

Reading in the Dark (Seamus Deane; 1996) The Guardian Fiction Prize winner recounts a young boy's struggles to unravel the truth of his own history growing up during the Troubles of Belfast.

The Sea (John Banville; 2005) The Booker Prize–winning novel is an engrossing meditation on mortality, grief, death, childhood and memory; it was made into a film in 2013.

Strumpet City (James Plunkett; 1969) Plunkett brings Dublin to life around the time of the 1913 Lockout in what is considered to be a masterpiece of 20th-century Irish literature.

The Butcher Boy (Patrick McCabe; 1992) A brilliant, gruesome, tragicomedy about an orphaned Monaghan boy's descent into madness. It was later made into a successful film by Neil Jordan.

she herself has suffered from and is admirably honest about. Former agony aunt Cathy Kelly turns out novels at the rate of one a year: her latest book is *Between Sisters* (2017), exploring the lives of two very different sisters.

Irish Poets

Ireland's greatest modern bard was Derry-born Nobel laureate Seamus Heaney (1939–2013), whose enormous personal warmth and wry humour flows through each of his evocative works. He was, unquestionably, the successor to Yeats and one of the most important contemporary poets of the English language. After winning the Nobel Prize in 1995 he compared the ensuing attention to someone mentioning sex in front of their mammy. Opened Ground – Poems 1966–1996 (1998) is our favourite of his books.

Dubliner Paul Durcan (1944–) is one of the most reliable chroniclers of changing Dublin. He won the prestigious Whitbread Prize for Poetry in 1990 for Daddy, Daddy and is a funny, engaging, tender and savage writer. Poet, playwright and Kerryman Brendan Kennelly (1936–) is an immensely popular character around town. He lectures at Trinity College and writes a unique brand of poetry that is marked by its playfulness, as well as historical and intellectual impact. Eavan Boland (1944–) is a prolific and much-admired writer, best known for her poetry, who combines Irish politics with outspoken feminism; In a Time of Violence (1994) and The Lost Land (1998) are two of her most celebrated collections.

To find out more about poetry in Ireland in general, visit the website of the excellent Poetry Ireland (www.poetryireland.ie), which showcases the work of new and established poets. For a taste of modern Irish poetry in print, try Contemporary Irish Poetry, edited by Fallon and Mahon. A Rage for Order, edited by Frank Ormsby, is a vibrant collection of the poetry of the North.

One of the most successful Irish authors is Eoin Colfer, creator of the Artemis Fowl series, eight fantasy novels following the adventures of Artemis Fowl II as he grows from criminal antihero to saviour of the fairies.

When James Joyce – unathletic and losing his eyesight – got into drunken fights while living in Paris in the 1920s, he would often hide behind his drinking companion, the much more physically imposing Ernest Hemingway.

Irish Landscapes

Irish literature, song and painting make it pretty clear that the landscape – spread across 486km north to south and only 275km from east to west – exerts a powerful sway on the people who have lived in it. This is especially true for those who have left, for whom the aul' sod is still a land worth pining for, and for many visitors the vibrant greenness of gentle hills and the fearsome violence of jagged coasts are an integral part of experiencing Ireland.

Cliffs & Stones

Massive rocky outcrops, such as The Burren in County Clare, are for the most part inhospitable to grass, and although even there the green stuff does sprout up in enough patches for sheep and goats to graze on, these vast, other-worldly landscapes are mostly grey and bleak. Nearby, the dramatic Cliffs of Moher are a sheer drop into the thundering surf below. Similarly, there is no preparing for the extraordinary hexagonal stone columns of the Giant's Causeway in County Antrim or the rugged drop of County Donegal's Slieve League, Europe's highest sea cliffs. Sand dunes buffer many of the more gentle stretches of coast. Smaller islands dot the shores of Ireland, many of them barren rock piles supporting unique ecosystems – Skellig Michael is a breathtakingly jagged example just off the Kerry coast (and featured in the recent Star Wars films).

In 1821 the body of an Iron Age man was found in a bog in Galway with his cape, shoes and beard still intact.

The rural farms of the west coast have a rugged, hard-earned look to them, due mostly to the rock that lies so close to the surface. Much of this rock has been dug up to create tillable soil and converted into stone walls that divide tiny paddocks. The Aran Islands stand out for their spectacular networks of stone walls.

Mountains & Forests

The west of Ireland is a bulwark of cliffs, hills and mountains and is the country's most mountainous area. The highest mountains are in the southwest; the tallest mountain in Ireland is Carrantuohil (1040m) in County Kerry's Macgillycuddy's Reeks.

The Irish frequently lament the loss of their woodlands, much of which were cleared by the British (during the reign of Elizabeth I) to build ships for the Royal Navy – and the indoor panels and seating of Westminster. Little of the island's once-plentiful oak forests survive today, and much

NATIONAL NATURE RESERVES

There are 66 state-owned and 10 privately owned National Nature Reserves (NNRs) in the Republic, represented by the National Parks & Wildlife Service (www.npws.ie), which are defined as areas of importance for their special flora, fauna or geology. Northern Ireland has more than 45 NNRs which are leased or owned by the Department of the Environment. These include the Giant's Causeway and Glenariff in Antrim, and North Strangford Lough in County Down. More information is available from the Northern Ireland Environment Agency (www.ni-environment.gov.uk).

THE BOG

The boglands, which once covered one-fifth of the island, are more of a whiskey hue than green – that's the brown of heather and sphagnum moss, which cover uncut bogs. Visitors will likely encounter a bog in County Kildare's Bog of Allen or while driving through the western counties – much of the Mayo coast is covered by bog, and huge swaths also cover Donegal.

of what you'll see is the result of relatively recent planting. Instead, the countryside largely comprises green fields divided by hedgerows and stone walls. Use of this land is divided between cultivated fields and pasture for cattle and sheep.

Plants

Although Ireland is sparsely wooded, the range of surviving plant species is larger here than in many other European countries, thanks in part to the comparatively late arrival of agriculture.

There are remnants of the original oak forest in Killarney National Park and in southern Wicklow near Shillelagh. Far more common are pine plantations, which are growing steadily. Hedgerows, planted to divide fields and delineate land boundaries throughout Ireland, actually host many of the native plant species that once thrived in the oak forests – it's an intriguing example of nature adapting and reasserting itself. The Burren in County Clare is home to a remarkable mixture of Mediterranean, alpine and Arctic species.

For information on parks, gardens, monuments and inland waterways, see www.heritageireland.ie.

The bogs of Ireland are home to a unique flora adapted to wet, acidic, nutrient-poor conditions, whose survival is threatened by the depletion of bogs for energy use. Sphagnum moss is the key bog plant and is joined by other species such as bog rosemary, bog cotton, black-beaked sedge (whose spindly stem grows up to 30cm in height) and various types of heather and lichen. Carnivorous plants also thrive, such as the sundew, whose sticky tentacles trap insects, and bladderwort, whose tiny explosive bladders trap aquatic animals in bog pools.

Mammals

Apart from the fox and badger, which tend to shy away from humans and are rarely seen, the wild mammals of Ireland are mostly of the ankle-high 'critter' category, such as rabbits, hedgehogs and shrews. Hikers often spot the Irish hare, or at least glimpse the blazing-fast blur of one running away. Red deer roam the hillsides in many of the wilder parts of the country, particularly the Wicklow Mountains and in Killarney National Park, which holds the country's largest herd.

The illustrated pocket guide *Animals of Ireland* by Gordon D'Arcy is a handy, inexpensive introduction to Ireland's varied fauna.

For most visitors, the most commonly sighted mammals are those inhabiting the sea and waterways. The otter, rarely seen elsewhere in Europe, is thriving in Ireland. Seals are a common sight in rivers and along the shore, as are dolphins, which follow the warm waters of the Gulf Stream towards Ireland. Some colonise the coast of Ireland year-round, frequently swimming into the bays and inlets off the western coast.

Bird Life

Many travellers visit Ireland specifically for the birding. Ireland is a stopover for migrating birds, many of them from the Arctic, Africa and North America. Additionally, irregular winds frequently deliver exotic blowovers rarely seen in Western Europe.

In autumn the southern counties become a temporary home to the American waders (mainly sandpipers and plovers) and warblers. Migrants from Africa, such as shearwaters, petrels and auks, begin to arrive in spring in the southwestern counties.

The reasonably rare corncrake, which migrates from Africa, can be found in the western counties, in Donegal and around the Shannon Callows, and on islands such as Inishbofin in Galway. In late spring and early summer, the rugged coastlines, particularly cliff areas and islands, become a haven for breeding seabirds, mainly gannets, kittiwakes, Manx shearwaters, fulmars, cormorants and herons. Puffins, resembling penguins with their tuxedo colour scheme, nest in large colonies on coastal cliffs.

The lakes and low-lying wetlands attract large numbers of Arctic and northern European waterfowl and waders such as whooper swans, lapwings, barnacle geese, white-fronted geese and golden plovers. The important Wexford Wildfowl Reserve holds half the world's population of Greenland white-fronted geese, and little terns breed on the beach there, protected by the dunes. Also found during the winter are teals, redshanks and curlews. The main migration periods are April to May and September to October.

Irish Birds by David Cabot is a pocket guide describing birds and their habitats, which outlines the best places for serious birdwatching.

The magnificent peregrine falcon has been making something of a recovery and can be found nesting on cliffs in Wicklow and elsewhere. In 2001, 46 golden-eagle chicks from Scotland were released into Glenveagh National Park in Donegal in an effort to reintroduce the species. The project has been afflicted by adverse weather and, sadly, by unknowns poisoning and shooting of the birds, but as of 2013 it has managed to survive courtesy of two separate nests that have produced a handful of surviving chicks between them. More recent reintroductions include the white-tailed sea eagle, with a pair called Saoirse and Caimin successfully breeding a chick in 2014 – the first native-born sea eagle in 110 years. For more information (and live cam action), check out www.goldeneagle.ie.

Environmental Issues

Ireland does not rate among the world's biggest offenders when it comes to polluting the environment, but economic growth has led to an increase in industry and consumerism, which in turn generate more pollution and waste. While the population density is among Europe's lowest, the population is rising. The last 30 years have seen a massive expansion of suburban developments around all of Ireland's major towns and cities; the biggest by far is, inevitably, around Dublin, especially in the broadening commuter belt of Counties Meath and

FRACKING

Fracking, or hydraulic fracturing, is banned in both the Republic and Northern Ireland. There's been great interest in the shale-rich areas of the Northwest Ireland Carboniferous Basin, roughly covering parts of counties Leitrim, Roscommon, Sligo, Cavan, Donegal and Fermanagh, with pro-fracking groups lobbying hard for the exploitation of the area's reserves of shale gas, but a 2016 report by the Environmental Protection Agency (EPA) found that while many of the environmental problems related to the process could be overcome, not enough was known to ensure the protection of human health. Similarly, the north's environment minister Mark Durkan banned fracking until such time as there is 'sufficient and robust evidence on all environmental impacts of fracking.'

Kildare. The collapse of the construction bubble in 2008 put an end to much of this development, but the rows of semidetached houses still remain. As more people drive cars and fly in planes, Ireland grows more dependent on nonrenewable sources of energy. The amount of waste has risen substantially since the early 1990s.

Needless to say, concern for the environment is growing and the government has taken some measures to offset the damage that a thriving economy can cause. Since 2007 the Sustainable Energy Authority of Ireland (www.seai.ie) has been charged with promoting and assisting the development of renewable energy resources, including solar, wind, hydropower, geothermal and biomass resources. As it stands, the country is only tapping a fraction of these: in 2013, 7.8% of the country's energy requirements (heat, electricity and transport) were being met by renewables.

The European Renewables Directive set Ireland a target of sourcing 16% of all energy requirements by 2020, as well as the management of grid access for electricity for renewable sources, and adherence to sustainability criteria for biofuels and bioliquids. It has long been clear that Ireland won't meet those requirements, which has earned them ongoing fines.

On a more practical level, a number of recycling programs have been very successful, especially the 'plastax' – a €0.24 levy on all plastic bags used within the retail sector, which has seen their use reduced by a whopping 90%.

While this is a positive sign, it doesn't really put Ireland at the vanguard of the environmental movement. Polls seem to indicate the Irish are slightly less concerned about the environment than the citizens of most other European countries, and the country is a long way from meeting its Kyoto Protocol requirement for reduced emissions. The government isn't pushing the environmental agenda much beyond ratifying EU agreements, although it must be said that these have established fairly ambitious goals for reduced air pollution and tighter management of water quality.

Sustainable Tourism

The annual number of tourists in Ireland far exceeds the number of residents (by a ratio of about 1½ to one), so visitors can have a huge impact on the local environment. Tourism is frequently cited as potentially beneficial to the environment – that is, responsible visitor spending can help stimulate ecofriendly sectors of the economy. Ecotourism is not really burgeoning in a formalised way, although EcoTourism Ireland (www.ecotourismireland.ie) is charged with maintaining standards for ecotourism on the island and promotes tour companies that comply with these standards. The rising popularity of outdoor activities such as diving, surfing and fishing creates economic incentives for maintaining the cleanliness of Ireland's coasts and inland waters, but increased activity in these environments can be harmful if not managed carefully.

Ireland's comprehensive and efficient bus network makes it easy to avoid the use of a car, and the country is well suited to cycling and walking holidays. Many hotels, guesthouses and hostels tout green credentials, and organic ingredients are frequently promoted on restaurant menus. It's not difficult for visitors to minimise their environmental footprint while in Ireland.

IRISH LANDSCAPES SUSTAINABLE TOURISM

Look for *Reading the Irish Landscape* by Frank Mitchell and Michael Ryan for info on Ireland's geology, archaeology, urban growth, agriculture and afforestation.

Ireland's National Parks

Burren (p346)

Connemara (p385)

Glenveagh (p461)

Killarney (p258)

Wicklow Mountains (p139)

Ballycroy (p418)

Sporting Ireland

For many Irish, sport is akin to religion. For some it's all about faith through good works such as jogging, cycling and organised team sports. For everybody else, observance is enough, especially from the living-room couch or the pub stool, where the mixed fortunes of their favourite teams are followed with elevated hope and vocalised despair.

Gaelic Football & Hurling

Gaelic games are at the core of Irishness; they are enmeshed in the fabric of Irish life and hold a unique place in the heart of its culture. Their resurgence towards the end of the 19th century was entwined with the whole Gaelic revival and the march towards Irish independence. The beating heart of Gaelic sports is the Gaelic Athletic Association (www.gaa.ie), set up in 1884 'for the preservation and cultivation of National pastimes'. The GAA is still responsible for fostering these amateur games. It warms our hearts to see that after all this time – and amid the onslaught of globalisation and the general commercialisation of sport – they are still far and away the most popular sports in Ireland.

Gaelic games are fast, furious and not for the faint-hearted. Challenges are fierce, and contact between players is extremely aggressive. Both sports are county-based games. The dream of every club player is to represent their county, with the hope of perhaps playing in an All-Ireland final in September at Croke Park in Dublin, the climax of a knockout championship that is played first at a provincial and then interprovincial level.

Football

There is huge support in Ireland for the 'world game', although fans are much more enthusiastic about Manchester United, Liverpool and the two Glasgow clubs (Rangers and Celtic) than the struggling pros and part-timers who make up the National League (www.fai.ie) in the Republic and the Irish League (www.irishfa.com) in Northern Ireland. It's just too difficult for domestic teams to compete with the multi-millionaire glitz and glamour of the English Premiership, which has always drawn off the cream of Irish talent.

At an international level, the Republic and Northern Ireland field separate teams but both struggle to qualify for major tournaments.

> Every county capital has a stadium where counties play representative Gaelic football and hurling matches. The league and championship seasons run roughly from February to late September and tickets for all but the biggest matches (usually at Dublin's Croke Park) are easy to get; see www.gaa.ie for schedules.

YOU SAY SOCCER, I SAY FOOTBALL

To distinguish it from Gaelic football, you'll often hear football referred to as 'soccer' (especially in Gaelic strongholds whereby doing so implies scorn on so-called 'garrison sports'), which will allay American confusion but only irritate the Brits. But Irish fans of Association Football (the official name of the sport) will always call it football and the other, Gaelic football or, in Dublin, 'gah' – which is just the pronunciation of the letters GAA (Gaelic Athletic Association).

RULES OF GAELIC FOOTBALL & HURLING

Both Gaelic football and hurling are played by two teams of 15 players whose aim is to get the ball through what resembles a rugby goal: two long vertical posts joined by a horizontal bar, below which is a soccer-style goal, protected by a goalkeeper. Goals (below the crossbar) are worth three points, whereas a ball placed over the bar between the posts is worth one point. Scores are shown thus: 1-12, meaning one goal and 12 points, giving a total of 15 points.

Gaelic football is played with a round, soccer-size ball, and players are allowed to kick it or handpass it, like Australian Rules. Hurling, which is considered by far the more beautiful game, is played with a flat stick or bat known as a hurley or *camán*. The small leather ball, called a *slíothar*, is hit or carried on the hurley; handpassing is also allowed. Both games are played over 70 action-filled minutes.

It's all a far cry from their respective moments of glory – the 1980s for Northern Ireland and 1988 to 2002 for the Republic.

In order to avoid competing (and losing) with the more popular English Premier League, whose season runs from mid-August to mid-May, the League of Ireland runs its season from April to November, the only European league to do so. Northern Ireland's Irish League still follows the British winter timetable.

Rugby

Although traditionally the preserve of Ireland's middle classes, rugby captures the mood of the whole island in February and March during the annual Six Nations Championships, because the Irish team is drawn from both sides of the border and is supported by both nationalists and unionists. In recognition of this, the Irish national anthem is no longer played at internationals, and is replaced by the thoroughly inoffensive *Ireland's Call*, a song written especially for the purpose.

At a provincial level, Leinster and Munster are major players on the European stage, having won the Heineken Cup (renamed the European Champions Cup in 2014) three times and twice respectively; Ulster are just a step behind with one win.

Golf

Scotland may be the home of golf, but Ireland is where golf goes on holiday.

With over 400 courses to choose from, there's no shortage of choice when it comes to teeing it up. These include a host of parkland (or inland) courses; worth checking out are the wonderful, American-style resort courses built over the last couple of decades, with immaculate, lawn-like fairways, white-sand bunkers and strategically placed water features ready to swallow the chunkily hit ball.

But the essence of Irish golf is to be found on seaside links, dotted in a spectacular string of scenery along virtually the entire coastline. Here, nature provides the perfect raw material, and the very best of them are not quite built into the landscape as found within it, much like Michelangelo 'found' his figures hiding in the blocks of marble.

Finally, a word about the Irish golfer. Clubhouse snobs and high-handicap etiquette junkies aside, the real Irish golfer is the man or woman who puts their shoes on in the car park and can't wait to tee it up on the first; they know all the safe spots to land the ball and see it as their duty to share local knowledge. If you land up in the club on your own and they're doing a little putting practice before heading out, they're the ones that will offer a twosome because it's just not

> Most counties are good at one Gaelic sport and not the other. Kilkenny, Waterford, Clare and Tipperary are traditionally hurling counties; Kerry, Meath, Mayo and all nine Ulster counties are better at football. Cork, Galway, Offaly, Wexford and Dublin have the privilege of being good at both sports.

right to play on your own. The Irish golfer is friendly, easygoing and always recognises that you will never win at golf, and that today's bad round is just for today and tomorrow will turn up something different. And they know that golf is played over 19 holes – sure what's the point of playing unless you can laugh about it all over a drink when the round is done?

Horse Racing & Greyhound Racing

A passion for horse racing is deeply entrenched in Irish life and comes without the snobbery of its English counterpart. If you fancy a flutter on the gee-gees you can watch racing from around Ireland and England on the TV in bookmakers shops every day. No money ever seems to change hands in the betting, however, and every Irish punter will tell you they 'broke even'.

Ireland has a reputation for producing world-class horses for racing and other equestrian events such as showjumping, also very popular albeit in a much less egalitarian kind of way. Major annual races include the Irish Grand National (Fairyhouse, April), Irish Derby (the Curragh, June) and Irish Leger (the Curragh, September). For more information on events, contact Horse Racing Ireland (www.hri.ie).

Traditionally the poor-man's punt, greyhound racing ('the dogs'), has been smartened up in recent years and partly turned into a corporate outing. It offers a cheaper, more accessible and more local alternative to horse racing. There are 20-odd tracks across the country, administered by the Irish Greyhound Board (www.igb.ie).

Irish academic Dr Fintan Lane's book *Long Bullets: A History of Road Bowling in Ireland* traces the sport to the 17th century.

Road Bowling

The object of this sport is to throw a cast-iron ball weighing approximately 800g along a public road (normally one with little traffic) for a designated distance, usually 1km or 2km, with speed, control and accuracy. The person who does it in the least number of throws is the winner. Participants traditionally bet during the game.

The ball is known as a bowl or bullet. A shot is a throw and a kitter-paw is a left-handed thrower. If you hear someone talking about their butt, they are referring to the throwing mark on the road. Breaking butt means someone has stepped over the mark before releasing the ball. *Faugh an Bheallach* is a traditional Irish battle cry and means you should get out of the way. A sop is a tuft of grass placed where the bowl should first strike the road and a score is a match.

The main centre for road bowling is Cork, which has 200 clubs, and, to a lesser extent, Armagh. Competitions take place throughout the year, attracting considerable crowds. The sport has been taken up in various countries around the world, including the US, the UK, Germany and the Netherlands, and a world championship competition has been set up (see www.irishroadbowling.ie). In Ireland the sport is governed by the Irish Road Bowling Association.

Survival Guide

Directory A–Z

Accommodation

From basic hostels to five-star hotels, you'll find every range of accommodation in Ireland. Advance bookings are generally recommended and an absolute necessity during the busy holiday period.

Hotels From chain hotels with comfortable digs to Norman castles with rainfall shower rooms and wi-fi – with prices to match.

B&Bs From a bedroom in a private home to a luxurious Georgian townhouse, the ubiquitous B&B is the bedrock of Irish accommodation.

Hostels Every major town and city has a selection of hostels, with clean dorms and wi-fi – some have laundry and kitchen facilities.

Booking Services

Daft.ie (www.daft.ie) Online classified paper for short- and long-term rentals.

Elegant Ireland (www.elegant. ie) Specialises in self-catering

castles, period houses and unique properties.

Imagine Ireland (www. imagineireland.com) Modern cottage rentals throughout the whole island, including Northern Ireland.

Irish Landmark Trust (www. irishlandmark.com) Not-for-profit conservation group that rents self-catering properties of historical and cultural significance, such as castles, tower houses, gate lodges, schoolhouses and lighthouses.

Lonely Planet (www.lonely planet.com/Ireland/hotels) Recommendations and bookings.

Stay in Ireland (www.stayinire land.com) Lists guesthouses and self-catering options.

B&Bs & Guesthouses

Bed and breakfasts are small, family-run houses, farmhouses and period country houses with fewer than five bedrooms. Standards vary enormously, but most have some bedrooms with private bathroom at a cost of roughly €40 to €60 (£35 to £50) per person per night. In luxurious B&Bs, expect to

pay €70 (£60) or more per person. Off-season rates – usually October through to March – are midweek prices.

Guesthouses are like up-market B&Bs, but bigger – the Irish equivalent of a boutique hotel. Facilities are usually better and sometimes include a restaurant.

Other tips:

➡ Facilities in B&Bs range from basic (bed, bathroom, kettle, TV) to beatific (whirlpool baths, rainforest showers) as you go up in price. Wi-fi is standard and most have parking (but check).

➡ Most B&Bs take credit cards, but the occasional rural one might not have facilities; check when you book.

➡ Advance reservations are strongly recommended, especially in peak season (June to September).

➡ Some B&Bs and guesthouses in more remote regions only operate from Easter to September or other months.

➡ If full, B&B owners may recommend another house in the area (possibly a private house taking occasional guests, not in tourist listings).

➡ To make prices more competitive at some B&Bs, breakfast may be optional.

BOOK YOUR STAY ONLINE

For more Ireland reviews by Lonely Planet authors, check out http://lonelyplanet.com/ireland/hotels/. You'll find independent reviews, as well as recommendations on the best places to stay. Best of all, you can book online.

SLEEPING PRICE RANGES

Accommodation prices vary according to demand – or have different rates for online, phone or walk-in bookings. B&B rates are more consistent, but virtually every other accommodation will charge wildly different rates depending on the time of year, day, festival schedule and even your ability to do a little negotiating. The following price ranges are based on a double room with private bathroom in high season.

BUDGET	REPUBLIC	DUBLIN	NORTHERN IRELAND
€/£	less than €80	under €150	less than £50
€€/££	€80–€180	€150–€250	£50–£120
€€€/£££	more than €180	over €250	more than £120

Camping, Caravanning & Canal Boats

Camping and caravan parks aren't as common in Ireland as they are elsewhere in Europe. Some hostels have camping space for tents and also offer house facilities, which makes them better value than the main camping grounds. At commercial parks the cost is typically somewhere between €15 and €25 (£12 to £20) for a tent and two people. Prices given for campsites are for two people unless stated otherwise. Caravan sites cost around €20 to €30 (£17 to £25). Most parks are open from Easter to the end of September or October.

An alternative to normal caravanning is to hire a horse-drawn caravan with which to wander the countryside. In high season you can hire one for around €850 a week. Search Fáilte Ireland's www.discoverireland.ie for a list of operators, or see www.irish horsedrawncaravans.com.

Another unhurried and pleasurable way to see the countryside (with slightly less maintenance) is by barge on one of the country's canal systems. Contact Fáilte Ireland for a list of rental companies.

Yet another option is to hire a boat, which you can live aboard while cruising Ireland's inland waterways. One company offering boats for hire on the Shannon-Erne Waterway is **Emerald Star** (☑071-962

7633; www.emeraldstar.ie; per week from €1100).

Hostels

Prices quoted for hostel accommodation apply to those aged over 18. A high-season dorm bed generally costs €12 to €25 (£10 to £18). Many hostels now have family and double rooms.

Relevant hostel associations:

An Óige (www.anoige.ie) HI–associated national organisation with 26 hostels scattered around the Republic.

HINI (www.hini.org.uk) HI-associated organisation with five hostels in Northern Ireland.

Independent Holiday Hostels of Ireland (www.hostels-ireland.com) Fifty-five tourist-board-approved hostels throughout all of Ireland.

Independent Hostel Owners of Ireland (www.independent hostelsireland.com) Independent hostelling association.

Hotels

Hotels range from the local pub to medieval castles. Booking online or negotiating directly will almost always net you a better rate than the published one, especially out of season or midweek (except for business hotels, which offer cheaper weekend rates).

The bulk of the country's hotels are of the midrange variety, with clean rooms and a range of facilities, from restaurants to gyms. The recent trend toward soffering free wi-fi is stubbornly resisted by

many, who still charge for the privilege.

House Swapping

House swapping can be a popular and affordable way to visit a country and enjoy a real home away from home. There are several agencies in Ireland that, for an annual fee, facilitate international swaps. The fee pays for access to a website and a book giving house descriptions, photographs and the owner's details. After that, it's up to you to make arrangements. Use of the family car is sometimes included.

Homelink International House Exchange (www.homelink.ie) Home exchange service running for over 60 years.

Intervac International Holiday Service (www.intervac-home exchange.com) Long-established, with agents in 45 nations worldwide.

Rental Accommodation

Self-catering accommodation is often rented on a weekly basis and usually means an apartment, house or cottage where you look after yourself. The rates vary from one region and season to another. **Fáilte Ireland** (☑Republic 1850 230 330, the UK 0800 039 7000; www.discoverireland.ie) publishes a guide for registered self-catering accommodation; you can check listings at its website.

Climate

Belfast

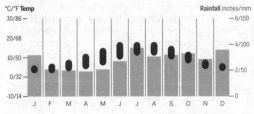

Dublin

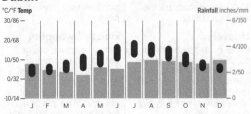

Galway

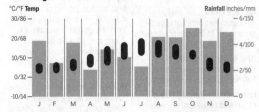

Children

Ireland loves kids. Everywhere you go you'll find locals to be enthusiastic and inquisitive about your beloved progeny. However, this admiration hasn't always translated into child services such as widespread and accessible baby-changing facilities, or high chairs in restaurants – especially in smaller towns and rural areas.

Although there are legal restrictions on children in pubs, restaurants technically should allow kids of all ages at all times. But in practice, many restaurants (especially in the higher bracket, but not exclusively so) would prefer if you left the kids at home, especially at busy times, when high chairs are suddenly unavailable: if you're booking ahead, be sure to specify if you need one.

When it comes to activities for the whole family, Ireland is much better placed than it was even a decade ago, as many providers recognise the important of catering to the whole family. Most activity centres offer kids' programs for all ages; many museums have kid-friendly exhibits and some even cater guided tours to suit younger ages.

Lonely Planet's *Travel with Children* has lots of useful information.

For further general information check out the following:

Lonely Planet (www.lonely planet.com/family-holidays) Useful and extensive resource on travelling with children.

eumom (www.eumom.ie) For pregnant women and parents with young children.

BabyGoes2 (www.babygoes2. com) Travel site with family-friendly accommodation worldwide.

Practicalities

Baby-changing facilities Only in larger cities, and then only in large shopping centres.

Babysitting agencies Only found in larger cities and in some of the more established, upmarket hotels; expect to pay between €12 and €20 per hour plus transport costs.

Car seats (around €50/£35 per week) Mandatory in rental cars for children aged nine months to four years.

Pubs Unaccompanied minors are not allowed in pubs; accompanied children can remain until 9pm (10pm May to September).

Transport Children under five travel free on all public transport.

Customs Regulations

Both the Republic of Ireland and Northern Ireland have a two-tier customs system: one for goods bought duty-free outside the EU, the other for goods bought in another EU country where tax and duty is paid. There is technically no limit to the amount of goods transportable within the EU, but customs will use certain guidelines to distinguish personal use from commercial purpose. Allowances are as follows:

Duty-free For duty-free goods from outside the EU, limits include 200 cigarettes, 1L of spirits or 2L of wine, 60ml of perfume and 250ml of eau de toilette.

Tax and duty paid Amounts that officially constitute personal use include 3200 cigarettes (or 400 cigarillos, 200 cigars or 3kg of tobacco) and either 10L of spirits, 20L of fortified wine, 60L of sparkling wine, 90L of still wine or 110L of beer.

Electricity

**Type G
230V/50Hz**

Embassies & Consulates

Following is a selection of embassies in Dublin and consular offices in Belfast. For a complete list, see the website of the Department of Foreign Affairs (www.dfa.ie), which also lists Ireland's diplomatic missions overseas.

Australian Embassy (☏01-664 5300; www.ireland.embassy. gov.au; Fitzwilton House, 7th fl, Wilton Tce, Dublin 2;

☏8.30am-4.30pm Mon-Fri; ☐37 from city centre)

Canadian Embassy (☏01-234 4000; www.canada.ie; 7-8 Wilton Tce, Dublin 2; ☏9am-1pm & 2-4.30pm; ☐37 from city centre)

Dutch Embassy (☏01-269 3444; www.netherlandsandyou. nl/your-country-and-the-nether lands/ireland; 160 Merrion Rd, Ballsbridge, Dublin 4; ☏8.30am-12.30pm & 1.45-4pm Mon-Fri; ☐4, 7, 8 from city centre)

Dutch **Consulate** (☏028-9077 9088; 14-16 West Bank Rd, c/o All-Route Shipping Ltd; ☏9am-1pm & 2-4.30pm Mon-Fri; ☐Mount Vernon House) in Belfast

French Embassy (☏01-277 5000; www.ambafrance-ie.org; 66 Fitzwilliam Lane, Dublin 2; ☏9-10am & noon-4pm Mon-Fri; ☐46A from city centre)

German Embassy (☏01-269 3011; www.dublin.diplo.de; 31 Trimleston Ave, Booterstown, Blackrock, Co Dublin; ☏8am-5pm Mon-Thu, to 2pm Fri, consular service 9am-noon Mon, Tue & Fri, 8.30-11.30am & 2-4pm Wed; ☒Booterstown)

Italian Embassy (☏01-660 1744; www.ambdublino.es-teri.it/Ambasciata_Dublino; 63-65 Northumberland Rd, Ballsbridge, Dublin 4; ☏10am-12.40pm Mon, Wed & Fri, 1.20-3.40pm Tue & Thu; ☐4, 7, 63, 84 from city centre)

UK Embassy (☏01-205 3700; www.gov.uk; 29 Merrion Rd, Ballsbridge, Dublin 4; ☏9am-5pm Mon-Fri; ☐4, 7, 8 from city centre)

US Embassy (☏01-630 6200; http://ie.usembassy.gov/ embassy; 42 Elgin Rd, Balls-bridge, Dublin; ☐4, 7, 8 from city centre)

US **Consulate** (☏028-9038 6100; https://uk.usem-bassy.gov/embassy-consulates/belfast; Danesfort House, 223 Stranmillis Rd; ☏8.30am-5pm Mon-Fri; ☐Broomhill Pk) in Belfast

Food

Booking ahead is recommended in cities and larger towns; same-day reservations are usually fine except for top-end restaurants – book those two weeks in advance.

Restaurants From cheap cafes to Michelin-starred feasts, covering every imaginable cuisine.

Cafes Open during the daytime (rarely at night), cafes are good for all-day breakfasts, sandwiches and basic dishes.

Pubs Pub grub ranges from toasted sandwiches to carefully crafted dishes as good as any you'll find in a restaurant.

Hotels All hotel restaurants accept nonguests. They're a popular option in rural Ireland.

Health

No jabs are required to travel to Ireland.

Excellent health care is readily available. For minor, self-limiting illnesses, pharmacists can give valuable advice and sell over-the-counter medication. They can also advise when more specialised help is required and point you in the right direction.

EU citizens equipped with a European Health Insurance Card (EHIC), available from health centres or, in the UK, post offices, will be covered

EATING PRICE RANGES

The following price ranges refer to the cost of a main course at dinner.

BUDGET	REPUBLIC	DUBLIN	NORTHERN IRELAND
€	less than €12	less than €15	less than £12
€€	€12–€25	€15–€28	£12–£20
€€€	more than €25	more than €28	more than £20

for most medical care – but not nonemergencies or emergency repatriation. While other countries, such as Australia, also have reciprocal agreements with Ireland and Britain, many do not.

In Northern Ireland, everyone receives free emergency treatment at accident and emergency (A&E) departments of state-run NHS hospitals, irrespective of nationality.

Insurance

Comprehensive travel insurance to cover theft, loss and medical problems is highly recommended. Worldwide travel insurance is available at www.lonelyplanet.com/travel-insurance. You can buy, extend and claim online anytime – even if you're already on the road.

Internet Access

Wi-fi and 3G/4G networks are making internet cafes largely redundant (except to gamers); the few that are left will charge around €6 per hour. Most accommodations have wi-fi service, either free or for a daily charge (up to €10 per day).

Legal Matters

Illegal drugs are widely available, especially in clubs. The possession of small quantities of marijuana attracts a fine or warning, but harder drugs are treated more seriously. Public drunkenness is illegal but commonplace – the police will usually ignore it unless you're causing trouble. Should you find yourself under arrest, you have the right to remain silent and contact either an attorney or your embassy.

Once you are charged and cautioned you will either be released on bail (known as 'station bail') or, in the event of a more serious offence, transferred from the police station to the District Court as early as possible (usually within 12 hours), where you will either be bailed or remanded in custody by the judge.

Contact the following for assistance:

Legal Aid Board (☑066-947 1000; www.legalaidboard. ie) Has a network of local law centres.

Legal Services Agency Northern Ireland (☑028-9076 3000; www.justice-ni.gov.uk/topics/legal-aid) Administers the statutory legal-aid scheme for Northern Ireland, but cannot offer legal advice.

LGBTQ Travellers

Ireland is a pretty tolerant place for gays and lesbians. Bigger cities such as Dublin, Galway and Cork have well-established gay scenes, as do Belfast and Derry in Northern Ireland. In 2015 Ireland overwhelmingly backed same-sex marriage in a historic referendum, whereas Northern Ireland is the only part of the United Kingdom where it's not legal.

While the cities and main towns tend to be progressive and tolerant, you'll still find pockets of homophobia throughout the island, particularly in smaller towns and rural areas. Resources include the following:

Gaire (www.gaire.com) Message board and info for a host of gay-related issues.

Gay & Lesbian Youth Northern Ireland (www.cara-friend.org.uk/projects/glyni) Voluntary counseling, information, health and social-space organisation for the gay community.

Gay Men's Health Project (☑01-660 2189; http://hse.ie/go/GMHS) Practical advice on men's health issues.

National Lesbian & Gay Federation (NLGF;☑01-671 9076; http://nxf.ie) Publishes the monthly Gay Community News (www.gcn.ie).

Northern Ireland Gay Rights Association (☑0771-957 6524; www.nigra.co.uk; Belfast LGBT Centre, 23-31 Waring St) Represents the rights and interests of the LGBTQ community in Northern Ireland. It offers phone and online support, but is not a call-in centre.

Outhouse (☑01-873 4932; www.outhouse.ie; 105 Capel St; ☐all city centre) Top gay, lesbian and bisexual resource centre. Great stop-off point to see what's on, check noticeboards and meet people. It publishes the free Ireland's Pink Pages, a directory of gay-centric services, which is also accessible on the website.

PRACTICALITIES

Newspapers Irish Independent (www.independent.ie), Irish Times (www.irishtimes.com), Irish Examiner (www.examiner.ie), Belfast Telegraph (www.belfasttelegraph.co.uk).

Radio RTE Radio 1 (88MHz–90MHz), Today FM (100MHz–103MHz), Newstalk 106-108 (106MHz–108MHz), BBC Ulster (92MHz–95MHz; Northern Ireland only).

Smoking It is illegal to smoke indoors everywhere except private residences and prisons.

Weights & Measures The metric system is used; the exception is for liquid measures of alcohol, where pints are used

Money

The Republic of Ireland uses the euro (€), while Northern Ireland uses the pound sterling (£), although the euro is also accepted in many places.

The best exchange rates are at banks, although bureaux de change and other exchange facilities usually open for more hours.

ATMs

Most banks have ATMs that are linked to international money systems such as Cirrus, Maestro or Plus. Each transaction incurs a currency-conversion fee, and credit cards can incur immediate and exorbitant cash-advance interest-rate charges. Watch out for ATMs that have been tampered with; card-reader scams ('skimming') have become a real problem.

Credit & Debit Cards

Visa and MasterCard credit and debit cards are widely accepted; American Express is only accepted by the major chains, and virtually no one will accept Diners or JCB. Chip-and-PIN is the norm for card transactions – only a few places will accept a signature.

Smaller businesses, such as pubs and some B&Bs, prefer debit cards (and will charge a fee for credit cards), and a small number of rural B&Bs only take cash.

Taxes & Refunds

Most goods come with value added tax (VAT) of 21% (20% in Northern Ireland), which non-EU residents can claim back so long as the store in which the goods are purchased operates either the Cashback or Taxback refund program (the Tax-Free Shopping refund scheme in Northern Ireland), usually indicated by a display sticker on the window.

To claim the VAT, you must fill in the voucher that comes with your purchase, which must be stamped at the *last point of exit* from the EU. If you're travelling on to Britain or mainland Europe from Ireland, hold on to your voucher until you pass through your final customs stop in the EU; it can then be stamped and you can post it back for a refund of duty paid.

Goods such as books, children's clothing and educational items are excluded from VAT.

Tipping

Hotels €1/£1 per bag is standard; tip cleaning staff at your discretion.

Pubs Not expected unless table service is provided, then €1/£1 for a round of drinks.

Restaurants For decent service 10%; up to 15% in more expensive places.

Taxis Tip 10% or round up fare to nearest euro/pound.

Toilet Attendants Loose change; no more than €0.50/50p.

Opening Hours

Banks 10am–4pm Monday to Friday (to 5pm Thursday)

Pubs 10.30am–11.30pm Monday to Thursday, 10.30am to 12.30am Friday and Saturday, noon to 11pm Sunday (30 minutes 'drinking up' time allowed); closed Christmas Day and Good Friday

Restaurants Noon–10.30pm; many close one day of the week

Shops 9.30am–6pm Monday to Saturday (to 8pm Thursday in cities), noon to 6pm Sunday

Photography

➡ Natural light can be very dull, so use higher ISO speeds than usual, such as 400 for daylight shots.

➡ In Northern Ireland, get permission before taking photos of fortified police stations, army posts or other military or quasi-military paraphernalia.

➡ Don't take photos of people in Protestant or Catholic strongholds of West Belfast without permission; always ask and be prepared to accept a refusal.

➡ Lonely Planet's *Guide to Travel Photography* is full of helpful tips for photography while on the road.

Public Holidays

Public holidays can cause road chaos as everyone tries to get somewhere else for the break. It's wise to book accommodation in advance for these times.

The following are public holidays in both the Republic and Northern Ireland:

New Year's Day 1 January

St Patrick's Day 17 March

Easter (Good Friday to Easter Monday inclusive) March/April

May Holiday 1st Monday in May

Christmas Day 25 December

St Stephen's Day (Boxing Day) 26 December

St Patrick's Day and St Stephen's Day holidays are taken on the following Monday when they fall on a weekend. In the Republic, nearly everywhere closes on Good Friday even though it isn't an official public holiday. In the North, most shops open on Good Friday, but close the following Tuesday.

Northern Ireland

Spring Bank Holiday Last Monday in May

Orangemen's Day 12 July

August Holiday Last Monday in August

Republic of Ireland

June Holiday 1st Monday in June

August Holiday 1st Monday in August

October Holiday Last Monday in October

Safe Travel

Ireland is safer than most countries in Europe, but normal precautions should be observed.

➡ Don't leave anything visible in your car when you park.

➡ Skimming at ATMs is an ongoing problem; be sure to cover the keypad with your hand when you input your PIN.

➡ In Northern Ireland, exercise extra care in 'interface' areas where sectarian neighbourhoods adjoin.

➡ Best avoid Northern Ireland during the climax of the Orange marching season on 12 July: sectarian passions are usually inflamed and even many Northerners leave the province at this time.

Telephone

When calling Ireland from abroad, dial your international access code, followed by ☎353 and the area code (dropping the ☎0). Area codes in the Republic have three digits, eg ☎021 for Cork, ☎091 for Galway and ☎061 for Limerick. The only exception is Dublin, which has a two-digit code (☎01).

To make international calls from Ireland, first dial ☎00, then the country code, followed by the local area code and number. Always use the area code if calling from a mobile phone, but you don't need it if calling from a fixed-line number within the area code.

In Northern Ireland, the area code for all fixed-line numbers is ☎028, but you only need to use it if calling from a mobile phone or from outside Northern Ireland. To call Northern Ireland from the Republic, use ☎048 instead of ☎028, without the international dialling code.

USEFUL CALLING CODES

	REPUBLIC	NORTHERN IRELAND
Country Code	☎+353	☎+44
International Access Code	☎00	☎00
Directory Enquiries	☎11811/11850	☎118 118/118 192
International Directory Enquiries	☎11818	

Mobile Phones

All European and Australasian phones work in Ireland and Northern Ireland; some North American (non-GSM) phones don't. Check with your provider. Prepaid SIM cards cost from €10.

➡ Both the Republic and Northern Ireland use the GSM 900/1800 cellular phone system, which is compatible with European and Australian, but not North American or Japanese, phones.

➡ SMS ('texting') is a national obsession – most people under 30 communicate mostly by text.

➡ Pay-as-you-go mobile-phone packages with any of the main providers start at around €40 and usually include a basic handset and credit of around €10.

➡ SIM-only packages are also available, but make sure your phone is compatible with the local provider.

Time

In winter Ireland is on Greenwich Mean Time (GMT), also known as Universal Time Coordinated (UTC), the same as Britain. In summer the clock shifts to GMT plus one hour, so when it's noon in Dublin and London, it's 4am in Los Angeles and Vancouver, 7am in New York and Toronto, 1pm in Paris, 7pm in Singapore and 9pm in Sydney.

Tourist Information

In both the Republic and the North there's a tourist office or information point in almost every big town; most can offer a variety of services, including accommodation and attraction reservations, currency-changing services, map and guidebook sales, and free publications.

In the Republic, the tourism purview falls to **Fáilte Ireland** (☎Republic 1850 230 330, the UK 0800 039 7000; www.discoverireland. ie); in Northern Ireland, it's **Discover Northern Ireland** (☎head office 028-9023 1221; www.discovernorthernireland. com). Outside Ireland, both organisations unite under the banner Tourism Ireland (www.tourismireland.com).

Travellers with Disabilities

All new buildings have wheelchair access, and many hotels (especially urban ones that are part of chains) have installed lifts, ramps and other facilities such as hearing loops. Others, particularly B&Bs, have not invested in making their properties accessible.

Public Transport

In big cities, most buses have low-floor access and priority spaces on board, but only 63% of the Bus Éireann coach fleet that operates on Commuter and Expressway services is wheelchair-accessible. Note, too, that many of its rural stops are not accessible.

Trains are accessible with help. Call ☎1850 366 222 (outside Republic of Ireland ☎+353 1 836 6222) or email access@irishrail.ie 24 hours in advance to arrange assistance with boarding, alighting and transferring at intermediate stations. Note that there is a limited number of wheelchair-accessible spaces on each train. Newer trains have audio and visual information systems for visually impaired and hearing-impaired passengers. Assistance dogs may travel without restriction. A full list of station facilities as at 2015 can be downloaded from www.irishrail.ie/travel-information/disabled-access.

Resources

➡ For an informative article with links to accessibility information for getting there and away, getting around and tourist attractions, visit www.ireland.com/en-us/accommodation/articles/accessibility/.

➡ Three review sites worth checking out – covering accommodation, eating and drinking, and places of interest – are https://mobilitymojo.com/, whose searchable database is expanding outside its base of Dublin and Galway; http://www.trip-ability.com/, which is expected to soon feature a booking facility; and www.accessibleireland.com/, which also hosts short introductions to public transport.

➡ Download Lonely Planet's free Accessible Travel guides from http://lptravel.to/AccessibleTravel.

➡ The **Citizens' Information Board** (☎0761 079 000; www.citizensinformationboard.ie) in the Republic and **Disability Action** (☎028-9029 7880; www.disabilityaction.org) in Northern Ireland can give some advice to travellers with disabilities.

Visas

If you're a European Economic Area (EEA) national, you don't need a visa to visit (or work in) either the Republic or Northern Ireland. Citizens of Australia, Canada, New Zealand, South Africa and the US can visit the Republic for up to three months, and Northern Ireland for up to six months. They are not allowed to work unless sponsored by an employer.

Full visa requirements for visiting the Republic are available online at www.dfa.ie; for Northern Ireland's visa requirements see www.gov.uk/government/organisations/uk-visas-and-immigration.

To stay longer in the Republic, contact the local *garda* (police) station or the **Garda National Immigration Bureau** (☎01-666 9100; www.garda.ie; 13-14 Burgh Quay, Dublin; ⊗8am-9pm Mon-Fri; 🚇all city centre). To stay longer in Northern Ireland, contact the Home Office (www.gov.uk/government/organisations/uk-visas-and-immigration).

Women Travellers

Ireland should pose no problems for women travellers. Finding contraception is not the problem it once was, although anyone on the pill should bring adequate supplies.

Rape Crisis Network Ireland (☎091-563 676; www.rcni.ie) In the Republic. App available.

Work

EEA citizens are entitled to work legally in the Republic of Ireland and Northern Ireland. Non-EEA citizens with an Irish parent or grandparent are eligible for dual citizenship (and the right to work), although this procedure can be quite lengthy – enquire at an Irish embassy or consulate in your own country.

Full-time US students aged 18 and over can get a four-month work permit for Ireland, plus insurance and support information, through **Work & Travel Ireland** (☎01-602 1788; www.workandtravelireland.org).

Most Commonwealth citizens with a UK-born parent are entitled to work in the North (and the rest of the UK) through the 'Right of Abode'. Most Commonwealth citizens under 31 are eligible for a Working Holidaymaker Visa: valid for two years, it allows you to work for a total of 12 months and must be obtained in advance. Check with the UK Border Agency (www.gov.uk/government/organisations/uk-visas-and-immigration) for more info.

Transport

GETTING THERE & AWAY

Entering the Country

Dublin is the primary point of entry for most visitors to Ireland, although some do choose Shannon or Belfast.

➡ The overwhelming majority of airlines fly into Dublin.

➡ For travel to the US, Dublin and Shannon airports operate preclearance facilities, which means you pass through US immigration *before* boarding your aircraft.

➡ Dublin is home to two seaports that serve as the main points of sea transport with Britain; ferries from France arrive in the southern ports of Rosslare and Cork.

➡ Dublin is the nation's rail hub.

Air

Airports

Ireland's main airports:

Cork Airport (☏021-431 3131; www.corkairport.com) Airlines servicing the airport include Aer Lingus and Ryanair.

Dublin Airport (Map p96;☏01-814 1111; www.dublin airport.com) Ireland's major international gateway airport, with direct flights from the UK, Europe, North America and the Middle East.

Shannon Airport (SNN;☏061-712 000; www.shannonairport.ie; ☏) Has a few direct flights from the UK, Europe and North America.

Northern Ireland's main airport:

Belfast International Airport (Aldergrove;☏028-9448 4848; www.belfastairport.com; Airport Rd) Has direct flights from the UK, Europe and North America.

Land

Eurolines (www.eurolines.com) has a daily coach and ferry service from London's Victoria Station to Dublin Busáras.

Sea

The main ferry routes between Ireland and the UK and mainland Europe:

➡ Belfast to Liverpool (England; eight hours)

➡ Belfast to Cairnryan (Scotland; 1¾ hours)

➡ Cork to Roscoff (France; 14 hours; April to October only)

➡ Dublin to Liverpool (England; fast four hours, slow 8½ hours)

➡ Dublin and Dun Laoghaire to Holyhead (Wales; fast two hours, slow 3½ hours)

➡ Larne to Cairnryan (Scotland; two hours)

CLIMATE CHANGE & TRAVEL

Every form of transport that relies on carbon-based fuel generates CO_2, the main cause of human-induced climate change. Modern travel is dependent on airplanes, which might use less fuel per kilometre per person than most cars but travel much greater distances. The altitude at which aircraft emit gases (including CO_2) and particles also contributes to their climate change impact. Many websites offer 'carbon calculators' that allow people to estimate the carbon emissions generated by their journey and, for those who wish to do so, to offset the impact of the greenhouse gases emitted with contributions to portfolios of climate-friendly initiatives throughout the world. Lonely Planet offsets the carbon footprint of all staff and author travel.

Ferry & Fast Boat Routes

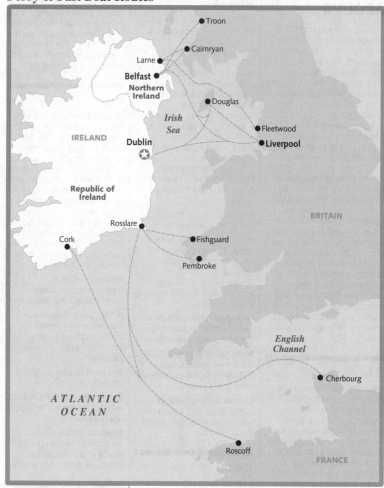

➡ Larne to Troon (Scotland; two hours; March to October only)

➡ Larne to Fleetwood (England; six hours)

➡ Rosslare to Cherbourg/ Roscoff (France; 18/20½ hours)

➡ Rosslare to Fishguard and Pembroke (Wales; 3½ hours). Competition from budget airlines has forced ferry operators to discount heavily and offer flexible fares.

A useful website is www. aferry.co.uk, which covers all sea-ferry routes and operators to Ireland.

Main operators include the following:

Brittany Ferries (www.brittany ferries.com) Cork to Roscoff; April to October.

Irish Ferries (www.irishferries. com) It has Dublin to Holyhead ferries (up to four per day year-round); and France to Rosslare (three times per week).

P&O Ferries (www.poferries. com) Daily sailings year-round from Dublin to Liverpool, and Larne to Cairnryan. Larne to Troon runs March to October only.

Stena Line (www.stenaline. com) Daily sailings from Holyhead to Dublin Port, from Belfast to Liverpool and Cairn-ryan, and from Rosslare to Fishguard.

GETTING AROUND

The big decision in getting around Ireland is whether to go by car or use public transport. Your own car will make the best use of your time and help you reach even the most remote of places. It's usually easy to get very cheap rentals – €10 per day or less is common – and if two or more are travelling together, the fee for rental and petrol can be cheaper than bus fares.

The bus network, made up of a mix of public and private operators, is extensive and generally quite competitive – although journey times can be slow and lots of the points of interest outside towns are not served. The rail network is quicker but more limited, serving only some major towns and cities. Both buses and trains get busy during peak times; you'll need to book in advance to be guaranteed a seat.

Air

Ireland's size makes domestic flying unnecessary, but there are flights between Dublin and Belfast, Cork, Derry, Donegal, Galway, Kerry, Shannon and Sligo aimed at passengers connecting from international flights. Flights linking the mainland to the Aran Islands are popular.

Bicycle

Ireland's compact size and scenic landscapes make it a good cycling destination. However, unreliable weather, many very narrow roads and some very fast drivers are major concerns. Special tracks such as the 42km Great Western Greenway in County Mayo are a delight. A good tip for cyclists in the west is that the prevailing winds make it easier to cycle from south to north.

Buses will carry bikes, but only if there's room. For trains, bear the following in mind:

➡ Intercity trains charge up to €10.50 per bike.

➡ Book in advance (www.irishrail.ie), as there's only room for two bikes per service.

Companies that arrange cycle tours in Ireland include the following:

Go Ireland (☑066-976 2094; www.govisitireland.com) Has guided and independent tours.

Irish Cycling Safaris (☑01-260 0749; www.cyclingsafaris.com; €810-845) Organises numerous tours across Ireland.

Lismore Cycling Holidays (☑087-935 6610; www.cyclingholidays.ie) Runs tours around the southeast.

Boat

Ireland's offshore islands are all served by boat.

Ferries also operate across rivers, inlets and loughs, providing useful short cuts, particularly for cyclists.

Cruises are popular on the 258km-long Shannon–Erne Waterway and on a variety of other lakes and loughs.

Bus

Private buses compete – often very favourably – with Bus Éireann in the Republic and also run where the national buses are irregular or absent.

Distances are not especially long: few bus journeys will last longer than five hours. Bus Éireann bookings can be made online, but you can't reserve a seat for a particular service. Dynamic pricing is in effect on many routes: book early to get the lowest fares.

Note the following:

➡ Bus routes and frequencies are slowly contracting in the Republic.

➡ The National Journey Planner app by Transport for Ireland is very useful for planning bus and train journeys.

The main bus services in Ireland:

Bus Éireann (☑1850 836 6111; www.buseireann.ie) The Republic's main bus line.

Translink (☑028-9066 6630; www.translink.co.uk) Northern Ireland's main bus service; includes Ulsterbus and Goldline.

Car & Motorcycle

Travelling by car or motorbike means greater flexibility and independence. The road system is extensive, and the network of motorways has cut driving times considerably. But also note that many secondary roads are very narrow and at times rather perilous.

All cars on public roads must be insured. If you are bringing your own vehicle, check that your insurance will cover you in Ireland.

BUS, TRAIN & FERRY COMBOS

It's possible to combine bus, ferry and train tickets from major UK centres to most Irish towns. This might not be as quick as flying on a budget airline but leaves less of a carbon footprint. The journey between London and Dublin takes about 12 hours by bus, eight hours by train; the London to Belfast trip takes 13 to 16 hours by bus. Both can be had for as little as £29 one way. Eurolines (www.eurolines.com) has bus-ferry combos while Virgin Trains (www.virgintrains.co.uk) has combos that include London to Dublin. For more options, look for SailRail fares.

ROAD DISTANCES (KM)

	Athlone	Belfast	Cork	Derry	Donegal	Dublin	Galway	Kilkenny	Killarney	Limerick	Rosslare Harbour	Shannon Airport	Sligo	Waterford
Belfast	242													
Cork	219	424												
Derry	209	117	428											
Donegal	183	180	402	69										
Dublin	127	167	256	237	233									
Galway	93	306	209	272	204	212								
Kilkenny	116	284	148	335	309	129	172							
Killarney	232	436	87	441	407	304	193	198						
Limerick	363	323	105	328	287	202	98	113	111					
Rosslare Harbour	201	330	208	397	391	153	274	98	275	211				
Shannon Airport	133	346	128	351	282	218	93	135	135	25	234			
Sligo	117	206	336	135	66	214	138	245	343	227	325	218		
Waterford	164	333	126	383	357	163	220	48	193	129	82	152	293	
Wexford	184	309	187	378	372	135	253	80	254	190	19	213	307	61

Car Hire

Advance hire rates start at around €20 a day for a small car (unlimited mileage). Shop around and use price-comparison sites as well as company sites (which often have deals not available on booking sites).

Other tips:

➡ Most cars are manual; automatic cars are available, but they're more expensive to hire.

➡ If you're travelling from the Republic into Northern Ireland, it's important to be sure that your insurance covers journeys to the North.

➡ The majority of hire companies won't rent you a car if you're under 23 and haven't had a valid driving licence for at least a year.

Motoring Organisations

The two main motoring organisations:

Automobile Association (AA; ♪Northern Ireland breakdown 00 800 8877 6655, Republic breakdown 1800 66 77 88; www.theaa.ie)

Royal Automobile Club (RAC; ♪Northern Ireland breakdown 0333 200 0999, Republic breakdown 0800 015 6000; www.rac.ie)

Parking

All big towns and cities have covered and open short-stay car parks that are conveniently signposted.

➡ On-street parking is usually by 'pay and display' tickets available from on-street machines or disc parking (discs, which rotate to display the time you park your car, are usually provided by rental agencies). Costs range from €1.50 to €6 per hour; all-day parking in a car park will cost around €25.

➡ Yellow lines (single or double) along the edge of the road indicate restrictions. Double yellow lines mean no parking at any time. Always look for the nearby sign that spells out when you can and cannot park.

Road Rules

Ireland may be one of the few countries where the posted speed limits are often much faster than you'll find possible.

➡ Motorways (marked by M+number on a blue background): modern, divided highways.

BORDER CROSSINGS

Border crossings between Northern Ireland and the Republic are unnoticeable; there are no formalities of any kind. However, this may change once Brexit occurs in 2019.

BUS & RAIL PASSES

There are a few bus, rail and bus-and-rail passes worth considering:

Irish Explorer Offers customers five days of unlimited Irish Rail travel out of 15 consecutive days (adult/child €160/80).

Open Road Pass Three days' travel out of six consecutive days (€60) on Bus Éireann; extra days cost €16.50.

Sunday Day Tracker One day's unlimited travel (adult/child £7/3.50) on Translink buses and trains in Northern Ireland, Sunday only.

Trekker Four Day Four consecutive days of unlimited travel (€110) on Irish Rail. Note that Eurail's one-country pass for Ireland is a bad deal in any of its permutations.

➡ Primary roads (N+number on a green background in the Republic, A+number in Northern Ireland): usually well-engineered two-lane roads.

➡ Secondary and tertiary roads (marked as R+number in the Republic, B+number in Northern Ireland): Can be very winding and exceedingly narrow.

➡ Tolls are charged on many motorways, usually by machine at a plaza. On the M50, pay the automated tolls between junctions 6 and 7 at www.eflow.ie.

➡ Directional signs are often not in evidence.

➡ GPS navigation via your smartphone or device is very helpful.

➡ EU licences are treated like Irish licences.

➡ Non-EU licences are valid in Ireland for up to 12 months.

➡ If you plan to bring a car from Europe, it's illegal to drive without at least third-party insurance.
The basic rules of the road:

➡ Drive on the left; overtake to the right.

➡ Safety belts must be worn by the driver and all passengers.

➡ Children aged under 12 aren't allowed to sit in the front passenger seat.

➡ When entering a roundabout, give way to the right.

➡ In the Republic, speed-limit and distance signs are in kilometres; in the North, speed-limit and distance signs are often in miles. Speed limits:

Republic 120km/h on motorways, 100km/h on national roads, 80km/h on regional and local roads, and 50km/h or as signposted in towns.

Northern Ireland 70mph (112km/h) on motorways, 60mph (96km/h) on main roads, 30mph (48km/h) in built-up areas.

➡ Drinking and driving is taken very seriously; you're allowed a maximum blood-alcohol level of 0mg/100mL (0.05%) in the Republic, and 35mg/100mL (0.035%) in Northern Ireland.

Hitching

Hitching is becoming less popular in Ireland. Hitching is never entirely safe, and we don't recommend it. Travellers who hitch should understand that they are taking a small but potentially serious risk. It's illegal to hitch on motorways.

Local Transport

Dublin and Belfast have comprehensive local bus networks, as do some other larger towns.

➡ The Dublin Area Rapid Transport (DART) rail line runs roughly the length of Dublin's coastline, while the Luas tram system has two popular lines.

➡ Taxis tend to be expensive: flag fall is daytime/night-time €3.60/4 plus €1.10/1.40 per kilometre after the first 500m.

➡ Uber is in Dublin but is not as popular as MyTaxi (www.mytaxi.com), a taxi app.

Train

Given Ireland's relatively small size, train travel can be quick and advance-purchase fares are competitive with buses.

➡ Many of the Republic's most beautiful areas, such as whole swaths of the Wild Atlantic Way, are not served by rail.

➡ Most lines radiate out from Dublin, with limited ways of interconnecting between lines, which can complicate touring.

➡ There are four routes from Belfast in Northern Ireland, one links with the system in the Republic via Newry to Dublin.

➡ True 1st class only exists on the Dublin–Cork and Dublin–Belfast lines. On all other trains, seats are the same size as in standard class, despite any marketing come-ons such as 'Premier' class.

Irish Rail (Iarnród Éireann; ☑1850 366 222; www.irishrail.ie) Operates trains in the Republic.

Translink NI Railways (☑028-9066 6630; www.translink.co.uk) Operates trains in Northern Ireland.

Train Routes

Portrush
Coleraine
Ballymoney
Larne Harbour
Larne
Derry
Ballymena
Whitehead
Antrim
Carrickfergus
Yorkgate
Bangor
Lisburn
Belfast Central
Lurgan
Portadown

Northern Ireland

Newry

Sligo
Colooney
Dundalk
Ballina
Ballymote
Boyle
Drogheda
Castlebar
Foxford
Carrick-on-Shannon
Balbriggan
Manulla Junction
Dromod
Skerries
Westport
Castlerea
Longford
Claremorris
Ballyhaunis
Edgeworthstown
Dublin Connolly
Roscommon
Mullingar
Howth
Republic of Ireland
Ballinasloe
Athlone
Enfield
Dublin Pearse
Woodlawn
Maynooth
Dun Laoghaire
Attymon
Clara
Dublin Heuston
Bray
Athenry
Tullamore
Kildare
Greystones
Galway
Craughwell
Portarlington
Newbridge
Wicklow
Ardrahan
Portlaoise
Athy
Rathdrum
Gort
Roscrea
Carlow
Arklow
Nenagh
Ballybrophy
Ennis
Birdhill
Templemore
Gorey
Castleconnell
Kilkenny
Muine Bheag
Limerick
Thurles
Enniscorthy
Limerick Junction
Thomastown
Tipperary
Carrick-on-Suir
Wexford
Charleville (Rathluirc)
Cahir
Tralee
Clonmel
Rosslare Strand
Farranfore
Mallow
Waterford
Rosslare Europort
Killarney
Banteer
Rathmore
Millstreet
Cork
Midleton
Glounthaune
Cobh

Language

Irish (Gaeilge) is the country's official language. In 2003 the government introduced the Official Languages Act, whereby all official documents, street signs and official titles must be either in Irish or in both Irish and English. Despite its official status, Irish is really only spoken in pockets of rural Ireland known as the Gaeltacht, the main ones being Cork (Corcaigh), Donegal (Dún na nGall), Galway (Gaillimh), Kerry (Ciarraí) and Mayo (Maigh Eo).

Ask people outside the Gaeltacht if they can speak Irish and nine out of 10 of them will probably reply, 'ah, cupla focal' (a couple of words), and they generally mean it. Irish is a compulsory subject in schools for those aged six to 15, but Irish classes have traditionally been rather academic and unimaginative, leading many students to resent it as a waste of time. As a result, many adults regret not having a greater grasp of it. In recent times, at long last, a new Irish curriculum has been introduced cutting the hours devoted to the subject but making the lessons more fun, practical and celebratory.

PRONUNCIATION

Irish divides vowels into long (those with an accent) and short (those without) and also disinguishes between broad (**a, á, o, ó, u**) and slender (**e, é, i** and **í**), which can affect the pronunciation of preceding consonants. Other than a few odd-looking clusters, such

as **mh** and **bhf** (pronounced both as w), consonants are generally pronounced as they are in English.

Irish has three main dialects: Connaught Irish (in Galway and northern Mayo), Munster Irish (in Cork, Kerry and Waterford) and Ulster Irish (in Donegal). The blue pronunciation guidelines given here are an anglicised version of modern standard Irish, which is essentially an amalgam of the three – if you read them as if they were English, you'll be able to get your point across in Gaeilge without even having to think about the specifics of Irish pronunciation or spelling.

BASICS

Hello.	Dia duit.	deea gwit
Hello. (reply)	Dia is Muire duit.	deeas moyra gwit
Good morning.	Maidin mhaith.	mawjin wah
Good night.	Oíche mhaith.	eekheh wah
Goodbye.		
(when leaving)	Slán leat.	slawn lyat
(when staying)	Slán agat.	slawn agut
Yes.	Tá.	taw
It is.	Sea.	sheh
No.	Níl.	neel
It isn't.	Ní hea.	nee heh

Thank you (very) much.
Go raibh (míle) maith agat. — goh rev (meela) mah agut

Excuse me.
Gabh mo leithscéal. — gamoh lesh scale

I'm sorry.
Tá brón orm. — taw brohn oruhm

I don't understand.
Ní thuigim. — nee higgim

WANT MORE?

For in-depth language information and handy phrases, check out Lonely Planet's *Irish Language & Culture*. You'll find it at **shop.lonelyplanet.com**, or you can buy Lonely Planet's iPhone phrasebooks at the Apple App Store.

Do you speak Irish?
An bhfuil Gaeilge agat? on wil gaylge oguht

What is this?
Cad é seo? kod ay shoh

What is that?
Cad é sin? kod ay shin

I'd like to go to...
Ba mhaith liom baw wah lohm
dul go dtí... dull go dee...

I'd like to buy...
Ba mhaith liom... bah wah lohm...
a cheannach. a kyanukh

another/ *ceann eile* kyawn ella
one more

nice *go deas* goh dyass

MAKING CONVERSATION

Welcome.
Ceád míle fáilte. kade meela fawlcha
(lit: 100,000 welcomes)

How are you?
Conas a tá tú? kunas aw taw too

..., (if you) please.
...más é do thoil é. ...maws ay do hall ay

What's your name?
Cad is ainm duit? kod is anim dwit

My name is (Sean Frayne).
(Sean Frayne) is (shawn frain) is
ainm dom. anim dohm

DAYS OF THE WEEK

Monday	*Dé Luaín*	day loon
Tuesday	*Dé Máirt*	day maart
Wednesday	*Dé Ceádaoin*	day kaydeen
Thursday	*Déardaoin*	daredeen
Friday	*Dé hAoine*	day heeneh
Saturday	*Dé Sathairn*	day sahern
Sunday	*Dé Domhnaigh*	day downick

SIGNS

Fir	fear	Men
Gardaí	gardee	Police
Leithreas	lehrass	Toilet
Mna	mnaw	Women
Oifig	iffig	Post
An Phoist	ohn fwisht	office

CUPLA FOCAL

Here are a few phrases *os Gaeilge* (in Irish) to help you impress the locals:

Tóg é gobogé.
Take it easy.
tohg ay gobogay

Ní féidir é!
Impossible!
nee faydir ay

Ráiméis!
Nonsense!
rawmaysh

Go huafásach!
That's terrible!
guh hoofawsokh

Ní ólfaidh mé go brách arís!
I'm never ever drinking again!
knee ohlhee mey gu brawkh ureeshch

Slainte!
Your health!/Cheers!
slawncha

Táim go maith.
I'm fine.
thawm go mah

Nollaig shona!
Happy Christmas!
nuhlig hona

Cáisc shona!
Happy Easter!
kawshk hona

Go n-éirí an bóthar leat!
Bon voyage!
go nairee on bohhar lat

NUMBERS

1	*haon*	hayin
2	*dó*	doe
3	*trí*	tree
4	*ceathaír*	kahirr
5	*cúig*	kooig
6	*sé*	shay
7	*seacht*	shocked
8	*hocht*	hukt
9	*naoi*	nay
10	*deich*	jeh
11	*haon déag*	hayin jague
12	*dó dhéag*	doe yague
20	*fiche*	feekhe

GLOSSARY

12 July – the day the *Orange Order* marches to celebrate Protestant King William III's victory over the Catholic King James II at the Battle of the Boyne in 1690

An Óige – literally 'the Youth'; Republic of Ireland Youth Hostel Association

Anglo-Norman – Norman, English and Welsh peoples who invaded Ireland in the 12th century

Apprentice Boys – *Loyalist* organisation founded in 1814 to commemorate the Great Siege of Derry in August every year

ard – literally 'high'; Irish place name

Ascendancy – refers to the Protestant aristocracy descended from the Anglo-Normans and those who were installed here during the *Plantation*

bailey – outer wall of a castle

bawn – area surrounded by walls outside the main castle, acting as a defence and as a place to keep cattle in times of trouble

beehive hut – see *clochán*

Black & Tans – British recruits to the Royal Irish Constabulary shortly after WWI, noted for their brutality

Blarney Stone – sacred stone perched on top of Blarney Castle; bending over backwards to kiss the stone is said to bestow the gift of gab

bodhrán – hand-held goatskin drum

Bronze Age – earliest metalusing period, around 2500 BC to 300 BC in Ireland; after the Stone Age and before the *Iron Age*

B-Specials – Northern Irish auxiliary police force, disbanded in 1971

bullaun – stone with a depression, probably used as a mortar for grinding medicine or food, often found at monastic sites

caher – circular area enclosed by stone walls

cairn – mound of stones over a prehistoric grave

cashel – stone-walled *ring fort*; see also *ráth*

céilidh – session of traditional music and dancing; also called 'ceili'

Celtic Tiger – nickname of the Irish economy during the growth years from 1990 to about 2002

Celts – *Iron Age* warrior tribes that arrived in Ireland around 300 BC and controlled the country for 1000 years

chancel – eastern end of a church, where the altar is situated, reserved for the clergy and choir

chipper – slang term for fish-and-chips fast-food restaurant

cill – literally 'church'; Irish place name; also 'kill'

Claddagh ring – ring worn in much of *Connaught* since the mid-18th century, with a crowned heart nestling between two hands; if the heart points towards the hand then the wearer is partnered or married, if towards the fingertip he or she is looking for a mate

clochán – circular stone building, shaped like an oldfashioned beehive, from the early Christian period

Connaught – one of the four ancient provinces of Ireland, made up of Counties Galway, Leitrim, Mayo, Roscommon and Sligo; sometimes spelled 'Connacht'; see also *Leinster, Munster* and *Ulster*

craic – conversation, gossip, fun, good times; also known as 'crack'

crannóg – artificial island made in a lake to provide habitation in a good defensive position

currach – rowing boat made of a framework of laths covered with tarred canvas; also known as 'cúrach'

Dáil – lower house of the parliament of the Republic of Ireland; see also *Oireachtas* and *Seanad*

DART – Dublin Area Rapid Transport train line

demesne – landed property close to a house or castle

diamond – town square

dolmen – tomb chamber or portal tomb made of vertical stones topped by a huge capstone; from around 2000 BC

drumlin – rounded hill formed by retreating glaciers

Dúchas – government department in charge of parks, monuments and gardens in the Republic; formerly known as the Office of Public Works

dún – fort, usually constructed of stone

DUP – Democratic Unionist Party; founded principally by Ian Paisley in 1971 in hardline opposition to *Unionist* policies held by the *UUP*

Éire – Irish name for the Republic of Ireland

esker – raised ridge formed by glaciers

Fáilte Ireland – 'Welcome Board'; Irish Tourist Board

Fianna – mythical band of warriors who feature in many tales of ancient Ireland

Fianna Fáil – literally 'Warriors of Ireland'; a major political party in the Republic, originating from the *Sinn Féin* faction opposed to the 1921 treaty with Britain

Fine Gael – literally 'Tribe of the Gael'; a major political party in the Republic, originating from the *Sinn Féin* faction that favoured the 1921 treaty with Britain; formed the first government of independent Ireland

fir – men (singular 'fear'); sign on men's toilets; see also *leithreas* and *mná*

fleadh – festival

GAA – Gaelic Athletic Association; promotes Gaelic football and hurling, among other Irish games

Gaeltacht – Irish-speaking region

gallóglí – mercenary soldiers of the 14th to 15th century; anglicised to 'gallowglasses'

garda – Irish Republic police; plural 'gardaí'

ghillie – fishing or hunting guide; also known as 'ghilly'

gort – literally 'field'; Irish place name

hill fort – a hilltop fortified with ramparts and ditches, usually dating from the *Iron Age*

HINI – Hostelling International of Northern Ireland

Hunger, the – colloquial name for the Great Famine of 1845–51

hurling – Irish sport similar to hockey

Iarnród Éireann – Republic of Ireland Railways

INLA – Irish National Liberation Association; formed in 1975 as an *IRA* splinter group; it has maintained a ceasefire since 1998

IRA – Irish Republican Army; the largest Republican paramilitary organisation, founded 80 years ago with the aim to fight for a united Ireland; in 1969 the IRA split into the Official IRA and the Provisional IRA; the Official IRA is no longer active and the PIRA has become the IRA

Iron Age – metal-using period that lasted from the end of the *Bronze Age*, around 300 BC (the arrival of the Celts), to the arrival of Christianity, around the 5th century AD

jarvey – driver of a *jaunting car*

jaunting car – Killarney's traditional horse-drawn transport; see also *jarvey*

Leinster – one of the four ancient provinces of Ireland, made up of Counties Carlow, Dublin, Kildare, Kilkenny, Laois, Longford, Louth, Meath, Offaly, West Meath, Wexford and Wicklow; see also *Connaught, Munster* and *Ulster*

leithreas – toilets; see also *mná* and *fir*

leprechaun – mischievous elf or sprite from Irish folklore

lough – lake, or long narrow bay or arm of the sea

Loyalist – person, usually a Northern Irish Protestant, insisting on the continuation of Northern Ireland's links with Britain

Luas – light-rail transit system in Dublin; Irish for 'speed'

marching season – *Orange Order* parades, which take place from Easter and throughout summer to celebrate the victory by Protestant King William III of Orange over Catholic James II in the Battle of the Boyne on 12 July 1690, and the union with Britain

Mesolithic – also known as the Middle Stone Age; time of the first human settlers in Ireland, about 8000 BC to 4000 BC; see also *Neolithic*

mná – women; sign on women's toilets; see also *fir* and *leithreas*

motte – early Norman fortification consisting of a raised, flattened mound with a keep on top; when attached to a *bailey* it is known as a motte-and-bailey fort, many of which were built in Ireland until the early 13th century

Munster – one of the four ancient provinces of Ireland, made up of Counties Clare, Cork, Kerry, Limerick, Tipperary and Waterford; see also *Connaught, Leinster* and *Ulster*

nationalism – belief in a re-united Ireland

Nationalist – proponent of a united Ireland

Neolithic – also known as the New Stone Age; a period characterised by settled agriculture lasting from around 4000 BC to 2500 BC in Ireland; followed by the *Bronze Age;* see also *Mesolithic*

NIR – Northern Ireland Railways

NITB – Northern Ireland Tourist Board

NNR – National Nature Reserves

North, the – political entity of Northern Ireland, not the northernmost geographic part of Ireland

NUI – National University of Ireland; made up of branches in Dublin, Cork, Galway and Limerick

Ogham stone – a stone etched with Ogham characters, the earliest form of writing in Ireland, with a variety of notched strokes

Oireachtas – Parliament of the Republic of Ireland, consisting of the *Dáil*, the lower house, and the *Seanad*, the upper house

Orange Order – the largest Protestant organisation in Northern Ireland, founded in 1795, with a membership of up to 100,000; name commemorates the victory of King William of Orange in the Battle of the Boyne

óstán – hotel

Palladian – style of architecture developed by Andrea Palladio (1508–80), based on ancient Roman architecture

paramilitaries – armed illegal organisations, either *Loyalist* or *Republican,* usually associated with the use of violence and crime for political and economic gain

partition – division of Ireland in 1921

passage grave – Celtic tomb with a chamber reached by a narrow passage, typically buried in a mound

penal laws – laws passed in the 18th century forbidding Catholics from buying land and holding public office

Plantation – settlement of Protestant immigrants (known as Planters) in Ireland in the 17th century

poitín – illegally brewed whiskey, also spelled 'poteen'

provisionals – Provisional IRA, formed after a break with the official *IRA* (who are now largely inconsequential); named after the provisional government declared in 1916, they have been the main force combating the British army in *the North;* also known as 'provos'

PSNI – Police Service of Northern Ireland

ráth – *ring fort* with earthen banks around a timber wall; see also *cashel*

Real IRA – splinter movement of the *IRA*; opposed to *Sinn Féin's* support of the Good Friday Agreement; responsible for the Omagh bombing in 1998 in which 29 people died; subsequently called a ceasefire but has been responsible for bombs in Britain and other acts of violence

Republic of Ireland – the 26 counties of *the South*

Republican – supporter of a united Ireland

republicanism – belief in a united Ireland, sometimes referred to as militant nationalism

ring fort – circular habitation area surrounded by banks and ditches, used from the *Bronze Age* right through to the Middle Ages, particularly in the early Christian period

RTE – Radio Telifís Éireann; the national broadcasting service of the Republic of Ireland, with two TV and four radio stations

RUC – Royal Ulster Constabulary, the former name for the armed Police Service of Northern Ireland *(PSNI)*

Seanad – upper house of the parliament of the Republic of Ireland; see also *Oireachtas* and *Dáil*

shamrock – three-leafed plant said to have been used by St Patrick to illustrate the Holy Trinity

shebeen – from the Irish 'síbín'; illicit drinking place or speakeasy

sheila-na-gig – literally 'Sheila of the teats'; female figure with exaggerated genitalia, carved in stone on the exteriors of some churches and castles; explanations include male clerics warning against the perils of sex to the idea that they represent Celtic war goddesses

Sinn Féin – literally 'We Ourselves'; a *Republican* party with the aim of a united Ireland; seen as the political wing of the *IRA* but it maintains that both organisations are completely separate

slí – hiking trail or way

snug – partitioned-off drinking area in a pub

souterrain – underground chamber usually associated with *ring* and *hill forts;* probably provided a hiding place or escape route in times of trouble and/or storage space for goods

South, the – Republic of Ireland

standing stone – upright stone set in the ground, common across Ireland and dating from a variety of periods; some are burial markers

Taoiseach – Republic of Ireland prime minister

teampall – church

trá – beach or strand

Treaty – Anglo-Irish Treaty of 1921, which divided Ireland and gave relative independence to the South; cause of the 1922–23 Civil War

tricolour – green, white and orange Irish flag symbolising the hoped-for union of the 'green' Catholic Southern Irish with the 'orange' Protestant Northern Irish

turlough – a small lake that often disappears in dry summers; from the Irish 'turlach'

UDA – Ulster Defence Association; the largest *Loyalist* paramilitary group; it has observed a ceasefire since 1994

uillean pipes – Irish bagpipes with a bellow strapped to the arm; 'uillean' is Irish for 'elbow'

Ulster – one of the four ancient provinces of Ireland; sometimes used to describe the six counties of *the North*, despite the fact that Ulster also includes Counties Cavan, Monaghan and Donegal (all in the Republic); see also *Connaught, Leinster* and *Munster*

Unionist – person who wants to retain Northern Ireland's links with Britain

United Irishmen – organisation founded in 1791 aiming to reduce British power in Ireland; it led a series of unsuccessful risings and invasions

UUP – Ulster Unionist Party; the largest *Unionist* party in Northern Ireland and the majority party in the Assembly; founded in 1905 and led by *Unionist* hero Edward Carson from 1910 to 1921; from 1921 to 1972 the sole *Unionist* organisation but is now under threat from the *DUP*

UVF – Ulster Volunteer Force; an illegal *Loyalist* Northern Irish paramilitary organisation

Volunteers – offshoot of the IRB that came to be known as the *IRA*

Behind the Scenes

SEND US YOUR FEEDBACK

We love to hear from travellers – your comments keep us on our toes and help make our books better. Our well-travelled team reads every word on what you loved or loathed about this book. Although we cannot reply individually to your submissions, we always guarantee that your feedback goes straight to the appropriate authors, in time for the next edition. Each person who sends us information is thanked in the next edition – the most useful submissions are rewarded with a selection of digital PDF chapters.

Visit **lonelyplanet.com/contact** to submit your updates and suggestions or to ask for help. Our award-winning website also features inspirational travel stories, news and discussions.

Note: We may edit, reproduce and incorporate your comments in Lonely Planet products such as guidebooks, websites and digital products, so let us know if you don't want your comments reproduced or your name acknowledged. For a copy of our privacy policy visit lonelyplanet.com/privacy.

OUR READERS

Many thanks to the travellers who used the last edition and wrote to us with helpful hints, useful advice and interesting anecdotes: Akos Szoboszlay, Alex Gee, Angelica Beschi, Brian Galligan, Chris Huffman, Elizabeth Cooke, Erika Gorman, Hazel Redmond, Ilse Adema, Joop Drop, Kevin Christie, Kyle Bush, Laura Manago, Manel Tauron, Marie Foster, Melanie West, Raymond Smith, Robin Gruwell, Ryan Williams, Sandra Hynes, Sara McGarity, Susan Hobson, Thorsten Thomas, Tom Lowe

WRITER THANKS

Isabel Albiston

Thanks to all the friendly staff at Northern Ireland's tourist offices who plied me with leaflets while on the road. Thanks in particular to James at Lonely Planet, Victoria Moore at Translink, Barry Flanagan and Caroline Wilson. Lastly, huge thanks to my parents for all your help.

Fionn Davenport

Thanks to everyone in Dublin who helped with research; to Laura for constantly picking me up from the airport; and to LP editors for indulging my every misstep.

Damian Harper

Thanks to everyone who came up with tips and suggestions and helped point me in the right direction along the Wild Atlantic Way. Much gratitude to Shannen, Declan Hassett, Auriel, James Peake, Damien M, Kieron, Fabio, Hans and a raised glass and a tip of the hat to the delightful people of Ireland who made the journey so pleasurable. Daisy, Tim and Emma – thanks as ever.

Catherine Le Nevez

Sláinte first and foremost to Julian, and to all of the Irish locals and fellow travellers throughout County Clare, County Galway, County Kerry and Counties Meath, Louth, Cavan & Monaghan. Huge thanks too to DE James Smart and everyone at LP. As ever, merci encore to my parents, brother, belle-sœur and neveu.

ACKNOWLEDGEMENTS

Climate map data adapted from Peel MC, Finlayson BL & McMahon TA (2007) 'Updated World Map of the Köppen-Geiger Climate Classification', Hydrology and Earth System Sciences, 11, 163344.

Cover photograph: Giant's Causeway, County Antrim, Francesco Carovillano/ 4Corners©

THIS BOOK

This 13th edition of Lonely Planet's *Ireland* guidebook was researched and written by Neil Wilson, Isabel Albiston, Fionn Davenport, Damian Harper and Catherine Le Nevez. The previous edition was written by Neil Wilson, Fionn Davenport, Damian Harper, Catherine Le Nevez and Ryan Ver Berkmoes. This guidebook was produced by the following:

Destination Editor James Smart

Product Editor Jessica Ryan

Senior Cartographer Mark Griffiths

Book Designer Gwen Cotter

Assisting Editors Imogen Bannister, Michelle Bennett, Nigel Chin, Katie Connolly, Pete Cruttenden, Andrea Dobbin, Katie Lynch, Chris Pitts

Cartographer Michael Garrett

Cover Researcher Naomi Parker

Thanks to Stephen Cluskey, Noelle Daly, Paul Harding, Martin Heng, Sandie Kestell, AnneMarie McCarthy, Genna Patterson, Kathryn Rowan, Ellie Simpson, Angela Tinson, Tony Wheeler

Index

Map Legend

Sights

- Beach
- Bird Sanctuary
- Buddhist
- Castle/Palace
- Christian
- Confucian
- Hindu
- Islamic
- Jain
- Jewish
- Monument
- Museum/Gallery/Historic Building
- Ruin
- Shinto
- Sikh
- Taoist
- Winery/Vineyard
- Zoo/Wildlife Sanctuary
- Other Sight

Activities, Courses & Tours

- Bodysurfing
- Diving
- Canoeing/Kayaking
- Course/Tour
- Sento Hot Baths/Onsen
- Skiing
- Snorkelling
- Surfing
- Swimming/Pool
- Walking
- Windsurfing
- Other Activity

Sleeping

- Sleeping
- Camping
- Hut/Shelter

Eating

- Eating

Drinking & Nightlife

- Drinking & Nightlife
- Cafe

Entertainment

- Entertainment

Shopping

- Shopping

Information

- Bank
- Embassy/Consulate
- Hospital/Medical
- Internet
- Police
- Post Office
- Telephone
- Toilet
- Tourist Information
- Other Information

Geographic

- Beach
- Gate
- Hut/Shelter
- Lighthouse
- Lookout
- Mountain/Volcano
- Oasis
- Park
- Pass
- Picnic Area
- Waterfall

Population

- Capital (National)
- Capital (State/Province)
- City/Large Town
- Town/Village

Transport

- Airport
- Border crossing
- Bus
- Cable car/Funicular
- Cycling
- Ferry
- Metro station
- Monorail
- Parking
- Petrol station
- S-Bahn/Subway station
- Taxi
- T-bane/Tunnelbana station
- Train station/Railway
- Tram
- Tube station
- U-Bahn/Underground station
- Other Transport

Routes

- Tollway
- Freeway
- Primary
- Secondary
- Tertiary
- Lane
- Unsealed road
- Road under construction
- Plaza/Mall
- Steps
- Tunnel
- Pedestrian overpass
- Walking Tour
- Walking Tour detour
- Path/Walking Trail

Boundaries

- International
- State/Province
- Disputed
- Regional/Suburb
- Marine Park
- Cliff
- Wall

Hydrography

- River, Creek
- Intermittent River
- Canal
- Water
- Dry/Salt/Intermittent Lake
- Reef

Areas

- Airport/Runway
- Beach/Desert
- Cemetery (Christian)
- Cemetery (Other)
- Glacier
- Mudflat
- Park/Forest
- Sight (Building)
- Sportsground
- Swamp/Mangrove

Note: Not all symbols displayed above appear on the maps in this book

OUR STORY

A beat-up old car, a few dollars in the pocket and a sense of adventure. In 1972 that's all Tony and Maureen Wheeler needed for the trip of a lifetime – across Europe and Asia overland to Australia. It took several months, and at the end – but broke but inspired – they sat at their kitchen table writing and stapling together their first travel guide, *Across Asia on the Cheap*. Within a week they'd sold 1500 copies. Lonely Planet was born.

Today, Lonely Planet has offices in Franklin, London, Melbourne, Oakland, Dublin, Beijing and Delhi, with more than 600 staff and writers. We share Tony's belief that 'a great guidebook should do three things: inform, educate and amuse'.

OUR WRITERS

Neil Wilson

Curator; Counties Wicklow & Kildare; Counties Wexford, Waterford, Carl Kilkenny; County Cork; Counties Limerick & Tipperary

Neil was born in Scotland and has lived there most of his life. Based in P shire, he has been a full-time writer since 1988, working on more than 8C guidebooks for various publishers, including the Lonely Planet guides tc Scotland, England, Ireland and Prague. Like most Lonely Planet authors fell into the guidebook-writing business by accident. Having fled the rat race of the oil ind soon after graduating as a geologist, he returned to university to do postgraduate resear academia turned out to be just as dull as industry, so like any sane person he gave it all up a penniless writer. The penniless bit was easy. On the writing side, he began by producing cles for a Scottish magazine, but was soon off to photograph Corfu for a guidebook.

Read more about Neil at
lonelyplanet.com/profiles/neilwil

Isabel Albiston

Belfast; Counties Down & Armagh; Counties Derry & Antrim; Counties F managh & Tyrone; Counties LondonDerry & Antrim After 6 years workin, the *Daily Telegraph* in London, squeezing in as many trips as annual leav would allow, Isabel left to spend more time on the road. A job as writer fc magazine in Sydney, Australia, was followed by four years living and wor in Buenos Aires, Argentina. Isabel started writing for Lonely Planet in 20 having been back in the UK just long enough to pack a bag for a research trip to Malaysia, has contributed to six LP guides. See her pics on instagram: isabel_albiston.

Read more about Isabel at
lonelyplanet.com/profiles/IsabelAlbi:

Fionn Davenport

Dublin Irish by birth and conviction, Fionn has been writing about his na country for more than two decades. He's come and gone over the years, pulled abroad to escape Dublin's comfortable stasis and by the promise adventure, but it has cemented his belief that Ireland remains his favour place to visit, if not always live in. These days, he has a weekly commute to Dublin from Manchester, where he lives with his partner Laura and the Trevor. In Dublin he presents Inside Culture on RTE Radio 1 and writes travel features for a of publications.

Read more about Fionn at
lonelyplanet.com/profiles/FionnDa\

OVER PAGE | **MORE WRITERS**

Published by Lonely Planet Global Limited
CRN 554153
13th edition – Mar 2018
ISBN 978 1 78657 445 9
© Lonely Planet 2018 Photographs © as indicated 2018
10 9 8 7 6 5 4 3 2 1
Printed in China

Damian Harper

Counties Mayo & Sligo; County Donegal; the Midlands Damian has been writing for Lonely Planet for over two decades, contributing to titles covering regions as diverse as China, Beijing, Shanghai, Vietnam, Thailand, Ireland, London, Mallorca, Malaysia, Singapore & Brunei, Hong Kong, China's Southwest and the UK. A seasoned guidebook writer, Damian has penned articles for numerous newspapers and magazines, including *The Guardian* and *The Daily Telegraph*, and currently makes Surrey, England, his home. A self-taught trumpet novice, his other hobbies include collecting modern first editions, photography and Taekwondo. Follow Damian on Instagram (damian.harper).

Read more about Damian at
lonelyplanet.com/profiles/DamianHarper

Catherine Le Nevez

County Kerry; County Clare; County Galway; Counties Meath, Louth, Cavan & Monaghan Catherine's wanderlust kicked in when she roadtripped across Europe from her Parisian base aged four, and she's been hitting the road at every opportunity since, travelling to around 60 countries and completing her Doctorate of Creative Arts in Writing, Masters in Professional Writing, and postgrad qualifications in Editing and Publishing along the way. Over the past dozen-plus years she's written scores of Lonely Planet guides and articles covering Paris, France, Europe and far beyond. Her work has also appeared in numerous online and print publications. Topping Catherine's list of travel tips is to travel without any expectations.

Read more about Catherine at
lonelyplanet.com/profiles/CatherineLe
Nevez